THE CHOSEN

BOOKS BY JEROME KARABEL

POWER AND IDEOLOGY IN EDUCATION
co-edited with A. H. Halsey

THE DIVERTED DREAM: COMMUNITY COLLEGES
AND THE PROMISE OF EDUCATIONAL
OPPORTUNITY IN AMERICA, 1900–1985
with Steven Brint

THE CHOSEN: THE HIDDEN HISTORY
OF ADMISSION AND EXCLUSION AT HARVARD,
YALE, AND PRINCETON

THE
CHOSEN

THE HIDDEN HISTORY
OF ADMISSION AND EXCLUSION
AT HARVARD, YALE, AND
PRINCETON

JEROME KARABEL

HOUGHTON MIFFLIN COMPANY
BOSTON · NEW YORK
2005

Copyright © 2005 by Jerome Karabel
ALL RIGHTS RESERVED

For information about permission to reproduce selections from
this book, write to Permissions, Houghton Mifflin Company,
215 Park Avenue South, New York, New York 10003.

Visit our Web site: www.houghtonmifflinbooks.com.

Library of Congress Cataloging-in-Publication Data
Karabel, Jerome.
The chosen : the hidden history of admission and exclusion
at Harvard, Yale, and Princeton / Jerome Karabel.
p.   cm.
Includes bibliographical references and index.
ISBN-13: 978-0-618-57458-2
ISBN-10: 0-618-57458-1
1. Universities and colleges — Atlantic States — Admission.
2. Education, Higher — United States — History.   I. Title.
LB2351.3.A85K37 2005
378.1'61'0973 — dc22   2005011133

PRINTED IN THE UNITED STATES OF AMERICA

Book design by Robert Overholtzer

MP 10 9 8 7 6 5 4 3 2

TO KRISTA, ALEX, SONYA, AND MISHA

and

To the Memory of My Parents,

DOROTHY AND HENRY KARABEL

Contents

Introduction

THE TASK OF THE WRITER, someone once said, is to render the strange familiar and the familiar strange. In America today, few customs are more familiar than the annual ritual in which our leading universities sort through tens of thousands of applications to determine which students will be among the fortunate few to be admitted. So familiar are the features of this process — the letters of recommendation, the personal interviews, the emphasis on extracurricular activities and scores on the Scholastic Aptitude Test (SAT), the boost given to athletes and alumni children, and the heavy stress on highly subjective qualities such as "character," "personality," and "leadership" — that they have come to be taken for granted.

Yet viewed from both a historical and a comparative perspective, the admission practices of America's top colleges and universities are exceedingly strange.[1] Just try to explain to someone from abroad — from, say, France, Japan, Germany, or China — why the ability to run with a ball or where one's parents went to college is relevant to who will gain a place at our nation's most prestigious institutions of higher education, and you immediately realize how very peculiar our practices are. Explaining where these strange practices came from and why they have proved so enduring is one of the primary objectives of this book.

Like the most prestigious universities of other nations, Harvard, Yale, and Princeton — the three institutions at the center of this book — admitted students almost entirely on the basis of academic criteria for most of their long histories. But this changed in the 1920s, when the traditional academic requirements no longer served to screen out students deemed "socially undesirable." By then, it had become clear that a system of selection focused solely on scholastic performance would lead to the admission of increasing numbers of Jewish students, most of them of eastern European background. This transformation was becoming visible at precisely the time that the nationwide movement to restrict immigration was gaining momentum, and it was unacceptable to the Anglo-Saxon gentlemen who presided over the Big Three (as Harvard, Yale, and Princeton were called by then). Their response was to invent an entirely new system of admissions — one at variance with their own traditions as well as with those of leading universities in other countries. It is this system that persists — albeit with important modifications — even today.

The defining feature of the new system was its categorical rejection of the idea that admission should be based on academic criteria alone. Though the view that scholastic performance should determine admission was not uncommon among the faculty, the top administrators of the Big Three (and of other leading private colleges, such as Columbia and Dartmouth) recognized that relying solely on any single factor — especially one that could be measured, like academic excellence — would deny them control over the composition of the freshman class. Charged with protecting their institutional interests, the presidents of the Big Three wanted the latitude to admit the dull sons of major donors and to exclude the brilliant but unpolished children of immigrants, whose very presence prompted privileged young Anglo-Saxon men — the probable leaders and donors of the future — to seek their education elsewhere. Such latitude was conspicuously missing from a policy of selection focused exclusively on academic excellence.

Chastened by their recent experience with the traditional system of admission examinations, which had begun yielding the "wrong" students, the leaders of the Big Three devised a new admissions regime that allowed them to accept — and to reject — whomever they desired. The cornerstones of the new system were discretion and opacity — discretion so that gatekeepers would be free to do what they wished and opacity so that how they used their discretion would not be subject to public scrutiny. In contrast to the old system, whose results were distressingly unpredictable, the new system allowed college administrators to adapt as conditions changed. Once this capacity to adapt was established, a new admissions regime was in place that was governed by what might be called the "iron law of admissions": a university will retain a particular admissions policy only so long as it produces outcomes that correspond to perceived institutional interests.[2]

The centerpiece of the new policy would be "character" — a quality thought to be in short supply among Jews but present in abundance among high-status Protestants. To the gentlemen who ran Harvard, Yale, and Princeton, "character" was shorthand for an entire ethos and way of being. Inherently intangible, "character" could only be judged by those who had it. Coupled with the new emphasis on such highly subjective qualities as "manliness," "personality," and "leadership," the gatekeepers of the Big Three had broad discretion to admit — and to exclude — applicants on the basis of highly personal judgments.

This shift in the 1920s, from objective academic criteria to subjective nonacademic criteria, was part of a broader redefinition of "merit." Yet, though both the intent and the consequence of this shift were to favor one group over another, it was presented in universal terms — a requirement in a society whose core ideology was equality of opportunity and whose national identity was that of a land where, unlike the class-bound societies of Europe, achievement rather than the prerogatives of birth would determine one's fate in life.[3] For the gatekeepers of the Big Three, the trick was to devise an admissions process that would be perceived — not least by themselves — as just. The ideology of "character" provided precisely such a legitimation.

Because graduates of Harvard, Yale, and Princeton have always been heavily overrepresented in the American elite, the stakes involved in who gains access to them have long been high.[4] (The White House has been occupied by a graduate of the Big Three during 44 of the 105 years covered in the book. By 2008 that number will increase to 47, for George W. Bush is a Yale man.)[5] In recent decades, competition for entry to the Big Three and other selective colleges has become so fierce and the public's obsession with these institutions so great that it has spawned an entire industry — a sprawling complex that includes coaching companies, guidebooks, private tutors, summer camps, software packages, and private counselors who charge fees up to $29,000 per student.[6] Beneath this industry is the belief — corroborated by a wide body of research — that attending a "prestige" college will confer important benefits later in life.[7] This growing preoccupation with college admissions is not irrational, especially in a society in which the acquisition of educational credentials has taken its place alongside the direct inheritance of property as a major vehicle for the transmission of privilege from parent to child. And as the gap between winners and losers in America grows ever wider — as it has since the early 1970s — the desire to gain every possible edge has only grown stronger.[8]

Given the high stakes involved, it is not surprising that the criteria governing selection to our leading colleges and universities have time and again become the object of bitter conflict. At the center of these struggles has been the definition of "merit" — the quality that most Americans agree should determine college admissions. But while, at least in public, there has been something approaching a consensus that in America "merit" — and not inherited privilege — should determine the distribution of educational opportunity, there has been no consensus on what "merit" is. In truth, there is no neutral definition of "merit"; however it is defined, it will benefit some groups while disadvantaging others.

This book examines the many definitions of "merit" that have governed admissions to Harvard, Yale, and Princeton since 1900, explaining why changes in criteria occurred, who gained and lost with each change, and what it meant for the country at large. This story is inextricably intertwined with the larger story of America during that time — how it changed from a nation dominated by a small group of privileged white men of Anglo-Saxon origin to one that has progressively incorporated previously excluded groups, including Jews, blacks, and women.

But this story is also the tale of the maintenance of a social order characterized by vast inequalities of wealth and power. Over the course of the twentieth century, some of the more farsighted leaders of the Big Three played no small part in preserving this system. One of the ways they did so was by using admissions policy to promote individual mobility at those moments when the reigning American ideology of equality of opportunity was being challenged by radical movements demanding greater equality of condition.[9]

This distinction — between *equality of opportunity,* the principle that the individual's chance to get ahead should not be limited by social origins or by ascribed characteristics such as race or gender, and *equality of condition,* the principle that inequalities of wealth, power, and status should be kept to the minimum level possible — runs throughout the history of the Big Three in the twentieth century and is central to the conceptual framework of this book.[10] In this sense, a meritocracy — that is, a society in which the principle of equality of opportunity prevails and those with the most "merit" govern — is not an expression of, but an alternative to, a more egalitarian society.[11]

In the United States, the meritocratic principle has enjoyed far more popular support than the principle of equality of condition. Yet the definition of "merit" that prevails in a given society, whether the United States today or ancient Greece, generally expresses the ideals and interests of its dominant groups.[12] In a warrior society, "merit" consists of courage and skill on the battlefield; in a society dominated by religion, "merit" is exhibited by knowledge of the sacred texts; in a Communist society (Maoist China would be an archetypal example), "merit" is composed of a combination of "redness" (loyalty to the ideals of socialism) and expertise useful to the regime.

The Big Three's definition of "merit" changed fundamentally several times in the past century. In 1900, "merit" was basically academic and measured by one's mastery of a traditional curriculum, including Latin and Greek. But in the 1920s, in the context of a powerful national movement to restrict immigration, this definition gave way to the ideal of the "all-round man" of sturdy character, sound body, and proper social background. An undergraduate who devoted his time to his club or his sports team was the ideal. He who spent time at his desk was labeled not merely "a grind" but "a greasy grind."

In the late 1950s, in an atmosphere of intense concern about "talent loss" sparked by the Cold War and *Sputnik,* the "all-round" man began to lose ground to the intellectually gifted applicant whose exceptional scores on the SAT and high grades were accompanied by excellence in one or more extra-curricular endeavors. It was in this period that the word "meritocracy" — a term introduced into the language in 1958 in Michael Young's brilliant satire, *The Rise of the Meritocracy*, to refer to a society in which advancement is based, not on the prerogatives of birth, but on talent and performance — first entered popular parlance.[13] To those such as the Yale alumnus William F. Buckley Jr., who favored preference for alumni sons and saw the Big Three as playing a key role in the perpetuation of the existing elite, meritocracy was a threat. But to those who favored an academic meritocracy along the lines of France's École Normale Supérieure or Japan's Tokyo University, both of which admitted students purely on the basis of scores or exams, Young's essay was a battle cry. Yet to Young himself, meritocracy — whether the academic variant favored by segments of the faculty or the more intangible and sub-jective type, including extracurricular activities and personal qualities such as "character" and "leadership," preferred by Big Three administrators — was itself the problem, for it deflected attention from the real issues of poverty and inequality of condition onto a chimerical quest for unlimited social mo-bility.

Young's critique of meritocracy found resonance in the more radical at-mosphere of the 1960s. But the main effect of the political and social upheav-als of the decade was to change the definition of "merit" yet again, provoking a seismic cultural shift that elevated the values of "diversity" and "inclusion" to a central place in the selection policies of the Big Three. It was in this con-text that vigorous race-based affirmative action was born and the barriers to the admission of women were finally pushed aside.

The history of admissions at the Big Three has thus been, fundamentally, a history of recurrent struggles over the meaning of "merit." Yet beneath the flux has been a consistent pattern: the meaning of merit has shifted in re-sponse to changing power relations among groups as well as changes in the broader society. This proposition — that the definition of "merit" is fluid and tends to reflect the values and interests of those who have the power to im-pose their particular cultural ideals — is the central argument of this book.

But to say that the prevailing definition of merit generally mirrors the val-ues and interests of dominant groups is not to say that it is always the case. Precisely because the definition of merit is so important, it is often contested. Especially during periods of political and social turmoil, outgroups may exert a powerful influence on university admissions by pressing for alternative definitions of merit consistent with their own world views and interests. This was what happened in the 1960s when, amid the social and political turmoil, an ideology that linked "merit" to "diversity" was elaborated and affirmative action was put in place. The history of admissions at the Big Three is a history, not only of elite dominance, but of resistance by subordinate groups. And because the ideology of equality of opportunity is so central to the legitimacy of the American social order, universities are particularly susceptible to pressures from movements dedicated to policies of inclusion that promise to put America's highest ideals into practice.

Although admissions decisions are made by educators, they are also deeply political. As Glenn Loury has aptly noted, elite universities are a "venue where access to power and influence is rationed."[14] As some of the most astute admissions deans at the Big Three have acknowledged in moments of candor, the allocation of scarce and highly valued places in the freshman class is an inherently political process, complete with interest groups (e.g., the athletic department, the faculty) and external constituencies (e.g., the alumni, important feeder schools, mobilized minority groups) vying for bigger slices of the pie.[15] Power — including the capacity to shape the very categories used to classify candidates for admission and to designate specific groups as warranting special consideration (e.g., legacies and historically underrepresented minorities, but not disadvantaged whites) — is at the center of this process. From this perspective, an admissions policy is a kind of negotiated settlement among contending groups, each wishing to shape admissions criteria and the actual selection process to produce the outcome they prefer.[16]

The story of admission and exclusion at Harvard, Yale, and Princeton provides a lens through which to examine some of the main events and movements of America in the twentieth century — the emergence of the United States as an imperial power, immigration restriction, anti-Semitism, the Great Depression, World War II, the dropping of the atomic bomb, the launching of *Sputnik*, the Cold War, the civil rights movement, the women's movement, the rise of Asian Americans, and the triumph of the market ethos. It unfolds through the eyes of several individuals who left a permanent imprint on American higher education. Among the people who figure prominently in the narrative are Endicott Peabody, the austere and aristocratic headmaster of the Groton School (1884–1940) who brought the gentlemanly ideals of the British upper class into American education and served as a lifelong mentor to Franklin Delano Roosevelt, and Woodrow Wilson, whose failed effort to eliminate the eating club system at Princeton, where he served as president from 1902 to 1910, enduringly shaped that institution's image while launching him on the path to the White House.

Joining them in the early years of the story will be the Harvard presidents

Charles W. Eliot (1869–1909) and A. Lawrence Lowell (1909–1933), two Boston Brahmins who between them presided over America's oldest and wealthiest university for more than sixty years. Though both had impeccable patrician backgrounds, the two men were bitter personal and political enemies, and their frequent clashes embodied a recurrent conflict within the Protestant elite between its progressive, inclusionary wing and its conservative, exclusionary wing. In the 1920s, they fought over religious quotas at Harvard, with the liberal Eliot, then almost ninety years old, struggling desperately to block Lowell's plan to limit Jewish enrollment. This epic battle was one of the formative episodes in the history of the Big Three.

From the Great Depression through midcentury and beyond, the dominant figure in American higher education — and the central character in our story — was James Bryant Conant, the brilliant chemist who succeeded Lowell as president of Harvard (1933–1953). Although conventionally identified as an arch-meritocrat, Conant was a complex man who created a powerful new synthesis in elite college admissions that drew on Eliot's commitment to equality of opportunity while leaving in place many of Lowell's policies designed to preserve Harvard's predominantly Anglo-Saxon character. Yet if Harvard's admissions practices under Conant were in many ways traditional, his widely read writings were not. Inveighing against the "hereditary aristocracy of wealth" and calling for the vigorous enforcement of meritocratic principles even if such enforcement meant downward mobility for the sons of the privileged, Conant's writings were surprisingly radical. Composed during the depths of the Depression, when assaults on the capitalist system both at home and abroad seemed to threaten its survival, these writings laid out a compelling vision of upward mobility through education — including access to the nation's leading private colleges — as an antidote to class consciousness and the growing appeal of socialism.[17]

Continuing Conant's legacy during the 1960s, another period of radical challenges to the existing order, was Kingman Brewster, the debonair president of Yale (1963–1977). A handsome patrician whose ancestors came to America on the *Mayflower*, Brewster exemplified the progressive wing of the Protestant Establishment, and some of the reforms he introduced at Yale were among the most radical in the history of the Big Three.[18] But Brewster, like Conant, was dedicated to the preservation of the existing order and saw a belief in the system's openness to merit as essential to its legitimacy. Also like Conant, he saw members of that powerful segment of the Protestant upper class opposed to necessary reforms — whether in admissions or in the larger society — as posing a threat to the survival of the free enterprise system.

No story of admissions to Harvard, Yale, and Princeton would be complete, however, without a discussion of the men who presided over the actual process of selection. Since the invention of the office of admission in the early 1920s, three deans of admission stand out for their influence not only on their institutions but also on their peers nationwide: Radcliffe Heermance of Princeton (1922–1950), Wilbur Bender of Harvard (1952–1960), and R. Inslee ("Inky") Clark of Yale (1965–1970). The longest-serving dean of admissions in the history of the Big Three, the redoubtable Heermance did more than any other man to refine the techniques of excluding "undesirables," and his distinctive personal imprint was visible in every Princeton freshman class for more than a quarter century. Bender, a Mennonite from Indiana appointed dean of admission by Conant near the end of his presidency, was perhaps the most colorful man ever to serve in such a position. A sophisticated modernizer who retained an attachment to upper-class prep school boys, whom he referred to as "the gentlemen," Bender fell victim to the push by the faculty for greater meritocracy after *Sputnik*. But before leaving, Bender issued a powerful critique of admissions by academic criteria alone that remains influential even today. And Clark, a member of Skull and Bones and a quintessential Yalie as an undergraduate, was the unlikely author of the "revolution" at Yale — a transformation of admissions so radical that it spawned a full-scale alumni revolt. Together, Heermance, Bender, and Clark — who spanned the spectrum from right to left — represent the full range of the Big Three's responses to the recurrent dilemmas posed by admissions.

In charting the transformation of Harvard, Yale, and Princeton over the course of the twentieth century, it becomes clear that change in admissions policy has come about primarily through their attempt to preserve and, when possible, to enhance their position in a highly stratified system of higher education.[19] Though often viewed as forward-looking and driven by their commitment to high ideals, the Big Three were more often deeply conservative and surprisingly insecure about their status in the higher-education pecking order and intensely preoccupied with maintaining their close ties to the privileged. Change, when it did come, almost always derived from one of two sources: the continuation of existing policies was believed to pose a threat either to vital institutional interests (above all, maintaining their competitive position) or to the preservation of the larger social order of which they were an integral — and privileged — part.

Perhaps the quintessential example of the pursuit of institutional interests was the decision by Yale and Princeton finally to admit women — a choice explained much less by their commitment to the principle of equality of opportunity than by their recognition that their ability to attract "the best boys" was gravely endangered by their all-male character. The clearest example of the fear of social disintegration was the adoption by the Big Three in the late 1960s of vigorous race-based affirmative action — again, a decision made less in response to the moral claims of the civil rights movement (which, after all, had been active since the mid-1950s) than to the palpable threat of social breakdown in the wake of the massive race riots of 1965–1968. To be sure, the men who presided over the Big Three took their ideals seriously and sometimes incurred considerable risks to abide by them. But a far more reliable guide to understanding their behavior than their professed principles is to see them as constrained managers not so very different from the heads of large corporations, whose primary task is to defend their organization's position in a highly competitive environment.

The evidence on which this story is based comes primarily from the archives of Harvard, Yale, and Princeton. In researching the story of admission and exclusion at the Big Three, I unearthed documents — some of them reported here for the first time — that included the correspondence of key administrators and admissions officers, internal memoranda, handbooks for admissions officers and alumni interviewers, internal statistical studies, and minutes of meetings of the admissions committee, the faculty, and the trustees. Particularly useful were annual reports on admissions dating from 1911 at Harvard, 1913 at Yale, and 1922 at Princeton. Also illuminating were various faculty reports on admissions, including background papers to assist the faculty in its deliberations. In addition, I consulted student newspapers, alumni magazines (including dissident conservative alumni magazines at Yale and Princeton), and administrative publications. To compile biographical information and statistical profiles, I examined freshmen face books, yearbooks, and reunion reports. Finally, I benefited greatly from access to the materials used by the Office of Civil Rights of the U.S. Department of Education in its two-year investigation (1988–1990) into charges of discrimination against Asian-American applicants to Harvard. These materials offered tremendous insight into both the actual mechanics of the admissions process and the relative weight of various factors in the ultimate decision to admit or reject individual applicants.

This book is divided into three parts, each covering roughly one-third of a century. In Part I, which begins as the nineteenth century gives way to the twentieth and ends during the early years of the Great Depression, I describe the birth of the college admissions system with which we are familiar today. But the character of this system cannot be understood without a grasp of both the system of exam-based admissions that preceded it and the ethos of the group that shaped the new system. Constructed by the Protestant upper class in response to "the Jewish problem," the new regime was a radical departure from traditional, academic selection practices. Part I describes how this system came into being — who favored it, who opposed it, and why it took the particular form that it did.

Part II, which begins in 1933 with the accession of James Bryant Conant to the presidency of Harvard and ends in the mid-1960s, explains how a system of admissions devised to preserve the prerogatives of the Protestant elite gradually evolved into something quite different. For it was during this period that a number of major reforms — among them, the growth of merit-based scholarships, the rising importance of the SAT, the reduction of discrimination against Jews and public school students, and the elaboration of an institutional ideology officially committed to equality of opportunity and the search for "talent" — were introduced, giving credence to the notion of rising "meritocracy" at Harvard, Yale, and Princeton. Yet it was also when Harvard adopted an unpublicized policy of limiting "intellectuals" to no more than 10 percent of the freshman class and enunciated the principle of the "happy bottom quarter" — a policy that reserved a substantial portion of the places in the class for students who were not distinguished academically but whose other talents made them appealing. As Part II ends, SATs and the number of scholarship students at the Big Three are rising, but the student body remains overwhelmingly white and — at Yale and Princeton — exclusively male.

Part III, which opens in the mid-1960s and carries the story forward to today, begins during a period of intense social and political conflict. In a few short years, the Big Three were enduringly transformed, adopting race-based affirmative action and then — in rapid sequence — coeducation and sex-blind admissions. So radical were these changes that they generated a concerted attempt at counterrevolution in the form of alumni revolts at Yale and Princeton. Part III explains why these changes took place and why attempts to reverse them ultimately failed. It concludes with a discussion of recent developments at the Big Three — among them, allegations of discrimination against Asian Americans, the continued conflict over affirmative action, the debate about what weight (if any) should be given to legacy status and athletic ability, and efforts to reduce the vast underrepresentation of students from working-class and poor families. These developments make it clear that the battle over the definition of merit remains as ferocious today as ever.

The origins of today's policies are more than a century old. The story begins, accordingly, in 1900, when, in the words of E. Digby Baltzell, "a British-American, white-Anglo-Saxon-Protestant (WASP) establishment . . . authoritatively ran the world."[20]

PART I

....

THE ORIGINS OF
SELECTIVE ADMISSIONS,
1900–1933

CHAPTER 1

Elite Education and the Protestant Ethos

O N A CLEAR FALL MORNING in late September of 1900, a lanky young man with patrician features and pince-nez glasses stood among the more than five hundred freshmen gathered to register at Harvard. Though neither a brilliant scholar nor a talented athlete, the young man had a certain charisma about him — a classmate later described him as "gray-eyed, cool, self-possessed, intelligent . . . [with] the warmest, most friendly, and understanding smile."[1] The freshman had been given a strong recommendation from his Latin teacher, who described him as "a fellow of exceptional ability and high character" who "hopes to go into public life."[2] His name was Franklin Delano Roosevelt, and in 1933 he became the fourth graduate of Harvard College to serve as president of the United States.

Franklin's acceptance at Harvard had been taken for granted. Having attended Groton, the most socially elite of America's boarding schools, he was sure to be admitted to Harvard; in 1900, 18 of his Groton classmates (out of a class of just 23) joined him in Cambridge.[3] There the Groton boys — along with their peers from St. Paul's, St. Mark's, Milton, and other leading private schools — dominated the upper reaches of campus life.

Even then, however, the children of the elite did not constitute the entire freshman class. Harvard, far more than Yale and especially Princeton, took pride in the diversity of its student body. In his address to new students, President Charles W. Eliot denounced as a "common error" the supposition that "the men of the University live in rooms the walls of which are covered with embossed leather." The truth, Eliot insisted, was quite the contrary: "the majority are of moderate means; and it is this diversity of condition that makes the experience of meeting men here so valuable."[4]

Though Eliot was downplaying the heavy representation of children of privilege at Harvard, there was in fact a surprising degree of heterogeneity among the students. More than 40 percent of Roosevelt's freshman class came from public schools, and many were the children of immigrants.[5] And of Harvard's leading feeder schools, the top position in 1900 was occupied not by Groton or St. Paul's (18 students) but by Boston Latin (38 students), a public institution that had long since lost its cachet as a school for the sons of Boston Brahmins.[6]

Yet the Harvard attended by public school boys was separated from the Harvard of Roosevelt and his friends by a vast social chasm. Its physical symbol was the divide between Mount Auburn Street's luxurious "Gold Coast, where the patrician students lived," and the shabby dormitories of Harvard Yard, some of which lacked central heating and plumbing above the basement, where the more plebeian students stayed.[7] Roosevelt was, by birth, a natural member of the Mount Auburn group; even before he enrolled at Harvard, he visited Cambridge with his future roommate, Lathrop Brown, to select a suitable spot on the Gold Coast. Their choice was Westmorly Court (now part of Adams House), an elegant structure that provided the young men with a high-ceilinged suite complete with two bedrooms, a sitting room, an entrance hall, and a bath.[8]

As the scion of a prominent family with long Harvard ties — his father, James, had graduated from Harvard Law School in 1851, and his distant cousin Theodore, then running for vice president of the United States, graduated from the college in 1880 — Roosevelt fit smoothly into the Gold Coast atmosphere. Though he had pledged to make a "a large acquaintance" at Harvard, young Franklin remained firmly within his milieu of origin. Taking his daily meals at an all-Groton table in a private dining hall, he spent many of his evenings at Sanborn's billiard and tobacco parlor, where he could meet "most of the Groton, St. M[ark's], St. Paul's and Pomfret fellows." He was also a regular on the Boston social circuit, attending teas, dinners, and debutante parties.[9]

Though Roosevelt's distinguished lineage guaranteed him a certain social success, it did not free him from the need to compete for a place in Harvard's rich and highly stratified extracurricular life — a realm of energetic activity that occupied a far more central place in the lives of most students than their studies. Occupying the apex of the extracurriculum at turn-of-the-century Harvard was football, and Roosevelt dutifully went out for the team. He was joined by 142 other students — well over a quarter of the entering class.[10] Trying out for the position of end, he stood 6'1" but weighed just 146 pounds. On October 13, 1900, Roosevelt — who had been a mediocre, if eager, football player at Groton — was notified that he had failed to make the team.[11]

Within days of being cut, Roosevelt decided to try his hand at another prestigious activity — the *Crimson*, Harvard's student newspaper. On October 19, he wrote to his parents, informing them that he was trying out for the newspaper and expressing the hope that "if I work hard for two years I may be made an editor."[12] But at the *Crimson*, as in football, he did not survive the fierce competition; vying for a slot among 86 candidates, he was passed over when the first crop of freshman was selected in February.[13]

Yet Roosevelt persisted in his efforts to make the paper, scoring a coup in April when his cousin Theodore, by then the vice president, visited Cambridge and told him that he would be lecturing the following morning in Professor Lowell's class in constitutional government. Franklin broke the story in the *Crimson,* and the following morning a crowd of 2,000 was milling about in front of Sanders Theatre, trying to attend the lecture. From this point on, Roosevelt's star began to rise, and in the autumn of 1902, he became the *Crimson's* assistant managing editor.[14]

As Roosevelt advanced at the *Crimson,* his success owed more to his doggedness than his journalistic talent, for he was an unremarkable writer. His family name was perhaps his greatest asset; in September 1901, after the assassination of William McKinley, Cousin Teddy became president of the United States. In Franklin's February 1903 campaign for managing editor (a position that led automatically to the presidency), a poster read: "For Managing Editor — Cousin Frank — the Fairest of the Roosevelts." Roosevelt won the election, ultimately serving as president of the *Crimson* from June to December of 1903.[15]

The *Crimson* valued hard work and talent, yet some of the same social cleavages that divided the campus were nevertheless visible. Remembering his days on the newspaper, Roosevelt's classmate Walter E. Sachs, later of the Goldman Sachs investment firm, recalled that he lived in a very different world from Roosevelt's. Whereas FDR ate at the Groton table on the Gold Coast and went to fashionable parties in Boston, Sachs and his friends lived in the Yard and ate cheap and disagreeable food at table 30 in Memorial Hall, which served 21 meals a week for $4.25.[16]

Yet Roosevelt got along with his fellow students on the *Crimson.* Though hardly a crusading president (he devoted his editorial energies to such issues as the deficiencies of the football team and the need for wider walkways in the Yard), he revealed a talent as a leader. Recalling that Roosevelt "liked people . . . and made them instinctively like him," his classmate and successor as *Crimson* president, Walter Russell Bowie, observed that "in his geniality was a kind of frictionless command."[17]

Though the *Crimson* presidency was a prestigious position, the pinnacle of social success at Harvard resided in membership in the Porcellian, the oldest and most exclusive of the "final clubs." On the face of it, Roosevelt seemed a perfect candidate — his father had been named an honorary member of Porcellian, and Cousin Theodore had also belonged. Roosevelt had also attended the right boarding school; of the sixteen juniors and seniors in Porcellian, five were Groton alumni.[18]

The Porcellian stood at the summit of Harvard's elaborate and rigid social hierarchy, which began to sort students from the moment the new freshmen arrived in Cambridge. By sophomore year, the class was officially divided into the social elect and the outsiders by the venerable Institute of 1770, which identified the one hundred members of the class most fit for "society." Elections were organized into groups of ten, with the first group chosen by the previous class, the "first ten" choosing the second, and so on until the tenth and final group had been selected. So exalted was election to the Institute that the Boston newspapers and the *Crimson* published the names of the students in the precise order in which they were admitted, a practice that continued through 1904.[19]

Roosevelt, however, was bypassed not only by the "first ten" but also by the four groups that followed. In late November, his roommate Lathrop Brown was chosen, and Roosevelt was in a state of intense anxiety. Finally, on January 9, 1902, he received word that he had been picked as "the first man among the 6th ten."[20] His election, albeit late, would give him automatic entrance to Delta Kappa Epsilon (also known as DKE or "the Dickey"), a secret fraternity that required its members to undergo arduous initiation rites that have been aptly described as "a curiously primitive rite of passage." But Roosevelt accepted these rites without complaint, writing to his mother that "I am about to be slaughtered, but quite happy nonetheless."[21]

Roosevelt's elation at being selected was understandable, for only the first seven or eight groups of ten from the hundred students admitted to the Institute of 1770 were invited to join the Dickey, and membership was a prerequisite for election to a final club. Nevertheless, the fact that fifty students had been placed ahead of a young man of such an unimpeachable background was surprising and a bad omen. FDR's placement may have reflected some personal qualities that caused irritation even within the Roosevelt family. On the Oyster Bay side of the clan (Theodore Roosevelt's side of the family), young Franklin had been given a variety of unflattering nicknames, including "Miss Nancy" (because he allegedly "pranced and fluttered" on the tennis court) and "Feather Duster" (a pun on FD deriving from his supposed resemblance to the "prettified boys" displayed on a well-known brand of handkerchief boxes). The gentlemanly and slight Roosevelt may have been viewed as somewhat lacking in those "manly" qualities then so highly valued — an impression consistent with a *Crimson* poster that referred to him as "Rosey Roosevelt, the Lillie of the Valley."[22]

Though friendly, hard-working, and well intentioned, Roosevelt was not universally liked by his peers. Some of them, including his Groton classmates, found him two-faced, a "false smiler," and — beneath the veneer of easy self-confidence — rather "pushy." Others, including some of the well-appointed women with whom he socialized, considered him shallow, excessively smug about his family's social standing, and priggish.[23] But whatever the sources of Roosevelt's weak social position within Harvard's Class of 1904, a rank of number 51 in the Institute of 1770 did not augur well for an invitation to the Porcellian Club, which accepted only eight new members annually.

Nevertheless, Roosevelt continued to hope that he would be elected.[24] Yet when the moment came, he was rejected.[25] It was a crushing blow — a deep humiliation for a young patrician who had taken for granted entry into the most rarefied social circles. Though he was elected to the Fly, another prestigious final club, it was little consolation. More than fifteen years later, when he was assistant secretary of the navy, Roosevelt told Sheffield Cowles (the son of Teddy Roosevelt's sister Anna) that his rejection by Porcellian had been the "greatest disappointment of my life" — a failure made still worse by the fact that two of Teddy Roosevelt's sons, Theodore Jr. and Kermit, had been elected to the club. Years later, Eleanor Roosevelt went so far as to claim that the incident had given her husband an "inferiority complex," albeit one that "had helped him to identify with life's outcasts."[26]

The Big Three in the Early Twentieth Century

In his intense preoccupation with social and extracurricular recognition, Franklin Delano Roosevelt was an emblematic student of his time. Not only at Harvard, but at Yale and Princeton as well, the academic side of the college experience ranked a distant third behind club life and campus activities. As a consequence, the competition for social position and the leadership of extracurricular activities could be — and often was — ferocious; in scholastic matters, however, the "gentleman's C" reigned supreme.

At the center of student consciousness was football, which had risen to extraordinary prominence in just three decades. Indeed, the term "Big Three" may be traced to the 1880s, when the three institutions established their dominance in collegiate football.[27] By 1893, the game between Yale and Princeton — then held in New York City — attracted 40,000 spectators and was such a compelling event that ministers cut short their Thanksgiving service to arrive at the game on time.[28] A decade later, Harvard Stadium — the first reinforced concrete structure in the world — opened to welcome 35,000 people to the Yale game. Harvard Stadium later expanded its seating capacity to 58,000, but it was its archrival Yale that in 1914 opened the largest football stadium in the nation, a shrine to football that seated 70,000 spectators.[29]

Although big-time college football has long since shifted to other schools and regions, Harvard, Yale, and Princeton were the preeminent powers in the nation at least through 1915. Yale, where the legendary Walter Camp (the inventor of the "All-American" team) served for many years as advisory coach, ran the leading football program in the country; between 1872 and 1909, the Yale Bulldogs won 324 games, lost 17, and tied 18.[30] For many Americans, the

Big Three were known primarily as football powerhouses; Frank Merriwell, the mythical Yale football hero of two hundred dime-store novels published between 1896 and 1916, became a gigantic mass phenomenon, with the series selling as many as 200,000 copies a week.[31]

Princeton, too, was a major force in football, winning or co-winning 9 national championships (compared to Yale's 14) between 1880 and 1915 and producing at least one All-American in every year but two between 1889 and 1914. Harvard, which lost regularly to Yale until a new coach changed its fortunes in 1908, fielded the weakest team of the Big Three.[32] According to Brooks Mather Kelley, "Yale's success against Harvard was so great that Cambridge men began to think of Yalies as nothing but muckers [hired professionals], while Yale men had serious doubts about the manliness of the Harvards."[33] Yet even Harvard was a major power, being designated national champion or co-national champion seven times between 1890 and 1913.[34] In 1919, Harvard — named co-national champion along with Notre Dame and Illinois — went to the Rose Bowl, where on January 1, 1920, it defeated Oregon, 7–6.[35]

But the Big Three were famous for far more than football. As America's most prominent colleges, they were widely viewed as training grounds for the nation's leaders. Between September 1901 and March 1921, no one occupied the White House who was not an alumnus of the Big Three. First Teddy Roosevelt (Harvard 1880), then William Howard Taft (Yale 1878), and finally Woodrow Wilson (Princeton 1879) served as president. Not since the early days of the Republic, when John Adams (Harvard 1755), James Madison (Princeton 1771), and John Quincy Adams (Harvard 1787) were elected to the presidency, had the nation seen anything like it.

Big Three alumni were also well represented among leading corporate chieftains. In one study of top executives in the early twentieth century, Harvard and Yale led the way; in another, Harvard ranked first, followed by Princeton, Columbia, and Yale.[36] Though self-made men such as Andrew Carnegie still loomed large in the world of corporate magnates, they overwhelmingly sent their own sons to elite private colleges. William Rockefeller (a brother and partner of John D.) and Edward Harriman, for example, were among the leading robber barons of the late nineteenth century, and neither had attended college. But their sons, William Rockefeller Jr. and Averell Harriman, both graduated from Yale. Even the great John Pierpont Morgan, a cultivated man from a privileged background, was not a college graduate; John Pierpont Morgan Jr., however, graduated from Harvard, where he founded his own final club (Delphic, also known as Gas) when he was slighted by the existing clubs.[37]

By the 1890s, Harvard, Yale, and Princeton had become iconic institutions, exerting a broad influence on the national culture and on the very definition of what it meant to be "a college man." Evidence of the public's interest in the Big Three was everywhere: in newspapers, in the crowds that flocked to football games, and in the campus portraits that had become regular features in national magazines such as *McClure's, Atlantic Monthly, North American Review,* and *Scribner's.*[38] Ernest Earnest, in his fine book *Academic Procession: An Informal History of the American College (1636–1953),* observed: "To an amazing degree the pattern set by Harvard, Yale and Princeton after 1880 became that of colleges all over the country. The clubs, the social organization, the athletes — even the clothes and the slang — of the 'big three' were copied by college youth throughout the nation."[39] Though Harvard, Yale, and Princeton may have faced stiff competition from other universities — notably Chicago, Columbia, and Johns Hopkins — in the battle for leadership in research and graduate education in the early years of the century, their dominance in setting the tone of undergraduate life was clear.[40]

Despite their growing prominence, however, Harvard, Yale, and Princeton faced serious problems. Yale had become the archetype of the elite private college through the immense popularity of Frank Merriwell and later of Dink Stover (the hero of Owen Johnson's 1912 novel, *Stover at Yale*), but deteriorating academic standards were a subject of intense internal discussion.[41] So, too, was the alleged decline in standards of deportment — a significant issue for an institution that prided itself on turning out "gentlemen." According to the Yale historian George W. Pierson, "Disorders, infractions, and petty irritations had been getting rather frequent and unnecessary." By 1902, "an unending stream of individuals had to be disciplined for cheating, or for drunken disorder, or for throwing bottles out the windows, or even for going sailing with low women."[42]

In 1903, a committee headed by Professor Irving Fisher issued a devastating report about the academic atmosphere at Yale. Scholarly performance, the report concluded, had been dropping regularly since 1896–1897, with the decline most marked among the highest-ranking students. The value system underpinning campus culture, which elevated social, athletic, and fraternal activities over scholarship, was at the root of the problem: "An impression is very strong and very prevalent that the athlete is working for Yale, the student for himself. To be a high-stand man is now a disadvantage rather than otherwise . . . In fact, hard study has become *unfashionable* at Yale."

"In general," the report went on, "the man who attends strictly to study (the 'grind') is regarded as peculiar or even contemptible. It is believed that a man should 'know men' at Yale; that 'study is a mistake.'" To support its sobering conclusions, the report offered an intriguing fact: whereas 26 of 34 of Yale's valedictorians had been tapped by one of Yale's prestigious senior societies between 1861 and 1894, only 3 of 9 had been tapped since.[43]

So anti-intellectual was the undergraduate culture at Yale that classes vied with one another for the honor of being the least studious. In 1904, the year-book boasted of having "more gentlemen and fewer scholars than any other class in the memory of man." But the Class of 1905, judged by the Fisher Committee to have been the worst in recent Yale history, bested its predecessor, offering the following ditty:

> Never since the Heavenly Host with all the Titans fought
>   Saw they a class whose scholarship
> Approached so close to naught.[44]

Meanwhile, the Yale senior societies continued to select their members on the basis of athletic talent, prominence in extracurricular affairs, and social background. And so great a public honor was election to a society that the question of who was (and was not) "tapped" on Tap Day was the subject of regular coverage in the *New York Times*.[45]

If intellect was not highly valued at turn-of-the-century Yale, it was perhaps even less esteemed at Princeton. Headed since 1888 by Francis Landley Patton, a Presbyterian theologian noted for his administrative laxity and his failure to enforce disciplinary and academic standards, Princeton had a reputation as the least academically serious member of the Big Three.[46] Patton himself hardly helped matters when he reportedly said at a faculty meeting: "Gentleman, whether we like it or not, we shall have to recognize that Princeton is a rich man's college and that rich men do not frequently come to college to study."[47] Patton also made a remark that was to haunt Old Nassau's reputation for years to come: Princeton was "the finest country club in America."[48]

A sense of the atmosphere at Princeton circa 1900 is provided by a newspaper account of a "rush" (a common event) that took place after the freshman-sophomore baseball game: "The first-year men won the game, and to celebrate the victory endeavored to parade the streets of Princeton under the protection of the junior class . . . a battle, in which fists and clubs were used freely, lasted for ten minutes. The sophomores, overwhelmed by numbers, slowly retreated, and a running fight ensued, which was stopped by the combatants becoming widely scattered over the campus. Many of the students were badly used up, but no serious injuries were inflicted."[49] Eugene O'Neill, who attended Old Nassau (as Princeton was often called by its alumni) a few years later before dropping out after nine months, found a similar atmosphere; "Princeton," he observed, "was all play and no work."[50] By the early twentieth century, being selected for membership in one of Princeton's eating clubs had become far more important to most students than their studies.[51]

So weak was Princeton's academic atmosphere that a faculty committee was formed in 1901 to investigate "the scholastic condition of the college."[52] Patton vigorously opposed its recommendation to raise academic standards, and by March 1902 a group of trustees began to look into the matter. It became apparent that Patton's end was near when, at a dinner at the Waldorf in New York, men from Harvard, Columbia, and Hopkins told several trustees in blunt terms that "Princeton was becoming the laughing stock of the academic world, that the President was neglecting his duty, the professors neglecting theirs, the students neglecting theirs, that Princeton was going to pieces."[53] In a matter of weeks, Patton had been forced to resign, and Woodrow Wilson, an eminent political scientist who had been on the faculty since 1890, was named president. Wilson spent much of the next eight years trying to raise his school's academic standards.[54]

Though Harvard was by far the most academically distinguished of the Big Three, it too suffered from a student culture largely hostile to academic exertion. As at Yale and Princeton, a faculty committee was formed at Harvard to identify the sources of low academic standards and to devise policies for elevating them. The committee, which was chaired by Le Baron Russell Briggs and included Harvard's future president A. Lawrence Lowell, concluded that the amount of time that students spent studying was "discreditably small."[55] Its analysis of replies to letters of inquiry from 245 instructors and 1,757 students revealed a surprising fact: the instructors believed that students spent twice as much time on their studies than they actually did. Even the better students were devoting only about 25 hours a week to academic work, including the 12 hours spent at lectures; the less committed students spent considerably less time on academic tasks.[56]

This was the era of Eliot's liberal — and much-criticized — elective system, and many students gravitated to the "snap" and "cinch" courses then abundantly available. So common was this practice that the students joked about "the Faculty of Larks and Cinches."[57] Henry Yeomans, a government professor who was himself an alumnus (1900), aptly described the atmosphere of the time: "Few, among either instructors or students, who knew the College about 1900, and who respected intellectual achievement, could be satisfied with conditions. A man who worked hard at his studies was too often called a 'grind.' As if the term were not sufficiently opprobrious, it was not uncommon to strengthen it to 'greasy grind.'" The problem, he believed, was made worse by "the development of a social cleavage between the men who studied and the men who played, or more commonly and worse, who loafed." In Yeomans's view, there could be little question about who set "the undergraduate standard of idleness: it was the rich and socially ambitious."[58]

The low academic standards at the Big Three were in no small part a product of just how easy it was to gain admission. A candidate had only to pass subject-based entrance examinations devised by the colleges. Like many American universities, Harvard, Yale, Princeton, and Columbia administered their own exams.[59] But the tests were not especially demanding, and a young man with modest intelligence from a feeder school like Groton could usually pass them with ease.[60] If he did not, however, he could take them over and over again to obtain the requisite number of passes.[61]

Even the unfortunate applicant who failed to pass exams in enough subjects could still be admitted with "conditions." In practice, this meant that he gained entrance by special action of the faculty. At each of the Big Three, admission with conditions became a common pathway to the freshman class; in 1907, 55 percent of those admitted at Harvard had failed to fulfill the entrance requirements.[62] Similarly, at Yale in 1909, the proportion of freshmen admitted with conditions was 57 percent; of these, 22 percent had one condition, 14 percent two, and 21 percent three.[63] Even Princeton, a smaller institution that was making a vigorous effort to raise its standards under Woodrow Wilson, admitted a clear majority of its students with one or more conditions; between 1906 and 1909, the proportion of students so admitted ranged from a low of 56 percent in 1909 to a high of 65 percent in 1907.[64]

Why would these eminent universities admit so many students who did not even meet their modest entrance requirements? Part of the answer is their eagerness to enroll what later came to be called "paying customers," for tuition provided the bulk of their income (over 60 percent at Harvard in 1903–1904).[65] But there was also a powerful sense of pride in sheer bigness, especially at Harvard and Yale. In the 1890s, *Harvard Graduates' Magazine* (*HGM*) bragged about how its enrollment had grown spectacularly and in the process outstripped Yale; in 1900, it boasted that Harvard had the largest undergraduate enrollment in the nation and that its total enrollment of over 4,000 placed it "among the great universities of the world, surpassed in population only by Berlin, Vienna, Madrid, and Paris." Harvard, *HGM* noted proudly, had passed England's two ancient universities, Oxford and Cambridge, which enrolled just 3,500 and 3,000 students respectively.[66]

Although Harvard, Yale, and Princeton were willing to allow the size of the freshman class to fluctuate from year to year to accommodate the growing number of students who could pass some or all of the required exams, there were powerful forces limiting expansion. In addition to escalating competition from smaller colleges, such as Dartmouth, Williams, and Amherst, there was an increasingly visible disconnect between the Big Three's traditional entrance requirements and the curricula offered by the nation's rapidly expanding public high schools.[67] Both Yale and Princeton required that candidates pass examinations in both Greek and Latin, thereby effectively excluding most high school graduates, for only a handful of public schools offered both languages.[68] Even Harvard, which under Eliot had abolished its Greek requirement in 1898, still required Latin — not a problem at well-established secondary schools such as Boston Latin and Philadelphia's Central High School, but still an insurmountable obstacle at most public schools.[69] The Big Three therefore found it hard to tap into the expanding pool of high school graduates — a point frankly admitted in 1909 in the *Princeton Alumni Weekly*, which noted that it did not recognize many of the subjects taught in public high schools while its own requirements, especially in classical languages, could not be fulfilled in most of them. Even the public schools in nearby New York City, the nation's largest urban center, did not offer the courses required by Princeton.[70]

Especially when coupled with the high cost of tuition, the net result of these requirements was that the students at Harvard, Yale, and Princeton were overwhelmingly from well-to-do backgrounds. Almost exclusively white (though in some years Harvard and Yale enrolled a handful of blacks) and composed largely of graduates of elite private schools, the student bodies represented the most privileged strata of society. Though Harvard — which had the most flexible entrance requirements and the most generous scholarship program — was a partial exception, the Big Three were strikingly homogeneous, not only in class and race, but also in religion and ethnicity.[71] At Princeton, whose country club reputation was not without justification, Catholics and Jews together made up only 5 percent of the freshmen in 1900; at Yale, which was in a city with a large immigrant population, the combined Catholic-Jewish population was just 15 percent in 1908.[72] Even Harvard, which was in a dense urban area with large numbers of immigrants from Ireland and southern and eastern Europe, the Catholic proportion of the freshmen was 9 percent in 1908, with Jews constituting roughly the same number.[73]

These were by no means trivial numbers, especially at Harvard and Yale, but it was clear that the same relatively compact social group predominated at each school: old-stock, high-status Protestants, especially Episcopalians, Congregationalists, and Presbyterians. The Big Three were, in short, overwhelmingly populated by white Anglo-Saxon Protestants, or WASPs — a term coined more than half a century later by the sociologist and chronicler of the WASP upper class, E. Digby Baltzell.[74]

The Protestant Upper Class and the Creation of a Cultural Ideal

As the nineteenth century ended, the Protestant upper class stood at the summit of a nation that was more powerful than ever before. For the first time in its history, the United States was a genuine global power; its population of 76 million far surpassed that of Great Britain, Germany, or France, and its economy was the most dynamic in the world. In 1898, the United States had made the fateful decision to enter into a war with Spain — "the splendid little war" that made the United States a colonial power, owning the Philippines, Guam, Hawaii, and Puerto Rico along with de facto control of Cuba.[75] The United States thus took its place among the great imperial powers in a world increasingly divided into zones controlled by the major European powers.

Though members of the Protestant upper class — notably Theodore Roosevelt, Henry Cabot Lodge, Elihu Root, John Hay, and Alfred T. Mahan — were at the forefront of the imperial project, the WASP elite was in fact bitterly divided over America's new imperial role. Indeed, it was graduates of Harvard and Yale who made up most of the members of the Anti-Imperialist League. And it was patricians such as William James, Thomas Wentworth Higginson, and Charles W. Eliot — joined by a diverse group that included Jane Addams, Samuel Gompers, Mark Twain, and Andrew Carnegie — who led the opposition to the annexation of the Philippines.[76] Condemning "Expansion, World-Power, Inferior Races, Calvination, Duty-and-Destiny" as "twaddle and humbug," the anti-imperialists ringingly reaffirmed America's tradition of anticolonialism — after all, the United States owed its very origins to its colonial struggle against Britain.[77]

Yet the proponents of a new and more muscular American global role carried the day, their cause strengthened by the brute reality that European powers had gained control of one-fifth of the world's land and one-tenth of its population between 1870 and 1900 and that recent years had seen the rise of Japan and Germany as colonial powers. In the wake of the new global position of the United States, many white Americans (though not Irish Americans), as the historian Nell Painter has noted, "renounced their traditional anglophobia (a legacy of the American Revolution and, especially, the War of 1812) to proclaim the kindredness of the English-speaking people and the natural superiority of Anglo-Saxons."[78] The ideology of Anglo-Saxonism, though hardly new, received a powerful boost from America's entry into the ranks of imperial nations. Among the core tenets of the ideology was the conviction that, not only blacks, Native Americans, and Asians, but also the burgeoning population of Italians, Jews, Poles, Irish, and other immigrants lacked the distinctly Anglo-Saxon talent for self-governance.[79]

During the three decades before 1900, the Protestant elite had become a true national upper class. Under the stimulus of rapid industrialization, urbanization, and nationalization of what had been a largely regional economy, the upper class developed a set of institutions that helped weld it into a national entity that bridged the cultural and social divide between the old patricians and the nouveaux riches of the Gilded Age. Among the upper-class institutions that either were invented or came to prominence in the 1880s and 1890s were the *Social Register* (its first edition was published in New York City in 1888), the country club, the exclusive summer resort, and the elite men's social clubs that arose in cities such as New York, Boston, and Philadelphia.[80]

Educational institutions — notably, boarding schools and the elite private colleges — played a critical role in socializing and unifying the national upper class. Indeed, it was only during this period that entry into the right clubs at Harvard, Princeton, and Yale — few of which predated the Civil War — became a student obsession. Meanwhile, the upper classes of the great eastern cities increasingly sent their children to the Big Three; by the 1890s, 74 percent of Boston's upper class and 65 percent of New York's sent their sons to either Harvard, Yale, or Princeton.[81]

Perhaps even more than the Big Three, the emblematic institution of the Protestant upper class was the private boarding school. Bringing together children as young as eleven from the upper classes of the major eastern metropolitan areas, the boarding school was the ideal instrument to shape the personal qualities and instill the values most esteemed by the Protestant elite. Educational and cultural ideals, Max Weber once observed, are always "stamped by the decisive stratum's . . . ideal of cultivation."[82] In the United States in the late nineteenth century, the "decisive stratum" was the WASP upper class and its ideal, that of the cultivated "gentleman" along British lines.

As early as 1879, the *North American Review,* a venerable magazine founded in Boston in 1815 that was one of the few American periodicals to compete with the great British quarterlies, published a two-part series, "The Public Schools of England." It was written by Thomas Hughes, the author of the popular *Tom Brown's School Days,* and it was intended to introduce an American audience to the peculiar British institution that had proved so successful in welding the aristocracy and the rising bourgeoisie into a cohesive ruling class.[83] Hughes proposed that private boarding schools on the British model be built in the United States to serve as a "stepping-stone . . . between the home of the American gentry and the universities."[84]

"It is not easy," he wrote, "to estimate the degree to which the English people are indebted to these schools for the qualities on which they pique themselves most — for their capacity to govern others and control themselves, their aptitude for combining freedom with order, their public spirit, their vigor and manliness of character, their strong but not slavish respect for public opinion, their love of healthy sport and exercise." "However discriminating a nation may be in spirit and character," he argued, "the time must come when it will breed a gentry, leisure class, aristocracy, call it by what name you will." The public schools had "perhaps the largest share in molding the character of the English gentleman." Two "nations of the same race, and so nearly identical in character and habits as the people of the United States and the English," Hughes concluded, would benefit from employing the same type of educational institutions to shape their leadership class.[85]

Less than four years later, a young Massachusetts patrician named Endicott Peabody proposed the establishment of a boarding school in New England almost exactly on the model described by Hughes. A member of a distinguished family whose roots went back to the Puritans, at the age of thirteen Peabody had moved to England, where his father joined Junius Morgan (the father of J. P. Morgan) as a partner in a banking firm. "Cotty," as the young man was called by friends, immediately entered Cheltenham, an English public school, and soon became a devoted Anglophile. The sturdy Peabody flourished at Cheltenham, joining enthusiastically in the athletic life of the school and becoming skilled in cricket, tennis, and rowing. After five years at Cheltenham, he went on to Trinity College at Cambridge, where he studied law and once again was a star athlete. Though born a Unitarian, Cotty developed a deep attachment to the Church of England during his time at Cambridge.[86]

By the time Peabody returned to the United States in 1880, he was as much British as American in both speech and demeanor. In search of a career, he initially followed the family tradition by joining Lee, Higginson and Company, a brokerage firm founded many years earlier. But he quickly became restive in business and soon enrolled at the Episcopal Theological Seminary in Cambridge. A competent but uninspired student, he briefly left the seminary before being ordained to serve as parson in the remote town of Tombstone, Arizona. Cotty then returned to complete his studies, and it was there, in the spring of 1883, that he conceived the idea of a school that would stress religious education and Christian life while striking a balance between the acquisition of culture and participation in athletics. His vision, shared by his fellow seminarian and lifelong friend Sherrand Billings, was of "a school where boys and men could live together, work together, and play together in friendly fashion with friction rare."[87]

For most twenty-five-year-old men, such a vision might be a distant dream, but Endicott Peabody was no ordinary young man. Tall, broad-shouldered, blue-eyed, and fair-haired, he was a striking presence whose enthusiasm, energy, and obvious decency left a strong impression. More than personal presence was needed, of course; founding a school, especially a boarding school on the British model, would require considerable resources. Cotty's family, fortunately, was at the center of a network of some of the wealthiest and most powerful patricians in the United States, so resources would prove no obstacle. Starting with his relative James Lawrence, who (along with his brother) donated ninety scenic acres of farmland for the school, Peabody put together a board of trustees that included J. P. Morgan, James and William Lawrence, Phillips Brooks, and his father, Samuel Endicott Peabody. Its site was approved by no less a figure than Frederick Law Olmsted, the renowned landscape architect. The Groton School opened its doors in the fall of 1884.[88]

Groton was the second of seven elite boarding schools — the others were Lawrenceville (1883), Hotchkiss (1892), Choate (1896), St. George's (1896), Middlesex (1901), and Kent (1906) — founded between 1883 and 1906.[89] It was a period of tremendous social change in America, and many of the transformations were deeply disturbing to the old Protestant upper class. Mass immigration and rapid urbanization, in particular, created a sense among patricians that they were losing control of the country, especially its cities. Increasingly, they withdrew to their own clubs and summer resorts.

The transformed urban environment of the late nineteenth century presented a distinctive set of problems for the rearing of upper-class children; whereas in previous years the elite had relied on private day schools and tutors to educate their offspring, they believed that the city had become an unhealthy place for children to grow up. One solution could be to send them to an undefiled rural or small-town setting in which Christian educators of solid character could be entrusted with their children's moral development.[90]

The official announcement of the opening of "a School for Boys in Groton, Massachusetts" made a direct appeal to these sentiments: "Every endeavor will be made to cultivate manly, Christian character, having regard to moral and physical as well as intellectual development . . . A farm of ninety acres, in a healthy and attractive situation near the town of Groton, 34 miles from Boston and in direct communication with New York, has been given the school, and upon this estate will be erected during the coming season a building with classrooms and dormitory." In a preface to the announcement, the trustees described the idea of Groton as "an attempt to found a boys' school in this country somewhat after the manner of the Public Schools of England"; they noted that the headmaster was a graduate of Cambridge University who had spent five years at Cheltenham. Like its British counterparts, which were "under the influence of the Church of England," Groton would be "under the influence of the Protestant Episcopal Church" and its headmaster, an Episcopalian clergyman.[91]

The tiny Groton School was an almost immediate success. Within five years of its founding, Theodore Roosevelt, who had declined Peabody's invitation to become one of the school's first teachers, wrote to the headmaster, telling him that he was "doing a most genuine service to America" and that "it has been a great comfort to me to think of small Ted [then ten years old] at your school."[92] In 1889, Peabody was asked to apply for the presidency of Columbia University (he declined), and in 1890, the prominent diplomat and future secretary of state John Hay asked Peabody to place his two sons on the list of students wishing to attend Groton. To support his request, he offered a list of references that included Oliver Wendell Holmes, Henry Adams, and Phillips Brooks. (In the end, Peabody placed the boys on the wrong waiting list, and they were forced to attend other schools.) Even Emily Post entered one son's name at birth for admission to Groton and the other's at age two.[93] By 1900, a veritable *Who's Who* of the American ruling class — Whitneys, Biddles, Adams, Saltonstalls, du Ponts, and Roosevelts — had entrusted their sons to Endicott Peabody and Groton.[94]

Social distinction was at the very center of Groton's magnetic appeal to the Protestant upper class. Peabody himself — with his patrician appearance, his gentlemanly demeanor, and his ardent commitment to the boys' cultivation of impeccable manners — attracted the scions of leading families. The men of wealth and power who entrusted their sons to him were well aware of his unique social position. To be sure, many other boarding school headmasters shared his background (if not his British education). But none of them could match his personal location at the crossroads of America's two most important investment banking firms of the era — the House of Morgan and Lee, Higginson and Company — in New York and Boston, the nation's two greatest financial centers.[95] To the Protestant elite, a Groton education meant, not only the inculcation of the right values, but also the fostering of intimate ties to "the right people." One of the principal motivations to send boys to Groton and like institutions seems to have been their parents' desire to rescue them from the life of luxury and self-indulgence that they feared the children were destined to lead unless vigorous countermeasures were taken. "Early Groton parents," wrote Peabody's biographer (and Groton alumnus) Frank Ashburn, were privately disgusted with the bringing up of well-to-do American boys of the period, "whom they considered 'spoiled ladies' men tied to women's apron strings."[96] Affluence, they believed, was rendering their sons soft and effeminate.

In response to these concerns, the "St. Grottlesex" schools imposed a regime of Spartan deprivation on their charges. At Groton, the students lived in small, barren cubicles almost totally lacking in privacy. Showers were cold, and weekly allowances were limited to a quarter, a nickel of which was to be donated at Sunday church services. Deprivation, Peabody firmly believed, was salutary; otherwise, the parental "tendency to overindulge their children" would lead to a "lack [of] intellectual and moral and physical fibre."[97]

What did not loom large among these parents was a commitment to intellect. "For scholarship as such," Ashburn observed, "many parents never gave a hang"; indeed, many of the most eminent among them had never attended college themselves.[98] What they correctly saw in Peabody was a man who considered character far more important than intellect. In hiring teachers, the rector (as everyone called him) valued intelligence, but he believed that "there were things distinctly more important" such as "fine character," a "lively manner," and a love of boys.[99]

At the core of Peabody's vision of Groton was the ideal of "manly, Christian character." Though the WASP elite was not particularly religious (Ashburn notes, "Some of the early fathers do not seem to have cared tuppence for religion, except as a thing to be generally encouraged and strengthened"), it found this vision congenial.[100] Especially appealing was the emphasis on "manly" character, for the elite (and not only the elite) was deeply worried that American men were losing their "manliness." A variety of forces were behind this fear — the closing of the frontier, the rise of white-collar employment, the decline of family farms and businesses, the paucity of opportunities in the decades after the Civil War to express valor on the battlefield, and the expanding role of women.[101] What Peabody implicitly promised was to turn their often fragile and overindulged sons into the kind of "manly" men fit to run the affairs of a great nation.

The idea of "manly Christian character" was a British import that may be traced back to the writings of Charles Kingsley (1819–1875), an Anglican clergyman, novelist, and Cambridge professor who exerted a profound influence on the young Peabody.[102] A passionate advocate of what came to be known as "muscular Christianity," Kingsley was a devoted English patriot and a stout defender of British imperialism. A proponent of a reformist strand of "Christian socialism," he believed that committed Christians were warriors on behalf of goodness whose responsibilities both at home and abroad could not be met without great "strength and hardihood."[103] Kingsley was a firm champion of vigorous athletics, for sports would instill the sturdy character and shape the strong body that permitted Christians to do God's work. Athletics, he believed, would offer England's privileged classes "that experience of pain and endurance necessary to bring out the masculine qualities."[104]

Kingsley was near the height of his influence when Peabody was a student at Cheltenham and Cambridge. Early in his college career, the young American read the *Life of Charles Kingsley,* which first gave him the idea of becoming a minister. Kingsley's biographer, Peabody later recalled, "set forth his subject's enthusiasm in connection with social problems" and "introduced me to a man of vigorous, virile, enthusiastic character; a gentle, sympathetic, and unafraid example of muscular Christianity, a 'very' gentil Knight."[105] Kingsley's distinctive version of muscular Christianity exerted an enduring impact on Peabody as well as on the headmasters of many other leading American boarding schools.[106]

As at the British public schools, Groton's vehicle for the development of manly Christian character was athletics. Competing in sports, Peabody believed, helped develop in students a multiplicity of virtues: loyalty, courage, cooperation, and masculine strength. By teaching young men to exert themselves to the fullest while playing within the rules, athletics would teach self-control and a sense of decency and fair play.

Though quite attached to crew and "fives" (a kind of squash imported from Eton), Peabody reserved his greatest enthusiasm for football. All boys, however physically slight or personally uninterested, had to play.[107] Football was, in Peabody's view, a deeply moral enterprise. Writing to a friend in 1909, he articulated his views: "In my work at Groton I am convinced that foot ball [*sic*] is of profound importance for the moral even more than the physical development of the boys. In these days of exceeding comfort, the boys need an opportunity to endure hardness and, it may be, suffering. Foot ball has in it the element which goes to make a soldier."[108] For Peabody, as for many of his contemporaries in the British and American upper classes, life was a ruthless Darwinian struggle between good and evil in which the morally superior — those who represented "civilization" against "barbarism" — would sometimes need physical force to impose moral order.[109]

With athletes occupying the apex of the student pecking order, both Christianity and character tended to be overshadowed by "manliness."[110] Ranking lower still was intellect — a quality that was viewed with suspicion as oriented to the self rather than the community. "I'm not sure I like boys who think too much," Peabody once said. "A lot of people think of things we could do without."[111]

In such an atmosphere, the boy of bookish or artistic inclination who lacked interest in — or talent for — manly sports was relegated to the lower ranks and sometimes despised. Remembering his years at Groton, Ellery Sedgwick, the editor of the *Atlantic Monthly* who later became a trustee, recalled "but a single instance of a boy who became the acknowledged head of the school wholly innocent of athletic supremacy and merely gifted with character and superlative intelligence." In a school in which "organized sport is the personification of manliness" and the belief widespread that "moral courage is a by-product of the physical struggle," Sedgwick observed, "the boy who seeks another path to his development presents to the master a picture of a shirker and not infrequently a poltroon as well."[112]

There was little room at Groton for the boy of artistic or intellectual inclination; as his biographer admits, Peabody "distrusted artists as a genus," believing them to be "a folk who have unreliable relationships with the world, the flesh, and the devil, with a consequent weakening of moral fiber."[113] Nor was there much room for the independent spirit; in a letter to the parents of a boy whom Peabody suggested "would get more from a different school," the young man, whose offenses were admittedly "very slight," seems to have been guilty of the crime of being "an individualist who has little in common with his surroundings."[114]

Peabody was fond of saying that a headmaster has "to be a bit of a bully" and needs to have the capacity to inflict pain.[115] But in Groton's system of authority and social control, it was often the students who used the harshest means to enforce conformity and to punish classmates judged deviant. For students deemed to be in violation of the school's rigid and sometimes mysterious code of etiquette or who were felt to be lacking the right "tone" (often by showing insufficient deference to upperclassmen), the punishment could be brutal.

George Biddle, of the Class of 1904, describes what would happen when a student was judged to run afoul of school norms:

> The heaviest of the fourth-formers — perhaps a dozen of them — grabbed the offender, jerked him off the ground, and ran him down the cellar-stairway to the lavatories in approved football rush . . . A first offender was given only about ten seconds. The water came from the open spigot with tremendous force and the stream could be concentrated in violence by thumb and forefinger. Besides the culprit was winded and frightened and held upside down during the pumping. He was being forcibly drowned for eight or ten seconds. Then he was jerked to his feet, coughing, choking, retching . . . If he hadn't had enough the first time he was put under again for ten seconds.[116]

Employed until the 1920s, "pumping" was carried out with the approval of the senior prefect (the school's highest-ranking student authority, appointed by the headmaster) and the knowledge of the rector himself. Among those students pumped in the early years at Groton were Teddy Roosevelt Jr. (who was judged "fresh and swell-headed"), the future secretary of state Dean Acheson ("cheeky"), and Peabody's own son, Malcolm ("bad tone").[117]

The harsh atmosphere was part of a larger system of socialization that imposed on the children of the privileged a willful regime of austerity and deprivation. These schools were hardening the sons of the elite for a life of command in which subordinates — whether inferior classes, ethnic or racial groups, or colonial "natives" — would often be disinclined to obey and would sometimes mount resistance. The system of power and control at the elite boarding schools was devised to expose the young men who went through them to the experience of both obedience and command, often under trying conditions. Having survived institutionalized bullying, the graduates would have the necessary toughness to succeed in their future leadership positions.[118]

The Groton ethos, like that of the leading British public schools, was an uneasy admixture of two seemingly contradictory systems of belief: gentility and social Darwinism.[119] On the one side, men such as Peabody were deeply committed to the nurturance of Christian gentlemen: men whose devotion to such virtues as honesty, integrity, loyalty, modesty, decency, courtesy, and compassion would constitute a living embodiment of Protestant ideals.[120] But on the other side, life was viewed as a struggle in which the battle went to the strong, and those individuals and nations not manly enough to participate would be left remorselessly behind in a world in which only the fittest survived. The Christian gentleman thus had no choice but to be aggressive and even ruthless in order to win.[121]

Peabody's most important ally in promulgating this ideology was Theodore Roosevelt, who had been preaching the virtues of "the strenuous life" since the 1890s. A close friend of Peabody's and the father of a student, TR was a frequent visitor at Groton, where he unfailingly preached the virtues of a life of gentlemanly service to the public. In a speech on Groton's twentieth anniversary, in 1904, President Roosevelt told the students: "You are not entitled, either in college or life, to an ounce of privilege because you have been to Groton — not an ounce, but we are entitled to hold you to exceptionable accountability because you have been to Groton. Much has been given you, therefore we have a right to expect much of you."[122]

Adherence to the philosophy of "the strenuous life," Roosevelt believed, implied a "duty toward the people living in barbarism to see that they are freed from their chains, and we can free them only by destroying barbarism itself."[123] The Christian gentleman, then, was impelled on both moral and practical grounds to take up what some have called the "gentleman's burden": the responsibility, in the wake of the Spanish-American War, to "fulfill duties to the nation and . . . to the race" and to "do our share of the world's work by bringing order out of chaos in the great, fair tropic islands from which the valor of our soldiers has driven the Spanish flag."[124]

Peabody, whose beloved Cheltenham had sent many of its graduates into the imperial civil service in India, shared Roosevelt's enthusiasm for America's fledgling empire. Indeed, even before the Spanish-American War ended, he wrote to Senator Henry Cabot Lodge, offering Groton as a source of the officials who would be needed to administer the empire.[125] Yet Peabody was not, as the historian James McLachlan has rightly noted, "a howling imperialist; he simply believed that if America was to have an empire, it should be a Progressive empire — honestly administered by well-educated gentlemen, pure, clean, and Christian."[126]

Peabody's proposal to Lodge was an expression of his abiding commitment to public service. Inscribed in the school's motto — Cui Servire Est Regnare, "To serve is to reign"[127] — the emphasis on service was at once a noble and altruistic ideal and an expression of a deeply embedded assumption that the type of young men who went to Groton would (and should) rule America. "In season and out," recalled Ellery Sedgwick, "public service was held up to every boy as a shining goal."[128] Yet the rector's dedication to public service was not purely disinterested, for public *service* is also a form of public *power*.[129] And to the extent that the power exercised by a small group was perceived as serving the public good, it would enjoy the legitimacy that was the condition of its survival.

Despite Peabody's constant exhortations, most Grotonians rejected the call to public service, choosing instead to pursue lucrative careers in the private sector. While the rector was urging his boys to "keep away from Wall Street," the financial centers of New York City held a special allure for "Grotties."[130] According to a study carried out by Groton, the majority of alumni worked in business, with a particularly heavy concentration in "finances, stocks, bonds, etc."; according to another study, Grotonians were especially well represented in finance and banking, with a striking presence in J. P. Morgan and Company and Lee, Higginson and Company.[131] A Groton alumnus from the Class of 1906 captured the depth of resistance to Peabody's efforts: "When he urged the boys to be true to themselves and drop out of their parents' income class, they simply did not hear him. They were going to make money enough to be able to send their sons to Groton."[132] Two students of the American establishment have put it well: for most Groton graduates, "service to God and Country was overshadowed by service to Mammon."[133]

Yet for a small but influential group, Peabody's call to service struck a chord. The Boston wing of the Social Gospel movement, the historian Arthur Mann has argued, could be divided into two main groups: "the moderates, who wished to Christianize capitalism; and the radicals, who wished to socialize Christianity."[134] No radical, Peabody clearly belonged to the first group, but he was sincere — as was TR — in his desire to soften the rough edges of a system too often dominated by greed. Inspired by the rector's quest for ameliorating reforms, a number of Groton alumni — among them, Averell Harriman, Dean Acheson, and Sumner Welles — dedicated their lives to public service.[135]

One young Grotonian who took Peabody seriously was Franklin Delano Roosevelt. Registered by his parents at Groton in 1883, before construction of the school had even begun (and when he was just a year old), FDR came from a family committed to the same ideal of manly Christian character as Peabody.[136] His father, James Roosevelt, so respected the rector that he wrote to him a few years before his son was scheduled to enter the school, asking if he could recommend "a New England man," if possible "a *gentleman* . . . with the culture and training of Englishmen, combined with the standard character of the American gentleman" to serve as a tutor.[137] Though Peabody's reply has been lost, a clearer statement of the social and cultural ideals the two men shared would be hard to find.

Like many of his classmates, young Franklin felt respect bordering on awe toward Peabody. But unlike many of his peers, he genuinely shared the rector's deeply felt religious beliefs. To FDR, as to Peabody, the essence of Episcopalian faith was "a pure, simple, unquestioning and unquestioned belief in God as a loving Father and in the consequent ultimate beneficence of universal processes."[138] According to Eleanor Roosevelt, her husband's deep religious faith — which she described as "simple," but "unwavering and direct" — was an important source of his self-confidence, his faith in his own judgment, and his belief that he and the people he represented would ultimately prevail.[139]

As a student, Roosevelt was active in the Groton Missionary Society, frequently visiting an eighty-four-year-old black woman who was the widow of a Civil War drummer and twice serving as a counselor in a two-week summer camp that Groton held for children from the slums of Boston and New York.[140] These activities reflected his devotion to Peabody's ethic, and they were the first step in a life devoted to public service. Yet Roosevelt's commitment to being of service to others was not entirely innocent of self-interest; in a paper written during his second year at Harvard, trying to explain why some of the great old Dutch families of New Amsterdam, but not the Roosevelts, had gone into decline, he suggested that their fall had occurred because "they lack progressiveness and the true democratic spirit." The Roosevelts, on the other hand, had retained great "virility" as a family because "they have felt that being born in a good position, there was no excuse for them if they did not do their duty by the community."[141]

Though Roosevelt was energetic and intelligent, he never gained Peabody's full approval while at Groton. True, the rector had written a generous note to his parents on his graduation, describing him as "a thoroughly faithful scholar and a most satisfactory member of the school throughout his course" from whom he would part "with reluctance." Nevertheless, Peabody had denied him the school's highest honor — being named a senior prefect.[142] More than three decades later, the rector offered his candid assessment of Roosevelt as a student: "He was a quiet, satisfactory boy of more than ordinary intelligence, taking a good position in his Form but not brilliant. Athletically, he was rather too slight for success. We all liked him."[143]

Yet Roosevelt remained one of his most loyal "boys," asking him to officiate at his wedding, sending all four of his sons to Groton, and saving every single one of the birthday cards that the rector sent him (as he did all Groton alumni) annually.[144] In 1932, when FDR ran for president, Peabody voted for Hoover, judging him an "abler man" even though he had been "very fond of" Franklin "ever since he was a small boy." Nevertheless, his position was to separate politics from personal sentiment: "I do not," he wrote to Ellery Sedgwick, "consider personal relationships when I am casting my vote for a Government official."[145] Perhaps to soften the blow to Roosevelt — that a man whom he so admired would fail to support him at the climactic moment of his political career — Mrs. Peabody sent him a letter of apology.[146]

Yet Peabody was proud of Franklin's ascension to the presidency, describing it as "very much in the tradition of the Groton School."[147] FDR, in turn, maintained a reverential attitude toward the rector, whom he invited to preside over religious services at St. John's Episcopal Church on inauguration day in March 1933. There Roosevelt sang hymns with the rector, who had asked for "Thy blessing upon thy servant, Franklin."[148] Roosevelt's public display of religiosity met with Peabody's strong approval, and the rector later wrote to him that "it is a great thing for our country to have before it the leadership of a man who cares primarily for spiritual things. At a time when the minds of men are distraught and their faith unsteady, a spiritual leader at the head of the nation brings fresh power to the individual and to the cause of Christ and His Church." "To us in this School," he added, "it is a great thing to be able to point to a Groton graduate, now in the highest position in the country, believing in the Church and devoted to its interests."[149]

Throughout his years in the White House, FDR and Peabody maintained a lively correspondence, with the president always beginning "My Dear Mr. Peabody" and the rector responding with "My Dear Franklin." As the New Deal unfolded, it became increasingly clear to Peabody that FDR was trying to introduce changes that embodied the moderate strand of Social Gospel reformism to which the rector adhered. In 1935 Peabody wrote to the president, praising him as a man with "one supreme purpose in mind, the guidance of this country in such a way that all its citizens who are minded to do honest work shall have a chance to secure a living free from anxiety and with an opportunity for the development of which they are capable." The rector singled out for praise the Social Security Act and the Civilian Conservation Corps, but it was FDR's larger vision — "that there should be throughout the land a greater emphasis laid upon the duty of the citizen to the community and this even among those who were formerly considering only their own interests" — that caused him to "most heartily rejoice."[150]

Though Peabody did not agree with all of Roosevelt's policies and rhetoric ("I do wish that Franklin had not denounced big business men as a class"), he defended him stoutly against his enemies, especially those who accused him of insincerity and a lack of integrity.[151] Having known him so long, the rector was secure in his evaluation: "While Roosevelt is not in my judgment a particularly aggressive person, I believe that when he is convinced that a thing should be done he has [the] courage to put it through."[152] Roosevelt was, in short, a man of sound character, and that was good enough for the rector.

Peabody's enthusiasm was not shared by the vast majority of Groton graduates. At a dinner at the Union Club in New York City given in honor of the rector as he was approaching his eighty-first birthday, he addressed the anti-Roosevelt mania among Groton graduates, telling the assembled: "Something has troubled me a good deal lately. Personally I don't pretend to know much about politics or economics. But in national crises like the present one, we get pretty excited and perhaps we give vent to expressions that later on we are sorry for. I believe Franklin Roosevelt to be a gallant and courageous gentleman. I am happy to count him as a friend."[153] Silence greeted his remarks — a fitting response, perhaps, for a group in which the sentiment was widespread that FDR was a "traitor to his class." But in Peabody's view, Roosevelt was rather its savior. In a context in which "change of a drastic nature was called for," the president's reforms "secured this country from the serious attacks made upon it by extreme radicals."[154]

By 1940, with the Nazis occupying France and poised to overrun Britain, the United States faced the greatest threat to its survival since the Civil War. Realizing the nation was in peril, Peabody and Roosevelt drew even closer, affirming the basic values they had long held in common. On April 25, 1940, FDR wrote to Peabody: "More than forty years ago you said, in a sermon in the old Chapel, something about not losing boyhood ideals in later life. Those were Groton ideals — taught by you — I try not to forget — and your words are still with me and with hundreds of others of 'us boys.'"[155] Less than six weeks later, with Paris about to fall to the Germans, Roosevelt wrote to the rector once again, assuring him that he was "deeply conscious of the great responsibilities resting on this country in the present dark hour of the world's history" and firmly "convinced that the people of the United States will not fail in upholding, and, if necessary in defending, the ideals which have made their nation great." Peabody responded immediately, praising the "high wisdom and magnificent courage" with which the president was confronting the "grave problems" facing the nation.[156]

Roosevelt was disappointed that Peabody, then eighty-three, was unable to preside over religious services at the start of his third term, in January 1941, but his response was magnanimous: "I count it among the blessings of my life that it was given to me in formative years to have the privilege of your guiding hand and the benefit of your inspiring example."[157] They remained in contact, exchanging notes in the immediate aftermath of the attack on Pearl Harbor and visiting in 1942. Although Peabody was twenty-five years his senior, Roosevelt apparently found it difficult to conceive that the sturdy headmaster was mortal, for when he wrote the directions for his funeral service, he requested that the rector preside. When the end finally came for Peabody, in November 1944, the person with him at his sudden death reported that they had been chatting pleasantly and that his last words were: "Franklin Roosevelt is a very religious man."[158]

Gravely ill himself, Roosevelt was shaken by Peabody's death and sent this wire: "The whole tone of things is going to be a bit different from now on, for I have leaned on the Rector all these many years far more than most people know."[159] Soon after, in his 1945 inaugural address, the president harkened back to something that "my old schoolmaster had said": that "things in life will not always run smoothly . . . [but that] the great fact to remember is that the trend of civilization itself is forever upward; that a line drawn through the middle of the peaks and valleys of the centuries always has an upward trend."[160] Remarkably, these words reprised the rector's sermon that FDR had heard almost forty-five years earlier, at the dedication of Groton's new chapel on October 15, 1900.[161] Things came full circle: three months after his own address, Roosevelt too was dead of a cerebral hemorrhage.

Though Roosevelt had been Peabody's most renowned student, the rector's standing in the larger community had been established long before FDR became a public figure. In 1904, with President Theodore Roosevelt delivering the keynote address and Franklin (recently graduated from Harvard) in attendance, Peabody presided at a festive celebration of Groton's twentieth anniversary. Prominent old Grotonians poured in from distant quarters, but the most visible sign of the school's remarkable success came from the presence of representatives from Harvard and Yale, both of which conferred honorary degrees on the rector. In granting Peabody a master of arts, Yale attached the citation: "What strength is to weakness, what experience is to ignorance or blind confidence, what light and faith are to darkness and doubt, what courage is to trembling fear, what the spiritual potter is to the pliant clay of youthful character, what Paul was to Timothy — that, all that, is the Head Master of Groton School to the young manhood blessed with his devoted instruction and companionship." Harvard, still the destination of most Groton graduates, did Yale one better, conferring on the rector a doctorate of sacred theology. Its citation read: "Endicott Peabody, graduate of the English Cambridge, clergyman, headmaster of a school for boys that stands for purity, manliness, and helpfulness."[162]

In two short decades, Groton had established itself as the nation's most prestigious boarding school, exerting an influence that went far beyond the small social group in which it originated.[163] Yet Groton and comparable schools rarely spoke in public of cultivating "Christian gentlemen"; instead, they called for building "character" — a way of freeing the values embodied in the notion of a gentleman from their association with a particular social class.[164] By conferring honorary degrees on Endicott Peabody — the quintessential Christian gentleman — Harvard and Yale were consecrating the educational and cultural ideals that he and his school represented. Implicit in these ideals was a particular definition of "merit" — one that considered "character," "manliness," and athletic accomplishment as important as academic excellence. Less than two decades later, when Harvard, Yale, and Princeton adopted selective admissions policies and for the first time imposed a limit on the size of the freshman class, it was this definition that profoundly shaped the admissions criteria — and the social composition — of the Big Three.

CHAPTER 2

The Big Three Before Selective Admissions

I F ENDICOTT PEABODY WAS the leading headmaster in the United States, then Harvard's Charles W. Eliot (1834–1926) was the nation's leading college president. But to say that he was the most renowned figure in American higher education is to vastly understate his importance, for his influence went well beyond the academy. Dubbed "First Citizen of the Republic" by Theodore Roosevelt (whose feelings toward him were, at best, ambivalent) and referred to by Harvard's philosophy professor Ralph Barton Perry as "adviser at large to the American people on things in general," Eliot was revered by both his peers in higher education and his fellow citizens.[1] When he retired in 1909 after forty years of service, he had succeeded not only in transforming Harvard but in changing the definition of a great university. No college president, before or since, has exerted a greater impact on the shape and character of American higher education.

Like Peabody, Eliot came from a distinguished Massachusetts family whose roots dated back to colonial times. The first Eliot arrived in America in 1669, and by the late eighteenth century the family had amassed a fortune in trade.[2] Even by the exacting standards of Boston's upper class, Eliot's lineage was distinguished. His grandfather, perhaps the wealthiest Bostonian of his time, had endowed Harvard's Eliot Professorship of Greek. His father, Samuel Atkins Eliot, served as mayor of Boston as well as treasurer of Harvard College and ex officio member of the Harvard Corporation, Harvard's governing body.[3] In a world in which a small and tightly connected group of families from the Protestant upper class effectively controlled both Harvard and Boston's major social institutions, Eliot was a Brahmin's Brahmin.[4]

Harvard: Eliot, Lowell, and the Clash of Visions

Though Eliot shared Peabody's background, his views on many matters differed sharply from those of the rector. A generally liberal and tolerant man, especially by the standards of his time and milieu, Eliot opposed the Spanish-American War, lending his name to a group of 85 Harvard professors against the fighting.[5] Eliot, unlike Peabody, remained loyal to his Unitarian origins and adopted a broadly ecumenical view, with a goodly dose of skepticism toward established religious dogmas, including those of his own church. A firm believer in freedom of religion, Eliot eliminated required chapel in 1886 — an action not taken until 1926 at Yale and 1964 at Princeton.[6] "Institutional Christianity," he once wrote, could "still be very un-Christlike."[7]

A progressive on many social and political issues, including immigration (he opposed restriction), sex education (he favored it), and foreign policy (he had a strong preference for diplomacy over force), he was among the most liberal members of the Protestant elite. But his decidedly liberal views on educational matters had the greatest impact on Harvard. During his presidency, student freedom grew dramatically; having little taste for regulating students, he cut the length of the student rulebook from forty pages to five while radically increasing the number of courses offered.[8] His most famous reform — one which had an enduring impact on American higher education — was the adoption of an elective system, in which students were almost entirely free to choose their own courses. Whether in the realm of curriculum or of private life, students at Harvard enjoyed a degree of freedom unknown at Yale or Princeton.[9]

Above all, Eliot was a democrat; unlike many Brahmins, he had a genuine faith in America's democratic institutions and in the role of education in fostering democratic self-governance.[10] As for Harvard itself, Eliot held a broadly inclusive view. To be sure, the university's mission was to train an elite, but it was to be an elite drawn from all segments of society. In his celebrated inaugural address, delivered on October 19, 1869, he articulated his vision: "The poorest and the richest students are equally welcome here, provided that with their poverty or their wealth they bring capacity, ambition, and purity. The poverty of scholars is of inestimable worth in this money-getting nation . . . The poor friars, not the bishops, saved the church. The poor scholars and preachers of duty defend the modern community against its own material prosperity. Luxury and learning are ill bedfellows."[11] Harvard, Eliot insisted, must be open, not only to the sons of the "city trader or professional man," but also to the boy whose father was a "farmer or mechanic, who finds it a hard sacrifice to give his boy his time early enough to enable him to prepare for college." To this end, Harvard offered more scholarships than any other college in the country so that "those who prove themselves men of capacity and character . . . never go away for lack of money."[12]

If Eliot perhaps exaggerated the degree to which nineteenth-century Harvard was open to talented young men regardless of financial circumstances, he was nonetheless deeply committed to keeping the university affordable so that students of limited means could attend. In 1904, he wrote to Charles

Francis Adams, a member of the Board of Overseers who had long been one of his sharpest critics:

> You said at the start of this discussion about raising the College fee that you wanted the College open to young men who had either money or brains. The gist of our difference lies, I think, in this restricted alternative. I want to have the College open equally to men with much money, little money, or no money, provided that they all have brains. I care no more than you for young men who have no capacity for an intellectual life. They are not fit subjects for a college, whether their parents have money or not. I am inclined to think that you would be more tolerant than I of the presence of stupid sons of the rich. I care for the young men whose families have so little money that it would make a real difference to them whether the Harvard tuition fee were $150 or $225. You do not seem to care for that large class. To my thinking, they constitute the very best part of Harvard College.[13]

Despite considerable financial pressure, Eliot held firm, and tuition did not rise again at Harvard until 1916.[14]

Though an ardent proponent of equality of opportunity, Eliot was no egalitarian. In his inaugural address, he stated flatly that "the community does not owe superior education to all children, but only to the elite — to those who, having the capacity prove by hard work that they have also the necessary perseverance and endurance."[15] This meritocratic credo, which guided Eliot throughout his life, was elaborated in his famous 1897 essay, "The Function of Education in a Democratic Society." In it he made clear that he saw the provision of upward mobility through education as a bulwark against movements for equality: "The freedom and social mobility which characterize the democratic state permit, and indeed bring about, striking inequalities of condition; and if the surface of democratic society should be leveled off any day, inequalities would reappear on the morrow, unless individual freedom and social mobility should be destroyed. The children of a democratic society should, therefore, be taught at school, with the utmost explicitness, and with vivid illustrations, that inequalities of condition are a necessary result of freedom."[16]

In another essay, "Equality in a Republic," Eliot left no doubt that the kind of equality he had in mind was fully compatible with a class society: "republican institutions," he wrote "do not prevent the existence, on the one hand of a very rich class, and on the other of a very poor class."[17] To Eliot, as to virtually all men of his social standing, private property was sacred and republican institutions should not interfere either with its accumulation or its transmission from generation to generation.[18]

A man of the Victorian era (he was three years old when Queen Victoria ascended to the throne and sixty-seven when she died), Eliot frequently used such words as "character," "gentleman," and "manly" in describing the ideal Harvard student. Yet though these were the very words Endicott Peabody used to articulate his educational ideals, they took on a different meaning in Eliot's hands. Eliot fervently believed in progress, and he wanted both Harvard and the broader educational system to prepare citizens for life in a democratic society. Good character, he believed, was equally available to Christians and non-Christians alike; it entailed "industry, persistence, veracity in word and act, gentleness, and disinterestedness" and called for the repudiation of "selfishness, greed, falseness, brutality, and ferocity."[19] Being a "gentleman," he insisted, was not a matter of birth or breeding; it was an earned status embodied in behavior, and in America it meant being a "democrat." A true gentleman was "considerate, generous, hard-working, and would never do anything to hurt . . . any human creature weaker than himself."[20] And the gentleman was most definitely not, wrote Eliot — in a passage that betrayed his feelings toward some of the Harvard students who considered themselves gentlemen — "an indifferent good-for-nothing, luxurious person, idling through the precious years of college life."[21]

Eliot's definition of "manliness" was also very different from that held by Peabody and Theodore Roosevelt. By embracing "gentleness" and rejecting "brutality" and "ferocity," he was articulating a more traditional notion in which honor and protection of the weak loomed large while brute force, though sometimes necessary, was the last resort.[22] To be sure, Eliot believed in "manly sports" and was himself a living example of commitment to strenuous exercise in the form of rowing (he had rowed for a Harvard team that broke a course record), horseback riding, and bicycling.[23] Indeed, in discussing the rise of intercollegiate athletes in 1881, he credited games and sports with transforming "the ideal student . . . from a stooping, weak, and sickly youth into one well-formed, robust, and healthy."[24] But within a decade he had changed his mind, believing that some sports had become excessively violent and were inherently unsportsmanlike.

The divergent views of Eliot and Roosevelt on collegiate football reveal conceptions of "manliness" that were linked to more fundamental differences about both the role of the university and the place of America in the world of nations. As early as 1895, Eliot had proposed the suspension of football, a sport that he denounced as "more brutal than prize-fighting, cock-fighting, or bull-fighting."[25] In response, Senator Henry Cabot Lodge, one of Roosevelt's principal allies in his quest for a more manly American foreign policy, proclaimed at a commencement dinner in 1896: "The time given to athletic contests and the injuries incurred on the playing field are the price which the English-speaking race has paid for being world conquerors." Yet Eliot stood his ground, insisting that war was utterly unlike "the bodily collisions which take place between foot-ball players" while noting pointedly that athletes tended to be mediocre students.[26]

Having inveighed against the evils of football for more than a decade, Eliot had a big opportunity to abolish the game in 1905. Twenty-one Americans had died playing the game the previous year, *McClure's* and *Collier's* had run exposés of the game's brutality and corruption, and a widely reproduced October 1905 photograph of a Swarthmore player whose face had been reduced to a bloody mess had created a national sensation. After the 1905 season, Columbia, Stanford, Northwestern, and California gave up football.[27] If Eliot, who had the support of the faculty and the Board of Overseers, was able to persuade Harvard to do the same, other institutions would surely follow.[28]

Sensing the gravity of the situation, Theodore Roosevelt — acting at the suggestion of none other than Endicott Peabody — called for a conference at the White House in October 1905 with the purpose of reforming, and thereby saving, the game. He believed that if the Big Three could agree on reforms, other colleges would follow their lead, so no other colleges were invited.[29] Leading the reform effort was Harvard's football coach William T. Reid Jr. '01, a close ally of Roosevelt's and the recipient of a $7,000 stipend and expense account — larger than that of any Harvard faculty member.[30] After the meeting, the participants issued a public statement, acknowledging that "an honorable obligation exists to carry out in letter and in spirit the rules of the game of foot-ball, relating to roughness, holding, and foul play."[31]

But the matter was far from settled, and in December Columbia's president, Nicholas Murray Butler, announced that Columbia was eliminating football. With the momentum seemingly favoring the abolitionists, the Intercollegiate Athletic Association, with Reid taking the lead, adopted a series of reforms (including the forward pass) designed to open up the game and make it less violent. Though Eliot still favored abolition, the Harvard Corporation, its opposition softened by the reforms, voted to keep the sport, with the president casting a negative vote.[32]

Long at odds with Theodore Roosevelt, whom he had once called "a degenerate son of Harvard," Eliot was not a graceful loser and continued to denounce the game in each of his final annual reports.[33] For his part, Roosevelt believed that Harvard would be "doing the baby act" if it abolished football, and he reportedly denounced Eliot as a "mollycoddle."[34] In February 1907, Roosevelt made clear what he believed was at stake in a speech before 1,900 students at the Harvard Union: "We cannot afford to turn out of college men who shrink from physical effort or from a little physical pain," for the nation needed men with "the courage that will fight valiantly alike against the foes of the soul and the foes of the body."[35]

In the end, what separated Roosevelt and Eliot on the question was a difference not only in their conception of "manliness" but also in their view of the role of force in human affairs. Intuitively, Roosevelt himself grasped the depth of their disagreement: "If we ever come to nothing as a nation," he complained to Henry Cabot Lodge, "it will be because of the teaching of Carl Schurz, President Eliot, the *Evening Post* and futile sentimentalists of the international arbitration type," who had succeeded in eating away what he called "the great fighting features of our race."[36]

Though Eliot had failed to eliminate football, he did accomplish his more fundamental goal of opening Harvard to a far broader range of students. "The essence of freedom," he had written in 1874, "is in equality of opportunities, and the opportunity of education should be counted the most precious of all."[37] Standing in the way, he believed, was Harvard's Greek admission requirement. Prodded by Eliot, Harvard took a first step toward abolishing Greek in 1886, and by 1898 the faculty had adopted a scheme "which made it possible for a boy to avoid either Latin or Greek without penalty in the form of harder work in other subjects."[38] Thus, even before the new century, Harvard had eliminated an exclusionary admission requirement that remained firmly in place at Yale and Princeton.

As the president of an institution whose fortunes were closely tied to the upper classes of New England and New York, Eliot publicly acknowledged the importance of educating the sons of the privileged, declaring in his inaugural address that "the country suffers when the rich are ignorant and unrefined" and that "inherited wealth is an unmitigated curse when it is divorced from culture."[39] In truth, he had little patience for many of the wealthy young men at Harvard, writing to a schoolmaster that "the striking things about the American boy from well-to-do families are his undeveloped taste and faculty for individual labor, the triviality of his habitual subjects of thought, the brevity of his vocabulary, and his lack of judgment and sense of proportion in historical, literary and scientific subjects."[40]

Eliot sponsored a variety of other measures that he hoped would attract a more diverse student body. Among the most important were the decision in 1905–1906 to replace Harvard's own exams with those of the College Entrance Examination Board (which tripled the number of locations where applicants could be examined) and a simultaneous bureaucratic reorganization that transformed the college's five separate admitting committees into a single committee. Following these reforms, a temporary decline in enrollments was reversed and the proportion of public school students began to increase.[41] In 1906, perhaps by sheer coincidence, one of the most illustrious classes in Harvard's history arrived in Cambridge; its members included John Reed, T. S. Eliot, and Walter Lippmann.[42]

In his commencement address in 1903, Eliot elaborated on his vision of a democratic and inclusive Harvard, declaring that "it is to the last degree undesirable that the colleges should be accessible only to the well-to-do."[43] He noted that fully one quarter of the students at Harvard either held scholarships or were working their way through college — which may explain how the sons of "wage-earners" composed 12.6 percent of undergraduates in 1904.[44] By the standards of the Big Three, Harvard was remarkably heterogeneous under Eliot; in 1908, his last full year in office, public school students constituted 45 percent of the freshman class, and one student in six was either Catholic (9 percent) or Jewish (7 percent).[45] A further sign of Harvard's cosmopolitanism was its openness to blacks, immigrants, and foreigners.[46] A homogeneous New England college when Eliot studied there in the 1850s, Harvard had by the early 1900s become genuinely diverse, a place where the "collision of views" that Eliot valued so highly was powerfully reinforced by the sheer variety of students.[47]

Yet Eliot's very success in diversifying Harvard also created a problem, for the much-discussed divide between rich and poor students would not have existed in a more homogeneous institution. Similarly, Eliot's transformation of Harvard from a regional college into the nation's preeminent research university led many observers to conclude that the rise of the graduate and professional schools had relegated the college to secondary importance.[48] Combined with the growing sentiment that Eliot's cherished system of free electives had led all too many students to choose a course of study that was neither rigorous nor coherent, there was a deepening sense that change, especially at the undergraduate level, was required.[49]

At the head of the forces opposing Eliot was A. Lawrence Lowell, who represented the conservative and exclusionary wing of the Protestant upper class as surely as Eliot represented its liberal and democratic wing.[50] Yet Lowell, who had been practicing law in Boston, had been summoned to Harvard by Eliot himself. In 1897, after the publication of Lowell's two-volume work, *Government and Parties in Continental Europe* (1896), Eliot asked him to join the faculty of the new Department of Government.

Though Lowell had written a long article a decade earlier in the *Harvard Monthly* that sharply criticized the elective system, Eliot recognized the forty-year-old as a man of exceptional intellect. By 1900 Lowell, who clashed repeatedly with Eliot in the coming years, had risen to the rank of full professor.[51] In 1909, despite Eliot's strong preference for another candidate, Lowell was named Harvard's new president — a post he would hold for nearly a quarter of a century. Among the many opponents of Eliot who greeted this appointment with enthusiasm was Endicott Peabody, who hoped that Eliot's departure would lead to a "more spiritual atmosphere at Harvard."[52]

Abbott Lawrence Lowell (1857–1943) came from one of the few Massachusetts families to enjoy a social standing higher even than that of the Eliots. Arriving in Boston in 1639, the Lowells were already sending their sons to Harvard by the early 1700s, and by later in that century a Lowell was a member of the Harvard Corporation. The family was highly cultured, and it produced an impressive array of parsons, jurists, scientists, and statesmen. But its economic foundation had not been fully laid until the first half of the nineteenth century, when Abbott Lawrence's (or "Lawrence," as he was called) two grandfathers built the major textile cities of Lowell and Lawrence. By the time Lawrence entered in 1873, he was among the sixth generation of Lowells to have attended Harvard.[53]

The brother of a celebrated poet (Amy) and a renowned astronomer (Percival), Lawrence was himself a formidable figure both intellectually and physically. Graduating second in his class with highest honors in mathematics, he published his undergraduate thesis under the auspices of the American Academy of Arts and Sciences. While excelling academically, he also established himself as the college's leading long-distance runner, winning races in the half-mile, mile, and two-mile competitions while irritating his opponents by looking over his shoulder as they trailed behind him. Like other young men from proper families, he belonged to the Institute of 1770 and Hasty Pudding.[54] But he was not by temperament a clubman, choosing not to join Porcellian, where generations of Lowells had been members.[55]

Graduating from Harvard Law School with honors in 1880, he formed a partnership in Boston with his brother-in-law Francis Cabot Lowell. Though the co-author of a book, *Transfer of Stock in Private Corporations,* Lowell had not found his true métier in the law. Perhaps the law had failed to fully engage his formidable intellect; perhaps it was the brusqueness, the arrogance, and the unshakable certainty of his own rightness that others were later to notice; whatever the reasons, even his own loyal biographer has acknowledged that he "did not succeed as a practicing attorney."[56] Scholarship, however, proved far more suitable for Lowell's energies, and his work in the emerging field of political science while still a lawyer put him on the path that culminated in the Harvard presidency.

Though he succeeded one of the true giants in the history of American higher education, Lowell made his own substantial mark as president of Harvard. In addition to mounting a courageous defense of academic freedom in the difficult years of World War I and its aftermath, he embarked on a series of reforms that completely changed undergraduate education.[57] Through the introduction of tutorials, concentration and distribution requirements, three-week reading periods, and general examinations, the quality of education — and of intellectual performance — in the college improved considerably. Genuinely concerned about the lives of undergraduates, Lowell was deeply troubled about the gap between the rich and the poor students at Harvard — an issue toward which the far more liberal Eliot had been curiously indifferent.[58] To close the chasm, Lowell believed it imperative that Harvard provide new residential facilities in which students from different backgrounds would live and learn together. Beginning with the opening of four freshman dormitories in 1914 and culminating in the inauguration of Harvard's residential house system in 1930 and 1931, Lowell transformed not only Harvard's physical landscape but also — and far more important — the very character of undergraduate life.[59]

Lowell, like Peabody, drew inspiration from Oxford and Cambridge. An enthusiastic student of English institutions and a firm believer that the "Anglo-Saxon race" had a special talent for the "art of self-government," he looked to Oxbridge as a model of what Harvard could be.[60] In contrast to Eliot's Harvard, which in his view had elevated the graduate and professional schools over the college, Lowell held out the ideal of an institution whose goal was "to produce a well-rounded manhood, men each as perfect as may be in body, mind, and soul."[61] Quoting Aristotle's view that "the fate of empires depends on the education of youth," he maintained that colleges should produce an elite that was socially as well as intellectually cohesive.[62]

That Oxford and Cambridge did not even award doctoral degrees and were relative backwaters in the production of new knowledge — the defining features of a true university to Eliot — was of little concern to Lowell.[63] Nor was their failure to produce experts with the kind of specialized knowledge that Eliot believed essential to the workings of a democratic society of particular concern.[64] On the contrary, the very success of Oxford and Cambridge in producing broadly educated generalists whose polished social skills prepared them for the task of governance was precisely what attracted Lowell to the Oxbridge model.[65] Lowell was primarily concerned with "the descendants of old, well-to-do American families," who were destined, in his view, to occupy positions of leadership in American life.[66] It was imperative that institutions like Harvard provide them with an undergraduate experience that would shape their character and friendships as well as their intellect.

Lowell's efforts to undo much of Eliot's legacy reflected their profound differences in basic social and political values. Nowhere was their difference more clear than on one of the defining issues of the era: the question of whether immigration, which had been increasing rapidly since the early 1880s, should be restricted.

Like many Boston Brahmins, A. Lawrence Lowell believed that the masses of immigrants pouring into the United States in the late nineteenth century posed a dire threat to American democracy and to the Anglo-Saxon character of the nation's culture. He became one of the early supporters of the Immigrant Restriction League, a group founded in 1894 by a group of Harvard-educated Bostonians who wished to convince the public of the "necessity of a further exclusion of elements undesirable for citizenship or injurious to our national character." In 1912, Lowell became the league's vice president.[67]

Underlying his decision to take on this role was his belief that the "new immigrants" from southern and eastern Europe were much less assimilable than the "old immigrants" from the British Isles and northern Europe. A believer in the superiority of Anglo-Saxon values and customs, he wished to preserve the cultural hegemony of old-stock Americans. But Lowell also had a more specifically political fear about the fate of American democracy, for he had long before come to the conclusion that "no democracy could be successful unless it was tolerably homogeneous."[68] In favoring a 1922 bill to limit permanently the percentage of immigrants from southern and eastern Europe, Lowell wrote, "The essential thing about any nation is its population, and . . . a nation subject to immigration in large quantities is lacking in duty to its posterity if it does not so select the stock that it will admit."[69] The president of the nation's most prestigious university had lent the full weight of his office to the cause of closing "the open door."

Though many members of the Protestant elite, including the presidents of Stanford, Bowdoin, and Western Reserve, shared Lowell's position, Eliot was not among them.[70] Optimistic by temperament and confident in the ability of American democracy to incorporate waves of immigrants, he became "the most impressive foe of the Immigration Restriction League" and "the mouthpiece for the most active opposition to Boston restrictionists."[71] Writing to a fellow Brahmin with whose views he strongly disagreed, Eliot declared that "the attitude of the Immigration Restriction League has struck me as vicious — economically, politically, and sentimentally." Immigrants, he insisted, had helped make America a great nation. "We need them," he wrote, "whether they are Jews or Gentiles, Greeks or barbarians, literate or illiterate, skilled or unskilled, children or adults."[72] Eliot's commitment to their cause had not always been so enthusiastic. While favoring unrestricted immigration for "all the European race" because it was capable of "complete assimilation," he had written in 1892 that there were other "races which cannot be assimilated — like the African, Chinese, and Japanese."[73] But even European immigrants posed problems, and in 1902 Eliot attributed "a good many problems in the United States" to "the difficulty of assimilating year after year large numbers of foreigners."[74] Yet by 1906 he had concluded that he could not "admit the doctrine that the United States should be reserved for the white race."[75]

At an age when most men become increasingly conservative, Eliot grew more and more liberal. In 1921, the eighty-seven-year-old had gone so far as to reject the prevailing ideologies of assimilation and amalgamation to which he had previously adhered, replacing them with the emergent theory that came to be known as "cultural pluralism."[76] "The United States," he wrote, would benefit from being "a country of many races, many religions, and many varieties of human nature, forming one liberty-loving stable democracy." In 1925, Eliot declared that the nation must "learn that alien immigrants should not be made as like as possible to Americans but should preserve their own peculiar gifts and merits as contributions to American life."[77]

A believer in the idea of progress, Eliot held to a vision of the United States that saw the inclusion of ever more groups in the American dream as a source of national strength. Lowell, in contrast, had a far bleaker sense of human possibility and saw group difference as a threat. With respect to his beloved country, Lowell felt defensive: Anglo-Saxon men had made the nation great, and outsiders would — unless thoroughly assimilated — undermine its character.

Unlike Eliot, Lowell was frequently harsh and repressive in defending the established order within Harvard and without, especially in dealing with challenges from outsiders. On the labor question, one of the central issues of the time, Lowell was instinctively hostile to workers. This became most dramatically visible in 1919, when he helped organize two hundred Harvard students to volunteer to maintain the public order during a Boston police strike; the police wanted the right to form a union.[78] Some years later, he caused the university great embarrassment when he fired a group of scrubwomen rather than comply with a demand from the Massachusetts Minimum Wage Commission to pay them 37.5 cents per hour. Harvard had just received a $5 million donation from an alumnus but insisted that it would not go above 35 cents.[79] Even faculty appointments were not immune to Lowell's attitude toward labor. In the case of Arthur Lovejoy, considered by many one of the nation's most eminent philosophers, Lowell vetoed his appointment to the Philosophy Department because Lovejoy had been an active supporter of the American Association of University Professors.[80] Lowell was also no friend of the education of women. In response to a casual suggestion that the law school become coeducational, he kicked the door in his office and declared stonily, "This isn't going to happen while I am president of this university."[81]

Lowell was particularly hostile to the growing number of radicals, especially those of immigrant origin, dedicated to changing the existing distribution of wealth and power. In one of the most heavily publicized acts of his presidency, he volunteered to serve as a member of a gubernatorial committee to investigate whether the controversial Italian anarchists, Nicola Sacco and Bartolomeo Vanzetti, had received a fair trial. Though many observers, including the Harvard Law School professor Felix Frankfurter, doubted the men's guilt, the "Lowell Committee" concluded that they were guilty of murder beyond a reasonable doubt. The men were executed on August 23, 1927; every year as long as Lowell lived, the anniversary of their death brought him "letters and telegrams, usually anonymous, of bitter, personal abuse."[82]

The most chilling example of Lowell's intolerance concerned men of his own milieu who were homosexual. When Lowell discovered that a longtime member of the Harvard faculty was homosexual, he immediately demanded his resignation. But the professor pointed out that he had devoted his life to Harvard and asked Lowell what he would do if he were in his shoes. Lowell's reply, corroborated by two sources, was direct: "I would get a gun and shoot myself."[83]

Despite his narrow views, Lowell continued in the early years of his administration to follow Eliot's path of seeking to broaden the range of backgrounds of Harvard's students. In 1910–1911, Lowell's second year in office, Harvard introduced a "New Plan" of admissions, targeted to public school students, that demanded only "an approved school [course] and examination in four subjects with satisfactory results." Neither Latin nor Greek was required, and a growing number of public schools were able to prepare students for the examinations. In a discussion with the principal of Andover, Lowell explained that under the New Plan, "it would be rather more difficult for the poor scholar who goes to a good preparatory school to get in, but would be more easy for the good scholar from a school that does not habitually prepare for Harvard."[84] On hearing about the New Plan, the steel magnate and philanthropist Andrew Carnegie wrote approvingly to Lowell: "I cannot repress my desire to congratulate you and Harvard University upon its action in linking the graduate of the high school with the university. There is now a clear path for the poor boy from the bottom to the top."[85]

Though only 83 students were admitted under the New Plan in 1911, their numbers grew rapidly to 224 in 1914 — nearly a third of the total number of admits.[86] One of the primary goals of the New Plan had been "to open the road to Harvard College to the pupils from good schools, and more particularly from good public schools, throughout the nation." In the program's first year, it was already clear that it had been successful, drawing to Cambridge boys from twelve states that had sent Harvard no students under the Old Plan.[87] Equally important, the New Plan's students, whom many feared would not be prepared for Harvard, outperformed their mostly private school peers, with over half of them garnering As and Bs in their freshman year compared to less than a third of Old Plan students.[88]

By 1913, public school graduates outnumbered those from private schools in Harvard's freshman class, 288 to 276.[89] A sense of the range of secondary schools is provided by a list of the top feeder schools to Harvard a year earlier: while several were well-known private schools such as Exeter (24), Milton (20), and Middlesex (18), the two largest feeders were Boston Latin (53) and Cambridge Latin (35), followed by Boston English (17).[90] In 1914, the retired president Eliot went so far as to claim that "a full quarter of all the students might properly be called poor; perhaps an eighth belong to families that might fairly be called rich; and the other five-eighths come from families that are neither rich nor poor."[91] These figures no doubt exaggerated the proportion of truly poor students at Harvard while underestimating the percentage from wealthy families. Yet scholarships were fairly common (one in five students from Boston Latin, Cambridge Latin, and English High held scholarships in 1911), and in 1912 Harvard opened a Student Employment Office to assist boys trying to work their way through college.[92]

Lowell's success in diversifying the student body had the ironic effect of widening the gap between rich and poor that had worried him since his days as a professor. The divide between the Gold Coast and the Yard was more than economic; it also corresponded to the increasingly visible split between WASPs and Jews. While upper-class Protestants dominated the Gold Coast, Jews — most of them public school boys from modest backgrounds — increasingly congregated in or near the Yard. One dormitory near the law school, Walter Hastings Hall, with a large number of Jews became known as "Little Jerusalem"; around the same time, the top floor of a freshman dorm in the Yard came to be called "Kike's Peak."[93] Meanwhile, the proportion of Jews continued to increase under Lowell, rising from 9.8 percent in 1909 (Eliot's final year as president) to 15.1 percent in 1914.[94]

For many years, Lowell had expressed his concern about the students' disparate living conditions and the effects they had on social cohesion. In a letter to Eliot in 1902, he had forcefully articulated his position:

> It seems to me that there is a growing feeling among some members of the faculty that the tendency of the wealthy students to live in private dormitories outside the yard, involves great danger of a snobbish separation of the students on lines of wealth, and is thereby bringing about a condition of things that would destroy the chief value of the College as a place for the training of character. I fear, that with the loss of that democratic feeling which ought to lie at the basis of university life, we are liable to lose our moral hold upon a large part of the students, and that this feeling can be maintained only when a considerable proportion of every section of students is living within the walls.[95]

Lowell never wavered in his views on the importance of common residential facilities, especially for freshmen. "Such dormitories," he wrote, "would give far greater opportunity for men from different schools and from different parts of the country to mix together and find their natural affinities unfettered by the associations of early education, of locality and of wealth; and above all it would tend to make the college more truly national in spirit."[96]

New freshman dormitories became one of Lowell's highest priorities, and by 1911–1912 funds had been secured for three of four proposed buildings. In 1914, amid much fanfare, these freshman halls, with housing for 489 students, opened their doors.[97]

All freshmen were required to reside in the freshmen dormitories, "except those who are permitted by the Assistant Dean of Harvard College to live elsewhere."[98] In reality, this clause meant that dorm space was "allotted by a mysterious yet undeniable system of caste including a Category X for Jews."[99] Perceived by many as bastions of the St. Grottlesex set, the new dormitories also excluded the handful of blacks then enrolled.[100] Though admission to Harvard was still nondiscriminatory in 1914, Lowell's freshmen dormitories were sites of carefully engineered Anglo-Saxon predominance. A precedent was set, and within a decade Lowell took measures to ensure that a majority of the student body would continue to come from old Protestant stock.

Yale: A National and Democratic Institution?

Though it was Harvard's closest peer, Yale was a very different institution in the early years of the twentieth century. Far more traditional than Eliot's Harvard, Yale did not eliminate its Greek requirement until 1904 and its Latin requirement until 1931.[101] Its conservatism was also evident in its decision to remain unabashedly Christian, retaining compulsory daily and Sunday chapel attendance until the mid-1920s.[102] It was no wonder, then, that Yale received the warm support of Endicott Peabody, who noted approvingly in 1909 that "much of the better half of our VI form goes to Yale this year" — a trend he attributed to Harvard's insufficiently spiritual atmosphere and "the great rift between the haves and have nots."[103]

At the center of Yale's self-definition was the belief that it was a national and democratic institution — an implicitly invidious comparison to Harvard, which it considered more regional and less democratic. On the question of geographical representation, Yale's claim was not without support; in 1904–1905, 27 percent of Yale's undergraduates came from outside the New England and Middle Atlantic states, compared with only 21 percent of Harvard's students. Particularly in the Midwest and the South, Yale's modest drawing power was nevertheless stronger than that of its chief competitor.[104]

Yale's claim to be more democratic, though contestable, was also not without foundation. Although Harvard drew substantially more students from public schools (42 vs. 28 percent in 1900), the gulf between the Gold

Coast and the Yard gave Cambridge a decidedly less democratic atmosphere than New Haven, where residential segregation was much less pronounced.[105] Yale, moreover, had no precise analogue to Harvard's final club system, where students from only the most elite social backgrounds were eligible.[106]

Yale's principal source of pride was its distinctive — and professedly meritocratic — social system. At the top of this system were the powerful and mysterious senior societies, which "tapped" students for membership in the spring of their junior year. According to the official ideology, membership was open to all students, and selection was on the basis of personal accomplishment rather than social origin.

To understand Yale's distinctive ethos, there is no better source than Owen Johnson's *Dink Stover* (1911), a classic collegiate novel that shaped the public's perception of Yale — and Yale's self-image — for decades to come.[107] In the book's opening pages, Dink, a clean-cut and magnetic athlete, says that Yale is "the one place where money makes no difference . . . where you stand for what you are." Soon an upperclassman explains to Dink Yale's social system and the senior societies that dominate it: "You'll hear a good deal of talk inside the college, and out of it, too, about the system. It has its faults. But it's the best system there is, and it makes Yale what it is to-day. It makes fellows get out and work; it gives them ambitions, stops loafing and going to seed, and keeps a pretty good, clean, temperate atmosphere about the place." Standing at the top of the system — which Stover "believed in . . . as an honest attempt to reward the best in the college life, a sort of academic legion of honor, formed not on social cleavage, but given as a reward of merit" — was the legendary Skull and Bones, the oldest and most prestigious senior society.[108] At the end of the book, the sturdy and courageous Stover receives — not without ambivalence — the ultimate honor: he is tapped for Bones, relieved "to be no longer an outsider, but back among his own with the stamp of approval on his record."[109]

Though only about 15 percent of Yale's students were elected to the six senior societies, they exerted a profound influence on the texture of undergraduate life.[110] From the moment a freshman arrived in New Haven, the game was clear: to rise to the top of the powerful, self-contained student culture, one had to "do something for Yale." In practice it meant a ferocious competition for leadership in extracurricular activities; being captain of the football team or editor of the *Daily News* virtually guaranteed one's election to a top senior society. A defining feature of Yale's social system — and perhaps the principal source of its democratic reputation — was that students from the most distinguished families had no guarantee of success. Even boys of relatively modest social origin could dream of membership in Bones; though the odds were stacked against them, extraordinary accomplishment combined with personal charisma could result in success on Tap Day. In this regard, Yale could hardly have been more different from Harvard — a point of great pride in New Haven.

For some scions of the upper class who wished to test their mettle against other talented and ambitious young men, Yale's very competitiveness was appealing and the possibility of failure exhilarating. One such young man was Averell Harriman, a Groton graduate and the son of one of America's wealthiest men. Reflecting on the tap system more than seventy years after his days at Yale, he said, "It gave me purpose . . . I scoffed at Harvard's Porcellian Club. It was too smug. But to get into Bones, you had to do something for Yale."[111] On May 12, 1912, an article in the *New York Times* reported that "one of the burning topics current on the [Yale] campus is 'Will Harriman go Keys?'"[112] In the end Harriman, later named in his yearbook to the top ten list for "Most Thorough Gentleman" and "Most Likely to Succeed," was tapped for Bones — an honor he shared with William Howard Taft, Henry Stimson, and Robert Taft, who had come before him, and Henry Luce, George H. W. Bush, John Kerry, and George W. Bush, who came after.[113]

It is difficult to exaggerate the grip that Yale's senior society system held over the undergraduates. In the battle for social position, noted Owen Johnson, academics were relegated to the periphery of student life: "The fierceness of the competition makes of the curriculum a secondary affair. In the large majority of cases, the tension of the conflict and all the multiplication of activities absorb all the energy. Classroom work is regarded as a necessary evil and a sort of vexatious obstacle imposed by the faculty."[114] In such an atmosphere, athletic excellence, especially in football, constituted the pinnacle of success; summarizing the situation, one particularly well informed observer noted that while "the professional spirit prevails in Yale athletics . . . the amateur spirit prevails in Yale scholarship."[115]

Even more than Harvard's, Yale's student culture was oriented toward business.[116] Many students had come to New Haven, in the words of Yale's historian George W. Pierson, "to learn not from books but from each other — not how to be scholars but how to succeed."[117] Infertile ground for nonconformists and individualists, the Yale "machine" (as even its friends sometimes called it) was effective in training leaders — the kind of men who would preside over America's major economic and political institutions. But Yale's ferocious competitiveness — described by Laurence Veysey as "a perfect parody of the American race for success" — was not without costs. Every year, the elation of the elected few was accompanied by feelings of disappointment and even humiliation of the many spurned by the senior societies despite their efforts. "The sense of social failure is so deep at Yale," one alumnus recalled, "that many graduates yearly leave New Haven never to return."[118]

Because its senior societies were more open and democratic than the final clubs at Harvard and the eating clubs at Princeton, Yale's pride in them was understandable. Election into Skull and Bones, in particular, had a definite meritocratic aspect. Coming from a family that was socially distinguished or wealthy (or, better yet, both) was a distinct asset, albeit not necessarily decisive. Henry Seidel Canby, who graduated in 1899 and spent the rest of his life at Yale as a faculty member after receiving a Ph.D. in 1905, described how the system actually worked:

> Money counted, social standing outside counted, yet the son of a shopkeeper could get as far on athletic prowess as the gilded child of privilege on his family momentum. Good looks counted also, more, I should say in the men's than in the women's colleges; and so did good clothes if worn in the collegiate manner which required the slovenly use of expensive and well-cut garments. Wit, and the gift of being amusing, especially when tight, were very helpful; and so was political sagacity. And . . . there were routes upward for boys who could write what the college magazine wanted, or make the kind of music that undergraduates liked; and a broad path, much trodden in my day, for the energetically pious who could organize religion, and sell God to the right kind of undergraduate. They were sure of a senior society.[119]

Yale's most prestigious society went to considerable lengths to have a "representative" character, annually including one or more men who were working their way through college. In contrast to Harvard, where excellence in scholarship was an outright liability in the competition for election to Porcellian or A.D., Bones by the 1910s typically took two to four members of Phi Beta Kappa every year.[120]

Yet private school boys had a definite advantage; in 1928, for example, just 2 of 60 entrants to the four most prestigious societies (Skull and Bones, Scroll and Key, Wolf's Head, and Elihu) had come to Yale directly from public schools.[121]

While Catholic students were active in extracurricular life and were occasionally admitted to senior societies, Yale's growing Jewish population fared less well.[122] Though active in the orchestra and debating (and in such groups as the Society for the Study of Socialism), Jews were excluded from the top positions in the major student organizations.[123] By 1911, anti-Semitism was clearly an issue on campus; that year, the Elihu Club passed by a vote of 13–0 a motion "that Jews should be denied recognition at Yale."[124] Between 1900 and 1930, more than 1,200 Jews entered Yale; none was elected to a senior society.[125]

Nevertheless, the meritocratic aura of the senior societies shaped Yale's identity. Membership became an important marker for selection to the ranks of those who ran the institution. Of 34 elected alumni fellows on the Yale

Corporation between 1872 and 1936, 17 had been members of Skull and Bones and 7 of Scroll and Key. University treasurers for all but five years between 1862 and 1910 were "Bones men," as were university secretaries for more than a half century between 1869 and 1921. Even the Yale presidency was usually occupied by a society man; during 68 of the 99 years between 1886 and 1985, Yale's chief executive was a member of Skull and Bones, Scroll and Key, or Wolf's Head. And the faculty was even more inbred, at least into the early twentieth century; between 1865 and 1916, a remarkable 80 percent were "Bones men."[126]

Notoriously insular, Yale was deeply wedded to its distinctive traditions. But by the turn of the century, it was becoming apparent that some of these traditions were ill suited to a society in transition. Between 1888 and 1896, the size of Yale's freshman class had grown faster than those at Harvard and Princeton; after 1896, however, Yale hardly grew at all while Princeton experienced a small increase in enrollment and Harvard expanded rapidly, passing Yale in total freshman enrollment in 1902. Yale was attracting more high school students than ever before, but the rate of increase was not keeping pace with the growth of public education. Worse still, Yale was losing ground to Harvard and Princeton in attracting students from its own feeder schools.[127]

Yale's difficulties were linked to the very traditionalism that had long been a source of institutional pride. In particular, the steadfast commitment of the college (though not the less prestigious Sheffield Scientific School, which was growing more rapidly) to both Greek and Latin as entrance requirements was a barrier to the growing number of public school graduates. Even Yale's cherished system of senior societies had become an obstacle to many; with "only one chance in six of getting into the social swim," some boys chose to enroll elsewhere.[128] The college's declining numbers, bluntly concluded a faculty committee investigating the matter, were rooted in "Yale's lack of touch with the outside world."[129]

Despite considerable faculty resistance, Yale dropped the Greek entrance requirement in 1904 "so fast that many schools did not hear about it until some time after the change had gone into effect."[130] Observing Yale's sudden about-face, *Harvard Graduates' Magazine* could not refrain from gloating. Yale had "clung to sectarianism in religion and conservatism in education" and had "stood by her ideals valiantly." But "in the long run these are not the ideals of the American people, and of late years . . . Yale has been getting rid of them as expeditiously and quietly as possible."[131]

The elimination of Greek was but the first step in Yale's efforts to keep up with its rivals. Having previously shunned the subject exams of the new College Entrance Examination Board (CEEB) as less rigorous than its own exams, Yale in 1907 publicly announced that it would accept the results of CEEB exams. By 1911, under pressure from alumni in the western states calling on Yale to modify its admissions requirements to bring it more "closely in touch with the educational conditions existing in the Western high schools . . . to the end that Yale's preeminence as a national university may be preserved," the administration reduced the number of required entrance exams, permitted exams in four new subjects, and ruled that "admission to Yale College would be granted without examination in special cases for exceptional scholarship."[132] Finally, in 1916 Yale joined Harvard and Princeton in abolishing its own examinations in favor of those administered by the College Board and introduced an even farther-reaching reform: a "New Plan" of admissions that required only "a satisfactory school record" and "comprehensive examinations in not more than four subjects."[133]

These reforms provided more opportunities to students from public schools and to those from distant states, but they did not fundamentally transform the composition of the student body. In 1916, just 26 percent of the entrants to Yale College (105 of 400 freshmen) were from public schools, and only 12 percent came from west of the Mississippi.[134] Yet Yale's intellectual atmosphere — perhaps reflecting the dynamic cultural and political debates of the period — showed a decided improvement.[135] Literary culture, in particular, flourished during this period, producing such writers as Archibald MacLeish '15, Stephen Vincent Benét '19, Henry Luce '20, and Thornton Wilder '20. In 1918–1919, these four men came together in a single writing course, joined by such figures as Philip Barry (who wrote the script for *The Philadelphia Story*) and Walter Millis (the author of *Why Europe Fights*). It was, said the historian Robin Winks, "as distinguished a group as was ever assembled in such a seminar."[136]

Although Yale had rebounded from its intellectual nadir just after the turn of the century, its atmosphere was still far less intellectual than that of its archrival in Cambridge. Henry Stimson, a devoted Yale alumnus who also graduated from Harvard Law School, compared the two: the teaching at Harvard "created a greater revolution in the power of my thinking than any teaching I got from Yale, while the faith in mankind that I learned on the campus at New Haven was greater and stronger than any such faith I achieved at Harvard."[137] Archibald MacLeish, a loyal Old Blue who captained the water polo team and was elected to Skull and Bones during his student days, was more harsh in his assessment: "I loved Yale deeply, but it wasn't an educational institution. It lacked the sort of thing I felt at once when I went to the Harvard Law School."[138] In truth, though Yale tended to compare itself to Harvard, it was in many ways more similar to Princeton, where the undergraduate college was the center of the institution. And Princeton — like its rivals to the north — was having serious problems adjusting to the new conditions of the twentieth century.

Princeton: The Finest Country Club in America

As the nineteenth century gave way to the twentieth, Princeton remained by far the most religious member of the Big Three. Since its founding in 1746, it had been a Presbyterian institution and the trustees mandated that only Presbyterian ministers could serve as president. Francis Lander Patton, who served from 1888 to 1902, was very much in the traditional mold. A British citizen born in Bermuda, he was a theological conservative who developed a reputation as a heresy hunter before being named to professorships at both Princeton Theological Seminary and Princeton College. (The university did not exist as such until 1896.) In his interview for the presidency, Patton insisted that "we must keep Princeton a Christian college" while also emphasizing his desire to make Old Nassau a true center of learning.[139]

Though more tolerant in university affairs, Patton believed that faculty members had an obligation to present a broad Christian viewpoint in the classroom. On appointing the future Princeton president Woodrow Wilson to the chair of Political Economics and Jurisprudence in 1890, Patton immediately informed him that his Christian perspective would have to be made more explicit in his teaching. Emphasizing that the trustees were determined "to keep this College on the old ground of loyalty to the Christian religion," he made it clear to Wilson that subjects were "to be dealt with under theistic and Christian presuppositions: & they [the trustees] would not regard with favour such a conception of academic freedom or teaching as would leave in doubt the very direct bearing of historical Christianity as a revealed religion upon the great problems of civilization."[140]

The son of a Presbyterian minister and a devout Presbyterian himself, Wilson accepted the position. But a few years later, Patton's rigidity about religious matters placed him in an embarrassing situation. While negotiating in the fall of 1896 with the eminent University of Wisconsin historian Frederick Jackson Turner, Wilson was asked directly if Princeton had any religious tests. He replied, "I think I can say without qualification that no religious tests are applied here. The president and trustees are very anxious that every man they choose should be earnestly religious, but there are no doctrinal standards among us." Yet in the end the trustees blocked the appointment, apparently because Turner was a Unitarian. Though unable to prove that religion was the basis of the decision, Wilson was outraged: "I am probably at this writing the most chagrined fellow on the continent!" he wrote to Turner, adding that "it is no doubt just as well that I have not now a chance to go elsewhere."[141]

While strict about religious matters, Patton was notoriously lax on academic standards. By the turn of the century, Princeton had become something of a joke among the professoriat: easy to enter and difficult to flunk out of, Old Nassau had become a magnet for lackluster students from privileged backgrounds. According to Moses Taylor Pyne, one of the most powerful trustees, "Study was not dignified, nor was it absolutely essential" during the Patton years. Examinations were based on the memorization of facts and relied heavily on coaching, leading one student to write on his paper: "This question is unfair. It requires thought." When asked early in his presidency how many students there were at Princeton, Wilson answered, "About 10 percent."[142]

Himself a gentleman on the English model, Patton was also lenient about the club-centered culture of luxury that was established by 1900. As recently as the early 1890s, Princeton had prided itself on Old Nassau's "democratic" character — a belief grounded in a unitary campus culture that supposedly minimized differences of wealth and judged students "by worth, not birth." But with the influx of wealthy students from private boarding schools and the growth of private eating clubs, Princeton's campus culture underwent a major transformation. By 1902, 11 private eating clubs had opened (compared to only 2 — Ivy and Cottage — in 1889), and more than half of the upperclassmen were members. Competition for entry into the clubs, especially the more prestigious ones, became a veritable obsession among freshmen and sophomores, and social pursuits occupied a far more central place in the lives of Princeton students than their academic studies. The failure to get into the right eating club could be devastating; in his autobiography, Ernest Poole described his feelings on learning that he had been blackballed by one of the top clubs: "The news came like a thunderbolt. With a cold sick feeling the bottom dropped out of my college life." The fate of those excluded altogether was even worse; they were branded, in the words of the *Princeton Alumni Weekly,* "queer, unlikable, and non-clubbable."[143]

But it was Princeton's declining academic standing rather than its growing reputation as the finest country club in America that triggered the faculty revolt that led to Patton's resignation. At a time when higher education was becoming more highly valued in the larger culture, Princeton was, in the words of George Marsden, "second to none in its lack of rigor."[144] Even the feeder schools to the Big Three were apparently dissatisfied; in 1900, while Yale attracted 154 students from nine leading boarding schools and Harvard 117, Princeton (admittedly a smaller institution) drew just 62, more than half of whom (34) came from a single school, Lawrenceville, which had been founded in 1883 for the express purpose of preparing students for Princeton.[145] So weak were academic standards in the John C. Green School of

Science (which at this time enrolled more students than the slightly more rigorous Academic Department, which offered the A.B.) that it was "regarded by the scientific fraternity as something between a joke and a scandal." For many students, it was considered "bad form to elect courses that actually required work." When a handful of professors attempted to enforce higher standards, "they found themselves confronted with empty benches."[146]

By late 1900, the faculty — especially its younger and more dynamic members — had had enough. Over Patton's objections, a committee was formed to investigate academic conditions and to generate proposals for reform. When Patton proved totally unresponsive to its recommendations, the rebellion escalated, soon reaching the board of trustees. Meanwhile, the board itself, which had historically been controlled by Presbyterian clergymen, had brought into its ranks a number of wealthy businessmen and prominent lawyers. These men, whose ethos reflected the growing power of large corporations, had little patience with either Patton's religious rigidity or his administrative inefficiency. With the assistance of some confidential maneuvering by Woodrow Wilson and a few other powerful faculty members, the trustees were persuaded that Patton had to go.[147]

After Patton's resignation was secured, the trustees moved immediately to name Wilson as his successor. In many ways he was the obvious candidate: a distinguished scholar, a gifted public speaker, an acclaimed teacher, and an alumnus (1879), he seemed exceptionally well suited to the job. Already one of Princeton's most eminent faculty members when appointed in 1890, he had risen to new heights with the delivery of an eloquent and memorable oration, "Princeton in the Nation's Service," at the school's sesquicentennial celebration in 1896. He had, moreover, shown exceptional discretion — at least in public — during the bitter power struggle between Patton and the faculty.[148]

The first man to hold the Princeton presidency who was not a minister, Thomas Woodrow Wilson was born into a devout Presbyterian family in 1856. His father, Joseph Ruggles Wilson, was a Presbyterian minister from Ohio who had completed his training at the Princeton Theological Seminary. His mother, Jessie Woodrow, was born in England, the daughter of a Presbyterian minister who had gone to Canada in 1835 and then Ohio in 1837. Married in 1849, Joseph and Jessie Wilson moved in 1855 to an important Presbyterian church in Staunton, Virginia. Tommy, as he was called until after his college days, was born the following year and spent his entire youth in the Deep South, primarily in Augusta, Georgia, and Columbia, South Carolina.[149]

The milieu in which Wilson was raised was both devoutly religious and profoundly southern. His father believed slavery to be sanctioned in the Bible and strongly supported the South during the Civil War. One of the leaders of the Southern Presbyterians when they separated from their northern breth-ren in 1861, the Reverend Wilson served as a chaplain in the Confederate Army. During the war, his church in Augusta served as an emergency hospital for wounded Confederate troops. Young Tommy witnessed all this and devel-oped a pride in the bravery of the Confederate soldiers as well as a lifelong reverence for General Lee.[150]

Wilson's views were deeply affected by his southern upbringing. The South, he often said, was "the only place in the country, the only place in the world, where nothing has to be explained to me." Although he did not share his father's enthusiasm for the "Lost Cause" and wrote a major historical work, *Division and Reunion, 1829–1889* (1893), that was one of the most bal-anced accounts of the Civil War and Reconstruction at that time, his views of blacks were characteristically southern. A defender of both segregation and the disenfranchisement of blacks, he believed African Americans to be "igno-rant and unfitted by education for the most usual and constant duties of citi-zenship." In private, his views were even more harsh; Wilson referred to blacks more than once as "an ignorant and inferior race."[151]

Wilson's top priority on assuming the presidency of Princeton was to raise academic standards as part of a broader commitment to educational re-form. On October 21, 1902, four days before his inauguration, he bluntly told the trustees that Princeton had "not kept pace" with Harvard and Yale "in university development" and that while it had failed to move forward, "other newer institutions, like Columbia, the Johns Hopkins [where Wilson received his Ph.D. in 1886], and the University of Chicago [had] pressed in ahead of her." Unless Princeton raised the money necessary for a major research insti-tution, it would have to "withdraw from university competition."[152]

Wilson could not bear to see his alma mater fall from the top ranks. As he had noted in "Princeton in the Nation's Service," the school had played a crit-ical role in the formation of the United States, and he believed that it was des-tined to play a central role in its future. But he was well aware that Princeton could not fulfill its mission unless he fundamentally reformed the institution at both the undergraduate and the graduate level. In his inaugural address, he made it clear that a first-rate graduate college was an essential part of his vi-sion: "We shall build it, not apart, but as nearly as may be at the very heart, the geographical heart of the university . . . The windows of the graduate col-lege must open straight upon the walks and quadrangles and lecture halls of the studium generale."[153]

But Wilson's first task was of necessity the undergraduate college, which enrolled over 90 percent of all students.[154] Wilson believed that more rigorous admissions standards were a precondition for raising the academic quality of the student body, and his views on admissions had a strongly meritocratic strand. In an address before the Phi Beta Kappa Society of Yale, he described a revealing incident:

> Not long ago a gentleman approached me in great excitement just after the entrance examinations. He said we had made a great mistake in not taking so and so from a certain school which he named. "But," I said, "he did not pass the entrance examinations." And he went over the boy's moral excellencies again. "Pardon me," I said, "you do not understand. He did not pass the entrance examinations. Now," I said, "I want you to understand that if the angel Gabriel applied for admission to Princeton University and could not pass the entrance examinations, he would not be admitted. He would be wasting his time."[155]

A perspective more different from that of Patton is hard to imagine.[156]

As Wilson frankly admitted in his annual Report of the President for 1907, the insistence on higher academic standards initially reduced the size of the freshman class from 391 in 1905 to 322 in 1906. But he saw it as a necessary consequence of raising academic quality: "Formerly, because our examinations were often less difficult or our standards less rigidly maintained than those of other universities of the same rank and reputation, a large number of ill-prepared and unstudious boys came to Princeton from the secondary schools, particularly the private schools. Now, it being generally understood that our requirements are rigidly insisted on and that poor preparation means almost certain failure at the term examinations after entrance, none but boys who can hope to meet our requirements are inclined to attempt our tests." According to Wilson, "the proportion of the present freshman class admitted without conditions is much larger than last year" and the "best secondary private schools are sending a larger number of their men to us." But he admitted that "such changes are always slow" — a point underscored by the fact that in 1906 only 42 percent of students were admitted without conditions.[157]

Wilson, however, was not a simple meritocrat. Close to his English family origins and Anglophilic in his cultural and political values, he looked to Oxbridge for inspiration as early as his undergraduate days. While editor of the *Princetonian* (the student newspaper), Wilson wrote an article praising Oxford and Cambridge for promoting "individual development and . . . independent thought" and noting with approval their role as "the great feeders of the two political parties" in a society in which "the young man who displays commanding talents is sure of an opening in public life." In an adumbration of themes that he would develop almost two decades later in "Princeton in the Nation's Service," he asked how Princeton could provide a setting in which "the educated young men of America" could become "as great a power in the state as are the educated young men of England?"[158] Visits to Oxford and Cambridge in the 1890s only increased his admiration for them and strengthened his conviction that they offered important lessons for Princeton.[159]

With Oxbridge rather than the great German universities as his model, Wilson's ideal college graduate was a broadly educated gentleman rather than the specialist expert favored by Eliot. Accordingly, when Wilson reformed the curriculum shortly after taking office, he rejected Eliot's system of free electives and launched a program in which all students were required to take a set of broad courses while choosing their general degree programs.[160] In a speech to the alumni in 1903, Wilson told them "to stop miscellaneous endeavors to turn every boy's footsteps toward Princeton" and "send only the choice spirits, the most useful, all-around Christian gentleman." Unlike Eliot at Harvard, which had abolished compulsory chapel in 1886, he continued required chapel services, dashing the hopes of many undergraduates. Religious services, the devout Wilson believed, were as much a part of life at Princeton as daily classes, and he led chapel services himself once or twice a week.[161]

Having reformed the curriculum and stiffened the requirements to enter and remain at Princeton, Wilson moved rapidly to reform the heart of the educational process — the relationship between teacher and student. Dissatisfied with education by lecture and recitation, he turned directly to the Oxbridge tutorial as a model. In this system, undergraduates met with tutors individually or in small groups to discuss the reading and to have their work supervised and assessed.[162] The Princeton version of this system would call the tutors "preceptors" and would place special emphasis on the personal qualities and teaching ability of the men chosen. According to Wilson: "The importance of the whole system lies in the character of the men who are being obtained . . . They are to be selected primarily upon their stand as gentlemen, men who are companionable, clubbable, whose personal qualities of association give them influence over the minds of younger men. If their characters as gentlemen and as scholars conflict, the former will give them the place."[163] The products of this system were to be not brilliant scholars but well-educated gentlemen who could take their place among the ranks of the nation's leaders.[164]

Yet Wilson soon developed a reputation as a principled and embattled opponent of social privilege, and it placed him on the path that would lead to his election as president of the United States in 1912. How this happened cannot be understood without an account of his epochal battle with Princeton's eating clubs — a battle that did not begin in earnest until 1906, his fourth year as president.

Perhaps by coincidence, 1906 was also the first year that Wilson, a conservative Democrat hostile to the populist wing of the Democratic Party represented by William Jennings Bryan, was first touted as a potential candidate for president.[165] The date of his rise to political prominence was February 3, 1906, the occasion a dinner in his honor at the Lotus Club in New York City. The principal speaker was George Brinton McClellon Harvey, the editor of *Harper's Weekly* and an enthusiastic supporter of Wilson since he had heard his inaugural address at Princeton in October 1902. Harvey's idea — which was shared by many conservative Democratic leaders — was that the eloquent and charismatic Wilson was just the man to wrest control of the party from its populist wing and to reverse the progressive policies of Theodore Roosevelt. Harvey concluded his peroration by declaring that "it is with a sense almost of rapture that I contemplate even the remotest possibility of casting a ballot for the president of Princeton University to become President of the United States."

Wilson was on the cover of the March 10, 1906, issue of *Harper's Weekly*, and Harvey reprinted his address at the Lotus Club, assuring his readers that the speech was not "a hasty or ill-conceived utterance." In April, the prestigious *North American Review* (also controlled by Harvey) ran a lead editorial praising Wilson as a potential presidential nominee.[166] And by year's end, Wilson was aware that an impressive array of powerful men — among them, the *New York Times* publisher Adolph S. Ochs, the *Louisville Courier-Journal* editor "Marse Henry" Watterson, the bank president J. H. Eckles, and the utilities magnate Thomas Fortune Ryan — were all interested in him as a possible presidential candidate.[167]

Though Wilson had long worried that the eating clubs posed a threat to his mission of placing academic pursuits at the center of life at Princeton, it was not until the late fall of 1906 that he finally turned to the issue. So severe was club mania that students from prep schools sending large delegations to Old Nassau often organized themselves for freshman club membership while still seniors in secondary school. At the same time, the proportion of Princeton upperclassmen in eating clubs grew to 75 percent, leaving those excluded feeling so rejected that they sometimes left college altogether.[168]

The obstacle that the clubs posed to raising Princeton's academic standing was motivation enough to move forward, and the fact that Wilson's reform efforts might lead to a public confrontation with a highly visible symbol of social privilege was hardly negative for a man who had felt the first stirrings of national political ambition. At a meeting of the board of trustees on December 13, 1906, Wilson laid out his diagnosis of the problem. The eating clubs, he said, had fostered "a sharp social competition . . . upon which a majority of men stake their happiness." As a consequence, "the spirit of the place has grown less democratic than it used to be." The many men who fail to be selected are "more and more thrust out of the best and most enjoyable things which university life naturally offers — the best comradeships, the freest play of personal influence, the best chance of such social consideration as ought to be won by natural gifts and force of character." Overall, he concluded, the clubs and the increasing "luxury of life" they promoted were a force for "disintegration" and "demoralization."[169]

Wilson's remedy was radical. In a meeting with the trustees on January 10, 1907, he proposed to adopt a Quadrangle Plan: students of all four classes would live together, under the supervision of a resident master and preceptors, in residential quadrangles with a common dining hall and a common room for social interaction. Clearly inspired by the colleges at Oxford and Cambridge, the Quad Plan, Wilson acknowledged, would be a death knell for the eating clubs, for it implied "either their abolition or their absorption."[170] Though the Quad Plan foreshadowed the house and college plans that would be put into effect a quarter of a century later at Harvard and Yale, in the context of Princeton it was nothing less than revolutionary. Wilson was proposing to eliminate the very institution that defined the Princeton experience for many students and alumni.

Given the opposition that such a bold plan might have been expected to cause, it is testimony to Wilson's enormous stature that the initial response was positive. At a June 10, 1907, meeting of the trustees convened to discuss the Quad Plan, Wilson drew in full on his tremendous authority as well as his formidable powers of persuasion. "A vital spontaneous intellectual life," he declared, was the supreme purpose of the university, but "Princeton's intellectual development and academic revitalization" were gravely endangered by the growing prominence of the eating clubs. "If the present tendencies of undergraduate organization are allowed to work out their logical results," he warned, "the University . . . seems in danger of becoming . . . only an artistic setting and background for life on Prospect Avenue."

Predisposed to defer to the man who had carried Princeton to new heights of prominence and dazzled by his extraordinary eloquence, the Board of Trustees — a body known for its conservatism — adopted Wilson's plan by a vote of 24–0, with a single abstention.[171] But Wilson's apparent triumph was short-lived. Virtually from the moment that the Quad Plan appeared in the *Princeton Alumni Weekly* of June 12, opposition mounted. Media coverage, though generally favorable, fanned the flames of alumni resistance. The *New York Times,* for example, headlined its story "Wilson to Abolish Clubs," followed by the subhead, "He Declares They Are a Menace to the Life of the University."[172] To many Old Tigers (as Princeton alumni were sometimes called), however, the eating clubs *were* the life of the university, and a not inconsiderable number remained active members after graduating, returning to stay there for football games and other occasions. To them, Wilson wanted to eliminate what was best about Princeton.

Though Wilson faced opposition from several prominent faculty members, including the dean of the Graduate School Andrew West and Professor of Logic John Grier Hibben (his successor as president of Princeton), a majority of the faculty supported the Quad Plan. On October 1, 1907, the faculty voted, 80–23, to reject a resolution for the preservation and reform of the club system — a great triumph for Wilson. Though his opponents emphasized that 49 of the 50 preceptors had voted on the side of the administration, the tenured faculty had supported him, albeit by the narrower margin of 31–22. But their verdict was clear: the clubs should go. To Oswald Veblen, a preceptor who had come to Princeton from the University of Chicago, the battle over the clubs was a struggle between those who wished to keep Princeton a college and those who wished to make it a genuine university.[173]

Shortly after Wilson first announced his proposal, his wife sardonically told the *New York Evening Post* that "he has ruined what was universally admitted to be the most agreeable and aristocratic country club in America by transforming it into an institution of learning."[174]

Yet by the time the faculty approved the Quad Plan, opposition had intensified where it mattered most — among the alumni, on whom Princeton increasingly depended for financial support.[175] A man's club, wrote Arthur H. Osborn '07 in a letter to Wilson, was his "second home." The clubman "cannot help but feel angry when he sees property of which he is at least part owner confiscated. It is contrary to the Constitution of Our Country."[176] Such sentiments were common among Old Tigers; Bayard Henry, a trustee who had initially supported the plan, concluded on reflection that even the idea of serving the same food to all students was "socialistic and not natural."[177]

Though Wilson had been careful in public to justify his Quad Plan on academic rather than social grounds, his opponents presented it as a misguided attempt to impose "democracy" on an unwilling population. Henry Fairfield Osborn 1877, the noted paleontologist and curator (later president) of the American Museum of Natural History, wrote to Wilson that he wanted Princeton to attract men "who have the good fortune to be born with some means and with natural advantages of home culture and refinements." The sons of the privileged, he argued, were destined to be more successful in life than the "sons of obscure men."[178]

On October 10, 1907, the Ivy Club, the oldest and most prestigious of Princeton's eating clubs, submitted a report on the proposed plan that was forthrightly elitist: "The work that Princeton should do for our country," it declared, "cannot be fully accomplished unless she attracts all grades of boys including the wealthier and more socially desirable boys into her halls." Wilson's scheme, the report argued, would have harmful effects on Princeton, for its insistence on forced mixing would inevitably lead the most "desirable" boys to enroll elsewhere.[179] The attitude underlying this report was encapsulated in a remark allegedly made by a Philadelphia matron: "No one is going to make my boy eat with muckers."[180]

For Wilson, the struggle over the plan was a moral crusade; in a letter to a friend, he described it as "a scheme of salvation" and confided that "my heart is in it more than anything else."[181] For the alumni, the stakes were equally high; Wilson's attack on the clubs, they correctly intuited, was an attack on an entire way of life that reveled in social exclusivity. Often clubmen as adults, they joined Princeton's eating clubs, then moved on to a larger pattern of club membership that included country clubs, summer resorts, and — at the capstone of the system — the metropolitan men's clubs that played such an important role in the maintenance of "gentlemanly control of social, political, and economic power."[182] From their perspective, the elaborate eating club system was an unsurpassed vehicle for socializing — and ranking — the next generation of gentlemen.[183]

So when Princeton's trustees convened on October 17, 1907, to decide the fate of the Quadrangle Plan, the tension in the room was palpable. Though the plan had the support of the majority of the faculty, alumnus and trustee opinion had turned overwhelmingly against it in the four months since the trustees had authorized Wilson to proceed. Especially damaging to Wilson's cause was the revelation by H. G. Murray, the secretary of the Committee of Fifty (a group of some of Princeton's wealthiest and most loyal alumni), that opposition to the Quad Plan was so fierce that it was endangering the school's finances. Since Wilson's announcement of the "quad scheme," he reported, contributions had slowed to a trickle (no more than $300), and cancellations amounted to thousands.[184] When Moses Taylor Pyne 1877 — a generous donor, the most influential trustee, and a member of some two dozen clubs in New York, and elsewhere — announced his opposition to the plan, its fate was sealed.[185] Three resolutions, all put forward by Pyne, passed with only one dissenting vote. They stated that the action taken by the board in June was no longer in effect, that the president should withdraw his Quadrangle Plan, and that the committee that had proposed it be disbanded. Though Wilson's friends on the board managed to pass a face-saving resolution recognizing that "the President's convictions have not changed," freeing him to continue to try to persuade the Princeton community of the plan's wisdom, Wilson himself described the result of the meeting as "complete defeat and mortification."[186]

The defeat of the Quadrangle Plan was a fateful moment in Princeton's history. For the next half century and beyond, the eating clubs constituted the centerpiece of Princeton's campus culture, defined its public identity, and exerted a profound influence in determining who would — and would not — apply to Old Nassau. Having survived Wilson's challenge, the club system emerged strengthened, with the number of eating clubs growing to seventeen in 1913 and membership reaching 90 percent by the 1930s.[187] Unlike Harvard and Yale, where the majority of students did not belong to a final club or a senior society, at Princeton, failure to be elected meant relegation to the outer margins of campus life. This gave status consciousness a pervasiveness at Princeton unlike anything at Harvard or Yale — a pattern reinforced by the clubs' organization into a well-understood hierarchy that made it possible to determine where each student ranked.

Ironically, Wilson's refusal to admit defeat reinforced the very country club image that he had worked so hard to eliminate. First in his continued battle for the Quad Plan, which continued into 1908, and later in his fight for a centrally located, research-oriented Graduate College, which lasted until 1910, Wilson increasingly presented his reforms as a battle of democracy against privilege. In a speech at the Princeton Club of Chicago on March 12, 1908, he launched a direct assault on the eating clubs, denouncing them for favoring private school boys and athletes while enforcing conformity. But the core of the speech was an eloquent defense of the great American ideals of equality of opportunity and classlessness. Expressing his "absolute sympathy with that order of life . . . under which every man's chance was rendered as free as every other's and under which there was no preferment of persons or classes in the lawmaking of the country," he expressed alarm that Americans were beginning to think in terms of classes.[188]

Having taken his crusade for educational reform outside the confines of the campus, Wilson had become an increasingly visible national political figure. By the summer of 1908, his name was being mentioned as a possible nominee for both president and vice president. In November, following the defeat of William Jennings Bryan's third candidacy for president, Wilson looked squarely at the possibility of a political career, telling a friend that "the fray would be delightful, and would be free of all the polite restraints of academic controversy."[189]

As recently as 1904, Wilson had been a conservative Democrat who denounced "populists and radical theorists" and called on the Democrats to create "a party of conservative reform." But by 1908 he had moved to the left.[190] While this shift may in part have been the product of an aspiring politician who recognized the power of appeals to the "people" against the "interests" in an era of muckraking and growing Progressive power, Wilson had also been genuinely offended by the power of the wealthy to frustrate his reforms at Princeton.[191] Shortly after the trustees voted down the Quad Plan, a sympathetic trustee urged Wilson to publicly denounce "the money spirit of the opposition." Though Wilson refrained from taking this step, there is little doubt that the plan's final defeat led him to believe that "University policy had become the victim of entrenched wealth."[192] By the summer of 1909, further embittered by the trustees' fierce opposition to his plan for a Graduate College, he privately disparaged "the restless, rich, empty-headed people" who had ruined his plans for Princeton.

In a note to Moses Pyne written on December 22, 1909, he expressed strong disapproval of a large donation from William Cooper Procter (of Procter and Gamble), declaring that "I cannot accede to the acceptance of gifts upon terms which take the educational policy of the University out of the hands of Trustees and Faculty and permit it to be determined by those who give money." Writing to a friend, Wilson was even more blunt; his proposal to build the Graduate College at the center of the campus, where it would symbolize the university's commitment to intellectual excellence, had been defeated "because money talked louder than I did."[193]

As Wilson became increasingly embittered, his public rhetoric escalated. In a speech at St. Paul's in June 1909, Wilson said that "sideshows" (the eating clubs) were swallowing the "main circus" (the university's academic offerings) and that wealthy people were to blame. A month later, in a Phi Beta Kappa address at Harvard, he attributed the proliferation of extracurricular activities to the lack of interest in books of the businessmen's sons then crowding the colleges. And on February 3, 1910, in an editorial in the *New York Times* virtually ghostwritten by Wilson, Princeton was presented as the chief battleground in the struggle between "democracy" and "privilege." At stake, said the editorial, was whether Americans' endowed universities would fulfill their "democratic mission" or be degraded into "mutually exclusive social cliques, stolid groups of wealth and fashion, devoted to non-essentials and the smatterings of culture."[194]

While genuinely angry at the moneyed men who, in his view, exerted a corrosive influence on America's leading institutions of higher education, Wilson recognized that his struggles for campus reform had elevated his public profile and catapulted him into the top rank of national political leaders. On February 28, 1910, his wife, Ellen, told him that "his defeat in the controversy over the Graduate College left him free again . . . to accept the nomination for governor and go into politics." His setback on the campus, she told him, "has strengthened you *immensely* throughout the country, it is said there have been hundreds upon hundreds of editorials and all *wholly* on your side." As the moment came for Wilson to decide whether to run for governor of New Jersey, he explained that the position was "the mere preliminary of a plan to nominate me in 1912 for the presidency."[195]

Wilson's resignation from Princeton was now only a matter of time. But before leaving, he landed one last blow against the forces that had thwarted his reforms. Having just learned of his humiliating defeat on the question of the Graduate College, Wilson delivered an impassioned speech before the Princeton alumni of Pittsburgh on April 16, 1910. It was the speech of an angry man who had decided to abandon the formal niceties of academe for the rough-and-tumble world of politics.

Taking a populist stance, Wilson launched a frontal attack on the Protestant churches, accusing them of "serving the classes and not the masses" and showing more regard "to their pew-rents than to the souls of men." The universities fared no better: "We look for the support of the wealthy and neglect our opportunities to serve the people." The strength of the nation, Wilson proclaimed, came not from the "handful of conspicuous men [who] have thrust cruel hands among the heartstrings of the masses of men upon whose blood and energy they are subsisting," but rather "from [the] great mass of the unknown, of the unrecognized men, whose powers are being developed by struggle." Wilson concluded with a heartfelt plea: "I have dedicated every power that there is in me to bring the colleges that I have anything to do with to an absolutely democratic regeneration in spirit, and I shall not be satisfied . . . until America shall know that the men in the colleges are saturated with the same thought, the same sympathy that pulses through the whole great body politic."[196]

This speech won Wilson no friends in Princeton and effectively destroyed whatever small chance he may have had to carry out his educational plans there.[197] In October, he formally submitted his resignation, and on November 8, 1910, he was elected governor of New Jersey by a landslide. His reputation as a defender of democracy against the power of wealth and privilege having been secured in no small part by his struggles at Princeton, Wilson was now on the road that would take him to the White House.

Wilson's accomplishments during his eight years as president of Princeton were considerable. Having inherited an institution whose academic reputation was in sharp decline, he restored its standing among America's leading universities. Wilson elevated Princeton's standards of admission and retention, and he implemented a program of curricular reform that combined a broad grounding in the liberal arts with opportunities for specialization and advanced work. Above all, he raised the quality of the faculty and of instruction, bringing talented and energetic instructors to the new preceptorial system. Of the 50 young men he brought to Princeton to serve as preceptors, 21 remained on the faculty until retirement; among them were some of the university's most distinguished professors.[198] Moreover, in this period the Princeton faculty became markedly less inbred, with the proportion of alumni dropping from 68 to 41 percent.[199]

Yet in many fundamental ways the Princeton that Wilson left in 1910 was remarkably like the institution that he had inherited. Though he had set out to make Princeton a major national center for graduate education, graduate enrollment had in fact been virtually static, while that of other major universities had been increasing rapidly.[200] Intellectually, Princeton, though improved, still remained something of a backwater when Wilson departed, especially compared to great research universities such as Harvard, Chicago, and Columbia.

Perhaps the clearest indication of just how little Princeton had changed was in the composition of its student body. The college most dominated by private schools when Wilson was inaugurated, it retained that status when he resigned, with only 20 percent of the freshman class coming from public schools.[201] Racially, Princeton remained as segregated as ever, with not a single black student; indeed, in response to a 1909 letter from "a poor Southern colored man from South Carolina" who expressed an interest in Princeton, Wilson responded that it would be "altogether inadvisable for a colored man to enter."[202] Finally, of the Big Three, Princeton remained the closest thing to a WASP preserve; in 1910, Catholics and Jews composed just 6 percent of freshmen, and nearly two-thirds of the new entrants belonged to just two Protestant denominations: the Episcopal and Presbyterian churches.[203]

In part, this lack of diversity reflected Wilson's preference for a "compact and homogeneous community."[204] To be sure, Princeton's location in a small and increasingly fashionable town was not a favorable setting for a heterogeneous student body. But the school's lack of diversity also reflected a conscious decision to exclude commuters from nearby Trenton, a city of nearly a hundred thousand that included large numbers of immigrants. This situation was in sharp contrast to that of both Harvard and Yale, who drew much of their variety from the relatively large number of local public school boys who did not live on campus.[205] The prospect of such boys enrolling at Princeton did not appeal to Wilson; in his view, students who attended Columbia, which had many commuters, were "simply going to a day school."[206] Finally, a relative lack of financial aid reinforced Princeton's homogeneity and aura of exclusivity; among the undergraduates, only about one in eight were on scholarship.[207]

Even E. E. Slosson, an outside observer sympathetic to Wilson, said of Princeton in 1910 that it was an institution that "offers one particular kind of college training to one rather limited social class of the United States." Summarizing the difference between Old Nassau and its Cambridge rival, Slosson said simply: "The aim of Princeton is homogeneity. Harvard's ideal is diversity." Princeton's "entrance requirements," he wrote, "its tuition fees and expensiveness, its limited range of electives, its lack of professional schools, its rules and customs, its life, traditions and atmosphere, shut out or fail to attract the vast majority of potential students."[208]

Yet it was this very image that drew many students to Princeton. Among those attracted by Old Nassau's mystique — its eating clubs, its beauty, and its aura of social exclusivity — was a handsome young man from St. Paul, Minnesota, named Francis Scott Key Fitzgerald (1896–1940). Though he had considered Yale, he preferred Princeton, for he imagined Princeton men as "slender and keen and romantic and the Yale men as brawny and brutal and powerful."[209] Gaining admission, however, did not prove easy, for Fitzgerald had attended a minor Catholic prep school in New Jersey, the Newman School in Hackensack. After initially failing the exams, he took them again in September, this time scoring close to the necessary number of credits. Though he had still not passed, students in his situation could go before a board of appeals and attempt to talk, or "bicker," their way in. This Fitzgerald did, and on September 24, 1913, he was able to wire his mother news of his admission.[210]

Fitzgerald's Princeton — or, more precisely, the indelible portrait of it that he painted in his novel *This Side of Paradise* (1920) — was to enduringly shape the university's reputation. When Fitzgerald entered in the fall of 1913, the Catholic Midwesterner was just one of 405 freshmen, albeit one with strong literary and social ambitions. Prep school boys, who dominated campus life, were themselves arrayed in a finely calibrated hierarchy.[211] At the top of the heap were St. Grottlesex graduates, the young men who defined appropriate modes of behavior, speech, and dress.[212] But for Fitzgerald, as for many freshmen, the personification of the Princeton ideal was the legendary football and hockey star Hobey Baker, a St. Paul's graduate whose exploits on the field were so heroic that he had attained demigod status. In *This Side of Paradise*, Baker served as the inspiration for "Allenby, the football captain, slim and defiant . . . aware that this year the hopes of the college rested on him."[213]

Like many underclassmen, Fitzgerald was obsessed with the eating clubs. But he had a romantic image of them. In his novel, Amory Blaine — the protagonist, who has much in common with Fitzgerald — memorably characterizes the individual clubs: "Ivy, detached and breathlessly aristocratic; Cottage, an impressive mélange of brilliant adventurers and well-dressed philanderers; Tiger Inn, broad-shouldered and athletic, vitalized by an honest elaboration of prep-school standards; Cap and Gown, anti-alcoholic, faintly religious and politically powerful; flamboyant Colonial; literary Quadrangle; and the dozen others, varying in age and position."[214] Fitzgerald's social success at Princeton was confirmed in the spring of 1915 when he was elected to the Cottage, a luxurious club whose president, Walker Ellis, has been described as the "effortless embodiment of all the qualities of elegance and superiority, which were the Princeton ideal." At the Cottage election dinner, Fitzgerald — who at this stage in his life rarely drank heavily — became so inebriated that he passed out cold.[215]

In his preoccupation with club membership, Fitzgerald was a typical Princetonian. At Yale, the competition for senior societies was fierce and overt, but at Princeton the emphasis was on grace, elegance, and good form. Above all, the aspiring member had to appear not to be trying too hard either in extracurricular activities or in the subterranean battle for social position; it was called "running it out" and was fatal to a student's chances for election to one of the better clubs.[216] "I think of Princeton," said Amory Blaine, "as being lazy and good-looking and aristocratic," distilling its ethos of debonair detachment.[217]

Nevertheless, some types of extracurricular accomplishment did count. After football, which stood at the top of the list, the most sought-after campus organization was the Triangle Club, an undergraduate group that annually produced a musical comedy, followed by the *Daily Princetonian* and the *Princeton Tiger*, the humor magazine.[218] Observant students understood the system; in *This Side of Paradise*, Amory Blaine quickly discovered that "writing for the *Nassau Literary Magazine* would get him nothing" but that "being on the board of the *Daily Princetonian* would get anyone a good deal." But the Triangle Club, which "every year took a great Christmas trip," was where "the most ingenious brains and talents were concentrated."[219]

Fitzgerald's prominence in the Triangle Club, where he wrote the plot and lyrics for the play *The Evil Eye*, smoothed his pathway into the Cottage Club. There he met and befriended the suave Walker Ellis '15, who served as president of both Triangle and Cottage.[220] But sheer accomplishment would get one only so far in the world of the eating clubs. Thus it was that Edmund Wilson '16, Fitzgerald's friend and collaborator on *The Evil Eye*, found himself in Charter, a respectable club but by no means an elite one. Wilson's social background was far superior to that of Fitzgerald, whose father had failed in the furniture and soap business before he inherited a comfortable sum of money from his mother. Wilson was descended from Cotton Mather, and his father was a Princeton graduate and a well-known lawyer who had sent young Edmund in 1908 to the Hill School, a major feeder to Old Nassau. But Wilson, destined to be one of America's great men of letters of the twentieth century, lacked Fitzgerald's magnetic good looks and conviviality. In many ways, he was the antithesis of the successful clubman; according to his biographer, "he had no interest in sports, did not play billiards or bridge, did not dance or drink, and did not know any girls to bring to the parties."[221]

The picture of Princeton that Fitzgerald left behind when he published *This Side of Paradise* to considerable acclaim was not one of brilliant and studious loners like Wilson but of graceful and aristocratic young men who led lives of elegance on a campus of "lazy beauty" and "handsome, prosperous big-game crowds."[222] The image that endured was encapsulated in a single, memorable phrase: what drew him most to Princeton, recalled Amory Blaine, was "its alluring reputation as the pleasantest country club in America."[223] For Princeton, which was constantly struggling to attain the level of academic respectability enjoyed by Harvard and Yale, the country club image proved a haunting one. Sensing just how much was at stake, Princeton's president John Grier Hibben took the unusual step of writing to Fitzgerald within weeks of the book's publication. On May 27, 1920, he wrote: "It is because I appreciate so much all that is in you of artistic skill and certain elemental power that I am taking the liberty of telling you very frankly that your characterization of Princeton has grieved me. I cannot bear to think that our young men are merely living for four years in a country club and spending their lives wholly in a spirit of calculation and snobbishness." Fitzgerald, who had dropped out of Princeton because of poor grades and ill health, replied politely a week later, conceding that "*This Side of Paradise* does over accentuate the gayiety [*sic*] and country club atmosphere of Princeton."[224] But the damage was already done; more than forty years after the book's publication, Princeton's administrators were still decrying its effect on the university's reputation.[225]

This country club reputation was not, in the end, entirely fair; Princeton, after all, housed some of the nation's most talented scholars and students, and it remained a leading university. But its aura of luxury and exclusivity — qualities not exactly foreign to the more urban Cambridge and New Haven — did give the college something of a country club flavor. And in one regard the metaphor was particularly apt: in its stance toward Jews, who were excluded from Princeton's eating clubs as surely as they were kept out of the country clubs that arose in the suburbs of America's cities in the late nineteenth and early twentieth centuries. In both cases, social exclusion — and the preservation of Anglo-Saxon dominance — was one of the main functions of the institution.[226]

As with Harvard's final clubs and Yale's senior societies, the exclusion of Jews from Princeton's eating clubs was part of a broader pattern of anti-Semitism. But anti-Semitism at Princeton was particularly early and intense, especially given its tiny number of Jewish students. In 1907, during the controversy over the Quadrangle Plan, a Jewish alumnus named Leon Michael Levy, who had attended Princeton from 1901 to 1903, wrote to Woodrow Wilson, blaming his departure on its "abominable system of club life." The eating clubs, Levy claimed, were responsible for the "social humiliation," "racial contempt," and "class prejudice" he suffered at Princeton. While there, he reported, his only friends were two other Jewish students and two Christians, one of whom he described as "an eccentric literary genius" and the other Princeton's "finest debater" (in all likelihood, Norman Thomas '05).[227]

In his account of Princeton in *Great American Universities*, E. E. Slosson wrote that "anti-Semitic feeling" seemed "more dominant than at any of the other universities I visited." "The Christian tradition of Princeton, the exclusiveness of the upper-class clubs, and the prejudices of the students," he explained, "keep away many Jews, although not all — there were eleven in the Freshman class." "If the Jews once got in," he was told, "they would ruin Princeton as they have Columbia and Pennsylvania."[228]

During the teens, casual anti-Semitism was part of Princeton's natural landscape. In *This Side of Paradise*, Fitzgerald does not give the one Jewish student a name, referring to him simply as "a Jewish youth"; a page later, Amory and his friend Kerry "filled the Jewish youth's bed with lemon pie."[229] Yet despite this hostile atmosphere, the number of Jewish students slowly grew, bringing the number of "Hebrews" (as they were called in the official statistics) to 4 percent of the freshmen class in 1918.[230] In New Haven and Cambridge, the growth in Jewish enrollment was much more pronounced. At Yale, the Jewish proportion of the freshman class rose to a historic high of 9 percent in 1917. And at Harvard, located in a metropolitan area where Jews numbered well over 100,000, Jewish students made up a remarkable 20 percent of the freshmen in 1918.[231]

This growing Jewish presence profoundly discomfited the men who ran the Big Three. Though a high proportion of these young men were competent or better academically, few of them were "gentlemen" by birth and only a handful had much likelihood of attaining that status (should they even desire to do so). Moreover, their numbers were increasing — a product both of the growth of the nation's Jewish population and of the rapid increase in the number of public schools that prepared students to meet the stiff entrance requirements. From the perspective of the Anglo-Saxon men who ran Harvard, Yale, Princeton, and like institutions, something had to be done soon or their schools would be overrun by culturally alien students.

Such sentiments were much in evidence in May 1918 at a meeting of the Association of New England Deans held at Princeton. The topic of the day was the rapid increase in the "foreign element," and the deans of Tufts, Bowdoin, Brown, and MIT all expressed concern about the growing number of Jews. But it was Dean Frederick Scheetz Jones of Yale (Class of 1884) who articulated their fears explicitly: "I think we shall have to change our views in regard to the Jewish element. We should do something to improve them. They are getting there rapidly. If we do not educate them, they will overrun us. We have got to change our policies and get them into shape. A few years ago every single scholarship of any value was won by a Jew. I took it up with the Committee and said that we could not allow that to go on. We must put a ban on the Jews. We decided not to give them any scholarships but to extend aid to them in the way of tuition."[232] Though no formal action was taken, the issue was now on the table: should measures be taken to limit the number of Jews?

For the Big Three, it was not a simple dilemma. At all three institutions, it was a time-honored tradition to admit essentially all male students who met their academic requirements. Furthermore, enormous efforts had been expended over the previous two decades to raise their standards of admission. But now, just as these efforts were beginning to bear fruit, the "wrong" students were passing the exams. Harvard, Yale, and Princeton thus faced a painful choice: either maintain the almost exclusively objective academic standards for admission and face the arrival of increasing numbers of Jews *or* replace them with more subjective criteria that could be deployed to produce the desired outcome. Their decision to do the latter was a great departure from their historic practices and bequeathed to us the peculiar admissions process that we now take for granted.

CHAPTER 3

Harvard and the Battle over Restriction

WHEN THE ASSOCIATION of New England Deans convened to consider the "Jewish problem" in the spring of 1918, it did so amid a rising wave of anti-immigrant sentiment. During the decade before America's entry into World War I in 1917, concerns had been growing about the unprecedented wave of immigrants pouring into the United States — a torrent that peaked at over 1.2 million in 1914, when the war in Europe temporarily stemmed the flow.[1] But the American decision to join the British and French in their battle against Germany gave new fuel to nativist sentiment, for it led to an obsession with "100 percent Americanism" — an obsession that cast a suspicious eye toward all Americans not of "Anglo-Saxon" origin.[2]

In June 1917, just two months after Congress declared war, it passed the Espionage Act, which provided penalties of up to twenty years in prison for those who demonstrated, spoke, or wrote against the war.[3] It was followed in May 1918 by the even more draconian Sedition Act, which, in the words of the historian Eric Foner, "criminalized spoken or printed statements intended to cast 'contempt, scorn, contumely or disrepute' on the 'form of government' or that advocated interference with the war effort."[4] Though Eugene Debs, the Indiana-born leader of the American Socialist Party, was sentenced to ten years in prison under these statutes, immigrants bore the brunt of the repression. Thousands of "enemy aliens" were arrested in 1918, and numerous foreign-language newspapers were banned from the mails.[5]

But anti-immigrant sentiment had been rising even before the Wilson administration decided to enter the Great War. In 1911, the famous Dillingham Commission (chaired by the Republican senator William P. Dillingham of Vermont) issued its 42-volume report, giving the restriction forces a legitimacy they had previously lacked.[6] Among the many contributions of the Dillingham Report to the nativist cause was its seemingly scientific documentation of the inferiority of the heavily Catholic and Jewish immigrants of southern and eastern Europe compared to their sturdier, more industrious, and predominantly Protestant "Teutonic" predecessors from Britain, Scandinavia, Holland, and Germany.[7]

Yet it was not until February 1917 — two months before America entered the war — that the restrictionists had their first major legislative victory. Overriding Woodrow Wilson's presidential veto, Congress passed the Immigration Act of 1917, which imposed a literacy requirement on immigrants for the first time in American history. Though ostensibly a neutral act targeted at individuals, the legislation in fact applied the principle of group exclusion to European immigrants — a status previously reserved, as Gary Gerstle has noted, to nonwhites.[8] The real purpose of the act was to cut the number of "new" immigrants from eastern and southern Europe — a point confirmed by Senator William P. Dillingham, the bill's chief architect, who acknowledged that he had endorsed the literacy test only after learning that it would reduce "new" immigrants by 30 percent while not cutting the flow of "old" immigrants at all.[9] When the bill passed on February 5, 1917, the patrician members of the Immigration Restriction League, which had been founded by three Harvard-educated Boston Brahmins in 1894, were so pleased that they held a quiet celebration dinner in Boston's exclusive Union Club.[10]

Social Upheaval and the Rise of Anti-Semitism

Of all the immigrant groups streaming into the United States, none aroused greater antipathy than the Jews of eastern Europe. As early as 1913 William Barclay Parsons, a Columbia University trustee who was one of the early leaders of the movement to limit the number of Jews in elite private colleges, wrote of them: "In character they are terribly persistent. They realize that there has been for 2000 years or more a prejudice against them, and they are always seeking after special privileges for themselves and their people . . . They form the worst type of our emigrants, they supply the leaders to anarchistic, socialistic and other movements of unrest. In the recent election the socialistic vote was confined largely to the East Side and to Brownsville, in Brooklyn, where they live."[11] A year later, Parsons's fears were seemingly confirmed when the Jews of New York City's Lower East Side elected Meyer London, the Socialist Party candidate, to Congress.[12]

Among the most conspicuous public opponents of America's entry into the war was Victor Berger, an Austro-Hungarian Jewish congressman from Milwaukee, then one of the nation's socialist strongholds. Unlike Meyer London, who had reluctantly gone along with American intervention, Berger militantly opposed the war and was sentenced to twenty years in prison under the Sedition Act. Reelected to Congress while headed to jail, he was barred from his seat by his congressional colleagues. Percy E. Quin of Mississippi (Democrat) called Berger "a more dangerous character . . . within the

United States" than any other person and condemned the "colony of Germans . . . in Milwaukee" for reelecting "that enemy of the Government to the Congress."[13]

Reinforcing these fears of Jewish radicalism was the Red Scare of 1919–1920. Provoked by the massive strike wave of 1919 and by the fear that the Bolshevik Revolution might be exported to the United States, the Red Scare led to the arrest of thousands of radical aliens and the deportation of hundreds. Among those deported were many Jews, including the famous anarchist Emma Goldman.[14]

To nativists, the Bolshevik Revolution became the archetypal symbol of radical threats — whether anarchist, socialist, or communist — to "100 percent Americanism." In the minds of many restrictionists, Jews were the primary carriers of the virus of revolutionary socialism; they had, after all, participated disproportionately in the Bolshevik Revolution and allegedly wished to spread communism worldwide.[15] (Leon Trotsky, who had stayed briefly in New York City during World War I, became a convenient symbol of the internationalist Jew dedicated to spreading the revolutionary bacillus globally.) The literacy requirement of the Immigration Act had proved useless against such revolutionaries; unlike the masses of uneducated immigrants who filled America's factories and mines, they were "literate, cerebral, and clever."[16]

In New York City, by then the population capital of world Jewry, stories circulated that "every Jewish immigrant would become a soldier in the revolutionary army then assembling in America."[17] Never mind that many more Jews were in flight from the Bolshevik regime than were trying to spread its revolutionary doctrines or that socialist Jews such as Victor Berger himself were principled anticommunists; in the context of the Red Scare, Bolshevism had become "Jewish Bolshevism" to much of the public.[18]

Reinforcing the hostility to Jews after World War I was the emergence of the doctrine of "scientific racism." Committed to proving the genetic inferiority of the new immigrants, scientific racism provided a respectable intellectual rationale for immigration restriction. Among its many subdoctrines was racial anti-Semitism, the belief that Jews were a distinct, inferior, and unassimilable race.[19]

The high priest of scientific racism was Madison Grant (1865–1937), a New York socialite and the author of the influential book *The Passing of the Great Race* (1916). Born into a wealthy family whose roots in America dated to colonial times, he was educated at private schools and tutored for several years in Dresden, Germany, before entering Yale; he graduated in 1887, then received his law degree from Columbia in 1890. Over six feet tall with an upright carriage and a meticulous dresser, the distinguished-looking Grant radiated self-assurance. Among his friends were Theodore Roosevelt, Elihu Root, and the renowned paleontologist Henry Fairfield Osborn.[20]

Though a lawyer by profession, Grant found his true passions elsewhere. A founder of the New York Zoological Society in 1895, the American Bison Society in 1905, and the Save-the-Redwoods League in 1919, he served from 1922 until his death as vice president of the Immigration Restriction League. Like many eastern patricians, especially those living in centers of mass immigration such as New York and Boston, Grant was deeply worried that America was losing its Anglo-Saxon character. And of the many immigrant groups streaming into the United States, none aroused in him greater animosity than the eastern European Jews then arriving in New York in unprecedented numbers.[21]

Threatened on one side by the throngs of eastern and southern European immigrants and on the other by the rise of nouveaux riches industrial barons, eastern patricians like Grant had been feeling an acute sense of cultural displacement and economic decline since the late nineteenth century. Perhaps the classic displaced patrician was the brilliant Henry Adams, who abandoned the traditional optimism of his class for the dark and defensive musings of a Brahmin resentful that the nation his ancestors had helped found no longer had a place for "a gentleman." To Adams, and to many of his fellow patricians, the Jew became the symbol of an irredeemably vulgar and acquisitive society. By 1890, the temperamental Adams — who a decade earlier had written of Jews without stigma — had taken the first steps down a path that would end in bitter anti-Semitism. Frustrated by his failure to receive the public recognition that he felt was his due and envious of the Jews' apparent adaptability, he became increasingly sour, writing to his brother Brook that even "a furtive Yacoob or Ysaac still reeking of the Ghetto, snarling a weird Yiddish . . . had a keener instinct, and intenser energy, and a freer hand than he — American of Americans."[22] For Adams, the Jew had become a scapegoat for all that he detested about his age, with the word "Jew" becoming interchangeable with "nouveau riche" or "capitalist" and "Jewish" a synonym for "greedy" and "materialistic."[23]

Grant lent his considerable stature as an intellectual and scientist as well as his formidable writing skills to the anti-immigration movement, endowing it with a legitimacy that it would otherwise have lacked. The leader of a Big Three triumvirate that included Henry Fairfield Osborn (Princeton 1877) and Lothrop Stoddard (Harvard '05), Grant was more responsible than any other person for popularizing the idea that important and biologically based racial differences existed *within* Europe. Drawing on the work of William Z. Ripley, the author of *The Races of Europe* and a professor of political economy at Harvard since 1901, he divided Europe's peoples into three basic groups:

the Nordics, the Alpines, and the Mediterraneans. Though each group was classified as Caucasian, there were fundamental differences among them.[24]

At the top of the racial hierarchy were the Nordics, a race of "great stature," "fair skin," and "high, narrow, and straight-nose" whose center of "greatest purity" was in Scandinavia. All over the world, Grant wrote, "the Nordics are . . . a race of soldiers, sailors, adventurers and explorers, but above all, of rulers, organizers, and aristocrats." The Alpine," centered in the Slavic nations of eastern Europe, is "always and everywhere a race of peasants, an agricultural and never a maritime race." Generally "submissive to authority both political and religious," those Alpines found in western Europe are "usually Roman Catholics." The Mediterranean, in turn, is "inferior in body stature to both the Nordic and the Alpine." Found largely in southern Europe, the Mediterranean race had major accomplishments in art to its credit, but "in literature and in scientific research and discovery the Nordics far excel it."[25]

Though convinced of the inferiority of blacks — he referred to African Americans as "a serious drag on civilization" from the time "they were given the rights of citizenship" — Grant was not primarily concerned with their threat to Anglo-Saxon dominance.[26] To be sure, the distinction among the "so-called Caucasians," the "Negroids," and the "Mongoloids" (from whom the American Indians were derived) was an important one.[27] But to early-twentieth-century America, the main threat came not from the nonwhite races but from the Alpines and Mediterraneans who were depleting the Nordic stock that had made the United States great.

According to Grant, "The settlers in the thirteen colonies were over-whelmingly Nordic, a very large majority being Anglo-Saxon in the most limited meaning of the term."[28] But America's racial stock, which had changed radically from the great days of the Revolutionary War, was now threatened by mongrelization, for the hard truth was that "the result of the mixture of two races, in the long run, gives us a race reverting to the more ancient, generalized and lower type." Though his fellow citizens suffered from "a widespread and fatuous belief in the power of the environment, as well as education and opportunity to alter heredity," the reality was that "speaking English, wearing good clothes and going to school do not transform a Negro into a white man."[29] "Americans will have a similar experience," Grant argued, "with the Polish Jew, whose dwarf stature, peculiar mentality, and ruthless concentration on self-interest are being engrafted upon the stock of the nation."[30]

Grant's anti-Semitism was not without a powerful cultural component. "The man of the old stock," he wrote, "is literally being driven off the streets of New York City by the swarms of Polish Jews." Above all, the Jew posed the threat of mongrelization. Partly "Asiatic" in origin and hence not genuinely

Caucasian, the Jew was contaminating America's racial stock. In one of his most memorable passages, Grant specified what was at stake in "racial mixing": "The cross between a white man and an Indian is an Indian; the cross between a white man and a Negro is a Negro; the cross between a white man and a Hindu is a Hindu; and the cross between any of the three European races and a Jew is a Jew."[31]

Though *The Passing of the Great Race* received little response when it was first issued in 1916, subsequent editions were published to great acclaim in the more receptive atmosphere of 1920 and 1921. Described by John Higham, the author of the classic work on American nativism, as the central intellectual inspiration for the resurgent racism of the early 1920s, Grant's book sold over 16,000 copies.[32] In addition to having a wide influence on the scholarly community, Grant's work received a warm reception in the media, receiving favorable mention in the *New York Times,* the *Boston Evening Transcript* (the preferred newspaper of the Boston Brahmins), and *Science,* the journal of the American Association for the Advancement of Science.[33] Most important, it was endorsed in 1921 in an editorial in the *Saturday Evening Post,* then America's most widely read magazine, with a circulation of 2 million.[34] Aided by a series of articles in the *Post* by the well-known writer Kenneth L. Roberts on the grave threat posed to America by European immigration, Grant's tripartite distinction among Nordics, Alpines, and Mediterraneans moved into the popular consciousness.[35]

Joining Grant in the pantheon of leading scientific racists was his close friend and ally Henry Fairfield Osborn (1857–1935). A member of an old Scottish Presbyterian family from New York's mercantile elite, Osborn grew up in a household closely connected to the leading political and financial figures in nineteenth-century New York City. The son of the president of the Illinois Central Railroad, Osborn studied in England with Thomas Huxley and Francis Balfour after graduating from Princeton in 1877. Receiving his Ph.D. in 1881, he joined the Princeton faculty, becoming a professor of comparative anatomy, biology, and zoology. In 1891, he accepted a joint appointment at Columbia and the Museum of Natural History. President of the museum from 1908 to 1933, he attained international renown as a paleontologist and the moving force behind one of the world's leading science museums.[36]

A devoted alumnus, Osborn was a vigorous defender of Princeton's eating clubs and a stout opponent of Woodrow Wilson's Quadrangle Plan. An active clubman himself, he belonged to the University, Century, Boone and Crockett, Princeton, and Half Moon clubs of New York and the Cosmos Club of Washington. Like his friend Grant (who served as a trustee of the Museum of Natural History), Osborn was obsessed with the threat that southern and eastern European immigrants posed to the nation's racial stock and to its Anglo-Saxon heritage. In his preface to the second edition of *The Passing of the Great Race,* he insisted that "heredity and racial predisposition are stronger and more stable than environment and education."[37] A leading member of the eugenics movement, Osborn looked to it "for the conservation of the best spiritual, moral, intellectual, and physical forces through heredity," for only through eugenics would "the integrity of our institutions be maintained in the future." Osborn was clear about what he thought was the greatest threat facing America: "The gradual dying out among our people of those hereditary traits through which the principles of our religious, political and social foundations were laid down and their insidious replacement by traits of less noble character."[38]

Like Grant, a fervent advocate of immigration restriction, Osborn believed that "the Anglo-Saxon branch of the Nordic race" was the group upon which "the nation must chiefly depend for leadership, for courage, for loyalty, for unity, and harmony of action, for self-sacrifice and devotion to an ideal."[39] He believed that the "Nordic tide which flowed into Italy" provided Raphael, da Vinci, Galileo, Titian, and Botticelli; even Columbus, he claimed, "was clearly of Nordic ancestry."[40] In his opening address to the Second International Congress of Eugenics, held in 1921 at the Museum of Natural History, Osborn sounded the alarm: just as "science has enlightened government in the prevention and spread of disease, it must also enlighten government in the prevention of the spread and multiplication of worthless members of society."[41]

The third and youngest member of the triumvirate of scientific racism was Theodore Lothrop Stoddard (1883–1950), a Harvard graduate (A.B. '05 magna cum laude, Ph.D. in political science in 1914) and the son of the prominent writer and lecturer John Lawson Stoddard. A member of an old Protestant family that had produced many ministers, Stoddard was a militant agnostic and considered himself a "scientific humanist." Already convinced by 1910 that "the key-note of the twentieth century world-politics would be relations between the primary races of mankind," he wrote his doctoral thesis on the bloody revolt of the blacks against the French colonists in Santo Domingo in the late eighteenth and early nineteenth centuries.[42]

A practicing journalist who had served as director of foreign affairs for the important magazine *The World's Work,* Stoddard was a devout disciple of his friend and mentor Madison Grant.[43] In 1920, he became famous almost overnight with the publication of his volume, *The Rising Tide of Color Against White World-Supremacy.* With a twenty-page introduction by Grant — who praised Stoddard as a "prophet" who "takes up the white man's world and its potential enemies as they are to-day" — the book put forward a bold thesis: the "white world," wracked by "internal Bolshevist disaffection," was "ill-prepared to confront — the rising tide of color" sweeping across broad sectors of the globe.[44] While emphasizing the global conflict between the "white man" and the "colored man" (yellow, brown, black, and red) to an even greater extent than Grant, he agreed with his mentor on the fundamental threat to the United States: the invasion by "hordes of immigrant Alpines and Mediterraneans, not to mention Asiatic elements like Levantines and Jews." The "melting pot," he declared flatly, was "an absurd fallacy," for "each race-type, founded ages ago, and 'set' by millenniums of isolation and inbreeding, is a stubbornly persistent reality." When different races intermarry, "the offspring is a mongrel — a walking chaos so consumed by his jarring heredities that he is quite worthless."[45]

In Stoddard's schema, the Jew was perhaps the most menacing figure of all. More Asiatic than white, Jews constituted a kind of vanguard for Asian barbarism in its timeless conflict with European civilization. Jews, Stoddard insisted, were a mongrel race, a people with "dwarfish stature, flat faces, high cheekbones, and other Mongoloid traits" — a set of characteristics that he traced to their putative origins among Mongolian Khazars.[46] The very archetype of the "Under-Man" who posed a threat to the civilized world, the Jew — "instinctively analytical, and sharpened by the dialectic subtleties of the Talmud" — had provided the leadership of the "largely Jewish Bolshevist regime in Soviet Russia."[47]

Released at the dawn of what E. Digby Baltzell has aptly called the Anglo-Saxon decade, *The Rising Tide of Color* was highly controversial even then. Yet though satirized by F. Scott Fitzgerald in *The Great Gatsby* (the dull and brutal Tom Buchanan praises "*The Rise of the Colored Empires* by this man Goddard"), the book was a great commercial success, going through fourteen printings by 1923.[48] Stoddard was considered an authoritative figure by many military officers, with his books standard reading at the Army War College, and he testified before Congress as an expert witness on immigration.[49] But the clearest sign of his influence came from the respect he received from President Warren G. Harding in a 1921 speech in Birmingham, Alabama: "Whoever will take the time to read and ponder Mr. Lothrop Stoddard's book on *The Rising Tide of Color* . . . must realize that our race problem here in the United States is only a phase of a race issue the whole world confronts. Surely we shall gain nothing by blinking at the facts."[50]

By early 1921, the racist and nativist ideas promulgated by Stoddard, Grant, and Osborn had come to dominate respectable opinion. In February 1921, Calvin Coolidge, as vice president–elect of the United States, endorsed their essential principles in an article in *Good Housekeeping:* "There are racial considerations too grave to be brushed aside for any sentimental reasons. Biological laws tell us that certain divergent people will not mix or blend. The Nordics propagate themselves successfully. With other races, the outcome shows deterioration on both sides. Quality of mind and body suggests that observance of ethnic law is as great a necessity to a nation as immigration law."[51] Later that spring, both the *New York Times* and the *Saturday Evening Post* published editorials sympathetic to these views.[52]

The stage was now set for the scientific racists to achieve their most cherished objective: the passage of a law that would restrict the immigration of "undesirable" peoples. In addition to the favorable cultural and intellectual atmosphere, economic and political conditions were ripe; by late 1920, the United States was suffering from both high unemployment and the lingering suspicion from the Red Scare that immigrants posed a radical threat to the American way of life.[53] At the epicenter of these nativist fears were Jews. According to testimony given to the House Immigration Committee by an official in the State Department, America was threatened by an inundation of "abnormally twisted" and "unassimilable" Jews — "filthy, un-American, and often dangerous in their habits."[54] Testimony delivered before the Senate Committee on Immigration on January 11, 1921, was even more explicit; according to Captain John B. Trevor, Harvard '02 and a friend of Madison Grant's who had worked for the Military Intelligence Division (MID) of the army, a map of New York City that coded in red neighborhoods with high levels of radical activity revealed that these districts were "chiefly inhabited by Russian Jews."[55]

Alarmed, the House and Senate passed by overwhelming margins a bill that imposed "the first sharp and numerical limits on European immigration."[56] Initially vetoed by President Wilson, who was by then a lame duck, it was signed into law by President Harding on May 19, 1921. Unlike the 1917 law, which had failed to stem the flow of "non-Nordic" immigrants, the 1921 law accomplished its goal. By 1923, the number of immigrants from eastern and southern Europe had dropped from 513,813 to 151,491. As a proportion of immigrants from all over the world, this group's share had shrunk from almost two-thirds to barely more than a quarter.[57]

Intended to preserve the predominantly Anglo-Saxon composition of the population, the Immigration Act of 1921 was also a self-conscious attempt to keep political radicals out of the United States. Devised in part to limit the entry of Italians (who were thought to produce anarchists like Sacco and Vanzetti), the new law was designed to drastically reduce the number of Jews from Poland and Russia — widely believed to be the primary carriers of the un-American ideology of socialism.[58] Though the law never explicitly mentioned Jews, there was little question at the time of its target. In *Jews in America*, published just two years after the immigration law of 1921 was enacted, the Pulitzer Prize–winning journalist Burton J. Hendrick did not mince words: the law was "chiefly intended — it is just as well to be frank about the matter — to restrict the entrance of Jews from eastern Europe."[59]

Anti-Semitism, though it had not yet reached high tide, was by 1921 surging across America.

Harvard: The Quota Controversy and the Quest for Restriction

As the nation moved to limit the number of Jewish immigrants, the Big Three confronted their own "Jewish problem." Harvard, just minutes away from the nation's fourth-largest concentration of Jews and long considered more open and democratic than Yale and Princeton, was particularly vulnerable to a "Jewish invasion."[60] By 1918, when the Association of New England Deans first discussed this issue, Harvard's freshman class was 20 percent Jewish. This was by far the highest proportion in the Big Three: three times the percentage at Yale, six times that at Princeton.[61]

A vice president of the Immigration Restriction League, President A. Lawrence Lowell was no friend of the Jews. But even had he been free of anti-Semitic sentiments, he would have had reason to worry about the consequences for Harvard of its growing Jewish presence on campus. For at a certain point, the arrival of the Jews would mean the departure of the sons of the Protestant upper and upper-middle classes whom Harvard most wished to enroll. Far more than an expression of cultural prejudice, Harvard's preference for these young men — which it shared with all the other leading private colleges — was quite rational from an organizational perspective. After all, who but the sons of the Protestant elite would provide the "paying customers," the gentlemanly atmosphere, and the future leaders in business and government — not to mention generous donors — on which Harvard's claims to preeminence ultimately rested?

For anyone who doubted the existence of a "tipping point" of Jewish enrollment beyond which the WASP elite would abandon a college, Columbia served as a sobering example. Located at the epicenter of European immigration, Columbia could hardly ignore New York's vast Jewish population, which dwarfed that of any other American city. As early as 1908, the headmaster of Horace Mann, a leading private school in New York, reported to Columbia's president Nicolas Murray Butler that the prevailing view among parents with children in private school was that "the University undergraduate body contains a prepondering element of students who have had few social advantages and that as a consequence, there is little opportunity of making friendships of permanent value among them. As a result, most of the parents sent their children out of the city for college."[62] One year later, a visitor to Princeton reported sentiment among the students that the Jews had already ruined Columbia.[63] And by the 1910s a college song offered a revealing glimpse into students' perceptions of Columbia:

> Oh, Harvard's run by millionaires,
> And Yale is run by booze,
> Cornell is run by farmers' sons,
> Columbia's run by Jews.
> So give a cheer for Baxter Street,
> Another one for Pell,
> And when the little sheenies die,
> Their souls will go to hell.[64]

By 1914, the "Jewish problem" was so great at Columbia that its dean, Frederick Keppel, openly acknowledged the widespread perception that the large number of immigrants had made it "socially uninviting to students who come from homes of refinement." While publicly insisting that "Columbia is not 'overrun' with Jews any more than it is with Roman Catholics or Episcopalians," Keppel privately admitted that "boys whose families are in New York society" had a strong tendency to go out of town for college and that no conceivable plans that Columbia could devise would attract them.[65] In truth, New York's upper class had begun to abandon Columbia as early as the 1890s. But the arrival of large numbers of Jews in the years after 1910 seems to have decisively accelerated the process; still attracting 16 percent of the sons of New York's elite between 1900 and 1909, the proportion dropped precipitously the following decade to 6 percent.[66]

By the time Columbia finally moved vigorously to repel the "Jewish invasion," it was far too late. Though the proportion of Jews, which had reached perhaps 40 percent, was reduced to 22 percent by 1921, the sons of the Protestant elite had abandoned Morningside Heights, never to return.[67] In the 1920s, just 4 percent enrolled at Columbia; meanwhile, 84 percent matriculated at the Big Three.[68] A contemporary observer, writing under the veil of anonymity, captured what had happened to the Columbia campus:

> As one casually observes the men of the College, one is struck by the complete lack of undergraduate atmosphere about any group of them. Singularly absent is the grace, the swagger, the tall attractive sleekness which, if it does not always dominate the usual college group, at least always touches it importantly. These men, one senses at once, are not of the highest caste, nor have they among them an influential sprinkling of members of the highest caste for their models . . . Seen quickly, there is even a certain grubbiness about them. One somehow expects them all to be Jews, for it is usually the Jewish members of such a group who lower the communal easy handsomeness.[69]

As the case of Columbia had demonstrated, the possibility of "WASP flight" was a clear and present danger for any institution with a substantial Jewish presence.[70]

The specter of Columbia was very much on the mind of President Lowell

as he confronted Harvard's "Jewish problem." With Columbia and NYU taking active measures to limit Jewish enrollment, Lowell moved in February
1920 to inquire about the number of Jews at Harvard College.[71] Although the
dean's office did not provide a precise estimate, Lowell had ample reason to
worry; a study of higher education enrollment patterns in 1918–1919 among
the leading private colleges revealed that only Columbia and the University of
Pennsylvania — the very institutions that many members of the eastern upper class believed had already been "ruined" by the Jews — had a higher percentage of Jewish students than Harvard.[72]

Though the proportion of Jews in Harvard's freshman class had ranged
from 13 to 20 percent between 1912 and 1919, Harvard retained its close connection to Boston's upper class throughout the 1910s. Indeed, the link between Harvard and Brahmin Boston was far tighter than the historical ties
between the upper classes of New York and Philadelphia with Columbia and
Penn, respectively.[73] By the 1910s, Harvard enrolled 85 percent of the sons of
the Boston upper class, whereas just 52 and 6 percent of their counterparts in
Philadelphia and New York matriculated at Penn and Columbia.[74] Harvard,
moreover, enjoyed a close relationship with the upper class of New York City,
which in recent decades had come to dwarf Boston in economic importance;
in the 1910s, nearly a third of the sons of New York's elite enrolled at Harvard.[75] To Lowell, Harvard's rising Jewish enrollment posed a threat to these
crucial relationships, making it imperative to bring the "Jewish invasion" under control.

In a letter to the Harvard philosophy professor William Earnest Hocking,
who had proposed enlisting the Jewish alumni to assist in eliminating the
"undesirable Jews" (as he claimed had already occurred at Williams),[76] Lowell
explained that his main concern was that the sheer number of Jews would
cause the flight of the Protestant elite and thereby "ruin the college":

> The summer hotel that is ruined by admitting Jews meets its fate, not because
> the Jews it admits are of bad character, but because they drive away the
> Gentiles, and then after the Gentiles have left, they leave also. This happened
> to a friend of mine with a school in New York, who thought, on principle, that
> he ought to admit Jews, but who discovered in a few years that he had no
> school at all.[77] A similar thing has happened in the case of Columbia College;
> and in all these cases it is not because Jews of bad character have come; but
> the result follows from the coming in large numbers of Jews of any kind,
> save those few who mingle readily with the rest of the undergraduate body.
> Therefore any tests of character in the ordinary sense of the word afford no
> remedy.[78]

Lowell's personal preference was "to state frankly that we thought we could
do the most good by not admitting more than a certain proportion of men in

a group that did not intermingle with the rest, and give our reasons for it to the public." But he also anticipated quite presciently that "the Faculty, and probably the Governing Boards, would prefer to make a rule whose motive was less obvious on its face, by giving to the Committee on Admission authority to refuse admittance to persons who possessed qualities described with more or less distinctness and believed to be characteristic of the Jews." For Lowell, however, it was crucial that "the Faculty should understand perfectly well what they are doing, and that any vote passed with the intent of limiting the number of Jews should not be supposed by anyone to be passed as a measurement of character really applicable to Jews and Gentiles alike."[79]

In frankly endorsing a double standard, Lowell was rejecting the argument that applying ostensibly neutral criteria such as "character" would be sufficient to reduce the number of Jews. On this issue, as on many others, Lowell was utterly forthright: his goal was restriction itself. In a letter to Julian Mack, a member of Harvard's Board of Overseers and a federal judge, Lowell made explicit some of the cultural assumptions behind his commitment to a Jewish quota: "It is the duty of Harvard to receive just as many boys who have come, or whose parents have come, to this country without our background as it can effectively educate: including in education the imparting, not only of book knowledge, but of the ideas and traditions of our people. Experience seems to place that proportion at about 15%."[80]

By the spring of 1922, when Lowell moved decisively, the proportion of Jews had already reached 21.5 percent. Unless immediate measures were taken, Lowell wrote in a letter on May 20, it would suffer the fate of Columbia. At Harvard, he warned, "the danger would seem to be imminent."[81]

Compared to rural and small-town institutions such as Dartmouth, Princeton, Williams, and Amherst — which had already taken measures to limit the size of the freshman class and overhaul their admissions policies — Harvard was particularly vulnerable.[82] An urban institution with a long tradition of openness to graduates of public as well as private secondary schools, Harvard was not insulated from the growing numbers of public school graduates who met its entrance requirements. Between 1900 and 1920, the number of male graduates from the nation's high schools had risen from 95,000 to 311,000 — an increase of over 300 percent.[83] The democratization of the opportunity to graduate from high school was a mixed blessing for institutions such as Harvard. While their numbers meant a much larger pool of academically qualified students, it also meant a surge in the number of applicants who lacked the social graces of an earlier generation.[84] Many of these students were from urban areas, and a disproportionate number of them — especially in the college preparatory track — were the children of Russian and Polish Jews.[85]

Left to his own devices, the authoritarian Lowell would have been more than willing to impose his own solution to the "Jewish problem." Indeed, that is precisely what he tried to do when he asked the Committee on Admission to admit as transfers only those "Hebrews . . . possessed of extraordinary intellectual capacity together with character above criticism" and to impose a higher standard for admission to the freshman class on members of the "Hebrew race." This was a covert attempt to impose a quota, but it was rejected by Chairman Henry Pennypacker, a graduate of Harvard (1888) who had served as headmaster of Boston Latin School from 1910 to 1920. Though Lowell's subordinate, Pennypacker told him that the group's members "felt that the Committee should not practice discrimination without the knowledge and assent of the Faculty," of which it was "merely the administrative servant."[86] The stage was thus set for a conflict between the autocratic Lowell and a faculty that, while hardly free of anti-Semitism, was reluctant to publicly endorse a policy of discrimination.

By this time, the faculty was actively involved in the debate about the "Jewish problem" that Lowell had initiated. At a meeting on May 23, Lowell's brother-in-law and personal friend, James Hardy Ropes, the Hollis Professor of Divinity, introduced a three-part motion; its most controversial elements instructed the Committee on Admission "to take into account the proportionate size of racial and national groups in the membership of Harvard College" and declared that "it is not desirable that the number of students in any group which is not easily assimilated into the common life of the College should exceed fifteen percent of the whole college." These proposals, which clearly had Lowell's support, generated a complex and at times bewildering array of amendments and countermotions, some of them supporting the basic thrust of Ropes's proposals and others opposed. Though the motion proposing a 15 percent quota on "any group which is not easily assimilated" (an unsubtle euphemism for Jews) was not approved, the meeting was a partial triumph for Lowell, for a slightly revised version of the other controversial element was passed by a vote of 56–44. It called upon the Committee on Admission, "pending further action by this Faculty . . . to take into account the . . . proportionate size of racial and national groups in the membership of Harvard College."[87] This was a dramatic departure from Harvard's historic commitment to nondiscrimination and, for that very reason, was warmly welcomed by Lowell.

Yet even before the faculty meeting, opposition to Lowell's efforts to limit Jewish enrollment had been growing. In addition to Mack, who had exchanged a series of increasingly tense letters with Lowell, further opposition was expressed by Jerome D. Greene, who had served as secretary to President Eliot (1901–1905) and then secretary to the Corporation (1905–1911).[88] Reportedly Eliot's top choice as his successor, Greene left Harvard to become an important banker in New York two years after Lowell took office.[89] On the Board of Overseers, he was generally thought to represent the views of Eliot, who remained a towering figure at Harvard (and a troublesome presence for Lowell) even though he had retired thirteen years earlier and was nearing the age of ninety.

After conferring with several Harvard officials, including Director of Admission Pennypacker, Greene wrote to Lowell, expressing his view that the "Jewish problem" resided less in any deficiencies among Harvard's Jewish students than in the response of their non-Jewish classmates to their very presence on campus: "The real kernel of this problem seemed to consist not in any question of the relative delinquency of the class of students in question as to either scholarship or conduct, but in the actual disinclination, whether justified or not, on the part of non-Jewish students to be thrown in contact with so large a proportion of Jewish undergraduates." Yet even Greene did not propose maintaining Harvard's policy of admitting students almost exclusively on the basis of academic criteria. Instead, he suggested a faculty study whose objective would be to devise a new policy of admissions "whereby numbers would be kept down or reduced, and the student body limited to the most promising individuals without reference to any question of race or religion." While insisting that these criteria be applied equally to Jews and Gentiles, Greene assured him that the consequence of the new policy "would undoubtedly be to reduce materially the number of those Jews who are of objectionable personality and manners."[90]

That men of goodwill like Greene apparently believed that Jews were far more likely than non-Jews to possess disagreeable personal qualities suggests that even principled opponents of Lowell were not immune to the anti-Semitic sentiments taken for granted in their milieu. Indeed, even Eliot, the leading public critic of Lowell's policy and long a defender of Jews and immigrants, believed that Jews had many "undesirable qualities" rooted in the "century-long persecution to which they have been subjected in the European and Asiatic countries through which they have been scattered."[91] In a 1919 article sympathetic to Zionism that he published in *The Maccabean*, Eliot described many Jews as having "feebled, stunted, undeveloped bodies, and morbid nervous systems" — qualities that made "the Jewish element of the population . . . dreaded at all the large public and private hospitals and dispensaries because it provides so many neurasthenic patients, the treatment of whom is always prolonged and tedious and not infrequently unsuccessful." According to Eliot, Jews' susceptibility "to sudden attack from their Christian neighbors . . . had the inevitable depressing effect on the spirit of the people," rendering them "subservient rather than independent, submissive rather than resistant." Lacking "the good elements in the martial spirit," Jews met "the indignities and cruelties to which they were subjected not with indignant protest but with lamentations, both public and private." Excluded from many occupations, "Jews in all generations developed skill in buying at low prices and in selling at high and also skill in lending money at high rates to impecunious Christians" — qualities that led to their acquiring "among Christians a reputation for being grasping and sharp in their money transactions." "The present Christian generation of European and American origin," Eliot wrote, "dread the clannishness of the Hebrew people who live among them." And although Christians considered "the refined, educated, and public-spirited Jew . . . a thoroughly satisfactory friend and neighbor, the coarse, ignorant, ostentatious Jew is a peculiarly disagreeable product of free institutions, especially if he be newly rich."[92]

This was the classic litany of complaints against Jews, and such sentiments were likely commonplace among the Harvard faculty. Yet faced with the full implications of its actions at the May 23 meeting, the faculty drew back from its implicit endorsement of discrimination. By May 29, Lowell had received four separate petitions requesting that he call a special meeting to permit the faculty to reconsider the motions it had passed less than a week earlier. One petition, signed by 31 faculty members, described the "action of the Faculty relating to controlling the percentage of the Jews in Harvard College" as "a radical departure from the spirit and practice of the College" and declared "that racial considerations should not influence the Committee on Admission before a careful and deliberate study of the whole question of the Jews shall be made by the Faculty."[93] Faced with broad sentiment within the faculty that the actions taken on May 23 were too precipitous and required reconsideration, Lowell had little choice but to call a new meeting.

By now the eyes of the public were fixed on Harvard, and the meeting of the faculty convened on June 2 was a historic one. Early in the meeting, Professor of Biological Chemistry Lawrence Joseph Henderson, a close ally of Lowell's who held strong anti-Semitic views, introduced a motion: "That the Committee on Admission be instructed, pending the report of the special committee, to keep the proportion of Jews in Harvard College what it is at present."[94] This motion would in fact mean the imposition of a Jewish quota. The faculty voted down Henderson's motion, 64–41 — a major setback for Lowell.[95] Yet the call to set a ceiling on Jewish enrollment was supported by some of Harvard's most eminent professors; among them were Albert Bushnell Hart (History), George Lyman Kittredge (English), Richard C. Cabot (Medicine and Social Ethics), and James Bryant Conant (Chemistry), the man who would succeed Lowell in 1933.[96]

Compounding Lowell's defeat was the faculty's decision to rescind by a vote of 69–25 the motions passed at the May 23 meeting.[97] But the faculty stopped short of rejecting Lowell's initiatives altogether, leaving in place the earlier decision to appoint a special committee "to consider principles and methods for more effectively sifting candidates for admission." A key concession, it implicitly recognized Lowell's major point: the "Jewish problem" facing Harvard was a genuine one. Never one to shrink from blunt public declarations, Lowell made it explicit in a statement that was incorporated into the minutes of the June 2 meeting: "The primary object in appointing a special Committee," he declared, "was to consider the question of Jews." If any member of the faculty did not concur, Lowell warned: "Let him speak now or forever after hold his peace."[98]

Utterly convinced of the rectitude of his position, Lowell was confident that he could persuade others that there was no alternative to a quota. But in addition to the equivocal response of the faculty, there was the overwhelmingly negative reaction of the press. Within days of the announcement of Lowell's plan, the *Boston Telegram* ran an editorial: "Down Hill from Harvard to Lowell." In New York, the *Times* responded with an article, "Discrimination Against Jews Suspected in New Harvard Policy on Admission."[99] And the *Nation*, despite its reference to "pushing young men with a foreign accent, accustomed to overcome discrimination by self-assertion," came out unequivocally against Jewish quotas. "A university which bars a persecution-scarred race," its editorial of June 14, 1922, declared, "cannot keep alive the traditions of intellectual integrity, of *noblesse oblige,* and of essential democracy which have made our elder universities play so great a role in American life — or it must open its doors frankly and fairly to all who can meet its requirements of scholarship."[100]

Lowell's proposal also created a storm of political controversy. In addition to an attack from Boston's mayor James Michael Curley ("If the Jew is barred today, the Italian will be tomorrow, then the Spaniard and the Pole, and at some future date the Irish") and a formal resolution of opposition from Samuel Gompers, president of the American Federation of Labor, the proposal also generated a call for a legislative committee, to be appointed by Governor Channing Harris Cox, to investigate whether Harvard was acting in violation of a bill already on the books that mandated equality of opportunity.[101] But Lowell was undeterred.

Believing that the meeting of June 2 had been a success, Lowell wrote to Professor Kittredge, offering his own assessment: "We . . . attained by far the most important object, which was that of making substantially every member of the Faculty understand that we had before us a problem, and that that problem was a Jew problem and not something else. We had also brought the Faculty to the point of being ready to accept a limitation of the number of

Jews, for their own benefit as well as that of the college, if the Committee should, on investigation, report that it is necessary. I have no doubt that they will so report, because I think I know the situation well enough to be persuaded that there is no other solution."[102] However confident Lowell may have been about the faculty's eventual decision, he was not about to delay all action until it had finished its deliberations. In January 1922, four months *before* the faculty began its debate, Lowell instructed the dean's office to use the allocation of scholarships to limit the number of Jews. In an internal memorandum, the dean's office reported that "Mr. Lowell feels pretty strongly that of the scholarships controlled by us the percentage allotted to Jews in their first year at Harvard should not exceed the percentage of Jews in the Freshman Class." In essence, Lowell had imposed a quota on the number of scholarships awarded to Jews regardless of academic performance and need. Though awards were still to be given "primarily on the basis of high scholarship," recipients henceforth were required to be "men of approved character and promise."[103]

At the same time, Harvard was also beginning to gather the information that would permit it to identify which applicants were Jewish. Starting in the fall of 1922, applicants were required to answer questions on "Race and Color," "Religious Preference," "Maiden Name of Mother," "Birthplace of Father," and "What change, if any, has been made since birth in your own name or that of your father? (Explain fully.)" Lest any Jews slip through this tightly woven net by failing to disclose their background (a pattern thought to be rather common, given their alleged lack of character), the high school principal or private school headmaster was asked to fill out a form that asked him to "indicate by a check [the applicant's] religious preference so far as known ... Protestant ... Roman Catholic ... Hebrew ... Unknown."[104]

While moving behind the scenes to stem the flow of Jewish students, Lowell was publicly taking great pains to constitute a visibly balanced Committee on Methods of Sifting Candidates for Admission. Realizing that this committee, which was entrusted with reviewing Harvard's admissions policies, needed to have Jews among its members if it was to have any public legitimacy, Lowell appointed three — Paul J. Sachs ('00, associate professor of Fine Arts), Harry G. Wolfson ('12, professor of Jewish Literature and Philosophy), and Milton J. Rosenau (Honorary '14, professor of Medicine) — to the thirteen-member body. Sachs and Wolfson had voted against Henderson's motion. But Lowell also appointed three men who had voted for the motion (Professor of Hygiene Roger I. Lee '02, Chairman of the Committee on Admission Henry Pennypacker '88, and Henderson himself) and a fourth (Dean Wallace B. Donham '98 of the business school) known to share his position.[105] Though the committee's members represented a wide range of views,

Lowell believed that it would in the end give his proposed policy of restriction a much-needed seal of approval.

Lowell managed to resist strong pressure to place Felix Frankfurter on the committee. The most visible Jewish member of the faculty, the brilliant law professor was an obvious choice. Such, in any case, was the view of Julian Mack, the sole Jewish member of the Board of Overseers, who urged Lowell to appoint him. In making the case for Frankfurter, who had been his close friend for more than a decade, Mack wrote: "If a Jewish member of any of the Faculties is to be on, I think it would be the unanimous judgment of those interested that Frankfurter, by training and by personal experience, is the most fitted to study and deal with the problem. While a Viennese by birth and belonging to the German Jewish, not the East European Jewish, element, he understands the latter as he has grown up side by side with them."[106] But Lowell, who had tangled with Frankfurter on a number of matters and despised his generally liberal political views, was not moved. "All members of the Committee ought," Lowell wrote to Mack, "to be persons in whom all Harvard men feel confidence, and you know that there are many people — including many on the Governing Boards of the University — who have not that feeling towards Professor Frankfurter. Many people with a high opinion of Professor Frankfurter's ability do not trust the solidity of his judgment."[107]

In refusing to appoint Frankfurter, Lowell was doing his utmost to ensure a favorable report from the committee.[108] A formidable debater with a strong personality, Frankfurter might well sway others to his viewpoint, which was strongly against restriction. Equally worrisome, the irascible Frankfurter had a powerful streak of independence and might issue a stinging dissent even if a majority of the committee supported Lowell — a trait that later became visible on the Supreme Court where he wrote 291 dissents.[109] There were still three Jews on the committee. But none of them posed the threat that Frankfurter would have; Sachs was an upper-class German Jew "far removed from the element" that Lowell was targeting, Wolfson was a "scholar pure and simple," and Rosenau was scheduled to be abroad while the committee would do much of its work. From Lowell's perspective, it seemed designed to produce the desired outcome but with enough variety to ensure public legitimacy.[110]

The committee's internal organization gave Lowell little reason to worry. Divided into four subcommittees, the larger committee assigned all three Jewish members to the subcommittee that would meet and correspond with prominent Jews as well as Harvard's Jewish alumni. Jews were not represented on the three other subcommittees, two of which — the subcommittee assigned to see how other colleges were handling their "Jewish problem" (chaired by Henry Pennypacker) and the subcommittee assigned to gather statistics about Jewish students at Harvard — were far more important than the one on which the Jewish faculty served.[111] The fourth subcommittee was enjoined to sample undergraduate opinion, which Lowell believed was largely in favor of restriction.[112]

Of the four, the Subcommittee to Gather Statistics arguably held the greatest potential for long-term impact. In order to count the number of Jews, one had to develop techniques for identifying them — techniques that could later be used to identify Jewish applicants. The subcommittee went about its work with a chilling enthusiasm. It consulted "the original enrollment cards or entries in admissions books" (which included the student's name, place of birth, father's name and occupation, mother's maiden name, home address, and school or college last attended), "bondsmen's names," and "individual college records (as obtained from the Senior Album)." Armed with this information, the group proceeded to classify each Harvard student into one of four categories: "J1," "J2," "J3," and "Other." A "J1" was assigned "when the evidence pointed conclusively to the fact that the student was Jewish," a "J2" when a "preponderance of evidence" suggested the student was Jewish, and a "J3" where "the evidence suggested the possibility that the student might be Jewish." This classification system provided the framework — right down to the tripartite distribution among "J1s," "J2s," and "J3s" — that would be used three years later to limit Jewish enrollment.[113]

After seven months, the subcommittee received a 104-page report with the conspicuously dry title "Statistical Report of the Statisticians."[114] But its contents were anything but dry. A remarkable investigation into the lives of Harvard students between 1900 and 1922, it was designed to provide the statistical evidence that Lowell hoped would clinch his case. Yet the results of the study, which had been conducted with great care, offered ammunition to both sides in the increasingly heated debate.

For those worried that the number of Jews at Harvard was rising, the study offered ample confirmation of their fears. Just 7 percent of freshmen in 1900, Jews had increased steadily over the entire period, rising to 10 percent in 1909, 15 percent in 1915, and 21.5 percent in 1922.[115] But nothing in the study suggested that this growth posed an *academic* problem for Harvard; on the contrary, the Jewish students outperformed their Gentile classmates by a considerable margin. Massively underrepresented among students reported for unsatisfactory academic records (15 percent of Jews vs. 37 percent of non-Jews), they were heavily overrepresented among those who received degrees with distinction (28 vs. 15 percent).[116] Were Harvard committed to raising the academic level of its student body, the proportion of Jews, the evidence suggested, should be increased rather than decreased.

Yet Lowell, aware of these numbers and inclined to dismiss them as the product of the Jewish students' greater dependence on scholarships, had never rested his case for quotas on academic grounds. Convinced that deficiencies in the "character" and ethical standards of Jews resulted in more frequent "discipline for offenses of a moral nature," he planned to press this issue.[117] Even before the faculty had begun to discuss the issue of quotas, Lowell had launched his own investigation. Having received a preliminary report on the misdeeds of Harvard's Jewish and non-Jewish students, he wrote back to the dean's office: "You have basely gone back on me. Somebody told me that of the fourteen men discussed last year for cheating and lying about it, thirteen were Jews. Now you make out that there were twelve of them, of whom only five were Jews. Please produce at once six more!"[118] Around this time, Lowell also told a distinguished alumnus that 50 percent of the students found guilty of stealing books from the library were Jewish. But when asked how many students had been apprehended, Lowell told him, "Two."[119]

The statistical report offered more systematic data on the distribution of offenses of a moral nature. Here Lowell found some apparent support; for the period covered, 4.7 percent of Jews, but only 3.0 percent of non-Jews, were found to be "under discipline." Though less likely to have been found guilty of drunkenness (0.1 vs. 0.5 percent), Jewish students were more likely to have committed "offences invoking dishonesty" (3.7 vs. 2.0 percent). These findings may, of course, have reflected genuine group differences in the propensity to commit such offenses; on the other hand, they may also have reflected a discriminatory pattern of treatment by the university authorities — a possibility compatible with the barely mentioned finding that over 25 percent of Jewish students "under discipline" were expelled compared to only 11 percent of non-Jews.[120] Though the numbers were small, the statisticians did not hesitate to draw out their implications: "The [higher] proportion of Jews under discipline . . . adds much to the strength of any case that could be based on the records."[121] In its final report, the committee as a whole wrote of the Jewish Harvard student in its cover note to President Lowell: "In morals, he seems to be more prone to dishonesty and sexual offenses, but much less addicted to intemperance."[122]

The findings on patterns of student participation in extracurricular and social activities also seemingly lent some support to Lowell. It was his belief that Jewish students were less likely to "do something for Harvard" than their Gentile classmates, and the results of the study confirmed that they were in fact less involved in the nonacademic side of college life. In athletics, which occupied such a central place in campus culture during the 1920s, non-Jews were almost twice as likely to participate as Jews: 48 vs. 25 percent. The discrepancy was even more pronounced off the playing field; there the figure was 33 percent for non-Jews and 11 percent for Jews.[123] But the meaning of these figures was not self-evident. It was possible that the relative paucity of

Jews in Harvard's extracurricular life reflected the lower participation rate of commuting students in general — a group among whom Jews were heavily overrepresented.[124] It was also possible that the Jewish students' low participation rate was in no small part a response to exclusion or hostility on the part of Gentile students.[125]

The committee's findings on social as opposed to extracurricular life in Cambridge offered ample confirmation of the hypothesis that anti-Semitism was a powerful force among the undergraduates. Segregation between Jewish and non-Jewish students was the rule rather than the exception; only 3.6 percent of Jews belonged to social clubs (other than the six Jewish fraternities), compared to 58.6 percent of non-Jewish students.[126] Particularly striking were the committee's findings on the final clubs; for the seven classes that entered Harvard between 1912 and 1918, not a single Jew was elected to any of the five most prestigious clubs: Porcellian, AD, Fly, Spee, and Delphic (Gas).[127] The total exclusion of Jews from the summit of Harvard's social system confirmed what many had long suspected: the sheer fact of being Jewish — regardless of background, education, and personal demeanor — remained a serious social handicap at Harvard.

Lowell hoped that findings like these would convince the "better class" of Jews, many of them of German background, that something needed to be done to stem the flow of "undesirable" Jews. This hope was not unrealistic; at Williams, well-established Jewish alumni had reportedly assisted the college in excluding their "less fit" brethren, and some years later their counterparts did the same at Dartmouth, expressing satisfaction that their alma mater was admitting only "the better type of Jews and not the Brooklyn and Flatbush crowd."[128] At Harvard, hostility on the part of upper-class Jews toward their working-class and immigrant ethnic brethren was hardly unknown. Jesse Isidor Straus, an eminent businessman with three generations of ties to Harvard, reported to Charles Eliot that the "catastrophe" (the bitter controversy over Lowell's proposed policy) had been caused by the increase in Jewish students commuting from East Boston. Though opposed to blanket quotas, he wondered whether "there might have been found some less obnoxious method of discriminating against *them*."[129]

If Lowell was hoping for a prominent Jew to come out in favor of his policy, few prospects seemed more promising than Walter Lippmann '10. Already a renowned writer, Lippmann was an upper-class German Jew who shared Lowell's visceral distaste for the immigrant Jews from Poland and Russia. About the Jewish masses, Lippmann had written: "I worry about upper Broadway on a Sunday afternoon where everything that is feverish and unventilated in the congestion of a city rises up as a warning that you cannot build up a decent civilization among people who, when they are at last, after centuries of denial, free to go to the land and cleanse their bodies, now huddle together in a steam-heated slum." Those Jews of modest origin who had been lucky enough to succeed fared even worse with Lippmann: "The rich and vulgar and pretentious Jews of our big American cities are perhaps the greatest misfortune that has ever befallen the Jewish people . . . They are the real fountain of anti-Semitism. When they rush about in super-automobiles, bejeweled and furred and painted and overbarbered . . . they stir up the latent hatred against crude wealth, and that hatred diffuses itself." Rejecting the cultural pluralism of fellow intellectuals such as Randolph Bourne and Horace Kallen, Lippmann believed that the only solution for Jews, who were more "conspicuous" than Gentiles, was total assimilation. In the words of his biographer Ronald Steel, "The good Jew should lie low, dress and behave unobtrusively and be as indistinguishable as possible from the crowd."[130]

Given these sentiments, it is not surprising that, when Harvard's "Jewish problem" erupted into public view, Lippmann's first inclination was to find a discreet way to reduce the number of Jews. Accepting Lowell's premise that it would be "bad for the immigrant Jews as well as for Harvard if there were too great a concentration," he went so far as to suggest that Massachusetts set up a state university led by Jews to "persuade Jewish boys to scatter." Later, in a draft of a letter to a member of the faculty's committee considering admission criteria, he wrote that "I am fully prepared to accept the judgment of the Harvard authorities that a concentration of Jews in excess of fifteen percent will produce a segregation of culture rather than a fusion." In the clash between the culture of Jews and that of Christians, he added, "My sympathies are with the non-Jew. His personal manners and physical habits are, I believe, distinctly superior to the prevailing manners and habits of the Jews."[131]

Yet, in the end, even Lippmann could not bring himself to endorse an outright quota. Contacted by both Judge Mack and Felix Frankfurter (who was very active behind the scenes), he arranged to meet with Laurence Henderson on October 25, 1922. While sharing his hostility to Polish and Russian Jews, Lippmann was appalled when Henderson — who professed to favor higher intellectual standards — proposed a loophole for students who could not pass the examination if they showed promise of being "business and social leaders." A higher required grade on the entrance examination, Lippmann said, "would be a form of selection wholly without offence to the Jewish people." Though sympathetic to the idea of recruiting students from a wider geographical area — a change that he realized might reduce the number of Jews from New York and Boston — he was opposed to any direct methods of restriction.[132]

By January 1923, as the committee was nearing the end of its deliberations, Lippmann turned militantly against Lowell's policy. In an editorial in the *New York World,* he wrote that at Harvard there had been "a change of soul at the top . . . In the place of Eliot, who embodied the stern but liberal virtues of New England, there sits a man who has lost his grip on the great tradition which made Harvard one of the true spiritual centers of American life. Harvard, with the prejudices of a summer hotel; Harvard, with the standards of a country club, is not the Harvard of her greatest sons."[133] In articulating these sentiments, Lippmann was expressing the views of not only the Jewish alumni of Harvard but of Jews nationwide. In carrying out its work, the committee had interviewed eighty "representative Hebrews on the subject of our Jewish problem." Though of diverse views, "all, or virtually all, were of one accord in vehement opposition to any system based on racial proportion."[134]

Not convinced that Lowell's distinction between "desirable" and "undesirable" Jews would not in the end be used against *all* Jews, Julian Mack and Felix Frankfurter had been successful in convincing Jews on and outside the committee that the best response to Lowell's attempts to divide the Jewish community was one of principled solidarity. But their success in temporarily blocking Lowell's initiative would have not been possible without the active and vigorous support of many distinguished Protestant alumni of Harvard. Particularly crucial was the support of Eliot, then eighty-eight years old, and Greene, Eliot's disciple and an influential member of the Board of Overseers. Throughout the controversy, Eliot and Greene were in close contact, united by their conviction that Lowell had violated fundamental Harvard principles. Believing Lowell to be flawed and untrustworthy, Eliot worked assiduously to block his efforts to impose a quota.[135] Assisted by the tireless and combative Greene and working closely with Mack and Frankfurter, he was able to convince the Board of Overseers that supporting Lowell's proposal would constitute an abdication of Harvard's best traditions.[136]

Completed on April 7, 1923, the final report of the Committee on Methods of Sifting Candidates for Admission was a major setback for Lowell. In the letter accompanying the report, Chairman Charles H. Grandgent wrote that of 100 "Harvard graduates not of Hebrew stock" (many of them "persons of high distinction"), "nearly all protested with earnestness . . . against the principle of racial discrimination." "A few suggested restriction," Grandgent wrote, but "hardly one favored frank limitation." Discussion "in the public and academic press," he noted, was of "like tenor."[137]

A man of extraordinary hubris, Lowell had made a grave error in making public his plan to impose a Jewish quota. As his counterparts at Yale and Princeton grasped intuitively, the public declaration of an intent to discriminate violated core American principles and was likely to lead to a bitter public controversy. This is precisely what happened at Harvard, with Jewish and non-Jewish foes of restriction mobilizing both inside and outside Harvard. Yet Lowell was utterly forthright about his intentions, making it impossible for Harvard to take measures in full public view that more prudent administrators elsewhere were already carrying out behind closed doors. It was a mistake that Lowell would not repeat.

To Eliot's great satisfaction, the committee's members were unanimous in recommending that "no departure be made from . . . the policy of equal opportunity for all regardless of race and religion," adding, "Any action liable to interpretation as an acceptance of the principle of racial discrimination would to many seem like a dangerous surrender of traditional ideals." In the context of 1923, this was a double rebuke to Lowell, for it overturned his policy of excluding African Americans from the freshmen dormitories at the same time that it repudiated his proposed Jewish quota.[138] The committee further stated that "even so rational a method as a personal conference or an intelligence test, if now adopted here as a means of selection, would inevitably be regarded as a covert device to eliminate those deemed racially or socially undesirable and . . . could not fail to arouse damaging suspicion." Finally, in an effort to thwart any attempt by Lowell to circumvent its stand, the committee expressed its opposition to "an arbitrary limitation of the number of students to be admitted" and specified that "if the size of our Freshman class is to be reduced, the reduction can best be accomplished by raising the standard for admission."[139]

To be sure, the report did not give the Mack-Eliot coalition everything that it wanted; in particular, it opposed the committee's recommendation that Harvard admit students "whose scholastic rank places them in the highest seventh of the boys of their graduating class" and "who have satisfactorily completed an approved school course" at "schools which do not ordinarily prepare their pupils for college examinations."[140] Designed to facilitate the admission of "a new group of men from the West and South," the top one-seventh plan seemed to men like Eliot and Frankfurter a thinly disguised attempt to lower the Jewish proportion of the student body by bringing in boys — some of them academically ill equipped for Harvard — from regions of the country where there were few Jews. Despite the opposition of a number of faculty members, however, the top seventh was formally approved at a special meeting of the faculty on April 24, 1923, by a vote of 73–20.[141]

Despite the faculty's approval of the top-seventh plan, Lowell realized that the report constituted a major defeat. While publicly professing support for the committee's work, Lowell wasted little time in working to undermine it. Barely two months later, he persuaded the Fellows of the Harvard Corporation to let him commission a faculty study to determine "whether it might be wise to limit the number of students admitted to the Freshman class to one thousand."[142] A ceiling on the size of the class, he realized, was the necessary precondition for addressing the "Jewish problem," for as long as Harvard had an absolute standard of admission, a discretionary selection policy using nonacademic as well as academic criteria would not be possible. Lowell's revival of the limitation idea — in direct contravention of the committee's guidelines — thus signaled the beginning of a new, more subtle campaign to restrict Jewish enrollment. It was precisely the kind of devious action that Rosenau had anticipated a few months earlier when he told Eliot that "Lowell and the Committee on Admission to Harvard College will exclude Jews all the same."[143]

Indeed, by the end of 1923, Lowell's Committee on the Limitation of Students issued a report recommending a limit of 1,000 on the size of the freshman class and introduced additional changes in the criteria for admission. Whereas selection decisions had been made almost solely on the basis of scholarship, the committee — which included Henry Pennypacker and James Bryant Conant — proposed using letters from teachers and personal interviews to shed light on the candidates' "aptitude and character."[144] It was a major victory for Lowell.

Recognizing the potential for discrimination in the new reliance on nonacademic criteria, Eliot and Mack launched a last-ditch effort to block the new policy before it was approved by the Board of Overseers. But despite letters from Eliot and Mack's decision to return from a trip to Florida for the express purpose of opposing the new policy, it passed easily at the board's meeting on February 25, 1924.[145] Though the Committee on the Sifting of Candidates for Admission had explicitly rejected the idea of "an arbitrary limitation of the number of the students to be admitted" and the use of "a personal conference" in making admissions decisions, the authors of the new policy insisted that "the proposals now made are not in conflict with any of the recommendations of that Committee."[146] The Board of Overseers stipulated that the limit "be reconsidered at the earliest possible time" and that the president of the board should appoint a Special Committee comprising members of the Corporation, the overseers, and the faculty to review and evaluate the policy of limitation.

While these stipulations suggested that the policy was a provisional one, this was not Lowell's interpretation. Seizing on the opening provided by the Overseers' action, he immediately wrote to Pennypacker that the admissions committee was now fully empowered to seek information on the "character" of candidates from "persons who know the applicants well" and that it was "under no obligation" to apply the top-seventh plan "to any school if it does not think it best to do so" and was "at liberty to withdraw the privilege from other schools."[147] Without saying so explicitly, Lowell was telling Pennypacker that he now had the authority to begin reducing the number of Jewish students as long as he did so discreetly.

In his continuing push for the restriction of Jews, Lowell was assisted by the growing momentum of the movement to further limit immigration. Since the passage of the Immigration Act of 1921, anti-Semitism, xenophobia, and racism were all on the rise. Propelled by the exponential growth of the Ku Klux Klan, whose membership peaked at over three million in 1924, and by the mass dissemination of anti-Semitic propaganda in Henry Ford's *Dearborn Independent*, hostility to Jews, blacks, and immigrants escalated from the already high levels of 1921.[148] The nativist wave, which had ebbed and flowed over the course of the nation's history, would reach its crest in 1924.

Adding fuel to the popular sentiment against immigrants were the writings of important Anglo-Saxon intellectuals, many of them alumni of Harvard, Yale, and Princeton. Joining Grant, Osborn, and Stoddard as scientific racism's most prominent proponents were the eugenicist Harry N. Laughlin and Princeton's professor Carl Brigham, himself a 1912 graduate of Princeton.[149] Laughlin claimed to have shown higher rates of genetically based "degeneracy" and "social inadequacy" among the newer immigrant groups, and he served as the "expert eugenics agent" for the House Committee on Immigration and Naturalization.[150] In 1923, Brigham published *A Study of American Intelligence*, a widely publicized work based on the testing of army recruits in World War I — the first mass testing of a population ever conducted. Using the categories of Nordic, Alpine, and Mediterranean developed by Madison Grant, Brigham offered seemingly scientific documentation for the intellectual superiority of Nordics. With considerable alarm, he reported that the average intelligence of Americans was declining — a product, he believed, of increasing immigration from southern and eastern Europe as well as miscegenation between white and black Americans. Contributing to this decline was the growing number of Jews, whom he classified as Alpines because they shared "the head form, stature, and color" of their Slavic neighbors. The results of his study, Brigham claimed, "disprove the popular belief that the Jew is highly intelligent," instead showing immigrant Jews to have I.Q.'s well below average. Unless the United States wished the average intelligence of its population to continue to decline, drastic action was needed. Such action, he wrote, would include not only a much more restrictive and selective immigration policy but also "the prevention of the continued propagation of defective strains in the present population."[151]

Also contributing to the nativist upsurge was the Yale alumnus Burton J. Hendrick (1895), whose widely read book, *The Jews in America*, was published in 1923. Though pleased to inform his readers that the Jew was not as serious an economic threat as many believed (a review of a list of rich New Yorkers revealed the good news that "the racial stocks which founded the United States one hundred and fifty years ago still control its wealth"), Hendrick believed that the Jew did pose a grave political threat. Declaring that "there is a great mass of radicalism among the Polish Jews" — a community that showed "enthusiasm for the doctrines of Karl Marx, in preference to the doctrines of Washington and Jefferson and Franklin and Lincoln and Roosevelt" — he maintained that they were "devoid of patriotism" and "unsympathetic with the thing known as Americanism." Jews, he argued, could best be judged by the newspapers they edited, published, and read — newspapers such as the *Forward* (circulation 160,000), which preached "political principles whose success means the destruction of the American system of government."[152]

Buoyed by the works of sympathetic intellectuals and scientists as well as popular support, the Immigration Restriction League was finally poised to realize its goal: the passage of legislation that would preserve America's predominantly Anglo-Saxon character. With the coalition supporting immigration restriction now ranging all the way from the crude racists of the Ku Klux Klan to the refined gentlemen of the Immigration Restriction League and with the nativist cause now invested with unprecedented intellectual and scientific respectability, the passage of new legislation was all but inevitable.[153] But the proposal favored by leading restrictionists in Congress — to reduce the number of immigrants from southern and eastern Europe by basing the annual quotas on the 1890 rather than 1920 census — seemed to many transparently discriminatory and hence faced strong political opposition. The solution was provided by John B. Trevor, the Harvard alumnus who had played a critical role in passing the Immigration Act of 1921. A truly fair immigration policy, he argued, should be based not on the number of foreign-born in the United States but on the national origins of the entire current population of the United States. By this standard, going back to the 1890 census was more than fair; it was actually generous, for it would allocate 15 percent of the slots for immigrants from the nations of southern and eastern Europe even though only about 12 percent of Americans traced their origins there. With this brilliant rhetorical sleight-of-hand assuaging the consciences of reluctant senators, the watershed Immigration Act of 1924 passed the Senate easily, with only six negative votes, and was signed into law by President Coolidge on May 26, 1924.[154] Reducing the number of immigrants from 350,000 to 150,000 per year while slashing the annual quota for southern and eastern Europeans to fewer than 20,000 (compared to its average annual prewar level of 738,000), the act constituted a historic triumph for the small band of patricians who, thirty years earlier, had formed the Immigration Restriction League.[155]

For Lowell, a former national vice president of the league, the passage of the immigration act was deeply gratifying. But as he surveyed the situation in Cambridge that year, he could not have been equally pleased with the progress of his campaign for restriction at Harvard. Despite his best efforts, Jewish enrollment continued to rise — a striking contrast to the situation at Yale and Princeton, which had moved quietly to limit the number of Jews. By 1924, their measures had succeeded in dramatically cutting Jewish enrollment — at Yale from 13.3 percent in 1923 to 10.0 percent, at Princeton from 3.6 percent to 2.0 percent.[156] Meanwhile, Harvard was nearly 25 percent Jewish and already having difficulty, Lowell believed, in getting applicants from western cities and the "great preparatory schools" because of its "reputation of having so many Jews."[157]

With an eye on his chief rivals, Lowell decided that he could no longer tolerate half-measures. The seriousness of the situation became fully apparent in the fall of 1925, when statistics from the dean's office reported that the proportion of Jewish freshmen had risen to 27.6 percent — not even counting the additional 3.6 percent in the "J3" category.[158] Ironically, it was the top-seventh plan — a measure intended to reduce the proportion of Jewish students — that was in good part responsible. Of the 276 students admitted under this plan, 42 percent were Jews. Designed to bring Harvard "a new group of men from the West and the South," the plan was in fact admitting more Jews from the Middle Atlantic states and New England.[159]

As Lowell was contemplating the disturbing figures, he was also receiving letters from alumni expressing concern that Harvard was being overrun by Jews. Among these letters was one from W. F. Williams '01, of Greenwich, Connecticut. Williams, who had attended a recent Harvard-Yale game, was profoundly troubled by the change in Harvard's atmosphere since his undergraduate days. As an expression of the sentiments held by a segment of the alumni, his letter is worth quoting at length:

> Naturally, after twenty-five years, one expects to find many changes but to find that one's University had become so Hebrewized was a feaful [sic] shock. There were Jews to the right of me, Jews to the left of me, in fact they were so obviously everywhere that instead of leaving the Yard with pleasant memories of the past I left with a feeling of utter disgust of the present and grave doubts about the future of my Alma Mater. One thought that kept recurring in my mind was as to what the future of the University would be when the Jew graduates of the present and future would have a possible preponderating vote for the Overseers and the right to fill the "Seats of the Mighty" in University Hall. A pleasant prospect to consider!
>
> My recent re-introduction to my University was when I left the street car at Beck Hall on my way to the Union to get my ticket for the game. Being uncertain what entrance to use I stopped a boy, evidently a student, to ask direc-

tions — he was a Jew. Rounding the corner of the Union, being still in doubt where to go I made enquiries from three other boys, also very evidentl (sic) students, — two Jews and a Negro, fraternizing. I was ushered to my seat at the game by a Jew and another of the same "breed" followed me to my seat and required me to sign my ticket. And not one of these appeared to be of the same class as the few Jews that were in college in my day but distinctly of the class usually denominated "Kikes."

Shades of my New England parents that Harvard University should come to such a pass that its graduates not only feel doubts about sending their sons to their University but that they are in many, many cases actually sending them elsewhere — on account of the Jews.

My business life has been spent in New York where one stumbles over Jews at every step and I am not anxious for my boys to come in contact with them until they absolutely have to. They are without doubt the Damned of God and the skunks of the human race. I grant you that there are many Jews like the Straus family who cannot be even remotely criticized, but generally speaking they're a menace to decent society and the American race. I cannot but feel that your New England blood must run cold when you contemplate their ever-increasing numbers at Harvard but what I cannot fathom is why you and the other Overseers don't have the backbone to put you (sic) foot down on this menace to the University . . .

The Jew is undoubtedly of high mental order, desires the best education he can get CHEAPEST, and is more persistent than other races in his endeavors to get what he wants. It is self evident, therefore, that by raising the standard of marks he can't be eliminated from Harvard, whereas by the same process of raising the standard "White" boys ARE eliminated. And is this to go on? Why the Psychology Test if not to bar those not wanted? Are the Overseers so lacking in genius that they can't devise a way to bring Harvard back to the position it always held as a "white man's" college?[160]

Lowell told Williams that he "had foreseen the peril of having too large a number of an alien race and had tried to prevent it," but that "not one of the alumni ventured to defend the policy publicly." He concluded by indicating that he was "glad to see from your letter, as I have from many other signs, that the alumni are beginning to appreciate that I was not wholly wrong three years ago in trying to limit the proportion of Jews."[161]

Yet Lowell still faced serious obstacles. Apart from the continued opposition of the redoubtable Eliot, he still had to gain the approval of the Special Committee on the Limitation of the Size of the Freshman Class.[162] Chaired by Henry James (1899), the son of the great philosopher William James and later the author of a two-volume biography of Eliot that won the Pulitzer Prize, the committee had the power to frustrate Lowell's plans.[163] Sensing that James might not share his views, Lowell turned his considerable energies to the task of convincing him that there was no realistic alternative to restriction.

Receiving a first draft of the Special Committee's report, which conspicuously failed to offer any specific measures to limit Jewish enrollment, Lowell responded with a confidential letter in which he noted that "questions of race," though "delicate and disagreeable," are not solved by ignoring them. Declaring that "the presence of Jews in large numbers tends to drive Gentiles elsewhere," he reminded James that "a few years ago many of us thought the proportion of Jews in Harvard College was reaching a dangerous point." Then, Lowell said, the figure was 21.7 percent; now it was more than 27 percent. Moreover, "the measures adopted at the time of the previous inquiry" — which included the limitation of the freshman class to 1,000, the creation of the top-seventh plan, and the use of letters and interviews to assess applicants — "have produced no effect."[164]

From Lowell's perspective, there was no alternative but to act immediately.

> To prevent a dangerous increase in the proportion of Jews, I know at present only one way which is at the same time straightforward and effective, and that is a selection by a personal estimate of character on the part of the Admission authorities, based upon the probable value to the candidate, to the college and to the community of his admission. Now a selection of this kind can be carried out only in case the numbers are limited. If there is no limit, it is impossible to reject a candidate who passes the admission examinations without proof of defective character, which practically cannot be obtained. The only way to make a selection is to limit the numbers, accepting those who appear to be the best.

The Overseers, Lowell told James, had only three choices: "They must either assume the responsibility for the increase in the percentage of Jews, or they must assume the responsibility of saying what should be done about it, or they must leave the administrative officers of the University free to deal with it." And should they choose the last option, which Lowell clearly favored, it would require "a limitation of numbers" that "must be continued as long as there is need for it."[165]

James's initial reaction was less than enthusiastic. "*Everything* in my education and bringing up," he wrote, "makes me shrink from a proposal to begin a racial discrimination at Harvard — there's no use my pretending this isn't the case." Yet he acknowledged that Lowell was "quite right in saying that a situation which contains serious and unfortunate elements ought to be faced again." He then assured Lowell that he would "endeavor to bring an open mind to its consideration and not to follow my predisposition blindly."[166]

Sensing James's irresoluteness, Lowell insisted that he was not proposing discrimination against the Jews but rather "discrimination among individuals in accordance with the probable value of a college education to themselves, to the University, and the community," carefully adding that "a very large proportion of the less desirable, upon this basis, are at the present time the Jews."[167] While hardly the kind of argument that would have persuaded Frankfurter or Mack, it apparently persuaded James. Declaring that he agreed in principle with Lowell's notion of "a sound and discerning 'discrimination' among individuals," he expressed confidence that "such a discrimination would inevitably eliminate most of the Jewish element which is making trouble." Then, revealing that he was himself not immune to the anti-Semitism common in his milieu, he added: "I don't think that all Jews are particularly intelligent by any means. What intelligence they have seems to ripen early. But apart from their precocity and a certain advantage it gives them in the way of a head start, I am not afraid of any competition." Nevertheless, James could not go along with those Overseers who advocated "a candid regulation excluding all but so many or such a proportion of 'Jews.'"[168] More subtle measures, he advised Lowell, would provide the best means of reducing the number of Jews at Harvard.

With James now on board and Judge Mack having completed his term as an Overseer, there was no one left to block Lowell's plans. When the Report of the Special Committee Appointed to Consider the Limitation of Numbers was approved by the Board of Overseers on January 11, 1926, Lowell had every reason to be pleased. In addition to endorsing a limit of 1,000 freshmen, it recommended that "the application of the rule concerning candidates from the first seventh of their school be discretionary with the Committee on Admission" — a provision that would make it possible to eliminate schools that sent too many Jews to Harvard. Equally important, the committee decisively rejected an admissions policy based on scholarship alone, stating that "it is neither feasible nor desirable to raise the standards of the College so high that none but brilliant scholars can enter" while stipulating that "the standards ought never to be too high for serious and ambitious students of average intelligence."[169]

When the faculty formally approved the report eight days later, Lowell was further elated, for they also approved measures making the admissions process even more subjective. In particular, the faculty called on Pennypacker to interview as many applicants as possible to gather additional information on "character and fitness and the promise of the greatest usefulness in the future as a result of a Harvard education." Henceforth, declared the faculty, a passport-sized photo would be "required as an essential part of the application for admissions."[170]

The actions of the faculty and the Committee on Limitation, Lowell realized, provided a tremendous opportunity to impose, at long last, the policy of restriction he had favored since 1922. But as he had learned from his bitter experience with the Committee on Methods Sifting Candidates for Admission, the wrong personnel could frustrate the best-laid plans. This time Lowell would ensure that the men on the Committee on Admission, which had final authority over applicants, shared his views. Toward this end, he appointed two new members, Kenneth B. Murdock and Robert DeCourcy Ward. The appointment of Ward was especially significant, for he had been one of the founders of the Immigration Restriction League and a critical congressional witness on behalf of the Immigration Act of 1924.[171] All in all, the Committee on Admission in 1925–1926 had seven members, four of whom had voted for Henderson's 1922 failed motion in favor of restriction and none of whom had voted against it.[172] And whereas the earlier committee on sifting candidates had three Jewish members, not a single Jew served on the Committee on Admission.

By the fall of 1926, a new admissions regime was in place. In a visit with Henry Pennypacker in late 1926, Dean Clarence W. Mendell of Yale learned that Harvard was "now going to limit the Freshman Class to 1,000 . . . After this year they are going to discontinue — for the East at least — the 'first seventh' arrangement which is bringing in as high as 40% Jews. They are also going to reduce their 25% Hebrew total to 15% or less by simply rejecting without detailed explanation. They are giving no details to any candidate any longer."[173]

Less than four months before Mendell's visit, Charles W. Eliot had died at the age of ninety-two. With Lowell no longer in his shadow, Harvard entered a new era.

CHAPTER 4

The "Jewish Problem" at Yale and Princeton

L OCATED IN A MIDSIZED CITY with a sizable Jewish population, Yale had its own "Jewish problem."[1] But unlike Harvard, where the proposed policy of restriction had become a matter of public controversy, Yale dealt with the issue behind tightly closed doors. Always attentive to developments at its older and wealthier rival to the north, the Old Blues who led Yale looked on with horror as Lowell's attempt to impose a quota created an ugly public row. This was simply not the Yale way of handling delicate and potentially volatile issues, and its administrators resolved that whatever path they would ultimately follow, they would do so outside the glare of public scrutiny.

Yale Confronts the "Hebrew Invasion"

Yale, too, was deeply worried about the rising number of Jewish students, and in 1921–1922 it began to discuss how it should respond. Having first raised the issue in 1918 at the meeting of the Association of New England Deans, Yale grew increasingly worried in 1921, when that fall's statistics revealed that over 13 percent of freshmen were Jewish — the highest figure in Yale's history.[2] The class that entered in 1921 was also the largest in the university's history at 866, and by November Yale's new president, James Rowland Angell, had formed a committee to study the question of limiting numbers.[3] In a matter of months, Angell had begun to gather systematic data on the number of Jews enrolled in recent years.[4]

The issues facing Yale were much like those facing Harvard, but there were a number of important differences. One of the most critical was that the office of the president was not nearly as powerful at Yale as at Harvard, where both Lowell and Eliot had dominated campus affairs. At Yale, as noted by the historian Marcia Graham Synnott, the president was *primus inter pares*, first among equals; he could consult, but he neither presided at faculty meetings nor directly initiated legislation. Unable by custom even to choose his own dean, President Angell was considered by the faculty to be an "outsider to the

Yale family" and hence was in a much weaker position than Lowell to direct Yale's response to the "Jewish problem."[5]

Though Angell would be important in shaping how Yale handled the question of restriction, the leading figure would be Robert Nelson Corwin, who served as chairman of Yale's Board of Admissions from 1920 to 1933. A descendant of an English family that arrived in Massachusetts in 1633, Corwin was a living embodiment of the Yale ideal of the all-around man. Born in Long Island in 1865, he prepped at Norwich Academy and entered Yale in 1883. As an undergraduate, he was a kind of Dink Stover figure, serving as captain of the 1886 national champion football team and being elected to Skull and Bones. But Corwin was also a talented scholar. After a brief stint teaching at the William Penn Charter School in Philadelphia, he went off to Germany, where he studied at the universities of Jena, Berlin, and Heidelberg before receiving his Ph.D. at Heidelberg in 1893. From there he went on to a meteoric career at Yale, where in 1899 he became professor of German and head of the German Department at the Sheffield Scientific School.[6]

A Congregationalist at a traditionally Congregationalist institution and the brother of two Yale alumni, Corwin was among the bluest of Old Blues. In 1888, he had married into a well-known Yale family, the Woolseys, whose Yale connections included his wife's father, her grandfather, seven uncles, and five brothers. Corwin was a consummate Yale insider, serving in a variety of administrative positions, including membership on the Governing Board of Sheffield and chairman of the University Board of Athletic Control. By the time he was named chairman of the Board of Admissions in 1920 (one year before Angell was installed as president), he had been a tenured full professor at Yale for more than two decades.

An admirer of Rudyard Kipling and William Graham Sumner, Corwin, like many old-stock Americans, viewed the changes sweeping across the United States in this period with considerable distaste. The growing presence of Jews at his beloved Yale was especially troubling. Corwin's visceral reaction to Jews was one of revulsion; a large proportion of them, he once wrote, were lacking in "manliness, uprightness, cleanliness, native refinement, etc."[7]

As chairman of admissions, Corwin was among the first administrators at Yale to suggest limiting numbers. Referring the question to the University Council on October 18, 1921, Corwin seemed to have had two related goals in mind: a ceiling on the sheer number of students, who were in fact straining Yale's educational capacities, and a reduction in the number of "undesirables." As he made clear in a memo in May 1922, such a limit would "make a selection necessary and logical among those satisfying the scholastic requirements," who in turn could be admitted upon "evidence of such personal characteristics as give promise that the candidate will profit by the opportunities and advantages offered at Yale and will be a credit to the institution."[8]

Acutely aware of developments at Harvard and other institutions, Corwin believed that their moves toward restriction required that Yale do the same: "In view of the fact . . . that Columbia has reduced the number of Jewish students by half and that Harvard is taking measures leading to the same result, and that several other eastern colleges are limiting numbers partly with this same end in view, it seems necessary that we should take some action if we are not to add to our present quota those who are refused admission to other universities which draw from the same source as we do."[9] Yet even had other institutions not already taken action, Corwin's antipathy to "Hebrews" (the term used by several of his colleagues) would almost certainly have led him to advocate a policy of restriction.[10]

Believing Jews — especially the New Haven boys, who constituted the majority of Yale's Jewish enrollment — to be an "alien and unwashed element" that "graduates into the world as naked of all the attributes of refinement and honor as when born into it," Corwin quite naturally wanted to stem their "infiltration" into Yale.[11] "Alien in morals and manners" and lacking the "ethical code" of their fellow students, the "Jewish boys" at Yale had a habit of "taking . . . all that is offered or available and giving little or nothing in return." Especially arousing Corwin's ire were the Jews who commuted to Yale. "The serious phase of the problem here as at Harvard," he wrote, "is the local Jew, who lives at home, knows nothing of dormitory associations, [and] sees nothing of Chapel or Commons."[12] Since Yale in Corwin's view had "about all of this race that it can well handle" and had already passed "the saturation point," a quota limiting "the number of Jews admitted to something below 10%" made perfect sense.[13]

Corwin's partner in combatting the "Hebrew invasion" was the Dean of Yale College Frederick Scheetz Jones. A graduate of Minnesota's Shattuck School and a Yale alumnus ('84), Jones was, like many Yale administrators, elected to Skull and Bones as an undergraduate. After a stint as dean of the School of Engineering and professor of physics at the University of Minnesota, he returned to New Haven, where he served as dean of the college from 1909 to 1927.[14] Within the administration, Jones was the first to declare the growing number of Jews on campus to be a problem, stating at the May 1918 meeting of the Association of New England Deans that Yale and like institutions were in danger of being "overrun by the Jews."[15] Summering in Cape Cod in 1922 near Harvard's Pennypacker, Jones dispatched the following note to his friend Corwin, who a few days earlier had asked him to convey to Pennypacker his "hope that the Hebraic question is not interfering with his summer's rest": "Yours rec'd. *Too many Freshmen!* How many Jews among them? And are there any *Coons?* Pennypacker is here and much disturbed over the Jew Problem. *Don't let any colored* transfer get *rooms* in College. I am having a big rest."[16]

As early as 1918, well before Yale had begun to move toward limiting numbers, Jones had taken the lead in denying Jews scholarship assistance in order to discourage them from attending.[17] By 1921–1922, it was the policy of the dean's office "not to award the honorary scholarships in upper years to Jews." Jones's justification was that the scholarships generally came from "foundations established by people who did not have in mind the support of Jewish students but rather the idea of aiding deserving students of the Christian religion."[18] Nevertheless, in Jones's view, further tightening in the allocation of financial aid to Jews was needed: "I should be disposed," he wrote to Corwin in May 1922, "to put a very definite limit, and a rather low one, on the amount of beneficiary aid that we grant to Jewish students, and I should not increase this as the proportion of Jews increased but would avoid offering financial inducements to Jewish students to come here in accepted numbers." By 1924, Jewish freshmen composed just 16 percent of scholarship and loan recipients at Yale College despite being 26 percent of the applicants.[19] And of all the scholarship and loan money awarded, Jews received just 11 percent — a clear indication that Yale was following Corwin's suggestion that Yale should award its financial aid to Christian students from families of "education and refinement" in the "solid middle class."[20]

The discriminatory allocation of financial aid was but one vehicle for stemming the flow of Jewish students — and hardly the most efficient. Far more critical to the success of the campaign for restriction was the imposition of a limitation of numbers, which, as Dean of Freshman Roswell P. Angier noted, "might give some ground for tackling the race question."[21] Recognizing the sensitivity of the issue, Corwin astutely suggested that "it would give us better publicity if we should speak of *selection* and of the rigid enforcement of high standards rather than of the limitation of numbers," which had "come to connote a special kind of limitation."[22]

Though Yale had started its deliberations on this question in October 1921, it still had not acted twelve months later. But the university had gathered more data, with a report from Dean Jones showing that while Jews outperformed their non-Jewish classmates academically, they were relegated to the margins of Yale's dense extracurricular life and were totally excluded from the senior societies. Nevertheless, as at Harvard, Jews did participate in some extracurricular activities, most notably the orchestra and debating. Another organization in which the Jewish students were heavily involved, Jones reported, was the Society for the Study of Socialism "The Jew," Jones concluded, "is as active in extra-curricular activities as he is encouraged to be."[23]

Chastened by Harvard's unpleasant experience in the spring of 1922, the Committee on Limitation of Numbers reported to the University Council in October 1922 that it had "requested that publicity in connection with its deliberations be avoided for the present." Corwin remained a strong proponent of limitation, and on January 9, 1923, he dispatched a memo calling not only for the freshman class to be limited to approximately 800 but also for "Personal Inspection of all Doubtful Candidates" and "Restriction of Scholarships," with most aid targeted to the "cultured, salaried class of native stock."

Finally, on January 19, 1923, the university "voted to informally approve of the proposal to limit the numbers of the entering Freshman Class."[24] Less than a month later, the Corporation officially voted to limit the number of freshmen to 850.[25] In announcing the new policy, Yale was careful to explain it in a manner consciously designed to avoid provoking the controversy that had wracked Harvard. The official announcement said simply: ". . . the university is not willing to receive more students than it can properly care for. With the present resources it is impracticable to provide for a number larger than this and still assure to each student adequate instruction . . . students will be selected primarily on the basis of scholastic attainment and promise." President Angell, in a statement issued soon afterward, sounded the same theme, insisting that "scholarship will be the prime consideration" in determining which applicants would be admitted under the new policy of limitation. Yet in the very next sentence, he added an important qualifier, declaring, "This does not mean that no attention will be paid to qualities of personality and character" — precisely the kind of subjective characteristics that were soon used to discriminate against Jewish applicants.[26]

Yet limitation of numbers, in and of itself, did not initially lead to a reduction in the proportion of Jews entering Yale. Criteria intended to reduce the number of Jews, *if neutrally applied,* might not have the anticipated effects. Corwin admitted as much in a remarkably frank statement made during the early stages of the discussion at Yale: "No college or school seems to have discovered or devised any general criteria which will operate to exclude the undesirable and uneducable members of this race. All which have been successful in their purpose have had to avail themselves of some agency or means of discrimination based on certain non-intellectual requirements."[27] Whatever the cause, the enrollment figures for 1923 demonstrated that limiting numbers would not be enough to reduce the flow of Jews to Yale; the proportion of numbers of the "self-styled chosen race" (as Corwin put it) rose that fall to 13.3 percent — the highest figure in Yale's history and more than double the percentage just five years earlier.[28] If the "Jewish invasion" was to be halted, it was now clear — as Lowell had been forthright enough to acknowledge before his plan went public — that only a frank double standard was likely to work.

By 1924 Corwin had moved toward an explicit quota. The goal of a Jewish enrollment of no more than about 10 percent had been enunciated two years earlier in a memorandum to the Corporation's Committee on Educational Policy.[29] Armed with the discretion that would permit it to deploy subjective judgments of "personality and character" as a basis of excluding applicants who met (or exceeded) Yale's academic requirements, the Board of Admissions had the necessary weapons to turn back the invasion of the "Hebrews." In the fall of 1924, the number of Jews in the freshman class dropped from 115 the year before to 88 — a figure that just so happened to constitute precisely 10 percent of all entering students.[30] Though Jewish enrollment continued to fluctuate a bit from year to year, it would be almost four decades before the proportion of Jews in the freshman class would reach the level attained in 1923.[31]

As Yale altered its admissions policies, it set in motion a broader debate about the definition of merit. When Harvard publicly announced in 1926 that its new admissions policy would place great emphasis on character and personality, the *Yale Daily News* praised its decision and put forward its own version of how Yale should select its students in a major editorial, "Ellis Island for Yale." It called on the university to "institute immigration laws more prohibitive than those of the United States government." Like their adult counterparts in the Yale administration, the students were well aware that limiting numbers could lead to an academic meritocracy — or, as the *Yale Daily News* put it, "a merciless competition for seats in the University," in which "the average undergraduate will be the abnormal brain specimen" — unless countervailing measures were taken. Yale's new policy, declared the *News,* should be based on "more consideration of the character, personality, promise and background of the individual in question."[32]

What the editors most feared was that an admissions policy "purely on the basis of scholastic standing" would leave little place for them and their kind; under such a regime, "Yale graduates will find no room for what children of theirs are not abnormal." Against the ideology of academic meritocracy, they offered the traditional upper-class ideal of "character and leadership" in "service to the nation." Though Jews were never mentioned explicitly, the *News* seems to have had them firmly in mind when it insisted, "The survival of the fittest should yield men who are equipped to do more than pass scholastic examinations or earn money." Committed to ensuring that Yale "continue with her past and present success in graduating men of the highest character into all walks of life," the paper praised Harvard's new policy requiring applicants to submit photos of themselves. But Yale's "Ellis Island," the *Daily News* suggested, "might go them [Harvard] one better and require applicants to submit photographs of their fathers also."[33]

The new definition of merit at Yale — one that was far less academic and far more subjective than the one that had prevailed as recently as 1921 — was firmly enshrined within a few short years. In a letter to a personal acquaintance inquiring about what it would take for her son to gain admission to Yale, President Angell wrote: "The all-important consideration is that your boy should achieve high standing in his work at the Parker School and should be able to present a four years' record of creditable deportment and development of character. Sound physique is hardly less essential." While "the creditable passing of the entrance examinations is a sine qua non," Angell said, "it is by no means the whole story." Also essential was that her son "grow in grace, in body and in character as rapidly as may be." Yale, he told her, was also in search of "boys of really fine personality."[34] If Angell's correspondent concluded that there was something ineffable about the ideal candidate for Yale, that was precisely the point: with objective standards now a thing of the past, the Board of Admissions could use its considerable discretion to admit those applicants who fit the profile of the "Yale man" while eliminating those deemed "undesirable."

Whether intended or not, one of the by-products of the changes that Yale introduced was to alter the composition of the student body as a whole. Having long prided itself on being the most "national and democratic" of the great private colleges, Yale by 1930 was in fact less national and decidedly less democratic than it had been before restriction. Always a prime destination for graduates of private schools, the university had become even less accessible to the growing ranks of graduates of public schools, whose proportion of the freshman class dropped from 24 percent in 1920 to 19 percent in 1930.[35] By 1930, Yale had become so reliant on a handful of top private schools to fill its class with students deemed socially desirable that the graduates of just eight of them — Andover (74), Exeter (54), Hotchkiss (42), St. Paul's (24), Choate (19), Lawrenceville (19), Hill (17), and Kent (14) — provided nearly a third of the freshman class.[36] At the same time, Yale's geographical reach had actually narrowed, with the proportion of students from west of the Mississippi dropping from 12 percent in 1920 to 7 percent in 1930.[37]

Even more striking was the increase in the proportion of alumni sons, whose share of the freshman class rose from 13 percent in 1920 to 24 percent in 1930.[38] In 1925, the Board of Admissions voted to assure the alumni that the "limitation of numbers shall not operate to exclude any son of a Yale graduate who has satisfied all the requirements for admission." In practice, the policy institutionalized a substantially lower standard of admission for the sons of Yale; by the late 1920s, legacies were judged "as having satisfied the scholastic requirements for admission upon their passing examination in fifteen units with a mark of 60 or above," but nonlegacies needed a mark of about 70.[39] One effect of this preference was to further reduce the admissions chances of Jewish applicants, who rarely were alumni sons, but its impact was much broader; by 1928 the proportion had risen to 22 percent. By this point even Corwin, worried that Yale had gone too far, wrote to Angell to inform him of the "evident feeling that any Yale affiliation carries with it certain admission ticket privileges" and to warn him about the "pitfalls of a double or doubtful standard of admission."[40] All in all, Yale was far more insular in 1930 than it had been a decade earlier.

Five years after the introduction of the quota, Corwin received a letter from Francis Parsons, a member of the Yale Corporation from Hartford, who wrote to express his displeasure about the number of Jewish names in a newspaper article listing the boys from Connecticut admitted to Yale that year; Parsons had taken the trouble to underline each and every name that sounded Jewish. Corwin responded sympathetically, writing that "the list as published reads like some of the 'begat' portions of the Old Testament and might easily be mistaken for a recent roll call at the Wailing Wall." Expressing the hope that the "Jewish representation in the present Freshman class . . . will not be far from ten per cent," Corwin added that he "should not put on black if it were less."[41]

Because of the large number of Jews wishing to attend Yale, Corwin assured Parsons that the "racial problem is never wholly absent from the minds of the Board of Admissions." While he envied institutions such as Princeton and the "large fitting schools" (boarding schools), which could rigorously limit the number of Jews because those in charge stood by their admissions offices regardless of the immediate consequences, it was not possible at Yale because "so great a proportion of our Jewish representatives are of local origin" and "some of our prominent local Jews hold key positions politically and financially." Nor should Yale follow the example of Harvard, which though "now . . . sawing wood and not saying a word," had earlier run into "rough weather by attempting to justify her proposed action before putting it into force." Instead, Yale should follow a middle course, limiting the number of Jews to roughly 10 percent "without publicity and firmly."[42]

One year after his letter to Parsons, Corwin wrote to Angell, proudly informing him that the Board of Admissions had attained new levels of success in limiting the number of Jewish freshmen. In the fall of 1930, just 8.2 percent of the class was Jewish — a result attained "without hue and cry and without any attempt on the part of those chiefly affected to prove that Yale had organized a pogrom." Statistics attached to the letter showed that Corwin had succeeded in part by reducing, but not eliminating, Jewish representation from New Haven, Hartford, and Bridgeport; they sent 48 boys to Yale in 1926, but just 28 in 1930. The main reason for the success of Yale's policy was, however, the remarkable lack of access provided to graduates of public schools in the nation's three largest centers of Jewish population: New York, Chicago, and Philadelphia. The home of more than 2.3 million Jews (roughly half of the nation's Jewish population) and more than 12 million people overall, the three cities sent a total of 13 public school graduates to Yale in 1930,[43] far fewer than the number (24) sent by St. Paul's, an Episcopalian boarding school in New Hampshire with a graduating class of 68.[44]

Compared to Harvard, where Jews sat on both the Board of Overseers and the Faculty of Arts and Sciences and where Protestants of the stature of Eliot and Greene opposed restriction, Yale saw remarkably little opposition. But the question of anti-Semitism soon became a subject of public controversy, thanks to the efforts of a Jewish undergraduate whose name, unbeknownst to him, had been underlined by Parsons in the newspaper clipping. His name was Eugene Victor Debs Rostow; a quarter of a century later, he was named dean of Yale Law School.

Born in Brooklyn, the son of a socialist, and a graduate of the New Haven public schools, Rostow entered Yale at the age of sixteen on a Sterling Memorial Scholarship. A brilliant student — he was elected to Phi Beta Kappa as a junior — he strived with considerable success to live up to the Yale ideal of the all-around man, playing on the water polo team, contributing to the *Lit*, and editing the *Hoot*.[45] But he was troubled by the anti-Semitism he saw around him, and in his junior year he published an article in the *Hoot* with the provocative title "The Jew's Position." In it, he noted bitterly that the faculties of the great private universities were "strictly sterilized against Hebrew contamination" and wrote of his own institution that "the bald fact remains, in spite of all the official disclaimers, that there is not one Jew on the faculty of Yale college." Yet even Rostow, who saw "conclusive proof of discrimination against Jews at admission" at "Harvard, Columbia, and Princeton," could not bring himself to believe that his beloved alma mater would engage in such a distasteful practice. Based "on the testimony of Dean Clarence W. Mendell, who is himself a member of the Admissions Committee," Rostow assured his readers that "there is not and has not been discrimination in this department." Despite what he admitted were a "number of suggestive incidents and no lack of faculty suspicion," Rostow concluded that Yale's "Board of Admissions . . . like the excellent Scholarship Committee" was "above callow prejudices."[46]

In truth, few Yale administrators were more aware than Mendell of just how systematically the school was discriminating against Jews in both admissions and financial aid. But its actual policy was a closely kept secret, and Mendell, who had visited Harvard and Dartmouth to see how they were handling their "Jewish problem," chose to lie to the trusting Rostow.[47]

Even President Angell, who had publicly denounced bigotry as an expression of "obstinate intolerance, ignorance, and at times even malice," was not above joking in private about Yale's discriminatory practices.[48] Less than a year after Rostow's article appeared, Angell responded to a letter from Corwin, containing ten years of statistics on Jewish enrollment at Yale, by thanking him for "the Hebraic record which you are kind enough to send me." While noting that "the oscillations are rather larger than I would have expected," Angell offered his own suggestion for reducing Jewish enrollment: "It seems quite clear that if we could have an Armenian massacre confined to the New Haven district, with occasional incursions into Bridgeport and Hartford, we might protect our Nordic stock almost completely."[49]

Behind Angell's chilling attempt at humor was his pride that Yale had solved a difficult problem without incurring any serious costs. By turning back the "Hebrew invasion" firmly and without publicity, Yale had dodged the twin dangers of acting too late (Columbia) and acting too forthrightly (Harvard). Never allowing the proportion of Jews anywhere near the levels reached at Columbia (40 percent) and Harvard (28 percent), Yale could avoid the perception that it had been "taken over" by the Jews. For an institution whose primary constituency remained the Protestant elite, handling the "Jewish problem" with such discretion would not go unrewarded. By limiting the number of Jews, Yale was able to retain the loyalty of New York City's upper class, by far the nation's largest; during the 1930s, 34 percent of the young men listed in New York's *Social Register* enrolled at Yale — a tiny increase from the previous decade. But the same could not be said of Harvard. During the 1930s, just 15 percent of the sons of New York City's upper class enrolled at Harvard — a precipitous decline from 32 percent in the 1920s.[50]

Princeton: The Club Tightens Its Membership Criteria

After World War I, the demand for access to American colleges and universities reached unprecedented heights. Like many leading private institutions, Princeton benefited from this growing demand. Before the war, an entering class of 400 was exceptionally large; by 1920, the number of freshmen had reached 467.[51] In 1921, the number of freshmen surged to 582 — the largest in Princeton's history.[52]

Perhaps because of its small-town location, rapid expansion at Princeton did not bring with it the diversification that accompanied growth at Harvard and Yale. Eighty percent of the entering class of 1921, for example, came from private schools, with Lawrenceville alone sending 56 students.[53] Nearly two-thirds of the class was either Episcopalian (34 percent) or Presbyterian (32 percent), and there was not a single nonwhite. There were, however, a sprinkling of Catholics (7 percent) and Jews (4 percent). Though well below the corresponding numbers at Harvard and Yale, the 23 Jews were nearly double the typical number before World War I and constituted a historic high.[54]

Also different from the situation at Harvard and Yale, the rising number of Jews seems not to have been the driving force behind Princeton's decision to limit the size of the freshman class. As far back as 1904, when only a handful of Jews were enrolled, Woodrow Wilson had suggested that Princeton might have to limit itself to 2,000 undergraduates in order to provide students with the best possible education while preserving its "homogeneity."[55] When John Grier Hibben, Wilson's successor, announced this policy in January 1921, he seemed to be thinking along similar lines. Citing the limited amount of dormitory space (only 1,275 students could be accommodated) and the strain on the educational facilities, Hibben issued a public statement, declaring: "We wish to limit the enrollment to that number which we can properly accommodate and still maintain the character of our Princeton life and educational policy."[56] Realizing that its niche in the increasingly competitive ecology of American higher education was quality rather than quantity, Princeton thus became the first of the Big Three to limit its numbers.

Yet limitation required a policy of selection; Princeton spent much of the next twelve months in a spirited internal debate about the content of the new admissions policy that would accompany limitation. To develop a proposal for selecting students under the new conditions, Hibben appointed a Special Committee on Limitation of Enrollment consisting of five members, including the university secretary Varnum Lansing Collins '92, university executive secretary and future senator from New Jersey H. Alexander Smith '01, and the renowned professor of modern language Christian Gauss. Their task was to issue a set of recommendations that would meet with the approval of both the faculty and the trustees.[57]

One of the committee's first acts was to look at the methods of selection elsewhere, including Dartmouth's new Selection Process for Admission and the increasingly visible Rhodes Scholarships.[58] Awarded to more Princetonians than to graduates of any other college in its first decades, the Rhodes Scholarship Program exerted a profound influence on Princeton's new admissions policy.[59] A product of the same elite Anglo-Saxon culture that dominated the Big Three, the Rhodes selection process provided one of the few available templates for a method of admission that would identify the leaders of the future. Coupled with the enormous prestige that Oxford and Cambridge enjoyed as the leading universities of the world's greatest empire, one could see why the Big Three continued to look to Oxbridge as a model in the early 1920s.[60]

Devised by Cecil Rhodes (1853–1902), the legendary British imperialist and diamond magnate, the Rhodes Scholarships embodied the same broad vision of "manly Christian character" that animated Rhodes's contemporary Endicott Peabody. Though Rhodes was less religious, both men were decisively shaped by the values of Victorian England and by the ideal of public service so central to Oxford and Cambridge when they attended college there in the 1870s.[61] But whereas Peabody's signal contribution was to bring the ideals of late-nineteenth-century elite British education to the United States, Rhodes's great innovation was the idea of bringing members of America's leadership class to England to be instilled with the imperial ideals of the British upper class. Yet underlying both projects was a shared goal: the cementing of the relationship between the elites of the world's two great Anglo-Saxon powers.

In a "Confession of Faith," written in 1877 when he was twenty-four years old and still an undergraduate at Oxford, Rhodes articulated the imperialist worldview that, a quarter of a century later, would underlie the Rhodes Scholarships: ". . . if we had retained America there would at the present moment be many millions more of English living. I contend that we are the finest race in the world and that the more of the world we inhabit the better it is for the human race. Just fancy those parts that are at present inhabited by the most despicable specimen of human beings, what an alteration there would be in them if they were brought under Anglo-Saxon influence . . . I contend that every acre added to our territory means in the future birth to some more of the English race who otherwise would not be brought into existence." That same year, in his first will, Rhodes laid out his goal: "The extension of British rule throughout the world," including "the ultimate recovery of the United States of America as an integral part of the British empire."[62]

Sixteen years later, Rhodes developed the idea of a system of scholarships at Oxford designed to promote the "Unity of the Empire." By 1898, Rhodes had decided that it was imperative that America be "brought under the umbrella of his imperially unifying idea," next to promising young men from South Africa, Canada, Australia, and New Zealand.[63] Having reflected for years on the matter of how winners of the scholarships should be chosen, Rhodes indicated that he did not want mere "bookworms" but competent scholars who demonstrated "fondness of and success in manly outdoor sports" as well as "brutality."[64] In addition, Rhodes Scholars should exhibit "moral force of character and of instincts to lead" and qualities of "manhood truth courage devotion to duty." So obsessed was Rhodes with choosing the right men for the awards that he specified the precise weight of the various criteria: "four-tenths for scholarship, two-tenths for athletics, two-tenths for manhood, etc. and two-tenths for leadership."[65]

When Princeton's Special Committee on Limitation of Enrollment issued the first draft of its report in March 1921, the influence of the Rhodes criteria was evident. In a list of qualifications, the committee called on each applicant to be assessed on "mental qualifications," "manhood qualifications," "physical qualifications," and "leadership qualifications." Since Princeton was looking to educate "leaders" and not mere "bookworms," there was also an emphasis on "executive" ability, as demonstrated in extracurricular activities. Finally, the committee proposed to give preference to sons of alumni and to collect data on "home influences" and "race and nationality."[66]

The proposed shift to subjective and nonacademic admissions criteria did not go unnoticed. There was, after all, another way to carry out selection under limited enrollment: to accept the applicants with the strongest academic credentials. Faced with the Special Committee's recommendations, which many faculty members believed had little to do with the university's core intellectual functions, the faculty came close to proposing just that. At a meeting on March 14, 1921, they passed a resolution stating their sense that "primary consideration be placed upon scholarship and that other considerations be regarded as secondary."[67]

With the faculty also opposed to a second proposal to shift control over entrance to Princeton from a standing faculty committee to a new Committee on Admissions to be appointed by the president, the Special Committee was forced to retreat and regroup during the summer. Taking the lead in putting together a compromise that would be acceptable to both the faculty and the trustees was H. Alexander Smith. A member of the Special Committee, Smith sought the counsel of Walter E. Hope '01, a politically astute New York lawyer who was also an alumni trustee. Fiercely opposed to admitting students purely on the basis of academic criteria, Hope believed that Old Nassau should educate "men of broader qualifications." To select such men, the Committee on Admissions would need great "elasticity" — a condition that could not, he warned, be met if the university was too explicit or public in its guidelines.[68]

Smith communicated Hope's views to the chairman of the Special Committee, Howard McClenhan, while conveying his belief that the trustees would "all see the importance of some evidence besides the mere passing of examinations" and would "also favor a large discretion to the Committee." Having secured the support of the Special Committee for his basic approach, Smith wrote to Hope in late November that he was "endeavoring to get the other members of the Dean's Committee to agree to the principle of a short report, emphasizing a broad authority in the committee," which would "be held responsible to Trustees and Faculty." Smith's essential idea was that the report's brevity and vagueness, combined with the great authority it invested in the new Committee on Admissions, would give the university the discretion it needed to select the students it preferred.

When the thorny issue of control was settled by a compromise — the president would appoint a full-time director of admissions while the faculty would appoint four members of its own to the committee — the stage was set for final approval. On January 9, 1922, the faculty approved the "Report of the Special Committee on the Limitation of Undergraduate Enrollment"; three days later the trustees did the same. In its final form, the report left the committee with extremely broad latitude, stating that "in determining admission to the University the primary considerations shall be scholarship and character."[69] Princeton thus became the first of the Big Three to build enormous discretion into the very heart of the admissions process — a landmark innovation that Yale and Harvard would soon adapt to their own purposes.

The man who would exercise the tremendous discretion granted the Committee on Admission was Radcliffe Heermance. Appointed director of admissions by President Hibben in October 1922, Heermance remained in that position until 1950, the longest tenure of a dean or director of admissions in the history of the Big Three. Called "the keeper of the Princeton gate" by *Newsweek,* a student publication wrote, as he neared retirement, that "the Princeton of the last 25 years has probably been influenced more by Dean Radcliffe Heermance than by any other single person or factor."[70]

Born in Rhinebeck, New York, on April 18, 1882, Heermance was the son of a lawyer descended from a Dutch family with roots in America dating back to the seventeenth century.[71] After graduating from Riverview Military Academy in 1900, he entered Williams College, one of the few schools to rival the Big Three in its appeal to the eastern upper class. At Williams, the strapping Heermance was a great success, voted "social leader" as well as "biggest bluff" by his classmates.[72] Standing six feet tall and of sturdy build, he won a varsity letter in football, played a major role in the Dramatic Club, and served as "prophet of the Class."

After graduating from Williams, Heermance then taught English at Lawrenceville and went on to receive master's degrees from Harvard in 1908 and Princeton in 1909. He joined the Princeton faculty that year, first as an instructor in English, then as assistant professor in 1912, and finally in 1922 as full professor. Though an unremarkable scholar, Heermance was a loyal and effective member of the Princeton administration, and his selection as its first director of admissions was well received. Well known and respected by Princeton's chief feeder schools, Heermance strengthened the personal and institutional relationships necessary for a steady flow of students who conformed to the image of "the Princeton man." In 1925, he was also appointed dean of freshmen — a position from which he assigned an adviser to students from the same prep school. Each adviser would, in turn, "visit the prep school in which he was interested at least once a year."[73]

Heermance was a larger-than-life presence for more than four decades. Burly and mustachioed, he cut an imposing figure — his formidable reputation no doubt burnished by the commission he received as major of infantry when he ran the ROTC program at Harvard during World War I. Known for his resounding voice, his forceful personality, his gentlemanliness, and his great physical vigor, he was described by a friend as "always conjuring a vision of a cavalry officer, sabre at point, at full gallop towards a line of green hills." To Frank Bowles, who served as admissions director at Columbia and was one of his many admirers, Heermance "stood for . . . integrity, humanity, unity, oratory, absolute assurance — a very fair picture of what an Ivy Leaguer should be but not often is."[74]

When Heermance took office in October 1922, he and his fellow members of the Committee on Admissions were well aware that the primary issue pre-occupying their counterparts at Harvard and Yale was how to limit the enrollment of Jews. Even at Princeton, the number of Jews in the freshman class had been on the rise, reaching a historic high of 25 in the fall of 1922.[75] Though the matter did not yet have the same urgency for Princeton as that felt by Harvard and Yale, it was nevertheless one of the first matters taken up by the committee. In a letter of November 23, 1922, to Delaware's chairman of Princeton's Endowment Fund, the university secretary, Varnum Lansing Collins, also on the committee, issued an appeal for assistance: "I hope the Alumni will tip us off to any Hebrew candidates. As a matter of fact, however, our strongest barrier is our club system. If the graduate members of the clubs will ram the idea home on the undergraduate bicker committees and make the admission of a Hebrew to a club the rarest sort of a thing, I do not think the Hebrew question will become serious."[76] Yet the number of Jews in the freshman class continued to rise, albeit modestly.

Both clubmen themselves, Collins and Heermance understood that the selection process at Princeton's eating clubs discriminated against Jews, thereby preventing their full participation in campus life. In a study of the class that entered Princeton in 1923, Synnott found that of the 23 Jews in the class, all of whom were born in the United States, only 1 belonged to an eating club; in contrast, of 27 Catholic students in the class, 21 belonged to an eating club.[77] Despite their marginal position in student life, Jews continued to apply to Princeton in significant numbers, and the Committee on Admissions thus had to decide whether their applications should be judged by the same criteria as those of other candidates.

Reporting on a visit to Princeton that he had taken in January 1923, just two months after Heermance's appointment, Yale's chairman of the board of admissions, Robert Corwin, described how the "Jewish problem" was handled at Old Nassau: "The restriction at Princeton is enforced in two ways, or by two agencies, — first and perhaps chiefly, by undergraduate sentiment, which refuses social honors to Jews, and secondly, by a rigid selection based upon a personal inspection of all doubtful candidates. This fall more than 250 such candidates appeared in person before the Committee on Admission. The Chairman of this Committee concedes that personal impression gained in this personal interview is frequently the deciding factor."[78] By 1924, the number of Jews in the freshman class had dropped to 13. Two decades would pass before Jewish enrollment would reach the modest level of the early 1920s, and even in the last years of the Heermance era, the proportion of Jews in the freshman class would never exceed 7 percent.[79]

In order to identify the kinds of boys whom Princeton wished to enroll and to screen out "undesirables," Heermance developed an elaborate selection process that pioneered many of the innovations that have shaped elite college admissions ever since. Perhaps the most important of these was Princeton's heavy reliance on the personal interview — an ideal device for assessing appearance, deportment, manners, and, not least, ethnic and religious background.[80] But Heermance and the Committee on Admissions also required, in addition to a letter from the headmaster or principal, three personal letters of reference. If the admissions process seemed to bear a distinct resemblance to that of the process for selection by a private club, where members needed to vouch for the personal qualities of the prospective invitee, it was no coincidence; an ideal writer of a letter of reference, Heermance suggested, would be "some Princeton graduate in the community" who could provide "a confidential statement concerning the boy's character and standing."[81]

To find the kind of young man Princeton most desired, Heermance introduced still another innovation: personal visits to the major boarding schools to interview prospective students.[82] He would then draw up "a card, similar to the 'tickler' card used in the army, containing information relative to scholarship, character, schools attended, method of admissions, parents' college associations, etc." Then all applicants would be divided into four groups:

Class 1   Very desirable and apparently exceptional material from every point of view.

Class 2   Desirable, good material.

Class 3   Doubtful, the emphasis to be placed on the results of final examinations.

Class 4   Undesirable from the point of view of character and, therefore, to be excluded no matter what the results of the entrance examinations might be.[83]

In addition to reserving the right to reject candidates who, no matter how brilliant their scholastic records, were deemed to be deficient in "character," the committee was careful to maintain the latitude to admit "exceptional cases" with weak academic records — providing a path for athletes and sons of prominent alumni whom Princeton wanted to accept for "institutional" reasons.[84]

While acknowledging the heavy weight accorded subjective, nonacademic qualities, Heermance had described an admissions process that was eminently defensible in public. How it actually worked was described by a Princeton trustee to Langdon P. Marvin, a member of Harvard's Board of Overseers and (until 1924) a law partner of Franklin D. Roosevelt's. Marvin then wrote to Lowell:

> At Princeton there are now 4 to 5% Jews. As you know, there is a limit of 600 students in the Freshmen Class, and the so-called applicants, meaning those who express their intention of going to Princeton, are about 1,500 a year. Every candidate is required to submit a very full school report and recommendation, and also two letters, preferably from Princeton graduates — something like letters required for admission to a club. On the information thus obtained, the Director of Admission, *Professor Radcliffe Heermance . . . grades all of the applicants, before they take any of the examinations, into Classes A, B, C, and D — a more or less social basis.* He then awaits the results of the examinations, and all of those in Grades A and B who pass the examinations are at once admitted, also those in Grade C, so far as there is room, but none of Grade D are admitted, no matter how high their examination marks. You will see that this gives a somewhat arbitrary basis of selection and regulation which permits the racial moulding of the College pretty much as may be desired, and there is consequently no Jew question at Princeton. The method seems never to have been questioned, at least not publicly [emphasis mine].[85]

Marvin sent his letter to Lowell in January 1926, and shortly thereafter Harvard finally took the measures — many of them borrowed from Princeton — that permitted it to cut Jewish enrollment almost in half, reducing it from 27.6 percent in the entering class of 1925 to roughly 15 percent.[86]

In its efforts to screen out "undesirables" and to attract the "right" kind of young men, the Office of Admissions received powerful assistance from Princeton's public image and from the student culture supporting it. In addition to F. Scott Fitzgerald's celebrated novel *This Side of Paradise*, which popularized the notion of Princeton as "the pleasantest country club in America," the best-selling author Upton Sinclair reinforced this elitist reputation in 1923 by referring to Princeton as "the most perfect school of snobbery in America" with "no Negroes" and "few Jews."[87] A widely read article that same year, "Harvard, Princeton and Yale," by the young Edmund Wilson captured the campus atmosphere; possessing "a certain grace and a debonair irony," Princeton students, he wrote, "walk back and forth to their meals at large eating-clubs, which look rather like country-clubs, while gold canopies of autumn leaves pave the sidewalks where they lounge." In the "lax and easy-going" ambiance of Princeton, "too great seriousness tends to be considered bad form or merely unnecessary."[88]

Whereas at Harvard a segment of the student body vigorously opposed Lowell on restriction, at Princeton the new admissions policy met with strong student approval. In a series of editorials published shortly after the trustees announced the plan to limit enrollment, the *Daily Princetonian* expressed its enthusiastic support and advocated that selection be based on such "vital factors as character, personality, physical ability, public spirit, and all that goes to make up leadership of the highest type." Princeton should "develop, not mere scholars, but *leaders* — men sound of body, mind, and spirit." To be sure, students with high scores on the entrance examination should be admitted, but only if "they were of good moral character, and were not in any way obviously undesirable." At the same time, students with weaker academic qualifications should also be admitted on the basis of "the applicant's athletic and extracurricular activities and . . . a personal interview." Finally, the sons of alumni should receive preference, for their families embody "the finest Princeton spirit" and "are linked to their Alma Mater by bonds of tradition and memory."[89]

The foundation of Princeton's distinctive student culture, of course, remained the eating club, which enjoyed a new wave of popularity in the 1920s. In the course of the decade, two new eating clubs were established, and the proportion of upperclassmen belonging to clubs reached 75 percent. Yet the pressures of the competition for membership grew so intense that they triggered a major revolt. In 1924, the president of the senior class, the chairman of the *Princetonian,* the presidents of all the clubs, and the captains and managers of all the athletic teams signed a petition calling on President Hibben to abolish "bicker week" (when the clubs interviewed prospective members), referring to it as a "slave market." But bicker week was not abolished, and the clubs emerged strengthened, with membership rising to 90 percent in the 1930s.[90] Meanwhile, the clubs themselves remained highly stratified, with one study showing that the four oldest and most prestigious clubs (Ivy, Cottage, Tiger, and Cap and Gown) recruited 72 percent of their members from just fifteen prep schools while only 18 percent of the membership of four newer and lower-status clubs came from these same schools.[91]

By 1930, Princeton — like Yale — was even more insular and dominated by prep school graduates than it had been a decade earlier. With Heermance firmly in command, the number of public school graduates in the freshman class had dwindled to 94 — fewer than the 102 alumni sons entering Princeton that year. The representation of "Hebrews," as they were called in the *Freshman Herald,* also dropped; just 11 entered in 1930, compared to 227 Presbyterians and 224 Episcopalians.[92]

At the same time that Princeton's social base was becoming ever more narrow, the academic quality of the freshman class was growing weaker and weaker. As Carl Brigham, who had joined the Committee on Admissions in

1926, forthrightly acknowledged in a confidential report: "At the depth of the depression, Princeton found it necessary to increase its number of 'paying guests' in order to help meet expenses. In 1932 the size of the incoming Freshman Class was increased to 659 although the number of applicants (773) was the lowest for many years." Meanwhile, Brigham, who had devised the Scholastic Aptitude Test (SAT) and convinced Princeton to become one of the first colleges in the nation to require it, witnessed the unpleasant spectacle of the SAT scores of Princeton freshmen dropping to record lows in the early 1930s. With the acceptance rate rising from 69 percent in 1928 to 79 percent in 1930, Brigham admitted that it would be "absurd to maintain that this increasing ratio of admissions to applicants would not result in a lowering of the general level of the entering classes."[93]

Yet as desperate as Princeton was for qualified students, it was not desperate enough to relax its pattern of discrimination against the small number of Jews who applied. In 1931, a year in which nearly 80 percent of applicants were accepted, just 5 of 28 Jews who had completed applications by May 21 enrolled that September; in 1924, the first year of the quota, the comparable figures were 13 of 27.[94] While Princeton continued to publicly deny that it limited Jewish enrollment, the evidence that it did so was unequivocal. An account by Robert M. Hutchins, the president of the University of Chicago, of a lunch he had with President Hibben between 1930 and 1932 reveals the sensitivity of the matter. Having been told by Hibben that about 200 Jewish students were enrolled at Princeton that year, Hutchins asked with evident skepticism about the number the year before. Hibben responded:

> "About two hundred."
> I said that was very odd and asked how it happened. He said he didn't know; it just happened.
> Mrs. Hibben was outraged and said, "Jack Hibben, I don't see how you can sit there and lie to this young man. You know very well that you and Dean Eisenhart get together every year and fix the quota."

Though Hibben retired in 1932, the policy of limiting the number of Jews persisted well beyond his administration. In 1935, with a new president, Harold Willis Dodds, in office, just 12 of the 58 Jews (21 percent) who had completed applications matriculated that September (when 69 percent of all applicants were admitted).[95]

The Birth of Selective Admissions

Until several years after World War I, Harvard, Yale, and Princeton followed the time-honored system for selecting students used throughout most of the world (and still followed in most countries today): applicants were required to take an examination, and those who passed were admitted. Though the performance of some students placed them in a gray zone from which they could be admitted "with conditions," the basic criteria remained objective and academic. To be sure, women were ineligible to apply, blacks were excluded from Princeton, and academic standards were often low. Moreover, the curricular requirements were suffused with class bias; at many public high schools, students simply did not have the opportunity to acquire the knowledge that would permit them to pass the exams. Yet for the growing number of students — many of them from immigrant and working-class backgrounds in the large urban centers — who attended public schools where they could prepare for the exams, the system was meritocratic in an elemental way: if you met the academic requirements, you were admitted, regardless of social background.

But in two important regards the American system was different from the system that prevailed in the great universities of continental Europe, then the acknowledged world leaders in research: the American system was decentralized, and private institutions occupied a major — indeed, a dominant — place within it. As such, it followed much more of a market logic than the tightly controlled system of countries such as France and Germany, where the number of university students was regulated by the state.[96] One consequence of the more market-oriented American system was that the number of students entering Harvard, Yale, and Princeton fluctuated, sometimes quite widely, from year to year.

Nevertheless, the system was operating quite smoothly until students deemed socially "undesirable" started to pass the examinations. Because of its location in New York City, which by the early twentieth century had the largest concentration of Jews in the world, this problem arose first at Columbia. As early as 1908, reference was made to the "undesirable students" enrolled at Columbia in an internal report. In 1910, the dean of Columbia College expressed his concern about "a number of ill-prepared and uncultured Jews" who were trying to gain admission.[97]

The creation of the country's first Office of Admissions, established at Columbia in 1910, was a direct response to the "Jewish problem." Headed by Adam Leroy Jones, it used subjective criteria in evaluating candidates as it attempted to create a favorable "mix" in the student body. Through an emphasis on qualities such as "character" and "leadership," which could not be quantified, as well as the strategic deployment of discretion in determining which candidates who had not passed all the exams might still be admitted, Jones was able to report that the students who enrolled under his tutelage were "very much more desirable" than the ones accepted in previous years.[98]

Yet because of Columbia's "position at the gateway of European immigration" (as Dean Frederick Keppel put it), even the creation of an Admissions Office and the new procedures was not enough to solve the "Jewish problem." Thus in 1919, when the Big Three still had no office of admissions, Columbia became the first major private college to impose a limit on numbers — a crucial step toward controlling the number of Jewish students. Finally, in 1921 Columbia imposed a quota, reducing the proportion of Jewish freshmen to 22 percent from 40 percent or more before the limit went into effect.[99]

It was therefore no accident that Columbia — not Harvard, Yale, or Princeton — was the first college to introduce four major changes in how it admitted students: the establishment of an office of admissions, the use of nonacademic criteria such as "character" and "leadership"; the imposition of a limitation of numbers, and finally the employment of an outright quota. For Columbia faced a problem in the teens that the Big Three did not have to confront until the 1920s: how to respond when academic standards of admission resulted in the large-scale enrollment of "undesirable" students. Though the timing differed in each case, the ultimate response of all four institutions was the same: the abandonment of a system of admission based almost exclusively on academic criteria.

The decision of the Big Three to replace this system with one that gave heavy weight to subjective factors was by no means inevitable. On the contrary, as the Harvard Committee on Methods of Sifting Candidates for Admissions pointed out in 1923, when it declared that "if the size of our Freshman class is to be reduced, the reduction can best be accomplished by raising the standard for admission," as noted earlier.[100] Even at Princeton, the most clublike of the Big Three, the faculty's initial response to limitation was to insist that selection should be based on scholastic qualifications.

In addition to its simplicity and transparency, such a system would also have been consistent with the traditions of the Big Three, which had long admitted students primarily on the basis of exam scores, and with the practices of leading universities across the world. But such a policy would not solve — and might well exacerbate — the "Jewish problem" facing these schools. For Jewish applicants tended to present strong academic qualifications, and raising the admission standard would almost certainly increase rather than reduce their number.

In a letter written in 1922, Harvard's president Lowell left no doubt that the traditional system of admission would have remained in place had there not been a "Jewish problem": "We can reduce the number of Jews by talking about other qualifications than those of admission examinations. If the object is simply to diminish the Jews, this is merely an indirect method of avoiding a problem in American life which is really important. This is the feeling of the most thoughtful people here, both Gentile and Jew. On the other hand, we are in no present danger of having more students in college than we can well take care of; *nor, apart from the Jews, is there any real problem of selection, the present method of examination giving us, for the Gentile, a satisfactory result.*"[101] The problem, in short, was not with the academic method of selection per se but with its outcome: it was now yielding too many Jews.

In drastically altering its admissions policy, Harvard exemplified what I have called "the iron law of admissions": an institution will abandon a particular *process* of selection once it no longer produces the desired *result*.[102] In the long history of admissions at the Big Three, there are many examples of the operation of this law — among them, the rise of affirmative action in the late 1960s. But the shift that took place in the 1920s — from a largely objective standard to a subjective and relative standard — was the most momentous, for it gave us the peculiar system of college admissions we still have today.

The new system of selection was far more complicated than the exam-based system that had preceded it, and implementing it required a new bureaucratic apparatus of information gathering and assessment. In addition to a director or dean, the new Office of Admissions would need to collect vast quantities of data formerly unnecessary.

The development of a procedure for identifying Jews was only the first step. For the first time, candidates were asked to fill out lengthy applications that included demographic information, a personal essay, and a detailed description of extracurricular activities that might demonstrate "leadership" and reveal something about their "character." The centerpiece of the new system was the personal letter of recommendation, especially those from trusted sources such as alumni and headmasters or teachers from the leading feeder schools. Finally, to ensure that "undesirables" were identified and to assess important but subtle indicators of background and breeding such as speech, dress, deportment, and physical appearance, a personal interview was required, a final screening device usually conducted by the Director of Admissions or a trusted alumnus.

The new policy permitted the rejection of scholastically brilliant boys considered "undesirable," and it granted the director of admissions broad latitude to admit boys of good background with weak academic records. The key code word here was "character" — a quality thought to be frequently lacking among Jews but present almost congenitally among high-status Protestants.[103] Indeed, it was precisely because of its strong emphasis on "character" that the Rhodes Scholarship selection process constituted a model for many Big Three administrators. In a 1922 letter to Lowell, Langdon P. Marvin made the connection between the Rhodes criteria and the "Jewish problem" explicit: the adoption of a "character standard somewhat in line with the

Rhodes conditions," he wrote, would suffice to prevent a "Jewish inundation."[104]

Transforming its admissions criteria in response to the "Jewish problem,"
Harvard exemplified a recurrent pattern in the history of elite college admissions: the particular definition of "merit" at a given moment expresses
underlying power relations and tends, accordingly, to reflect the ideals of
the groups that hold the power of cultural definition. In the case of the shift
from intellect to character that took place in the 1920s at the Big Three, the
redefinition of merit was part of a larger mobilization by old-stock Protestants to preserve their dominance by restricting both immigration and the
educational and occupational opportunities available to recent immigrants
and their children.

Yet it would be wrong to suggest that the new definition of merit was
nothing more than a device to limit Jewish enrollment. The ideal of the all-
around man that came to dominate elite college admissions had deep roots in
the history and culture of the American upper class. Long before there was
any "Jewish problem," the Groton ideal of the manly, Christian gentleman
had established itself in the Protestant elite as the embodiment of the truly
educated man. So when the men who ran the Big Three turned to Groton and
the Rhodes Scholarship to help define "merit," they were articulating cultural
and educational ideals that expressed their deepest values.

But the cultural ideals of the Protestant elite were not those of America's
growing Jewish population, and the institutionalization of these ideals in the
new definition of merit harmed Jewish interests. Especially at Harvard, where
Lowell's stance became known to the public, Jews mounted a spirited resistance. Defending both their ideals and interests, they struggled to maintain
the traditional admissions policy while making it clear that they would not
object to a limit *if* selection were based on academic criteria alone. Joined by
prominent Gentile allies such as Charles Eliot and Jerome Greene, Lowell's
opponents struggled mightily to preserve a policy that they believed embodied Harvard's best traditions and the nation's noblest ideals.

The struggle over admissions policy that began in the 1920s marked the
beginning of a battle over the definition of merit between WASPs and Jews
that did not end until half a century later; even today, it influences the admissions practices of the nation's elite colleges. What gave the battle its special intensity was the high stakes involved for both groups. For old-stock Protestants, the rising position of Jews in the economy, the professions, and higher
education constituted a challenge, not only to their economic interests, but
also to their cultural dominance. For Jews, the movement to impose restrictions on their educational and economic opportunities constituted an assault, not only on their prospects for upward mobility, but also on their de-

vout belief — or, more precisely, their fervent hope — that America truly was the land of opportunity. For both groups, the clash over the definition of merit had powerful symbolic as well as material dimensions; it was, at bottom, a conflict over whose cultural ideals would be validated by the nation's most highly regarded academic institutions as their admissions offices decided which human qualities to reward and which to penalize.

Fearful that Jews would overtake them in the economy, upper-class Protestants were even less confident that they could win a head-to-head scholastic competition in higher education.[105] In an exchange with a Jewish alumnus of Dartmouth who was helping the administration weed out "undesirable" Jewish applicants but wanted to preserve slots for the truly brilliant candidates from public schools, the director of admissions, E. G. Bill, wrote that he could not comply because "the alumnus had no idea of how many of those students were already applying." Dartmouth's president Ernest M. Hopkins was even more alarmed, warning the alumnus that "any college which is going to base its admissions wholly on scholastic standing will find itself with an infinitesimal proportion of anything else than Jews eventually."[106]

While worried — often well beyond the actual threat — by the competitive success of Jews in business and higher education, members of the Protestant elite remained confident of their superiority in other important domains. Believing that Jews were poor physical specimens, they were convinced that admissions criteria stressing physical as well as mental fitness would redound to their advantage. Even among those relatively sympathetic to Jews, the belief in their debility was virtually universal; according to Theodore Roosevelt, "The great bulk of the Jewish population, especially the immigrants from Russia and Poland, are of weak physique and have not yet gotten far enough away from their centuries of oppression and degradation" to become physically strong.[107] In truth, "fondness for and success in . . . outdoor sports" — as the Rhodes Scholarship criteria put it — were less common among urban Jews than among Protestant boys educated in boarding schools.[108]

Closely connected to this belief was the charge that the Jew was deficient in "manliness." Thought to be excessively bookish, he was seen as lacking the physical strength, the erect carriage, and the straightforwardness of the "manly" American; instead, the Jew (and especially the immigrant Jew) was distinguished by "the furtive manner, the stoop, the hunted look, and the martyr air."[109] Above all, the Jew allegedly lacked the courage to engage in violence in defense of the nation — perhaps the defining feature of "manliness" in this era.[110]

While suffused with anti-Semitism, the image of the "unmanly Jew" pointed to a genuine and deeply rooted difference between the culture of immigrant Jewry and that of men such as Endicott Peabody and Cecil Rhodes.

Lacking both a state and a military, Jews had, in the words of Martin Green, "no tradition of virile adventure."[111] Raised in a milieu in which the scholar traditionally occupied the highest place and manliness was judged more by learning than physical prowess, immigrant Jews had a fundamentally different notion of what it meant to be a man than did upper-class Protestants.[112]

But in the eyes of a segment of the Protestant elite, the Jews' real sin was their allegedly active effort to subvert America.[113] This fear of immigrant radicalism was a powerful force behind the Immigration Acts of 1921 and 1924. At both Harvard and Yale, administrators noted with dismay the disproportionate presence of Jews in student socialist societies. And at Dartmouth, which drew from an applicant pool that overlapped heavily with that of the Big Three, hostility to the politics of Jewish undergraduates was even more pronounced; according to President Hopkins, "The unhappiness of soul and the destructive spirit of revolt . . . characteristic of the Jewish race at all times under all conditions" threatened to destroy the spirit of Dartmouth. Denouncing the "specious and superficial radicalism" of the Jewish students, he insisted that "the jaundiced mulling of that small portion of our undergraduate body which loves to line up against the wailing wall is little indicative of the spirit which education is supposed to produce and is little representative of the traditions of the American college."[114]

The very extremity of such remarks suggests that the conflict between WASPs and Jews in the 1920s was far more than a simple clash over access to choice positions in higher education and the economy. While conflicting material interests were an essential component of the struggle, so too were these profound and psychologically freighted differences in culture and way of life. To Yale's Admissions Board chairman Robert Corwin and to many of the WASP elite, the Jew was a fundamentally distasteful being who could not be assimilated.[115]

In the final analysis, it was Corwin's definition of merit — and not the more purely intellectual one favored by Eliot, Mack, and Frankfurter — that prevailed at the Big Three. Though the Jews and their allies had tradition on their side as well as the fundamental American ideal of equality of opportunity, their opponents drew strength from the larger movement for restriction then sweeping across the nation. Within the WASP elite, Eliot's view was decidedly in the minority, and even those Big Three administrators who were not personally anti-Semitic could not deny the overwhelming evidence from Columbia and elsewhere that the presence of "too many" Jews would in fact lead to the departure of Gentiles. Given the dependence of the Big Three on the Protestant upper class for both material resources and social prestige, the "Jewish problem" was genuine, and the defense of institutional interests required a solution that would prevent "WASP flight."[116]

The response of elite private colleges to the "Jewish problem" was one of the turning points in the history of American higher education. Had the principled position held by Eliot and his allies prevailed, the Big Three's policy of admitting students almost exclusively on the basis of academic criteria might still be with us. Instead, the traditional policy was abandoned and, in the process, both the procedures and the criteria used in admissions at elite private colleges nationwide were forever altered.

The creation of a new system of admissions occurred in the midst of one of the most reactionary moments in American history — a few years in the first half of the 1920s defined by rising xenophobia and anti-Semitism, widespread political repression, the emergence of the Ku Klux Klan as a genuine mass movement, the growing prominence of eugenics and scientific racism, and the imposition by Congress of a racially and ethnically biased regime of immigration restriction. Many of the features of college admissions with which we are all familiar — the emphasis on "character," the preference for alumni sons and athletes, the widespread use of interviews and photos, the reliance on personal letters of recommendation, and the denigration of applicants whose sole strength is academic brilliance — have their roots in this period.

Though all of these features are now taken for granted as a natural feature of the academic landscape, many of them are in fact extraordinarily strange. Americans, for example, accept as normal that highly subjective qualities such as "character" and "personality" should figure centrally in the admissions process — a policy that seemed to many at the time it was invented to be an open invitation to prejudice and discrimination. Americans also take for granted that the ability to throw, kick, or hit a ball is a legitimate criterion in determining who should be admitted to our greatest research universities — a proposition that would be considered laughable in most of the world's countries. And Americans also tolerate a system in which our most selective institutions of higher education routinely grant preference to the children of alumni and major donors — a practice that viewed from a distance looks unmeritocratic at best and profoundly corrupt at worst.

All in all, the admissions process at America's leading colleges and universities has striking affinities to the system of selection to a private club. Given its historical origins, this resemblance is less than fully coincidental.

Though the system still bears the marks of its origins in the response of the elite colleges to the "Jewish problem," it has proved remarkably resilient. Its strength lies in its tremendous flexibility — a capacity, grounded in the tremendous *discretion* built into the system combined with the *opacity* that has shielded those exercising this discretion from public scrutiny. By emphasizing the inherently subjective character of admissions decisions, the new system of selection left the elite colleges free to adapt to changing circumstances by admitting — and rejecting — pretty much whomever they wished. As power relations between social groups changed, Harvard, Yale, and Princeton were thus able to alter their criteria and procedures to produce the desired outcome. Though it was designed for the specific purpose of limiting Jewish enrollment, the system could as easily be used for purposes of inclusion as well as exclusion — a potential that was most dramatically realized with the rise of affirmative action in the late 1960s.

One of the unintended consequences of the manifold changes was a more general narrowing of the range of backgrounds in the freshman classes at the Big Three. Historically the most open and democratic member, Harvard under Lowell had become increasingly insular. With 85 percent of its students wealthy enough to pay their own way and the vast majority of those on scholarship receiving less than half their expenses, even Harvard's alumni magazine worried openly about whether financial aid was keeping pace with the rising cost of college and whether Harvard was doing enough to "keep careers open to talent."[117] At the same time, the shortage of applicants raised serious questions about the academic level of the student body — a problem exacerbated by the paucity of scholarships.

One loyal Harvardian who shared both these concerns was a rising young professor of chemistry named James Bryant Conant. Selected by the Corporation in 1933 to succeed Lowell, Conant inherited an admissions machinery brilliantly constructed to manage the "Jewish problem." Conant's task was to modernize this machinery while keeping Jewish enrollment below the level that would provoke "WASP flight." His solution — an innovative synthesis of the policies of Eliot and Lowell that combined a shift toward greater meritocracy with the jealous guarding of the discretion that permitted the Admissions Office to continue to limit the number of "undesirables" — was to leave a permanent imprint on the admissions practices of the elite colleges.

PART II

THE STRUGGLE OVER MERITOCRACY, 1933–1965

CHAPTER 5

Harvard's Conant: The Man and His Ideals

F EW MEMBERS OF the Protestant elite were more troubled by the growing social and economic exclusivity of the nation's leading private universities during the Great Depression than James Bryant Conant, Harvard's president from 1933 to 1953. A brilliant chemist who was himself an
alumnus (A.B. '13, Ph.D. '16), Conant (1893–1978) is one of the towering figures in the history of American higher education.[1] Many of the hallmarks of
meritocratic ideology that we now take for granted — the principle that admission to college should be based, not on family background, but rather on
talent and accomplishment; the policy of need-blind, full-aid admissions;
and the heavy reliance of selective colleges on the SAT — may be traced in
good part to Conant's ideas and actions during his tenure as president of
Harvard.[2]

One of Conant's first acts as president was to establish a program of National Scholarships, designed to bring talented young men from across the
country to Harvard. "We should be able to say that any man with remarkable
talents may obtain his education at Harvard," he wrote in his first President's
Report, "whether he be rich or penniless, whether he comes from Boston or
San Francisco."[3] The holder of a Harvard National Scholarship should, if sufficiently needy, look to the university to pay all his expenses, including tuition, room, board, and other costs. It was a remarkable change for an institution that, when Conant took office, awarded no full scholarships and only a
handful that covered even half the expenses of a year at Harvard.[4]

Perhaps the greatest innovation of the program was the principle of the
"sliding scale." In a letter to Frederick Lewis Allen (Harvard '12), the editor of
Harper's Magazine and an old friend, Conant explained the new policy:
whereas previously, "the more brilliant the boy, the larger the sum of money
. . . the new policy is to make the award on merit . . . and then to adjust the stipend according to the need."[5] Though limited in scope, Harvard's National
Scholarship Program established important precedents that decades later became standard practice at America's leading private colleges and universities.[6]

An obvious question arose: how would winners be selected? Conant's answer was that the decisive factor should be "potential for success in college work": the "new scholarships were to be awarded only to those who were expected to be the top-ranking scholars of the class on graduation." This definition of merit sent the message that the quality Harvard valued most was academic excellence. Conant conceded when challenged by Thomas N. Perkins, a member of the Corporation, that it ignored qualities of great importance that were not measured by grades in courses and "would miss many future leaders of the nation." Nevertheless, Conant insisted that scholastic talent, measured by the ability "to graduate *magna* or *summa cum laude*," should be the primary qualification for National Scholarship awardees.[7]

Perkins was reluctantly willing to accept Conant's definition of merit, but he immediately raised another question: could Harvard predict which students would be most successful academically? The very survival of the program, Conant realized, depended on a positive answer to this question. To find a solution, he appointed a subcommittee in 1934 of two assistant freshman deans, Wilbur J. Bender (later dean of admissions at Harvard, 1952–1960) and Henry Chauncey (later president of the Educational Testing Service, from its founding in 1948 to 1970). Both of them were deeply impressed by the SAT, recently developed by Princeton's Carl Brigham, and Conant accepted their recommendation that all applicants for National Scholarships be required to take it.[8]

By 1937, the College Entrance Examination board, at the request of Harvard, Yale, and Princeton, had developed a new one-day version of the SAT to serve as a scholarship examination. In the morning, students took an SAT consisting of two parts, one verbal and the other mathematical; in the afternoon, they took "achievement tests" in particular subject areas. The exam was so well received that many colleges began to use it for candidates not applying for scholarships as well, and the number of students taking it increased from over 2,000 in 1937 to over 4,000 the following year.[9]

Harvard's criteria for National Scholars — which, in addition to SAT scores, included grade point averages (GPA), class rank, recommendations, and a personal interview — proved extremely successful in identifying high-performing students. Of the original 10 National Scholars from the Class of 1938, 5 graduated summa cum laude, 3 magna cum laude, and 2 cum laude; 8 were inducted into Phi Beta Kappa.[10] With each additional group of National Scholars who compiled outstanding records, it seemed increasingly clear that it was possible, with the assistance of the new science of psychometrics, to predict which applicants would prove to be brilliant scholars.

Very early in his presidency, Conant laid out a bold, new vision for America's leading universities. Quoting Jefferson, Conant maintained that institutions such as Harvard had a solemn responsibility to "cull from every condition of our people the natural aristocracy of talents and virtue and prepare it by education at the public expense and for public concerns." Privately endowed colleges had a duty to provide generous scholarships so that youth of great ability but little money could attend.[11] "Only thus," Conant declared, "can the road to the top be kept open and the spirit of democracy . . . prevail in our halls of learning."[12]

In the years to come, Conant would expand and deepen his critique of America's colleges and universities, with profound consequences for both their identities and their practices.

A Man of Many Paradoxes

As president of Harvard, "Conant early established himself," *Newsweek* reported in a glowing cover story, "as the No. 1 man in American education."[13] Yet he remains an elusive figure. A radical democrat who favored the cultivation of a "natural aristocracy," an advocate of confiscatory inheritance taxes who vigorously espoused free enterprise, and a committed proponent of peace who helped spearhead the development of poison gas in World War I and the atomic bomb in World War II, Conant was a man of many paradoxes.[14]

Though born in Boston in 1893, Conant was fond of saying, "I make no claim of being a proper Bostonian."[15] Compared to Eliot and Lowell, Conant had a modest background. He grew up in middle-class Dorchester, then a rapidly growing suburban Boston neighborhood. Five miles from Harvard Square, Dorchester was a different world from the elegant Boston neighborhoods such as Beacon Hill from which Harvard traditionally drew its leaders.

Conant's parents, Jeanette Orr Bryant and James Scott Conant, were not themselves upper class, but their Yankee backgrounds sharply distinguished them from the Irish, Italian, and Jewish immigrants then pouring into Boston. On his mother's side, young Bryant (as his family called him) was descended from William Bradford, the second governor of the Plymouth Colony, and related to John Alden, who had arrived in America on the *Mayflower*. On his father's side, he was the ninth generation in a line of direct descent from Roger Conant, the founder of Salem, Massachusetts, in 1626.[16] Throughout his life, he remained proud of his New England heritage and served as a member of the executive committee of the "extremely select Association of Grandchildren of the Eighteenth Century."[17]

Conant's father grew up in the town of Bridgewater, the son of a poor shoe cutter, but he worked his way into the prosperous middle class by founding his own photography firm in 1876. He also took advantage of the construction boom in Dorchester, becoming a real estate speculator and a builder of two-story, two-family houses.[18] His efforts must have been quite successful, for as Bryant reached high school age, the family considered enrolling him in fashionable Milton Academy.[19] When James Scott Conant passed away in 1927, he left an inheritance of well over $100,000 — a considerable sum at the time.[20]

Conant's parents, who practiced Swedenborgianism during the boy's childhood but drifted toward Unitarianism as he grew older, took a keen interest in his education.[21] When Bryant took the entrance examination for Roxbury Latin, a prestigious six-year college preparatory school, he scored high in reading, geography, and grammar but was rejected because he had failed the spelling section.[22] Conant's mother, by all accounts a forceful woman, implored the authorities to admit him despite his deficiency, citing his excellence in other subjects. They relented, making Conant one of only 35 students admitted out of 90 who took the exam.[23]

Conant's extraordinary promise as a scientist was visible early in his years at Roxbury Latin. In his second year, he met Newton Henry Black, a gifted science instructor who had graduated from Harvard in 1896.[24] Black sensed in Conant a kindred spirit, who shared his passion for chemistry and an abiding commitment to the scientific method.

Already conducting small experiments at home by the age of ten, Bryant had persuaded his father to construct a laboratory for him in the vestibule of their house.[25] Once at Roxbury Latin, Black served as an exemplary mentor for the precocious "towhead with a Dutch cut and a broad collar," giving freely of his time.[26] Just after his fifteenth birthday, Conant wrote to his sister, then studying art in Paris, that an ideal gift for him on her return would be a copy of *Schule der Chimie*, a two-volume work by Ostwald.[27] By Conant's senior year, his instructors were effusive in their praise, with one describing him as "perhaps the most brilliant fellow we ever had" in physics and chemistry and Black himself proclaiming him "the most promising boy I have had in my ten years here at the school."[28]

But not all subjects came as easily to the adolescent Conant. In 1905–1906, he ranked just sixteenth in a class of thirty-two, with mostly B's and C's in nonscientific subjects.[29] His response was to work harder, imposing on himself the exceptional discipline that became one of his greatest strengths. Each year, Conant carefully calculated his rank in the class. Slowly but surely, he moved to ninth in 1907 and finally to first just in time for graduation in 1910. In recognition of his achievements, the faculty selected him to give the class oration at commencement. Instead, the seventeen-year-old Conant presented a complex chemistry experiment in full public view, performing it with lucidity and grace.[30]

Though a wizard in science, Conant did not fit the stereotype of the "meatball." Popular with his classmates, the lanky adolescent played football, served as editor-in-chief of the student newspaper, and garnered acclaim as the heroine, complete with blond wig and petticoats, in the school play *Maître Courbet*.[31] Overall, his classmates and teachers agreed that Conant was "a damned likable kid."[32]

Underneath Conant's genial exterior, however, pulsed a spirit of grand ambition and fierce determination. Intent on becoming a university professor of chemistry, he would not enter Harvard as an ordinary student. Early in his senior year at Roxbury Latin, Black had written on Conant's behalf to the distinguished chair of Harvard's Chemistry Department, Theodore William Richards, predicting that Conant was "bound to be heard from later as a scholar and a man."[33] Black's goal was not only to gain admission for his protégé but also to secure his exemption from first-year chemistry and permission to take advanced classes normally closed to freshmen. After some hesitation, the department granted Black's request, citing Conant's "extraordinary ability."[34] It was not the last time that Conant benefited from the goodwill of a well-placed sponsor, and he took full advantage of the special opportunities that Harvard afforded him.

Conant soon demonstrated that he would deliver on the brilliant future that his mentors had predicted. He excelled in his studies, capturing the attention not only of Richards, the nation's most eminent chemist, but of a dynamic new faculty member, Elmer Peter Kohler, who had recently come to Harvard from Bryn Mawr.[35] Kohler was so impressed with the aspiring chemist that he agreed to work with him on a piece of research and offered him a teaching assistantship in his course in organic chemistry while he was still an undergraduate. In June 1913, less than three years after enrolling, Conant completed his degree magna cum laude, having been elected to Phi Beta Kappa and named an honorary John Harvard Scholar.[36]

But Conant was well aware that academic excellence hardly guaranteed social acceptance at the Harvard of his day.[37] On the contrary, being designated a "grind" — a very real possibility for an intensely studious young man like Conant — would mean relegation to the margins of student life.[38]

With dogged determination and on the advice of his sisters as well as two older Harvard cousins, as a freshman Conant set out to win election to the *Harvard Crimson*.[39] In his personal diary, which regularly recorded his grades on lab work, a weather report, and his social and academic ambitions, he wrote in the spring of 1911: "chased *Crimson* hard," even sleeping through an hour exam in English.[40] Though failing as a freshman, in his second year he succeeded, writing in red in his diary on January 7, 1912: "Big punch! An editor at last."[41] Years later, he estimated that his campaign to join the *Crimson* "nearly wrecked a half-year of work."[42]

"What made all the effort worthwhile," Conant wrote in his memoirs, "was the fact that success opened the doors to my election to a highly selective literary club, the Signet."[43] Founded in 1870 as a protest against the exclusivity of the Hasty Pudding Club, the Signet had a tradition of "occasionally electing the unclubbed intelligentsia."[44] In this "invitation-only watering hole for faculty, students, and alumni," writes Conant's biographer James Hershberg, "the affable, quick-witted, relaxed (at least outwardly) undergrad honed social skills, collected friends and acquaintances, and began to build a reputation as a chemist who felt equally at ease discussing politics, philosophy, literature, and other topics far removed from formulae and test tubes."[45] As Conant himself said, the Signet was where "I found my general education."[46]

Though ignored by the exalted Institute of 1770, Conant was tapped for membership in Delta Upsilon,[47] an unpretentious fraternity that was a haven for students from nonpatrician (albeit relatively privileged) backgrounds. At DU Conant socialized with ambitious and energetic young men including Joseph Kennedy, the father of the president, and Robert ("Bob") Benchley, who became one of America's top humorists. Conant's friends and acquaintances at DU, many of whom went on to prominent careers in business, law, and the media, proved valuable sources of advice and information for years to come.[48]

Conant had gained a respectable place in Harvard's complex and highly competitive social hierarchy. This was no small accomplishment, and it had been realized only with painstaking effort. A highly self-conscious and controlled individual, Conant carefully constructed his public personality to produce — much as in the science lab — the desired outcome.[49] "Smile, damn it, smile!!," he scribbled in his freshman diary, underlining the first smile four times and the second ten times.[50] Such stern injunctions seemed to work, with the tightly wound young man apparently popular not only with his classmates but also with socially appropriate young ladies.[51] John Marquand, a friend and fellow rooming-house boarder who later became a popular novelist, marveled at Conant's ability to be "brilliant without being grubby" and his capacity "to learn everything without the slightest damage to his poise and popularity."[52]

After graduation, Conant took a summer job at the Midvale Steel Company in Philadelphia, where Frederick Winslow Taylor was trying to put some of his ideas about scientific management into practice.[53] Refusing to forsake the academy, Conant turned down several attractive offers in industry. One such offer — to the top post in the research division of an Ohio rubber company — came in 1915, when he was still a graduate student.[54]

As far back as his days at Roxbury Latin, Conant had set his sights on completing a Ph.D. at Harvard under the supervision of Professor Richards, who in 1914 became the first American to win a Nobel Prize.[55] In the end, his thesis was supervised jointly by Richards and Kohler. An ambitious work in two parts, one in organic chemistry and the other in physical chemistry, it was approved in June 1916. Conant was just twenty-three years old; he had completed his undergraduate and graduate work in six years.[56]

In normal times, Conant would almost certainly have gone to Germany on completing his Ph.D., to study with the great masters in the world capital of research in chemistry. But in 1916, Europe was wracked by war and America was heatedly debating whether to intervene. Conant was skeptical of the war fever then sweeping Harvard and much of the country, and he considered salvaging his plan for postdoctoral study in Europe by combining enrollment at Zurich's famous Institute of Technology with enlisting for a few months in the American Ambulance Service as a noncombatant. When he learned that the service required a minimum commitment of a year, however, Conant quietly abandoned his idea of postdoctoral study, "not ready to invest that much time away from the chemistry lab.[57]

The war presented chemists with new opportunities in industry, and Conant seized the moment. Joining two Harvard friends, Chauncey Loomis and Stanley Pennock (an all-American guard on a champion Harvard football team), Conant formed a company designed "to manufacture those chemicals which were selling at fabulous prices because their importation from Germany had ceased." In theory, at least, "vast profits were in store for those who engaged in such an operation." Conant planned to return to the academy as soon as the war was over, having earned a "comfortable bankroll to supplement what I knew would be a meager salary."

The founders of LPC Laboratories knew that the window for profits was narrow, and they hurried to begin production. In August 1916, Loomis and Conant attempted a pilot operation in a one-story building they had rented in the Queens section of New York City, but succeeded only in setting it on fire, completely destroying it in the process. Meanwhile, Conant received a "startling" letter from Harvard, offering him a position as instructor in organic chemistry; his partners generously consented to his returning to Cambridge, altering the business arrangement but retaining him as a partner.[58]

The men collected the insurance and reopened the enterprise, renamed Aromatic Chemical, in an abandoned slaughterhouse in Newark, New Jersey. On November 17, 1916, a disastrous explosion occurred, killing Stanley Pennock and two employees, Max Stern, a plumber, and Samuel Welte, a merchant. Loomis, who had desperately tried to avert the accident, miraculously survived, having been blown through a door into a muddy ditch.[59] Back in Cambridge, Conant, who heard the news while lecturing, was shocked and stricken with guilt.[60] Writing about the tragedy later, he concluded that "the procedure had been formulated erroneously" and that it had been "no one's fault except my own."[61] "This tragic experience with applied chemistry should have discouraged me for a lifetime," wrote Conant in an unusual display of introspection. "In fact it did not: within eighteen months I was to become involved again (as a chemist in military uniform) in developing a new manufacturing process for a certain chemical — this time a poison gas."[62]

Conant's conversion from failed businessman to successful military officer took place with remarkable rapidity. In April 1917, he had unhappily watched President Wilson's speech asking Congress to declare war on Germany. His distress, he admitted, was less at Wilson's violation of his campaign platform of noninvolvement than at the war's "effect on my own personal plans." Having "miraculously gotten my foot on the bottom rung of the Harvard academic ladder," Conant was anxious to hang on.[63] But by June he had followed a colleague in chemistry from MIT to Washington, D.C., where he began to work on poison gas for the federal Bureau of Chemistry. Soon Conant became head of a research team at American University and a first lieutenant in the Sanitary Corps of the army.[64]

The program of research in chemical warfare had its roots in the shocking blow that Germany had delivered to the Allies on April 22, 1915, when it used poison gas in direct violation of the Hague Convention. In July 1917, three months after the United States entered the war, Germany escalated matters by using mustard gas, a viscous substance five times more toxic than phosgene, the gas used previously.[65] Under these dire circumstances, Conant turned his considerable talent and energy to the Allied cause, hoping to develop "the great American gas which would win the war."[66]

Sensing his exceptional ability not only as a chemist but also as an administrator, in July 1918 the Chemical Warfare Service promoted the calm and diplomatic twenty-five-year-old to major, dispatching him immediately to supervise a top-secret project in Cleveland.[67] There Conant showed himself to be unusually skilled as a quiet leader of men.[68] His task was to bring Lewisite, a gas so toxic that even the most minute exposure was said to cause "intolerable agony and death after a few hours," to mass production as quickly as possible.[69]

Reflecting on the matter in *My Several Lives,* he explained: "I did not see in 1917, and do not see in 1968, why tearing a man's guts out by a high-explosive shell is to be preferred to maiming him by attacking his lungs or skin. All war is immoral."[70] For his work in bringing Lewisite into production two months ahead of schedule, Conant was awarded a Commendation for Unusual Service. Of greater importance in the long run, Conant's wartime experience put him in contact with leaders in the military, business, and science, and stimulated ambitions that went well beyond being a successful professor of chemistry.[71]

From Faculty Member to Harvard President

Shortly after receiving his discharge from the army, Conant was offered a full-time faculty position by Harvard. Though the University of Chicago had courted him vigorously and made him a handsome offer, he had his heart set on tenure at Harvard and took a humble assistant professorship as a step toward this goal.[72]

Conant's personal life also changed dramatically at this time when he became engaged to a shy and bookish young woman with strong interests in the arts and literature. A graduate of the exclusive Misses May's finishing school, Conant's fiancée had studied art history at Boston's Museum of Fine Arts.[73] Her name was Grace ("Patty") Thayer Richards, and she was the daughter of Theodore William Richards, by far the most eminent member of Harvard's Chemistry Department.

Conant's marriage was a long and generally happy one, and there is no reason to believe that his feelings were anything but genuine. Yet it must have occurred to Conant that his wife would bring much to the union. Her father had married the daughter of a prominent Harvard Divinity School professor, and Richards's own family background was impeccably upper class.[74] In the Harvard milieu, his union with Grace Thayer Richards, whom he wed on April 7, 1921, could only be an asset.

Shortly after becoming engaged, Conant looked into the distant future and confessed to his future wife that he had "three ambitions": "to become the leading organic chemist in the United States; after that . . . to be president of Harvard; and after that, a Cabinet member, perhaps Secretary of the Interior."[75]

Conant methodically accumulated the range of knowledge and contacts that would help him realize these ambitions. In 1922, he helped found the Shop Club, where every month he would join a few dozen Harvard faculty members for dinner and an informal presentation of their research. There he met distinguished colleagues from across the university, impressing them with the breadth of his knowledge and his powerful curiosity.[76] Just as the Signet had established Conant the undergraduate as more than a narrow chemist, the Shop Club established Conant the faculty member as a cultivated man with wide-ranging interests. This reputation, and his resulting friends and acquaintances, proved crucial a decade later when a search was undertaken to find a successor to President Lowell.

Conant's first major test as a faculty member came in 1922, during the controversy over Lowell's attempt to impose a quota on the number of Jewish students at Harvard. The moment of decision came at a faculty meeting on June 2, when Lawrence J. Henderson, the prominent professor of biochemistry and the uncle of Conant's wife, put forward a resolution "to keep the proportion of Jews at Harvard College what it is at present," pending a report of a special committee on admissions.[77] Conant voted in favor of the resolution, but he left behind no record of his views on the controversy over Jewish quotas that wracked Harvard in the 1920s.[78] Yet one thing is clear: when it came time to take a stand, Conant voted with the minority of the faculty who favored restricting Jewish enrollment.

Meanwhile, his rise through the faculty ranks was meteoric. Promoted to associate professor in 1925 on his return from a sabbatical in Germany, Conant then received a lucrative offer from the California Institute of Technology that included a full professorship, four private assistants, and funding for four fellowships. In response, Harvard promoted him to full professor, raised his salary, reduced his course load, and increased funding for his laboratory and graduate students. This effort to keep him in Cambridge was led by Lowell himself, who had warned prophetically: "If you go to California, they will end up making you president."[79]

After deciding to stay in Cambridge, Conant continued his ascent, publishing eighty scientific papers between 1926 and 1933. In 1929, he was appointed to the Sheldon Emery Chair of Organic Chemistry, making him the most eminent scholar in his field in America's leading university. Two years later, at thirty-eight, he was named chair of Harvard's Chemistry Department. And in 1932 he received both the William H. Nichols Medal of the American Chemical Society and the Charles F. Chandler Medal at Columbia University.[80] When Lowell announced his impending retirement in November 1932, Conant was at the top of the academic ladder, earning a deserved reputation as a gifted scientist who seemed a good bet to win a Nobel Prize.[81]

Yet Conant did not fit the Brahmin profile of the two men who had presided over Harvard since 1869. His only administrative experience had been as chairman of the Chemistry Department for a mere two years. Nevertheless, when the six Fellows of the Corporation who would pick Lowell's successor gathered in December 1932, they surprised one another by each placing Conant's name on their list of prospects.[82]

The story of how Conant was selected over such patrician luminaries as Elihu Root Jr. and Henry James (the son of the philosopher and the nephew of the novelist) is a complex one and not without intrigue.[83] But it does not fit the oft-told Algeresque tale of the outsider, rising through sheer talent and energy to the highest position in American higher education. To be sure, Conant was a man of formidable talent and energy. But he was also a descendant of the original Puritan settlers of New England, had attended a fine prep school, had parents who were able to build him a private laboratory when he was a child, and had a sister, Marjorie, who had gone to Paris to study painting.[84] From the perspective of both Conant and the Boston Brahmins, a social gulf separated them; from the perspective of the broader society, he was a member of the Anglo-Saxon elite, and the social distance between him and Boston's fabled upper class was barely discernible.

Conant's rise to the top tier of contenders took place early in the search process after a meeting with Robert Homans, a member of the Corporation who, under the guise of canvassing Conant's views on a successor, was really assessing Conant. The professor forthrightly offered his opinions on Harvard's strengths and weaknesses, making it clear that, in his view, Lowell's emphasis on undergraduate tutorials had filled the younger ranks of the faculty with "mediocre men" and had led to "standards of promotion that were not high enough" and were taking "Harvard downhill."[85] There were few positions in American universities where a professor could carry on research, he told Homans, and to "fill one of these positions with a second-rate person was to betray a trust — to be guilty of almost criminal negligence." Conant then shared his thoughts on the survival power of universities by reviewing the history of Oxford and Cambridge during the Puritan rebellion of the mid-seventeenth century.[86] Homans was dazzled by the erudite professor, exclaiming at dinner that evening to his son George, "I think we've got our man."[87]

Conant was now a leading candidate for the presidency, and the members of the Corporation sought to assure themselves that he would be a good choice. A visit from his old friend Charlie Curtis ascertained that he would take the job if it were offered (though he told Curtis that he "certainly did not want the job").[88] The Corporation decided that it needed more details on Conant's family and youth and dispatched Lawrence Henderson to gather information. Henderson carried out his rather awkward mission while Conant was out of town. When Conant returned a few days later, Henderson told him that President Lowell had called him to his office to discuss the possibility of Conant's becoming the next president of Harvard.[89]

The search process was now in its final stages. But doubts remained, with Grenville Clark '03, one of the Corporation's most influential members, expressing a preference for "a more mature and more experienced man of greater demonstrated ability to take on so many-sided a job" and Thomas Perkins reporting: "What I hear about Conant seems to indicate that to choose him would be to take a big risk."[90]

Crucial testimony that Conant would be up to the job came from extended interviews with Simon Flexner, director of the Rockefeller Institute for Medical Research, and James P. Baxter III, a professor of diplomatic history at Harvard. Flexner reported that while Conant had not spoken much at board meetings, he always had something noteworthy to say and was a sharp judge of his colleagues. Baxter's testimony was more forceful; in his view, Conant was "almost a genius," so knowledgeable about topics of general interest that he could match Baxter's own specialist knowledge of "Woodrow Wilson's state of mind on the eve of the Great War."[91]

In the end, the vote of the Corporation was unanimously for Conant.[92] But acclaim for the decision was not universal. Felix Frankfurter was so upset that he expressed regret that he had not acceded to President Roosevelt's wish that he leave academe and become solicitor general.[93] (Frankfurter would, a few years later, leave Cambridge for the U.S. Supreme Court, and for the next twenty years Conant would be president of Harvard.) The austere meritocrat, just forty years old, had realized his second great ambition. He would now have the chance to make his mark on Harvard and on the country.

The new president wasted no time in expressing his position on controversial educational issues. "Harvard's success," he wrote in his first President's Report to the Board of Overseers just a few months after taking office, "will depend almost entirely on our ability to procure men of the highest caliber for our student body and our faculty." In order to bring top students to Harvard College, he proposed a sharp increase in the institution's "woefully inadequate" scholarship funds.[94]

The selection process for admission should, if anything, be more stringent than it had been under Lowell. Conant was interested in "quality not quantity" and "to this end" favored allocating "financial aid in larger amounts to more carefully selected men." "The ideal," he declared, "would be fellowships sufficient to provide for 10 or 15 percent of each class." Keeping the percentage at this point would guarantee that "no one need fear lest our fellowships be so large in number that we pauperize the student body."[95]

Conant's idea of providing scholarships large enough to draw "to the College and to our graduate schools several hundred of the most brilliant men throughout the country each year" seems commonplace today, but it was a revolutionary concept in 1934.[96] Yet as a perceptive *New York Times* profile of Harvard's new president observed, the realization of Conant's principles would require a "degree of ruthlessness in the removal of cherished clutter . . . and even amiable individuals entrenched in the clutter."[97]

The centerpiece of Conant's strategy was his program of National Scholarships, which embodied the critical principles that Conant hoped would spread to other major American universities: ability rather than inherited privilege should determine educational advancement; the most talented students, however poor, should receive scholarships large enough to permit them to attend the best institutions; these awards should be generous enough so that recipients could concentrate on their studies and extracurricular activities rather than time-consuming jobs; such awards should be made solely on merit, and the amount determined by need (the "sliding scale"); America's leading universities should become genuinely national institutions; and, perhaps most important, sheer academic brilliance should be recognized as a crucial component of merit.[98]

Conant was careful to assure Harvard's various constituencies that the National Scholarships would not be too radical a departure from previous practices. On the crucial question of whether they would be awarded on the basis of academic ability alone, Conant's answer was a resounding no; "high character" would be "essential."[99] The cultivation of brilliant scholars was not the primary goal: "the aim," he told the Board of Overseers, is to educate "future leaders of professions, of business, and of public affairs."[100] The vast majority of freshmen would continue to be selected through traditional processes. "The ideal for the future," Conant declared in a major 1936 address, "would seem to me to be something like a hundred National Scholarship holders in each entering class of a thousand."[101]

In a major article, "The Mission of American Universities," Conant emphasized "that there are many walks of life where real intellectual capacity is required — where what is commonly called brains counts heavily."[102] From his perspective, the task of the educational system was to identify students of differing innate capacities and to channel them into the type of schooling that corresponds to their level of intellectual ability as well as their proper place as adults in the division of labor. "At least half of higher education," he wrote, "is a matter of selecting, sorting, and classifying students."[103]

A Spokesman for Higher Education

In May 1938, Conant took his educational credo to the public for the first time in a widely read article in *Harper's Magazine*, "The Future of Our Higher Education." Identifying himself with the Jeffersonian tradition of universal schooling and its emphasis on the paramount importance of equality of opportunity, he took strong position against the tradition of what he called "Jacksonian Democracy" — a powerful strand in American thought and practice that he deemed excessively egalitarian. "Jacksonian Democracy," he wrote, "affirmed that all men were born equal, envied intellectual pre-eminence, and preached the doctrine of equal educational privilege for all."[104]

Jeffersonians emphasized the identification and education of an elite, a "natural aristocracy of talent and virtue." For Conant, the main point in the Jeffersonian tradition is its belief that this "natural aristocracy" is to be found

among all segments of the population, including the poor and the uneducated. In order to fulfill its democratic mission, the nation's system of higher
learning must identify this natural elite and give it the resources necessary to
obtain the best possible education.

But the realities of American higher education, Conant believed strongly,
fell far short of the Jeffersonian ideal. Far too many talented young people
were excluded from college because of economic or geographical barriers, to
the detriment of both "the professional leadership of the country" and "the
advancement of knowledge and its application to the needs of society."[105] To
address this problem, Conant pointed to the principles of the National Scholarships and suggested applying them to colleges and universities nationwide.
Fellowships should be awarded solely on merit, with the amount of the award
based on a "sliding scale." Above all, the number of scholarships should be
massively increased, for "a selection of a group of promising students from all
economic levels for higher education in the universities is essential for the
continued vitality of a democracy."[106]

Conant explained that the implementation of his Jeffersonian program
would involve a significant redistribution of privilege. The problem with
American higher education was not that enrollment was too restricted but
that "there are too many rather than too few students attending the universities of the country."[107] Conant believed that "the country at large would benefit by an elimination of at least a quarter, or perhaps one-half, of those now
enrolled in advanced university work, and the substitution of others of more
talent in their place."[108] Realizing this ideal would therefore involve both the
inclusion of more talented students of modest backgrounds and the elimination of large numbers of less able students, many of them from privileged
backgrounds.

As president of an institution with close ties to the upper class, Conant
was careful not to carry his meritocratic logic too far. Acknowledging that
higher education had a long tradition of accommodating an "aristocratic element," representing "the passing of power and wealth from generation to
generation," Conant insisted that "their education must be fitted into the
general scheme." For the legitimation of this deeply anomalous position
within the larger Jeffersonian framework, he turned to Charles Eliot, whose
commitment to intellectual excellence was beyond reproach. Conant reminded his readers that Eliot, in his inaugural address in 1869, had proclaimed: "[T]his College owes much of its distinctive character to those who,
bringing hither from refined homes good breeding, gentle tastes, and a manly
delicacy, add to them openness and activity of mind, intellectual interests,
and a sense of public duty . . . To lose altogether the presence of those who in
early life have enjoyed the domestic and social advantages of wealth would be

as great a blow to the College as to lose the sons of the poor. The interests of the College and the country are identical in this regard. The country suffers when the rich are ignorant and unrefined. Inherited wealth is an unmitigated curse when divorced from culture."[109] Nothing less than the good of the nation required that Harvard and like institutions admit the sons of the privileged, even when their merits fell well short of qualifying them for the "natural aristocracy." To do otherwise would permit a dangerous philistinism to prevail in the American elite.

But what of the vast majority of young people who were neither natural nor hereditary aristocrats? Not destined for membership in the economic, political, or cultural elite, they "should receive a training which not only equips them for work but prepares them for life as well-rounded, intelligent, and useful citizens in a democratic society." Conant's education schema included universal elementary education for all and "universal opportunity for secondary education."[110] But its core was the principle of differentiation — different types of schooling for students destined to occupy different positions in the division of labor.

Opposed to radically increasing the number of students in higher education, Conant nonetheless recognized the power of the democratic impulses calling for the expansion of opportunities to attend college. His ingenious plan for reconciling the growing popular demand for higher education with his principle of differentiation was to advocate an increase in the number of two-year junior colleges, where "a general college education can be given at greatly reduced cost locally, since students live at home."[111] In this model, only a small proportion of junior college students would go on to a university; for the vast majority, the junior college would be a final destination, where they received vocational training or perhaps the rudiments of a liberal education.[112]

Beneath Conant's relentless advocacy of tracking in both secondary and higher education was a deep-seated fear. "I doubt if society can make a graver mistake," he warned, "than to provide advanced higher education of a specialized nature for men and women who are unable subsequently to use that training." Writing in 1938, Conant was haunted by the specter of Nazism: "The German experience in the decade after the war should warn us against the perils lying in wait for a nation which trains a greater number of professional men than society can employ."[113]

Nazism and the Totalitarian Threat

Long preoccupied with Germany, Conant was appalled that the nation that had given the world Goethe and Beethoven was now a Nazi dictatorship posing a manifest threat to world peace. In a reflective statement to his class-mates in February 1939 in preparation for the twenty-fifth reunion of Har-vard's Class of 1914, he wrote: "With Munich fresh in our minds and a February crisis apparently brewing as I write, it is hard not to turn one's thoughts back to the summer of 1914 without having the question arise, must it all happen again?"[114]

The question was answered when German troops attacked Poland on September 1, 1939. Speaking to Harvard's students in late September, Conant proclaimed that that "every ounce of our sympathies is with those fighting the Nazis." With the "fate of humanity's experiment with free institutions" at stake, he warned that "the forces of violence must be beaten back by superior violence yet without engendering bitterness or hate."[115] On September 28, in a widely publicized letter to Alf Landon, the nominal head of the Republican Party, he came out "strongly in favor" of repealing the arms embargo, ex-plaining that if the Nazis defeated France and England, "the hope of free in-stitutions as a basis of modern civilization" would be "jeopardized."[116]

Conant's interventionist stance in 1939 and 1940 flew in the face of power-ful isolationist sentiment both on campus and off. In response to his letter to Landon, the *Harvard Crimson* attacked him for "earning an unenviable place in the road gang which is trying to build for the United States a super-high-way straight to Armageddon." A flood of letters, both pro and con, descended on Conant from around the country. "Men like you have no right [to be] at the head of an American institution of learning," wrote a woman who signed herself "a daughter of the American Revolution and *proud* of it." "Harvard's large Jewish enrollment," she suggested, must have "something to do with your un-American utterance regarding what our policy should be toward those two dead beat nations, England and France."[117] Eight months later, in May 1940, a *Christian Science Monitor* poll of Harvard students revealed that 91 percent were unwilling to go to war to join the cause of the Allies and 62 percent opposed even the extension of aid, fearing that it might bring the war closer to home.[118]

The prospect of war with Germany led Conant to deepen and broaden his critique of American education, for he saw in the nation's schools and univer-sities a democratic force that could serve as a bulwark against the totalitarian threat. In a remarkable speech, "Education for a Classless Society," delivered at the University of California at Berkeley in March 1940 and published in the *Atlantic Monthly* two months later, Conant for the first time linked his views on education to a broader social and political philosophy.[119] He did so at a time when the American social order faced the greatest threat to its survival since the Civil War. Over the previous decade, America had witnessed unem-ployment rates as high as 25 percent; the rise of organized movements to stop evictions ("rent riots") in New York, Chicago, and other large cities; general strikes in San Francisco and Minneapolis; the formation of the Congress of Industrial Organizations (CIO) and the growth of union militancy; an upsurge in membership in the Communist Party; the invention of the sit-down strike in 1936–1937; the murder of ten picketing strikers by the police at Republic Steel in Chicago in 1937 (the "Memorial Day Massacre"); and the establishment of a Popular Front against fascism that brought together Communists, liberals, radicals, and Socialists.[120] Among intellectuals, radical and even socialist ideas attained unprecedented influence; in literature, works challenging the status quo, such as John Steinbeck's *Grapes of Wrath,* Clifford Odet's *Waiting for Lefty,* and Richard Wright's *Native Son,* set the tone. It was during this period that even as principled an anti-Stalinist as John Dewey wrote that liberalism would have to acknowledge that "the liberty of individuals" would require measures to "socialize the forces of production."[121] In such a context, Conant's fear that the American system of free enterprise might be endangered was not irrational.

Conant's intention in writing "Education for a Classless Society" was to put forward a distinctively American alternative to the increasingly influential socialist vision of a society without classes. Placing himself firmly within the Jeffersonian tradition, he described its essence as three interrelated elements: "passion for freedom of the mind . . . a belief in careers open to all through higher education, and a faith in universal schooling."[122] The very survival of America as a free society, he argued, depended on the ability of the educational system to break the barriers of hereditary privilege.

Conant saw the Jeffersonian tradition as threatened by growing fascist aggression abroad and the hardening of class lines at home. The latter threat was particularly worrisome, for its roots long predated the rise of fascism. In the half century since 1890, Conant contended, the great American ideal of classlessness — "a continuous process by which power and privilege may be automatically redistributed at the end of each generation" — had become less and less of a reality.[123]

Conant believed that with the closing of the frontier, the growth of large cities and slums, the increase in tenant farming and migratory labor, and the rise of mass unemployment, a new and more class-ridden social order had emerged. "We are seeing throughout the country," he noted with alarm, "the development of a hereditary aristocracy of wealth." "Ruthless and greedy exploitation of wealth of both natural and human resources by a small privileged class founded on recently acquired ownership of property," he warned, "has hardened the social strata and threatens to provide explosive material beneath."[124]

The emergence of "a hereditary aristocracy of wealth" was, of course, a gross violation of the Jeffersonian ideal. But Conant's immediate concern was that a society with too much hereditary privilege "soon produces class consciousness." "Extremes of wealth and poverty," he added, "accelerate the process."[125]

The United States, Conant believed, was unique among the great powers in that it remained, however precariously, both "free" and "classless." In contrast, "Russia today is classless, but not free; England free, but not classless; Germany neither free nor classless."[126] Conant's antidote to class struggle was increased social mobility. What was needed was not, he emphasized, "a radical equalization of wealth" but a "more equitable distribution of opportunity." As long as each generation believed that it could "start life afresh" and that "hard work and ability would find their just rewards," America would be immune to the twin European afflictions of class consciousness and political extremism.[127]

America's vast system of public high schools was the cornerstone of Conant's plan to create a more fluid society. In the United States, unlike in Europe, students headed for different parts of the division of labor were not educated in separate schools. But in order to handle the "horde of heterogeneous students" that "has descended on our secondary schools," Conant believed that "extreme differentiation of school programs" would be "essential."[128] Improved testing and more discriminating guidance were necessary "to cull from every condition of our people the natural aristocracy of talent and virtue."[129] Once culled, these natural aristocrats would attend America's leading universities, where they would receive the type of education befitting future members of the elite.

In a rhetorical move that became a staple of his essays addressed to the larger public, Conant presented himself as a plainspoken progressive, firmly rooted in a distinctively American tradition that rejected both radicalism and reaction. Conant was cautious by temperament, and his political instincts naturally gravitated toward the center. As he saw it, the "extreme Right" had an undue admiration for the classbound educational system of England and opposed educational and economic reform that would undermine class consciousness by increasing social mobility. For its part, the "socialistic Left" imported alien European ideologies of class struggle into the United States and displayed a singular insensitivity to tyranny by concentrating power in the state. What both the Left and the Right had in common, Conant argued, was an aversion to the great Jeffersonian tradition.[130]

As an alternative to a forced choice "between potential Bourbons and latent Bolsheviks," Conant proposed a revitalization of the tradition of indigenous "American radicalism."[131] This radicalism, he was careful to point out, was in no way in conflict with capitalism; on the contrary, through the "spreading of private ownership" and "the stimulation of small enterprises," it promised to help save capitalism.[132] Social justice received only passing reference in Conant's political program; while admitting that "even free schools offer little opportunity to famished youngsters," Conant — writing in the midst of the Great Depression — did not go beyond the idea of supplying food and clothing to those who most needed them.[133] Nevertheless, Conant's tone was resolutely progressive: "If the American ideal is not to be an illusion, the citizens of this Republic must not shrink from drastic action." To defend the distinctively American version of the "classless" society against challenges from both Left and Right, the support of "reformers and even fanatical radicals" would be necessary.[134]

Controversy on the Charles

Conant's progressive rhetoric reached its zenith in a highly controversial article in the May 1943 *Atlantic Monthly,* "Wanted: American Radicals." Much had changed since the appearance of "Education for a Classless Society" exactly three years earlier: the Germans had turned on their Soviet allies, the Japanese had attacked Pearl Harbor, and the United States had become engaged in a "total war" against the Axis powers. Conant's own life had changed as well; an interventionist in 1940, he was now an integral part of the war effort. Lending his formidable scientific and administrative talents to the government as chairman of the National Defense Research Committee, he was to organize the nation's civilian scientific resources, both human and material, to develop the weapons that would win the war.[135] A critical member of the so-called Top Policy Group, Conant was centrally involved in the Manhattan Project to develop the atomic bomb and served as chief adviser to General Leslie Groves, its head.[136]

While shouldering these responsibilities, Conant remained president of Harvard and took the time to write a sympathetic article, "American Radicals."[137] He did so because he believed that the fate of freedom in the United States depended ultimately not only on superior weapons but also on superior ideas. With victory over fascism now on the horizon, Conant was already turning his attention to the postwar world. There the primary threat to freedom, he believed, would come from the domestic Left.

To turn back the socialist menace, Conant looked to the indigenous American radical — the spiritual descendant of Whitman, Emerson, Thoreau, Jackson, and Jefferson, who would be "respectful but not enthusiastic about the ideas of Marx, Engels, and Lenin."[138] His thesis by now was familiar: a third choice was needed between what he called American "reactionaries" and European "radicals." But the militancy of his insistence that genuinely radical change would be needed if the American system was to survive was new.

Particularly worrisome to Conant was the impending demobilization of the 11 million men in the armed forces, which, if handled improperly, "could well sow the seeds of a civil war within a decade." He hoped that the future of the returning soldiers would be determined by "their merit, their talents, their character, and their grit." But if they came to feel that their opportunities were governed by "accidents of geography and birth, there will be many who will become frustrated and embittered — particularly if the general level of prosperity should fall."[139]

To the authentic American radical, the only way to prevent the growth of a "caste-ridden society" that would pose a "danger for the liberty of all" was to take drastic measures to ensure equality of opportunity.[140] Committed to "wielding the axe against the root of inherited privilege," the American radical "will be resolute in his demand to confiscate (by constitutional methods) all property once a generation." To do so, he "will demand really effective inheritance and gift taxes and the breaking up of trust funds and estates." "And this point," Conant emphasized, "cannot be lightly pushed aside, for it is the kernel of his radical philosophy."[141]

To make equal opportunity a reality, much more social mobility, both upward *and* downward, would be required. In a United States governed by authentic American radicals, Conant proclaimed, we would "with enthusiasm put a son of management who does not have the capacity for desk work in the way of earning an honest living as a manual worker." Coming from the president of a wealthy private university heavily dependent on gifts from the wealthy, this was provocative rhetoric indeed. But Conant did not stop there. He insisted that the American radical "will not place a higher value on property rights than human rights, for his forbears never did." (Jefferson, Conant noted pointedly, had written "life, liberty, and the pursuit of happiness" into the Declaration of Independence, not "life, liberty, and property.")[142]

To many of Harvard's most loyal supporters, this time Conant had gone too far. Among the ruffled alumni was Thomas W. Lamont, a loyal and generous graduate of Exeter and Harvard (Class of 1892), the chairman of J. P. Morgan, and one of the nation's wealthiest men.[143] In a polite but pointed eight-page letter to Conant, Lamont made clear his discontent. Conant's "American radical," he wrote, was a "destructive sort of chap" who would "strike a death blow to individual enterprise." Lamont rejected the notion that a castelike system was developing in the United States, but he reserved his deepest displeasure for Conant's proposal to confiscate all property once a generation. "By confiscating inheritances," Lamont contended, "your Radical would undermine the profit system . . . the system under which in three hundred years America grew from a wilderness to a land in which men are free, and men have more nearly equal opportunity than ever before, a land in which the average man lives better, healthier, and wealthier than ever man has anywhere."[144]

Conant responded in a seventeen-page letter that is an invaluable source for understanding the private thoughts behind his public pronouncements. In it, he revealed the passions and fears that fueled his commitment to educational and social reform. At the outset, Conant made explicit that he and Lamont differed on the seriousness of the disease afflicting America; whereas for Lamont it was nothing more than a "disagreeable cold," for Conant it "was pneumonia with a possible prognosis of death."[145]

Conant left no doubt that the terrible affliction that threatened the American system was the sharpening of class lines and the growth of what he called "industrial feudalism," a type of European system in which the children of the privileged became owners and managers and the children of manual workers were relegated to life in the working class. In the twentieth century, he argued, industrial feudalism had often "led to either Communism or Nazism."[146] In the United States, the way out of this predicament was to "follow the lines of our national history" through a "conscious repudiation of feudalistic tendencies and renewed emphasis on the essential American ideal of a fluid society."[147]

Conant went on to lay out an astute analysis of the class divisions in American society. The fundamental class boundary in the United States was the one between "manual workers" and "professional and business groups." Very few children of workers in "textile mills, automobile plants, steel works, mines," and similar settings were, he contended, "mounting the ladder of professional or managerial responsibility."[148] Even in companies like AT&T, which "run on the merit system," the choice of managers "operates within a relatively small group," for only "college graduates (and preferably graduates of the better colleges)" can get their feet "at the bottom of the management ladder." Under such conditions, the working class, Conant feared, would lose faith in the American dream. "If the great mass of people without property" do not believe that opportunity awaits their children, freedom and private enterprise could be destroyed in a clash of "haves" and "have nots."[149]

Conant was frank in acknowledging that the opportunity for a boy to attend Harvard was profoundly shaped by the class character of the larger society. Drawing on data from the Class of 1940, he informed Lamont that the top 2.7 percent of the population — those with incomes of $5,000 or more — provided 60 percent of Harvard's students. Only 16 percent came from the nearly 90 percent of families with incomes of less than $2,500.[150] Conant concluded that Harvard in fact provided little in the way of opportunity to the great majority of the population.

Unless ways were found to reverse the trend toward sharpening class divisions, Conant believed that "in the present temper of the times private enterprise is likely to go." The underlying problem, he wrote, was that "industrial feudalism and universal suffrage are an unstable mixture and will sooner or later blow up." Threatening to ignite the explosion was the very real prospect of a postwar economic downturn; "another crash and depression," Conant fretted, "would critically endanger the continuation of free enterprise, which to me is the basis of a free society."[151]

Always looming in the background was the threat of what Conant called "the Russian experiment" — a threat that in 1943 appeared to him more ideological than military. World War II had only exacerbated this threat, for "the vast contributions of the Russian people under a collectivist dictatorship to the defeat of Hitler [were] almost immeasurable" and had increased the appeal of the Soviet model.[152] If "we fail to work out a satisfactory adaptation of the American system to the needs of the post-war years," he warned, "the influence of Russian success" could well be "profound."[153]

Yet for all his blustery rhetoric about confiscating all property once a generation and building a "classless society," Conant's "American radical" was actually a rather tame fellow. Drastic inequalities were not a problem for him as long as the opportunity to become rich was more equally distributed; the American radical, Conant explained to an Oklahoma newspaper editor, "would be quite willing to have incomes soar to the skies."[154] In truth, Conant's "American radical" was strikingly silent on some of the main issues that Roosevelt's New Deal had begun to address: the right of workers to organize, the problems of persistent mass poverty and unemployment, and the need to construct a rudimentary American welfare state.[155] One critic's pointed assessment of Conant's "American radical" was not far from the mark; Conant used "the language of the left," wrote Max Lerner, "to express the ideas of the Center."[156]

Ironically, since Conant's purpose in writing the *Atlantic Monthly* article had been to articulate a set of ideas that would help preserve free enterprise, businessmen were enraged by it. Lamont, whose response had been measured, reported to a friend that Conant "had stirred up a hornet's nest" and that "the Harvard crowd was generally buzzing with the whole thing."[157]

Members of Harvard's inner circle were deeply troubled by the article. Where, they wondered, did the president of a rich private university dependent on inherited wealth get off espousing a radical redistribution of property once a generation? Adding to their irritation was a feeling that Conant had avoided taking responsibility for his own views by hiding behind his hypothetical "American radical." One Corporation member doubtless spoke for many alumni when he tartly suggested that "this is not a dignified or sportsmanlike way to put yourself on record."[158]

Though the details remain murky, the ferocious controversy provoked by the *Atlantic Monthly* article seems to have played an important role in a little-known effort to remove Conant from his position as Harvard's president. In a 1974 interview, Paul Buck, Harvard's provost under Conant, described the atmosphere during this period as one of "crisis": Conant's "American radical would have first among his list of objectives the confiscation of inherited wealth. (Laughter.) Whew! Well that hit the Corporation — Bill Claflin[159] was especially offended, he says, 'Here I sit on the largest private endowment in the country.' Henry James was very much upset. He went to the country for seclusion so he could write an answer to it. Later he was persuaded not to do it, it was just going to add fuel to the fire, but this was a shocking experience." Buck's advice to Conant was to let the matter rest. "You've made a mistake, Jim," he said, "and you can't do anything in a case like this."[160]

In truth, by the time "Wanted: American Radicals" appeared, Conant's position with the Corporation had already been weakened by a growing perception that his attention was far more focused on Washington than Cambridge.[161] Particularly troubled by Conant's near total absorption in national affairs was Henry Shattuck (A.B. '01, LL.B. '04), the influential former treasurer of the Corporation and since 1942 its senior Fellow. A partner in the eminent Boston law firm of Ropes and Gray and a Republican member of the Massachusetts legislature,[162] Shattuck had also been disturbed by the talk of confiscation in the essay.[163] Convinced that Conant would be "happier" in Washington, Shattuck proposed that he be asked to take a leave of absence and that Buck be appointed in his place.[164]

Buck transmitted this idea to Conant, who was horrified at the prospect. Unable to tell Buck or the Corporation exactly what he was doing in Washington (even his wife was kept in the dark about his involvement in the Manhattan Project), Conant explained that "I've got to have the title to get this important work done." The ever-loyal Buck replied, "Well, that's very simple, then," and promised to tell Shattuck that he "would not go along with his plan."[165] Faced with Buck's opposition and Conant's cryptic but portentous reference to the "important work" he was doing in Washington, Shattuck dropped the idea.[166]

Educational Statesman

Having survived a serious challenge to his presidency, Conant emerged from the war as American education's leading spokesman. Once the Manhattan Project became public, Conant could no longer be viewed as simply the president of America's leading university; he was now the educational statesman who, at a time of great national peril, had brilliantly harnessed the scientific resources of America's universities to the cause of victory over fascism.

Though his stature reached new heights, Conant never again pressed the limits of respectable political discourse as far as he had in the *Atlantic Monthly* article. He was now more prudent in his calls for reform. No more would readers hear him cackling with delight at the thought of the son of a businessman being relegated to the working class to earn an "honest living." The notion of confiscating property once a generation was now strictly taboo.

Prudence did not mean, however, that Conant had lost his capacity to write forceful and even brilliant analyses of American education. In November 1945, three months after Japan's surrender ended World War II, he laid out his educational and social vision for the postwar world in a series of lectures at Columbia University, "Public Education and the Structure of American Society."[167] These lectures, which were published the following year in book form, were Conant's most elaborate formulation to date of his ideas on education and American society.

The lectures started from the premise that the goal of American education was to foster the development of a "free and harmonious people operating an economic system based on private ownership but committed to the ideals of social justice." Stratification, Conant believed, was inevitable in an industrial society. A sound educational policy would keep the tensions inherent in an unequal society from exploding into disastrous political and social upheavals. In his view, the stakes could hardly have been higher: "the chances of a non-revolutionary development of our nation in the next fifty years seem to me to be determined largely by our educational system."[168]

As in his earlier writings, "fluidity" remained the key to avoiding a social upheaval. But what was new was Conant's argument that the degrees of "visibility" and "complexity" of a system of stratification were crucial in determining the stability of the social order. The way to preserve the American system of free enterprise and democracy, Conant maintained, was to minimize the visibility of its stratification structure and to maximize its complexity. To illustrate his point, he offered an illuminating and sophisticated comparison of the American army in World War II and the Prussian part of the German army in World War I. On the face of it, he noted, the two organizations seemed similar: relatively simple though elaborate structures, a clear chain of command, precise definitions of each individual's position, and high visibility of the system of rank embodied by external insignia. Yet the American army, with its nonhereditary officer corps and its less regimented style, seemed "a very democratic one" while the Prussian army was "the epitome of militarism." An important source of the very different aura of the American army, Conant believed, was that it had "deliberately fostered a climate of opinion which 'played down' rather than glorified a man's position in the social structure."[169]

Conant underscored the lesson of this comparison: "*Without changing essentially the organization of the army, it was possible to modify to a surprising degree the visibility of its social structure.*"[170] His plan was to apply this principle to civilian life. Through universal secondary education, comprehensive high schools, the expansion of opportunities to attend college, and vigorous efforts to emphasize the "social equality of a great variety of occupations" and diverse fields of study, Conant hoped to blur the boundaries between social classes.[171]

American leftists, he believed, were committed to increasing the transparency of the class divisions inherent in the existing order to pursue their goal of turning the masses against capitalism. Conant's mission was exactly the opposite: to promote educational reform, "both by action and by talk," that would render these same divisions as invisible as possible.[172]

The meritocratic order that Conant espoused would be highly stratified and extremely competitive.[173] "Classless" only in the sense that high fluidity and complexity, combined with low visibility, would obscure the underlying structure of social and economic inequality, its real commitment was to equality of opportunity, not equality per se. Yet even on the question of opportunity, Conant was withering toward those who took seriously the quintessentially American idea that any child could, "with the aid of proper education, become anything he desires." Such thinking denied the "reality of intellectual talent": "Only in matters connected with organized sport does the average American think clearly about the significance of innate ability . . . Yet when it comes to studies, parents often expect the school and college to accomplish the equivalent of turning a cripple into a football player."[174] To Conant, this powerful "Jacksonian" strand in American thinking represented egalitarianism gone wild.[175]

Conant's lectures represented the crystallization of years of serious reflection on the problems of American education, and they contained the seeds of virtually all the ideas that he expressed in a prolific body of writing on educational reform over the next two decades. Already in 1946 a figure of such stature that a cover story in *Time* magazine touted him as a potential candidate for president, Conant reached an even greater influence with the advent of the Cold War in 1947–1948.[176] His long-standing message — that America could simply not afford the loss of talent caused by large-scale inequality of opportunity — now had special resonance in the context of America's escalating conflict with the Soviet Union.[177]

Conant had long believed that Soviet communism posed a grave ideological threat to the United States, but the Soviets' explosion of an atomic bomb in 1949 and Communist North Korea's invasion of South Korea in 1950 convinced him that it posed a serious military threat as well.[178] As chair of the report on national security for the National Education Association's prestigious Educational Policies Commission (EPC), Conant pressed the point that an embattled America could ill afford to waste invaluable "human resources." In the EPC's 1951 report, *Education and National Security,* Conant's imprint was highly visible. "The safety of America," it argued, as well as "the prospects of peace in the world," might well be determined by educational decisions made in the next few years.[179]

The Soviet threat, coupled with the public's memory of the crucial role that nuclear scientists played in winning World War II, gave powerful new impetus to Conant's argument in favor of special attention for talented students. With the Soviet system scouring its vast population for young people from any social background or region who had the ability to become nuclear physicists, the United States had no choice but to do the same. *Education for the Gifted,* another report by the EPC that bore Conant's mark, called on the American people to "invest a larger portion of their economic resources in the education of individuals of superior talent."[180]

Having privately decided, five years in advance, to retire as Harvard's president in 1953, Conant made a calculated decision to provoke one final major controversy.[181] His target — the proposed use of public monies to support private elementary and secondary schools — was, he acknowledged in his memoirs, "carefully defined" so that he would fire his shots and then "withdraw from the field of battle."[182] His message, which was published in the May 3, 1952, *Saturday Review,* made sure an explosive controversy would ensue: "The greater the proportion of our youth who attend independent schools, the greater the threat to our democratic unity. Therefore, to use taxpayers' money to assist such a move is, for me, to suggest, that American society use its own hands to destroy itself."[183] In a matter of days, the predicted counterattack — with shots being fired from both parochial and elite private schools — was in full swing.

With what he later described as "malice aforethought," Conant included in the article the following provocative sentence: "I cannot help regretting that private schools have been established in the last twenty years in certain urban areas where a generation ago a public high school served all the youth of the town or city." He then compounded the offense by noting "the 'snob aspect' of some of these new independent schools."[184] The spectacle of Harvard's president mischievously tweaking some of the very private schools that sent Harvard many of its students was strange by any standard. But his underlying message was serious: the emergence of a dual system of education in the Untied States would, especially at a time of great national threat, "weaken the unity of the community."[185]

Having begun Harvard's presidency with some fairly simple ideas about extending opportunity to the academically talented, Conant ended twenty years later with a richly elaborated plan for educating all Americans.[186] Rooted in a principled commitment to democracy and free enterprise, he provided a comprehensive analysis of the relationship of education to society and a detailed platform for reforming the schools so that their practices were more closely aligned with the nation's basic ideals. In an era when both left and right had mounted serious challenges to the American system, Conant remained steadfast in his faith that the educational system was a vast democratic resource that, properly deployed, would ensure the nation's survival.

The emerging ideology of meritocracy had found in Conant a brilliant and tireless advocate, and his writings had an immense impact on the structure and practices of America's schools and universities. From the nation's growing reliance on standardized tests to the increased availability of scholarships, from the founding of the National Science Foundation to the passage of the National Defense Education Act, Conant's influence was everywhere visible.

CHAPTER 6

The Reality of Admissions Under Conant

TODAY, MORE THAN A HALF century after Conant stepped down as Harvard's president, his reputation as the man who brought meritocracy to Harvard (and, by dint of Harvard's influence, to American higher education in general) is stronger than ever. According to the eminent Harvard sociologist David Riesman, his administration reflected a move toward the democratic kind of meritocracy represented by the Harvard National Scholarships.[1] Seymour Martin Lipset agrees, crediting Conant (and his provost, Paul Buck) with "a new emphasis on pure achievement, meritocracy," which, in turn, was related to the triumph at postwar Harvard of "the academic culture over the 'clubby culture' (linked to family social status, social life, and athletics)."[2]

James G. Hershberg, in his major biography of Conant, identifies "his successful encouragement of a meritocratic, a socially, ethnically, and geographically more diverse student body" as "probably his most significant legacy to the college." Hershberg portrays Conant as a staunch foe of the privileges of the Protestant Establishment: "Determined to diversify the college, opening more positions for talented youths from around the country, and consequently cutting into the spaces traditionally reserved for the upper-class offspring of New England alumni," he had embarked on a "search for 'new blood' over 'blue blood' [that] was bound to alarm the aristocrats."[3] Nicholas Lemann, in his influential account of the history of standardized testing, is even more unequivocal; the larger-than-life Conant who bestrides *The Big Test* felt an "animus against the American elite of the mid-twentieth century." His goal, Lemann writes, was nothing less than to "dethrone" the existing upper class, a group he found "suffocatingly narrow," and to "replace it with a new elite chosen democratically on the basis of its scholastic brilliance."[4]

If, as Hershberg contends, Conant had little patience with "privileged sloth," he had strong sympathy for "the "meatballs" — "the ambitious, lower-middle-class local students, the first- and second-generation ethnic immigrants who worked overtime to overcome prejudices (and quotas)."[5] Jews were, from this vantage point, major beneficiaries of Conant's democratic convictions. The contrast with Lowell could not have been more stark. Whereas Lowell had imposed a strict limit on the number of Jews at Harvard, Conant "discarded any semblance of quotas."[6] In his essay on the history of Jews at Harvard, Henry Rosovsky, a Jewish refugee from Europe and a former dean of the Faculty of Arts and Sciences, states that postwar Harvard "welcomed us with open arms."[7] In the prevailing interpretation, Conant's lack of prejudice toward Jews and his animosity toward the privileges of the Protestant upper class derived from the same source: a bedrock commitment to equality of opportunity as guaranteed by meritocratic selection.

The problem with this interpretation of Conant is that it is based far more on his pronouncements than on his deeds. At the level of public rhetoric, Conant was a progressive, sometimes even a radical; at the level of practice, he was surprisingly conservative, continuing many of the exclusionary policies put in place by Lowell while softening their rough edges. During his presidency, Harvard's admissions policy continued to be tilted toward the privileged at the same time that it discriminated against Jews and other socially "undesirable" students. A careful examination of these practices reveals a very different man than the stout defender of meritocracy traditionally portrayed — a man who, despite his eloquent denunciations of hereditary privilege, went to great lengths to make sure that Harvard would continue to serve the wealthy and the powerful.

Conant's Dean of Admission

The sudden death of Henry Pennypacker, Harvard's chairman of the Committee on Admissions since 1920, two months after Conant took office, gave the new president an opportunity to select a chair who would share his vision of a more meritocratic Harvard. Pennypacker, widely esteemed for his "manly character" and "sympathetic understanding of boys," was the very embodiment of the cultural ideals of the Protestant upper class.[8] A graduate of Exeter and Harvard, where he took a degree in Latin and won the intercollegiate shot-put, he had faithfully implemented Lowell's policy of restricting the number of Jews. The timing of his death provides a window into the president's priorities on the matter of selection.

Never one to make a major decision lightly, Conant informed himself fully on the state of admissions at Harvard. One of the documents he received was a stunningly forthright memorandum from Anne MacDonald, who had been the assistant to Pennypacker and to the acting chairman after Pennypacker's death. The memo provided a detailed portrait of how admissions decisions were being made when Conant came into office. Central to the process was the personal interview — a highly charged event that, MacDonald emphasized, "must be very carefully handled with sympathy and understanding," especially in dealing with those frequent cases that were "hopeless from the start." Some interviews were more sensitive than others: "The interviews with rejected Hebrews or their relatives are particularly precarious, and one needs to be constantly on the alert. A single false step might easily bring the University to the front pages of the morning papers." Luckily, MacDonald reported, "for the last ten years, or since the restriction, we have been particularly fortunate in settling these cases."[9]

When Conant received MacDonald's memo, he was already considering as Pennypacker's successor Richard Gummere (Ph.D. '07), the headmaster of the William Penn Charter School in Philadelphia. The sixth generation of a distinguished line of Quaker schoolmasters dating from 1779, Gummere had an impeccable social background.[10] A graduate of the Haverford School and Haverford College (where his father had been an eminent professor of English), he had also attended the Marburia School in Switzerland. Before going to the William Penn Charter School, he taught at Groton and served as professor of Latin at Haverford. He was also a talented athlete and had played on the nation's first soccer team at Haverford.[11]

Gummere had first come to the attention of the Harvard administration in 1922. That spring, at the height of the controversy over Lowell's proposal to impose a Jewish quota, Pennypacker had contacted Gummere, asking how best to handle the delicate matter of Jewish applicants. Gummere's response was forthright:

> I feel that Doctor Edsall [a Harvard faculty member] has stated the case very correctly and intelligently, as far as the experiences of the Penn Charter School in the Jew problem are concerned. Such action was taken very definitely, and a very limited number of Jews is admitted; in fact, it is at present almost infinitesimal. We are particularly careful not to make any issue of the matter, and when people of that persuasion wish to be admitted, and we either have enough in the school, or do not feel that the applicant is satisfactory, we employ the same methods of keeping them out of the school as we would any unsatisfactory candidate of any denomination. As a matter of fact, I admitted only one Jew last fall, and plan to admit none this coming fall.

He then requested that Pennypacker "regard this letter, especially the figures given in the last sentence, as entirely confidential" and expressed his hope that "your own problem will work out satisfactorily."[12]

But before appointing him to a sensitive position, Conant wanted more information, so he made inquiries among trusted members of the WASP establishment who knew the candidate personally. One such inquiry was made by A. C. Hanford, the dean of the college, during a conversation with Alan Valentine, Yale's dean of admissions.[13] In a letter to Conant, Hanford reported that "Valentine had high regard for Gummere as a man" and that "he stood very well in the community." But he also said that "Gummere let his emotions influence him too much and said that he used to have some rather painful conferences with him regarding boys of very limited ability whom Gummere supported most warmly." Valentine, Hanford said by way of summing up, "was, therefore, inclined to question a little his standards."[14]

Hanford's report that the dean of admissions at Harvard's chief competitor considered Gummere somewhat soft on standards did not deter Conant from offering him the position of chairman of the Committee on Admission. On May 18, 1934, the *Harvard Crimson* reported that Richard Mott Gummere, president of the Headmaster's Association, had been named chairman, effective September 1, 1934. To permit him to complete his duties in Philadelphia, Harvard granted Gummere a leave of absence for the fall semester.[15]

Before his term began, Gummere prepared a fascinating, nineteen-page document, "Confidential Report to President Conant on Harvard Admissions Problems." The report makes clear that Conant had spoken with Gummere in some detail about his views on admissions and that the two men agreed on fundamentals. Perhaps most crucial, they shared the conviction that Harvard had to be careful not to alienate its traditional clientele — or, as Gummere put it, the "several groups on whose cooperation and good will the continued stream of applications and the 'selling' of Harvard to the best type of boy depends [*sic*]."[16]

Gummere assured Conant that "I am entirely in harmony with your aim to make Harvard a national university, without losing the flavor of its tradition." But what did he mean in practice? In a section of his report about "the type of student that Harvard wants," Gummere was direct: "The 'sons of alumni' type might represent, as you remarked to me, forty percent of an entering class — required to conform to a reasonable minimum requirement, and making up a group from which the 'manager' type and the class officers and the later businessman would come."[17] Such students, the great majority of whom would come from eastern private schools, would help preserve Harvard's refined social atmosphere, pay their own fees, and maintain Harvard's close ties to the economic elite (and future donors).

The report also affirmed Gummere's commitment to "attract first-class scholars."[18] But he dismissed the recent statistics published by Harvard showing public school boys to be heavily overrepresented in Phi Beta Kappa and among those receiving summa cum laude and magna cum laude degrees. This superiority, he suggested, "may be ascribed to the fact that one does not find many public schools boys at Cambridge who can afford to neglect their studies for the sake of social contacts . . . If the private-school group, from places like Exeter and Milton, decided in caucus to go after Phi Beta Kappa, they could reverse these figures in a single year."[19]

When deciding whom to admit and whom to reject, Gummere stated that "the college must know the schools, and especially the headmasters and principals, as intimately as possible." For applicants from far away, it was critical to receive personal assessment from "reliable Harvard people."[20] College Board examinations and other measures of academic performance were useful, "but no mechanical or automatic way of selection is possible." Finally, on the critical question of how to balance the different types of candidates, Gummere suggested following the path laid out by Lowell: "I do not see what we can do here except to walk wisely and intelligently, as Harvard has done with the Jew problem."[21]

In selecting Gummere, Conant sent a reassuring message to Harvard's traditional constituencies. Here, after all, was a man of impeccable social credentials who was also the president of the association of leading prep schools. Conant's choice also revealed his intentions as president: reform would take place, but only within carefully circumscribed limits. To be sure, Harvard would search for new sources of academic talent but in a fashion studiously designed not to offend its traditional clientele. Under Gummere, the upper-class students who had historically given Harvard much of its cachet would receive special consideration from the Committee on Admission. For these students, the academic requirements for admission would remain minimal.

At the same time, Harvard would open its doors to a limited number of students of "remarkable talents," regardless of their ability to pay. But they would be a minority of the freshmen class — no more than 10 or 15 percent.[22] The recipients of scholarships would have to meet high academic standards, but (as Conant emphasized time and again) "character," "leadership," and athletic ability would also be taken into account. Conant and Gummere agreed that it was imperative "not to let the public think we are out for scholars only."[23] A sound admissions policy would, in short, be a "balanced" one, and its administration would require considerable discretion and judgment.[24]

Harvard Admissions from the Great Depression to World War II

The first decade of Gummere's term showed striking continuity with the policies laid down by Lowell and Pennypacker, including the establishment of a fixed number of places in the freshman class and a clear statement to both applicants and the public that candidates would not be accepted on academic ability alone. Instead, a multiplicity of nonacademic criteria — alumni parentage, athletic talent, geographical diversity, and vague qualities such as "character" and "leadership" — played a pivotal role in determining admittance. This system, as we have seen, had been put in place to limit the number of Jews. But it also allowed private colleges and universities to produce the kind of student body they desired while shielding themselves from external scrutiny. Under Gummere, who served until 1952, Harvard's system of selective admissions continued to do both.

The admissions office during the early years of the Gummere era was not the highly bureaucratic and professional apparatus that it became by the mid-1950s. Essentially a two-person operation run by the chairman and his powerful assistant, Anne MacDonald, the committee relied heavily on personal interviews, which provided an opportunity to assess a candidate's social graces and personality.[25]

Reflecting on the Gummere years, Paul Buck described the chairman "as an old-fashioned type of admissions man who played golf with the headmasters and took them to lunch at the Tavern."[26] Dining informally with men he trusted, Gummere could identify the applicants who conformed to his notion of "the best type of boy."[27] The information exchanged at these intimate gatherings also helped him identify "undesirable" applicants, including those deficient in "character."

At the same time that the committee was making every effort to attract candidates from the leading boarding schools, other young men who had shown an interest in Harvard were discouraged from applying. In 1938–1939, for example, there were "3,000 serious applicants for admission," but only 1,895 were "approved . . . for final consideration." To makes these decisions, Gummere enlisted "the Hygiene Department's assistance in looking over the records of candidates." In addition, he reported, "increased emphasis is being put on the preliminary interviews."[28] Rather than subjecting undesirable applicants, many of them Jewish, to a formal rejection, the committee preferred to discourage them — politely but firmly — from submitting a final application.

When subtlety failed, the committee was not beyond resorting to stronger measures. In an effort to attract "capable boys from schools which do not ordinarily prepare their pupils for college examinations" and thereby to increase geographical diversity, Harvard under Lowell had adopted a "top-seventh" plan. Designed to bring to Cambridge more small-town students, most of whom were expected to be Protestant, the plan had the totally unintended effect of providing another avenue of entry for Jewish students.[29] Gummere developed an innovative solution to this problem. In a letter responding to an inquiry from Radcliffe Heermance, Princeton's director of admissions, Anne MacDonald explained Harvard's policy: "If we seem to be getting a preponderance of an undesirable type from any particular locality, we cut out the whole locality. There are times, consequently, when we are not very popular in certain quarters, and there is much wailing and gnashing of teeth, but we stand to our guns."[30] As part of this policy, Harvard specifically excluded from its "top-seventh" plan applicants from high schools in Long Island, eastern New York, and New Jersey.

The admissions process left plenty of room for personal intervention in favor of — or against — particular candidates. Thus A. C. Hanford wrote to MacDonald on behalf of an Ohio applicant, one William Johnson, reporting that "I do not know the young man personally, but I have become very well acquainted with the father, who is the most loyal and active alumnus in the state of Illinois." In another case, Hanford wrote about another applicant whose father was a Harvard professor and a librarian at one of its professional schools. Reporting that "our families have spent summer vacations at the same camp in New Hampshire," he assured the committee that "James is a boy of good character and first-rate ability." Though not athletic, he had done a "good deal of horseback riding at a ranch" in Arizona to which his father sent him and is in good health. Both boys were accepted.[31]

But not all applicants with Harvard connections were welcomed. In 1936, Irving B. Rosenstein, who had graduated first in his class at Harvard, contacted Dean Hanford about two young men who were applying for admission. Hanford took notes during his conversation but did not pass on an endorsement. Instead, he wrote directly to Gummere, stating that "I do not know either Goldberg or Rabinowitz, and I realize that we have quite enough applicants of this type." Nevertheless, Hanford continued, "I felt it my duty to pass along the information that Rosenstein had given me regarding the two boys."[32]

In another case that year, Jerome Greene, secretary to the Harvard Corporation, explained to John D. Lynch, the mayor of Cambridge, why a young man named S. A. Goldstein,[33] who reportedly had high marks on his College Board exams, had been turned down. Mr. Goldstein, Greene reported, "came just under the 'weighted average,' which takes all pertinent factors into account." Harvard, he declared, had "no reason to suppose that he is not a creditable representative of his race, many members of which are admitted to Harvard each year." He closed his letter by assuring Mayor Lynch that "no personal discrimination against him was involved."[34]

Greene was not wrong when he wrote that Harvard admitted a considerable number of Jews — far more, in fact, than Yale and Princeton. That said, the best available evidence shows that discrimination was both widespread and systematic. On the basic issue of the quota that Lowell had quietly put into effect, the record leaves little doubt that Conant and Gummere continued to set a ceiling on Jewish enrollment for at least a decade.[35]

By the time of Lowell's retirement, the proportion of Jews in the freshman class — which had been 28 percent as late as 1925 — had plunged to under 15 percent. When Conant arrived in 1933, just 12 percent of the freshmen applying to the Houses were Jews; under Conant and Gummere, the numbers ranged from 14 to 16 percent between 1935 and 1941.[36] As late as 1942 — almost a decade into Conant's tenure — a quota was still clearly in place. According to an internal memorandum, of 886 nonscholarship applicants eligible for admission in May 1942, "about 100 will be lost on account of the 'quota.'"[37] Even in the midst of World War II and with qualified students (especially ones who could pay) in short supply, Harvard continued to impose a quota on Jews.

There is no clear evidence that Harvard had a parallel limit on the number of blacks in the late 1930s and early 1940s. Such a limit was hardly necessary, however, for the number of blacks who had the means and the inclination to apply to Harvard was tiny. Those who did enroll during the 1930s represented the continuation of a long-standing pattern of black interest in Harvard; during the more than seven decades from 1870 (when Harvard graduated its first black) through 1941, it is estimated that roughly 165 blacks matriculated.[38] Though this averages out to just two or three a year, it was far higher than at Yale, which also had a long history of educating blacks, not to mention Princeton, which remained totally segregated until the end of World War II.

While Harvard had a reputation for openness to blacks, the few who matriculated in the early Conant years did not receive a warm welcome. A rare insight into Harvard's attitude toward blacks during this period is provided by the response to a 1935 letter from a Mr. Loevinger, inquiring about blacks' access to Harvard's dormitories — a sensitive issue that had exploded into a very public one in the 1920s.[39] Unsure of how to respond, Harper Woodward, secretary to President Conant, wrote to Dean Hanford, admitting that "the problem of formulating a thoughtful and tactful reply has given me some trouble." Perhaps, he mused, "it would be best to send as little information as possible, or perhaps none at all?"[40]

Hanford wrote back promptly. Acknowledging that "there are no Negro undergraduates now living in the dormitories or Houses," he insisted that Harvard had no "rule or policy" preventing them from doing so. His explanation for this pattern of de facto segregation was economic; the absence of African Americans was primarily because "most of them pay very little for a room and single rooms are fairly expensive." In any case, Hanford concluded, "most of them realize that they are better off living outside."[41]

In response to an inquiry in the spring of 1939 from Dean Addison Hibbard of Northwestern University, Hanford reported that only five blacks were registered in the entire college. But by then a black student resided in the freshmen halls, and Hanford reported that he had been admitted to Adams House for the following year.[42] Nevertheless, six years into Conant's tenure, blacks made up less than one quarter of one percent of the student body — a sharp downturn even from the conservative Lowell administration. In 1922, at roughly the midpoint of Lowell's presidency, seventeen blacks were enrolled at the college.[43]

It is clear that blacks simply did not figure in Harvard's never-ending quest for "paying customers." In a 1938 confidential memorandum, Conant expressed grave concern about the "size of the pond in which the privately supported colleges are fishing." Drawing on government statistics, Conant set out to estimate the number of "potential freshmen (white, male) each year" from families with incomes over $5,000 — the floor for students able to pay Harvard's costs without financial assistance. He estimated that there were only about 15,000 such young men in the country, and "not more than 50 percent of the children of the group would be 'good bets' for Harvard": a "small pond" that contained no more than 7,000–8,000 students out of roughly 1,000,000 young men of college age.[44]

Throughout Conant's tenure, these two themes — the paucity of competent students who could pay their own way and the urgency of attracting a sizable portion of them — set the limits of Harvard's admission policy.[45] But not all qualified students who could pay their own way were highly sought after; some such students — especially those of Jewish origin and relatively unassimilated eastern European backgrounds — were welcome only in limited numbers. More was at work here than simple ethnic prejudice. Harvard could not afford — or so its leaders believed — to enroll too many Jews lest they reduce its appeal among its traditional upper-class clientele. For in the end, Harvard depended on such "paying guests" not only for tuition but also — and far more critically — for the donations that formed the foundation on which the preeminence of the private colleges rested.

Seen in this light, the presence of admissions practices inconsistent with Conant's meritocratic public pronouncements makes perfect sense. The strong preference for the children of alumni, for example, reflected an unsentimental assessment of likely economic return; loyalty on the part of the institution would be more than repaid, Harvard believed, by the generosity of alumni. It is hardly surprising, then, that a father who had attended Harvard virtually guaranteed his son's admission; as late as 1951, 94 percent of legacies were admitted.[46]

Harvard's pronounced preference for the graduates of leading private schools followed the same logic. Apart from offering a steady supply of "paying guests," such schools educated just the sort of young men Harvard most wished to enroll. In 1940, of the 77 applicants from the St. Grottlesex schools, only 1 was rejected. The larger elite boarding schools fared just as well; of 137 applicants from Andover, Exeter, Choate, Hotchkiss, Hill, and Lawrenceville, 2 were denied admission.[47]

In stark contrast, public school students — including those from some of the nation's finest high schools — were not sought out, and their applications were far more likely to be rejected. In 1940, just 11 students applied from three large, highly selective urban high schools in the Northeast: Bronx High School of Science and Stuyvesant High School, both in New York City, and Central High School, in Philadelphia. Of these 11, 4 were rejected — more than the number turned away from 213 applicants from the top dozen boarding schools. Even Boston Latin, with its strong historic ties to Harvard, was not exempt from this pattern; of 59 applicants to Harvard in 1940, 14 failed to gain admission.[48]

Applicants from public schools had to meet a higher academic standard for admission than those from private schools, and they outperformed them academically once at Harvard. The results of a study of the freshman classes between 1939 and 1941 suggest that the degrees of preference given to private school students must have been considerable; public school students were twice as likely to make the Dean's List and only half as likely to be designated academic failures as prep school graduates.[49] Harvard frankly acknowledged that recruiting the most academically talented freshmen class was not its goal. Gummere put the matter well in his 1940–1941 report: "It is as much to the credit of a slower-witted student that he should pass creditably as it is for a naturally brilliant boy that he should rank on the Dean's List."[50]

It is impossible to ignore the many ways in which Harvard's admissions practices during the Conant years were systematically tilted toward the privileged, but it is also true that Harvard was moving gradually toward greater inclusiveness. One indication was the increase in the proportion of the freshmen from public schools: 49 percent of those admitted in 1941 compared to roughly 40 percent in 1932 and in 1933, Lowell's last two years.[51] Possibly related to this increase was the modest rise in the academic quality of the freshmen during roughly the same years.[52] Above all, there was Conant's innovative and widely publicized program of National Scholarships — the embodiment of his commitment to equality of opportunity.

The National Scholarship Program

From its very beginning, the National Scholarship Program embodied two contradictory principles: on the one hand, a nationwide search for brilliant students, regardless of financial means, and on the other, a set of geographical restrictions on where to look for such students.

The roots of this contradiction may be found in Harvard's quest for a geographically diverse study body, which began in the 1920s as one of a series of measures designed to limit the number of Jews. Harvard's "highest seventh" plan was the first expression of this commitment to "geographical diversity."[53] This plan, in Conant's words, contained "all-important limitations [that] excluded would-be candidates who went to school in New York and Boston and nearby communities."[54]

The National Scholarship Program followed the same logic: it would seek top-ranking scholars from anywhere but the Middle Atlantic states — the center of the nation's Jewish population.[55] Conant wished to attract brilliant students to Cambridge, yet the criteria for selection were carefully designed to include highly subjective attributes such as "unimpeachable character" and "strong personal qualities."[56] The continuity with the restrictive measures introduced by Lowell is striking and produced the same result: a selection process that gave Harvard wide latitude to ensure that National Scholarship recipients would be the "right kind of boys."

In the competition, Jewish applicants faced a triple handicap: the geographical qualifications eliminated most of them, the selection criteria included subjective (and nonscholarly) qualities that they were generally thought to lack, and the people making the final decision were largely in sympathy with Harvard's policy of restriction. Nevertheless, the possibility remained that somehow — as had in fact happened with the "highest seventh" plan — more Jews would survive the selection process than Harvard deemed desirable. A 1936 letter by Grenville Clark, a prominent New York lawyer and a key member of Harvard's Corporation, broached the delicate issue of the number of Jews among the winners of the National Scholarship. In a draft of a response to Clark (written for A. C. Hanford, dean of the college), Henry Chauncey indicated that although he shared Clark's concerns about the "Jewish problem," he believed that his fears about the program were unfounded: "It is difficult to estimate with any exactness the racial origins of the Prize Fellows. I have run through all their applications and have made a memorandum of what seemed to be the likely ancestry of each man. I doubt if it is worth while [*sic*] to ask an expert on genealogical and racial problems to give us any more definite report. I imagine that some of the names may have given Mr. Clark the idea that we had a pretty large percentage of Jews. Fortunately, this is not the case. Wise is probably the only Jew, and Mr. Briggs speaks of him as 'the finest kind of Jewish stock.'" To further assure Clark, Chauncey suggested that he be given the opportunity to peruse "the applications of this year's Prize Fellows some time when he is passing through Cambridge."[57]

Though blacks in the 1930s were hardly likely to inundate Harvard with applications for National Scholarships, they too apparently were not the type of student the program hoped to attract. When the first announcement of generous prize fellowships went out, the managing editor of *The Crisis*, a respected publication whose editor-in-chief was W.E.B. Du Bois, asked President Conant "what the attitude towards colored students will be in the matter of these scholarships."[58] Vernon Munroe Jr., secretary to the president, responded for Conant, but he avoided answering the question. Instead, he emphasized that the proposals "constitute a mere suggestion for a plan the details of which have not been formulated and the funds for which are not yet available."[59] Even had this statement been true — and because the names of the first prizewinners were announced just a few months later, it is suspect — it did not preclude a clear statement of principle declaring that Harvard would not discriminate on the basis of race, ethnicity, or religion in awarding the fellowships. But Munroe made no such declaration, writing instead, "Until the proposals have achieved a more concrete form, Mr. Conant regrets that he is unable to answer the questions which you have raised."[60]

Though the program discouraged black applicants and discriminated against those Jews who did apply, it did allow students from relatively modest backgrounds to attend Harvard. Of the 34 winners in 1938, for example, 15 had annual family incomes under $2,500, with 9 of them under $2,000. The fathers' occupations were diverse: 4 farmers, a toolmaker, an auto mechanic, 4 professors, 1 physician, 2 attorneys, and 2 schoolteachers, and 13 from a wide gamut of business pursuits, ranging from the vice president of a manufacturing company to the proprietor of an automobile body repair shop. As intended, a good number of the winners came from small towns: 8 from communities under 10,000 and 9 more from towns of 10,000–50,000.[61]

The National Scholarship Program succeeded in finding students whose exceptional talents would be confirmed by their performance at Harvard. Of the 10 recipients who graduated in 1938, 5 graduated summa cum laude, 3 magna cum laude, 2 cum laude, and 8 were elected to Phi Beta Kappa.[62] Among the early winners were some men who were the truly brilliant students Conant had in mind; one of them, chosen in 1935, was an Illinois public high school graduate named James Tobin, who went on to win the Nobel Prize in economics.[63]

Though only 253 students were awarded National Scholarships between 1934 and 1942, the program had a much larger impact on both Harvard and the nation.[64] At Harvard, where a "gentleman's C" was still a mark of status among the students who set the tone of campus life, the National Scholarship enshrined the principle that the highest awards would be bestowed only on those students with distinguished academic records. By guaranteeing that truly exceptional students could attend Harvard regardless of their need, the program attracted strong candidates from distant regions who would otherwise never have thought of applying to a "rich man's college." In 1937, for example, 46 "runners up" in the competition were given freshman scholarships and matriculated at Harvard. In addition, 22 students who failed to receive the scholarship were admitted and ultimately enrolled.[65]

At the national level, perhaps the greatest impact of the program was to strengthen the role of standardized tests in college admissions.[66] In 1937, Harvard, along with Yale, Princeton, and eleven other colleges, set up special one-day scholarship examinations to be administered under the auspices of the College Entrance Examination Board and the American Council on Education. Consisting of a test of verbal and mathematical aptitude in the morning and a series of objective achievement tests in the afternoon, these exams were required for all National Scholarship candidates. Though only 2,005 students nationwide took these tests at their first administration on April 24, a historic precedent had been established.[67] The results of these tests would henceforth be a crucial factor in determining who would obtain scholarships at the leading private colleges and universities. Academic excellence would be judged by "objective" standards, and in the case of Harvard, a few young men of exceptional ability would receive scholarships generous enough to permit them to attend, regardless of family background. For a fortunate few, a core principle of meritocracy — that of need-blind admissions — was now a reality.

Yet if the program was an important move toward greater equality of opportunity, the process that selected the awardees fell far short of Conant's professed meritocratic ideals. Officially committed to strengthening Harvard's appeal in distant regions, the program had, by 1941, come to include Massachusetts, which already provided Harvard with roughly 40 percent of its freshmen.[68] In 1942, 9 of the 35 National Scholarships went to Massachusetts students, including graduates of Groton, Middlesex, Deerfield, and Andover.[69] At the same time, students from New York State, with a population almost three times that of Massachusetts and which supplied Harvard with well under half as many freshmen, remained ineligible.[70] Clearly, more was at work here than a simple quest for "geographical diversity."

By 1942, the National Scholarship Program attracted an unprecedented 887 applicants and had been extended to sixteen states. But the war had already begun to interrupt the flow of students, and Harvard decided to discontinue the program for the duration of the conflict.

Admission Dilemmas During Wartime

Harvard's top priority during World War II was to help America win the war while maintaining as steady a flow of students as circumstances would permit. On December 14, 1941, one week after the attack on Pearl Harbor, Harvard and a group of other elite private colleges agreed to eliminate the cumbersome June subject examinations of the College Entrance Examination Board and to require instead the Scholastic Aptitude Test (SAT) for all applicants, not just scholarship candidates.[71] As with other temporary adaptations to wartime, the requirement became a permanent feature of the admissions process. Undertaken at a moment of national emergency, it was a momentous shift: the abolition of the old-fashioned essay examinations and their replacement by the streamlined and more "objective" SAT planted the seeds of the test-based meritocracy that arose after the war.

With men of all social classes serving in the military and a spirit of shared sacrifice among civilians, the wartime atmosphere provided openings for those who wished to challenge prevailing patterns of privilege.[72] But although Conant's meritocratic pronouncements reached new rhetorical heights, Harvard's actual practices continued to exclude the socially undesirable. By 1943, however, attracting the right kind of "paying guests" had become particularly difficult, for the applicants "consisted mainly of those below the draft age, and those classified in 4-F or designated for work along special lines," and the draft age had been lowered.[73] Applications plummeted from 2,185 in 1942 to 1,540 in 1943, yet Harvard actually increased its rejection rate from 13 to 27 percent. Perhaps as a consequence, the proportion of public school graduates among those admitted — which had reached an unprecedented 57 percent in 1942 — plunged to 42 percent in 1943, where it remained for the duration of the war.[74] The many dislocations caused by the war did not, however, prevent the Committee on Admission from planning for the future. By the summer of 1943, with America's triumph in sight, Gummere began work on a confidential — and astonishingly blunt — report, "Problems of Admissions to Harvard College." Among those receiving the report was Paul Buck, Conant's powerful right-hand man and since 1942 dean of the faculty.[75]

Gummere acknowledged Harvard's serious image problems: "One section of the USA thinks of us as millionaires, another as Phi Beta Kappas only, another as alien to Southern points of view, another as too radically democratic. "A certain type of boy believes that there is no 'club' or social reward for undergraduate prominence." "Your chairman," he wrote plaintively, "is weary of being told . . . that the *college* part of Harvard University is inferior in spirit and unity and the 'preparation of the whole man' to the small college or to certain other universities — especially Yale."[76]

"To be very frank," Gummere continued, "we are not attracting enough good average boys who are intelligent but not top scholars — the type who will make conscientious alumni later on."[77] His solution was to reach out for help through the "key-men" alumni program, established in 1942 so that designated graduates could interview prospective applicants and transmit their candid appraisals of candidates to the Committee on Admission. The aim was to "encourage all boys of ability and character and 'all around' qualities to come to Harvard," with an "emphasis on 'paying guest' candidates" in the "key-men" program's first year.[78]

Busy trying to recruit "average good schoolboys," Harvard was at the same time turning away less socially desirable applicants from another quarter. In 1942, admission decisions had been carried out within the framework "of a quota for a certain type"; one internal document estimated that the number of Jews lost to this quota was 100. Of the students admitted, it was acknowledged that "there will be a good many who would not have been approved for admission in previous years."[79]

Yet even in the face of a serious shortage of candidates, Harvard remained more than willing to reject applicants it felt would detract from the College's social atmosphere. In an appendix to his report, Gummere reported that as of May 1943, 211 of 1,126 candidates for admission had been rejected. Who were these students whom Harvard shunned even as it could not fill its normal freshmen class? Gummere was euphemistic but clear: "*Nearly all* rejections as of May, 1943, were 'Group III.' This is a dangerous situation: if it keeps up, we are sitting on a volcano. We must have more candidates not Group III."[80] Even at the height of a war against a fanatically racist, anti-Semitic enemy, it seemed that nothing — not even the reports of the extermination of European Jews already making their way into the newspapers — could dislodge Harvard's policy of restricting Jewish enrollment.[81]

But even as Harvard clung to the status quo in some areas, the disruptions caused by the war produced change in others. Perhaps the most visible change was the entrance absorption of Radcliffe women into Harvard.[82] Conant acknowledged that since the "last thing in the world that I desired when I took office was to open Harvard College to 'young ladies,'" this change was accepted only with great reluctance.[83] Yet the depletion of the faculty had left Conant with little choice, and in the spring of 1943 Radcliffe women were permitted to attend selected upper-division classes alongside Harvard men for the first time. Within a few years, Harvard and Radcliffe, both of which continued to maintain separate admissions offices, were effectively coeducational, at least in terms of classroom instruction. The new policy soon became taken for granted and was popular among the students, but Conant was never entirely comfortable with it; according to campus legend, he once returned to Harvard Yard during the war and was distressed to see women in the classroom, only to be reminded by Buck that he himself had approved the historic agreement.[84]

The war also brought changes in the personnel of the admissions office. Buck took a strong interest in the operation of the Committee on Admission and increased administrative oversight through new appointments to its ranks, including Assistant Dean Henry Chauncey. Equally significant was the death of Anne MacDonald in June 1944. Though her status as a woman prevented her from ever enjoying a title higher than assistant to the chairman, MacDonald had been a formidable and decidedly old-school presence.

Years later, Buck recalled that "I discovered very soon that Dick Gummere really didn't admit people . . . it was that Miss MacDonald . . . that funny old lady."[85] So shocked was Buck at the reports of her power that he directed Chauncey to see that the whole committee examined the files of all applicants. A new regime, still formally headed by Gummere but under the administration's close supervision, was being established.

Veterans and the "New" Harvard

Well aware that the war's end would trigger a surge in applications from veterans as well as the return to Cambridge of many of the 3,500 men who had left to serve in the military, Harvard began planning in earnest for the postwar era while battles continued in Europe and the Pacific.[86] In 1945, Buck made a crucial appointment, bringing Wilbur Bender, an assistant dean with Henry Chauncey in the 1930s, back to Harvard as counselor for veterans. Buck so wanted Bender to take the job — and to have him preside over the process of determining which of thousands of veterans hoping to attend Harvard would be admitted — that he promised that Bender would become dean of Harvard College as soon as Hanford, who was nearing retirement, stepped down.[87] In 1952, Bender moved from his position as dean of the college to become Gummere's successor as dean of admissions. In these capacities — counselor for veterans, dean of the college, and dean of admissions — Bender became what the honorary LL.D. awarded him in 1961 proclaimed: "an architect of the post-war Harvard."[88]

Bender's background verged on the exotic. Born in 1903 to a "farming family in Elkhart, Indiana," Wilbur J. Bender was one of seven children and a Mennonite — a church he described as "a small, fundamentalist, pacifist sect."[89] After the premature death of his father, who had served as the executive officer of the Mennonite Board of Missions and Charities, the sixteen-year-old Bender (already a high school graduate) needed to support himself. He took a variety of jobs, including section hand for the New York Central Railroad, factory worker, chauffeur, and semiprofessional basketball player. After two years at Goshen College, a Mennonite institution in Goshen, Indiana, he left for financial reasons and taught for two years in the Indiana public schools. A scholarship permitted Bender to attend Harvard as a transfer student, and he spent two years there, graduating magna cum laude in 1927.

After two years of teaching in a private school in Williamstown, Massachusetts (the home of Williams College), he returned to Harvard, taking a master's degree in American history in 1930. In 1931, still a graduate student, he became an assistant dean under Dean of Freshmen Delmar Leighton. As a "baby dean," he was instrumental (along with Henry Chauncey) in developing the techniques used to select the winners of the National Scholarship Program. His excellent work on Conant's pet project did not escape the attention of the president, who approved of him "wholeheartedly."[90] Buck, then a rising instructor in history, also came to know and admire the dynamic young man.

In 1936, still hoping to complete his doctorate in American history at Harvard, Bender accepted a job at Andover. But in 1942, at thirty-nine, he left to become a lieutenant in the Naval Reserve and to direct the V-12 program at Tufts University. His decision to join the navy made him the first member of his pacifist Mennonite family in ten generations to wear a uniform, though he never saw sea duty. After his discharge in September 1944, he returned to Andover to teach. Within a year, however, he was back at Harvard.[91]

Bender had an unusual background for a Harvard dean, but what made his appointment still more remarkable were his unabashedly progressive political views. Writing to his Harvard classmates in the late 1930s, Bender noted proudly that "I am probably the only member of my class who is also a member of the American Federation of Labor." A member of the American Civil Liberties Union and the American Association of University Professors, he reported that he was "about ready to take a Ph.D. at Harvard with a thesis on the history of American middle class radicalism after the Civil War."[92] Earning his livelihood at the time at Andover, he jokingly described his tasks as "trying to make a few of the sons of the upper bourgeoisie safe for democracy."

Bender's views may have softened a bit after the war, but they remained decidedly liberal. In one of his first acts as counselor for veterans, Bender issued a plea to Buck, Gummere, and other important administrators to leave space in the college for veterans with no previous Harvard connections, arguing that otherwise "Harvard would lose possibly its best chance in history to get able students, regardless of their economic status."[93] Where the G.I. Bill was concerned, Bender's position contrasted sharply with that of Conant, who had initially opposed the measure as excessively democratic; the G.I. Bill, Bender told a reporter from the *Boston Herald*, was "a statesmanlike piece of social legislation."[94] In 1947, just as he was about to assume his duties as dean of the college, he gave a speech at a reunion of his class in which he pointedly emphasized that he was an atypical Harvard man: "not a Bostonian, not an athlete, not a club man, not a Republican."[95] After describing his modest background in considerable detail, he concluded that portion of his speech with a simple statement: "As far as I can tell, I am a free man and a Democrat."

In other ways, Bender was the consummate insider: a graduate of Harvard College, an assistant dean under both the Lowell and the Conant administrations, and a teacher for more than half a decade at Andover, one of Harvard's top feeders. By the time he returned to Cambridge in 1945, Bender knew Harvard's traditions intimately and respected them deeply. A true loyalist, he would bring change to the institution that had launched his ascent, but only with extreme caution.

As the person in charge of screening the 20,000 veterans interested in attending Harvard, Bender had wide latitude to discourage men from applying, and he did not shrink from exercising it. In an article on veterans in the *Harvard Alumni Bulletin,* he reported, "Every effort has been made to discourage formal application and thus to avoid formal rejection of men who had no real chance of admission in the present competition."[96] As he explained in a speech to the Harvard Club: "We are concerned about character and a lot of intangible qualities which it is easier to list than to detect — leadership, personal force, warmth of personality, emotional stability. We have admitted men who are going to have a tough time making C's because we were impressed by their non-academic qualifications and felt they were going to do something in the world. We are concerned about geographic distribution. We very definitely put into the scale that an applicant had a Harvard father. And athletic ability."[97] Now being applied to veterans, these were the same criteria that had been used under both Lowell and Conant.

The flood of applicants gave Harvard an unprecedented opportunity: to select its freshmen class from a huge pool of highly qualified applicants. Though the official statistics for the fall of 1946 showed an acceptance rate of almost 55 percent, the reality was that there were more than ten applicants for every place.[98] Of those veterans accepted, virtually all of them could enjoy the generosity of the G.I. Bill. For these men, need-blind admissions — a longstanding dream of Conant's that would not become institutional policy until the mid-1960s — was already a reality.

The massive infusion of federal dollars permitted Harvard to enroll the most diverse student body in its history. The entering class of 1946 was the high-water mark; half the freshmen class and almost three-quarters of the 5,400 students in the college (compared to only 3,500 before the war) had served in the military.[99] By all accounts, the veterans brought to the campus a degree of maturity and seriousness never before seen in Cambridge.[100] They included students whose ethnic and class origins made Harvard more heterogeneous than ever before, and there is no reason to doubt President Conant's description of them as the most able, mature, and promising students Harvard had ever had.[101]

Yet it is easy to exaggerate how different the "new" Harvard was from its predecessor.[102] Three-quarters of the veterans had, after all, been admitted before their military service, and many of them had attended Harvard before the war. As Bender noted, they were "a normal Harvard population."[103] Moreover, in admitting the nonveteran half of the class, Harvard maintained its exclusionary practices. While 80 percent of the applicants from the leading prep schools were admitted, only 33 percent of the applicants from the three highly selective urban high schools with large Jewish populations gained entry.[104] Even those veterans who had previously neither attended nor been admitted to Harvard had relatively privileged backgrounds. Of those, for example, who entered in 1947, the average parental income was $7,400, compared to $4,950 for scholarship students and $2,620 for all American families. Over 40 percent had attended private schools, the vast majority of which were in New England.[105]

Presented with a large and diverse group of candidates who could, by virtue of the G.I. Bill, pay their own way, Harvard responded in a characteristically measured fashion, moving incrementally to broaden its social base while protecting its traditional constituencies. After the torrent of veterans entering in 1946, the flow quickly slowed, turning before long into little more than a trickle. Thus, whereas veterans made up 48 percent of those admitted in 1946, their numbers dwindled to 11 percent in 1947 and 1948 and a mere 3.5 percent in 1949.[106]

An Official Admissions Ideology

Perhaps the most enduring effect of the veterans was that they forced Harvard to reflect on what kind of students it most wanted. Provost Paul Buck and Wilbur Bender, dean of Harvard College, explicitly put forth an official ideology of admissions in three widely read articles in the *Harvard Alumni Bulletin* in 1946, 1948, and 1949.[107] Treated as a trilogy, they offered value-based rationales for admitting some students while rejecting others. Though generated in the context of the postwar pressures of the mid- and late 1940s, the ideas they expressed provided an architecture for admissions policy that largely endures today, not only at Harvard, but at virtually all of the nation's elite private colleges and universities.

In his 1946 essay "Balance in the College," Buck identified Harvard's fundamental admissions task: the articulation of a "clear idea of what we want and an equally clear idea of what we don't want."[108] Citing Presidents Eliot and Conant for authority, Buck put forward his core concept of "balance," of Harvard as a place where, in the words of its quasi-official historian Samuel Eliot Morison: "rich men's sons and poor, serious scholars and frivolous wasters, saints and sinners, Puritans and papists, Jews and Gentiles will meet in her Houses, her Yard, and her athletic fields, rubbing off each other's angularities and learning from friendly contact what cannot be learned from books."[109] One of the great dangers facing Harvard, Buck believed, was that excess pressures for entry from groups reflecting only one element of this mix could destroy Harvard's delicate but essential "balance."

Buck's remarks leave little room for doubt about what he meant: because of its reputation for intellectual excellence and equal opportunity, Harvard was in danger of being overpopulated by the "sensitive, neurotic boy." As an example of the threat to Harvard, Buck cites the "large metropolitan public high schools of New York and New Jersey," from which "95 percent of the applicants for Harvard . . . are of one category — bright, precocious, intellectually over-stimulated boys." The "larger private schools from these same states are no better," for they are "weighted with the delicate, literary type boys who don't make the grade socially with their better balanced classmates who, in turn, head for Yale or Princeton."[110]

In contrast to these "floppy ducklings," Harvard should seek out sturdy young men of "the healthy extrovert kind . . . so much admired by the American public." Such individuals are usually not outstanding students; "many boys of the kind we want [are] in the second quarter of classes."[111] But the presence of such boys on campus is essential if Harvard is to attract, as Buck put it in 1948, "a student body balanced in its composition and its potentialities for later contributions to all phases of American life."[112]

Buck is clear that "applicants of the kind we most desire" are unlikely to require scholarships. Unlike Harvard's search for National Scholars, Buck was convinced that "our approach to [finding] such new boys should be by some appeal other than the financial one." In pursuing such students, special care must be taken not to alienate the traditional feeder schools: "We must do nothing to disturb the cherished relations we have with those schools who understand us and have stood behind us through thick and thin."[113] In a similar vein, he worried that the National Scholarship Program, so highly publicized in the West and Midwest, might dissuade "the good (as distinct from top-flight) high school student with the resources to pay his own way."[114]

A balanced Harvard would not, Buck maintained, wish "to stop the flow of the studious or sensitive type boy." Indeed, Harvard should capitalize on its appeal to "the exceptional boy, even if he is a bit 'queer' from the standpoint of his fellows."[115] But they were not the students most sought after by Harvard.

Bender expressed his views on admissions in a spirited 1949 piece, "To the Critics of Harvard." He believed that Harvard must have a "floor, a minimum standard below which we will not go no matter how beautiful a character a boy has, nor how fast he can run, nor who his father is." But standards would not be set too high, and they would be applied flexibly; "we admit boys with IQ's well below others who we reject when we believe that they have . . . intangible qualities in high degree." He recognized that many of them would be

"C" students — a group that over the years had produced "some of our most distinguished and useful graduates."[116]

Bender was forthright in acknowledging that, as long as they met the academic minimum, certain types of applicants would receive preference as a matter of institutional policy. In characteristically colorful language, he declared that "we do discriminate in our admissions policy . . . and I hope we always will."[117]

Among those singled out as beneficiaries of this "discrimination" were the children of Harvard graduates, athletes, and applicants from the West and South and farms and small towns. Bender assured the readers of the *Alumni Bulletin* that alumni percentage was a definite consideration in admissions. At the same time, "there is nothing automatic about being admitted because you are the son of an alumnus." Control remained "in the hands of the Admissions Committee, which makes final judgment on the boy and determines what is in the best interest of the College." But "other things beings equal, the son of an alumnus will be admitted."[118]

Harvard also gave official preference to athletes. Bender described athletic ability as more than a "tie-breaker"; instead, it was a "decided plus factor." To be sure, Harvard would "not admit a man, no matter how great a football player he may be, unless he is intellectually qualified and of sound character." That said, the underlying message strongly supported athletes and athletics; Harvard, Bender maintained, "would be a poor place without football" and had "no intention of going the way of Chicago."[119]

One more group was given preference: those wealthy enough not to need financial assistance. Buck had been explicit about attracting students who had the resources to cover their expenses, but Bender made only a fleeting reference to applicants who are able to "pay their way."[120] Yet the implication of their remarks was clear: students requiring scholarships would have to meet higher standards than those who did not. Since this policy contradicted the meritocratic ideals expressed in Conant's many writings as well as Buck's emphasis on "democratic selection," Harvard officials, including Bender, hardly wished to dwell on the matter.[121]

Where in Bender's admission schema was the scholastically brilliant boy whom Conant so emphasized in his public statements? Harvard, Bender wrote, "would take long chances on the rare boy who appears to have real intellectual brilliance," but will reject those applicants judged to have "serious defects of character or personality." The number of such "mental giants" was in any case quite limited; as a rough estimate, he noted that only 2 percent of Harvard's students were straight "A."[122]

The official admissions ideology elaborated by Bender and Buck received a kind of codification in an October 1, 1949, announcement sent out to prospective applicants. The Committee on Admission, the statement reported, "attaches much weight to character, personality and breadth of interest." In the competition for entry, "*students are not accepted on the basis of scholarly attainment alone.*" While "intelligence ratings, rank in class, and test results are important," such factors "are not the only criteria." In selecting students, "the Committee sets a high value on extracurricular interests and contributions to school and community life."[123]

Between the lines of the articles by Buck and Bender was an ideology that was incompatible not only with academic meritocracy but with meritocracy itself, however broadly defined. For meritocracy, if it means anything, is a system in which scarce rewards are allocated on the basis not of background but of individual accomplishment. Yet background — whether in parentage, capacity to pay, boarding school attendance, or place of residence — loomed large in Harvard's admissions policy. This contradiction between the official ideology of "democratic achievement" and the stark reality of institutionalized preference for the members of privileged constituencies was one of the defining features of Harvard admissions under Conant.

Preference for the Privileged

Harvard's public statements in the postwar years consistently emphasized its commitment to equality of opportunity, yet its internal discussions repeatedly returned to an unpleasant, if little publicized, truth: America's wealthiest institution of higher education depended on large numbers of "paying guests" to meet its expenses. Though the postwar boom was already under way, the bottom line for Harvard in the late 1940s was basically unchanged: each year, it would have to fill at least 75 to 80 percent of the seats in its freshman class from that very small segment of American society that could afford an Ivy League education.

Bender was so worried by Harvard's dependence on the wealthy that he confessed to his peers at his twentieth reunion that he feared economic pressures might become so great that eastern private colleges would have to either "shrink in size or drop standards way down to take in and keep any moron who can pay the freight."[124] To minimize the chances of Harvard's ever facing such a grim choice, Bender and other Harvard administrators carefully crafted an admissions policy that was systematically tilted in favor of those who could afford to pay. Some scholarship applicants would gain admission, but they would have to show evidence that they were likely to be in the top half of the class and that they possessed some of the "intangible qualities" that Harvard wanted.[125]

Favoring wealthy applicants over those who applied for scholarships was

hardly the only way in which Harvard's policy privileged the already privileged. Even more desirable was an applicant of bona fide upper-class origin —
in Bender's words, "the St. Grottlesex type, or at any rate the sons of the economic and social upper crust."[126] They not only covered their own expenses
but in many cases possessed the kind of wealth that might someday contribute to Harvard's endowment. And as we saw earlier, the very presence of "upper-crust" students on campus made Harvard more appealing to other children of privilege. Bender put the matter bluntly: upper-class families wanted
their offspring to attend colleges with "a certain snob appeal." In attracting
them, Harvard faced stiff competition from other private colleges, especially
"Yale, Princeton, Amherst and Williams."[127]

Harvard's response was virtually to guarantee admission to those who
met minimal standards. In 1950, of the 48 students who applied from three
leading St. Grottlesex schools (Groton, St. Paul's, and St. Mark's), Harvard accepted 46.[128] Bender's assessment of how Harvard was faring in the competition for these students is revealing: "There is a general impression that Harvard has lost ground in the last generation in its appeal to the nice boys, by
which is generally meant the St. Grottlesex type . . . We still attract more than
our share of the others who come here because of family or tradition. But we
don't get as many as we should of the solid middle group from this kind of
school — the good healthy . . . extrovert who can pay his own way."[129] In truth,
Harvard still had a strong appeal to the traditional New England upper class;
of Boston families in *The Social Register* with sons who graduated from college in the 1940s, 61 percent attended Harvard, compared to only 7 and 1 percent at Yale and Princeton, respectively. Yet troubling signs appeared elsewhere on the eastern seaboard: Yale had displaced Harvard as the leading
choice of the New York elite (25 vs. 20 percent for both Harvard and Princeton), and Princeton was vastly more popular among the sons of the Philadelphia upper class (35 vs. 2 percent for Harvard and 14 percent for Yale).[130]

In its quest to attract the "well-rounded" young man, Harvard worked
hard to maintain its historically strong ties with the leading prep schools. As
part of this effort, Harvard introduced the Harvard Prize Fellowships, intended for the graduates of New England boarding schools that had sent 5 or
more students to Cambridge in any two of the previous five years. In 1950,
Harvard awarded 23 Prize Fellowships, with 6 going to Exeter and 6 more to
Andover.[131] A year later, Henry S. Dyer, the director of Harvard's Office of
Tests, proposed a reform that would more directly involve the prep schools
for the purpose of "cementing our relations with the better private secondary
schools in such fashion that we would attract from those schools a larger
number of *paying guests*."[132]

By 1950, the connection between Harvard and the leading prep schools was as strong as it had been before the war. Of the 278 students from the top boarding schools who applied that year, 245 were accepted. This rejection rate of only 12 percent constituted a marked decrease from the 20 percent who had been rejected in 1946, at the peak of the veterans' surge. For Exeter and Andover, perennially two of Harvard's top feeders, the acceptance rate was a stunning 94 percent.[133]

Harvard's postwar admissions policy gave systematic preference to still one more privileged group: the sons of alumni. Bender's 1949 article in the *Harvard Alumni Bulletin* maintained that being the child of an alumnus would serve as a tiebreaker, "other things being equal." But the actual policy gave considerably greater weight to Harvard parentage. In a 1949 memo, "Harvard College Admission Policy," marked "Confidential for Use of Schools and Scholarship Committees," the section under "Harvard parentage" states flatly that "it is customary to admit sons of alumni provided they are qualified academically and appear to have a good character, a stable personality, and a sincere desire to obtain a liberal education at Harvard."[134]

In 1952, almost two decades into Conant's term as president, fewer than 13 percent of legacy applicants were rejected.[135] Special consideration was also given to applicants with relatives other than fathers who had gone to Harvard; such ties, members of the Schools and Scholarships Committees were told, have "a somewhat smaller effect on the [Admission] Committee's decisions, but [they are] taken into account."[136] Remarkably, a majority of the freshmen entering in the fall of 1947 from private schools had either fathers or near relatives who were Harvard College alumni.[137]

Despite Conant's meritocratic rhetoric and Harvard's stated desire to become a "democratic, national institution" and a "vehicle for social mobility,"[138] the admissions policy in the last years of the Conant administration systematically favored the most privileged segments of American society. In truth, Harvard did more than give preference to socially elite applicants from exclusive boarding schools; it actively solicited their interest and fretted over the ones who chose to go elsewhere.

Since Harvard saw its mission as training the leaders of the next generation, admitting students whose backgrounds made it likely that they would occupy top positions in America's most powerful economic and political institutions seemed a good bet. A purely academic meritocracy might appeal to certain professors and intellectuals. But from Harvard's perspective, any policy that would reject a future FDR simply did not make sense. Harvard's policy of extending preference to the already privileged was perfectly rational from an institutional point of view. But it was not publicly defensible. Under Conant's leadership, Harvard presented a carefully cultivated democratic face to the public while quietly doing what it felt necessary to preserve its close historic ties to the privileged groups whose goodwill remained indispensable to its welfare.

Harvard's Quest for Athletes

It is easy to understand why Harvard was unwilling to state openly its preference for upper-class candidates. Its reticence on the advantage given to outstanding athletes is somewhat more perplexing. After all, athletic excellence reflects personal achievement rather than the privileges of birth and is a widely recognized form of individual "merit" (albeit not of the academic sort).

In Harvard's official statement to applicants in 1949, athletic ability is not even mentioned, though there is a passing reference to "extra-curricular interest."[139] Two years later, in a statement issued jointly by Conant and the presidents of Yale and Princeton, Harvard went so far as to deny that excellence in sports was even a factor in admissions. Reaffirming the Big Three's policy of not granting athletic scholarships, the statement went on to say that in allocating "opportunities for admission and financial assistance," students "shall be neither privileged nor favored because of their athletic ability."[140] This insistence on absolute neutrality toward athletes betrayed an uneasiness about the role of nonacademic criteria in institutions that considered themselves first and foremost centers of academic excellence.

In fact, internal documents from all three institutions reveal that talented athletes were more than welcome and that being a varsity-level athlete, especially in football, could compensate for a weak academic record. Shortly after the war, Bender told the audience at the annual dinner of the Harvard Club that if "any of you know big boys who can run and pass and kick, and are decent citizens and gentlemen . . . send them along."[141] A few years later, Bender, by then chairman of the Committee on Admission, bluntly told the Board of Overseers that "it is a fact that if we did not place considerable emphasis on our recruiting and admissions and award scholarship assistance on athletic ability we couldn't stay in the Ivy League."[142]

In the confidential admissions guidelines issued to the Schools and Scholarship Committees of the Associated Harvard Clubs, the Committee on Admission stated clearly that "outstanding athletic ability is a strong point in favor of a candidate."[143] In a personal letter to Charles C. Buell of St. Paul's School,[144] Dean Hanford laid out Harvard's policy:

> Everybody here is extraordinarily sorry if there has grown up a feeling that Harvard is not interested in the student if he is a football player. This is just not true . . . We are interested in all-around students of good character and personality, and the man who has taken part in football and other athletics is

more than welcome provided we can be convinced that he can do at least satisfactory work — not honor work, but be able at least to meet the minimum requirement. In fact, *we lean over backward to accept such students if they present evidence of having what seems to be at least an even chance of having a satisfactory record.*

"The great difficulty," he explained, "is that in too many cases the applicant turns up with a very spotty school preparation and examination scores in the three hundreds."[145]

Harvard's strong preference for athletes was part of a larger policy in which physical characteristics played an important role. In the confidential guidelines given to the Schools and Scholarship Committees, the third criterion was "Health and Athletic Activities," which stated that "the presence of any significant health problems should be reported to the Committee."[146] Behind this focus on physical appearance was a decided preference for young men with all-American looks.

Assessments of the candidate's appearance was a routine feature of interview reports. An applicant from a leading Midwestern country day school, for example, was described as a "large, wholesome, attractive boy." Despite "difficulty with spelling and difficulty in passing examinations," this boy, who was "president of his class and a leader in school," was admitted.[147] Boys deemed less physically attractive, many of whom seem to have come from modest social backgrounds, generally fared less well.

Ambivalence Toward Top Scholars

Despite — or perhaps because of — its reputation as a mecca for brilliant students, Harvard's attitude towards top scholars was deeply ambivalent. Admittedly, Harvard did accept a modest number of students primarily on the basis of their scholastic brilliance, and some of them were even offered scholarships. But precisely because of Harvard's reputation, the number of such students had to be strictly limited.

Fundamental to Harvard's admissions policy — and to its highly equivocal stance toward the most academically accomplished applicants — was the question of institutional mission. Bender expressed the views of Harvard's top administrators, including Conant, when he wrote that Harvard's task went far beyond training "the future scholar or scientist or the brilliant intellectual"; it also had a responsibility to groom "the successful businessman . . . or governor." Especially in attracting the upper-class students who were sought by all the elite private colleges, Harvard had to be very careful lest its image be reinforced as a place "full of long-haired esthetics [*sic*], of pansies and poets and various la-de-da types" as well as "parlor pinks, communists, fellow travelers, etc."[148] Such perceptions, Bender warned, could prove disastrous for Harvard.

In the United States, as Richard Hofstadter noted long ago, anti-intellectualism has always been a powerful and pervasive cultural current.[149] Certainly, such sentiments were not absent among the members of the Associated Harvard Clubs. At a joint Cambridge meeting of the representatives of the Harvard Schools and Scholarships Committees and members of the Harvard administration, for example, a member of the Cincinnati Harvard Club named Lawson explained how applicants referred to as "Quiz Kids" were handled. Quiz kids, he noted, had been called "greasy grinds" when he was an undergraduate. "They worked hard, and they were wizards in the classroom," he admitted, "but they weren't worth a lot to the school." The Cincinnati chapter, Lawson reported, did not "particularly like Quiz Kids, even if they do run top notch on the College Entrance examinations and they are coded 97 and they have a straight A average in high school. Whenever any of these young men are interviewed by the Harvard Club of Cincinnati," he declared, "I am not going to recommend them for a scholarship no matter how hard they have worked."[150]

Harvard's ambivalence was especially visible on the issue of scholarships. Able to award financial assistance to only about one-fifth of the freshman class, the criteria for allocating Harvard's limited scholarship resources raised the issue of institutional priorities perhaps even more sharply than the criteria for admissions. And in distributing its resources, Harvard demonstrated that attracting top scholars was by no means its primary goal.

The decision to appoint Francis Skiddy von Stade Jr. '38 as director of scholarships in 1946 reveals Harvard's priorities during Conant's final years. A graduate of St. Paul's, where he had been captain of the polo team, von Stade became something of a legend as the last undergraduate to arrive in Cambridge with his own polo ponies. A patrician of impeccable background, he succeeded in gaining entry to the Porcellian.[151]

Von Stade, like other Harvard administrators, emphasized the absolute necessity of finding "paying guests" for the great majority of places in the freshman class.[152] Scholarships were not for scholars alone; after a boy had established that he was academically competent, "the question of individual personality become paramount." Varsity potential, von Stade reported, was an important factor: "The Committee considers athletic capacity as an asset of equal merit with some other less virile pursuits."[153] As director of scholarships, he apparently pursued athletes vigorously, noting with pride that interviews with every scholarship applicant from Boston Latin had yielded "the fastest man in New England" and "one of the better backs on the freshman football team."[154]

In 1948, Harvard relaxed its academic standards for scholarships. Von Stade heartily approved, writing to Conant that it would "reduce grade-chasing" and "serve to aid men whose greatest strength lies not so much in the scholarly line of endeavor as it does in the direction of useful citizenship." To find such men, von Stade turned to the loyal alumni who represented the local Schools and Scholarship Committees. Because of the passage of antidiscrimination legislation in Massachusetts, which von Stade believed was "going to force a great many schoolmen to hedge their references on boys," alumni evaluations were needed "more than ever before" and would be "extremely vital."[155] The stakes were very high. According to von Stade's own estimates, of 1,344 scholarship applicants in 1951, "between 900 and 1,000 boys were turned down because of lack of funds."[156]

According to the standard interpretation of Conant, one of his greatest achievements was to bring to a definitive end the policy of systematic discrimination against Jews that had begun under Lowell. In reality, his policy toward Jews was hardly free of discrimination. To be sure, he did relax the rigid quota of 15 percent adopted under Lowell, and the proportion of Jews increased substantially during his administration. But Harvard's long-standing policy of holding Jews to different and higher standards than other applicants very much remained in place under Conant. So, too, did the criteria emphasizing character and other "intangibles" that had been devised in the 1920s to limit Jewish enrollment.[157]

The "Jewish problem" posed difficult dilemmas for the presidents of the elite private colleges, even after World War II.[158] Bender was the one Harvard administrator who did not mince words: the "belief that Harvard has a high proportion of Jews" was a disadvantage in attracting "boys who can pay their own way," especially those of the "St. Grottlesex type." Young men from this group tend "to herd together in safest folds where they can associate with others of their own kind." Harvard was hardly their only option; faced with what they perceived as an excessive number of Jews, they could find a more congenial atmosphere at Princeton, Williams, Yale, or Dartmouth.[159] "All of these places," he noted pointedly, "restrict the number of Jews to 5% or less, with the possible exception of Yale."[160]

Given this intense fear of alienating its traditional constituencies, it is hardly surprising that postwar Harvard did not move to eliminate discrimination against Jews. Instead, it embarked upon a characteristically cautious policy of gradually relaxing restrictions on Jewish enrollment while being careful to keep in place measures to ensure continued "balance" in the college, including the old effort to attain "geographical diversity."

This quest meant that applicants from distant regions, especially the South and West, would be given preference in the admission process.[161] What

Harvard did not admit in public, however, was that this policy would continue to be used to limit the number of students from the Middle Atlantic states. Of candidates for admission reviewed in May 1949, for example, those from New York, New Jersey, and Pennsylvania were admitted at a rate of 35 percent — far lower than the rate of 56 percent for all applicants.[162]

The May 1949 acceptance rate for New England — which enrolled many fewer Jewish students than the Middle Atlantic region — was 60 percent for Massachusetts and 65 percent for the other New England states. Yet New England posed the greatest threat to Harvard's aspirations to be a genuinely national institution; the home of only 8.4 million people (6 percent of the nation's population), New England was the source of 42 percent of Harvard's admits in 1949. The Middle Atlantic states, though containing three times the population (27.5 million) of New England, contributed only 22 percent.[163]

Harvard's policy clearly reflected more than a desire to produce a diverse freshmen class; after all, the St. Grottlesex students so prized by Harvard came overwhelmingly from either the Middle Atlantic states or New England. Yet 73 of the 86 students who applied from these schools in 1950 were accepted. That same year, Bronx Science (New York City), Stuyvesant (New York City), and Central (Philadelphia) fared much less well, with only 17 of 52 gaining admission.[164] Seventeen years after Conant had taken office, Lowell's policy of discrimination against Jews and favoritism toward the Protestant upper class was still very much in place.

Such discrimination was hardly new, but Jews were less inclined to tolerate it after the war. Having shared in the sacrifices that led to the Allied victory, Jews — like blacks — mobilized to fight for full inclusion in American society. In the wake of the extermination of 6 million Jews, the struggle against anti-Semitism, already a well-established tradition among American Jewry, took on an added urgency. As Deborah Dash Moore notes, "University and medical school quotas, restrictive covenants, the want ads listing 'Christian only' would all be challenged as un-American practices."[165]

In October 1946, several Jewish alumni wrote to Conant, protesting Harvard's policy and calling for "fair and open selection."[166] That same year, Massachusetts passed a Fair Employment Practice Law that — though not specifically addressing the issue of admissions — sent a message that continued discrimination on the basis of race, religion, or national origin could cause serious problems for Harvard.[167]

Three years later, the Massachusetts legislature enacted the Fair Educational Practices Law, which Harvard and other private colleges had vehemently opposed. It repeated the same ban against discrimination as the earlier law but this time specifically addressed the issue of the selection of applicants for admission to an educational institution.[168]

The Fair Educational Practices Law was passed in the midst of perhaps the largest political offensive against anti-Semitism in American history. It began with the March 1944 decision of several major Jewish organizations to establish the National Community Relations Advisory Council (CRC), whose goals were both the passage of antidiscrimination legislation and changes in public attitudes.[169] This assault on anti-Semitism enjoyed the support of many non-Jews and often worked together with the larger civil rights movement to attack discrimination against African Americans, Catholics, and other minorities.

In the late 1940s, assaults on anti-Semitism seemed to be coming from everywhere. In the federal government, the President's Commission on Higher Education published a landmark study, *Higher Education for American Democracy* (1947), which specifically denounced quotas directed against Jews and Negroes as "un-American"; in Hollywood, *Gentleman's Agreement* (1947), starring Gregory Peck, painted a devastating portrait of genteel anti-Semitism and won an Oscar for Best Picture in the process; in journalism, Carey McWilliams published a widely read exposé, *Mask for Privilege* (1948); and in higher education itself, the American Council on Education published a major study of discrimination in college admissions, *On Getting into College* (1949).[170] In addition, the American Jewish Committee sponsored a series of books called *Studies in Prejudice*, the best known of which was Theodor A. Adorno's *The Authoritarian Personality* (1950). By 1949, fair employment legislation had passed in a number of states, including New York, New Jersey, Connecticut, Rhode Island, Oregon, and Massachusetts. And by 1952, public opinion polls began to show a marked decline in anti-Semitism.[171]

Faced with this sea change in the cultural and political atmosphere, Harvard had little choice but to respond. While publicly denying that its admissions policy discriminated against Jews, Harvard moved quietly to inform those involved in admissions that some adjustments would have to be made. Meeting with representatives of the Schools and Scholarship Committees shortly after the passage of the new act, Bender told those assembled that "you should not ask or give information at any time about race, religion, color, or national origin." Any alumni representative who, in his report, does "something like writing and saying 'This is the finest member of the Negro race I have ever seen' or 'This boy is planning to become a Jewish rabbi,'" he warned, "embarrasses us greatly." Since such remarks are "forbidden in the law," everyone "must be super careful now."[172]

At the same time, Bender saw "no reason why the law should make any difference in any of our basic policies and certainly not in our admission or scholarship policies." The law — whose specific wording reflected intense lobbying from private colleges and universities — stated that it was "not intended to limit or prevent an educational institution from using any criteria other than race, religion, color or national origin in the admission of students." In practice, this meant that Harvard was free to continue to use not only nonacademic criteria such as athletic ability, alumni parentage, and geographical diversity, but also the "intangible qualities" that had been used to limit the number of Jews. Precisely because such qualities remained critical, Bender believed that it was "more important than ever before that we have good interviews and good assessment of intangible qualities that a candidate may possess."[173]

Despite his insistence that Harvard was already in full compliance with the Fair Educational Practices Act, Bender in fact was quite worried about its possible impact. For one thing, "we don't know who will do the enforcing" and "the amount of trouble this law may cause for us." More worrisome was the specter of "isolated individuals with a chip on their shoulder": rejected applicants, perhaps "disgruntled or neurotic," who "may create difficulties." Alumni representatives, Bender advised, should be extremely cautious with a candidate who "looks like perhaps a touchy individual or has a difficult personality or where he belongs to one of the minority groups that might make trouble."[174]

In the end, Harvard's strategy was to gradually reduce discrimination against Jews while keeping intact the policies that had limited Jewish enrollments in the past and would continue to do so in the future. Throughout the Conant administration and beyond, all of Lowell's policies from the 1920s — the emphasis on character and other intangible qualities, the reliance on personal assessments from trusted sources, the preferences for the children of alumni and for applicants from outside the Northeast — remained in place. But now the implementation of these policies would be carried out in a fashion somewhat friendlier to Jewish applicants. Yet discrimination was still prevalent; the statistics for the entering freshmen of 1950, whether for individual high schools such as Bronx Science or for the Middle Atlantic states as a whole, leave little room for doubt.

Nonetheless, there seems to have been a modest increase in the chances of Jewish applicants in Conant's final years as a result of the new law. In May 1949, applicants from the Middle Atlantic states were admitted at a rate of 63 percent of the whole pool. A year later, with the legislation in effect, applicants from this region were accepted at a rate of 74 percent of all applicants.[175] By 1952, according to a study of students at eleven universities across the country, 25 percent of the students enrolled at Harvard were Jewish — more than at any of the other institutions, including Cornell (23 percent), which had a large contingent of students from New York City.[176] This was a marked increase over the 15 percent admitted when Conant took office. Yet at the end of the Conant years, Jewish enrollment still fell short of the 28 percent in 1925 — the last year before the imposition of Lowell's restrictive measures.[177]

There is no documentary evidence that Conant personally harbored anti-Semitic sentiments. But it is also clear from the historical record that he voted in 1922 with the minority of the faculty who favored limiting the number of Jews, that in 1934 he appointed a man with a well-known commitment to restrictive measures, that Harvard continued to impose a quota on Jewish enrollment into the 1940s, and that in 1952 (as will be shown in Chapter 9) — in one of his last acts as president — he selected as the new dean of admissions a man who had a personal distaste for many of Harvard's Jewish students and who was deeply worried that their presence would drive away the upper-class Protestant boys whom Harvard most wished to enroll. This was not, in short, the record of a principled opponent of anti-Semitism, and it does not square with Conant's enduring reputation as the man who eliminated the last vestiges of discrimination against Jews at Harvard.

The timing of the changes in Harvard's policy toward Jews under Conant suggests that the improvements that did take place were not the product of a commitment to the principle of equality of opportunity, but a measured response to the political and legal pressures of the postwar years. Restrictions on Jewish enrollment had come into being in the 1920s as part of a powerful movement led by WASPs to maintain their dominance in America's elite colleges, and they were relaxed a quarter of a century later only as a result of a powerful countermovement of the excluded. The motivation behind Harvard's response to this movement in the waning years of the Conant administration was captured well by a college president of the time who remarked: "Whenever colleges have become more liberal and wise in their selection of students other than those who are white and Gentile, they have done so, not because of a zeal for fair play and democracy, but because they were forced to by the pressure of organized and unorganized opinions upon their public-relations policy."[178]

Conant's Legacy

Frequently radical in his public rhetoric, especially on issues of equality of opportunity, Conant was strikingly cautious in practice. On the issue of Jews, for example, Conant did not wish to confront the matter directly, fearing that it would be "dynamite" for the university.[179] Yet when conditions changed after World War II, Harvard under his leadership moved quietly to loosen the restrictions on enrollment of Jews while keeping in place mechanisms that would prevent their numbers from rising so high as to threaten "balance" in the College.

If the increase in Jewish enrollment was the most visible symbol of Harvard's becoming a more democratic and inclusive institution, Conant's National Scholarship Program had the greatest long-term impact. Its great innovation was to articulate in the most forceful terms a principle that became a central tenet of meritocratic ideology: outstanding students should be able to attend the nation's leading private universities, regardless of their ability to pay. Though now taken for granted, it was a truly radical principle at the time. His second core principle, that the National Scholarships would cover all expenses for applicants with demonstrated financial need, including tuition, room, board, and incidentals, gave birth to the "sliding scale": National Scholars who needed less than a full scholarship would be given awards commensurate with their resources; well-to-do awardees would receive only a small honorific stipend. Thirty years later, Harvard applied these principles to the entire pool of applicants for the first time in its history. These policies — need-blind admissions and need-based financial aid — today constitute the foundation of admissions policy at Harvard and its principal rivals.[180]

Conant also advanced the principle — at the time a contested one — that scholastic excellence should be the primary criterion for allocating rewards. To act on this principle, he used a new test administered by the College Entrance Examination Board. By requiring that all candidates for National Scholarships take the Scholastic Aptitude Test (SAT), Conant gave a huge boost to the emerging national movement for the "scientific" evaluation of academic potential. Before long, the SAT was required of all applicants to leading colleges. By the time Conant stepped down in January 1953, standardized (and ostensibly objective) tests had become a pillar of the emerging system of college admissions. Yet Harvard's continued need for "paying guests" was the stark material reality underpinning its entire policy. Harvard remained heavily dependent on its ability to attract the offspring of the eastern upper class; this obdurate fact was never far from Conant's mind. However genuine his meritocratic convictions may have been, putting them fully into practice would have to wait.

If a consistent strand in Conant the thinker was an insistence on the urgent necessity of allowing "merit" rather than "accidents of birth" to determine the distribution of educational opportunity, an equally consistent pattern in Conant the actor was a pronounced tendency to defer to the prerogatives of privilege. Far from being the scourge of the "Brahmin power structure" depicted by Hershberg, Conant was in truth its reluctant protector.[181] In his powerful 1940 essay "Education for a Classless Society," Conant warned that America was witnessing the development of a "hereditary aristocracy of wealth"; as president of Harvard, however, he was preoccupied with attracting the sons of this very aristocracy. A firm proponent in principle of the Jeffersonian ideal of a "natural aristocracy," in practice he looked to America's closest approximation of a European aristocracy — the established upper-class Protestant families of the Northeast — for the material and symbolic support that would sustain Harvard's position as America's leading university.

What this strategy for maintaining Harvard's preeminence meant in practice was a policy of vigorous affirmative action for the privileged — "paying guests," sons of alumni, graduates of leading boarding schools, and scions of "upper-crust" families. On this fundamental matter, Harvard's admissions practices under Conant showed striking continuity with Lowell's practices. Even in Conant's final years, when admissions had become more competitive than ever before, traditional elite constituencies benefited from massive preference.[182]

In the end, Conant's admissions policies did not repudiate the policies established by Lowell but refined and elaborated on them. On the fundamental issues — that admission would not be based on academic ability and achievement alone; that "character," "leadership," and other intangible qualities would weigh heavily in the admissions process; that athletes, the sons of alumni, and applicants from distant regions (with small Jewish populations) would receive preference — Conant and Lowell were in agreement. The Harvard that Conant left in 1953 was not so very different from the Harvard he had inherited from Lowell twenty years earlier.

CHAPTER 7

Reluctant Reform Comes to Yale

I N THE LATE SPRING OF 1933, a proud Yale administration faced a crisis that had been brought on by the Great Depression: a shortage of paying freshmen for the fall's entering class. For Yale, which in the 1920s had been more popular among prospective students than Harvard, the paucity of "paying guests" was humiliating.[1] Yet as the Depression continued to deepen, more students than ever before declined offers of admission in 1932 and even more seemed likely to do so in 1933.[2]

Faced with the possibility of a shortfall of tuition at a time of grave fiscal crisis, the Yale Corporation made a conscious decision to lower academic standards to ensure a class of normal size. Imposed over the objections of the Board of Admissions, this policy, wrote one administrator, "necessitated literally scraping the bottom of the admissions barrel and admitting more than one hundred candidates who would ordinarily have been rejected." Though the Board of Admissions warned that the enrollment of so many weak students would have a deleterious effect on both the quality of scholarship and Yale's reputation, the Corporation refused to budge.[3]

That fall, 904 freshmen matriculated, the largest entering class in Yale's history. Predictably, the policy generated many human casualties; the Class of 1937 quickly shrank to 838 and suffered from high academic mortality right up through graduation.[4] It was not the first time that institutional interests — in this case, of a nakedly economic character — would trump academic standards, nor would it be the last. But in its unusual transparency, it served as a reminder of an important, albeit less visible, truth: particular admissions policies are likely to remain in place only as long as they produce outcomes that correspond to organizational interests.

The Yale Ethos

Though perhaps 20 percent of Yale's students received scholarships in the 1930s, its reputation as a "rich man's college" was not undeserved.[5] Graduates of prep schools — between 70 and 80 percent of freshmen — set the tone of undergraduate life, and the campus had more than its share of the sons of corporate magnates. More than 30 percent of the freshmen in the late 1930s were themselves the sons of Yale men, with perhaps half having a Yale grandfather, uncle, or older brother.[6]

The opening in 1933 of elegant, neo-Gothic residential colleges modeled on Oxford and Cambridge did nothing to detract from Yale's aristocratic reputation. August Heckscher '36, a member of the first Yale class to live in the colleges, described them as "sumptuous enclaves where students were to live . . . with their own dining halls and libraries." More than forty years later, he vividly evoked the opulent atmosphere of the period: "In fact, we *were* pioneers, being the very first to be served in the vaulted halls by uniformed waitresses standing deferentially while we wrote our choice from a varied menu, and also the first in these luxurious conditions to embark upon scholarly and literary flights with the faculty members who regularly sat down with us."[7]

Hecksher's idyllic portrait notwithstanding, academic values hardly reigned supreme in campus life. On the contrary, an undergraduate unduly preoccupied with his studies would be designated a "grind" and relegated to the bottom of the student hierarchy. A disproportionate number of such academically oriented students were Jews, many of them on scholarships that required a rank in the top quarter of their class to be renewed, which only reinforced their marginalization in campus life.[8]

Yet Yale was not without some democratic features and a certain publicspiritedness. Its prestigious secret societies — led by Skull and Bones, Scroll and Key, and Wolf's Head — honored achievement as well as background.[9] As in the Dink Stover era before World War I, accomplishment in extracurricular activities virtually guaranteed a student's being tapped for a place in one of the six societies, an honor limited to roughly 10 percent of the class. In this specific sense, Yale's "democratic spirit" — often contrasted with the more exclusionary social atmosphere of Harvard and Princeton — was not entirely mythical.[10]

Students would spend countless hours competing for leadership in campus organizations so that they could "do something for Yale" — an ethos that fit well with its role as the nation's leading source of corporate leadership.[11] Professor Henry Seidel Canby '99, speaking both from experience and observation, said that college life was "geared to the needs of an industrial, get-rich-quick country." The extracurriculum, he argued, "educated specifically for the harsh competitions of capitalism, for the successful often unscrupulous pursuit by the individual of power for himself, for class superiority, and for a success measured by the secure possession of the fruits of prosperity."[12]

But there was more to Yale than the admittedly striking affinities between its value system and the code of the modern business executive. Central to its identity was also a powerful emphasis on community leadership and an abiding commitment to public service. Paul Moore '41, who for many years served as the Episcopal bishop of New York City, described the ethos as one in which the Puritan ethic and the American business ethic came together in the nineteenth century, giving it "a sturdy chauvinistic spirit." When Moore was an undergraduate, "you were expected to 'pull your weight' as a Yale citizen," going out for "athletics, or singing, or debating or Dwight Hall, the organization sponsoring good work." So strong was the "do something for Yale" ethos that failing to participate in such activities meant that "you would not be tapped for a senior society, a dreadful thought meant to strike fear in our heart." Yale's fundamental mission, Moore believed, was "to forge a serious public-spirited young man who would take his place in industry, law, academic life or public service."[13]

The embodiment of the Yale ideal was the handsome, personable, and intelligent (though not studious) young man of high character who was also an exceptional athlete. Sports loomed larger in undergraduate life at Yale than at Harvard, and Yale's athletic success helped shape its distinctive identity. As late as 1927, Yale was co–national football champion (with Illinois), and in 1936 and 1937 it produced two consecutive Heisman Trophy winners, Larry Kelley and Clint Frank. Reminiscing about his student days, the former Wisconsin senator William Proxmire '38 reported that "the real preoccupation of Yalies was not literature or science — not even business or women," but sports. "Yale football," he continued, "was the *pièce de résistance* . . . To many — probably most — Yale meant Kelley and Frank and football."[14]

Another factor giving the campus a different flavor from Harvard was Yale's stronger orientation to business — an orientation reflected in the higher proportion of Yale men going into careers in the corporate world.[15] Yale was also shaped by its location in a midsized city rather than a major metropolitan area. The larger number of commuters — and of Jews[16] — at Harvard was in part a product of its proximity to Boston, and the visible presence of local students, many of them working and lower middle class, contributed to its reputation as both grittier and more cosmopolitan than its rival in New Haven.

The already considerable difference between Yale and Harvard of the early decades of the century widened with James Bryant Conant's ascent to Harvard's presidency. Conant's public rhetoric, if not his practice, was militantly meritocratic, and his widely publicized National Scholarship Program sent the message that Harvard was looking for top scholars and would pay to attract them. As growing numbers of young men entered the competition for these scholarships, the perception grew among students and schoolteachers alike that Harvard was more interested than Yale in the student whose primary strength was scholastic brilliance.

Harvard's academic image was somewhat overdrawn, but this was a nuance generally lost on the public. According to the Yale historian George W. Pierson, "It was true that Harvard put the emphasis on brains, whereas Yale wanted the all-around boy, with brains, social talents, and some athletic ability." Whether as a consequence of conscious policy or of Harvard's reputation (or both), "to the distress of the Yale faculty . . . [Harvard] captured more of the really bright students." Yale, benefiting from the widespread rumor among high schools outside the Northeast that "Harvard was interested only in brains . . . perhaps captured more than its share of potential community leaders."[17]

Like other elite private colleges, Yale was at once a beneficiary and a prisoner of its public image. To members of the "Yale family" and to those close to it socially and culturally, what distinguished it was its democratic campus life, its emphasis on hard work and leadership, and its steadfast adherence to the ideal of the well-rounded, public-spirited young man. F. Scott Fitzgerald captured elements of this image when he compared his own alma mater, Princeton, to a lazy spring day while characterizing Yale as "November, crisp and energetic."[18]

To many far from the Yale family, however, it appeared to be a rich man's school, insular and singularly unwelcoming to outsiders. The striking paucity of applicants from America's burgeoning public high schools — in 1936, just 542 out of well over 400,000 male high school graduates — was in no small part a product of Yale's reputation.[19] When Edward S. Noyes took office that same year as the new chairman of the Board of Admissions, the stark reality was that Yale, like Harvard and Princeton, continued to have difficulty filling its freshmen class with enough students who could meet its rather minimal academic qualifications and pay their own way. To address this problem, Noyes embarked on a strategy of strengthening ties with Yale's most reliable source of just the kind of young men it sought: the nation's leading boarding schools.

Mecca of the Prep Schools

In selecting Noyes as chair of its Board of Admissions, Yale turned to someone with deep roots within the Yale family. Edward S. Noyes '13 was the son of an alumnus, Edward M. Noyes '79, a prominent Congregational minister in Newton, Massachusetts.[20] Noyes was also a descendant of James Noyes, one of the Congregational ministers who had founded Yale, and had numerous other relatives who were Old Elis. Even in an institution noted for relying on its own, Noyes could hardly have had a more distinguished Yale pedigree.[21]

A personification of the Yale ideal, Noyes won several swimming medals as an undergraduate, was active in the glee club and the orchestra, and graduated Phi Beta Kappa. After a few years teaching English, German, and Latin at private schools, he returned to Yale, receiving a master's degree in 1920 and a Ph.D. in 1924, becoming an associate professor of English with a specialty in Alexander Pope. A longtime reader in English for the College Entrance Examination Board, Noyes seemed just the man to bring order to a Board of Admissions that had suffered from instability since the retirement in 1933 of Robert N. Corwin.[22]

Noyes was appointed by President James Rowland Angell on July 1, 1936, Angell's last year in office. One of his top priorities was to solidify Yale's relations with the elite private schools. In his first Annual Report to the President and Fellows of Yale, he reported proudly that he had "visited thirty-two private and public schools, including most of the eastern institutions from which Yale regularly receives delegations of students." These visits provided "excellent opportunities to meet, in the most natural way, headmasters and teachers, and to discuss with them problems of admission both specific and general."[23]

In the fall of 1937, the first class admitted under Noyes entered Yale College. Of 859 freshmen, a remarkable 351 — more than 40 percent of the class — came from just a dozen boarding schools. Leading the pack was Andover, with 89 students; other schools included Hotchkiss (40), Exeter (30), Taft (29), Choate (27), Hill (27), Kent (26), and St. Paul's (21). That same fall, Harvard enrolled 265 students — barely 25 percent of the class — from its top dozen private school feeders.[24] It was no wonder, then, that by 1937, "Yale's relations with the leading prep schools were in better shape than anyone could remember."[25]

The appeal of prep school boys to Yale was the same as at Harvard and Princeton: typically, they had solid academic preparation, came from old Protestant families whose status would contribute to the genteel social atmosphere of the campus, were of good "character" and had "leadership" potential, and could pay for their schooling. This last attribute was not negligible, especially during the Depression, and Noyes — much like his opposite number at Harvard, Richard Gummere — was always searching for "paying guests" with the right cultural attributes.[26]

It is less apparent why Yale held a powerful allure for these young men. After all, New Haven lacked the idyllic small-town appeal of Princeton or the big-city attractions of Boston and Cambridge; a graduate of the Class of '41 was not far off the mark when he described New Haven as "smoky, dirty, dull, small . . . just gray and dreary urban Connecticut."[27] From an academic perspective, Yale, though stronger than Princeton, ranked well behind Harvard, trailing in one 1935 survey Chicago, Columbia, and Berkeley as well.[28] Harvard's superior academic standing was not, moreover, simply a function of its outstanding doctoral programs and research facilities (generally of little concern to upper-class young men) but also of its renowned professional schools in business, law, and medicine.[29]

Yet Yale remained the great mecca for young men from the leading boarding schools, drawing far more of them than Harvard and Princeton. In 1940, 302 students from the dozen top prep schools came to New Haven; only 207 went to Cambridge and 213 to Princeton. Put another way, 42 percent of the graduates of top schools who attended one of the Big Three chose Yale. Strikingly, given Princeton's deserved reputation as a haven for preppies, the 35 percent proportion of the freshman class at Yale came from the leading twelve boarding schools, compared to 33 percent at Princeton.[30] Harvard, by far the most heterogeneous of the three, drew only 20 percent of its students from these schools.[31]

One possibility is that Yale was even more willing to admit the weaker students from these schools than its rivals. But in 1940 Harvard admitted 98.6 percent of the students (210 of 213) who applied from those top boarding schools — hardly a sign that its standards for prep school students were more stringent than Yale's.[32]

Although much evidence suggests that Harvard and Princeton also worked hard to attract these students, there can be no doubt that Yale under Noyes went out of its way to establish warm relations, not only with schools that customarily sent delegations to New Haven, but also with "schools which seemed most to merit cultivation although they have in the recent past sent relatively few candidates to Yale."[33] Noyes made it a priority to visit the leading boarding schools, in one year personally visiting the campuses of Andover, Exeter, St. Paul's, Groton, Hotchkiss, Kent, Lawrenceville, Hill, Choate, Taft, Deerfield, and 24 other private schools. In those cases where he could not visit the school personally, he sent his right-hand man, Edward T. Hall, who made trips to St. Mark's, Middlesex, Milton, and five other institutions.[34]

Part of Yale's appeal was undoubtedly its image as a genteel college with a rich extracurriculum, excellent athletic teams, and strong school spirit. Unlike Harvard, which suffered from a reputation of favoring "brains," Yale seemed to be a place where a well-rounded young man could flourish. And unlike Princeton, whose exclusive and insular atmosphere seemed perhaps all too familiar, Yale seemed to strike a happy balance between a gentlemanly social life and the opportunity to prove one's mettle outside academics.

The contrast with Harvard was particularly striking. Harvard, complained Wilbur J. Bender, was viewed by many of the most desirable students as "a place only for grinds . . . a big-city college full of muckers and public-school boys and meatballs." Notably lacking at Harvard, according to this image, were "virile, masculine, red-blooded he-men."[35]

To be sure, Yale could hardly be accused of being a haven for "public school students and meatballs." During the thirties, an average of sixteen boys from New York City's vast public school system — just seventy miles from New Haven — enrolled at Yale. This was substantially fewer than the number who matriculated from St. Paul's, which had a graduating class of fewer than ninety students. In Philadelphia, a city of nearly two million about the same distance from Yale as St. Paul's, an average of one public school graduate went to New Haven every two years.[36]

If graduates of the top boarding schools could be confident that they had chosen a college with relatively few public school "muckers," they could be equally assured that many of their classmates would have Yale in their blood. In 1940, the Alumni Board of Yale reported that "sons of Alumni comprise a substantially higher proportion of the undergraduates at Yale than at Harvard, Princeton, or Dartmouth."[37] By the late 1930s, nearly one-third of Yale freshman had alumni fathers.

The Board of Admissions under Noyes did a fastidious job of keeping the number of socially undesirable students to a minimum. All applicants, Noyes emphasized in a confidential 1939 memo, were required to meet "the necessary qualifications of character, conduct, and personality." To ensure that these requirements would be met, "the confidential reports from their schools are carefully studied." In borderline cases, he added, "the Board gives all possible preference to the sons of Yale men and to those applicants who are most warmly recommended by their headmasters or principals."[38]

One of the purposes of this policy was to avoid offending the upper-class families on whom Yale depended, and it seems to have been largely successful. Harvard was less effective in screening out the "meatballs," and their presence detracted from Harvard's social appeal. "There is a general impression," fretted Wilbur Bender, "that Harvard College has lost ground in the last generation in its appeal to . . . the sons of the economic and social upper crust."[39] That Bender's concern was not misplaced is confirmed by changes in the pattern of college choice in the upper class: whereas in the 1910s, Harvard attracted more of the sons of New York *Social Register* families than Yale by a margin of 32 to 25 percent, by the 1930s Harvard's share plummeted to 15 percent while Yale's rose to 34 percent.[40] The presence at Harvard of relatively large numbers of social outsiders — and their relative absence at Yale — is the most likely cause of this reversal.

Yale's fear that too many socially undesirable students might drive away its most prized constituencies was not without foundation. To prevent this from happening, the Board of Admissions held to its ideal of the well-rounded gentleman. The threat of contamination, however, could not be kept at bay by the neutral application of established criteria, for it was still possible that too many members of stigmatized social groups would qualify for admission. The "racial problem," Robert N. Corwin had written, was "never wholly absent from the minds of the Board of Admissions," for Yale would "become a different place when and if the proportion of Jews passes a certain as yet unknown limit."[41] It was the job of the board to see that Yale never reached that limit.

Handling the "Jewish Problem"

In the 1920s, Yale had moved much more quietly than Harvard to restrict the number of Jewish students, and as a consequence it had avoided the bitter public controversy that erupted in Cambridge. But Yale's discretion was not to be confused with a lack of resolve. On the contrary, Yale followed a highly disciplined policy of limitation, keeping the Jewish enrollment from return-ing to its peak of 13.3 percent in 1925 and 1927 for well over thirty years.[42] Pres-ident Angell (1921–1937), who publicly denounced "national and especially racial prejudice" as "perhaps the most socially and morally disintegrating of all the forms of bigotry," vigorously supported restricting the number of Jews.[43] In 1934, in proposing a plan similar to Harvard's top-seventh plan to admit applicants from the upper fifth of their classes, Angell cautioned that in order to "avoid a possible influx of undesirable racial groups, it might be necessary to limit the privilege to schools not in metropolitan centers, at least not in the eastern centers."[44]

Noyes was appointed chairman of the Board of Admissions by Angell, and his views on the Jewish question were fully consistent with Yale's policy.[45] Conservative in his beliefs and cautious in temperament, Noyes was fero-ciously protective of those traditions that he deemed essential to Yale's repu-tation. In his Report to the President for 1938–1939, he reported proudly that "representatives of the Board of Admissions have refused to speak to school assemblies or to carry on propaganda of any sort." "This is in marked con-trast to the practice of some colleges," he acknowledged, "but Yale has every-thing to gain by maintaining this contrast."[46]

Noyes realized that the outbreak of World War II might lead to a shortage of qualified applicants. In a memorandum to the president and provost on December 13, 1941, he cautioned against lowering admission standards. Any such lowering, he warned, "would before long be followed by a decrease both in the number and in the caliber of boys who want to come to Yale." His con-clusion was clear: any actions that "seriously impair our reputation as a uni-versity with high standards for admission" threatened "to kill the goose that lays the golden eggs."[47]

Noyes was acutely aware that a decline in "social standards" in the form of Jewish enrollment could pose every bit as much of a threat to Yale's reputation as a weakening of academic standards. The advent of war, it seemed, had only exacerbated the "Jewish problem." He wrote:

> Selective Service has increased the problem of Jewish applications for Yale, as for many other colleges. For any or all of a number of reasons, Jewish boys apparently finish secondary school at an earlier age than Gentiles. It may be that they mature earlier; it may be that they permit themselves — or are permitted — fewer distractions; it may be that they are [p]ushed as fast as possible by their families. In any event, the proportion of Jewish applicants among those candidates who might be expected to matriculate has increased far beyond the proportion of Jewish applicants to the whole group of applicants. Moreover, even in the "young" group, the matriculants, the Jewish boys are younger. Thus, for example, the proportion of Jews in the class matriculating in July, 1943, was slightly under 10%. By the end of the summer term, 133 of these Freshmen had left to enter service; when the class reached its Sophomore year, the proportion of Jews had jumped to 23%, and the increase in proportion will continue as long as the class remains in college.

Noyes's solution was "to adopt standards of selection from this group more severe than in the past, in order to prevent it from reaching an undue proportion in the residential colleges."[48]

Yale's discrimination against Jewish applicants intensified even as America's struggle against Nazi Germany was reaching its climax. In a carefully worded letter to President Seymour on June 23, 1944, Morris Feldman '24 of Newark, who had been Seymour's student, observed that several of the sons of his friends, "boys from cultured homes," had been turned down by Yale at a time when its treasurer had reported that the draft had so limited the number of available applicants that "almost any draft exempt student with the proper educational background could secure admission to the Freshman Class." "Stories are multiplying," Feldman reported, of "cases where the University has turned down what would to the ordinary mind be an excellent candidate, without even the courtesy of an interview." Despite being a "loyal alumnus" who has "tried to combat what I considered to be idle gossip and unfair innuendo," he admitted that he had "a most uneasy feeling," especially given the "University's desperate need for non-military students," that "possibly there may have been a change in the University's policy to one of the exclusion, or at least rigid limitation of Jewish students."[49]

Seymour's response was remarkably frank. While insisting that the "same standards of selection are applied to all applicants as individuals regardless of their social, regional, or religious backgrounds," Seymour admitted that Yale's commitment to remain "a truly national institution, representative of the country as a whole . . . may, in certain circumstances, involve some temporary restriction on the numbers selected from one or another of the nation's population groups in order to prevent distortion of the balanced character of the student body." Yale, he insisted, had no "rigid quota" on Jews or "any other well defined racial or religious group" and annually admitted a "substantial number of Jewish boys." Nevertheless, limitations on the number from particular groups would sometimes be necessary "to keep the various elements in the incoming classes in some rough approximation to the proportions which obtain throughout the national population."[50]

Seymour was "confident that this policy, though designed in the interest of the University, is also of clear benefit to the Jewish students at Yale." In an argument reminiscent of one that Lowell made in the 1920s regarding Harvard, Seymour went so far as to claim that Yale's restrictions served to prevent "prejudice against any minority or racial group." Although wartime conditions had led to the rejection of a "number of Jewish boys who in normal circumstances might well have received favorable consideration," these rejections served a larger purpose, he argued, for they were necessary to preserve "some reasonable balance with those of other elements in the student body." Yale's policy of "balance," he claimed, was not without support in the Jewish community; indeed, Seymour reported that many "of my Jewish friends have told me it is because of this balance that they want their boys to come to Yale."[51]

Noyes received a copy of Seymour's letter to Feldman and hailed it as "a very fine statement of our Board's policy."[52] Yet it offered little insight into the reality of Yale admissions. In truth, Yale was not preoccupied with keeping the student body "in some rough approximation to the proportions which obtain throughout the national population"; this was, after all, an institution that took over 40 percent of its freshmen from a dozen elite boarding schools attended almost entirely by upper- and upper-middle-class Protestant young men. Clearly, the disproportionate presence of some social groups enhanced Yale's social standing while that of others would detract from it. Jews were firmly in the latter category, which is why every year more students came to New Haven from Hotchkiss than from the combined public school systems of New York, Boston, and Philadelphia.[53]

Just how far Yale was willing to go to protect its social standing was revealed during the latter years of World War II, when the campus faced an acute shortage of students. During the depths of the Great Depression, as was shown earlier, Yale had been willing to sacrifice academic standards so that the freshman class would not fall under 850 students. But during World War II, when enrollments plummeted below 700 in 1943–1944 and 1944–1945, Yale made a conscious decision to turn away qualified Jewish students.[54] "The proportion of Jews among the candidates who are both scholastically qualified and young enough to matriculate," wrote Noyes in his report for 1944–1945, "remains too large for comfort."[55] Fearing a decline in its social status, Yale deemed it better to suffer the short-term material losses caused by a shortage of students than to risk the enduring losses that would follow from a decline in its reputation. In the language of sociology, Yale judged its symbolic capital to be even more precious than its economic capital.[56] In order to preserve it, the "Jewish problem," which Noyes reported was "spreading West and South to a degree unknown a few years ago," would have to be kept under rigorous control.[57]

Yale's Opposition to Legislation Against Discrimination

As World War II ended, Yale faced a growing political mobilization against anti-Semitism and racial discrimination. A letter to Seymour from the recently tenured Yale law professor, Eugene Rostow (A.B. '33, LL.B. '37) shortly after V-E Day foreshadowed the atmosphere that the Allied victory would produce:

> Our experience with Hitlerism in all its forms has changed the meaning of anti-Semitism and other kinds of group discrimination. They are no longer merely unattractive social sins, but a powerful symbol, a political weapon, a tool of violence. The University should not condone them, nor further their spread, by example or otherwise. It is more important than ever that the University, like other institutions which mold attitudes and opinions, take a bold lead in vindicating its educational principles in every possible way . . .
>
> There is another aspect of the question. The war has quickened the process of social change. New man [sic] and new classes are demanding equal opportunities. The fair employment practice statutes are a profound and, as I believe, a healthy sign of the times. The great private universities, which have so far led in the development of American scholarship and education, must meet the challenges of new social needs and conditions. We are a national trust, and our responsibilities in the field of educational policy are the very heavy obligations of creative, constructive leadership. The policies which govern our action should rest on principle, without equivocation or compromise. And we must realize that in our time the need for trained men is so great, and our national resources of ability and character so limited, that the community can no longer afford the waste of allowing a poor student to displace a good one.[58]

Yale, Rostow argued, "should base its admission policy on educational and professional criteria alone."[59]

When New York City threatened Columbia with a lawsuit alleging discrimination against blacks and Jews and raising the possibility of the loss of its tax-exempt status, Yale took notice. By May 1946, Yale for the first time enunciated a policy of giving applicants of "outstanding intellectual capacity"

top preference. In addition, the new policy explicitly prohibited racial and religious quotas. At the same time, Yale reaffirmed its commitment to a diverse
student body and indicated that for the many qualified applicants who were
"not of the highest intellectual capacity," emphasis would continue to be
placed on the promise of "leadership and effective influence and service in
the life of the community after graduation."[60]

Though a strategic retreat, this carefully designed policy left Yale with
considerable room to exercise "discretion" in selecting its freshmen. Yale used
it to pursue its institutional interests as it saw them — which meant continued restrictions on the number of Jews. Over the period covering the entering
classes of 1946 through 1950, Jewish enrollment averaged 10.2 percent — a
slight decline from the 10.7 percent who enrolled in the five years before the
war.[61] A measure of the strength of Yale's commitment to excluding those
Jews who did not fit the image of the "Yale man" is that only seven students
from the large and heavily Jewish Bronx High School of Science — arguably
the nation's most academically distinguished high school at the time — entered Yale between 1950 and 1954. In contrast, Andover sent 275 students to
New Haven during the same period.[62] The charged atmosphere of postwar
America had pushed discrimination farther beneath the surface, but a Jewish
quota — or something very much like it — was still clearly in place.[63]

Committed to discrimination, Yale had little choice but to oppose the numerous attempts by civil rights groups to persuade the Connecticut legislature to pass a law banning discrimination. The climactic struggle came in
1949–1950 after similar legislation had passed in Massachusetts and several
other states. In April 1949, Governor Chester Bowles, on receipt of a study
by the Connecticut State Inter-Racial Commission, stated flatly that "the
record of our private non-denominational colleges in this field of discrimination seems a rather dismal one." At a time when "our democratic way of
life is challenged by the totalitarian concept of the Communists," he warned,
"forthright, vigorous action" needed to be taken "to eliminate discrimination
wherever it exists."[64]

The legislation then before the Connecticut House and Senate, Yale argued in a public statement in March 1950, was both unnecessary and potentially harmful.[65] While claiming principled opposition to discrimination, the
university contended that "lasting improvement can only be accomplished
. . . by education, and not by legislation." In any case, discrimination simply
did not occur in Connecticut's private colleges and universities; on the contrary, the institutions had a "proud record" on the issue, belying "all suggestions of parochialism and prejudice." Admissions was not a matter for blunt-
edged legislation, for it "requires skill, judgment and experience."[66]

The statement's final point was that "the proposed law might easily do more harm than good." Should such legislation pass, in due time a "sensitive boy" who has been rejected for admission to college because he "cannot meet the competition of many applicants for few places" would file a lawsuit.[67] The resulting proceedings would "do great damage to the community," for they would arouse "race prejudice, always existing, though generally dormant." And what would become of the "sensitive boy" who set these drastic repercussions in motion? In all likelihood, he would be "spoiled for life."[68]

Though these arguments were less than compelling, they provided a public rationale for the successful effort by Yale and other powerful private institutions in Connecticut to thwart repeated attempts by civil rights groups to pass a Fair Educational Practices Act. Yale went to extraordinary lengths to block such legislation, even attempting to enlist carefully selected Jewish students to testify on its behalf. In 1951, facing still another antidiscrimination bill before the Connecticut legislature, Yale's chief counsel, Frederick W. Wiggin, wrote to Yale's rabbi, Joseph Gumbiner, requesting a list of "prominent Jewish students" who might be "presentable and effective witnesses."[69]

Though Rabbi Gumbiner, who had been at Yale since 1949, could hardly have failed to notice that the proportion of Jews in the freshmen class in 1950 was a suspiciously low 7.2 percent, he complied with Wiggin's request.[70] Among the eight students he selected was Anthony M. Astrachan, a scholarship student from New York's Stuyvesant High School and the associate editor of the *Yale Daily News*.[71] Writing in 1982 about his years at Yale, Astrachan '52 recounts how surprised he was when the university lawyer invited him to lunch. Perhaps, wondered Astrachan, he was "being scouted for a senior society."[72]

It quickly became apparent, however, that Wiggin was interested in hearing Astrachan's views on the proposed legislation. When the New Yorker made it clear that he thought "Yale would face serious trouble if she didn't change her homogeneous ways," it became equally clear that he would not make a good witness. Wiggin, Astrachan recalled, was "indignant at the idea that a bill . . . might be thought necessary, since the university was already about nine percent Jewish, one half of one percent black," and "we have a Buddhist and a Moslem in almost every class."[73]

The record does not show whether any of the other students on Rabbi Gumbiner's list ever testified before the Connecticut legislature. But Yale succeeded in turning back every attempt at passing the legislation, defeating renewed efforts in 1953, 1955, and 1957. By 1959, John Q. Tilson Jr., a member of the Wiggin and Dana law firm, informed Yale's treasurer, Charles S. Gage, that "for the first time I can remember, there are no bills on fair educational practices" before the Connecticut General Assembly. Yale had been more successful than any other Ivy institution in keeping the "Jewish problem" under strict control. As late as 1961–1962, Jews constituted just 12 percent of the student body.[74] With Princeton and Dartmouth, both renowned for their anti-Semitism, having permitted Jewish enrollments to reach roughly 15 percent, Yale stood alone as the most gentile college in the Ivy League.[75]

The Question of African Americans

Black civil rights groups had been among the staunchest allies of the many Jewish organizations that had struggled in vain to pass a Fair Educational Practices Act. African Americans had good reason to be skeptical about Yale's professed commitment to color blindness; after all, only seven blacks had graduated from the college between 1924 and 1945.[76] Many alumni remembered when blacks were not permitted to play on its athletic teams; in one particularly flagrant incident, Coach Tad James denied a truly great football prospect named Cato Baskerville a chance to make the team.[77] In the fall of 1945, just after the Japanese surrender and the end of the war, only five black undergraduates were enrolled at Yale.[78]

But blacks were far more distant than Jews from the milieu of elite private colleges, and conscious discrimination was hardly necessary to limit their numbers. "In contrast to the Jewish situation," wrote a student of Yale admissions who had interviewed Chairman Noyes in December 1947, "it is a source of sincere regret to the Yale Board of Admissions that there is not a larger number of qualified Negro applicants."[79] And it was true that as early as 1945, Yale, which prided itself on its openness to black students, conducted an inquiry into "why there were not more Negroes in the University." An interracial group looked into the matter and concluded that Yale's admission policy was not at fault; there was a lack of applications from African Americans. They attributed this paucity of applications to three reasons: blacks did not enjoy the benefits of adequate secondary schooling and tended to be ill prepared academically, many were not aware that Yale was open to them, and many could not afford to study there.[80]

Nevertheless, Yale made genuine efforts to increase the number of black students. In striking contrast to Princeton, where 62 percent of the undergraduates polled in 1942 came out against the admission of African Americans, the Yale student body voted in 1945 by a majority of 87 percent (with 5 percent against and 8 percent no opinion) to earmark funds from the Yale Budget Drive Fund (the undergraduate "community chest" effort) specifically for scholarships for blacks. By 1947–1948, the program had made available $8,320 (part of it from the United Negro College Fund) for scholarships for black freshmen — 17 percent of the total Yale Budget Drive Fund of $49,432.[81]

Yale did change as a result, but not very much. In 1948–1949, four blacks entered Yale, and in 1950 four others received bachelor's degrees.[82] One of the black graduates was Levi Jackson, the popular captain of Yale's football team. Jackson, the first black tapped for Skull and Bones, instead chose to stay with his friends by joining Berzelius.[83] Commenting on his election to Skull and Bones, Jackson had joked, "If my name had been reversed, I would never have made it."[84] Jackson's quip may have been true, but in 1949 Skull and Bones, for the first time in its 117 years, had tapped a Jew.[85] But Jackson's remark pointed to a deeper truth about Yale at midcentury: at the very time it was seeking to open the door a crack wider to the nation's black population, it continued to patrol the entryway lest too many Jews gain admittance.

The Growing Role of Public High Schools

The number of students from public schools increased at a rapid rate after World War II. Between 1934 and 1940, the nation's public schools contributed just 203 students per year of all Yale freshmen. But by 1947–1953, these numbers had more than doubled to 415 students annually — from 24 to 37 percent of all freshmen.[86]

This transformation reflected a conscious decision on Yale's part to expand its student base. The pivotal moment took place in the midst of the war, when a drastic shortage of the kind of students Yale wished to enroll led to a decision, at President Seymour's suggestion, to establish a new Joint Committee on Enrollment and Scholarships.[87] This committee, in which alumni interviewers played a major role, would be devoted to finding good candidates from public high schools outside the great Jewish population centers of the Northeast. By 1944–1945, alumni were already writing reports to the Board of Admissions "on the vast majority of candidates from public high schools outside of New Haven."[88]

Yale did not embark casually upon its decision to increase the number of high school graduates, and it took careful measures to ensure that the change would be gradual. Crucially, the growth in the number of public school boys was not accomplished at the expense of the private school boys, for the postwar expansion of enrollments made it possible to avoid a zero-sum conflict. With the average number of entrants growing from 845 in the seven years before the war to 1,111 between 1948 and 1952, Yale was able to increase the number of private school graduates in the freshman class from 597 to 672 per year.[89] At the same time, Yale also went to great lengths not to offend its alumni as it opened its doors more widely to the public schools, keeping in place a long tradition of giving preference to legacies. As late as 1950, the dean of freshmen publicly described Yale's policy as one in which "every break is given to a Yale son"; for them, "the scholastic standards are less rigorous . . . many more gambling cases are admitted, there are less rigorous de-mands that the boys be outstanding personally, and no attention is paid to geographic considerations."[90]

Yale was equally careful to guarantee that the public school graduates it did accept would conform to the profile of the "all-around boy."[91] Unlike the great state universities, which generally accepted students solely on the basis of their academic record, Yale was committed to interviewing as many candi-dates as possible before granting them admission. In a process committed to picking boys on the basis of "personality," "character," and "leadership" as well as scholastic promise, the interview provided indispensable information.

Though Yale already possessed letters of recommendation from high school principals, they were, according to the dean of freshmen, "often either too meager as to be useless or so flattering as to be suspect" — a striking con-trast to "the detailed and informative comments of the headmasters of most of the private schools." Indeed, one reason that Yale had established the Alumni Board's Committee on Enrollment and Scholarships was that it had been "completely baffled" in its "attempts to evaluate the high school boy as a person." All too frequently, from Yale's point of view, "the paragon of all the virtues, according to the high school, turned out to be meek, mild, and undis-tinguished."[92]

Yale's alumni representatives made every effort to evaluate the candidate as a whole person, submitting detailed reports based, not only on "lengthy in-terviews," but also on "further information gathered from the school, from the parents of the other young people in the community, and from people for whom [the applicant] had worked."[93] The report called for "a list of the activ-ities of each boy, a sort of pen portrait of the boy, and finally a rating of the boy as A+, A, and so on down." Yale did "not hesitate to admit a lad with a relatively low academic prediction whose personal qualifications seem out-standing rather than a much drabber boy with higher scholastic predica-tions."[94]

The competition for admission among high school boys was tough. In 1950, when Yale's overall acceptance rate was 46 percent, only 24 percent of the applicants (439 of 1,800) interviewed by alumni gained admission.[95] But getting in was only half the battle, for most of the public school graduates needed financial aid. How Yale allocated its scholarships went a long way to-ward determining which of them would come.

Scholarships and the Yale Ideal

Perhaps even more than its admission decisions, how a college chooses its scholarship recipients reveals its true priorities. For unlike "paying guests," scholarship students are a drain on, not a contributor to, the economic resources of the university. Yet long before the advent of need-blind admissions in the 1960s, elite colleges routinely deemed the presence of some students so desirable that it helped defray their expenses. At Yale, an elaborate scholarship program had long been an integral part of its claim to being a national and democratic institution.

Several years before Harvard instituted its National Scholarship Program, Yale established University Regional Scholarships in 1928 for outstanding students from three areas — the Far West, the South Atlantic, and the Southwest. All three were places from which Yale drew few students, and all three had small Jewish populations. The criteria were based on those used by the already famous Rhodes Scholarships:

1. Manhood, force of character, and moral leadership
2. Literary and scholastic ability
3. Physical soundness and vigor as demonstrated by interests in sports and in other ways.[96]

These criteria corresponded to a striking degree with the ideal "Yale man," and they confirmed the move away from the strictly exam-based criteria that had been used before the limitation of numbers and selective admissions in 1923. The first University Regional Scholarships were awarded to the entering Class of 1932, and by 1936–1937 Yale was maintaining 30 students annually on these funds.[97] But the total number of students on one sort of scholarship or another in the 1930s was far more, averaging 178 per year — roughly 20 percent of each entering class.[98]

After World War II, Yale faced an atmosphere that was more democratic and more competitive than the one during the interwar years. Dedicated to maintaining its position vis-à-vis its rivals, Yale reaffirmed its commitment to enrolling "a student body that is second to that of no other institution." To attract such a student body — one "whose quality transcends any economic or geographic bounds" — would require an expansion of its scholarship program.[99]

By the late 1940s, with the flow of entering veterans on the G.I. Bill having slowed to a trickle, the issue of scholarships had become a preoccupation of the Yale administration. In 1949, Yale announced to the public that its extensive scholarship program would be dedicated to bringing to New Haven two distinct kinds of boys: "true scholars" and "fine citizens." Candidates in each group would be measured by different standards, with character, personality, leadership in school affairs, and the like "deemed to be of 'tremendous importance'" in the latter group. The number of scholarships for "true scholars," Yale made clear, would be substantially smaller than the number for "fine citizens."[100]

Rector Endicott Peabody, the legendary headmaster of Groton from 1884 to 1940, who introduced the ideals of the British upper class into American education. This gentlemanly ethos would later profoundly shape the definition of "merit" used by Harvard, Yale, and Princeton in selecting students.

Franklin Delano Roosevelt, circa 1900, when he enrolled at Harvard with eighteen of his twenty-three Groton classmates. He became president of the *Crimson* but failed to make the Porcellian Club — an event that he described more than fifteen years later as "the greatest disappointment of my life."

A formal dinner at one of the Princeton eating clubs in the 1890s. Between 1895 and 1907 the number of eating clubs increased from five to fourteen.

Woodrow Wilson, president of Princeton from 1902 to 1910. Wilson's battle with Princeton's eating clubs, which he considered a force for "disintegration" and "demoralization," ended in defeat but established his reputation as a principled opponent of social privilege and set him on the path that led to the White House.

ABOVE LEFT: F. Scott Fitzgerald, a member of Princeton's Class of 1917, lounging. His bestselling novel *This Side of Paradise* (1920), which described Princeton as "the pleasantest country club in America," enduringly shaped the college's reputation. ABOVE RIGHT: The British imperialist Cecil Rhodes in 1900. Committed to the extension of influence of the "finest race in the world," he established the Rhodes Scholarships (first awarded in 1904) to promote the "Unity of the Empire." The criteria Rhodes elaborated for awarding the scholarships — "moral force of character and instincts to lead," "success in manly outdoor sports," and a hostility to mere "bookworms" — exerted a powerful influence on the admissions policies adopted by the Big Three in the 1920s.

The Cottage Club, which Fitzgerald joined in 1915. In *This Side of Paradise*, Amory Blaine, the novel's protagonist, describes Cottage as an "impressive mélange of brilliant adventurers and well-dressed philanderers."

Abbot Lawrence Lowell, Harvard's president from 1909 to 1933. A man of surpassing arrogance, Lowell replaced the college's exam-based system of admissions with a more subjective one, emphasizing "character," "leadership," and "personality." The purpose of the new policy, he stated frankly, was to limit the number of Jews, and in 1926 he imposed a quota.

Charles W. Eliot at ninety in 1924. President of Harvard from 1869 to 1909 and generally considered the nation's leading educator, he led the opposition in the epochal battle between 1922 and 1925 to block Lowell's quota scheme. A consistent defender of "poor scholars," Eliot had little patience for "the stupid sons of the rich."

CLOCKWISE FROM TOP LEFT: Madison Grant, Henry Fairfield Osborn, and Lothrop Stoddard. Grant (Yale, Class of 1887), Osborn (Princeton, Class of 1877), and Stoddard (Harvard, Class of 1905) were leading proponents of the doctrine that became known as "scientific racism," and their writings laid the intellectual groundwork for immigration restriction and the adoption of Jewish quotas by the Big Three. The United States, Grant wrote in *The Passing of the Great Race,* was threatened by marginalization, particularly by the "Polish Jew," whose "dwarf stature, peculiar mentality, and ruthless concentration on self-interest are being engrafted upon the stock of the nation." Osborn, president of the Museum of Natural History from 1908 to 1933, wrote the preface to the second edition of Grant's book, and Grant in turn wrote the introduction to Stoddard's racist classic, *The Rising Tide of Color Against White World Supremacy.*

ABOVE LEFT: Radcliffe Heermance, director of admissions at Princeton from 1922 to 1950. Committed to limiting Jewish enrollment, he developed a new admissions policy that included interviews, two letters of personal recommendation, and a social ranking of applicants. In 1939 he pulled a black student from the registration line and told him that he was not wanted at Princeton.

ABOVE RIGHT: Robert Corwin, chairman of the Board of Admissions at Yale from 1920 to 1935. The architect of Yale's Jewish quota of 10 percent, he believed that Jews were lacking in "manliness, uprightness, cleanliness, native refinement, etc."

LEFT: Henry Pennypacker, chairman of the Committee on Admission at Harvard from 1920 to 1933. A graduate of Exeter and Harvard (Class of 1888) and the former headmaster of Boston Latin School, Pennypacker faithfully implemented Lowell's anti-Jewish policies. During his tenure, Harvard kept a careful count of the number of Jews, distinguishing between "J1s" (definitely Jewish), "J2s" (probably Jewish), and "J3s" (possibly Jewish).

James Bryant Conant, age forty, in 1933, his first year as president of Harvard. An eloquent and tireless proponent of equal opportunity, he was often radical in his public rhetoric and quickly developed a reputation as a committed meritocrat. But Harvard's admissions policies during his tenure, from 1933 to 1953, frequently diverged sharply from that rhetoric and exhibited many continuities with the exclusionary practices put in place by Lowell.

Conant as the senior statesman of American education. Hailed by *Time* as a possible presidential candidate and by *Newsweek* as "U.S. Education's No. 1 Man," he left Harvard in 1953 to serve as high commissioner and then ambassador to Germany. When he returned home in 1957, he became a leading educational spokesman, writing a series of influential books, including *Slums and Suburbs* and *The American High School Today*.

Richard Gummere, chairman of the Committee on Admission at Harvard from 1934 to 1952. Hand-picked by Conant, he had come to Harvard's attention in 1922 because of his exemplary handling of the "Jew problem" as headmaster of a private school in Philadelphia.

Wilbur Bender, dean of admissions and financial aid at Harvard from 1952 to 1960, was widely considered responsible, along with Conant, for "Harvard's transformation from a college for well-bred Easterners to a diverse meritocratic university." In truth, Bender had a fondness for the St. Grottlesex boys, whom he called "gentlemen," and a dislike for "intellectuals," whose numbers he wished to limit to 10 percent.

Genuinely brilliant students, Yale maintained, would be accepted and given financial aid: "Applicants of *truly outstanding* intellectual capacity . . . need not fear their chances of receiving scholarship assistance at Yale." In contrast to the "fine citizens," the "true scholars" were relatively easy to identify: on the basis of "a strictly accurate statistical device . . . it is possible to predict quite reliably the academic success at Yale of each applicant."[101] But the number of students chosen, both scholarship and paying, on the basis of sheer scholastic promise would be limited; boys of unusual capacity "did not account for more than ten percent or so of any class."[102] Like Harvard, Yale was in effect imposing a 10 percent quota on the number of the class chosen on the basis of academic excellence.[103]

Predicting which candidates were most likely to become "fine citizens" was difficult. Yale relied heavily on the reports of the alumni interviewers, for they provided frank evaluations of less tangible qualities such as personality and character. The "student who has actively served his community . . . to the benefit of his school and locality" was an especially likely recipient of a scholarship.[104]

The expansion of Yale's scholarship program after World War II made it possible for more public school boys to come to New Haven than ever before. Of the 386 high school graduates in the entering class of 1950, 61 percent received scholarship assistance compared to 15 percent among private school graduates.[105] In increasing the proportion of the class on scholarship, Yale had a dual purpose: not only to make Yale more democratic but also more national. And Yale succeeded, reducing the proportion of scholarship recipients from the six northeastern states from 80 percent of all awardees in the later 1920s to 55 percent by the early 1950s.[106]

For the students who did receive scholarships — in 1952, only 300 young men out of 1,650 applicants — life at Yale could prove difficult.[107] Insisting that financial assistance was not a right but "a privilege that carries with it corresponding responsibilities," Yale required that scholarship students work during term time or forfeit their entire award. For freshmen, work usually involved fourteen hours a week in the university dining halls, serving food, taking tickets, and cleaning tables.[108]

Though such labor may have been an improvement over the days in the not-so-distant past when scholarship students lived in the cheapest possible rooms and scrubbed floors or washed dishes,[109] it was a striking contrast to Harvard's policy, which allowed scholarship boys to refuse to work, the only penalty being a reduction in the size of the award.[110] Furthermore, Yale's work requirement also applied to upperclassmen, who graduated from their freshmen jobs in the dining hall to "bursary" employment scattered around the campus. Overall, Yale's underlying attitude was summed up by the dean of freshmen when he described scholarship holders as "deeply conscious of their good fortune in being at Yale."[111]

In addition to the time pressure imposed by the work requirement, scholarship recipients at Yale (as at Harvard) were under the added pressure of having to perform well academically or risk losing their awards. Yale's official policy was to renew the scholarship only of the student who does "not rest on his laurels,"[112] which meant "a top quarter scholastic ranking" for recipients of the University Regional Scholarships; for others, especially those with "outstanding qualities of character and personal leadership," renewal would be granted if the student ranked in the top half of his class.[113] It was not surprising, therefore, that scholarship students, who had already met a higher standard at the point of admission, outperformed their classmates by a considerable margin. A study of the Classes of 1940 and 1941, for example, revealed that 55 percent of scholarship holders won academic honors compared to less than a third of their fellow students.[114] The same pattern could be seen in students elected to Phi Beta Kappa: in 1950, more than half of the seniors were drawn from the ranks of scholarship recipients.[115]

Yale was justifiably proud of its scholarship program, considering it the foundation of its long-standing claim to being "both a *national* and a *democratic* institution."[116] Compared to Harvard and Princeton, a larger proportion of the Yale freshmen class in the early 1950s was on scholarship: roughly a third, in contrast to about a quarter at Harvard and Princeton. But it was also true that Yale was the most expensive of the Ivy League colleges, costing $300 more per year than its main competitors.[117] In truth, all of the Big Three were still primarily "rich men's colleges" at midcentury, drawing two-thirds to three-quarters of their students from that small segment of American families — probably not more than 5 percent — who could pay their own way.

Within these limits, Yale pursued with great vigor promising students who needed scholarships. As a result, postwar Yale was more diverse than it had been during the interwar years, increasing the percentage of public school graduates to almost 40 percent by the early 1950s and enrolling a larger percentage of its students from outside New York and New England.[118] But Yale's range of students on campus did not increase commensurately, for the criteria governing the allocation of scholarships had been consciously designed to bring to New Haven more of the type of "all-around boy" who was already present in abundance. "The toughest decision facing the Committee on Enrollment and Scholarships," wrote the editors of the *Yale Alumni Magazine*, came when "choosing between an all-around boy with a lower academic standing but high personal qualifications and a much less colorful boy with higher proven scholastic ability."[119] Yale's preference for the former as well as its manifest ambivalence toward "true scholars" was one of several factors contributing to the slippage in intellectual preeminence that was already becoming visible in the final years of the Noyes era.

Preferred Categories and the Persistence of Privilege

By the late 1940s, concerns were growing at the highest administrative levels that Yale's intellectual standing was in decline. William Clyde DeVane (B.S. '20, Ph.D. '26), the widely respected dean, expressed his worries in his Annual Report to the President for 1947–48: "What I want for Yale College is an intellectual eminence that is as great as her athletic or her social or her eminence in activities of all sorts . . . I would have Yale turn out more leaders of the intellectual life of our country. For the man of activity we unquestionably provide a superb training — none better. For the man of intellectual achievement I am afraid we are surpassed by Harvard, Columbia and Chicago, in that order."[120] For an institution that had considered itself, with Harvard, the nation's preeminent institution of higher learning, the admission that it had been surpassed intellectually by two other institutions — one not even in the Ivy League — must have been deeply humbling.

A big part of the problem was the exceptionally ingrown character of the Yale faculty: as late as 1950, half its members had Yale degrees. As Kabaservice points out, "Standards for appointment and promotions tended to emphasize citizenship rather than scholarship, clubbability rather than real merit," and "inheritance, wealth, background and social standing" remained "significant criteria." In such an atmosphere, "dark blossoms of anti-Semitism and anti-Catholicism flourished" in many departments.[121]

Yale's admissions policy only compounded the problem. Under the administration of Charles Seymour (B.A. '08, Ph.D. '11), Yale's president from 1937 to 1950, the selection of students was consistently and powerfully tilted toward the usual handful of preferred categories: athletes, alumni sons, and boarding school graduates, many of whom had less than sterling academic qualifications.

Seymour, an accomplished mountaineer who had rowed at King's College, Cambridge, before graduating from Yale, had a special fondness for sportsmen.[122] In a candid 1948 letter to Noyes, he declared that "Yale is definitely interested in having superior athletes in all fields in larger numbers." To realize this objective, the university was "prepared to take more gambling chances on the admission of athletes of superior personality, whose scholastic record offers likelihood that they can meet college standards but without distinction." "Ability and achievement in competitive athletics," wrote Seymour, "give about as reliable an index of leadership potentiality as can be found." Particularly "in dealing with candidates whose qualifications are not primarily intellectual," Yale should adhere to the following principle: "the lower the scholastic record the more stress should be laid upon personal qualifications, and among those qualifications notably, athletic leadership."[123]

Despite facing a large surplus of qualified candidates in the late 1940s for the first time in its history, Yale still was admitting virtually every legacy it thought had a decent chance of graduating. As long as these applicants showed "evidence of reasonable ability for successful work in Freshman Year," secured a "full recommendation from their school," and made Yale their first choice, they would be offered a place in the freshman class.[124]

So lenient was Yale's policy toward legacies that, as of 1948–1949, "of those up for action before the Freshman Rules Committee, an alarmingly high proportion has been of Yale sons." Noyes acknowledged that "there are not a few in the Freshman Class who would not have been admitted, had they been judged on equal terms with other applicants." Ever prudent, however, Noyes shrank from the thought of seriously modifying the policy, concluding, "No immediate change in the Board's procedure is recommended," for "to put alumni sons on precisely the same platform as other applicants may never be wise."[125]

In 1950, when well over half of all applicants were rejected, fewer than one quarter of alumni sons were denied admission. This high rate resulted in a freshman class in which Yale sons made up 24 percent of all students. With the freshman class at Harvard and Princeton made up of legacies at only 18 and 16 percent, respectively, Yale was demonstrably the most inbred of the three.[126]

Many, though not all, of these sons came from a larger category: the traditional feeder schools. Though attendance at one of these institutions could no longer guarantee admission, Yale in the final years of the Seymour administration continued to look to them for the majority of its students.

Fourteen years after Noyes's 1936 appointment, the mechanics of the admissions process remained heavily slanted toward the private schools. Each year Yale would send a representative — usually Noyes himself — to interview interested boys. Few public schools enjoyed the same courtesy. During the May meeting of the Board of Admissions, Noyes himself "consulted by telephone with the headmasters or college advisors of a dozen schools regarding their lists of applicants, and found most sympathetic cooperation." If a candidate was rejected, Yale reconsidered any case when the headmaster or principal requested it. Of the 60 students for whom such reconsideration was requested in the spring of 1950, 20 were granted admission and a number of others were placed on a waiting list.[127]

The result of this painstaking cultivation of close relations with the major boarding schools was an entering class in 1950 in which almost two-thirds of the freshmen came from private schools. So extreme was the preference that a committee of the Alumni Board, in a confidential report on the performance of the admissions office under Noyes, wrote that the Board of Admissions "fails to exercise a proper and desirable degree of selectivity in admitting from private schools and particularly from the larger schools." "Small wonder," the report continued, "that the [private] schools like our admissions policy or that some schools officials admit privily [*sic*] that it is easier to get their boys into Yale than into any of her active competitors."[128]

The consequences for academic standards were decidedly negative. High school graduates consistently outperformed their peers from private schools, attaining higher grades and leaving for academic reasons only a third as frequently.[129] The magnitude of this difference is visible in the reports that Yale routinely sent to its feeder schools on the performance of their graduates; in the case of Choate, for example, fewer than 10 percent of those who entered Yale between 1946 and 1948 (with average SATs of 548 verbal and 591 math scores) ranked in the top quarter of their class.[130] At a time when Yale's intellectual standing in the top ranks of American universities was increasingly precarious, its continued preference for less qualified boarding school boys was a liability it could ill afford.

New Pressures and the End of the Noyes Era

Though a distinguished historian, the gentlemanly and diplomatic Seymour was not the right man to lead Yale through a period of intensifying competitive pressure. After thirteen years of an administration characterized by "hesitancy, timidity, and conservation," Yale was, according to Kabaservice, "beset by serious financial problems, administrative paralysis, and weakness outside the humanities."[131] Within Yale itself, Alfred Whitney Griswold uncharitably described the often immobile Seymour "as descended from a long line of bronze statues."[132] In Cambridge, the verdict was harsher still: Seymour, said Wilbur J. Bender, was a "provincial, pontifical nonentity."[133]

Meanwhile, Yale's Board of Admissions was having problems of its own adapting to the postwar environment. Sheer numbers had pushed pressure for admission to unprecedented heights, and some of Yale's most cherished traditional constituencies now had to compete with large numbers of applicants outside the "Yale family." At the same time, changes in the policy of the College Board, which until 1949 required that students list their first choice of college, were making it harder to predict how many students would actually enroll in the freshman class. In 1950–1951, when the College Board no longer required that candidates list preferences, Yale and its sister institutions entered a new and forbidding world in which they would have to compete with one another — and with "lesser" colleges — for the most desirable students.[134] The effects of the new College Board policy were dramatically visible in 1951, with the proportion of students accepting Yale's offer of admission plummeting from 81 to 62 percent.[135]

For Noyes, a gentleman of the old school for whom it was a point of pride that Yale did not recruit students, the increasingly intense competition among colleges must have been bewildering and distasteful. Noyes believed deeply that appearing too eager to attract students could destroy one of Yale's most precious assets — its standing as an institution too lofty to have to seek out applicants or convince those admitted to come. Recruiting, in his view, would make the "Board an office of propaganda and procurement."[136]

Inheriting the problem of admissions (among other difficulties) was Yale's new president, Alfred Whitney Griswold. Taking office in July 1950, Griswold was, like his predecessors, a quintessential Yale man. A descendant of Eli Whitney (Yale 1792) on his mother's side and of six colonial governors of what later became the state of Connecticut on his father's, Griswold attended the Hotchkiss School and graduated from Yale in 1929. While an undergraduate, he served as managing editor of the college humor magazine, the *Yale Record*, and wrote for the *Yale Daily News*. Voted the "wittiest" and "most original" member of his class, "Whit" (as he was called by his friends) was elected to Psi Upsilon fraternity and to Wolf's Head, a prestigious senior society.[137]

After a summer stint on Wall Street following graduation, he returned to Yale to teach Freshman English and never left. Griswold received a Ph.D. in 1933 in the new field of History, the Arts and Letters, writing the first dissertation in American Studies in the country. The author of two major books, *The Far Eastern Policy of the United States* (1938) and *Farming and Democracy* (1948), he was promoted to full professor in 1948. Something of a nonconformist by Yale standards, he was one of a very few Democrats on the faculty and a strong supporter of the New Deal.

But Griswold was also something of an old boy, fond of drinking and singing with his prep school friends as a graduate student and a loyal member of Wolf's Head as a young faculty member. He did not stray from his patrician background in his choice of a spouse, marrying a multimillionaire's daughter, Mary Brooks, whom he had met while summering on Martha's Vineyard.[138] Though a respected faculty member, Griswold seemed an unlikely candidate for the presidency: he was not only relatively young but rather unknown by Yale standards. He did not seek the presidency and was not even aware he was being considered on the day of his election; indeed, that very afternoon he had been in New York to go to the theater, and after lunch with a friend, the president of Mount Holyoke, he remarked to his wife, "Thank God we're not in *that* racket."[139]

Griswold had long been a friend of Wilmarth S. Lewis's, a member of the Yale Corporation's committee charged with selecting a new president. In addition, in 1947 he had impressed Ted Blair, an important committee member and former football captain, when he drafted a report that led to the establishment of the University Council. This alumni advisory body played a major role in raising the money that permitted Yale to remain a great university. He also had support from the formidable Dean Acheson (Groton '11, Yale '15), then the nation's secretary of state. On February 11, 1950, he was formally elected president. When so informed, the surprised Griswold hesitated to accept, but his protestations were overridden by Dean Acheson, who told him, "Pull up your socks, boy, and get on with it."[140]

Griswold brought a new perspective to the Yale presidency. Deeply committed to academic excellence, he was less enthusiastic about the extracurricular activities for which Yale was renowned, often deprecating them as "Bonesy bullshit" and "that Dink Stover crap."[141] Even athletics did not escape his skepticism. Not much of an athlete himself, he insisted that sports should be subordinate to academics, denounced athletic scholarships as "the biggest swindle perpetrated on American youth," and played a leading role in maintaining the amateur character of Ivy League sports.[142]

Yet on the crucial issue of admissions, Griswold's views were in the end not very different from those of Noyes. The Yale man of the future, Griswold assured an alumni gathering, would not be a "beetle-browed, highly specialized intellectual, but a well-rounded man."[143] A devout believer in the humanities and a militant foe of vocationally oriented disciplines and specialists, he was viewed with suspicion, even dislike, by Yale's scientists. Described by the historian Roger Geiger as "out of harmony with the postwar research economy," Griswold did little to encourage scientists to obtain federal support and was held responsible by them for alleged discrimination in undergraduate admissions against fledgling scientists.[144] If support for the nascent postwar meritocracy was the hallmark of the forward-looking college president, Griswold must be counted firmly among the ranks of the traditionalists.

Despite his support for the New Deal, Griswold was conservative socially and culturally. He supported the faculty's 1952 decision to impose a requirement, for the first time in Yale's history, that undergraduates wear coats and ties at meals. The new code was needed, claimed its supporters, to combat the "sloppiness" and "disorderliness" of the "ill-bred," nontraditional students who were now more numerous on campus.[145] Of a piece was his denunciation, in his *Report to the Alumni for 1952–53,* of the public schools as the "rotten pilings" of the American educational system.[146] Faced with evidence that the graduates of these schools were outperforming their private school peers and scoring higher on tests of scholastic aptitude, Griswold suggested that

Yale had lowered its standards to accommodate these boys' lack of preparation. The solution was a return to admissions standards driven by the curriculum — a change that would strongly favor graduates of private schools.[147]

Almost from the moment he came into office, Griswold was barraged by critics of Noyes and of the Board of Admissions. A recurrent theme was that Noyes was utterly lacking in public relations skills. An active Connecticut alumnus did not mince words: "Whether you like it or not, Yale has a selling job to do today and it requires an A1 man to do the job . . . Ed Noyes is just not properly qualified to fill that job and never will be." Especially at a moment when "a big drive for the alumni fund" was in the offing, Yale could simply not afford "poor public relations."[148]

In February 1951, a pair of troubling reports arrived from the Alumni Board's influential Committee on Enrollment and Scholarships and painted a devastating portrait of the Board of Admissions. In particular, Noyes's opposition to "propaganda" and "procurement" came in for sharp denunciation; as one report observed, it was "completely unrealistic" and ignored "the fact that whatever the situation may have been twenty-five or thirty years ago, today we face well-organized competition for really top-flight boys not only from those whom we choose to consider our natural rivals, but from institutions of lesser breed." The very purpose of the creation of this committee in 1944 was, the report noted, "to secure the applications of the really first-rate high school graduates" — to accomplish, in short, "through alumni contacts what the Board of Admissions was unwilling or unable to do." Yet despite the tireless efforts of alumni, this goal had only been partially realized — an outcome that the report attributed in no small measure to the impression consistently conveyed by the Board of Admissions that Yale was a college to which "many are called but few are chosen."[149]

A further blow was delivered from within the Board of Admissions itself. In June 1951, Albert "Baldy" Crawford '13, the chairman of the Scholarship Committee and a personal friend of Noyes's from college days, lent his voice to those who argued that Noyes's policies were harming the university. Explicitly echoing a criticism of the Committee on Enrollment and Scholarships, he charged that Noyes relied far too heavily on Yale's statistical formula for predicting freshman grades (which "in Mr. Corwin's time [was] regarded with derision") and too little on "character." Crawford formally resigned from the Board of Admissions, making sure to enclose a copy for Yale's president.[150]

Though Griswold apparently did not accept Crawford's resignation,[151] it was now only a matter of time before Noyes would be relieved of his duties. The end came in 1953 after Griswold received still another letter of complaint, this one from W. H. Hopkins, president of the important Washington, D.C., alumni club. The charges were all too familiar: Noyes, Hopkins wrote, lacked "competence in the public relations field" and had alienated promising private school boys by conveying the impression that they were being "patronized."[152] A few months later, shortly after Yale experienced the lowest yield of admits (56.6 percent) in its history, Noyes was put on sabbatical leave and "promoted" to the position of director of Yale's Master of Arts in Teaching program.[153] After seventeen years, Noyes's days were over.

The Yale that Noyes left behind remained in many ways a deeply traditional, insular institution. Of the freshmen entering in 1953, the last admitted under his direction, alumni sons made up well over a fifth — an even higher percentage than at Princeton (18 percent) and Harvard (18 percent).[154] Private school graduates continued to predominate, constituting just over 60 percent of the freshmen, compared to 55 percent at Princeton and 47 percent at Harvard.[155] The major boarding schools continued to send large delegations to Yale; with Andover (89), Hotchkiss (40), and Exeter (30) leading the way, a dozen schools contributed a fourth of all entering students.[156] Finally, and perhaps most important, being a "paying guest" remained a major asset; in 1952, when 51 percent of all applicants were admitted, only 300 of 1,650 scholarship candidates (18 percent) received awards.[157]

As Noyes stepped down, the "Jewish problem" remained high on Yale's agenda; continued discrimination kept Jewish enrollment at 12.6 percent in the freshmen class of 1953 — hardly a significant change from 11.2 percent in 1937.[158] Similarly, the proportion of blacks had barely changed, with African Americans continuing to account for less than one half of one percent of the freshman class.[159] And the most fundamental discrimination of all — the total exclusion of the female half of the population — remained effectively invisible; the very idea of coeducation was not even a matter for discussion.

Yet not far beneath Yale's familiar surface, a different institution was beginning to emerge. The most far-reaching change was that, for the first time, public school students were coming to Yale in unprecedented numbers, making up 40 percent of the freshmen in 1953 — a sharp increase over the 26 percent of the freshmen of 1937, the first admitted under Noyes.[160] Largely as a result, Yale had also expanded its geographic reach, almost tripling the proportion of students from west of the Mississippi at the same time that the New England share dropped from 60 to 47 percent.[161] None of these changes could have occurred, of course, without an increase in scholarships, which in 1952 were awarded to almost 30 percent of the entering students.[162]

Even Yale's most treasured constituencies had to settle for a smaller slice of the pie as the Noyes era came to an end. A comparison of the freshman class of 1937 and 1953 reveals a pattern of gradual but undeniable change under Noyes. Legacies made up over 30 percent of all entering students in 1937;

by 1953, their share had dropped to 22 percent.[163] Private schools showed a similar pattern of decline; the source of 76 percent of all freshmen in 1937, their portion had dropped to 60 percent in 1953.[164]

A new Yale — one a bit more compatible with its cherished self-image as a national and democratic institution — was in the process of being born. Present among the freshmen in 1953 were a considerable number of students who would have been quite unlikely to attend the old Yale. Among them were Calvin Trillin, a graduate of Southwest High School in Kansas City and a Jew, and André Schiffrin, a scholarship boy from New York City and the son of Jewish refugees from France. When Noyes's final class of freshmen graduated, Trillin was chosen to deliver the Class History and Schiffrin, the Class Oration.[165] Yet for Yale's future, the most important member of the class was a freshman from a public high school on Long Island whose father had not even attended college: R. Inslee Clark Jr., the man who, as Yale's dean of admissions from 1965 to 1970, presided over the most radical transformation ever witnessed in an Ivy League institution.

CHAPTER 8

Princeton: The Club Expands Its Membership

I N 1933, as James Bryant Conant was assuming the presidency of Harvard, Princeton too was inaugurating a new president. But unlike Conant, who confessed his ambition to become president of Harvard to his fiancée thirteen years before being offered the job, Harold Willis Dodds, Princeton's choice, was taken unawares.[1] "It was a surprise to me, and quite a shock," he later recalled. Nevertheless, Dodds concluded that he simply could not turn it down: "I felt I either had to accept the offer or leave town."[2]

The son of a professor of Bible Studies at Grove City College, a Presbyterian institution in Pennsylvania, Dodds (1899–1980) was a far more surprising choice for a Big Three presidency than Conant. Unlike his immediate predecessors at Princeton, Woodrow Wilson '79 and John Grier Hibben '82, Dodds had not attended Princeton as an undergraduate, though he did take a master's degree in politics there in 1914; in contrast, Conant had compiled a distinguished undergraduate record at Harvard, where attendance at another undergraduate institution (in Dodds's case, Grove City College) would have meant exclusion from consideration for the presidency. But perhaps the greatest difference between the two men was that Conant was already an eminent scholar thought by many to be destined for a Nobel Prize when chosen as president. Dodds, though a full professor since 1927, had yet to publish his first book.[3]

Though lacking Conant's brilliant and wide-ranging intellect, Dodds was not without his strengths. Having taught at Western Reserve after completing his Ph.D. in politics at the University of Pennsylvania in 1917, he became secretary of the National Municipal League in 1920 and came to the attention of Secretary of State (and later Chief Justice of the Supreme Court) Charles Evans Hughes. Hughes developed a great respect for the young executive and involved him in a variety of Latin American issues. Having lectured at a number of eastern colleges, Dodds was appointed to the Princeton faculty in 1925, and in 1930 he was named chairman of the new School of Public and International Affairs (now the Woodrow Wilson School). At the age of forty-four, he was named to the presidency, which he held until 1957. Though not charis-matic, Dodds developed a reputation as a flexible and quietly competent ad-ministrator who oversaw the transformation of Princeton from what was es-sentially a college to a genuine university.[4]

The Princeton that Dodds inherited had many of the qualities of an ex-clusive, self-perpetuating private club. Even more than Yale and Harvard, Princeton drew its students from a narrow segment of America's privileged classes. In 1932, the year before Dodds took office, just 15 percent of the enter-ing freshmen came from public schools, then graduating 375,000 young men annually.[5] Over 18 percent came from that minuscule segment of the popula-tion whose fathers had attended Princeton.[6]

Throughout the interwar period, Princeton remained highly dependent on a small number of prep schools to fill the freshman class. Just fifteen schools provided nearly half the freshman class in 1932. The top feeder was nearby Lawrenceville, which alone provided Princeton with 62 students — nearly 10 percent — of the freshmen. Next was Exeter (31), and third was Mercersburg (27), which was not generally ranked among the leading schools. In truth, Princeton's top feeders were a mixture of the elite boarding schools (Hotchkiss, 26; St. Paul's, 22; Hill, 16; Andover, 15; Choate, 13; Kent, 10) and others that were not quite top tier (Hun, 21; Loomis, 16; Gilman, 16; Blair, 13; Newark Academy, 13; Peddie, 11).[7] While these schools may have varied sharply in social prestige, they had one thing in common: they supplied the kind of young man Princeton most wanted: well-mannered upper- or upper-middle-class Protestant boys who could pay their own way.

Princeton's reputation as the nation's most snobbish college was grounded in the dominant role played in the social life of the campus by lux-urious private eating clubs, themselves arrayed in a highly elaborate hierar-chy.[8] At Harvard and Yale, there were, to be sure, exclusive clubs that occupied a somewhat parallel position — at Harvard, the final clubs, joined by perhaps 10 percent of the class and at Yale, the somewhat more open senior societies, which admitted a roughly similar proportion of students. But at Princeton, as many as 90 percent of all upperclassmen were members of the eating clubs in the 1930s, giving the campus a distinctively genteel aura.[9]

Reinforcing Princeton's country club atmosphere was the reality that membership was restricted. Ineligible for membership in the interwar years was the nation's entire black population. Though a handful of African Ameri-cans had attended Princeton in the eighteenth and nineteenth centuries, not a single black had entered as an undergraduate in the twentieth.[10] The ostensi-ble reason for this long-standing policy was Princeton's tradition of enrolling students from the South, but in truth Princeton had long been a heavily northern institution; when Dodds took over, the proportion of the student body that was southern was very small — of the 659 freshman who entered in 1932, just 67 were from below the Mason-Dixon Line, and of them, 43 were from Maryland and the District of Columbia.[11]

"Hebrews," as they were then called at Princeton, were also unwelcome, but unlike blacks, their attendance was not prohibited. Nevertheless, the eating clubs, which often excluded Jews from membership as "unclubbable," served as a powerful disincentive for them to even apply because they would most likely be relegated to the margins of student life. The result was a remarkably homogeneous student body. Year after year, over 60 percent of the freshmen came from just two Protestant denominations, Episcopalian and Presbyterian. In 1932, a typical year, there were 225 Episcopalians (33 percent) and 204 Presbyterians (30 percent) in an entering class that was over 87 percent white and Protestant.[12]

Perhaps even more striking than the racial and religious homogeneity of the students was their level of economic privilege. Each year the *Freshman Herald* listed statistics on fathers' occupations, and each year the result was the same: wealthy businessmen and lawyers predominated, respectable but not lucrative professions such as minister and professor were modestly represented, and farmers and working men — a strong majority of the male labor force nationwide — were hardly present at all. In 1932, the top occupations were executive (69), lawyer (66), merchant (45), manufacturer (41), banker (38), and broker (37); nonbusiness professions included minister (10), superintendent (6), teacher (5), and professor (4); farmers numbered only 4, while workers, if broadly defined, numbered just 16.[13]

In an era when well under 10 percent of men and an even lower percentage of women attended college, almost two-thirds of Princeton's freshmen had a parent who had been to college, often at elite institutions. Among the fathers, the most common were Princeton (126), Penn (23), Harvard (15), Columbia (12), and Cornell (12); among mothers, the top institutions were Smith (16), Bryn Mawr (11), Vassar (9), and Wellesley (9).[14]

Nevertheless, as Dodds prepared to take office, Princeton's fiscal situation was precarious, and the academic level of the freshman class was declining. To cover expenses, Princeton had just admitted the largest freshman class in its history, and Director of Admissions Radcliffe Heermance acknowledged that it had "been necessary to take into consideration the financial standing of the applicant."[15] In his confidential report, Brigham had suggested that Princeton could find stronger students "from states remote from the Northeastern seaboard . . . [who] represent a very desirable type," but had cautioned that attracting such students would depend "on the provision of substantial scholarship funds."[16] In the meantime, Princeton had to make do with the pool of students recruited from its traditional constituencies — the same pool from which over 30 percent of the entering freshmen of 1928 had failed to graduate in four years."[17]

Dodds Expands the Pool

Less than two years after his inauguration, Dodds moved to reduce Princeton's dependence on private schools and to increase its national representation. At a meeting of the Committee of Admissions on June 14, 1935, he called for more high school applicants and an evaluation of Harvard's top-seventh plan. But Heermance opposed this suggestion, complaining that such a system might lead to the enrollment of too many Jews and that most of the students admitted would require financial aid.[18]

Though officials at Harvard had privately assured Heermance that the "Jewish problem" could be managed, the matter required constant vigilance, for Jews are "unable to be loyal to anything" and frequently deny their origins. (In one of his annual reports to the president, Heermance observed that ten Jews had been admitted, "seven of which admit being Jews".)[19] Yet Dodds still believed the plan of "admission without examination" was worth the risk, and in 1936 it was passed by the Princeton faculty. Heermance's concern proved unfounded; during the plan's first five years, the percentage of "Hebrews" in the freshman class never exceeded 2.3 percent.[20]

The official rationale for Princeton's abandonment of the requirement that all applicants take the College Board exams (a requirement which, by the mid-1930s, Princeton was alone in maintaining) was that it deprived the school "of the chance to pass upon the qualifications of many boys who are exactly the type that [the] University wants and needs." Noting that the percentage of students from west of the Alleghenies had actually been greater twenty or thirty years earlier, Princeton argued that the College Boards, which it had adopted in 1916, had led to a rise in scholastic standards "but at the expense of national distribution." Admission without examination, it was hoped, would attract "men of exceptional achievement and promise from certain schools in the West and South, and possibly from certain rural high schools in the East."[21]

If the intent of the new policy, which was called Plan C, was to expand Princeton's geographical reach and increase the number of public school students, then it must be counted a success. In 1938, in its second year of operation, 42 students were admitted under Plan C, 31 of them from public schools.[22]

By 1941, 57 students gained admission under Plan C — 15 of them from the South, 12 from the Southwest and Pacific coast, and 29 from the Midwest (the one remaining student was foreign).[23] By 1936, a record 73 students were admitted via Plan C. In 1936, the last year the College Boards were required, only 6 percent of the freshman class came from the Midwest, the South, the Southwest, and the Pacific coast combined; by 1941, the proportion had almost tripled to over 17 percent.[24] The trend in the proportion of freshmen from public schools was in the same direction, though not nearly as pronounced: just 19 percent of entering students in 1936, high school graduates had risen to over 23 percent by 1941.[25]

Yet it is easy to exaggerate how much Plan C actually changed Princeton, for the boys it brought to the campus — "of exactly the type that Princeton wants and needs" — turned out to be not very different from the boys already there. In the Annual Report of the Committee on Admissions for 1937, all 29 of the Plan C students are profiled, and they are a decidedly Princetonian group. Almost half of them (13) reported involvement in sports (8 at the varsity level), and many of the others showed evidence of "leadership" in school affairs. Though more of them applied for financial aid than was customary, there do not seem to have been many disadvantaged students among them; indeed, 5 of them came from a single high school, New Trier, in Chicago's affluent northern suburbs that was known for its academic excellence.[26] There does not seem to have been a single Jewish, Italian, Polish, or Irish surname among them.[27]

Much like Harvard's National Scholarship Program, what Plan C did do, however, was attract a new pool of talented and ambitious Protestant boys, most of them upper middle or middle class, from outside the eastern seaboard. And much like the Harvard National Scholars, the students admitted under Plan C did well academically: 25 of the 29 had above average grades, with 1 achieving high distinction, and 11 others gaining honor standing.[28] From Princeton's perspective, the Plan C students were a most welcome addition, for they made Princeton more of a national institution without upsetting its character as an overwhelmingly Protestant institution attractive to the scions of the eastern upper class.

Princeton's experience suggested that the presence of more public high school students was not necessarily a threat to its elite character and might even enhance it. But a lack of scholarship funds had kept some of the most promising Plan C admits from attending Princeton and threatened its competitive position with both Harvard and Yale. Indeed, even before Plan C went into effect, Heermance warned Dodd that the lack of resources for scholarships was causing Princeton to lose "many outstanding candidates who keenly desired admission" and was damaging to its efforts "to maintain our prestige in many schools because we cannot give adequate financial aid to their best students."[29]

The administration's solution was ingenious: Princeton would strengthen its ties with its alumni both to raise funds for scholarships and to deploy its far-flung network of graduates to search for talented boys throughout the country. But the key innovation was the establishment in 1940 of an Annual Giving Program.

The program began modestly, raising $80,000 in 1940–1941 from 18 percent of the alumni and a few friends of the university. Sensing that an important precedent had been established, Dodds told the class agents involved in the first fund drive: "You men have started something which may well be the most effective force for progress at Princeton." By 1941–1942, 25 percent of the alumni participated, raising $102,000, and by 1949–1950, the half-million-dollar mark had been passed.[30]

Over time, Princeton developed unsurpassed ties with its alumni, with more than 72 percent — the highest figure for any college in the United States — participating in 1958–1959.[31] But in conceiving the Annual Giving Program, Princeton's purpose was not simply to raise money but also to involve the alumni in its search for promising students, especially in public high schools. Both goals were accomplished. In addition, the Schools Committees, part of local Princeton Alumni clubs, played a major role in transforming Princeton's applicant pool from "alarmingly small" in 1941 to the larger and stronger one that emerged after the war.[32]

The "Negro Question"

Unlike Harvard and Yale, Princeton had long had a systematic policy of excluding blacks. In 1910, E. E. Slosson, in a widely read survey of fourteen leading universities, reported that at Princeton "negroes . . . are shut out by reason of their race, an injustice which is unique among the universities."[33]

Princeton's policy of excluding blacks continued through the interwar years. In 1939, a black student named Bruce Wright — a graduate of New York's Townsend Harris High School, then the best public secondary school in the city — was accidentally admitted and awarded a full scholarship.[34] When Wright came to enroll, he was pulled from the registration line by an upperclassman, whose task was to help the freshmen, who told him, "The dean of admission would like to see you." Wright was escorted to the office of Radcliffe Heermance, who, he later recounted, looked at him "as though I were a disgusting specimen under a microscope." "The race problem," Heermance declared, "is beyond solution in America . . . If you're trying to come here, well, you're going to be in some place where you're not wanted." He concluded the meeting by suggesting that Wright go to a college of "his own kind."[35]

The son of a man who worked several jobs, Wright described himself as "shattered" by this encounter. Yet he persisted in his effort to register, writing to Heermance and asking him to explain why he was being denied entrance despite having been accepted. Heermance responded on June 13, 1939:

> Dear Mr. Wright:
>
> Princeton University does not discriminate against any race, color or creed. This is clearly set forth in the original charter of the college and the tradition has been maintained throughout the life of the University . . .
>
> Let me give you a purely personal reaction and I speak as one who has always been particularly interested in the colored race and I have always had pleasant relations with your race both in civilian life and in the army. I cannot conscientiously advise a colored student to apply to Princeton simply because I do not think he would be happy in this environment. There are no colored students in the university and a member of your race might feel very much alone.
>
> There are, moreover, a number of southern students enrolled in the college. This has been a tradition of long standing at Princeton, and as you know, there is still a feeling in the south quite different from that existing in New England. My personal experience would enforce my advice to any colored student that he would be happier in an environment of others of his race.[36]
>
> Yours sincerely,
> Radcliffe Heermance

Mr. Wright did not register at Princeton, enrolling instead at Lincoln University, a black college in Pennsylvania. He won a Bronze Star and a Purple Heart in World War II and went on to a distinguished career as a lawyer; in 1983, he was elected a justice of the Supreme Court of the State of New York.

Princeton's policy of total exclusion of African Americans was not without its critics even then. It became especially difficult to defend in the context of the rise of Hitler, and one of Princeton's most distinguished alumni, Norman Thomas '05, pressed the issue. A former Presbyterian minister and the leader of America's Socialist Party, Thomas chose the *Princeton Alumni Weekly* to launch his attack in March 1940.[37] Reminding his fellow alumni of Princeton's motto, "For the nation's service," and of the struggle against fascism, he accused the school of maintaining "a racial intolerance almost worthy of Hitler and wholly alien to any idea of a university or even a college in a democracy." "Harvard, Yale, Columbia, Chicago, indeed all leading American colleges and universities except Princeton," he noted tartly, enrolled African Americans. Princeton's continued policy of exclusion, he concluded, is "relevant to deep-seated social prejudice, but not to a democracy, to a social club, perhaps, but not to a university."[38]

Despite some vocal support from alumni, Thomas's broadside had no immediate effect. While Thomas worried about the struggle of the democracies against fascism, the men who ran Princeton remained preoccupied with maintaining its traditional character. Just months after Thomas's letter appeared, Heermance reported his vision of the freshman class to President Dodd: it was to be 90 percent "clubbable."[39] Heermance was apparently not alone in his commitment to the old Princeton, for in 1941 a panel of deans stated that they did not want Princeton to become a university only for "high stand men" (students who would perform well academically).[40] The traditional Princeton would not, it was clear, change without pressure.

Though the student body was roughly 85 percent Republican, it was a handful of liberal students who demanded change.[41] In the fall of 1942, with the United States officially at war with Nazi Germany, the *Daily Princetonian* launched a sustained attack on "White Supremacy at Princeton." Denouncing its policy as perpetuating a "racial theory more characteristic of our enemies than of an American university," a front-page editorial acidly observed that "Princeton is in the anomalous position of maintaining racial supremacy and at the same time declaring itself on behalf of democracy when actually the two are in no way compatible." In the context of the war, only the admission of blacks, they argued, was consistent with "the conviction long held by Princeton men that Princeton means leadership as well as scholarship." Should the university refuse to abolish its policy of racial exclusion, the only appropriate course of action, the paper suggested, would be to acknowledge that it has "no further justification for its existence than to serve as a finishing school for boys of the 'nicer type.'"[42]

Within days, the question "Should Negroes Be Admitted to Princeton?" was debated in front of the student body under the auspices of the Whig-Cliosophic Society. Representing the affirmative were Francis L. Broderick '43, chairman of the *Daily Princetonian,* and Powell Whitehead Jr. '43, editorial co-chairman; representing the negative side were Lemuel C. Hutchins '43, president of the Princeton Senate, and Wallace J. Williamson III '43.[43] Broderick and Whitehead based their argument on principle, contending that discrimination was contrary to democratic values, that Princeton could not realize its avowed goal as a national university training men to be leaders in a democracy without admitting students from all racial groups, and that it needed, once and for all, to recognize the fundamental equality of mankind. Hutchins and Williamson rested their arguments on practical grounds. Were Princeton to admit black students, it would, they claimed, be making promises it could not fulfill because "more than 50 percent of the advantages of Princeton are secured outside the classroom, and Negroes would inevitably be excluded from these activities." The particular educational problems of African Americans, they argued, would best be solved by building more and better institutions of higher education for blacks.[44]

While Hutchins and Williamson claimed that a concern for the well-be-

ing of blacks was the source of their opposition to admitting them to Princeton, a number of letters to the *Daily Princetonian* revealed that some of the
opponents of integration had less elevated motives. According to Joseph D.
Bennett '43, who described himself as a proponent of conservatism, limited
government, and aristocracy and/or constitutional monarchy, "the admission
of Negroes to the suffrage, or to white universities" would be "further to de-
grade the body of electors to the level of the Negro . . . The Negroes are not
improved by their admission to a group with relatively high standards, but
the group is corrupted to the lower level of the new members."[45] Two days
later, four freshmen published a letter noting that Princeton had long had "a
policy of excluding Negroes from its campus" and that these policies "were
endorsed as regards Negroes, by its leaders, including Woodrow Wilson."
"Ever since slavery," they said, "the Negro has lacked initiative"; otherwise,
"there would be no problem today, for the Negro would have risen as the
American has risen." Calling upon the *Daily Princetonian* to reconsider its
position "before further arousing the student body," the freshmen made their
own position clear: "as for us, we hope the day will never come when Negroes, as they now exist and live, will wave their hats with our sons 'in praise
of old Nassau.'"[46]

Such sentiments were by no means uncommon among the undergraduates. A 1942 survey of student opinion conducted by the *Nassau Sovereign* revealed that 62 percent opposed the admission of African Americans.[47] And
even among the 38 percent who believed that blacks should be admitted,
more than a third also favored limits on them once they enrolled, including
dormitory segregation, exclusion from the eating clubs, the imposition of
higher standards than those used for whites, and definite quotas.

The students who favored exclusion offered a number of justifications:
blacks would not be happy at Princeton; there are plenty of good colleges that
would welcome them; private colleges are not obligated to admit all academically eligible students; and students would not like their "sisters and dates" to
be forced to associate with blacks. Interestingly, Princeton's southerners —
who at this point were only 10 percent of the undergraduates, with more than
two-thirds coming from the Baltimore and Washington region rather than
the Deep South[48] — were slightly more liberal than the northerners, supporting the admission of blacks at a rate of 40 percent (compared to 37 percent for
northerners) and attaching conditions only 25 percent of the time (compared
to 39 percent for northerners).[49]

Clearly, the student body was deeply divided on the matter, but the proponents of integration continued to press the issue. Their strategy was to ask
the Undergraduate Council to "take definite action on the Negro issue." But
the council was no less divided than the student body as a whole, and on Oc-

tober 21, 1942, a resolution calling for the immediate admission of African Americans was rejected, 7–6. Though a second resolution calling for the admission of "qualified Negro students" to the Graduate School did pass at the same meeting (also 7–6), the opponents of discrimination had failed in their effort to have the Undergraduate Council officially declare its opposition to Princeton's policy of racial exclusion at the undergraduate level.[50]

Chastened but undeterred, the *Daily Princetonian* appealed to the Board of Trustees. In an editorial, "A Time for Greatness," the newspaper called on the trustees "to decide whether this University shall prolong a policy of racial discrimination against which every democratic principle is unalterably opposed." Citing its own poll of faculty, showing that 79 favored the admittance of blacks and 24 were opposed, it asked the trustees to make "a real decision."[51] A decision to make "no statement," the editorial warned, "must be placed alongside actual opposition to the admission of Negroes, a vote for Princeton's determination to maintain its practice of white supremacy."[52]

But the trustees, after hearing a report from President Dodds, were apparently not in the mood for greatness and took no action.[53] Despite a concerted and impassioned assault by student activists, Princeton's policy, unique among the nation's leading universities, remained in place.

Princeton Enters the Postwar World

World War II and its aftermath brought many changes to Princeton, not least among them the introduction of a small number of blacks into the student body. What student activists had been unable to accomplish was imposed by the federal government, which in 1945 sent four African Americans to Princeton as part of the navy's V-12 program for training officers. Though three of the four students failed to become members of the eating clubs that continued to dominate campus life, they seem to have been reasonably well received. One of them, Arthur J. Wilson'48, became captain of the basketball team in 1945–1946, going on to receive a bachelor's degree in 1948.[54]

The arrival of the V-12 students did not, however, foreshadow a progressive increase in the number of blacks at Princeton. As conditions returned to normal after the war, few black students applied to Princeton and even fewer were admitted. Indeed, in the seven classes that entered between 1946 and 1952, the total number of black students who entered may not have exceeded four. In 1953, when Harvard and Yale routinely enrolled several African Americans, not a single black student matriculated at Princeton. Though Princeton was officially open to "qualified Negroes," there were no blacks among the freshmen entering in 1954 and 1955.[55]

In other ways, however, postwar Princeton was quite a different institution from its prewar counterpart. The underlying source of change was the sheer increase in the number of applicants, many but by no means all of them veterans. For the first time, Princeton had a clear surplus of highly qualified applicants. As late as 1941, virtually every applicant who was white, gentile, and able to pay his own way was admitted. But by 1946, with many more talented applicants than the school could possibly accommodate, the old policy of almost automatic admission for candidates with a good social background was simply no longer viable.[56]

Yet it would be misleading to see Princeton as simply responding to an unprecedented crush of applicants, for the growth in the pool — especially after the veterans' surge in 1946 and 1947 had run its course — was in no small part the product of a conscious decision to increase the number of candidates from the nation's public schools. The vehicle for implementing the new policy was again the far-flung network of Alumni Schools Committees, which were reorganized in 1946. In 1947, Dodds asked the alumni "to tell us about the boys we cannot miss, for we will be guided more than ever before by your recommendations," and they seem to have honored his request.[57]

By the summer of 1947, 50 alumni associations had formed Schools and Scholarships Committees involving 400 alumni to assist in recruiting and interviewing candidates — the great majority of them from public schools — for admission to Princeton. By 1948, the number of Schools and Scholarships Committees had grown to 70, and by 1955, nearly 100 committees involving over 800 alumni interviewed more than 2,500 applicants.[58]

According to Charles W. Edwards '36, who joined the Committee on Admissions in 1946 and succeeded Heermance as director in 1950, the Alumni Schools Committees were more responsible than any other factor for the growth in the number of applications to Princeton and for their increasing geographical diversity.[59] Given Princeton's history as the Ivy League school most dominated by prep school graduates (between 1927 and 1946, Lawrenceville alone sent 1,186 students), the transformation of the student body in the decade after World War II was nothing short of remarkable.[60] Public school students, who made up only 17 percent of all entrants between 1928 and 1937 and just 25 percent between 1938 and 1947, rose to 39 percent of all Princeton freshmen by 1950.[61] By 1955, they made up half of all freshmen, making Princeton far more open to public school students than Yale, which drew over 60 percent of its students from private schools that year.[62]

Though the alumni interviewers were a conservative lot, their participation in an admissions process designed to bring new talent to Princeton gave them a vested interest in seeing that the boys they judged to be most promising — many of whom were from backgrounds quite different from their own — would gain admission. Since almost all of them were from public schools, the Schools and Scholarship Committee was brilliantly designed to deploy the labors of loyalists from the old Princeton to create a new and more inclusive Princeton. Generally considered — not without justification — to be a powerful source of reaction, the alumni of Old Nassau became, almost despite themselves, a force for real (if gradual) progress in making Princeton less insular.

When Princeton turned, in the period immediately before and after World War II, to its alumni for assistance in increasing its endowment and in selecting its students, it did so in part to keep from falling behind its chief rivals. Though in competition for many of the same students, Princeton had fewer financial resources at its disposal than Harvard and Yale, which in 1946 ranked number one and number two nationally in total endowment ($160 million and $108 million, respectively). In contrast, Princeton ranked twelfth, with a relatively paltry endowment of $34.9 million — a gap that was explained partly, but by no means wholly, by its smaller size. Also ranking ahead of Princeton in endowment were not only such renowned universities as Chicago and Columbia, but also schools of markedly lower status, such as the University of Rochester, the University of Texas, and Duke. Perhaps even worse from Princeton's perspective, several small liberal arts colleges with which it competed directly — notably Amherst and Williams — possessed a larger endowment per student.[63]

In looking to its alumni for help, Princeton was turning to a group distinguished not only by its exceptional loyalty but also by a level of conservatism unusual even in the old Ivy League. Overwhelmingly Republican, the alumni body was largely composed of upper- and upper-middle-class Protestants — more than a third of them Episcopalian — who had attended private secondary schools and belonged to private eating clubs at Princeton.[64] On the face of it, they did not seem a promising group to help raise the academic level of the student body and make it more national.

In truth, the emphasis on such qualities as "character" and "personality" gave both alumni and staff interviewers wide latitude to exclude applicants considered socially undesirable and to give a boost to those with whom they felt some cultural affinity. Every candidate was rated both academically and personally ("grades I through V"). Writing in 1946, Heermance reported proudly that "*there has been no significant change in admissions policy for 20 years.*"[65]

As before the war, a bad personal rating could ruin a candidate's chance for admission. In 1948, only 8 freshmen had a rating of IV on "character and personality," and not one had a rating of V.[66] In 1950, only a single freshman out of 768 freshmen had a personal rating below III, and once again none had a rating of V. That year, Princeton for the first time reported separate personal ratings for public and private school graduates; surprisingly, though most of the men who assigned these subjective ratings were themselves alumni of prep schools, public school graduates received a slightly higher mean rating on "character and personality" than private school graduates.[67]

The enormous discretion of the Committee on Admissions was used to craft a student body that, while more diverse in terms of secondary school and geographical origin than before the war, continued to embody the type of sturdy, all-around boy long identified with Princeton.[68] Of the 754 freshmen in 1953, almost a fourth (182) had been members of the football team, and more than one in seven (115) had been president of his school or class.[69] Though the class was also strong academically, with 88 valedictorians, there was still plenty of room for students who had not distinguished themselves academically, especially if they were deemed to have desirable personal or social qualities. Most of these students seem to have come from private schools; whereas 96 percent of public school graduates ranked in the top quarter of their class, only 68 percent of prep school graduates had the same standing. And for the freshman class as a whole, more than half (52 percent) scored under 600 on the verbal section of the SAT.[70]

Heavily overrepresented among that considerable segment of the student body admitted for primarily nonacademic reasons were the sons of alumni. Indeed, the foundation of the implicit bargain forged between the alumni and the administration was a recognition that if the alumni were to give both their wealth and their labor to assist Princeton in recruiting a more diverse and academically accomplished student body, Princeton would have to give them something in return. While the Dodds administration was careful to cultivate in the alumni a feeling of participation in the formation of admissions policy and in the admissions process itself, its most valuable resource by far was its control over the fate of legacy applicants. Immediately after the war, in a speech to the class agents of the Princeton University Fund, Heermance explained just how strong a preference Princeton gave alumni sons: in 1946, the most competitive year in Princeton's history, 82 percent of all alumni sons were admitted and constituted 26 percent of civilian admits. The contrast with the legions of veterans who applied that year was striking; of the 15,000 to 17,000 men who applied or inquired, 2,000 were judged to have met Princeton's criteria, but only 750 — under 38 percent — were offered admission.[71]

Princeton's policy toward legacies dated back to the 1920s, and it continued virtually unchanged for more than a decade after World War II. Dodds had been forthright in acknowledging the policy of preference for alumni sons: "We had always recognized that young men with a sound Princeton heritage have a certain claim on us."[72] Given that Princeton's plan for securing its economic future rested heavily on its alumni and especially on its Annual Giving Program, its policy of vigorous affirmative action for legacies was a logical expression of fundamental institutional interests.

While candid in admitting that alumni sons would be given an edge in the admissions process, Princeton was understandably reluctant to publicize its true policy: all legacies judged capable of doing the required work would be admitted (presuming, of course, that they were of sound "character"). Instead, the standard public description was that "*other factors being equal, the Princeton son gets the preference.*"[73] In fact, legacy applicants were frequently admitted over far stronger candidates who lacked a Princeton affiliation. As late as 1958, in a brochure distributed to the alumni, Princeton described its policy bluntly: "Actually, the Princeton son does not have to compete against non-Princeton sons. *No matter how many other boys apply, the Princeton son is judged on this one question: can he be expected to graduate?* If so, he's admitted."[74] As proof that its policy was "as lenient as possible," Princeton went so far as to report the lagging academic performance of legacies once enrolled; half of the bottom quarter of the freshman class, it reported, was composed of alumni sons, and five of the nine freshmen who failed at midyear were legacies.[75]

In order to make sure that alumni sons did not get lost in the rising tide of applicants, familial connections were clearly indicated on the summary card used by the Committee on Admissions in evaluating each candidate. Should a legacy candidate be provisionally rejected, his application would be "put in a special pile and given a second thorough examination to make sure the reasons for rejection are good."[76] The result was an acceptance rate for legacies more than twice as high as that for other applicants. In 1947, for example, 75 percent of legacies were accepted compared to only 30 percent of the entire pool of 2,500 applicants.[77] Had alumni sons been accepted at the same rate as other candidates, their numbers among those admitted would have been reduced from 209 to 83.

From 1948 through 1953, the acceptance rate for legacies was at least double that of other applicants, and in most years the gap was even greater. On average, students with fathers who had attended Princeton constituted over 18 percent of the freshman class between 1948 and 1953.[78] Each year, the *Freshman Herald* — which for many years included statistics on students' religious background, father's occupation, and the specific colleges attended by both parents[79] — contributed to Princeton's singular aura as the Ivy League college that most resembled a self-perpetuating private club. But the truth of the matter was that Princeton's policy of applying radically lower standards toward legacies was shared by its supposedly more meritocratic rivals, Harvard and Yale. Harvard, its eloquent public rhetoric of meritocracy notwithstanding, gave even greater preference to alumni sons under Conant than Princeton under Dodds. In 1952, Harvard admitted 87 percent of its legacies; at Princeton that year, the rate was just over 70 percent.[80] Though no comparable figures at Yale are available, the percentage of freshmen who were alumni sons was even higher than at Princeton, averaging 22 percent for the classes entering between 1948 and 1953.[81]

Tension with the Prep Schools

Princeton's admissions policy, like Harvard's and Yale's, had long given preference to the graduates of the leading boarding schools. Yet it was also the policy of Princeton under Dodds "to encourage and increase the entrance of high school graduates."[82] This policy began in the 1930s with the introduction of the admission without examination program, and over time it transformed the school's character. Composed of three-fourths private school boys as late as 1942, Princeton increased the proportion of public school graduates to 28 percent in 1946, 35 percent in 1949, and 44 percent in 1952.[83] The preppiest of the Big Three before World War II, Princeton by 1952 enrolled a higher percentage of public school boys than Yale (41 percent) and almost as many as Harvard (48 percent).[84]

According to a frank discussion in the annual Report to the President by the Committee on Admissions, there were repercussions. In 1951, Charles William Edwards, the new director of admission, complained that things had "reached a point where many of our rejections cause bitterness and misunderstanding," with such sentiments "most apparent this past year with the independent schools." "Over and over again," he reported, "schools felt that we must be prejudiced because we did not admit more of their particular candidates."[85]

In 1953, he addressed the increasingly negative feelings of the boarding schools with unusual candor: "It is my belief that perhaps involuntarily we still 'favor' certain schools such as Andover, Exeter, and Lawrenceville and Deerfield, and yet these schools and others feel that Princeton is the most difficult college for their graduates to enter."[86] From the available evidence, it seems that both parts of Edward's statement were true: Princeton did continue to favor prep school applicants at the same time that they sometimes found it harder in some ways to gain admission there than at Harvard and Yale. Certainly, Princeton showed no lack of concern about maintaining good relations with the private schools. "The feeling in many boarding schools that Princeton is 'the hardest college to get into,'" wrote Edwards, "is something that should be carefully considered." Noting that Princeton had cut the delegations from the prep schools, Edwards mused, "Perhaps it is time to reconsider our policy."[87]

Part of the problem was Princeton's size. Though Yale and Princeton had roughly the same number of applicants, Yale was able to accept 500 candidates more than Princeton's 1,145. Harvard was even larger, admitting 1,805 students in 1951 — over 60 percent more than Princeton. Nevertheless, as Edwards noted, "It is hard for a school to understand an admission by Harvard or Yale and a rejection by Princeton."[88]

Striving to maintain its strong ties with the private schools, Princeton continued to admit their candidates at a higher rate than the candidates from public schools. In 1955, the first year that the annual report of the Committee on Admissions provided statistics on candidates from the two types of schools, 51 percent of applicants from private schools were admitted compared to only 38 percent from public schools.[89] Worried nonetheless, Princeton used its alternate list "in many cases . . . to add the one boy about whose rejection a specific school felt badly." Such actions, Edwards noted with satisfaction, "helped immeasurably in our relationships with schools."[90]

Though the major boarding schools continued to send sizable delegations to Princeton in the early 1950s, they recognized that the pathway to Old Nassau had narrowed. As recently as 1940, twelve leading prep schools provided a third of the freshmen class but by 1952 they provided less than a fifth. The top feeders still sent large numbers to Princeton in 1952: 37 from Exeter, 30 from Lawrenceville, 20 from Andover, and 18 from Hill. But this was in every case a decline from 1940, when the numbers were, respectively, 44, 54, 23, and 25.[91] For feeder schools with less prestige, the decline was even more dramatic: Mercersberg, which had averaged 22 students a year between 1927 and 1946, dropped to 9 in 1952, and Gilman, which had averaged 17, fell to 8.[92]

The unrivaled citadel of prep school dominance before the war, Princeton in 1953 for the first time admitted more public school than private school graduates.[93] Though their students still received considerable preference, the boarding schools could no longer assume that Princeton belonged to them.

The "Hebrew" Question

The decline in the number of prep school graduates admitted to Princeton after the war was the product of a largely autonomous decision reached by its top administrators. The same cannot be said of the growth in Jewish enrollment. The growing presence of "Hebrews" — the term for Jews used by the *Freshman Herald* through 1949 — reflected the rise of powerful forces that mobilized against the anti-Semitism then taken for granted that had limited the proportion of Jews in the freshman class to no more than 3 percent before the war.[94]

Even the notoriously anti-Semitic Heermance was forced in the context of World War II and its aftermath to relax Princeton's long-standing Jewish quota. As at Harvard and Yale, the shortage of qualified applicants — especially men too young to be drafted — led to a marked increase in the percentage of "Hebrews" in the freshman class: from 2.6 percent in 1942 to 4.8 percent in 1943 to 8.1 percent in 1944. As normal conditions returned, Jewish enrollments once again dropped, though to levels a bit higher — 4.7 percent in 1946 and 3.1 percent in 1947 — than those before the war.[95]

By 1948, Princeton's admissions policy was under political and legal assault. Early that year, Carey McWilliams, a renowned writer who later became editor of *The Nation,* launched a sweeping assault on anti-Semitism in his book *A Mask of Privilege,* declaring flatly that "Princeton maintains a tight Jewish quota of less than 4 percent of its enrollment."[96] An indignant Dean Heermance categorically denied the charge. "Absolutely untrue," he told the *Daily Princetonian.* "We've never had a quota system, we don't have a quota system, we never will have a quota system."[97]

Had the offensive been confined to writing by intellectuals, it might well have had little effect. But it was joined by a political and legal assault whose goal was the passage of the Fair Educational Practices Act before the New Jersey legislature.[98] Like Harvard and Yale, Princeton opposed such a law, claiming that New Jersey colleges "are remarkably free from discriminatory practices." "Coercive legislation," it solemnly warned, is no substitute for "the voluntary action of the educational institutions themselves" and would constitute "an infringement of the freedom of the independent college."[99]

But the New Jersey legislature, under pressure from a wide range of civil rights organizations and well aware that New York's legislature had passed a similar law that spring, was undeterred and in 1949 passed the legislation.[100] Even before it passed, Princeton felt the growing political pressure and in 1948 admitted the largest percentage of Jews — 6.8 percent — in its peacetime history. By 1950, the question about religious affiliation, a fixture on Princeton's application since the 1920s, was finally deleted.[101]

The growing number of Jews posed problems for Princeton, where campus life had been premised on cultural homogeneity. In particular, the selective and exclusionary eating clubs, which even after the war remained the center of social life, constituted a crisis waiting to happen, for those students left out were relegated to a painfully visible second-class status. Though Jews were sometimes accepted by clubs, especially ones far below the top of Princeton's rigid hierarchy, they were far more likely to be considered "unclubbable" than their gentile peers.

Perhaps not coincidentally, the first class to mount a campaign to guarantee that 100 percent of students who wished to join an upper-class eating club would be offered admission to at least one of them against the clubs' anti-Semitic policy was the freshman class of 1948, which included the unprecedented number of 54 Jews. In November 1949, before the annual Princeton "bicker" (when sophomores were interviewed by the clubs in a scramble for a membership "bid" to the most prestigious one that would have them), 610 members (out of 795) of the class declared in a petition that they would boycott all of the clubs unless every classmate who wished to join received at least one bid. They argued that "we members of the sophomore class feel it necessary for us to demand that all men admitted to Princeton be accepted into the social system of the upper-class years as well as the academic life of the university."[102]

In the context of Princeton, the petition was considered a radical act, especially by the alumni still active in the clubs. Sensing a potential crisis, the Board of Trustees moved quickly, approving at its February 1950 meeting the creation of a university-subsidized eating club with open admission. Don Oberdorfer, a Jewish member of the class who became editor of the *Daily Princetonian,* years later described what happened next: "Nassau Hall, suddenly confronted with the prospect of economic as well as social crisis, suggested the creation of a subsidized nonselective club to take any sophomores left out by the selective bicker process. In a class meeting, we voted down this eighteenth club as a 'dumping ground' for leftovers, and affirmed our optimism that the existing clubs should and would accommodate us all."[103] The controversy aroused strong passions on all sides, and after an intense struggle involving the administration, the Graduate Inter-club Council, club members, and a steering committee of the sophomore class officers, the insurgent students triumphed. On March 9, 1950, the *Daily Princetonian* announced in a banner headline: "ALL SOPHS GET BIDS."[104]

The struggle for the "100 percent principle" revealed that the full incorporation of Jews into Princeton would not be easy, but that change was possible. Yet the 100 percent goal was never fully accepted by the eating clubs themselves, and eight years later, in the notorious "dirty bicker" of 1958, 23 students — 13 of them Jewish — found themselves without a single bid.[105] Anti-Semitism was hardly dead at the Big Three, but even Princeton could no longer afford to ignore the claims of Jews both on and off campus.

The Dodds and Conant Administrations Compared

When Harold Willis Dodds and James Bryant Conant took office in 1933, they were assuming the leadership of two very different institutions.[106] In many ways, Dodds and Conant themselves seemed to embody the differences in the ethos of the two institutions. Dodds was deeply religious; Conant paid lip service to a vaguely defined Protestantism but was by temperament a rationalist and a skeptic. Politically, Dodds was the far more conservative, using the occasion of a speech to the National Alumni Association to denounce "Big Government" and "the grave evils in policies of public spending and government aid."[107] Conant, in contrast, was a strong supporter of Franklin Roosevelt and expressed a certain sympathy for the "American radical."[108] But perhaps their most fundamental difference — one that corresponded to the much greater emphasis on graduate training and research at Harvard — was that Conant was a great scholar.

Conant's meritocratic public pronouncements powerfully reinforced Harvard's reputation as an institution open to talent, regardless of background. One would expect that Harvard's admissions policy would have moved much more rapidly against discrimination than Princeton's. Yet Princeton, which began with a far more exclusive policy, altered its admissions practices far more profoundly than did Harvard between 1933 and 1953. To be sure, Harvard remained more open and meritocratic than Princeton when Conant left office. But the gap between the two schools had narrowed greatly, and the unheralded Dodds had orchestrated changes that made Princeton a very different place from the one he had inherited.

One of Dodds's great accomplishments was to break the stranglehold that the prep schools had possessed over access to Princeton under his predecessor, John Grier Hibben. In 1930, 33 percent of Princeton's freshmen came from the dozen top prep schools; by 1950, it was 23 percent, and the absolute number had declined from 206 to 175.[109] At Conant's Harvard, stability rather than change was the rule: the same dozen schools supplied an identical 18 percent of freshmen in both 1930 and 1950, and the absolute number had actually increased, from 181 to 212[110] — hardly the figures one would expect from a college led by a man one observer described as harboring an "animus against the American elite of the mid-twentieth century."[111]

The strong preference that Harvard gave alumni sons is further evidence that Conant's rhetoric was more meritocratic than Harvard's practice. In 1951 and 1952, near the end of Conant's tenure, 532 legacies applied to Harvard College, and just 10 percent were rejected.[112] In the same period, Dodds's Princeton showed a far greater willingness to turn away alumni sons, rejecting slightly over 25 percent.[113]

In 1953, perhaps the most widely known difference between Princeton and Harvard was the former's far more exclusionary stance toward Jews. Long a bastion of anti-Semitism, Princeton limited the proportion of Jews in the early 1930s to less than 2 percent of the entering class.[114] Harvard, which under Lowell had moved rigorously to reduce Jewish enrollment from a peak of 25 percent in 1925, nevertheless continued to enroll a class that remained roughly 10 to 15 percent Jewish in the early 1930s, even after the restrictions adopted in the late 1920s had taken full effect.[115]

The proportion of Jews at Harvard rose to approximately 25 percent in 1952; this figure, though still short of the percentage reached a quarter of a century earlier, signified a major improvement in the fortunes of Jewish applicants under Conant.[116] Yet despite Harvard's relatively high percentage of Jews, anti-Semitic discrimination remained a central feature of Harvard's admission policy even in the last years of the Conant administration when applicants from academically selective urban high schools faced a combined rejection rate of 68 percent, compared to 36 percent for all applicants and a mere 15 percent for the overwhelmingly Protestant young men from the St. Grottlesex schools.[117]

Princeton under Dodds was even more anti-Semitic than Harvard. Yet given that Princeton attracted far fewer Jewish applicants, it seems to have moved more dramatically to reduce discrimination in admissions than Harvard under Conant. In both institutions, the pivotal event in weakening (through by no means eliminating) discriminatory practices was the mobilization against anti-Semitism after World War II and the ensuing passage of fair educational practices laws. But Princeton had much further to go than Harvard, and it changed more rapidly in the decade after the war.

By the late 1940s, 6–7 percent of Princeton's entering freshmen were Jewish — a low figure, but a historic high for Princeton.[118] After the passage of New Jersey's antidiscrimination legislation in 1949, forcing Princeton to stop asking about religious background on the application, data on the number of Jews in the freshman class became impossible to find. Nevertheless, there is strong evidence that barriers to Jews continued to fall in the 1950s, for by the spring of 1958, Princeton was about 14 percent Jewish.[119] This number was, of course, well below that of Harvard's, but there was no denying that the gap between the two had narrowed considerably. While the percentage of Jews at Harvard had been more than six times greater than at Princeton when the two men took office, it was only about two to one when Conant prepared to leave two decades latter.[120]

Yet on one fundamental issue the Dodds administration had done little to free Princeton from the burden of its history. Though three black students enrolled in the entering freshman class of 1949 in the wake of the passage of New Jersey's Fair Educational Practices Act, Princeton soon reverted to its old ways, enrolling few blacks in the early 1950s and none in the class entering in 1953.[121] Harvard, while hardly a model of racial diversity, was decidedly more open to African Americans, enrolling perhaps five or six blacks a year in the early 1950s.[122]

Princeton's continued exclusion of blacks in the 1950s was a great blot on Dodds's otherwise surprisingly progressive record. On the issue of scholarships, for example, Dodds was a democrat, arguing consistently that a geographically and economically diverse student body was in the interest of both Princeton and the nation. That he did not consider this mere rhetoric is confirmed by the fact that almost a third of the class that entered in 1952 received financial aid — a figure that slightly surpassed the proportion of freshman receiving aid that same year at Harvard, which was much better endowed.[123]

Academically, the two colleges were quite similar — a striking finding in light of Harvard's long-standing reputation as the far more intellectually serious institution. In truth, neither school's academic standards in the early 1950s were particularly high. In 1952, median SATs at Harvard were 583 verbal and 598 math, with the students in the tenth percentile of all freshmen scoring just 474 verbal and 469 math.[124] Princeton did not report statistics in the same format, but its SAT scores seem to have been comparable; in 1952, mean SATs at Princeton were 571 verbal and 619 math, with 15 percent of freshmen scoring under 500 on the verbal and 7 percent under 500 on the math.[125]

Though neither Harvard nor Princeton came close to approaching the meritocratic ideal that had been so brilliantly articulated in Conant's writings, both institutions had taken important steps toward greater equality of opportunity. Yet despite Conant's radical public rhetoric, it was Dodds's Princeton that had changed far more. Princeton, a patrician and anti-Semitic enclave of modest academic standards when Dodds took office, was transformed under his leadership into an increasingly diverse and open institution. By the time Conant left Harvard in January 1953, Princeton had become arguably more selective than both Harvard and Yale — no small accomplishment for an uncharismatic man whom the dean of Harvard College had dismissed as "a nice mediocrity."[126]

If Dodds's leadership contributed to Princeton's transformation, the striking convergence of the two schools that took place was in good part a product of powerful forces that affected both institutions: new legal and political constraints, a changed cultural and economic landscape, major demographic shifts that included the rapid expansion of the applicant pool, and dramatically increased competition among private colleges. Whatever their personal ideologies, the men who ran America's leading universities had little choice but to adapt to these changes.

CHAPTER 9

Wilbur Bender and His Legacy

I N THE ANNALS of the Big Three, there has never been a dean of admission more colorful — or more broadly influential — than Harvard's Wilbur J. Bender. Though he was chairman of the Committee on Admission for only eight years (1952–1960), he was the key figure in shaping Harvard's admissions during the decade and a half after World War II. According to a 1977 report on the composition of the student body written by Henry Rosovsky, dean of the faculty: "Harvard's transformation from a college of well-bred Easterners to a diverse national university owes a great deal to one president (Conant) and one dean (Bender)."[1] Bender's policy statements — which brilliantly articulated the viewpoint that admissions should be based on far more than academic performance and that intangible personal qualities should often be the deciding factor — still continue to exert a major impact at virtually all of the nation's selective private institutions.

By the time Bender was named to replace Richard Gummere, the longtime chairman of the Committee on Admission was sixty-eight years old — two years beyond the normal administration retirement age.[2] But beyond his age, Gummere was by background and temperament ill equipped to deal with the more democratic and competitive postwar atmosphere. As early as 1947, Paul Buck, the provost, wrote to President Conant, stating that "Gummere certainly is not entirely in tune with the direction along which Harvard is moving."[3] Though Buck did not cite details, elsewhere he bemoaned Gummere's unwillingness to visit schools outside New England at a time when Harvard was trying hard to become more of a national institution.[4] By the early 1950s, the world of admissions had become, as the *Harvard Alumni Bulletin* observed, "one of stiff competition for students among academic institutions," and the gentlemanly, aristocratic Gummere was not comfortable "selling" Harvard.[5] By the time he retired, Harvard's "yield" ratio (the ratio of matriculants to admits), which had usually been over 90 percent before the war, had dropped to 63 percent.[6]

Perhaps sensing that the Office of Admission would provide a wider canvas for his talents, Bender asked Buck for the opportunity to succeed Gummere.[7] He assumed the deanship at an especially propitious time, for the Conant administration was ending, and the new president, Nathan M. Pusey, would not be in place until the fall of 1953.[8] For a master administrator like Bender, this relative power vacuum provided extra space to lay down the foundations of a new order in admissions.

Bender never forgot that Harvard had opened its doors to a bright, energetic young man from the provinces and gave him critical financial aid. When as dean of admission he described "able, ambitious boys, usually scholarship boys and usually the only boys from their school" as Harvard's "most promising group," he may well have had in mind applicants not unlike his younger self.[9]

Intensely competitive and described by a friend as a "positively dangerous" squash partner, Bender was deeply devoted to his alma mater and committed to moving vigorously to improve its position vis-à-vis its chief rivals.[10] In order to realize this objective, he believed that nothing less than a full-scale review of Harvard's admission policy was required.

Bender's Vision

In September 1952, less than three months after taking office, Bender wrote just such a review. His vehicle was a confidential forty-three-page "Comprehensive Formal Statement of Harvard College Admission Policy," submitted for discussion at a dinner of the Committee on Admission and Scholarships and Financial Aids.[11] In this extraordinary document, by far the frankest and most revealing discussion about admissions in Harvard's history, Bender laid out the hidden logic behind the school's practices and the personal vision that would guide his term as dean.

The social and political context of Bender's "Comprehensive Formal Statement" in 1952 could hardly have been more different from that of Conant's classic 1940 essay, "Education for a Classless Society." American politics had turned sharply to the right in the intervening years, with Republicans retaking the White House that fall for the first time in two decades and gaining a majority in both Houses of Congress. Whereas Conant wrote during a period of union mobilization, pervasive leftist influence on both elite and popular culture, and deep concern about the threat of fascism, Bender wrote when unions were on the defensive, radical workers and intellectuals were commonly accused of subversion, and communism was widely viewed as a grave peril. The previous four years, in particular, had been deeply troubling. In 1948, Communist regimes were installed in Czechoslovakia and Hungary; in 1949, the Communists took power in China, and the Soviet Union successfully tested an atomic bomb; in 1950, Communist North Korea invaded South

Korea and was joined later that year by armies from Red China as American troops pushed north toward the Chinese border; in 1951, Julius and Ethel Rosenberg were found guilty of conspiring to transmit classified military documents about the atomic bomb to the Soviets.[12]

Stepping into the middle of this charged atmosphere was Senator Joseph McCarthy of Wisconsin. In a speech in Wheeling, West Virginia, he famously claimed to have in his hands "a list of 205 — a list of names that were made known to the Secretary of State as being members of the Communist Party who nevertheless are still working and shaping policy in the State Department."[13] Then, in a pointed attack on the eastern elite, he pointed to the primary source of subversion: "It is not the less fortunate, or members of minority groups who have been selling this nation out, but rather those who have had all the benefits the wealthiest nation on earth has to offer — the finest homes, the finest college educations, and the finest jobs in the government we can give. This is glaringly true in the State Department. There the bright young men who are born with silver spoons in their mouth are the ones who have been worse [sic]."[14] Harvard, noted a student of McCarthyism, "symbolized two groups which he [McCarthy] defined as un-American and corrupting of basic values, the cosmopolitan high-status internationalist eastern WASP elite and the intellectuals."[15] For McCarthy, the ultimate embodiment of the subversive aristocrat was Secretary of State Dean Acheson, a graduate of Groton, Yale, and Harvard whom he described as a "pompous diplomat, with his striped pants and his phony British accent."[16]

Bender was keenly aware of the accusations that Harvard was a hotbed of Communists, subversive intellectuals, homosexuals, and (heavily overlapping with the three aforementioned groups) Jews when he wrote his "Comprehensive Formal Statement." In drafting it, he adopted the posture of the sophisticated pragmatist: a man who, while not giving short shrift to ideals, accepted that Harvard was constrained by powerful external forces. A master of institutional *realpolitik,* Bender knew that the university, though often viewed as an ivory tower, was driven by *interests* as well as *values.*[17] "One could write a beautiful statement of admission policy which would be logical and high-principled within itself," he observed, "and have little relation to the complicated and illogical realities of Harvard and the college admissions picture generally."[18] Should an administration neglect its interests in the pursuit of worthy but unattainable ideals, great harm was likely to befall both the institution and the individuals responsible.

Bender posed the fundamental issue crisply: "What kind of student body do we want at Harvard and how do we get it?" The starting point would be "an analysis of the kinds of people who come to Harvard now and their reasons for coming." Using existing patterns of enrollment as a baseline, the admissions office could then "state the kind of realistically ideal student body we want to have and a program for getting from here to there."[19]

Realistic idealism is, of course, an oxymoron, and for Bender realism was to be the guiding principle. Writing when Harvard still accepted almost two-thirds of its applicants,[20] Bender saw grave danger in wandering too far from the traditional elite constituencies. Yet despite the obvious benefits to Harvard of enrolling the children of the upper class, Bender was decidedly am-bivalent about their place in Harvard College. Not one to mince words, he ad-mitted that Harvard's social elite "exercised a far stronger influence on the University, on the alumni, and perhaps on society than their numbers and in-dividual talents alone would justify." Moreover, it might turn out to be a de-clining social class: "Will current national, social and economic policies," Bender wondered, "gradually eliminate this group anyhow and thus solve our problem?"[21]

Despite these misgivings, Bender was unwilling to subject the social elite to the same standards as those for other applicants. What this meant in prac-tice was the perpetuation of Harvard's established policy of giving them strong preference and treating the leading prep schools with care. "Creation of hostility or bad relations with any of these schools," Bender warned, "could damage us seriously."[22]

Also still receiving preference were the sons of alumni. Harvard's policy limited its "freedom of choice"; by Bender's own estimate, preferential treat-ment was responsible for "forty or fifty sons of alumni admitted each year." In his view, this was a bit excessive; over time, he hoped that Harvard could "set [its] standards somewhat higher."[23] Yet it remained a permanent feature of institutional policy. Harvard, as Bender never tired of pointing out, was "op-erating in a real and complicated world" and could not afford the luxury of following "some beautiful blue-print."[24]

"Harvard," Bender wrote, was "*one of the few colleges with 'snob' appeal.*" Accordingly, it attracted the children of the "upper-upper" class throughout the country, but particularly students from the Northeast. Typically, these young men had graduated from a "'snob' school like Groton, St. Mark's, St. Paul's and Milton."[25] Constituting about "ten percent of the College, almost entirely paying guests,"[26] these young men provided the recruits for Harvard's prestigious final clubs. It was possible, Bender acknowledged, that "a third or half of this group, strictly on their merits in terms of SAT scores, character and personality, was not particularly desirable." But if Harvard rejected them, it "would lose most of the rest of the group, including a lot of able and desir-able students."[27]

Bender favored a policy that ensured the perpetuation of preference for the sons of the privileged. But he did so less as an expression of his values than a concession to political and material realities.[28] His favorite candidate was that public school boy, usually on scholarship, who was the sole student admitted from his high school and came to Harvard from a remote community. Such a boy, Bender believed, displays exceptional "independence" and "mettle" and "contribute[s] an unusual amount of leadership to the college."[29] Seeking these boys out was consistent with Harvard's well-established policy of favoring geographical diversity (lest "the percentage of boys from metropolitan centers . . . become undesirably large").[30] Bender also favored those students, regardless of background, with "outstanding qualities of character and personality," as exemplified by such traits as "integrity, responsibility . . . warmth, charm, independence, courage, initiative" and "capacity for leadership, force, vigor, solidity."[31]

Admitting that it was "probably pure prejudice," he confessed a preference for "the boy with some athletic interests and abilities, the boy with physical vigor and coordination and grace." So that Harvard could compete with its rivals, Bender favored giving athletic ability "considerable weight in both recruiting and selection."[32]

Bender's soft spot for athletes was more than personal preference. The "well-publicized football defeats of recent years," he believed, contributed to Harvard's reputation as a school with "no college spirit, few good fellows and no vigorous, healthy social life" and a surfeit of "pansies," "decadent esthetes," and "precious sophisticates." Nothing would do more to counteract this terrible image than a more visible presence of athletes on campus and more victories on the field, especially in "the great American game of football."[33]

Few things could do more to improve Harvard's position than a successful intercollegiate athletic program. "Yale or Dartmouth," he wrote, "may have to make a special effort to balance their collegiatism, their cheerful extroverts and careerists and Nordic blondes with intellectualism." But Harvard's problem was "to keep intellectualism in balance" lest it lost its "appeal for the normal American boy."[34]

From Bender's vantage point, Harvard's strongest appeal was for "the studious, the intellectual, the esthete," and this was more of a problem than an opportunity. Harvard's vital interests were endangered by the image that "the only person who belongs at Harvard is the valedictorian, the obvious intellectual, the white-faced grind."[35] Though he favored cautiously increasing the number of "brilliant students," Bender warned that such a move could "easily boomerang and damage the overall quality of the student body." Even the National Scholarship Program may have been counterproductive: "by emphasizing our concern for top students, it gave the impression that all we wanted was this kind of person and scared off other highly desirable students."[36]

The underlying difference between "desirable students" and the "top brains" was that the latter would become "scholars, scientists, teachers," while the former were destined to hold major levers of political and economic power in American society. Bender put the issue bluntly: "If we go too far out in left field, we lose our capacity to influence and contribute to American life." In the end, enrolling too many intellectuals would make Harvard "too isolated from America."[37]

Not far beneath the surface of Bender's anxiety was the gnawing worry that an admissions policy tilted heavily toward academic performance would result in too many Jews. This anxiety was sometimes expressed in a coded fashion: Harvard might be overrun with "the too early sophisticated metropolitan type," the "neurotic at odds with his community."[38] Elsewhere, though, Bender is explicit: Harvard has a strong appeal for "intellectual, musical or esthetic individuals . . . coming largely from metropolitan centers" and "there is a high percentage of Jewish boys in this group."[39] While this group included a considerable number of "our most interesting and potentially significant students," it also contained "some of our most unattractive and undesirable ones, the effeminates, the precious and affected, the unstable."[40]

"It is also alleged," Bender reported, "that we are dominated by Jews, that we are Godless, that we have a high percentage of mental breakdowns and suicides, that in general we are an unhealthy, overly and sterilely intellectualized place out of touch and out of sympathy with the main healthy currents of American life." "The charges may not be true," he wrote, "but again they may." Whatever the reality, such perceptions posed a serious threat to Harvard, for they could cause "students from upper-income, business backgrounds" to abandon Harvard for "colleges like Yale, Princeton, Dartmouth, Williams, etc."[41]

The threat of excessive intellectualism was also intertwined with the image of Harvard as a haven for "pansies" and "communists." Homosexuals, in particular, had long been a preoccupation of Bender's; as far back as 1947, he had worried about Harvard's reputation as a college full of "pansies and poets and serious la-de-da types" as opposed to "virile, masculine, red-blooded hemen."[42] In the minds of Harvard's many critics, "communism," "homosexuality," "intellectualism," and "neuroticism" constituted an interrelated syndrome that cut Harvard off from mainstream America. It was no wonder, then, that Bender wished to improve Harvard's techniques for evaluating "intangibles" and, in particular, its "ability to detect homosexual tendencies and serious psychiatric problems."[43]

The concrete embodiment of what could happen to Harvard if it went too far down the wrong path was the University of Chicago, which had a particularly strong appeal for "the hot-house intellectual" and "the glib verbal-

254   The Struggle over Meritocracy, 1933–1965

ists."[44] Though Chicago was arguably Harvard's chief rival as America's leading research university, Bender did not even list it among Harvard's rivals for
the most desirable students.[45] By creating a campus tilted toward excessive intellectualism, Chicago had violated Harvard's cardinal principal of "balance."
Consequently, Chicago appealed neither to the children of the social elite nor
to the overlapping (but not identical) group of young men destined to run
America's major institutions.[46]

Chicago's disastrous public image of hothouse intellectualism, Bender
believed, was in no small part a product of its decision to abandon intercollegiate athletics.[47] Harvard could not afford to make the same mistake. Precisely
because of its reputation, Harvard needed not only to retain intercollegiate
athletics but to start winning.[48]

Nevertheless, Bender's vision of Harvard was at the same time more open
to "top brains" and more socially inclusive than that of his predecessor.
Though no one was more aware of the dangers of excess intellectualism than
Bender, in the end he favored raising the academic level of the student body
and insisted that all applicants, regardless of even "their athletic ability or
their potential financial contributions," meet Harvard's "minimum standards
of eligibility for admission." Like Conant, he ultimately came down on the
side of increasing the proportion of "brilliant students" ("the boys who are
going to be the scholars and scientists and top lawyers"), though only from 5
to 10 percent.[49] Still — and this is crucial to understanding admissions at Harvard both before Bender and after, 90 percent of the students were to be selected on other grounds.

Conant, who wrote comments in the margins of Bender's report, did not
agree on every particular. Where Bender wrote, for example, "we can in good
conscience choose the athlete" when considering "two candidates approximately equal on most grounds," Conant jotted down: "too strong."[50] And
when Bender, arguing on behalf of the proposition that the National Scholarships, "by emphasizing our concern for top students . . . gave the impression
that all we wanted was this kind of person and scared off many other highly
desirable applicants," stated that "Mr. Conant now tends to accept this view,"
Conant's response was a simple: 'I don't!'"[51]

Yet Conant had not erred in appointing Bender as the guardian of his legacy in admissions, for on fundamental matters the two men were in firm
agreement. Both had a realist view of admissions, and both felt that Harvard's historic closeness to the Protestant upper class was one of its greatest strengths and was in Harvard's vital interest as well. They agreed, moreover, on the decidedly unmeritocratic policy that followed from this decision
to maintain close ties with upper-crust families: restrictions, albeit weaker,
would still be imposed on groups whose presence on campus might deter

the most "desirable" students. At the same time, Bender, like Conant, was a cautious reformer who genuinely wished to make Harvard's student body more national, more socially inclusive, and more academically adept.

The Early Years

One of Bender's first moves was to consolidate power via bureaucratic reform. Unlike Gummere, who served as chairman only of the Committee on Admission, Bender arranged to put himself in charge of financial aid under the title of dean of admissions and financial aids. In his first annual Report to the President, Bender noted, "Before 1952, admissions, Freshman Scholarships, and employments, loans, and scholarships for upperclassmen were handled by various offices working more or less independently of each other."[52] Now, all of these functions has been consolidated in a single office.

In the more complex and competitive environment of higher education in the 1950s, admissions could no longer, Bender realized, be a "one-man operation."[53] He was fully committed to building an admissions office that was both more professional and more bureaucratic, thereby accelerating the process of rationalization of the admissions process that had begun under Conant.[54] The realization of any coherent plan, he believed, would require a "real team of all those working on admissions and financial aid, with no unnecessary jurisdictional barriers, as little overlapping and duplicating as possible and no situations where the right hand doesn't know what the left hand is doing."[55] Bender moved quickly to bring in a first-rate staff consisting of men who "were not slaves to past practices," including Richard G. King, who had been director of the Office of Tests, and a promising young graduate student in economics and former Harvard National Scholar, Fred Glimp '50 (who would later succeed him).[56]

Having consolidated his power base, Bender set about trying to establish more control over the alumni's Schools and Scholarships Committee, which had taken on an increasingly important role after the war.[57] The alumni were both a resource and a problem — Harvard needed them to recruit and interview candidates, especially in distant regions, but some of them believed that they should have the final say over candidates from their territory. Since Harvard depended on the alumni for scholarship support, which included Harvard Club scholarships targeted to local students, the issue was delicate.

Bender proposed to handle the problem by clarifying the relationship between the local committees and the main office in Cambridge. The Committee on Admission would continue to use alumni representatives in recruiting and screening applicants, but it would see that the "right men" were involved and communicate with them regularly.[58]

The chief vehicles for what Bender called "the indoctrination of the alumni representatives" were a "new handbook spelling out our policies as simply and clearly as possible," a "regular newsletter going out to all Schools and Scholarship Committee members as well as individual representatives several times a year," and "regular meetings in Cambridge and possibly regional meetings."[59] The revised *Schools and Scholarship Committee Handbook* became a kind of bible for alumni workers. A tightly written 56-page document, it left ample space for judgment but little room for confusion.

The *Handbook* sent a clear message that any applicants, including even the most brilliant ones, were to be rejected if there was evidence of "serious weakness of character" or "serious personality problems." However, Harvard did want to increase the number of truly outstanding students "who graduate Magna or Summa Cum Laude and who are likely to become scholars, scientists, or top professional men." Since "some very promising boys are very queer-looking ducks indeed at seventeen," interviewers should be careful not to confuse "mere shyness or surface immaturity" with "instability." "And the greater the talent," the *Handbook* stated, "the more willing we are to take chances on apparent personal idiosyncrasies."[60]

The vast majority of applicants, however, would not be given such latitude. For them, "other factors are of considerably greater importance than academic factors," including "Harvard parentage," "geographic distribution," "outstanding qualities of character," and "unusual attractiveness of personality." The *Handbook* made clear the committee's preferences: "We don't believe that the academic difference between a 'C plus' and a 'C minus' student at Harvard is as significant as other kinds of difference."[61]

The allocation of scholarships would place a similar degree of emphasis on nonacademic qualities. Since scholarships were in short supply (only about one freshman in four would be eligible), both the academic and the nonacademic qualifications for them would be "considerably higher than for admission." The more Harvard wanted the student, the bigger the scholarship. For those fortunate enough to be awarded scholarships, renewal was by no means automatic: in deciding which recipients to drop, Harvard asked for reports not only from instructors and advisers but also from coaches, House staffs, employers, and others. Even a strong academic performance did not guarantee renewal: "a high-ranking student may be denied aid," the *Handbook* noted, "and a Group IV student [1½ Bs and 2½ Cs or better] given large aid on the basis of judgments about his non-academic personal qualities."[62]

Since Harvard's basic admissions problem was one of image, the solution required better "public relations."[63] A conscious effort to improve this image had already begun in 1951, as Bender was completing his term as dean of the college, with the release of the film *Invitation to Harvard,* which was carefully crafted to counter the perception of Harvard as overly intellectual. Opening with shots of Harvard Yard and the Charles River, the film moves on quickly to the football team, complete with several minutes of play ("On a crisp fall afternoon, you'll sense a new excitement in the air").[64] The viewer is then treated to shots of basketball, diving, swimming, wrestling, fencing, squash, baseball, crew, tennis, and track and field.

Extracurricular life at Harvard involved more than just sports, the film points out; it included the *Lampoon* (the humor magazine), the *Advocate* (the literary magazine), and the *Crimson* (the student newspaper). The film then moves on to the important question of social life, noting Harvard's proximity to "two excellent women's colleges — Wellesley and Radcliffe," one of its clear advantages over Yale and Princeton. Only after some shots of the elegant life at Harvard's residential Houses does the issue of academics appear, and then only for a few minutes. Then it is back to a more detailed portrait of life in the Houses: "Social life, carried on with gayety and moderation, makes the Harvard House a happy place to live, and the background for a balanced program of work and recreation."[65]

The revised Rollo Book of 1952, sent out to all candidates for admission, reinforced the image of balanced student life conveyed visually by *Invitation to Harvard*. Harvard, the information bulletin boasted, "has one of the finest college athletic plants in the country," an extensive intramural sports program in which "the goal is athletics for all," and a "rich variety of extra-curricular organizations and activities which provide opportunity for recreation and the expression and development of special talents."[66] Harvard was not, the Rollo Book insisted, "a rich-man's college": "More than half of the students earn a significant part of their college expenses and about thirty per cent receive financial aid from the College in the form of scholarships, beneficiary aid, or loans."[67] Contrary to another widespread stereotype, the student sought by Harvard was "not necessarily brilliant." Though "superior academic ability" was an important factor, "other factors weigh heavily in the selection: character, maturity, motivation, capacity for leadership, and geographic distribution."[68]

Despite the shift in rhetoric, change in Harvard's actual practices came only gradually. Nevertheless, Bender's accession to the chairmanship of the Committee on Admission and on Scholarships and Financial Aids did produce some identifiable shifts in the character of the student body. In his first year in office, Bender raised incoming freshman median scores on the SAT from 583 to 609 on the verbal section and 598 to 625 on the mathematical section.[69] At the same time, the percentage of entering freshmen from private schools declined from 52 percent in 1952 to 47 percent in 1953.[70] This was the first time in Harvard's peacetime history that public school graduates outnumbered private school graduates. Yet after this initial movement toward greater academic meritocracy, progress slowed and in some cases even went into reverse. Though SAT scores continued to inch upward, there were worrisome signs of retreat from that part of Bender's vision that called for "a Harvard College democratically open to talent wherever found."[71] In a frank discussion of the class that entered in 1954, Bender acknowledged that limited funds had forced Harvard to reduce the percentage of scholarship holders from 32 percent in 1953 to 28 percent. Overall, it was his impression that "this year we lost to other colleges a larger than normal proportion of our best all-round candidates, both scholarship winners and paying customers."[72]

Between 1953 and 1957, the proportion of freshmen from private schools rose from 47 to 50 percent.[73] The admissions figures from the top boarding schools show a consistent pattern of strong preferential treatment. In 1955, when 52 percent of all applicants were rejected, 70 percent from a dozen leading prep schools were admitted. For the six St. Grottlesex schools, the figure was 74 percent. And for Exeter and Andover, which formed a category or "docket" of their own, the figure was a remarkable 79 percent.[74]

Financial considerations were a factor in Harvard's continued special treatment of graduates of the top boarding schools, but so too were social and cultural ones. In a speech to Harvard's Board of Overseers on March 8, 1954, Bender expressed his concern that prep school students had dropped below 50 percent of the freshman class. If they dropped down to a third or a quarter, he wondered, "would Harvard lose its social prestige entirely then and more and most of the remainder of our gentlemen go to Yale, Princeton, Williams, and so on?" Such a shift "would mark the end of the Clubs, the end of the non specialists, and the man of action."[75]

One way of avoiding such an eventuality, of course, was to give continued preference to the elite boarding schools, and this remained systematic policy through Bender's years in office. But admitting these students would not get them to come unless Harvard's social atmosphere remained comfortable. Perhaps for this reason, or perhaps simply because Bender did not like the social and personality type generated by the great urban high schools of the Northeast, Harvard continued to impose stringent standards on applicants from New York's Bronx High School of Science and Stuyvesant and Central High School of Philadelphia, admitting only 18 percent in 1955.[76]

Part of the lower admission rate for heavily Jewish public schools may have been because many of their students had to meet the higher standards for scholarship applicants. But a disproportionate need for financial assistance cannot explain an 18 percent admission rate, for over 40 percent of all scholarship candidates received offers of admission.[77] In a letter to McGeorge Bundy, then dean of the faculty, Bender said that his ideal was "a Freshman

Class selected on its merits with whatever financial aid . . . necessary being provided."[78] At Harvard in the mid-1950s, this ideal remained quite distant from reality.

The Debate over Scholarships

Though America in the 1950s was becoming ever more affluent, Harvard continued to lack the funds necessary for all the scholarship applicants it would have liked to support. In his letter to Bundy, Bender expressed his concern that Harvard seemed to be falling behind Yale and Princeton in the proportion of the freshman class on scholarship. Any further reduction, he warned, "will lessen our selectivity and hurt quality."[79] Over half the students who were admitted to Harvard but declined to come, Bender noted in the annual report for 1955, "were scholarship candidates who were denied scholarship assistance." Perhaps even more troubling was "that one third of the superior candidates who were judged worthy of scholarship assistance went elsewhere to college."[80]

Ironically, at the very time that Harvard was becoming more meritocratic (as judged by rising SATs and GPAs), the student body was becoming less socioeconomically diverse. From a historic high of 32 percent of freshmen on scholarships in 1953, the figure dropped to 23 percent in 1957.[81]

In a 1958 memo to the Committee on Admission, Richard King, associate director of admissions and financial aids, reported that he was especially concerned about "the potential scholarship applicants who don't even apply in the first place." Noting that over the previous few years, we "have been receiving fewer applications (both relatively and absolutely) from needy students and have been helping more families which . . . are less needy than the ones we were helping four or five years ago," King pointed to increasing tuition, the application fee imposed in 1955, and earlier application deadlines as likely sources of decline in the number of candidates from families of limited means.[82]

In facing this dilemma, Harvard was assisted by the sudden emergence of merit-based national scholarship programs funded by corporations and foundations.[83] The first major program was the General Motors National Scholarship, which in 1955 selected 70 male winners (and only 30 females), 20 of whom chose Harvard, by far the most of any college. In 1956, the much larger National Merit Scholarship Corporation began its awards. That year, 402 National Merit Scholarships were awarded to boys, 57 of whom matriculated at Harvard — again, the largest group entering any single college;[84] moreover, in 1956, "in addition to 262 [students] who received Harvard awards, 84 other scholarship applicants received substantial help from non-

Harvard sources."[85] Many of these students were able but needy and would otherwise have drained Harvard's limited resources for financial aid.

Though Harvard's expenditures for financial aid scholarship money continued to rise during the 1950s, the economic level of the students' families went up rather than down. In 1956, when the median family income in the United States was $3,900, the median scholarship recipient at Harvard came from a family with an income of $6,000 — a figure in the top 30 percent of all American families.[86] As had long been true, the great majority of students continued to be recruited from the top 10 percent of the income distribution — a segment whose income was growing more rapidly between 1949 and 1956 than that of any other group. The underlying issue, as King noted, was the very definition of merit used by Harvard: boys from socioeconomically advantaged homes were more likely "to make a good impression in a 20-minute interview than their less fortunate contemporaries," and they were likely to be deemed intelligent, at least "as measured by standardized tests, or scholastic aptitude, as measured by the SAT." The net result was that "the odds are pretty well stacked against the very needy student, because he will probably not look as good on paper (or at least on the papers we ask for) as his socio-economically favored competitor."[87]

Plagued by limited scholarship funds, Harvard turned increasingly to long-term loans to fill the gap. In 1948–1949, undergraduates received just $10,000 in loans, compared to $500,000 in scholarships; by 1955–1956, loans had risen 2,000 percent, to $200,000, while scholarship expenditures increased by a relatively modest 70 percent, to $850,000.[88] The director of the Financial Aid Office, John U. Monro '34, believed that loans had many virtues: they could be used as a substitute for term-time employment, when students preferred not to work, and they were "an excellent means for helping families of fairly substantial income, temporarily embarrassed by having two or three youngsters in private schools or colleges at the same time." "Considering the income expectations of most of our graduates," he concluded, "there seems good reason to depend on loans, and to an increasing degree, in the years ahead."[89]

King also endorsed the idea of increasing the relative weight of loans to scholarships in 1957. In a clear expression of the Zeitgeist of the fifties, he argued that higher education was "the only major business in this country which has not gone in heavily for credit extension, yet we could get into it easily and benevolently." "We don't need to give away as much money as we now do to the scholarship holders enrolled at our institution, particularly the less needy ones."[90] Not long after King's article appeared, Monro proposed — in the context of rapidly rising tuition charges, which had increased from $400 in 1947 to $1,000 in 1957 and a projected $1,250 in 1958 — an even greater reliance on loans. "Our admission drawing power," he wrote in a January 1958 memorandum to the Committee on Admission and Scholarship, "is such that we can and should start including loans as a regular part of our financial offering to most scholarship freshmen."[91]

Fred Glimp, a junior member of the committee, weighed in with several powerful counterarguments. Like his mentor, Bender, Glimp was a scholarship boy from a background unusual for a Harvard student. A graduate of Boise High School in Boise, Idaho, Glimp had joined the army air corps in 1944 and served with an air force supply unit in Germany. One of the many veterans admitted to Harvard, Glimp initially found it difficult, receiving a B, C, D, and E on his first hour exams. But he was a good baseball player, and his success on the freshman team gave him a feeling of competence. Glimp's academic performance soon took a turn for the better, and as an upperclassman he was awarded a Harvard National Scholarship. In 1950, he was elected to Phi Beta Kappa, graduating magna cum laude in economics.[92]

The trend toward an even greater reliance on loans troubled Glimp, who since 1956 had been serving as assistant director of admission and scholarships while pursuing a doctorate in economics. In a memo to his fellow committee members, he argued that the projected shift "would fundamentally alter the face and heart of Harvard" and "would be tragically short-sighted and insensitive." The essential threat was financial: the donations on which Harvard depended "turn to an important extent on the sense of loyalty and obligation of those in whom Harvard once invested on little more than a simple faith in their qualifications." Though personally experienced in dealing with the "seemingly ungrateful, insatiable parents of scholarship holders" and aware that a few recipients themselves showed "a lack of appreciation," he insisted that such cases were exceptional; more important, "for fund-raising purposes," it is not the disgruntled or unappreciative who matter but the "Neil McElroys, Roy Larsons, and William Stanislaus Murphys."[93] In Glimp's view, Harvard would in the end be making a grave mistake if it relied too heavily on loans, for the "intangible entanglement of having received aid without strings attached is hard to measure but it is strong and it touches checkbooks."[94]

The long-term harm that a loan-centered financial aid policy would do to Harvard's finances was not the only reason that Glimp opposed it. Education, in his view, was at bottom most about "investing" the precise amount of money that would yield the maximal "return." Harvard had an obligation to provide an environment conducive to genuine concern for the "useless" studies that "refine the individuals' reflective interests and give depth and breadth to his powers." This was not, Glimp noted tartly, an atmosphere likely to flourish in the context of "a growing attitude that loyalty and support have been discharged with the last loan payment."[95]

What Glimp feared — a financial aid program that "shifted emphatically from gift aid toward loans" — did not come to pass. And the young man who passionately opposed the shift would soon be promoted to director of freshmen scholarships. By 1960, at the age of just thirty-four, Glimp would be dean of admissions and financial aids — a remarkable rise for a young man from the provinces who, barely a decade earlier, had been earning some extra money as an undergraduate chauffeur for James Bryant Conant.[96]

The Revolt of the Scientists

The faculty at Harvard and other elite colleges had long complained about the academic quality of the student body and the preferential treatment accorded alumni sons, prep school graduates, and athletes. These complaints took on greater weight as federal grants won by faculty members, especially scientists, came to play a growing role in the economics of the leading research universities. The value of academic research to the nation had been dramatically demonstrated by the Manhattan Project, and the postwar university increasingly depended on federal grants and contracts. The consequence was "further to enhance the status of the academician, who is now a prime fund raiser for his institution."[97] With talented researchers in short supply, the voice of the faculty — especially that segment of it that had the greatest capacity to attract federal monies — came to be heard more loudly than before.

By 1957, faculty power had been rising for over a decade, and faculty members everywhere sought to apply more meritocratic standards in selecting undergraduates. That fall, their efforts received a powerful boost from an unexpected source when, on October 4, the Soviet Union launched *Sputnik*, the world's first satellite. For the United States, locked in a bitter Cold War with the Soviet Union, the threat posed by *Sputnik* was palpable. Should the Soviets gain scientific and technological superiority over the United States, military superiority would, Americans feared, inevitably follow, thereby threatening the survival of the nation. That was the lesson drawn from World War II, for it was the atomic bomb that had finally brought the conflict to an end.[98]

In the wake of *Sputnik*, the federal government undertook a series of bold initiatives, including the passage of the National Defense Education Act (NDEA) and the establishment of the National Aeronautics and Space Administration (NASA), to ensure American superiority in science and technology.[99] Funding for the National Science Foundation more than tripled in a single year, increasing from $40 million to $134 million.[100] Overall, "the post-Sputnik surge of federal research funding had indisputably inaugurated a golden age for academic science."[101]

Harvard's scientists seized the opportunity to increase pressure on the Admission Office. In 1958, Professor Gerald Holton,[102] a German-born physicist who had recently gained tenure, attacked Harvard's admission policy. In a letter to the dean of the faculty, McGeorge Bundy, he criticized the lack of rigorous prerequisites for courses in mathematics, science, and foreign languages. Holton argued that Harvard was emphasizing an ill-defined concept of "ability" at the expense of competence in specific subject areas and characterized the admissions policy as one that "gives the appearance of having been designed to attract to Harvard College that twentieth-century version of the Noble Savage, the proverbial student from West Podunk High who has remarkable ability, but who has remained unspoiled by contact with hard knowledge in the several main fields of thought." The solution, Holton believed, was "to reinstitute a prerequisite of examined achievement and competence . . . in at least the following fields on the elementary level: mathematics, one experimental science, and one foreign language."[103]

Bender's main opposition came, however, from a group led by the renowned and formidable chemist George Kistiakowsky. A Russian émigré born in Kiev in 1900, Kistiakowsky had served in the Russian White Army before moving to Berlin, where he received a Ph.D. in chemistry in 1925.[104] After a brief stint at Princeton, he was lured to Harvard by Conant, who was then chairman of the Chemistry Department. The two men quickly became close professional and personal friends.

When war broke out in Europe, Kistiakowsky was the first member of the Harvard faculty to be awarded contracts from the new federal Office of Scientific Research and Development. He worked closely with Conant on the Manhattan Project, heading the explosives section of the National Defense Research Committee (NDRC).[105] When Conant asked him to leave the NRDC in early 1944 to come to Los Alamos, he did so without hesitation. And when the historic Trinity test of the first atomic bomb took place at Alamogordo, New Mexico, on July 15, 1945, Kistiakowsky was there with Conant as the great explosion shook the desert.[106]

Kistiakowsky personified the new alliance that had emerged during and after World War II between Big Science and the federal government. With his enormous prestige enhanced by his membership on President Eisenhower's Science Advisory Committee, he joined Harvard's Committee on Admission in 1957 as one of several faculty representatives.[107] He did not like what he saw there, and at a 1958 faculty meeting he launched a frontal assault on Bender's policies. Kistiakowsky claimed that Harvard's promotional materials, especially the Rollo Books, emphasized an outmoded, gentlemanly concept of liberal education at the expense of serious training in the sciences. More scientists and engineers, he argued, were urgently needed by the nation, and

Harvard was not producing its "fair share" of them. He proposed a far more academically rigorous admissions policy limited to the top 1 percent of the nation's high school seniors, with the SAT playing a central role in determining who would belong to this elite group.[108]

Bender was an articulate man, and he rose to defend Harvard's policies. Kistiakowsky's intemperate public attack was a sharp departure from Harvard's tradition of settling internal differences quietly and in private, and it angered him. In full view of the faculty, Bender denounced Kistiakowsky as an arrogant and impossible member of the committee.[109] In the gentlemanly world of Harvard, their exchange constituted a mutual declaration of war.

In his Report to the President for 1957–1958, Bender elaborated his differences with the two groups of scientists. The proposal of Holton's group, which complained that freshmen were poorly prepared, would in his view lead "to a serious decline in the quality of the Harvard student body, by cutting Harvard off from fresh and vigorous sources of talent throughout the country." The actual effect of their proposal would be to impede the committee's capacity "to identify curiosity, creativity, energy, drive, independence and capacity for growth, qualities which are at least as important in determining the promise of a student body as the amount of mathematics or French a student knows." Furthermore, it would make it more difficult to address "the question of the diversity of qualities, interests and backgrounds needed in the making of an optimal student body, and the question of Harvard's relationship with the country and the democratic process."[110]

The second group — the one led by Kistiakowsky, though he was never mentioned by name — came in for even harsher criticism. According to Bender, it "demanded a revision of Rollo that would emphasize science far more than before and minimize the 'nonsense about liberal education' contained in it." But the attack exhibited "a curiously unscientific approach to the problem," for it never specified what a "fair share" of the scientists would be, nor did it offer any evidence of whether their numbers had increased at Harvard or how their proportion of the student body compared to that of other leading liberal arts colleges.[111] "Perhaps," Bender mused, "the time has come . . . to define our purpose as the production of chemists or economists or anthropologists rather than educated men." "But if the definition is to be changed," he noted pointedly, "it should be done by the faculty as a whole and not on the authority of a small group of scientists."[112]

The Special Committee on College Admission Policy

Harvard's response to the intensifying conflict was the time-honored one of establishing a committee to look into the matter. Appointed by McGeorge Bundy, the Special Committee on College Admission Policy was a distinguished one. Chaired by Franklin L. Ford, a rising young historian who would soon succeed Bundy as dean of the faculty, its members constituted something of an all-star list of the Harvard faculty: Crane Brinton '15, a renowned historian and, since 1942, chairman of the Society of Fellows; Walter Jackson Bate '39, Ph.D. '42, the author of a classic biography of Samuel Johnson and a former Junior Fellow; Samuel Stouffer, who founded Harvard's Laboratory of Social Relations and was the principal author of the landmark study *The American Soldier;* Alvin Pappenheimer Jr. '29, Ph.D. '32, a professor of biology and editor of the journal *Immunology;* Edgar Bright Wilson Jr., the Theodore William Richards Professor of Chemistry, a former Junior Fellow and a close ally of Kistiakowsky's, with whom he had worked on the atomic bomb. Other than Bender himself, the sole member of the committee from the administration was John Monro, by now dean of the college.[113]

For those who wished to push Harvard much further down the road toward academic meritocracy, the times could hardly have been more favorable.[114] Since *Sputnik*, a sense of national crisis had been growing about the capacity of the American educational system to keep up with the Soviet Union in producing scientists and engineers. Sounding the alarm with particular force was Vice Admiral Hyman G. Rickover, the author of the bestselling book *Education and Freedom.* Calling on the educational system to emphasize the identification and training of the academically gifted, Rickover quoted Alfred North Whitehead to underline his central point: "The rule is absolute, the race which does not value trained intelligence is doomed."[115]

In this atmosphere, the pressure to do something to counteract Soviet advances in education and science was overwhelming. At the federal level, the response was swift. In 1958, Congress passed the National Aeronautics and Space Act and the NDEA, both of which channeled substantial resources to the nation's research universities. The latter legislation, adopted in response to what Congress referred to as an "educational emergency," had especially important long-term effects, for it broke a stalemate that had been thwarting federal aid to higher education. With it, a new era of federal support for research universities was born. Resources surged into higher education; the percentage of the gross national product devoted to university research, a paltry 0.07 percent in 1953, grew to 0.12 percent in 1960 and 0.20 percent in 1964.[116] At Harvard, federal support almost tripled in the decade between 1953 and 1963, increasing from $36 million to $100 million.[117]

Another important change was a shift in the policy of the College Board on the disclosure of SAT scores. Before 1958, secondary schools and colleges received the results of the SAT, but students did not.[118] After *Sputnik* and the ensuing national obsession with the identification of gifted students, withholding this information seemed less defensible.

With the release of the SAT scores, the balance of power between colleges and applicants was altered in a subtle but profound way. For the first time since the advent of selective admissions, students and their families had an objective and uniform yardstick to help them assess whether colleges and universities were living up to their professed ideals of equality of opportunity. If elite private colleges wished to continue to favor the rich and the well-born, their actions would now be more visible.

As the Admission and Scholarship Committee convened in the spring of 1958 to conduct the annual business of selection, it faced heavy pressure — from an increasingly assertive faculty, from applicants empowered by knowing their SAT scores, and from the growing national obsession with scientific brilliance — to give greater weight to scholastic talent than ever before. The freshmen who enrolled that fall showed every sign of being the strongest class academically in Harvard's history. In one year, median combined SATs had risen by 50 points, from 1285 to 1335 — the second-largest increase ever recorded at Harvard.[119] At the high end of the distribution, freshmen in the ninetieth percentile scored 1,532 (the figure was 1,490 the year before). In a related trend, the number of students from public schools reached an all-time high of 54 percent (just 50 percent the year before) — a development that could only be welcomed by faculty calling for more meritocracy.[120] At the same time, Harvard had also expanded its program of admitting particularly brilliant students directly from the eleventh grade, accepting a record 12.[121]

The academic quality of the freshman class was rising, and Harvard was remarkably successful in attracting the students it wanted. In 1958, 74 percent of those admitted to Harvard matriculated there, a striking increase from the 61 percent just three years earlier and by far the highest in the Ivy League.[122] Harvard was somewhat perplexed by this, speculating that new financial aid policies and "more favorable nation wide publicity . . . than at any time in recent memory" were responsible for its growing popularity.[123] Whatever the reasons, the results in 1958 were dazzling; more winners of National Merit Scholarships entered Harvard than the rest of the colleges of the Ivy League combined, and nearly 10 percent of the freshmen were either General Motors or Merit Scholars.[124]

With statistics like these, one might think the faculty would be grateful to Bender for bringing to Cambridge an ever more able student body. Indeed, such sentiments existed, especially among faculty members who had been in Cambridge long enough to remember what Harvard had been like before the war.[125]

Yet other faculty members correctly believed that Harvard was still systematically favoring the sons of the privileged. As evidence, they could cite data from the Admission and Scholarship Committee's own Annual Report to the President. In 1958, 20 percent of the entering freshmen were the sons of

alumni; they were admitted at a rate of 69 percent compared to just 39 percent for all applicants.[126] Had they had the figures, they also could have cited
the admissions rates for applicants from the top boarding schools that same
year, which were almost two in three at a time when applicants from selective
public high schools in New York and Philadelphia were admitted in less than
one case in four.[127]

Then there was the touchy issue of athletes.[128] Harvard's fortunes in
sports, especially in football, had improved dramatically under Bender, but
good results on the playing field were simply not possible if the same academic standards were applied to athletes as to other students.[129] In 1958, the
Admissions Office compiled data on what they called "the Pigskin Tribe":
football players who had entered Harvard in 1952, 1955, 1957, and 1958. In
these four years, median verbal SATs in the group ranged from 530 to 575, and
23 percent scored below 500. Of the 236 members in this category, 17 percent
had projected rank lists (PRLs) of 5.0 or below (3½ Cs and ½ D) with an additional 45 percent having PRLs of 4.0 to 5.0.[130] If faculty members suspected
that Harvard was relaxing its normal standards for athletes, especially in contact sports, such data confirmed their concern.

That a gulf separated the outlook of the faculty meritocratic wing from
that of the Admissions Office was evident in a confidential memo that Bender
circulated to the Admissions and Scholarship Committee shortly before the
Faculty Special Committee on College Admission Policy began its deliberations. Bender's basic thinking had not changed much since his "Comprehensive Formal Statement" in 1952, despite the new environment of the late 1950s.
Bender posed the fundamental issue starkly: "Should our goal be to select a
student body with the highest possible proportions of high ranking students,
or should it be to select, with a reasonably high range of academic ability, a
student body with a certain variety of talents, qualities, attitudes and backgrounds?"[131] A growing segment of the faculty favored the former approach,
but Bender believed that nonacademic qualities should continue to play a
major role in Harvard admissions. "Are there any good ways," he asked, "of
identifying and measuring goodness, humanity, character, warmth, enthusiasm, responsibility, vitality, creativity, independence, heterosexuality, etc, etc.,
or should we care about these anyhow?" Quoting an unnamed colleague, he
argued that "above a reasonably good level of mental ability, above that indicated by a 550–600 level of SAT score, the only thing that matters in terms of
future impact on, or contribution to, society is the degree of personal inner
force an individual has."[132]

Bender reminded his colleagues that Harvard was not free to admit
whomever it pleased: "we have to deal with the schools and the alumni and
the families and the candidates with which or with whom we have to deal,

however much we might like to operate in a vacuum, without pressures and prejudices, our own and others, affecting our decisions." He remained deeply concerned about finances, but also mused whether the elite constituencies that Harvard had always depended on might not be the ones that would carry it into the future. "Are the hard-nosed high school graduate [*sic*] rather than the senior of inherited wealth going to be the ones who will enlarge our endowment in the future?"[133]

Bender had hit on a central dilemma: in a changing society, would Harvard be best served by continuing to favor the children of the upper class or should it attach itself to a potentially rising class of academically talented boys from the nation's public schools? "Are we interested in keeping Harvard an institution which will be socially acceptable for young gentlemen to attend?" he asked. "Or are young gentlemen a vanishing rose and would we be better off without them?"[134] How the Special Committee answered these questions would reveal a great deal about Harvard's strategy for maintaining its preeminence in a world in which the Protestant upper class was already showing signs of losing its hegemony.[135]

From the moment the Special Committee convened in the spring of 1959, it was apparent that the central issue was whether it would endorse the policies of the Bender regime or suggest that Harvard embark on a fundamentally different path. That Bender had little confidence in the committee was clear in its first meeting when he asked "whether decisions about the make-up of the future classes at Harvard should be made by the Faculty alone or whether this was not also a proper area of concern for Harvard's alumni at large, perhaps represented in committee appointed through the Board of Overseers." This was clearly an attempt to find a decision-making body more sympathetic to his views, and it is hardly surprising that it received a firm (if polite) negative response.[136]

Though the committee was carefully balanced to give voice but not undue weight to the views of scientists (it included just two, a chemist and an immunologist), its composition as a largely faculty body (only two members, Bender and Monro, came from the administration) ensured that it would be more than a rubber stamp for the prevailing policies. Representing the faculty opinion most opposed to Bender's philosophy was E. Bright Wilson, a brilliant and intellectually elitist chemist who had attained the rank of full professor at the age of thirty-eight and was a member of both the National Academy of Sciences and the American Academy of Arts and Sciences. A man of militantly meritocratic views, he favored the ruthless elimination of academically weak students and their replacement with those of greater academic ability and seriousness.[137] At the committee's second meeting, Wilson proposed a sharp reduction in "boys from the City of Cambridge, many of whom are hopelessly outclassed at Harvard, as well as playboys who just don't care."[138] That there might be important institutional reasons to admit such boys — a point repeatedly emphasized by Bender — was of little concern to Wilson.

In an attempt to adjudicate the views embodied by Bender and Wilson, the committee turned, in good academic fashion, to gathering data. Over the course of its eleven months of deliberation, statistics were collected on the academic performance of many groups: public vs. private school students, athletes vs. nonathletes, alumni sons vs. other students, local students vs. those from outside Greater Boston, and scholarship students vs. those paying their own way. Not since the 1920s, when Harvard struggled with the "Jewish problem," had admissions undergone such an extensive review. And, again as in the 1920s, Harvard was the first of the Big Three to address publicly the difficult issues admissions faced in an era when accusations of favoritism and discrimination had become conspicuous features of the political landscape.

The person who supplied the statistics was Richard G. King, the associate director of admissions and freshman scholarships, who was also the secretary to the committee.[139] In a remarkable presentation on September 29, 1959, he submitted data comparing the backgrounds of students from the Classes of 1957 and 1958 who graduated with high honors or better versus those who had failed or dropped out. King noted that the study generated a profile of the academically successful student at Harvard: "parents probably in the professional class but impecunious enough to need a small scholarship award, home outside New England, public rather than private secondary school — a school small to medium size or of very large size (i.e., a small city or a very large city high school, but not a suburban high school), academic interest in science prior to entrance but not necessarily on graduation from college, professionally oriented goals at entrance, high abilities and good adjustments to Harvard." He offered a portrait of the unsuccessful Harvard student as well: "father a Harvard college graduate now a high salaried business executive, living in a suburban community in New England, from a select or semi-select private secondary school, either undecided as to career or planning to enter 'business,' and relatively low test scores, PRL, rank in class, etc."[140]

Analyzing statistics from 79 secondary schools that had placed four or more students in three Harvard classes, King reported a massive difference between public and private schools in both average rank and the proportion graduating with honors. "The most obvious fact to observe," he noted, "is how much better the large contingent public schools tend to do than the large contingent private schools." King pointed to both "admission factors and motivational factors," candidly admitting that "the 'select' feeder schools which we have cultivated and which cultivates [*sic*] us over a long period of time tend to fall more often in the bottom half than the top half of Table 1."[141] This was something of an understatement, for not one of the 30 top institutions was an eastern boarding school.[142] Some of the St. Grottlesex schools, in particular, had especially poor records, with St. Mark's, St. Paul's, and Middlesex ranking 63rd, 65th, and 76th, respectively.[143] Overall, of the 15 lowest-ranking institutions, 13 were private schools, with the only exceptions — Cambridge High and Latin and Rindge Technical High School — both beneficiaries of Harvard's politically savvy policy of giving preference to hometown boys.

What was most striking about the schools at the top was not only that they were public but where they were located. Ten of the top 12 schools were in New York City — by far the nation's largest center of Jewish population.[144] Both of the others — Philadelphia's Central High School and Washington's Wilson High School — enrolled large numbers of Jewish students. Since the 1920s, when Lowell first imposed a quota, it had long been suspected that Jewish applicants were held to higher standards than their gentile peers. Thirty years later, this was apparently still the case, especially for Jews from the Middle Atlantic states, where well over half of the nation's Jews still lived.[145]

King's "Study of Magnas, Summas, Flunk Outs, and Drop Outs — Classes of 1957 and 1958," also presented at the September 29, 1959, meeting, reinforced the conclusion that Harvard under Bender was far from an institution based on merit.[146] He noted that "the New England private schools supply over 40% (187/463) of our flunk-outs and drop-outs, but less than 20% (68/344) of our magnas and summas." Overall, public high schools produced more graduates with high honors or better than flunkouts or dropouts; in contrast, the private schools produced less than half as many summas or magnas as academic failures.[147] Striking differences were also visible by parental occupation; to take but two examples, the ratio of summa or magna graduates to flunkouts or dropouts was 5 to 1 for the sons of store owners and over 0.5 to 1 for the sons of business executives.[148] Even at the "new" Harvard, hailing from the old upper class was still a crucial advantage in gaining a place in the freshman class.

King's studies stimulated a sharp debate between Wilson and Bender. For Wilson, the implications were clear: Harvard should move expeditiously to eliminate the bottom 10 percent of the class. But that conclusion was not self-evident to Bender; according to him, the students who flunked out were by no means the ones with the lowest College Board scores but "tended to be slightly above the middle of the class in ability terms but were apt to have various psychoneurotic or personal problems." And "if we were to eliminate all candidates showing neurotic tendencies," he argued, "we would probably eliminate a number of our Group I's as well as some of our drop-outs."[149]

Nevertheless, even Bender conceded that Harvard needed to deal rigorously with applicants from schools at the bottom of the school performance study. In fact, Harvard had already been doing so for at least half a dozen years. "The question," Bender stated, was simply "how do you get from here to there?" and "how fast do you do it?" At this point in what must have been a tense meeting, Chairman Ford asked whether "our present bottom 10% hurts us in getting the 10% that we were most interested in." According to Bender, the experience of the University of Chicago[150] strongly suggested that "when one attempted to eliminate the 10% who are at the bottom of the academic scale but who have other strong qualifications, one no longer got the academic top 10%."[151] What this meant in plain English was that even the academically brilliant preferred to attend an institution with social cachet — an element of Harvard's historic atmosphere that would be lost without a critical mass of "gentlemen."[152]

Brinton, a former Rhodes Scholar with a broad historic and comparative perspective on higher education, posed a sharp question to clarify the issue at hand: "Do we want an École Normale Supérieure, a 'cerebral school' aimed solely at preparing students for the academic professions?" Bender's answer was a resounding no. But to Wilson the matter was not so clear: the basic issue was which students "could take advantage of the unique intellectual opportunity which Harvard has to offer." In a barb clearly aimed at Bender, Wilson proclaimed that "he just did not accept potential financial return . . . as the basis for showing favoritism to Harvard sons who were less well qualified academically than other admission candidates."[153]

Having been under assault by segments of the faculty for almost two years — first by Holton, then by Kistiakowsky, and now by Wilson — Bender apparently decided that he had had enough. In a meeting of the committee a month after this testy exchange, he announced his resignation as dean of Admissions and Financial Aids, and stated that he would prefer neither to affix his signature to the final report of the subcommittee nor to withhold his vote of approval.[154] His departure was set for July 1, 1960, and he agreed to continue to meet with the subcommittee until it completed its mission. No longer a formal member, he was now free to express publicly his dissent about the direction it proposed to take Harvard. That Bender positioned himself to do so could hardly have escaped the attention of those who were to write the final report.

Final Deliberations: The Search for Consensus

With Bender's departure decided and his signature no longer a possibility, the committee now faced the difficult task of forging a consensus. As chair, Ford had primary responsibility for seeing that the committee avoid an embarrassing public split. The greatest threat came from Wilson, whose position in favor of a rigorous academic meritocracy was shared by an important segment of the faculty. Ford now had to incorporate enough of Wilson's proposals into the final report to keep him from dissenting publicly while rejecting those that would clash with Harvard's fundamental institutional interests.

Ford's job was not made any easier by new statistics that were released at the same meeting at which Bender's resignation was announced. Though King had been unable to attend the meeting because of illness, he supplied figures showing that Harvard sons represented about 20 percent of the freshman class though they made up only about 10 percent of applicants — the result of a substantially higher admission rate among legacies: 63 percent in 1959 versus 38 percent for all applicants. One predictable consequence was that they were more likely to drop out and flunk out and less likely to earn academic honors.[155]

Perhaps because King was absent, the committee minimized the implications of these findings. The minutes of the meeting report that "there is no evidence that the Harvard sons, *as a group*, are essentially inferior as students to the College population as a whole." Director of Admissions David Henry went even further, stating that "the favoritism shown Harvard sons by the Admissions Committee has never gone beyond . . . a slight and exceedingly vague 'plus' in certain cases of marginal admits."[156]

So off the mark were these comments that despite his illness, King wrote to Chairman Ford to set the record straight immediately. "The advantage," he insisted, "is clearly more than a slight and vague 'plus' as you yourself must be aware if you sat on any of the New England private school dockets." "I don't see any point," he continued, "in pretending that the favoritism is merely marginal when in fact it is more than that." King concluded that legacy preference should be further reduced: "I think we should probably turn the thumbscrew one thin turn more now that the Program [fund-raising] drive is over."[157]

The issue of athletes was equally delicate.[158] Of the freshmen with "known football potential" who matriculated in 1955, 1956, and 1957, 56 percent (89 of 160) had PRLs of 4.0 or lower, with 15 percent having PRLs of 5.0 to 6.0. Moreover, in these same three years, 57 percent of the football players received scholarships, compared to only about 25 percent of all the freshmen.[159] And like alumni sons, the overall academic performance of athletes was below average, with 63 percent in the bottom half of the class and only 10 percent in the top quarter.[160] Nonetheless, Ford's attitude toward athletes remained positive; in his view, "the problem here did not seem immensely acute, though there would always be some concern with respect to varsity prospects in the contact sports, particularly football and hockey."[161]

As the committee approached the end of its deliberations, a number of questions remained unresolved. How would the final report handle the volatile issue of alumni sons? Of private versus public school applicants? Geographical diversity? Athletes? Ford's attempt to find a position between the poles of the debate represented by Wilson and Bender is visible in his "Working Notes for the Report," distributed to the committee in November 1959. In this twenty-two-page document, Ford squarely faces the possibility of public division: "Split votes, frankly reported, may in some instances be the only way to place such issues squarely before the Faculty."[162]

Echoing Bender, Ford noted the existence of "practical limitations which restrict our ability to pick and choose," citing "financial limitations on families and our scholarship program," "public attitudes," and "the desire to stay on good terms with particular schools, Harvard clubs, and individual parents." "How frank," he asked, "can we be in our report about these diplomatic problems?"[163]

Ford tried to walk a fine line, but it was clear from the "Working Notes" that his sympathies resided more with Bender than with Wilson. Selection, he argued, should be decided "on the basis of a wide range of qualities, some testable, some not." Above all, Harvard should avoid using any "single mechanical criterion" and continue "to play hunches" and "to take some chances with selecting applicants in the face, or in the absence, of test scores." With respect to the confidential studies of school performance prepared by King, Ford argued that they should "be read and viewed with extreme caution." Although these studies did reveal a huge gap between students from the "big city, especially New York high schools" and leading boarding schools, this "should be no surprise." After all, the students from "tremendously competitive big city high schools" are "primarily the proven academic winners, boys who are probably more highly motivated and more ruthless in their demands upon themselves than are the members of any other distinguishable groups in the college."[164]

Although students from the elite boarding schools tended to perform poorly at Harvard, Ford was not eager to reduce their numbers. Acknowledging that the "percentage of public school graduates at Harvard is almost certain to rise," he asked, "How hard do we want to push it?" Speaking for the committee, he reported that "many of us have discovered in our thinking a strong, but not very rationally developed, commitment to the idea of mixture in this as in so many other regards."[165] Translated into policy, this meant that boarding school applicants, though no longer totally insulated from competition with high school students, would continue to receive preference. So, too, would athletes and alumni sons, though Ford admitted that the latter was "one of the hottest potatoes we have to pick up" and intimated that a reduction in the magnitude of favoritism for legacies might be in order.[166]

Ford's paper elicited a variety of responses from members of the committee, but by far the most negative one came from Wilson. In a pair of letters that constituted something of a manifesto for the wing of the faculty favoring strict academic meritocracy, Wilson explicitly advocated admitting fewer private school students and commuters, eliminating all preferences for athletes, and (if funds permitted) selecting "the entering class regardless of financial need on the basis of pure merit."[167] The issue of athletes particularly vexed Wilson, who stated flatly: "I would certainly rule out athletic ability as a criterion for admission of any sort," adding that "it bears a zero relationship to the performance later in life that we are trying to predict." He also argued that "it may well be that objective test scores are our only safeguards against an excessive number of athletes only, rich playboys, smooth characters who make a good impression in interviews, etc."[168] As a parting shot, Wilson could not resist accusing Ford of anti-intellectualism; citing Ford's desire to change Harvard's image, Wilson asked bluntly: "What's wrong with Harvard being regarded as an egghead college? Isn't it right that a country the size of the United States should be able to afford one university in which intellectual achievement is the most important consideration?"[169]

Admission to Harvard College

Before submitting the final version of the report for publication, Ford sent a draft to McGeorge Bundy, then dean of the faculty. "It is an admirable document," he wrote Ford, "and I do not know whether to be more impressed by its wisdom, its style, or the rapidity of its composition."[170]

The diplomatic Bundy did, however, have one important reservation: the handling of the ever-delicate Jewish question. "Without meaning to open Pandora's Box," he wrote, "I hope you will tell me someday whether you and your colleagues really looked hard at the question of our process of choice and judgment among boys from metropolitan high schools, a large number of them Jewish." In a formulation befitting the WASP gentleman from Groton that he was, Bundy made a pointed observation: "I am satisfied that we have an honorable record here, but I am not quite certain that we are as perceptive or as generous as we should be."[171] If the committee was inclined to minimize the implications of the school performance data submitted by King, Bundy was not: lingering anti-Semitism, he clearly implied, was still hurting the admission chances of Jewish applicants from large urban high schools.

When *Admission to Harvard College: A Report by the Special Committee on College Admission Policy* (also known as the Ford Report) was published to considerable fanfare in February 1960, there was no indication that the committee had responded in any way to Bundy's concern about the issue of Jews.

On the contrary, it blithely noted that only one region — the Middle Atlantic — was underrepresented in the allocation of scholarship funds, contributing 30.5 percent of registered freshmen but receiving just 19.7 percent of scholarship funds. "We obviously under-subsidize the Middle Atlantic region, which is to say, New York in particular," the report noted. In contrast, several other regions — notably, Mountain, Pacific, and Central — "are receiving the strongest financial support relative to the size of their representation." "In presenting the above statistics," however, "the Committee sees no reason to criticize the combination of judgments which they reflect."[172]

Although Bundy's comments evoked little response, the same cannot be said of Wilson's unremitting efforts to push the committee toward a greater reliance on academic criteria. Responding to Ford's "Working Notes," Wilson had called for a number of specific changes: "an increase in the proportion of high school students," "a decrease in the number from certain schools which have consistently shown a poor performance," "no lessening of standards for local candidates," "a further reduction in Harvard sons," and "reduction of the preference for athletes." Were Wilson to have his way, Harvard's admission practices would be fundamentally transformed.

The committee gave Wilson and the segment of the faculty that he represented some of what they wanted, but not so much as to limit the flexibility that gave the admissions office ample room to pursue Harvard's institutional interests. Perhaps the most obvious concession was a statement specifying, "We must direct our efforts toward training our share . . . of the truly brilliant members of American society." The report made a clear reference to Wilson himself, recounting, "As one member of the Committee put the matter early in our deliberations: 'Harvard must keep trying to push its top one percent of brilliant students up to two percent of comparable quality.'"[173] Yet elsewhere, the report noted that of the 161 applicants with the highest PRLs (3.9 percent of all candidates), 27 were nevertheless rejected.[174] Clearly, Harvard would retain the right to reject applicants, however brilliant.

Wilson also seemed to have an impact on the hotly contested preference for commuters. At one of the committee's earliest meetings, in a direct response to a question from Wilson, Bender indicated that "the Committee felt a particular 'political' obligation to the City of Cambridge, but that there were also political pressures from other parts of the Greater Boston community that the Admission Committee had to take into account."[175] In truth, as Harvard became an increasingly national institution, the proportion of commuters had long been declining. Massachusetts residents, a far larger group of students than those from Greater Boston, made up 55.1 percent of the Class of 1929 but only 21.3 percent of the Class of 1963.[176] Still, a policy of residual preference for local boys remained in place, and Wilson wanted it removed.

Ford's draft of the report went a long way toward this position: "A greatly increased effort should be made to attract qualified applicants from Boston and its suburbs, but there should be no relaxation of standards in favor of such applicants." But the published version must have satisfied Wilson even more: "A greatly increased effort" was softened to "A continuing effort" while the core principle — identical standards — remained in place.[177]

On the issue of public versus private school students, the Ford Report moved in Wilson's direction with qualifications: "The Committee cannot escape, nor does it wish to avoid, the conclusion that Harvard should continue to admit an increasing proportion of its freshmen from among qualified graduates of public schools." At the same time, it was important to maintain the "diversity" provided by private school graduates, for "gifted students" obtain a better education "by living in an undergraduate population representing a wide variety of school backgrounds." Moreover, private school students "contribute a great deal to the intellectual atmosphere of Harvard," even though many of them are "not oriented toward academic or professional training, and so are not interested in striving for degrees with honors."[178] Ultimately, the committee candidly acknowledged that the continuing high percentage of private school boys was in part a function of sheer money: "the cut-off line . . . is fixed not by school background but by the limit of our financial resources." Even in 1960, considerable numbers of public school graduates, though offered admission, were "unable to register because of lack of scholarship funds."[179]

The Ford Report's treatment of legacies may not have gone as far as Wilson would have liked, but it did recommend that "the applications of 'Harvard sons' should be scrutinized with increasing rigor" and that "parentage should not be a basis for the preferential acceptance of weak candidates." Yet the careful words left considerable room for special treatment. Lest there be any confusion, the report explicitly stated that "some degree, probably a quite substantial degree, of family continuity, is vital to any college" and noted the importance of alumni to both recruiting and financial support.[180]

"There can be such a thing," the committee observed, "as *too little* alumni pressure on admissions." Fortunately, Harvard — unlike Columbia and Chicago — did not suffer from this difficulty. "The alumni problem," the committee had noted in private deliberations, was "in itself an index of 'desirability' of the mother institution."[181] Harvard could be proud that its admissions policy had not interfered with the maintenance of its tremendous social prestige — in contrast to those of some institutions that had unduly emphasized academics and hence admitted too many students of dubious social background.[182]

The Ford Report's recommendation on athletes could not have satisfied

Wilson. Although it states that "no applicant should be brought to Harvard in the face of clearly indicated weaknesses which would prevent his making his way as a student in the college," it also reported that "the majority of the Committee members agree with the policy followed at present by the Admission Committee," described rather disingenuously as "giving just as much attention to the athletic rating as to any other extra-curricular excellence, *once the question of intellectual competence has been squarely faced.*"[183] But Harvard's current policy on athletes was, as Wilson repeatedly emphasized, totally unacceptable to him.[184] While paying lip service to rigorous academic standards for admitted athletes, it was in fact a ratification of the status quo; athletic ability, especially in contact sports such as football, was given far more weight — despite official university policy to the contrary — than "artistic, musical, or dramatic ability."[185]

The committee also took up a number of issues not critical to Wilson. One of the most important was the question of the students' social and economic backgrounds. Though Harvard's professed ideal was "one of seeking to break through all barriers which separate gifted boys from the chance to capitalize on their gifts," the proportion of freshmen on scholarships had barely risen from the roughly 25 percent, where it had long been (in 1953, it was 27 percent), despite rising tuition. Perhaps as a consequence, those students awarded scholarships were less disadvantaged than their predecessors; whereas the median family income of a scholarship holder was $4,800 in 1952, it had risen by 1959 to $7,700. The committee offered a frank assessment: "The faculty should not, under present conditions, expect too much socio-economic diversity in the college. The long-established predominance of business and professional family backgrounds remains essentially unaltered."[186]

In truth, during the very period when Harvard was hailed as being increasingly meritocratic, the proportion of working-class students actually declined. Between 1954 and 1958, when median combined SATs rose from 1,242 to 1,285, the percentage of freshmen from working-class backgrounds dropped from 10 to 7 percent.[187] As the committee stated: "We are still able to bring to Cambridge only a few students from low income groups and almost none from the lowest." But instead of proposing to change this situation, the report rationalized it: "[I]t is easily possible to ask a talented boy to jump further, in terms of educational demands and cultural surroundings, than his background will permit." What this meant concretely was that "maximum need" scholarships would be awarded rarely and with great caution.[188]

The committee did not propose that Harvard make one of its highest priorities the provision of enough scholarship money to remove financial factors from admissions.[189] Though such a policy was obviously a precondition for the realization of meritocratic ideals, *Admission to Harvard College* explicitly stated that it would not be feasible: "Although we still indulge in a relatively small number of undeniably 'weak admits,' the Committee believes that there exists at present no reason to exclude them, without the prospect of abler full tuition-paying replacements."[190] The elementary aspiration articulated by Wilson — that Harvard should have the "scholarship funds to pick the entering class regardless of financial need on the basis of pure merit and then take care of those who needed help" — was not endorsed by the committee.[191] Equality of opportunity at the nation's wealthiest university would have to wait.

Formally approved by the faculty on April 11, 1960, the Ford Report was a landmark document. Just as Harvard was the first of the Big Three to issue a report on the "Jewish problem" in the 1920s, so too was it the first to develop policies designed to handle the impending crush of applicants that would accompany the arrival of the first wave of the baby-boom generation. But unlike the 1920s, when Harvard was justly accused of imposing policies that limited the number of outsiders, this time the report was filled with the rhetoric of inclusion and equality of opportunity. The Harvard "philosophy of admissions," the report ringingly declared, "must preclude, without qualifications, any discrimination against a boy on the basis of his ethnic background, his religion or his family's station in life."[192]

Compared to the prevailing policy, the recommendations of the Ford Report constituted a step toward greater meritocracy. Whether the issue was alumni sons, candidates from Greater Boston, athletes, or high school vs. private school graduates, the unifying theme was a reduction, if not the outright elimination, of preferences traditionally granted privileged categories.[193] The report was suffused with meritocratic language: "Harvard should go on making every effort," it declared, "to attract candidates who offer the highest promise of distinguished intellectual achievement."[194]

In an article published in the *Harvard Alumni Bulletin* shortly after the Ford Report was approved, McGeorge Bundy emphasized that nonacademic factors would weigh heavily in allocating the vast majority of places in the freshman class. Echoing the report, he wrote that "truly remarkable minds are rare." But for the 98–99 percent whose minds were judged by Harvard to be less than truly remarkable, other factors such as "warmth, tenacity, moral courage, and practical judgment" would prove critical.[195]

Though the Ford Report repeatedly emphasized the importance of attracting brilliant students to Cambridge, its main thread was to reaffirm that many factors, rather than the single factor of intellect, would determine whom Harvard would admit. Bundy reported that this issue had been settled definitively: "When in Faculty meetings a few men who believe deeply in the single criterion of intellectual promise attempted to amend the Report, they were clearly defeated on a voice vote." And even when the report stated that "Harvard's advantages lie, above all, in the realm of intellect," it was in no way a repudiation of Harvard's traditional policy of balance: "When the Ford Committee praised the 'realm of the intellect,' it did not mean to praise only would-be scholars or self-conscious 'intellectuals.'"[196]

Praised by Bundy as a "careful, fair, and deeply responsible study," the Ford Report was a quintessentially Harvard document: measured, well researched, cautiously reformist, and subtly protective of Harvard's institutional interests.[197] Proposing no radical new departures, it nudged Harvard gently in the direction of greater meritocracy. While calling for elevating the intellectual level of the student body, it made it clear that a purely academic meritocracy was not what it had in mind. The foundation remained Harvard's belief that its primary mission was not to educate scholars, writers, and scientists, but to train the "men of affairs" who would occupy positions of leadership in business and government. So concerned was the Special Committee about Harvard's efficacy in producing elites that it specifically recommended that "the University should undertake an investigation of possible correlations between admission data and outstanding performance in all fields of human endeavor."[198] And the results of such a study would almost surely confirm what both the committee and the administration strongly suspected: a policy of strict academic meritocracy would have excluded many future leaders in the economy and the polity.

Bender's Attack on the Ford Report

At Harvard's highest levels, *Admission to Harvard College* was rightfully viewed as a masterful handling of many difficult issues. Ford had enhanced his standing within Harvard, and when McGeorge Bundy left Cambridge to become special assistant for national security to President Kennedy, the forty-two-year-old historian was named his successor as dean of the Faculty of Arts and Sciences. But Wilbur Bender, who had already announced his resignation, was deeply unhappy with the report and took the unusual step of making his disagreement public. His frankest response, however, was confidential: "Comments on the Report of the Subcommittee on College Admission Policy," an impassioned criticism of the final draft of *Admission to Harvard College*. Because of its "blunt language" (Bender's own description), it is the best source for understanding his thinking as his career at Harvard was coming to a close.[199]

For Bender, who loved Harvard and had devoted much of his life to it, the failure of the report was that it had not "come to grips with the fundamental problem of selection": "whether our eventual goal for Harvard is an American *École Normale,* or the nearest approach to it we can get."[200] In Bender's reading, "it is implied, but not directly stated" that Harvard should emulate this model, which admits students purely on the basis of their performance on an exam and serves as a training ground for many of France's leading academics and intellectuals.[201] Professors, in particular, were especially prone to take this view: "My guess is that many, perhaps most, of the faculty would support such a policy, and many would assume that the case for it was obvious and irrefutable."[202]

To Bender, however, the vision of a freshman class selected solely on the basis of academic criteria was nightmarish. "Would we have a dangerously high incidence of emotional problems, of breakdowns and suicides? Would we get a high proportion of rather precious, brittle types, intellectuals in quotes, beatniks, etc.?" "Do we really want," he continued, "a college in which practically everyone was headed for a career as a scholar, scientist, college teacher or research doctor?"[203]

For years, Harvard's policy had been a carefully crafted one of balance between public and private school students, between scholars and "gentlemen," and between future members of the intellectual elite and the economic elite. But the report threatened to upset this balance, which would have disastrous consequences, for it would "divorce entirely the future scholar from contact with the future businessman, politician, etc."[204]

The Ford Report did not — much to the dismay of Wilson and his allies — in fact endorse the model of an academic meritocracy.[205] Yet it did issue a number of recommendations that, if implemented, would undeniably move Harvard some distance in that direction. Three issues sharply separated Bender from the committee: the treatment of the overlapping categories of "gentlemen," candidates from the leading boarding schools, and alumni sons. In each case, the committee had, in Bender's view, failed to grasp that Harvard's special relationship with traditional elites was an integral part of what had made it great in the past and would permit it to remain great in the future.

"For the past century," Bender observed, Harvard "has been one of three or four colleges in the country which have had a special appeal to the upper income and socially elite families of the country and particularly of the Eastern seaboard." Whether one approved or not, this historic relationship was "one element in the special style and flavor of Harvard" and in the distinctive combination of "gentlemen and scholars" that was very much part of it.[206]

In Bender's view, perhaps the committee's most serious deficiency was its failure to consider the possibility that there was a "connection between this special combination and the greatness of Harvard."[207] The committee had, in short, skirted a question fundamental to Harvard's future: "Do we now want to liquidate the gentlemen, or further greatly curtail them?"

Acknowledging that such a policy was "now perhaps for the first time both a possible and in many ways a reasonable thing to do," Bender was deeply worried about the price that Harvard would pay: "To be crude about it, where will the future financial support of Harvard come from, and who among the businessmen and politicians of the future will defend the independence, freedom and integrity of Harvard? Can we look forward confidently to other means of financing the Harvard of 1990? The 82 million of the Program is coming largely from the "gentlemen" of the past, not the scholars, and a future student body made up largely of prospective Ph.D.'s will not add much, presumably, to our endowment." Admitting the possibility that "the 'gentlemen' will disappear anyhow" and that "the big money will be in the hands of other kinds of people, possibly including Harvard Ph.D.'s who came to us as bright, impoverished scholars from small town high schools," Bender nevertheless believed that it would be reckless for Harvard to abandon its traditional ties to the elite.[208] More than endangering Harvard's finances, it would also threaten to destroy its distinctive campus atmosphere (and hence its privileged niche in the ecology of elite higher education) and its opportunity to educate some of the leading businessmen and politicians of the next generation.

Regarding legacies, Bender wrote: "Let's face this one squarely and either abolish the preference or stand on it, and not be apologetic or shame-faced about it."[209] He was clearly on the side of those who wished to continue favoring Harvard sons and though the report did not disagree with him on this point, he apparently found its language less than reassuring.[210] Fearful that the Special Committee's implicit agenda reflected a larger movement to abolish preferences for legacies altogether, he suggested taking the matter out of the hands of the faculty: "it would be wise," he wrote, "to discuss this issue with those responsible for the alumni relations of the College and also with the governing boards."[211]

Bender also believed that the report dealt with athletes inadequately. Admitting that "both this and the Harvard son problem are sources of potential embarrassment if discussed candidly in a public document," he nonetheless called for an internal discussion in which the issue of athletes was "faced squarely and realistically." Though the committee called for giving athletic ability weight as "a significant extra-curricular activity," Bender feared that the report's main thrust was toward the elimination of preference.[212]

In the end, Bender's deepest worry was that the Ford Report was pushing Harvard in a direction that would separate it from the "men of affairs" who made their mark on American life. Bender believed that the professors who constituted the Special Committee adhered to a dangerously erroneous theory about what led to the highest levels of success in America. To test his hypothesis that Harvard's most brilliant students were not its most "distinguished graduates," he carried out his own study of exceptionally successful alumni.

The twenty-six men studied were a veritable *Who's Who* of the American elite: among them was a former secretary of defense, the president of Commonwealth Edison and Electric Bond and Share, the publisher of the *Minneapolis Star and Tribune,* the senior partner of Davis Polk, and (not least) the general chairman of the Program for Harvard College. Twenty-two were private school graduates, with St. Paul's (four) and Groton (three) leading a list of the nation's most elite boarding schools.[213] These men had not compiled particularly distinguished academic records at Harvard; the majority of them had relatively poor grades.[214] A casual inspection suggested "a much higher than average participation by the above in athletic and other extracurricular activities" — precisely the kinds of students likely to be excluded by the École Normale model.[215]

Bender's Parting Critique

In a document written not long after he left Harvard, Bender elaborated on his theme that a "top-one-percent" policy would cut Harvard off from men of power and reduce "Harvard's total impact on society."[216] "Two of the top four major candidates for the two top positions in the 1960 presidential campaign," he observed, "were ... Harvard graduates and from Boston"; furthermore, "they were both Harvard sons and private school graduates and thus included in the two groups which have been the favorite whipping boys of some of the most vociferous critics of the present admission policy." "It is likely that one or both of them," he noted pointedly, "would be denied admission to Harvard if the top-one-percent policy were adopted."[217]

Bender had done much to adapt his alma mater to the first era in its history characterized by a large surplus in the number of qualified applicants. As he noted with pride in his "Final Report to the President," what happened under his watch was "the greatest change in Harvard admissions, and thus in the Harvard student body, in a short time — two college generations — in our recorded history."[218] In 1952, the year before he took office, just 30 percent of applicants were rejected; by 1960, when he left, that number had more than doubled, to 63 percent. As applications increased, so too did the academic level of the freshman class, with combined median SATs rising almost two hundred points from 1,181 to 1,377 between 1952 and 1960. The freshman who ranked in the ninetieth percentile of the class in 1952 would have dropped to the fiftieth percentile eight years later.[219]

In other ways, however, change had been exceedingly slow during the Bender years. The Admissions Office had maintained its "drawing power in those schools which traditionally have had very close ties to Harvard — Andover, Exeter, Milton and Groton, for instance and which continue to send us large delegations of excellent candidates, in some cases larger than ever before."[220] The proportion of freshman legacies in the freshman class remained undiminished; indeed, between 1952 and 1960, their percentage rose from 17 to 18 percent.[221] Meanwhile, the socioeconomic composition of the student body became, if anything, more elite, with the percentage of freshmen whose fathers had not attended college cut from 37 to 18 percent and the median family income of scholarship holders rising from the fifty-eighth percentile ($4,900) of American families to the seventy-fifth ($7,800).[222] Clearly, rising academic standards had not led to greater social inclusivity; with tuition increasing rapidly and the proportion of scholarships steady (just 25 percent of the freshman class), the proportion of American families who could finance a Harvard education was — by Bender's own estimate — just 5 to 10 percent.[223]

For Bender, Harvard's distinctive atmosphere was inextricably intertwined with the presence in each class of a critical mass of "gentlemen." Bender's problem was that the "gentleman" was already in decline. Culturally and economically hegemonic when he joined the Harvard administration in the early 1930s, the Protestant upper class of the Northeast no longer enjoyed the supremacy it had once taken for granted.[224] New groups — Jews, Catholics, and the nouveaux riches of the South and West — were rising and eager to stake their own claims in the economy and the polity.

Also rendering Bender's attachment to the "gentlemen" increasingly obsolete was the concurrent (and not unrelated) rise of what the sociologist Alvin Gouldner has called the "new class."[225] Composed of intellectuals and what Gouldner calls technical intelligentsia, the new class core was comprised of highly educated professionals whose claims to income, power, and status derived not from property, but from knowledge and expertise. Dependent for its reproduction on the transmission of cultural rather than economic capital (unlike the "old class," which still largely relied on the direct transmission of property), the ascendancy of the new class infused the old American ideology of equality of opportunity with new life, for its own spontaneous ideology emphasized advancement through academic achievement rather than hereditary privilege. Buttressed by the increasingly critical role of knowledge in the postindustrial economy, the expansion of the state, the ever more visible role of science in national defense, and the rapid expansion of higher education, the new class posed a growing challenge to the power and the worldview of the old upper class.

In this new environment, Bender's fondness for the academically undistinguished scions of the upper class and his antipathy toward the scholastically brilliant had come to seem antiquated. Accusing the proponents of meritocracy of favoring "graduate school admission criteria and goals," Bender warned that such a policy had already been shown to yield "a lot of singularly unimpressive human beings in the crop which enters each year."[226] Though a high I.Q. did not necessarily make it likely that an individual would be "unstable or unattractive or physically uncoordinated or have a bad character or a high feminine component," he noted, in an apparent attempt at humor, that "there is some profane amateur opinion that the percentage of bearded types tends to go up with the increase of average I.Q."[227]

Bender contended that "the student who ranks first in his class may be genuinely brilliant," but in truth "the top high school student is often, frankly, a pretty dull and bloodless, or peculiar, fellow." The valedictorian, he continued, "may have focused narrowly on grade-getting as compensation for his inadequacies in other areas, because he lacks other interests or talents or lacks passion and warmth or normal healthy instincts or is afraid of life."[228]

These vintage Bender sentiments embodied a set of values that were more and more out of step with the times. A former colleague observed two years after Bender's untimely death in 1969 that he was a man of strong biases in favor of "country boys," "westerners," and "athletes," and against "effete, eastern soft, rarefied intellectualism," "valedictorians," "ballet dancers," "New Jersey suburbia," and "Bronx School of Science."[229] These prejudices, consonant with Harvard's ethos in the early 1930s, had by 1960 become a serious liability. At a time when the very survival of the nation might depend on discovering the brilliant, if unrefined, boy from a modest social background who might invent the next atomic bomb, Bender's hostility to "scientists as withdrawn, scrawny, not personable, excessively intellectual" was a luxury that Harvard — and perhaps America — could no longer afford.[230] Together with the anti-Semitism present in what his colleague generously construed as "anti-urban" sentiments, one can see why Bender was no longer the man for the job.

Bender's great misfortune was to be a traditionalist when meritocratic ideology reached high tide.[231] The central tenet of a meritocracy — that advancement in the educational system should be governed by demonstrated academic achievement — seemed to have history on its side. In such an atmosphere, the idea of admitting students to colleges purely on the basis of academic criteria had become so commonsensical that even the *New York Times,* in an editorial, "Ivy League Admissions," came out in favor of determining admissions "on a strictly objective basis — an average of entrance examination scores or the like."[232]

From today's vantage point, Bender's vocal insistence on the preservation of preferences for the privileged seems hopelessly backward-looking. But his departure did not represent the symbolic defeat of the forces at Harvard favoring the maintenance of outdated policies: Harvard's admissions remained, with a few minor modifications, what they had been during Bender's years. Though Bender lost many of his specific battles with the Special Committee, he won the larger war. For the admission policy he abhorred — variously called the "top-one-percent policy," "graduate school criteria," and "single-factor admissions" — would never be put into effect.

The cause that Bender fought for has remained Harvard's basic admissions policy until the present day.[233] In the aftermath of his historic assault, the forces at Harvard favoring selection on academic criteria alone were routed, never to recover. Just how thorough a defeat they suffered would become apparent over the next several years as the new dean of admissions, Fred Glimp, a Bender protégé, moved Harvard even further away from the model of the École Normale.

The Glimp Years

Fred Glimp's social origins were even more modest than Bender's: he was the son of an Okie with a ninth-grade education. Legend has it that Glimp was accepted by Harvard because a secretary spotted his photo and thought he looked nice. Harvard's faith in Glimp, whatever its basis, was not misplaced.[234]

After serving as Bender's assistant from 1954 to 1958 and as director of freshman scholarships from 1958 to 1960, Glimp was appointed Bender's successor at the comparatively young age of thirty-four. Glimp's main accomplishment during his seven years in the post was to institutionalize the philosophy that Bender had articulated while further diversifying the student body.[235]

In the 1961 revised edition of the "Schools and Scholarship Committee Handbook," a basic document sent to all alumni interviewers and staff, Glimp made it clear that he shared Bender's philosophy: "We do not believe," he declared, "that a college of 4500 Group I students would be the ideal college or provide its students the best possible educational experience, even if educating career scholars were Harvard College's sole task, which it is not."[236] In the 1962 edition of the Rollo Book, sent out to all prospective applicants, candidates whose sole strength was academic were put on notice: "The obsessive grade-grubber, the person who is afraid of life and the arrogant or precious intellectual are not likely to profit greatly here."[237]

In his first few months in office, Glimp took this general orientation and extended it in a new direction. In a statement distributed to all staff and alumni interviewers, he raised anew the issue: "Any class, no matter how able, will always have a bottom quarter. What are the effects of the psychology of feeling average, even in a very able group? Are there identifiable types with the psychological or what-not tolerance to be 'happy' or to make the most of education while in the bottom quarter? Are they boondockers? Are they Harvard sons? Are they St. Grottlesex types?"[238] Wouldn't it be better, he implied, if the students at the bottom were content to be there? Thus the renowned (some would say notorious) Harvard admission practice know as the "happy-bottom-quarter" policy was born.[239]

Another important change was an increase in the number of freshmen on scholarship: from an average of 282 between 1956 and 1959, and 316 in 1960, to 345 in 1961. This increase, which had long been favored by Bender and explicitly recommended by the Ford Report, was made possible by President Pusey's decision to support the new level of scholarships out of the unrestricted income of the faculty.[240] Harvard now had 29 percent of freshmen on scholarship, placing it in a tie with Yale for second in the Ivy League, behind only Princeton, at 33 percent. In terms of size of the average scholarship, however, Harvard was well ahead of its rivals, spending $1,320 per student, compared to $1,166 at Princeton and $1,106 at Yale.[241]

By 1965, just over a third of all freshmen were on Harvard scholarships, and 7 percent received renewable outside aid.[242] Though Harvard was not yet able to adopt a policy of need-blind, full-aid admissions, it was very close to being able to remove finances as a consideration in determining who could come to Harvard.

Classification and Power

In assessing the 5,000–7,000 applicants competing annually for just 1,400–1,500 slots, the Admissions Office used a complex system of classification to process each candidate. The design of this system was a fateful matter, for systems of classification are also systems of power, favoring some groups while disadvantaging others.[243] For this reason, the very categories of classification systems are often objects of struggle between groups; witness the checkered history of racial classification in the United States and the creation of a multiracial category by the Census Bureau in 2000.[244]

During the Glimp and Bender years (and beyond), the most consequential classificatory scheme at Harvard was the "docket system," whose origins may be traced to the emphasis on geographical diversity that was part of the attempt to address the "Jewish problem" in the 1920s.[245] Harvard's docket system was divided into twenty-two groups, ranging from the huge (Docket B, which covered eight Rocky Mountain states) to the very small (Docket P, limited to Boston Latin, and Docket Q, which covered the rest of metropolitan Boston). This system also included four separate categories solely for private schools: Exeter and Andover (Docket L), "Select New England private schools" (Docket M), other New England private schools (Docket N), and private schools in the Middle Atlantic states (Docket R). That private schools had four dockets of their own in a system primarily organized according to geography was testimony to the preferred status they continued to enjoy.[246]

While the docket system was not, strictly speaking, a quota system, it did generate "targets" for each docket that proved strikingly close to the actual number of students admitted each year. Targets for Docket M ("Select New England private schools"), for example, varied narrowly from 127 to 131 between 1961 and 1965; the actual number of admissions varied from 129 to 134. Other, less favored dockets had similarly predictable patterns; for example, Docket S, comprising the public schools of metropolitan New York City, metropolitan Philadelphia, and New Jersey, and including roughly twice as many applicants as Docket M, had targets ranging from just 82 to 94 during the same five years, with the number of actual admits varying from 85 to 91.[247] Inscribed in the system was a set of categories of favored and disfavored groups; applicants from the upper Midwest (Docket D, covering North and South Dakota, Minnesota, and Wisconsin) were accepted in 1965 at a rate of over one in four while those candidates in Docket S were accepted at a rate of one in seven. But the most favored dockets of all were private school dockets M and L, with, respectively, 44 and 46 percent acceptance rates compared to just 20 percent for all applicants.

The structure of this system ensured that competition would be almost entirely within rather than between dockets.[248] The generous targets for some dockets were designed to insulate applicants from competition with other dockets while the abstemious targets for others were intended to guarantee that the number of students admitted would not upset Harvard's delicate "balance." Clearly, a candidate's docket substantially enhanced — or diminished — his chance of admission. Inscribed in the docket system was the set of outcomes that Harvard wished to see: disproportionately large delegations from the leading private schools, a sizable representation from regions far from the Northeast, and limits on the number of public school students from the Middle Atlantic states, especially metropolitan New York City and Philadelphia.

A second system of classification rated each applicant individually along four dimensions: personal, academic, extracurricular, and athletic. In addition, applicants were further rated by school principals and teachers and by those who had interviewed them — staff members, alumni, or both. With all of the information in hand, each candidate would be assigned an overall rating from one ("Clear Admit. Exceptional in some way or other, strong in all respects") to nine ("Clear reject. Serious weakness").[249]

Several aspects of this scheme are striking. First, academic ranking was but one of the four dimensions. Second, athletic ability, which could easily have been subsumed under the extracurricular ranking, was considered so important that an entirely separate rating was given to all applicants, including the many who had shown little or no evidence of athletic talent. Third, and most significant, there was a separate ranking for the highly subjective "personal" dimension — clearly an attempt to get at the "intangible" qualities so important to Bender and Glimp.

In contrast to the other three dimensions, the coding guide distributed to the admissions staff offered relatively little insight into the criteria used to rank applicants on "personal" characteristics. For a student to receive a "1," for example, he must be considered "Tops in all respects"; a "2" if he was "very appealing; unusually forceful; effective; human, or whatever." A candidate who is "generally not appealing and whose negative characteristics outweigh positive" ones receives a "5," and one who gives a "generally poor impression" and seems to be "unstable or offensive" is assigned a "6."[250]

The criteria at the personal level may have been unclear, but the consequences were not. A personal rating of "4" (the apparently neutral, "Generally acceptable, nothing strong positively or negatively"), for example, was fatal to a candidate's admission chances, with a rejection rate of 98 percent. A personal rating of "1" was a virtual guarantee of admission, with a rejection rate of just 2.5 percent.[251]

According to Harvard's own statistical studies, the personal rating was a stronger predictor of which candidates would ultimately be admitted than the more objective academic rating. This subjectivity was one of the great assets of the personal rating, for it permitted admissions officers to exercise the discretion they valued so highly. Some people, as Bender wrote in his "Final Report to the President," were "singularly unimpressive human beings"; others were apparently just the kind of boys that Harvard most wanted.[252] The great virtue of the personal rating was that it permitted the Admissions Office to distinguish — with the spuriously mathematical precision implicit in ranking a human being on a scale of 1 to 6 — between the two.

Favored and Disfavored Categories

A third major scheme divided applicants into twelve categories. The "typology," as Harvard called it, was an integral part of each student's file: accordingly, the first reader assigned the candidate a code letter that was a shorthand for the social type he was thought to embody. This code letter — for example, "A" for "All-American" ("healthy uncomplicated athletic strengths and style, perhaps some extra-curricular participation, but not combined with top academic credentials") — would accompany the candidate's file until a decision was made to "admit" or "deny."[253]

The codes provided a lens through which applicants would be seen and appraised. Every applicant would be placed in one of the categories, with those hardest to type placed in the residual category of "other":

1. S First-rate scholar in Harvard departmental terms.
2. D Candidate's primary strength is his academic strength, but it doesn't look strong enough to qualify as an S (above).
3. A All-American — healthy, uncomplicated athletic strengths and style, perhaps some extracurricular participation, but not combined with top academic credentials.
4. W Mr. School — significant extracurricular and perhaps (but not necessarily) athletic participation plus excellent academic record.
5. X Cross-country style — steady man who plugs and plugs and plugs, won't quit when most others would. Gets results largely through stamina and consistent effort.
6. P PBH [Phillips Brooks House] style: in activities and personal concerns.[254]
7. C Creative in music, art, writing.
8. B Boondocker — unsophisticated rural background.
9. T Taconic — culturally depressed background, low income.[255]
10. K Krunch — main strength is athletic, prospective varsity athlete.[256]
11. L Lineage — candidate probably couldn't be admitted without the extra plus of being a Harvard son, a faculty son, or a local boy with ties to the university community.
12. O Other — use when none of the above are applicable.

With minor modifications, this typology was still in place at least through 1988.[257]

The typology was a perfect embodiment of the philosophy of admissions articulated by Bender and further elaborated by Glimp, in which a complex array of nonacademic considerations prove decisive. Broadly speaking, these characteristics can be broken into three groups: those that favored the socially and culturally disadvantaged (B and T), those that favored privileged groups (L), and the remainder, which favored applicants on the basis of either personal qualities (X and P) or their accomplishments in extracurricular activities (W or C) or athletics (A or K).

How this system operated in practice can be seen with greatest clarity among those students who were accepted despite weak academic records. In a remarkable study of the entering freshmen of 1966, the Admissions Office reported on the characteristics of the 209 students who had received academic ratings of 5 ("Marginal. Might pass with great effort, on motivation for academic works questionable") or 4 ("Capable of passing record but probably not honors work"). Of these 209 students, 44 were from the Lineage category, an additional 19 were Taconic or Boondocker, and another 19 had been placed in Cross-Country. But the biggest type by far was athletes, with 60 All-American types and 22 from the Horse (elsewhere called Krunch) category. In sharp contrast, just 5 Creative, 4 PBH types, and 12 Wheels (another term for Mr. School) managed to enter Harvard in 1966 with academic ratings of 4 or 5.[258]

The Ford Report had called for the reduction, though not the elimination, of the preferential treatment accorded legacy applicants. But five years later, this preference remained massive: an applicant with an academic 3, for example, gained admission about 25 percent of the time, but 67 percent of legacies with the same rating were admitted.[259]

If a purely academic meritocracy was incompatible with Harvard's wish to favor alumni sons and athletes, so too was it in conflict with Harvard's growing effort to reach out to the disadvantaged. This effort, which began with Conant and expanded under Bender, gained momentum with Glimp's accession to the position of dean of admissions. Coming from his own relatively disadvantaged background, Glimp wished to make the opportunity to attend Harvard available to low-income and rural students.

By 1966, 10 percent of the Harvard freshman class (118 students) was composed of students who qualified for Federal Opportunity Grants — a considerable accomplishment, given that they were awarded only to students whose families were below the poverty line.[260] A study by Humphrey Doermann two years earlier offered an illuminating profile of the types of low-income students who entered Harvard. In 1965, the largest group (49) consisted of sons of laborers and factory workers, followed by students from rural backgrounds (32), with an additional group (25) described simply as "disadvantaged." In order to accept these students, Harvard had to be flexible in applying its academic requirements: of the 106 students in the study, 21 percent had SAT verbal scores below 572, placing them in the bottom decile of Harvard students. Though Doermann emphasized that the study's results suggested "that one consequence of attempting to raise, consciously, our aptitude test score distribution would be to decrease disproportionately the already-small delegation [of low-income students]," he also acknowledged that over 80 percent of the 121 students in the bottom verbal SAT decile were *not* from such backgrounds.[261]

As Harvard well knew, any increase in the required academic minimum would also eliminate some of the "paying guests" on whom it still depended. In a remarkably forthright memorandum, "Small Size of the Pool of Bright

AND Prosperous College Candidates in the United States," Doermann estimated that "the national supply" of male high school graduates scoring verbal 600 or better from families earning $15,700 or more (an estimate of the
top 2.5 percent and top 5 percent levels) was roughly 10,000 male students.[262]
Simply lowering the cut line to 550, he estimated, would increase the supply
to perhaps 20,000. On the other hand, were Harvard to raise the academic
minimum to an SAT of verbal 620 and a family income of $15,000 (roughly
the "no-need" line), Doermann's best estimate was that there were only 5,000
to 7,000 such students nationwide. Were Harvard to further constrict the
pool of potential "paying guests," it would do so at its own peril.[263]

Harvard's consistent and forceful opposition to the pure academic meritocracy model was not about its commitment to diversity and the disadvantaged. The larger issue at stake — and one that long predated Harvard's commitment to diversity — was whether Harvard would be free to pursue its
institutional interests as it defined them.

The Happy-Bottom-Quarter Policy and the Fate of the "Intellectuals"

In his final report to the president, Glimp described "the notion behind the
efforts and decisions of the last seven years" as "a natural extension of the
changes under Dean Bender's chairmanship."[264] Yet this description does not
do justice to the innovativeness of Glimp's "happy bottom-quarter" policy.
Glimp's goal was to identify "the right bottom-quarter students — men who
have the perspective, ego strength, or extracurricular outlets for maintaining
their self-respect (or whatever) while making the most of their academic opportunities at a C- level."[265] But who were the lucky 300 or so individuals who
would be offered a ticket to Cambridge despite their modest academic credentials? Reading Harvard's public discussions of the matter, one could conclude that the main purpose of the "happy-bottom-quarter" was to guarantee
that the student body would be socioeconomically and racially diverse. But
disadvantaged students at Harvard, perhaps 9 percent of the class, clearly did
not constitute the majority.[266] Nor did the limited number of African Americans, with many of them overlapping with the category of "disadvantaged"
and a number of them undoubtedly not in the academic bottom quarter.[267]
The conclusion is unavoidable: though the "happy-bottom-quarter" policy
did contribute to diversity, it was not primarily about offering opportunities
to blacks or to poor and working-class students.

Glimp's commitment to a "happy bottom-quarter" was part of a conscious decision to continue to accept students who scored in the 500s — and
sometimes even lower — on the verbal SAT.[268] According to Harvard's own
estimates, squeezing out the bottom tenth of the class would narrow the po-

tential pool of admits by 75 percent.[269] The issue of the size of the pool had long been something of an obsession; as noted earlier, Conant had worried that Harvard was fishing in too small a pond as far back as the 1930s.[270] Three decades later, the Admissions Office remained preoccupied with the same issue, proposing to solve it by setting — as Bender had suggested — a reasonably (but not unduly) high academic floor and then selecting from those above it on primarily nonacademic grounds.

What was the effect of this policy on aspiring scholars and intellectuals — the very candidates most sought by the faculty? Officially, Harvard's answer was clear: it claimed to "have admitted at once the small number of really brilliant students who appeared to possess sound character and personality."[271] In reality, Harvard rejected one candidate in seven with an academic rating of 1 — a category so stratospheric that it was reserved to only the top 2 percent of all applicants between 1960 and 1964.[272] Apparently, serious problems of "character or personality" were not uncommon among the academically brilliant.

In 1952, Bender had proposed reserving about 10 percent of the class for "top brains"[273]; fourteen years later, with the number of applicants having grown by more than 3,500, Glimp did not wish to increase this number. In a 1966 memo to his fellow members of the Admission and Scholarship Committee, he acknowledged, "The handful of men who seem likely to startle some part of the faculty have a special claim on us," but estimated their number at only 100 to 150.[274] With 1,200 places in the class (and over 1,400 admissions slots), this was essentially the same 10 percent target Bender had proposed. Thus in 1966, near the zenith of the supposed trend toward meritocracy, 9 out of 10 admissions decisions at America's most renowned research university were based on factors other than sheer scholastic brilliance.

In fact, the prospects of the most academically talented applicants declined during the Glimp years.[275] In 1960, academic 1's and 2's were accepted at a combined rate of 63 percent; by 1964, that rate had dropped to 52 percent. Yet during these same years, the combined acceptance rate of personal 1's and 2's actually climbed from 67 to 69 percent. In 1964, for the first time, a majority of academic 2's — 549 individuals — were rejected by Harvard.[276] Had all of them been accepted (as well as all of the 84 academic 1's), there would still have been well over 250 places remaining in the freshman class.

This shift away from academic factors under Glimp had a strong negative impact on certain types of students. Whereas in 1960 applicants from the Bronx High School of Science, Stuyvesant, and Philadelphia's Central High School were accepted at a rate of 26 percent, by 1965 that rate had been cut in half, to 13 percent.[277]

Had Harvard been an academic meritocracy, it would have accepted far more boys from the Bronx Sciences and the Central High Schools than from the Grotons and the St. Paul's. In 1963, both Bronx Science (48) and Central (45) alone had more National Merit Scholarship semifinalists than the six St. Grottlesex schools combined (32).[278] But Harvard in the 1960s remained, as before, much more interested in attracting the polished young man who attended St. Grottlesex than his less refined, if more academically talented, peer at the selective urban high schools. With personal factors carrying increasing weight while academic factors were declining in significance, Harvard in 1965 was in many ways less meritocratic than it had been five years earlier.

During the Glimp years, it became increasingly clear that the Harvard that Bender had long feared was coming into being would never do so.[279] Instead, the Glimp era produced a Harvard in which a "happy-bottom-quarter" would be a matter of institutional policy and pure "intellectuals" were limited to roughly 10 percent of the class. The ideology of academic meritocracy had had its moment at Harvard, and it had been decisively defeated.

CHAPTER 10

Tradition and Change at Old Nassau

I F HARVARD IN THE 1950s was worried about its image as a college "dominated by Jews" and "full of pansies," Princeton was afflicted by no such problem.[1] In no danger of being overrun by "top brains" and "grinds," Princeton's problem was quite the opposite: its image as a genteel and anti-intellectual country club, filled with — in the words of the inimitable Bender — the highest proportion of "extremely nice Nordic blondes, best dressed and best mannered."[2] In an era when colleges were increasingly ranked on the basis of academic values, Princeton's long-standing image as an eating club–dominated bastion of gentlemanly sociability — a place where brilliant scholars would be uncomfortable — had become a serious liability.

When the College Board decided in 1949 to permit students to apply to several colleges without naming a first choice, Princeton's image took on added importance. For the first time, Princeton — and Harvard and Yale as well — would have to compete to attract the students it had admitted. As late as 1950 (the last year the old system was still in place), 85 percent of those admitted to Princeton enrolled in the fall; by 1953, that figure had plummeted to 61 percent.[3]

The person assigned the difficult task of adapting Princeton to this new environment was Charles William Edwards, named in 1950 as successor to the redoubtable Radcliffe Heermance, the only director of admissions the school had ever known. Edwards '36 had impeccable family credentials: his father '06, uncle '00, and brother '33 were all alumni. A graduate of the Noble and Greenough School, near Boston, Edwards played football while serving as class president and literary editor of the school paper. As an undergraduate at Princeton, he compiled an unremarkable academic record but was very active in extracurricular activities. The president of Tiger Inn, one of the more elite eating clubs, he played varsity rugby and earned class numerals in both cross-country and track. An Episcopalian and a Republican, Edwards was also a member of the Right Wing Club at Princeton.[4]

After graduation, Edwards returned to Noble and Greenough, where he taught history for six years until enlisting in the American Field Service in 1942, where he trained in Syria with the British army. A combatant in the climactic battles of the African and Italian campaigns, he rose to the rank of major before returning to Princeton in 1945. Named assistant director of admissions in 1946, he became Princeton's second admissions director in the summer of 1950.[5]

The Issue of Alumni Sons

At the outset, Edwards faced two major problems that had not confronted his predecessor: a vigorous competition among applicants for a place in the freshman class and an increasingly intense competition among the colleges (and especially among the Big Three) to persuade those admitted to come. One of Edwards's greatest assets was Princeton's loyal and closely knit alumni body. By 1955, 800 to 900 alumni in nearly 100 Alumni Schools Committees interviewed more than 2,500 candidates for admission.[6] That same year, the million-dollar mark in annual giving was passed for the first time. By 1958–1959, the proportion of alumni contributing to Princeton annually surpassed 72 percent — the highest figure attained by any American college to that point.[7]

Yet the alumni were also a serious problem, for they contributed to the image — and the reality — of Princeton as a private club. Notoriously involved in campus affairs long after they graduated (with some of them still visiting their eating clubs regularly), the alumni took for granted that their sons would receive a strong preference in the admissions process. Some even felt that the admission of their offspring was an alumni right. In his "Report to the President" for 1954, Edwards referred to three such fathers whose sons had failed to gain admission despite a legacy acceptance rate of over 80 percent; "all three," he wrote, "held in the main to the thesis that no son of a Princeton alumnus should be rejected . . . regardless of his record in school." Such a viewpoint, Edwards reported with dismay, "is not as limited among alumni as one would suppose."[8]

Through its assiduous cultivation of its alumni, Princeton had played no small part in creating the atmosphere in which such attitudes could survive. The character of campus life itself contributed to sentiments of alumni entitlement; as late as 1954, the *Freshman Herald* still listed, name by name, "Members of the Class Whose Father Attended Princeton University as Undergraduates" (for example: John C. Danforth, son of D. Danforth, Class of 1920).[9] Of the 149 sons of Old Nassau in the Class of 1958, many were destined to join their fathers' eating club.

In 1958, as Harvard was preparing to appoint a faculty committee to review admissions practices that deviated from meritocratic ideals, Princeton issued an official document that declared unequivocally that "the Princeton son does *not* have to compete against non-Princeton sons." In a pam-

phlet, "Answers to your questions about the ADMISSION OF PRINCETON
SONS," the question of standards was dealt with directly: "*No matter how
many other boys apply, the Princeton son is judged from an academic standpoint
solely on the one question: Can he be expected to graduate?* If so, he's admitted."[10] Edwards reaffirmed this policy in his "Report to the President" for
1958, stating simply: "If it was felt that a boy in this category could successfully meet the demands of a Princeton education he was admitted."[11]

Though Edwards accepted Princeton's policy, he more than once expressed deep ambivalence about its wisdom. The consequence of the policy
was, as he was well aware, that legacies were heavily overrepresented among
Princeton's weakest students. Alumni sons, though constituting 19 percent of
all freshmen in 1954, accounted for half of the 34 boys with Converted School
Grades (CSGs) of 4− or below.[12] And of "41 boys about whom there is slight
doubt as to their motivation, incentive or general maturity," 21 were Princeton sons. "It is exceedingly difficult," complained Edwards, "to know just
where the line should be drawn in this area."[13]

By 1957, Edwards's stance had moved from ambivalence to open criticism.
Observing that the legacy applicant "does not meet the 'competition' for the
number of places available as do all other candidates," he reported that of the
26 freshmen with CSGs of 4− or below, 21 were alumni sons. This was too
much for his sense of decency and fair play: "In spite of widespread feeling to
the contrary," he wrote, "it would almost seem that Princeton sons receive too
much priority." This conclusion was "borne out by the fact that among the
cases appearing each year before the Discipline Committee and the Committee on Examinations and Standing Princeton sons appear out of proportion
to their representation in the undergraduate body."[14]

Despite recurrent reservations — in 1961 he asked still again "whether or
not a Princeton son should be admitted if he is clearly inferior on either academic or personal bases to many applicants who are rejected" — the policy of
admitting all minimally competent legacies was still in place when Edwards
stepped down in 1962.[15] In his last five years, when the admission rate was
roughly one-third, slightly over two-thirds of alumni sons were admitted.[16]
Some Princeton fathers were not satisfied. "The alumni," an admissions officer told a journalist in 1962, "feel their boy has to be a genius to make it."
The faculty, for their part, believed that "any idiot whose father went to
Princeton can get in."[17]

The Student Body

Though Princeton in the 1950s was no longer the prep school enclave that it
had been before World War II, alumni of the major boarding schools still set

the tone of campus life. Each year "delegations" of boys arrived from the great boarding schools; the typical freshman from a public high school was a "singleton." In 1954, well over a fifth of the class came from just 9 preparatory schools; the top 3 — Lawrenceville, Exeter, and Deerfield — sent delegations of 32, 24, and 21, respectively.[18] Despite the growing presence of public school graduates, 56 percent of the freshmen in 1954 had attended private secondary schools.[19]

Prep school graduates were at a distinct advantage, for they came with a network of friends and acquaintances that facilitated their entry into the more prestigious eating clubs. At the top of the social hierarchy, the archetypal young man was the alumnus of an elite boarding school, Episcopalian or Presbyterian, and his father had attended Princeton. At the bottom was his social and cultural opposite: the graduate of a public school, perhaps Jewish, who needed a scholarship in order to attend.

Prep school boys and alumni sons were not, of course, the only types favored by Princeton's admissions policy. Like Harvard and Yale, Princeton gave strong preference to candidates who displayed athletic talent in secondary school. But only Princeton regularly listed in its annual reports on admissions the number of freshmen who had been varsity football, basketball, or hockey players in high school. In 1957, 200 freshmen were reported to have played varsity football in secondary school — more than 25 percent.[20] If the image of the Princetonian remained that of an athletic and gentlemanly young man, the school's admissions policy had played no small part in sustaining it.

Like its Big Three rivals, Princeton continued to place great emphasis on intangible nonacademic qualities in admissions. "Teachers and scholars," stated Radcliffe Heermance in a special 1953 report to the president and trustees looking back on his 28 years of experience, "are inclined to be unduly influenced in favor of an applicant who presents a record of distinguished academic achievement." Instead of focusing narrowly on academic talent, those selecting the freshman class should emphasize "the basic qualities which make up the useful life . . . : unselfishness, loyalty, friendliness, cooperation, courage to stand on one's own feet, and the will to help others."[21] It was the old ideology of "character" in modern form, but its purpose was essentially unchanged: to give the admissions office the necessary discretion to admit the types of boys whose social and personal characteristics made them a good fit for Princeton and to exclude those whose presence might undermine its distinctive but delicate campus atmosphere.

The vehicle for putting this policy into practice was Princeton's rating system, which assigned every candidate a score between 1 (high) and 5 (low) on "academic promise" and "character and personal promise."[22] At times, the character rating provided an opportunity to discuss nonacademic attributes, often discovered during personal interviews, of seemingly little relevance to admissions. After reading the data in one applicant's file, for example, an admissions officer turned to Edwards and asked:

> "Does this say fat, Bill?"
>
> "Oh, yes," Edwards said, unperturbed. "This is the fat boy. Guidance counselor thinks he should demonstrate self-control by losing more weight."
>
> "Good Lord, yes," Farrell said. "I saw him. He weighs more than three hundred pounds. Walks like a penguin."

Despite his obesity, the candidate — who had applied to the School of Engineering and had high test scores — was admitted ("One fat engineer, coming up," muttered an admissions officer).[23]

At times, however, nonacademic qualities judged to be negative could prove fatal to a candidate's chances.[24] In a profile in the alumni magazine of six young men who had applied to Princeton in 1958, one applicant was rejected despite the interviewer's remark that he "might be a potential genius." The candidate, who had a very high CSG (2+) and ranked third in a class of 724, was judged to be "bright" but "narrowly bookish." Perhaps his greatest defect, however, was that he "was critical of all in authority." Having made a "very negative personal impression" in the interview, the boy was rejected despite being by far the strongest applicant academically of the six candidates described.[25]

Nevertheless, some things at Princeton had in fact changed. Most obvious was the influx of public school students, whose proportion in the freshman class had risen from 21 percent in 1940 to 39 percent in 1950 to 51 percent in 1958.[26] With the growth in the number of public school graduates came a substantial increase in the number of Jewish students. Barely 1 percent of freshmen in 1940, Jews constituted roughly 14 percent of all undergraduates by 1958.[27] Yet, despite the altered composition of the student body, campus social life — and the eating club system that stood at the center of it — had hardly changed at all. It was a formula for trouble, as the notorious "Dirty Bicker" of 1958 would dramatically demonstrate.

The Princeton Social System in the 1950s

In 1950, the eating clubs had responded to the growing student demand for acceptance into Princeton's social system by announcing the "100 percent principle": every sophomore who wished to join a club would receive a bid from at least one institution. Each year those unfortunate students — perhaps thirty or so annually — who went through Bicker yet failed to receive an invitation from any of the seventeen clubs became known as "100 percenters." With the cooperation of the Inter-Club Committee (ICC), these outcasts would then be scattered among the eating clubs, with the most prestigious less willing than the others to take in even one or two of them.[28]

But there was considerable (if far less than unanimous) support among the students for the 100 percent principle, and it was honored each year through the mid-1950s.[29] Yet the alumni, who controlled the Graduate Boards of the clubs and hence their finances, were not comfortable with the growing diversity of the student body. In the 1950s they began to interfere in the selection of undergraduate members — a matter that had traditionally been a prerogative of the undergraduates themselves.

In an extraordinary report directed to President Dodds and the trustees, a Special Committee of the alumni Graduate Inter-Club Council (GICC) pinpointed the problem:

> When the present club system was developed and when the membership bodies of the various clubs were being established, the admissions policy was, in general, the selection of the all-round boy with very heavy favoritism on those who attended eastern preparatory schools. In the past few years the pressure for admission has required stiffer qualifications. As a result the percentage of preparatory school boys has dropped from around 90% to under 50% and boys of very diversified background and training are now being admitted. It must be realized that this radical change in the type and complexion of the undergraduate body presents problems to a club system operating on the free and voluntary elective system.[30]

Ironically, the Special Committee's proposed solution was identical to that proposed by many of the students, including the most liberal: "that the University establish, effective September 1957, adequate eating and social facilities for upperclassmen who do not join clubs."[31]

Such a facility was necessary, the GICC believed, because the 100 percent principle inevitably led to "the efforts of the undergraduates to ram uncongenial eligibles into clubs." This was a serious matter, for the club system had its origin in the mutual groupings of congenial friends and its foundation was the "free and voluntary selection of its membership."[32] One of the great virtues of the system from the alumni's point of view was that it gave the student crucial experience in "learning to get along with his fellowmen." Just as "a student must 'deliver the goods' to get his Bachelor's Degree or his 'P' [athletic letter] . . . so he must sell himself to his college mates in order to merit an invitation to join an upperclass club." "Being invited to join one of the clubs," the GICC firmly believed, "is a privilege to be won and not a place to be drawn for or assigned."[33]

Were an adequate alternative facility available, the GICC estimated that

50 to 75 students out of a class of 750 would wish to join. This group would be composed of:

a) subjective or introvert type personalities who are interested in their academic work to the exclusion of about everything else
b) some Do-gooders who consider the club system undemocratic and who prefer the wider association with their college mates to the more intimate club life
c) students who could ill afford the more expensive rates at the private clubs

Many of these students "would be happier in such a place than they would be in a club having been forced into the club mold." Despite the expressed worries of the "100 percenters" and other students, "this new facility need not be a 'garbage can.'"[34]

To make sure that the administration understood, the GICC warned, "To destroy the club system would be to diminish the Princeton spirit and to reduce substantially the amount of annual giving."[35] President Dodds had tried hard to accommodate the alumni, but they posed a serious problem: their opposition to the 100 percent principle threatened the delicate equilibrium then in place on the volatile issue of discrimination by the eating clubs. In 1955, the alumni interfered in the selection process itself, using the Graduate Boards to veto bids to students deemed "uncongenial." According to Raymond W. Apple '57, writing in the *Daily Princetonian*, the last stages of the Bicker process that year manifested "a spirit of racial discrimination . . . now bluntly explicit."[36]

The leadership of the undergraduate clubs had worked hard to maintain the 100 percent principle, proposing a rotation plan for students without a bid. Though supported by 16 of the 17 clubs (Cottage was the holdout), the rotation plan did not pass because of the opposition of 10 of the Graduate Boards.[37] Nevertheless, the 100 percent principle was maintained in 1956, following 20 strenuous but ultimately successful hours of effort by the ICC to place more than 20 "100 percenters."[38]

After extended negotiations with the GICC, the administration, backed by the trustees, managed in the fall of 1956 to convince the Graduate Boards that neither they nor the administration would be involved in club selection "for an experimental period of three years."[39] In addition, the university announced that it would establish a temporary facility in Madison Hall, previously a part of Commons, to provide meals and amenities to upperclassmen not in the clubs — less than the full-fledged eating and social facility proposed by the alumni but a concession nonetheless.[40]

To outside observers, the Bicker of 1957 seemed to go smoothly, meeting the goal of 100 percent membership for the eighth consecutive year. But that year's Bicker was among the most tense in Princeton's history. A club leader who witnessed an incident the night before Open House night described the scene:

> It was about eleven the night before Open House and the last calling period had just finished. On my way back from Prospect Street I happened to stop for almost 45 minutes to talk to two classmates in front of Witherspoon Hall. We stood outside even though it was a damp and misty night. Soon I began to notice that a number of undergraduates were arriving singly and in small groups at the neighboring dormitory . . .
> We entered the dorm where the meeting was in progress and it was impossible to depict accurately what we saw. The meeting was composed entirely of Jewish boys, most of whom were sophomores. There were somewhere between one hundred and one hundred and fifty present and they were crowded into rooms on two floors, but most of them were just standing around with bewildered and blank faces. A few were in tears. Some were very angry. The emotional intensity which pervaded the meeting was beyond description.[41]

In the end, a group of 15 or so student leaders managed to calm their anxious and unhappy classmates, but the message was clear: the 100 percent principle was in imminent danger of breaking down.

The hierarchy among the eating clubs remained as rigid as ever. At the top stood Ivy, founded in 1879, and so exclusive that it was not until 1951 that it approved its first member known to have graduated from a public high school.[42] But by 1956 its image had softened a bit; its members, while still having a reputation as well-to-do and well-mannered prep school graduates, were described as "friendly" and "respected" young men of "good character" who did not "live up to the aristocratic, snobbish label of yesteryear."[43] In 1958, the chairman of the ICC — and the person most responsible for seeing that Bicker would honor the 100 percent principle — was Steven C. Rockefeller, the great-grandson of John D. Rockefeller and the president of Ivy.[44]

At the bottom of the hierarchy was Prospect, described by the novelist Geoffrey Wolff '60 as a "club so profoundly at the bottom of the food chain that it cut *nobody*."[45] In some ways, Prospect was not even an eating club in the traditional sense: it was a student cooperative whose members did "almost all the work of the club, including waiting on tables and maintenance."[46] Moreover, Prospect was one of just 2 clubs not even on Prospect Street; it was on an adjacent street, next door to Terrace, another low-status club. The newest of the 17 clubs, founded in 1941, Prospect was also the cheapest, charging its members a rate about a third less than that of the other eating clubs.[47]

Prospect was by far the most Jewish of the clubs — both a reflection and a source of its inferior status. The official estimate was that its membership was half Jewish, but the names of the 41 Prospect seniors in 1958 suggest that the proportion of gentiles may well have been exaggerated. In striking contrast to the Big Five (Ivy, Cottage, Cap and Gown, Tiger Inn, and Colonial), the students at Prospect were overwhelmingly public school graduates, most of them from New York and New Jersey.[48] Particularly well represented were alumni of such heavily Jewish city high schools as Midwood and James Madison in Brooklyn, DeWitt Clinton and Science in the Bronx, Weequahic in Newark (Philip Roth's alma mater), and Central in Philadelphia. Prospect's president in 1958 — and the person most responsible for trying to ensure its survival in an increasingly precarious situation — was Myron Margolin, a graduate of Plainfield (New Jersey) High School, where he had been class valedictorian.[49]

It was an open secret at Princeton that the vast majority of Jewish students were concentrated in four of the lowest clubs in the hierarchy (among them, Prospect, Court, and Terrace) and that those clubs higher in the social ladder limited the number of Jews issued invitations lest they risk dropping a few rungs. The issue of whether there were actual quotas was more controversial, but even the president of the ICC acknowledged that three clubs used quotas — all of them, ironically enough, among the four clubs with large numbers of Jews.[50] The logic behind quotas was laid out bluntly, if regretfully, by Thomas Carnicelli '58, who argued that they were a reasonable adaptation to a campus rife with anti-Semitism:

> I would first like to set two hypothetical situations at opposite poles. At one pole is a situation which I consider a desirable goal: a number of Jewish boys accepted and happy in every club on the Street, having been judged in Bicker solely on the basis of their worth as individuals . . . At the other pole is what I have previously called "the worst possible thing which could happen to Princeton," an all-Jewish club.
>
> I believe that a quota may serve as a means of avoiding the second, negative pole, in the context of the present system of social values which prevails at Princeton. This system of social values is frequently disgusting, totally at variance with the ideals of a liberal university. It places a social stigma on the Jew, merely because he is a Jew. *There are quotas only against Jews, because no other minority group at Princeton carries such a social stigma . . .*
>
> *Quotas can only be justified in the context of the present system of social values at Princeton.* They arise as necessary defenses against the pernicious effects of these values. It may conceivably be that clubs with quotas are the least discriminatory of all the clubs. They are the only ones who consider enough Jewish boys to be faced with the necessity of limiting their numbers . . .

Carnicelli looked forward to the day when quotas would be "unnecessary, unjustifiable and, I should hope, non-existent." But that would not happen until "the social stigma attached to the Jewish boy is eradicated."[51]

Certainly, the sense that Jews carried a stigma at Princeton was no figment of Carnicelli's imagination. But the stigma was more complex than a blanket hostility, utterly without regard to individuals. As defenders of the club system were fond of pointing out, all the clubs supposedly had at least one Jewish member, and "the outstanding Jewish boy, like any others, will be taken into Prospect Street's best clubs" (Ivy actually had two Jewish members).[52] Nevertheless, a subtle but powerful cultural anti-Semitism was widespread; most Jewish students, the judges during Bicker agreed, had personal and cultural attributes that made them "uncongenial" clubmates.

A member of the Class of 1957, who had served as Bicker chairman of his eating club ("one 'just above' the middle in social standing"), explained how Jews ended up in the low-status clubs:

> The "name" of one's club depends in large measure upon the number of prep-school graduates and tweed-clad extroverts that are among its members. The Princeton club is primarily for the social side of life. There is no room for the nondrinker, the silent introvert, or the man who spends so much time on studies that he neglects the social life which is so much a part of college. Whatever my personal prejudice, or lack of it, I had to resist the admission to the club of those types who by the traditional standards were not suitable for a social organization. Such persons were generally brilliant high-school graduates who had to combat the handicap of inadequate secondary-school preparation by concentrating on academic work to the exclusion of most other pursuits. Even the so-called prejudice against Jews, I found, was not so much an opposition to them as such, as to the fact that most of them (either because they were "grinds" or because they felt ill at ease among prep-school socialites) were simply poor mixers and did not fit well into a purely social organization.

From the perspective of this recent graduate, "the 'country club' appellation sometimes flung at Princeton is no more than the envious viciousness of the socially self-conscious individual who resents the idea that you can be superbly educated and have fun at the same time."[53]

From an administrative point of view, the great accomplishment of the 100 percent solution of 1950 was that it integrated every interested upperclassman into an eating club, thereby avoiding the potential public relations nightmare of outcast students charging that they had been victims of discrimination. From the perspective of the eating clubs, the 100 percent principle permitted the club leadership to feel that it was taking responsibility for seeing that all students had a place in campus life while preserving a cherished tradition. But the 100 percent Bicker was inherently unstable, for it depended on two distinct conditions, both of them precarious: the willingness of the clubs to share the burden of placing the "100 percenters" and the willingness of Princeton's growing Jewish population to accept being heavily concentrated in the lowest-status clubs. By 1958, both of these conditions had become increasingly problematic.

With respect to the first condition, The student leadership had become more and more skeptical about the 100 percent principle; in 1956, Archibald L. Gillies, the chairman of the ICC and president of Ivy, had threatened to hold a "natural Bicker," with no promise to reach 100 percent. Though Gillies managed through strenuous effort to place all eligible sophomores, he was so displeased by the experience that he met secretly with President Dodds and convinced him to sign a letter he had drafted calling for the university to provide attractive alternatives to the eating clubs. In Gillies's view, the ideal situation would be one in which only a minority of upperclassmen wished to be in the eating clubs, which would serve as a supplement to the university's own eating and social facilities — as mere "icing on the cake."[54]

While commitment to the 100 percent principle was wavering from above, support from below was also weakening. Indeed, the Jewish community that was arguably the principal beneficiary of 100 percent Bicker — after all, it was Jews who, though making up only a seventh of the student population, constituted roughly half of the up to forty students annually without bids[55] — was by the mid-1950s increasingly ambivalent about it. Although the policy provided a place for students who would otherwise be pariahs, the price tag was acceptance of the markedly inferior status of Jews in the club hierarchy — an inferiority that, many of them believed, was a product of clear-cut discrimination.

The "Dirty Bicker" of 1958

The chain of events that culminated in the infamous "Dirty Bicker" had its origins in the inherent conflict between the principle of club selectivity and the principle of 100 percent. The decision that precipitated the crisis was made, appropriately enough, by Prospect, the club at the very bottom of the hierarchy and the one with the least to lose. With the avowed intention of breaking the Bicker system, Myron Margolin announced that his club would be open for the first time to all students in 1958.[56] This move further lowered Prospect's already abysmal status; it was in effect a decision to leave the system. According to the ICC chairman, Steven Rockefeller, "Now sophomores started to think that a bid at Prospect was no bid at all and that Prospect was really not even a club."[57]

Margolin, for his part, stood by his offer of membership in Prospect to anyone in the sophomore class, but he introduced a critical qualification: the club would open itself only to those who wished to join and would not consider students who had shown no interest.[58] This raised the question of how to define a "100 percenter" — was it, as in previous years, a student who had failed to receive a bid from any of the clubs, *or* did Prospect's new policy of "open admission" mean that, by definition, there would no longer be any "100 percenters"? While the ICC eagerly seized on the latter interpretation as a way of formally complying with the 100 percent principle, Margolin insisted that a student who did not wish to join Prospect and had not received a bid was a "100 percenter" unless another club offered him a place.

Not counting those who chose Prospect, there were 143 sophomores who had not received a bid by Friday night, February 7, the evening before the climactic Open House when new members would be ushered into their clubs. By Saturday morning, the number of men without bids (popularly known as "men in trouble") had dropped to 86, still an extremely large number. On Saturday afternoon, the ICC convened a meeting to develop a strategy for handling the problem, but three of the clubs announced they would refuse to take even one "100 percenter." By this point, it was apparent that the goal of 100 percent was in serious trouble, but Rockefeller responded to the crisis by redoubling his efforts.[59]

At a meeting of the sophomore class held late Saturday afternoon, those students without a bid were instructed to arrive at 9:30 P.M. at the back door of the Ivy Club, where the ICC would determine their fate. It was a bitterly cold evening, and around nine a group of "men in trouble" began to assemble. While a festive atmosphere reigned inside Ivy, where new members lit up cigars and put on their club ties, the "100 percenters" — who at one point numbered as many as 40 — paced on the unheated porch, painfully aware that their fate rested in the hands of their social betters. To make matters worse, when an unauthorized *Harvard Crimson* photographer managed to get into the club, the doors were locked, leading the porch to immediately be dubbed the "cage."[60]

By the time the ICC reassembled at eleven, the number of sophomores without bids had dropped to 35, with 4 "100 percenters" opting to join Prospect. To make the meeting as open as possible, Rockefeller and the ICC took the unusual step of inviting major campus leaders, including the president of the Undergraduate Council, two former sophomore class presidents, two editorial writers from the *Daily Princetonian,* and the president of Hillel, the Jewish student organization. After an intense discussion, the ICC decided to encourage the remaining men to join Prospect. But most of them resisted, feeling that they were being "railroaded" into an inferior club. Increasingly irritated by the stance of the men without bids, some of whom were displaying "antagonistic" attitudes, the ICC suspended its efforts to place them. "It was too much to ask every club," Rockefeller later argued, "to take two one hundred percenters."[61] As the discussion continued without resolution, the president of Hillel jumped on a chair and read a petition — soon signed by 15 sophomores — stating simply: "I feel I have been discriminated against because of race or religion." Despite this accusation, the ICC would not budge, and at 2:10 A.M. it announced its decision: it would not take responsibility for the men without bids and place them among the remaining clubs.[62]

By Sunday evening, the ranks of the 35 men without bids had dwindled to 23, with 6 grudgingly signing up with Prospect, 4 obtaining last-minute invitations from other clubs, and 2 opting to join Wilson Lodge, the interim alternative facility.[63] Of the 23 students left, 15 were Jews — a point emphasized in the frenzy of media coverage that followed. Also noted by the media was the embarrassing fact that 7 of the 16 National Merit Scholars in Princeton's sophomore class found themselves among the 41 men who had gathered on Ivy's back porch.[64] After ten days of furious activity, what came to be known as the "Dirty Bicker" of 1958 was history.

Though Bicker was now finished, the question remained: in a class of 740 students, what had distinguished these 23 men from their classmates? Clearly, Jewishness was involved, but it could hardly have been the sole factor; after all, at least 75 Jewish students did receive invitations from the clubs — mostly from clubs other than Prospect.[65] Perhaps in the end the real question was not how the "100 percenters" differed from their peers but whom did the Bicker system elevate and whom did it relegate to the margins of campus life? In particular, what qualities separated those invited into one of the Big Five eating clubs from those consigned to clubs at the bottom?

At the center of Bicker was a peculiar Princeton ritual in which prospective club members ("eligibles") were instructed to wait patiently in their rooms, evening after evening, for visits from club delegations.[66] Edward Said '57, the renowned intellectual and cultural critic, describes in his memoir how the system operated:

> We were all trapped in a hideous eating club system, so that after sophomore year we all had to become club members through an appalling system called Bicker or, in effect, we would perish. Socially, Bicker meant that for two weeks in the February of your second year you were shut up in your room for entire evenings awaiting delegations from each of the clubs. Gradually their number decreased as more and more candidates were weeded out (Jews, non-prep-school boys, badly dressed people), whereas in the case of athletes (jocks), St. Paul's and Exeter graduates, or the children of famous parents (Batista, Firestone, DuPont) the visits of the now importuning clubs intensified.

Each year, Said recounts, "a group of twenty to thirty would be left unchosen at the end, and public meetings would be held apportioning the '100 percenters' — the students no one wanted, most of them Jews — among the various magnanimous heads of the clubs."[67]

During the designated Calling Periods, students were warned that the failure of an "eligible" to be in his room at the specified time could result in the denial of a club bid. In the words of the club's guidebook, "Common Sense About Clubs": "Don't leave a note saying you are in the Library and are any place else and will return. Bicker committee-men are not Mounties."[68] Even the faculty acquiesced to the all-consuming character of Bicker; Said, a serious student, recalls that he was "surprised how obligingly our teachers took the fact that for those two Bicker weeks no one did any reading."[69]

The purpose of the visits by the delegations from the eating clubs was to identify "congenial" potential clubmates, and they could be as brief as a few minutes. According to Wolff, who experienced the Bicker of 1958 firsthand, the process could be brutal: "Every club came once at least to every suite, but the winnowing was quick and ruthless. Club members recognized their types, and after each interview gave a grade to the sophomore, from the highest (1: "ace") to the lowest (7: flagrant neglect, "fleg-neg," "lunchmeat," "banana," "wonk," "wombat," "turkey"). It frequently happened that from a room of six sophomores only one was wanted by a particular club, or three were wanted, or five. The desirables were courted avidly, sometimes double-teamed, while the unwanted was treated to small talk by a specialist at dumping."[70] Since the result of Bicker was sometimes to separate friends who had hoped to join a club together, one of its byproducts was to strain — and sometimes shatter — existing friendships.[71]

In a matter of just a few minutes, each sophomore would be assessed on such matters as his appearance, his mannerisms, his interests, and his social skills. In a memorable scene in Wolff's novel *The Final Club*, the protagonist, Nathaniel Clay, has been called on by a delegate from the Colonial Club. Early in the meeting, a member of the delegation notices that Nathaniel's tweed jacket was "badly dimpled." When Nathaniel confirmed that he had indeed committed the sin of using a wire rather than a wood hanger, the meeting came to an abrupt end. This was not the first of Nathaniel's cultural missteps, and at the end of Bicker he found himself a "100 percenter" — one of just "twenty-three Princeton sophomores with whom no Princeton juniors or seniors wished to break bread."[72]

Wolff describes Bicker's rules of decorum as "runic" and its scoring system as "Byzantine."[73] But there was — as Wolff himself intuited — an underlying social logic, for Bicker expressed in condensed form the qualities that Princeton's student culture most valued and most scorned. Though the cues were sometimes subtle and difficult to decode (especially for outsiders), the process was designed to subject the entire sophomore class to judgment on the basis of well-defined social and cultural criteria.

At the top of the value system stood the gentleman athlete — the handsome young man of excellent social background who was also a "good mixer."[74] The archetypal top clubman had attended a fine private school and was cultivated in both appearance and demeanor. Intelligent but definitely not an intellectual, he exuded casual self-assurance.

At the bottom stood the unfortunate sophomore who was in many ways the antithesis of the top clubman. Socially awkward and often introverted, he was unduly studious and decidedly unathletic. Having been raised in modest circumstances and educated at a public school, he was utterly lacking in the easy self-confidence of a top clubman. At least in stereotype a poorly dressed and physically unattractive student known for his lack of appeal to young women, he did not like to drink and had a not undeserved reputation for being a "poor mixer."

This value system long predated the arrival of a significant number of Jews at Princeton, and its underlying character was perhaps not so much anti-Semitic as anti-intellectual. Nevertheless, there could be no denying that Jews fared poorly in such a system. Part of the problem, some Jewish students insisted, was sheer anti-Semitism — a problem no doubt exacerbated by the existence of implicit and sometimes explicit quotas in a number of clubs. But perhaps the deeper problem was that the clubs' criteria had been designed at the turn of the century by Protestant gentlemen to select "congenial" club-mates and had changed little since. Even if applied in a thoroughly nondiscriminatory manner, these criteria tended to relegate Jews and members of other marginal groups to clubs at the bottom rungs of the ladder.[75] The discomfiting truth was that Jews and WASPs often differed in both their values and their ways of being in the world. If the most desirable men from the point of view of Princeton's eating clubs were to be well-bred and athletic gentlemen who liked to drink and eschewed excess study, then few Jews were likely to qualify.

How much of the disproportionate concentration of Jews among "100 percenters" and students clustered in the lowest-ranking clubs was due to outright discrimination and how much to the neutral application of culturally skewed criteria is, in the end, impossible to determine. But what is clear is that those students — Jewish and gentile alike — at the low end of the club totem pole sometimes suffered greatly. Steven Rockefeller forthrightly acknowledged the pain that they experienced: "The experience of being rejected by Princeton's only social system left many one hundred percenters with a deep seated feeling of resentment and bitterness, and a dangerous sense of failure and insecurity. It was a terribly depressing and discouraging experience for them and it is hard to imagine the disillusionment and humiliation involved. It seems quite impossible to justify the last ten years of Bicker when this human factor is seriously considered." The existing system, Rockefeller concluded, "represents a lack of sensitivity to the well-being of the individual student, it creates a strained atmosphere on the campus and it embarrasses Princeton publicly."[76]

The initial response of Robert Goheen '40, Princeton's new president and the only head of Old Nassau ever to have belonged to an eating club, to the Bicker of 1958 was less charitable than that of Rockefeller.[77] Claiming that the allegations of discrimination were exaggerated, he insisted that such charges obscured "the plain facts that there are today members of the three major faiths of this country in each of the seventeen eating clubs."[78]

A few days later, in response to an Open Letter from the Undergraduate Council, Goheen defended the clubs even more vigorously: "The University welcomes the voluntary association of men having common interests who can dine together and enjoy the society of their fellows in congenial groups of relatively small size. In the University, as in life generally, such free association of men is a normal and healthy process and necessarily implies the right of selective invitation." Emphasizing that "an overwhelming proportion of the sophomores of each faith have been accepted in clubs," Goheen maintained that none of Princeton's clubs practiced the "total exclusion of any minority group." Nevertheless, if in fact "certain individuals were excluded because of their religion and for no other reason," then he deplored the practice. Princeton's eating clubs, he declared, "should pattern this policy on that of the University, which selects its students and its faculty solely upon their merits as individuals."[79]

Having done his part to defend the clubs, Goheen took the occasion of a meeting of the National Alumni Associations, fortuitously scheduled two weeks after the end of Bicker, to publicly announce his plans for cautious reform. While leaving the existing clubs unchanged — including their cherished right to select their own members — he disclosed a plan to construct alternative social and eating facilities for undergraduates, so that students could "have a satisfactory experience without the stark and absolute choice between a club and nothing."[80] After years of foot-dragging — and in the context of intense student pressure and a spate of unfavorable publicity — Princeton's administration finally committed itself to providing a genuine alternative to the club system.

If Goheen's response reflected the view of a consummate Princeton insider, the perspective expressed in an award-winning *Harvard Crimson* article, "The Quest at Princeton for a Perfect Cocktail Soul," reflected that of an outsider who looked at the strange ritual of Bicker with the sensibility of an anthropologist studying an exotic tribe. Bicker, of course, was an easy target for satire, and the *Crimson* reporter did not hesitate to take aim: it was, he observed tartly, a process in which "the wrong color of socks, a grammatical skip or affectation, [or] a pun or wisecrack in questionable taste" could ruin a young man's chances to enter the club of his dreams. But underneath the breezy satirical tone of the article was a powerful indictment of the club system: "the code of values" it expressed did nothing less than condemn "certain personality traits, ethnic groups, and even scholarship, intellectualism, and originality themselves."[81]

As a social system, the eating clubs embodied "social insulation, a striving for comfortable groups, [and] the frank institutionalization of arbitrary and unreflective prejudices." Ironically, those who suffered the most, contended the *Crimson*, "are not necessarily those scores of students who are dumped in undesirable organizations or left altogether out in the cold" but "the hundreds who happily make the respectable and especially the most desirable clubs on the street." For it is "they who have consented without apparent compunction to build their prestige, success, and social contentment on the hypocrisy, mendacity, inhumanity, servility, pettiness and sheer unreason upon which Princeton's club system and Bicker procedure are obviously reared."[82]

The freedom of Harvard students from such a system "should in no wise be interpreted as evidence for the stouter moral fiber of the undergraduate body compared to that encamped around Nassau Hall." Instead, it was a product of "a philosophy of education which viewed the student social structure as a primary concern and area of legitimate jurisdiction for a great university" — a philosophy that resulted in the House system, which was built on the principle of diversity, "a principle which was the inverse of selectivity."[83] In the increasingly meritocratic atmosphere of the late 1950s, Princeton's club system had become a major liability in the competition for the most "desirable" students. The main beneficiary would be Harvard, the only Big Three institution where students could graduate barely aware that selective student clubs even existed.[84]

Princeton's Position Declines — and the Faculty Responds

The "Dirty Bicker" of 1958 was a public relations disaster, and its impact was immediately visible in the decline in the proportion of those admitted who chose to attend Princeton. In 1958, for the first time in Princeton's history, the yield rate fell below 60 percent; moreover, as Edwards admitted in his annual report, "for the first time among the 525 boys declining admission (461 last year) the percentage of those who were rated as being the very best candidates was higher than among those that came." It was clear that the Bicker controversy was to blame: "There seems no doubt that unfavorable publicity in the national press had a significant effect on the final choice of Princeton by boys admitted to Princeton and one or more other colleges." A disturbing indicator of Princeton's deteriorating position was its need to admit sixty boys from the Alternate List — "the largest number on record."[85]

Though 1958 was a particularly bad year, Princeton's problems had actually begun a few years earlier. As late as 1951, Princeton's yield was considerably higher than Harvard's, with 70 percent of admits choosing to come, compared to 61 percent at Harvard. By 1955, Princeton's yield had dropped rather sharply to 62 percent, yet it was still marginally higher than Harvard's 61 percent. But by 1957 Harvard had forged ahead, with a yield of 69 percent compared to 63 percent at Princeton.[86] Though it is not clear exactly what factors produced this change, there is little question that the continued dominance of the eating clubs deterred some students from coming to Princeton.[87] A historian of club life at Princeton captured the underlying issue with exceptional clarity: "By 1958 the entire sophomore class could no longer be pushed, shoved and contorted to fill the framework for upperclass life formed in the nineteenth century and perpetuated by the 17 clubs."[88]

In the aftermath of the "Dirty Bicker," the difference in yield rates between Princeton and Harvard rose to 14 points (59 vs. 73 percent) — double the margin from the year before.[89] Yet even these figures do not reveal the full magnitude of the gap. In 1958, the third year of the prestigious National Merit Scholarships, Harvard enrolled 94 freshman Merit Scholars; Princeton, just 15. Worse still, while Harvard was number one in the nation, Princeton was an abysmal tenth, trailing not only such long-standing competitors as MIT and Yale but also Northwestern and Michigan.[90]

How much of Princeton's relative decline was a product of the decisions of the Admissions Office and how much of it was a consequence of its inability to get top students even to apply increasingly preoccupied the faculty, and in 1959 it created a Faculty Subcommittee on Admission Policy and Criteria. Charles C. Gillespie, a historian of science who was a member of the original committee and subsequently chaired it, was blunt: "The committee was set up," he reported, "because the faculty was dissatisfied with the entering class."[91]

Princeton in the 1950s was not the great research university that Harvard was, and the faculty seemed to have had neither the stature nor the influence of its Harvard counterparts.[92] Nevertheless, it did mobilize, and in 1959 it established a policy that applicants with verbal or math SATs over 780 or an average of 750 could not be refused by the admissions staff without additional review by a faculty committee. The concern behind this rather mechanistic measure was that the Admissions Office might be giving preference to "well-rounded" students over their more academic classmates.[93]

The Faculty Subcommittee on Admission Policy and Criteria issued its report in September 1960, just seven months after the Harvard Special Committee on College Admissions Policy released its own report. In contrast to Harvard's magisterial 56-page published document, the Princeton faculty contented itself with 8 double-spaced typed pages.[94] Yet in substance the two reports did not differ significantly, with both calling for more emphasis on academic criteria and special consideration for exceptionally brilliant students. The Princeton report was especially forceful on the latter issue, saying *"that there is a need to take more risks in the admission of clearly exceptional applicants, even if this should mean a slight increase in the incidence of scholastic failures and personal difficulties, and the accompanying expenditure of faculty and administrative time and attention."* The Princeton subcommittee was also concerned that "applicants of outstanding ability may occasionally be passed over in favor of 'well-rounded' men of lower intellectual capacity" and recommended that *"all applicants of the very highest rank in school (and certainly those in the top 2 or 3 percent of large schools) be regarded as eligible for admission, and rejected only when the grounds are clear and demonstrable."*[95]

The subcommittee well understood the underlying issue : the "problem, bluntly stated, is not how to select the best candidates from those seeking admission, but how to induce more first-rate students to apply, and no less important, to accept admission." But it was a difficult dilemma because of Princeton's image as an institution "sometimes wary of brilliant scholars because they may not adapt well to the conditions of campus life." In the competition for top scholars, Princeton's rival in Cambridge was faring particularly well — a pattern due in part to "a tendency in secondary schools to encourage the really exceptional student to apply to Harvard, on the ground that he will be best off there." Princeton, the Faculty Report acknowledged, faced a public relations problem and suggested that *"ways must be found to remove misconceptions, and to present a more accurate image of Princeton to the secondary schools and to the public at large."*[96] Yet beneath the concern was the realization that Princeton's unfortunate image contained elements of truth. According to Gillespie: "We want to see what we can do about changing the image if it's inaccurate — and what we can do about changing the University if, as I think is true, some of the image *is* accurate."[97]

Edwards did not disagree with the substance of the faculty analysis. Princeton's growing inability to win the head-to-head competition for students was a source of considerable frustration to him. Yet he clearly resented what he considered unwarranted faculty intrusion into the admissions process. In 1959, just when the faculty was beginning to assert itself, he argued in his annual report "that 'admission' has become a profession in itself and that unless one has a thorough training and indoctrination, it does more harm than good to have members of the faculty actually participate."[98] By 1961, he was even more emphatic: while conceding that "liaison between faculty and the Admissions Office should be maintained as strongly as possible," he told the president that "this should not be carried to the point where faculty committee members decide on individual cases." The faculty did have an appropriate role in reviewing policy and procedure, but "it should not be set up as a review board on specific cases of admission or rejection."[99] Precisely such a review board had been set up for cases of boys whose scores on standardized tests marked them as exceptional.

Even so, direct faculty involvement in admissions did not alter Princeton's relative lack of appeal to top scholars: of 150 applicants with records that placed them in the top one half of one percent of high school students, only about 70 would come to Princeton.[100] Starting in the late 1950s, virtually every annual report bemoaned the lower yield rate of the academically strongest candidates. In 1962, when 65 percent of all those admitted accepted Princeton's offer, only 58 percent with CSGs of 2+ or better, 55 percent of valedictorians, and 49 percent of students selected as University Scholars chose to matriculate.[101]

Each year, the competition with Harvard and Yale seemed to go more and more poorly. In 1960, Princeton lost 107 to Harvard and 70 to Yale; by 1962, those numbers had risen to 122 and 87.[102] Perhaps even more disturbing, the gap in overall yield between Old Nassau and Harvard had risen to a staggering 17 percent (82 vs. 65 percent) in 1962, when Princeton had led just seven years earlier.[103] Even among the elite prep schools that had been most closely tied to Princeton, Harvard and Yale now exerted considerably greater attraction; in 1960, Princeton's top nine feeder schools sent 130 students — far fewer than to Harvard and Yale, which enrolled 167 and 182, respectively.[104]

In 1962, Edwards announced his resignation, telling a visiting journalist, "I don't think I could live through another admission season." Reflecting on his tenure a few days later, he spoke movingly of the pain caused to the thousands of highly qualified applicants who were rejected nonetheless and said simply, "Somebody has got to find a better answer than I know."[105] The person whose task it became was another son of Old Nassau, E. Alden Dunham '53.

The Dunham Years

E. Alden Dunham, a graduate of Montclair (New Jersey) Academy, was a quintessential "all-around" man. A three-year member of the varsity tennis team, he also played intramural football and basketball and was a member of Cap and Gown, an eating club with a reputation for being a close-knit, self-assured community with more than its share of "campus wheels" and athletes.[106] He was also an outstanding student, graduating Phi Beta Kappa with highest honors in English.[107]

In his entry in the senior yearbook, Dunham described himself as a Protestant Episcopalian and a member of the Republican Party expecting to enter either teaching or business. In May 1954, he married Louise Green (Vassar '54), the daughter of Robert M. Green '13, a former trustee of Princeton and former chairman of the National Alumni Associations. Through his marriage, Dunham acquired six brothers-in-law — all Princeton alumni.[108]

After graduation, he served for three years in the navy, taught at Andover for a year, and in 1958 received an M.A.T. at Harvard. At this point, he made what turned out to be a fateful career decision, becoming special assistant to James B. Conant, then president emeritus of Harvard. Conant, who remained the leading luminary in American education, described Dunham in his memoirs as his "right-hand" man and credited him with coining the phrase "social dynamite" to describe the conditions in the nation's urban slums.[109] Dunham helped Conant prepare his widely read studies *The American High School Today; The Child, The Parent, and the State;* and, the best known, *Slums and Suburbs.* At the same time, Dunham entered graduate school at Columbia, receiving a doctorate in educational administration from Teacher's College.

Though not yet thirty-one when he became director of admission in the summer of 1962, Dunham entered the job with the stature of a man closely associated with Conant. With his doctorate in hand, he was well situated to accomplish what would clearly be one of his major tasks: repairing the frayed relations between the Admissions Office and the faculty. Dunham emphasized in his first annual report that "the task of policy formation principally lies with the faculty." At the same time, he insisted that the faculty, having established general policy, "must delegate its authority to the Committee on Admission."[110] So successful was Dunham in coopting the faculty that by 1964, the *Daily Princetonian* was able to say that the members of the faculty committee on admission had "become more or less a rubber stamp for his policies."[111]

The *Daily Princetonian*'s rather vivid portrait of Dunham describes him as a "tall, somewhat handsome" man who "could be a successful executive of a large corporation." Dunham was not a corporate executive, but he had concentrated power for himself in the manner of a top CEO. Though the admissions staff had been formally decentralized, "the final decisions all come back to Mr. Dunham; he accepts every boy admitted to Princeton." Not an easygoing man and considered by some to be lacking in warmth, especially on first meeting, Dunham was nevertheless widely recognized as a highly competent and determined administrator.[112]

The talented and energetic Dunham faced numerous challenges. One of the most difficult was the issue of African Americans; Princeton was lagging well behind Yale and especially Harvard at a time when the elite private colleges had decided that diversity required an increase in the number of black students. Like all of his Ivy League counterparts, Dunham favored a larger black presence on campus. In explaining his position, he pointed to two reasons: first, "the addition of more American Negroes and other underprivileged groups to the campus would contribute to the diversity of the student body and enrich the residential experience of all," and second, "at this particular point in American history it behooves all educational institutions to do what they can toward upgrading the status of the Negro in our free society."[113]

Yet Dunham was characteristically cautious about the actual prospects for black students. "The basic problem," he wrote, "is a lack of well-qualified candidates" — a reality that "all the good will in the world is not going to change . . . for many years." But Princeton faced particularly acute problems of its own — its long-standing southern reputation and the small-town atmosphere. "Given a choice," admitted Dunham, "many Negroes prefer Harvard or Yale, where abolitionism was much stronger and where the anonymity of a large city is close at hand."[114]

Nevertheless, Princeton embarked on a conscious effort to enroll more African Americans, and in Dunham's first year, it admitted 11, 5 of whom chose to come.[115] Though supported by the trustees, Dunham's policy was controversial. In particular, some southern alumni opposed it, with one of them threatening, "If this active recruitment continues, there will be increased withdrawal of support from the University by the alumni in the area not only financial, but moral."[116] Yet by 1966 18 blacks (2.2 percent of all freshmen) entered Princeton — still fewer than at Harvard and Yale, but a vast increase over the 1 or 2 black students who entered annually in the last five years of the Edwards era.[117]

One of the most delicate issues facing Dunham was the perennial problem of alumni sons. The alumni were always a major source of funds, with the Annual Giving Program — Princeton's largest source of unrestricted operating income — providing over $2 million in 1964–1965.[118] In addition, the Admissions Office depended heavily on 1,400 alumni in 141 schools committees for both recruiting and interviewing applicants, so it had a powerful interest in maintaining good relations with them.[119] At no other college were the alumni more interested in the well-being of their alma mater — and in how the Admissions Office treated their sons.

Dunham faced the same problem as his peers at Harvard and Yale. With the competition for places rapidly intensifying with the arrival of the first wave of the baby boom, the preference given to legacies was forcing the Admissions Office to turn away far more qualified applicants in what was be-coming a zero-sum game. To a man whose public position was that Princeton should make every effort to avoid "impeding rather than promoting social mobility through education," the policy of admitting barely qualified legacies was deeply anomalous.[120] By the fall of 1964, Dunham told the *Daily Prince-tonian* that the old policy toward alumni sons "is becoming increasingly dif-ficult to live with."[121] Holding up the specter of a class consisting entirely of legacies, all capable of doing the work, he was clearly laying the groundwork for a more stringent policy.[122]

But like his mentor Conant, Dunham was not a man to ignore powerful institutional interests, and he moved only gradually. In 1965, the proportion of alumni sons admitted dropped to 54 percent, from 59 percent a year earlier, and then in 1966 the proportion dropped to 47 percent.[123] Yet legacies still had a huge advantage over other applicants, who were admitted at a rate of just under 20 percent. Though the official ideology was that alumni sons should be "given preference in admission in comparison with other candidates who have roughly equal qualifications," the folders of legacies still received "spe-cial attention . . . in the form of additional readings and reviews."[124] This pref-erence remained a powerful force under Dunham, with legacies enjoying an admittance rate more than double that of other applicants throughout his administration.[125]

Though himself a private school graduate, Dunham indicated from the outset that applicants from prep schools should expect no special consider-ation. "It seems inevitable," he wrote in his first annual report, "that the inde-pendent schools will be increasingly squeezed in the future as their enroll-ments remain constant but public school enrollments bulge and as Princeton increasingly through its alumni schools committees attracts students nation-wide."[126] Princeton may in fact have become tougher toward applicants from the leading boarding schools, but the top prep school boys increasingly pre-ferred Yale and especially Harvard to Princeton. The *Daily Princetonian* was blunt about Princeton's difficulty in attracting "the bright — the really bright — prep school student": "As a rule, the very top students in most Eastern prep schools go to Harvard, though they may have been admitted to Princeton as well. Princeton will often get the student who, though intelligent, was a notch below his Harvard-bound classmate. Princeton professors who know the prep schools are the first to deplore the loss; some feel it is the old problem of Princeton's image in the prep schools." "It may be awhile," predicted the pa-per, "before Princeton is competing on equal footing with Harvard for the number-one scholars of Exeter, Groton, and Lawrenceville."[127]

The case of Lawrenceville, which had long been Princeton's top feeder school, was symptomatic. As late as 1954, Lawrenceville sent 36 boys to

Princeton and 9 to Harvard, but by 1965 the pattern was reversed, with 14 going to Harvard and 11 to Princeton.[128] By the mid-1960s, Princeton had clearly lost some of its appeal to the graduates of the elite boarding schools; of the 15 leading institutions, just 98 students went to Princeton in 1965, 207 to Harvard, and 173 to Yale.[129]

Princeton's numbers were not the result of a more stringent admissions policy. In fact, the data from 11 major prep schools show that in 1968, when Harvard, Yale, and Princeton were admitting about 20 percent of all applicants, the overall admission rate for these schools was higher at Princeton (48 percent) than at Yale (44 percent) and Harvard (44 percent). The report concludes that "the results should clearly set to rest any charges that our colleges are not interested in these schools."[130]

In fact, Princeton's declining appeal to prep school students from the top prep schools was part of a more general difficulty: its declining competitiveness vis-à-vis Harvard. While Princeton was holding its own fairly well with Yale, attracting 47 percent of students admitted to both institutions during the Dunham years, the same was not true of Harvard. Between 1963 and 1966, 638 students were accepted at both Princeton and Harvard; just 19 percent of them chose Princeton.[131] Worse still, from Princeton's point of view, many top scholars were not even applying.[132]

Princeton's decreasing ability to compete with Harvard was, in turn, part of a still broader problem — that, as Dunham candidly admitted in his first annual report, "Princeton loses many of its top men." In 1963, when Princeton's overall yield rate was 69 percent, "only 56 percent of admits with CSGs of 2 plus or better accepted admission."[133] Three years later, Dunham's last year, the situation was worse; of 187 admitted students with an academic rating of 1, just 42 percent chose to enroll.[134] Whatever the reasons for the difficulties — the persistent image of Princeton as a country club, the reputation for homogeneity, the location in a small town, the absence of the professional schools and large graduate programs that defined a great research university, or (though rarely discussed at the time) the continued exclusion of women — Princeton continued to have trouble attracting the most brilliant young scholars.[135]

The Admissions Office could do only so much. But the one area where it did control was in determining which of its applicants it would admit. Princeton's 1–5 system of evaluation ranked each candidate in two distinct areas: academic promise, and character and personal promise. As Dunham acknowledged, "Reducing people to numbers is a gross oversimplification." The nonacademic dimension was, he believed, especially problematic, for "combining judgment of character and particular nonacademic talents in one grade is especially difficult."[136] Nevertheless, each Princeton applicant — and by the mid-1960s there were more than 5,000 of them — was assigned two numbers, both of which powerfully affected his chances of admission. In 1966, 66 percent of nonacademic 1s were admitted compared to only 9 percent of nonacademic 4s.[137]

Personal interviews played a major role in determining a candidate's nonacademic rating.[138] Few students were admitted in the absence of the kind of screening permitted by an interview; in 1965, just 56 students in a freshman class of 826 students had not been interviewed by either an alumnus, a staff member, or both. Interestingly, those applicants who had been interviewed by both had an admission rate of 32 percent (by far the highest); those unfortunate candidates interviewed by neither were admitted at a rate of just 11 percent.[139]

The qualities that generated a high nonacademic rating remain rather murky, but one thing seems clear: athletic ability was a major asset. In his official 1965 statement on admissions, Dunham twice referred to "physical energy" (right beside "strength of character") as among the "qualities sought in every young man admitted to Princeton."[140] Though Princeton, unlike Harvard, did not rank every applicant on athletic ability, outstanding talent in sports — and even simple participation at the varsity level, especially in sports socially defined as "manly" — was an important plus.[141]

The academic rating was also a powerful factor in shaping admission decisions. Especially since the Faculty Report of 1960, the Admissions Office had been under considerable pressure to admit more top scholars. By 1965, Princeton's official policy stated clearly that "those relatively few applicants with extraordinary intelligence and sound character are readily admitted."[142] But the actual policy was quite different; in 1966, a third of academic 1's — students so outstanding that they were among the top 282 of more than 5,600 applicants — were rejected.[143] Had Princeton admitted all of them, there still would have been almost 1,000 places still available. Instead, Princeton rejected 95 of them, admitting weaker students judged to have superior nonacademic qualifications.

It is possible that all 95 of these young men were of "unsound" character. But it is more likely that they were deemed personally unappealing, though exactly why is not clear. One faculty member familiar with Dunham's policies offered the following observation: "I feel that the real oddball is still being passed up . . . I'm from Harvard, and the students there are just uglier than Princeton students. We are afraid of the real nut."[144] Dunham's own view is implicit in his characterization of men rated 4/1: they are "superb scholars, some of whom may be risks from the nonacademic point of view." In 1966, over two-thirds of the applicants so rated were denied admission.[145]

In striking contrast, the applicant who was weak academically but judged exceptional in his nonacademic qualities (the 1/4) fared well in the Dunham years. In 1966, 64 percent of the applicants with 1/4 ratings were accepted — almost double the rate of 4/1 candidates.[146] Dunham's description of the policy was straightforward: "the less a candidate offers academically, the more he must offer nonacademically."[147]

During Dunham's tenure, the number of applicants to Princeton soared from 4,289 to 5,628. With over 90 percent of these students capable of surviving academically, Princeton — like Harvard during the Glimp years — increasingly turned to nonacademic factors to determine which candidates would be admitted.[148] Between 1964 and 1966, the proportion of academic 1's accepted dropped from 75 to 66 percent; during these same years, the proportion of nonacademic 1's admitted rose from 74 to 77 percent. Even more striking, however, was that admission rates for 1/4 candidates increased from 54 to 64 percent, whereas 4/1 admissions declined from 42 to 32 percent.[149]

Though Princeton did not carry out the type of statistical studies of the determinants of admissions decisions conducted at Harvard, the data reveal that the same pattern prevailed at both institutions: nonacademic factors carried greater weight than academic ones, and their relative importance seemed to increase over time. Dunham firmly believed that "the difference between success and failure at Princeton in subsequent careers" was to a great degree a function of "qualities of personality about which we know too little and certainly cannot adequately measure — motivation, persistence, independence, breadth of interests, ability to relate to others, sense of humor, to mention just a few."[150] In the end, Princeton's mission was to educate leaders in many different walks of life. Dunham — like Bender and Glimp — was convinced that only an admissions policy that gave considerable weight to nonacademic factors could accomplish this goal.

Even with more than twice as many applicants as in 1951, the student body that resulted from such a policy was not so different from the one that had arrived in Princeton fifteen years earlier. In 1966, as Dunham left office to assume a position with the Carnegie Foundation, the typical Princeton student remained a well-to-do white Protestant from a private boarding school or an affluent suburban high school.[151] Data from a 1966 survey of entering students (answered by almost 98 percent of freshmen) revealed just how homogeneous the student body remained. About 95 percent white, the freshman class was just 2 percent black, with an additional 1.4 percent "Oriental" and 1.5 percent "Other." Jews, roughly 15 percent of the student body in 1960, had dropped to approximately 12 percent under Dunham.[152] Despite the increasing rhetoric about enrolling more "disadvantaged" students, most of the freshman class hailed from privileged backgrounds; at a time when the median national family income was barely $7,500, the median Princeton student came from a family with an income well in excess of $15,000. If anything, the educational backgrounds of Princeton parents were even more privileged, with over two-thirds of the fathers having graduated from college compared to just one man in seven nationwide.[153]

At the end of the Dunham era, the image problem that had plagued Princeton was more serious than ever before. At a time of great turmoil in the nation's cities and on its campuses, Princeton remained a bastion of tradition — an all-male, overwhelmingly white campus, where 90 percent of the upper-classmen still belonged to private eating clubs. In 1966, Princeton seemed hopelessly out of step with the times.

In 1964, the *Daily Princetonian* reported that "faculty members realize that to get diversity, Princeton must consciously attempt to shake off the image of homogeneity."[154] But the problem, in the end, was not Princeton's image; it was the reality of an institution still mired in the past.

CHAPTER 11

Yale: From Insularity to Inclusion

VEN BY IVY LEAGUE standards, Yale in the 1950s was an exceptionally insular institution, and this insularity was visible in President Griswold's decision to appoint Arthur Howe Jr. '47 as chairman of the Board of Admissions in 1953. Howe, like Griswold, was a graduate of the Hotchkiss School and had a fine Yale pedigree — his father, Arthur Howe Sr. '12, was captain of the football team, an All-American, and a member of Skull and Bones.[1] Howe Jr. apparently inherited some of the athletic ability of his father. After graduating from Hotchkiss in 1938, he spent a year at Rugby, the renowned British public school, and made the prestigious First Fifteen of the rugby team at the very home of the sport.[2]

When Howe entered Yale in 1939, "the dominant element of undergraduate life," he acknowledged, "was not formal intellectual activity." Though students often enjoyed their professors, "much time and energy went elsewhere, into social, esthetic, and a great variety of other extra-curricular activities."[3] Howe flourished in this atmosphere, joining the Yale Political Union and Delta Kappa Epsilon and participating in football, rugby, and swimming. But the war had already begun in Europe, and in November 1941 he joined the volunteer ambulance corps of the American Field Service. Howe served under the British Eighth Army in the Middle East and Europe until 1944, when, now a major, he received a medical discharge.[4]

Howe spent five of the next six years teaching at Hotchkiss, with a stop in 1946–1947 to return to Yale, where he completed two years of course work in one to receive his degree. At Hotchkiss, he had come under the influence of George Van Santvoord (Hotchkiss '08, Yale '12), the school's legendary headmaster and a close friend of A. Whitney Griswold, long a member of Hotchkiss's Board of Trustees. Shortly after being installed as Yale's president, Griswold phoned Howe in England, where he was spending a year at Oxford, to offer him a position as assistant dean in the Freshman Year Office. Howe accepted, and just two years later Griswold appointed him chairman of the Board of Admissions, a position he held until 1964. Throughout his term in office, Howe got along famously with his fellow Hotchkiss alumnus. Griswold, he recounted, "hired people whom he trusted and set them to it . . . as long as one worked for Whit, there were never any enemies out back."[5]

The Yale over which Griswold presided was a profoundly conservative institution. *Time* magazine, itself a redoubt of Old Elis, wrote on the occasion of its 250th anniversary in 1951, "Yale is a dynasty, perhaps the most inbred of all the ivy league colleges." According to *Time*, "55% of its faculty are Yale men." As Geoffrey Kabaservice noted, "The habit of promoting from within meant that the standards for appointments and promotions tended to emphasize citizenship rather than scholarship, clubbability rather than real merit."[6]

At the same time that other leading universities were eagerly embracing the new opportunities provided by federal grants and the growth of "big science" in the years after World War II, Griswold reaffirmed Yale's commitment to the traditional liberal arts, led by the humanities. Scientists, elsewhere the leading edge of the more meritocratic universities then emerging, remained peripheral players at Yale and complained that Griswold did not support (and perhaps impeded) their efforts to obtain grants from foundations and federal agencies.[7] Deeply distrustful of federal sponsorship of university research, Griswold has been aptly described as "out of harmony with the postwar research economy." By the late 1950s, Yale was beginning to face serious difficulties in both recruiting and retaining top scientists.[8]

Though still one of the nation's leading colleges, Yale in the 1950s was suffering from a certain provincialism. Nicholas Lemann, who characterized the Yale of that time as more "like a very big boarding school" than "a major international research university," captures the prevailing atmosphere well: "Yale had an engineering school and a medical school, but in the pure sciences it was barely in the game. Its best academic departments were English and history; even in these the leading professors were themselves graduates of boarding schools and Yale (rather than members of the world academic royalty like the professors Clark Kerr had brought to Berkeley), who had intense, familial, character-molding relations with the undergraduates. Triple-named Episcopalians set the tone of the faculty: Chauncey Brewster Tinker, William Lyon Phelps, Samuel Flagg Bemis, Norman Holmes Pearson."[9] High-status Protestant boys from boarding schools set the tone among the students as well; in 1954, 57 freshmen came to Yale from Andover alone, joined by 35 from Exeter and 32 from Lawrenceville.[10]

In *Remembering Denny,* his affecting memoir of a college friend, Calvin Trillin '57 recalls that "Yale could strike a high school boy from the provinces as something like a foreign country — a rather intimidating foreign country." In his entering class, 61 percent of the students were from private schools, 39 percent from public schools. Trillin paints a vivid portrait of the difference:

"The Eastern boarding school people had their own way of dressing — what was called the Ivy look did not spread to the rest of the country until a year or two later — and their own way of talking . . . They set the tone: cool, understated, wearing through at the elbows." Though public school graduates like Trillin believed that "a lot of the rich Eastern people were at Yale because of some entitlement of family or class or money and that we were there because, in ways that were perhaps not immediately apparent, we somehow deserved to be," he acknowledged that in the mid-1950s, "Yale seemed very much *their* place."[11]

A feature of Yale's campus atmosphere in the fifties was the powerful role still played by the selective senior societies. Though only about 10 percent of the class was "tapped," the societies' ostensibly democratic selection criteria — that students would be admitted not on the basis of family background but on what they had accomplished at Yale — meant, as Trillin shrewdly observed, that "absolutely everyone was being judged."[12] This continued to give a certain competitive edge to life at Yale, especially in extracurricular activities — a noteworthy contrast to Princeton, where the wrong social background precluded entry into the more prestigious eating clubs.

One thing that Yale's senior societies did have in common with Princeton's eating clubs was anti-Semitism: it was not until 1957 that Wolf's Head, one of the more prestigious societies, first offered membership to a Jew (and even then, only over the vigorous opposition of the club's alumni). By the late 1950s, Yale had fewer Jews (12 percent) than Princeton (14 percent).[13]

Prep Schools and the Quest for the "All-Around" Man

The foundation of Yale's distinctive culture was its close relationship with the private boarding schools. The most expensive of the Ivy League colleges (albeit by a narrow margin), Yale also had the highest proportion of prep school graduates. In 1954, Howe's first year as chairman, 61 percent of the freshmen came from private schools; that same year, the proportions at Princeton and Harvard were 55 and 46 percent, respectively.[14] If these figures attested to Yale's continued appeal to private school boys, they also testified to the appeal these boys held for Yale.

In Arthur Howe Jr., the boarding schools had a loyal friend. He knew the schools well and trusted their judgment. Moreover, he shared their ethos, with its emphasis on character, leadership, and the development of sound bodies as well as sound minds.

Given the increasingly contentious issue of college admissions criteria, this ethos had an uneasy relationship with the emergent academic meritocracy, which emphasized intellectual excellence over more intangible qualities such as "personal force" and "integrity."[15] The prevailing view — and one from which Howe did not dissent — was that boarding school graduates possessed these intangible qualities more than their public school peers, especially insofar as they embodied potential for future leadership. Howe, noting that the boarding schools had felt the growing competition of the postwar years, argued forcefully in his 1955 "Report to the President" that it would be "undesirable to further limit the places which are being offered to their students."[16]

Acting quickly on his own recommendation, he devised a system in which applicants from designated secondary schools — almost all of them private — would receive an early rating of A (admission virtually guaranteed), B (still in the running), or C (rejection effectively guaranteed).[17] In determining these ratings, Yale would rely heavily on the recommendations of the headmaster, supplemented by staff interviews with the candidate.

The foundation of this system was the trust and mutual understanding between admissions officers and boarding school administrators, who shared a common culture. In the program's first year, Howe reported that he was pleased with its performance. His confidence was based in part on the receipt of frank appraisals of candidates from trusted sources: "It has become apparent that we frequently acquire from conversations information that would not be reported to us in writing."[18]

Howe convinced Harvard and Princeton to adopt the ABC system; as a result, a large block of places in the freshman class was reserved for private schools in a time of rapidly increasing competition. By placing such heavy weight on the headmasters' judgment, the system perpetuated their definition of merit — character, leadership, and well-roundedness — when this definition was more and more subject to criticism.[19] The result was continued special treatment for the graduates of the top private schools: in 1955, only fifteen leading schools provided 275 members — 27 percent — of Yale's freshman class.[20] And in 1957, 1958, and 1959, the top ten feeder schools to Yale were — without a single exception — all private schools.[21]

The cornerstone of Howe's admissions policy was the requirement that applicants exhibit both "brains and character." Character was connected, in turn, to the crucial yet equally exclusive quality of "personal promise." In assessing the latter, the Admissions Office would look for evidence of a boy's "industry," "persistence," "self-discipline," "sense of responsibility" and — interestingly — "his ability to participate in group activities."[22] An apparent inability to get along with others was a distinct drawback, if not an outright cause of disqualification.

Howe's most important source for assessing intangible qualities was "more-or-less back-door information we could solicit out of the school, or out of a trusted teacher who would confide in us." But "confidential, trusted sources" existed only in those schools that had long, close and long-standing relationships with Yale,[23] almost all of which were private schools. This reliance placed the growing number of public school applicants at a distinct disadvantage.

Yale remained committed to its ideal of the "well-rounded" man — the athletic and intelligent student who displayed "character" and "leadership." Years after his departure from Yale, Howe vigorously defended the "classical concept of well roundedness — the golden mean." "We weren't going to throw this out," he said years later, "just because uninformed theorists accused us of catering to mediocrity through the concept."[24] On the contrary, Yale — even more than Harvard — remained committed to selecting students of "character and intelligence and not one without the other."[25]

This ideal increasingly came under attack over the course of the decade. In 1957, in a series of editorials in the *Yale Daily News*, it was subjected to a withering assault. One lead editorial was blunt: "The 'well rounded man,' a concept on which Yale seems solidly and pugnaciously to stand, seems to have exerted a wholly disproportionate influence on admissions thinking and trends." Citing discussions at a recent meeting in New Haven of the Yale Alumni Committee on Enrollment and Scholarships, the paper reported that "a man was judged to be 'too smart' for Yale; his predicted average was 85, but he failed, according to his headmaster, to 'get along with his fellows.'"[26]

A better policy, the *Daily News* contended, would replace the emphasis on balance with a focus on "distinction." In any case, the existing policy was not defensible: "Candidates are often admitted on the basis of a combination of just-barely adequate academic stature and what a sociologist (or even Arthur Murray) might describe as 'social skills.'" Equally indefensible was the policy of admitting athletes primarily because they were athletes: "no adequate rationalization for the large number of skilled football players who continue to gain admission has ever been brought forward (doesn't a flair for cricket contribute to the class's balance in an extraordinary degree?)."[27]

The solution, the paper argued, was to "insist that intellectual distinction in at least one area should override all other considerations; we cannot afford to play second fiddle to Harvard in this area." Quite simply, Yale had to stop discouraging applicants "because they were 'too bright,' or rather because their intellectual attainments were not complemented by talents of a political, athletic or artistic type."[28]

The issue of Yale's standing vis-à-vis that of Harvard, hardly an issue in 1950, became a subject of great concern by the end of the decade. In a 1959 article in the *Daily News*, a student asked a series of pointed questions: "Why doesn't Yale compete for Harvard intellectuals? Why doesn't Yale get more

National Merit Scholarship winners? Why is Yale a rich man's college, or is it a rich man's school? Is Yale just a well-rounded mediocrity?" These questions, the author noted, "are a symptom in themselves."[29]

The *Daily News* reporter acknowledged that Harvard had four times as many National Merit Scholars in the Class of 1961 as its rival in New Haven, which had a modest 26. Equally troubling, the notion that Yale was a "rich man's college" turned out to have considerable truth: 65 percent of the students still paid their own way, but only about 4 percent of the nation's families (those with incomes over $15,000) could afford to do so.[30]

Underlying Yale's growing insecurity was the distasteful fact that its appeal to top applicants was declining; whereas in 1951, 62 percent of the admits at both Yale and Harvard ultimately enrolled, by 1957 Yale's yield rate dropped to 58 percent while Harvard's rose to 70 percent.[31] As the 1950s ended, Yale remained one of the nation's preeminent colleges. But its position with respect to its chief competitor had undeniably declined, and the question of whether its traditionalist admissions policy had contributed to this problem could no longer be ignored.

The Process of Admissions at Yale

In a much-discussed article in *The New Yorker* in 1960, Katherine Kinkead offered a close look at how Yale determined who would be admitted that year.[32] Though she was not permitted to attend the meetings at which the final decisions were made, Kinkead was able to look at the folders of individual applicants, complete with written comments from alumni interviewers, teachers, and headmasters as well as members of the admissions staff. In addition, she conducted lengthy interviews with the staff members and was notified which of the applicants whose folders she had read were accepted and which rejected. Nothing like this article had ever appeared about any of the Big Three, and it offered an unprecedented portrait of the informal criteria that continued to shape Yale admissions at the dawn of the 1960s.

One of the most striking features of Kinkead's account is just how seriously Yale took the notion of "personal promise." In search of the "real person" behind the file, the Admissions Office fastidiously combed through the comments of alumni and staff interviewers, teachers, and headmasters. Examining the applications herself, Kinkead reported that she "was continually astonished at how sharply the personalities of the boys whose photographs stared out at me were conveyed by their answers to the form questions and by the comments of their various teachers and interviewers."[33] Each candidate was rated on a scale of 1–9 for "personal promise." Kinkead's account makes clear that "promise as a person," as opposed to "promise as a student," was often the decisive factor in determining an applicant's fate.

But what did "promise as a person" mean? According to Waldo Johnston '37, an admissions officer in charge of liaison with the alumni, Yale was looking for insight into "the *spirit* of a candidate — the selflessness, integrity, and honesty that are so badly needed in this day of false ideals."[34] If this sounds a lot like the old patrician ideal of "character," it is not a coincidence; Howe told Kinkead, "You can sum up what we're after as brains *and* character." In emphasizing "personal promise," Yale's real agenda was the same as Harvard's: to avoid selecting students on academic criteria alone and to maintain the flexibility in admissions criteria to permit the selection of boys who would serve Yale's institutional interests.[35] "If high academic ability were the only criterion," said Howe, "we would have to eliminate quite a few future presidents of the country . . ."[36]

The admissions committee viewed evidence of "manliness" with particular enthusiasm. One boy gained admission despite an academic prediction of 70 because "there was apparently something manly and distinctive about him that had won over both his alumni and staff interviewers."[37] Another candidate, admitted despite his schoolwork being "mediocre in comparison with many others," was accepted over an applicant with a much better record and higher exam scores because, as Howe put it, "we just thought he was more of a guy."[38] So preoccupied was Yale with the appearance of its students that the form used by alumni interviewers actually had a physical characteristics checklist through 1965.[39] Each year, Yale carefully measured the height of entering freshmen, noting with pride the proportion of the class at six feet or more (24.8 percent in 1960).[40]

The other side of the Admissions Office's emphasis on a "sound body" was its palpable distaste for candidates deemed one-sidedly intellectual. In an interview with Kinkead, Howe confessed his concern about the "grade-hound": "Sometimes I lie awake nights worrying about whether we've been kidding ourselves with taking a lot of brainy kids who are too egocentric ever to contribute much to society. Or have we been taking a lot of twerps who have read the how-to-get-into-college books, listened to their counselors, and learned to take tests?"[41] Howe was not alone in his distaste. Assessing a candidate from a large, excellent public school who had a 95 average and SATs of 796 verbal and 750 math and whose projected average at Yale was 87, a Yale interviewer described him as "uninteresting" and a "grade-grubber," stating flatly that "I would prefer to see this lad go to Harvard." In the end, the boy, whose file revealed that he had some artistic talent, was rejected by Yale.[42]

In evaluating the more than 4,500 candidates for admission in 1960, Yale exhibited a strong interest in their family backgrounds. Sheer wealth was definitely a factor. Howe stated the issue sharply: "Which would you admit, the millionaire's son who is rather supercilious now and is only mediocre academically but will one day fall heir to the means of doing great good for society, or the grade-hound?"[43] He recounted the case of the son of a Pittsburgh family, major Yale benefactors, who had a predicted average of 57 and who had flunked out of his first prep school and ranked dead last in his second. Yale reluctantly declined to admit the boy but counseled his family that joining the army might do him good. Two years later, after his military service and several months at a private tutoring school, Yale accepted him just before the opening of school.[44]

Not surprisingly, students from less elite backgrounds were not given the same consideration. Some of the admissions officers — all but one of whom were Yale graduates — liked to meet the parents of applicants, and their interactions with them could prove consequential. In one particularly memorable case, a businessman had been unusually gracious in obtaining some foreign books for a member of the admissions staff, only to announce that his son had his "heart set on Yale" and "One good turn deserves another." The admissions officer acknowledged that the applicant was "a great kid" but believed that the incident offered "some insight into the boy's home life and background." Despite the boy's qualifications, he was rejected, for the committee "couldn't help wondering how far he had absorbed his father's standards."[45]

In other cases, however, a modest family background could be a real advantage. Assistant Director of Admissions Arthur Farwell Tuttle Jr. '45 — the son of Arthur Farwell Tuttle '15 and the grandson of Henry Nelson Tuttle '81[46] — enjoyed meeting the candidates' parents, noting, "With luck, we occasionally stumble upon something we would want very much to know." He recounted the case of a boy who came in "with his father and mother, both of them simple, uneducated people." "That lad," he reported, "did everything he could to let me know how proud he was of them."[47] Though Kinkead does not record the ultimate disposition of the case, it is clear that Tuttle saw the incident as evidence that the candidate was just the kind of poor but virtuous boy — the young man of "good character" — that Yale had long sought.

Yale's traditionalist scholarship policy did not make it easy for students of modest backgrounds to survive in New Haven. "Scholarship recipients were," according to Johnston, "expected to have even higher academic and personal promise than applicants not requesting aid," and they faced greater pressure than their wealthier classmates.[48] Yale's philosophy was built on the belief that requiring work in return for a scholarship was good for the character of recipients. As Howe put the matter in a radio interview, Yale wished to communicate that in America "you don't get something for nothing."[49]

In the mid-1950s, freshmen on scholarships were required to work up to 14 hours a week washing dishes or waiting tables in the dining hall.[50] By 1960, the number of required hours seems to have been reduced to about 10, but the work had not changed. These boys also faced the possibility of losing their scholarships altogether if their academic performance did not meet Yale's standards for recipients of financial aid. "Straight gift scholarships (with employment)," stated the official policy, "are ordinarily not granted to those students who stand below the top quarter of their class."[51] But for undergraduates judged to be exceptional in "character and leadership" — and one suspects that not a few varsity athletes were among them — "special Scholarships (with employment) . . . are available on a straight gift basis to students who rank above the bottom 20 percent of their class."[52]

The Jewish Question Revisited

Just as Kinkead was conducting her study, the volatile issue of whether Yale discriminated against Jewish applicants was being raised yet again. Pressing the matter was a loyal and well-connected alumnus, William Horowitz '29, who had become a prominent businessman and was chairman of the Connecticut State Board of Education.[53] A classmate of President Griswold's, Horowitz had asked to meet with him, and on April 5, 1960, he handed him a letter describing why he believed that Yale still had a Jewish quota. He presented figures showing that the number of Jews entering Yale between 1951 and 1959 had never exceeded 143, with the figure varying within the narrow range between 105 and 122 in every year but 1958. Horowitz also submitted figures for Yale's medical school — which enrolled 12 to 20 Jewish students between 1952 and 1959 in classes of 80 — that led him to the same conclusion: Yale still set a ceiling on Jewish enrollment.[54]

Griswold's notes from the meeting reveal that he denied Horowitz's allegations, insisting that "the numbers listed in his letter were the result of a search for human beings of specific characteristics rather than the result of an application of a predetermined quota for Jews." He also insisted on the "tremendous improvement in the position of Jews at Yale that had taken place" since he and Horowitz were undergraduates — a point on which the latter "agreed without reservation."[55] Maintaining that Yale's policy "would continue to be to find students of the proper qualities whether they were Jews or non-Jews," he could not resist expressing some skepticism about the numbers in the letter, noting that they "include only orthodox professing Jews."[56]

Yale's policy unquestionably held Jewish applicants to a higher standard than that for non-Jews. In 1955, Basil D. Henning,[57] a respected member of the History Department and master of Saybrook College, delicately raised the issue to Howe, expressing concern "about the boys with high predictions whom we reject." But Henning could not bring himself to propose to eliminate the policy; he realized, he wrote, that "in most cases you and Don are right in bopping these predominantly Brooklyn boys, but I still feel a little uneasy."[58] Henning's suspicion was not off the mark; in Griswold's first five years in office (1950–1954), only 7 students came to Yale from Bronx Science, 275 from Andover.[59]

Four years later, when Rabbi Richard J. Israel came to Yale from UCLA to direct the B'nai B'rith Hillel Foundation, the issue of discrimination against Jews was raised again from the inside. Arriving in 1959 from UCLA, Rabbi Israel quickly sensed that the number of Jews at Yale was suspiciously low.[60] But it was only after more than a year of investigation that he found:

> a somewhat guilt-ridden member of the admissions committee . . . [who] made a clear unequivocal statement about the undergraduate admissions policy . . . He has told us that there is a plain and open double standard for Jews and that many candidates otherwise qualified are rejected solely and exclusively on the grounds of their presumed . . . Jewishness.
>
> There is nevertheless no quota as such. The administration is . . . unaware of the number of Jewish students in Yale College. They simply have a policy of "conscious self-restraint." That is to say, they automatically turn down a "suitably" large number of Jews.[61]

Rabbi Israel approached Howe, but the dean denied the rabbi's claim that the percentage of Jews in recent years had hovered in the range of 10 to 12 percent. Howe asserted that there were large numbers of Jews who did not declare themselves, and he proceeded to identify five, "all but one appearing to be the children of intermarriage (as determined by the mother's name)." From Israel's point of view, these students were "only definable as Jews by a kind of Hitlerian definition."[62]

Frustrated by this encounter, Rabbi Israel turned to Yale's dynamic young university chaplain, William Sloane Coffin Jr., for assistance. Coffin '49 — the son of William Sloane Coffin '00 and the nephew of Henry Sloane Coffin '97 — was a graduate of Andover, chairman of the Yale Chapter of the American Veterans' Committee, and a member of Skull and Bones.[63] In part by dint of his unimpeachable background but even more because of his undeniable charisma, Coffin was a major influence at Yale. He liked Israel (who considered him "a goy for whom there is hope"), and when Yale's rabbi came to him, he did not hesitate to help.[64]

Coffin decided to take up the matter with President Griswold, "who seemed reluctant to do much until I told him that 'the conscience of Yale' was not about to go to sleep on this one." This angered Griswold, who asked tartly, "Well, what do you want me to do?" Coffin responded that he wanted Griswold to "start an investigation to find out why there are so few Jews in Yale College."

> "Do your own investigating," he said angrily.
> "I will," I said, "if you'll put it in writing that you want me to."

Suddenly he relaxed. He had an infectious grin which he now gave me. "Go to hell, Coffin," he said. Within twenty-four hours I had a letter and Yale had a new policy.

From his own investigation, Coffin concluded that "anti-Semitism at Yale was not overt as once it had been, but there were no Jews on the admissions committee, in the admissions office and few among the alumni recruiters."[65]

Coffin's account suggests an overnight change in Yale's policy, but the most authoritative account concludes that it took place over the ten months between May 1961 and February 1962. Perhaps the critical moment came in November 1961, when Rabbi Israel presented data from the Hillel Directory of each of the Ivy colleges to Coffin's predecessor, Sidney Lovett, showing that Yale had the lowest Jewish enrollment in the Ivy League. Yale's 12 percent placed it behind not only Columbia (45 percent) but also Princeton (15 percent), Dartmouth (15), and Harvard (21).[66] Lovett turned the data over to Griswold, who then discussed the matter with Howe, Coffin, a faculty representative to the admissions committee, and Lovett himself. By March 1962, Griswold had approved a policy effective for the class that would enter that fall, calling for the removal of "economic, social, religious or racial barriers to the fulfillment of . . . the democratic ideal of equal opportunity."[67]

Yet anti-Semitism within the Admissions Committee itself remained a serious problem. R. Inslee Clark '57, who joined the committee in 1961–62, has described its anti-Semitism: "It was incredible. It was deeply ingrained, more so than for other minorities, because the others weren't even part of the applicant pool . . . One of the reasons nobody wanted to go to Brooklyn Tech or Bronx Science or Stuyvesant was because those schools were where the Jews were. And I would hear, 'They all have 95 averages and 700 college boards. Do you want to get them stirred up to apply to Yale and then have to turn them down?'"[68]

Around this time, when two junior members of the committee asked why a group of students with Jewish-sounding surnames from the district for which they were responsible had all been voted down, veteran members replied, "Well, we could fill all of Yale with them. But we can't, of course."[69]

Yet soon Yale was no longer at the bottom of the Ivy League in Jewish enrollments. After the passage of the new admissions policy, change was immediately evident. The Jewish proportion, just 10 percent of the class that entered in 1961, rose the following year to 16 percent — the highest figure to that point in Yale's history.[70] Though Jewish applicants were still not treated the same as gentiles, the barriers were clearly coming down. More radical change would have to await a shift in the admissions criteria themselves — a shift that would, within a few years, produce a student body unlike any Yale had ever seen.

Faculty Discontent and the Push for Reform

In the aftermath of *Sputnik*, members of the Yale faculty, like their counterparts at Harvard, joined to push the Admissions Office to adopt a more meritocratic policy. As at Harvard, scientists were in the vanguard.[71] But it was not only scientists who were unhappy with Yale's admissions policy. R. Inslee Clark, in an interview years later, captured the tension well: "There was a feeling in the early Sixties (and perhaps even more in the Fifties) that the faculty and the Admissions Office were not in synch; that the faculty was always anxious for brighter and brighter kids, particularly more scientists and engineers, but frankly, just brighter people."[72]

The faculty's impression that its views were not in harmony with those of Howe was accurate. In Howe's report to the president for 1959–1960, the tension between the Admissions Office and the faculty was palpable. "In a major university community," Howe wrote, "professional status is primarily related to intellectual achievement, with relatively little regard for other considerations." As a consequence, "there has been a marked lessening of the University's demonstrated concern for manners, morality and selflessness . . ." The "most intolerant and intolerable of all students," he contended, "is the one admitted primarily for his intellectual capacity, but whose insecurity and lack of personal values have negated academic potential and substituted a protective covering of flaunted cynicism."[73]

From Howe's perspective, the tension was in good part a status conflict. "A few of Yale's distinguished scholars had slipped," in Howe's view, "into a faddish but largely outmoded perception of independent schools" — a misperception rooted "in their own social discomfort in relations with wealthy, exclusive 'preppies' of a previous generation."[74] Whatever the source of the faculty's views (and they were not homogeneous), Howe felt increasing pressure. "In my last two or three years," he recalled, he "heard . . . voices calling for a new Yale, quickly." In particular, there was a call for "more intense recruitment of the intellectually brilliant with less concern for human qualities that were not predictable."[75]

The faculty's belief that applicants from leading boarding schools received preferential treatment was widespread and not unjustified. In 1959, 69 percent of the applicants from Andover were admitted — in a year when under a third of all applicants were accepted. While Harvard and Princeton also admitted Andover graduates at a high rate (64 and 58 percent, respectively), they were much less likely to accept academically undistinguished candidates. Of the Andover students in the bottom half of the class, Yale accepted 14 compared to 5 at Princeton and 3 at Harvard. And of Andover graduates from the bottom quarter of their class, Yale took 4 while Harvard and Princeton took just 1 each.[76]

One consequence of this favoritism was Yale's lower proportion of public school students — only 44 percent in 1960, compared to 56 percent at Harvard and 53 percent at Princeton. Legacies, too, occupied a more favored position at Yale, making up 24 percent of the freshmen class, compared to 20 percent at Princeton and 18 percent at Harvard.[77]

In contrast to the faculty, who in the late 1950s played a minor role in admissions, the alumni were central to the actual process of selecting students. Of the 4,000 or so students who applied to Yale, roughly 3,000 would be interviewed by alumni around the country.[78] In most cases, especially for candidates outside the Northeast and from public schools, the alumni interview would be a candidate's only interview.

The influence of well-connected alumni in the selection process gave Yale admissions an "old boy" flavor. How it worked can been seen in the case of a young man from Wyoming whose girlfriend introduced him to Thomas Stroock '48, a rising oilman and a friend of George H. W. Bush '48. Stroock took a liking to the young man, a Protestant lad who played halfback and outside linebacker on the football team and was president of his senior class, and called the Admissions Office to tell them to take him. The young man, a graduate of Natrona County High in Casper, was admitted to Yale with a rare full scholarship. But he did not fare well. Not a diligent student, he flunked out — no easy task when the failure rate was under 2 percent.[79] But flunking out did not prevent the young man, Dick Cheney, from going on to a successful career.[80]

With an admission policy that emphasized nonacademic factors heavily and continued to favor traditional elite constituencies, it was not surprising that the intellectual atmosphere at Yale was less than scintillating. Even the students remarked on the problem;[81] in a report, "Academic Indifference at Yale," 15 members of the Aurelian Society described "the lack of real interest in the intellectual life of the University on the part of all too many students" — students who "get away with little work and a fairly respectable 'gentleman's average.'" The report noted acidly that "much time is spent at Yale in activities better done in country clubs, businesses or during vacation."[82]

It was not an altogether comfortable atmosphere for the most academically inclined students. In an era when academic knowledge was growing ever more prestigious, Yale's traditionalist admissions policies were increasingly outmoded. Paradoxically, their effect was to reduce Yale's attractiveness among the very students it most wished to enroll: the top graduates of the leading boarding schools. By the late 1950s, even Andover's college placement officer was recommending Yale for jocks who met minimum academic standards and Harvard for intellectually serious students.[83] In 1960, for the first time in memory, the number of Andover graduates going to Harvard (50) surpassed the number going to Yale (34).[84]

The problem of Yale's image at the boarding schools was part of a much larger problem: Yale's declining position vis-à-vis Harvard.[85] In truth, the ablest students, whether from private or public schools, were increasingly choosing Harvard. This pattern became clear by the late 1950s and was a growing concern among both alumni and faculty.[86] In 1960, Yale was attracting slightly under two-thirds of the students it admitted; at Harvard, the yield rate, which had been rising since 1956, surpassed four-fifths.[87]

So disturbing was this decline that Dean Howe, in a memorandum to the Board of Admissions, admitted his concern that Yale's preoccupation with the matter had produced a "massive inferiority complex."[88] Conceding that Harvard was "the institution foremost in all our minds when we become concerned about the Yale image," he proceeded to enumerate some of the advantages of its Cambridge rival. Among Harvard's assets were "its wealth, age, distinction, and aggressive publicity program," "its relationship with Radcliffe," and "the greater size and diversity of its Graduate level programs." Nevertheless, Howe insisted, "Yale has an undergraduate student body, which by a broad definition of 'quality,' compares favorably with Harvard's; and in a narrower definition with the emphasis solely on intellectual achievement, stands only a little behind Harvard."[89]

Howe's protestations notwithstanding, the sense in New Haven was that Yale's position was slipping. The reason was not altogether clear; after all, Harvard had been older and wealthier in 1950, when the yield rates of the Big Three were virtually identical, and coeducational classes with Radcliffe dated back to World War II.[90] Perhaps Harvard forged ahead because of a cultural and political shift among academically talented youth that accelerated with the launch of *Sputnik* but had its roots in World War II and the early days of the Cold War — a shift away from the traditional ethos of the all-around gentleman toward a more cosmopolitan "new class" ethos, centered on sheer intellectual achievement. Whatever the sources of Harvard's ascendance, the response in New Haven was one of deepening consternation.

In the forefront of the opposition to Yale's traditionalist policies was the faculty, which, like other faculties in research universities, had increasingly been selected on meritocratic grounds after World War II. Well aware that their colleagues at Harvard had issued a report in 1960 calling for greater emphasis on academic criteria in admissions, the faculty put increasing pressure on Griswold to move Yale in the same direction. In response to what Howe described as "new internal demands with some of the more outspoken faculty seeking faster rapid changes in the College," Griswold appointed a faculty committee to examine the education of first-year students in Yale College.[91]

The Committee on the Freshman Year, as it was formally called, moved quickly to place under its purview "the ways in which the freshman class is assembled."[92] Chaired by Leonard Doob — an eminent psychologist known for being willing to oppose Griswold, if necessary — the committee was an intellectual powerhouse that included some of Yale's most distinguished faculty.[93] It included Eugene Rostow'33, LL.B. '37, who had written President Seymour a strong letter of protest about Yale's policy of discrimination toward Jews in 1945,[94] William Clyde DeVane'20, Ph.D. '26, the respected dean of Yale College, and G. Evelyn Hutchinson, the brilliant Sterling Professor of Zoology.[95] Whatever the committee's ultimate recommendations, the prestige of its members guaranteed their serious consideration.

The Doob Report was written in the wake of Yuri Gagarin's pioneering space flight of April 1961, a moment when it seemed that superiority in science and technology might well determine the fate of the Cold War.[96] Issued in April 1962, the report opened by stating, "The changes wrought by time, by developments in scholarship, science, and technology, and by the position occupied by the United States have imposed new responsibilities upon Yale and a few other comparable universities in this country." "Yale is no longer an 18th-century academy or a 19th-century college," it noted, "but it is a university of the 20th century in one of the great nations." As such, its primary mission was "the task of advancing knowledge and of training future scholars."[97]

Calling for a "change in emphasis" at Yale — which implied that Yale should make "more scholarly demands" on its undergraduates — the report insisted that "the students we educate should exemplify and radiate the power and grace of learning." The implications of such a shift in emphasis were clear: "More of the graduates of Yale College, we think, must become professional scholars and teachers." Noting that as far back as 1946, Yale's official admissions policy "affirmed that students of outstanding intellectual capacity shall be given first preference," the report recommended an "explicit directive" to see to it that this policy would actually be put into effect.[98]

The committee's two principal recommendations called for Yale to adopt the precepts of academic meritocracy as its framework for admissions:

1. Candidates whose records show exceptionally high promise of continuing intellectual achievement should be sought out and admitted without regard for any other criteria save those indicated of emotional maturity and good character.

2. All other applicants for admission should be considered in the light of the fact that Yale is first and foremost an intellectual enterprise and that, consequently, those being educated here must be equipped with intellectual powers equal to the demands of the educational process at every stage.[99]

The implications were twofold: first, that admitting academically brilliant students should be the top priority, and second, that no applicants whose admission was based in part on nonacademic characteristics — implicitly but unmistakably including athletes, legacies, and "fine boys" from the best boarding schools — should be permitted to attend Yale unless their academic qualifications were strong.

Behind the recommendations of the Doob Report lay an atmosphere of mutual distrust between the faculty and the Admissions Office.[100] The administration, for its part, mistrusted the faculty, fearing that if they "commandeered the admissions process, they would admit students for academic reasons alone."[101] The faculty, in turn, believed that the 1946 policy of giving first preference to the intellectually strongest students had never been put into effect. Years later, Doob himself recalled that the committee, and especially Evelyn Hutchinson, repeatedly remarked on "the fact that almost no students from the Bronx School of Science were admitted, and that these were serious, lower-class, New York boys."[102]

So suspicious was the committee of the Admissions Office that it initially suggested that the office be taken out of the control of the president and be made part of the administrative structure of Yale College — the pattern at the rest of Yale. But Griswold warned Doob that he needed to retain personal control of the admissions process. The result was a compromise: the president would retain control, but the faculty would be more active in the selection and recruitment process and would have its members annually appointed to the Committee on Admissions.[103]

The committee also called for eliminating Yale's requirement that scholarship students work on campus — a policy that placed Yale at a competitive disadvantage with Harvard, which had eliminated its work requirement some years earlier.[104] Finally, the report recommended the admission of women, not "on a token basis but as a substantial proportion of each class." But this recommendation was placed firmly in the category of "ultimate" rather than "immediate," and it was made clear that "there should be no reduction in the number of men admitted to Yale College."[105] In any case, the admission of women was not the committee's top priority; on the contrary, it was Doob's hope that the proposal for coeducation would serve as a "smokescreen . . . that would deflect attention from what he saw as the urgent recommendations of the report."[106]

On May 19, 1962, the Yale Corporation formally approved all of the recommendations that called for immediate action. But the admission of women, while approved in principle, was indefinitely delayed.[107]

The Doob Report was a watershed document, for it insisted that Yale would have to change in fundamental ways if it were to fulfill its responsibilities to the nation. It was a meritocratic manifesto, but implementing it would require the full cooperation of the administration. Here the faculty had ample reason for concern, for President Griswold, though supporting the Report in public, was reported to have been unhappy about it in private. According to Howe, "The idea that the College would make a major shift toward becoming part of a great research university, focusing on producing scholars and teachers, just never seemed to me to be in Whit's book."[108] Howe's response, too, was largely negative; in an interview conducted three decades later, he said, "It had raised false expectations of changes that were either unattainable or undesirable, some reflecting faddish notions of the Sixties from which the University is still recovering."[109]

In the end, the implementation of the Doob Report did not remain in the hands of men who were less than enthusiastic about it. In 1963, Griswold succumbed to stomach cancer after a two-year battle. His untimely death at the age of fifty-six left much of Yale in mourning; Howe was particularly shaken.[110] The following year, Howe, too, left Yale, no longer in sync with a new and more progressive administration.

The Dawn of the Brewster Era

Yale's recently appointed provost, Kingman Brewster Jr., who had left his professorship at Harvard Law School to come to Yale in 1960, was one of the Doob Report's strongest supporters. According to Doob himself, Brewster exhibited "a personal interest in getting the Report through."[111] And Howe, whose leadership of the Admissions Office had been implicitly criticized, reported that "Kingman warmly endorsed the Report."[112]

Appointed acting president immediately after Griswold's death and officially named Yale's eighteenth president in October 1963, Brewster shepherded through another major reform in the battle to make Yale more meritocratic. On April 19, 1963 — the day that Griswold died — Howe wrote a memo to the Governing Board of Admissions about "the possibility of our divorcing admissibility from financial need." While it had long been Yale's "avowed policy to reach admissions decisions without reference to whether candidates requested financial assistance," the reality, Howe acknowledged, was that "the Admissions Committee has not fully observed its avowed policy." In practice, Yale favored the student who "will not cost us anything" over one who "would require substantial assistance." Especially hurt were applicants with "extremely high need," for Yale was well aware that such students cost more than the average scholarship recipient.[113]

Though Griswold also favored divorcing admissions from financial status, it was Brewster who was in charge when the Corporation finally approved the policy of "need-blind" admissions, making Yale the first university to separate admissions decisions from requests for financial aid and to promise to provide adequate scholarship assistance to those admits who needed it.[114] Born in 1919 to a family whose roots went back to the *Mayflower*, Kingman Brewster Jr. was a patrician's patrician. Descended from Elder William Brewster, who came to the Massachusetts Bay Colony from England in 1620, he was the son of Kingman Brewster, a prominent lawyer who had graduated from Amherst and Harvard Law School. His mother also had a distinguished lineage. Descended from Huguenots who came to America in 1635 and the daughter of a prosperous and respected businessman, Florence Besse was a graduate of Wellesley, with an M.A. from Radcliffe. So wealthy was her father that, when he died in 1930, he bequeathed to his heirs over $4.5 million.[115]

Brewster's father, who became an important lobbyist in Washington, held political views well to the right of the Republican mainstream. Bitterly hostile to the New Deal and to brain trusters, the senior Brewster held racist and anti-Semitic views not uncommon in his milieu. According to Geoffrey Kabaservice, the elder Brewster "believed that Smith College (where his daughter Mary was a student) was a hotbed of communism, and that Franklin Delano Roosevelt was secretly a Jew named Rosenfeld."[116]

But Brewster was not raised primarily by his father. In 1923, when he was four, his parents separated and later divorced. Young Kingman remained in contact with his father — who, despite his harsh political views, was a man of tremendous charm — but was raised by his mother, an enlightened and energetic woman who did not share his father's attitudes. After spending several years with the Besse family in Springfield, Massachusetts, the Brewsters moved to Cambridge in 1930. There Florence married Edward Ballantine, a Harvard professor and composer she had known since childhood. Though Ballantine did not wish to act as Kingman's father — a role occupied by his uncle Arthur Besse, a liberal Republican and civic-minded businessman who had attended Lawrenceville and Harvard — he enjoyed a good relationship with the boy and introduced him to a number of important figures in the musical and cultural worlds of Cambridge and Boston.[117]

Moving to Cambridge, young Kingman was enrolled in the Belmont Hill School — a private school founded by Harvard professors in search of appropriate education for their children. Though not especially bookish, Kingman was a good student who liked to read. Devoting most of his time to extracurricular activities, he was editor-in-chief of the school newspaper and a leader of the debate team. His crowning achievement at Belmont Hill was winning a major debate on "whether capitalism is more conducive to war than socialism." Taking the affirmative, Brewster, whose team had not lost a debate in three years, led his school to a victory over a formidable Groton team that included McGeorge Bundy, William Bundy, and Franklin D. Roosevelt Jr.[118]

Tied to three distinguished families, Kingman traveled easily in elite circles. Among the people he met either at his Cambridge home or at the family home in Martha's Vineyard were Elihu Root Jr., Walter Lippmann, Felix Frankfurter, Max Eastman, and Roger Baldwin, the founder of the American Civil Liberties Union. Young Kingman was especially close to Baldwin, Harvard '04, who had gone to prison for draft resistance during World War I. To Brewster, Baldwin was the personification of the courageous and independent reformer who had stood up for civil liberties in a difficult time.[119]

Brewster regularly socialized with many of these luminaries at the family's summer home in Martha's Vineyard. A fierce if gentlemanly yachtsman, Kingman sailed with his cousins up and down the East Coast, developing a reputation in the junior yachting world of the mid-1930s. He exhibited great talent, with his team twice winning the award for the best small-boat racer in the twelve-to-eighteen age bracket in the United States and Canada.[120]

Though a living embodiment of what the French call "jeunesse doré," Kingman Brewster Jr. was not the kind of young man content to while away his time enjoying the privileges that were his birthright.[121] In 1936, after finishing secondary school a year early thanks to private tutoring from a Harvard student, Brewster volunteered his services to the reelection campaign of George W. Norris, a progressive, iconoclastic Republican senator from Nebraska.

One of the leading figures of the Progressive movement and the author of the Norris–La Guardia Anti-Injunction Act of 1932 and the Norris-Rayburn Rural Electrification Act of 1936, Norris represented a liberal, independent strand of Republicanism much admired by Brewster. Renowned for his integrity, Norris had risked his political career by crossing party lines and endorsing Al Smith in 1928 and Franklin Delano Roosevelt in 1932. But what may have most attracted Brewster to the senator was that, like Baldwin, he had taken a strong stance against American intervention in World War I and suffered vilification as a consequence. Norris was running as an Independent in 1936, and this, too, must have appealed to Brewster. When the campaign was over, the seventeen-year-old could say that he had had a small part in a historic event, for Norris triumphed over his Republican opponent to become the only Independent in either house of Congress.[122]

Even Brewster's choice of Yale, which he entered in the fall of 1937, showed an independent streak; of his Belmont Hill classmates, 24 of 26 matriculated at Harvard. It did not take long for the handsome and charming Brewster to establish himself as a major figure on the Yale campus. The recipient of the Freshman Debating Prize, he also succeeded during his first year in gaining a place on the *Yale Daily News,* where he later served as chairman of the board. Brewster was also active in the Political Union, the Elizabethan Club (the literary society), and the Aurelian Honor Society. It was thus no surprise when a semiserious poll of the senior class voted him to have "done the most for Yale." And it was no accident that his classmates dubbed him and his roommate, Bill Jackson, "the senators."[123]

Academically, Brewster did well, graduating cum laude. But his standing among his classmates was rooted in his prominence in the public intellectual life of the campus. "He was always up there in the stratosphere," one contemporary recalled, "with guys like Mac Bundy and the deeper thinkers."[124] There was little doubt that he would be "tapped" for Skull and Bones.[125] When Brewster did the unthinkable — turning down his place in Bones — he became a legend in Yale undergraduate lore.[126]

Like many students at the time, Brewster was an ardent opponent of America's intervention into World War II. A founding member of the America First Committee (AFC) in 1940, he was a national spokesman for student antiwar sentiment, co-authoring an article for the *Atlantic Monthly* and testifying before the Senate.[127] Though the AFC has rightly been portrayed, especially in its later stages, as a bastion of conservative isolationism, Brewster criticized its domination by conservatives, telling its head, Robert Douglas Stuart Jr.: "You need laborites and progressives. It would be awful if the Committee turned out to be the instrument of one class." Ultimately, the National Committee did include progressives like Robert M. La Follette Jr. and Chester Bowles, but Brewster resigned in the spring of 1941, telling Stuart that the passage of the Lend-Lease Act had settled the matter of America's ends and a pressure group could only serve as a vehicle of obstruction.[128] By the time he gave the Class Oration in 1941, Brewster had come to accept the inevitability of war, telling his classmates that he took it "as a matter of course that those of us who have known the best of American life will not fail in its defense." "We are called, in last resort," he declared, "precisely *because* we see a higher purpose to man than power and a nobler capacity than sheer force, and we are determined that this concept of nearly two thousand years shall not die."[129]

When the Japanese air force attacked Pearl Harbor on December 7, 1941, Brewster joined Yale Naval Unit Number Three, where he became an aviator and rose to the rank of lieutenant. Serving for four years on the East Coast and in Brazil, Brewster never engaged in combat despite his efforts to transfer to an aircraft carrier that served as a base for night-flying bombers. Nevertheless, flying itself was extremely hazardous; of the 10 men in Brewster's unit, 4 died in crashes.[130]

After the war, Brewster enrolled at Harvard Law School and made *Law*

Review — an honor reserved for the top 20 students in a class of over 300. Brewster worked as note editor and graduated magna cum laude. Of equal importance, he met his mentor there: Professor Milton Katz, who years later remembered him as "one of the outstanding young men of his class — a rigorous mind capable of analytical work and, with that, the imagination to excel in many fields."[131]

His first job after graduating was to accompany Katz to Paris to serve as his assistant at the European headquarters of the Marshall Plan. Though he flourished in the job, Brewster stayed only one year, returning in 1949 — at Katz's advice — to be a research associate in MIT's Department of Economics and Social Science. Then, to his great pleasure, he was offered an assistant professorship at Harvard Law School in 1950. At the age of thirty-four, though he had written only a single article, Brewster was promoted to full professor.[132]

While not one of the law school's most renowned scholars, Brewster was an important figure on campus by virtue of his charisma, his solid scholarship (he was the author of a major work, *Antitrust and American Business Abroad*, 1958), and his tremendous accumulation of social capital. A good friend of McGeorge Bundy, who had been dean of Harvard's Faculty of Arts and Sciences since 1953 and head of the Harvard chapter of the American Association of University Professors, Brewster was a known and respected figure in the Harvard community.[133]

Though lacking administrative experience, Brewster was asked to become provost at Yale in the fall of 1959. The offer, which he was quick to accept, had much to do with his long friendship with Griswold — it went back to his teenage years, when he came to know Griswold on Martha's Vineyard, where both families had homes. Griswold considered Brewster perhaps the brightest undergraduate he had ever taught. So close were the two of them that on the night Brewster turned down Skull and Bones, he bicycled to Griswold's house, expecting that his friend and mentor would be pleased. Instead, Brewster learned from Griswold's wife that, at that very moment, he was busy participating in tap night activities at Wolf's Head, his own secret society.[134]

When Brewster married Mary Louise Phillips, an attractive and intelligent Vassar junior whose father was an alumnus of Yale and Yale Law School, he wrote a heartfelt letter to Griswold, saying, "I can think of no one whose matrimonial state gave me more strength than did you for that trembling waddle to the altar." The two men remained close, and when Brewster joined the Harvard faculty, they would often sail together off Martha's Vineyard. So when Griswold offered him the job of provost (Yale's number two post), it was irresistible.[135]

Assuming his new position in the fall of 1960, Brewster quickly impressed the faculty, students, and younger members of the Corporation with his intelligence, his style, and his consultative way of making decisions. When Griswold died, Brewster was his logical successor. Nevertheless, Yale conducted a lengthy, open, and (for Brewster) agonizing search that lasted five months. On October 11, 1963, the Yale Corporation offered Kingman Brewster Jr. the presidency by a vote of 13–2; the opposition came from two senior members of the Corporation who feared that the liberal Republican from Massachusetts would push too hard for change in their beloved institution.[136]

From the moment he became president, Brewster received correspondence on admissions issues from within and without the Yale community. Less than three weeks after taking office, Leon Himmelfarb of West Hempstead, Long Island, wrote, asking whether it was true that "Yale has definite restrictive quotas in operation against Jews, Negroes and other minority groups." Brewster, relying on a response drafted by Howe, assured Mr. Himmelfarb "without qualification that Yale has no quotas for any minority or majority group" and that, to the best of his knowledge, "Yale has at no time in its history had such restrictions."[137]

At the same time, Brewster received a letter from Andrew Robinson '27, the vice president of a major corporation. "There is a very strong feeling among many of our alumni, with which I concur," Robinson wrote, "that this near-sacred mission of the University ['developing men of character, leadership and accomplishment'] is hanging somewhat in the balance due to a policy of admissions which has accented out of proportion the academically-gifted young man, at the sacrifice of the individual possessing far better-than-average scholastic capability, yet having those qualities of leadership and extra-curricular capabilities that mean so much in achieving success in business, professional and political life." Robinson warned Brewster that "it would be tragic if . . . our fervent efforts to enlist the highest qualified students scholastically resulted in a serious diminution of those less perfect academically but with the potential of making a greater contribution to society and to Yale University."[138]

In some of his earliest speeches as president, Brewster showed a shrewd awareness of the contradictory pressures he faced while insisting that it was in Yale's and the nation's interest to move admissions policy in a more meritocratic direction. "The complication of the modern world and the specialized knowledge required for its understanding," he told the Cincinnati Yale Club at its 100th Anniversary Dinner, "make it certain that the trained intelligence will assume an even greater importance in the struggle for leadership." Having stressed themes dear to the hearts of the faculty members who had written the Doob Report, he then sent an important signal to advocates of the Old Yale: "It is the fate of Presidents as well as Deans of Admission to have to bear the brunt of a two-front war. On one flank will be urged upon us men of high character and low intellect; on the other will be pressed the cause of young men of high intellect and moral callousness." Brewster believed Yale should "remain a place where some of those of highest intellectual and moral capacity of each succeeding generation may find *both* these capacities excited, challenged, and stretched to their limit."[139]

Yet in a speech in Dallas the following month, Brewster struck a vintage Conant theme, firmly taking the side of those calling for new policies that would eliminate the privileges of birth: "So until we can say that there are no longer any financial obstacles to access to any level of higher education to which a person would both aspire and qualify, we cannot say that we are adequately protecting the nation; we cannot say that we are doing our best to compete with totalitarianism, which Fred Barghoorn described; we cannot say that we are making the most of our economic potential as described by Jim Tobin; but perhaps more important than these, we cannot say that we are living up to the American ideal of equality of opportunity."[140]

Meanwhile, on the campus, Brewster was receiving a crash course in the politics of admissions. The issue was that of alumni sons, whose proportion had dropped below 20 percent for the first time in thirty years. At the suggestion of Charles M. O'Hearn '24, who led Yale's fundraising efforts, Howe urged Brewster both to continue Yale's policy of favoring legacies when "things were appropriately equal" and to introduce a new policy giving greater preference to the sons whose fathers "whole record of service both to Yale and to American society" was particularly distinguished.[141] After "some rather cold-blooded discussion of the problems inherent in recognizing degrees of Yale son preference," Howe reported, "the Committee agreed that this was the only feasible approach to the problems that faced us." It was, he argued, "a matter of self-interest on Yale's part." Howe reported that "some of the discussion was . . . a bit of a shock for the new Faculty members of the Admissions Committee (Messrs. Martz, Napier, Taft, and Walker)." The dean of admissions singled out Horace Taft '49 — a member of the Physics Department, the son of Senator Robert A. Taft '10, and the grandson of William Howard Taft '78 — as "the most shaken by the worldly considerations which seem to play a role in admission policy." But Howe stressed that in the end, "each of these men concurred with the thinking that emerged from the meeting."[142]

The response of Yale's new president to Howe's memorandum was quintessential Brewster. "It seems to me it is quite right," he wrote back, "for the Admissions Office to obtain *factual* information from the Alumni and Development offices with respect to the relationship to Yale of an applicant's family." But "in no case should the *opinion* about the chances of admission be solicited from or volunteered by these two offices." Yale "should certainly avoid," Brewster continued, "discriminating among alumni sons on the grounds of the fathers' contribution, except where the situation is obviously 'equal in every other way.'" Finally, Brewster recorded his agreement "with the standards by which we now discriminate between alumni sons and non-alumni sons," but he recommended that "even these might be *relaxed* if we are confident of a high potential in one or another kind of academic role," a suggestion that gave the Admissions Office even more latitude than Howe had requested.[143] Howe had a green light for his new policy, but Brewster had gone on record as supporting it only if it was carried out with appropriate decorum.

Though Brewster and Howe had reached apparent agreement on the thorny issue of alumni sons, their relationship was less than warm. In February 1964, a month after the above exchange, Howe announced that he was taking a year's leave of absence, a move that became permanent when he left Yale to assume the presidency of the American Field Service.[144] Howe left voluntarily, but he later said of his relationship with Brewster that "our perspectives and styles were sufficiently different that neither one of us regretted my departure."[145]

Taking his place as acting dean of admissions in what was obviously a holding move was sixty-eight-year-old Alton Rufus Hyatt '18.[146] New principles for the admission of alumni sons had been enunciated by Howe and Brewster, but what they would mean in practice was still not clear. On the one hand, Yale sons would continue to be favored, but only when "things were approximately equal." On the other hand, consideration of particular cases would look at "the father's whole record of service both to Yale and to American society." The clear implication was, as Howe admitted, "the differential treatment of alumni sons," but the question remained: just how much advantage would the sons of particularly prominent fathers enjoy?[147]

The answer came in the case of a Yale son from a leading boarding school who had compiled an undistinguished record there, not once making the honor roll. A mediocre student, the young man scored just 566 on the SAT verbal — a score that would have placed him in the bottom 10 percent of a Yale freshman class.[148] Though popular with his classmates, he did not have any particularly outstanding extracurricular talents. So weak was his overall record that when the school's college placement counselor examined the young man's grades and College Boards, he gently suggested that he apply to some "safety schools" in addition to Yale.

But the candidate came from a distinguished Yale family, with Old Blue ties going back several generations. His father, a wealthy businessman, had been a great success at Yale, graduating Phi Beta Kappa and being elected to

Skull and Bones. Perhaps even more important, his grandfather, also a member of Skull and Bones, was a prominent politician who had served as a member of the Yale Corporation. Clearly, this was no ordinary Yale family.

When decision time finally came in April 1964, this Yale son was the happy recipient of a letter of admission. His name was George W. Bush.[149] The Old Yale, it seemed, was still very much alive, though perhaps not altogether well.

PART III

INCLUSION AND THE PERSISTENCE OF PRIVILEGE, 1965–2005

CHAPTER 12

Inky Clark, Kingman Brewster, and the Revolution at Yale

THE DEAN OF ADMISSIONS at any first-rate university college," Brewster once said, "has the toughest job of anyone in the society."[1] While something of an exaggeration, the remark suggests that he was well aware of the swirl of contradictory pressures that would face Howe's successor — and of the strategic importance of the job for Yale's future. In selecting a new dean of admissions, Brewster faced a basic choice: Would Yale admissions continue on the largely traditionalist path laid down by Howe and Griswold? Or would it embark on a strategy of fundamental change, with all the risk and uncertainty that such a path would entail?

When Brewster began his search in the fall of 1964, change was everywhere in the air. The historic civil rights march on Washington had taken place just a year earlier, the Great Society was in full flower, and a student movement was stirring on the nation's campuses. Even at Yale, the demand for change in admissions was receiving powerful reinforcement from respectable quarters. Perhaps the most powerful voice came from the prestigious University Council's Committee on Admissions; noting the "ferment . . . stirring among creative young Americans these days," it urged the college to seek out "brilliant and restless minds" and to admit "candidates from the disadvantaged, depressed, and even despised corners of our society."[2]

One of the candidates for dean of admissions was R. Inslee ("Inky") Clark Jr. '57, a twenty-nine-year-old who had joined the Committee on Admission in 1961 and was its youngest member. Brewster ostensibly invited him to "come over and share some ideas" about a number of people whom he said he was considering for the position. One of them was Ned Hall, the respected headmaster of the Hill School.[3] Clark knew Hall from his visits to the school as a junior admissions officer, and his appraisal was blunt: "Mr. Brewster, every time I'm at the Hill School and there is a discussion about somebody who should be getting into Yale and who is not, he would always push for the same kind of person. The push was always for the well-rounded, pleasant, jovial, athlete type. It was never for the abrasive kid. It was never the scientist. It was never the egghead. It was never the oddball. And I said, 'I don't mind that, but it's so predictable. I think if you appoint somebody like that, that's what you're going to end up with in your class: lots of people like that.'"[4] Clark's implication was clear: he would like to see Yale take a very different direction.

As the interview progressed, it became clear to Clark that he was under consideration. When Brewster asked whether he thought of himself as more of an architect or an engineer, Clark responded, "I think of myself as an architect . . . I want to design." He went on to say that he would like to "design quite a different student body from the one we have now," one that would be an "intellectually stronger and more diverse student body." But making this a reality, Clark insisted, would require a different kind of admissions staff and the total removal of financial aid as a consideration in admissions.[5]

So when Brewster offered Clark the job, he knew the general direction in which the young admissions officer planned to take Yale. Little in Clark's background foreshadowed the drastic changes that he introduced. Although Clark's father had not attended college and Clark was himself the graduate of a public school, Garden City High School on Long Island, Clark's mother had graduated from Vassar. Like all his predecessors as dean, Clark was of solid Protestant stock and his profile at Yale was that of a quintessential Old Blue. A member of the varsity golf team and a frequent name on the Dean's List, he was also president of St. Elmo's fraternity, president of the Interfraternity Council, editor-in-chief of the yearbook, and a member of Skull and Bones.[6]

After graduation, Clark taught at the Lawrenceville School, where he also served as a housemaster and a coach. But having been commander of the Campus Air Force Reserve Officer Training Corps (ROTC) as an undergraduate, Clark had a two-year military obligation. He fulfilled it as an air force lieutenant in Newburgh, New York, where he was able to attend the Maxwell School of Public Affairs at Syracuse University on nights and weekends, receiving a master's degree in 1959. Clearly extraordinarily energetic, he also obtained a master's degree in history at Columbia after returning to Lawrenceville for another year of teaching. By 1961, when he joined the Yale admissions staff at the age of twenty-six, Clark had in four short years discharged a two-year military commitment, acquired two master's degrees, and gained two years of teaching experience in a boarding school.[7]

A number of important markers — his membership in Skull and Bones, his status as a varsity athlete, his presidency of the Interfraternity Council, and even his handsome WASP appearance — suggested that the Old Yale might find a valuable ally in Clark. For this reason, his appointment as dean of admissions was greeted coolly by the many members of the faculty who believed that Yale needed serious reform. Shortly after the choice was announced, Paul Weiss, a philosophy professor, wrote to Brewster, saying that he had been "hearing from a number of people — both those who know him [Clark] and those who know only about him — that the appointment of the new admissions man was a serious error."[8] C. Vann Woodward, perhaps the most eminent of Yale's many distinguished historians, expressed his concern that the "new Dean of Admissions looks, from where I sit, rather much like the Yale 'Image'" — an image that he believed needed to be changed.[9] And William Sloane Coffin Jr., the university's popular and charismatic chaplain, went so far as to tell Clark in person: "I don't think you're the kind of person that I would have wanted for this position."[10]

Responding to Coffin, Clark requested a chance to demonstrate that he was serious about making major changes. It was enough to win Coffin over, but Clark was well aware that altering Yale's traditional policies would not be easy, and shortly after being appointed, he asked Brewster if he could spend the spring observing how other colleges and universities handled admissions. He "wanted to test the water a little bit out there with some people to see what they thought: what they thought of Yale, what they thought about Yale admissions, what they thought should be done, could be done, etc."[11]

Clark was careful to visit not only Yale's traditional competitors — Harvard, Princeton, Stanford, Dartmouth, Amherst, and Williams — but also institutions of quite different character, such as Berkeley and NYU, to see a wide range of admissions philosophies and practices. "Berkeley was a totally different admissions process from Yale's. That was at one end of the spectrum. The other end was the Amherst or Williams kind of approach, which was very, very personal, very subjective, and very weighted — particularly at Williams, I thought — toward maintaining the kind of college that Williams was in the Fifties and the Sixties: very white, very New Englandy, very genteel, very much the place for the well-rounded kind of person. This also reflected, frankly, the people who were running the admissions program at Williams. So there I saw the two totally opposite approaches to admissions."[12] Clark concluded that Yale should avoid both poles, with Berkeley's form of meritocracy rejected as impersonal and by-the-numbers and Williams's approach (much closer to Yale's traditional practices) rejected as unduly subjective and too heavily weighted toward the perpetuation of existing elites.

But it was Clark's visit to Harvard, Yale's chief competitor, that left him with the most indelible impression. During the previous decade, Harvard had forged ahead of Yale in direct competition for students, and by 1965, 86 percent of applicants accepted at both institutions chose Harvard.[13] So Clark was not surprised that Fred Glimp, Harvard's dean of admissions, evinced little inclination to tamper in any way with an admissions system whose summit Harvard occupied.

Nevertheless, Glimp's reaction to Clark's plan to reform Yale was revealing. According to Clark, Harvard's dean generally applauded the ideas and directions he was proposing but said, "Boy, that's going to be a tough road for Yale to go down." Glimp's face, Clark recalled thirty years later, took on "that kind of wry, wonderful, Harvardian look . . . as if to say, 'Boy, you are young and green, and you're going to get slaughtered.'"[14] The next five years —which became known as the Inky Clark era at Yale[15]— would show that Glimp was not wrong.

A New Admissions Regime

Even before he formally took office in July 1965, Clark moved quickly to enlist the support of the faculty by asking Brewster for permission to constitute an Advisory Board "to help lay down guidelines for Yale admissions policy." The faculty's support, he realized, was critical; he would need a counterweight to Yale's traditional constituencies, and the faculty shared his goal of enrolling a student body at once stronger intellectually and more diverse socially. The members of the committee —a distinguished group that included John W. Hall, Griswold Professor of History; James Tobin, Sterling Professor of Economics and a member of the first cohort of Conant's Harvard National Scholars; and D. Allen Bromley, professor of physics and director of the Nuclear Structure Laboratory— ensured that it would be a serious force. Given Yale's checkered history on the issue of quotas, the fact that two of its members had obvious Jewish surnames —Harry W. Wasserman, chairman of the Chemistry Department, and Alvin Eisenman, professor of graphic design— sent a message that a new era was beginning.[16]

In choosing Clark and in forming the Advisory Board, Brewster had in mind a vision that owed a great deal to the meritocratic ideals articulated by Conant.[17] In a speech to the Yale Club of Southern California in 1965, Brewster sounded a familiar theme of Conant's by identifying "the history of western civilization in general and Anglo-American civilization in particular" with the "struggle for the enlargement of the capacities and opportunities of all men." Echoing Conant, Brewster believed that "resentments will be minimized and responsible energy will be maximized" to the extent that equality of opportunity prevails: "if, by and large, people feel that success is related to effort, at worst to luck, and in any case, is seldom rigged by private status or political favor."[18]

The Admissions Policy Advisory Board, chaired by Tobin, did not dally in laying out new guidelines that reinforced the meritocratic direction favored by Clark and Brewster, issuing a Preliminary Report in December 1965 that pushed Yale toward radical reform. The report began by reaffirming the admissions criteria laid down by the Doob Report: intellectually brilliant candidates "should be sought out and admitted without regard for any other criteria save those indicative of emotional maturity and good character," and all other applicants "should be considered in light of the fact that Yale is first and foremost an intellectual institution." Knowing that the Doob Report had never been put into effect, the board pointedly called for giving it "more operational precision."[19]

Among the report's many recommendations (which, it emphasized, had been "firmly and unanimously agreed on") were a series of measures designed to make Yale's professed meritocratic ideals a reality. Some of these recommendations — for example, greater faculty participation in admissions (including increasing the number of faculty members on the Admissions Committee from four to eight) and not entering on the candidate's summary card the overall judgment of readers until all the readers had finished the reviews — would introduce important changes into the admissions *process*.

Other recommendations, however, were implicitly or explicitly designed to introduce changes into the substantive *outcomes* of the process. Among the more significant was the removal of all "information regarding a candidate's financial need, or even whether he has applied for aid," from his folder, the abolition of "the numerical rating . . . of non-academic personal qualities," and an increase "in the number of applicants and admissions from New York and other eastern metropolitan areas" (a thinly veiled reference to the issue of continued discrimination against Jews).[20] The board also firmly endorsed an important reform that Clark had already put in place: the elimination of "the A, B, C grouping of candidates from selected secondary schools."[21]

The support that Clark received from the board was critical, for it empowered him to move aggressively to change other practices that had long been in place. One of his first acts as dean was to eliminate from the alumni interview form the checklist of physical characteristics of candidates interviewed. In Clark's view, the checklist was a remnant of an earlier time when "there was a certain image to a Yale man, a Princeton man," and had the effect of discriminating against Jews, intellectuals, and scientists.[22] He also introduced a radical reduction in the importance given to the applicant's predicted academic average — a measure that had been used since the 1920s. Although in principle a predicted GPA could be useful as Yale tried to raise the academic level of its student body, in practice it was based on how students from the applicants' secondary school had performed at Yale in the past — not a problem for candidates from traditional feeder schools, who could reasonably be evaluated, but impossible to calculate for the growing number of applicants from public schools. For a decade, Yale had handled this problem by deflating the projected GPA for applicants from unfamiliar secondary schools while assigning a "plus factor" to candidates from private schools with tough grading systems, such as Hotchkiss.[23] Recognizing that this system institutionalized discrimination against students from unknown public schools, Clark made it the official policy of the Admissions Committee to ignore the predicted academic average for candidates from such schools.[24] No longer would boarding school students enjoy an advantage built into the admissions process.

With the support of the Admissions Policy Advisory Board, Clark also moved quickly to implement another crucial change that would help level the playing field: the total elimination of family financial status as a factor in admissions. Even before Clark's appointment Yale had adopted a policy of need-blind admissions; the number of students on financial aid rose in 1964 to 41 percent from just 35 percent a year earlier.[25] But when Clark took office, an applicant's folder still included information on whether he was applying for financial aid and how much he would need to attend Yale. In practice, this meant that when considering a candidate, a member of the Admissions Committee would see that it would "cost" Yale $8,000 to bring him to New Haven.[26] So the admissions decision was not truly "need blind."[27] Clark removed this information for the class that entered in 1966, and, for the first time, Yale admitted students without any regard to their capacity to pay. Though Harvard quietly adopted a similar policy not long after, Yale was the first university to proclaim a totally need-blind admissions policy publicly and to provide sufficient assistance to permit all admitted students to attend.[28]

These reforms were consistent with Clark's goal of producing an intellectually stronger and more diverse student body. But having been a member of the Committee on Admissions since 1961, he realized that all of the changes he had introduced, however promising they looked on paper, might never be fully implemented unless the staff supported them. And here there was reason for concern, for the staff was filled with Old Blues who represented traditional Yale; in 1964–1965, all eleven staff members had gone to Yale, with three the sons of alumni and a fourth (the acting dean of admissions) the brother of three Yale graduates.[29]

Though personally friendly with many members of the Admissions Committee (years later, Clark reported that he "dearly loved those people as human beings"), he felt that he had no choice but to dismiss most of them: "In order to fulfill the kind of mission or destiny that I felt for the University and for the Admissions Department, it could not be achieved with the people that were there. They were very, very stuck in their ways and they were very, very sure about the kinds of people that should be at the University. I mean, some of the comments that were made at the Admissions Committee meetings would appall you — statements about certain kinds of backgrounds of people, certain kinds of schools, etc. They were appalling. I'm not saying that this didn't occur at other universities, but it was certainly inappropriate for the kind of direction and move that we were on.[30]

So Clark hired an almost entirely new staff — younger, larger, and more diverse, with more graduates of public schools, more people who had not attended Yale, and — for the very first time — a black admissions officer.[31] By the time the first admissions cycle under Clark reached its midway point in December 1965, a new direction was clearly in place. Virtually everything that could change — the criteria, the actual process, and the staff itself — had changed before a single applicant was considered.

Though the new regime had yet to admit a single student, a certain apprehension was in the air. In an interview with the *Yale Daily News,* Clark declared — ominously for those wedded to Yale tradition — that "the old notion of the 'feeder school' supplying most of the class is no longer applicable."[32] But questions about the new policy, which emphasized diversity and "special talent" over the "all-around" man, abounded. Would Yale, asked the paper, be able to "produce the leadership that they always have in the past?" Would the new policy "lead to a new and different type of alumni who will not be so willing to donate funds as the past Yale graduates?" Was it true that the new policy "does not weight athletic prowess very heavily?"[33] And would the alumni sons and boarding school boys who had virtually defined the "Yale man" be overlooked by the new men in power?

Prep Schools and the End of Preference

As late as 1962, as the Howe era was ending, private school graduates still outnumbered those from public schools at Yale — a pattern that had disappeared at Harvard in 1953 and at Princeton in 1958. Even so, the numbers were down from the days of Ned Noyes, in the late 1940s and 1950s, when prep school boys constituted close to two-thirds of the freshman class.[34]

Under the interim administration of Alton Hyatt in 1964 and 1965, the position of the prep schools continued to erode. In both years, public school graduates outnumbered their prep school peers, though boys from private schools still constituted 48 percent of entering students as late as 1965.[35] Major feeder schools, though not as central to Yale as a decade earlier, still sent sizable delegations to New Haven: 43 from Andover, 22 from Exeter, 21 from Hotchkiss, 13 each from St. Paul's and Choate, and 11 each from Lawrenceville and Hill.[36]

In Clark's view, these numbers reflected in no small part the systematic preference that Yale gave to the leading boarding schools. Its most visible expression was the system of early notification of students from selected schools, almost all of them private. Having participated in the system as a junior admissions officer, Clark had come to disapprove of it strongly: "I thought to myself, 'This isn't fair. This isn't right. Every applicant ought to be treated exactly the same in terms of the procedure for admission to one of the top universities of the world.'"³⁷ To Clark, the ABC system symbolized what was wrong with Yale admissions: "In the early Sixties — and I'm sure this was true in the Fifties and before — there were a handful of New England boarding schools that were handled with kid gloves by Yale. Normally the dean of admissions himself visited these schools, and would bring one or two of the most senior members of the staff, who were private school people. They would normally stay for two or three days. They would be wined and dined by the faculty, and there would be a lot of schmoozing going on, and there would always be a headmaster's reception — you know, that kind of thing."³⁸ In his first year in office, Clark — moving in concert with Princeton — eliminated it. Interestingly, Harvard — with its more meritocratic public image — refused to abolish the ABC ratings, deciding that the existing system, inegalitarian though it was, served its institutional interests.³⁹

The prep schools were displeased by Clark's abolition of the system, but his difficulties were seriously compounded by a number of less than diplomatic public remarks. His most serious faux pas took place at Andover, for decades Yale's most important feeder school. In the past, Dean Howe and his two assistants had spent three days in Andover, culminating in a three-hour discussion about individual applicants with the college placement officer. In Clark's first year, however, Yale conducted all the interviews in a single day, sending twelve admissions people, none of them familiar from previous meetings.⁴⁰ To Andover, this was a signal that Yale no longer cared about its students.

But the story that swept rapidly across the prep school world concerned not the mechanics of interviewing but what Clark had said at Andover. Just the week before, Harvard had visited Andover, and a student had asked, "How does Harvard feel about the bottom of the class at Andover?" Since it was the period of Glimp's "happy bottom-quarter" policy, the answer was that there were plenty of Andover students in the bottom quarter who would be welcomed at Harvard, especially if they were athletes or alumni sons. Clark, unaware of this exchange, was asked the same question at a large meeting, but his answer could not have been more different. In an interview years later, Clark recalled his response: "I said, in effect, Yale can do a lot better than the bottom quarter at Andover. We're looking for the top kids at Andover. If you haven't performed well at Andover, what makes you think you're going to perform well at Yale?"⁴¹ The implications were unmistakable: whatever the policy at Harvard and other Ivy League schools, students with mediocre aca

demic records at Andover — and, by extension, other top boarding schools —
would no longer be accepted at Yale.

When the 1966 admissions cycle was completed, the worries of Andover
and other boarding schools about Clark were amply confirmed. In 1965, 43
Andover graduates enrolled at Yale; in 1966, the number plummeted to 22.
Similar declines were visible at St. Paul's, where the Yale delegation dropped
from 13 to 6, and at Groton, where it dropped from 6 to 3. Overall, the number of Yale freshmen from the leading boarding schools declined from over
160 in 1965 to barely 100 in 1966.[42] No single year in Yale's history had ever
witnessed anything like this.

The boarding schools, whose success had come to be measured by the
proportion of their class accepted at Ivy League schools, were threatened and
angry. Matthew Warren, the longtime rector at St. Paul's, was so disturbed
that he arranged a private meeting with Brewster to find out why "Yale is so
modestly interested in us." Brewster responded that Yale had "recently expanded the scope of its admissions search" and was "receiving applications
from more and more secondary schools and, as would be expected . . . discovering more brilliant young men of the finest character from across the nation." Nevertheless, Brewster reported, candidates from St. Paul's in the top
two quintiles had a "very good chance of being admitted to Yale" (6 of 9 such
applicants were chosen in 1966). Even students in the third quintile had a
good chance of gaining admission, though "only those who show particular strength in non-academic areas." But under the new admissions policy,
Brewster acknowledged that "very few will be admitted from the bottom
quintiles."[43]

This was almost certainly greater consideration than candidates from the
most competitive public schools would receive. Nevertheless, it constituted a
major change, and it did not satisfy St. Paul's. Later that spring, Brewster received a letter from Edward Palmer '16, a former member of both the Yale
Corporation and the St. Paul's Board of Trustees and a prominent banker.[44]
Claiming that his remarks were "based on talks with friends close to Andover,
Exeter and St. Mark's and others, and definite first-hand facts learned at St.
Paul's," Palmer reported "an increasing and cumulative tendency for the
better boys in all these schools to go to Harvard."[45] Part of the problem was
the perception of Yale at the top prep schools. "If Yale is interested in getting
the really good boys from the school," Palmer told Brewster, "they certainly
make no effort to show it."[46]

"When I reflect on my Corporation days and who were its most effective
members," Palmer wrote, "I think of Whit Griswold, Henry Sherrill, Dean
Acheson, Morris Hadley, and Lefty [Wilmarth S.] Lewis." All of them "as well
as the most recently elected members of the Yale Corporation," he pointedly

reminded Brewster, "had prepared at private schools." "I wonder," he added, "whether they would have ended up at Yale if the present attitudes of the respective admissions departments had existed then." "Yale's present policy," he warned, "is costing her a good deal of the cream of the crop, present and future."[47]

Despite such criticism, Clark stood his ground. A particularly tense confrontation occurred at Choate, a prestigious Connecticut boarding school that was the alma mater of John F. Kennedy and Adlai Stevenson. As recently as 1962–1964, an average of 13 Choate students went on to Yale annually; in 1966, the number dropped to 2. Nevertheless, Clark did not hesitate to attend a Choate faculty meeting that he later described as "very, very stormy" to explain in blunt detail why the students were finding it so hard to get into Yale.[48]

In an interview with Choate's student newspaper, Clark explained that the talent of the student body was simply not that high and that the school's "most qualified students turn to the other top Ivy League Colleges before Yale." The Yale Admissions Office, Clark went on, was in contact with 8,000 of the nation's 25,000 secondary schools and was able to visit 1,500 of them. As an example, he cited the Bronx School of Science, where a graduating class of roughly 900 included as many as 200 boys whom "Yale should be interested in."[49] If Choate wanted to get more boys into Yale, Clark suggested, it should be "beating the bushes" for the country's most talented students, converting itself in the process into "a great national high school."[50]

Meanwhile, as the administrators and alumni of Yale's traditional feeder schools bemoaned its new, more meritocratic policies, educators in public schools welcomed them. Not long before, Yale had assiduously avoided sending recruiters to schools such as Bronx Science and Stuyvesant; now it was treating them as potential sources of some of Yale's most desired recruits. This new interest in urban schools with large numbers of working-class and middle-class Jewish students was, in turn, part of a broader commitment that took Yale to religious schools, rural schools, and inner-city schools with predominantly black and Latino populations.

Yale's reception at these schools was not always warm. Clark got a frosty welcome at Chaminade, a large Catholic high school on Long Island with a strong academic reputation, and in some of New York City's public schools, which remembered Yale's absence in previous years. At Abraham Lincoln High School in Coney Island, the college counselor, Abraham Lass, asked Clark: "'Where have you been for twenty years?' I said, 'I'm sorry.' He said, 'Don't expect me to give you my top Jewish kid — he's going to City or Columbia. Don't ask me for my best scientist — he's going to MIT. Where has Yale been?'"[51] Yet Yale persisted, intensifying its efforts in urban areas. Clark told the *New York Times* that "there's really as much diversity in taking Harlem, Park Avenue and Queens" as in sending our "recruiting people to out-of-the-way places like Nevada."[52] Yale's new presence was yielding results: Clark proudly reported in his first year that "there is a large jump in the number of boys we are taking from such New York City schools as Erasmus, Stuyvesant, Yeshiva of Flatbush, and Bronx Science." In 1965, he noted, Yale accepted only 1 boy from Bronx Science; in 1966, the number rose to 7.[53]

Yale's new policy radically transformed the composition of the student body. Private school boys, 56 percent of all entrants as late as 1960, had by 1967 dropped to just 39 percent of Yale freshmen; Yale now had a lower proportion of private school students than Harvard (41 percent).[54] Just two years into the Clark administration, the fortunes of the leading boarding schools had declined so dramatically that a previously unthinkable question was now being asked: Was Yale discriminating against applicants from prep schools? Though this perception was widespread, especially among prep school headmasters and alumni, the truth was that candidates from public and private schools were now being treated on an equal footing.[55] At an institution where, just a quarter of a century earlier, five prep schools contributed more students to the freshman class than all of the nation's public schools combined, simple equal treatment was nothing less than revolutionary.[56]

The Decline of Alumni Privilege

If the large delegations of boys from major boarding schools was a chief source of Yale's historic image as a school for all-around gentlemen, the exceptionally high proportion of alumni sons ensured that an aura of continuity and tradition would pervade the campus. As late as 1960, nearly one freshman in four was the son of an alumnus of Yale College; if one counts the sons of parents who had attended a Yale graduate or professional school, the figure rises to 26 percent.[57] Even Harvard (18 percent) and Princeton (21 percent) could not match these figures.[58]

But as the pressure on Yale admissions rose in the 1960s with increasing numbers of applicants, the Howe administration, which was generous toward legacies, had little choice but to reduce their number in the freshman class. By 1963, the last entering class for which Howe was fully responsible, alumni sons had declined to 19 percent. Of equal significance, almost half of legacy applicants were rejected that year. Nevertheless, for the applicants whose fathers had attended Yale College (186 of the 199 alumni sons who matriculated that fall), the admission rate remained 53 percent, compared to just 37 percent for the sons of fathers who had attended a Yale graduate or professional school and 31 percent for nonlegacy candidates.[59]

By the time Clark took over, the position of legacies had slipped a tad further, with the overall admission rate (including the sons of parents who had attended the graduate and professional schools) dropping to 43 percent in 1965 and the proportion of the freshman class at 18 percent.[60] But this gradual decline had not prepared Yale's alumni for what would happen in 1966. Suddenly, even the sons of Yale College graduates were being accepted at a rate of just 37 percent — remarkably, a bit lower than the rate for the sons of graduate and professional school alumni.[61] In a single year, the number of freshmen whose fathers were alumni of the college dropped from 15.7 percent a year earlier to just 12.7 percent of the freshman class. In 1967, the situation of college sons deteriorated still further, with their proportion in the freshman class plummeting to 10.6 percent.[62] Had Clark intended to provoke Old Elis, he could hardly have picked a more effective course of action.

The reaction of the alumni was swift and furious. Rejection letters had hardly been delivered before the administration was swamped with protests. On April 20, 1966, an aggrieved Old Blue wrote to Yale's secretary, Reuben Holden, complaining that his son had been rejected while several lower-ranking boys at the private day school he attended had been accepted, with Yale's Admissions Office offering the interesting explanation that the boy "lacked aggressiveness." The unhappy father claimed to have been told that "this year absolutely no consideration was given to the fact that an applicant had a Yale father."[63] Nevertheless, the 36 percent admission rate of alumni sons was still well above the rate of 23 percent for applicants whose fathers had not gone to Yale.[64] Even under Clark, special treatment for legacies was still built into the admissions process, with alumni sons recommended for admission during the first round exempted from further scrutiny, unlike nonlegacy applicants, who were required to undergo further review. And alumni sons judged "borderline" in the first round received formal consideration in the second review.[65]

But to Yale alumni this was not enough; far more salient was that their sons were being rejected at unprecedented rates and that their proportion of the freshman class was declining rapidly. By the fall of 1966, Yale's Alumni Board had formed a special committee to begin an official study of the matter, with its purview extending to the related issue of the sharp decline in the number of private school graduates admitted. Heading the committee was George Cook III, an impeccable embodiment of the Old Yale: boarding school graduate, captain of the Yale track team, executive of a large corporation, and resident of Darien, Connecticut.[66]

In October 1967, the Cook Committee issued its "Report to Alumni on [the] Alumni Board's Study of Admissions," and shortly thereafter a version of it was soon mailed to the alumni. Having spoken to 150 Yale Club presidents and 200 Alumni Schools Committee chairmen, the committee fully understood the depth and breadth of alumni dissatisfaction. In its report, the committee noted that "many alumni appear to be worried that Yale is changing from the good thing that it was to something different and not so good." While taking on such issues as "brains vs. character," ("does Yale only take eggheads or is credit given for character, personality, and extra-curricular achievements?"), athletes ("look at the recent record. Does Yale still care about the success of its teams?"), and the quality of the admission staff ("have they the requisite maturity?"), the report focused on the intertwined issues of private versus public school ("is the high school boy favored over the one from a private school?") and the handling of alumni sons.[67]

The report acknowledged that "the steady decline in the percentage of private school students in each class compared to public school acceptances has created a widely held opinion that there is a deliberate movement against the established independent schools." While the committee insisted that this decline did not reflect "a deliberate decision," the figures in the report cast doubt on this claim. Between 1960 and 1967, the proportion of private school boys at Yale declined from 56 to 38 percent; at Princeton, the decline was 47 to 38 percent, and at Harvard, the proportion remained steady at 41 percent. While conceding that in Clark's first year, "the manner in which a few private schools were dealt with showed lack of tact," the report noted that Yale's relationship with the private schools had improved significantly by 1967. In explaining why these schools were sending so many fewer students to Yale, the report pointed to "the pressure from a greater number of outstanding applicants from a broader base of good public schools" and the provision of "adequate financial aid."[68] But this explanation went only so far; after all, these same trends were present at Harvard as well, but somehow Yale's competitor had managed to maintain a steady number of boys from private schools.

On the combustible issue of alumni sons, the report tried to assure Old Blues that the Admission Committee attached "particular importance to the application of a legacy" and described its "prevailing attitude" as "one of 'let's find reasons to take him' rather than the converse." But from an alumni perspective, the figures constituted a stark indictment of Yale's policy. In 1961, Yale led the Big Three in legacies with 28 percent, with Princeton at 21 percent and Harvard at 19 percent. Six years later, the order was the exact reverse: Harvard, 20 percent; Princeton, 16 percent; and Yale, 14 percent. Further, these figures seriously underestimated the weakness of the position of alumni sons at Yale, for only the Yale statistics (as the report admitted in a footnote) included the sons of parents who had attended graduate or professional school.[69] The truly comparable figure for Yale was just 10.6 percent.[70] Though the report did not make the comparison, the simple fact was that alumni preference was far stronger at Harvard and Princeton than at Yale. In 1966, the admissions rate of legacies was 2.6 times the rate of other applicants at Harvard and 2.4 times higher at Princeton. But at Yale it was a mere 1.4 — confirmation of the widespread perception that alumni parentage no longer carried much weight in New Haven.[71]

If the intent of the Cook Report had been to calm the relationship between Yale and its alumni, it was a failure. In the *Yale Alumni Magazine* of December 1967, Joseph E. Muckley '30 wrote that the report contradicted its claim that the admissions process "seems to give due credit to the values which tradition, loyalty, and familiarity lend." Kenneth E. Ryan '27, prophetically citing the possibility of a future financial crisis, called for a "review of the Corporation's policies to permit the admissions at Yale of more alumni sons." Ryan couched his argument in terms of "hard-headed prudent judgment" and warned about the likely consequences of Yale's policy: "a Yale graduate who is a grandparent or parent of an applicant for admission cannot be counted upon to support Yale with optimum generosity and good will" if legacy candidates "eminently suited in every way for admission to a great university continued to be rejected."[72]

Until the fall of 1967, the issue of alumni sons had been largely an internal affair, but it changed that October when William F. Buckley Jr. '50, one of Yale's most renowned alumni and a leading conservative writer, announced that he would run an insurgent campaign to gain a seat on the Yale Corporation. Buckley explained to the *New York Times* that he was running in part because of his opposition to Yale's admissions policies. Yale, he said, had ceased to be the "kind of place where your family goes for generations" and had been transformed into an institution where "the son of an alumnus, who goes to a private preparatory school, now has less of a chance of getting in than some boy from PS 109 somewhere."[73] Yale's new admissions policies, Buckley stated, were "egalitarian hocus-pocus."[74]

Worried that these views were likely to resonate with many alumni, Yale nominated Cyrus Vance '39, a well-known and widely respected diplomat, to run against Buckley. Vance, a graduate of the Kent School, a member of Scroll and Key, and a varsity hockey player at Yale, was a quintessential Establishment figure: a partner at a major New York law firm who had served as secretary of the army and deputy secretary of defense under Kennedy and Johnson.[75] Buckley knew that Vance was a formidable opponent, but he was intent on winning. As part of his campaign, he wrote an article for the April issue of the *Atlantic Monthly* in which he laid out his case. One of the more memorable passages zeroed in on the issue of alumni sons: "it is true that a Mexican-American from El Paso High School with identical scores on the achievement tests, and identically ardent recommendations from their headmasters, had a better chance of being admitted to Yale than Jonathan Edwards the Sixteenth from St. Paul's School."[76] Artfully, Buckley had woven together in a single sentence a panoply of alumni grievances: the rise of the public schools, the growing presence on campus of racial and ethnic minorities, and the decline of alumni privilege. A large mailing of reprints of the article, Buckley told the *Times,* would be sent to Yale alumni.[77]

Despite these efforts, Vance was victorious, reportedly by a "substantial margin."[78] Yet the Yale administration had been seriously shaken by Buckley's challenge. In November 1967, a month after Buckley had announced his candidacy, Brewster promised the Development Board that he would look into the question "of why it is that Yale's admissions are currently yielding a less responsive opportunity for Yale sons than Princeton and Harvard seem to be yielding to Harvard and Princeton sons" and try to "find out whether this is a trend, if this has a source, if it in fact cannot be cured without getting into the double standard or the quota business."[79] Even after Buckley's defeat, the Development Board remained so concerned that it passed a resolution calling on the Admissions Office to reactivate the old ABC system for students from selected secondary schools, adopt a policy to ensure that each class would be composed equally of private and public school students, and offer admission to 50 percent of the sons of Yale College graduates who applied.[80] Though this resolution — clearly designed to turn back the clock — was never put into effect, it was testimony to the existence of powerful forces within Yale that believed that Clark's policies posed a threat not only to Yale's traditions but also to its most vital interests.

The End of Anti-Jewish Discrimination

When Clark joined the Admissions Office in 1961, Jewish enrollment in the freshman class stood at 11 percent — the lowest of any Ivy League college.[81] Though at the time Yale visited many secondary schools nationwide and lavished great attention on the eastern boarding schools, it generally avoided public schools in nearby New York City and Long Island, still the home of over 40 percent of the nation's Jewish population.[82] Nevertheless, the New York–Long Island area — considered the "jungle" by Howe's admissions staff — still produced many Yale applicants. Born in Brooklyn and raised on Long Island, Clark volunteered for recruiting and interviewing responsibilities in the area, even though his colleagues considered it one of the "crummiest" regions in the nation.[83]

Faced with evidence that Yale was still using something very much like a quota to limit the number of Jews, Griswold had in 1962 called for the removal of any remaining religious barriers to admission. Yet Jewish enrollment had increased only modestly: from roughly 11 to 12 percent during the years between 1953 and 1962, it rose to about 16 percent in 1962 and stayed at that level for the next three years. Given Yale's urban location and its proximity to New York City, this was a relatively low number — and one that was well below Harvard's, not to say Penn's and Columbia's.[84] Although the quota had been lifted, the culture of Howe's Admissions Office remained distinctly unfriendly to Jews.[85]

In replacing much of the admissions staff at the same time that he doubled its size, Clark wanted especially to eliminate the atmosphere of "deeply ingrained" anti-Semitism that he had witnessed as a young admissions officer.[86] Suddenly, Yale was recruiting at the very New York City schools that it had avoided so assiduously in the past. In doing so, Yale was following a directive from the Admissions Policy Advisory Board, which had explicitly called for more "applications and admissions from New York and other eastern metropolitan areas."[87]

Yale's historic emphasis on "geographical diversity" had been rooted in no small part in its desire to limit the number of Jewish students, and the elimination of geographical factors in admissions removed an important barrier to Jewish enrollment.[88] So, too, did the radical reduction in preference for alumni sons and prep school boys, which opened up more spaces for applicants from different backgrounds.

Taken together, the impact of these changes was to bring to a definitive end Yale's long history of anti-Semitic discrimination. In a single year, the Jewish proportion of the freshman class nearly doubled, rising from 16 percent in 1965 to roughly 30 percent in 1966.[89] Clark recalled that Yale's rabbi was flabbergasted by the transformation, saying, "I don't believe what's happening. I don't understand what's happening. I think it's wonderful. But I don't quite understand it."[90]

Brewster and Clark had been aware that the policies they were following would increase the number of Jewish students substantially and that this increase would not be warmly received in many quarters. Why were they willing to live with consequences, including alumni dissatisfaction, that would have deterred many university administrators? Part of the answer, surely, is that Brewster, like his friend McGeorge Bundy, was part of that segment of the WASP upper class that consciously rejected anti-Semitism as morally indefensible and incompatible with their larger commitment to progressive reform.[91] For Clark, too, anti-Semitism was a moral issue — and one of the main reasons that, once appointed dean of admissions, he quickly moved to replace most of the existing staff.

Yet in other circumstances, administrators who were not personally anti-Semitic had pursued policies designed to limit the number of Jews. But the situation facing Brewster and Clark in the mid-1960s was fundamentally different from the one their predecessors had faced — and one that left far more space for reforms that would increase Jewish enrollments. One key change was that anti-Semitic attitudes had declined sharply between the 1930s and the 1960s, with some of the largest declines occurring among the well-to-do, city dwellers, and residents of the eastern states — the very populations most relevant to institutions such as Yale.[92] By the spring of 1966, when the first class of "Inky's boys" entered Yale, the civil rights movement had utterly transformed the moral landscape, making discrimination of any kind morally unacceptable. At the same time, a growing student movement, thrust into the public eye by Berkeley's Free Speech Movement of 1964 and given added momentum by the burgeoning antiwar movement, was bringing traditional policies into radical question.[93] Finally, the Watts riots, which shook Los Angeles in the summer of 1965, seemed to demonstrate that the perpetuation of injustice could threaten the survival of the system itself.

Brewster and Clark moved decisively to take advantage of the openings created by these developments to pursue reforms, but not all members of the Yale community welcomed their efforts. Shortly after the 1967 publication of an article in the *New York Times* describing these policies, Ashby Porter '09 wrote to Brewster, contending that there was a "great danger in concentrating the admissions in a narrow strip along the Atlantic Coast and particularly in New York City." The part of the article noting an increase in the number of Jews at Yale did not escape Porter's attention, and it did not please him. While expressing "great respect for the brilliant minds of many Jewish men who have been leaders in science and industry," he also told Brewster that "Jews as a class are clannish, self-centered, rather selfish and do not rank high in public service." Drawing on statistics in the *Times* article observing that Columbia and Penn undergraduates were about 40 percent Jewish, he warned that "many gentiles might well hesitate to enroll in an institution where the Jewish population is so heavy."[94]

Alumni dismay about the number of Jews at Yale, though rarely articulated publicly, was often a subtext of other grievances, such as Yale's alleged emphasis of "brains" over "character." On occasion, however, the issue rose to the surface. In early 1973, shortly after the *Yale Alumni Magazine* published an article estimating that a third of Yale undergraduates were Jewish, an alumnus from the Class of 1912 wrote to his class secretary.[95]

> Dear Dick: In the January issue of *YAM* is an article . . . by the rabbi appointed apparently by the Hillel people and [it] is very well written from the Jewish standpoint. Jewish students at Yale are now in the majority . . .
> This imbalance is the result achieved by Clark and his extremists who made up the team admitting students to the Freshman Class a few years ago. They turned down scores of sons of Yale men who richly deserved to succeed

their fathers and scoured the ghettos of New York and elsewhere to recruit freshmen. That is what has today made Yale a Jewish university . . .

These facts are why . . . I cannot go along with your thoughts that I should help support Yale of today. The place we knew and loved has been wrecked by three men, Brewster, Coffin, and Clark. Let them look to those they have recruited for the money to run Yale today. It saddens me to prophesy that Yale will soon be just another public institution, thanks to the lack of foresight of the Corporation and the willfulness of three men, who have made Yale a Jewish haven. I write you thusly so you . . . will know why I am today supporting to the best of my ability those colleges which my grandsons have been forced to attend.[96]

Yale did not, of course, have anything approaching a Jewish majority, either then or at any other point in its history. Yet though the letter writer's grasp of the numbers was obviously limited, he was not wrong on one fundamental point: the changes wrought by Brewster and Clark meant that the Yale that he "knew and loved" was truly no more.

The Redefinition of Merit and the Transformation of the Student Body

In meetings across the country with alumni of all ages, Clark was repeatedly peppered with questions: "Why does Yale now favor blacks over alumni sons? Why do you like Jews better than Christians? Why don't you like athletes? Why is it better to go to a public school today than to a private school?"[97] Clark denied the charges, insisting that Yale was now treating everyone the same. But part of what had made Yale "Yale" was precisely the strong preferences historically given its traditional constituencies. Now that this had changed, it was no wonder that beneficiaries of the old policies had come to believe that Clark was systematically favoring Jews over Christians and public school boys over the graduates of leading boarding schools.

Yet of perhaps even greater significance than equal treatment was a subtle but profound change in the kind of boy Yale was seeking. What had really changed in the mid-1960s was how merit itself was defined. And it is only by grasping the true character of this change that one can understand why the new policy so fundamentally transformed the Yale student body.

For Brewster and Clark, the point of departure for Yale's admissions policy was the Doob Committee's belief that "Yale is first and foremost an intellectual enterprise." But a very different notion of Yale's mission had dominated its public statements in the decade after World War II. As noted earlier, in 1949 the *Yale Alumni Magazine* published an influential article, "The Essence of Yale," which maintained flatly that the education of "fine citizens," most of them "rather unscholarly," was Yale's "majority function."[98] To be sure, Yale would also educate some "true scholars," but their number would be small. Most of Yale's limited scholarship resources would be allocated to the "fine citizens," with awards made primarily on the basis of "character, personality, leadership in school affairs, and the like."[99]

The conception of merit behind these policies did not change fundamentally during the Howe regime (1954–1964). On the contrary, Howe did his best during a period of rapid increase in the number of applicants to maintain the status quo, retaining strong preferences for the traditional constituencies. As late as 1960, he did not hesitate to publicly express overtly anti-intellectual views.[100]

By the time Clark took over in 1965, Yale was actively recruiting "brainy kids," having altered its ideal from "well rounded" individuals to a "well-rounded" class. Among the students most sought after were brilliant specialists, not a few of them young scientists. Yale had redefined merit for many reasons, but enrolling more Jews was not one of them. Nevertheless, these changes had the effect of elevating the value of some forms of cultural capital disproportionately possessed by Jewish applicants. For the new definition of merit had unambiguously elevated scholastic excellence into the primary — albeit not the only — criterion for admission. Nonacademic qualities, Yale emphasized, would still be important, but they would no longer be permitted to serve as vehicles of social exclusion. Addressing the issue, the Admissions Policy Advisory Board bluntly expressed its belief that "in the past, at Yale and elsewhere, 'character' and 'leadership' have sometimes been rubrics under which favoritism has been shown to families of certain economic, religious, ethnic, and scholastic backgrounds."[101]

The emphasis was now on what Clark called "talent searching." Very simply, Yale's goal was to find the "most promising secondary school graduates in the country." This meant that Yale would have to recruit widely, especially in inner-city and rural schools, to "thoroughly do away with those images that might suggest that Yale 'is a place for rich kids,' 'is not for the creative person,' 'has a quota system,' 'is no good for the sciences.'"[102] The "egghead" and the "oddball" were now considered essential to a well-rounded class.

For Yale, the college that had given the nation "Dink Stover," this was an epochal change in the meaning of merit. Not long before Clark took office, a faculty committee had foreshadowed this change by calling for the admission of more of those they called "bright rebels" and "creative intellectuals." Such people, the committee noted, are "not always pleasant" and enrolling more of them might mean "more drop-outs, more beards, more complainers, and more flunkouts" and "(possibly also more creative) riots."[103] Nevertheless, such students were critical to Yale's cultural and intellectual vitality. Clark's policies put the committee's proposal into practice and brought to Yale a variety of people rarely seen in the past. Stewart Alsop (Groton '32, Yale '36), a prominent journalist, concisely described what had happened in *Newsweek:* "The cheerful prep-school boys in tweed coats who once dominated the Yale campus have been replaced by brilliant high school radicals with scraggly beards."[104]

Even the physical characteristics of Yale freshmen changed — a consequence, perhaps, of Clark's decision to abolish the "physical characteristics checklist." No sooner had Clark made this change than an unhappy Cleveland alumnus wrote to him in protest. His concern was that "chopping the check list of boys' physical characteristics [might] lead to the acceptance of some candidates who just don't belong in the Yale environment and whose acceptance by the Admissions Committee may lead to an unhappy experience at Yale for the boy himself." "Yale has done pretty well in years past," he argued, "by selecting normal, above-average young men without looking for eggheads or queer characters."[105]

There is no way to estimate the number of eggheads admitted to Yale, but it is possible to report on what happened to the height of the freshmen after the checklist was eliminated. According to official Yale statistics, between 1965 and 1966 (when the first Clark class arrived in New Haven), the proportion of freshmen six feet tall and over dropped from 26.0 to 20.6 percent. The average height also declined from 70.4 to 70.0 inches — the largest drop in a single year since Yale began keeping these records in 1883.[106]

Height aside, how different were "Inky's boys" from their predecessors in the Howe years? While the numbers of legacies and boarding school graduates were dropping to historic lows, the academic level of the class was rising to unprecedented heights.[107] In 1966, the median verbal SAT rose to 697, a 22-point increase over the previous year's and the highest ever at Yale. By way of comparison, a student with a 634 verbal SAT, the median score in 1958, would have ranked below the 25th percentile in 1966; moreover, a student with a 534 verbal SAT in 1958, which would have placed him in the 10th percentile, very likely would have been rejected in 1966, when the 10th percentile was scoring nearly 600 on the SAT verbal.[108] Meanwhile, as Clark was eliminating the bottom of the freshman class of the Old Yale, he was admitting more National Merit Scholars — 278 in 1968, more than double the number in 1963.[109]

At the same time, the number of students admitted primarily for their athletic ability was slipping.[110] Although Brewster insisted that athletic ability remained "explicitly in the deliberations of the Admissions Committee," he also noted that "Yale refuses to permit a double standard for the admission of athletes as less good students because they are great as athletes."[111] According to Charles Lindblom, a faculty member on the Admissions Committee in the spring of 1966, "Athletic skill appeared to become an issue in an inconsequential number of cases."[112] By 1969–1970, the first year that all of Yale's varsity teams were filled with "Inky's boys," Yale came in sixth in the Ivy League and had a losing season overall (in all varsity sports combined) — its first in Ivy League history.[113]

Of all Clark's changes, one of the most fateful was the increase in the proportion of the freshman class from families of modest means and the simultaneous decrease in the percentage from the Protestant upper class. Yale's "need-blind" policy transformed the student body, increasing the proportion of freshmen on financial aid from a third in 1958 to just over a half in 1966.[114] In the same period, the amount of freshman financial aid more than doubled, to nearly a million dollars annually, and the burdensome requirement that scholarship recipients work up to 14 hours weekly was abolished. Privileges of background — whether Yale heritage, upper-class origins, boarding school training, or sheer money — carried less weight than ever before.[115]

The Yale that had come into being under Clark and Brewster, while committed to an admissions policy that rewarded individual achievement over the prerogatives of birth, adhered to a definition of merit that recognized that some environments facilitated academic excellence, conventionally defined, while others thwarted it. Given Yale's deepening commitment to racial and class diversity, this understanding was critical, for the gap in scores on the increasingly influential SAT between an upper-middle-class applicant from Scarsdale and a working-class applicant from Bedford-Stuyvesant was almost guaranteed to be considerable. In an official statement published in the *Yale Alumni Magazine,* Clark made clear that the Admissions Office viewed academic achievement in a social context. "When looking at an applicant's scores," he wrote, "it is necessary to consider his background, his community, his home life, and the schools he has attended. A boy from a disadvantaged area might have a severe handicap on certain objective tests."[116] With this revised definition of merit as a guiding principle, Yale admitted far more blacks in Clark's first year than at any other time in its history; in 1966, it enrolled 35 black freshmen, compared to 23 a year earlier and just 2 in 1958.[117]

Taken together, all of these changes meant that Yale, arguably the least meritocratic of the Big Three in the late 1950s, had by the late 1960s forged ahead of Harvard in the extent to which it embodied meritocratic ideals. The evidence left little room for doubt that privileges of birth now counted for less at Yale than at Harvard. In 1969, four years after Clark took office, the legacy–nonlegacy admissions ratio at Yale was 1.83; at Harvard it was 2.75.[118] Attendance at a boarding school was also more of a factor in Cambridge than in New Haven. In 1968, when Harvard took only 18.5 percent of its applicants, 69 of 130 (53 percent) of candidates from the six St. Grottlesex schools were admitted and 63 came; at Yale, just 29 students from these schools enrolled in

1968.[119] At Choate, where the best students were reportedly more likely to apply to Harvard than Yale, the figures were even more striking: Harvard — 61 applied, 28 accepted, 25 enrolled; Princeton — 30 applied, 17 accepted, 13 enrolled; Yale — 28 applied, 5 accepted, 3 enrolled.[120]

As the college with the highest yield rate, 84 percent in 1964, Harvard had little incentive to change, for it was getting the students it most wanted. Harvard's leaders were quite satisfied with the status quo and — with full awareness of what they were doing — rejected efforts by Brewster and Clark to convince them to abolish the ABC system of early notification. As Clark put it years later, "Harvard felt that it had a very, very good thing going with its feeder schools and that there was no particular reason to change." Its resistance, he observed, reflected the simple logic of institutional self-interest: "I don't think there was anything in it for Harvard."[121]

While Harvard continued to adhere to Glimp's "happy bottom-quarter" policy, Yale was going down a road much closer to the ideal of meritocracy. By 1966, median SATs (combined verbal and math) at Yale were, in a reversal of the historic pattern, higher than at Harvard: 1,408 versus 1,385; of equal significance, the median SATs of the 10th percentile at Yale were 1,201, compared to 1,144 at Harvard.[122] And while Yale was moving to raise admissions standards for athletes, Harvard continued to give them strong preference.[123] At annual meetings in the late 1960s where the Ivy League colleges would swap information on their athletes, Yale's suspicions about Harvard were confirmed: in terms of grades and test scores, Yale's athletes were much more representative of the entire student body than their peers in Cambridge.[124] Indeed, athletes were the single biggest beneficiary of Harvard's "happy bottom-quarter" policy, though legacies and boarding school graduates were not far behind.[125]

To say that Brewster's and Clark's Yale had become more meritocratic than Harvard and Princeton is not, however, to say that it had become a meritocracy, much less the kind of pure *academic* meritocracy favored by faculty members like Tobin.[126] Though the legacy advantage during the Clark years was weaker than at any other time before or since and far weaker than at Harvard and Princeton, it was an advantage nonetheless — a preference based on an accident of birth and incompatible with the most basic tenet of meritocracy.

While genuinely "need-blind" in its admissions decisions, Yale under Clark still drew a clear majority of its students from the most affluent segments of American society. At a time when roughly 5 percent of American families could afford the $3,000 that Yale charged for tuition, room, and board, 58 percent of students were able to attend without a scholarship.[127] Built into the very definition of merit used by Yale and other top private colleges were academic standards that had the effect, if not the intent, of favor-

ing the children of the affluent. As Harvard's Humphrey Doermann documented in the mid-1960s, relatively few students from the bottom 50 percent
of the income distribution had the SAT scores necessary to compete for a
place at an elite private college.[128] Yale was aware of such studies, and perhaps
for this reason it moved quickly to repair the damage done to its relationships
with prep schools caused by Clark's "arrogance" and "brashness" during his
first year as dean.[129] But to those many alumni who claimed that Clark was
engaged in "reverse discrimination" against private schools, Brewster had a
ready answer: independent schools, though enrolling only about 2 percent of
high school graduates, still constituted 42 percent of Yale freshmen.[130]

Although the Yale faculty did not seem particularly concerned with the
overrepresentation of the children of the privileged even under Clark and
Brewster, it *was* troubled by the continued emphasis on personal qualities.
The Admissions Policy Advisory Board had explicitly called for the abandonment of the "numerical rating (on a one to nine scale) of non-academic personal qualities," believing the scale to be of "little value . . . in predicting conspicuous achievement in the Yale community."[131] Just beneath the surface was
the question of whether "merit" was to be defined in largely objective academic terms, as favored by most of the faculty, or in more subjective personal
terms, as preferred by the administration, which needed the latitude to protect institutional interests.[132] And on this issue, the administration did not
back down; in 1970, Yale continued to rate each candidate on two 1–9 scales,
"the first, an estimate of academic achievement and potential" and "the second, an estimate of personal promise," with applicants whose two ratings
added up to 12 or more points generally admitted.[133]

Tension between the faculty and administration arose as well on the related issue of athletes. While applauding the higher academic standards applied to athletes with varsity potential under Clark, the faculty wanted to reduce still further the weight given athletics. In the view of the Advisory
Board, athletics was relevant *only* to the extent that it shed light on "important dimensions of character," such as "leadership, cooperation, loyalty, purpose, perseverance, and integrity." Lest there be any misunderstanding, the
board stated that relevant evidence of such qualities can be "provided just as
well by fencing as by football, just as well by boys light in weight and short in
stature as by the physically well-endowed, just as well by leaders in weak
inter-school or intramural competition as by all-state stars."[134] Here, too, the
administration thought that the faculty was taking the ideal of academic
meritocracy too far and refused to change Yale's policy. In 1967, Clark's second year in office, 100 freshmen — 10 percent of the class — had been captains of varsity teams in high school, an increase of 16 over the group admitted three years earlier by Howe.[135]

After Clark's first year, the Advisory Board complained that "one-sided intellectual talents" tend to "lose out to unobjectionable candidates for whom success is fairly certain but also fairly certain to be routine."[136] Charles Lindblom, a faculty member who served on the Admissions Committee in 1966 and wrote a memo to James Tobin just after completing his service, was more blunt: "The category of students referred to in the Doob Report — students to be admitted on the basis of intellectual excellence without regard to any other characteristics except moral integrity — turns out to be a very tiny category . . . roughly 1 percent of the applicants and in any case, not more than 3 or 4 percent." Members of the Admissions Committee (including some faculty representatives), he reported, tend "to look at intellectuality in a secondary school student as a possible undesirable abnormality."[137] When Lindblom pressed this point he was quickly called into Brewster's office.[138] At the meeting, which Lindblom believed was held at Clark's request, Brewster said, "Ed, you know, I think I've put you on too many committees lately. I really think I've been unfair to you and I think the most burdensome committee you're on is the Admissions Committee, and so I'm going to let you off of that."[139] Radical though Brewster and Clark may have been compared to their peers, both past and present, they were not about to permit the vision of a pure academic meritocracy to become a reality at Yale.

Brewster, Clark, and the Creation of a New Elite

To say that Brewster and Clark did not create an academic meritocracy on the model of the École Normale Supérieure is not, however, to say that the changes that they introduced were inconsequential. On the contrary, the new admissions policy — and the new definition of merit at the center of it — profoundly transformed the Yale student body.

Yet it was not enough for Brewster and Clark simply to have an *inclination* to create a new admissions policy. They also needed the *capacity* to make it a reality. Had they come to power a decade earlier with the same ideas, they would not have been able to put them into effect because objective conditions were not ripe. But by 1965 a radically new admissions policy was possible, though hardly inevitable.

Perhaps the most fundamental change was that new material circumstances made "need-blind" admissions — the indispensable precondition for any genuinely meritocratic policy — feasible for the first time. The crucial ingredient was a huge infusion of federal research money, which increased from 4.6 percent of Yale's budget in 1954–1955 to 22.9 percent in 1964–1965.[140] As recently as 1960, Harvard's Wilbur Bender, warning against taking the logic of meritocracy too far, had argued that it was not the scholars who contributed money to Harvard and that Harvard lacked resources to offer scholarships to more than about 25 percent of its entering students.[141] Yet just four years later, Yale — buoyed by the huge increase in federal dollars as well as by the growth in foundation grants — was able to announce a "need-blind" admissions policy.

The increase from the federal government was critical, for it reduced Yale's dependency on its traditional constituencies. In 1954–1955, when Yale's Alumni Fund contributed $5.3 million, the federal government awarded just $1.0 million in grants and contracts; ten years later, the pattern was reversed, with the federal government providing $12.7 million and the Alumni Fund $9.2 million.[142] The result was a shift in the balance of power between the alumni and the faculty, for it was only the faculty who could gain access to the river of federal grants and contracts that had begun to flow. And the faculty, unlike the alumni, favored an admissions policy in which intellectual accomplishment was the primary, if not the sole, factor.

Powerful demographic trends also facilitated the adoption of a more meritocratic admissions policy. When Clark entered Yale as a freshman in 1953, the admission rate was still near 50 percent, and in 1955 it remained 45 percent.[143] This was the period when the low birthrates of the Depression years were still limiting the number of young men of college age. But in the mid-1960s, with the arrival of the first children of the postwar baby boom, the number of male high school graduates exploded — from 613,000 in 1954 to 1,314,000 in 1965.[144] By then, the number of applicants to Yale had surged to over 6,000 (compared to fewer than 4,000 in 1954), and the admissions rate had dropped to 23 percent.[145]

This huge increase reduced Yale's reliance on its traditional private feeder schools. With more and more good public schools, especially in the nation's growing suburbs, Yale was less dependent than ever before on maintaining a steady supply of applicants from the major boarding schools. Increasing affluence had produced an expanded national upper middle class, and Yale could now find large numbers of public school graduates who were both "highly qualified" and (in a phrase then still current) "paying customers."

Economic and demographic trends provided the broad historical backdrop to the changes introduced by Brewster and Clark, but the social and political turmoil of the mid-1960s gave added impetus to their reform impulses. When Clark formally took over as dean in July 1965, it was a historic moment. In June, President Johnson delivered his famous speech at Howard University in which he announced that America sought "not just equality as a right and a theory, but equality as a fact and as a result"; on August 6, he signed the Voting Rights Act of 1965, and five days later, on August 11, the Watts riot erupted in Los Angeles.[146] Earlier that spring, 20,000 to 25,000 people had gathered in Washington to protest the Vietnam War — the largest peace march in American history.[147] Meanwhile, a radical student movement was growing on American campuses, with its most visible representatives — the Students for a Democratic Society (SDS) — now boasting chapters across the nation. Rarely had the conditions for fundamental social change — including a change in how America selected its elite — seemed so favorable.

From Brewster's perspective, the turmoil of the mid-1960s presented Yale with a fundamental dilemma: how "to keep Yale up to date" in a period characterized by an "exponential rate of change" while at the same time "trying to keep Yale, Yale."[148] A genuine reformer, but hardly a radical, Brewster saw Yale's essential mission as a training ground for the leaders of the next generation — a place to educate men who "become truly outstanding in whatever they undertake . . . whether it be in the art and science of directing the business or public life of the country" or "the practice of one of the professions or the advancement of art or science or learning."[149] Clark concurred with Brewster's frankly elitist vision: in order to remain a "truly world-important institution," Yale wished to select the young man who is "likely to be a leader in whatever he ends up doing."[150] But success, especially in a period of dizzying social and technological change, was by no means assured. A failure to keep pace in admissions could, Brewster believed, send Yale on a rapid downward spiral. "I do not intend to preside," he said in an off-the-record comment shortly after his inauguration, "over a prep school on Long Island Sound."[151]

Brewster did have a theory of how society was changing — and of the implications of these changes for Yale's admissions policy. Drawing on the idea of a "postindustrial" society already circulating in sophisticated circles, he argued in one of his first speeches as Yale's president that the "specialized knowledge" required by a complex modern society "make[s] it certain that the trained intelligence will assume an even greater importance in the struggle for leadership."[152] The consequences of this analysis for admissions policy were clear: "academic excellence is . . . more than ever before the first business of any university or college which would seek to hold its claim to national, let alone world importance."[153] While "character" was still relevant, Yale would have to place greater emphasis on sheer intellect if it wished to educate the leaders of the future.

Brewster elaborated on these ideas in a presentation to the Educational Policy Committee of the Yale Corporation in mid-March 1966. He identified the emergent postindustrial social structure as one characterized by "increasing organization and professionalization of a society dominated by organized services rather than competition of truly independent proprietors." Such a society was one of "unpredictable change" and an "ever-receding frontier" of knowledge and, as such, would require the "capacity to break new ground or at least adapt to it."[154] In a 1966 article in the *Yale Alumni Magazine,* Brewster spelled out the implications for admissions of the changes then transforming America: "Any double standard which consciously permitted admission of a boy less promising in place of another of greater promise would start Yale on a downward slide — not just the downward slide in terms of image or lustre, but the downward slide in terms of our ability to attract over the generations ahead the best teachers and the best students."[155]

The emphasis on intellect and meritocratic principle in the new admissions policy constituted a real shift for Yale, and it aroused powerful resistance. Early in Clark's tenure, the issue came to a head when he was asked to appear before the Corporation to explain the new policy. The climactic moment took place when a prominent banker raised his hand after Clark's presentation and said: "'Let me get down to basics. You're admitting an entirely different kind of class than we're used to. You're admitting them for a different purpose than training leaders.' Clark responded that the America of the 1960s was different from what it once had been and that more national leaders would be coming from more groups, including more women. The Corporation fellow was unsympathetic: 'You're talking about Jews and public school graduates as leaders. Look around you at this table. These are America's leaders. There are no Jews here. There are no public school graduates here.'"[156] The underlying issue could not have been articulated with greater clarity: would Clark and Brewster's move toward academic meritocracy identify and train the leaders of tomorrow, or would it cut Yale off from the very groups that had made it a great university?

The debate between Clark and the Corporation harkened back to a similar debate at Harvard a few years earlier. In arguing against what he called the "top-one-percent policy," Bender said that an admissions model that relied too heavily on intellect would detach Harvard from "men of affairs" in business and politics and thereby reduce Harvard's "total impact on society."[157] Both to assure its economic future and to continue to educate the men most likely to run the nation's major economic and social institutions, Harvard needed to continue to favor traditional elite constituencies: "gentlemen," graduates of boarding schools, and alumni sons.

Such views were common among Yale alumni, and they were well represented on the Yale Corporation. But they were less compelling in 1965 than they had been five years earlier. Much had changed in the intervening years — the weight of federal dollars, the power of the faculty, the sheer number of applicants, and (not least) the general political and cultural atmosphere. To Brewster and Clark, the admissions policy favored by men like Bender was more than a violation of the American principle of equality of opportunity —

it was a backward-looking strategy that tethered Yale to a group in decline at the same time that it prevented it from strengthening its ties to rising groups likely to play prominent leadership roles in the future.

Weakening Yale's ties to its traditional constituencies was, to be sure, not without risk, but so too was maintaining them in a period of rapid and unpredictable social change. Brewster, who, Geoffrey Kabaservice reports, sometimes liked to think of himself as "an intellectual investment banker," realized that Yale now had the capacity — and the need — to diversify its portfolio, dumping stocks that showed signs of slipping and investing in an array of newer stocks that, while perhaps riskier, promised higher rates of return.[158] How Yale admitted its students, Brewster believed, had an importance that went well beyond Yale, for the perceived fairness of its selection process reflected on the fairness — and ultimately the legitimacy — of the system itself. As he wrote in a letter to a former member of the Corporation, disenchanted with the new admissions policy, Yale was "along with only a handful of other privileged institutions . . . an obvious and visible avenue to special opportunity — social, financial, professional and political, as well as intellectual." The belief that this opportunity was not open to all constituted a threat to the legitimacy — and perhaps ultimately to the survival — of the capitalist system itself. "More important to our nation than the race to the moon or the level of GNP or the number of cars in every garage is our ability to convince ourselves and the world that under a politically free, private property, contractually organized economic system, success depends more on merit, less on private status or public favor, than in any totally organized or politically dictated society. It is terribly important to keep alive the widespread confidence that success in America is a function of merit and effort." At stake in the battle over admissions, Brewster wrote, was something much larger than Yale: "the quality of the nation, not as a welfare state but as an opportunity society — depends mightily on how we decide who is to have the privilege of Yale."[159]

Like Conant in the 1930s, Brewster was writing at a moment in history when challenges to the established order seemed to threaten the survival of the American system. For Brewster, the main danger was the escalating racial conflict that threatened to tear the society apart; in the absence of "true emancipation," Brewster wrote in a letter to an alumnus, "the whole country" might "go up in the flames of racial hate."[160] For Conant, writing in the midst of depression and then war, the main threat was escalating class conflict; without serious measures designed to produce "a more equitable distribution of opportunity" and renewed faith in the American dream, the system of "private enterprise" could be destroyed in "a clash of 'haves' and 'have nots.'"[161] For both Conant and Brewster, domestic threats were reinforced by challenges from abroad to the "American way of life" — in Conant's case, by

Nazism and Communism; in Brewster's, by a variety of alternatives to capitalism, many of them ill defined, that held a powerful appeal among many radicals in the 1960s. And in both cases, the antidote to these threats was the same — a conspicuous commitment to equality of opportunity through education that would convince the excluded that they had a stake in the existing system.

Despite widespread perceptions to the contrary, especially among Old Blues, Clark was certainly correct when he observed that neither he nor Brewster was a "radical, disruptive, or far left" type of person. Instead, they were part of a larger group "anxious to change the University as the nation was changing, for the better."[162] Brewster, in particular, was the very model of the patrician reformer — a familiar type in American history dedicated to changing the system in order to preserve it. Like Franklin Roosevelt and Teddy Roosevelt before him, Brewster believed that the reactionary wing of the business class posed a threat, through its steadfast opposition to necessary reforms, to the survival of the system of "free enterprise." And like the Roosevelts, Brewster, in his efforts to impose reforms designed to serve national rather than sectional or class interests, was frequently reviled as a traitor to his class.[163]

Nothing in Brewster's objective circumstances impelled him to embark on the path of meritocratic reform. Yet it was not a coincidence that Brewster and Conant, two of the greatest reformers in American higher education, presided over their institutions during the two periods in the twentieth century — the thirties and the sixties — when social upheavals most seriously threatened the existing order. Nevertheless, there were also important differences between the two periods; perhaps the most noteworthy was that Brewster faced mobilizations around the issues of race and gender that Conant could hardly have imagined. As Inky Clark astutely observed, the logic of meritocratic inclusion could not stop with white men: "You should not and you cannot isolate one group and say, 'They cannot use these facilities, these attributes, these wonderful opportunities.' That's part of the meritocracy."[164]

Racial Conflict and the Incorporation of Blacks

A S THE ADMISSIONS COMMITTEES of Harvard, Yale, and Princeton convened in the spring of 1960 to select the next freshman class, a
wave of protests led by students from black colleges swept across the
South. On February 1, four black students from North Carolina Agricultural
and Technical College, all of them wearing a jacket and tie, sat down at the
whites-only lunch counter of a Woolworth's in Greensboro, North Carolina,
and asked to be served. When they were denied service, they refused to leave,
using a sit-in tactic that had already been deployed in more than a dozen cities since 1957.[1] Returning the next day, they were joined by 23 classmates; by
the weekend, the A&T football team had joined the protest, insisting on their
right to be served.[2] Within six weeks, sit-ins led by students had spread to
every southern state except Mississippi.[3] By April, a conference was called by
Ella Baker, the acting executive director of the Southern Christian Leadership
Conference (SCLC), to bring the student activists together. Out of this meeting emerged an organization that would do much to shape the decade: the
Student Nonviolent Coordinating Committee (SNCC).

The sit-in movement emerged six years after the Supreme Court's historic
1954 *Brown v. Board of Education* decision that declared segregated schools
unconstitutional, but its roots may be traced to the tradition of direct action
that began in Montgomery, Alabama, on December 1, 1955, when Rosa Parks
refused to sit in the back of a bus. A black boycott of Montgomery's bus system was organized in the following days, led by the Reverend Martin Luther
King Jr., then twenty-six years old. Speaking before a large crowd at the Dex-
ter Avenue Baptist Church, King brilliantly captured the mood of his flock:
"And you know, my friends, there comes a time when people get tired of being trampled by the iron feet of oppression. There comes a time, my friends,
when people get tired of being thrown across the abyss of humiliation where
they experience the bleakness of nagging despair . . . We are here — we are
here because we are tired now . . . And we are determined here in Montgomery — to work and fight until justice runs down like water, and righteousness
like a mighty stream."[4] By the time the struggle in Montgomery was finally
won on December 21, 1956, King had become a figure of national stature.[5]

As the struggle for civil rights intensified in the late 1950s, it became increasingly clear that racial problems threatened to undermine the position of the United States in the Cold War. Soviet propaganda took special delight in publicizing every embarrassing incident, and Governor Orval Faubus's use of the National Guard in Little Rock, Arkansas, to keep black children out of school was especially useful in its efforts to portray the United States as a citadel of racial oppression. The international situation was a central backdrop to the growing debate over the race question; even Secretary of State John Foster Dulles (Princeton '08), though hardly a liberal, recognized the harm that discrimination was causing U.S. foreign relations and urged support for civil rights legislation. Senator Jacob Javits of New York summarized the situation clearly: "The great contest between freedom and communism is over the approximately 1.2 billion largely Negro and Oriental population who occupy the underdeveloped areas of the Far East, the Middle East, and Africa. One of the greatest arguments used by the Communist conspirators against our leadership of the free world with these peoples has been that if they follow the cause of freedom, they too will be subjected to segregation which it is charged that we tolerate within certain areas of the United States; federal civil rights legislation is the best answer. The people are, therefore, watching with the most pronounced concern our present international struggle on civil rights."[6] In August 1957, the Eisenhower administration finally passed a civil rights bill, its provisions watered down by powerful southern members of Congress. Another civil rights bill followed in 1960, but it too fell far short of a serious commitment to transform America's racial order.[7]

The men who ran Harvard, Yale, and Princeton were, of course, aware of these developments. But as of 1960, the struggle for civil rights had not led them to see why they should alter their admissions practices to include more blacks. All three institutions were, after all, formally committed to the principle of nondiscrimination, and at least at Harvard and Yale, a modest number of African Americans had graduated over the years.[8]

As a result, blacks were barely visible on campus, constituting just 15 of the more than 3,000 students who entered Harvard, Yale, and Princeton in 1960. Harvard, which long had enjoyed a reputation for nondiscrimination, enrolled the most blacks — 9 in a class of 1,212 freshmen.[9] Yale, which prided itself on its tradition of openness, enrolled 5 black students out of a freshmen class of 1,000.[10] And Princeton, which had not enrolled its first black student until 1945 and was still considered by far the least hospitable of the Big Three, had only a single African American in its freshman class of 826 students.[11]

A decade later, all three institutions had been radically transformed. Over 280 African Americans were part of the freshman class — 83 at Yale, 103 at Princeton, and 98 at Harvard.[12] No change in the history of these tradition-bound institutions — save, perhaps, the admission of women to Yale and

Princeton in 1969 — had ever taken place so rapidly. How and why this radical transformation occurred is inextricably intertwined with the racial politics of the decade.

Yale: From Neutrality to Affirmative Action

In the spring of 1960, Dean of Admissions Arthur Howe Jr. received a letter from a Tennessee man inquiring whether there had been any alteration in Yale's admission policy with respect to race. Howe's response was prompt and to the point: "There has been no change in Yale's admissions policies with reference to Negroes. We shall continue to expect them to meet the same standards required of other applicants."[13]

That same spring, the case of a black applicant from a large industrial city in the East revealed what the "same standard" principle meant in practice. A young African American had applied to Yale; he was number one in his class of 500, carried a straight-A average since the seventh grade, was the varsity quarterback, captain of the number two basketball team in the state, and the school's first black president of the Student Council. He had compiled this record in the face of extremely adverse circumstances; according to the alumni interviewer, "His parents are almost illiterate — his father an unemployed invalid and his mother a laundry worker." Moreover, the Admissions Office, which placed great emphasis on evidence of "character" and "leadership," was aware that he had so impressed members of his own community that "the area's leading Negroes are guaranteeing five hundred dollars a year towards his college expenses." But the young man had not done well on his College Boards, averaging only 488 on the SAT. Yale — which at the time was very concerned about picking the "right boy" among black applicants to ensure graduation — concluded that he was too great a risk to warrant acceptance.[14] His rejection, an admissions officer said regretfully, was "part of the price we pay for our academic standards."[15]

Yet even at Yale the atmosphere in the early 1960s had changed from that of just a short time earlier. For one thing, the nation had a dynamic new president in John Fitzgerald Kennedy — a man who had presented himself during the presidential campaign as an advocate of civil rights and, once in office, moved quickly to sign an executive order establishing the Presidential Commission on Equal Opportunity.[16] For another, the struggle of the civil rights movement had continued, sometimes advancing and sometimes blocked by ferocious resistance. In January 1961, two students, one male and one female, successfully integrated the University of Georgia; four months later, Freedom Riders were beaten and arrested in Alabama.[17]

Yale was among the first Ivy League colleges to respond to the charged atmosphere, and in 1961–1962 Howe hired Charles McCarthy '60, a graduate of Loomis and a member of Skull and Bones, to recruit qualified blacks by cultivating relations with high schools known to enroll significant members of academically talented black students.[18] Other Ivy League schools were impressed with McCarthy's efforts, and at the 1962 meeting of Ivy admissions officers, they asked Howe if it would be possible to share McCarthy's contacts with other Ivy League colleges.[19] The result was the Cooperative Program for Educational Opportunity, which was joined by the eight Ivy League colleges as well as the Seven Sisters.[20] Nevertheless, even at Yale, progress remained slow; in 1962, just six African-American freshmen arrived in New Haven.[21]

As the "race question," in both North and South, became more salient, it increasingly drew the attention of political elites. In 1961, James Bryant Conant, still the nation's best-known educator, had famously written in his 1961 study, *Slums and Suburbs,* that America "was allowing social dynamite to accumulate in our large cities."[22] Since then, the racial situation had, if anything, worsened, with James Meredith's attempt to enroll at the University of Mississippi in September 1962 provoking a near-insurrection. So ferocious was the resistance to Meredith's presence on campus that Kennedy ultimately had to call in 500 federal troops to restore order. The toll was a measure of the fierceness of the mob's opposition to integration — 2 bystanders dead and 160 injured, 28 of them by gunshots.[23]

In the fall of 1962, President Kennedy summoned the leaders of five major universities, including Harvard and Yale, to the White House. Representing Yale was Kingman Brewster Jr., who attended in place of President Griswold, already gravely ill. According to Arthur Howe, who heard about the meeting from Brewster, Kennedy told the group, "I want you to make a difference . . . Until you do, who will?"[24] By the time Brewster became acting president in April 1963, the urgency of the situation — and the potential for racial violence in the North — had become clear. One sign of the times was the publication in early 1963 of James Baldwin's bestseller *The Fire Next Time.*[25] Baldwin, the son of a preacher, drew his title from a slave song: "God gave Noah the rainbow sign. No more water, the fire next time!" His message was unmistakable: either America would find a way "to end the racial nightmare" or racial conflagration would follow.

Like many members of the Establishment, both inside and outside academe, Brewster was deeply worried that America's unresolved racial conflicts might tear the nation apart. For this reason, as well as his deep admiration for Martin Luther King Jr.'s commitment to racial justice and nonviolence, Brewster decided to award King an honorary doctorate in 1964. At the time, King was tremendously controversial, considered by many to be a lawbreaker and a dangerous radical, [26] and Brewster's choice provoked outrage among many alumni. Responding to the protest of Thomas B. Brady '27, a justice on the Mississippi supreme court, Brewster wrote: "the effort to cure racial injustice should not be allowed to fester into a war between the races. Therefore it is especially important for the institutional symbols of white privilege to let it be known that they share this cause."[27]

Even more impassioned in defending Brewster's decision was the Yale Corporation member J. Irwin Miller '31, a Phi Beta Kappa graduate who went on to get an M.A. from Oxford in 1933.[28] A former president of the Irwin-Union Bank and the current chairman of the board of Cummins Engine Company, Miller was a religious man (he had served as president of the National Council of Churches of Christ and as chairman of the trustees of Christian Theological Seminary), and King's appeal to Christian values resonated deeply with him. In a letter to a disgruntled Old Eli, he wrote:

> I am extraordinarily proud of our university for honoring Rev. Martin Luther King. I say this as a graduate, but also as a person who has been engaged in business management for more than 30 years, and as a veteran of World War II.
>
> The menace and threat of world-wide communism is a very real one. In my opinion we combat it best by making our own country so strong and healthy . . . that the communist virus finds no fertile soil among us.
>
> This means, among other things . . . the extension of equal freedom, dignity, and opportunity to every segment of our people. We have no sickness in our nation more apt to turn mortal than that which denies the full fruits of a free society to those of Negro ancestry. Rev. King represents in my opinion the most responsible and Christian effort of Negroes to gain what they never should have been denied.[29]

From the perspective of Miller and of the many like-minded men of the Establishment, taking strong measures to rectify racial injustice was not simply a moral imperative; it was also a matter of enlightened self-interest at a time when the existing order was under challenge both internationally and domestically.

But awarding an honorary degree was one thing; changing long-standing, deeply embedded admissions practices another. Though Yale was now committed to recruiting more African Americans, a variety of barriers — social, academic, economic, cultural, and psychological — stood in the way.

The problem for well-intentioned institutions like Yale was that the supply of "qualified" blacks was extremely limited, given the prevailing definition of merit. According to a study conducted in the mid-1960s by Humphrey Doermann, Harvard's director of admissions, only 1.2 percent of the nation's male black high school graduates could be expected to score as high as 500 on the verbal section of the SAT and a mere three-tenths of one percent as high as 550.[30] Since the floor of acceptable SAT scores had been rising rapidly at Yale — by 1965 students in the tenth percentile of the freshmen class had verbal SAT scores of 591 (up from 506 in 1957)[31] — it followed that the pool of eligible black candidates was tiny: perhaps as few as 400 nationwide if a score of 550 was the cut-off point.[32] It was therefore hardly surprising that in 1964 Yale — despite vigorous efforts to identify qualified black candidates and to help them meet Yale's standards[33] — enrolled only 14 African-American freshmen — fewer than 2 percent of the class.[34]

A decade after *Brown v. Board of Education,* Yale and other elite private colleges found themselves at a crossroads: unless they altered their admissions criteria, they would not be able to enroll substantial numbers of black students. Having tried to increase African-American numbers through recruitment and outreach, they were coming up against the limits of these policies. Yet reconsidering their admissions criteria — which they believed (not without justification) were more meritocratic than ever before — was a step that they were loath to take. To do so would be to raise the troubling possibility that the admissions standards of which they were so proud might not be racially neutral after all and their cherished notion of who was "fit" for an Ivy League education might have to be modified.

As late as the fall of 1964, Yale reaffirmed its commitment to "color-blind" standards; at a meeting on October 26, the Governing Board of the Committee on Admissions expressed "no interest in suddenly opening the gates solely to increase the number of Negro and foreign students, unless they were qualified according to the same criteria used to judge all other candidates."[35] Just ten days earlier, the Committee on Admissions had itself decided against enrolling "Negro and other underprivileged candidates" by lowering admissions standards, with Georges May, the dean of Yale College, expressing "strong opposition" to using a double standard for admission.[36]

What changed after 1964 was that Baldwin's "fire next time" suddenly ignited in several urban centers. The pivotal event was the Watts riot in Los Angeles in August 1965. Though there had already been disturbances in New York; Philadelphia; Rochester; Paterson, New Jersey; and other (mostly eastern) cities in the summer of 1964, the scale of the rebellion in Watts was terrifyingly different. Over the course of six days, 34 people were killed and 1,072 injured (the great majority of them black), 4,000 arrested, and 977 buildings destroyed or damaged. To restore order, 14,000 National Guardsmen, 700 sheriff's deputies, and 1,000 Los Angeles police officers were deployed — a show of force necessitated by the more than 30,000 people estimated to have engaged in the riot, surrounded by at least 60,000 sympathetic spectators.[37] Ominously for the prospect of racial peace, the Watts riot began just five days after President Johnson signed the Voting Rights Act of 1965, the symbolic high point of the civil rights movement's struggle to remove legal barriers to racial equality.

The growing social disorder — embodied also by racial disturbances in nineteen other cities, the assassination of Malcolm X in January 1965, and growing antiwar and student movements — provided an important backdrop to Kingman Brewster's decision to appoint Inky Clark as Yale's dean of admissions.[38] Clark realized that a change in the definition of merit was required if black enrollment was to increase substantially: either more flexible academic standards would be applied to black candidates or Yale would remain overwhelmingly white. Given Clark's and Brewster's priorities, the latter was unacceptable, and they moved rapidly to make their promise of a more racially diverse Yale a reality.

The most important step was to admit that Yale's seemingly neutral academic standards were, in the end, not neutral at all. For the first time, the Admissions Office acknowledged that a candidate's academic profile was profoundly influenced by the opportunities that had been available to him. By 1965–1966, the first year of the Clark era, the Admissions Committee made it standard procedure — at least for African Americans — to "seriously consider the possibility that SAT scores might reflect cultural deprivation rather than lack of intelligence."[39]

Coupled with this new recognition of the social context was a willingness to undertake "risks" that had been unacceptable a few years earlier. Amid the racial turmoil of the mid-1960s, rigid adherence to the status quo began to look risky. Only reform, reasoned enlightened patricians like Brewster, could preserve the essentials of the American way of life at a time that racial violence was threatening to tear the nation apart. Even the faculty, whose fervent commitment to high academic standards had pushed Yale toward greater meritocracy, was willing to depart from established practices in the changed atmosphere. "We must be prepared," wrote the Admission Policy Advisory Board, "to take more risks than we would with students whose whole home and school backgrounds have prepared them for college and for college entrance exams." And in justifying its position, the faculty used the same argument made by Brewster and Clark[40]; in fulfilling its "national obligation to participate actively in the education of Negroes . . . it is necessary to allow for the handicaps of inferior preparation and to look behind the usual quantitative measures of academic achievement for high intellectual capacity and motivation."[41]

Empowered by Brewster and the faculty to be flexible in considering minority applicants, Clark moved quickly. Expanded recruiting was integral to his plan; in 1965–1966, 15 admissions officers, including the first black mem-

ber of the Admissions Committee in Yale's history, visited close to 1,000 secondary schools in search of "talent."[42] With timely assistance from the federal
government, which initiated Educational Opportunity Grants for exceptionally needy undergraduates, Yale also sharply increased its financial aid as part
of its commitment to genuinely need-blind admissions.[43] And as part of its
search for promising African-American applicants, Yale began working more
closely with organizations that targeted minority students, including the National Scholarship Service and Fund for Negro Students, A Better Chance
program (ABC), and the New York College Bound Corporation, as well as the
Cooperative Program for Educational Opportunity.[44]

The result of all these efforts was that black numbers at Yale reached a record high, with 35 African Americans in the 1966 freshman class — a significant increase over the previous high of 23 in 1965. Yet even this number
fell well short of Clark's goals, for African Americans still made up only 3.4
percent of entering students. Even more distressing, further progress proved
difficult; in 1967, the number of black applicants declined slightly, as did the
number of black admits and matriculants. Two years into Clark's term and
despite energetic efforts to recruit a more diverse student body, just 31 African
Americans enrolled at Yale — barely 3 percent of the freshman class.[45]

Meanwhile, national developments were increasing the pressure on Yale
and other leading private colleges to do something about America's deteriorating racial situation. In the summer of 1967, an unprecedented wave of race
riots shook the nation; by year's end, 82 racial disturbances had erupted in
71 different cities.[46] On July 12, a riot broke out in Newark — a declining eastern industrial city not unlike New Haven — that lasted 6 days, took 23 lives,
and required 3,000 troops to quell.[47] In the immediate aftermath, William
Lichten, a Yale physics professor, wrote to President Brewster, noting the shift
among northern Negroes from "apathy . . . to peaceful protests and demonstrations to . . . riots and violence" and pointing to the rapid growth of New
Haven's black population, which raised the prospect of Yale's becoming "a
white island in a black sea." As a matter of both elementary justice and institutional self-interest, Yale, he argued, had to do more.[48]

Just days after Lichten's letter arrived, an even bigger race riot exploded in
Detroit. In 8 days, 43 people died (33 blacks, 10 whites), 2,500 stores were
looted, burned, or destroyed, and 7,200 people were arrested — double the
number arrested in Watts. Whole sections of the city were burned, and order
was not restored until units from the 82nd and 101st Airborne Divisions of
the U.S. Army as well as National Guard troops were deployed.[49] After this
uprising, *Newsweek* described the riots as "a symbol of a domestic crisis
grown graver than any since the Civil War." *U.S. News and World Report* asked
simply: "Is Civil War Next?"[50]

By 1967–1968, signs of a new mood among African Americans were visible everywhere. At the symbolic level, the term "Negro" was giving way, especially in militant circles, to "black" — a shift attributable in no small amount to the rise of "black power," which Stokely Carmichael introduced in June 1966.[51] Perhaps most troubling to liberals like Brewster, the civil rights movement's commitment to nonviolence was increasingly being contested by firebrands who promised to use "any means necessary," including violence, to achieve racial justice.[52] New groups willing to brandish weapons in public, like the Black Panthers, became prominent; at the same time, old groups such as SNCC dropped their commitment to nonviolence and increasingly adopted a stance of racial separatism.[53] These developments seemed to suggest that the idea that America might be on the brink of a new civil war was not outlandish.[54]

The apprehensions that these events provoked in the heart of the Establishment were manifest in one of the landmark documents of the period: the Report of the National Advisory Committee on Civil Disorders, a body that had been appointed by President Johnson in the immediate wake of the Newark and Detroit riots. Chaired by Otto Kerner,[55] the Democratic governor of Illinois and a graduate of Brown, the committee had as its vice chairman one of the leading lights of the liberal Establishment: John V. Lindsay, the mayor of New York City and a fellow of the Yale Corporation. The other members made up something of a *Who's Who* of the power elite: Senator Edward W. Brooke (Republican, Massachusetts), the first black man to serve in the Senate since Reconstruction; Senator Fred Harris (Democrat, Oklahoma), a well-known liberal; Charles B. Thornton, the CEO of Litton Industries; Roy Wilkins, executive director of the National Association for the Advancement of Colored People; and I. W. Abel, president of the United Steelworkers of America.[56] Given the prominence of the members of the commission and the urgency of its topic, its report was guaranteed to receive enormous publicity.

The group issued a summary of its report (which quickly became known as the Kerner Report) on March 1, 1968, and the full text two days later. Within three days, Bantam Books' first edition of 30,000 copies had sold out. By July, more than 1.6 million copies had been sold.[57] This was an extraordinary outpouring of public interest, but even more remarkable was the bluntness of the commission's conclusions. "Our nation," warned the report on its first page, "is moving toward two societies, one black, one white — separate and unequal." The danger posed to the nation could hardly have been greater: "Discrimination and segregation have long permeated much of American life; they now threaten the future of every American."[58]

Most shocking of all was the commission's conclusion that blame for the nation's social troubles rested squarely on the doorstep of white America. In one of its most memorable passages, the report insisted: "What white Americans have never fully understood — but what the Negro can never forget — is that white society is deeply implicated in the ghetto. White institutions created it, white institutions maintain it, and white society condones it."[59] Considering the riots themselves, the report stated bluntly, "White racism is essentially responsible for the explosive mixture which has been accumulating in our cities since the end of World War II."[60]

"The frustrations of powerlessness," it warned, "have led some to the conviction that there is no effective alternative to violence as a means of expression and redress, as a way of 'moving the system.'"[61] Yet the situation was not without hope, for even the rioters "appeared to be seeking . . . full participation in the social order and the material benefits enjoyed by the majority of American citizens."[62]

Because of this desire to "share in both the material resources of our system and its intangible benefits — dignity, respect and acceptance . . . deepening racial division is not inevitable."[63] But reversing the movement toward separation would require vigorous measures dedicated to "the realization of common opportunities for all within a single society."[64] And in this effort, colleges and universities had a critical role, for the integration of the educational system and the expansion of opportunities for higher education was, the commission insisted, "essential to the future of American society."[65]

The Kerner Report came out at precisely the moment that Yale was accepting the class that would enter in the fall of 1968,[66] and it accurately captured the new mood of militancy — and urgency — on the campus. A Black Student Alliance of Yale (BSAY) had been formed in 1964 (initially the organization had no name) primarily as a social organization for the 14 black freshmen who entered that year, but by 1967–1968 it had grown both in number and in racial consciousness. By the fall of 1967, it issued a critique of the Yale curriculum, telling the administration that much of what was offered had a "lily-white" complexion. After a breakfast meeting in December 1967 with John Hay Whitney '26, a fellow of the Corporation and the publisher of the *New York Herald Tribune*, a full-scale meeting was called on February 15, 1968, of the BSAY and top administrators, including Brewster and Clark.[67] Among the students' many complaints was their dismay at the inefficiency of Yale's efforts to recruit African Americans; according to them, either the "admissions process isn't turning up or isn't admitting qualified black students."[68]

The result of this mobilization by the BSAY, which included roughly 90 percent of the black undergraduates, was an unprecedented effort to bring more black students to New Haven.[69] Approximately 1,200 schools were visited in 1968 (up from fewer than 1,000 in 1966), and recruitment in inner-city schools was expanded. As a result of student pressure, the BSAY "became actively involved in recruiting black students with the full blessing and cooperation of the Admissions Staff."[70] The number of black applicants shot up by 34 percent, rising to a record 163; according to the director of admissions, the increase could be "attributed, to a great degree, to the activities of this special group."[71] The net impact was that 43 African Americans enrolled in the fall of 1968 — still just 4 percent of all freshmen, but a record number nonetheless.[72]

Yet just as Yale was completing its selection of the most racially diverse student body in its history, an unprecedented outbreak of riots shook the nation's cities — resulting in 39 deaths and 20,000 arrests — apparently confirming the worst fears of the commission. The precipitating event was the April 4, 1968, assassination of Martin Luther King Jr., America's preeminent civil rights leader and the best hope for those who remained committed to nonviolence. Certainly, the response to King's assassination in the nation's ghettos gave little comfort to those in the civil rights movement, both black and white, who sensed that King's message was being superseded by the loudening chorus of voices embracing violence as a legitimate means in the struggle for liberation. To suppress the disorders — the worst since the Civil War — 75,000 federal troops and National Guardsmen were called up.[73]

But statistics alone do not describe the fear that the riots evoked in the nation's power centers. In Washington, D.C., senators and congressmen could see smoke rising from the multitude of fires set not far from the White House; some were so worried that they wanted the president to declare martial law, and they fretted that the Marines surrounding the Capitol had not been issued ammunition.[74] According to *Newsweek,* within hours of the assassination, "roving bands of teenagers . . . were already darting into Washington's downtown shopping district" and "fires were beginning to light the night sky." On the scene was Stokely Carmichael, a bitter opponent of King's nonviolent stance, brandishing what looked like a pistol and urging the crowd to "Go home and get your guns." "When the white man comes," warned Carmichael, "he is coming to kill you." "The plundering and burning lasted until dawn, then subsided," wrote *Newsweek,* "only to resume with far greater intensity [the] next day."[75]

By morning, the situation was so far beyond the control of Washington's 2,900-man police force that President Johnson had little choice but to call out federal troops.[76] A defiant mood prevailed among the rioters, with looting and burning sweeping 14th Street and 7th Street, two of the city's main thoroughfares. An eyewitness account captured the atmosphere: "Parts of Washington looked as though they had been hit by enemy bombing planes. Huge columns of smoke rose hundreds of feet. The shriek of sirens on police cars, the constant tinkle of shattering glass, the acrid smell of the tear gas — all helped give the scene in the capital of the U.S. the appearance of an inferno."[77]

Looting came within two blocks of the White House itself; troops had to be stationed on the White House grounds.[78] Surveying the uprising in Washington and elsewhere, a British journalist wrote, "The riots were on a scale unprecedented except for a country on the verge of revolution."[79]

Just two weeks after the rebellion in Washington was brought under control, self-styled student revolutionaries at Columbia University staged their own uprising. Taking place at an Ivy League institution in New York City, the media capital of the world, the revolt at Columbia generated enormous publicity. By the time the insurgency ended, the SDS slogan of "Two, three, many Columbias" reverberated not only across America's campuses but around the world.[80]

The events at Columbia showed that the student movement had reached a new level of militancy and one that posed a genuine threat to the power of the university authorities. The revolt began on April 23, 1968, when radical students occupied Hamilton Hall, locking the dean in his office (he was released 26 hours later).[81] One of the students' demands was an end to war-related research, but the issue with the most traction was the demand that Columbia end the construction of a gymnasium in a public park next to the campus, in Harlem. The gym, which was offering just 15 percent of its facilities for the use of the residents of the densely populated ghetto neighborhood, actually planned a separate entrance for them. From the perspective of the student militants, the entire project reeked of a "quasi-colonial disdain for the black community."[82]

In no small part because of the gymnasium, Columbia's black students became thoroughly involved in the protests despite their decided skepticism about the white radicals. Though the predominantly white students of SDS had led the initial occupation of Hamilton Hall, the black students of the Student Afro-American Society (SAS) soon asked them to leave, finding them too unruly for their taste. The white students complied and showed their solidarity by following the advice of the SAS, which told them, "If you want to do something that's relevant, grab as many buildings as you can." Meanwhile, the black students continued their occupation of Hamilton.[83]

Though fearful that calling in the police might trigger a riot in Harlem, the Columbia administration did just that after the eighth day of the occupation. The black students, who had consistently been more organized than their white counterparts, showed the same discipline in ending the sit-in, marching out in drill formation to waiting vans — where the police arrested them.[84] But the white students in the other buildings resisted (passively in most cases, but in one case attempting to block the door), and the police responded violently. In the end, more than 200 people were injured and 705 arrested (524 of them students). As Daniel Bell, then on the Columbia faculty, pointed out, almost 10 percent of the undergraduates at Columbia had been arrested.[85]

For the men who ran Yale, Harvard, Princeton, and other elite universities, the revolt at Columbia was sobering. It was not simply a matter of a rebellion at a fellow Ivy League institution (though that was disturbing, to be sure); equally distressing was the *manner* in which the revolt unfolded, complete with the use of force, the appearance of an ominous (if fragile) alliance between black and white militants, and — not least — the total collapse of gentlemanly notions of "civility." As campus revolts, including building occupations, spread nationwide over the next few weeks to virtually every type of institution — among them, such prestigious colleges as Stanford and Northwestern — the thought that they might well be next was very much on the minds of each member of the Big Three.[86]

At Yale, the Brewster administration was strongly committed to the proposition that flexible reform and an atmosphere of open communication could avoid the kind of disorder that had shaken Columbia and Berkeley. But as the 1968–1969 academic year began, it soon became apparent that Yale was not immune to the mood of racial militancy visible on other campuses. Early that fall, a group of militant blacks marched directly to Brewster's home and demanded that Yale increase the number of black students to be admitted that year. Brewster, who excelled in face-to-face meetings, convinced the students that their cause was his cause and enlisted their help. As Kurt Schmoke '71 (later a Rhodes Scholar and the mayor of Baltimore) recalls their meeting: "Brewster was absolutely a master at co-opting the student body. There is no other way of putting it."[87]

Yet the matter of exactly how Yale would increase black enrollment that fall had still not been resolved. In early January, 30 BSAY members met with Dean Clark, demanding that 12 percent of the incoming class be blacks (roughly the black proportion of the population nationwide). In addition, they demanded that the Admissions Office fund BSAY members to visit urban neighborhoods to ensure that the number of African-American applicants would increase to a level that would make it possible for Yale to attain the 12 percent goal.[88]

These were radical demands, but after a series of meetings with Clark and Brewster, an accord was reached. Though Clark had agreed in early January 1969 that 12 percent of the incoming class would be black *if* enough qualified candidates applied, Brewster — who had always opposed quotas — made clear in a letter to the BSAY that the 12 percent figure was not a guarantee: "While we do believe in these special efforts, we cannot hold out the promise of achieving any target if it would mean admitting students who, in the eyes of the admissions committee, would not be likely to meet Yale's requirements."[89] Nevertheless, he left open the possibility that the next freshman class *might* be 12 percent black and, in the meantime, acceded to the demand that Yale fund the recruiting trips requested by the BSAY. Brewster and Clark also agreed to extend the normal January 1 application deadline to February 24[90] — a major concession, reflecting the threat of disruption that lurked not far in the background.

The BSAY mobilization, coming at a moment of tremendous social and political turmoil, pushed Yale farther than it had ever gone before and propelled black enrollment to an unprecedented level. Spurred in part by the post-deadline recruiting trips, applications from African-American men numbered 387, more than double the 163 just a year earlier, accompanied by 138 black women in what would be Yale's first year of coeducation. Black admissions also rose to record heights: 120 men (compared to 55 in 1968) and 35 women. All in all, 96 blacks (71 men and 25 women) — 8 percent of the freshman class — entered Yale in 1969. Only four years earlier, just 2 percent of the freshman class was African American.[91]

The remarkable increase in black enrollments that took place during the Clark years was not without its costs. Searching vigorously in ghetto schools previously well outside the Yale orbit and willing to take risks that would have been unthinkable during the Griswold-Howe administration, the Admissions Committee was now taking students whose backgrounds made their adjustment to Yale — where affluent white students still set the tone — quite difficult. Of the blacks who entered Yale in 1966, 35 percent did not return after their freshman year[92]; how many left in subsequent years is unknown. Yet if Brewster's and Clark's goal was to create a new stratum of black leadership, their objective was realized. By the early 1970s, a steady flow of African-American Yale alumni was streaming into the nation's top graduate and professional schools and moving into important positions in the professions, business, and government.

The shift toward a more racially diverse student body was also not without financial cost. Need-blind admissions, which was expensive, had been a precondition for the diversification of the student body. And black scholarship recipients were, on average, poorer than their white peers. By 1970–1971, "Yale was spending over $800,000 a year for blacks . . . about half its financial aid budget."[93] There were hidden costs as well, for Yale's vigorous effort to recruit blacks was one of several policy shifts during the Clark years that estranged large segments of the alumni, costing Yale a not inconsiderable sum in lost donations.[94]

Nevertheless, once Yale had made its commitment to increase black enrollment, the policy proved irreversible, spreading rather quickly to other racial and ethnic minorities. Already, in Clark's first year as dean, Yale was looking for students from a variety of historically underrepresented groups; according to a *New York Times* article on Ivy League admissions in 1966, "The New Haven college will have a few Puerto Ricans in its Class of 1970, and a full-blooded American Indian too."[95] By 1968, in addition to recruiting in inner cities and in Puerto Rico, Yale was actively seeking Native Americans, even sending representatives to Indian reservations.[96]

By 1969–1970, Asian Americans were also included among the groups whose recruiting trips were paid for by Yale — a product of vigorous protests by the Asian-American Students Association (AASA).[97] The AASA had complained about Yale's admissions policies in a letter to the Undergraduate Admissions Committee in November 1969; by January, it reported that it was "deeply concerned about the Committee's failure to recognize that the majority of Asian-American high school students come from lower-income brackets and predominantly Third World communities." The letter went on to declare: "We demand that these students be judged on criteria other than 'white middle-class' since they have faced the same inadequacies in their secondary education as other minority groups."[98] In his report for 1970–1971, the dean of admissions proudly noted that 31 Asian Americans had matriculated at Yale that fall alongside 77 blacks, 22 Mexican Americans, and 6 Puerto Ricans.[99] As the 1960s came to an end, affirmative action at Yale was no longer for blacks only.

The Integration of Old Nassau

In the early 1960s, it was no exaggeration to describe Princeton as a de facto segregated institution. Though Old Nassau no longer actively discriminated against black applicants, it did nothing to seek them out. Given Princeton's terrible reputation in the black community, few blacks even bothered to apply.[100] In 1960, just 1 African American entered in a freshman class of over 800; 1 more matriculated in 1961.[101]

Yet some undergraduates were dissatisfied with Princeton's racial composition, and in January 1962 a student conference at the Woodrow Wilson School passed a resolution calling for "an energetic program of recruiting qualified American Negro students." While acknowledging that "the University does not intentionally discriminate in considering the applications of Negroes," it maintained that "many qualified Negro students are not aware of the fair consideration which their applications would find here." Specifically, the students proposed that the class that would enter in 1963 be "at least two percent" Negro.[102]

Though modest and carefully worded, the proposal received a lukewarm response from the administration. Insisting that "we try to keep everything as fair as possible," one university official argued that "rather than discriminate against the colored student, there is more of a danger here of us leaning forward to accept him and then running the risk that he won't be able to remain here." Adopting the same stance as Yale at the time, the official warned that failure for blacks was especially problematic: "When a Negro student flunks out here, it is a tougher loss for us than, for example, a John Jones."[103]

Questioned about the small number of blacks on campus, one Princeton official said, "If we've got six, that's fine with me," adding that "I know that they were admitted regardless of their color."[104] Even President Goheen, a man known for his decency, shared the lack of concern that pervaded the campus, once calling the NAACP the "N.A. double-C.P." and another time misnaming the National Scholarship Service and Fund for Negro Students, a key organization for colleges interested in increasing their black enrollment.[105] Goheen's response to the undergraduates' proposal of at least 2 percent black students, though modulated, was in the end negative: while in favor of "the admission of well-qualified Negro students to Princeton," he sharply criticized any notion of a numerical goal. Echoing the position of color-blindness then shared by northern liberals and conservatives alike, he reaffirmed that "the fundamental operation of the University's admissions policy . . . must be toward the individual — towards individuals as persons — not toward social statistics."[106]

Yet patterns that were acceptable to men like Goheen in 1962 had become unacceptable by September 1963 — a shift due to the bloody events in Birmingham (including the deaths of four black schoolgirls in a church bombing) and the sense of urgency conveyed by the historic August civil rights march on Washington.[107] In the fall of 1963, in the annual "Report to Schools" sent to 4,000 of the nation's secondary schools, the Office of Admissions announced for the first time in its history that "Princeton is actively seeking qualified Negro applicants . . . Efforts of school people in steering toward Princeton qualified Negroes will be appreciated."[108] After the call went out, President Goheen gave it his personal endorsement, noting, "For the past decade, we have been terribly concerned about what we could do for students from undeveloped countries. It took a shock [the civil rights crisis] to make us realize our problems at home."[109]

Princeton's newfound willingness to seek out black students coincided with the arrival of E. Alden Dunham '57 as director of admission.[110] Conant's special assistant for four years, Dunham was keenly aware of America's racial problems and the potentially explosive situation in the nation's ghettos.[111] Yet like his mentor, Dunham was a cautious man, believing that only incremental change was possible.[112]

Nevertheless, Dunham was genuinely committed to bringing more African Americans to Princeton, and he was able to increase the number of black applicants from 20 in 1963 to 72 in 1964. Yet in 1964, only 12 blacks entered Princeton's freshman class. Dunham was forthright in admitting that Princeton was facing an uphill battle in its efforts, citing three reasons for the small number of black matriculants: "First, Negroes are a minority, so that there are fewer to begin with. Second, they tend to congregate on a low rung of the socio-economic ladder, a fact that further reduces the number of qualified candidates. This is a socio-economic phenomenon, not a matter of race. Just as there are few qualified whites from slum areas, so there are few qualified Negroes. The net result is a small pool of able boys to be spread among many colleges. The third factor is the long Southern tradition at Princeton, together with a small-town atmosphere. Given a choice, many Negroes prefer Harvard or Yale, where abolitionism was much stronger and where the anonymity of a large city is close at hand."[113]

Though Princeton no longer overtly discriminated against black students, its entire atmosphere was inhospitable. In the early 1960s, its social life was still dominated by eating clubs, and blacks were relegated to the periphery of campus life; as late as 1963, none of the three black upperclassmen (out of five black undergraduates) were members of an eating club.[114] Extracurricular life could be equally unwelcoming; in 1964, a student group ironically called the Princeton Committee to Promote Racial Reconciliation was formed to promote the conservative viewpoint that argued that informed people could favor continued racial segregation. As its first action, the committee placed a book on sale — *Race and Reason,* by Carleton Putnam '24 — that argued that the genetic limitations of blacks made successful integration impossible. Though the committee had only 15 members, its leader, Marshall I. Smith '66, claimed that more than a third of the student body supported its stand on racial matters. As evidence, he cited a recent debate at the prestigious Whig-Clio Club where over a fourth of those present endorsed a resolution affirming the existence of racial difference.[115]

Convincing black students to attend such an institution was not going to be easy, but Old Nassau pressed on. In 1964, Princeton hired Carl A. Fields as the first black administrator at an Ivy League institution — a clear sign that it wished to break with its unhappy racial history.[116] In 1965, Dunham issued a strong public defense of Princeton's policy of seeking out "qualified Negroes" in the alumni magazine, arguing that Princeton had long "felt a responsibility to be responsive to the nation's need for men who can fulfill important leadership roles" and that, "from the national point of view, the call for Negro leadership at this time in our history is clear."[117] The same year, the Admissions Committee institutionalized special consideration for black applicants by giving them a special category (and round in the admissions process) next to such groups as alumni sons and Naval ROTC candidates.[118]

In 1966, Dunham publicly endorsed the same position on the evaluation of the academic qualifications of African Americans as that articulated by Brewster and Clark at Yale: "There is a special concern about evaluating applications from disadvantaged students. Just as the College Board takes pride in its record of providing through its testing program a means for upward mobility on the part of middle-class Americans, there is now a realization that the nature of present examinations may impede the extension of educational opportunity for the disadvantaged. Test score interpretation becomes ever more difficult for these students than for the typical applicant."[119] By interpreting the scholastic records of "disadvantaged" applicants in the context of the opportunities available to them, Dunham provided the latitude to define "merit" flexibly in assessing black candidates — a necessity if Princeton was to have any chance of substantially increasing the number of its African-American students.

The result of this more contextual definition of merit was that Princeton, which had long given preference to traditional elite constituencies, now had a rationale for giving special consideration to blacks and other "disadvantaged" candidates for admission. Legacies, prep school boys, and athletes, Princeton was well aware, had traditionally been admitted with far weaker academic qualifications (at least as measured by such indicators as average SATs) than that small segment of the class admitted on almost exclusively academic criteria. In the mid-1960s, they were joined by African Americans. Many of the black students admitted under Dunham were in fact doubly disadvantaged: the majority of them, in sharp contrast to their classmates, came from working-class backgrounds.[120] Not surprisingly, their SAT scores were lower than the Princeton average: roughly 550 verbal and 590 math for blacks who entered Princeton from 1963 to 1966, compared to about 650 verbal and 695 math for the class as a whole.[121]

When Dunham took office, he wrote that all educational institutions, including Princeton, had "an opportunity and responsibility [to] do what they can toward upgrading the state of the Negro in our free society."[122] Two years later, after the passage of the Civil Rights Act of 1964 and the awarding of the Nobel Peace Prize to Dr. King, he expressed his hope that Princeton could help "in a small way" to meet "the call for Negro leadership."[123] Yet despite Dunham's efforts, the number of blacks at Princeton increased only modestly. By 1965, the freshman class included 16 African Americans; in 1966, the number increased to 18 — still just 2 percent of the class.[124]

Nevertheless, when Dunham left Princeton in 1966 to join the Carnegie Corporation, he left behind a changed institution. Though the well-rounded man was hardly a creature of the past, a different ideal — that of "the well-rounded class" — had come to frame admissions policy. In place of the socially adept, well-rounded man, specialist types from increasingly diverse

backgrounds now made up much of the student body. So different was the atmosphere that the prestigious Big Five Clubs — Ivy, Cottage, Cap and Gown,
Colonial, and Tiger Inn — could not find enough "suitable" boys and had to
use other criteria, such as athletics and special talents. Club seniors were already unanimous by 1965 in appraising the first class admitted by Dunham as
"the worst ever." As a result of changes in the composition and character of
the student body, social distinctions in Princeton's tradition-laden eating
clubs were becoming increasingly blurred.[125]

Meanwhile, though still only a very small proportion of the student body,
black students were for the first time present in sufficient numbers to constitute an organized group. In the spring of 1967, about two-thirds of the 40 African-American undergraduates formed the Princeton Association of Black
Collegians (PABC). Their choice of "black" rather than "Negro" reflected the
growing mood of militancy among the African-American students, and the
PABC soon staged its first protest. When Alabama's governor George Wallace
came to address the Whig-Clio Society and began his customary racist attack,
the black students rose in a body and left the auditorium.[126] That spring,
when the number of blacks accepted unexpectedly dropped from 32 to 23, a
number of students in the PABC made their displeasure known to members
of the administration.[127]

By the time school resumed in the fall of 1967, the atmosphere had grown
palpably more tense. Over the summer, the situation in racially divided Newark — New Jersey's largest city, less than an hour's drive from Princeton —
had exploded into a full-scale riot. The rebellion in Newark lasted six days
and involved so many sniping incidents (152 by one count) that the scene in
parts of the city resembled guerrilla warfare. Order was not restored until the
National Guard was deployed, and by the time the riot was finally suppressed,
26 people had died.[128] Less than a week after relative calm returned to Newark, the even larger riot in Detroit broke out.

Princeton responded to the tumultuous events of the summer of 1967 by
issuing, early in the fall in its annual "Report to Schools," another call for
more African-American applicants — the first such appeal since 1963. Delicately noting that "the need for Negro leadership is particularly urgent at the
present time," the Admissions Office promised "to interpret fairly credentials
of students from non-traditional backgrounds, realizing that their test scores,
academic records, and leisure time activities are often different."[129] Meanwhile, even Princeton was showing itself to be not immune to the surge in
campus radicalism sweeping the nation. In October, the Princeton chapter of
SDS, just two years old, organized its first disruptive protest — a sit-in at the
Institute for Defense Analysis (IDA), a nonprofit corporation conducting research for the Pentagon on university land in a building leased from the uni-

versity. Claiming that the IDA was an off-campus facility, Princeton allowed the police to handle the sit-in. Thirty students were arrested, "most of whom went limp and had to be dragged or thrown into police vehicles."[130] At tradition-bound Princeton, which prided itself on a gentlemanly tradition of civility, the specter of a serious campus uprising led by student radicals was now on the horizon.

Whatever the concerns aroused by SDS, it was the threat of black radicalism, both on and off campus, that was the moving force behind the intensification of Princeton's effort to recruit more black students in 1967–1968. Under pressure from both the PABC and the events of the previous summer, Princeton made a decision to move decisively to increase black enrollment. In a clear sign of change at the Admissions Office, Princeton not only accepted late applications from black candidates but actively encouraged them; in the end, 143 blacks applied in 1968, up from 83 in 1967. These applicants, in turn, received special consideration and greater flexibility in the interpretation of their academic records; the result was that the African-American admissions rate soared to 53 percent — almost double the rate of a year earlier. In 1968, 44 blacks entered Princeton — a radical change for a college that had just one black entrant in 1961 and had never before exceeded 18 in a single class.[131]

Princeton's public statements left little doubt that the increasingly violent racial disturbances that shook the nation's cities in the summer of 1967 were the main cause of the change in its admissions policy. The 1968 "Report to Schools" noted: "After 1967, the year of the riots, the increases [in] . . . the number of black students admitted and enrolled in selective colleges . . . were dramatic."[132] In his second report as director of admissions, John T. Osander '57,[133] who succeeded Dunham in 1966, noted that Princeton "admitted a larger number of black students than our larger and more liberal-minded competitors, Harvard and Yale" and expressed his hope that "what we did in 1968 should provide some indication to the black community that we take the Civil Disorder Commission's charges of white racism seriously."[134] "At the most practical level, if integration and non-violence are in the best self-interests of the white community," Osander wrote, "then it is essential that strong programs of action are taken to provide truly equal rights and truly equal conditions for all people."[135]

Princeton's vigorous affirmative action policy was part of a broader effort to change what Osander called its "conservative, upper-class image."[136] Diversifying the racial composition of the student body was necessarily at the center of this effort, and by the late 1960s, Princeton had broken decisively with its past. The academic year 1968–1969 saw, if anything, an even more energetic effort to transform the racial character of the student body than 1967–1968, itself a record year. Hovering in the background was the threat of disruption; in the spring of 1968, Princeton's black students threatened to close down the campus when Goheen initially rejected their proposal to cancel classes and hold seminars as a tribute to Martin Luther King Jr. on the day of his funeral, and in March 1969, 51 students in the PABC organized an eleven-hour occupation of an administration building to protest Princeton's refusal to rid itself of investments in corporations doing business in South Africa.[137]

Amid an atmosphere of increasing student militancy and social breakdown in the nation's cities, Princeton altered its admissions policies yet again. The most visible change was the historic decision to admit women, but 1968–1969 was also the year Princeton began to recruit Mexican Americans, Puerto Ricans, and Native Americans and expanded its efforts to recruit more "disadvantaged" whites.[138] After years of attempting to change its image, Princeton's efforts were finally bearing fruit; once again, the number of African-American applicants more than doubled, rising from 143 to 325.[139] This increase allowed Princeton to become somewhat more selective in assessing black candidates, dropping their rate of admission to 34 percent from 53 the year before.

A mere decade earlier, alumni sons were the main beneficiaries of "affirmative action."[140] By the late 1960s, special consideration, largely the province of the privileged in previous decades, had been formally expanded to blacks and other minorities. Of the 120 African Americans admitted in 1969, 75 had academic ratings of 4 or 5 — a pattern made possible by the increasingly contextual definition of "merit" that had been put in place over the past few years.[141]

Princeton's efforts to recruit blacks peaked in 1970, when the African-American proportion of the freshman class reached 10.4 percent — the highest figure ever attained, before or since, at a Big Three institution. From a stance of strict neutrality in 1962, Princeton had moved in a few short years to a strategy of using all the means at its disposal to increase black enrollment: appeals to secondary schools for more applicants, recruiting visits to areas with large minority populations, expanded contacts with community organizations, and the direct involvement of undergraduates from the PABC in recruiting students.[142] A minority presence was now built into the admissions process itself, with blacks on the Admissions Committee and a single member of the staff writing assessments of all candidates deemed "disadvantaged." Finally, and most significantly, the criteria by which black and other disadvantaged candidates were judged now took into account the limited opportunities that they typically had had to acquire the kind of academic record that would lead to admission under ostensibly color-blind criteria.

Having started the decade well behind Harvard and Yale, Princeton was now ahead of them in recruiting African Americans — no small accomplish-

ment for a college that did not take its first black until 1945 and failed to enroll a single black freshman for three consecutive years in the 1950s.[143] Princeton's success in transforming itself was part of a conscious decision to alter its
admissions practices fundamentally. Reinforcing this decision was the recognition that a critical mass of black students would do a great deal to address
the continued perception that Princeton was, as Osander bluntly put it,
"wealthy, conservative, isolated, rural, indolent, snobbish, and non-intellectual." This image problem, he noted, was compounded by "the Princeton eating and social system [which] made it harder to attract a meritocratic rather
than an aristocratic student body."[144] If, in the increasingly ferocious competition for top students of the late 1960s, a traditionalist image of upper-class
gentlemanliness was a serious handicap, Princeton's decision to recruit black
students demonstrated better than any other change that "Old Nassau" was
no more.

The incorporation of blacks into Princeton was the leading edge of a
broader strategy of transformation. Long perceived as a bastion of the WASP
upper class, Princeton became a pioneer in institutionalizing special consideration for all disadvantaged students, including whites. By 1969, 29 students
classified as "non-black disadvantaged" were admitted; 20 of them chose to
enroll.[145] Other minorities were also becoming visible at Princeton; by 1971,
the Union Latino-Americana was, according to the Admissions Office, providing "an excellent model for student involvement in admission recruiting
work."[146] The 1971 admissions report presciently predicted that "as the numbers of Latinos, American Indian, Asian, and other minority group students
on campus increase, we can expect such students to be interested in increased
enrollment for all Third World student groups."[147] A year later, Princeton was
issuing statistics on the number of freshmen from five separate minority
groups: Latino (22), Chicano (14), Oriental (27), Indian (five), and black
(113). Together, these Third World students, as they were then called, made up
16.5 percent of the freshman class of 1972 — a clear refutation of Princeton's
deeply ingrained image as a white institution.[148]

Despite these dramatic changes, Princeton had retained its traditional
character in other ways. Unlike Yale, which had radically reduced the degree
of preference for alumni children, Princeton continued to treat them delicately, offering them admission at a rate roughly 2.5 times higher than that of
other applicants between 1966 and 1970.[149] Overall, these students who entered Princeton in these years remained a strikingly privileged lot; among the
freshmen in 1970, just 8 percent had fathers who were workers (skilled, semiskilled, and unskilled) or farmers — groups that still constituted a majority of
the labor force.[150] Two-thirds came from families with incomes over $15,000
— a level reached by just 18 percent of American families in 1970.[151] At the

time the least wealthy of the Big Three, Princeton could not offer financial aid to all admits who needed it. Though admission was officially need-blind, Princeton lacked the resources to make it "full-aid"; in 1968, it had to deny financial aid to 70 admits who, by its own calculations, were in need of scholarship assistance.[152]

Harvard and the Black Question in the 1960s

Of the eight Ivy League colleges, none enjoyed a better reputation in the African-American community in 1960 than Harvard, which had a long history of being open to blacks dating back to 1865, when Richard T. Greener entered the college.[153] Between 1865 and 1941, approximately 165 black students enrolled at Harvard, slightly more than two a year.[154] The level of black enrollment increased markedly in the 1940s and 1950s, with at least 97 blacks matriculating between 1939 and 1955.[155] Though this meant that just 6 or so African Americans a year entered classes generally numbering well over 1,000, it was the largest group at any Ivy League college.

Harvard's "favored status within the Negro community," wrote the author of a 1962 paper on "Negroes in the Ivy League," was primarily due to "the reputation she gained from her many successful Negro graduates and from her long tradition of equality on the campus."[156] Though Harvard's record was in truth not without blemishes, especially during the Lowell years,[157] it had largely been free of the overt racial discrimination seen at Princeton and many other elite colleges.[158] By the late 1950s, Harvard was actively (if quietly) seeking to increase the number of African-American students on campus. One of its principal assets in this effort was a close relationship with the National Scholarship Service and Fund for Negro Students (NSSFNS). In the final years of the Bender administration, which ended in 1960, perhaps as many as half of Harvard's black students had learned about the college through the NSSFNS.[159]

In Bender's last year, Harvard established an innovative program that looked for students (especially from the South) from economically and culturally impoverished homes. Funded in 1959 by the Taconic Foundation in New York and nicknamed the "Gamble Fund," the initiative was not specifically targeted at blacks.[160] But they were major beneficiaries, with 18 black students — a majority of them supported by the fund — enrolled in the program's first three years. To help them adjust to college, Harvard sent the students to Andover in the summer before their freshman year. In a few cases — especially for those who had attended particularly weak schools — students were sent to Andover for a full year of preparation.[161]

According to one well-informed observer, something like what came to be known as affirmative action was already institutional policy: "Without question Harvard does go out of its way . . . [and] will take a boy with inadequate test scores if there are indicators he will develop."[162] Many of the African Americans admitted in these years were disadvantaged by class as well as race; in 1961, 90 percent received scholarships, compared to 25 percent of all undergraduates.[163] Between 1959 and 1961, 10 low-income (family income under $5,000) black students entered Harvard; 6 graduated on schedule and a seventh within six years.[164]

By 1963, Harvard had enough black students — 55 undergraduates, by one estimate — to stimulate the formation of the Association of African and Afro-American Students (generally known at Harvard simply as "Afro").[165] In the next few years, Harvard continued to make significant, if gradual, gains in black enrollment — an achievement facilitated by the Glimp administration's conscious decision to seek greater social and racial diversity and to "give less weight to the so-called objective factors (rank in class and test scores) and more weight to other evidence, not only of intellectual promise but of other qualities and kinds of promise as well."[166]

In 1965, 42 black freshmen matriculated at Harvard — an impressive figure compared to Yale (23) and Princeton (12).[167] All of them scored above 500 on the verbal section of the SAT, and their median score was about 600 — relatively high figures, given that only about 1.2 percent of all black high school graduates had scores over 500.[168] The black freshmen were from far less advantaged backgrounds than their white classmates; in 1965, when roughly a third of Harvard freshmen received scholarships, the figure among African-American freshmen was 88 percent.[169] Especially by Harvard's standards, many of the black freshmen were outright poor; almost half came from families with incomes under $5,000 — putting them in the bottom 30 percent of American families.[170] Harvard's pioneering efforts in the early and mid-1960s thus made an important contribution not only to racial diversity on the campus but also to class diversity.

Further progress proved difficult, however; black enrollment at Harvard stagnated between 1965 and 1968. Indeed, after a small increase in 1966, the black proportion of Harvard's freshmen declined slightly in 1967 and again in 1968.[171] The reasons are not clear, but increased competition from other elite colleges may have been a factor. Perhaps also relevant was Harvard's admissions ideology, which spoke frequently of the "disadvantaged" and of "diversity" but generally avoided any specific mention of race. Harvard was certainly searching for talented black students, but it was doing so quietly and cautiously within an official ideology of "color-blindness."

At Harvard, as on so many other campuses, the assassination of Martin Luther King Jr. in April 1968 precipitated a crisis. Tensions were evident at the service held shortly after King's death at Memorial Church. Inside were 1,200 mourners, almost all of them white; outside, 80 blacks held an alternative service organized by Afro.[172] At the end of the service, in a tense confrontation, the students presented the administrators walking out of the church with a list of demands. Among them was a call for changes in Harvard's admissions policy toward blacks.[173]

Afro wanted Harvard to "admit a number of Black students proportionate to our percentage of the population as a whole" — roughly 12 percent.[174] Harvard did not accede to this demand, but Chase Peterson '52, the new dean of admissions, quickly agreed to meet with the angry students.[175] Admissions decisions had already been made for the class that would enter in the fall of 1968, but Harvard could alter its admissions practices for the next year. By April 29 — less than four weeks after King's death — Peterson announced his commitment to enrolling a substantially higher number of black students in a joint statement with the Ad Hoc Committee of Black Students.[176]

Concretely, the agreement reached between the administration and the students called for the better representation of blacks on the Admissions Office staff, direct involvement of undergraduates in recruiting African-American students, and bringing more black candidates to visit Harvard before admissions decisions. These were important concessions, but the most crucial victory was the extraction of a specific promise to increase substantially the number of black students. While insisting that "we are not responding to a crisis so much as to a void that exists at Harvard,"[177] Peterson was in fact negotiating in an atmosphere in which the threat of campus disruption was palpable.[178]

Though Peterson affirmed in his annual report for 1967–1968 Harvard's long-standing position that it "will never admit a young man simply to fill a quota," the decision had already been made to raise by a sizable margin the number of black students who would enter in 1969.[179] While continuing to oppose quotas publicly, the Admissions Committee privately accepted the notion that a "critical mass" of black students would be needed to provide one another with moral and social support. If formal quotas had been rejected, numerical targets would nonetheless frame Harvard's admissions policy toward blacks.[180]

In 1969, admissions decisions were made in an atmosphere of acute racial and political tension.[181] So tangible was the threat of a student revolt that, as Peterson said, "There was a serious question as to whether the admissions office itself would be attacked and whether we would be able to complete our procedures and mail our letters by April fifteenth."[182] His concern was understandable; on April 9, radical students had occupied University Hall, where they remained until the police forcibly expelled them the following day in a bloody assault in which 48 people were injured seriously enough to require medical care. In all, the police arrested 196 people, 145 of them Harvard or Radcliffe students.[183]

Shortly after these tumultuous events, a confrontation took place between militant black students and the administration over the form of a proposed Department of Afro-American Studies. Though the crisis ended on April 22 when the Harvard faculty voted, 251–158, in favor of a proposal acceptable to the students (and considered an "academic Munich" by some of the faculty), there was little doubt that some sort of "militant action" would have followed had it been rejected.[184] Even an armed takeover of a building — an action that had shaken Cornell just a few days earlier — was not out of the question.[185]

Threatened as never before by militant students, both black and white, the Admissions Office — though not a specific target of either of the spring confrontations — fundamentally altered its practices.[186] In a first step toward making good on its promises, it hired its first black admissions officer, John Harwell, a former Chicago public school teacher then working for the Urban League. Harwell — who apparently had been recommended by Jeff Howard '69, the head of Afro — was personally called by Peterson. After some initial skepticism, he became convinced that he could make a contribution, and came to Harvard in the fall of 1968. At the same time, black students helped to recruit African-American applicants, assisted by committed alumni who visited inner-city schools never before approached by Harvard.

Though no official policy change was announced, the admissions criteria were altered to take still greater account of the limitations of background and schooling that shaped the qualifications of many black candidates. A student who had "survived the hazards of poverty" and who showed that he "is clearly intellectually thirsty" and "still has room for more growth" would be given preference. The presence of such students, Peterson argued, would make the campus both more diverse and more intellectually stimulating.[187] Diversity, both racial and social, was thus not only a social necessity but an educational one.

With the "diversity rationale" for affirmative action firmly in place (the very rationale that would later carry the day in the historic *Bakke* decision in 1978), Harvard set about making good on its promise to increase the number of black students. The first class admitted after the agreement, selected in 1969, had far more black students than any previous class. Of the 1,202 freshmen who enrolled at Harvard that fall, 90 were African Americans — a 76 percent increase over the 51 black freshmen in 1968.[188]

The next two years showed that 1969, far from being an aberration, marked the beginning of the institutionalization of blacks as a powerful interest group in the competition for slices of the admissions pie. Though there does not seem to have been a quota in the strict sense of the word, a target of at least 100 black admits seems to have been established.[189] In 1970, 108 blacks were admitted, of whom 98 chose to attend. The following year 109 blacks were accepted; 90 matriculated.[190] Though Harvard continued to deny that it had a quota, the African-American proportion of the freshman class leveled off at around 7 percent after 1968 — almost double the previous high.[191]

In honoring the agreement on black admissions that it had made in the tumultuous atmosphere of 1968, Harvard had little choice but to accord to African-American candidates the same special consideration previously re-served for groups such as alumni sons and athletes. In 1971 — a representative year — legacies and athletes were admitted at rates 2.3 and 2.1 times higher, respectively, than nonathletes and nonlegacies; blacks were admitted at a rate just 1.2 times higher than nonblacks.[192]

A more revealing measure, however, is the probability of admission once one controls for the academic rating given candidates. In 1971, of all the appli-cants rated 2 or 3 (on a scale of 1–5, with 1 as the highest), alumni sons and athletes were admitted at 2.2 and 2.8 times higher than their "unmarked" counterparts. From this perspective, the degree of preference accorded black candidates rated academic 2 or 3 — who were admitted at a rate 2.6 times higher than nonblack candidates — was slightly less than that given athletes but a bit more than that accorded legacies.[193]

As with other groups given special consideration, blacks had somewhat weaker academic credentials than average Harvard freshmen. But unlike many other preferential categories — notably legacies and graduates of lead-ing boarding schools — blacks came, on average, from families far less eco-nomically and culturally advantaged than most Harvard students.[194] In 1969, when the effort to recruit inner-city blacks was at its peak, as many as 40 per-cent of African-American freshmen came from lower-class backgrounds.[195] As at Yale and Princeton, the median SAT scores of black freshmen were lower than those for the class as a whole: 1,202 in 1969 compared to 1,385 for all entrants.[196] Yet admissions at Harvard had for some time been determined at least as much by nonacademic factors as academic ones, and black appli-cants — perhaps reflecting the fact that they generally had overcome more obstacles on the way to college than white candidates — received higher "per-sonal ratings" than whites. In 1971, for example, 30 percent of black candi-dates for admissions received personal ratings of 1 or 2 — a level reached by only 19 percent of nonblack applicants.[197]

Though Harvard worked hard to identify outstanding candidates, both black and white, whose exceptional personal strengths might compensate for relatively weak academic records, its efforts to reach out to disadvantaged stu-dents were not without complications. In a highly controversial 1973 article in the Harvard alumni magazine, Martin Kilson, one of the few tenured African Americans on the Harvard faculty, estimated that as many as 40 percent of black freshmen arrived in Cambridge with academic deficiencies. To prove his point, Kilson cited statistics showing that only 48 percent of black students made the Dean's List (ranks I–III) while 82 percent of their white classmates did so.[198]

But by the time Kilson's article appeared, Harvard was already moving away from its attempts to recruit blacks from the inner city and impoverished rural areas. According to the Office of Admission, roughly 75 to 80 percent of the blacks admitted in 1973 were *not* from disadvantaged backgrounds.[199] As early as 1970, Peterson noted, "We have learned . . . that we cannot accept the victims of social disaster however deserving of promise they once might have been, or however romantically or emotionally an advocate (or a society) might plead for him."[200] Having gone to the ghetto, Harvard quickly realized that blacks from relatively privileged backgrounds made the transition more easily than the working-class and poor blacks to what was still an overwhelmingly white institution.

Well ahead of its Big Three rivals in its openness to black students in 1960, by the decade's end Harvard had lost its advantage. Even before its retreat from its efforts to recruit inner-city blacks, Harvard had been characteristically cautious in its affirmative action policy lest it stray too far from its traditional practices. In 1970, Princeton achieved its highest percentage of blacks — 10.4 percent. Harvard, which had more distinguished black alumni than any other elite college, was just 8.1 percent black.[201] In the competition for the top African-American students, Yale, which had long trailed well behind Harvard, was closing the gap; indeed, in the competition for National Achievement Scholars, Yale enrolled 75 in 1970 compared to Harvard's 81 — a virtual tie. Given the smaller size of Yale's student body, it may very well have meant that Yale had forged ahead in Achievement Scholars per capita.[202] Harvard remained, by any standard, a popular choice among the most sought-after black students, but its status as the most racially diverse college in the Ivy League was by 1970 a relic of the past.

Race, Political Mobilization, and Institutional Change

Few changes in the history of Harvard, Yale, and Princeton have been more profound than those produced by the black struggle for racial justice in the 1960s. In a short decade, the Big Three had become exemplars of racial diversity by 1970, enrolling not only a critical mass of blacks but also growing numbers of Latinos, Native Americans, and Asian Americans. Invisible in 1960, blacks — and, increasingly, other minorities as well — were now "insiders," serving as members of the Admissions Committee and as student recruiters for colleges that had more and more come to consider racial diversity a critical component of institutional excellence.

How was it that African Americans — who constituted well under 1 percent of the student body in 1960 — came to take their place beside such privileged categories as legacies, graduates of top boarding schools, and athletes? The conventional explanation — that "a rising concern over civil rights" led the elite colleges to begin recruiting blacks — is true as far as it goes, for the civil rights movement did stimulate a deeper awareness of racial injustice among the men who ran the nation's leading colleges.[203] Nevertheless, as late as 1964 — a full decade after *Brown v. Board of Education* and nine years after the Montgomery bus boycott — the Big Three remained less than 2 percent black.[204] Clearly, the civil rights movement, morally compelling though it was, had not in and of itself been enough to fundamentally alter the admissions practices of Harvard, Yale, and Princeton.

What changed after 1964 was the growth of disruptive activity, both on and off campus. The watershed event was the Watts riot of 1965, but it was not until the uprisings in Newark and Detroit two years later that it became clear that Watts had foreshadowed an even greater breakdown in America's major cities. Then, in the spring of 1968, when more than a hundred cities broke out in riots after the assassination of Martin Luther King Jr., it seemed as if the entire nation was on the verge of unraveling.

Meanwhile, the New Left was also challenging the status quo on and off campus. By 1968, the opposition to the Vietnam War had become a genuine mass movement, and growing segments of it were adopting disruptive tactics. SDS, in particular, had a powerful presence on many campuses and focused increasingly on issues of racism and university complicity with the war.

Administrators at Harvard, Yale, and Princeton had struggled for a decade to admit a critical mass of black students. So when the black students mobilized in 1968 to fight for more admission slots for African Americans, they were not pushing in a different direction from the one that the Big Three had already embarked upon. Instead, they were simply demanding a bigger slice of the admissions pie — or so the men who ran these colleges could tell themselves. That, in contrast to some of the calls for revolutionary change coming from the predominantly white New Left, was a demand they could accommodate.[205]

There is little question that the mobilization of black students on campus was a major factor behind the sharp increases in black enrollment in 1968 and especially 1969. Yet the mobilization would not have had nearly as powerful an impact in the absence of the urban riots that preceded it. Indeed, it was Princeton, shaken by the riots in Newark and Plainfield in the summer of 1967, that moved first to transform its admissions practices toward African Americans.[206] Explaining in its annual report for 1967–1968 that "the events of last summer nationally, and the appeal of the National and State Commissions made it imperative that we move off . . . [the] plateau [of 15 or so black matriculants annually]," Princeton more than tripled the number of blacks in the entering class of 1968, enrolling a record 44.[207]

Though the terrifying wave of riots in the wake of Martin Luther King Jr.'s assassination took place too late to affect the freshman class that entered that fall, it did jolt the educational establishment. In 1969, the number of black admits at the Ivy League colleges surged a record 89 percent — a dramatic testimony to the power of the riots to alter established practices. Pressured by militant black students capitalizing on the momentum for change produced by the riots and the threat of further disorder, Harvard and Yale joined Princeton in altering their normal procedures in the search for more African Americans. The result was a 101 percent increase in black admits at Harvard and a 121 percent increase at Yale.[208] In the fall of 1969, 224 blacks matriculated at the Big Three — a remarkable 386 percent increase over the 58 who enrolled in 1964.[209] What the civil rights movement had been unable to accomplish — a fundamental alteration of racially neutral admissions practices that had the effect, if not the intent, of limiting black enrollment to token levels — the riots had made possible.

To accomplish their goal of rapidly increasing the number of black students, the Big Three had no choice but to modify the increasingly academic definition of merit that had come to predominate in the 1950s and 1960s. The dilemma facing them was embodied most visibly by rising SAT scores. At Harvard, for example, the median verbal SAT score had risen from 563 in 1952 to 697 in 1967.[210] But black SATs were on average a standard deviation lower than those of whites.[211] Clearly, if merit was to be defined by applicants' scores on the SAT, then blacks would be few in number at the Big Three.

But the conflict between "meritocracy" and what came to be known as "affirmative action" was in many ways more apparent than real. Harvard, Yale, and Princeton had never been pure academic meritocracies, and each of them had long given considerable weight to nonacademic qualities in admissions decisions. In the past, however, departures from purely academic criteria had generally served to further advantage the already privileged or to facilitate the admission of candidates who served institutional interests. What was new about the admission policies of the late 1960s was that special consideration was being deployed in a systematic and vigorous way on behalf of the historically excluded. In this specific sense, the institutionalization of preferential treatment for African Americans alongside other privileged categories was a genuinely historic change, for it marked a shift away from the logic of "social closure" toward one of social inclusion.[212]

In explaining why they were willing to take such a major step, the Big Three colleges made much of the notion of "diversity" and occasionally referred to the historical injustices visited upon African Americans. But the dominant theme in the texts of the period was neither diversity nor compensation for past injustices, but rather the need for "Negro leadership."[213]

Institutions such as Harvard, Yale, and Princeton had, of course, been in the business of training leaders for centuries, and there was little doubt at the time that more of the nation's future leaders would be African American than ever before. Yet what gave the call for Negro leadership its urgency was a sense that a fateful struggle for the soul of the nation's black population was being waged in the 1960s. On one side of this struggle stood the apostles of nonviolence and integration, led by Martin Luther King Jr.; on the other stood the proponents of violence and separatism — an increasingly influential current embodied by such diverse figures as Malcolm X and (later in the decade) Stokely Carmichael, H. Rap Brown, and Huey Newton.

As early as 1964, farsighted leaders such as Brewster saw what was at stake and decided to come down decisively on the side of nonviolence and integration. The awarding of an honorary doctorate to Dr. King that spring, despite fierce opposition from a segment of the alumni, was a powerful symbol of Yale's stance. In explaining his decision to an irate Old Blue from Georgia, Brewster made clear his worry that an increasingly restive black population might go down the wrong path: "King, like Wilkins,"[214] he wrote, "is violently opposed by the hoodlum wing of the colored spokesmanship and is looked upon as the one Negro leader whose opposition to violence has not lost him the following of the majority of the colored population."[215]

In committing themselves to substantially increasing black enrollment, the Big Three were demonstrating that they were serious about helping to construct a black leadership stratum in business, government, and the professions. But the black leaders that reformers like Brewster and Clark had in mind were to be "responsible" rather than "extreme" and to serve as bridges between the white establishment and the increasingly disaffected black population of the nation's ghettos. The construction of such a leadership stratum, they hoped, would serve to improve the collective condition of African Americans and to bring about racial justice. At the same time, the very existence of a visible black elite was also designed to strengthen both the stability and the legitimacy of an increasingly beleaguered social order. Geoffrey Kabaservice has put it well: "by expanding equality of educational opportunity, elite universities such as Yale would . . . act as a countermeasure to revolution by furthering social mobility and strengthening the case for change within the system."[216]

The changes in admission practices introduced in response to the demands of the black movement had profound and reverberating effects on the character of the Big Three. The most obvious of these was the incorporation of other "people of color"; with the doors opened to blacks, it was just a matter of time before other minorities, including Latinos, Native Americans, and Asian Americans, would mobilize and demand their share of the admissions pie.[217] At Yale, which had been a leader in the inclusion of nonblack minorities, Latinos, Native Americans, and Asian Americans together made up 7.4 percent of the freshman class in 1972; at Princeton, these same groups constituted 5 percent of the freshman class.[218] Harvard lagged behind its rivals in reporting statistics on nonblack minorities, but finally did so in 1976; that year, Latinos, Native Americans, and Asian Americans contributed 109 students (6.7 percent) to the freshman class.[219]

The most profound and far-reaching impact of the black struggle for racial justice was to delegitimize long-standing admissions practices that favored the privileged. In an atmosphere in which the claims of the excluded occupied the moral high ground, it became increasingly difficult to justify policies that favored WASPs over Jews, prep school students over high school students, and the affluent over those who needed scholarship assistance. With the notable exception of alumni sons, whom the Big Three deemed still essential to their vital institutional interests,[220] elite constituencies that had long been given preference in the admissions process saw their privileges considerably eroded in the 1960s.[221] At the same time, groups that had traditionally been discriminated against — Jews, graduates of public high schools, and scholarship applicants — came to be treated in a far more evenhanded fashion. Paradoxically, then, the black struggle for inclusion — often thought to be in fundamental conflict with the logic of meritocracy — contributed to the emergence of admissions policies at Harvard, Yale, and Princeton that were far more meritocratic in 1970 than in 1960.

The movements of the 1960s had been dedicated to the elimination of barriers. By the end of the decade, perhaps the most fundamental barrier of all — the one that excluded the female half of the population — had finally been breached. Yet at the beginning of the decade, the refusal by the nation's three most prestigious colleges to accept applications from women was so taken for granted that it was not even considered a form of discrimination. Clark, who presided over Yale's transformation in the late 1960s, offered a succinct explanation of why this age-old barrier had to go: "The real reason was that Yale's resources should be available to the most worthy, most desirable people in society: men, women, Blacks, whites, Christians, Jews, etc. . . . In other words, you can't go right up to the issue of coeducation and then take a different stance."[222] Yet however inevitable coeducation may look in retrospect, its adoption was the object of bitter controversy at the time. Just how bitter will become apparent as we turn to how and why Yale and Princeton finally came to admit women — and how they and Harvard ultimately came to admit students without regard to sex.

CHAPTER 14

Coeducation and the Struggle for Gender Equality

A S THE 1960S OPENED, there were few signs that it would be the decade that would finally bring coeducation to Yale and Princeton after more than two centuries of exclusion. While a civil rights movement dedicated to the emancipation of the nation's black population was gaining momentum by 1960, no comparable movement existed among women. An ideology of domesticity — the belief that women would find fulfillment in the home through marriage and motherhood — continued to hold sway, its power reinforced by the emphasis on tradition and "security" characteristic of the Cold War era.[1] Even highly educated young women generally adhered to traditional gender values; in 1961, a study of the aspirations of college seniors showed that most female students, while highly respectful of classmates who attained scholarly or scientific distinction, "themselves mostly wanted to be mothers of 'highly accomplished children' and wives of 'prominent' men."[2]

The situation in higher education was in some ways worse than it had been before World War II. In 1930, women constituted 43 percent of all undergraduates and 18 percent of doctoral recipients; in 1960, they made up 36 percent of undergraduates and 10 percent of doctoral recipients.[3] As the Kennedy administration began, the high-status professions continued to be male preserves; of students enrolled in law school in 1961, just 3.6 percent were women.[4] And at most of the elite undergraduate schools, the exclusion of women was still the norm, not only at Harvard, Yale, Princeton, Dartmouth, and Columbia, but also at Williams, Amherst, and Wesleyan (the "Little Ivies").[5]

Within what the Big Three called the "leadership stratum," women were virtually nonexistent. In C. Wright Mills's classic 1956 work, *The Power Elite,* the exclusion of women was so taken for granted that Mills — an outspoken radical but a product of his times on matters of gender — did not even mention their absence among corporate and military leaders.[6] President Kennedy's New Frontier cabinet had not a single female, and the Senate included just two: Maureen Newberger of Oregon, who had succeeded her late husband, and Maine's Margaret Chase Smith.[7] If the mission of Harvard, Yale, and Princeton was, as its top administrators insisted, to educate the next generation of America's leaders, the admission of women seemed a distraction from their main purpose.

Yet beneath the surface of a seemingly stable system of male domination, important changes were already in motion. Among the most significant was the growing female participation in the labor force. By 1960, 35 percent of women over the age of sixteen were working — 24 million people, almost a third of whom had children.[8] And more mothers of preschool children were working — 19 percent in 1960, up from 12 percent a decade earlier.[9]

This increase in female labor force participation reflected the growing need for white-collar employees in an emergent postindustrial society, but it was given added impetus by the imperatives of the Cold War. Like the push in the late 1950s for greater meritocracy among men, the Cold War provided an ideological rationale for greater equality of opportunity for women.[10] In 1957, the Eisenhower administration's Commission on Scientists and Engineers announced that "long established prejudices against women in engineering and science need to be broken down not only among employers, supervisors, and coworkers, but among women themselves."[11] That same year, the National Manpower Council, a Columbia University panel funded by the Ford Foundation, complained that "of all the young women capable of doing college work, only about one fourth graduate from college, and only one woman out of every three hundred capable of earning a Ph.D. degree actually does so."[12] The implication was clear: the loss of talent caused by discrimination against women in both the educational system and the labor market was a threat to national security that could no longer be tolerated.[13]

Though the forward-looking recommendations of the National Manpower Council — which included the expansion of public child care and maternity leave programs, which would provide both job security and income — did not evoke an immediate response, they entered the public domain when the extreme domesticity of the 1950s had reached its peak and soon began to decline.[14] After 1957, the age at which couples married began to rise and birthrates began to fall.[15] These changes accelerated after 1960, when the FDA approved the birth control pill. As Sarah Evans has pointed out, the pill's effect was to broaden "the possibilities of recreational sex, enjoyed for its own sake in contexts not linked to procreation or even domesticity."[16]

Yet for all the changes occurring in women's lives, the notion of separate male and female spheres remained deeply ingrained. Despite a barrage of articles in 1960 in such media mainstays as the *New York Times, Newsweek, Time, Redbook,* and *Harper's Bazaar* about the "trapped housewife," no alternative language or ideology existed to challenge traditional sex roles.[17] Meanwhile, Harvard, Yale, and Princeton remained bastions of male domination. Emblematic of the temper of the times was the speech delivered annually to incoming freshmen by Radcliffe's president, Wilbur K. Jordan; a Radcliffe education, he told them, would train them to be excellent wives and mothers and perhaps even to win the ultimate prize: marriage to a Harvard man.[18]

Yale: The Long Road to Coeducation

Apart from West Point and Annapolis, perhaps no American college was more assertively "male" in its reputation and self-image than Yale. Yale's identity was inextricably joined to the notion of the "Yale man" — that gentlemanly, athletic, intelligent (but not intellectual), competitive, and good-looking young man who gave the college its distinctive character. By 1950, women had begun to enroll (albeit in modest numbers) in Yale's graduate and professional schools, but their presence at Yale College remained unthinkable. Even the faculty, though ostensibly open to talented women, remained a male preserve; as late as 1961, the Yale College faculty did not include even one female full professor.[19] In 1966, the university's publicity office described attendance at Yale as an opportunity to learn what it is to "Be a Man" (the title of a film about Yale, released that year, by Murray Lerner).[20]

Nevertheless, the idea of admitting women to Yale College had been broached as far back as the spring of 1956. It was first raised by Thomas Mendenhall, an associate professor of history, at an alumni meeting in Milwaukee, where he reportedly mentioned that it was only a matter of time before Yale became coeducational. His casual remark found its way into the *New York Times,* and it did not elicit a warm reception from Old Elis. Mendenhall then distanced himself from his reported remarks, claiming that, in speculating about the future of Yale, he had merely indicated that he "wouldn't be surprised if Yale had a female admit some twenty-five years from now."

A far more serious controversy developed in the fall of 1956. On September 28, Arthur Howe Jr., the new dean of admissions, delivered a speech to the faculty advocating the admission of women to Yale College, arguing that it would raise the academic level of the student body, attract outstanding young students who preferred coeducational schools, and reduce the disintegration of the Yale community on weekends as students left to visit distant women's colleges. In defending his proposal, Howe also invoked the nation's "increasing need for professionally educated women and the advancing position of women in our present system."[21]

The alumni's response was swift and overwhelmingly negative. Looking back years later, Howe said, "It was hot news that this bastion of male dominance was going coed. You can imagine what happened at the President's office the next day, and the fundraisers, the alumni office, and the admissions office. The phones were ringing for days.[22] President Griswold issued a press release at once, insisting that the possibility of admitting women was "discussed on a purely theoretical basis," that Yale was "nowhere near deciding the question in principle," and that, in any case, "the possibility of putting any such policy into practice is even more remote."[23]

Sensing that the disclaimer had failed to stem the rising tide of publicity about the possibility of admitting women, Griswold issued a second press release the following day, stating that Yale was "far from being convinced that it [admitting women] would be the right course of action." "There is not the remotest possibility," it continued, "of its taking place at Yale in the foreseeable future." Even the dean of Yale College, William C. DeVane, was enlisted in the effort, despite his reported endorsement of Howe's recommendation. The possibility of coeducation, he said, was a "remote one" and "will continue to remain for some time in the realm of theory and opinion."[24]

Yale felt it had to distance itself so decisively from what was, after all, only a proposal because of the intensity of the alumni response — something that could not be ignored at a time that alumni contributions still constituted a far more significant source of revenue for Yale than federal funds. Griswold was not personally enthusiastic about coeducation; he was a product of the "Old Yale" and considered coeducation a threat to its traditional character.[25] But whatever his personal sentiments, Griswold could not be indifferent to the anger expressed by Old Elis, who were not beyond threatening to withdraw promised testamentary bequests.[26]

Though the storm of controversy provoked by Howe subsided relatively quickly, it foreshadowed many of the arguments against coeducation that would be made when the issue reemerged in the 1960s — for example, the claim that admitting women could reduce Yale's "prominence, influence and prestige."[27] What is most striking about the alumni response was its deeply visceral character. The coeducation proposal, wrote one Old Blue, was "horrendous news"; "the very thought of it," wrote another, "has made me miserable" and was the cause of the loss of "much sleep."[28]

Even the undergraduates opposed coeducation. They organized a Keep Yale Male campaign, and the *Daily News* expressed the fear that coeducation would "come down the chimney, like a plague," and lead to the "emasculation" of the college.[29]

Clearly, Howe's proposal was culturally and economically premature.[30] If proposals for coeducation were to be given serious consideration in the future, they would have to be put forward in a more favorable environment.

The hostile reaction to Howe's proposal quashed serious discussion of coeducation at Yale until the publication of the Doob Report in 1962. On the issue of women, the Doob Committee sounded the theme of "talent loss," which was central to Cold War arguments for equality of opportunity: "In the young women of the nation we have a huge supply of talent for which our educational institutions have insufficiently provided, and our country has imperfectly utilized. We think Yale has a national duty, as well as a duty to itself, to provide the rigorous training for women that we supply for men, and we recommend that the University keep in its view for ultimate adoption the entrance of women to the freshman class." But the report added two qualifications: "first, women should not be admitted on a token basis but as a substantial proportion of each class; secondly, there should be no reduction in the number of men admitted to Yale College."[31]

Despite its strong language, the report was not quite the ringing endorsement of coeducation that it seemed at first glance. For one thing, the proposal to admit women was placed in the category of a "long-range recommendation": what was elsewhere referred to as an "ultimate" (rather than an "immediate") recommendation.[32] Second, the insistence that the number of men at Yale College not be reduced meant that coeducation would have to wait until the money to finance expansion was available. Finally, as Leonard Doob himself admitted, the recommendation to admit women was included in good part to "deflect attention away from our recommendation concerning the Freshman Year."[33]

In addition to the predictable alumni protests, support for coeducation was notably lacking among the undergraduates.[34] In 1961, the proportion of Yalies saying that they would attend a coeducational school if they had it to do over again ranged from just 15 percent of freshmen to 40 percent of seniors.[35]

In April 1962, the month the Doob Report was released, another poll revealed that while many students supported a separate women's college strongly affiliated with Yale, they were mostly opposed to having women in the classroom.[36] The following year, a poll of freshmen found three-quarters opposed to coeducation. An unscientific survey conducted by the *Yale Daily News* found that antediluvian attitudes toward women were not uncommon.[37] While several students expressed support for coeducation (one going as far as to say "We shouldn't have to worry about the Yale tradition of 'manliness'"), others were bitterly opposed. A member of the sophomore class was concerned about Yale's reputation: "The image of the Yale man that has been so many years in the making of the highly sophisticated, intelligent, worldly, all-around stud . . . a female wouldn't fit into this"; another sophomore argued that standards would fall: "Girls are intellectually inferior to boys. The class intelligence would go down." And a freshman made the classical "distraction" argument: "With girls around here we would never get any work done . . . They would just be a pain in the neck."[38]

Yet within eighteen months, signs were visible that the tide was beginning to turn. Though sexist attitudes were still widespread among the undergraduates,[39] in October 1963 students staged a demonstration at Woodbridge Hall for the admission of women. Calling themselves the Lucinda Foote Committee — after a twelve-year-old girl who had been excluded from Yale in 1783 despite having passed the required exams in Latin and Greek — the protestors dubbed their demonstration a "March on New Haven for Equality in Ivy League Admissions."[40]

The new assertiveness among the undergraduates who favored coeducation was given added impetus by the civil rights movement. At a moment when blacks and their allies in the civil rights movement occupied the moral high ground in their struggle to dismantle the old ideology of "separate but equal," it was increasingly difficult to exclude people from educational opportunities purely on the basis of gender. At the same time, the prevailing ideology of meritocracy rendered the continued exclusion of women — who, by any standard, constituted a goodly proportion of the most brilliant students — more and more anomalous. Arthur Howe Jr., who had recently announced his resignation as dean of admissions, put the matter sharply in May 1964: "a great university such as Yale," he told alumni at a meeting in Philadelphia, "just cannot go on endlessly excluding half of the population."[41]

In the three years since the Doob Report's publication in 1962, Yale's landscape had been dramatically altered. Though the movement that came to be known as "second-wave" feminism was not yet visible, the situation of American women was obviously changing — a transformation that was marked by the appearance of the Report of the Presidential Commission on the Status of Women in 1963, the adoption by Congress of the Equal Pay Act of 1963, the publication of Betty Friedan's *The Feminine Mystique* that same year, and the passage of Title VII, barring discrimination on the basis of sex, in the Civil Rights Act of 1964.[42] Meanwhile, a mass movement to change America — which included the civil rights movement, the student movement, the antiwar movement, and the emergent counterculture — was beginning to transform the atmosphere on the nation's campuses. If the Doob Report had appeared in a climate still inauspicious for a change as profound as coeducation, the expectant atmosphere of the mid-1960s was a far more favorable one for reforms that challenged "tradition."

Still another factor conducive to coeducation was a subtle but important change in relations between the sexes in the first half of the 1960s. Referred to by *Newsweek* as "The Morals Revolution on the U.S. Campus," it irretrievably altered the texture of the relations between men and women.[43] Under the sexual regime of the 1950s, inequality between men and women was taken for granted; one consequence was that sexual relations between Yale undergraduates and "townies" and even prostitutes — relations that embodied this inequality — were not uncommon. But in the 1960s, such relations were much less acceptable.[44]

As the 1960s progressed, undergraduates found Yale's traditional pattern of male-female relations undergoing a radical change.[45] With the advent of "the pill" and more Yale undergraduates having sexual relations with their girlfriends, a growing number of students came to feel that what went on between them was none of the university's business.[46] A protest at Yale in November 1964 called for an end to "parietals," regulations that permitted women to visit students' rooms during a limited number of hours. Calling themselves the "Visiting Hours for Women Committee," the protesters called for unrestricted privileges and garnered 1,600 signatures on a petition they were circulating. In the winter of 1965, the Brewster administration expanded the range of visiting hours, but this did not solve the problem, for the rules still called for students to be dismissed if found with women in their rooms outside the designated hours. A compromise of sorts was reached — the rules would remain on the books while not being vigorously enforced — but it satisfied no one.[47]

Had all of these developments not been enough, Yale's decreasing competitiveness with Harvard might well have been sufficient in and of itself to put coeducation on the agenda. Once Harvard's equal in the competition for the students deemed most desirable, Yale had been falling behind its Cambridge rival since the mid-1950s. By 1965, Harvard lost only one admit in seven to other institutions, but Yale lost one in three.[48] Even more disturbing, Yale was losing 86 percent of students admitted to both institutions.[49]

Yale's own study in 1965 of admits who chose other institutions confirmed what Yale administrators had long suspected: its all-male character was a serious drawback. Of the 362 admits who replied, 110 and 104, respectively, listed "proximity to girls' colleges" and "coeducational undergraduate programs" as factors in their decision to turn down Yale. Of the 178 who chose Harvard, the proportion citing these factors was even higher, with 56 percent mentioning "proximity to girls' colleges" and 40 percent "coeducational undergraduate programs." An even larger proportion of those who chose Harvard — 76 percent — explained their choice as influenced by a "college community larger and more interesting." Yale could not move to a more cosmopolitan area, but it *could* admit women. If it wished to narrow the gap with its ancient rival — and with Harvard attracting as many Yale admits as the rest of the nation's colleges combined, this was an urgent priority — no measure held more promise than coeducation.[50]

Arthur Howe, who had resigned as dean of admissions shortly after Brewster took office, had long warned Yale of the handicaps that single-sex education imposed in the contest for the best students. At the 1956 meeting in which he proposed coeducation, he told the faculty that the all-male school was "harmful, academically and socially."[51] Having visited many coeducational colleges, he concluded: "The brightest and best in those schools all too frequently were not applying to Yale, and the reason given most frequently by students and counselors alike was our lack of coeducation. There was a feeling that coeducational institutions were more natural, more realistic, more progressive . . . It bothered me to lose strong prospects to what were often "lesser" places."[52]

His successor, Inky Clark, was every bit as committed to coeducation but faced far less opposition both on and off campus. Clark argued forcefully to Brewster that their shared ambition of putting Yale in the forefront of higher education was incompatible with its maintenance as a single-sex institution. In March 1966, Clark's first year in office, the Yale Corporation announced that it recognized "the need for high quality education for women" and was "interested in exploring how Yale might contribute to meeting this need beyond what it already does through its graduate and professional schools." But the Corporation explicitly stated that it "would prefer a 'coordinate college' approach rather than the expansion of Yale College to accommodate women" and attached two conditions to any future reform: it "would not favor admitting women if it required reducing the number of men in Yale College" (echoing the Doob Report) and "the addition of women would have to be underwritten by sufficient funds to maintain the quality of the University."[53]

While well short of a decision to approve coeducation, the announcement was historic. In January 1966, Yale embarked on an exploration of the possibilities of cooperation with Vassar, including "the desirability and possibility of relocating Vassar College in New Haven."[54] The appeal of the "coordinate college" model was clear: it would bring a partner with a considerable dowry in the form of its endowment; it would avoid the expansion of Yale College while importing women into the larger community; and — not least — it would help to neutralize the opposition of alumni and other important constituencies.

The proposed union with Vassar enjoyed Brewster's warm personal support. Not a supporter of full coeducation, Brewster nevertheless believed that Yale could not maintain its standing unless it brought women to New Haven.[55] His primary concern, as he remarked at a meeting of alumni, was "not so much what Yale can do for women but what women can do for Yale."[56]

Philosophically, Brewster believed that women were in many ways fundamentally different from men and that their needs would best be served by an education that acknowledged these differences. Their "ambitions and careers," he wrote, "may be quite different from [those of] most of the male students in Yale College," adding that even those "women of the highest intellectual capacity and interest may seek to make their vocational contribution through marriage, family, and community service on [a] vocational or part-time basis rather than by the pursuit of a full-time calling, academic or otherwise."[57] It was therefore a major disappointment to him when the talks about moving Vassar to New Haven collapsed, a victim of opposition by Vassar's alumnae and faculty as well as its trustees' realization that the proposed marriage would almost certainly be at the expense of Vassar's identity. On November 20, 1967, Vassar's trustees issued a brief statement that they had "decided the college should remain in its birthplace."[58]

Yet even before the breakdown of the negotiations with Vassar, there were signs that other segments of the Yale community were more supportive of full coeducation than Brewster. In October 1966, the Admissions Policy Advisory Board, chaired by Professor James Tobin, called on the Corporation to make coeducation "a high priority among plans for the university's future." Declaring, "In the context of contemporary America, the older system of separate education appears outmoded," the Tobin Committee noted that "many Yale undergraduates today find their lives confining, their seclusion unrealistic, and the rhythm of work and pleasure distractingly abrupt."[59]

Even the members of the Corporation, who had already expressed their preference for coordinate education in their initial announcement of March 1966, had grown more sympathetic to full coeducation than Brewster. Indeed, while Brewster was touting the proposed merger with Vassar, his closest advisers were apparently counseling against it.[60] Among the most farsighted members of the Corporation was a liberal corporate magnate, J. Irwin Miller. In a speech to alumni in June 1967, Miller contended that "Yale is a great place now precisely because it is changing radically and creatively in response to a wildly changing environment."[61] He noted the growing sentiment among young men "that says 'We want an educational experience that is somehow comparable to the experience in the world outside'" and warned that "the quality of admission to Yale and Princeton will undergo a long, slow decline unless there are women."[62] In the end, it was Corporation members like Miller who convinced Brewster to embrace full coeducation. As Brewster himself acknowledged: "I changed my mind . . . it was the trustees who led me, not vice versa."[63]

Even after the negotiations with Vassar collapsed, Brewster clung to the idea that there might be a way of enrolling women at Yale short of full coeducation. In May 1968, six months after Vassar rejected Yale's offer, his preferred alternative was a "cluster-coordinate" institution "consisting of three educationally separate women's divisions, whose organizing principle might be programs cutting across traditional departments, aiming for a broad sophistication in a cluster of disciplines rather than preparation for specialized or professional graduate work." Brewster hoped that reforming Yale in this way might "revive the humane spirit in the pursuit of liberal learning as an end in itself" — a task for which women were peculiarly suited since most of them were "out from under the shadow of professional or graduate ambition."[64]

But Brewster's sentiments were increasingly out of harmony with the times. The year 1968 was the apex of a period of upheaval punctuated by campus uprisings, ghetto revolts, huge antiwar demonstrations, and a burgeoning counterculture. In this environment, anything less than full coeducation seemed like a dubious compromise on an issue of fundamental principle: the ideal of equality of opportunity applied to women, too.

The growing number of students in favor of coeducation were quick to capitalize on the insurgent atmosphere of the period. In October, the Yale chapter of SDS explicitly rejected the coordinate model, insisting that "full coeducation . . . is the only acceptable answer."[65] Three weeks later, a group of 750 students marched to Brewster's home, demanding immediate coeducation.[66] Though the issue of how many women would be admitted does not seem to have been raised, an organization called the Coed Action Group was demanding the "admission of men and women in approximately equal numbers to each incoming class," with 500 women to enter in 1969.[67] SDS echoed this demand, proposing that "an even number of men and women . . . be admitted and housed on the present Old Campus."[68]

The demand for equal numbers reflected the impact of the nascent feminist movement. Invisible to the public just a year earlier, second-wave feminism burst onto the national scene after months of intense discussion — and conflict — within the New Left.[69] Limited at first primarily to a tiny group of women who had been active in the civil rights movement, by the fall of 1968 the woman's movement had become a presence on elite college campuses like Yale.[70] Though the movement had not yet produced the works — among them, Germaine Greer's *The Female Eunuch,* Robin Morgan's *Sisterhood Is Powerful,* and Kate Millet's *Sexual Politics* — that would contribute to the rise of feminist consciousness among millions of women, its elemental call for equality could not be ignored.[71]

In the end, the driving force behind the decision to embrace coeducation was the desire — shared by all Yale administrators, whatever their personal views — to preserve Yale's position at a time when a rapidly changing environment threatened to push it into decline. The most insistent voice was that of Inky Clark, whose office was most affected by Yale's refusal to accept

women. In his Report to the President for 1967–1968, written in the wake of
the failed merger with Vassar, Clark issued a forceful appeal for action:

> I would use the occasion of this Report to formally emphasize the need for ed-
> ucating a substantial number of women undergraduates at Yale. Though I
> have never, nor would never, advocate the education of women undergradu-
> ates primarily because it would assist the Admissions department in attracting
> the most able men undergraduates, there is no question but that we are handi-
> capped in our present position. In nationwide terms the yield from our ac-
> cepted group of applicants is high, yet it is not as high as it might be or should
> be. Further, while one might argue that certain applicants are attracted to Yale
> because it is male on the undergraduate level, my feeling is that this number
> is very small and that by and large we are not now seeing some applicants
> who would be extremely attractive to us, because of the present arrangement
> . . . Speaking strictly from an admissions standpoint, a decision to educate
> women at Yale . . . is not only desirable, but virtually essential.[72]

His subtext was unmistakable: unless Yale wished to fall even further behind
Harvard, it had no choice but to admit women.

A few months later, Clark again stressed the urgency of immediate action:
"Our department has a tremendous stake in what is going on in this area, for
obviously we are in competition with our rivals for top boys all over the
country, and the question of women at Yale is a factor. It becomes even more
of a factor as some institutions announce plans of one kind or another."[73]
This time the reference was clearly directed at Princeton.

In mid-September 1968, Princeton released a study with the rather un-
gainly title "Report on the Desirability and Feasibility of Princeton Entering into the Education of Women at the Undergraduate Level." Coming from
a committee chaired by Professor Gardner Patterson, an economist at the
Woodrow Wilson School, the report was a bombshell, for it unequivocally
endorsed full coeducation at a major competitor with an even more conservative reputation than Yale's.[74] Within days of its appearance, Brewster acknowledged the Patterson Report as "a most extensive and thoughtful and
impressive analysis and argument" about an institution whose similarities
with Yale were sufficient to make the study "very apposite." Giving it special
significance, Brewster noted, was that it offered an "analysis of the financial
picture and argumentation for and against varying degrees of coeducation as
against coordinate education . . . far more thorough than anything developed
at Yale," as well as a section that dealt "straightforwardly with the conjectures
about the effect of coeducation upon alumni and other financial support."[75]

The Patterson Report shifted the balance of forces at Yale decisively in favor of full coeducation. Princeton was not just another college; it was, after
Harvard, Yale's chief rival, and it was doing distressingly well in the competition for top students. Between 1965 and 1968, Yale lost more than 350 young

men to Princeton — 46 percent of all the applicants admitted to both institutions.[76] Already far behind Harvard, Yale was in imminent danger of falling behind Princeton too. The very possibility must have been almost too much to contemplate for the proud Old Blues of the Yale Corporation, and the decision to go coeducational was now virtually inevitable.

Just two months after Princeton released the Patterson Report, Yale announced that it would admit undergraduate women for the fall of 1969.[77] Brewster admitted that the decision was "somewhat precipitate" but maintained that it capitalized upon "a 'can do' mood of responsible optimism" among students, faculty, and administrators.

In truth, Princeton's announcement that it was moving toward coeducation left Yale with little choice. Brewster hinted as much in his announcement, noting that Yale's "sense of competitive rivalry was whetted by the public release of the Princeton Report." The statesmanlike Brewster was also forthright in acknowledging the moving force behind the decision: the belief that "coeducation would improve the quality of Yale College and Yale's ability to attract the students it most wants."[78] As Elga Wasserman, who served as special assistant to the president on the education of women, acknowledged, "In order to be able to continue to attract the top men, they had to take in women. They wanted to make Yale a better place for the men."[79]

Yale's ultimate goal, Brewster reported, was to enroll at least 1,500 undergraduate women while leaving the male enrollment at 4,000 — a ratio of 2.7 men for every woman. Opportunities to attend Yale would thus be extended to women but "without reducing the number of young men."[80] Though a quota on the number of women was a clear violation of the ideology of meritocracy, it was critical in defusing the opposition. Had the advocates of coeducation insisted in 1968 on redistributing rather than expanding the admissions pie, it is not at all clear that they would have prevailed.

The consequence of the decision not to reduce the number of men was that women faced higher standards in the competition for admission. In 1969, 22 percent of male candidates were accepted, compared to just 10 percent of their female counterparts.[81] The ability level of Yale women was correspondingly higher, and they consistently earned better grades than the men.[82] Yale held considerable appeal to young women, especially in the early years of coeducation, and the yield rate in 1969 was a healthy 80 percent.[83] Even more impressive, Yale outdrew Radcliffe among those students accepted by both institutions, with 60 of 95 choosing Yale.[84] The male yield rate rose as well, increasing to 66 percent in 1969 from 59 percent a year earlier.[85] If one of the primary purposes in accepting women was to improve Yale's position in the competition for the best students, the first years of coeducation were a striking success.

Yet it was not long before the obvious lack of equity in maintaining different and higher admission standards for women became an issue. Indeed, the first group of female undergraduates had not even arrived when Elga Wasserman put forward a far-reaching recommendation. "There should be no difference," she wrote, "in the criteria for admission and financial aid for men and women."[86] Though on the surface nothing more than an affirmation of the traditional American ideal of equal opportunity, it was a radical suggestion in the context of Yale in 1969. Putting it into effect would not be possible without a substantial reduction in the number of men admitted — the very change that Brewster had promised not to make when coeducation was announced.[87]

The committee received important support from the Office of Admissions. In an interview a few months before his departure, Clark advocated "a substantial increase in the number of women in Yale College — as soon as possible." "Ideally," he added, "the female quota should be abolished."[88] In his final Report to the President, Clark admitted that "the sheer ratio now existing means that the males taken in near the end of the process are not as strong as a number of women who must be rejected," and he argued for "equal opportunity for a Yale education" rather than the existing "predetermined ratio."[89]

At the same time, the emerging feminist movement on campus began to press for full equality. In the fall of 1969, Carol P. Christ, a teaching fellow in Religious Studies, wrote to Brewster and other members of the administration calling for the admission of an equal number of men and women.[90] The following spring Paula Johnson, an instructor in English who had served on the Admissions Committee, sent Brewster a letter accusing Yale of massive discrimination against female applicants. The policy of limiting the number of entering women resulted in the rejection of "outstanding young women" in favor of "less exciting" young men. Yale's quota, Johnson charged, "results in a crueler double standard than the simple exclusion of women ever did."[91]

Nevertheless, Yale moved slowly in increasing the number of women. In 1971, the number of female freshmen inched upward to 275 from 232 the previous year — still only 27 percent of the number of men.[92] Yale was a prisoner of its own commitments: it had promised not to reduce the number of men, but it could increase female enrollment only at the cost of overcrowding. The administration had assumed that the problem would be addressed by increasing the number of undergraduates, from 4,000 to 6,000, leaving a ratio of 2 men for every women.[93] But by 1971 the strategy had become doubly problematic: a growing segment of the community favored a ratio approximating 50–50 at the same time that opposition to expansion was rising.

In response, Brewster decided in April to appoint a faculty committee to study undergraduate education and to address the issue of the male-female ratio in the context of a plan about the ultimate size of the college.[94] The distinguished committee was headed by the renowned professor of political science Robert Dahl. In the two and a half years since the original decision to admit women, much had happened, not least the presence of a much larger bloc of women on the Yale campus who could press their own interests. But perhaps the greatest change was in the larger society, where feminism (then usually called "women's liberation") was becoming a mass movement and public attitudes were changing radically.

A marginal phenomenon when Yale adopted coeducation, the women's movement could be found in every major American city by 1971. "Consciousness-raising" groups had spread with astonishing speed to campuses and small towns alike, resulting in growing numbers of women who considered themselves feminists.[95] Feminist arguments were now a presence in the mass media, and the obvious justice of their cause — that women, too, deserved equal rights — was attracting converts from both parties.[96] In a reflection of the new national mood — and of the power of a constituency representing potentially half the population — both houses of Congress passed the Equal Rights Amendment (ERA) in 1972.[97] Particularly stunning was the magnitude of the victory: 354–23 in the House, 84–8 in the Senate. Within three days of the Senate's passage, six states had ratified the ERA, and by early 1973 twenty-four more had followed.[98]

Public opinion on women's issues changed rapidly, too. Between 1967 and 1972, for example, nationwide support for the employment of married women rose sharply, from 44 to 64 percent.[99] Among students at private universities, a parallel shift occurred; between 1967 and 1972, the proportion agreeing with the statement "The activities of married women are best confined to the home and family" fell from 46 to 27 percent.[100] Support nationwide for a qualified female candidate for president rose from 57 percent in 1967 to 66 percent in 1971 while the proportion of the population favoring large families dropped from 35 to 23 percent between 1966 and 1971.[101] Countless other examples could be cited, but the basic trend was clear: support for gender equality — and for policies that would advance it — surged between the late 1960s and the early 1970s.

At Yale, the most fundamental obstacle to reducing the number of men was the deep-seated belief that the university's most fundamental mission was to educate "leaders" and the taken-for-granted assumption that women were much less likely to attain this status. Even before Brewster had made the final decision to admit women, the issue of leadership and its implications for Yale's gender composition had come up in a confrontation between SDS and Henry Chauncey, Brewster's special assistant. In response to SDS's demand for immediate coeducation and a 50–50 percentage, Chauncey had said no. "I don't think that there's anything we're more committed to," he told the students gathered in his office, "as educating the number of males we presently do." The reason, he bluntly told them, was that "the society in which we live, rightly or wrongly — and I think wrongly — sees the men as the leaders."[102]

In truth, Yale's admissions policy — like those of Harvard and Princeton — had for some time embodied an uneasy compromise between two competing logics: an educated guess about who *would* be in the elite of the future and a determination about who *should* be in this elite. In the case of women, these two logics were on a clear collision course. Even those female applicants with outstanding "merit" — and hence who deserved admission if Yale was to be an authentic meritocracy — were less likely to become leaders than men with weaker qualifications, given the existing patterns of power in business and government.[103]

The first coeds had barely arrived in New Haven when feminists on campus raised the critical question: were female students also regarded by Yale as future leaders? Carol Christ posed the issue sharply: "Are women being educated to aid men in fulfilling these roles in society, or are women being educated to take these roles of leadership alongside men?" For Christ, the latter was "the only reason which . . . justifies admitting women to Yale," and she urged Brewster to exercise "the potential Yale has for influencing society to accept and to expect women to become its leaders."[104]

Brewster had claimed in his 1966 statement on admissions that "there are relatively few institutions whose education does conspicuously offer a special career advantage." On what grounds, then, were women to be denied this advantage? Moreover, the opportunity to attend Yale "must be convincingly open to free, competitive admission based on merit." This ethos had infused Yale's admission policy since the mid-1960s, and by 1972 it was taken for granted. Excluding people on grounds other than "merit" — and a gender quota seemed to do precisely that — had become increasingly indefensible. Whether women were, statistically, as likely as men to become leaders was not the point; what was relevant was that they were just as meritorious as men.[105] Treating them otherwise not only violated the principle of equal opportunity but also contributed to the perpetuation of the unjust system that kept them down.

By early 1972, even insiders were publicly making the argument that the continuation of the quota on women was incompatible with Yale's stated commitment to excellence. In a letter in the *Yale Alumni Magazine*, five veteran members of the Admissions Committee (four of them faculty) reported that "the present quotas" forced them repeatedly "to withhold admission from women who were more compelling candidates than some of the men we had admitted four hours earlier." Stating their demoralization at seeing "a quota system jeopardize the search for excellence" and their anguish in working "with a policy that conflicts with our highest hopes for Yale College," they warned, "To continue to offer women only the spaces available after filling the quota of 1,025 men and to deny admission to hundreds of Yale's strongest applicants is seriously to weaken Yale's commitment to coeducation and quality."[106] A few weeks later, a group of Yale students, faculty, and administrators calling itself the Ad Hoc Committee on Coeducation issued a report recommending that "the Yale Corporation adopt a policy of equal opportunity for admissions for women and men." Yale's chaplain, William Sloane Coffin, who had participated in the deliberations of the committee, endorsed its recommendation, noting, "The underlying assumption at Yale has been that it is not as important to educate women as it is to educate men." The report offered Yale "a marvelous opportunity" to "pioneer" sexual equality in its admissions policies.[107]

Although defending a gender quota was by this point ideologically hopeless — after all, who in 1972 would defend a quota limiting the number of Jews, public school graduates, or even students needing scholarship assistance? — Brewster was still moving cautiously. Stating that "to reduce the number of men in any context other than an overall reassessment of the Yale College would be to do exactly what we said in 1968 we would not do" and stressing the importance of "widespread alumni confidence in the reliability of our words and our intentions," Brewster insisted that a final decision on the issue of the sex ratio would have to await the deliberations of the Dahl Committee as well as those of a second study that would determine whether further expansion was feasible.[108] Offering nothing more in the short run than an increase of 50 women in the class that would enter in the fall of 1972, Brewster did promise to resolve the issue at the Corporation's November meeting. But he emphasized that it would not be acceptable "to have the decision made as a result of pressure — student or alumni — rather than as a matter of conviction."[109]

Whatever hopes Brewster may have harbored that expansion would permit him to keep the same number of men were dashed by the Dahl Committee, which concluded that "the college is as large as it can be . . . and the number of students in residence at Yale College should not be increased beyond the present 4800." On the issue of admissions, the committee was frank: "When a limited number of places are arbitrarily reserved for women in the freshmen class, admissions standards for women are more demanding than those for men. Many women are denied admission even though they are better qualified than some of the men admitted." The committee's solution was for Yale to honor the principle of equal opportunity that it had long avowed, recommending that "admission to Yale College should be granted on the basis of qualifications without regard to sex." Yet sex-blind admissions did not necessarily mean a 50–50 ratio; on the contrary, since national data (including statistics from the University of Chicago) suggested that more men tended to apply to selective private institutions, the committee announced its expectation that admission without regard to sex "would result in a student body of approximately 60 per cent men and 40 per cent women."[110]

After a series of meetings in the fall of 1972 by faculty, students, and alumni on the committee's recommendations and the future of coeducation, the matter of the quota on women finally came before the Corporation on December 9. After considering all the arguments, the Corporation voted to announce that "it is Yale's objective to admit students on their merits without setting numerical quotas for the number of men and women." Yet it also voted "to seek an increase in the number of women in the Class of 1977 by somewhere between one hundred and one hundred thirty" — a decision that still reflected the logic of a quota (albeit an expanded one). Compounding the sense that the Corporation had not left the idea of numerical targets behind was the statement that it expected "that the reduction in the number of men would be no less than ten percent, no larger than fifteen percent" — a feeling reinforced by its declaration that a majority of its members would favor an ultimate ratio "in the vicinity of sixty percent men and forty percent women." Even on the most important point — whether admissions should be genuinely sex-blind — the Corporation was equivocal: "We believe that the gender of the applicant should not be the deciding factor in a candidate's chance of admissions" — a formulation that left open the possibility that it could still be taken into account.[111]

The Corporation was nevertheless clear on three major points: Brewster's former commitment not to reduce the number of men no longer held, "students should be admitted to Yale College on the basis of their merit and potential," and "rigid quotas, minimums or ceilings described in terms of sex" were to be avoided.[112] The class admitted in 1973 reflected the transitional character of the policy, with the number of females at 451 (up 123 from the previous year) and the number of men at 862 (down 158).[113] Despite the consistency of these figures with the targets set by the Corporation, admission in 1973 seems to have been largely nondiscriminatory, with men and women accepted at 26 and 25 percent, respectively.[114]

By 1974, Yale had finally adopted genuinely sex-blind admissions. Just as the Dahl Committee had predicted (and the Corporation hoped), many fewer women applied to Yale, resulting in a freshman class that was still only 36 percent female. By 1979, however, with men no longer protected from competition with women, female enrollment had surged, reaching 46 percent. Coeducation, which had been approved in 1968 with assurances that it would not reduce the number of men, was now doing just that; indeed, a mere decade later, men had lost 334 places in the freshmen class — nearly a third of their enrollment in Yale's last years as an all-male institution.[115] Though sixteen more years would elapse before females constituted a majority of the entering students, Yale by the mid-1970s was — to the consternation of many an Old Blue — no longer the "Mother of Men" but a college where women increasingly shaped both its identity and its character.[116]

A Tiger, Not a Dinosaur: Princeton Goes Coeducational

Of all of America's research universities in 1960, Princeton was the last remaining male institution. Even Yale had 400 women in its graduate and professional schools as far back as 1956.[117] By the early 1960s, women made up about 20 percent of graduate students at the other Ivy League universities[118]; meanwhile, Princeton did not admit its first female graduate student until April 1961, when Sabra Follett Meservey, a graduate of Barnard with a M.A. from Columbia and the wife of a Princeton physics professor, was admitted to the program in Oriental Studies. Her admission, Dean Donald R. Hamilton hastened to assure the community, was a "special case." "Princeton," he announced, "may admit other women in the future as special cases, but does not plan to make general admissions of women graduate students."[119]

The undergraduates at Old Nassau were, in general, quite conservative, and until the mid-1960s they generated little pressure to admit women. Even during World War II, with enrollments plummeting as Princetonians joined the armed services, undergraduates did not welcome the matriculation of women even as special students acquiring skills to help the war effort. In 1942, when 23 women were permitted to enroll in a special mapmaking course taught by Professor Philip R. Kissam, the *Daily Princetonian* expressed its negative verdict sardonically: "But this is too much — that after 196 years of male seclusion behind these cloistered walls, Princeton's stern academy should be invaded by women . . . C'est la guerre. It has asked us for our energy and our rubber, but now it asks too much. The sanctuary of the monastic orders of bengals whose harsh cloth was worn by such pillars of masculinity as Aaron Burr and Light Horse Harry Lee has been blasted open to the painted Goddess of modernity . . . (A most unfortunate coincidence of nomenclature that Prof. Kissam should be placed in charge of instruction.)"[120]

Undergraduate women did not enroll again at Princeton until 1963, when five women attending other colleges were admitted to a "critical languages" program, developed during the Cold War to permit students to spend their junior year at Princeton studying such languages as Russian, Chinese, Japanese, and Arabic. The reception given the women was decidedly mixed. "It disgusts me to be in competition with girls," said one undergraduate. "If I'd wanted to compete I would have gone to Stanford." Not all students agreed; one told the *Daily Princetonian,* "I think this is a much needed reform in Princeton's attitude toward women, and I hope we will move faster in the future, to change the present ridiculous situation."[121]

By the mid-1960s, Princeton's capacity to attract the most sought after students was in visible decline. As at Yale, this trend was especially evident in competition with Harvard, where men and women attended classes together. In 1955, Harvard lost 85 students to Princeton; by 1965, the number had dropped to 32. Meanwhile, 124 students admitted to both Princeton and its Cambridge rival in 1965 chose Harvard — a ratio of almost 4 men to 1.[122] Overall, Harvard's yield rate in 1965 was 86 percent; Princeton's was a comparatively weak 68 percent.[123] Yet just ten years earlier, Princeton had enjoyed a slight edge in overall yield: 62 vs. 61 percent.[124] The conclusion seemed obvious: unless something was done, Princeton's standing on the highest rung of America's colleges could soon be a thing of the past.

The mid-1960s was also the moment when attitudes among Princeton undergraduates shifted strongly toward coeducation. In January 1965, the *Daily Princetonian,* editorializing in the immediate aftermath of a decision by the trustees not to extend visiting hours for women, described the undergraduate's experience at Princeton as "an unhealthy one which is based on a fundamental divorce between his intellectual and social lives." In a jibe clearly directed at President Goheen's remarks the previous month that "Princeton doesn't have any social problems that coeducation would cure," the editorial concluded by affirming that "coeducation is the solution for Princeton's social illness."[125]

If undergraduate opinion was shifting in favor of coeducation, the same could not be said of the administration. Despite the students' pleas, Goheen announced in February 1965 that "the University has no plans for coeducation." Backing off slightly from his earlier statement, however, he acknowledged that "coeducation would solve some problems," but "it would also create many."[126] When the *Daily Princetonian* pointedly offered the administration a $500 contribution toward coeducation, Goheen's response left little doubt about his lack of enthusiasm. "The university's first responsibility," he declared, "lies in educating men; taking in a thousand women would use up classroom seats that should be filled by men."[127]

By the spring of 1966, Princeton was aware that the Yale Corporation had announced the possibility of establishing a "coordinate" relationship with a woman's college and that a *Yale Daily News* poll of undergraduates had shown strong support for coeducation. When Yale publicly embarked on its efforts to bring Vassar College to New Haven in December 1966, Princeton grew alarmed that its closest rival might gain a competitive edge. An article by Michael W. Miles, an undergraduate, in the *Princeton Alumni Weekly* captured the growing panic: "Men in the Admissions Office, meanwhile, envision a serious threat to Princeton's competitive position among the Big Three; for, while Princeton has in the recent past attracted five out of every ten students admitted by both it and Yale, this ratio could change radically for the worse with both Yale and Harvard sold out to the suffragettes."[128] Reporting that "some thought that 'an undergraduate rebellion' was needed to move the University to action," Miles noted acerbically that "this was when only the quality of student life was affected by monasticism and before University prestige became a potential factor." And prestige, he observed, "has a magical appeal for policy-makers everywhere."[129]

Educated at Lawrenceville and Princeton, Goheen was once described by an administrator as "never a coeducationist at heart"[130]; he was, however, sensitive to the changes taking place around him — and to Princeton's interests. With his own new provost (and future Princeton president) William Bowen privately telling him that "the all-male Princeton cannot be, it cannot last"[131] and with students protesting Princeton's stubborn refusal to admit women, Goheen began to quietly reconsider his position.[132] At a trustees' meeting in January 1967, he noted Yale's merger talks with Vassar and confidentially acknowledged that "Princeton in a few years might find itself the only major university not significantly engaged in the education of women" and therefore in a position of increasing competitive disadvantage.[133] In February, Goheen began ill-fated secret talks with Sarah Lawrence College, in Bronxville, New York, about a possible merger, and in March he received a confidential faculty report on the perennial Princeton issue of eating clubs that explicitly recommended coeducation.[134] That same month a student group favoring the admission of women distributed a poll answered by 1,400 students; responses reportedly ran 95 percent in favor of coeducation.[135] Later that spring, a slate of students favoring coeducation swept the undergraduate elections.[136]

Sensing that the ground was shifting under him, Goheen changed positions, telling a reporter from the *Daily Princetonian* in May 1967, "It is inevitable that, at some point in the future, Princeton is going to move into the education of women. . . . The only questions now," he added, "are those of strategy, priority, and timing."[137]

Though Goheen claimed that he had thought the interview was "off the record" and its publication the product of an "overly zealous" reporter, he had intended to bring the matter before the trustees for some time. On June 12, 1967, after apologizing to the trustees for the story and for a recent *New*

York Times article on the failed merger with Sarah Lawrence, he reported that he had come to favor coeducation. His first reason was the critical one — admitting women, he said, would help admissions. Noting that Yale, Williams, and Wesleyan were all actively considering coeducation, he shared with the trustees a letter from William L. Pressley '31, president of the Westminster Schools of Atlanta. Princeton's all-male character, Pressley told Goheen, was the reason that no one from his school would be attending Princeton that fall. Goheen cited two other reasons for the admission of women: their presence would "add to the intellectual and cultural life of the university" and "the more extensive and active role of women in the modern world." "Can one think of an all-male Princeton twenty years hence and see it as other than anachronistic?" The answer, he told the trustees, "must be 'No.'"[138]

A couple of weeks before the June 12 trustees' meeting, Goheen had written to Gardner Patterson, a professor of economics and former director of the Woodrow Wilson School, asking him to lead a committee to study the desirability and feasibility of admitting women. Though the invitation hit Patterson, he later recounted, "like a bolt out of the blue," he accepted Goheen's offer, asking only that the committee "include at least one skeptic, but no cynics please." Telling the trustees that "a University with so profound a sense of obligation to the world can no longer . . . ignore the educational needs of one half the human race," Goheen formally asked the trustees for permission to have Patterson conduct the study. As expected, the trustees agreed, but with one proviso: Patterson was to study "both the pros and cons" of coeducation.[139]

Though Patterson, a Midwesterner who had attended the coeducational University of Michigan as an undergraduate, claimed that he was initially undecided about coeducation and probably would have answered a poll about the issue in the negative (after all, "Princeton was doing all right — why change it?"), it did not take him long to conclude that the admission of women was both desirable and feasible.[140] During the fall, the committee conducted polls of the faculty and students that showed strong support for coeducation: 91 and 82 percent, respectively. Particularly revealing was the students' answer to the question "If Princeton were to remain all-male, would you advise an academically qualified younger brother to accept admission?" Fifty percent of Princeton's juniors and 56 percent of seniors answered no — a devastating indictment of the status quo.[141]

In January 1968, Patterson gave an oral progress report to the trustees, the content of which was published a few weeks later in the *Princeton Alumni Weekly*. Though a prefatory note by Goheen insisted that "no commitments have been made or decisions reached" and Patterson himself described the committee as "still very much in the middle of its investigation," the direction of Patterson's thought was clear. On the critical question of the effects of the admission of women "on the quality and quantity of male applicants," he reported that preliminary evidence suggested that "Princeton's attractiveness for men would increase for quite a few, would not be changed for some, and would decrease for virtually none."[142]

Patterson did not hesitate to raise a number of troubling questions: "What would Princeton be missing, if anything, by having nothing to do with the education of a sector of the population whose role in society is changing toward greater participation outside the home? Is there a basic problem of discrimination with which a national institution must concern itself?" Finally, given that "it seems quite likely that . . . before long it [Princeton] will be the only major all-male university in the land," Patterson asked a disconcerting question: "If this were to become one of the most distinguishing characteristics of Princeton, would it be much more difficult to remain in the forefront?"[143]

In the six months between Patterson's interim report to the trustees and the committee's final report in July 1968, compelling additional evidence accumulated in favor of coeducation. Perhaps the most powerful new piece of information came from a February poll sent out to over 4,600 secondary school seniors at "superior" public and private schools. Disguised as a sampling of student opinions on a variety of issues, the poll never mentioned Princeton. Some 78 percent of the respondents favored coeducation and 5 percent preferred single-sex institutions. Among men in the top two-fifths of their class, support for coeducation was even more decisive, with 81 percent saying it would make a school more attractive and 3 percent saying it would make it less attractive (15 percent said it would make no difference; 1 percent had no opinion).[144]

During these months, the Admissions Office was forcefully pressing its position in favor of coeducation. In a letter to Provost (and committee member) William Bowen, Director of Admission John T. Osander wrote: "I feel very strongly that there is no single step the University could take that would increase our recruiting potential more than the addition of women students."[145] Princeton's image, Osander realized, had become a serious problem in recruiting top students.[146] Admitting women would be just the kind of dramatic reform (along with the vigorous recruiting of blacks) that would help counteract this image.

Of the Ivy League colleges, Princeton alone suffered a drop in the number of applicants in 1968: down 3.5 percent in a year when increases at the other schools ranged from 3 to 12 percent.[147] Between 1965 and 1968, Osander reported, only Princeton and Dartmouth — the two Ivies that were small and rural, as well as restricted to men — had witnessed application increases of less than 1 percent while applications rose 18 percent at Columbia and 13 percent at Harvard. Furthermore, Princeton's competitive position was declining; of the 154 students admitted to both Princeton and Harvard, 132 chose Harvard.[148]

In polling Princeton's various constituencies, Patterson was careful not to poll all alumni on the grounds that such a poll would be "meaningless unless the alumni had the facts, and they couldn't have the facts until they read his report."[149] Important trustees reinforced his resistance; the reason, according to the *Daily Princetonian* reporter who studied the decision to admit women in meticulous detail, was that "they didn't want their hands tied by an alumni vote." Instead, Princeton polled two alumni subgroups deemed by Patterson as having "something to contribute" (and even they were in good part a response to pressure): those in educational occupations and those on the Alumni Schools Committee. As expected, alumni working in the field of education were relatively supportive of coeducation, with 69 percent in favor of admitting women "if feasible" and 59 percent saying that coeducation would make them "more enthusiastic about sending a son to Princeton." But the Alumni Schools Committeemen — a key constituency directly involved in recruiting and interviewing applicants — was far more skeptical; only 34 percent favored coeducation even "if feasible."[150] Their opposition, though not highlighted in the Patterson Report, in fact reflected the sentiments of a substantial proportion of alumni — sentiments that led to an open revolt by a segment of the alumni in 1969.[151]

The depth of opposition to coeducation among many alumni (especially the older ones) was apparent from a torrent of letters received by the Patterson Committee. Serving as the lightning rod for the opposition was the committee's Arthur J. Horton, who forwarded many of the letters to Patterson.[152] These alumni opposed coeducation on many grounds, but among the most common arguments were that women do not use their education as profitably as men later in life, that coeducation would mean the loss of the camaraderie of an all-male atmosphere, that expansion would be detrimental to the university, and, not least, that the decline in alumni loyalty that would result would lead to a decline in annual giving.

A sampling of the letters reveals the tenor of the opposition:

> By the nature of our fundamental social system, the percentage of women who use their educations outside the home is low, even at the professional school level . . . insofar as the goal of the university is to place its chosen in positions and careers of responsibility, its productivity is many times greater if it sticks to the education of men . . .[153]

> Our world today is much separated by sex. Look at the business world and the housewife world. Sure we have women in industry, but there is a barrier . . . To me a male institution builds up a little greater Spartan personality. When

things become tough, when we fail to make the grade, we have to live alone with it. This builds character.[154]

The coed intellect that Princeton would like to attract might be found, on the average, to be too bookish to be a good date for the Princeton man.[155]

Those who took the trouble to write letters were, of course, among the most vocal opponents of coeducation, but they may well have reflected a majority of the alumni; a poll taken in April and May 1969 found that 55 percent of over 18,000 respondents were opposed to the admission of women.[156]

Patterson was well aware of the strength of the alumni opposition, but he did not allow it to prevent him from advocating coeducation in his magisterial 288-page report, "The Education of Women at Princeton," which he delivered to the Board of Trustees on July 12, 1968. The report, summarized in a 52-page version in the *Princeton Alumni Weekly*, argued that women would improve the intellectual, cultural, and social atmosphere of the campus and that coeducation would expand opportunities for Princeton to serve the nation. Its principal argument, however, was that it was essential for Princeton to become "increasingly attractive to the best men applicants" and that admitting women would "appreciably increase that attractiveness."[157]

As befit an economist, Patterson was especially worried about Princeton's declining "market share" in its battle with its chief competitors, Harvard and Yale. But there was also a purely financial element in his concerns. He candidly noted that while "Princeton does not, of course, demand that all students pay the full charges," nevertheless, "many must if the present scholarship funds are to be adequate." Drawing on Humphrey Doermann's research at Harvard, Patterson noted that the pool of men with SAT verbal scores of 650 or better and family incomes of $16,000 or more (roughly what was needed to cover Princeton's expenses) was just 6,000 students nationwide.[158] The implications of this finding were alarming, for it meant — as Conant had discovered thirty years earlier — that the pool of students who were both smart (at least as measured by SATs) and rich was distressingly small. Admitting women, Patterson knew, would not only make Princeton more attractive to the most desirable young men; it would also double the size of the pool of high-scoring applicants who could pay their own way.

Patterson was not about to be deterred by loyal but (in his view) ill-informed alumni. Still, in the course of the report he answered all of their major criticisms. The *Daily Princetonian* succinctly summarized the substance of his response:

Yes, coeducation might destroy "male camaraderie," but it would increase pride in Princeton as a leading institution. Yes, a larger university would not be as intimate, but much of Princeton's intimacy was lost after World War II, and expansion would not depersonalize the socially diverse campus. Yes, women in the classroom might distract a small percentage of men, but time wasted on numerous weekend road-trips would be saved.

Yes, it might be important for the United States to have an all-male university, but it was just as important for Princeton to admit women if it wanted to keep its status as a leading educational institution. Yes, men "use" their education more, but participation in the labor force by women is increasing. Yes, Princeton will change drastically from the university the Class of 1940 knew, but not much more drastically than it had already changed since 1920.[159]

Though Arthur Horton publicly disagreed with Patterson's conclusion, even he commended the quality of the report.[160] The other eight members of the committee unequivocally endorsed Patterson's findings and recommendations: "We urge the university to make an affirmative decision on a program for the education of women," they wrote, and to "do this as quickly as possible."[161]

It seemed only a matter of time before Princeton would end its all-male tradition. But doing so, its leadership realized, was a momentous matter, and it was important to try to bring along those members of the "Princeton family" still opposed. The trustees moved deliberately, announcing in mid-September that they had received the Patterson Report and would appoint a special committee to study it.[162] At Goheen's request, the chair would be Harold H. Helm '20, a Princeton trustee for twenty-one years, chairman of the trustees' Finance Committee, and former chairman of the Chemical Bank–New York Trust Company.[163] Since Helm's first disposition on the matter of coeducation was mildly negative, Goheen realized that gaining his support would be crucial in convincing the full Board. Serving as vice chairman was Laurence S. Rockefeller '32, a strong advocate of coeducation who, it was rumored, had secretly committed $4 million for the admission of women as far back as 1967.[164]

Having moved to neutralize potential opposition on the Board of Trustees, Goheen also tried to coopt the alumni through a series of meetings in twenty-six cities around the country where William Lippincott '41, executive director of the Alumni Council, would try to "sell" the idea of coeducation. Goheen himself attended six of these meetings and found more or less what he expected: a considerable number of alumni who strongly opposed the admission of women, a group of roughly equal size who supported it, and a broad group in the middle. Whether Goheen succeeded in altering alumni opinion, no one could claim that he had not made a good-faith effort to listen to their views.[165]

In late September 1968, the Undergraduate Assembly endorsed coeducation, 46–2, and a week later the faculty approved the Patterson Report with only a handful of voices in opposition. But the final blow to the opposition came in mid-November, when Yale announced that it was going coeducational and that women would be admitted for the fall of 1969. Sure enough, within days of Yale's announcement, news was leaked that Princeton's trustees had a "contingency" plan for the admission of women in the fall of 1969 and might formally approve coeducation as early as January.[166]

The pressure to move — and to move quickly — to admit women was quickly becoming unstoppable. Having made a concerted attempt to change its conservative, "preppie" image through the admission of blacks and a larger number of public school graduates, Princeton was now at risk of becoming an anachronism. Indeed, the likelihood that the men's college was destined to become a "dinosaur or dodo, irrelevant to the interests of modern life" was the theme of an editorial by John Davies '41 in the *Princeton Alumni Weekly*, the first it had published in fourteen years — a sign, it said, of "the urgency of the issue." Citing the opinion of "a seasoned observer of the Princeton scene," Davies argued that "a Princeton without girls in the 1970's would be an anachronism, in the 1980's ludicrous. . . . For any friend of Princeton to oppose coeducation is the equivalent of a Ford Motor Company director advocating, 'Let's Bring Back the Edsel.'"[167]

On January 11, 1969, the trustees announced that they had "approved in principle the University undertaking the education of women at the undergraduate level."[168] By a vote of 24–8, the Board had made what it called "the largest single decision that has faced Princeton in this century." In explaining his decision, the chairman of the Special Trustees Committee on the Education of Women, Harold Helm, pointed to "the strong recommendation made by the faculty . . . and the unqualified belief in it of the administration." Yet fully a quarter of the Board members voting (four members were absent) refused to approve coeducation even "in principle."[169] This was in striking contrast to Yale, where the Corporation's vote just two months earlier had been unanimous.

It was still unclear exactly when Princeton would admit women. At a press conference on January 13, Goheen said it was unlikely to be in 1969 "because of the problems of facilities and financing."[170] But he soon changed his mind. Five distinguished women representing five major institutions — Radcliffe, Stanford, UCLA, Sarah Lawrence, and the University of Chicago — unanimously advised that Princeton admit women that fall if at all possible and that it adopt full coeducation rather than a coordinate arrangement. "Don't settle for building the kind of thing that we are trying to escape from," Radcliffe's president Mary Bunting advised Goheen — powerful testimony to Radcliffe's feelings of inequality in its mixed coordinate-coeducational relationship with Harvard.[171]

Bunting's advice was reinforced in March when a special faculty-administration-student committee on the implementation of the trustees' decision, including Goheen, Patterson, Bowen, and the future Harvard president Neil L. Rudenstine '56, came out firmly in favor of coeducation, citing both educational and financial considerations. The committee's report systematically analyzed the costs and benefits of five distinct models of the education of undergraduate women. Rejecting the models of Barnard, Radcliffe, and Pembroke, none of which was fully coeducational in both instruction and residence, the committee embraced the model embodied by Stanford, which avoided "any connotation of 'segregation' and thus is attractive on grounds of principle to those who believe that it is important that men and women students learn how to know each other simply as 'people.'" Another advantage of "Model 4" was that its "operating and capital costs would be less than the corresponding costs of any of the other models."[172]

In embracing this model, the committee was aware that it was going further in integrating women than many alumni thought appropriate. Admitting that it was hard "to estimate the extent, seriousness, and duration of possible alumni antipathy to Model 4," the committee predicted that its adoption would require at the very least "a greater effort to explain the University's position." Yet in endorsing the Stanford model, a central factor of which was "an established ratio of women to men students" (30 percent women, 70 percent men, in the case of Stanford), the committee had self-consciously rejected "Model 5" — with sex-blind admissions, the only one that would "satisfy individuals who are opposed to any discrimination against women students."[173]

Followed by many major state universities, Model 5 had "no established ratio of women to men students," but it was rejected because it would mean "a significant reduction in the absolute number of men students admitted." True, Model 5 was the only model that "treats all applicants equally" and had "much to be said for it in terms of general principle." But general principle, the committee concluded, would have to give way in this case to the protection of institutional interests. A reduction in the number of male undergraduates was likely to trigger "an adverse reaction from some alumni . . . especially in view of the repeated assurances to the contrary which have been given."[174] Still in need of private contributions, Princeton — like Yale — did not want to unduly offend its alumni. The solution, as at Yale, was to keep male enrollments level by protecting male applicants from direct competition with women.

Anticipating that the trustees might still decide to admit women in 1969, the Admissions Office had begun to accept applications from women in February, carefully suggesting to potential candidates that "you file forms only if you realize that we may not be able to consider your application."[175] Meanwhile, Yale was already examining almost 3,000 applications from women, some of whom would be accepted that spring. Finally, on April 19 — just days after Yale had sent out letters of acceptance to its first women — the trustees made the decision: for the first time in Princeton's 223-year history, women would be admitted as undergraduates. But the undergraduate male enrollment of 3,200 was not to be reduced and the number of women would be modest — just 90 or so freshmen that fall and a "first plateau" of 650 coeds by the 1973–1974 academic year.[176]

Coeducation did not enable Princeton to overtake Harvard or Yale, but it did (as Patterson had predicted) lead to an increase in the quantity and quality of applicants. Between 1968 and 1970, the number of male candidates for admission increased 15 percent. At the same time, Princeton had an entirely new pool of talented applicants to pick from — more than 2,000 women by 1970. Moreover, the arrival of women coincided with gains in head-to-head competition with Harvard; in 1970, 46 men admitted to Harvard chose to enroll at Princeton — more than twice the number taken from Harvard in 1968, though 77 percent of the students admitted to both institutions still preferred Harvard (down from 86 percent in 1968). Yet as Princeton narrowed the gap with Harvard, it actually fell further behind Yale, which had moved more quickly to increase female enrollment. In 1970, when the second group of freshmen women arrived at both Princeton and Yale, Old Nassau was the choice of only 34 percent of the students accepted by both colleges — a decline from 45 percent in 1968.[177]

Princeton was now coeducational, but discrimination was still embedded in the admissions process. Committed to not reducing the number of men and allowing only modest expansion, it had little choice but to hold the women who applied to higher standards. In 1970, with a "fixed ratio" of 4 men for every woman, this meant that only 14 percent of the female applicants were accepted, compared to 22 percent of the men. Had women been accepted at the same rate as men, it would have meant 168 extra letters of admission, with over 100 of these women likely to enroll.[178]

The result of the fixed ratio was that the women who were admitted to Princeton were even more elite both academically and socially than their male classmates. This was not the intention of those who set the quota on women, but rather a natural consequence of a policy whose extreme selectivity meant that women with exceptionally high levels of capital — cultural, economic, and social — were the most likely to meet the exacting admission standards.[179] Thus, in 1970, over half of the freshmen women had fathers with a graduate degree; among men, the proportion was just over a third. Similarly, over 60 percent of the women came from families with incomes over $20,000; among men, the figure was 49 percent. And while 30 percent of the women had fathers who were physicians, lawyers, and college professors, the figure for men was just 16 percent.[180]

While the degree of male advantage in the admissions process declined in 1971 and 1972, the continued unequal treatment of female applicants was becoming less acceptable both at Princeton and in the larger society. Timothy Callard, the new director of admission,[181] though pleased at the number of "applications from outstanding candidates who, in the past, would not have even considered Princeton because of its former all-male, upper-class, white-Anglo-Saxon-Protestant image," was uneasy about the fact that "the competition for women remained somewhat stiffer than that for men."[182] Expressing his preference for a sex-blind admission process, Callard noted that an increase in the number of female applicants would make it "extremely difficult not to discriminate against women and still try to enroll a class of 800 men and only 300 women."[183]

The issue of whether Princeton could continue to have a quota on women had almost been settled by Congress's passage of Title IX, banning discrimination on the basis of sex at any higher education institution receiving federal assistance. But an amendment to the Higher Education Act of 1972 that would have withdrawn federal assistance from any private college that discriminated against women in admissions, submitted by Representative Edith Green (Democrat, Oregon), was narrowly defeated.[184] Though institutions like Princeton thus still could continue to treat female applicants differently, the political climate was clearly changing.[185] Should Princeton fail to adopt sex-blind admissions, it might soon find itself forced to do so by congressional edict — an unappealing prospect indeed for Princeton's new administration, headed by William Bowen, who had succeeded President Goheen in 1972.[186] By 1973, those in charge realized that quotas on women had become untenable politically, ideologically, and perhaps even legally.[187] The "concept of treating men and women equally," the Report of the Commission on the Future of the College observed, "has established itself powerfully in the past three or four years . . . Many people now feel — and we share this view — that a policy of quotas by sex, however justifiably applied up to now, is intrinsically undesirable."[188]

With Yale having already adopted sex-blind admissions, the days of quotas at Princeton were clearly numbered. Apart from the possibility that the "Green Amendment" would be passed, there was a serious case that discriminatory admissions policies were illegal under *existing* law because they violated the "equal protection" clause of the Fourteenth Amendment.[189] Supporting the argument that sex-based quotas were illegal was a recent New Jersey court decision, which added the category of sex to the existing antidiscrimination law.[190] While the legal situation was far from settled, prudence dictated — and Princeton was by any standard a prudent institution — the elimination of an admissions policy that discriminated on the basis of sex as soon as possible.[191]

On January 19, 1974 — nine months after the publication of the Report of the Commission on the Future of Yale College and thirteen months after Yale had abandoned its quota — Princeton's trustees announced that, effective immediately, the university would adopt sex-blind admissions. Citing the very real possibility that Princeton's practices could be judged illegal, the trustees took the high ground in explaining why they had rejected any legal challenge that might permit them to maintain the status quo: "We would not want to be in the position of arguing in the courts for a principle — the maintenance of quotas based on sex — in which we do not believe."[192] They noted that the new policy did imply a modest reduction in the number of men: perhaps 40 to 70 a year.[193] In the end, the drop in the number of men proved even smaller than predicted: during the five years between 1974 and 1978, an average of 762 men matriculated annually — just 34 fewer than during the last two years of the quota.[194]

By 1974, just five years after it had admitted its first group of women, Princeton had a higher proportion of women than Harvard in the freshmen class. So, too, did Yale; its freshman class was 36 percent female, compared to 30 percent at Harvard and Radcliffe.[195] Long the only member of the Big Three that admitted women, Harvard had fallen behind its rivals. That it would respond to the changed situation was a given; the only questions were when and how.

A Challenge for Harvard

Founded in 1879 as a "sister" institution to Harvard, Radcliffe was the weak younger sibling. Plagued by a modest endowment and lacking its own faculty, it suffered at times from indifference and even disdain from the Harvard administration; during the Depression, Lowell hinted more than once that Radcliffe was a burden on the university. But under the pressure of World War II, which deprived Harvard of most of its students, the schools grew closer, and in 1943 Radcliffe students attended classes with their Harvard peers for the first time. Yet the institutions maintained separate administrations; in Conant's memorable phrase, "Harvard was not coeducational in theory, only in practice."[196]

Throughout the postwar years, Harvard and Radcliffe continued to have separate admissions offices, and it was not until 1963 that Radcliffe women were awarded Harvard degrees.[197] During the mid-1960s, just as Yale and Princeton were beginning to consider the possibility of admitting women,

Radcliffe and Harvard began a process of exploring the idea of incorporating Radcliffe within Harvard, much as Pembroke had been incorporated within Brown. But the talks foundered on Radcliffe's unwillingness to be absorbed by the Harvard administration and by Harvard's disinclination to absorb Radcliffe's growing deficit. According to Radcliffe's president, Mary Bunting, her Board of Trustees felt that it had not had sufficient time to consider all of the ramifications of a possible merger — a sign that it probably "wasn't yet time."[198]

But by 1969 the landscape had changed: both Princeton and Yale had become coeducational. In what could hardly have been a coincidence of timing, the Radcliffe trustees voted in February to begin discussions about a merger with Harvard.[199] Radcliffe's concerns that Yale and Princeton's decision would weaken their competitive position were confirmed that spring, when 60 Radcliffe admits chose to attend Yale and 13 to attend Princeton.[200] Perhaps of even greater significance, Harvard, too, was losing more students to Yale and Princeton: 64 and 28, respectively, in 1969, compared to 40 and 20 in 1968.[201] By 1970, Harvard's overall yield rate, which stood at 86 percent in 1967 and 1968, had dropped to 78 percent — its lowest level in more than a decade.[202]

Yet Harvard was slow to respond to the new situation. Though the distance separating it from its rivals had narrowed, it was deeply reluctant to alter a system whose summit it had long occupied. This resistance was particularly manifest in a study of the Harvard-Radcliffe relationship chaired by Dean of Admissions Chase N. Peterson.

Completed in January 1970, the Peterson Report was a spirited defense of the status quo.[203] Its essential argument was that Harvard faced an admissions "trilemma": it could increase the size of Harvard and Radcliffe by 60 percent (from 6,000 to 9,600, enrolling an equal number of men and women), decrease male enrollment by 40 percent, or maintain the existing male-female ratio of four to one. The main threat was what the committee called "admission sex equality," and it posed the issue in the starkest possible terms: "*We cannot have our present size and our present enrollment and an equal sex admission ratio. What we should have and what we would like to have is not, in this case, what we can have.*"[204]

Since no one was seriously proposing expanding Harvard by 3,600 students, the committee's real concern was that a merger of the two institutions would result in a substantial reduction in the number of men. The committee vigorously opposed such a merger, correctly sensing that after any union between Harvard and Radcliffe, "it is unlikely that a fixed and unequal admissions ratio will be held, regardless of what the historical and practical considerations are or of what we now say."[205] Virtually every conceivable argument against reducing the number of men was put forward: it would force Harvard "into less diversity at a time when we are being asked for more,"[206] it would

ABOVE LEFT: Francis Skiddy von Stade, Jr., the embodiment of patrician Harvard, kept his own polo ponies as an undergraduate (Class of 1938). He was a Harvard administrator from 1940 until 1976, serving in various posts, including director of scholarships and master of Mather House. As dean of freshmen, he was a vigorous opponent of those who wished to make Harvard more inclusive, expressing particular reservations about "poor boys from very poor cultural backgrounds" and "Negroes."

ABOVE RIGHT: McGeorge Bundy was dean of Harvard's Faculty of Arts and Sciences from 1953 to 1961, when he left Cambridge to serve as President Kennedy's special assistant for national security. A Boston Brahmin, Groton graduate, and member of Skull and Bones at Yale, Bundy belonged to that wing of the Protestant upper class that opposed anti-Semitism. He was rumored to have been behind Bender's resignation as dean of admissions.

LEFT: Fred Glimp, the dean of admissions and financial aid at Harvard from 1960 to 1967, was the architect of Harvard's "happy-bottom-quarter" policy; he continued Bender's policy of limiting "intellectuals" to roughly 10 percent of the freshman class.

ABOVE: Alfred Whitney Griswold was president of Yale from 1950 to 1963. Even though he eliminated the Jewish quota in 1962, Yale remained a conservative institution under his tenure, dominated by prep-school graduates and continuing to hire much of its faculty from within its own ranks. BELOW: Skull and Bones is the most prestigious of Yale's senior societies. Its members have included William Howard Taft, Henry Stimson, Potter Stewart, Averell Harriman, Robert Taft, Henry Luce, William F. Buckley Jr., George H. W. Bush, John Kerry, and George W. Bush.

GEORGE HERBERT WALKER BUSH (Poppy) was born in Milton, Mass., June 12, 1924. He is the son of Prescott Sheldon Bush, '17, and Dorothy Walker Bush, a brother of Prescott S. Bush, Jr., ex-'44, and a nephew of James S. Bush, '22, George H. Walker, Jr., '27, John M. Walker, '31, and Louis Walker, '36.

In 1942, after graduating from Andover, Bush entered Naval Aviation. He later served as pilot in the Pacific and was awarded the D.F.C. He was discharged as a lieutenant (j.g.) in September, 1945, and entered Yale in November. Bush, who has majored in economics, was awarded the Francis Gordon Brown Prize in 1947. He was on the University baseball team for three years, being captain in Senior year, and on the University soccer team in 1945; he has both a minor and major "Y." He was secretary of the 1946 Budget drive and in 1947 served on the Undergraduate Athletic Association, the Undergraduate Board of Deacons, and the Interfraternity Council and was elected to the Triennial Committee. He belongs to Delta Kappa Epsilon, the Torch Honor Society, and Skull and Bones.

He was married in Rye, N. Y., January 6, 1945, to Barbara Pierce, Smith ex-'47, daughter of Marvin and Pauline Robinson Pierce. Their son, George Walker, was born in New Haven, July 6, 1946. Bush may be addressed at Grove Lane, Greenwich, Conn.

George Herbert Walker Bush, an archetypal "all-around man," in the Yale yearbook for the Class of 1948. After serving as a congressman, ambassador to the United Nations, and director of the Central Intelligence Agency, Bush served as cochairman of the $370 million Campaign for Yale and helped bring it to a successful conclusion. In 1989 he became the second Yale undergraduate to serve as president (the first was William Howard Taft).

George W. Bush playing rugby as a Yale undergraduate. At Andover, his record — an SAT verbal score of 566, no outstanding extracurricular talents, and not a single appearance on the honor roll — was so weak that the dean of students suggested he apply to some schools less competitive than Yale. But Bush was no ordinary legacy — his grandfather was a U.S. senator and had recently been a member of the Yale Corporation — and in April 1964 he was admitted. The caption in the Yale yearbook, where the photo first appeared, reads: "George Bush delivers illegal, but gratifying right hook to opposing ball carrier."

Kingman Brewster Jr.'s controversial tenure as president of Yale, from 1963 to 1977, transformed the university, doubling the number of Jews, quadrupling the number of blacks, and admitting women as undergraduates for the first time. But Brewster was no radical and wished to preserve the established order by reforming it. The survival of the American free-enterprise system, he believed, depended on "widespread confidence that success is a function of merit and effort."

ABOVE LEFT: R. Inslee Clark Jr., whose five years (1965–1970) as Yale's dean of admissions triggered an alumni revolt. On his watch the preference for traditional privileged constituencies was radically reduced and merit itself was redefined. With the alumni in open rebellion and the university in financial disarray, Clark resigned in 1970, leaving behind a legacy of fear among the elite colleges that the cost of encroaching on alumni privileges and trying to put meritocratic ideals into practice was simply too high. ABOVE RIGHT: William Sloane Coffin Jr., Yale's university chaplain from 1958 to 1975. An antiwar activist and a crusader for civil rights, he pressed Griswold to eliminate the Jewish quota. Of Brewster, who had stood by him despite repeated calls by angry alumni for his removal, Coffin once said, "I was never sure if Kingman believed in God, but I was sure God believed in Kingman."

ABOVE LEFT: Black students from Harvard's Association of African and Afro-American Students ("Afro") meet on April 22, 1969, as the faculty considers their demands for a program in Afro-American Studies. The faculty meeting took place in an atmosphere in which the threat of violence was palpable; armed black students had taken over a building at Cornell just a few days earlier, and the dean of admissions reported that earlier in the month there had been a "serious question whether the admissions office itself would be attacked." After two hours of tense discussion, the faculty approved Afro's demand by a vote of 251–158. ABOVE RIGHT: Radcliffe students demonstrating in favor of sex-blind admissions at commencement in 1971. At the time Harvard men outnumbered Radcliffe women, who faced much higher standards for admission, by roughly four to one. By 1975, facing political pressure from within and the likelihood that the courts would declare quotas on women illegal, Harvard adopted sex-blind admissions, the last member of the Big Three to do so.

A demonstration in New Haven on May 1, 1970. On April 16 Abbie Hoffman, one of the Chicago Seven, had announced that radicals converging on New Haven to protest the trial of Black Panther Bobby Seale intended to burn Yale down. Seven days later Brewster famously said that he was "skeptical of the ability of black revolutionaries to achieve a fair trial anywhere in the United States." His remarks, which outraged many alumni, failed to satisfy the radicals. But Brewster was a master of cooptation, and his decision to house and feed the demonstrators helped defuse an explosive situation.

William F. Buckley Jr., who ran for a seat on the Yale Corporation in 1967 on a platform of restoring the old Yale. Thrust into national prominence by his controversial 1951 assault on his alma mater, *God and Man at Yale*, he was a militant critic of Clark and Brewster's admissions policies, complaining that "the son of an alumnus, who goes to a private preparatory school, now has less chance of getting in than some boy from PS 109 somewhere."

Shelby Cullom Davis, a banker, philanthropist, and man of letters, at a Princeton dinner. In 1964 he contributed more than $5 million to put Princeton's $53 million capital campaign over the top. Disturbed by coeducation and by other changes in Princeton's admissions policy, in 1972 Davis founded the Concerned Alumni of Princeton (CAP), a conservative group strongly opposed to the administration. Of Davis's vision, President William Bowen said, "There's not one chance in a million that the basic direction of the university will change. I could get struck by lightning, but even so there'd be no change in coeducation, no change in faculty, and chapel wouldn't become compulsory again."

Derek Bok was president
of Harvard from 1971
to 1991. In both the *Bakke*
and Michigan cases, he
and William Bowen played
leading roles in defending
affirmative action. In his
book *Universities in the
Marketplace,* published in
2003, he argued that the
growing commercialization
of American universities
poses a threat to their
fundamental mission.

William Bowen, president
of Princeton from 1972
to 1987, was coauthor
with Bok of the influen-
tial study of affirmative
action *The Shape of
the River.* In 2004, in a
series of lectures at the
University of Virginia, he
came out in favor of
class-based affirmative
action, arguing that the
nation's elite colleges need
a "thumb on the scale"
to increase the number
of socioeconomically dis-
advantaged students.

Fred Hargadon, dean of admissions at Princeton from 1988 to 2003. In the face of growing criticism of early decision as reinforcing the advantages of the already privileged, Hargadon vigorously defended Princeton's program. During his tenure the proportion of Jews mysteriously dropped to about 10 percent — a result, many faculty believed, of a subtle shift in admissions policy away from sheer intellectual excellence toward athletic ability, geographical diversity, and other nonacademic factors.

William Fitzsimmons, dean of admissions at Harvard since 1986. In 2000 he and colleagues released a paper expressing concern about growing stress on college applicants, noting that "many seemed liked dazed survivors of some bewildering lifelong boot-camp." Fitzsimmons, who for more than two decades had been worrying about the declining socioeconomic diversity of the student body, was able to announce in 2004 that Harvard was adopting a new policy exempting families with incomes under $40,000 from having to contribute to their child's college expenses.

raise ethical (and perhaps legal) issues about the use of specific Harvard endowments, it would distort undergraduate enrollment in a number of departments, and it would require the rejection of so many strong male applicants that it would raise the danger that "even superior [male] applicants in the future will be discouraged from applying."[207] Beneath these concerns was the same worry that had plagued Yale and Princeton: it would cause a reduction in alumni support — support that, for Peterson, a graduate of the all-male Middlesex School and president of the Porcellian Club as a Harvard undergraduate, was the financial underpinning of Harvard's cherished independence.[208]

The Peterson Committee relied heavily on the argument that the only alternatives to the status quo were a drastic expansion of the student body or a radical reduction in male enrollment. But this argument was deeply flawed, for there was an alternative — for Harvard to make admission decisions without regard to sex. As a study by Dean Whitla (the director of Harvard's Office of Tests and a member of the committee) showed, such an admissions policy would in all likelihood have increased the percentage of females in the freshman class to just 24 or 25 percent.[209] But Peterson, opposed to *any* reduction in the number of men, preferred not to focus on this very reasonable alternative to the status quo: sex-blind admissions, combined with modest expansion.

The Peterson Committee was not wrong in its belief that a merger would make it impossible to maintain the 4–1 male-female ratio nor in its observation that "at no time have the pressures without and within been of greater intensity than they are today."[210] Precisely this kind of pressure made itself felt in February 1970 when three representatives of the National Organization of Women (NOW) met with President Nathan Pusey to propose to change the sex ratio to one to one. The NOW representatives, all of them former or current Harvard students, specified that if Harvard and Radcliffe merged, women should make up half of the student body, even if it meant reducing the number of men. Pusey rejected the idea of any such decrease — a position that, while defensible in early 1970, would soon become both politically and legally untenable.[211]

Harvard's rigid resistance to increasing female enrollment gave way shortly after a young and vigorous new president came into office in July 1971. Succeeding the aging and decidedly uncharismatic Pusey, Derek Bok was just forty years old and something of an academic wunderkind. The grandson of Edward Bok, a Dutch immigrant who came to America as an impoverished six-year-old and went on to found a publishing empire that included the *Ladies' Home Journal,* Bok was a Phi Beta Kappa graduate of Stanford and a magna cum laude graduate of Harvard Law School, where he served as an editor of the *Harvard Law Review.*[212] During a year in Paris as a Fulbright

Scholar, he met Sissela Myrdal, a daughter of the renowned Swedish economist Gunnar Myrdal, author of the classic study of race, *An American Dilemma*, whom he married in a ceremony performed by Pierre Mendès-France, a former French prime minister. After two years in the U.S. Army, when he managed to do some graduate work in economics, Bok joined the Harvard Law School faculty in 1958, becoming a full professor just three years later. Bok's specialties were labor and antitrust law, and in 1962, he wrote *Labor Law* with Archibald Cox. In 1968, he was appointed dean of the law school, a position in which he developed a reputation as a skilled mediator and an advocate of expanded opportunities for minorities.[213]

As Bok took office as president, he could not help but notice that Harvard had suffered a remarkable decline in the number of applicants: from over 8,400 in 1968 to fewer than 6,800 in 1971.[214] While part of this drop could have been attributed to the bad publicity surrounding the seizure of University Hall by radical students in April 1969 and the subsequent police bust, it seemed likely that a portion of it was caused by increased competition from its newly coeducational rivals, Yale and Princeton. Recognizing that the status quo was no longer serving Harvard's interests, Bok moved quickly to alter the traditional 4–1 ratio of men to women to 2.5 men for every woman. This change, which was announced just four months after Bok took office, was to go into effect for the freshman class that would enter in the fall of 1972.[215]

Bok planned to absorb much of the growth in female enrollment through expansion, but he realized that it would require some reduction in the number of men. In October 1971, Harvard announced a projected reduction of 50 men in the class that would enter in 1972 — an estimate that proved high, for only 37 fewer men enrolled that fall than in 1971. Over the next two years, however, the number of men continued to drop, declining to 1,109 in 1974 from a peak of 1,229 in 1971.[216] Still, this was a reduction of less than 10 percent — a modest decrease, given the political atmosphere of the times on issues of gender equality.

Meanwhile, the number of women in the freshman class grew to 463 in 1974 — an increase of 37 percent over 1971.[217] Yet the new ratio of 2.5 to 1 still set an upper boundary on women, constituting precisely the type of quota that would have been deemed unacceptable if applied to Jews or blacks. As at Yale and Princeton, the contradiction between the official ideology of equal opportunity and the stark reality of a gender quota caused increasing unease on campus. Even before the first freshman class admitted under the new ratio arrived in the fall of 1972, Harvard's new dean of admissions, Fred Jewett '57, expressed his disapproval of the ceiling on female enrollment.[218] "Ideally," he said, "you ought to be considering people without regard to sex."[219]

Pressure for gender equality was also mounting from students and other constituencies.[220] In an April 1973 editorial, the *Crimson* laid out the argument for a student body that would be 50 percent female:

> . . . Simply to talk of "non-discrimination" in an institution intent on enrolling more men than women is naïve. Harvard's applicant pool is so overqualified that any numerical limit on acceptances means arbitrary choice. The question centers on the principles that will guide such choices. Harvard's past practice demonstrates that, if possible, sexism will be one of those principles . . .
>
> By enrolling equal numbers of men and women . . . Harvard will demonstrate both its ability and willingness to provide a healthy educational community without sexual discrimination. Under those conditions non-discrimination would yield a one-to-one student body. Until students and alumni demand equal admissions by deliberate policy or Congress passes legislation which will force Harvard toward accepting as many women as men, the University will continue to discriminate against women. No one should be satisfied with Harvard's admissions policy until equal numbers of men and women are admitted.[221]

For many militant proponents of gender equality, the goal was less a nondiscriminatory process than what was believed to be a just outcome: a class with equal numbers of men and women. From this perspective, the problem with the 2.5–1 ratio was not that it was a predetermined ratio, but rather that it was the wrong ratio.

The *Crimson*'s campaign for a class that was 50 percent female continued in 1974. Maintaining that Harvard had a responsibility to advance the cause of gender equality, an editorial argued:

> Harvard is very conscious of its role as a social force in America; the University sees itself, for instance, as making disadvantaged students upwardly mobile. So by the same logic, Harvard should try to work toward a society where women have the same opportunities as men by producing equal numbers of qualified male and female graduates. One of the tired old justifications of admissions policies skewed in favor of men is that Harvard has a responsibility to educate male leaders. But Harvard's real responsibility is to work toward a society where both men and women are leaders. In the same way, the argument that male graduates give Harvard more money than female graduates works on the assumption of inequalities that Harvard should be trying to end, not adapting itself to.[222]

Only a 1–1 admissions policy, the *Crimson* concluded, could realize Harvard's mission as a force for genuine equality of opportunity.

The Bok administration was opposed to proposals to mandate a 50 percent female freshman class. In part, this resistance reflected a principled opposition to quotas of any sort rather than selection on the basis of "merit." But it also reflected a desire not to reduce the number of men too drastically lest it endanger Harvard's economic future; Radcliffe women, the administration was well aware, were not particularly generous toward their alma mater, giving to Radcliffe at a rate of 39 percent — among the lowest of the women's colleges.[223] Then there was the delicate issue of Harvard's definition of itself as educator of those in positions of "leadership" in a society in which women remained far less likely to attain such positions. To be sure, by 1973, no one in the Harvard administration would publicly utter the sentiments expressed four years earlier by Dean of Freshmen F. Skiddy von Stade '37: "When I see bright, well-educated, but relatively dull housewives who attended the Seven Sisters, I honestly shudder at the thought of changing the balance of males versus females at Harvard . . . Quite simply, I do not see highly educated women making startling strides in contributing to our society in the foreseeable future. They are not, in my opinion, going to stop getting married and/ or having children. They will fail in their present role as women if they do."[224] But the concern that a radical reduction in the number of men might compromise its ability to fulfill its mission of educating "leaders" had by no means disappeared.

From the point of view of the administration, the optimal solution was not a 50–50 freshman class but sex-blind admissions. It was a seemingly neutral principle that embodied meritocratic ideals; at the same time, it ensured (at least in the short term) a class that would be roughly two-thirds male, for more than twice as many men than women applied to Harvard at the time. In the fall of 1973, Bok and Radcliffe's president, Matina Horner, appointed a committee to recommend the best admissions policy. Though Bok continued to insist that he would "reserve public judgment" until the committee issued its findings, he delivered a speech before the committee's first meeting that left little doubt that he favored a sex-blind or, as he preferred to call it, "equal access" policy. President Horner and Dean Jewett were even more explicit, both telling the *Crimson* that they favored a sex-blind policy.[225]

Nevertheless, as the 16-member committee — which was headed by Karl Strauch, a physics professor, and included three other faculty members, 4 deans, 4 alumni, and 4 students — convened in December 1973, the option of a 1–1 ratio was still very much alive. Indeed, with virtually no one in favor of continuing the 2.5–1 ratio, the committee had only two options: either an explicit target of a freshman class that would be half female or sex-blind admissions.[226] And the 50–50 solution, in addition to editorial support from the *Crimson,* enjoyed strong backing from feminists, many of whom believed that only a guarantee of half the admissions slots would protect female applicants from discrimination in an institution still dominated by men. So concerned were students about the issue that Commencement protests were staged on behalf of a 1–1 ratio.[227]

After more than a year of discussion, the Strauch Committee came down firmly on the side of sex-blind admissions. Though several committee members expressed the fear that a sex-blind policy would favor men and limit female enrollment to no more than 40 percent, the argument that a 1–1 ratio was a quota and that "any kind of quota, in particular one based on race, religion, or sex, was inconsistent with the role of an institution serving the public in a free society" carried the day.[228] A university dedicated to the education of both men and women, the committee argued, "must provide equality of opportunity in admissions and intellectual development for both sexes." The Strauch Committee's principal recommendation followed logically: "An admission policy of equal access [to] be instituted as soon as possible, that is for the admission for the Class of 1980."[229]

The Strauch Committee was fully aware that sex-blind admissions would not do much to alter the ratio of men to women. Noting that between 1970 and 1974, Harvard averaged about 7,650 applicants annually while the Radcliffe applicant pool expanded from 2,548 to 3,388, the committee called for "vigorous recruiting efforts" to further increase the number of female applicants. Judging by the experience of "other universities similar to Harvard with a tradition of equal access admissions," the committee expected "a 1.5:1 ratio [60 percent men, 40 percent women] . . . within a reasonable period."[230] It also called for "equal access to financial support" and strongly endorsed "the present policy of admission without consideration of ability to pay, and the offer of sufficient financial [aid] to all who may need it."[231]

With the release of the Strauch Report in February 1975, Bok got just the recommendation he wanted. With little dissent — save a protest from Professor of Government Harvey Mansfield, who accused the committee of "proposing a fundamental change on the basis of an abstraction, namely the equality of women" — the faculty endorsed the report on April 8, and the Governing Boards of Harvard and Radcliffe followed suit quickly thereafter.[232] Effective July 1, 1975, the Admissions Offices of Harvard and Radcliffe were merged, and as of 1976, admission to the freshman class would be sex-blind for the first time in Harvard's 340-year history.

Strauch had been correct when he predicted that the implementation of the report would lead to no sudden or drastic changes in the student body; the proportion of men in the freshman class remained at 65 percent in 1976 and 1977.[233] By 1980, the number of applications from women had risen to over 5,500, and they constituted 40 percent of the freshman entering class — the proportion predicted by Strauch. That same year, the number of men in the class dropped to 971 — a decline of 19 percent from the last years of the traditional 4–1 ratio, when a minimum of 1,200 slots were reserved for men.[234]

Though Harvard had moved with characteristic caution, by the mid-1970s it had finally met the challenge posed by coeducation at Yale and Princeton. Yet it had lost one of its principal advantages — its historic connection with Radcliffe and, since 1943, the presence of women in the class-rooms. In 1976, Harvard still had the highest yield rate of the Big Three: 74 percent. But this was a far cry from 1968, when Harvard was the only coeducational member of the Big Three and enjoyed a yield rate of 86 percent — a position that was lost forever.[235]

Women, Institutional Interests, and the Logic of Inclusion

From today's vantage point, it is difficult to grasp just how thoroughly male the Big Three were in 1960. Apart from the obvious fact that Yale and Princeton did not admit any female undergraduates and even Harvard relegated them to a separate and much smaller institution, there was the assumption that one could speak of the Yale man, the Princeton man, and the Harvard man, casually confident that it was men — and men alone — who defined these institutions. Decisively reinforcing this feeling was the faculty itself, with no female full professors at Yale and Princeton in 1960 and just one woman out of a tenured faculty of 400 at Harvard.[236]

It was not until the mid-1960s that the idea of coeducation began to receive serious consideration at Yale and Princeton. Propelling it was less the conviction that women deserved equal opportunity than sheer institutional self-interest. As the data mounted on the reasons that admitted students chose not to enroll, the choice facing Yale and Princeton became clear: either admit women as undergraduates or risk falling behind Harvard and other institutions that included women.

Yet, this realization was not in and of itself enough to dislodge a tradition more than 200 years old. What gave the push for coeducation powerful (albeit indirect) momentum was the progressive opening of the Big Three to African Americans; this shift was behind the adoption of an ideology of inclusiveness that was in conflict with the continued exclusion of women. By 1968, with the influence of the black and student movements growing, the contradiction between the institutions' professed ideology of equal opportunity and the refusal to even accept applications from half the population had become too transparent to sustain. It could be argued (and was) that just as the Big Three were limited to men, so the Seven Sisters were limited to women. But by this time it seemed a hollow argument, reminiscent of the separate-but-equal doctrine that the civil rights movement had so thoroughly discredited.

In 1968–1969, the barriers that had excluded women for so long at Yale and Princeton were finally cast aside. But the decision to go coeducational by no means constituted the triumph of equal opportunity, for the terms of the agreements stipulated that women would be added to the existing freshman class without reducing the number of men.

Yale and Princeton (and, later, Harvard as well) were concerned that cutting the number of men would reduce the number of "leaders" they educated at the same time that it would cause a decrease in alumni contributions. Though the role of women in America was obviously changing — a point made by the Patterson, Dahl, and Strauch reports alike — a certain skepticism about the likelihood that women would enjoy the same opportunities as men in the economic and political elite was not unwarranted. Institutional self-interest, especially if materially defined, thus militated against any reduction in the number of men — a point repeatedly emphasized by the alumni and development offices of the Big Three.

But universities, like other institutions, have more than material interests: they also possess — to borrow a phrase from Max Weber — ideal interests.[237] Especially in universities, which pride themselves on their commitment to ideas and to the transmission of values, overt contradictions between their ideals and their practices are particularly costly, depriving them of the legitimacy and prestige that are their most precious resources. The quotas limiting the number of women presented an especially grave dilemma; arguably rational from the perspective of material interests, they were profoundly costly to the defense of the institutions' ideal interests. For as feminists and their allies never tired of pointing out, ceilings on female enrollment were the antithesis of the values of meritocracy and equal opportunity for which Harvard, Yale, and Princeton claimed to stand.

From an administrative point of view, abandoning the fixed ratios that had insulated men from competition with women had its risks: it could further estrange the alumni, reduce contributions from future alumni, and decrease the proportion of graduates who became "leaders." Yet in the end, the men who presided over the Big Three had no choice but to adopt sex-blind admissions. For even had they been inclined to resist powerful political and legal trends, maintaining a gender quota would contradict their identity as institutions committed to the ideals of equality of opportunity and social inclusion. By the early 1970s, these ideals were essential to the universities' definitions of themselves. Derek Bok identified the contradiction at the heart of the matter: "If we seek a student body that combines diversity with the highest intellectual talent," he asked, "why should any group be subject to a predetermined and seemingly arbitrary limit?"[238]

For Yale and Princeton, whose self-definition and public identity had been defined in no small part by their male character, the adoption in rapid succession of coeducation and sex-blind admissions constituted a profound transformation in the very fabric of college life. Even at Harvard, where the change was less drastic, the shift to sex-blind admissions was historic, for men would now have to compete with women for places in the freshman class. Yet once the barriers were removed, women's integration into the Big Three proceeded rapidly.

Female Yalies, Princetonians, and Harvardians were, after all, the daughters, sisters, and neighbors of the men who had historically attended the Big Three, and only their gender had prevented them from enrolling. Once the doors were opened, they were deemed to possess no less "merit" than their brothers. For some years, the Big Three had privately bemoaned the paucity of secondary school graduates nationwide who could meet their exacting standards and pay their own way. Now, in women (or, more precisely, in the affluent segment among them), they had a vast new pool — and the only one not yet tapped — of high-ability applicants who did not need scholarship assistance. "Paying customers" had long been welcome at the Big Three, and women proved no exception.

Many women did, of course, need scholarships. But in contrast to African Americans, women did not require disproportionate financial assistance; in fact, the proportion of them on scholarship, at least in the early years, was slightly lower than that among men.[239] Though the struggles of blacks had helped pave the way for the entry of women into the Big Three by discrediting the rationales that had long justified exclusion and discrimination, blacks were less well situated than women to take advantage of the new opportunities. Concentrated among the disadvantaged and heavily underrepresented among the privileged, blacks as a group lacked access to the elite schools and family-based cultural capital that produced high school seniors with the greatest "merit," at least as conventionally defined. They thus required "affirmative action," and as the political tumult of the late 1960s receded, so too did their representation at Yale and Princeton. Constituting 8 percent of the freshman class at Yale in 1969, they dropped to 5 percent in 1978; at Princeton, a similar pattern prevailed, with black enrollment peaking at 10 percent in 1970 and declining to 8 percent in 1978.[240] Meanwhile, women required nothing more than nondiscrimination to progress in a system that placed heavy weight on SAT scores and high school grades. Between 1970 and 1978, their proportion of the freshman class doubled, rising from 19 to 39 percent at Yale and from 18 to 35 percent at Princeton.[241]

Though women and blacks had reached Yale and Princeton through different routes, their presence was discomfiting to alumni nostalgic for the colleges of their youth. Other changes — the decline of the prep schools, the tougher academic standards for alumni sons, the decreased emphasis on "character" and the increased emphasis on "brains," the visible presence of student radicals on campus, and (though it was rarely said aloud) the growing number of Jews — were equally disturbing. For many Old Elis and Tigers, the institutions they cherished had fallen into the hands of those unworthy of its great traditions. Their effort to take it back generated a revolt whose goal was to turn back the changes of the 1960s.

CHAPTER 15

The Alumni Revolt at Yale and Princeton

THE ALUMNI'S FORMAL INVOLVEMENT in the affairs of Yale and Princeton has deep roots, dating back, in the case of Yale, to the late nineteenth century. In 1890, the Yale Corporation voted "to establish a fund to be known as the Alumni University Fund" in response to "a widespread sentiment among Yale graduates in favor of some systematic endeavor to increase the resources of the University."[1] Some sixteen years later, the Corporation authorized the establishment of the Alumni Advisory Board to "meet the desire of Yale graduates in different parts of the country for representation on the councils of the University."[2]

Yale was the first college to institutionalize its efforts to raise money from its alumni, and it was one of the first to give preference to the sons of alumni when selecting students.[3] In 1925, in the midst of a concerted effort to limit the number of Jewish students, Yale's Board of Admissions passed a resolution: "the limitation of numbers [that is, the imposition of a ceiling on the size of the freshmen class] shall not operate to exclude any son of a Yale graduate who has satisfied all the requirements for admission."[4] Already 17 percent of the freshman class in 1925, legacies increased to 30 percent of entering students by 1931 — the highest in the Ivy League.[5]

Though alumni played an important role in the admissions process, their influence rested principally on the money they contributed to Yale — and on Yale's dependence on that money. By 1964–1965, more than 35,000 contributors donated more than $9 million — about 16 percent of all expenditures in 1965.[6] But the greater significance of these contributions resided in their capacity to strengthen the endowment — the foundation of Yale's eminence. As Yale's top administrators were well aware, no capital campaign — present or future — could succeed without the enthusiastic support of the alumni.

Princeton witnessed a parallel pattern of alumni involvement. In 1888, it published its first alumni directory, and in 1900 it founded the *Princeton Alumni Weekly*. Four years later, it established a Committee of Fifty to raise funds for "the immediate necessity and future involvement of the University."

Renamed the Graduate Council in 1909, this body launched Annual Giving in 1940.[7]

As at Yale, Princeton's alumni were actively involved in recruiting and selecting students. But Princeton differed from its New Haven rival in one important respect: the alumni's considerable involvement in its elaborate system of private eating clubs. While only 10 percent of Yale alumni were tapped for senior societies, at Princeton virtually everyone belonged to an eating club. And at least into the 1950s, alumni remained active in their eating clubs, sometimes dining there on football weekends and other occasions. These clubs, moreover, were private institutions, legally and financially controlled not by Princeton University, but by governing boards dominated by Old Princetonians.[8]

In this atmosphere, some alumni felt a sense of ownership that went beyond mere shareholding — in their minds, Princeton belonged to them. Sensing this ferocity of commitment to the Old Princeton among many alumni, Princeton moved more cautiously than Yale to transform itself during the tumultuous years of the late 1960s. As a result, the alumni rose up at Princeton almost three years later than at Yale, where the revolt was triggered when the first letters of admission went out to "Inky's boys" in the spring of 1966.[9]

The Old Blues Attempt a Counterrevolution

E. E. Slosson, in his classic *Great American Universities* (1910), noted that in the eastern colleges, "the alumni seem to be, as a whole, a conservative, even a reactionary, influence, opposing almost any change, wise or unwise." Citing Yale as an example, he observed that alumni "as a body are inclined to regard their Alma Mater as a relic of happy schooldays and as such to keep it intact and unaltered, so that when they return they may find it as they remembered it."[10] As the Yale alumni revolt of the 1960s and 1970s revealed, Slosson's observations retained their currency more than half a century later.

In an article in the *Yale Daily News* on April 15, 1966 — just as letters of rejection and admission were being sent to the 5,800 applicants — Inky Clark told the newspaper that the proportion of students from public high schools was likely to rise and that the "in grown" prep schools would be disappointed in the future. Noting Yale's commitment to "diversity," he reported that it would see an increase in "risk" cases (very bright students from disadvantaged backgrounds) and in the number of black students. As part of this push for greater diversity, Yale visited 1,000 schools in 1966, up from 600 the year before. Among them were some heavily Jewish public schools in New York City — rich sources for precisely the kind of "promising science and engineering students" previously shunned by Yale. Many of the students now accepted by Yale — who came, Clark reported, from such places as "Bedford-Stuyvesant, the Bronx, and parts of New Jersey" — would be offered "substantial scholarships."[11]

By 1966, a revolt of the alumni had broken out, though it was unclear from the letters sent to Kingman Brewster that spring and summer whether Old Blues were more upset by the decision of the Admissions Office to turn down boys who in the past would have been accepted or to accept boys who previously would have been rejected.[12] What was clear, however, was that alumni discontent was widespread and a revolt was already unfolding; Brewster himself wrote to prominent alumni, trying to explain the logic of the changes he and Clark had introduced and not hesitating to appeal to "Yale's ambition to make an outsized mark on the quality and direction of the nation and the world."[13] So eager was Brewster to mollify angry alumni that he was not beyond discretely criticizing Clark himself, admitting that he did not like the interview that his new dean of admissions had given the *Yale Daily News* shortly after his appointment and noting, "He is young; he is new; he has only one year under his belt." Nevertheless, in the end Brewster defended Clark, telling a wealthy alumnus that "I am completely satisfied that he is doing his conscientious best to carry out policies I thoroughly believe in."[14]

That fall, Brewster wrote an article on admissions in the alumni magazine; although delicately phrased, it further fanned the flames.[15] A characteristic response came from Sanford Dickson '50, a physician at Sloan-Kettering in New York. Writing to a fellow alumnus in the Office of the Provost, he forcefully expressed his dismay:

> After considering all that has been written by Mr. Inslee Clark, President Brewster, and yourself, I find that I cannot convincingly rebut what the Yale Admissions Committee is currently doing. The Committee can easily produce a reasonable (if simplistic) argument in behalf of its present policies. However, I just don't happen to agree with these policies. I think that what I object to most is that in striving to become a so-called "national" university, Yale has apparently decided to deny that it has any obligation to the sons of its alumni or to the eastern preparatory schools which have in the past supplied Yale with large numbers of students. Yale not only refuses to give these boys any preference regarding admission but may even discriminate against them.

While recognizing that the large increase in the number of applicants had placed the Admissions Office in a "strong bargaining position," Dickson strongly condemned "the attitude that . . . Yale . . . can afford to ignore the natural desire of its alumni for their sons to be given the same opportunity that they had."[16]

Though supporting the "special effort to favor the Negro," Dickson was particularly exercised by Yale's "talent search" policy of looking "in every corner of every cranny of the country for every gifted white student who can somehow be enticed to come to Yale . . . when there are already more well-qualified candidates than Yale can accept." Recent graduates of the supposedly more meritocratic Yale were, in his view, often "conceited, arrogant, demanding, overly impressed with their ability and competence, and unwilling to put in a good day's work." Yet Yale, he argued, was spurning the alumni sons and private school boys, the majority of whom "have a heritage of believing and participating in some form of public (as well as patriotic) service." Why, he asked, was it Yale's policy to "go digging around Berkeley or elsewhere for eccentrics with some special talent and a high SAT score? . . .Until I see some indication that the Admissions Office has had a change of heart," he concluded, "I am going to continue withholding further contributions to Yale" — a position, he reported, that was shared by "a fair number of my contemporaries who have also stopped contributing for more or less the same reasons as myself."[17] In June 1967, Turner Dunbar '38, one of many alumni who solicited donations for the Alumni Fund, wrote to Brewster: "In recent contacts with classmates and other alumni I sense a very real surge of criticism regarding the type of boy Yale is seeking and admitting and some of us wonder what kind of alumni these young men will make and what they will contribute to our society. I also wonder how the Yale Alumni Fund will be doing 15, 20, and 25 years from now."[18]

By the fall of 1966, the alumni were sufficiently disturbed that they established, through the Alumni Board, a special committee to examine Yale's admissions policies.[19] After the public relations disaster of 1965–1966, Clark made an effort to mend fences with the alumni and the prep schools.[20]

But Brewster was not about to leave the issue of whether Clark had "gotten the message" to chance.[21] In a lengthy letter on March 15, 1967, he laid down guidelines for the class to be admitted that spring.[22] On the critical issue of legacies, Brewster's message was diplomatic but clear: "The only preference by inheritance which seems to me to deserve recognition is the Yale son. Tradition, loyalty, familiarity deserve to be given weight."[23] Though addressed to Muyskens, Yale's new director of admissions (and hence the number two man in the Admissions Office) Brewster's missive was clearly intended for Clark, to whom the letter was copied. It was also widely circulated within Yale and enclosed with Brewster's personal responses to disgruntled alumni to reassure them that the administration was taking their concerns seriously.[24]

But Clark was not an easy man to move, and the students admitted in 1967 looked very much like the 1966 group that had so enraged the alumni. Indeed, in many ways 1967 was the peak of the Clark revolution, with the proportion of alumni sons in the freshman class dropping to an all-time low of

12 percent.[25] Though the legacy admission rate had climbed marginally from 37 to 38 percent, the number of alumni sons applying to Yale dropped by more than 17 percent. Particularly worrisome to Yale was the trend among those alumni sons admitted to go elsewhere. In 1967, 21 percent of them did just that, up from a mere 7 percent in 1965 — the year before Clark's appointment.[26] After just two years, alumni estrangement had reached new heights: under Clark, Yale was not only rejecting unprecedented numbers of legacies but also creating an atmosphere on campus that made it less appealing even to those who had survived the fierce competition for a place in the freshman class.

When the archconservative William F. Buckley announced his candidacy for a position on the Yale Corporation in the fall of 1967, it was at the high point of the Clark revolution. A major thorn in Yale's side since 1951, when he published *God and Man at Yale* at the age of twenty-six, Buckley was running on a counterrevolutionary platform.[27] The restoration of alumni privilege was at the center of his candidacy. "I think of the alumni as the constituency of the University," he told the *Yale Daily News*. "Without parochializing Yale, it ought to be considered more their school."[28]

Though Buckley's candidacy was ultimately defeated, it seems to have affected Yale's handling of applications from alumni sons in a way that Brewster's letter to Muyskens had not. Well aware that the Corporation, the Alumni Board, and Brewster were looking over his shoulder in his third year as dean, Clark grudgingly responded to the pressure. In 1968, 44 percent of the legacy applicants were accepted — still a lower percentage than Harvard's (46 percent) or Princeton's (56 percent), but a sizable increase over the previous year (38 percent) and almost double the 23 percent rate for nonlegacy applicants.[29] Yet even this concession was short-lived, for in 1969 the proportion of alumni sons dropped yet again, to 36 percent — the lowest in Yale's history.[30]

Despite the temporary increase in 1968 in the admission rate for legacies, tensions with the alumni continued to build. Ever since Brewster announced that Yale was exploring a union with Vassar, a segment of the alumni had recoiled from the very idea that their male sanctuary would be invaded by women. And when Yale finally decided in November 1968 to go coeducational, it did so — unlike Princeton — without having extensively consulted with the alumni.

This decision imposed additional strains on Yale's already tense relations with its alumni, but it was not — again in contrast to Princeton — the principal source of their disaffection. For even before Yale made the decision to go coeducational, alumni estrangement was already widespread. "Among the alumni," Nicholas Lemann has written, "a cult of Clark hatred quickly developed."[31]

From the perspective of many alumni, Clark's definition of merit was narrowly intellectual, self-consciously hostile to alumni sons, graduates of leading boarding schools, and athletes, and at bottom an assault on Yale's historic character. Though the battle through the spring of 1968 was a seemingly narrow struggle over which young white men to admit (blacks still constituted just 4 percent of the freshman class), it was ferocious nonetheless.[32] As the alumni knew intuitively, it was a struggle for the soul of Yale. And as of 1968, it was a struggle that they were losing.

The sense that they were losing control over their alma mater led the alumni to form still another committee in the fall of 1969. Chaired by Martin Dwyer Jr. '44 and called the Commission on Alumni Affairs, it was charged with making "an independent and constructively critical inquiry into the way alumni participate in the direction of the University" at a moment when Yale's financial situation was increasingly precarious.[33] Ever since Brewster had assumed the presidency in October 1963, Yale had been operating at a loss, and by 1969 the deficit had grown to almost $900,000 — more than triple that of two years earlier. Ominously, the endowment — the foundation of Yale's economic security — had also dropped, decreasing by $24 million between 1968 and 1969. Most disturbing of all, however, was a decline of 1,100 in the number of donors to the Alumni Fund between 1967–1968 and 1968–1969 — one of the few such drops in Yale's history and a clear sign of deepening alumni estrangement.[34]

Particularly disturbing to the Old Blues most actively involved in Yale's affairs was the manifest tension between the Admissions Office and the roughly 1,900 alumni who served on 260 Alumni Schools Committees throughout the country.[35] Aware from the outset that his initiatives would generate opposition, Clark had tried in his first year to establish greater control of the alumni by consolidating the traditionally influential Committees on Enrollment and Scholarships in the Admissions Office and redesignating them Alumni Schools Committees.[36] Clark had also attempted to curb the influence of the alumni by turning to a new source for recruiting that was more in tune with his policies: the undergraduates themselves. By 1967–1968, the Undergraduate Schools Committee included 360 students, many of whom interviewed applicants, especially minorities, during the Thanksgiving and Christmas vacations.[37]

The alumni sensed that they were being pushed to the margins of the admissions process, and they were not happy. According to the Dwyer Commission, there was widespread dissatisfaction with how the Office of Admissions was handling local Alumni Schools Committees because their recommendations were often ignored. A study of candidates interviewed by both alumni and the staff of the Admissions Office revealed that their ratings were based on different criteria and that disagreements were greatest precisely in those cases where the personal evaluation counted the most. These differences were particularly pronounced at the extremes. Of those rated in the bottom 10 percent by the Admissions Office — "real losers," in the parlance of the staff — 40 percent were rated strong or exceptionally strong by alumni interviewers; conversely, more than 40 percent of those with the highest possible staff ratings were judged average or lower than average by the Alumni Schools Committees.[38]

In this atmosphere, some alumni interviewers simply quit. One of them was a former team captain and a loyal alumnus who felt that he did not understand what kind of person the new Yale was looking for — a conclusion he had reached after six consecutive years in which he had recommended students for admission only to have every one of them ultimately rejected. Another expressed the views of many of his fellow committeemen when he said: "The great majority of men who freely give of their valuable time to work on Alumni Schools' Committees across the country are successful men as measured by their attainments in life since they left Yale. They are men who have competed in the 'battle of life' and come out victorious. They daily make complicated and difficult judgments involving vast sums of money, people and materials and they have to be right. Yet it would appear on the basis of this year's results, in my own area at least, we might better have spent our time at tennis, golf or at the movies, for the Admissions Committee disregarded our work and recommendations almost in toto."[39] His remarks echoed those of B. H. Prentice '05, who, in one of the earliest critiques of Clark's policies, argued that the most distinguished leaders produced by Yale — "the Stimsons, the Tafts, the Achesons" — had been successful because they possessed qualities "more meaningful than mere intellectuality."[40]

In response to the surging wave of discontent among Old Blues, the Dwyer Commission proposed increased alumni influence on admissions by moving "the system away from the personal recruitment of applicants by the admissions staff" and toward increased "reliance on the ASC [Alumni Schools Committees] to handle the interviews and provide the majority of qualified candidates."[41] But by the time the report came out in December 1970, it had been overtaken by events, most notably the resignation of Inky Clark and the founding of an alumni group whose goal was to reverse many of the changes introduced by Brewster.

The announcement of Clark's resignation was particularly significant, for Clark was the embodiment of the admissions policies that had so inflamed the alumni. Officially, his departure was entirely voluntary; in an interview with the *Yale Daily News*, Sam Chauncey, Brewster's special assistant, said that Clark would have been appointed to another five-year term had he so desired.[42] According to Clark, he had approached Brewster in 1968–1969, his fourth year in office, for help in seeking another job; Brewster offered his support, and in July 1970 Clark became headmaster of the prestigious Horace Mann School in New York City. But as Clark candidly admitted, pressures were building, and in a new term "there would . . . have been some retrenchment brought on possibly by financial constraints and pressure from alumni." Speaking of Brewster, whom he admired deeply, Clark acknowledged: "I never was sure, in the time that we were there together, that he totally approved of all the things we were doing, because some of the things we were doing were hurting some other things that had to be done from a president's viewpoint. After all, as president you have to raise money, the alumni have to love you, and heads of schools in New England who have always sent their children to you have to love you, too." Alumni discontent, by his admission, had gained momentum in his first year in office and had grown "by leaps and bounds in years #2, 3, 4, and 5."[43] By 1970, with Yale in increasing financial trouble, the handwriting was on the wall: it was time for Clark to go.

Clark's departure no doubt produced elation among the disgruntled alumni, but it was not enough to temper their growing anger at Brewster. Relations between Brewster and the alumni had been strained since 1966, when the new direction in admissions became visible, and were further strained by the 1968 decision to admit women. But by the spring of 1970, the focal point of discontent was Brewster's allegedly soft stance toward student radicals — a perception reinforced by his apparent sympathy for a student strike in early May that began as an expression of solidarity with the Black Panthers then being tried in New Haven. When Brewster publicly declared on April 23 that he was "appalled and ashamed that things have come to such a pass in this country that I am skeptical of the ability of black revolutionaries to achieve a fair trial anywhere in the United States," alumni outrage exploded.[44] According to the *New York Times*, Brewster's remarks "contributed to a 25 per cent drop in attendance at the three-day alumni reunion" in June and "led many alumni to withhold donations to the university's current fund drive."[45]

Brewster's remarks on the Black Panthers had been made in a context in which Yale's very survival seemed at risk. Several weeks earlier, Brewster had received word that somewhere between 50,000 and 500,000 demonstrators would stage a rally in New Haven on May 1 that would include radicals whose announced intent was to "Free Bobby [Seale]" and to "Burn Yale." At a rally in Boston on April 15, Abbie Hoffman, one of the Chicago Seven, had publicly declared that the radicals' goal was to go to New Haven to burn Yale down. There was a possibility, of course, that this was mere rhetoric, but the demonstrators from the Boston rally had marched into Cambridge and went on a rampage in Harvard Square. Anxiety in New Haven, already considerable, began to soar.[46]

Brewster made his famous statement at a faculty meeting whose purpose was to decide how to respond to the thousands of radicals poised to descend on New Haven just seven days later. Carefully negotiating his way between the radical and liberal factions of the faculty (no strong conservative position was expressed at the meeting), Brewster orchestrated the passage of a resolution stating that faculty "should be free to suspend their classes" — a crucial watering down of an earlier and more radical resolution calling for the "suspension of the normal academic functions" and recommending that faculty "should suspend their classes."

A master of cooptation, Yale's president also took the unusual step of not only leaving the campus open as the demonstrators arrived in town but organizing Yale to house and feed them. When the demonstrations — which had provoked such hysteria that roughly a third of the undergraduates left town — ended peacefully, it became clear that the debonair and gentlemanly Brewster had once again defused a potentially disastrous situation. "I was never sure if Kingman believed in God," the former Yale chaplain William Sloane Coffin said years later, "but I was sure God believed in Kingman."[47]

Though Brewster's actions helped keep the peace in New Haven under extremely trying circumstances, they also provoked a great deal of outrage, especially among conservatives. Vice President Spiro Agnew called for Brewster's resignation, asking Yale alumni to demand "a more mature and responsible person" to serve as president.[48] Even the judge who presided at the trial of the Black Panthers joined in the chorus of criticism; after finding that the charges against the Panthers could not be sustained, he described his decision to acquit them as "a direct answer to a careless and sad comment made by the president of Yale University that he was skeptical of the ability of black revolutionaries to get a fair trial."[49]

Brewster responded forcefully, albeit privately, to the judge's remarks:

> The Panther shoot-out turns out to be a police shoot-in, and the dismissal of fabricated charges against the Panther defendants is celebrated by the Judge as proof that the President of Yale University is wrong in his skepticism! Splendid; I'm glad to be proved wrong. Meanwhile, the victims of that shoot-in are still dead, and the police officers who killed them will apparently not be prosecuted — in part because the living victims of the shoot-in so despair of justice at the hands of white society as to be unwilling to appear before a grand jury.
>
> The fault for the uproars on our campuses and streets do not lie with the young and the blacks. If it lies anywhere, it lies with us, with our generation. One of the reasons the young and downtrodden create their disturbing commotions is that people our age delude themselves about the quality of existing institutions and hence put off and put down those who seek orderly change.[50]

His response expressed one of his cardinal convictions: that — as he had written in a letter to President Nixon's attorney general, John Mitchell, a few months earlier — his task as president of a great university was "to convince restless students that their best chance to improve the quality of society is to work within, not against, the political and legal system, even if the objective is radical reform." But if the system seemed rigid, he warned, it would "drive constructive reformers into the ranks of the destructive radicals."[51]

It was Brewster's openness to far-reaching reform as well as his evident sympathy for many of the causes that the radical students were espousing that helped Yale avoid the types of disruptive student uprisings that had shaken Harvard, Columbia, and Cornell. Described by students as a "charismatic listener," Brewster was masterful at conveying to militants that he was taking their views seriously and making strategic concessions when necessary.[52] This talent was especially evident in Brewster's dealings with militant students from the Black Student Alliance of Yale (BSAY), who extracted important concessions from him and, in return, supported him at critical moments, including in the spring of 1970.[53] But from the perspective of white radicals, Brewster's tactics were the classic ones of divide and rule; describing the struggles of the period, the SDS leader Mark Zanger (the model for "Megaphone Mark" in *Doonesbury*) recalled that "the administration legitimized [the BSAY] and delegitimized us at every turn."[54]

By a coincidence of timing, Brewster's greatest trials occurred in the middle of a review of his performance by the Yale Corporation. Begun in September 1969 at Brewster's suggestion, the review had promised to be routine. But as financial problems deepened and the events of April and May made Brewster a figure of national controversy, the review turned into a more serious matter. Nevertheless, the likelihood of a negative verdict remained negligible, for Brewster came from the same social milieu as the men who made up the Corporation and was a personal friend of several of them; the committee's vice chairman was William P. Bundy '39, the brother of McGeorge Bundy '40, perhaps Brewster's best friend.[55] After an exhaustive process, including interviews with more than a hundred people connected with Yale, the Corporation unanimously concluded that there was "remarkable and widespread" support for Brewster and that he should continue as president.[56]

If the Corporation was unanimous in its support, the same could not be said of the alumni. To be sure, Brewster had his supporters among them, especially among the more recent graduates. But many Old Blues had long been unhappy with him, and his apparent sympathy for the student strikers was the final straw. In August 1970, a group called Lux et Veritas, Inc. (LEVI), was formed, claiming that Yale was "in the process of losing the support of many of its alumni, alumni whose loyalty up to the recent past has been the envy of every other university." As evidence, the organization's founders noted that contributions to the Alumni Fund had dropped below 50 percent in 1970 for the first time in many years, adding, "It is no secret that the capital development campaign results are below expectations at the present time."[57]

The catalyst behind LEVI was Thomas Slater, a conservative undergraduate who, after the May Day events, had founded "Operation Watchdog," a project that accused Yale of surrendering to "leftwing radicalism" in pamphlets distributed at alumni reunions later that spring.[58] Serving as co-chairmen of LEVI were John W. Castles III '45, captain of the wrestling team and a member of Scroll and Key, and J. William Stack Jr. '40, captain of the football team and a member of Skull and Bones.[59] Both were exceptionally active alumni, with Castles the former chairman of the Alumni Fund and Stack serving as a class agent for thirty years. Joining them as founding members were Louis Loeb '19, the chairman of his twenty-fifth reunion, Charles S. Gage '25, a former treasurer of Yale, and John D. Garrison '31, a former president of the New York Yale Club.[60] Whether their views represented those of most alumni, the LEVI board was, by its very composition, sending Brewster a message: some of the alumni with the greatest capacity to raise money for Yale were deeply disaffected.

Though LEVI claimed that its purpose was "to encourage a better understanding between all elements in the Yale community . . . to secure optimum alumni support (financial and otherwise), understanding and confidence in the University . . . [and] to promote the welfare and best interests of Yale," its true goal was to turn back the clock.[61] Its 1972 report on Yale admissions evinced a powerful nostalgia for the period around 1950, when "boys of unusual intellectual capacity . . . [did] not account for more than ten percent of any class" and Yale did "not hesitate to admit a lad with a relatively low academic prediction whose personal qualifications seem outstanding, rather than a much drabber boy with higher scholastic predictions."[62] The report accused Inky Clark of a multiplicity of sins — among them, the drop in the number of legacies and boarding school graduates, the "decline in athletic prowess" at Yale, and the use of a "double standard" in the admission of minority students.[63]

This was standard conservative fare, but LEVI went on to challenge the meritocratic consensus then well established, not only at Yale, but at its principal competitors as well. Yale's need-blind financial aid policy — considered a crowning achievement by those committed to equality of opportunity — was, according to the report, "imposing on Yale a material financial burden without even the justification of a commensurately high yield." And the increasing number of Jews was subject to implicit criticism; under the old policy, which favored boys with the greatest "all-around promise," the proportion of Jews hovered around 10 percent, but now, according to *New York* magazine, Yale was 30 percent Jewish. By virtually abandoning the goal of geographical diversity, Yale had opened itself to the possibility of becoming even more Jewish; after all, as the report noted (quoting the *New York Times*), nearby "metropolitan New York is the home of 40% of the nation's 5.6 million Jews."[64]

In its companion report on coeducation, LEVI complained that "the alumni body was in no way consulted . . . when a jury-rigged measure of co-education was introduced by fiat into Yale's undergraduate life," and it noted "the existence of a significant body of alumni opinion which questions fundamentally the desirability of any coeducation at all at Yale at the undergraduate level." Yet, though the report took the position that full coeducation "has placed a deleterious pressure upon educational, social, and financial resources at Yale, and has lowered the quality of education at Yale College," it stopped short of calling for a return to an all-male Yale.[65]

Part of the reason that LEVI did not come out in outright opposition to the admission of women was that its own random sample of Yale undergraduates found that "an overwhelming number, more than 80% of those who responded, favored immediate 'full' coeducation, either by establishing a formal 1–1 ratio or through 'sex-fluid' admissions procedures."[66] Even as conservative an organization as LEVI recognized that a call for the exclusion of women threatened to undermine whatever credibility it had. Instead, the report argued that the interests of both men *and* women would be better served by a coordinate arrangement of the type Brewster initially favored rather than the fully coeducational model that Yale ultimately adopted. Though opposed to sex-blind admissions, the report did not endorse a specific ratio of men to women, coming out in favor instead of "a steady growth . . . in the number of women at Yale; but not at the price of a drastic cutback in male enrollment."[67] By 1972, even Lux et Veritas recognized that the presence of women at Yale was destined to be stronger rather than weaker in the future.

Though Brewster was civil publicly toward LEVI ("I obviously am actively interested in any effort to improve communication between the University and the alumni . . . [and] count many of you among my long standing friends"),[68] privately he was furious. In a letter to Charles S. Gage '25, the usually unflappable Brewster wrote: "I was pained as well as surprised to see you as a sponsor of a group whose members I knew were extremely bitter in their criticism of me and many recent Yale policies." Although he expressed a willingness to talk in person about Gage's concerns, Brewster ended the letter on a note that was hardly conciliatory: "You know I will never question your own ultimate motivation as far as Yale is concerned. I trust you will never question mine."[69]

LEVI evoked an even less charitable response in some alumni. After reading its report, Jonathan Straus '56 wrote back, accusing LEVI of favoring "the traditional criteria for admission to exclusive social clubs: athletic ability, nepotism, and mediocrity . . . Your malicious commentary on the admission of Jews, Negroes, and other minorities," he continued, "barely conceals a vicious anti-Semitism and racism." Urging the members of LEVI to "grow up," the outraged Straus concluded his attack by recommending that they "get off the back of our university and return to your restricted clubs to reminisce about the golden days of 'old boy' dominance." Straus sent a copy to Sam Chauncey, whose response indicated just how hostile the Yale administration felt: "You've said all I wanted to say, but my position prohibits it. So thanks for being so frank to them and so supportive to us."[70]

Despite the Yale administration's antipathy toward LEVI, it could not afford to be unresponsive to disaffected alumni. By 1970, Yale was in deep financial trouble. Between 1969 and 1970, the deficit had doubled to more than $1.7 million; at the same time, the endowment had plunged from more than $521 million to less than $420 million — a loss of almost 20 percent in a single year.[71] By the summer of 1970, Brewster publicly admitted that "if the present shrinkage were to continue for another year, we would have to either abandon the quality of what we're doing, abandon great discernible areas of activity, or abandon the effort to be accessible on the merits of talent, not of wealth or of race or of inheritance."[72]

Admissions was at the center of the deteriorating relations between the alumni and the administration, and Clark's departure presented Brewster with an opportunity to reassert control. In an unusual move, he appointed Sam Chauncey director of university admissions — a brand-new position. This made Chauncey the superior of John Muyskens, the mild-mannered Canadian who had served as Clark's director of admissions. Chauncey's official task was to "provide liaison and coordination between the undergraduate, graduate and professional schools," but his real job was to undo some of the damage of the Clark era while maintaining the broad direction that had been established in the late 1960s.[73]

The son of Henry Chauncey, the imposing president of the Educational Testing Service, Sam Chauncey was a graduate of Groton and Yale '57.[74] Nicholas Lemann offers a vivid portrait of the younger Chauncey: "He was never an outstanding student and he did not cut the same spectacular figure as his father. He was smaller, quieter, less commanding and exuberant. He had fine, tight, organized features that did not stand out. He was fit but not a star athlete. His virtue was precisely his good selfless character, along with an acute observational eye that his father lacked. Henry Chauncey unreflectively took up a leading position in society, while Sam Chauncey tended more to watch and to assess from a spot further from the rostrum."[75] A moderate reformer,

Sam was also a Yale loyalist with a keen sense of power relations. "No Yale president," he once said, "was ever so unrealistic as to believe that there were not institutional reasons for admitting certain people."[76]

A deliberate man, Chauncey did not move precipitously to alter the admissions policies of the Clark era. But by his second year, he recognized that Yale would have to make some adjustments if it was to remain competitive in the new, more austere fiscal environment.[77] In a January 1972 memorandum intended for internal consumption, Chauncey described the situation as one of "real chaos" and called on the Corporation's subcommittee on admissions to "establish the groups who need to be represented at Yale" and to "give the Admissions Office and Committee some indication of the number in each group."[78] This was a fundamentally political model of the admissions process, not unlike the one that had guided Bender at Harvard, and it called upon the Admissions Office to see to it that slices of the admissions pie be allocated with due attention to the power of the major constituencies.

The issue that most preoccupied Chauncey was the one that most threatened Yale's financial future: the continued tensions between the alumni and the administration. "Each year," he complained, "I find cases of applicants — sometimes alumni sons and daughters — who have been turned down and I cannot for the life of me see why." His principal recommendation called for increased attention to legacies: "Finally, *Yale must take stock of its relationship with its alumni.* There is no doubt that the financial situation in which Yale and her fellow private colleges find themselves is very serious. There is also little doubt that Yale will have to turn to her alumni for more in the way of capital and operating support if this financial situation is to change and improve. Support depends on loyalty and loyalty depends in many cases on family continuity . . . It is my genuine hope," he continued, "that we can see this year an increase in the number of sons and daughters in the class of 1976," adding that he would "make every effort possible to . . . see that the staff and Committee are sensitive to this area."[79]

Chauncey's concern was understandable. In 1971, Yale's deficit had risen for the fifth consecutive year — this time to a record of more than $2.5 million.[80] A letter from John E. Ecklund '38 of the Treasurer's Office made clear just how desperate the administration felt: "At this juncture, I do not believe anything will clear the atmosphere between Yale and her alumni on the subject of admissions except results, by which I mean a substantial increase in the number of sons and daughters of alumni of the undergraduate schools admitted and enrolled . . . I think that this substantial increase *must occur this spring,* that is, in 1972. The University Capital Budget Committee is working on a recommendation for a national Yale fund-raising campaign to begin as soon as possible. A visible change in admissions policy in regard to the alumni sons and daughters is indispensable and it will come too late if it comes in 1973. It must come in 1972." Though "thoroughly in accord" with Chauncey's "understanding that Yale will depend heavily on its alumni for its financial future," Ecklund suggested that he "not put it on paper as bluntly as that." Instead, Yale needed "a higher-sounding formula" that should "reflect a higher ideal."[81]

Chauncey took Ecklund's counsel to heart. In a speech on May 12, 1972, to the Cleveland Yale Club, he noted that the reduction in the number of undergraduate legacies had "seriously affected alumni morale and support." In a delicately worded statement, he argued that legacies should receive "special consideration" so that "we may maintain that continuity of loyalty so important to our future." Chauncey's strategy was to increase the number of legacy applicants, some of whom, he suggested, may have been discouraged from applying because "we have created an image that Harvard had in the 1950s — that Yale is a place for intellectual snobs and is looking only for the 'super brights'... Yale must also," Chauncey recommended, "make special efforts to increase the yield of alumni children"; in the most recent year, he noted with alarm, "27 sons and 11 daughters of Yale graduates went to Harvard after being admitted to Yale."[82] Though the editor's introduction to the published version of the speech noted that "both Harvard and Princeton offer more attractive financial packages than Yale, Chauncey said nary a word about Yale's need for financial support from alumni."[83]

Yet despite Yale's financial woes, the Admissions Committee was surprisingly unresponsive to Chauncey's request for greater "sensitivity" toward legacies. In 1972, it admitted 38 percent of them, a marginal change from the previous year's 37 percent. This was an increase from the last two years of Clark's term, but it was not nearly enough to mend the frayed alumni relations.[84] In the spring of 1972, Chauncey and Brewster accepted the resignation of John Muyskens, the last link to the Clark years.[85]

The choice of a new dean of admissions was obviously critical. After a long search, Brewster and Chauncey settled on Worth David '56. A graduate of the Hill School, a traditional Yale feeder, David embodied the ideal of the "all-around man," competing on the wrestling team and joining St. Anthony Hall, a fraternity. Already married as an undergraduate to Edwina Carnesale (a graduate of Dean Junior College), David later taught history and mathematics at Suffield Academy, a private school in Connecticut, and obtained a master's degree at Wesleyan. After working at Harvard as a special Teaching Fellow and then as an educational consultant, he was appointed principal of Clayton High School in suburban St. Louis.[86]

David brought to his new job his experience in both public and private schools and a readiness to implement the new admissions agenda that

Chauncey and Brewster wished to put in place after the turmoil of the Clark years. In one of his first acts as dean, he informed members of the Alumni Schools Committee that he "would attempt to translate into practice those reforms put forward by Mr. Chauncey."[87] Above all, this meant an increase in the number of alumni children. In a memo to the Yale Corporation's Sub-Committee on Admissions, David stated flatly that "the class of 1977 should include a minimum of 195 Yale sons and daughters . . . at least 15% of the matriculants."[88] But he recognized that it would not be easy and requested Brewster's help. "First is the question of definition of special hospitality with respect to alumni sons and daughters. Given the University's present financial difficulties, I sense very little need to point out to the faculty the importance of alumni to the University. Nonetheless, it would be helpful if you would reiterate your position as expressed in your Annual Report." David also asked Brewster to pressure the committee to fulfill "the University's obligation to traditionally oppressed minorities" and to admit applicants of "athletic distinction." Admitting that "all of this sounds somewhat ridiculous when made explicit," the new dean nonetheless expressed his hope that Brewster would "tell the Committee that athletic distinction should be a significant factor in the selection process."[89]

Pressure on the administration — and on David, in particular — to alter the admissions policy in order to alleviate Yale's financial difficulties increased during the 1972–1973 academic year. In December, Parker Williamson III, vice chairman of a major financial corporation and a member of the Yale Development Board, sent J. Richardson Dilworth '21, the head of the Corporation's Sub-Committee on Admissions, a blunt letter about the problems facing Yale.[90] Citing Lux et Veritas's report as "worthy of very careful study," he urged the President and Fellows of the Yale Corporation to take full responsibility for the admissions policy and its implementation rather than leaving it "in the lap of Inky Clark and now Sam Chauncey":

> Until your committee and all the Fellows recognize this and do something about it, our Lloyd Cutler, who is now Chairman of the Yale Development Board, will have an insurmountable task in trying to raise large amounts of money from our alumni.
>
> At the Yale Development Board meeting this Fall . . . we were told that organization for the new capital program would begin in 1973; 1974 and 1975 will be the years of the big push. I can only repeat that this is a very early timetable, if we at the same time wish to convince the alumni that the admissions policy has changed. I say again, until they are so convinced the Yale Development Board has one tough job on its hands.[91]

Supporting Williamson's point, an estranged Old Eli, angry that his daughter had been deprived of the opportunity to "have been the fifth generation of Wellingtons at Yale," protested that since "Yale in the past ten years has abandoned her sons and daughters for the public market, I cannot find it in my heart to march down this one-way street blindly and without reasonable reciprocity." Claiming that many alumni felt as he did, he warned that "Yale's long-term interests are not being advanced by these policies."[92]

In his first year in office, David established a clear objective on the issue of alumni children: to admit a minimum of 280 applicants to yield a minimum of 195 matriculants.[93] When the final figures came in, he had surpassed his target, admitting 314 and enrolling 207 — 25 of them from the waiting list.[94] Still, the administration worried that the increase was not sufficient to mend relations with the alumni. In a June 1973 letter to Dilworth, Chauncey suggested that the Admissions Office — in addition to setting and meeting specific goals with respect to legacies — "identify Yale College children separately from Yale University children." Chauncey also worried about the decline in Yale's athletic performance though he was cautiously optimistic about the possibilities of improvement: "Ink Clark's rather tough attitude" toward athletes had been replaced by Worth David's "sensible attitude toward the admission of students with athletic talent." Even the "Jewish question" was apparently still alive among some Old Blues, though Chauncey hastened to assure Dilworth that Jews had never been classified as a "minority" and that candidates were judged "without regard to religion."[95]

By the summer of 1973, the administration had arrived at a critical juncture. Yale remained in a deep financial crisis and was embarking on a major capital campaign to regain its footing. But changing the meritocratic admissions policies of the Clark and Brewster years would not be easy, for the faculty was now part of the admissions process and strongly disapproved of efforts to turn back the clock. Indeed, from the faculty's perspective, the move toward meritocracy was an unfinished revolution, still thwarted by unwarranted preferences given to powerful constituencies. In a letter to Brewster in May 1973, faculty members who had served on the Admissions Committee that year complained forcefully about "a clear sense of anti-intellectualism on the part of the admissions staff. Insisting that "candor is in order" in those cases "where admissions officers feel pressure because of outside influence (alumni, athletes, etc.)," the committee members complained of feeling "manipulated" because of the "frequent support of candidates whose qualifications were without substance." "The major charge of a great university," they sternly reminded Brewster, "is intellectual inquiry."[96]

At the same time that the faculty was pushing for more meritocracy, powerful forces within Yale and outside were pushing for less. In the 1960s, with the economy booming and federal grants growing, Yale had become less dependent on its alumni; in 1973, as the stock market tumbled and inflation surged, Yale's endowment dropped by $78 million (13 percent of its total value) and its dependence on its alumni correspondingly increased.[97] Signs of Yale's deteriorating situation were everywhere; the nation's leader in raising funds between World War I and World War II, it had dropped behind Harvard and Stanford in recent years. Ominously, by the early 1970s, Yale was losing some of its most distinguished faculty members in the humanities to Harvard and Princeton.[98]

In October 1973, as preparations for launching the $370 million Campaign for Yale were in their final stages, Brewster made his choice. At a meeting of the Yale Development Board, the Yale Alumni Fund, and the Association of Yale Alumni, he announced that Yale would make a special effort to enroll more alumni children:

> If Yale is going to expect her alumni to care about Yale, then she must convince her alumni that Yale cares about them . . . Alumni would like to feel that Yale wants their children if they are qualified and wants them badly enough so that they will go out of their way to encourage applications, will make time for a supportive interview, and if a child is admitted will make a real effort to persuade that child to come . . . The Yale Corporation has great confidence in Dean David and has directed him to see to it that every effort be made to attract, to admit, and to gain the acceptance of every qualified alumni son and daughter . . . The test will ultimately be by the performance of the dean, the staff, and the committees, and it is the job of the AYA to monitor that performance.[99]

Brewster also made concessions on the issue of athletes, another source of alumni disaffection. "Yale students," he declared, "should not go into game after game . . . with a feeling that they don't stand a chance." Accordingly, the Yale Corporation would "instruct the Dean of Admissions to give positive weight to athletic distinction if an athlete is otherwise qualified."[100]

These concessions must not have come easily to Brewster, who had invested ten years in making Yale a more open, meritocratic, and intellectually rigorous institution. But he wished to leave Yale in a sound financial condition before retiring, and there was no way to do this without restoring policies that ran counter to the values he had done so much to advance. In a November letter to Worth David, Brewster showed that he was serious about keeping his pledge to the alumni. Concretely, Brewster instructed David to have legacy applicants who had been judged "possible" admits in the early evaluation process to receive a special third reading.[101]

The statistics on the class entering in 1974 made it clear that a new admissions regime had finally been put in place. Almost half (49 percent) of the applicants whose fathers had attended Yale College were admitted — the highest figure in a decade.[102] All in all, 230 legacies — 18 percent of the class — enrolled at Yale.[103] This was 83 more alumni children than just two years earlier — an increase of 56 percent since David took office. And it was a sizable slice of the Yale admissions pie; in comparison, the *total* number of African-American students in the class was 81.[104]

Yet aggregate figures, however striking, do not convey the degree of preference given to legacies, especially to those from families deemed critical to Yale's financial future.[105] The Campaign for Yale closely coordinated its activities with those of the Admissions Office, and in June 1974 a staff member, Steven E. Carlson '73, proudly reported to Brewster that "the Admissions Office is now bending over backwards to accept alumni children."[106]

After reviewing several pages of statistics, Carlson offered his assessment of the new policy: "Please take note the *consideration given to alumni children is substantially on the upswing, particularly in the class of 1978 where the children of Yale College alumni have a 1 in 2 chance of being admitted, just as they did in 1964 for the class of 1968.* There has been a real change in Admissions Office procedure under Worth David." Noting that the historic preference for legacies "has been based on Yale's desire to please the alumni (including the very wealthy ones)," he then asked a fundamental question: "How much preference do wealthy alumni children receive? The acceptance rate of different applicants to the class of 1977 is instructive here. For everyone, there was a 24.2% chance; for Yale University and Yale College alumni children respectively 37.9% and 38.7%; but for Development Office preferred candidates — 3, 4, or 5-stars — there was a 76.2% chance, twice as good as other alumni children and three times better than the mass of applicants."[107] Clearly, in the eyes of Mother Yale, not all her sons were equal. Yet this very inequality reflected a conscious administrative decision, made under difficult circumstances, to do what it thought was best for Yale. "Please bear in mind," Carlson wrote to Brewster, "that twenty years from now, my generation will reap the whirlwind of a renewed aristocracy at Yale."[108]

The Revolt of the Tigers

Princeton's approach to change, unlike Yale's, was gradual and carefully designed to maintain the loyalty of its alumni. While Yale was sharply reducing the advantages enjoyed by legacies and the private school graduates, Princeton maintained its traditional policies. Indeed, the admission rate for legacies at Princeton actually rose from 54 percent in 1965 to 56 percent in 1968, and alumni sons made up over 20 percent of the freshmen class in both years. Private school boys also fared well; constituting just 36 percent of the entering class in 1965, their share rose to 40 percent of all freshmen in 1968.[109]

The contrast with Yale could hardly have been greater, yet by the spring of

1969, an important segment of the Princeton alumni was in open revolt. In the interim, Princeton had finally decided to admit women — a change that was simply too much for many alumni despite a concerted effort by the administration to placate them.

On February 6, 1969 — less than four weeks after the trustees announced their historic decision to admit women — a group of disgruntled alumni calling itself the Alumni Committee to Involve Itself Now (ACTION) was founded. In its first public announcement on March 12, ACTION claimed 500 members and promised to run insurgent candidates in the elections that spring for new alumni members of the Board of Trustees.[110]

As George Hamid Jr. '40, vice chairman of ACTION, put it, "Male isolation" had been "the big, contributing aspect to the success of his education."[111] ACTION's chairman, Jere Wescott Patterson '38,[112] was even more direct: "Let's be frank. Girls are being sent to Princeton less to educate them than to pacify, placate, and amuse the boys who are now there."[113] Underlying ACTION's hostility to coeducation was a feeling of revulsion at Princeton's alleged moral decline. "Why, if I could tell you what went on in Princeton dormitories," Hamid confided to a reporter. But after hesitating he added, "I better not go into that."[114]

Yet coeducation was by no means the only source of discontent among Old Tigers. They were also upset by student protests calling for divestment from South Africa and the closing of the Institute for Defense Analysis, the faculty decision to deny credit for ROTC courses, the decline of the eating clubs, and the more meritocratic admission policies of the period, but the end of Princeton's male tradition was the catalytic issue.[115] In a remarkable letter to the *Princeton Alumni Weekly*, fourteen of the founders of ACTION laid out their concerns. In addition to "the headlong rush into coeducation," these worries included: "Militant activist groups, Morality and dope, Support for the continuation of the Trustees, Continuance of Military and Naval Science courses for credit, Involvement of the University in government research, University investments, and others."[116] Amid these concerns was a powerful sense of nostalgia. "In our time," Hamid told the *New York Times,* "a Princeton man had the reputation of being a dashing, undisciplined fellow." But this reputation, he added, never conflicted with Old Nassau's motto, "Princeton in the Nation's Service."[117]

In a last-minute attempt to block the admission of women, a group of 15 graduates from Ohio organized a poll of alumni attitudes on the issue. The poll, which was mailed on April 10, 1969, to all undergraduate alumni and counted on May 8 by Ernst and Ernst, revealed that alumni opposition was perhaps even more widespread than the administration had acknowledged. Of the 55 percent of alumni who responded to the questionnaire, 57 percent wished to maintain Princeton's male tradition. The results also revealed a powerful correlation with age: while support for coeducation was common among recent graduates, a strong majority of alumni from before World War II were in opposition.[118]

Meanwhile, the administration quietly decided to go forward. Having said publicly in January that the first coeds were unlikely to arrive that fall, President Goheen and the trustees shifted course and on April 19, 1969, announced that women would be admitted immediately. In the intervening months, the Admissions Office had received over 500 applications from women; the moment the trustees announced their decision, letters of acceptance were sent to 135 of them.[119] By early May, when the alumni finally released the findings from their poll, coeducation was a fait accompli.[120]

Though publicly civil, the alumni and administration were engaged in a bitter conflict. In a letter to Herbert Hobler '44, one of ACTION's candidates for the Board of Trustees, Goheen had written that ACTION's behavior violated the discreet and gentlemanly Princeton way of doing things: "despite differences within the family, Princeton alumni and trustees have traditionally tried to pull together without enforcing the views of any constituency . . . I cannot believe," he added pointedly, "that the University is well served by fragmenting its alumni according to views on a single issue or set of issues."[121] ACTION was equally provocative. Alumni pressure to force the administration to hear the "majority" voice, Hamid told a local newspaper, would be largely financial. Though ACTION did not officially advocate withholding donations from Princeton's Annual Giving, Hamid noted that the number of individual donors was down and that Princeton had run a deficit of $1.7 million the previous year.[122]

The centerpiece of ACTION's strategy was its effort to place two of its members on the Board of Trustees. Its nominees, who gained their positions on the ballot on the basis of alumni signatures, were Hobler, a Princeton businessman and an elder of the Presbyterian Church, and Arthur Langlie '52, a Seattle lawyer, an active Republican, and a former deacon of the Presbyterian Church.[123] Both men, upstanding embodiments of the Old Princeton, had been active in alumni affairs. Yet they fought uphill battles, for they lacked the imprimatur of official nominees in an institution that valued tradition and harmony. When the ballots were counted, both were defeated, as were four of the six official nominees, including Donald Rumsfeld '54, then a fourth-term congressman from Illinois.[124]

But the ACTION revolt was far from over. At the June 1969 reunion, Jere Patterson spoke before an audience of 150. Among the issues he identified as deserving rigorous examination by "concerned alumni" were recent changes in admissions, discipline, ROTC, eating clubs, faculty, curriculum, and university decision making. While ACTION did not call for the dismissal of President Goheen or Dean of Students Rudenstine, it proposed to review their performances under the motto "Shape up or ship out." Outside the meeting, a student entrepreneur was selling orange and black student buttons with the inscription "Bring Back the Old Princeton."[125]

In the fall of 1969, ACTION sponsored a poll of alumni attitudes on a variety of sensitive issues, including campus protests, ROTC, curriculum, and admissions policy. Conducted by the Opinion Research Corporation, a respected Princeton firm, the study revealed that a strong majority of alumni favored a hard line on campus disorders and believed that Princeton had an obligation to offer ROTC to students who wanted it. But some of the study's findings were unexpected; perhaps the biggest surprise was that five in eight alumni approved of Princeton's making "reasonable exceptions" to its admissions requirements "in order to admit a significant number of deprived applicants." Despite the generally professional character of the poll, Goheen expressed his unhappiness with it, claiming that it was "not an exploration of the opinion of Princeton alumni made from an unbiased standpoint, but rather an attempt to measure what proportion of Princeton Alumni may share the particular concerns represented by the ACTION organization."[126]

By late 1970, as the student protests waned, ACTION had lost some of its momentum. Yet it was still busy trying to undo some of the changes of the 1960s, and it continued to express its estrangement from the administration. At a time when Princeton, like Yale, was suffering from serious financial problems, Patterson emphasized the costs of alumni disaffection in an interview in the *Princeton Alumni Weekly:* "Present policies at Princeton are bound to cost the university millions in reduced annual giving, decreased special gifts, and altered wills. Major contributors are increasingly withdrawing support, not for market reasons, but simply out of dismay and disgust. Some feel their contributions have been misused and that today's Princeton isn't what they want to help maintain or expand."[127] Recent trends gave added weight to these observations; in 1969–1970, as both the federal government and private foundations reduced their support and Princeton suffered from a $2.4 million deficit, the number of alumni contributing to Annual Giving dropped by more than 5 percent and the amount donated decreased by nearly $500,000.[128]

Patterson was relatively moderate on the issue of admissions, acknowledging that the policy still favored the sons of alumni and that he "would certainly not want to see . . . Princeton not have boys of diverse background in each class." But like many members of ACTION, he was profoundly unhappy about the decline of the eating clubs — a trend that he rightly saw as part of a broader movement away from selectivity. This "downgrading of some aspects of selectivity," he observed, "accounts for no small degree of alumni discontent." Then, in a plaintive cry for the Princeton of old, Patterson expressed sentiments no doubt shared by many of the disaffected alumni: "A pall of mediocrity seems to be descending upon the university. Regard for not only academic but personal excellence seems to be downgraded. The concept of an elite seems to be something to be quietly buried or denied: Princeton should be dedicated to generating not only excellence of mind but of conduct and character and responsibility. It should never pander to the mediocre or to pressures to pull the top down to meet the bottom or middle."[129] Though Princeton had never gone as far down the road toward the elimination of hereditary privilege as Yale under Clark and Brewster, ACTION's lament was strikingly similar to that felt by many an Old Blue: the all-male, gentlemanly sanctuary they knew and loved had been replaced by a heartless and soulless institution that valued brains over character and equality over excellence.

ACTION faded from view in 1971, but in the summer of 1972 another group of angry alumni formed a new organization, Concerned Alumni of Princeton (CAP) to try to reverse Princeton's policies. CAP can be traced to a letter in the February 22, 1972, *Princeton Alumni Weekly* from Shelby Cullom Davis '30, who was then serving as ambassador to Switzerland. Davis argued that "Princeton's unique character lies in its relatively small and homogenous alumni body, which has lavishly supported Princeton's schools' programs and finances throughout the years." After sharply criticizing the president-elect, William Bowen, for calling for the rapid increase in the number of women students, Davis appealed to his fellow graduates: "the alumni should realize the way Princeton is headed before it is too late and Princeton becomes just another one of a number of faceless American universities, without unique character."[130] In a second letter in May, Davis reported that he had received two dozen responses from alumni: 22 in favor and 2 opposed (including one "high administration official"). He closed with a call to action: "It is not too late to reverse the trend if the alumni make their wishes known in a massive way and an alumnus or group of alumni in America assume the mantle of leadership in a crusade to keep Princeton Princeton."[131]

In Shelby Cullom Davis, the administration faced a formidable adversary. An investment banker of immense wealth, Davis had donated more than $5.3 million to Princeton in 1964 — at the time the largest single contribution that was not given anonymously in the university's history and one that put a three-year $53 million capital campaign over the top. In addition to his exceptional generosity, Davis had long been active in Princeton's affairs, serving on the Advisory Council of the History Department since 1941 and as class secretary for seventeen years. Given his extraordinary record of service to Princeton, Davis might have reasonably expected to be offered a seat on the Board of Trustees or to be given an honorary degree. But neither honor came his way — an omission that may have vexed him.[132]

The son of George H. Davis, Princeton 1886, Shelby Cullom Davis was a Presbyterian and a graduate of Princeton's top feeder school, Lawrenceville. A member of the Charter Club at Princeton, he graduated with highest honors in History and went on to receive an M.A. from Columbia and a doctorate in political science from the University of Geneva. An accomplished man of letters, he had written five books before the age of thirty-five as well as articles for such publications as the *Atlantic Monthly* and the *Financial Times.* But it was above all as a businessman that Davis made his mark. The founder and managing partner of Shelby Cullom Davis & Co., he transformed a $100,000 loan in 1947 into a fortune of more than $800 million by the early 1990s. A longtime Republican, he was appointed ambassador to Switzerland by President Nixon in 1969 and served there until 1975.[133] Proud of his patrician background, Davis had served as governor of the Society of Mayflower Descendants of the State of New York and was a member of ten elite social clubs, including the Knickerbocker (New York), Bar Harbor (Maine), and Everglades (Palm Beach, Florida).

Yet even a man with such impeccable social credentials was apparently not immune to the status anxieties produced by the cultural and political turmoil of the 1960s. This feeling was betrayed in still another letter to the *Princeton Alumni Weekly* in October 1972, just as the existence of CAP was announced. Davis claimed the support of the "silent majority" of the alumni and reported with great dismay that one result of the administration's policies was that some undergraduates were labeling Princeton "Rutgers South."[134]

Joining Davis in founding CAP was another well-connected Old Tiger, Asa S. Bushnell '21. The son of a prominent Ohio banker, John Ludlow Bushnell, Princeton 1894, Asa Bushnell had prepared for college at Hill, another leading Princeton feeder school. An Episcopalian and a Republican, he served as president of the Cottage Club. After graduation, he was the editor of the *Princeton Alumni Weekly* from 1925 to 1930 and graduate manager of athletics from 1927 to 1937. Bushnell then became commissioner of the Eastern Collegiate Athletics Conference (ECAC), a position he held for three decades as the "recognized czar of intercollegiate athletics" — a reputation no doubt enhanced by his long service as secretary of the U.S. Olympic Committee. Ever the Princeton loyalist, Bushnell was president of his class as an undergraduate and later served as class secretary, class representative on the Alumni Council, and class vice president. "No one has done more to nurture nostalgic memories," said Bushnell's entry in the reunion report for 1966, which praised him as the member of the Class of 1921 who has "done the most" for Princeton.[135]

With Davis and Bushnell at the helm of CAP, the organization moved quickly to do something that ACTION had never accomplished: it established its own forum with the alumni by starting a magazine, *Prospect* (echoing the name of the street where Princeton's eating clubs were located), as a conservative alternative to the *Princeton Alumni Weekly*. In *Prospect* the disaffected alumni had an invaluable instrument, for it allowed them to elaborate and disseminate their criticism of Princeton's policies, putting added pressure on the administration. The first issues appeared in the fall of 1972 and were mailed to over 10,000 alumni.

Prospect was edited by T. Harding Jones '72, who met Davis when both men were vacationing at Northeast Harbor, Maine, in the summer of 1972. A member of the College Young Republicans angered by what he considered a left-wing bias of the faculty, the Ohio-born Jones was the founder and executive director of a group called Undergraduates for a Stable America. Sensing a kindred spirit, Davis saw in Jones just the man to edit *Prospect*.[136] Described by the *New York Times* as "well-financed," *Prospect* operated on a budget of roughly $200,000 a year. Princeton officials believed (but could not confirm) that Davis underwrote half of its total expenses.[137]

Prospect's inaugural issue tried to disguise its conservative ideological orientation, stating that it hoped "to provide a moderating influence with Princeton's best interests and its future in mind." "The goals of this magazine," it wrote in its mission statement, "are to *inform* alumni fully and accurately, to encourage expression of alumni *views*, to foster greater alumni *influence* in decision making, and to achieve a Better and Stronger Princeton." It promised to "offer detailed reports of significant occurrences on campus" and to "present in-depth studies of vital questions having to do with University policies and practices." *Prospect*'s objective, it assured the alumni, "is not to interfere, but to be of genuine service."[138]

Prospect had put together a distinguished Advisory Committee, which included the legendary basketball player, Rhodes Scholar, and future U.S. senator Bill Bradley '65. But after seeing the first issue, with such articles as "Goheen Heads McGovern Faculty Committee," "Undergraduates for a Stable America," and the "The Prospect for ROTC," Bradley announced his resignation in a short letter. Stating that "I cannot concur with the views presented," he complained that he had expected "a more representative cross-section of opinion."[139] What Bradley had sensed — and what became abundantly clear in the next few issues — was that *Prospect* would be a forum for a right-wing critique, not only of recent developments at Princeton, but of broader trends in American higher education.

Like ACTION, CAP accused the administration of effectively disenfranchising the alumni and of tolerating (if not actively cultivating) a faculty that was lopsidedly liberal in its views and a student body that was unpatriotic, disrespectful of traditional moral norms, and all too willing to engage in disruptive campus actions. Underlying all these concerns was the sense that Princeton was changing in ways antithetical to its best traditions — a change exemplified by the altered composition of the student body. This feeling led to a preoccupation with Princeton's admissions policy, and articles on the issue of who should be admitted — and who should not — became a staple in the pages of *Prospect.*[140]

In October 1973, a year after its inaugural issue, *Prospect* published a formal statement of the objectives of CAP. Declaring their intent of "preserving, and further improving, all that is best in a Princeton education" (by which "we mean an understanding of and respect for what it has meant to be a Princeton scholar and a Princeton gentleman"), CAP touted the virtues of a traditional Princeton education, which "gave a young man a sense of duty toward and respect for his country and its traditions, a respect for religion and the importance of God in our daily lives, a broad knowledge of Western civilization, the importance of honor and honesty in one's relationships, the independence to be able to take a courageous stand, and long standing friendship with and membership in an association of men who have shared in the traditions of Princeton." After alleging that the faculty was "overwhelmingly of one political and cultural bias (namely leftist)," CAP then issued its manifesto on admissions, declaring that it wanted

> a student body which . . . represents far better than Princeton does today, a fair cross-section of the future leadership of this country — not only in scholarly endeavors, or in political or economic philosophy, but in business, government, the professions, science (applied as well as pure), and the armed forces. Educational and traditional reasons should play a far greater role than sociological, untried reasons for making certain decisions. Princeton should not become . . . a haven only for young men and women intent upon leading America by dominating its intelligentsia . . . We must look for the young men and women who, twenty or thirty years from now, will likely be heading not only the nation's philosophy departments, but its major business enterprises, its government, the top civilian posts in its military organizations, its communications industries, and others.[141]

The statement's implication was unmistakable: Princeton's current admissions policy was tilted far too heavily toward the recruitment of "intellectuals," many of them critical of the American social order. Princeton was thereby failing to fulfill its essential mission: the education of future leaders in business and government.

To further their call for change, CAP commissioned a poll on alumni attitudes. The poll revealed the familiar generational split: alumni of the classes of 1960 to 1972 approved of Princeton's admissions policies by a margin of 61 to 20 percent, graduates from the classes of 1929 or earlier disapproved, 55 to 27 percent, with the classes from 1930 through 1959 more or less evenly split at 41 percent in favor and 45 percent against." Most striking, however, was the degree of opposition to Princeton's decision to admit more women and blacks. On the issue of race, just 36 percent of all alumni thought that "achieving racial balance" should be given "a great deal" or a "fair amount of weight" in evaluating candidates for admission; in contrast, 65 percent believed that "status as a son/daughter of an alumnus" should be given such weight and 63 percent believed "athletic ability" also merited such weight. On the issue of sex-blind admissions, the alumni showed a similar lack of enthusiasm, with 38 percent in favor of limiting women to 30 percent or less of the freshman class, whereas 33 percent favored either sex-blind admissions (25 percent) or "about 50 percent" (8 percent). Of the remaining 29 percent, 15 percent favored "other" (presumably no women at all), 7 percent had no opinion, and 7 percent, "about 40 percent."[142]

In an article in *Prospect* before the results of the poll were available, Shelby Cullom Davis expressed alarm at the growing number of women and minorities:

> What student population will build a strong Alumni body? Again, the record furnishes the answer:
> A student body which, in addition to its intellectual and physical achievements, takes interest and pleasure in associating together over the years as classes and classmates, through many and various ways, such as reunions, class luncheons and dinners . . . What sort of a student body should this be that will, in effect, "hang together" over the years? May I recall, and with some nostalgia, my father's 50th reunion, a body of men, relatively homogeneous in interests and backgrounds, who had known and liked each other over the years during which they had contributed much in spirit and in substance to the greatness of Princeton.
> I cannot envisage a similar happening in the future with an undergraduate student population of approximately 40% women and minorities, such as the Administration has proposed.

But the trend, Davis argued, was "by no means irreversible." Just as "Princeton's women population has increased from 0 to 170 to 400 to 755 to a goal of 1200, so too can it similarly decline. There is nothing sacrosanct about these numbers." Davis favored a reversal of the current policies and a return to the overwhelmingly white, male Princeton of the past: "Why should not a goal of 10%–20% women and minorities be appropriate for Princeton's long term strength and future?"[143]

The growing racial and gender diversity of the student body was not *Prospect*'s only complaint. An article by John H. Thatcher Jr. '53,[144] a longtime alumni interviewer and alumni schools committee chairman, expressed dismay about the personal qualities of the students being admitted to Princeton:

> Certainly one thing does appear to be happening — increasing numbers of students *are* being admitted to Princeton whose personality, character, and maturity are substantially less than the optimum expressed in the University catalogues and brochures. Several indices point to this — the jump in the number of Princeton students caught stealing from the University Store, the increasing difficulties in enforcing the Honor System, the growing defacement of books on reserve in the library, etc. In some respects, the worthwhile goal of diversity at Princeton would appear to have been achieved only by lessening the normally high amounts of character and personality of entering Freshman classes.

Responsibility for the declining proportion of students of "high character," Thatcher argued, resided in "shifting priorities and faculty-administration pressures on the Admission Office," the increased influence of faculty evaluators directly involved in assessing candidates, and the "relegation of the formerly large role alumni schools committeemen played in the admissions process to one that currently consists largely of information-servicing and recruiting."[145] To reverse the trend, he suggested a restoration of the role of alumni interviewers. Through their "personal evaluation and character estimation," Princeton could identify those candidates who should be rejected on personal grounds.

CAP did not, however, stop with general critiques of the admissions policy. Unlike ACTION, which launched its campaign against the admission of women when it was already too late, CAP forcefully expressed its opposition to sex-blind admissions *before* the trustees had reached a final decision. In mid-December 1973, as the trustees prepared to address the matter, the Executive Committee of CAP unanimously declared its opposition both to any expansion of the undergraduate student body and to the idea of admitting qualified applicants without regard to sex. In a formal statement that drew on the results of its poll, CAP declared:

> *Thus, a majority of alumni believe that there should be no increase in the number of women and only a small number — one fourth of alumni — believe that there should be no guidelines at all. Concerned Alumni of Princeton opposes adoption of a sex-blind admission policy.*

The Executive Committee was extremely concerned about the possibility that Princeton would go back on a promise made to alumni that the traditional class of 800 male undergraduates would be maintained if coeducation was adopted. It was only with this promise that alumni tolerated the action of the Administration in establishing coeducation . . . should it appear that this deliberation over enlarging the undergraduate enrollment and the establishment of a sex-blind admissions policy that would break a promise made to alumni, . . . is only a charade, our hoped for reconciliation of an alumni body already battered by policies adopted against its will, may be placed out of reach.

CAP's statement ended with a sharp warning to the trustees: "alumni cannot be expected to stand by while promises are broken and actions are taken which are clearly against their will."[146]

Yet in January 1974, despite the fervent protestations of CAP, Princeton's trustees announced the adoption of a policy of sex-blind admissions.[147] Acknowledging that there had been "a general understanding throughout the University community and the alumni body when coeducation was adopted in 1969, that there would be no decline in the number of male students enrolled," the administration defended its decision by noting, "Conditions do change, however, and the Trustees have an obligation to serve the long-term interests of the University in ways that are consistent with current and prospective needs."[148]

Nevertheless, CAP soldiered on in its struggle against sex-blind admissions, for it was not a campaign that it could afford to lose if it were to have any chance of winning the larger war to bring back the Old Princeton. In the end, the defeat CAP suffered on this issue was its Gettysburg; it would continue to fight to restore the status quo ante, but its major counteroffensive had been repulsed and the unhappy end was now in sight.

The rejection of its demand to limit (and, preferably, to reduce) the number of women was but one of many defeats. One of CAP's primary objectives was to reduce the number of students accepted almost exclusively on the basis of "brains," but the Admissions Office was moving precisely in the opposite direction; indeed, one of the themes of every annual report from 1972 through 1975 was that Princeton was not enrolling a sufficient number of academic "1's" (roughly, the top 700 of more than 10,000 applicants) and needed to find ways to improve the yield of top scholars.[149] On the issue of minorities, too, the Admissions Office showed no signs of reducing its efforts; on the contrary, it remained preoccupied with the task of identifying, attracting, and competing successfully for talented candidates from minority cultures, not only blacks, but also "Puerto Ricans, Mexican Americans, students from other Spanish-speaking backgrounds, Native Americans, and Asian Americans."[150] On the question of athletes — a particular concern of CAP's[151] — the Admissions Office continued to demand higher academic qualifications and reported proudly that higher standards had led to a reduction in the number of admitted athletes from 350 to 310 and a drop in the number with academic ratings of "4" or "5" from 183 to 144.[152]

After years of unremitting effort, the insurgent alumni had clearly failed in their efforts. In the fall of 1976, four years after *Prospect* first appeared, the freshman class embodied the New Princeton that the Old Tigers found so distasteful. Over a third female (and with 56 fewer men than two years earlier), it was 18 percent minority, with blacks alone composing 10 percent of the class.[153] Almost 60 percent of the freshmen had attended public schools, and Jews — who had been limited to 3 percent when most of the leadership of CAP had attended Princeton — now constituted 19 percent of the class.[154] Devoted alumni such as Shelby Cullom Davis had insisted that Princeton's greatness was rooted in its tradition of homogeneity, but by the mid-1970s the administration and trustees had made a very different wager: the university's future would rest on the diversity of its student body.

The Limits of Alumni Power and the Decline of the Protestant Establishment

Despite its many failures, the alumni revolt did, however, have one conspicuous success: the restoration of legacy preference at Yale and its maintenance at Princeton. At Yale, the results were particularly dramatic. In 1976, as the restoration entered its third year, 47 percent of legacy applicants were admitted — almost double the rate of other candidates and a higher percentage than that accepted in 1965, the last year before the arrival of Inky Clark.[155]

At Princeton, the push for meritocracy had never gone as far as it had at Yale, and the degree of preference for alumni children never really diminished. To be sure, a rising number of alumni sons were rejected because of the growing number of applicants; still, until 1969, Princeton had accepted a majority of legacies in every year but one (1966, when the admission dipped to 47 percent, only to rise to 51 percent in 1967 and 56 percent in 1968).[156] It was perhaps for this very reason that the alumni revolt did not really develop at Princeton until 1969, three years after the first stirrings of rebellion at Yale. Even then, Princeton — increasingly sensitive to alumni sentiments because of the rising chorus of protests about coeducation — was careful not to tamper with legacy preference. Admissions rates for alumni children never fell much below double the rate for other applicants, and in the mid-1970s preferences for legacies actually increased. In 1975, 48 percent gained admission — a rate 2.3 times higher than other applicants.[157]

Yet while the alumni had been able to protect their most direct interest — maintaining preference for their own children — the revolts at Yale and Princeton had failed to accomplish their broader objective — restoring the admission policy of old. Like Princeton, Yale by the mid-1970s had been permanently transformed. In 1976, public schools provided over 60 percent of all entrants, and women made up almost 40 percent of the freshman class. Minorities contributed over 13 percent of freshmen, and Jews — just 11 percent of the class as recently as 1961 — now constituted about a third of the undergraduate body. But the ultimate blow to the Old Yale was the end of the tradition of educating "one thousand male leaders"; in 1976, just 796 men enrolled in the freshman class — a drop of 22 percent from five years earlier.[158]

Ironically, many of the administrators who presided over the transformation of Yale and Princeton came from the same social milieu — WASP, upper or upper middle class, northeastern, and private school educated — that spawned the alumni revolt. But this segment of the WASP elite believed that both morality and institutional self-interest required that universities change with the times. The claims of the excluded and the victims of discrimination — blacks, women, Jews, and the poor — were, they concluded, fundamentally just. At the same time, men such as Kingman Brewster were deeply committed to maintaining Yale's position as a training ground for the leaders of the future and worried that if Yale retained its traditional practices, it might become, as he had memorably put it, "a finishing school on Long Island Sound."[159]

At bottom, Brewster was anything but an egalitarian. "As long as exclusion is on merit," he told a Commencement audience at Johns Hopkins, "there is no way of avoiding the exclusivity of excellence . . . No sentimental egalitarianism, racial or otherwise, can be permitted to lower the standards for the relatively few institutions which are capable of really superior intellectual accomplishment." A great university, Brewster concluded, "should not shy away from the obvious truth that there is not much room at the top compared to the room at the bottom."[160]

His goal as president, Brewster was fond of saying, was "to keep Yale Yale and still keep it up to date." To those less than sympathetic to the changes that he and Clark had made — among whom was the longtime university secretary Ben Holden '40 — he had a ready answer.[161] "What he [Ben] doesn't understand," Brewster told a trusted aide, "is that in order to preserve the Yale he cares about, the values that are very important to Yale, we have to make these changes. And if we didn't, we would lose much more."[162]

A substantial segment of the alumni, especially its younger members, also recognized the need for such change and fully supported the reforms, including the new admissions policies, favored by Brewster and Goheen.[163] Much to the consternation of groups such as CAP, this support extended to the men who had ultimate control of the institution: the Board of Trustees.

The depth of discontent with CAP at the highest levels of Princeton's power structure became visible in 1975 when the trustees released their long-awaited Alumni Affairs Committee Report. After criticizing CAP as a disloyal opposition, the committee rendered its verdict: "We think CAP's methods are unworthy of its ends and that its opposition has been carping, not constructive. We have no way to make a quantitative estimate of CAP's effects, but we are confident that it has hurt the University far more than it has helped. By sowing doubt, discontent, and disaffection, CAP has probably cost the University financial and volunteer support it otherwise would have had, and it has undoubtedly generated adverse national publicity."[164] In the gentlemanly world of Princeton, this was an unusually sharp denunciation, and it sent a clear message: CAP was damaging the institution it professed to love, and responsible alumni — whatever their differences with the administration and trustees on particular issues of policy — should not participate in it.

The alumni revolts at Yale and Princeton revealed a split in the heart of the Protestant Establishment at a time that its authority was under assault and its influence waning. Long past its interwar apogee by the time President Kennedy was inaugurated in 1961 but still largely intact, the Establishment was profoundly shaken and increasingly divided by the cultural and political rebellion of the 1960s. On one side of the divide was what might be called the Progressive Establishment — exemplified by such men as Kingman Brewster, who believed that the preservation of the system of private enterprise and the continued legitimacy of the American political order required vigorous reforms that responded to the concerns of the excluded and the disaffected.[165] On the other side were men such as Shelby Cullom Davis, who believed that the traditional practices of the Establishment had served the nation (and Princeton) well and that the reforms introduced by men such as Brewster posed a grave threat, not only to the nation's elite private universities, but also to the American way of life.

According to one influential interpretation, the demise of the Protestant Establishment was a case of class suicide, its fall precipitated by its own actions. In the words of one observer, "Nothing compelled the Harvards and the Yales to change their ways. They did it on their own; they kicked things off by volunteering to make room for a new elite."[166] But the truth is more complex, for the power of the Protestant Establishment had been weakened by World War II, which E. Digby Baltzell has rightly described as "the most leveling and homogenizing war in our history."[167] The Establishment's dirty little secret was that its continuity was premised on the exclusion of outsiders, and in the aftermath of World War II, its quasi monopoly on many of the best positions in higher education, the economy, and government became increasingly illegitimate. From this perspective, the rise of meritocracy and inclusion as the governing principles of the Big Three was less a gift bestowed by the Protestant Establishment than a product of the struggle against discrimination. By the time women were finally permitted to enter the male sanctums of Yale and Princeton, the Protestant Establishment's ability to justify the exclusion of an entire category of people had disintegrated.

The 1960s and their aftermath were unkind to both the liberal and the conservative wings of the Protestant Establishment. Having vested its claim to authority in its code of honor, integrity, service, duty, and sacrifice, its legitimacy was shattered by an unhappy series of events beginning with the Bay of Pigs and the Gulf of Tonkin and culminating with the Pentagon Papers and finally Watergate.[168] By the early 1970s, the central claim of the Establishment — that it was composed of men of superior character and judgment — seemed almost ludicrous. For these were the men who, not without subterfuge, had led the nation into a bloody and divisive war in Southeast Asia that threatened to tear the country apart.

The tumultuous domestic and international events of the 1960s proved more than a weakened Establishment could handle. And while the "best and the brightest," in the ironic phrase coined by David Halberstam, proved unequal to the challenges before them, their children further undermined their authority by turning against the war and — unlike their fathers — evading military service whenever possible.[169] If duty and sacrifice were at the heart of the Establishment code, then that code was now dead. This point was made forcefully in a memorable article, by James Fallows, who noted that while 35 men from Harvard's Class of 1941 died in World War II, not a single member of the Class of 1970 died in Vietnam.[170]

By the late 1960s, the Protestant Establishment was declining precipitously both in popular legitimacy and in self-confidence. Yet it was in this context that its conservative wing launched its revolt to bring back the Yale and Princeton of old. A cry of protest from a declining social group, it could hardly have picked a less propitious moment to call for a restoration, for this was a period when privileges of every sort were being called radically into question. But the revolt of the alumni was not simply about defending the interests of a beleaguered WASP elite (though this was undeniably part of the rebellion); it was also an attempt to defend the manners, mores, and morals to which the members of this elite had dedicated their lives. By elevating "brains" over character, narrow specialists over "the all-around man," public school boys over boarding school graduates, political activists over gentlemanly clubmen, and (in their view) Jews over Protestants, blacks over whites, and women over men, the new admission policies of Yale and Princeton were creating a world turned upside down. A new definition of "merit," they correctly sensed, had been imposed, and the qualities that they believed mattered most in life now counted for less than ever before.

The essence of the dispute was perhaps best captured in an interview that Shelby Cullom Davis gave to the *New Yorker*. President William Bowen, he observed, had stated that Princeton's "central, fundamental commitment" was "to the life of the mind." For Davis, however, "there are or ought to be many other fundamental, central things in an American university, including moral values." In the new Princeton, he noted acidly, "it apparently doesn't matter anymore what anyone does or who sleeps with whom."[171]

This was not, to say the least, a view that was likely to prevail in a great modern research university poised between the demands of a powerful faculty and a multiplicity of external forces, including the federal government, private foundations, and mobilized social groups. President Bowen encapsulated the viewpoint of university administrators in 1977 when he said: "What CAP wants me to do I really don't know. There's not one chance in a million that the basic direction of the university will change, I could get struck by lightning, but even so there'd be no change in coeducation, no change in the faculty, no change in admissions, and chapel wouldn't become compulsory again. I keep saying to Shelby Davis and the others, 'Tell me of any great university in the world that operates the way you would seemingly have us operate.'"[172] And Bowen was right. For regardless of who has been president, no university — and certainly not Princeton or Yale — has returned to the policies favored by men like Davis.

If the attempt to turn the clock back failed, it was not for lack of effort; at Princeton, the alumni revolt, which began in 1969, did not come to an end until *Prospect* published its final issue in 1985.[173] Contrary to the claim of David Brooks, the author of a perceptive study of the transformation of the American elite, the Protestant Establishment did *not* give up its power without a fight.[174] The alumni revolt at Yale and Princeton — waged by a powerful segment of the WASP elite — was at its deepest level nothing less than an attempt to defend both the values and the interests of the Protestant Establishment by regaining control of two of the institutions most crucial to its reproduction.

Yet this was a revolt that was doomed to failure. Unlike alumni, who can afford to be stuck in the past, college presidents must make a sober assessment of the forces that will shape the future. As far back as 1957, Harvard's farsighted dean of admissions, Wilbur Bender, wondered whether the "gentlemen" — the children of patrician WASP backgrounds whose interests he had done so much to protect — might be a "vanishing rose."[175] Less than two decades later, the rose, still alive, was showing every sign of withering. If the Big Three were to remain as influential in the future as they had in the past, they would have to look outside the Protestant Establishment for new sources of talent and ambition.

CHAPTER 16

Diversity, the Bakke Case, and the Defense of Autonomy

Y 1975, HARVARD, YALE, and Princeton had transformed themselves, enrolling a student body whose broad contours would be easily
recognized even today. Yet just fifteen years earlier, though already in
transition, the Big Three looked very much as they had before World War II
— overwhelmingly white, exclusively male, and largely Protestant. Indeed, on
the eve of President Kennedy's election, they were still de facto segregated institutions — less than 1 percent black and, in the case of Princeton, enrolling
just 1 African-American freshman in a class of 826.[1] The leading boarding
schools, though no longer able to assume that their graduates could choose
whichever college they preferred, continued to send large delegations to the
Big Three. Even anti-Semitism, though officially taboo, was still practiced in
1960; Harvard rejected three-quarters of the applicants from the Bronx High
School of Science and Stuyvesant that year (compared to just 31 percent from
Exeter and Andover) while Yale limited the Jewish presence in the freshman
class to one student in eight.[2]

Like the 1920s, the 1960s and early 1970s were a period of epochal change
at Harvard, Yale, and Princeton. But whereas the 1920s was dedicated to exclusion, the period between 1960 and 1975 witnessed a growing commitment
to inclusion. By 1976, women made up over a third of all freshmen at each of
the Big Three (almost 40 percent at Yale); students of color (African Americans, Latinos, Asian Americans, and Native Americans) contributed over 15
percent; and Jews ranged from a low of 19 percent at Princeton to a high of
perhaps 33 percent at Yale.[3] In barely a decade, a level of diversity previously
unimaginable had become a firm institutional commitment.

Though the conservative alumni's attempt to turn back the clock had
been repulsed, after 1975 the Big Three were not inclined to press further
down the road of inclusion. On the contrary, attempts to recruit students
from the inner cities were trimmed back; in the words of Morton Keller and
Phyllis Keller (who had been Harvard's senior associate dean for academic affairs): "It was generally agreed that during the late 1960s and early 1970s inad-

equately prepared black students were admitted to everyone's disadvantage."[4] African-American enrollments plateaued and in some cases declined; at Princeton, blacks had made up 10 percent of the freshmen in 1970 and 1972, but by 1974 their number had settled in the vicinity of 8 percent.[5] Reinforcing the sense that it was a period of consolidation rather than radical new initiatives was a growing feeling of financial constraint as the boom years of the 1960s gave way to the slow growth and stagflation of the 1970s.

One consequence of the rapid changes made between 1965 and 1975 was that the Big Three had become much more alike. Having spent much of the century guarding their distinctive traditions and identities, they had by the mid-1970s come to embrace a common ideal of diversity and to adopt strikingly similar admissions policies.[6]

The New Admissions Formula

By the mid-1970s, the formula — that is, the new admissions criteria and practices — used by the Big Three had been fully institutionalized: need-blind admissions, no discrimination against women or Jews, and special consideration for historically underrepresented minorities as well as athletes and legacies. Admission was in the end the outcome of a highly subjective process dedicated to assessing the personal as well as the academic characteristics of the applicant. This emphasis on personal qualities was still inscribed in the evaluation process, with each institution assigning candidates one numerical rating for academic and another for nonacademic characteristics (in the case of Harvard, there remained three distinct nonacademic ratings: personal, extracurricular, and athletic). In many cases, it was the nonacademic rating that determined whether the candidate was admitted — a pattern confirmed at Princeton in 1975 when applicants with a nonacademic/academic rating of 1/4 were admitted at a substantially higher rate (88 percent) than those with a rating of 4/1 (74 percent).[7]

As in an earlier decade, the Big Three gathered detailed information, not only on extracurricular accomplishments, but also on highly subjective personal qualities — those attributes that Harvard's Wilbur Bender had referred to in the 1950s as the "intangibles." Apart from the candidate's essay, photograph, and letters of recommendation from headmasters, teachers, and counselors, Harvard, Yale, and Princeton relied heavily on the impressions gleaned from personal interviews with admissions staff and/or alumni representatives for information about the person behind the folder — his or her demeanor, appearance, speech, social skills, affect, and personal presence (or lack thereof).

The Big Three's strong emphasis on nonacademic characteristics reflected both a vision of their mission and a theory about the sources of success in

American life. In terms of mission, all three schools were still deeply committed to identifying and training the elite of the next generation — the leaders of America's major social institutions. And in terms of theory, the men who ran these institutions believed — contrary to the perspective of many faculty — that there was little if any correlation between the scholastic brilliance of applicants and the likelihood that they would assume positions of political and economic leadership.[8] On the contrary, as admissions officers were fond of noting, some of the most renowned alumni were hardly stellar students; as Bender had pointed out in 1961, it was not clear that either Franklin D. Roosevelt or John F. Kennedy would have been admitted to Harvard under the prevailing standards.[9]

The Big Three — and other leading private institutions as well — were unanimous in firmly rejecting a French or Japanese type of admissions policy, based solely on academic criteria. But Harvard, Yale, and Princeton went much further. In the 1970s and later, only a small segment of the entering class was admitted on sheer academic brilliance; at Harvard in 1978, the figure was just 150 in a freshman class of over 1,600.[10] Even the most brilliant students could be rejected, as had long been Harvard's policy, if deemed to suffer from "serious defects of character or personality."[11]

In 1971, Harvard had tested a "merit model" of admissions, and the results showed that it "would benefit high-scoring graduates of schools in metropolitan New York, Philadelphia, and Chicago, at the expense of lower-scoring alumni sons, graduates of the select and not-so-select New England private schools, athletes, and black applicants."[12] From an institutional point of view, this was not an acceptable outcome.

Thus an essential component of the formula was the heavy emphasis on elusive personal qualities. A sense of how subjective a process it was is provided by Harvard's "Rating Code Guide for the Class of 1975," the guidelines given to admissions officers. Every candidate was to be assigned a personal rating from "1" (high) to "6" (low). An applicant with a personal rating of "2" was described as "Very appealing: unusually forceful, effective, humane or whatever." But the unfortunate candidate assigned a personal rating of "6" — the kiss of death for a Harvard applicant, regardless of academic record — fell into the following category: "Genuinely poor impression, personality difficulties, very immature, unstable or offensive."[13]

This extraordinary emphasis on highly subjective qualities — pursued right down to the assignment of a single number reflecting the institution's summary assessment of the candidate as a human being — was central to the admissions process of the Big Three. Though peculiar from the perspective of many faculty, the system had important institutional advantages. Apart from permitting the admissions office to act on its not unjustified belief that brains alone were a poor predictor of success later in life, the weight given to nonacademic factors permitted gatekeepers to balance interest groups against one another in selecting a class.[14] To do this, they needed to protect their autonomy and their discretion, both of which were well served by a complex admissions process designed to be flexible, subjective, and opaque.

The Assault on Affirmative Action

Ironically, it was at the very moment that universities began to use their discretion on behalf of the disenfranchised that cries of "reverse discrimination" echoed through the nation's media. As early as 1971, articles began to appear in leading magazines and newspapers, claiming that the special consideration given to blacks in university admissions and faculty hiring was the moral equivalent of the racism that the civil rights movement had struggled so hard to eradicate. With astonishing speed, a flood of articles with titles like "The Return of the Quota System," "Discrimination Against the Qualified?," "The Decline of Merit," "Do Colleges Practice Reverse Bias?," "A Breakdown in Civil Rights Enforcement?," "The Tyranny of Reverse Discrimination," and "The Idea of Merit" flooded the journals of thought and opinion.[15] Universities, which had long used their autonomy to perpetuate existing racial, gender, and class hierarchies and had elicited little criticism, now found that autonomy under assault by those who claimed to speak on behalf of the principle of "merit."

The assault on "affirmative action" — the term then used by universities (and employers) attempting to reach out to minorities — was not limited to the media. In addition to the growing opposition to "racial preferences" (the term preferred by opponents of race-attentive policies), a concerted effort was made to press the issue of "reverse discrimination" in the courts. In higher education, the issue first rose to national prominence when Marco DeFunis, a Phi Beta Kappa graduate of the University of Washington, sued its law school in 1971, charging that it had rejected him in favor of less qualified minority students.[16] DeFunis had been turned down the previous year as well, and in the summer of 1971 he filed a civil suit in the court system of the state of Washington, claiming that he had been deprived of Equal Protection of the Law under the Fourteenth Amendment because the university had accepted members of favored racial groups despite their inferior academic records. As a remedy, DeFunis proposed that the court order the university to admit him forthwith.[17]

In September 1971, a Washington trial court upheld DeFunis's claim and ordered the University of Washington Law School to admit him in time for the 1971–1972 academic year. Basing its decision on the Fourteenth Amendment, the court concluded that the "only safe rule is to treat all races alike" and that "there should be a remedy for the wrong" inflicted on DeFunis. The university complied with the court order, and DeFunis enrolled that fall. At the same time, however, it also appealed the ruling, requesting that the case go directly to the Washington supreme court, bypassing the state court of appeals because of the constitutional character of the issue at stake.[18]

In May 1972, as the public campaign against affirmative action was gaining momentum, the case was argued before the state supreme court. But the court's ruling in March 1973 dealt a blow to the forces against affirmative action by upholding the legality of the University of Washington's admissions practices in a 6–2 vote. In a decision that was welcomed by the higher education community, including the Big Three, the court's majority maintained that the university had a "compelling state interest" in producing "a racially balanced student body at the Law School" both for educational reasons and in order to train minority lawyers in a multicultural society. Especially significant for elite institutions such as Harvard, Yale, and Princeton, which were eager to preserve their autonomy in choosing their student bodies, was the court's argument that the Equal Protection Clause of the Constitution, while not requiring efforts to remedy racial unbalance, permitted the University of Washington to take voluntary actions to do so. Nevertheless, a warning note was sounded in the opinions of the two dissenters (one of whom was the chief justice), who ringingly declared, "Racial bigotry . . . will never be ended by exalting the rights of one group or class over that of another."[19]

DeFunis was well into his second year of law school when the court issued its ruling, and the University of Washington showed no sign of trying to oust him in the wake of the decision. Having been labeled a bigot by some of his classmates, DeFunis had little inclination to press the matter further. But when his attorney pointed out that the law school was now legally free to dismiss him if so inclined, he decided to appeal. After the state supreme court denied his request for a rehearing, his lawyer took the matter to the U.S. Supreme Court. In June 1973, Justice William O. Douglas agreed to issue a stay, blocking execution of the decision, and in November 1973 the Supreme Court agreed to hear the case.[20]

Because of the enormity of what was at stake, the *DeFunis* case attracted an exceptional number of amicus briefs. In the end, 30 briefs representing 60 organizations were filed; 22 took the side of the law school and 8 the side of DeFunis.[21] Harvard weighed in on the side of the University of Washington, filing a 52-page brief in February 1974.[22]

The *DeFunis* case was bitterly controversial; it so frightened the Nixon administration that it denied Solicitor General Robert Bork (who supported DeFunis) permission to file a brief.[23] But Harvard, fearing the potential consequences for its own admissions practices if a decision favored DeFunis, decided to take a strong position. Making its case was the Establishment icon and Harvard Law School professor Archibald Cox (St. Paul's '30, Harvard '34, Harvard Law School '37), whose already considerable reputation for integrity and fairness had been reinforced by his firing as Watergate prosecutor in October 1973 during Nixon's infamous "Saturday Night Massacre."[24] Having served as solicitor general during the Kennedy and Johnson administrations, Cox had argued before the Supreme Court on such landmark cases as *Baker v. Carr* (on reapportionment), *Heart of Atlanta* (public accommodations for all), and *South Carolina v. Katzenbach* (which upheld the Voting Rights Act).

In selecting Cox, Harvard was sending a message that it considered the *DeFunis* case to be a matter of the utmost seriousness.[25] Harvard's brief begins by declaring: "This case has vital importance for all colleges and universities throughout the United States." Noting that Harvard was "the oldest and one of the largest privately endowed institutions of higher education" in the United States," Cox then suggested — not without a touch of immodesty — "that relating Harvard's varied experience and resulting philosophy to the legal issues will help to provide the necessary perspective."[26] Given his stature, Cox could count on the Court — which numbered three graduates of Harvard Law School (William Brennan, LL.B. '31, Harry Blackmun, LL.B. '32, and Lewis Powell, LL.M. '32) and two graduates of its archrival, Yale Law School (Potter Stewart, LL.B. '37, and Byron "Whizzer" White, LL.B. '46) — to take his arguments seriously.[27]

Cox's brief had at its center the argument that the state should not encroach on the autonomy traditionally granted to universities in deciding on admissions. "Harvard's long experience in the area of undergraduate education," it claimed, "highlights the dangers of substituting an iron rule of law for the discretion of academic authorities to make a conscious selection of qualified students from the greatest variety of cultural, social, and economic backgrounds in order to improve the educational experience of the whole student body."[28] Using the race of an applicant from a historically disadvantaged minority as a "tip factor" in admissions was necessary, the brief maintained, to produce the "diversity" that was the sine qua non of a quality education. "A hard-and-fast rule forbidding an institution to give favorable consideration to membership in a minority race or other minority group in selecting an entering class from qualified applicants," Cox argued, "would severely constrict the freedom of academic authorities" to choose the student body that would best enable it to fulfill its educational mission. Noting that Harvard College selected less than 15 percent of its entering class purely "on the basis of extraordinary intellectual potential," Cox expressed the fear that "if promise of high scholarship were the sole or *even predominant* criterion,

Harvard College would lose a great deal of its vitality and the quality of the educational experience offered to all students would suffer."[29]

The threat to Harvard posed by the *DeFunis* case thus went well beyond the issues of blacks and other minorities; it raised the specter of an encroachment on the institutional discretion that Harvard believed indispensable to the protection of vital institutional interests. In the worst case, a ruling for DeFunis might lead to the Court's imposing the model of pure academic meritocracy that Bender and his successors at Harvard had so definitively rejected.

As the Supreme Court convened on February 24, 1974, to hear oral arguments in *DeFunis,* the stage was set for a historic decision with profound implications for the distribution of educational opportunities in America and the freedom of universities to set their own admissions criteria. However, by this time DeFunis was in his final semester of law school, and the University of Washington had publicly stated that it would permit him to graduate whatever the ruling. On April 23, 1974, the Supreme Court finally issued its decision: by a bare majority, 5–4 (with Burger, Blackmun, Rehnquist, Stewart, and Powell in the majority), the justices declared the case moot, contending that because DeFunis would be graduating in any event, there was no issue before the Court that demanded resolution.[30]

The majority's refusal to rule on the constitutional issues elicited a sharp dissent from the Court's minority. Written by Brennan, with the concurrence of Douglas, White, and Marshall, the dissent accused the majority of "striving to rid itself of this dispute" and of doing so in a fashion that "clearly disserves the public interest." The dissenters noted that "few constitutional questions in recent history have stirred as much debate" and predicted that "they will not disappear" but "must inevitably return to the federal courts and ultimately again to this Court."[31]

Of the four dissenters, only one — William O. Douglas, perhaps worried that his failing health would prevent him from ever ruling on the constitutional issues at stake — took the unusual step of issuing a full opinion on the merits of the case.[32] His views could hardly have been reassuring to Harvard and other leading universities. Indeed, if Douglas's opinion was a harbinger of the future, the selective colleges had reason to be doubly worried. On the one hand, the liberal justice defied their expectations that he would endorse race-attentive admissions ("There is no constitutional right for any race to be preferred . . . [DeFunis] had a constitutional right to have his application considered on its merits in a racially neutral manner"). On the other hand, he brought radically into question the standardized tests that had come to play such a large role in the admissions process at elite colleges.[33] Insisting that all applications be considered "*in a racially neutral way,*" Douglas issued a blistering critique of the Law School Aptitude Test (LSAT), denouncing it as an example of "mechanical criteria which are insensitive to the potential" of minority applicants. "Abolition of the LSAT," he suggested, "would be a start" down the constitutionally required road of race neutrality.[34]

Seemingly poised to resolve once and for all the question of whether universities could give weight to race in college admissions, the *DeFunis* case in the end settled nothing. Yet just as the dissenters had predicted, the issue of race-sensitive admissions soon found its way into the courts. Among the many Americans who had eagerly awaited the Supreme Court's ruling, none was more attentive than a young white man in California who had twice been rejected by the University of California at Davis Medical School. The lawsuit that he filed two months after the Supreme Court's nondecision in *DeFunis* led to the most important civil rights ruling since *Brown v. Board of Education.*

Institutional Discretion and the Ideology of Diversity

In June 1974, a thirty-four-year-old white man of Norwegian ancestry filed suit against the University of California at Davis Medical School, claiming that it had rejected him in favor of less qualified minority students. Allan Bakke, who had a burning ambition to become a doctor, had done well at the University of Minnesota, where he had majored in mechanical engineering and graduated with a GPA of 3.51.[35] But his qualifications, though strong, were not quite good enough to gain him admission to any of the eleven medical schools to which he applied. Though age had been one of the factors operating against him, he had come close to being admitted to UC Davis, making it to the interview stage in 1973 — an accomplishment attained by only one in six applicants.[36] When he was again rejected by UC Davis in 1974, he decided to file a lawsuit.[37] His essential claim was that UC Davis's policy of reserving 16 percent of the entering class for minorities "who are judged apart from and permitted to meet lower standards of admission" than white applicants denied him equal protection of the law.[38]

Bakke gained a partial victory in Yolo County (where UC Davis is located) court, when Judge F. Leslie Manker declared, "This court cannot conclude that there is any compelling or even legitimate public purpose to be served by granting preference to minority students in admission to the medical school when to do so denies white persons an equal opportunity for admission."[39] Yet the judge stopped short of ordering that UC Davis admit Bakke, concluding that it was unclear whether he would have been admitted in the absence of the medical school's special program for minorities. Judge Manker was, moreover, reluctant to substitute his own assessment for that of the university on a matter as complex and delicate as admissions, writing,

"The admission of students to the Medical School is so peculiarly a discretionary function of the school that . . . it should not be interfered with by a court, absent a showing of fraud, unfairness, bad faith, arbitrariness or capriciousness, none of which has been shown."[40] While Harvard and other institutions following the case could not have been pleased by Judge Manker's decision to declare race-attentive admissions illegal, his emphasis on the "discretionary function" of universities in making admissions decisions affirmed one of the central claims of Harvard's brief in *DeFunis.*

Whatever reassurance Judge Manker may have given Harvard dissipated, however, when the California supreme court issued a sweeping 6–1 ruling in favor of Bakke in mid-September 1976. Writing for the majority, Stanley Mosk, the former attorney general of the state of California and a twelve-year veteran of the state supreme court, declared: "We conclude that the program, as administered by the University, violates the constitutional rights of nonminority applicants because it affords preference on the basis of race to persons who, by the University's own standards, are not as qualified as nonminority applicants denied admission."[41] Arguing that special admissions programs such as the one at Davis might be "counter-productive," the court stated that "the principle that the Constitution sanctions racial discrimination against a race — any race — is a dangerous concept fraught with potential for misuses in situations which involve far less laudable objectives than are manifest in the present case."[42] On the crucial issue of whether Davis's program was constitutional, the court's opinion was an unequivocal no. "To uphold the University," Mosk wrote, "would call for the sacrifice of principle for the sake of dubious expediency and would represent a retreat in the struggle to assure that each man and woman shall be judged on the basis of individual merit alone."[43]

After denying the university's request for a rehearing of the case, the California supreme court issued its final decision on October 28, 1976: "On appeal the University has conceded that it cannot meet the burden of proving that the special admission program did not result in Bakke's exclusion. Therefore, he is entitled to an order that he be admitted to the University." This ruling was immediately challenged in the courts by the University of California.[44]

Though the court's decision did not directly affect Harvard and other elite private universities, the threat it posed was clear: if taking race into account in selecting students was unconstitutional, then they, too, might well be subject to lawsuits from aggrieved white applicants who had been rejected. So when the University of California filed a brief on December 14, 1976, with the U.S. Supreme Court, asking that the decision be overturned, the question immediately arose: should Harvard and other leading private universities file an amicus brief supporting the University of California?

Although Harvard had filed a forceful amicus brief in *DeFunis,* it did not take the lead in responding to the challenge posed by *Bakke*. That role fell to the University of Pennsylvania, where Louis Pollak, dean of its law school and a longtime civil rights activist, persuaded Penn's president, Martin Meyerson, that the university should file a brief. Pollak's concerns, shared by many other university administrators, were twofold: first, that the *Bakke* decision, if upheld, would make institutions of higher education highly vulnerable to lawsuits claiming "reverse discrimination," and second, that the imposition of a strict color-blind admissions policy would set back hard-won minority gains. Central to the brief drafted by Pollak and Penn's legal counsel Stephen Burbank was the claim that *Bakke* threatened the autonomy traditionally granted universities and their faculties in making admissions decisions.[45] It was essentially the same argument that Cox had made in Harvard's brief on *DeFunis*.

With the brief in draft form, Meyerson contacted the other Ivy League presidents about filing a joint document. At a February 1977 meeting of the Council of Ivy Presidents, Harvard and Columbia agreed to join Penn. But the other Ivies — apparently because of disagreements about the matter among the trustees and faculties — decided not to join the brief.[46] This was an especially puzzling choice in the case of Princeton; President William Bowen was a committed advocate of affirmative action who, shortly before the Supreme Court heard oral arguments in the *Bakke* case, published an eloquent defense of race-attentive admissions that echoed many of the arguments made in the "Ivy" amicus brief.[47] Joining Penn, Columbia, and Harvard in filing the brief was Stanford, a fraternal institution that Bakke had seriously considered suing before choosing UC Davis, whose status as a state institution made it more vulnerable to a legal challenge.[48]

The decision by elite private universities to intervene in *Bakke* was far more than an expression of their rather recent commitment to racial and ethnic minorities; it was also a self-conscious attempt to defend the discretion that permitted them to favor key constituencies — some of them relatively weak in academic merit — whom it wished to admit for institutional reasons. To be sure, the brief submitted by Harvard, Penn, Columbia, and Stanford did refer to the "need for highly trained minority persons" (required for "diversifying the leadership of our pluralistic society") and to the importance of a racially diverse student body for the accomplishment of "important educational objectives."[49] But the heart of the argument, laid out on the brief's second page, was a plea for the Court to exercise "judicial restraint" by recognizing that "colleges and universities, with rare exceptions, have been accorded freedom from external influence and intrusion" and "can flourish only so long as educators have substantial independence."[50]

The argument was carefully crafted to appeal to the Court's reluctance "to substitute its judgment for that of educators": "The guiding principle of freedom under which American colleges and universities have grown to great-ness is that these institutions are expected to assume and exercise responsibil-ity for the shaping of academic policy without extramural intervention. A subordinate corollary principle — critical for this case — is that deciding who shall be selected for admission to degree candidacy is an integral aspect of ac-ademic policy-making."[51] Citing a 1957 opinion of Justice Frankfurter, the brief listed as one of the "four essential freedoms" of a university "the capac-ity to determine for itself on academic grounds . . . who may be admitted to study." "Educators," it continued, "need to be free to make decisions reflecting their professional judgments . . . not subject to the restraints of a judicially imposed strait jacket." A ruling in favor of Bakke, the brief concluded, would constitute a serious violation of judicial restraint, for it would "displace the traditional authority of university faculties, officers, and trustees, who ac-cording to our traditions have primary responsibility to determine academic policy."[52]

The University of California chose Archibald Cox to present its case. Though not part of its original legal team, Cox was called into the case in March 1977 after the university rejected the pleas of minorities — fearful that the rigidity of the Davis program and the paucity of facts in the official record of the case might result in a Supreme Court ruling that would eliminate all affirmative action programs — not to file an appeal in the case. In choosing Cox, a longtime advocate of affirmative action and a man with the stature to command the respect of the Supreme Court, the university showed that it was making a good-faith effort to protect the interests of minorities in what promised to be a landmark case.[53]

In the meantime, an unprecedented flow of amicus briefs was pouring into the Court. By mid-July 1977, the pile of documents related to the case stood over a foot tall and was growing rapidly.[54] Ultimately, 57 amici were filed — more than any case in history. Nearly three-fourths came down on the side of the University of California against Bakke.[55]

The major newspapers and magazines were full of articles on both sides of the debate. One of the most visible was a lengthy cover story in the *Atlantic Monthly* by the former Harvard dean and then current Ford Foundation president McGeorge Bundy, "The Issues Before the Court: Who Gets Ahead in America?" In the article — which reportedly influenced the vote of Justice Harry Blackmun — Bundy passionately argued the case for affirmative ac-tion, insisting that diversity was a legitimate objective of the admissions pro-cess, that the autonomy historically granted universities was superior to state interference, and that a ruling in favor of Bakke "would place the great moral authority of the Court on the wrong side of a fundamental issue, on which it has a hard-won right to speak for the national conscience."[56]

On October 12, 1977, the Court convened to hear oral arguments in *Re-*

gents of the University of California v. Allan Bakke. Hundreds of people, some of whom had been waiting all night, had gathered on the steps of the Supreme Court, hoping to gain entry, and nearly 100 reporters were present.[57] Wearing his trademark bow tie and the traditional cutaway coat, Cox spoke first. Addressing the justices as a gentleman among peers, the patrician Cox began by declaring that the case before the Court "presents a single vital question: whether a State university, which is forced by limited resources to select a relatively small number of students from a much larger number of well-qualified applicants is free, voluntarily, to take into account that a qualified applicant is black, Chicano, Asian, or Native American in order to increase the number of qualified members of those minority groups trained for the educated professions."[58] The stakes, he emphasized, were high: "The answer which the Court gives will determine, perhaps for decades, whether members of those minorities are to have the kind of meaningful access to higher education in the professions, which the universities have accorded them in recent years, or are to be reduced to the trivial numbers which they were prior to the adoption of minority admissions programs."[59]

Cox's presentation was leavened with humor, and his responses to the cordial but sometimes pointed questions from the justices were poised and straightforward. Carefully staking out a moderate position, and at one point registering his opposition to any "notion of group entitlement to numbers regardless of either ability of the individual . . . or of their potential contribution to society," he nonetheless insisted, "There is no racially blind method of selection which will enroll today more than a trickle of minority students in the nation's colleges and professions." But his central argument stressed the wisdom of allowing universities rather than the courts to make educational decisions: admission standards at the University of California, he argued, had been "left to the different colleges, and very wisely I think because autonomous institutions, each trying to solve this problem in their own way, may give all of us the benefit of the experience of trial and error, creativity."[60] Cox returned to this theme in his closing remarks, urging the Court to exercise judicial restraint by allowing the universities to retain their historic discretion and independence.[61]

After more than eight months of tense internal deliberations, the Court finally announced its decision on June 28, 1978. Speaking for the Court was Justice Lewis F. Powell. Acknowledging that "we speak today with a notable lack of unanimity," he reported the unusual result: "There is no opinion joined in its entirety by five members of the Court." Nevertheless, the divided Court did reach a verdict: the California supreme court was upheld in ordering Bakke to be admitted to the Medical School at UC Davis, but it was reversed insofar as it had prohibited Davis from considering race as a factor in admissions.[62]

In truth, the bitterly divided Court had barely managed to render a verdict. In the opinion of four of the justices — Stevens, Burger, Stewart, and Rehnquist — the decision of the California supreme court, which would have effectively ended affirmative action in higher education, was upheld because "the University's special admissions program violated Title VI of the Civil Rights Act of 1964 by excluding Bakke from the Medical School because of his race."[63] But in the opinion of the Court's more liberal justices — Brennan, Marshall, Blackmun, and White — the Davis program violated neither Title VI nor the Constitution. Arguing that "we cannot . . . let color blindness become a myopia which masks the reality that many 'created equal' have been treated within our lifetimes as inferior both by the law and their fellow citizens," the justices concluded that "government may take race into account when it acts not to demean or insult any racial group, but to remedy disadvantages cast on minorities by past racial prejudice." Accordingly, the judgment of the California supreme court should be reversed "in all respects."[64]

Though Brennan had written on behalf of the four justices who upheld the Davis program, the historic import of the case was such that each of the concurring justices felt compelled to write a separate opinion laying out his personal views. Marshall, the legendary civil rights lawyer who had argued the plaintiff's case in *Brown v. Board of Education* and the Court's sole African American, noted pointedly that "it is more than a little ironic that after several hundred years of class-based discrimination against Negroes, the Court is unwilling to hold that a class-based remedy for . . . discrimination is permissible."[65] But it was Blackmun, a Nixon appointee, who issued perhaps the most eloquent defense of compensatory affirmative action: "In order to get beyond racism, we must first take account of race. There is no other way. And in order to treat some persons equally, we must treat them differently. We cannot — we dare not — let the Equal Protection Clause perpetuate racial supremacy."[66]

The deciding vote was in the hands of Justice Lewis Powell Jr. A gentlemanly Virginian and a Nixon appointee, Powell had been raised in the segregated South. Born in 1907 in Richmond, he attended all-white schools and graduated from Virginia's Washington and Lee College in 1929, going on to receive a law degree there in 1931. He then enrolled at Harvard Law School for a master's degree in law — a not uncommon move at the time for a graduate of a provincial institution who wished to enhance his credentials. While in Cambridge, he attended an intimidating but memorable seminar in administrative law taught by Felix Frankfurter, the already renowned future Supreme Court justice. From Frankfurter — and from another seminar taught by the law school's dean, Roscoe Pound — Powell imbibed a valuable lesson: legal decisions should be based not on the rule-bound formalism that he had been taught at Washington and Lee but on the actual consequences that these decisions would produce in society. Yet this potentially progressive approach (known at the time as "sociological jurisprudence") was always tempered for Powell by his instinctual respect for authority and judicial precedent.[67]

Temperamentally inclined to favor the status quo, Powell was not among that small group of whites who had risen up against the Jim Crow system that had prevailed in the South. He embarked on a conventional and extremely successful career as a corporate lawyer in his native Virginia. Quickly becoming a senior partner in a major law firm, he temporarily left his practice to volunteer for service in World War II, where he served in Army Air Force Intelligence, attaining the rank of full colonel and receiving the Bronze Star and the French Croix de Guerre with Palm.[68] After the war, he went on to further prominence, becoming a millionaire, and was elected president of the American Bar Association in 1964–1965.

Always active in civic affairs, Powell served as chairman of the Richmond School Board from 1953 to 1961 and as a member of the Virginia Board of Education from 1961 to 1969. His own carefully worded assessment of his service in these positions was that it had taken place when the pace of desegregation had been "necessarily more measured than civil rights leaders would have liked."[69] But this was a rather generous interpretation of his role in the years after the *Brown* decision, for when Powell stepped down as chairman of the Richmond School Board in 1961, after eight years of service, only 2 of the city's 23,000 black children attended school with white children. And during his two terms with the state Board of Education, Powell's sympathetic but fair-minded biographer reports that "he never did any more than was necessary to facilitate desegregation . . . [and] never spoke out against foot-dragging and gradualism."[70]

Powell nevertheless had a not unjustified reputation as a political moderate — a reputation burnished by his behind-the-scenes role in opposing the strategy of massive resistance to desegregation that enjoyed widespread support in Virginia in the 1950s.[71] Yet he adhered to a quite conservative political ideology. Just how conservative his views were is revealed in a remarkable confidential memo that he wrote to his friend and neighbor, the director of the National Chamber of Commerce, Eugene B. Snyder Jr., on August 23, 1971 — just two months before his nomination to the U.S. Supreme Court. In it, Powell expressed his alarm that the movements of the 1960s — symbolized by such figures as Ralph Nader ("the single most effective antagonist of American business") and Charles Reich (the author of *The Greening of America*) — had launched a "broadly based and consistently pursued" assault on the "American economic system." Urging "businessmen to recognize that the ultimate issue may be *survival* — survival of what we call the free enterprise system," he proposed a multipronged approach to defend capitalism: one that included the campuses, the national television networks, the courts, the political arena, stockholder power, and print media, including scholarly journals, books, and popular magazines. Foreshadowing the conservative political and ideological countermobilization of the 1970s and 1980s, Powell issued an urgent call to corporate America: "It is time for American business — which has demonstrated the greatest capacity in all history to produce and to influence consumer decisions — to apply their great talents vigorously to the preservation of the system itself."[72]

On the subject of affirmative action, however, he was well aware that it was a profoundly divisive issue — one that stood astride America's most dangerous cleavage.[73] If a way could be found to resolve the issue without exacerbating the nation's bitter racial divisions, Powell — who took pride in his ability to balance conflicting interests — would be the man to articulate it.

With four justices strongly in favor of race-attentive affirmative action and four others firmly opposed, Powell devised an ingenious way — hailed by some in the press as "Solomonic" and an act of "judicial statesmanship" — of splitting the difference.[74] Joining the conservative justices in ordering Bakke admitted and in rejecting the claims of compensatory justice, he aligned himself with the liberals on the crucial issue: whether race could be a factor in college admissions. While declaring the Davis plan to be a violation of the Constitution's Equal Protection Clause ("The guarantee of equal protection cannot mean one thing when applied to one individual and something else when applied to a person of another color"), Powell concluded that "the portion of the judgment that would proscribe all consideration of race must be reversed."[75]

Had Powell faced the issues raised by *Bakke* in 1970, he would almost surely have come down on the other side.[76] But by the time *Bakke* reached the Supreme Court, affirmative action had become part of the fabric of American higher education. In 1977, the elimination of affirmative action would have meant a radical alteration of the status quo — a deeply unappealing prospect for a man who believed that law should be an instrument of social stability.[77]

Having decided against banning affirmative action, Powell still faced the thorny question of specifying when race could be taken into account. His answer was that universities could consider race when doing so was necessary to obtain "the educational benefits that flow from an ethnically diverse student body."[78] This was precisely the justification that Harvard had long used in legitimating its admissions policies, and Powell was quick to recognize the public relations value of linking his opinion to the practices of the nation's oldest and most prestigious university. Pointing to Harvard served another function as well; universities needed to know what was now legally permissible, and Harvard provided a concrete example of a program that passed legal muster. In Powell's view, Harvard's policy avoided all the pitfalls of the Davis program: it eschewed quotas, followed a unified process in which minority candidates competed against nonminority applicants, and used criteria flexible enough to consider race as just one factor among others, including geography or life spent on a farm. For Powell, the "Harvard way" was the very model of how to consider race within the bounds of the law and the Constitution — a model enshrined in law by his unusual decision to reprint in full Harvard's own description of its admissions policy as an appendix to his opinion.[79] Princeton, too, was cited by Powell as having a model admissions policy, and his opinion quoted extensively from Bowen's article in the *Princeton Alumni Weekly,* "Admissions and the Relevance of Race."[80]

To be sure, the sharp distinction that Powell drew between the Davis program and Harvard was exaggerated, for Harvard also gave substantial preference to racial minorities. Indeed, none of the other eight justices found Powell's argument convincing, and even his own clerks reportedly found the distinction "embarrassing," believing it to be "elitist to condemn tiny Davis but praise Harvard for doing the same thing with better manners."[81] Powell's opinion nevertheless accomplished its main goal: to force universities to abandon quotas while permitting them to consider race in shaping its student body.[82]

Whatever its intellectual shortcomings, Powell's opinion was generally praised in the media, with Harvard Law School's Alan Dershowitz hailing it as "a brilliant compromise."[83] But not all supporters of affirmative action were pleased, for Powell had sharply rejected one of the central arguments of proponents of race-attentive admissions: race may be taken into account "to remedy disadvantages cast on minorities by past racial prejudices."[84] Casually dismissing the argument of "societal discrimination" as "an amorphous concept of injury that may be ageless in its reach into the past," Powell turned instead to the "attainment of a diverse student body" as the "compelling state interest" that would justify considering race in college admissions.[85]

Yet the "diversity defense" of affirmative action is in many ways a profoundly conservative argument, for it preserves the status quo in higher education. By consciously rejecting arguments that claim that the very criteria used to measure "merit" perpetuate racial and class privilege and by eschewing justifications of affirmative action as an appropriate remedy for past and ongoing discrimination, the diversity defense obscures some of the main reasons that leading colleges and universities adopted affirmative action in the first place: to right the wrongs of the past and to integrate the elite of the future.[86] However shrewd Powell's defense of affirmative action on diversity grounds may have been legally and politically, it came at a high cost, for it eroded the moral foundations on which affirmative action had been built.

Neither liberals nor conservatives were satisfied by Powell's compromise, but one group had reason to be elated: the leaders of the nation's elite private universities. Institutions such as Harvard now had the sanction of the nation's highest court to continue the policies that they long had followed in selecting students. "Diversity," a flexible ideology that in the past had been used to limit the number of Jews but was now being deployed to increase the numbers of historically underrepresented minorities, had been elevated by Powell's opinion to the status of a "compelling state interest." But the stakes in *Bakke* had always gone well beyond affirmative action; in the end, what was in question was nothing less than the freedom of universities to select their own students. In explaining Harvard's decision to participate in the *DeFunis* and *Bakke* cases, Derek Bok wrote that the university joined the litigation to defend itself and the principles in which it believed "against any effort from outside the University to overrule our policies and limit our authority to use our own judgment in admitting students to this institution."[87] From this perspective, *Bakke* was a victory of historic proportions — one that would protect institutional autonomy in admissions for years to come.

The Controversy over Asian Americans

While Harvard was preparing its brief in *Bakke*, a new and unexpected racial problem appeared. This time the group at issue was Asian Americans. Yale had been recruiting Asian Americans since the days of Inky Clark, in the late 1960s, and Princeton began to recruit Asian Americans in the early 1970s, but Harvard had remained insistent that Asian Americans were not underrepresented and hence not in need of affirmative action.[88] As late as the fall of 1976, the administration did not recognize Asian Americans as a minority and refused to allow them to participate in the college's Freshman Minority Orientation.[89]

Yet the wave of pan-Asian identity that swept across the nation's campuses in the 1970s finally reached Cambridge, and in 1974–1975, a group calling itself the Coalition of Asian Americans (CAA) was formed at Harvard. For two years, however, the administration refused to recognize it as a minority organization. The CAA grew more militant and began staging protests, accusing Harvard of a double standard: Harvard included Asian Americans in its affirmative action compliance reports to the federal government while it denied them minority status. By the spring of 1977, the CAA had become the Asian-American Association and was issuing demands, among them, that Asian-American recruitment should be expanded and formally incorporated into the Admissions Office's affirmative action program. By 1978, the proportion of Asian Americans had increased from 3.6 to 6.5 percent of the freshman class — a result of the successful mobilization of Asian-American students.[90]

The increasing presence of Asian Americans at Harvard and other elite campuses reflected the change in the composition of the American population set in motion by the Immigration Act of 1965, which finally eliminated the restrictive quotas of the Immigration Act of 1924. "Just as we sought to eliminate discrimination in our land through the Civil Rights Act [of 1964]," declared a congressman who strongly supported the new law, "today we seek by phasing out the national origins quota system to eliminate discrimination in immigration to this nation composed of the descendants of immigration."[91] The consequence was a surge of Asian and Latin American immigrants, with the proportion of immigrants from Europe and Canada declining precipitously.[92] The size of the Asian-American population, which numbered fewer than 1 million in 1960, grew rapidly from roughly 1.5 million in 1970 to more than 3.6 million in 1980. By 2000, there were 11.9 million Americans of Asian descent — roughly double the number of Jews nationwide.[93]

Like Jews, Asian Americans tended to have above-average academic records, and they were particularly well represented among the most successful students.[94] With a rapidly increasing population, it was natural that more Asian Americans would apply to the elite colleges. Between 1976 and 1985, for example, the number of Asian-American applicants to Harvard more than tripled, from 461 to 1,677. At the same time, the Asian-American proportion of the freshman class rose rapidly, from 3.6 percent in 1976 to 10.8 percent in 1985.[95]

This extraordinary growth lent itself to conventional success narratives, and by the mid-1980s articles such as "The Triumph of Asian-Americans: America's Greatest Success Story" had become commonplace in the media.[96] Classified as a "model minority," especially by conservatives eager to discredit affirmative action and to reaffirm America's reputation as the "land of opportunity," the implicit but invidious comparison to Latinos and especially blacks was never far beneath the surface. But Asian Americans rarely joined this narrative, for they were increasingly concerned that they, too, were victims of discrimination. Unlike conservatives, however, their grievance was not that they were victims of reverse discrimination because of affirmative action for blacks and Latinos, but that they were being held to higher standards than whites, who still held the vast majority of places at the nation's leading colleges.[97]

Between 1983 and 1986, Asian Americans leveled charges of discrimination at a number of top universities — among them Berkeley, Brown, Stanford, Princeton, and Harvard. At Brown, the Corporation Committee on Minority Affairs (COMA) conducted a thorough internal investigation of the matter. Like the Big Three, the Brown admissions process relied heavily on subjective judgments of applicants' nonacademic qualities. Addressing this issue, COMA's report found: "It was clearly stated by all admission staff to whom we spoke that Asian-American applicants receive comparatively low non-academic ratings. These unjustified low ratings are due to the cultural bias and stereotypes which prevail in the Admissions Office. Such bias and stereotypes prevent admission officers from appreciating and accurately evaluating the backgrounds and nuances of the Asian-American cultural experience." While making clear that it did not "claim intentionally unfair treatment on the part of individuals or in the stated admission policies of the University," the report acknowledged that "the admission practices used to implement these policies have resulted in . . . unfair treatment." It concluded: "An extremely serious situation exists . . . and immediate remedial measures are called for.[98]

Similar internal investigations at Princeton and Stanford revealed that Asian Americans were admitted at lower rates than whites, but among the private colleges it was only at Harvard that allegations of discrimination resulted in a formal federal investigation.[99] The roots of the controversy dated back to at least 1983, when Margaret Chin, a Harvard undergraduate who had worked in the Admissions Office, co-authored a report, "Admissions Impossible," under the auspices of the first East Coast Asian Student Union. Surveying data from 25 universities, the report claimed that while Asian-American applications were soaring, enrollments were barely increasing. At Harvard, Chin and other student activists raised the issue of the lower admission rate of Asian-American applicants with the admissions staff, who attributed it to their allegedly weaker qualifications. But internal research led the students to believe that Asian-American candidates were on average *more* qualified than other applicants. By 1983, they had come to the conclusion that Harvard, like other elite private institutions, had set an informal ceiling on Asian-American enrollment.[100]

An examination of the available data, however, did not lend itself to easy conclusions. True, the acceptance rate for Asian Americans at Harvard was lower than that for white applicants, and their proportion of the freshman class had hovered in a suspiciously narrow range (between 10 and 12 percent) between 1982 and 1986. Harvard had its own explanation for this situation. According to the former dean of admissions Fred Jewett, "Arguments over numbers ignore a whole range of personal qualities," especially since Harvard had an official policy of "choosing people who bring talents underrepresented in the applicant pool." Contending that "the academic interests of

Asian students are heavily weighted toward science" and that their geographical concentration in California, New York, and Hawaii disadvantaged them in light of Harvard's quest for a broad national student body, Jewett also estimated that 40 to 50 percent of the Asian students with high SAT scores nationwide applied to Harvard, implying that Asian Americans were less scarce (and hence less valuable) than other groups in an institution committed to diversity. This factor was accentuated by their greater propensity to accept Harvard's offer of admission (80 percent for Asian Americans compared to 75 percent for whites and 55 percent for blacks). In addition, Jewett noted, Harvard's long-standing policy of giving preference to alumni sons and daughters had an unintended negative effect on Asian-American applicants. Controlling for legacy applicants, he suggested, would reduce the differential in admission rates between Asians and whites.[101]

Jewett's defense was resourceful, but the political landscape had shifted beneath him. By the end of 1986, three years of pressure from Asian-American students and faculty had placed the question of anti-Asian discrimination on the public agenda, and in early 1987 a *New York Times* article catapulted the issue to national prominence. It quoted a professor at Berkeley, Ling-Chi Wang, who explicitly compared the treatment of Asian Americans to the (now-discredited) quotas that had been imposed on Jews in the 1920s.[102] This framing cast the admissions practices of some of the nation's leading universities in a harsh new light, and the media responded with a new wave of coverage. Within days, all four major networks — CBS, NBC, ABC, and CNN — called Professor Wang.[103] For the first time, allegations of anti-Asian discrimination were in the mass media.

Still, it was one thing to charge institutions such as Harvard with discrimination and quite another to provide concrete evidence proving these charges. It had long been known, for example, that Asian-American applicants faced higher rejection rates at Harvard than whites, but this fact was not in and of itself proof of discrimination; after all, it was possible that, just as Harvard claimed, they might have weaker qualifications. But this argument suffered a serious blow in the spring of 1987 when the *Public Interest*, a prestigious neoconservative policy journal, published an article showing that admitted Asian-American applicants had combined SAT scores of 1467 (742 verbal and 725 math) compared to 1355 (666 verbal and 689 math) for Caucasians — a 112-point difference.[104] At least with respect to academic qualifications, the evidence seemed clear: just like Jews before them, Asian Americans had to meet a different and higher standard than other applicants.[105]

Aware of the intensifying public scrutiny, Harvard issued a statement in 1987, declaring "most emphatically that no . . . quotas exist for any group here."[106] In early 1988, the Admissions Office took the unusual step of denouncing claims of discrimination as "media speculation" and a statistical fiction. A two-page statement by Susie Chao '86, director of minority recruitment, and Dean of Admissions William Fitzsimmons contended: "While Asian Americans are slightly stronger than whites on academic criteria, they are slightly less strong on extracurricular criteria. In addition, there are fewer Asian Americans in our applicant pool who are alumni/ae children or prospective varsity athletes. When all these factors are taken into account, the difference in admissions rates for the two groups disappears."[107] But the criticism continued unabated, including within Harvard itself, where an Asian-American undergraduate wrote an article in the *Crimson* that emphasized the "stark difference" between the acceptance rates of Asian and white applicants and suggested that Harvard was guilty of "subtle, even nonintentional discrimination."[108]

In July 1988, unbeknownst to the public, the Office of Civil Rights (OCR) of the U.S. Department of Education began investigating the treatment of Asian-American applicants at Harvard and UCLA.[109] When the *Washington Post* finally broke the story in November, it said the investigation was intended to "determine whether the institutions are employing illegal quota systems to limit the number of Asian American students they enroll." According to Gary L. Curran, a spokesman for the Department of Education, the investigation would not limit itself to the question of ceilings or quotas but would be a comprehensive examination of admissions practices. The inquiry, he reported, had been triggered not by complaints from specific individuals but by news reports and the expressed concerns of advocacy groups.[110]

The OCR investigation lasted more than two years amid ever-growing media scrutiny of the elite universities' admissions practices. In 1989, ABC television's *20/20* aired a story alleging that Harvard (along with Brown, Berkeley, and UCLA) discriminated against Asian-American applicants, and two members of Congress submitted a resolution to the House of Representatives calling on universities to review their admissions policies. Harvard claimed that the increasing pressure from Asian-American activists and the federal government had changed nothing; reviewing the results of its 1989 admissions process, Chao insisted, "We would have made the same decisions without the compliance review going on."[111] Yet the data show a rising admission rate for Asian Americans, whose timing corresponds strikingly to growing external pressure: admitted at just 64 percent the rate of whites in 1986, the rate had risen to 84 percent by 1989. In 1990, just as the compliance review was ending, the overall Asian-American admission rate — 11.3 percent as recently as 1986 — reached 16.9 percent. This was nearly equal to the rate of admission of white applicants.[112]

Harvard had resisted the OCR investigation as best it could, only grudgingly giving it access to the data indispensable to an independent investigation.[113] Though the Department of Education held in its hands the ultimate sanction — the withdrawal of federal funds from institutions in violation of the nondiscrimination clause of Title VI of the 1964 Civil Rights Act — Harvard nevertheless played an important role in shaping the investigation. The only relevant comparison, Harvard and OCR agreed, was the one between Asian-American applicants and whites; the delicate matter of how Harvard handled black and Latino applicants compared to Asian Americans was off limits. Harvard also extracted from OCR a promise not to release the data it obtained. Vigilant about the possibility of negative publicity and fiercely protective of its discretion in admissions decisions, Harvard summarized its agreement with OCR as follows: the data tapes "will not be made available to others," and OCR "will resist any efforts to obtain them under FOIA [the Freedom of Information Act]."[114]

After two years of investigation, OCR announced its findings in October 1990. Focusing on ten groups admitted from 1979 through 1988, it found that Asian Americans had been admitted at a significantly lower rate for each of the past seven years (1982–1988). Inferior qualifications did not explain this difference; on the contrary, based on a painstaking quantitative and qualitative analysis of Asian and white applicants, it concluded that "the two groups were similarly qualified." Yet OCR rejected discrimination in assessing the qualifications of candidates as a cause of the different admission rates: "there was no significant difference between the treatment of Asian American applicants and the treatment of white applicants."[115]

How, then, could one explain the lower admission rate of Asian Americans? OCR's answer was that while Harvard treated Asian and white applicants similarly, its admissions policy included two "tips," or "plus factors," which put Asian Americans at a disadvantage: the preferences given to legacies and to recruited athletes. According to its statistical analysis, the "[Asian-American] disadvantage is virtually eliminated if legacies and recruited athletes (groups with few Asian Americans) are removed from the Asian American and white samples." Further evidence, OCR claimed, was provided "by the comparable Asian American and white admit rates when legacies and recruited athletes were removed from the sample."[116]

Far from settling the matter, this finding raised the question whether these preferences were themselves discriminatory. But OCR rejected this line of argument, concluding that the preferences for "children of alumni and recruited athletes are legitimate institutional goals, and not a pretext for discrimination against Asian Americans." OCR determined, moreover, "that there are no alternatives to these preferences that could effectively accomplish the same legitimate goals." Grounding its reasoning explicitly in Powell's opinion in *Bakke,* OCR then defended institutional autonomy, replicating the very argument that Harvard itself had submitted in *Bakke:* "if schools are to possess a desirable diversity, officials must retain wide discretion, with respect to the manner of selecting students." The investigators' final verdict read: "OCR finds that Harvard's use of preferences for children of alumni, while disproportionately benefiting white applicants, does not violate Title VI of the Civil Rights Act of 1964."[117]

It was a huge triumph for Harvard, validating its denial of discrimination at the same time that it vindicated its long-standing defense of institutional discretion. But Asian-American activists expressed strong displeasure at the OCR decision. "I think OCR cleared Harvard on the basis of inadequate information," said Berkeley's Ling-Chi Wang, adding that "OCR has accepted very general explanations without actually making a link between the admissions policy and alumni giving." But from OCR's perspective, Harvard had met the two basic criteria for establishing the legality of a policy that had a disparate impact on a particular ethnic group: it was not using the policy to limit the enrollment of members of the group, and there was an identifiable connection between the policy and a legitimate educational goal. An OCR spokesman noted that Harvard was "an institution that has been around for several hundred years" and was following "a practice that is widespread." It was not the OCR's intention, he declared, "to set the world on its head" by declaring that common institutional policies "are going to be treated all of the sudden as violations."[118]

Image and Reality in Harvard Admissions

Though a great legal victory for Harvard, the OCR investigation received extensive media coverage and left in its wake considerable damage to Harvard's public image. For in the aftermath of the investigation, some admissions practices that Harvard preferred to keep behind closed doors came under intense public scrutiny.

Officially, Harvard's policy was that athletic talent was simply another "plus factor," no different in character from musical or artistic talent. But the data on recruited athletes left little doubt that Harvard accorded them a great deal of preference. From 1981 through 1988, recruited athletes were admitted at a rate of 49 percent compared to 19 percent for all applicants. According to statistics compiled by OCR, there was a 132-point gap in the mean SAT scores between athletes and admitted applicants who were neither athletes nor legacies — 1273 compared to 1405.[119] All in all, 300 recruited athletes were accepted in the entering class of 1989 — over 13 percent of all admits.[120]

While the statistical evidence punctured Harvard's claim that athletic talent was merely another plus factor, it was the textual evidence gleaned from comments by readers in the applicant's file that was most damaging. OCR's final report offered some examples:

> "A shaky record and so-so scores don't bode well for [the applicant's] case . . . nice personal qualities, and he'd make a fine addition to the team if the coaches go all out for him, but that's what it would take."

> ". . . a straightforward case hanging on athletic ability. Easy to do if a needed '1' [athletic rating], pretty ordinary if not."

> "If she's a '1' [athlete] she's one to compare on 'the list.' Otherwise I'm afraid the mediocre scores will work against her."

As OCR concluded, "These comments suggest that an applicant's athletic ability and Harvard's need for such an athlete on its teams (reflected in the coaches' 'lists'), can be crucial if not decisive in determining whether to admit the applicant."[121]

OCR's findings about legacy applicants were, if anything, even more embarrassing. For unlike athletic skill, which is arguably a form of merit, being the child of an alumnus was nothing more than an accident of birth. Nevertheless, Harvard gave strong preference to legacies, admitting them between 1981 and 1988 at a rate of 36 percent — more than double the rate for all applicants. According to data reported by OCR, admitted legacies ranked lower than admits who were neither legacies nor athletes on every important rating: personal, extracurricular, academic, teacher, counselor, and alumni (they did, however, enjoy a tiny advantage on the athletic rating).[122] Though the SAT gap (36 points) between legacies and other admits was much smaller than in the case of athletes, it was hardly surprising; after all, legacies typically came from culturally and economically privileged families who sent their children to excellent secondary schools.

OCR carefully examined the readers' comments in applicants' files to determine how much weight was given to legacy status. That it was considerable was clear:

> "Well, not much to say here. [Applicant] is a good student, w/average EC's [extracurricular], standard athletics, middle-of-the-road scores, good support and 2 legacy legs to stand on . . . Let's see what alum thinks and how far the H/R [Harvard/Radcliffe] tip will go."

> "Dad's . . . connections signify lineage of more than usual weight. That counted into the equation makes this a case which (assuming positive TRs and Alum IV) is well worth doing."[123]

> "This is a good folder, but without the lineage it seems shy of an absolutely clear hook."

"We'll need confirmation that dad is a legit, S&S [Alumni Schools and Scholarship Committee participant] because this is a 'luxury' case otherwise."

"Without lineage, there would be little case. With it, we will keep looking."

"Not a great profile but strong enough #'s and grades to get the tip from lineage."[124]

In each of these cases the applicant was admitted, leading OCR to conclude that "being the son or daughter of an alumnus of Harvard/Radcliffe was the critical or decisive factor in admitting the applicant." In addition, OCR suggested that there is "some evidence to suggest that certain alumni parents' status may be weighed more heavily than others."[125] While OCR was referring to the greater preference for applicants whose parents served on Schools and Scholarships Committees, a more important source of differential treatment may well have been financial — a pattern strongly suggested by David Karen's study of 1980 applicants, which showed that the legacy advantage was substantially reduced for those alumni children who applied for financial aid.[126]

Since both athletic and legacy preferences had a negative impact on Asian Americans, OCR called on Harvard to justify them. In the case of athletes, Harvard stated that "our coaches tell us again and again that it would be impossible to field a varsity level team without recruiting athletes." At the same time, Harvard maintained that its policy was to give "athletic excellence the kind of positive weight we give a myriad of other non-athletic excellences"[127] — a dubious proposition supported by no empirical evidence.

Harvard's justification for alumni preferences was refreshingly candid: "Harvard alumni support the college by devoting immense amounts of time in recruiting and other volunteer activities, by contributing financially, and by informing other people . . . about the College. If their children are rejected by Harvard, their affection may decline; if their children are admitted, their involvement with the College is renewed." In addition, "alumni provide the bulk of the scholarship funds provided to all students." On the legal question of whether Harvard could accomplish its legitimate educational and institutional goals through means "which might have a less severe impact on Asian-American applicants," Harvard replied that "tips for lineage . . . could not be eliminated without a severe effect" on its "strength and vitality" as well as its "ability to achieve . . . [its] educational objectives."[128]

Harvard's justification of legacy preferences was enough to satisfy OCR, but it failed to protect the university from a barrage of criticism. The *Crimson* was the first to launch an assault, denouncing legacy preferences as "the most egregious vestige of aristocracy remaining at Harvard." Not long afterward, an op-ed piece appeared in the *New York Times* assailing alumni preference as "affirmative action for the privileged" and contending that if legacies were admitted at the same rate as other applicants, then the number of places freed up would have exceeded the total number of blacks, Mexican Americans, Puerto Ricans, and Native Americans in the entire freshman class. Also joining the fray was the *Washington Monthly,* which ran a cover story, "Why Are Droves of Unqualified, Unprepared Kids Getting Into Our Top Colleges?" Its answer: "Because their dads are alumni."[129]

Dean of Admissions William Fitzsimmons responded to the criticism from the *Crimson,* accusing the newspaper of "insensitivity" and "negative stereotyping" in its treatment of legacies and recruited athletes. Emphasizing that the OCR investigation had not only exonerated Harvard of discrimination against Asian Americans but also praised the university for its adherence to the principles of "justice and equality," Fitzsimmons reaffirmed Harvard's rejection of "a one-dimensional [that is, purely academic] selection process" and its continuing commitment to identifying "a more diverse array of talents, skills, and qualifications than test scores alone could do." Such a policy, he argued, was indispensable if Harvard was to have a racially and socioeconomically diverse student body.[130]

But the *Crimson* remained unconvinced and published a blistering point-by-point critique the very next day. In particular, the newspaper rejected the Admissions Office's claim that legacies were admitted "when all other factors are substantially equal" — a proposition clearly undermined by the higher legacy admission rate (roughly three times the norm) and by the fact that alumni children lagged behind nonlegacies "in every single area of comparison."[131] Yet even the *Crimson* had no answer to the Admissions Office's trump card: Harvard continued to occupy the preeminent position in American higher education and was more successful than any other institution in attracting top students. On behalf of this proposition, Fitzsimmons offered an impressive array of empirical evidence: Harvard had the most National Merit Scholars in its class, with 314 (compared with 203 and 169 at the institutions ranking two and three), the most National Achievement Scholarships for African Americans, with 55 (compared with 34 and 29 at the next institutions), and the most Westinghouse Science Talent Search finalists, with 11 (out of just 20 nationwide).[132] These figures were remarkable, but before the criticism triggered by the OCR investigation, Harvard had never felt the need to disclose them publicly.[133]

The guiding public justification for Harvard's admissions policy in the 1990s was its deep commitment to diversity. This rationale was laid out with great elegance by President Neil Rudenstine in a carefully researched 62-page essay, "The President's Report, 1993–1995."[134] Formerly a professor of English at Princeton, where he had served as provost under William Bowen, Rudenstine reached all the way back to John Milton, who had written in the *Areopagitica,* "Where there is much desire to learn, there of necessity will be much arguing, much writing, many opinions; for opinion in good men is but knowledge in the making." Deploying John Stuart Mill and Cardinal Newman in his excavation of diversity's intellectual lineage, he described it as "integral to learning at a profound level." According to Rudenstine, the ideal of diversity had been a leitmotif of Harvard since at least 1859, when Harvard's president, C. C. Felton, argued that bringing students to Cambridge from all parts of the country and from foreign lands "must tend powerfully to remove prejudices by bringing . . . [students] into friendly relations."[135]

In Rudenstine's erudite but selective history of diversity at Harvard, Presidents Eliot and Conant loom large, but President Lowell, who governed Harvard for nearly a quarter of a century, rates only a single paragraph — an understandable choice, given that Lowell had introduced Jewish quotas to Harvard and justified them in good part in the name of diversity. But Rudenstine's main objective was to defend race-attentive affirmative action as the logical contemporary expression of Harvard's abiding commitment to diversity. Rejecting the argument (as had Bowen and Bok before him) that affirmative action may be justified "as an attempt to compensate for patterns of past societal discrimination," he rooted his case firmly in Lewis Powell's decision in *Bakke*. And, like Powell, he concluded that using race as a "plus" factor could be defended morally and legally on purely educational grounds: "the presence of minority students contributed — along with the presence and contributions of other students — to diversity and therefore to the total educational environment of an institution, as well as to the education of all its members."[136]

Rudenstine knew that one of the great benefits of Powell's decision was that it permitted the continuation of policies that "preserve an institution's capacity — with considerable flexibility — to make its own determinations in admissions." Avoiding a "narrow and numerical . . . definition of qualifications," admissions decisions should be the product of informed human judgment and hence are necessarily subjective. For Rudenstine, these subjective judgments should assess such qualities as "character," "energy," "curiosity," and "determination," as well as the applicant's "willingness to entertain the idea that tolerance, understanding, and mutual respect are goals worthy of persons who have been truly educated."[137]

Rudenstine's vision was noble, but a perusal of the readers' comments unearthed during the OCR investigation reveals a decidedly less elevated, if eminently human, tendency to judge candidates on more superficial grounds. Among the handwritten remarks uncovered by OCR were the following:

short with big ears

coffee house intellectual type

offbeat, eccentric

Ken is driven, almost compulsive

a young man with spiked hair

seems a tad frothy

This young woman could be one of the brightest applicants in the pool but there are several references to shyness and the alumni IV [interviewer] is neg[138]

The fate of these applicants is not known, but it was Harvard's policy to give the personal rating at least as much weight as the academic rating in making the ultimate decision to admit or reject.[139]

Despite the bad publicity generated by the OCR investigation, Harvard emerged with its autonomy intact. As with its intervention in *Bakke*, Harvard's fundamental goal had been to protect its discretion in admissions. Now, after more than a decade of potential legal challenges, its capacity to use its own criteria and judgment had been secured. Whatever the political fallout, Harvard was free to continue its policy of granting substantial preference to legacies and recruited athletes. Perhaps even more important, its ability to give heavy weight to nonacademic factors, including highly subjective ones such as "character," "personality," and "leadership," had been sanctified in separate rulings by the Supreme Court and the U.S. Department of Education.

Harvard used this latitude to select a freshman class far different from the one that a policy of pure academic meritocracy would have produced. In addition to the preference for legacies and athletes, Harvard also continued the policy of vigorous affirmative action for historically underrepresented minorities that it had begun in the 1960s. In 1991, when the white acceptance rate was 17 percent, the percentage of black and Latino candidates admitted was 26 and 20 percent, respectively.[140] According to data gathered by the Consortium on Financing Higher Education (COFHE), there was a sizable gap in mean SATs between racial and ethnic groups; while whites in the freshman class averaged 1400, blacks averaged 1290 and Latinos, 1310.

Asian Americans had the highest average SATs of all: 1450 out of a possible 1600.[141] In 1991, the Asian-American/white admission ratio stood at 84 percent — a sharp downturn from 98 percent in 1990, when the scrutiny from OCR was at its peak. Though the Asian-American/white ratio never again dropped to the 64 percent level of 1986, it never returned to its 1990 zenith.[142] Despite Asian Americans' growing proportion of the national population, their enrollment also peaked in 1990, at 20 percent of the freshman class, where it more or less remained through 1994. But in 1995, it declined to 18 percent, and by 2001 it had dropped below 15 percent.[143]

*   *   *

While Harvard retained its top status, it never quite regained the position it had occupied in the mid-1960s. By the 1970s, Yale and Princeton were co-educational, and competition was increasing from other universities, including Stanford. In 1967, when Harvard's yield rate peaked at 86 percent, it lost fewer than 200 admits to other institutions; by 1975, its yield rate had dropped to 74 percent, and it lost nearly 400 students to other colleges and universities. The 1980s witnessed a continued erosion in Harvard's position, with the yield rate — though still higher than those of its competitors — reaching a modern low of 70 percent in 1982.[144] Meanwhile, Stanford was emerging as a major rival, attracting 104 Harvard admits in 1984, second only to Yale (128) and ahead of Princeton (97). Nevertheless, in head-to-head competition with Stanford, Yale, and Princeton, Harvard continued to attract two to three times as many students as it lost.[145]

By the mid-1990s, it was apparent that Harvard had weathered the challenge mounted by its rivals over the previous two decades. The overall yield rate had returned to more than 75 percent by 1994, and in 1995 Harvard reported that the number of students lost to its principal eight competitors (defined as "the universities to which Harvard had lost ten or more students in at least one year" during the previous decade) dropped from 415 in 1990 to 271 in 1995.[146] Even Stanford, which had by this time arguably replaced Yale as Harvard's principal rival, was losing ground; winning a third of the students accepted at both institutions in the mid-1980s, it was now attracting only one in five.[147] At the same time, Harvard's reputation was rising worldwide: in less than ten years, the number of international applicants had more than doubled, from 740 to 1,825.[148]

Yet while Harvard's appeal had never been broader, the socioeconomic background of its student body was narrowing. Concern about the declining number of working-class students at Harvard dated back at least to the days of Bender, but by the early 1980s the issue had become a major worry. It particularly preoccupied Dean Fitzsimmons, himself a graduate of a parochial school in a working-class suburb of Boston who had received a scholarship to Harvard, then gone on to earn a doctorate in the sociology of education.[149] In 1982, while serving as director of admissions, he highlighted the problem of Harvard's declining socioeconomic diversity:

> Over the past several years, Harvard and Radcliffe have witnessed an alarming decline in the number of applicants from families in which the parents had not attended college. Three years ago, nearly 26% of the applicants to the Class of 1983 came from families in which the father had not attended college. This figure dropped to 21% for the Class of 1984, 19% for the Class of 1985, and 16.3% for this year's applicant pool . . . If our student body comes to be drawn increasingly from the ranks of the privileged, our role in educating the most

talented persons from across the country and the world will be diminished. Prospective students from modest economic backgrounds must not come to feel that Harvard and Radcliffe are closed to them. If they do, and if the same thing were to happen at other private colleges, we could end up with substantial economic and racial segregation in our system of higher education.[150]

In 1987, Fitzsimmons (by then dean of admissions) expressed his concern once again, calling on Harvard to "give careful scrutiny in the future to the children of parents who have not attended college."[151] And in 1992 he noted with distress "the erosion of need-blind admissions and the diminished ability of colleges to meet the full financial needs of their undergraduates"; he then quoted a *Washington Post* article that fretted that "the nation's elite schools appear to be returning to their earlier twentieth century days as bastions of the rich."[152]

Despite these repeated expressions of concern, the proportion of Harvard students from disadvantaged backgrounds continued to decline. In 1952, over 37 percent of the freshmen had fathers who had not attended college; by 1996, the proportion had dropped to less than 11 percent.[153] Fathers' occupations reflected the same trend; in 1954, the proportion in blue-collar jobs (foreman, factory hand, laborer) was roughly 10 percent; by 1996, it had dropped to under 5 percent. Such trends partly reflected higher educational levels in general and a movement from blue-collar to white-collar work. But these shifts could not explain the extraordinary overrepresentation of the children of highly credentialed professionals (physicians and dentists, attorneys, university professors and administrators) who, though constituting less than 3 percent of the labor force, made up nearly a third of Harvard freshmen in 1996.[154]

Similar trends were apparent at a number of elite colleges, but Harvard was lagging behind many of its competitors. According to a study of Pell grants, federal awards generally given to families with incomes under $35,000, Harvard ranked behind 18 of 26 of the nation's most prestigious universities (including Yale and Stanford) in the proportion of low-income students, with just 9 percent receiving Pell grants.[155] Though Harvard raised issues about the study's methodology, its own data revealed that fewer than 10 percent of undergraduates came from families with incomes under $40,000 in 2001–2002.[156] At the other end of the spectrum, 54 percent of Harvard students came from families able to pay the more than $38,000 per year in total expenses without scholarship assistance, and even the 46 percent on scholarship were a surprisingly affluent group, with median family incomes between $80,000 and $90,000. Over a third of scholarship recipients came from families with annual incomes of over $100,000 — a figure that placed them in roughly the top 10 percent of American families.[157]

Equally distressing to those committed to a diverse student body, Harvard's capacity to attract top black students was eroding. In 2002, just 6.8 percent of the freshman class was African American, a substantial drop from the 9 percent who entered in 1993 and a lower figure than the percentage at Yale, Princeton, Stanford, and Columbia. Part of the reason was the decline in yield rate among black students from 74 percent in 1996 to 61 percent in 2002. For the first time in twenty years, Harvard no longer had the highest yield rate for African Americans, having been surpassed by Stanford, with a yield of 64 percent.[158]

Yet despite these troubling indictors of declining class and racial diversity, Harvard was in many ways prospering more than ever. In 2002, almost 20,000 students applied for admission; nearly 90 percent of them were rejected. In head-to-head competition with its rivals, Harvard was still number one, enjoying a yield rate of almost 80 percent — by far the highest in the nation.[159] Furthermore, it had never been richer; its endowment — $4.9 billion in 1990 — had risen to $19 billion by 2000 — far and away the largest of any university in the history of the world.[160]

Though Harvard's position looked unassailable from the outside, the pressures of escalating competition from other schools may have been taking a toll. How else to explain the existence of a peculiar category known in the Admissions Office as "the Z-list"? Every year, a *Crimson* investigation revealed, Harvard admits approximately twenty students on the condition that they agree to take a year off before enrolling. These students are anything but random; perhaps as many as 72 percent of the Z-list are legacies, and the great majority are products of private schools.[161] While the motives behind the Z-list remain murky, financial and political considerations are apparently important; according to a counselor at Milton, a prestigious private school near Boston that in some years supplies 25 percent of the students on the Z-list, "institutional needs" and "pull" ("connections") often moved students onto the list. Though the Z-list students were, as the *Crimson* readily acknowledged, only a tiny proportion of the entering class, the list's very existence represented an affront to Harvard's professedly meritocratic principles. Especially at a time of mounting concern about the declining diversity of the student body, the list stands as both a strange anachronism and a vivid reminder that Harvard, despite its seemingly impregnable position, responds even today to the prerogatives of wealth and power.

CHAPTER 17

Money, the Market Ethos,
and the Struggle for Position

A S YALE AND PRINCETON confronted the same competitive pressures felt by Harvard, they did so in an environment increasingly shaped to the ethos of the market. For the wealthy, the 1980s and 1990s were remarkable decades. The Dow Jones Industrial Average, just over 759 in April 1980, rose to 11,722 in January 2000 — an increase of over 700 percent, controlling for inflation.[1] But this jump was modest compared to what happened to the NASDAQ over the same period. Barely 200 at its high point in 1980, it rose to the astonishing height of 5,000 in 2000.[2] The accumulation of so much wealth in such a short time was unprecedented in the annals of history, and it strengthened the position of those who wished to extend the logic of the market to institutions that had traditionally been strongholds of nonmarket values.[3]

Like museums, hospitals, and other nonprofit organizations, institutions of higher education were deeply affected by the shift in the Zeitgeist toward the glorification of markets.[4] This was the period that witnessed the rise of highly publicized systems of college rankings — above all, the influential annual survey of "America's Best Colleges" in *U.S. News and World Report*. The growing prominence of the rankings contributed to the fierce competition for students, faculty, and resources among the leading colleges and reinforced the metaphor of the student as a "consumer" purchasing a brand "product" from the "business" that the university had become. In this context, noted Alvin P. Sanoff, former managing editor of the *U.S. News* annual ranking issue, "The elite schools are like warring software companies, each trying to beat the other," and the "pressure on admissions folks and on schools to get the best candidates is enormous."[5] Just how weighty these pressure were became clear as even venerable institutions such as Yale and Princeton struggled to maintain their position in the increasingly competitive marketplace of higher education.

*   *   *

Because of its location in a decaying urban neighborhood, where race relations were tense, and enjoying neither the cosmopolitan attractions of Cambridge-Boston nor the idyllic, small-town appeal of Princeton, Yale — which had long prided itself as a training ground for America's leaders — faced a very real threat of decline.[6] By the mid-1970s, it was, moreover, mired in deep financial difficulties.[7] In 1975, Yale's endowment stood at $517.7 million — barely a 10 percent increase over the $457.1 million of a decade earlier. Meanwhile, the endowment at Harvard had virtually doubled during the same ten years, rising from $567.3 million to $1.118 billion.[8]

Yale: Leadership and the Specter of Decline

There were many reasons why Yale had run into financial difficulties, but one of the most critical was the deterioration in relations with the alumni during the Brewster years. In 1977, when President Carter appointed Brewster ambassador to Britain, he quipped that his departure might be worth as much as $100 million to Yale's fundraisers.[9]

But even Yale's about-face on legacies was not enough to repair fully the damage done by the admissions policies of the late 1960s and early 1970s. Indeed, the Campaign for Yale, launched with great publicity in April 1974 with the objective of raising $370 million in three years, fell short of its goal; it finally achieved success only after Brewster had left office and George Herbert Walker Bush (who had just finished his term as director of the CIA) and Lloyd Cutler became co-chairmen.[10]

By the late 1970s, with Brewster safely in England and A. Bartlett Giamatti (Andover '56, A.B. Yale '60, Ph.D. Yale '64) the president, relations with alumni became much warmer. In 1979–1980, the Yale Alumni Fund set a new record by collecting $12 million, the largest sum ever reported in a single year by any annual alumni fund drive.[11] At the same time, the belief that Yale had pressed too hard for meritocracy under Brewster and Clark became crystallized as the new conventional wisdom. "We probably went too far — certainly further than any other college in the United States," said the university's officer for development and alumni affairs, John Wilkinson.[12] By decade's end, the alumni restoration was complete. In 1980, the children of alumni (including those who attended a Yale graduate or professional school) constituted 24 percent of the freshman class — the highest level in almost twenty years.[13]

The improvement in relations between the alumni and the administration that took place under Giamatti strengthened Yale's financial situation, but it did not alter the sense that Yale was slipping vis-à-vis its principal rivals. Princeton, which as recently as 1970 was losing students also admitted to Yale at a ratio of almost 2–1, was gaining ground; by 1980, more than 43 percent of joint admits were choosing to enroll at Old Nassau.[14] In 1981, 41 percent of the students admitted to Yale chose to go elsewhere — a proportion distressingly close to the 43 percent who declined Princeton's offers. Meanwhile, Harvard was losing only 26 percent of its admits to other institutions.[15]

Around this time, Stanford, too, began to challenge Yale as the nation's second most prestigious undergraduate institution. Already enjoying a higher yield rate (roughly 62 percent) in the late 1970s than Yale and Princeton, Stanford became even more prominent in the 1980s, buoyed by the growing importance of Silicon Valley, the high visibility of Stanford and Hoover Institute scholars in the Reagan administration, and the sheer economic and cultural dynamism of an increasingly global California.[16] Though no data are available on head-to-head competition between Yale and Stanford, Princeton's own statistics reveal that, starting in 1982, the majority of students admitted to both Princeton and Stanford chose to attend the latter, with the proportion rising to nearly 2 in 3 by 1990.[17] It was during this period that Yale also lost ground. By 1988, Stanford enrolled 34 percent more National Merit Scholars than Yale, a reversal from a decade earlier, when Yale led Stanford by almost the same margin.[18]

By the early 1990s, the sense that Yale was in disarray was widespread. Among its many problems was a crumbling physical plant, which Yale officials estimated would cost $130 million to renovate. By 1991–1992, Yale was once again running a deficit, and it was making plans to lay off 140 employees as part of a downsizing strategy. Even Yale's renowned athletic program was not immune to the growing financial pressures, and in 1991 it dropped its varsity wrestling and water polo teams in an effort to save $550,000 from its athletic budget.[19]

Amid deepening financial difficulties, relations with Yale's labor unions, which had long been strained, reached a new low. Exacerbating the conflict was a slickly produced union pamphlet, "Am I Blue? A Report on the Threat to Excellence at Yale," which was sent to the parents of Yale students and many alumni. In it the unions portrayed a university suffering from disastrous decline, "blatant disregard for academic traditions," "short-sighted decisions," and "the factory-like conditions one expects to find at an inferior institution, not at Yale."[20]

Presiding over the school during this troubled time was Benno C. Schmidt, a Yale law professor and former dean of Columbia Law School.[21] In 1986, Schmidt had replaced the popular and gentlemanly Giamatti, who had left Yale in 1985 to become the commissioner of Major League Baseball. Any new president would have faced a difficult situation, but Schmidt made matters worse by proposing a 15 percent cut in the size of the faculty and the outright elimination of entire departments (including large ones, such as Sociology and Applied Physics) as a solution to Yale's financial woes. Believing that both its interests and the principle of faculty participation in university decision making were under assault, the faculty rose up in what the *Yale Daily News* described as "an historic attempt by the professors of the College to question the legitimacy of the completed actions of a sitting president."[22] At a climactic faculty meeting on March 5, 1992, Schmidt heard prominent faculty members methodically attack his plan for dealing with Yale's financial problems while presenting an alternative of their own, which would entail far less drastic cuts. Within weeks, Schmidt's provost and dean, both of whom had been closely associated with his plan, announced their resignations. In May, Schmidt made a sudden, surprising announcement that he would be leaving Yale to become president and chief executive officer of the Edison Project, a venture to create 1,000 profit-making elementary and high schools nationwide.[23] One can only imagine what James Bryant Conant, who considered public schools the foundation of American democracy and who had devoted the last decades of his distinguished career to their improvement, would have thought of Schmidt's decision.

Coming on the heels of Yale's highly publicized financial difficulties and labor troubles, Schmidt's resignation triggered a new wave of bad publicity. Suffering as well from what the alumni magazine called "New Haven's persistent urban woes," Yale began to show signs of slippage. With prospective students asking such questions as "Is Yale going bankrupt?," the number of applicants dropped from nearly 12,000 in 1990 to just over 11,000 in 1992. Yield rates, which were 58 percent in 1990, also declined, dropping to 54 percent in 1992.[24] Asked to explain Yale's declining appeal to accepted students, Director of Admissions Margit Dahl cited two factors: the "size of financial aid packages and quality of life in New Haven."[25]

By 1993, Yale's economic crisis was so severe that talk of abandoning need-blind admissions — the pillar of the more meritocratic policies of the 1960s — became a matter of public record. Pinched by recession, declining federal support for higher education, and rising costs for labor and high-tech scientific equipment, Yale was one of many institutions to examine whether it could afford to continue policies adopted under far more favorable economic conditions.[26] In 1990, Brown (which had the smallest endowment of the Ivy League colleges) had abandoned need-blind admissions, and by 1993 Columbia, Cornell, and Amherst were considering doing the same. But neither of Yale's principal competitors, Harvard and Princeton, was seriously contemplating abandoning need-blind admissions, leaving Yale with little choice but to reaffirm the principle enunciated by Kingman Brewster in 1966: the university must demonstrate "a visible willingness to help all worthy students or else we will price Yale out of the market for national leadership."[27]

Though immensely wealthy compared to most universities, Yale was lagging behind both Harvard and Princeton in endowment per student — a serious problem as it tried to keep pace.[28] In May 1992, just as Schmidt was leaving office, Yale announced the largest fund drive ever undertaken by an American university: a campaign to raise $1.5 billion. By the time the campaign went public, Yale had already received pledges of $571.2 million, 38 percent of its goal. And by the time the campaign ended five long years later, Yale had raised $1.7 billion — "the largest amount in the history of higher education."[29]

But while the campaign was in progress, Yale had to make some major adjustments. Among the many cuts made was one that seriously compromised Yale's commitment to equality of opportunity: in 1990, as the depth of the crisis was becoming clear, its policy of need-blind admissions for non-Canadian foreign students was dropped, a victim of Yale's growing popularity in Eastern Europe and China. In 1993, just 20 percent of the 650 international students who applied for admission and scholarship assistance were accepted — a rate of 3 percent in a year in which 23 percent of all applicants were admitted.[30] Many of the foreign candidates were rejected, Yale acknowledged, for lack of funds despite their "sound qualifications." Yet at the very moment that Yale was turning away worthy foreign applicants, Harvard was recruiting them; in 1990, Dean Fitzsimmons reported proudly, "This year again foreign students will be here in greater numbers than ever before, comprising over 6% of the incoming class . . . [This] demonstrates a positive response to the efforts of a pilot program initiated by President Bok to make Harvard a more international university."[31]

The need to reject qualified foreign applicants could not have pleased Yale's new president, Richard Levin, who took office in 1993. A San Francisco native with a 1968 B.A. from Stanford and a 1974 Ph.D. in economics from Yale, Levin was Yale's first Jewish president. Though one of the few presidents not to have attended Yale College, he had spent his entire academic career in New Haven, having served as chairman of the Economics Department and dean of the Graduate School before assuming the presidency.[32] With the forces of globalization becoming ever more visible in the early 1990s, Levin called in his inaugural address for Yale to become "a world university." Updating the time-honored view of Yale as a training ground for the next generation's elite, he expanded its traditional vision from a national to a global one, urging Yale to "aspire to educate leaders for the whole world."[33]

This was a grand vision, but Levin had more immediate problems as he took office. Though in his view, the college remained "the premier undergraduate educational opportunity in America," its attractiveness to top high school students was still slipping.[34] At one meeting of prospective students, reported an admissions officer, a parent stated that "a Yale undergraduate [told her] you have a one-in-four chance of being a victim of violent crime" on the Yale campus.[35] In 1993, applications suffered a 10 percent decline from three years earlier and the lowest figure since 1983. At the same time, the number of applications to Harvard continued to rise, increasing to 13,029 in 1993 — a gain of 6 percent over the previous year.

With Yale's image taking a beating in the press, the yield rate continued to drop.[36] While Yale's new dean of admission, Richard Shaw, a Dartmouth graduate and a former director of admissions at the University of Michigan who had come to New Haven in 1992, tried to make the best of a bad situation ("I feel good about holding stable"), he was also trying to improve Yale's public image.[37] As an outsider, Shaw could see that "the assumption that students admitted to Yale will automatically come here doesn't hold any more" and firmly believed that "we don't have to carry a message of arrogance to be effective."[38] By the fall of 1993, Shaw had put together what Levin (who acknowledged "Yale's need to advertise") described as "an elaborate, glossy, beautifully laid out book."[39]

Stimulated in part by this concerted public relations offensive, the number of applicants rose in 1994 by 21 percent over the previous year. This was an impressive rise, but Yale was still having difficulty convincing the students it admitted to enroll. In 1994, the yield dropped to 53 percent — the lowest rate in almost twenty years.[40] For Yale, as well as for Princeton and Stanford, the underlying problem was the same: Harvard, with a yield rate of 75 percent, was winning in head-to-head competition for joint admits and winning big.[41]

In the mid-1960s, Yale had led the way in abolishing the "ABC system," the policy of early notification initiated by the Big Three in the mid-1950s for applicants from leading private schools and a handful of top suburban public schools. By the mid-1970s, as the egalitarian tides of the previous decade receded, a new system of early notification was put in place at all the Ivy League colleges.[42] Under this system — in principle open to everyone, but in reality used primarily by students from the more privileged segments of American society — candidates would apply early and be notified by around mid-December whether they had been accepted. Known as "early action," this system did not require admitted students to enroll, but let them wait until spring to choose a college.

With increasing numbers of applicants taking advantage of early action, this system remained in place in more or less unaltered form until the mid-1990s. Especially at Harvard, the system served institutional interests; 90 percent of those admitted under early action ultimately accepted the offer.[43] But at Yale and Princeton, large numbers of early action admits matriculated elsewhere; at Yale in 1994, 126 applicants admitted under early action enrolled at other institutions.[44] These defections contributed to Yale's low yield rate, which in 1994 stood a full 22 points below that of Harvard.[45]

The yield rate, long a concern of university administrators, had taken on greatly added importance with the rising influence of the *U.S. News and World Report*'s annual ranking of colleges, which gave considerable weight to yield in determining the rank of an institution. According to James Fallows, editor of *U.S. News* from 1996 to 1998, "everyone involved with college admissions and administration recognizes that the rankings have enormous impact." Among the factors believed to be affected, Fallows noted, are "the number of students who apply to a school, donations from alumni, pride and satisfaction among students and faculty members, and even the terms on which colleges can borrow money in the financial markets."[46]

In early 1995, Yale and Princeton concluded that early action was doing them more harm than good. Recognizing that the system did not serve their interests in an increasingly competitive marketplace in which Harvard controlled the largest share, they determined that they could no longer afford the luxury of giving applicants early admission, only to have them decline later. So Yale and Princeton moved to a system of early decision, leaving Harvard the only member of the Big Three with an early action program.[47] Under the terms of early decision, students could apply to only one college early and had to make a binding commitment to enroll if accepted. According to Dean of Admissions Richard Shaw, Yale had assured itself of "another 100 students early on."[48]

Yale's move produced immediate dividends. In 1995–1996, the program's first year, 415 students were accepted under early decision, ensuring that almost 30 percent of the freshman class would be admitted with a virtually 100 percent yield.[49] Though Yale's performance in the "open market" — those students not admitted under early decision and hence not bound to enroll at a particular institution — remained modest (the yield rate among such admits was only about 51 percent), the overall yield rate rose substantially. In 1996, 60.7 percent of all admits chose to enroll — an increase of more than 5 percent over 1995 and the highest yield rate in more than two decades.[50]

Yale's shift to early decision marked a period of rebound from the doldrums of the early 1990s. In part because of the higher yield rate achieved by early decision, Yale once again rose to the top position in the *U.S. News* rankings, where it had stood in 1988 and 1989 before dropping to third place in 1990.[51] But more important was the decided improvement in Yale's financial situation associated with the successful completion of its much-publicized $1.5 billion fundraising campaign. Also contributing to Yale's improved fiscal condition was the booming economy and especially the spike in the stock market in the mid- and late 1990s. In 1990–1991, Yale's endowment had stood at $2.59 billion; nine years later, it had almost quadrupled, to $10.05 billion.[52] By the fall of 2000, as Yale headed into its tercentennial year, the alumni magazine reported that, after years of budget deficits, "Yale seems to be in better shape than at any time in decades."[53]

With its newfound wealth, Yale was finally able to take concrete steps to realize the vision of Levin's "world university." In November 2000, on the eve of its 300th anniversary, Levin announced that Yale would establish a Center for the Study of Globalization, begin a World Fellows Program ("a small-scale reverse Rhodes Scholarship of sorts"), and implement a policy of need-blind admissions for international students.[54] The last step was especially crucial — with Yale now aspiring "to educate leaders for the whole world," nothing less than a purely meritocratic admissions policy for foreign applicants would do. In 2001, the need-blind policy for international students went into effect, and its impact was immediately visible. Foreign students, just 5 percent of Yale freshmen in 1999, rose to 9 percent. By 2002, one Yale freshman in ten was an international student.[55]

Yale's commitment to a genuinely diverse student body was also apparent in the relatively high number of low-income and minority students on campus. In a study of Pell Grant recipients in 2001–2002 at the nation's leading universities, Yale showed itself to be more open to students of modest economic means than its Big Three rivals: 10.1 percent of Yale undergraduates had received Pell Grants, compared to 7.4 percent at Princeton and 6.8 percent at Harvard.[56] And in 2002 Yale led the Ivy League in the proportion of blacks in the freshman class, very narrowly edging out Princeton, 8.5 to 8.4 percent. Harvard, whose freshman class had been 9 percent as recently as 1995, dropped to 6.8 percent.[57]

Yale's meritocratic ethos, which had reached its zenith in the Clark-Brewster era, continued to shape policy during the Levin years. While alumni children still enjoyed a sizable statistical advantage over nonlegacies, Princeton and Harvard admitted legacies at a substantially higher rate despite their lower overall rate of admission. In 2002, 39 and 35 percent of legacies were admitted at Harvard and Princeton, respectively, compared to 29 percent at Yale.[58] The legacy-nonlegacy regular admission rates among the Big Three were even more striking: while legacies were admitted at a ratio 2.4 times higher than nonlegacies at Yale, the ratios at Harvard and Princeton were 4.1 and 3.4, respectively.[59]

Yet despite Yale's need-blind admissions policy and its relatively meritocratic treatment of legacy applicants, the socioeconomic composition of the student body remained heavily tilted toward the affluent. While Yale reported that 42 percent of the freshman class in 2002 received financial assistance from the university, this meant that 58 percent did not — a remarkable figure, given that only about 5–7 percent of American households could afford $35,000-plus in annual expenses.[60] Perhaps even more striking was the extraordinarily privileged family educational backgrounds of Yale freshmen; in 2001, more than 68 percent came from households in which a parent held a graduate degree, while only 8 percent came from a noncollege household.[61] Consistent with their economically and culturally privileged backgrounds, Yale freshmen disproportionately came from the nation's finest public and private schools. Though only about 11 percent of secondary school graduates nationwide are from private schools, the figure at Yale has been 43–47 percent in recent years — about the same as Princeton but higher than Harvard, where roughly 37 percent are private school graduates.[62]

Concerned about the increasingly affluent character of the student body, Yale began to look for new ways to increase diversity.[63] In the fall of 2002, Levin announced that Yale would eliminate its early decision policy and in 2004 replace it with early action. Explaining his decision, Levin cited a number of reasons, among them that "American high school students have too much pressure on them too early."[64] But a critical factor was his conviction that early decision programs favored the affluent and were thus incompatible with Yale's meritocratic principles. "Very conclusive research by three Harvard economists," Levin said, "showed Early Decision was discouraging applications by students with financial need and that it was tending to bias selection against those students. That cuts completely against the grain of everything we've tried to do for the last 40 years — including need-blind admissions and making the school more accessible."[65]

In announcing its decision to move to early action, Yale was joined by Stanford eight hours later. But the one institution that held steadfast in its commitment to the old policy was Princeton, which had gained ground on Yale by admitting half the class through early decision, guaranteeing a high yield rate.[66] By 2001, Princeton's yield rate had surpassed that of Yale (71 compared to 65 percent), and Princeton had for the first time gained the number one position in the *U.S. News* annual ranking.[67] Princeton's ascent had also been fueled by its emergence as the richest member by far of the Big Three; in 2000, its endowment was more than $1.3 million per student — 44 percent more than Yale and 26 percent more than Harvard.[68] In its struggle against its ancient rivals, Princeton would not hesitate to use its wealth as a weapon.

Princeton: Wealth, Image, and the Battle for Institutional Mobility

In the mid-1970s, Princeton was one of the nation's best-endowed universities, but it was not the almost unimaginably wealthy institution it has since become. Indeed, in 1976, Old Nassau was lagging behind its rivals in the financial packages it offered, reporting that its "self-help expectations continue to be very high in comparison with those of many of our major competitors, let alone most of the colleges and universities in the country."[69] As late as 1997, an internal study of students who declined Princeton's offer of admission found that "the number and the percentage of students choosing to decline admission . . . in order to enter non-Ivy-MIT institutions (which are not bound by any financial aid–overlap agreements) reached their highest levels in five years." Overall, the study revealed that "the number and percentage of students declining Princeton's offer of admission who cited financial reasons for their decisions rose dramatically from 139 or 11.7% last year to its highest level in five years (i.e., 180 or 16.2%)."[70]

Since the late 1950s, Princeton had also suffered from a relatively low yield rate. In 1974, the proportion of admits choosing to enroll dropped below 50 percent for the first time, where it remained in 1975 and 1976 (when it reached an all-time low of 47 percent). Princeton was doing particularly poorly in direct competition with Harvard; in 1977, of 540 applicants admitted by both institutions, 81 percent chose Harvard.[71] Yale, too, continued to rank ahead of Princeton, attracting 55 percent of 350 joint admits. Even Stanford, which had been behind Princeton in head-to-head competition in the early 1970s, had pulled even; in both 1976 and 1977, the number choosing its rising California rival was virtually identical (61 vs. 62 in 1976, with a tie at 62 in 1977).[72] If these trends continued, there was a very real possibility that Princeton would soon slip to the fourth position among the nation's elite private colleges.

Particularly distressing, especially to the faculty, was Princeton's inability to enroll the most brilliant students — the kind of students with dazzling records whose stock had soared with the rise of meritocracy over the previous quarter century. In 1979, Princeton attracted just 34 percent of the 457 academic "1"s it had admitted. Worse still, "the yield for 2/1s [students with nonacademic ratings of "2" and academic ratings of "1"] was only 18%."[73] In an era in which the most valued currency was sheer academic brilliance, Princeton was largely unsuccessful in attracting the very best young scholars.

In truth, Princeton was ambivalent about the admission of the scholastically brilliant. Responding to faculty complaints about the increasing rate of rejection for academic "1"s (from 9 percent in 1977 to 30 percent in 1981), Dean of Admission James Wickenden stood his ground: "It is my strong feeling that we should not automatically admit all Academic 1s. While these candidates have superb SAT scores and transcripts unblemished by Bs, some have such limited interests that one wonders about the contribution they would make to a residential college community."[74] In 1985, the new dean of admission, Anthony M. Cummings, put it this way: "Princeton has always wanted to train the next generation of leaders. We look for qualities of leadership and integrity as well as intellectual qualities."[75]

This was the same rationale that Bender had articulated in the 1950s for limiting the number of "intellectuals" at Harvard but with one crucial difference: while Harvard was a magnet for the academically brilliant, Princeton continued to have problems convincing those academic "1"s it did admit to come. In addition to suffering from its small-town location, Princeton was handicapped by its eating clubs, which had shown surprising resilience after declining sharply in the late 1960s and early 1970s.[76] The club system was still harmful to its efforts to recruit Jewish students and racial minorities, and in his Report to the President in 1980, Dean Wickenden bluntly stated, "A less discriminatory selection process for the clubs would have enormous public relations benefits for the University."[77] In 1983, Wickenden's last year as dean, 269 of 485 of the admitted academic "1"s chose to enroll elsewhere. Two years later, with the definition of an academic "1" narrowed to require that the applicant excel in all scholastic areas and not just one (such as physics or mathematics), the number of "1"s admitted dropped sharply to 256, with just 42 percent enrolling at Princeton.[78]

Amid widespread faculty concern about Princeton's inability — or unwillingness — to attract more brilliant students, the university also faced a wave of negative publicity about alleged discrimination against Asian Americans. In 1981, Dean Wickenden had privately reported that he was "concerned about Asian Americans being admitted at the lowest rate of all minorities in spite of the fact that the academic credentials of this group are much stronger than those of the other sub-groups."[79] By 1985, 17 percent of all applicants to Princeton were admitted, but only 14 percent of Asian Americans. But a Princeton study that was never made public concluded that, though Asian Americans had higher academic ratings than whites in four of the five years examined, there was no bias. "One of the things working against Asian-American" applicants, said Cummings, was that they were underrepresented among groups given preference for admission, such as alumni children, athletes, and blacks.[80] This was essentially the same argument that Harvard made a few years later, though it was careful to leave the higher admission rate for blacks (29 percent in 1987 compared to 15 percent for all Harvard applicants) out of the discussion.[81]

There was truth to Cummings's claim that Asian Americans were hurt by Princeton's preferential admissions policies for legacies, athletes, and historically underrepresented minorities, but in fact *all* groups falling outside these three categories suffered from reduced chances of admission in what was increasingly a zero-sum game. With roughly one Princeton freshman in six the child of an alumnus, Princeton's policy of preferential treatment for legacies was especially consequential. Throughout the 1970s and 1980s, their admission rate was well over double that of other applicants. In some years, the ratio reached more than 3–1; in 1985, for example, 47.8 percent of alumni children but only 15.5 percent of nonlegacy candidates were admitted.[82]

As with legacies, Princeton's policy toward athletes was still one of strong preference. In 1979, Wickenden provided a fine-grained description of how the process worked: "Because the admission staff alone cannot determine which of the applicants are likely to make the greatest contribution to the athletic programs of the University, we rely upon the assessments of the various coaches. The Department of Athletics provides names of athletically talented candidates in each sport, with an assessment of each individual's athletic ability. As in all other cases, the Admission Committee is not bound by these evaluations, but they are referred to frequently as we make fine distinctions among fairly similar candidates."[83] In 1978, Princeton admitted 422 "well-identified" student athletes, of whom 259 enrolled. This meant that over 22 percent of the freshman class was made up of athletes — a number that dwarfed the 194 legacies who enrolled that year.[84] Though the Ivy League had decided to raise the academic quality of admitted athletes in 1979 and in 1981 had established an Academic Index (consisting of SATs, achievement tests, and a converted rank score) to facilitate comparisons between institutions, the problem persisted. Among the Ivy league colleges, Wickenden reported, Princeton made a "relatively good showing"; nevertheless, as he forthrightly admitted, Princeton was still failing to live up to the most basic tenet of the 1954 Ivy agreement: "the academic credentials of the admitted athletes . . . [should be] representative of the class as a whole."[85]

Minorities were the smallest of the three groups receiving special consideration, but they nevertheless constituted a sizable segment of the freshman class — roughly 13 to 15 percent between 1980 and 1985.[86] As with legacies and athletes, many minority applicants would no doubt have been admitted without any preferential treatment. Yet given its starkly racist past, Princeton felt a special responsibility to guarantee that its student body would be racially diverse. Indeed, the most critical single measure of progress at Princeton — and the best hope for changing its image — was the number of black students it enrolled. In this regard, Princeton fared relatively well; in 1984, for example, 9 percent of all freshmen were black, compared to 8 percent at Harvard and 6 percent at Yale.[87] Princeton also did well in terms of attracting highly qualified black students; in 1985, the combined SAT scores for African-American freshmen was 1208, compared to 1240 at Harvard, which historically had a far better reputation among blacks.[88] Nevertheless, the yield rate among African-American admits was on the decline in the mid-1980s. In 1987, just 33 percent of admitted black students chose to enroll at Princeton — a striking contrast to the 64 percent rate among blacks at Harvard.[89]

Long an issue, Princeton's position vis-à-vis its competitors was becoming an institutional obsession by the mid-1980s. Among the school's many concerns was its low yield: 55 percent in 1983, compared to 71 percent at Harvard, 61 percent at Stanford, and 58 percent at Yale.[90] Particularly worrisome was its declining status compared with Stanford. In 1985, the annual report of the dean of admission referred to "the extraordinary emergence of Stanford as competition for large numbers of commonly admitted students." That year's statistics revealed that Stanford was winning the competition, with 155 students admitted at both institutions choosing to enroll at Stanford, compared to only 102 matriculating at Princeton.[91]

At the same time, Princeton was making modest gains in its competition with its New Haven rival. Though Yale attracted more joint admits than Princeton (135 of 229 in 1985), this ratio was better than the one a few years earlier and was the lowest number of admits lost to Yale at any time in the previous decade.[92] Moreover, Princeton had virtually pulled even with Yale in the number of National Merit Scholars enrolled (163 vs. 167 in 1985) — one of many signs that it had been doing better than in earlier years in attracting top scholars.[93]

By 1987, Cummings reported that "we have considerably narrowed the difference in our competitive position relative to Yale," but Stanford was enrolling "fully three-fifths of the common admittees." After four years as dean of admission, Cummings insisted that "it would be difficult to maintain that there are appreciable differences in competitive position among Princeton, Stanford, and Yale." He concluded: "While Harvard continues to enjoy preeminence, its three principal peer institutions jointly occupy the 'number two' position."[94] But this interpretation was rather questionable, for Princeton continued to lag behind Harvard, Stanford, and Yale in the competition for joint admits and, as of 1987, still had the lowest yield among the four institutions.

It was in this context that Princeton went outside the ranks of its own faculty in selecting a president for the first time since 1868. In a move freighted with symbolism, Princeton selected Harold Shapiro, a Jew and a naturalized immigrant born in Montreal, as its president in April 1987.[95] For a school long considered a citadel of anti-Semitism, the decision to end its uninterrupted line of WASP presidents was a further sign that it was serious about its commitment to diversity and equal opportunity. The symbolism was not lost among Princeton's Jews. "This shows that Princeton has come a long way," said the president of Hillel, Arie Katz, who added, "If you would have asked Jewish students at Princeton in the 1960's if they could picture Princeton with a Jewish president, I'm sure they would have said no."[96]

Shapiro, an economist with a 1956 A.B. from McGill and a 1964 Ph.D. from Princeton, had been a professor of economics at the University of Michigan before assuming its presidency in 1980. There he developed a reputation for handling racial tensions well — an important factor in Princeton's decision to hire him.[97] Like his predecessor, William Bowen, Shapiro was a respected professional economist and a moderate liberal politically.

When he took office in January 1988, Shapiro inherited one of the nation's leading universities but one that, despite Cummings's protestations to the contrary — stood behind Harvard, Stanford, and Yale. The person who had presided over Stanford's Office of Admission during its meteoric rise was Fred Hargadon. In April 1988, Hargadon was named Princeton's new dean of admission by Shapiro, then in only his fourth month in office.[98]

The son of a first-generation Irish immigrant with an eighth-grade education, Fred Hargadon was Princeton's first dean of admission without a Princeton degree. He grew up in a small town just outside Philadelphia where his father worked in an automobile factory, and after high school he worked and was then drafted. Hargadon seemed on a working-class trajectory, but after his stint in the army he took advantage of the G.I. Bill and enrolled at nearby Haverford College. Following some graduate work in Russian studies at Harvard and Cornell, he taught political science at Swarthmore, where he moved to the admission office, soon becoming its head. Hargadon might have stayed at Swarthmore permanently, but was recruited in 1969 by Stanford to serve as its dean of admission. He stayed at Stanford for fifteen years, leaving in 1984 to become a senior executive at the College Board.[99]

Though hailed by Shapiro as "the best person in admissions in America . . . the dean of admission deans," even Hargadon could not immediately alter Princeton's competitive position.[100] In fact, during his first year in office, Princeton's situation actually deteriorated a bit, with the proportion of joint admits choosing Yale over Princeton rising to 61 percent in 1989, up from 54 percent a year earlier. Meanwhile, Old Nassau continued to lag behind Stanford and Harvard, which attracted, respectively, 66 percent and 77 percent of joint admits.[101] While well ahead of such rivals as MIT and Brown, Princeton still was fourth in its appeal to the most sought-after students.

According to Shapiro, an important factor in Hargadon's selection was his outstanding record in attracting more women and minorities to Stanford. Although convincing more blacks and Hispanics to come to Princeton proved difficult, the number of women increased rapidly. Explicitly rejecting the argument that the prominence of science and engineering accounted for the relatively low number of Princeton women, Hargadon set out to enlarge the pool of female applicants and to ensure that they would receive equal treatment in the admissions process.[102] Between 1988 and 1994, the proportion of female applicants grew from 40 to 44 percent, and their percentage of the freshman class rose from 39 to 44 percent.[103]

Hargadon was struck in his first year by how different Princeton was from Stanford from the viewpoint of an admissions dean.[104] Stanford had roughly 1,600 places to fill, compared to no more than 1,150 at Princeton. At the same time, the pressures to admit students from important constituencies — whether alumni children, athletes, minorities, engineers, or potential scholars — were similar at the two institutions. What this meant in practice was that a high proportion of the class at Princeton was filled with members of politically powerful constituencies even though "unaffiliated candidates" (as Hargadon called them) constituted the largest segment of the applicant pool. As a consequence, admissions at Princeton had a more intensely zero-sum character than at Stanford, and the power of organized constituencies effectively limited the latitude of the dean of admission.

A savvy administrator, Hargadon quickly realized that he would have to enlarge his zone of discretion if he was to place his own imprint on the Princeton student body. One of his first moves was to put more distance between the Office of Admission and the powerful Alumni Schools Committees (ASCs), which interviewed about half of all applicants. Noting that "Stanford didn't have anything like them," Hargadon publicly took the position that the ASCs were a great resource — "2,000 people out there to help get a lot of messages out."[105] Privately, however, he expressed concern about their lack of racial and gender diversity. "It is perhaps inevitable," he wrote, "that the relationships between such a large volunteer effort and the admission office are frequently characterized by a certain amount of tension." This tension was exacerbated by his decision to break tradition by not sending out to ASC members "likely" and "unlikely" cards on the candidates interviewed until very late in the process and by a corresponding reduction in the time ASC members and the Admissions Office staff spent on the phone while they were reading applications. Both these changes expanded the autonomy of the Admission Office and were consistent with Hargadon's view that the ASCs needed greater clarity on "the extent and the *limits* to the role that they play in admissions."[106]

Hargadon also increased the discretion of the Admission Office and, in particular, its senior staff, including himself. In one of several reforms of the admissions process, Hargadon changed the system of review for final decisions, requiring that all applicants, after readings by two staff members, have their files forwarded for review by the dean and other senior admissions officers.[107] With a 17-member admissions staff, this reform meant that power was concentrated among the officers with the closest ties to the administration and the most experience.[108] In the end, no one would be admitted or denied without the direct involvement of Hargadon himself or his most trusted lieutenants.

Another important reform was a change in the system of evaluating applicants. While every candidate still received both an academic and a non-academic rating, Hargadon's view was that there needed to be a more sharply drawn "line between the evaluation of an applicant's credentials and the decision whether to offer that applicant admission."[109] The problem was most acute in the case of those candidates rated as academic "1's" — a group of particular importance to the faculty, who pressured the Admission Office to accept virtually all of them. Hargadon's solution was to massively expand the category, rendering it effectively impossible to admit all of the candidates receiving the revised academic "1" rating.

Hargadon claimed that the reason for relaxing the standards for an academic "1" was to facilitate efforts "to discern the intellectually inclined among the much larger group of extremely able applicants to be found among the [academic] 2s or 3s," but it also had the effect of increasing the power of the Admission Office compared to that of the faculty.[110] Under Hargadon's predecessor, receiving an academic "1" essentially guaranteed admission; in 1988, 98 percent of such candidates had been offered a place in the class, and in 1987, the figure had literally been 100 percent.[111] This had been a crucial concession to the faculty. But what seemed self-evidently reasonable to faculty was, from Hargadon's point of view, an encroachment on his discretion as dean. Complaining of the faculty's tendency to place "so much emphasis on the applicant-admit ratio" among academic "1"s, Hargadon did not hesitate to exercise his discretion to turn down some of the most brilliant applicants. In 1989 — when, even under the expanded definition, academic "1"s still constituted the top 6 percent of all applicants — well over a third of these outstanding scholars were rejected.[112]

Hargadon's reforms did not lead to any significant changes in the number of legacies, athletes, or minorities, but they did have an effect on the composition of the student body. Among the most visible changes was a decline in the number of Jewish students to the lowest level seen since the 1960s.[113] The decline had begun before Hargadon arrived, dropping from a peak of around 20 percent in the late 1970s to about 15 percent in the mid-1980s.[114] Beginning in 1986, the numbers began to fall further, declining to about 13 or 14 percent in the 1986–1988 period, the last three years of the Cummings era. After Hargadon's arrival, the rate of decline began to accelerate, with the proportion of Jews falling to 12 percent in 1989 and 10 percent in 1990.[115]

By the early 1990s, when the trend became visible, concerned faculty organized a meeting with Dean Hargadon. Hargadon said that he firmly opposed discrimination against any group and did not even know the religion of applicants to Princeton. But the critical question, as a number of faculty pointed out, concerned not his intentions (which they presumed to be good) but whether the policies he pursued had the unintended effect of reducing the number of Jewish students. In offering his own explanation for the downturn, Hargadon noted that the proportion of Jews among all college applicants had declined, dropping to 2 percent, according to data from the American Council on Education and Higher Education Research Institute of UCLA. But this could not explain why Princeton's closest rivals enrolled so many more Jews — 29 percent at Yale and 21 percent at Harvard, according to statistics provided by Hillel. Nor did Princeton's small-town setting provide a compelling explanation; after all, Amherst College, an important competitor, was also in a small town, but its Jewish enrollment was 16 percent.[116]

It is possible that the drop in Jewish enrollment may simply have reflected Princeton's declining attractiveness among Jewish students rather than any change in admissions policy. According to Edward Feld, Princeton's campus rabbi from 1973 to 1992, there was a "shift in the student mood back to the older Princeton" in the 1980s — a shift symbolized by "the reinvigoration of the clubs [which] brought back a sort of older style at Princeton which was more conservative, more elitist."[117] This resurgence was particularly unwelcome to many women, especially those with feminist sensibilities, and may explain why in the 1990s 12 percent of the men were Jewish while the figure for women was only about 8 percent. In the 1970s, the nadir of the eating clubs' influence and membership, 16 percent of men but 18 percent of women were Jewish.[118]

Yet the most powerful force responsible for the declining percentage of Jews at Princeton was, in all likelihood, subtle but consequential changes in admissions criteria. Among the faculty, there was a widespread perception that Hargadon placed greater emphasis on a number of factors — athletic ability, geographic diversity, and increased recruitment at suburban high schools — that had the effect, albeit not the intent, of reducing the number of Jews. According to the *Daily Princetonian,* a number of professors believed that the decline in the number of Jews was "inevitably linked to . . . an overall decline in the intellectual quality of the student body" — a perception reinforced by Hargadon's willingness to reject a much higher proportion of academic "1"s than his predecessor.[119]

Overall, the admissions policy under Hargadon placed slightly less emphasis on purely academic qualifications and a bit more on nonacademic factors — a formula that harmed groups whose primary strengths were intellectual. Jews were not the only group affected. Asian Americans also presented profiles whose strongest component was a high level of scholastic accomplishment. Hargadon recognized this; in a *Princeton Alumni Weekly* interview, he acknowledged that many Asian-American families encouraged their children to concentrate on academics and that Princeton's emphasis on "energy level outside the class, or taking part in activities . . . has turned out for many Asian-American students to be a handicap."[120] Not surprisingly, the gap in the admission rates for Asian Americans and whites grew during Hargadon's tenure; 86 percent of the admission rate of whites in the half-decade before his arrival, the Asian-American rate dropped to 70 percent during his first five years in office.[121]

Not particularly popular with the faculty, Hargadon remained focused on Princeton's competitive position.[122] But six years into his term, Princeton remained well behind Harvard and Stanford (though gaining on Yale). In 1994, it was still losing more than 43 percent of its admits — 885 students — to other institutions. And as had long been the case, most of these students enrolled at one of Princeton's three main rivals: Harvard (274), Stanford (126), or Yale (91).[123]

Since the 1970s, Princeton — like Harvard and Yale — had offered applicants the "early action" option. This system did not work well for Princeton, however, where 142 of the early action admits matriculated at another institution in 1994.[124] Recognizing this, Hargadon announced in early 1995 that Princeton was replacing its early action program with an early decision program of the type offered by less prestigious competitors. For Princeton, which was already filling nearly half the freshman class with early action admissions, the move to early decision was a sure-fire way to increase its yield, which lagged 18 points behind Harvard (57 vs. 75 percent in 1994).[125]

The benefits of early decision to Princeton were immediately visible: the yield, which stood at 57 percent from 1992 through 1994 and 60 percent in 1995, soared to 66 percent in 1996. Almost half of all freshmen — 556 students — were admitted under early decision, and every single one of them enrolled. Meanwhile, the number of students lost to Princeton's main rivals plummeted by over 30 percent, from 414 in 1995 to 286 in 1996.[126]

The move to early decision served the institutional interests of Princeton, Yale, and Stanford, for it increased their yields and stabilized their "market share" of top students by limiting the competition. But it did not serve the interests of students, who could not compare financial packages from different institutions. There was, moreover, a growing perception that colleges favored early decision applicants over regular candidates for admission — a concern powerfully reinforced by the same 2001 study of fourteen highly selective colleges that had turned Yale's president, Richard Levin, against early decision. The study's conclusion, which was reported in the *New York Times,* was that applying early was worth the equivalent of an extra 100 SAT points in increasing the likelihood of gaining admission.[127] If any students were well served by the growth of early decision programs, they were the economically and culturally privileged candidates from the best private and public schools —

a powerful irony for universities publicly committed to the ideals of inclusion and "diversity."[128]

Like most other universities with early decision programs — Cornell and Penn being notable exceptions — Princeton has generally maintained that it gives no preference to early decision candidates.[129] Until recently, it was impossible to assess this claim definitively, though the fact that early decision candidates were admitted to Princeton at a rate three to four times higher than other applicants aroused suspicion.[130] The final version of the Harvard study of early admissions (published as *The Early Admissions Game*) confirmed these suspicions. Reporting results on early versus regular applicants in 1999–2000 at some of the nation's most selective universities, including Harvard, the study found that the sheer fact of applying early conferred a substantial advantage at all of them save MIT, where the benefit was modest.[131] But at Princeton the advantage — well over 100 points — was particularly large. For a hypothetical Princeton early decision applicant who was average in terms of activities and type of high school attended, the increase in admission rate conferred by applying early was the highest of any of the institutions studied: 68 vs. 10 percent. At Harvard and Yale, in contrast, the gap was much smaller: 29 vs. 11 percent at Harvard (early action) and 44 vs. 18 percent at Yale (early decision).[132]

Princeton's choice to fill almost half its class through early decision applicants may have been unfair to regular candidates, but it boosted Old Nassau's competitive position. By 2000, Princeton's yield rate had risen to 69 percent (three points higher than Yale's), and the number of students lost to Yale had dropped to 56.[133] Perhaps because it had benefited so greatly from its extensive use of early decision, Princeton was more deeply committed to the policy than its New Haven counterpart.

In December 2001, the different postures of Yale and Princeton became publicly visible when Yale's Richard Levin suggested that perhaps early decision "doesn't benefit students at all" and declared, "If we got rid of it, it would be a good thing."[134] The split between the two ancient rivals escalated in late 2002 when Yale announced that it was ending its early decision program and reverting to an early action program, which involved no binding commitments. Stanford — which had been considering such a move — announced within hours that it would do the same.[135] Since Harvard had never abandoned early action for early decision, Princeton was now the odd man out. But far from joining its closest competitors in a deescalation of the admissions race, Princeton's President Shirley Tilghman — the first woman to head a member of the Big Three — insisted that Yale's decision would have no bearing on Princeton's policy.[136] Old Nassau was not about to reverse a policy — even one that was in direct conflict with its professed commitment to equality of opportunity — that had improved its relative position.

A similarly hardball stance characterized Princeton's position on the delicate matter of using financial incentives in the competition for students. Beginning in 1958, the Ivy League colleges and MIT had met annually to share financial aid data to adjust offers to commonly admitted applicants so that financial considerations would play as small a role as possible in a student's choice. But in May 1991, the Justice Department formally charged what had come to be called the "Overlap Group" with a violation of antitrust laws prohibiting "collusion." In response, the Ivy League institutions signed a consent agreement that ended the case against them but compelled them to stop holding the annual "Overlap Group" meetings.[137]

At the time, many Ivy League colleges, including wealthy ones such as Yale, were struggling to maintain their policy of need-blind, full-aid admissions. But within a few years, the economic boom of the 1990s had sent their endowments soaring. All private universities benefited from this enormous accumulation of wealth, but none more than Princeton. In 1990, Princeton's endowment stood at a healthy $2.475 billion; by 2000, it had risen well over 300 percent, to $8.649 billion — an astonishing increase in a single decade. Yale, Harvard, and Stanford had also gained from this windfall, but Princeton was by far the richest of the three, given its much smaller size. The figures for endowment per student in 2000 offer a sense of Princeton's extraordinary wealth: $1.321 million, vs. $1.049 million at Harvard, $0.915 million at Yale, and $0.651 million at Stanford.[138]

Princeton did not hesitate to take advantage of its edge. Already a need-blind, full-aid institution, it announced in February 2001 that it would offer enhanced financial aid packages to make a Princeton education more "affordable."[139] The keystone of the new program was to eliminate all loans from financial aid packages — a symbolically powerful but relatively inexpensive way to make its offers more attractive. In fact, loans had constituted only 8 percent of Princeton's $10 million budget for freshman financial aid in 2000 — a minuscule sum for an institution that could collect well over $300 million annually on its endowment at an interest rate of just 4 percent. Students' families — half of whom received no scholarship assistance whatsoever — still paid the great bulk of the total expenses for room, board, and tuition: 71 percent in 2001. This was down from 77 percent in 1997 (the last year before Princeton began to improve its financial aid offers), but it was not nearly as dramatic a change as the public fanfare that accompanied Princeton's announcement suggested.[140]

Though modest, these improvements that Princeton introduced into its aid packages in 2001 achieved the desired impact. Princeton's yield rate, which had been hovering around 68 percent for several years, rose to 71 percent in 2001 and to 74 percent in 2002.[141] This was the highest yield that Old Nassau had seen in more than fifty years, and it placed just behind Harvard at

79 percent in 2002. At the same time, the number of admits choosing to enroll at Princeton's closest competitors dropped to the lowest levels in memory. In 2002, Princeton lost only 142 admits to Harvard, 51 to Stanford, and just 39 to Yale — a combined decline of more than 40 percent from 1995, the last year before the adoption of early decision.[142] The most visible symbol of the success of the new policy was that Princeton vaulted in 2001 to the number one position in the *U.S. News* annual rankings and remained there in 2002 and 2003.[143]

To be sure, the top *U.S. News* ranking did not mean that Princeton had passed Harvard in the competition for the nation's top students. But it did mean that it had narrowed the gap with Harvard and that it had in some ways pulled ahead of Yale, if not Stanford.[144] Yet it had done so in good part by deploying its tremendous financial resources, in the process violating a well-established norm among elite private universities that "buying" students constituted a serious impropriety. Nevertheless, Princeton was in no mood to abandon the very policies that had advanced its relative standing.

In response, Yale and Stanford — both of them well endowed but neither quite as wealthy as Princeton — tried to reassert the traditional norm.[145] In a statement signed by 26 other leading private colleges and universities, Yale and Stanford reaffirmed their commitment to need-blind admissions and to ensuring that low-income students could attend their institutions. They also explicitly denounced the growing trend toward merit-based rather than need-based aid and the related trend of using financial means to compete for the most desirable students. The signatories read like a *Who's Who* of the nation's most prestigious institutions of higher education, including not only Yale and Stanford but also Columbia, Cornell, Penn, Swarthmore, Rice, Northwestern, Williams, Chicago, and Amherst. Conspicuously absent, however, were the nation's two wealthiest universities, Princeton and Harvard.[146] Able to make offers that their competitors could not match, they were not going to be bound by musty notions of gentlemanly behavior. Had Yale and Stanford possessed the same resources, there is little reason to believe that they would not have done the same.

By century's end, an intense preoccupation with competitive position had become, more than ever, a driving force in admissions policy at all four institutions. But at Princeton, the issue had become a genuine obsession. So it was perhaps not entirely coincidental that, in April 2002, an associate dean of admissions at Old Nassau was caught breaking into Yale's confidential on-line admission system. Claiming that he had entered the site only to assess the security of such systems, his real purpose seems to have been to snoop on several Yale applicants who had also applied to Princeton — one of whom was a Houston high school senior named Lauren Bush, a niece of President Bush.

In its account of the incident, the *Wall Street Journal* noted that "Yale and Princeton in particular have been intensely competitive in recent years, lobbing financial-aid changes back and forth in a contest in which Princeton is widely considered to be more aggressive, even as it has become more generous."[147] Not long before a magnet for the languid gentlemen so brilliantly portrayed by F. Scott Fitzgerald, even Princeton had now become an institution on the make.

CHAPTER 18

The Battle over Merit

H AD FRANKLIN DELANO ROOSEVELT returned to Harvard in the fall of 2000, precisely a hundred years after he had patiently waited in line in front of Sever Hall to register as a freshman, he would have been shocked. As he looked around, he would have seen immediately that nonwhites (half of them Asian Americans) made up over a third of the freshman class. Even more striking would have been the presence of women, now walking confidently through the Yard, where they constituted nearly half of the students.[1]

Less noticeable, perhaps, would have been the extraordinary growth in the number of Jews, whose proportion of the freshman class had tripled from 7 percent in his time to over 20 percent a century later.[2] But what Roosevelt would have grasped above all was that Harvard was no longer the private property of his social group: white, Anglo-Saxon, Protestant men, largely from the upper classes of New England and the mid-Atlantic states. Once the unquestioned rulers not only of Harvard (where they made up approximately 85 percent of students when FDR was an undergraduate) but of virtually all the major institutions of American life, WASP men were now a small and beleaguered minority at Harvard — no more than 20 percent of freshmen.[3]

The transformation of Harvard, Yale, and Princeton from enclaves of the Protestant upper class into institutions with a striking degree of racial, ethnic, and religious diversity was by any standard historic. Yet beneath this dramatic and highly visible change in the physiognomy of the student body was a surprising degree of stability in one crucial regard — the privileged class origins of students at the Big Three. By 2000, the cost of a year at Harvard, Yale, and Princeton had reached the staggering sum of more than $35,000 — an amount that well under 10 percent of American families could afford. (In 2004, annual expenses had risen to well over $40,000 per year.) Yet at all three institutions, a majority of students were able to pay their expenses without financial assistance — compelling testimony that, more than thirty years after the introduction of need-blind admissions, the Big Three continued to draw most of their students from the most affluent segments of American society.[4]

While "paying customers" still constituted the majority of students in 2000, students from modest backgrounds continued to be vastly underrepresented not only at the Big Three but at highly selective colleges nationwide.[5] At Princeton, which offered the most generous financial aid packages in the Ivy League, students from families in the bottom 50 percent of the income distribution (that is, below the 1997 median income of $40,000, with annual adjustments for inflation) made up just 10 percent of the freshman class; at Harvard, the number was a bit higher, at roughly 12 percent, but the majority of scholarship recipients had family incomes of over $70,000 per year, with nearly a quarter of them reporting incomes in excess of $100,000.[6] At Yale, though no statistics are available on the income distribution of the freshman class, the paucity of students from families with limited education suggests a similar pattern; in 2001, just 8 percent of Yale freshmen came from homes where neither parent had attended college.[7]

Despite their consistent emphasis on "diversity," highlighted recently in an amicus brief submitted to the Supreme Court in the Michigan case on affirmative action, the Big Three are notoriously lacking one of its most critical dimensions: class diversity.[8] In a study of the proportion of low-income students (as measured by the proportion of federal Pell Grants) at the nation's leading universities in the *U.S. News and World Report* rankings, the Big Three were found to be among the nation's least economically diverse schools. Of the 40 universities studied, Harvard and Princeton ranked 39th and 38th respectively, with Yale at 25th. While the three top universities in economic diversity were all public institutions (UCLA, UC Berkeley, and UC San Diego), the next two — the University of Southern California and New York University — were private. And one university in the top ten, California Institute of Technology, is among the most selective private institutions in the nation.[9]

The Big Three and other highly selective private colleges have not been unaware of the paucity of students from poor and working-class backgrounds at their institutions. In their landmark study, *The Shape of the River,* William Bowen and Derek Bok report that only 1 percent of white students at the most selective institutions come from low socioeconomic backgrounds.[10] While troubled about this finding, the authors — former presidents of Princeton and Harvard — make it clear that they believe there is little that can be done. Committed to maintaining "high academic qualifications" as measured by grades and test scores, they conclude that "the problem is not that poor but qualified candidates go undiscovered, but that there are simply very few of these candidates in the first place." Selective institutions, they write, "continue to contribute to social mobility, but they do so primarily by giving excellent educational opportunities to students from middle-class backgrounds." Though a number of scholars have proposed class-based affirmative action, Bowen and Bok reject such an approach, arguing that it would be "harmful to academic standards" and "probably prohibitively expensive."[11]

In accepting as inevitable the strikingly small number of students from low socioeconomic backgrounds at the nation's leading universities, Bowen and Bok express an attitude of resignation common among the gatekeepers of the elite private colleges. But such resignation is unwarranted, for there is in fact a significant pool of students from disadvantaged backgrounds with "high academic qualifications," at least as measured by the SAT. In 2004, the number of students with family incomes under $30,000 who scored 650 or higher on the math and verbal sections was 12,755 and 6,995, respectively; for students from homes where neither parent had more than a high school degree, the parallel figures were 22,477 and 14,812. In a nation in which more than 1.4 million students took the SAT in 2004, this is a modest pool. For purposes of comparison, however, it is worth noting that it is far larger than the comparable pool of African Americans with scores over 650: 2,962 (math) and 3,039 (verbal) in 2004.[12]

Yet despite the smaller pool of high-scoring black students, elite college administrators have shown no such resignation with respect to race, having noted with alarm that a race-neutral policy would reduce black enrollment at elite private colleges to perhaps 2 percent or less.[13] Indeed, it was the prospect of such a reduction that led to a massive mobilization on the part of the nation's most prestigious universities to preserve race-based affirmative action in the face of serious legal and political challenges.[14] The point here is not that class-based affirmative action should replace race-based affirmative action; it is rather that the radical underrepresentation of students from modest socioeconomic backgrounds at the nation's elite colleges is a serious problem demanding immediate attention. Bowen himself has recently recognized this, reversing his position and issuing a compelling call for the adoption of class-based affirmative action — a "thumb on the scale" for applicants from lower socioeconomic categories, to be put in place alongside (and not as a substitute for) the race-attentive policies that have long existed at the selective colleges.[15] Harvard's president, Lawrence Summers, has issued a similar appeal for preferences for the socioeconomically disadvantaged, noting in a major speech before the American Council on Education that "in the most selective colleges and universities, only 3 percent of students come from the bottom income quartile and only 10 percent from the bottom half of the income scale."[16]

Viewed from the perspective of a key argument of this book — that admissions policy tends to reflect power relations among major social groups — the heavy emphasis on race in the admissions decisions of the elite colleges and the relative lack of attention historically accorded class is hardly surprising. While there has been little political mobilization in recent decades on the issue of class inequality, the issue of racial injustice spawned the nation's greatest political mobilization of the twentieth century — the civil rights movement. With the foundations of the social order seemingly at risk of crumbling in the late 1960s, important concessions were extracted by racial minorities and then institutionalized. The imprint of that pivotal period is with us still, inscribed in the definition of merit we now take for granted. That no parallel redefinition of merit occurred with respect to social class — an equally powerful source of inequality of opportunity — reflects the fact that subordinate social classes in the United States today lack the political power attained by racial and ethnic minorities after years of arduous struggle.[17]

The new and more academic definition of "merit" that emerged at the Big Three in the decades after World War II did not raise the number of poor and working-class students in the freshman class. On the contrary, the increasingly rigorous academic requirements for admission — among them, the rising scores on the SAT, generally considered a clear sign of rising "meritocracy" — may well have been associated with a decline in opportunities for students from modest backgrounds. At Harvard, in the eleven years between 1952 and 1963 — a period when average combined SATs rose from 1181 to 1401 — the proportion of freshmen whose fathers had not attended college plummeted from 38 to 16 percent.[18] Though part of this decline could surely be attributed to rising rates of college attendance during the interwar period (when most of the fathers of students entering Harvard between 1952 and 1963 would have attended college), the magnitude of the drop was far too large for it to have been the primary explanation for such a dramatic change.[19]

If the growing emphasis on high grades and high test scores in the early decades of the Cold War further reduced the already meager chances of students of low socioeconomic status to enter the Big Three, it did promote a certain degree of social mobility. But the main beneficiaries were the children of families that, while lacking the wealth of the old upper class, were richly endowed with cultural capital. In 1956, the sons of business executives (22 percent of all freshmen) outnumbered the sons of professors (5 percent) by a ratio of more than 4 to 1; in 1976, the sons of professors — who constituted perhaps one-half of one percent of the American labor force — made up more than 12 percent of Harvard freshmen, compared to 14 percent for the sons of business executives.[20] At Princeton, a similar shift was visible; whereas in 1954 the sons of businessmen outnumbered those of elite professionals by a ratio of 2.5 to 1 (50 to 20 percent), by 1976 the gap had narrowed to 1.4 to 1 (32 to 23 percent).[21]

Under the more academically demanding admissions regime that prevailed by the 1960s, the scholastically brilliant children of the middle and upper middle class enjoyed greater opportunities than ever before to enter Harvard, Yale, and Princeton. At the same time, the less academically talented children of the old elite were finding it increasingly difficult to gain access to colleges where admissions had until recently been taken for granted. This shift toward what the sociologist Alvin Gouldner has called the "new class" was part of a genuine redistribution of opportunity in which cultural capital, especially in the years after *Sputnik*, increasingly displaced sheer economic capital as the principal pathway to the Big Three.[22] To be sure, children of wealth and social standing remained vastly overrepresented. But unless they could demonstrate a high level of academic accomplishment, even the children of the old upper class faced the prospect of rejection. The specter of downward mobility now extended to the most privileged sectors of the old elite — a development that would enduringly transform the atmosphere of the Big Three.

Equality of Opportunity and the Preservation of the American Social Order

Throughout the twentieth century, the men who presided over the Big Three were acutely aware that the legitimacy of the American social order — and of the position of the elite private colleges within it — was vulnerable to challenge from below. To be sure, the American system of free enterprise has for long periods of the nation's history seemed impregnable. But there were also periods of profound upheaval when the existing order seemed precarious — most notably during the Progressive Era, the Great Depression, and the 1960s. It is during just such periods that liberal reformers dedicated to changing the system in order to preserve it tend to rise to prominence. At the Big Three, the men who embodied this strand of liberal reformism were Charles W. Eliot, James Bryant Conant, and Kingman Brewster.

Though quite different in temperament and personality, Eliot, Conant, and Brewster shared a bedrock belief in private property and the American economic system. That this system produced vast material and social inequalities did not particularly trouble them; as Eliot observed in his essay "The Function of Education in a Democratic Society": "The children of a democratic society should . . . be taught at school, with the utmost explicitness and vivid illustrations, that inequalities of condition are a necessary result of freedom."[23] More than four decades later, Conant expressed a similar perspective when he called for "frank recognition of the profit motive" and said that he was "quite willing to have incomes soar to the skies."[24]

For Eliot, Conant, and Brewster, the primary threat to the legitimacy of the existing order came not from large-scale inequalities of condition, which they believed to be an inevitable and just byproduct of the American system of free enterprise, but from inequalities of opportunity. While accepting the tremendous inequalities in reward characteristic of the distinctive American version of capitalism, they saw the ideology of equal opportunity as a bulwark against radical movements calling for the redistribution of wealth and, in some cases, the elimination of the free enterprise system itself. "Continuous perpetuation from generation to generation of even small differences," Conant wrote in the thirties, "soon produces class consciousness."[25] With faith in the American dream of upward mobility diminishing, the nation was in danger of descending into a clash between the propertied few and the propertyless many. The outcome of such a clash, Conant feared, would be the end of private enterprise.[26]

Brewster likewise concluded that only a vibrant belief in the age-old American proposition that everyone, no matter how humble the circumstances of his or her birth, had a chance to rise to the top could legitimate the increasingly visible gap between rich and poor in the United States. Yet, as in the 1930s, the American dream of upward mobility was under vigorous assault as a myth deflecting attention from an unjust system, and by the late 1960s the established order seemed to be tottering. For Brewster, as for Conant, the solution was to infuse the ideology of equal opportunity with new vigor. A failure to do so, Brewster warned, could threaten "the survival of our way of life."[27]

In the view of liberal reformers like Brewster, Conant, and Eliot, the nation's leading universities have a special responsibility to make real the American dream of upward mobility through education, for they provide a crucial pathway into the elite for talented boys from families of limited means. Writing at a time when bloody urban race riots had shaken the foundations of American society and raised the specter of a collapsing social order, Brewster was explicit in making the connection between a belief in the promise of equal opportunity and the survival of the system. As one of only a handful of institutions offering a highly visible route to the most elite sectors of American life, Yale and similar universities needed to follow an admissions policy that appeared fair and open. Especially in "a politically free, private property, contractually organized economic system," wrote Brewster in a passage quoted earlier, "it is terribly important to keep alive the widespread confidence that success in America is a function of merit and effort."[28] Anything less, he firmly believed, would bring into question the legitimacy of the system itself.

The reformist impulse at the Big Three was thus also a preservationist impulse, dedicated to making the changes that would permit the free enterprise system to survive. Devout believers in equal opportunity as a matter of both principle and prudence, the liberal reformers worked to make their institutions more open to talented young men, whatever their social origins. Out of their cumulative efforts came many reforms — among them, Harvard's National Scholarships, the rise of need-blind admissions, and the search for talented students in the nation's ghettos and rural areas — that gave renewed force to the old ideology of equal opportunity. How effective such measures were in reinforcing the traditional American belief in upward mobility through education is difficult to say; they were, after all, no more than a small piece of a vast system of higher education whose very structure — with its immense system of open-access community colleges, its lack of sharp boundaries between different kinds of institutions, and its provision of second and third chances to succeed — at once embodies and reinforces the national ideology of equal opportunity.[29] Yet it is worth noting the observations of Paul Sweezy, a member of the old elite (Exeter '27, Harvard '31, Harvard Ph.D. '37) who became a Marxist in the 1930s. In a sharp critique of C. Wright Mills's *Power Elite,* Sweezy castigated the renowned radical for his complete failure "to understand the role of the preparatory schools and colleges as recruiters for the ruling class, sucking upwards the ablest elements of the lower classes and thus performing the double function of infusing new brains into the ruling class and weakening the potential leadership of the working class."[30]

Sweezy's comments express the classical Marxist viewpoint, but one hardly needs to be a Marxist to acknowledge the crucial importance of upward mobility through education in legitimating the American social order. Indeed, in its 2003 decision in the landmark affirmative action case, *Grutter v. Bollinger,* no less an institution than the U.S. Supreme Court explicitly recognized that the legitimacy of the larger social order was at issue in the admissions decisions of its leading universities. In a 5–4 decision upholding the admissions policy of the University of Michigan Law School, with the majority opinion written by Justice Sandra Day O'Connor (B.A. Stanford '50, LL.B. Stanford '52), the Court declared: "In order to cultivate a set of leaders with legitimacy in the eyes of the citizenry, it is necessary that the path to leadership be visibly open to talented and qualified individuals of every race and ethnicity. All members of our heterogeneous society must have confidence in the openness and integrity of the educational institutions that provide this training . . . Access to legal education (and thus the legal profession) must be inclusive of talented and qualified individuals of every race and ethnicity, so that all members of our heterogeneous society may participate in the educational institutions that provide the training and education necessary to succeed in America."[31] Though Conant and Brewster were long deceased, the decision ringingly affirmed the argument that they had made decades earlier: the legitimacy of the American social order depended in good part on the public's confidence that the pathways to success provided by the nation's leading universities were open to individuals from all walks of life.

Like the *Bakke* decision a quarter of a century earlier, the *Grutter* decision was a tremendous victory for the elite universities. For it affirmed not only the legality of the race-based affirmative action programs that had become central to the identity and mission of the nation's leading universities, but also the deference that the Court had granted to the tradition of institutional autonomy on which the admissions policies of institutions like Harvard, Yale, and Princeton ultimately rested. Declaring that "our holding today is in keeping with our tradition of giving a degree of deference to a university's academic decisions," the Court emphasized that "universities occupy a special niche in our constitutional tradition" and registered its preference for leaving the "complex educational judgments" involved in admissions decisions to the "expertise of the university." These were, of course, precisely the arguments made in favor of university autonomy by Harvard's Archibald Cox in *Bakke,* and their affirmation twenty-five years later in a decision that specifically invoked Justice Powell's opinion "recognizing a constitutional dimension, grounded in the First Amendment, of educational autonomy" was a spectacular triumph.[32]

Especially gratifying to the Big Three — and to Harvard, in particular — was the Court's decision to cite the very same "Harvard plan" that Justice Powell had cited as a model of "the flexible use of race as a plus factor." By holding up Harvard's undergraduate admissions policy (which had changed little in the intervening twenty-five years) as exemplary, the Supreme Court was in effect putting its seal of approval not only on the use of race as a factor in selection decisions, but on a policy that used many criteria — including highly subjective ones — in determining whom to admit and reject. Combined with its ringing defense of university autonomy, the Court's approval of the "Harvard plan" left little doubt that the admissions officers of the elite colleges would continue under *Grutter* to possess both the discretion and the opacity to pursue institutional interests as they saw fit.

But the Harvard plan cited by Justice Powell and Justice O'Connor also had a more specific meaning, for it constituted a decisive repudiation of the academically based policy favored by Charles W. Eliot, Harvard's greatest president. Noting that "the Committee on Admissions could use the single criterion of scholarly excellence and attempt to determine who among the candidates were likely to perform best academically," Harvard explicitly rejected this approach, insisting that under such a policy "the quality of the educational experience offered to all students would suffer."[33] Now, the Supreme Court, in its ruling in the Michigan case, was formally sanctifying Harvard's approach because of its emphasis on "individualized consideration." Also upheld as a model was the admissions policy of the University of Michigan Law School, whose selection process was described as a "highly individualized, holistic review of each applicant's file, giving serious consideration to all the ways an applicant might contribute to a diverse educational environment."[34] Not coincidentally, this was precisely how most of the nation's elite private institutions officially described their admissions policies.

Power, Merit, and the Politics of Admissions

Though nothing in the Supreme Court's recounting of the admissions policies of Harvard and the University of Michigan Law School was inaccurate, it constituted a partial, quite sanitized description of the selection process at elite universities. To be sure, such institutions do conduct "holistic" reviews of applicants, and they are genuinely committed to "diversity" (though racial diversity is far more important to them than class diversity). But the actual selection process at elite institutions is far more political than such accounts would suggest, and the admissions pie tends to be divided into slices whose size is closely connected to the power of major constituencies. As various accounts of the admissions process make clear, students who have a "hook" — most notably, legacy status, athletic talent, or membership in a historically underrepresented group — have a sizable advantage over those who do not.[35] At Princeton, members of these three groups are referred to as "tagged categories" and fill roughly 40 percent of the places in the freshman class. In practice, this means that the vast majority of candidates who are not legacies, athletes, or members of targeted minority groups compete for the remaining 60 percent of places in what an internal study group acknowledged is a balkanized and "tightly constrained admissions process."[36]

In truth, key constituencies — coaches, counselors at feeder schools, the development office, influential alumni, the faculty, and organized minority groups — shape both the criteria used in the selection process and the decisions on individual applicants.[37] In this regard, it is worth comparing the antiseptic discussion of "diversity" and "holistic" review in the *Grutter* opinion with the forthright description of admissions offered by John T. Osander, former director of admission at Princeton:

> ... the pressures on the admission office from various special interest groups continue somewhat uniformly: faculty, alumni, coaches, parents, school prin-

cipals or headmasters, may lobby from different points of view, but all do so against each other in competition for a set number of places. There has not been a year in which the admission office has suddenly ignored any one of these special interests. In fact, the weaving pattern from year to year suggests that even a slight dip one year brings a kind of pressure that pushes up that measurable item the next year at the probable expense of some other variable. In other words, the patterns suggest that what is referred to as admission "policy" is actually a slowly evolving set of practices that more or less seem to balance, or at least satisfy, a variety of pressures.

Noting that this "rather conservative process corresponds to the observed practice of measuring — during the decision period — a whole variety of factors against the results of the previous year," Osander acknowledged that "an entirely new and inexperienced staff could very well pick from the applicant group a student body with quite different individual and group characteristics." But such a change was unlikely to occur, he observed, for "it could not be done . . . without seriously upsetting the wide series of relationships that have been built up and maintained through the years with that variety of involved publics who are so very much responsible for generating the interest of applicants in Princeton."[38]

Because of the Big Three's dependency on powerful external constituencies, the tilt of their admissions policy has historically been toward the privileged. For it is the children of the established elite who are most likely not only to be the big donors of the future but also to supply the prominent alumni whose very success reinforces the prestige of the elite colleges. Yet Harvard, Yale, and Princeton have also been well aware that it is possible to overinvest in traditional elites, especially when they show signs of decline. The solution was to diversify the institutional portfolio to strengthen its connections to rising social groups — a strategy followed most dramatically by Yale in the late 1960s when, in the context of the emergence of postindustrial society and the increasing prominence of science and technology, it shifted its policy toward the brilliant children of the "new class" of credentialed professionals while eliminating the last vestiges of anti-Semitism.

Yet at certain historical moments — especially in periods of social crisis, when the legitimacy of the system itself is in question — the elite colleges will reach out beyond the privileged to the disenfranchised.[39] They do so not because the visible presence of previously excluded groups adds to the diversity of their students' educational experience, but because it reinforces a belief — crucial to the preservation of the social order — that success in America is a function of individual merit rather than family background. Both the origins and the institutionalization of race-based affirmative action may be traced to a recognition by the elite colleges that the continued exclusion of a highly visible and restive segment of the population would undermine the legitimacy of the nation's major social institutions.[40]

These three tasks — the recruitment of the children of the traditional elite, the incorporation of talented members of rising social groups, and the inclusion of a sufficient number of the children of the disenfranchised to maintain the system's legitimacy — have framed the admissions policy of the Big Three. But in recent decades, as inequality has grown and insurgent movements have receded, the pressure to further incorporate the disadvantaged has waned at the same time that the efforts of the privileged to maintain their privileges have intensified. So great has been the pressure on elites that in large cities like New York, Boston, and Washington, the competition to get into the preschool that will supposedly put Junior on the track to Harvard has become fierce. An ever more ferocious competition for admission into the "right" kindergarten follows, complete with test scores, letters of recommendation, and interviews. In recent years, the frenzy has become so great that parents have begun to hire private counselors, at fees of $500 to $4,000, to guide them through the kindergarten admissions process and to prepare their four-year-olds for interviews and aptitude tests.[41]

The rush for the best preschools and kindergartens is just the beginning of a long process in which privileged but anxious parents try to maximize their children's chances of gaining admission to Harvard, Yale, Princeton, and other prestigious colleges.[42] Apart from the perennial battle to gain entry into the most prestigious elementary and secondary schools, there is the question of the child's nonacademic development, for one-sidedly intellectual students, however brilliant, are generally viewed unfavorably by the leading colleges. So the quest to develop skills — athletic, musical, or artistic — that will later serve as "hooks" to attract the attention of elite college gatekeepers begins at ever-earlier ages, with expensive private lessons and summer camps viewed by many parents as indispensable. By secondary school, aspirants to the Big Three and similar colleges are busy filling their résumés with extracurricular activities that demonstrate "leadership," "character," and commitment to "service." Not to be ignored are the SATs, for weak scores can ruin the chances of otherwise promising candidates; hence the growth of a vast industry of coaching firms like Stanley Kaplan and Princeton Review and the rise of SAT tutors for the affluent.[43] Finally, there is the culmination of this entire process — the act of selecting which colleges to apply to and determining how to maximize the candidate's chances of gaining admission. Increasing numbers of students — including many at some of the nation's leading private schools — have decided that the stakes are so high and the decisions of gatekeepers so mysterious that it is imperative to obtain the assistance of high-priced college consultants, the most sought after of whom charge fees that approach $30,000 per candidate. So great is the pressure on college applicants that Harvard Dean of Admissions William Fitzsimmons and two colleagues recently released a paper on "burnout" expressing concern that too many students "seemed like dazed survivors of some bewildering lifelong boot camp."[44] For college placement counselors, too, the pressures to get students into the Big Three and other elite universities can at times prove too much. In 1996, the college counseling office at the Middlesex School discovered that a former college placement counselor and faculty member (himself a graduate of Middlesex and Harvard), who was then on sabbatical teaching at Harvard, had falsified figures in the catalogue, exaggerating the numbers of students who had enrolled at the Ivy League universities, Stanford, and other prestigious colleges. When he returned to Middlesex in the fall of 1997, the headmaster confronted him about the matter. He confessed and requested a leave of absence. But a friend reported that he "fell apart" after the meeting. A week later he undressed, waded into the ocean, and drowned himself. His suicide note apologized and read in part: "Please use part of my funds to compensate the school for their financial expenses related to my actions . . . I cannot compensate for all the other damage I have caused."[45]

The underlying source of the enormous stress surrounding college admissions is that even the privileged classes are no longer confident that they can pass their position on to the next generation. True, the children of families with high levels of cultural and economic capital enjoy a tremendous advantage in the competition for admission to the elite colleges, and they continue to occupy the vast majority of places in the freshman classes at institutions like Harvard, Yale, and Princeton. But under the current system, they, too, have to compete, and the majority of them are destined to fail in their quest for admission to the Big Three. Even those families that manage to get their children into the preparatory schools with the closest historic ties to the Big Three are unlikely to succeed; Groton, Exeter, and St. Paul's, which as recently as 1954 sent roughly two-thirds of their graduates to Harvard, Yale, or Princeton, saw the proportion of their graduates there drop by 2000 to 22, 14, and 10 percent, respectively.[46] As a consequence, deep apprehension about college admissions now extends to the highest reaches of the upper class. At the same time, the children of the working class and the poor are about as unlikely to attend the Big Three today as they were in 1954.[47] It is no exaggeration to say that the current regime in elite college admissions has been far more successful in democratizing anxiety than opportunity.

To acknowledge that today's system of admissions has not broadened opportunity for socioeconomically disadvantaged students is not to deny that it is far more meritocratic than the system in place in 1950. Nor is it to suggest that the shift in admissions toward individual achievement and away from family background was inconsequential. On the contrary, the shift to a more meritocratic system of selection at the nation's leading colleges has had enormous consequences both for the distribution of opportunity and for the public's perception of the fairness of the process by which rewards are distributed in America. One needs only think of what would have happened had the Big Three and other leading colleges *not* changed — had they remained de facto white institutions closed to women and rife with anti-Semitism — to grasp the magnitude of the transformation that has occurred since World War II.

Compared to the ancien régime in admissions, still largely in place in 1950, the system that had emerged by the mid-1970s was in many ways an embodiment of meritocratic ideals. In a context profoundly shaped by the competitive pressures of the Cold War, one barrier to talent after another fell — first the favoritism toward applicants from private schools, then discrimination against Jews, and then the multitude of obstacles to African Americans and other minorities. By the end of the 1960s, Harvard, Yale, and Princeton had taken a series of dramatic steps — introducing need-blind admissions, creating race-based affirmative action, and (at Yale and Princeton) eliminating age-old barriers to the enrollment of women — to open their gates to students who did not conform to the old profile of the upper-class, prep-school-educated WASP young man who had for so long set the tone of campus life.

With the advent of sex-blind admissions in the mid-1970s, the character of the Big Three had been irrevocably altered. In the last quarter of the century, the incorporation of new groups of talented students continued, first with the rapidly rising enrollments of Asian Americans and then, at the century's end, with the extension at Harvard and Yale of the core meritocratic principle of need-blind admissions to applicants from not only the United States but the entire world.[48] Meanwhile, the more meritocratic standards of the new regime in admissions had by every measure elevated the intellectual level of the student body at the same time that they had virtually eliminated the once numerous group that Charles W. Eliot had indelicately referred to as the "stupid sons of the rich."[49]

Yet the current admissions system, though a decided improvement over the system that preceded it, is not a meritocracy. Most eloquently articulated in the American context by James Bryant Conant, the meritocratic ideal requires that "each generation may start life afresh and that hard work and ability . . . find their just rewards." Drawing on Jefferson's famous appeal to "cull from every condition of our people the natural aristocracy of talent and virtue" (which Jefferson believed "nature has sown as liberally among the poor as the rich"), Conant wrote that the "American ideal" demands a "continuous process by which power and privilege may be automatically redistributed at the end of each generation."[50] To Conant, as to other meritocrats, widespread social mobility through education was essential to the American dream, and the nation's leading colleges had a solemn obligation to admit students on the basis of individual talent and accomplishment, not family privilege.

By this standard, the current practices of Harvard, Yale, and Princeton fall well short of the meritocratic ideal. Most obviously, there is the matter of preference for alumni children — a peculiar practice more suited to a feudal aristocracy than a society that prides itself on its commitment to equality of opportunity. Then there is the institutionalized tilt toward applicants connected to powerful constituencies — whether feeder schools, the development office, or the athletic department. But the deeper problem is inherent in the meritocratic project itself — the very definition of "merit" systematically favors the privileged over the disadvantaged. Though in principle open to everyone, the elite colleges are in truth a realistic possibility only for those young men and women whose families endow them with the type of cultural capital implicitly required for admission.

The modest number of poor and working-class students at the Big Three is not an intended consequence of the prevailing definition of merit any more than is the vast overrepresentation of the children of privilege. It is a product of a powerful, if hidden, social process common to all societies — that the qualities that come to define "merit" tend to be attributes most abundantly possessed by dominant social groups. This is not to say that the privileged will always be able to transmit their privileges to their offspring under the existing system; on the contrary, one of the defining features of a school-mediated system of class reproduction (as opposed to a system based primarily on the direct transfer of property) is that, as Pierre Bourdieu has noted, it can reproduce the privileges of the class system as a whole only "by sacrificing certain members of the [dominant] class."[51] Under this system, a limited amount of social mobility, both upward and downward, is not only possible but necessary.

But the existing system of ostensibly meritocratic selection does not, pace Jefferson and Conant, find that "nature" has sown talent "as liberally among the poor as the rich." Instead, it finds that "merit" is heavily concentrated among the scions of the privileged. Yet the apparent openness of the system — the availability of scholarships, the widely publicized efforts to recruit among the "disadvantaged," and the highly visible racial and ethnic diversity of the student body — gives credence to the American dream of upward mobility through education. Transforming hereditary privilege into "merit," the existing system of educational selection, with the Big Three as its capstone, provides the appearance if not the substance of equality of opportunity.[52] In so doing, it legitimates the established order as one that rewards ability and hard work over the prerogatives of birth.

The problem with a "meritocracy," then, is not only that its ideals are routinely violated (though that is true), but also that it veils the power relations beneath it. For the definition of "merit," including the one that now prevails at America's leading universities, always bears the imprint of the distribution of power in the larger society. Those who are able to define "merit" will almost invariably possess more of it, and those with greater resources — cultural, economic, and social — will generally be able to ensure that the educational system will deem their children more meritorious. In this specific sense, the ideal of a meritocracy — a system in which power plays no role in defining "merit" and in which rich and poor alike enjoy genuinely equal opportunities to succeed — is inherently unattainable.

Inclusion and the End of Privilege

If the ideal of a pure meritocracy is destined never to be realized, it does not follow that attempts to render the system more meritocratic are doomed to failure. Just as the admissions regime that emerged in the decades after World War II was more meritocratic than the one that preceded it, so, too, is it possible that the system of the future could more closely approximate the meritocratic ideal. Indeed, the strange system of elite college admissions that we have inherited from the past may prove surprisingly vulnerable to public scrutiny and debate. Many of the features we have long taken for granted were created at particular historical moments; the time has come to eliminate or modify several of them. It is with the goal of stimulating further scrutiny and debate that I offer several possible avenues of reform.

LEGACIES

Despite the colleges' insistence that preference for alumni children comes into play only as a tiebreaker among equally qualified candidates, favoritism for legacies is alive and well at the Big Three. This preference reached a historic low during the Clark-Brewster years at Yale, but the ensuing alumni revolt led to a restoration of the traditional policies in the mid-1970s. Though a majority of legacies are now rejected, they still receive substantial preference. A report from a 1998 Princeton study, which found that legacies were offered admission at a rate more than three times higher than other applicants, concludes, "*While the percentage of legacies in the entering class has gone down over the past decade, the relative admissions advantage for legacy applicants has actually increased.*"[53] More recent data from Harvard suggest a similar pattern; in 2002, 40 percent of legacies were admitted, compared to 11 percent of the other applicants.[54]

This policy has come under attack in recent years as a kind of affirmative action for the privileged.[55] Given that most legacies are affluent and white, this charge is not without foundation. But the main problem is that legacy preference flagrantly violates the core American principle of equality of opportunity, which requires that rewards be based on individual accomplishment.[56]

Historically, one of the main arguments for favoring legacies was that private institutions depended heavily on the largesse of their alumni; however, with the endowments of Harvard, Yale, and Princeton in 2004 at $22.6, $12.7, and $9.6 billion, respectively, this argument — which was never one of high principle — has become much less persuasive.[57] The time has come to consider whether legacy preference has any place in universities publicly committed to equality of opportunity. As a first step, the passage of legislation — such as the bill drafted by Senator Edward Kennedy (himself a legacy, Harvard '56) — that would require universities "to publish data on the racial and socioeconomic composition of legatees" would seem warranted.[58] So, too, would a requirement that universities disclose the admission rates of legacies and nonlegacies to cast a spotlight on a policy that Senator James Edwards has rightly characterized as "a birthright out of 18th-century British aristocracy, not 21st-century American democracy."[59]

EARLY ADMISSIONS

Early decision and early action programs, used by virtually all of the highly selective private colleges, also pose a threat to equality of opportunity, although less overtly than legacy preference. The problem with these programs is twofold: students who use them enjoy an advantage in the admissions process, and students admitted on early decision (though not early action) are obliged to attend the accepting institution and hence cannot compare financial aid offers.[60] Both patterns further advantage the already advantaged. It is generally affluent and well-informed students who benefit from the boost given to early applicants; moreover, the inability to compare financial aid packages precludes many students who need scholarship assistance from applying early. Students from less affluent families — who often attend schools where both information and counseling are in short supply — thus face a playing field slanted even more against them as a result of early admission.

Scrutiny of these programs has increased sharply over the past few years as journalistic investigations and scholarly studies have exposed many of their inherent problems.[61] As noted earlier, Yale's Richard Levin took an important step in December 2001 by publicly acknowledging the discriminatory character of early decision programs.[62] Eleven months later, he announced that Yale would eliminate its program, effective the following year.[63]

Yet Yale did no more than replace its early decision program with an early action program and announced, moreover, that it would not permit candidates for early action to apply to other early admissions programs. While Harvard announced a policy similar to Yale's (as did Stanford), Princeton retained its old policy of early decision. Though Harvard's dean of admissions stated that he would be pleased to see early admissions eliminated altogether (a viewpoint also held by Yale's Levin), no leading private institution has been willing to move first. This is, of course, a collective action problem (what game theorists call "a prisoner's dilemma"), for an institution that moved alone would be at a competitive disadvantage.[64] Nevertheless, from the viewpoint of equality of opportunity, there is no substitute for eliminating early admission programs and replacing them with a standard notification date for all applicants. In the absence of such action, sunshine legislation calling for greater transparency would be appropriate. Just as Congress requires colleges to release graduation rates by race, so it could require that institutions with early admission programs publicly disclose the racial and socioeconomic backgrounds of the students so admitted, the acceptance rate for early and regular candidates, and the proportion of places in the freshman class filled by early applicants.

ATHLETES

Viewed from a distance, one of the strangest features of admissions at the Big Three is the heavy preference for talented athletes. They are, after all, among the leading research universities in the entire world, and the ability to throw, catch, kick, hit, or bounce a ball would not at first glance seem to be a relevant qualification.[65] Yet the policy has deep roots, its origins dating back to the football mania that swept the Big Three in the late nineteenth century. By the 1920s, a preference for prospective varsity athletes (especially in football) had become institutionalized in the context of a broader move away from an admissions policy based on academics alone. Though the Ivy League has made vigorous efforts — including a ban on scholarships specifically for athletes — to keep the competition for outstanding athletes within bounds, the preference they get in the admissions process remains substantial. The stakes remain high because athletes are apportioned a sizable slice of the admissions pie; at Princeton in 1997–1998, for example, varsity athletes constituted 22 percent of all the men.[66]

As admissions to the Big Three and other elite private colleges has become even more competitive, the effective allocation of so many slots to athletes has become the object of an intense debate.[67] In the forefront of those questioning this practice has been former Princeton president (and current Mellon Foundation president) William Bowen, who has coauthored two major studies on college athletes.[68] Even for those aware of the power of membership in a preferred category in admissions, the results of the latest study are astonishing; at Ivy League schools, slots are reserved for potential team members and coaches basically get to select who will fill them as long as their candidates meet the college's minimum academic standards. As a result, recruited athletes make up the vast majority of a team in many sports — among men, 89 percent in hockey and 83 percent in football, and among women, 75 percent in basketball and 70 percent in swimming. Among male hockey, football, and basketball players, their average combined SAT score is lower than that of nonathletes by 177, 165, and 144 points, respectively.[69]

Recognizing that the recruitment of athletes has compromised their core academic mission, the Ivy League has recently taken some measures to bring the situation under control. In June 2003, the Ivies voted to cap the number of athletes admitted each year to play in the 33 sports sponsored by the league, to raise the academic requirements for admission, and to reduce the number of places reserved for football players from 35 to 25 per college.[70] But more drastic reform is needed, for too many applicants are still admitted almost exclusively on the basis of their athletic ability.[71] According to the Big Three's official ideology, skill in athletics is a legitimate form of "merit," but one that should be no more valued in the admissions process than exceptional ability in music, art, drama, dance, and debate. Putting this ideology into practice would not necessarily reduce the number of students participating in varsity athletics (indeed, it would probably increase the number of "walk-ons").[72] It would, however, almost certainly reduce the number of recruited athletes, freeing up precious places in the freshman class for students more willing and able to take advantage of the intellectual opportunities available in great research universities.

CLASS DIVERSITY

In the brief that Harvard, Yale, Princeton, and five other leading private universities submitted to *Grutter v. Bollinger*, one of the central arguments was that student diversity was essential to the fulfillment of their core educational mission. Insisting on "the compelling pedagogical interests" served by "a diverse and inclusive education experience," the brief went on to cite Charles W. Eliot's declaration that Harvard students should be the children of the "rich and poor" and the "educated and uneducated" in order to represent the full diversity of American society.[73]

A century after Eliot's statement, the Big Three are conspicuously lacking in significant representation of the "poor" and the "uneducated." Though hailing diversity as indispensable to their mission (according to the former Harvard president Neil Rudenstine, "diversity . . . is the substance from which much human learning, understanding, and wisdom derive"), the Big Three, as noted earlier, are in fact among the least economically diverse of the nation's major research universities.[74] As for highly selective institutions in general, a recent study found that students from the top percentile of the socioeconomic distribution are twenty-five times more likely to attend a "top-tier" college than students from the bottom quartile. Only 3 percent of students at highly selective institutions come from families in the lowest quartile; in contrast, blacks and Hispanics — who form a roughly similar proportion of the population — make up about 12 percent of the student body.[75]

The lack of class diversity at the nation's leading universities reflects the relative powerlessness — indeed, the invisibility — of the American working class. Unlike black and brown students, students of working-class origin have never mounted a serious effort either on or off campus to demand a larger slice of the admissions pie. The paucity of working-class students at the Big Three and other highly selective institutions contradicts their professed commitment to both diversity and equality of opportunity and threatens to undermine their legitimacy by reinforcing their image as citadels of privilege. Nor do they receive the kind of preference still accorded legacies and recruited athletes — groups that, according to a study of 19 selective colleges and universities (3 of which were Harvard, Yale, and Princeton) by William Bowen, are 30 and 20 percentage points more likely to be admitted, controlling for SAT scores. Indeed, contrary to the repeated claims of elite colleges, "applicants from low socioeconomic backgrounds, whether defined by family income or parental education, get essentially no break in the admissions process."[76]

But remedying the massive underrepresentation of poor and working-class students will not be easy. It will require, at the very least, a forthright acknowledgment of the problem as well as the adoption of specific measures to address it.[77] Class-based affirmative action programs of the type developed at the University of California in the wake of Proposition 209 (which banned race-based affirmative action) would be a useful first step. Yet any serious attempt to attain greater economic diversity will require a reassessment of the very meaning of "merit." For by conventional definitions, the privileged *are* the meritorious; of all students nationwide scoring over 1300 on the SAT, 66 percent come from the top socioeconomic quartile and only 3 percent from the bottom quartile.[78] As in the case of race, only a redefinition of "merit" that acknowledges the profound differences in educational opportunity holds a real possibility of bringing more than token class diversity to the Big Three.[79]

Taken together, these four measures would bring the Big Three a bit more into conformity with their professed ideals but would not dramatically transform them. Yet the tendency of universities to place institutional interests over the interests of students and the broader society suggests that even such modest measures are unlikely to be implemented unless powerful pressure — whether internal, external, or both — is applied. Real change does not come without cost; it is possible, for example, that the elimination of early admission programs might place the Big Three at a competitive disadvantage in the "positional arms race" in higher education and that this disadvantage might even be reflected in a drop in the despised but feared national rankings.[80] But is it too much to ask the leaders of our most prestigious institutions of higher education — institutions that constantly proclaim their commitment to the ideals of meritocracy and inclusion — that they exhibit the same integrity and firmness of character they demand of their applicants?

The Dark Side of Meritocracy

That the quasi-meritocratic admissions system of today is a major improvement over the more overtly discriminatory and hereditary system of the past is a proposition that few people this side of William F. Buckley would deny.[81] Under the admissions regime that prevailed as late as the 1950s, anti-Semitism was widespread, applicants from boarding schools received massive preference, women were not permitted to apply to the Big Three, blacks were totally absent, and the sheer act of applying for a scholarship could damage a candidate's chance for admission. The more meritocratic system of today is, by any standard, far more equitable and just than the system it replaced.

A reasonable principle for allocating scarce slots in higher education and employment, meritocracy is nevertheless seriously flawed as a governing societal ideal. It is well worth remembering that to Michael Young, the brilliant scholar and social reformer who coined the term, a "meritocracy" was a dystopia — a society in which the great ideal of equality had been abandoned in favor of a relentless competitive struggle for success that would culminate in a social order just as hereditary as the one that preceded it but less open to the quest for social justice.[82]

In Young's great satire, *The Rise of the Meritocracy,* advancement is based on merit (defined as "intelligence and effort" or "I + E = M") rather than background. Having learned that "the best way to defeat opposition is to win over its leaders," England's ruling class recognized that this meant "appropriating and educating the able children of the lower classes."[83] This goal was strikingly similar to the Jeffersonian ideal that the "best geniuses . . . be raked from the rubbish annually and be educated." The upward mobility via education that followed from expanded educational opportunities, Young believed, created "new conditions [under which] the lower classes no longer have a distinctive ideology in conflict with the ethos of society, any more than the lower orders used to in the heyday of feudalism."[84] As a consequence, the great historic demand of the Labour Party for equality of condition was replaced by a clamor for equality of opportunity. This was, of course, one of the principal objectives of the meritocratic project favored by Eliot, Conant, and Brewster, but to Young the abandonment of the demand for equality of condition was a political and historical tragedy.

In Young's view, equality of opportunity — the sacred principle of American meritocrats — meant "equality of opportunity to be unequal."[85] Under the meritocracy, individual mobility for the talented children of the working class was a real possibility. "But for the working class as a whole the victory was a defeat."[86] Perhaps worst of all, from Young's perspective, was the effect that meritocratic competition had on winners and losers alike. In the meritocracy, Young writes, "the upper classes are . . . no longer weakened by self-doubt and self-criticism," for "the eminent know that success is just reward for their own capacity, for their own efforts, and for their undeniable achievement . . . As for the lower classes," they "know that they have had every chance" and have little choice but to recognize that their inferior status is due not as in the past to a denial of opportunity, but to their own deficiencies.[87]

Though a meritocracy initially fosters considerable social mobility, Young observes that over time it produces an "elite [that] is on the way to becoming hereditary; the principles of heredity and merit are coming together."[88] This is what seems to have happened at the Big Three, where the children of the culturally capitaled enjoy a massive advantage in the competition for admission and the children of families not so endowed find themselves effectively excluded from the race before it begins.

Young also proved prescient in predicting that a seemingly meritocratic society would prove far more tolerant of economic inequality than more obviously classbound societies. In the United States, where two-thirds of the population agree that "people have equal opportunities to get ahead," only 27 percent favor "a government-guaranteed minimum standard of living"; in the United Kingdom, where meritocratic ideology is less powerful and class differences remain more visible, just 42 percent of the people believe they have equal opportunity, and 50 percent favor a government-guaranteed minimum.[89] In another recent survey, only 28 percent of Americans, but 63 percent of British and 82 percent of Italians, favored government action to reduce income inequality.[90]

But Americans do not simply have a value preference for equality of opportunity over equality of condition; despite a powerful body of evidence to the contrary, they believe there is more social mobility in the United States than in other advanced industrial societies.[91] A particularly dramatic piece of evidence comes from a poll taken on the eve of the 2000 election: it showed that 19 percent of Americans believed they were in the top 1 percent of the income distribution and an additional 20 percent were confident that they would be one day.[92] No wonder, then, that in putatively meritocratic America, public spending on higher education, which is seen as an essential provider of opportunity, ranks among the highest of 21 countries, while spending on social welfare, which is associated with a safety net for those who fail in an open competition, ranks among the lowest.[93] Overall, writes Seymour Martin Lipset, the United States is a "welfare laggard," exhibiting higher levels of poverty and inequality than any other advanced Western country.[94]

In June 2001, an eighty-five-year-old Michael Young, ailing and within a few months of his death, wrote a final assessment of the argument about the meritocracy that he had laid out more than four decades earlier. Noting that *The Rise of the Meritocracy* was "a satire meant to be a warning," Young registered strong disapproval of those who have taken the term "meritocracy" and transformed it into a social and political ideal. On the contrary, the book had been written to sound an alarm against an emergent trend in the British Labour Party to abandon its historic commitment to greater equality for the less noble ideal of equality of opportunity.

In the intervening years, Young wrote, much that he had feared had come to pass — the rapid growth of inequality, the political disenfranchisement of the masses by an ever more business-oriented Labour Party, the emergence of a new stratum of "meritocrats" who believe that "they deserve whatever they can get" and "actually . . . have morality on their side," and the rise of a "new class" of privileged credential holders possessing the means to reproduce itself.[95] Viewed from across the Atlantic, the trends he described sound strikingly — and distressingly — familiar. Nevertheless, the struggle for a more meritocratic university system — and for a more meritocratic society — is still worth waging. But Americans, whether at the Big Three and similar universities or well removed from them, would do well to heed Young's final warning: we neglect the dark side of meritocracy at our collective peril.

Notes

The starting point for anyone interested in history of admission and exclusion at Harvard, Yale, and Princeton must be the annual reports of the office of admission, which provided both indispensable statistical information and revealing discussions about the changing dilemmas facing those in charge of selection. In addition, the student newspapers often proved extremely illuminating, as did the alumni magazines. For the purpose of tracing the changing atmosphere at the Big Three, the yearbooks were also a telling source. Using them in conjunction with the freshman face books and the reunion reports made it possible to trace the trajectories of Big Three alumni, including many of the individuals who figure prominently in the narrative.

Primary documents in the archives of Harvard, Yale, and Princeton were an essential source for understanding the hidden dynamics of admissions. In analyzing the causes and consequences of shifts in policy, there is no substitute for the often astonishingly frank internal discussions of why some changes were adopted and others spurned. Changes in the definition of "merit" were crucial to these shifts, and in examining them, I have relied on a wide variety of materials. Especially useful were the correspondence files of college presidents and deans of admission; internal memoranda; minutes of meetings; promotional materials such as catalogues, brochures, and films; statistical studies of the admissions process and of the subsequent performance of matriculants; handbooks for alumni interviewers and the admissions staff; reports of faculty committees on admission policy, including background papers; and internal documents from the admissions offices, including rating schemes, typologies of applicants, and procedures used in evaluating candidates for admission. In those cases where the authors of the archival document cited were not employees of Harvard, Yale, or Princeton (often, but not always, alumni unhappy with changes in policy), I have generally used pseudonyms to protect their privacy.

Some sources, both primary and secondary, were used so frequently that I refer to them with abbreviations. These include

CHE	Chronicle of Higher Education
DP	Daily Princetonian
HAB	Harvard Alumni Bulletin
HC	Harvard Crimson
HM	Harvard Magazine
HU	Harvard University

HUA	Harvard University Archives
NYT	New York Times
PAW	Princeton Alumni Weekly
PU	Princeton University
PUA	Princeton University Archives
YAM	Yale Alumni Magazine
YDN	Yale Daily News
YU	Yale University
YUA	Yale University Archives

Finally, there is a selected bibliography immediately after the endnotes. Those who wish to examine a full list of the sources used, including archival citations for primary documents, may do so at http://sociology.berkeley.edu/faculty/KARABEL.

Introduction

1. In social science, the notion that scholars have a responsibility to make the strange familiar and the familiar strange has exerted its greatest influence in anthropology, notably in the work of Clifford Geertz, Melford Spiro, and George and Louise Spindler. See Clifford Geertz, *Interpretation of Cultures* (New York: Basic Books, 1973); Melford Spiro, "On the Strange and Familiar in Recent Anthropological Thought," in *Cultural Psychology: Essays on Comparative Human Development*, ed. James W. Stigler et al. (Cambridge: Cambridge U.P., 1990), 47–61; and George Spindler and Louise Spindler, "Roger Harker and Schonhausen: From Familiar to Strange and Back Again," in *Doing the Ethnography of Schooling: Educational Anthropology in Action*, ed. George Spindler (Prospect Heights, Ill.: Waveland Press, 1988), 23–24. But the idea seems to have originated in the realm of literature and, in particular, in the work of T. S. Eliot, who attributes to Samuel Coleridge the view that great poetry involved "making the familiar strange, and the strange familiar" (T. S. Eliot, "Andrew Marvell," *Times Literary Supplement*, 31 March 1921).

2. "Admissions policy" means the *criteria* (academic, cultural, personal, etc.) that govern decisions of inclusion and exclusion, the *procedures* for assessing applications, and finally the *practices* of the office of admissions, which may not correspond to the official criteria and procedures. The phrase "iron law" is borrowed from the German sociologist Robert Michels, who argued in his 1911 classic, *Political Parties* (New York: Free Press, 1962 [1911], 15), for the "iron law of oligarchy," which states that organizations, in-

cluding those dedicated to democratic goals, are inherently oligarchic.

3. Yet in one crucial regard — the elite's need to justify its privileges — the American elite was no different from those of other nations. As Max Weber has written: "The fortunate is seldom satisfied with the fact of being fortunate. Beyond this, he needs to know that he has a *right* to his good fortune. He wants to be convinced that he "deserves" it, and above all, that he deserves it in comparison with others . . . Good fortune thus wants to be "legitimate" fortune" (H. H. Gerth and C. Wright Mills, eds., *From Max Weber: Essays in Sociology* [New York: Oxford U.P., 1946], 271).

4. In this book, "elite" refers to the individuals who occupy the leading positions in major organizations in the economy, the polity, and the culture. This definition is slightly different from the one used by C. Wright Mills in *The Power Elite* (New York: Oxford U.P., 1956) and more recently by contemporary followers of Mills such as Richard Zweigenhaft and G. William Domhoff, who focus on "those who run and manage large corporations . . . and serve in the government as appointed officials and military leaders" (*Diversity in the Power Elite: Have Women and Minorities Reached the Top?* [New Haven, Conn.: Yale U.P., 1998], 1). Mills and Zweigenhaft and Domhoff all consider military leaders to be integral members of the power elite and exclude from their definition those who preside over the nation's major cultural institutions.

5. The classical study of the educational backgrounds of elites in various sectors of the American elite is George W. Pierson, *The Education of American Leaders: Comparative Contributions of U.S. Colleges and Universities* (New York: Praeger, 1969). For more recent evidence on the role of selective colleges in providing pathways to the elite, see Michael Useem and Jerome Karabel, "Pathways to Top Corporate Management," *American Sociological Review* 51, April 1986, and Zweigenhaft and Domhoff, *Diversity in the Power Elite*. Our own study of the "inner cabinet" — the secretaries of defense, state, treasury, and the attorney general — found that since 1900, one-third of the 134 individuals who have held these positions received their undergraduate education at Harvard, Yale, or Princeton.

6. For revealing looks at the growth of private college counselors (now called "college consultants"), see Ralph Gardner Jr., "The $28,995 Tutor," *New York*, 16 April 2001, and also Patricia M. McDonough et al., "Access, Equity, and the Privatization of College Counseling," *Review of Higher Education* 20, no. 3 (Spring 1997): 297–317.

7. The literature on the effects of college rank on earnings and other outcomes is ably summarized in William Bowen and Derek Bok, *The Shape of the River: Long-Term Consequences of Considering Race in College and University Admissions* (Princeton, N.J.: Princeton U.P., 1998). After reviewing a broad range of studies, including their own, their basic conclusion is that "even after controlling for ability as best one can, highly significant economic returns are gained by attending a more selective college or university." For a dissenting view, see Alan Krueger and Stacy Berg Dale, "Estimating the Payoff to Attending a More Selective College: An Application of Selection on Observables and Unobservables," *Quarterly Journal of Economics* 117, no. 4 (November 2002): 1491–1527.

8. On the growing inequality in the distribution of wealth and income in the United States, which ranks as the least egalitarian of the advanced societies, see Robert H. Frank and Philip J. Cook, *The Winner-Take-All Society: Why the Few at the Top Get So Much More Than the Rest of Us* (New York: Penguin, 1996) and Edward N. Wolff, *Top Heavy: The Increasing Inequality of Wealth in America and What Can Be Done About It* (New York: New Press, 2002).

9. Writing from a political perspective antithetical to that held by the men who presided over the Big Three, Karl Marx reached a similar conclusion about the deradicalizing effects of upward mobility on the working class. "The more a ruling class is able to assimilate the most prominent men of the dominated classes," he wrote in *Das Kapital*, "the more stable and dangerous its rule" (*Capital: A Critique of Political Economy*, vol. 3 [Chicago: Charles H. Kerr, 1909], 706).

10. See the provocative and lucid discussion of "Meritocracy and Equality," in Daniel Bell, *The Coming of the Post-Industrial Society* (New York: Basic Books, 1973), 405–55. Though my own position differs from Bell's, his essay (first published in the Fall 1972 issue of the *Public Interest*) is an exemplary discussion of the many social and political issues at stake in the debate over meritocracy.

11. In thinking about the difference between the principles of equality of opportunity and equality of condition, an image of two buildings — one a sleek skyscraper, the other an edifice housing the same number of people but closer to the ground — may be helpful. Those who favor equality of opportunity are primarily occupied with the fluidity of movement between upper and lower floors; there may be a huge distance (i.e., level of inequality) between the second and seventy-ninth floors, but as long as there is a fast elevator (i.e., extensive social mobility) to move people from the lower floors to the upper floors, the structure presents no problems. But to proponents of equality of condition, such a structure would by its very nature be undesirable because of the vast distance between top and bottom; far preferable from this point of view would be a well-designed structure of perhaps five or six stories, with no sharp division in accommodation between upper and lower floors and ample public space to encourage social contact and cooperation among the residents.

12. In conceptualizing the relationship between "merit" and power, I am particularly indebted to the work of Max Weber and Pierre Bourdieu. In his classic discussion of bureaucracy, Weber notes that cultural ideals are "stamped by the structure of domination and the ruling stratum." And in his brilliant analysis of "the pedagogy of cultivation" in Confucian China, he emphasizes that the specific type of cultivated man produced by the educational system ultimately depends on the "decisive stratum's respective ideal of cultivation." In Weber's conception of society, every "structure of domination" has a characteristic system of legitimation and a corresponding set of cultural ideals that tend to express the ethos and worldview of the dominant groups. Within this framework, the very definition of "merit" embodies underlying power relations and tends to reflect the cultural ideals of those groups that hold the power of cultural definition (Gerth and Mills, *From Max Weber*, 243–46). For a similar perspective, see also the work of Pierre Bourdieu, which emphasizes the role of what he calls "the cultural arbitrary" in expressing

"the objective interests (material and symbolic) of the dominant groups or classes" (Pierre Bourdieu and Jean-Claude Passeron, *Reproduction in Education, Society and Culture* [Beverly Hills, Calif.: SAGE, 1977], 9). See also Bourdieu's study of the French system of higher education, *The State Nobility: Elite Schools in the Field of Power* (Stanford, Calif.: Stanford U.P., 1996).

13. Michael Young, *The Rise of the Meritocracy, 1870–2033: An Essay on Education and Equality* (London: Thames & Hudson, 1958; Harmondsworth, U.K.: Penguin, 1961). Citations are to the Penguin edition. Born in 1915, Michael Young was the son of an Irish mother and an Australian father, both of them in the arts and frequently short of money. After graduating from Dartington Hall, a progressive school, he attended the London School of Economics, from which he graduated in 1939 with a degree in law. As director of research for the Labour Party from 1945 to 1951, he drafted the influential party platform, *Let Us Face the Future*, which helped defeat Winston Churchill and bring Labour to power in 1945. In 1954 he founded the Institute of Community Studies, and it was there that he wrote (with Peter Wilmott) a classic study, *Family and Kinship in East London*. But the initial response of publishers to a draft of *The Rise of the Meritocracy* was not positive, and eleven of them rejected it. Yet the book was finally published in 1958 and it went on to become an international bestseller, translated into twelve languages and selling 500,000 copies. In addition to coining the term "meritocracy," Young was a great social innovator, counting among his inventions the Open University, the Consumer's Association, the Advisory Centre for Education, and the School for Social Entrepreneurs, a business school for the nonprofit sector whose partners included OxFam and Amnesty International ("Lord Young of Dartington," *Guardian*, 16 January 2002; "Obituary: Lord Young of Dartington," *Independent*, 16 January 2002; Margalit Fox, "Michael Young, 86, Scholar; Coined, Mocked 'Meritocracy,'" *New York Times* [hereafter *NYT*], 25 January 2002; "Obituary of Lord Young of Dartington Creator of the Open University," *Daily Telegraph*, 16 January 2002).

14. Loury continues, "As a result, the selection of young people to enter prestigious educational institutions amounts to a visible, high-stakes exercise in civic pedagogy. These 'selection rituals' are political acts, with moral overtones. Their perceived legitimacy is crucial in our stratified society, where one's place in the status hierarchy can turn on access to elite institutions. (Consider, for example, what would it mean for our civic life if, due to the expense, only wealthy families could send their children to the most prestigious institutions.) It therefore matters a great deal — not just for the colleges and universities in question, but for all of us — how these admissions decisions are made" (foreword to Bowen and Bok, *Shape of the River*, xxii).

15. Wilbur J. Bender, "Comprehensive Formal Statement of Harvard College Admission Policy (Confidential)," 18 September 1952, HUA, 14, 24–30; John Osander, "Report to the Faculty," 1967–1968, PU; Henry Chauncey, "Yale Undergraduate Admissions," 21 January 1972, 3–4, YUA.

16. In conceptualizing the admissions process as an intensively political one, in which the power to shape the classification schemes used in evaluating applicants is a crucial determinant of outcomes, I have benefited greatly from David Karen's groundbreaking article, "Toward a Political-Organizational Model of Gatekeeping: The Case of the Elite Colleges," *Sociology of Education* 63, no. 4 (October 1990): 227–40, and Penny Hollander Feldman's excellent study, "Recruiting an Elite: Admissions to Harvard College" (Ph.D. diss., Harvard Univ., 1975).

17. James Bryant Conant, "Education for a Classless Society: The Jeffersonian Tradition," *Atlantic Monthly*, May 1940, 598. See also "The Future of Our Higher Education," *Harper's Magazine*, May 1938, 561–70, and "Wanted: American Radicals," *Atlantic Monthly*, May 1943, 41–45.

18. For an illuminating recent treatment of Brewster, see Geoffrey Kabaservice, *The Guardians: Kingman Brewster, His Circle, and the Rise of the Liberal Establishment* (New York: Henry Holt, 2004).

19. In emphasizing the central importance of a university's position within a stratified and segmented system of higher education, I am indebted to Bourdieu's concept of "field" — a metaphor that emphasizes the relational and power dimensions of interactions among organizations or individuals in a particular domain (e.g., religion, art, higher education) governed by its own relatively autonomous laws. In order to understand the admissions practices of the Big Three, the main insight of field analysis is that the actions of each member cannot be understood apart from the fiercely competitive dynamic of the larger field, which includes not only socially proximate institutions such as Dartmouth, Williams, and Stanford but more socially distant ones such as Columbia, MIT, Chicago, and Penn. For the application of the field concept to higher education, see Pierre Bourdieu, *The State Nobility*, and *Homo Academicus* (Stanford, Calif.: Stanford U.P., 1988 [1984]); and for a lucid discussion on the place of field analysis in Bourdieu's larger framework, see David Swartz, *Culture and Power: The Sociology of Pierre Bourdieu* (Chicago: Univ. of Chicago Press, 1997), 117–42, and Pierre Bourdieu and Loic Wacquant, *An Invitation to Reflexive Sociology* (Chicago: Univ. of Chicago Press, 1992), 94–115.

20. In the same book, Baltzell describes this period as one in which "a small class of British gentlemen, allied with a rising class of American business Brahmins, authoritatively led the world in an era of Anglo-Saxon imperialism" (*The Protestant Establishment: Aristocracy & Caste in America* [New York: Vintage, 1964], 11, 17).

1. Elite Education and the Protestant Ethos

1. George Biddle, "As I Remember Groton School: A Chapter of Autobiography, 1998–1904," *Harper's*, August 1939, 296.

2. John Bethell, "Frank Roosevelt at Harvard," *HM*, November–December 1996, 40. In my portrait of FDR's years at Harvard, I have drawn liberally on the excellent accounts in Bethell as well as on James MacGregor Burns, *Roosevelt: The Lion and the Fox* (New York: Harcourt, Brace, 1956); Kenneth S. Davis, *FDR: The Beckoning of Destiny, 1882–1928* (New York: Putnam's, 1971); Geoffrey C. Ward, *Before the Trumpet: Young Franklin Roosevelt, 1882–1905* (New York: Harper & Row, 1985); and Ted Morgan, *FDR: A Biography* (New York: Simon & Schuster, 1985).

3. Groton data from Michael Tronic, head librarian

of the school. Two of Roosevelt's more adventurous classmates went to Yale, and two others saw no need to attend college at all.

4. "Reception to New Students," *Harvard Crimson* (hereafter *HC*), 9 October 1900.

5. Whereas 41 percent of Harvard freshman in 1900 came from public schools, the figures at Yale and Princeton were 28 and 16 percent, respectively. These statistics are based on my own study of the individuals who entered these schools in the fall of 1900. For Harvard, the secondary schools attended by this class were taken from the *Twenty-fifth Anniversary Report: Class of 1904*. For Yale, the list of students entering in 1900 was taken from the *Preliminary List of Officers and Students of Yale University, 1900–1901* (New Haven, Conn.: Tuttle, Morehouse & Taylor, 1900); their secondary schools were taken from the *Yale Class Books, Tenth Anniversary Records*, and *Twenty-Fifth Anniversary Records* for the classes of 1903–1907. For Princeton, the secondary schools attended by the entering class of 1900 were taken from the *Nassau Herald: Class of 1904*; "Princeton Undergraduate Alumni Index 1748–1920," Seeley Mudd Ms. Library Online Database, www.princeton.edu/~mudd/databases/alumni.html (accessed 11 November 2003); and "Registrars Entrance Records," 1888–1900, PC. For all three institutions, students receiving private tutoring were listed under private schools.

6. Tied with Boston Latin as Harvard's leading feeder school in 1900 was Phillips Exeter Academy, a private school in New Hampshire founded in 1783 that was far more affordable — and far more diverse socially — than Groton or St. Paul's. In an illuminating discussion of the leading boarding schools, E. Digby Baltzell describes the "St. Grottlesex" schools (St. Paul's, St. Mark's, St. George's, Groton, Kent, and Middlesex) as "the most fashionable" and Exeter and Andover as "the least exclusive socially"; this description echoes a 1912 article that refers to "the great democratic schools of Andover and Exeter" as distinct from the "select fashionable schools." For empirical evidence from the early twentieth century consistent with these descriptions, see Steven B. Levine, "The Rise of American Boarding Schools and the Development of a National Upper Class," *Social Problems* 28, no. 1 (October 1980); Owen Johnson, "The Social Usurpation of Colleges: Part II — Harvard," *Collier's Magazine*, 25 May 1912, 14; E. Digby Baltzell, *Philadelphia Gentlemen: The Making of a National Upper Class* (Glencoe, Ill.: Free Press, 1958), 307. (A paperback edition of *Philadelphia Gentleman* was published in 1962 by Collier Books under the title *An American Business Aristocracy*.)

7. Samuel Eliot Morison, *Three Centuries of Harvard* (Cambridge, Mass.: Harvard U.P., 1936), 419–22.

8. Davis, *FDR*, 127.

9. Burns, *Roosevelt*, 17; Ward, *Before the Trumpet*, 214–16; John Bethell, *Harvard Observed: An Illustrated History of the University in the Twentieth Century* (Cambridge, Mass.: Harvard U.P., 1998), 41.

10. "Freshman Football: 143 Candidates Out — Usual Lack of Heavy Men," *HC*, 29 September 1900.

11. Davis, *FDR*, 143.

12. Morgan, *FDR*, 75.

13. Davis, *FDR*, 144; Ward, *Before the Trumpet*, 232.

14. Bethell, "Frank Roosevelt," 43; Ward, *Before the Trumpet*, 232.

15. Morgan, *FDR*, 84; Davis, *FDR*, 158.

16. Morgan, *FDR*, 78.

17. Ward, *Before the Trumpet*, 239; Bethell, "Frank Roosevelt," 44.

18. Bethell, "Frank Roosevelt," 43.

19. Among the most status-conscious of American colleges, Harvard had a long history of ranking students by the social standing of their families. According to Kenneth Davis, "In the mid-eighteenth century the college president personally listed students when they enrolled, in order of their social rank or, to be precise, according 'to the Dignity of the Familie whereto the student severally belonged' — a list that was printed in the college catalogue and that determined precedence in such matters as table seating and service, position in academic processionals, even recitations in class." Though the listing was officially abandoned in the late eighteenth century, it continued well into the nineteenth, with President John T. Kirkland finding it useful to keep up a method of listing his students "other than alphabetically." Though President Eliot rejected this system outright, by the 1870s the Institute of 1770 had come to perform the same function (Davis, *FDR*, 135; Cleveland Amory, *The Proper Bostonians* (New York: Dutton, 1947), 297; Morison, *Three Centuries*, 421–26).

20. Ward, *Before the Trumpet*, 234.

21. Davis, *FDR*, 79–80.

22. Bethell, "Frank Roosevelt," 41–42.

23. Ward, *Before the Trumpet*, 235; Davis, *FDR*, 153; Morgan, *FDR*, 81.

24. So proud was Theodore Roosevelt of his membership in Harvard's most exclusive club that, when informing Kaiser Wilhelm about the engagement of his daughter Alice to Nicholas Longworth, he felt compelled to mention that "Nick and I are both members of the Porc, you know" (Amory, *Proper Bostonians*, 304).

25. Since the process of election to Porcellian was secret, with a single member able to veto a candidate by placing a small black ball in a box, it remains unknown to this day why Franklin Roosevelt was not admitted. One possibility is that it had nothing to do with him personally but was the consequence of a recent, widely publicized scandal involving his relative and childhood playmate, James Roosevelt Jr. (known as "Taddy"), a Groton graduate who had dropped out of Harvard to marry a Hungarian-born dance hall girl and prostitute named Sadie Messinger, known in the press as "Dutch Sadie." Another common theory is that his association with Theodore Roosevelt may have worked against him. For accounts of the Porcellian episode, see Ward, *Before the Trumpet*, 217–22, 235; Morgan, *FDR*, 81; and Davis, *FDR*, 155–56.

26. Ward, *Before the Trumpet*, 235–36; Morgan, *FDR*, 81.

27. Marcia Graham Synnott, *The Half-Opened Door: Discrimination and Admissions at Harvard, Yale, and Princeton, 1900–1970* (Westport, Conn.: Greenwood Press, 1979), 3. See also the entry under "Big Three" in Alexander Leitch, ed., *A Princeton Companion* (Princeton, N.J.: Princeton U.P., 1978), 53–54. The appellation "Big Three" was common parlance for half a century before the concept of the "Ivy League" appeared. While references to the "eastern ivy colleges" first appeared in the fall of 1933, it was not until February 8, 1935, that Alan Gould, the sports editor for the Associated Press, used the precise term "Ivy League." A year later, the editors of the student news-

papers at seven of the eight colleges that later became the Ivy League (Harvard, Yale, Princeton, Dartmouth, Pennsylvania, Columbia, Cornell, and Brown) called for the formation of an athletic conference of that name. Yet a 1938 effort to formally constitute the group failed because Harvard and Yale refused to go along, preferring that the Big Three remain closed. In 1945, the presidents of the eight colleges established the Intercollegiate Agreement to link the institutions in football, but Harvard, Yale, and Princeton insisted that "Ivy League" not be used. Nevertheless the public began to identify the schools as belonging to the Ivy League, and on February 11, 1954, the existence of the Ivy League was formally announced (Mark F. Bernstein, *Football: The Ivy League Origins of American Obsession* [Philadelphia: Univ. of Pennsylvania Press, 2001], xii–xiii, 168, 180, 212). See also John Robert Thelin, "Images of the Ivy League, 1890 to 1960: The Collegiate Ideal and the Education of Elites in American Culture" (Ph.D. diss., Univ. of California at Berkeley, 1973), 197–226.

28. Frederick Rudolph, *The American College and University* (New York: Vintage, 1962), 375; Thelin, "Images of the Ivy League," 177–78.

29. Brooks M. Kelley, *Yale: A History* (New Haven, Conn.: Yale U.P., 1974), 302; Marcia Graham Synnott, "A Social History of Admissions Policies at Harvard, Yale, and Princeton, 1900–1930" (Ph.D. diss., Univ. of Massachusetts, 1974), 21.

30. Kelley, *Yale*, 301–2.

31. Mark A. Branch, "The Ten Greatest Yalies Who Never Were: Frank Merriwell," *Yale Alumni Magazine* (hereafter *YAM*), February 2003.

32. The designation of national champions before 1936, the first year of the Associated Press poll, is based on the Dickinson mathematical system (named after Frank Dickinson, an economics professor at the University of Illinois), which draws on three retroactive historical polls taken by the Helms Athletic Foundation, the College Football Researchers Association, and the National Championship Foundation ("National Champions: The Early Years," in *The 1999 ESPN Information Please Sports Almanac*, ed. Gerry Brown and Michael Morrison [New York: Hyperion ESPN Books, 1998], 162–63). For more lists of national football champions, see Bernstein, *Football*, 278–79, and David DeLassus, "Recognized National Championships by Year," College Football Data Warehouse, cfbdatawarehouse.com/data/national_championships/nchamps_year.php (accessed 1 July 2003).

33. Kelley, *Yale*, 302.

34. DeLassus, "Recognized National Championships by Year."

35. Bethell, *Harvard Observed*, 95.

36. Mabel Newcomer, *The Big Business Executive* (New York: Columbia U.P., 1955), 74, 111; William Miller, "The Business Elite in Business Bureaucracies: Careers of Top Executives in the Early Twentieth Century," in *Men in Business: Essays in the History of Entrepreneurship*, ed. William Miller (Cambridge, Mass.: Harvard U.P., 1952), 286–305.

37. On John Pierpont Morgan Jr.'s establishment of the Delphic Club, see Amory, *Proper Bostonians*, 308 and Morison, *Three Centuries*, 425–26. The educational background of the Harrimans and Rockefellers is drawn from various editions of *WWA*. John D. Rockefeller Jr. graduated from Brown in 1897.

38. John R. Thelin, *The Cultivation of Ivy: A Saga of the College in America* (Cambridge, Mass.: Schenkman, 1976), 9. For an example of the attention lavished on the Big Three in the 1890s, see the detailed portraits of Harvard, Princeton, and Yale in *Scribner's Magazine*: Edward Martin, "Undergraduate Life at Harvard," *Scribner's Magazine*, May 1897; James Alexander, "Undergraduate Life at Princeton — Old and New," *Scribner's Magazine*, June 1897; and Henry Howland, "Undergraduate Life at Yale," *Scribner's Magazine*, July 1897.

39. Ernest Earnest, *Academic Procession: An Informal History of the American College, 1636–1953* (Indianapolis: Bobbs-Merrill, 1953), 204.

40. In a much-cited study (James M. Cattell, *A Statistical Study of American Men of Science* [New York: Science Press, 1906], 561) of the educational backgrounds of 1,000 eminent men in science, the Columbia University psychologist John M. Cattell found that Harvard College, with 106, was the leading undergraduate source, followed by Yale (52), Michigan (35), Cornell (31), Columbia (28), Johns Hopkins (27), MIT (26), Princeton (23), and Amherst (23). But at the doctoral level Johns Hopkins (102) was first by a large margin, followed by Harvard (57), Columbia (38), Yale (28), Cornell (26), and Chicago (23), with Princeton, which had opened its graduate school only in 1901, well behind at 4. In his influential book, *Great American Universities* (New York: Macmillan, 1910), E. E. Slosson offered portraits of 8 institutions in addition to the 6 universities cited in the text: Stanford, California, Michigan, Wisconsin, Minnesota, Illinois, Cornell, and the University of Pennsylvania.

41. Owen Johnson, *Stover at Yale* (Boston: Little, Brown, 1912). A year before its publication as a book, *Stover at Yale* appeared as a serial in *McClure's Magazine* (Robert J. Higgs, "Yale and the Heroic Ideal, Götterdämmerung and Palingenesis, 1865–1914," in *Manliness and Morality*, ed. J. A. Mangan and James Walvin [New York: St. Martin's, 1987], 160–75).

42. George W. Pierson, *Yale College: An Educational History, 1871–1921* (New Haven, Conn.: Yale U.P., 1952), 233–34.

43. Pierson, *Yale College*, 240–41.

44. Thelin, *Cultivation of Ivy*, 12; Pierson, *Yale College*, 240.

45. For a sense of the frenzy surrounding Tap Day at Yale, see, for example, the *NYT* article "Yale Juniors Now in Fix of 'Stover,'" 12 May 1912, which had three separate subtitles: "Tap Day Exercises Will Be Held Thursday and Class Is Feverish with Excitement," "A Vanderbilt for Bones," and "Harriman's Son Picked as One of the Fortunate — Philbin of New York Also Regarded as Slapped." For other examples of typical *NYT* coverage, see "Tap Day at Yale — A Senior Society 'Turns Down' Gould, the Coming Football Captain — Young Vanderbilt Elected," 24 May 1901, and "Taft's Son Elected to Skull and Bones," 28 May 1909.

46. For portraits of Patton, see David W. Hirst, "Patton, Francis Landey," in Leitch, *Princeton Companion*, 354–57, and August Heckscher, *Woodrow Wilson* (New York: Scribner's, 1991), 134–35.

47. William K. Selden, *Club Life at Princeton: An Historical Account of the Eating Clubs at Princeton University* (Princeton, N.J.: Princeton Prospect Foundation, 1994), 16.

48. Henry W. Bragdon, *Woodrow Wilson: The Academic Years* (Cambridge, Mass.: Belknap Press, 1967), 272.

49. "Rush at Princeton — Lively Contest Between Freshman and Sophomores," *NYT,* 7 October 1900. For the coverage of another "rush" at Princeton the same year, see "Princeton 'Rush' a Draw — Sophomores Fail to Prevent Freshman from Wearing Spring Hats," *NYT,* 27 April 1901.

50. Arthur Gelb and Barbara Gelb, *O'Neill: Life with Monte Cristo* (New York: Applause, 2000), 221, 223, 230.

51. On the eating clubs at Princeton during this period, see Selden, *Club Life at Princeton,* 10–24; M'Cready Sykes, "Gentlemen: — the 'Nineties," *Princeton Alumni Weekly* (hereafter *PAW*), 6 February 1931; and C. Wadsworth Camp, "At the Turn of the Century: 1900–1910," *PAW,* 27 February 1931.

52. Ray Stannard Baker, *Woodrow Wilson: Life and Letters, Princeton 1890–1910* (Garden City, N.Y.: Doubleday, Page, 1927), 133.

53. Bragdon, *Woodrow Wilson,* 275.

54. For a brief but useful portrait of Wilson, see Arthur S. Link, "Wilson, [Thomas] Woodrow," in Leitch, *Princeton Companion,* 512–15.

55. Henry Aaron Yeomans, *Abbot Lawrence Lowell, 1856–1943* (Cambridge, Mass.: Harvard U.P., 1948), 75; Bethell, *Harvard Observed,* 19.

56. Slosson, *Great American Universities,* 18–19.

57. Bethell, *Harvard Observed,* 19.

58. Yeomans, *Abbott Lawrence Lowell,* 67–68.

59. Slosson, *Great American Universities,* 5.

60. By 1908, so many parents had attempted to register their boys to enter Groton in 1920 that the rector had to tell a parent trying to submit his son's name that his chances of gaining a place were small because more than 100 boys were already on the list for a class of 30. But those ultimately admitted would have a clear path to Harvard, if so inclined; of 405 Groton applicants to Harvard between 1906 and 1932, only 3 were rejected (Frank D. Ashburn, *Peabody of Groton: A Portrait* [Cambridge, Mass.: Riverside Press, 1967], 99, and *Fifty Years On: Groton School, 1884–1934* [New York: At the Sign of Gosden Head, 1934], 132).

61. As late as 1915, Harvard's Committee on Admission reported on a boy who took exams in several subjects three times before passing them. Though the young man "had every advantage of special preparatory schools and expensive and expert tutors, his record indicated as clearly as anything that he either would not or could not do the work of the quality that the College has a right to expect." Nevertheless, Harvard was required to admit him because he had indeed passed the requisite exams. In his first year, he accumulated three failures, one unsatisfactory pass, and one satisfactory grade (Committee on Admission, "Report of the Chairman of the Committee on Admission to the President," 1914–1915, HU, 287).

62. Slosson, *Great American Universities,* 5–6.

63. Entrance Committee, "Entrance Examinations," in "Report to the President of Yale University," 1913–1914, YU, 135.

64. Untitled article in *PAW,* 6 October 1909, 20.

65. Hugh Hawkins, *Between Harvard and America: The Educational Leadership of Charles W. Eliot* (New York: Oxford U.P., 1972), 279.

66. "The University: The Autumn Outlook," *Harvard Graduates' Magazine,* December 1900. In 1900–1901, Harvard enrolled 2,499 undergraduates (including 507 at the Lawrence Scientific School) and 4,297 students overall (Slosson, *Great American Universities,* 33).

67. On the growing concern, especially at Harvard and Yale, that they were losing students to other private colleges, see Hawkins, *Between Harvard and America,* 279; Pierson, *Yale College,* 238–39; and Thelin, *Cultivation of Ivy,* 15.

68. Pierson, *Yale College,* 186–91; Slosson, *Great American Universities,* 85; John P. Hoskins, "The Princeton Entrance Requirements as Compared with Those of Harvard and Yale," *PAW,* 1 December 1909, 153.

69. John Hays Gardiner, *Harvard* (New York: Oxford U.P., 1914), 56–57. In 1911, Harvard adopted the "New Plan," which broadened its curricular requirements for admission and permitted applicants to substitute French or German for Latin (Synnott, "Social History of Admissions," 129).

70. Hoskins, "Princeton Entrance Requirements," 168.

71. As early as 1895, when annual expenses were $400 to $500, Harvard awarded 125 scholarships ranging from $90 to $300 per year (Thelin, "Images of the Ivy League," 24).

72. Synnott, *Half-Opened Door,* 130–43, 178–82; Daniel A. Oren, *Joining the Club: A History of Jews and Yale* (New Haven, Conn.: Yale U.P., 1985), 320.

73. On the percentage of Jews at Harvard between 1900 and 1922, see Synnott, *Half-Opened Door,* 96. The figure on Catholics is from Bethell, *Harvard Observed,* 27.

74. The premier scholar of the Protestant upper class, Baltzell (1915–1996) was himself a "proper Philadelphian," raised in the fashionable Chestnut Hill section of the city. A graduate of St. Paul's and Penn, he served as a navy pilot in World War II and obtained a doctorate at Columbia in 1952. While several sources credit him with devising the term WASP, his widow claimed only that he had "explicated and defined it in his writings." Among his major works are *The Protestant Establishment: Aristocracy & Caste in America* (New York: Vintage, 1964); *Philadelphia Gentlemen: The Making of a National Upper Class* (Glencoe, Ill.: Free Press, 1958); and *Puritan Boston and Quaker Philadelphia: Two Protestant Ethics and the Spirit of Class Authority and Leadership* (New York: Free Press, 1979). It was *The Protestant Establishment* that introduced the term "WASP" into popular parlance. On Baltzell's life, see Eric Pace, "E. Digby Baltzell Dies at 80; Studied WASP's," *NYT,* 20 August 1996; Karl Vick, "He Defined the WASP — and Stung It," *Washington Post,* 20 August 1996; Godfrey Hodgson, "Obituary: E. Digby Baltzell," *The Independent (London),* 26 August 1996; and Tom Long, "E. Digby Baltzell, 80; Sociologist Known as 'Upper-class Populist,'" *Boston Globe,* 19 August 1996.

75. On the Spanish-American War and the debates leading up to it, see Warren Zimmerman, *First Great Triumph: How Five Americans Made Their Country a World Power* (New York: Farrar, Straus, 2002), and Kristin Hoganson, *Fighting for American Manhood: How Gender Politics Provoked the Spanish-American and Philippine-American Wars* (New Haven, Conn.: Yale U.P., 1998).

76. On the anti-imperialist movement, see Robert L. Beisner, *Twelve Against Empire: The Anti-Imperialists, 1898–1900* (New York: McGraw-Hill, 1968); Zimmerman, *First Great Triumph,* 329–61; Hoganson, *Fighting for American Manhood,* 164–72; and Nell Irvin Painter, *Standing at Armageddon: The United States, 1877–1919* (New York: Norton, 1987), 155–62.

77. The quote is from Painter, *Standing at Armageddon*, 155.

78. Ibid., 148–49.

79. Ibid., 149–52.

80. Baltzell, "'Who's Who in America' and 'The Social Register': Elite and Upper Class Indexes in Metropolitan America," in *Class, Status, and Power: Social Stratification in Comparative Perspective,* ed. Reinhard Bendix and Seymour M. Lipset, 2nd ed. (New York: Free Press, 1966); Baltzell, *Philadelphia Gentlemen,* 19–24; Baltzell, *Protestant Establishment,* 113–42; Steven B. Levine, "The Rise of the American Boarding Schools: A Study in the Influence of Elite Education on the Structure of the Upper Class" (senior thesis, Harvard Univ., 1978), 62–66.

81. In the late nineteenth and early twentieth centuries, the Philadelphia upper class was less closely tied to the Big Three than the elite of Boston or New York, preferring to send its sons to the University of Pennsylvania. But by the 1920s, Philadelphia's patricians had largely abandoned Penn, which was attended by only 14 percent of their sons, compared to 55 percent at the Big Three (40 percent at Princeton, 8 percent at Yale, and 7 percent at Harvard) (Richard Farnum, "Patterns of Upper-Class Education in Four American Cities: 1875–1975," in *The High Status Track: Studies of Elite Schools and Stratification,* ed. Paul W. Kingston and Lionel S. Lewis [Albany: State Univ. of New York Press, 1990], 53–73).

82. Max Weber, "The Chinese Literati," in *From Max Weber: Essays in Sociology,* ed. H. H. Gerth and C. Wright Mills (New York: Oxford U.P., 1946), 427. See also Max Weber, "Bureaucracy," in *From Max Weber,* ed. Gerth and Mills, 243.

83. On the British public schools, which were in fact privately endowed institutions, see Rupert Wilkinson, *Gentlemanly Power: British Leadership and the Public School Tradition* (London: Oxford U.P., 1964). Other excellent works from the vast literature on this subject include T. W. Bamford, *Rise of the Public Schools: A Study of Boys' Public Boarding Schools in England and Wales from 1837 to the Present Day* (London, Wisc.: Thomas Nelson, 1967); John Wakeford, *The Cloistered Elite: A Sociological Analysis of the English Public Boarding School* (London: Macmillan, 1969); J. R. de S. Honey, *Tom Brown's Universe: The Development of the English Public School in the Nineteenth Century* (New York: New York Times, 1977); and Elizabeth Krumpe, "The Educational Ideas of the Clarendon Headmasters from 1860 to 1914" (Ph.D. diss., Boston Univ., 1983).

84. Thomas Hughes, "The Public Schools of England, Part I," *North American Review,* April 1879, 352. An alumnus of Rugby, one of the oldest and most elite British public schools, Hughes (1822–1896) was deeply influenced by Rugby's renowned headmaster, Thomas Arnold (the father of Matthew Arnold). In 1857, he published *Tom Brown's School Days,* a classic portrayal of the life of a British schoolboy; it did much to establish the image of British public schools as places where team sports such as rugby played a critical role in the building of character. One of the founders of Christian Socialism, Hughes served as a Liberal member of Parliament from 1865 to 1874. See "Thomas Hughes (1822–1896)," Tom Brown's School Museum, www.geocities.com/Paris/Rue/1896/hughes.html (accessed 20 June 2004), and John Simkin, "Thomas Hughes," Spartacus Educational, www.spartacus.schoolnet.co.uk/REhughes.htm (accessed 20 June 2004).

85. Hughes, "Public Schools, Part I," 370–71; Thomas Hughes, "The Public Schools of England, Part II," *North American Review,* July 1879, 52. See also Edward N. Saveth, "Education of an Elite," *History of Education Quarterly* 28, no. 3 (Autumn 1988): 367–86.

86. Ashburn, *Fifty Years On,* 7–10; Ashburn, *Peabody of Groton,* 11–33.

87. Ashburn, *Fifty Years On,* 14–15.

88. Ashburn, *Peabody of Groton,* 34, 65–68.

89. Levine, "Rise of American Boarding Schools," *Social Problems,* 64. The other boarding schools classified among the leading dozen by sociologists and historians are Philips Academy, Andover (1778), Phillips Exeter Academy (1783), the Hill School (1851), St. Paul's (1856), and St. Mark's (1865).

90. Levine, "Rise of American Boarding Schools," *Social Problems,* 69–73; James McLachlan, *American Boarding Schools: A Historical Study* (New York: Scribner's, 1970).

91. Ashburn, *Peabody of Groton,* 67–68.

92. TR's beloved first wife, Alice Lee, was a first cousin of Endicott Peabody's (McLachlan, *American Boarding Schools,* 242).

93. Ibid., 258–59.

94. For the names of every Groton graduate during the school's first fifty years, see Ashburn, *Fifty Years On,* 185–93.

95. I am indebted for this insight into Peabody's distinctive social location to McLachlan, *American Boarding Schools,* 268.

96. Ashburn, *Peabody of Groton,* 71.

97. McLachlan, *American Boarding Schools,* 277.

98. Ashburn, *Peabody of Groton,* 70.

99. McLachlan, *American Boarding Schools,* 278–79.

100. *Peabody of Groton,* 70.

101. Among the many fine works in the burgeoning literature on the crisis of "manliness," the best are Gail Bederman, *Manliness and Civilization: A Cultural History of Gender and Race in the United States, 1880–1917* (Chicago: Univ. of Chicago Press, 1995); Kim Townsend, *Manhood at Harvard: William James and Others* (Cambridge, Mass.: Harvard U.P., 1996); Hoganson, *Fighting for American Manhood;* and Clifford Putney, *Muscular Christianity: Manhood and Sports in Protestant America, 1880–1920* (Cambridge, Mass.: Harvard U.P., 2001). For more general treatments of the history of manhood in the United States, see E. Anthony Rotundo, *American Manhood: Transformations in Masculinity from the Revolution to the Modern Era* (New York: Basic Books, 1993), and Michael Kimmel, *Manhood in America: A Cultural History* (New York: Free Press, 1996).

102. Kingsley's principal ally in the movement to build manly Christian character was none other than Thomas Hughes, the author of *Tom Brown's School Days* (1856) and the aforementioned pair of articles on British public schools that appeared five years before the founding of Groton. On Hughes and Kingsley and the American response to their ideas, see Putney, *Muscular Christianity,* 11–25.

103. Though he was one of the founders of the movement for Christian Socialism, Kingsley, as Frank Freidel has noted, "had more interest in social reform than socialism and a closer affinity to Toryism than radicalism" (*Franklin D. Roosevelt: The Apprenticeship* [Boston: Little, Brown, 1952], 38). Burns contends that the rector's socialism somewhat resembled that of his Cambridge teacher Charles Kingsley, who "ended up

more interested in better sanitation than in economic or social reform" (Burns, *Roosevelt*, 15).

104. Ibid., 11–14.

105. Ashburn, *Peabody of Groton*, 38.

106. So deep was Peabody's admiration for Kingsley that he looked to the example of his life for guidance in romance. In 1882, as he was courting his first cousin and future wife, Fanny Peabody, he wrote to a friend: "Such a companionship and such true sympathy as Charles Kingsley and his wife had together w'd be my dream" (letter of 11 December 1882, quoted in Ashburn, *Peabody of Groton*, 61).

107. Biddle, "As I Remember Groton School," 293.

108. As they prepared for the climactic annual football game against their arch rival, American boarding school boys in the period commonly sang "Onward, Christians Soldiers" in chapel on Saturday morning before the match (Armstrong, "The Lessons of Sports," 324; letter of 23 November 1909 reprinted in Ashburn, *Peabody of Groton*, 195).

109. On the specific connection between "manliness" and "civilization" in the United States in this period, see the pathbreaking study by Bederman, *Manliness and Civilization*.

110. Armstrong, "The Lessons of Sports," 322.

111. Quoted in Walter Isaacson and Evan Thomas, *The Wise Men: Six Friends and the World They Made* (New York: Simon & Schuster, 1986), 47.

112. Ellery Sedgwick, "Three Men of Groton," *Atlantic Monthly*, July 1946.

113. Ashburn, *Peabody of Groton*, 88. In his illuminating memoir of his years at Groton ("As I Remember Groton School," 297), George Biddle, who later became an important artist, registers his agreement with Ashburn, concluding that the school's "effect was to stifle the creative impulse."

114. Ashburn, *Peabody of Groton*, 172–73. Dean Acheson remembers the atmosphere at Peabody's Groton as one of rigidity and repression: "The organization of boarding school . . . devoured my early freedom. School life was organized from the wakening bell to the policed silence which followed lights-out. All was organized — eating, studying, games, so-called free time, the whole thing. One could understand and accept rendering unto Caesar the things which were Caesar's, the control of one's external life. The mind and spirit were not Caesar's; yet these were demanded too. And I, for one, found it necessary to erect defenses for the last citadel of spiritual freedom (*Morning and Noon* [Boston: Houghton Mifflin, 1965], 24).

115. Ashburn, *Peabody of Groton*, 86. In his first year at Groton, Averell Harriman '09 told his father, the great rail magnate E. H. Harriman, that Peabody "would be an awful bully if he weren't such a terrible Christian" (Rudy Abramson, *Spanning the Century: The Life of W. Averell Harriman, 1891–1986* [New York: Morrow, 1992], 76).

116. Biddle, "As I Remember Groton School," 294; Armstrong, "Lessons of Sports," 326.

117. On the matter of his son's pumping, Biddle reports that "the Rector was splendid about it" ("As I Remember Groton School," 293–94).

118. Of Groton's environment, Arthur Schlesinger Jr. has written that "to survive unhappiness at Groton was to be capable of anything" (*The Age of Roosevelt: The Crisis of the Old Order, 1919–1933* [Boston: Houghton Mifflin, 1956], 321). Writing of Dean Acheson, Isaacson and Thomas reach a similar conclusion: hav-

ing survived humiliating taunts and pumping "with a stiff upper lip, the bullying tactics of Senator Joseph McCarthy and others would seem pale in comparison" (*Wise Men*, 55).

119. I am indebted here to the penetrating study by J. A. Mangan, *Athleticism in the Victorian and Edwardian Public School: The Emergence and Consolidation of an Educational Ideology* (Cambridge: Cambridge U.P., 1981), especially 135–39. See also J. A. Mangan, *The Games Ethic and Imperialism: Aspects of the Diffusion of an Ideal* (New York: Viking, 1985); J. A. Mangan and James Walvin, eds., *Manliness and Morality: Middle-Class Masculinity in Britain and America, 1800–1940* (New York: St. Martin's Press, 1987); and J. A. Mangan, ed., '*Benefits Bestowed*'?: *Education and British Imperialism* (Manchester, U.K.: Manchester U.P., 1988).

120. "Being a gentlemen is a responsibility," Peabody once wrote, adding that it is not "something which happens" but rather something which "must be accomplished." Though "a lot of people seem to think that it is wrong to have good manners and to be decent and to live up to standards," the rector firmly believed that one should never apologize for being a gentleman (McLachlan, *American Boarding Schools*, 286).

121. Mangan, *Athleticism*, 135.

122. Quoted in McLachlan, *American Boarding Schools*, 293.

123. Quoted in Bederman, *Manliness and Civilization*, 189.

124. "The Strenuous Life," a speech before the Hamilton Club, Chicago, 10 April 1899, in Theodore Roosevelt, *The Strenuous Life* (New York: Review of Reviews Company, 1910), 9–10.

125. Though Lodge was noncommittal in his reply, insisting that America's new possessions would be "districts or territories" but not British-style "colonies," he suggested that "if we take the Philippines or any part of them . . . we shall need there for the district government . . . a class of men precisely like those employed by England in India" (McLachlan, *American Boarding Schools*, 294).

126. Ibid., 295. Though by no means an extreme imperialist by the standards of the era, Peabody did believe "that the Anglo-Saxon race should be the predominant one for the good of the world" (quoted in Ward, *Before the Trumpet*, 190).

127. According to Nicholas Lemann (*The Big Test: The Secret History of the American Meritocracy* [New York: Farrar, Straus, 1999], 15, 353), this translation was generally used until at least the 1920s but later became embarrassing; it was often rendered as "to serve Him is to reign" rather than "to serve is to reign." Peabody's own preferred translation was the tenuous "whose service is perfect freedom" (see Isaacson and Thomas, *Wise Men*, 48).

128. Sedgwick, *Three Men of Groton*, 70.

129. I am indebted for this formulation to McLachlan, *American Boarding Schools*, 295.

130. The quote about Wall Street is from George W. Martin, "Preface to a Schoolmaster's Biography," in *Views from the Circle: Seventy-Five Years of Groton School*, ed. The Trustees of Groton School (Groton, Mass.: Groton School, 1960), 141. In the official history of Groton, released on the school's fiftieth anniversary in 1934, Ashburn discusses the contributions of Grotonians to the corporate world: "Occasionally a

business man, such as Richard Whitney, '07, who was President of the New York Stock Exchange, does become nationally important and hold in his hand the seeds of good and evil. We are too close to estimate with any assurance of success the truth of the causes for which or against which he and some of his Groton compeers fought. The important thing seems to be that they have been there, in the heat of battle, and that other men have seen hope in them, as shown by their being given responsibility and power." Not long after this passage was written, Whitney, who had ferociously opposed the Security and Exchange Act and other New Deal regulations, found himself in prison at Sing Sing, where Peabody visited him with some regularity (Ashburn, *Fifty Years* On, 166; Baltzell, *Protestant Establishment*, 242).

131. Ashburn, *Fifty Years On*, 165–66; Levine, "The Rise of American Boarding Schools," *Social Problems*, 84.

132. Martin, "Preface to a Schoolmaster's Biography," 141–42.

133. Isaacson and Thomas, *Wise Men*, 48.

134. Arthur Mann, *Yankee Reformers in the Urban Age* (Cambridge, Mass.: Harvard U.P., 1954), 77.

135. For a list of early Groton graduates with prominent careers in public service, see Ashburn, *Fifty Years On*, 173–78.

136. Davis, *FDR*, 57–59; Ward, *Before the Trumpet*, 170–71.

137. Ward, *Before the Trumpet*, 173.

138. Davis, *FDR*, 113.

139. Freidel, *Franklin D. Roosevelt: The Apprenticeship*, 40; Ward, *Before the Trumpet*, 191.

140. Morgan, *FDR*, 62–63; Ward, *Before the Trumpet*, 192.

141. Davis, *FDR*, 153.

142. This honor was bestowed on 8 of the 22 members of Roosevelt's graduating class. See Morgan, *FDR*, 64–66; Davis, *FDR*, 125.

143. From a letter of 19 December 1932; quoted in Ashburn, *Peabody of Groton*, 346.

144. In a letter to Peabody on 10 February 1936, Roosevelt wrote: "If you had not sent me a birthday card I should have been really worried. Do you know that I have every one of them that you have sent me since the earliest days after I graduated?" (Ashburn, *Peabody of Groton*, 352). On Roosevelt's wedding and his request that Peabody preside at the ceremony, see Davis, *FDR*, 191.

145. Ashburn, *Peabody of Groton*, 346–47.

146. Morgan, *FDR*, 366.

147. Ward, *Before the Trumpet*, 207.

148. Morgan, *FDR*, 373, 70. Peabody also presided over religious services at FDR's second inauguration and apparently took part in services held through 1942 on the anniversary of the president's first inauguration.

149. Ashburn, *Peabody of Groton*, 348.

150. Ibid., 347.

151. Ibid., 351.

152. Ibid., 347.

153. Biddle, "As I Remember Groton School," 300.

154. Ashburn, *Peabody of Groton*, 350. The goal of Social Gospel educators, Arthur Mann has argued, was to imbue "the Boston seminarian and collegian with the idea that he stood between the plutocrat and the proletarian" and that the task of the "altruistic and refined" gentleman was "to safeguard society against

subversion from extreme and antithetical elements" (*Yankee Reformers*, 114).

155. Ibid., 352. "As long as I live," Roosevelt wrote in 1934, "the influence of Dr. and Mrs. Peabody means and will mean more to me than that of any other people next to my father and mother." A year later, he lent his considerable prestige to a movement to obtain an honorary degree for Peabody from Cambridge University, writing to the U.S. Ambassador to Britain that the rector was "the unquestionably outstanding Head Master in the United States" (Ward, *Before the Trumpet*, 189; Davis, *FDR*, 112).

156. Ibid., 352–53.

157. Ibid., 354.

158. Ashburn, *Peabody of Groton*, 421.

159. Morgan, *FDR*, 57.

160. Ward, *Before the Trumpet*, 191–92.

161. For a detailed description of this sermon, several passages of which were marked by the young Roosevelt, see Davis, *FDR*, 130. The chapel dedicated that day had a quite conscious purpose: "This chapel," said Bishop William Lawrence at the opening ceremony, "with its pointed arches and carved finials, will suggest to the worshipping boys all that is finest and most chivalrous in the history of the Anglo-Saxon people" (McLachlan, *American Boarding Schools*, 275).

162. Ashburn, *Peabody of Groton*, 174–76.

163. Quoted in Ashburn, *Fifty Years On*, 17.

164. I am indebted for this insight into the connection between the older image of the "gentleman" and the notion of "character" to McLachlan, *American Boarding Schools*, 273.

2. The Big Three Before Selective Admissions

1. Richard Smith, *The Harvard Century: The Making of a University to a Nation* (Cambridge, Mass.: Harvard U.P., 1986), 27–28; John T. Bethell, *Harvard Observed: An Illustrated History of the University in the Twentieth Century* (Cambridge, Mass.: Harvard U.P., 1998), 16.

2. Henry James, *Charles W. Eliot: President of Harvard University, 1869–1909*, vol. 1 (Boston: Houghton Mifflin, 1930), 4–12.

3. Hugh Hawkins, *Between Harvard and America: The Educational Leadership of Charles W. Eliot* (New York: Oxford U.P., 1972), 3.

4. For a detailed account of the close connection between Boston's Brahmin families and Harvard in the nineteenth century, see Ronald Story, *The Forging of an Aristocracy: Harvard and the Boston Upper Class, 1800–1970* (Middletown, Conn.: Wesleyan U.P., 1980), and Peter D. Hall, *The Organization of American Culture, 1700–1900: Private Institutions, Elites, and the Origins of American Nationality* (New York: New York U.P., 1984), 178–206. For a more general historical treatment of Boston's upper class and its distinctive ethos, see E. Digby Baltzell, *Puritan Boston and Quaker Philadelphia: Two Protestant Ethics and the Spirit of Class Authority and Leadership* (New York: Free Press, 1979).

5. Smith, *Harvard Century*, 44, 55.

6. Marcia Graham Synnott, *The Half-Opened Door: Discrimination and Admissions at Harvard, Yale, and Princeton, 1900–1970* (Westport, Conn.: Greenwood Press, 1979), 30. On the complex history of required religious services at Princeton, see the entry under

"Chapel, the University," in Alexander Leitch, ed., *A Princeton Companion* (Princeton, N.J.: Princeton U.P., 1978), 85–89.

7. Synnott, *Half-Opened Door*, 28. Disturbed by Eliot's lack of religiosity and by the lack of spiritualism in Cambridge, Peabody wrote in 1892 to a friend who shared his interest in attracting young men to the ministry: "I confess the condition of Harvard college to-day restrains my hopefulness and I doubt if you can have anything else so long as President Eliot is at the head!" Frank D. Ashburn, *Peabody of Groton: A Portrait* (Cambridge, Mass.: Riverside Press, 1967), 109.

8. Smith, *Harvard Century*, 42.

9. For this very reason Groton students, who had led highly regimented lives in boarding school, found it far harder to adapt to Harvard than to Yale or Princeton, where they were much less likely to get into trouble (Ashburn, *Peabody of Groton*, 117–118).

10. James, *Charles W. Eliot*, 288; Hawkins, *Between Harvard and America*, 144–45.

11. Charles W. Eliot, "Inaugural Address as President of Harvard College, October 19, 1869," in *Charles W. Eliot: The Man and His Beliefs*, ed. William A. Neilson (New York: Harper & Bros., 1926), vol. 1, 20.

12. Eliot, "Inaugural Address," 18–19.

13. James, *Charles W. Eliot*, 150–51.

14. The son of Charles Francis Adams 1825, who had declined the Harvard presidency before it was offered to Eliot in 1869, Charles Francis Adams 1856 was a contemporary of Eliot's, a member of Harvard's Board of Overseers since 1882, a prominent lawyer, and a distinguished scholar in his own right. See also Bethell, *Harvard Observed*, 8, 22.

15. Eliot, "Inaugural Address," 19.

16. Charles W. Eliot, "The Function of Education in Democratic Society," in Neilson, *Charles W. Eliot*, vol. 1, 111. In his magisterial study, *The Emergence of the American University* (Chicago: Univ. of Chicago Press, 1965), 89, Laurence Veysey writes that "Eliot saw educational reform as a means of preventing social engulfment and annihilation. Like the English Tories of his own day, he was willing to give the lower classes a kind of franchise in order to avoid revolution. Intellectually a liberal, he was in these other terms a tory democrat." Henry Lee Higginson, who was perhaps Harvard's most generous donor during the Eliot years, was even more explicit about the role of education as a counterweight to the potentially radical consequences of democracy: "Democracy has got fast hold of the world, and *will* rule. Let us see that she does it more wisely and more humanly than the kings and nobles have done! Our chance is *now* — before the country is full and the struggle for bread becomes intense and bitter. Educate, and save ourselves and our families and our money from mobs!" (Cleveland Amory, *The Proper Bostonians* (New York: Dutton, 1947), 173).

17. Eliot, "Equality in a Republic," in Neilson, *Charles W. Eliot*, 2: 745.

18. Ibid., 745, 750.

19. Eliot, "The Function of a Democratic Society," in Neilson, *Charles W. Eliot*, 1: 97–114.

20. Eliot, "The Character of a Gentleman," in Neilson, *Charles W. Eliot*, 2: 539–41.

21. Ibid., 542–43.

22. For an insightful analysis of the complexity of the debate about manliness at Harvard in the late nineteenth and early twentieth centuries, see Kim Townsend, *Manhood at Harvard: William James and Others* (Cambridge, Mass.: Harvard U.P., 1996).

23. Bethell, *Harvard Observed*, 16. Eliot had spoken of the "sons of Harvard" as belonging to "the aristocracy which excels at manly sports" ("Inaugural Address," 21).

24. Samuel Eliot Morison, *Three Centuries of Harvard* (Cambridge, Mass.: Harvard U.P., 1936), 409. In his early years as president, Eliot was not beyond arguing that outdoor sports "provide invaluable safeguards against effeminacy and vice" (Bethell, *Harvard Observed*, 28).

25. Ibid., 28–29; Hawkins, *Between Harvard and America*, 114.

26. Ibid., 114–15.

27. Rudolph, *American College and University*, 376–77.

28. For accounts of the movement to eliminate football at Harvard and other institutions, see Ronald Smith, "Harvard and Columbia and a Reconsideration of the 1905–06 Football Crisis," *Journal of Sport History* 8, no. 3 (Winter 1981); Ronald Smith, *Sports and Freedom: The Rise of Big-Time College Athletics* (New York: Oxford U.P., 1988), 191–208; Mark F. Bernstein, *Football: The Ivy League Origins of an American Obsession* (Philadelphia: Univ. of Pennsylvania Press, 2001), 79–84; Michael Oriard, *Reading Football: How the Popular Press Created an American Spectacle* (Chapel Hill, N.C.: Univ. of North Carolina Press, 1993), 170; Bethell, *Harvard Observed*, 28–31; Townsend, *Manhood at Harvard*, 109–11, 104; and Hawkins, *Between Harvard and America*, 114–15.

29. When word leaked about the meeting, Columbia attempted to obtain an invitation, but President Roosevelt refused lest he would have to invite Penn and other colleges (Bernstein, *Football*, 79).

30. Bethell, *Harvard Observed*, 29.

31. Bernstein, *Football*, 80.

32. Ibid., 84.

33. Bethell, *Harvard Observed*, 309.

34. Rudolph, *American College and University*, 377; Hawkins, *Between Harvard and America*, 115.

35. Morris A. Beale, *The History of Football at Harvard* (Washington, D.C.: Columbia, 1948), 171–73.

36. Smith, *The Harvard Century*, 44. The Prussian-born Carl Schurz, who had served as a United States senator from Wisconsin from 1869 to 1875 and then as secretary of the interior for Rutherford B. Hayes, was a leading anti-imperialist spokesman in the late 1800s and early 1900s. For a revealing portrait of Schurz, see Robert Beisner, *Twelve Against Empire: The Anti-Imperialists, 1898–1900* (New York: McGraw-Hill, 1968), 18–34.

37. Hawkins, *Between Harvard and America*, 173.

38. John Gardiner, *Harvard* (New York: Oxford U.P., 1914), 56–57; Hawkins, *Between Harvard and America*, 174.

39. In the same speech, Eliot argued that the "College owes much of its distinctive character to those who, bringing hither from refined homes good breeding, gentle tastes, and a manly delicacy, add to them openness and activity of mind, intellectual interests, and a sense of public duty" ("Inaugural Address," 20–21).

40. Bethell, *Harvard Observed*, 26–27.

41. Hawkins, *Between Harvard and America*, 176; Bethell, *Harvard Observed*, 27.

42. For a list of some of the other Harvard 1910 luminaries, see ibid., 56.

43. Hawkins, *Between Harvard and America*, 171.

44. John B. Langstaff, ed., *Harvard of Today from the Undergraduate Point of View* (Cambridge, Mass.: Harvard Federation of Territorial Clubs, 1913), 11; Hawkins, *Between Harvard and America*, 170.

45. Committee on Admissions, "Report of the Chairman of the Committee on Admissions," 1910–1911, HU, 225; Bethell, *Harvard Observed*, 27.

46. In 1908, Harvard College included approximately 29 blacks and 60 foreigners. Of all the undergraduates, 19 percent were either foreign-born or the sons of immigrants. The figure on blacks is calculated from a personal communication from Caldwell Titcomb in a letter dated 18 August 1999; Eliot estimated that there were about 38 black students at Harvard in 1907, but Bethell reports that there were "about two dozen black students in 1908." The figures on foreigners and on foreign-born and sons of immigrants are calculated from Synnott, *Half-Opened Door*, 38, 53. Hawkins, *Between Harvard and America*, 192; Bethell, *Harvard Observed*, 27.

47. Eliot's discussion of the salutary effects of a "collision of views" is cited in Neil Rudenstine, *The President's Report 1993–1995*, January 1996, HU, 11. One indication of just how diverse views had become in early-twentieth-century Harvard was the formation of an active chapter of the Intercollegiate Socialist Society (ISS), whose members included Walter Lippmann and Heywood Broun. The chapter had nearly 100 members and was named by the national office of the ISS in 1911 as the strongest chapter in the nation (Seymour M. Lipset and David Riesman, *Education and Politics at Harvard* [New York: McGraw-Hill, 1975], 119).

48. Of Eliot's many accomplishments, most historians believe that his greatest was the transformation of Harvard from a somewhat provincial college into the very model of a great research university. Yet Harvard's preeminence was by no means preordained; on the contrary, other universities — above all, Johns Hopkins — initially set the standard of excellence among doctorate-granting institutions. As late as the 1880s, Johns Hopkins conferred more than three times as many doctorates as Harvard (141 vs. 40). However, by the 1900s, Eliot's last decade in office, the balance had shifted in Harvard's favor; Harvard granted 372 doctorates compared to Hopkins's 297 (calculated from James, *Charles W. Eliot*, 2: 345). In 1910, the Columbia University psychologist James Cattell ranked American scientists and placed Harvard first, well ahead of Chicago, Columbia, and Johns Hopkins, respectively. See James M. Cattell, "A Further Statistical Study of American Men of Science," *Science* 32, no. 827 (4 November 1910): 633–48; James M. Cattell, "A Further Statistical Study of American Men of Science," part 2, *Science* 32, no. 828 (11 November 1910): 672–88.

49. For a discussion of the escalating criticism during Eliot's last years in office, see Hawkins, *Between Harvard and America*, 272–82.

50. For an illuminating comparison of the two men and their views to which I am much indebted, see Synnott, *Half-Opened Door*, 26–57. See also the more detailed comparison of Eliot and Lowell in Marcia Graham Synnott, "A Social History of Admissions Policies at Harvard, Yale, and Princeton, 1900–1930" (Ph.D. diss., Univ. of Massachusetts, 1974), 174–301.

51. Henry Yeomans, *Abbot Lawrence Lowell, 1856–1943* (Cambridge, Mass.: Harvard U.P., 1948), 48–58;

Smith, *Harvard Century*, 66–67; Bethell, *Harvard Observed*, 14.

52. Ashburn, *Peabody of Groton*, 212. On the decision of the Harvard Corporation — which included among its six voting members Lowell's brother-in-law and a relative of his wife's — to select Lowell as president, see Yeomans, *Abbott Lawrence Lowell*, 83–91. As tradition dictated, Eliot recused himself during the deliberations about his successor.

53. Yeomans, *Abbott Lawrence Lowell*, 3–16; Bethell, *Harvard Observed*, 40–41; Amory, *Proper Bostonians*, 43–44. For a history of the Lowell family from the 1630s to the 1940s, see Ferris Greenslet, *The Lowells and Their Seven Worlds* (Boston: Houghton Mifflin, 1946).

54. On Lowell's undergraduate years, see Yeomans, *Abbott Lawrence Lowell*, 36–42; Smith, *Harvard Century*, 66; and Bethell, *Harvard Observed*, 41.

55. When the Porcellian Club (then called the Pig Club) was founded in 1791, one of its first members was Francis Cabot Lowell (Amory, *Proper Bostonians*, 302).

56. Yeomans, *Abbott Lawrence Lowell*, 44. The devoted Yeomans '00 had been a student of Lowell's, his colleague in the Department of Government, and for a time dean of the college during his administration.

57. In 1919, when there was a move within the Board of Overseers to dismiss Harold Laski, a socialist faculty member whose views Lowell abhorred, Lowell told a reporter that "if the Overseers ask for Laski's resignation, they will get mine!" Faced with this unappealing choice, the Overseers backed off. And when there was a movement the following year to dismiss the law professor Zechariah Chafee, who had written a book criticizing the government prosecutions under the Espionage Act of 1918, Lowell led the defense and won a narrow victory before the Board of Overseers, 6–5 (Yeomans, *Abbott Lawrence Lowell*, 315–23). On Lowell's spirited and eloquent defense of academic freedom, see also Lipset and Riesman, *Education and Politics*, 135–42.

58. A devout believer in maximum student freedom in both curricular and extracurricular matters, Eliot opposed the construction of additional student dormitories. "One could wish that the University did not offer the same contrast between the rich man's mode of life and the poor man's that the outer world offers," he sighed, "but it does, and it is not certain that the presence of this contrast is unwholesome or injurious. In this respect, as in many others, the University is an epitome of the modern world" (quoted in Smith, *Harvard Century*, 49).

59. On the reforms that Eliot introduced into undergraduate education at Harvard, see Yeomans, *Abbott Lawrence Lowell*, 121–98; Smith, *Harvard Century*, 72–76, 93–95; Bethell, *Harvard Observed*, 24–25, 42–50, 102–6, 113.

60. Abbott L. Lowell, "The Colonial Expansion of the United States," *Atlantic Monthly*, February 1899, 152.

61. Bethell, *Harvard Observed*, 43.

62. Lowell's quote from Aristotle is cited in Smith, *Harvard Century*, 93.

63. Oxford and Cambridge did not award their first doctoral degrees until 1917 and 1920, respectively.

64. Like many Progressives, Eliot was a devout believer in the contributions that experts could make to the construction of a more rational and humane social order. "Confidence in experts, and willingness to

employ them and abide by their decisions," he wrote, "are among the best signs of intelligence in an educated individual or an educated community; and in any democracy which is to thrive, this respect and confidence must be felt strongly by the majority of the population" ("Function of Education," 107). On the conflict between the ideal of the "expert" often associated with the German university and that of the "gentleman," the characteristic product of the English university (especially Oxbridge), see Duke, *Importing Oxbridge*, 63–64. In his classical essay "The 'Rationalization' of Education and Training" (in *From Max Weber: Essays in Sociology*, ed. H. H. Gerth and C. Wright Mills [New York: Oxford U.P., 1946], 243), Weber argues that the rise of bureaucracy leads to the ascendancy of the "specialist type of man" (the "expert") over the "cultivated man" (the "gentleman").

65. On the influence that the Oxbridge model exerted on Lowell, see Abbott L. Lowell, "Inaugural Address, Delivered in Front of University Hall, on Wednesday Forenoon, October 6, 1909," in *At War with Academic Traditions in America* (Westport, Conn.: Greenwood, 1934), 40; Alex Duke, *Importing Oxbridge: English Residential Colleges and American Universities* (New Haven, Conn.: Yale U.P., 1996), 95; Lipset and Riesman, *Education and Politics*, 133–134; and Bethell, *Harvard Observed*, 45, 49.

66. Yeomans, *Abbott Lawrence Lowell*, 68.

67. Barbara M. Solomon, *Ancestors and Immigrants: A Changing New England Tradition* (New York: John Wiley, 1956), 105, 204.

68. Synnott, "Social History," 202.

69. Ibid., 205.

70. In addition to Stanford's president David Starr Jordan, Bowdoin's William DeWitt Hyde, and Western Reserve's William F. Thwing, the Immigration Restriction League counted among its active members Professors John R. Commons and Edward A. Ross of the University of Wisconsin, leaders in their respective disciplines of economics and sociology (Solomon, *Ancestors and Immigrants*, 123).

71. Ibid., 187–88.

72. Synnott, "Social History," 210. So enthusiastic was Eliot about the recent wave of immigrants that in 1907 he volunteered his services to the president of the Society for Italian Immigrants, writing to him that "the more Italian immigrants that come to the United States the better . . . The only way that I can help you is to state these opinions wherever and whenever I can appropriately do so. That help I propose to give steadily" (Solomon, *Ancestors and Immigrants*, 187, 259).

73. Letter of 21 November 1892, in *Charles W. Eliot*, ed. James, vol. 1, 54.

74. Hawkins, *Between Harvard and America*, 183.

75. Synnott, *Half-Opened Door*, 37.

76. The inventor of the term "cultural pluralism" was Horace Kallen. Born in Germany and the son of an Orthodox rabbi who came to the United States in 1887, Kallen (1882–1974) went on to receive an A.B. from Harvard in 1903 and a Ph.D. in 1908. In a 1915 article in the *Nation* and a 1924 book, Kallen laid out a form of pluralism that emphasized the integrity and autonomy of immigrant ethnic groups. Also instrumental in elaborating this idea was Randolph Bourne, a 1912 Columbia graduate who was heavily influenced by Kallen. On Kallen and Bourne, see David Hollinger, *Postethnic America: Beyond Multiculturalism*

(New York: Basic Books, 1995), 11, 12, 92–96; on Kallen, see also Sarah Schmidt, *Horace M. Kallen: Prophet of American Zionism* (Brooklyn: Carlson, 1995). The seminal works on cultural pluralism include Horace Kallen, "Democracy Versus the Melting Pot," *Nation*, 18–25 February 1915; Horace Kallen, *Culture and Democracy in the United States* (New York: Boni & Liveright, 1924); and Randolph Bourne, "Trans-National America," *Atlantic Monthly*, July 1916.

77. Synnott, "Social History," 220, 224.

78. Smith, *Harvard Century*, 83; Bethell, *Harvard Observed*, 93.

79. Smith, *Harvard Century*, 89–90.

80. Lowell also vetoed the appointment of Bertrand Russell on grounds of personal character (ibid., 85–86).

81. On Lowell and women, including the case of Madame Curie, who was denied an honorary degree during the Lowell years, see ibid., 85.

82. At Lowell's eighty-second birthday party in December 1938, it was only the intervention of the university's head of security that prevented him from seeing a hand-lettered placard that virtually hid his giant birthday cake: "Sacco and Vanzetti Might Have Lived to Be Eighty-Two, Too" (Smith, *Harvard Century*, 99). On Lowell's role in the Sacco and Vanzetti case, see Yeomans, *Abbott Lawrence Lowell*, 483–96; Bethell, *Harvard Observed*, 101; and G. Joughin and Edmund Morgan, *The Legacy of Sacco and Vanzetti* (New York: Harcourt, Brace, 1948), 302–9. For Frankfurter's perspective, see Felix Frankfurter, *The Case of Sacco and Vanzetti: A Critical Analysis for Lawyers and Laymen* (Boston: Little, Brown, 1927).

83. This incident is recounted in Smith, *Harvard Century*, 85. According to a recent history of homosexuality at Harvard, the professor in question was in all likelihood the distinguished professor of art history Arthur Kingsley Porter (Douglass Shand-Tucci, *The Crimson Letter: Harvard, Homosexuality, and the Shaping of American Culture* [New York: St. Martin's Press, 2003], 125–29). On July 8, 1933, Porter drowned while on vacation in County Donegal, Ireland ("A. Kingsley Porter Drowned Off Ireland; Archaeologist Lost from Boat in Storm," *NYT*, 10 July 1933). For further evidence of Lowell's repression of gays, which included his presiding over a "Secret Court" in 1920 that resulted in the expulsion of several homosexual students, see Amit Paley, "The Secret Court of 1920," *HC*, 21 November 2002, and "In Harvard Papers, a Dark Corner of the College's Past," *NYT*, 30 November 2002.

84. Synnott, "Social History," 129–30.

85. Andrew Carnegie to Lawrence Lowell, 19 January 1911, quoted in ibid, 131.

86. Committee on Admission, "Report of the Chairman of the Committee on Admission," 1914–1915, HU, 270. "Admits" refers to applicants who received offers of admission whether or not they matriculated.

87. Yeomans, *Abbott Lawrence Lowell*, 206–7.

88. Committee on Admission, "Report of the Chairman of the Committee on Admission," 1914–1915, HU, 291.

89. "The University: The Winter Term," *Harvard Graduates' Magazine*, March 1914, 444.

90. Geoffrey Kabaservice, "Kingman Brewster and the Rise and Fall of the Progressive Establishment" (Ph.D. diss., Yale Univ., 1999), App. H. A study of Har-

vard entrants from 1906 to 1915 revealed the following ranking of feeder schools: Boston Latin (381), Exeter (302), Cambridge High and Latin (254), Noble and Greenough (232), Milton (179), Andover (168), Middlesex (146), St. Mark's (141), Groton (139), Volkmann (133), St. Paul's (131), English High (Boston) (129), Newton High (122), and Roxbury Latin (107) ("College Enrolment Broadened: Number of Men from Public Schools and from West Increased," *HC,* 8 February 1916).

91. Charles Eliot, "Why a Student Should Choose Harvard," *Harvard Graduates' Magazine,* September 1914, 52.

92. "Public and Private School Scholarships," *HC,* 16 December 1911; Morris Gray Jr., "How Students Pay Their Way," *Harvard Graduates' Magazine,* December 1913, 281–83.

93. Bethell, *Harvard Observed,* 24; Smith, *Harvard Century,* 87.

94. Synnott, *Half-Opened Door,* 96.

95. Abbott Lawrence Lowell to Charles Eliot, 2 April 1902, quoted in Yeomans, *Abbott Lawrence Lowell,* 165–66.

96. Ibid., 169.

97. Ibid., 170–73.

98. Yeomans, *Abbott Lawrence Lowell,* 173.

99. Smith, *Harvard Century,* 74.

100. Yeomans, *Abbott Lawrence Lowell,* 175; Synnott, *Half-Opened Door,* 34.

101. George Pierson, *Yale College: An Educational History, 1871–1921* (New Haven, Conn.: Yale U.P., 1952), 186–200; Harold Potter Rodes, "Educational Factors Affecting the Entrance Requirements to Yale College" (Ph.D. diss, Yale Univ., 1948), 110.

102. Daniel A. Oren, *Joining the Club: A History of Jews and Yale* (New Haven, Conn.: Yale U.P., 1985), 104.

103. Ashburn, *Peabody of Groton,* 212.

104. George Pierson, *A Yale Book of Numbers: Historical Statistics of the College and University, 1701–1976* (New Haven, Conn.: Yale U.P., 1983), 80.

105. The public school figures are derived from my study of the entering classes of 1900 at Harvard and Yale. For Harvard, see *Twenty-fifth Anniversary Report: Class of 1904,* HU. For Yale, consult *Preliminary List of Officers and Students of Yale University, 1900–1901* (New Haven, Conn.: Tuttle, Morehouse & Taylor, 1900), and *Yale Class Books, Tenth Anniversary Records,* and *Twenty-Fifth Anniversary Records* for Classes of 1903–1907, YU. Though less residentially segregated than Harvard, turn-of-the-century Yale did have a private dormitory, known as "the Hutch," in which wealthy students congregated. See Pierson, *Yale College,* 235, 239.

106. In six classes (1905–1910) at Harvard, the combined membership of Porcellian and A.D. (the two most prestigious clubs) included not a single student from a public high school nor anyone from the relatively democratic boarding schools of Andover and Exeter. Between 1907 and 1910, 76 of 88 members came from Boston and New York alone. On the exclusionary character of Harvard's final clubs, see Owen Johnson, "The Social Usurpation of Colleges, Part II — Harvard," *Collier's,* 25 May 1912.

107. Calvin Trillin '57 grew up in Kansas City and recounts the story of how his father, growing up in a poor Russian-Jewish immigrant family in St. Joseph, Missouri, read *Stover at Yale* as a young man. He

named his son Calvin "because he believed, incorrectly, that it would be an appropriate name for someone at Yale" (Calvin Trillin, *Remembering Denny* [New York: Farrar, Straus, 1993], 34). Owen McMahon Johnson (1878–1952), the author of *Stover at Yale,* was the son of Robert Underwood Johnson, a writer who was an editor of *Century* magazine and, later, ambassador to Italy. A graduate of Lawrenceville, Johnson entered Yale in 1896 but disliked its snobbery, its senior societies, and its curriculum. Though editor of the *Yale Literary Magazine,* he failed to be tapped by a secret society. Best known for a series of novels that became known as the Lawrenceville stories, *Stover at Yale* was one of his most ambitious works. Its publication was followed by a much-discussed five-part series in *Collier's* in 1912, "The Social Usurpation of Our Colleges." Johnson was a Republican until 1932, when he became a Democrat and supported Roosevelt. He ran unsuccessfully as a Democratic candidate for Congress in 1936 and 1938. For biographical information on Johnson, see *WWA, 1926–1927;* Robert Gale, "Johnson, Owen McMahon," *American National Biography Online,* www.anb.org (accessed 12 April 2003); and J. M. Brook, "Owen Johnson," *Dictionary of Literary Biography Yearbook: 1987* (Detroit: Gale Research, 1988), 316–25. More than half a century later, Yale's president Kingman Brewster discussed the contemporary relevance of *Stover* in his foreword to Owen Johnson, *Stover at Yale* (1912; New York: Collier Books, 1968).

108. Ibid., 10, 25, 335.

109. Ibid., 384. For a fine discussion of *Stover* and the Yale "code," see Nicholas Lemann, *The Big Test: The Secret History of the American Meritocracy* (New York: Farrar, Straus, 1999), 142–43. On *Stover,* see also Robert J. Higgs, "Yale and the Heroic Ideal, *Götterdämmerung* and Palingenesis, 1865–1914," in *Manliness and Morality,* ed. J. A. Mangan and James Walvin (New York: St. Martin's Press, 1987), 160–75; Brook, "Owen Johnson," 316–25; and David Lamoreaux, "*Stover at Yale* and the Gridiron Metaphor," *Journal of Popular Culture* 11, no. 2 (Fall 1977): 330–44.

110. On Yale's distinctive culture in the early decades of the twentieth century, see the illuminating portraits in Lawrence R. Veysey, "Yale Students in a Changing Society," *YAM,* November 1969; Johnson, "Social Usurpation, Part III — Yale," 8 June 1912; and Edmund Wilson, "Harvard, Princeton, and Yale," *Forum,* September 1923.

111. Walter Isaacson and Evan Thomas, *The Wise Men: Six Friends and the World They Made* (New York: Simon & Schuster, 1986), 82.

112. "Yale Juniors Now in Fix of 'Stover,'" *NYT,* 12 May 1912.

113. Isaacson and Thomas, *Wise Men,* 82. Among the many other prominent Yale alumni who belonged to Skull and Bones were William F. Buckley Jr., McGeorge Bundy, Potter Stewart, and William Sloane Coffin Jr.

114. Johnson, "Social Usurpation, Part III — Yale," 23.

115. Edwin E. Slosson, *Great American Universities* (New York: Macmillan, 1910), 47.

116. In the last paragraph of *Stover,* Brockhurst, an intellectual and critic who is not elected to a senior society, describes Yale as "a magnificent factory on democratic business lines." Elsewhere, speaking of American higher education in general, he argues that

"our universities are simply the expression of the forces that are operating outside. We are business colleges purely and simply, because we as a nation have only one ideal — the business ideal" (Johnson, *Stover at Yale*, 238, 385–86).

117. Pierson, *Yale College*, 25.

118. Veysey, "Yale Students," 28.

119. Henry S. Canby, *Alma Mater: The Gothic Age of the American College* (Murray Hill, N.Y.: Farrar & Rinehart, 1936), 70–71. Canby's observations about Yale were based on a half century of experience. Graduating from Yale in 1899, he received his Ph.D. in 1905 and taught there from 1900, rising to the rank of full professor in 1922. He was the author of many books, including *College Sons and Fathers* (1915), *Everyday Americans* (1920), and *The Age of Confidence* (1934), and served as editor of the *Saturday Review of Literature* (1924–1936).

120. Johnson, "Social Usurpation, Part III — Yale," 13, 25. At Harvard, the combined membership of Porcellian and A.D. for the Classes of 1905–1910 produced only one member of Phi Beta Kappa (Johnson, "Social Usurpation, Part II — Harvard," 14.

121. Oren, *Joining the Club*, 87.

122. On Catholics at early-twentieth-century Yale, see Synnott, *Half-Opened Door*, 130–33.

123. No Jew, for example, served as chairman of the *Yale Daily News* (hereafter *YDN*) until Calvin Trillin '57, in 1956. See Oren, *Joining the Club*, 162; see also Synnott, *Half-Opened Door*, 145–47.

124. Oren, *Joining the Club*, 37, 342.

125. According to figures reported in Oren, 1,294 Jews entered Yale between 1900 and 1929. Though Synnott reports that a Jew was elected to Elihu early in the century, Oren, who has written the definitive history of Jews at Yale, concluded that "no Jews entered a senior society prior to 1937" (*Joining the Club*, 320–21, 342; Synnott, *Half-Opened Door*, 145).

126. These figures are drawn from Oren, *Joining the Club*, 23–24.

127. Pierson, *Yale College*, 238–39; Rodes, "Educational Factors," 107.

128. Pierson, *Yale College*, 239.

129. Rodes, "Educational Factors," 107.

130. Ibid., 110.

131. "Harvard, The National University," *Harvard Graduates' Magazine*, September 1904, 210.

132. Rodes, "Educational Factors," 113, 117–19.

133. Pierson, *Yale College*, 402, 410; Rodes, "Educational Factors," 125–26.

134. Calculated from Pierson, *Yale Book of Numbers*, 94.

135. See Henry May, *The End of American Innocence: A Study of the First Years of Our Own Time* (New York: Columbia U.P., 1992), for a vivid portrait of the cultural politics of the years just before America's entry into World War I.

136. Robin W. Winks, *Cloak & Gown: Scholars in the Secret War, 1939–1961* (New York: Quill–William Morrow, 1987), 28.

137. Henry Stimson and McGeorge Bundy, *On Active Service in Peace and War* (New York: Harper & Bros., 1948), xv.

138. Bernard Drabeck and Helen Ellis, eds., *Archibald MacLeish Reflections* (Amherst, Mass.: Univ. of Massachusetts Press, 1986), 17. Elsewhere, MacLeish reported on a conversation with a Harvard professor who was lecturing at Yale, whose view was that the

"Yale undergraduates are a) more gentlemanly, b) more homogeneous, and c) less mature by a year than Harvard dittos" (R. H. Winnick, ed., *Letters of Archibald MacLeish, 1907–1982* [Boston: Houghton Mifflin, 1983], 58). Other Yale alumni who agreed with this view included Sinclair Lewis '07, who advised a nephew with literary aspirations to go to Harvard rather than Yale, and Dean Acheson '15 (Richard Lingeman, *Sinclair Lewis: Rebel from Main Street* [New York: Random House, 2002], 21; Isaacson and Thomas, *Wise Men*, 87).

139. George Marsden, *The Soul of the American University: From Protestant Establishment to Established Nonbelief* (New York: Oxford U.P., 1994), 219; Henry Bragdon, *Woodrow Wilson: The Academic Years* (Cambridge, Mass.: Belknap Press, 1967), 202; and Thomas Jefferson Wertenbaker, *Princeton: 1746–1896* (Princeton, N.J.: Princeton U.P., 1946), 344–46.

140. Marsden, *Soul of the American University*, 220.

141. Ibid., 221–22.

142. The anecdote about the student complaint was one of Wilson's favorites (Don Oberdorfer, *Princeton University: The First 250 Years* [Princeton, N.J.: Trustees of Princeton University, 1995], 102). See also Ray Stannard Baker, *Woodrow Wilson: Life and Letters Princeton 1890–1910* (Garden City, N.Y.: Doubleday, Page, 1927), 150; Bragdon, *Woodrow Wilson*, 274; and Marsden, *Soul of the American University*, 223.

143. Bragdon, *Woodrow Wilson*, 272–73. See also William K. Selden, *Club Life at Princeton: An Historical Account of the Eating Clubs at Princeton University* (Princeton, N.J.: Princeton Prospect Foundation, 1994), 16–18, and Marsden, *Soul of the American University*, 222.

144. Marsden, *Soul of the American University*, 223.

145. The nine leading boarding schools studied are Groton, Hill, Hotchkiss, Lawrenceville, Andover, Exeter, St. George's, St. Mark's, and St. Paul's. If one includes three additional top boarding schools (Taft, Milton, and Pomfret), Yale gains an additional 25 students (to 179), Harvard an additional 26 (to 143), but Princeton only a single student (to 63). This information was drawn from my study of the entering classes of 1900 at Harvard, Yale, and Princeton. For Princeton, the secondary schools attended were taken from the *Nassau Herald, Class of 1904*; "Princeton Undergraduate Alumni Index 1748–1920," Seeley Mudd Ms. Library Online Database, www.princeton.edu/~mudd/databases/alumni.html (accessed 11 November 2003); and "Registrars Entrance Records," 1888–1900, PC. For Harvard, the secondary schools were taken from the *Harvard Class of 1904: Twenty-fifth Anniversary Report*. For Yale, the list of students was taken from the *Preliminary List of Officers and Students of Yale University, 1900–1901*, and the secondary schools for these students were taken from the class books, tenth-year reunion reports, and twenty-fifth-year reunion reports for the classes of 1903–1907.

146. The quotes are from Bragdon, *Woodrow Wilson*, 274.

147. Ibid., 274–76; Oberdorfer, *Princeton University*, 101.

148. Bragdon, *Woodrow Wilson*, 275; "Princeton in the Nation's Service" in Leitch, *Princeton Companion*, 385–87.

149. Kendrick Clements, *Woodrow Wilson: World Statesman* (Chicago: Ivan R. Dee, 1999), 1–3.

150. August Heckscher, *Woodrow Wilson* (New

York: Scribner's, 1991), 12; Clements, *Woodrow Wilson*, 3; Bragdon, *Woodrow Wilson*, 5, 11.

151. Clements, *Woodrow Wilson*, 6–7; Bragdon, *Woodrow Wilson*, 11–12.

152. Synnott, *Half-Opened Door*, 165.

153. Bragdon, *Woodrow Wilson*, 286.

154. In 1901, Princeton enrolled only 117 graduate students — most of them attached to the Presbyterian Theological Seminary — out of a total of 1,370 (John A. Thompson, *Woodrow Wilson: Profiles in Power* [London: Pearson Education, 2002], 44; Varnum Lansing Collins, *Princeton* [New York: Oxford U.P., 1914], 410).

155. Baker, *Woodrow Wilson*, 150–51.

156. On Patton's views, see Marsden, *Soul of the American University*, 223, and Selden, *Club Life*, 16.

157. "Report of the President," 1906–1907, PU, 16–17.

158. Woodrow Wilson, untitled editorial, *Daily Princetonian* (hereafter *DP*), 26 April 1877.

159. Baker, *Woodrow Wilson*, 80–81, 90–93; see also Duke, *Importing Oxbridge*, 9, 81–82.

160. Clements, *Woodrow Wilson*, 32.

161. Bragdon, *Woodrow Wilson*, 289, 299.

162. Thompson, *Woodrow Wilson*, 45.

163. Woodrow Wilson, "Press Club Banquet," *DP*, 17 April 1905.

164. On how the preceptorial system, which was introduced in the autumn of 1905, actually worked in practice, see Bragdon, *Woodrow Wilson*, 304–8, 359–60.

165. "Privately expressing the wish that Bryant . . . be 'knocked into a cocked hat,' Wilson maintained publicly that he was 'the most charming and lovable of men personally, but foolish and dangerous in his political beliefs'" (Bragdon, *Woodrow Wilson*, 344).

166. Baker, *Woodrow Wilson*, 197.

167. On the very night of Harvey's speech, Wilson sent him a warm letter of thanks for his remarks, writing that it was "most delightful to have such thoughts uttered about me." Though Wilson claimed that he was not taking "at all seriously the suggestion made by Colonel Harvey," the idea of his nomination for the presidency received a warm response in many newspapers and magazines across the nation (Arthur Link, *Wilson: The Road to the White House* [Princeton, N.J.: Princeton U.P., 1947], 98–102; Bragdon, *Woodrow Wilson*, 338–339).

168. Bragdon, *Woodrow Wilson*, 317–18.

169. Selden, *Club Life*, 20. See also Baker, *Woodrow Wilson*, 220, and Bragdon, *Woodrow Wilson*, 316.

170. Bragdon, *Woodrow Wilson*, 319–20.

171. Baker, *Woodrow Wilson*, 229–30; Link, *Wilson*, 46–48; Bragdon, *Woodrow Wilson*, 320–21.

172. "Wilson to Abolish Clubs," *NYT*, 25 June 1907; Bragdon, *Woodrow Wilson*, 321; Link, *Wilson*, 48.

173. Bragdon, *Woodrow Wilson*, 324–25; Link, *Wilson*, 53–54.

174. Thompson, *Woodrow Wilson*, 46.

175. In the nineteenth century, Princeton had primarily depended on Presbyterian associations for financial support. But this had changed in 1900, when the alumni were first empowered to elect trustees, and in 1904, when the "Committee of Fifty" was created to raise funds for "the immediate necessities and future development of the University." As early as 1902, Wilson had noted with dismay Princeton's growing dependence on alumni donations, calling it "a very unsound, a very unsafe business situation." Yet Wilson's cherished preceptorial system was extremely expensive and would not have been possible without generous alumni donations — which underscored the reality that, as Henry Bragdon noted, "a few wealthy alumni . . . had a potential veto on educational policy" (Selden, *Club Life*, 19–20; "Alumni Council," in Leitch, *Princeton Companion*, 10; Bragdon, *Woodrow Wilson*, 308).

176. Arthur H. Osborn to Woodrow Wilson, 9 July 1907, in Arthur S. Link, ed., *The Papers of Woodrow Wilson*, Vol. 17: 1907–1908 (Princeton, N.J.: Princeton U.P., 1974), 266–67. See also the discussion of the alumni's reaction to Wilson's plan in Synnott, *Half-Opened Door*, 168.

177. Bragdon, *Woodrow Wilson*, 302.

178. Henry Fairfield Osborn to Woodrow Wilson, 17 September 1907, in Link, ed. *Papers of Woodrow Wilson*, 389–91; Synnott, *Half-Opened Door*, 168.

179. At the time Wilson presented his Quadrangle Plan to the trustees, nearly a third of them were regular or associate members of the Ivy Club (Selden, *Club Life*, 24).

180. Bragdon, *Woodrow Wilson*, 323–24. In the parlance of the time, a "mucker" was a person of low or vulgar origin.

181. Ibid., 322.

182. E. Digby Baltzell, *The Protestant Establishment: Aristocracy & Caste in America* (New York: Vintage, 1964), 136.

183. After a trip to the United States in 1904, Max Weber observed that for wealthy American businessmen, "affiliation with a distinguished club is essential above all else . . . He who did not succeed in joining was no gentleman" (Gerth and Mills, *From Max Weber*, 310–11). On the importance of metropolitan clubs in the social organization of the American upper class, see Baltzell, *Protestant Establishment*, 135–42, and E. Digby Baltzell, *Philadelphia Gentleman: The Making of a National Upper Class* (Glencoe, Ill.: Free Press, 1958). On the parallelism between the hierarchy of final clubs at Harvard and the hierarchy of men's clubs in Boston, see Amory, *Proper Bostonians*, 300–301.

184. Adding to the weight of Murray's announcement was that Princeton was already running an annual deficit of about $100,000 — a product in good part of the expensive preceptorial system. The year 1907 was, moreover, one of panic on Wall Street, and the wealthy men on the Board of Trustees were genuinely worried about Princeton's financial situation (Bragdon, *Woodrow Wilson*, 323–26).

185. Selden, *Club Life*, 24.

186. Baker, *Woodrow Wilson*, 260–62; Bragdon, *Woodrow Wilson*, 225–26.

187. By 1948, over 99 percent of Princeton upperclassmen belonged to eating clubs (Selden, *Club Life*, 35, 34, 98).

188. Baker, *Woodrow Wilson*, 270; Bragdon, *Woodrow Wilson*, 331.

189. Thompson, *Woodrow Wilson*, 50.

190. Ibid., 50.

191. Ibid.; Clements, *Woodrow Wilson*, 53.

192. Bragdon, *Woodrow Wilson*, 330–31. The first indication that Wilson was becoming disenchanted with the wealthy men who controlled Princeton came in the summer of 1907, when it became apparent that the opposition to his Quad Plan was mounting. In a conversation with his brother-in-law, Stockton Axson, Wilson said that "these people are not fighting me out

of reason; they are fighting on the basis of their privilege, and privilege never yields" (Clements, *Woodrow Wilson*, 40).

193. Ibid., 46–47.

194. In a letter to the *Times* editor Henry B. Brougham, Wilson described the issue as a fight between "a college life in which all the bad elements of social ambition and unrest intruded themselves, and a life ordered upon a simpler plan under the domination of real university influence and upon a basis of real democracy." For details of Wilson's involvement in the *Times* editorial, see Bragdon, *Woodrow Wilson*, 371–72, and Link, *Wilson*, 74–76.

195. Clements, *Woodrow Wilson*, 48; Bragdon, *Woodrow Wilson*, 387; Thompson, *Woodrow Wilson*, 51.

196. Bragdon, *Woodrow Wilson*, 377; Baker, *Woodrow Wilson*, 340–341; Link, *Wilson*, 83.

197. Baker, *Woodrow Wilson*, 341–342.

198. Oberdorfer, *Princeton University*, 107.

199. Among the positions below professional rank, just 28 percent held Princeton degrees in 1910–1911, compared to 78 percent when Wilson was inaugurated in 1902 (Bragdon, *Woodrow Wilson*, 361).

200. Heckscher, *Woodrow Wilson*, 197. Between 1902–1903 and 1909–1910, the total number of graduate students increased less than 10 percent, from 124 to 134 (Slosson, *Great American Universities*, 109).

201. "Report of the President," 1909–1910, PU, 15.

202. Synnott, *Half-Opened Door*, 174.

203. "Report of the President."

204. Synnott, *Half-Opened Door*, 172.

205. In 1910, Trenton's population was 96,815, compared to Cambridge's 104,839 and New Haven's 133,605. Yet in 1900, while the public high schools of Cambridge and New Haven provided Harvard and Yale, respectively, with 20 and 31 students, Trenton's public schools sent not a single student to Princeton. In 1920, three students from Trenton High School enrolled at Harvard, nearly 300 miles away; that same year, Princeton once again enrolled no public school students from Trenton. The statistics on the entering classes of 1920 at Princeton were calculated from *Nassau Herald: Class of 1924* and registration cards from the fall of 1920 provided by PU. For Harvard's entering class, I consulted *Twenty-Fifth Anniversary Report: Class of 1924, Freshman Redbook: Class of 1924*, and the *Class Album: Class of 1924*. The population figures for 1900 are from James Langland, *The Chicago Daily News Almanac and Year-book 1915* (Chicago: Chicago Daily News, 1914), 157–59. The statistics on the entering class of 1900 at the Big Three are from my study of them, cited in note 5 of Chapter 1.

206. Synnott, *Half-Opened Door*, 173.

207. In addition to applying for the limited number of scholarships, Princeton students could also seek work through the Bureau of Student Self-Help, which in 1913 assisted 169 students (Collins, *Princeton*, 392). But under Wilson, Princeton students — unlike their peers at other New England colleges — did not wait on tables; it was in Wilson's view labor "ordinarily rendered by negroes" and would inevitably lead students so employed to lose "self-respect and social standing" (Synott, *Half-Opened Door*, 173).

208. Slosson, *Great American Universities*, 1904.

209. F. Scott Fitzgerald, quoted in Arthur Mizener, *The Far Side of Paradise: A Biography of F. Scott Fitzgerald* (Boston: Houghton Mifflin, 1951), 261. As Mizener has noted, Fitzgerald's image of Yale men as

"brawny and brutal and powerful" seems to have informed the portrayal in *The Great Gatsby* of Tom Buchanan, "one of the most powerful ends that ever played football at Yale."

210. Ibid., 29; Andrew Turnbull, *Scott Fitzgerald* (New York: Scribner's, 1962), 44.

211. Only 18.5 percent of Princeton's entering class of 1913 came from public high schools. In Fitzgerald's freshman class were 154 Presbyterians, 131 Episcopalians, 36 Catholics, and 12 "Hebrews" ("Report of the President," 1913–1914, PU, 33–34).

212. John D. Davies, *The Legend of Hobey Baker* (Boston: Little, Brown, 1966), 58.

213. The quote is from F. Scott Fitzgerald, *This Side of Paradise* (1920; New York: Scribner's, 1953), 42, and is cited in Davis, *Legend of Hobey Baker*, 69. Page references are to the 1953 edition. Davies's book is the best treatment of the life of Hobey Baker and of the mythical status he attained. A fighter squadron commander in World War I, he died at the age of twenty-six in December 1918 with his discharge papers in his pocket while testing a repaired plane. So great was Baker's legend that when an artificial ice rink was announced as his memorial, contributions poured in from 1,537 men from thirty-nine colleges, including 172 from Harvard and 90 from Yale ("Baker Memorial Rink," in Leitch, *Princeton Companion*, 37–38). Fitzgerald once said that in Hobey Baker he found "an ideal worthy of everything in my enthusiastic admiration, yet consummated and expressed in a human being who stood within ten feet of me" (Mizener, *Far Side of Paradise*, 6).

214. Fitzgerald, *This Side of Paradise*, 44.

215. Years later, he told a friend that "though I might have been more *comfortable* in Quadrangle, for instance, where there were lots of literary minded boys, I was never sorry about my choice" (Mizener, *Far Side of Paradise*, 50). See also Turnbull, *Scott Fitzgerald*, 57, and Matthew Bruccoli, *Some Sort of Epic Grandeur: The Life of F. Scott Fitzgerald* (Columbia, S.C.: University of South Carolina Press, 2002), 54–55.

216. Describing the Princeton ethos, Fitzgerald writes that "standing for anything very strongly . . . was running it out," as was "talking of clubs" (*This Side of Paradise*, 25). For an excellent discussion of the ideal Princeton man and how he differed from his counterparts at Yale and Harvard, see Kenneth Davis, *The Politics of Honor: A Biography of Adlai Stevenson* (New York: Putnam, 1957), 65–66.

217. Comparing Princeton to its Big Three rivals, Blaine says, "I want to go to Princeton. I don't know why but I think of all the Harvard men as sissies, like I used to be, and all Yale men as wearing big blue sweaters and smoking pipes" (Fitzgerald, *This Side of Paradise*, 25).

218. Bruccoli, *Epic Grandeur*, 32.

219. Fitzgerald, *This Side of Paradise*, 45.

220. Bruccoli, *Epic Grandeur*, 45; Mizener, *Far Side of Paradise*, 46–47.

221. Jeffrey Meyers, *Edmund Wilson: A Biography* (Boston: Houghton Mifflin, 1995), 1–26. Though Wilson once said that the eating clubs were "hopelessly dull," he often returned to the Charter Club, where he stayed on his many trips to Princeton in search of peace and quiet (Arthur Mizener, introduction to Davies, *The Legend of Hobey Baker*, vii). On Wilson's close but complicated relationship with Fitzgerald, whom he initially considered "ignorant, shallow, and

foolish," see Meyers, *Edmund Wilson*, 26–27, and Turnbull, *Scott Fitzgerald*, 58–60. When Fitzgerald died in April 1940 without having completed *The Last Tycoon*, it was Wilson who edited the manuscript and had it published the following year.

222. Fitzgerald, *This Side of Paradise*, 42–43.

223. Ibid., 36.

224. In his letter to Hibben, Fitzgerald wrote that "I have had no fault with Princeton that I can't find with Oxford and Cambridge," adding, "The men — the undergraduates of Yale and Princeton — are cleaner, healthier, better-looking, better-dressed, wealthier and more attractive than any undergraduate body in the country." But while he loved Princeton "better than any place on earth," his time there wasn't particularly happy and "his idealism flickered out with [the defeat of] Harry Strater's anticlub movement" (Bruccoli, *Epic Grandeur*, 125–26). On the anticlub movement of 1917, which initially reduced club membership by 25 percent and then petered out during World War I, see Selden, *Club Life*, 28–29; Mizener, *Far Side of Paradise*, 58–59; and "Princeton's Anti-Club Fight Stirs the University," *NYT*, 21 January 1917.

225. In 1962, Princeton's director of admissions, C. William Edwards, told a visiting journalist, "You can't begin to estimate the harm F. Scott Fitzgerald did us with his idea of Princeton as a country club" (Mayer, "How to Get into Princeton," 16).

226. For an excellent analysis of the historical function of country clubs, see Baltzell, *American Business Aristocracy*, 394–403, and Baltzell, *Protestant Establishment*, 123–24, 213–14, 355–62.

227. In the end, Levy transferred to the University of Pennsylvania, where he received an LL.B. in 1906 (Synnott, *Half-Opened Door*, 183–84).

228. Slosson, *Great American Universities*, 105.

229. Fitzgerald, *This Side of Paradise*, 47–48.

230. "Report of the President," 1917–1918, PU, 50.

231. Oren, *Joining the Club*, 320; Synnott, *Half-Opened Door*, 96. My estimate of the Jewish population of Boston in 1918 is based on statistics in the *American Jewish Year Book, 5681: September 13, 1920, to October 2, 1921* (Philadelphia: Jewish Publication Society, 1920), 22: 373–74.

232. "Meeting of Association of New England Deans Held in Princeton," minutes, 9–10 May 1918, YUA, 21–22.

3. Harvard and the Battle over Restriction

1. Bureau of the Census, *Historical Statistics of the United States: Colonial Times to 1970*, Bicentennial Edition, Part 1 (Washington, D.C.: Government Printing Office, 1989), 105.

2. On 100 percent Americanism, see John Higham, *Strangers in the Land: Patterns of American Nativism, 1860–1925* (New Brunswick, N.J.: Rutgers U.P., 1992), 204–12. Eric Foner, *The Story of American Freedom* (New York: Norton, 1998), 187.

3. Howard Zinn, *The Twentieth Century: A People's History* (New York: Perennial, 2003), 84–85; Nell Irvin Painter, *Standing at Armageddon: The United States, 1877–1919* (New York: Norton, 1987), 335.

4. Foner, *American Freedom*, 177. See also Higham, *Strangers*, 210.

5. Foner, *American Freedom*, 177; Higham, *Strangers*, 210.

6. Gary Gerstle, *American Crucible: Race and Na-*

tion in the Twentieth Century (Princeton, N.J.: Princeton U.P., 2001), 55.

7. See, for example, the entries on various nationalities in *Reports of the Immigration Commission, Dictionary of Races or Peoples* (Washington, D.C.: Government Printing Office, 1911). On the secession of the "Anglo-Saxons" from the larger "Teutonic" race in which they had claimed membership before America's entry into World War I, see Higham, *Strangers*, 201–2.

8. Long before the Immigration Act of 1917, the principle of group exclusion had been applied to both the Chinese (the Chinese Exclusion Act of 1882) and the Japanese (the Gentlemen's Agreement of 1907) (Gerstle, *American Crucible*, 96).

9. Ibid., 97.

10. Higham, *Strangers*, 203–4. The three founders of the Immigration Restriction League, all Harvard 1889, were Prescott Hall, Robert DeCourcy Ward, and Charles Warren, who acted with the assistance of Joseph Lee 1883 and Richards M. Bradley 1882. From the outset, two men — Hall and Ward — dominated its activities. See Barbara M. Solomon, *Ancestors and Immigrants: A Changing New England Tradition* (New York: John Wiley, 1956), 40. Higham, *Strangers*, 102–3; Marcia Graham Synnott, *The Half-Opened Door: Discrimination and Admissions at Harvard, Yale, and Princeton, 1900–1970* (Westport, Conn.: Greenwood Press, 1979), 96, 182.

11. Harold Wechsler, *The Qualified Student: A History of Selective College Admission in America* (New York: John Wiley, 1977), 138. Wechsler includes a fascinating, detailed account of Columbia's pioneering efforts, beginning around 1910, to limit the number of Jews in the freshman class.

12. For a vivid profile of London, who was born in eastern Europe and whose father ran an unprofitable anarchist print shop, see Irving Howe, *World of Our Fathers: The Journey of the East European Jews to America and the Life They Found and Made* (New York: Harcourt, Brace, 1976), 315–19.

13. Gerstle, *American Crucible*, 102.

14. On the "Red Scare," see Painter, *Standing at Armageddon*, 376–82; Gerstle, *American Crucible*, 92–94, 98–99; and Foner, *American Freedom*, 179.

15. That Russian Jews were disproportionately drawn to movements of the left, including socialism and communism, in the early twentieth century is a staple of the historical literature. But the best evidence indicates that the majority of Jewish socialists at the time of the Russian Revolution were in fact Mensheviks (members of the more reformist faction) rather than Bolsheviks (the more radical faction, led by Lenin); see Robert J. Brym, *The Jewish Intelligentsia and Russian Marxism: A Sociological Study of Intellectual Radicalism and Ideological Divergence* (London: Macmillan, 1988). For a useful account of the disproportionate participation of Jews in organizations and movements of the left, see Arthur Liebman, *Jews and the Left* (New York: John Wiley, 1979), and Yuri Slezkine, *The Jewish Century* (Princeton, N.J.: Princeton U.P., 2004).

16. Gerstle, *American Crucible*, 100.

17. Higham, *Strangers*, 279.

18. Gerstle, *American Crucible*, 100–1; Higham, *Strangers*, 278–81.

19. The classic works on scientific racism are Thomas Gossett, *Race: The History of An Idea in America* (New York: Oxford U.P., 1997); Stephen Jay

Gould, *The Mismeasure of Man* (New York: Norton, 1981); and Daniel Kevles, *In the Name of Eugenics: Genetics and the Uses of Human Heredity* (Cambridge, Mass.: Harvard U.P., 1995). For a detailed analysis of where Jews fit into the schemas of the scientific racists, see Robert Singerman, "The Jew as Racial Alien: The Genetic Component of American Anti-Semitism," in *Anti-Semitism in American History,* ed. David Gerber (Urbana: Univ. of Illinois Press, 1986), 103–28.

20. See *Dictionary of American Biography; American National Biography;* "Madison Grant, 71, Zoologist, Is Dead," *NYT,* 31 May 1937; Higham, *Strangers,* 155–56; and Gossett, *Race,* 353–54.

21. Higham, *Strangers,* 156.

22. Solomon, *Ancestors and Immigrants,* 40.

23. For insightful analyses of the social and psychological foundations of Adams's anti-Semitism, see E. Digby Baltzell, *The Protestant Establishment: Aristocracy and Caste in America* (New York: Vintage, 1964), 90–93, and Solomon, *Ancestors and Immigrants,* 36–41.

24. Madison Grant, *The Passing of the Great Race* (New York: Scribner's, 1924), 13–36. At times, however, Grant was less inclined to grant Alpines and Mediterraneans the fully Caucasian status that he granted Nordics. "The term 'Caucasian race,'" he wrote, "has ceased to have any meaning except where it is used, in the United States, to contrast white populations with Negroes or Indians or in the Old World with Mongols" (ibid., 65).

25. Ibid., 167–68, 142–43, 227–29.

26. Ibid., 82; see also Matthew Frye Jacobson, *Whiteness of a Different Color: European Immigrants and the Alchemy of Race* (Cambridge, Mass.: Harvard U.P., 1998), 82.

27. Grant, *Passing of the Great Race,* 33–34.

28. Ibid., 83.

29. Ibid., 16–18.

30. Grant also wrote of Jews: "These immigrants adopt the language of the native American, they wear his clothes, they steal his name and they are beginning to take his women, but they seldom adopt his religion or understand his ideals and while he is being elbowed out of his own home the American looks calmly abroad and urges on others the suicidal ethics which are exterminating his own race" (ibid., 16, 91).

31. Ibid., 18.

32. Higham, *Strangers,* 272; "Madison Grant, 71."

33. Higham, *Strangers,* 272; Gossett, *Race,* 362; George McDaniel, "Madison Grant and the Racialist Movement," *American Renaissance,* December 1997.

34. Higham, *Strangers,* 271; Joseph Bendersky, *The "Jewish Threat": Anti-Semitic Politics of the U.S. Army* (New York: Basic Books, 2000), 162.

35. Bendersky, "Jewish Threat," 162. In 1922, Roberts's articles from the *Saturday Evening Post* were collected into a widely read book, *When Europe Leaves Home* (Indianapolis: Bobbs-Merrill, 1922). In his widely read volume, Roberts concluded that America had been "founded and developed by the Nordic race, but if a few more million members of the Alpine, Mediterranean and Semitic races are poured among us, the result must inevitably be a hybrid race of people as worthless and futile as the good-for-nothing mongrels of Central America and Southeastern Europe" (quoted in Gossett, *Race,* 402).

36. *American National Biography;* "Dr. Henry F. Osborn Dies in His Study," and *NYT,* 7 November 1935; and *WWA, 1926–1927.*

37. Osborn, preface to 2nd ed. of Grant, *Passing of the Great Race,* xi.

38. Ibid., vii–ix.

39. Ibid., xi.

40. Quoted in Gossett, *Race,* 389.

41. Quoted in Edwin Black, *War Against the Weak: Eugenics and America's Campaign to Create a Master Race* (New York: Four Walls Eight Windows, 2003), 237.

42. Gosset, *Race,* 390–91. On Stoddard, see also *American National Biography;* "T. L. Stoddard, 66, Author of 12 Books," *NYT,* 2 May 1950; and *WWA, 1944–1945.*

43. With a circulation of 140,000 in 1918, the *World's Work* included worldwide news and comment, biographical sketches, and political cartoons (Irving Weingarten, "The Image of the Jew in the American Periodical Press, 1881–1921" (Ph.D. diss., New York Univ., 1980), 36–37). Stoddard served as director of foreign affairs for the magazine from 1918 to 1920.

44. Lothrop Stoddard, *The Rising Tide of Color Against White World-Supremacy* (New York: Scribner's, 1922), xi, 221.

45. Ibid., 165–66.

46. Madison Grant, introduction to ibid., xxi. Elsewhere, Stoddard referred to the "Negroid strain . . . in Jewry; to it the frizzy or wooly hair, thick lips, and prognathous jaws appearing in many Jews are probably due" (Singerman, "The Jew as Racial Alien," 117). As for Franz Boas, the great German Jewish anthropologist who led the intellectual counteroffensive against racism, Stoddard dismissed his arguments as "the desperate attempt of a Jew to pass himself off as white" (Jacobson, *Whiteness of a Different Color,* 184). On the intellectual assault on scientific racism, which by the 1930s had gained the upper hand, see Elazar Barkan, *The Retreat of Scientific Racism: Changing Concepts of Race in Britain and the United States Between the World Wars* (New York: Cambridge U.P., 1992). On the historical context of Boasian anthropology, see the fine article by Gelya Frank, "Jews, Multiculturalism, and Boasian Anthropology," *American Anthropologist* 99, no. 4 (December 1997): 731–45.

47. Bendersky, "Jewish Threat," 159. A biological determinist to the end, Stoddard believed that "Bolsheviks are mostly born and not made."

48. Baltzell, *Protestant Establishment,* 200–201. Of *The Rise of the Colored Empires,* Tom Buchanan said: "Well, it's a fine book and everyone ought to read it. The idea is if we don't look out the white race will be — will be utterly submerged. It's all scientific stuff; it's been proved . . . This fellow has worked out the whole thing. It's up to us, who are the dominant race, to watch out or these other races will have control of things" (quoted in Gossett, *Race,* 397).

49. Bendersky, "Jewish Threat," 26.

50. "Harding Supports New Policy in South," *NYT,* 27 October 1921.

51. Quoted in Kenneth Ludmerer, "Genetics, Eugenics, and the Immigration Restriction Act of 1924," 70.

52. Higham, *Strangers,* 271.

53. Ibid., 308.

54. Ibid., 309.

55. As an officer in MID's New York office, Trevor had prepared an "Ethnic Map of New York" to serve as a guide for army officers in suppressing a potential

Bolshevik-type uprising. Complementing this map was Trevor's "Plan for the Protection of New York in Case of Local Disturbances," developed in cooperation with the New York National Guard. Calling for the deployment of regular army units with 10,000 soldiers to defend Manhattan and 4,000 more to defend Brooklyn, Trevor was most worried about the Lower East Side (designated "A = Russian Jews" on the map), "the district most strongly permeated with the Bolshevik movement" (Bendersky, "*Jewish Threat*," 123–29, 147). For brief portraits of Trevor, who served as a trustee of the Museum of Natural History with Madison Grant and Henry Fairfield Osborn, see Higham, *Strangers*, 314, and Bendersky, "*Jewish Threat*," 66; see also *WWA, 1944–1945*.

56. Higham, *Strangers*, 311.

57. Gerstle, *American Crucible*, 103–4.

58. During the fiscal year 1920–1921, 119,000 Jews immigrated to the United States (Higham, *Strangers*, 309; Gerstle, *American Crucible*, 102).

59. Burton Hendrick, *The Jews in America* (Garden City, N.Y.: Doubleday, Page, 1923), 2.

60. In the U.S. Government 1926 Religious Census, the first ever conducted, Boston was reported as having 90,000 Jews, placing it fourth in the country. First was New York with 1,765,000, second was Chicago (325,000), and third was Philadelphia (270,000). Bureau of the Census, *Religious Bodies: 1926*, vol. 1 (Washington D.C.: Government Printing Office, 1930), 360. The second and last Government Religious Census was conducted in 1936.

61. Synnott, *Half-Opened Door*, 96, 182; Daniel A. Oren, *Joining the Club: A History of Jews and Yale* (New Haven, Conn.: Yale U.P., 1985), 320.

62. Elsewhere in the report, Horace Mann's headmaster, Virgil Prettyman, wrote that "the conditions and environment in which youth is to pass into manhood, the associations and friendships which may be formed within the student body, are popularly esteemed not less important factors in the value of a college education than the academic training and knowledge that may be acquired. Every undesirable student admitted is not an advantage but a detriment to the University" (Wechsler, *Qualified Student*, 148). Prettyman's views expressed in lay terms an idea with striking affinities to the concept of "social capital" as articulated on a more theoretical level by Pierre Bourdieu. For a discussion of his concept of social capital, see Pierre Bourdieu and Loic Wacquant, *An Invitation to Reflexive Sociology* (Chicago: Univ. of Chicago Press, 1992), 119.

63. Edwin E. Slosson, "Princeton University," *Independent*, 4 March 1909, 476.

64. Quoted in Stephen Steinberg, *The Ethnic Myth: Race, Ethnicity, and Class in America* (Boston: Beacon Press, 1989), 233.

65. Frederick Paul Keppel, *Columbia* (New York: Oxford U.P., 1914), 179; Wechsler, *Qualified Student*, 153, 181.

66. While only 6 percent of the scions of New York City's upper class attended Columbia in the 1910s, 73 percent attended the Big Three: 32 percent at Harvard, 25 percent at Yale, and 16 percent at Princeton (Richard Farnum, "Patterns of Upper-Class Education in Four American Cities: 1875–1975," in *The High-Status Track: Studies of Elite Schools and Stratification*, ed. Paul William Kingston and Lionel S. Lewis [Albany: State Univ. of New York Press, 1990], 60).

67. The figures for 1919 and 1921 are from "May Jews Go to College?" *Nation*, 14 June 1922, 708, and are cited in Wechsler, *Qualified Student*, 163–64. Though Farnum has expressed skepticism about whether Jewish enrollment at Columbia ever reached 40 percent, Yale's director of admission reported in 1922, after conferring with the dean of Columbia, that the proportion of Jews had been "reduced from about forty percent to about twenty." See Marcia Graham Synnott, "A Social History of Admissions Policies at Harvard, Yale, and Princeton, 1900–1930" (Ph.D. diss., Univ. of Massachusetts, 1974), 18; Richard Farnum, "Prestige in the Ivy League: Meritocracy at Columbia, Harvard, and Penn, 1870–1940" (Ph.D. diss., Univ. of Pennsylvania, 1990), 125.

68. The University of Pennsylvania, located in another of the nation's great centers of Jewish population, showed a parallel but even more precipitous decline, dropping from 52 percent in the 1910s to 14 percent in the 1920s. Whereas in the 1910s only 19 percent of the sons of Philadelphia's upper class enrolled at a Big Three college, by the 1920s the proportion had risen to 55 percent. The shift was in good part a product of the abandonment of Penn for Princeton, with the proportion at Old Nassau rising from 11 percent in the 1910s to 40 percent in the 1920s (Farnum, "Patterns of Upper-Class Education," 62).

69. M. G. Torch, "The Spirit of Morningside," *Menorah Journal*, March 1930, 255.

70. In 1984, I defined "WASP flight" as "the proclivity of upper-class Protestants to abandon an institution (e.g., a college, club, neighborhood, or vacation resort) in the face of entry into it by members of a low-status ethnic group. Structurally, it is strikingly similar to 'white flight,' — a term that has been used to describe the tendency of whites to flee public schools facing large-scale integration. In the cases of both 'WASP flight' and 'white flight,' there is evidence that institutions may reach a 'tipping point' beyond which the further entry of members of the 'outgroup' (typically Jews in the first case and blacks in the second) will cause members of the dominant group to abandon them" (Jerome Karabel, "Status-Group Struggle, Organizational Interests, and the Limits of Institutional Autonomy: The Transformation of Harvard, Yale, and Princeton, 1918–1940," *Theory and Society* 13). I have drawn on this article at several points in this chapter.

71. Synnott, *Half-Opened Door*, 16–19, 59.

72. *American Jewish Year Book, 5681: September 13, 1920, to October 2, 1921*, vol. 22 (Philadelphia: Jewish Publication Society, 1920), 387–90.

73. On the unusually close historical link between Harvard and Boston's upper class, see Ronald Story, *The Forging of an Aristocracy: Harvard & the Boston Upper Class, 1800–1870* (Middletown, Conn.: Wesleyan U.P., 1980), and E. Digby Baltzell, *Puritan Boston and Quaker Philadelphia: The Protestant Ethic and the Spirit of Class Authority and Leadership* (New York: Free Press, 1979), 246–80.

74. As far back as the 1880s, just as mass immigration from eastern and southern Europe was becoming visible in the large cities of the Northeast, there was a powerful tendency among the upper classes of Boston, New York, and Philadelphia to send their children to boarding schools in rural and small-town settings (Steven Levine, "The Rise of American Boarding Schools and the Development of a National Upper

Class," *Social Problems* 28, no. 1 [October 1980]; Baltzell, *Protestant Establishment*). But Boston's upper class remained faithful to Harvard, sending 78 percent of its sons there in the 1880s. The parallel figures for Philadelphia (Penn) and New York (Columbia) in the 1880s were 49 and 25 percent, respectively (Farnum, "Patterns of Upper-Class Education," 57, 60, 62).

75. Ibid., 60.

76. In his letter to Lowell, Hocking expressed particular concern about the increasing numbers of "rootless and religionless Jews" Hocking to Lowell, 18 May 1922, HUA).

77. The case of the New York City school referred to by Lowell — in which growing Jewish enrollment led to the flight of Christian students, reportedly then leading to the departure of many Jews — is described in detail in Henry A. Yeomans, *Abbot Lawrence Lowell, 1856–1943* (Cambridge, Mass.: Harvard U.P., 1948), 210–12.

78. Lowell to Hocking, 19 May 1922, HUA.

79. Ibid.

80. Lowell to Mack, 29 March 1922, HUA. Characteristically, the fact that Judge Mack was not only a Jew but was actively involved in Jewish affairs (ex-president of the American Jewish Congress, president of the Palestine Development Council) did not deter Lowell from writing him a letter that implied that Jews were less than fully American while explicitly proposing a quota. Nevertheless, Lowell may have had a sense of common class membership with Mack, who belonged to seven different social clubs, including the Cosmos Club of Washington, D.C., the Harvard Club of Boston, and the City Club in his home city of Chicago (*WWA, 1926–1927*).

81. Lowell to Tucker, 20 May 1922, HUA.

82. The proportion of undergraduates at these institutions in 1918–1919 was 2.8 percent at Dartmouth, 2.6 percent at Princeton, 1.9 percent at Amherst, and 1.4 percent at Williams (*American Jewish Yearbook, 1918–1919*, 386–89).

83. Bureau of the Census, *Historical Statistics*, Part I, 379.

84. At Columbia, it was the failure of the high school "to eliminate students . . . considered socially unqualified" that led to the adoption of selective admissions and of measures specifically designed to reduce the number of Jews. A generation earlier, when only an elite few graduated from high school, Columbia had been happy to "relegate [this function] to the secondary school" (Wechsler, *Qualified Student*, 133).

85. George S. Counts, *The Selective Character of American Secondary Education* (Chicago: Univ. of Chicago Press, 1922), 112.

86. Synnott, *Half-Opened Door*, 61.

87. Synnott, "Social History," 321–24. I have drawn extensively in the following section on Synnott's richly detailed discussion on the deliberations of the Harvard faculty in the spring of 1922 on "the Jewish problem."

88. On the exchange of letters between Mack and Lowell, see letters from Lowell to Mack, 29 March 1922, 31 March 1922, 4 April 1922, 7 June 1922, HUA; letters from Mack to Lowell, 27 March 1922, 30 March 1922, 6 June 1922, 9 June 1922, 13 June 1922, HUA.

89. John Bethell, *Harvard Observed: An Illustrated History of the University in the Twentieth Century* (Cambridge, Mass.: Harvard U.P., 1998), 40. A prominent banker, Greene had strong ties to the centers of financial power in both New York and Boston, with links to both John D. Rockefeller and the firm of Lee Higginson & Co.

90. Synnott, "Social History," 310–11.

91. Charles Eliot, "Zionism," in *A Late Harvest* (1919; Boston: Atlantic Monthly Press, 1924), 253. While concurring with Lowell that Jews had many disagreeable attributes, Eliot differed fundamentally from him in seeing these "undesirable" traits as products of oppression. Unlike Lowell, who believed that many Jews, especially those from eastern Europe, were unassimilable, Eliot was convinced that in the freer atmosphere of the United States, they would shed the negative qualities rooted in their history and become fully American. In his many writings on Jews, Eliot also stressed their many positive contributions to Western history. For all these reasons, the Jewish community at Harvard and elsewhere considered him a loyal friend and frequently published his writings. For examples of Eliot's writings on Jews, see Charles Eliot, "The Potency of the Jewish Race," *Menorah Journal*, June 1915, 141–44; Charles Eliot, "Three Lines of Action for American Jews," *Menorah Journal*, February 1918, 1; and Charles Eliot, "The Jewish Contribution to Modern Social Ethics," *Menorah Journal*, June 1919, 149–51.

92. Eliot, "Zionism," 253–57. Four years earlier, Eliot had warned, "If the [Jewish] race is to meet successfully the test of liberty, it will get over its apparent tendency of the moment towards materialism and reliance on the power of money" ("Potency of the Jewish Race," 144).

93. Synnott, "Social History," 326–34.

94. In a 1922 conversation with Julian Mack and Paul Sachs, both Jewish, Henderson referred to "the very objectionable and morally inferior" behavior and manners of many students of "the new Russian or Polish Jewish element" (Synnott, *Half-Opened Door*, 89).

95. Synnott, "Social History," 334–35.

96. "Minutes of Special Meeting of the Faculty of Arts and Sciences," 2 June 1922, HUA.

97. Synnott, "Social History," 324–25.

98. Ibid., 335–36.

99. Ibid., 356; "Discrimination Against Jews Suspected in New Harvard Policy on Admission," *NYT*, 2 June 1922.

100. "Jews have retained an extraordinary respect for learning," wrote the *Nation*, despite "all their hunt for money" ("May Jews Go to College?").

101. Synnott, "Social History," 357–58; "Governor Orders an Inquiry at Harvard Under Law Calling for Equal Opportunity," *NYT*, 7 June 1922.

102. Lowell to Kittredge, 3 June 1922, HUA.

103. Synnott, *Half-Opened Door*, 59.

104. Ibid., 258. As Michel Foucault has demonstrated, the gathering of knowledge by bureaucratic organizations is never a neutral process but rather an exercise of power; in the case of Harvard's admissions practices, the generation of the knowledge of an applicant's religious background was a precondition for the exercise of the power to discriminate. By the fall of 1922, this power was in the hands of administrators committed to turning back "the Jewish invasion." Of Foucault's many writings on surveillance, knowledge, and power, see especially *Discipline and Punish: The Birth of the Prison* (New York: Vintage, 1979) and *Power/Knowledge: Selected Interviews & Other Writings 1972–1977* (New York: Pantheon Press, 1980). For a

brilliant study that demonstrates how seemingly neutral forms of knowledge such as maps and censuses can be used as instruments of control, see James C. Scott, *Seeing Like a State: How Certain Schemes to Improve the Human Condition Have Failed* (New Haven, Conn.: Yale U.P., 1998).

105. Synnott, *Half-Opened Door*, 70.

106. Mack to Lowell, 6 June 1922, HUA. Born in Vienna in 1882, Frankfurter came to the United States in 1894. The son of a retail fur merchant, he lived on the Lower East Side, attended public schools, and graduated from City College in 1902. In 1903, he entered Harvard Law School, where he was first in his class and a member of the *Law Review*. In 1914, he was appointed professor of law at Harvard. During his quarter of a century at the Law School, no other Jew was appointed to the faculty. In 1939, Frankfurter left Harvard to join the Supreme Court, where he served until 1962. See Leonard Baker, *Brandeis and Frankfurter: A Dual Biography* (New York: Harper & Row, 1984), 41–44, 490; and Seymour Martin Lipset and David Riesman, *Education and Politics at Harvard* (New York: McGraw-Hill, 1975), 149; *WWA, 1926–1927*.

107. Lowell to Mack, 7 June 1922, HUA. In questioning Frankfurter's "judgment," Lowell was echoing a charge made six years earlier against Frankfurter's mentor, Louis Brandeis, the first Jew to serve on the Supreme Court. In a statement signed by William Howard Taft, Elihu Root, and five other past presidents of the American Bar Association, Brandeis was described "as not a fit person to be a member of the Supreme Court of the United States" by reason of his "reputation, character, and professional career." Brahmin Boston (but not Charles W. Eliot) was overwhelmingly against Brandeis's appointment, and Lowell himself joined 54 other Bostonians in a petition opposing his selection (Baltzell, *Protestant Establishment*, 192–93).

108. Even after Lowell had informed Mack of his decision not to appoint Frankfurter, Mack continued to press the issue, warning Lowell that "to leave off the Committee the one Jew of the Faculties who is uniquely fitted for this work would carry an obvious danger" (Mack to Lowell, 13 June 1922, HUA).

109. As a member of the Supreme Court, Frankfurter also wrote 263 opinions and 171 concurrences (Baker, *Brandeis and Frankfurter*, 491).

110. If Lowell was hostile to Frankfurter, it is clear from their correspondence that the feeling was mutual. In a testy exchange of letters when the committee was being constituted, Frankfurter accused Lowell of claiming to welcome "a Jewish member who shares Judge Mack's views" while in fact preferring someone who "passively" entertained them rather than a member who had "the power to render them effective by one's training and experience" (Frankfurter himself). When he wrote of someone who "passively" held Judge Mack's views, Frankfurter seems to have meant Wolfson, whom he described as "a naïve and bookish man, without talent or training which would enable him to share effectively the direction of such an inquiry" (Frankfurter to Lowell, 29 June 1922, HU). See also Frankfurter to Lowell, 19 June 1922, 21 June 1922, HU, and Lowell to Frankfurter, 20 June 1922, 24 June 1922, HU. But Frankfurter may have underestimated the Lithuanian-born Wolfson, who had written to Lowell criticizing the possible use of interviews in admissions, saying that "outward appearance is a proper

test for selecting book agents, bond salesmen, social secretaries and guests for a week-end party," but not "a proper test for the selection of future scholars, thinkers, scientists, and men of letters" (Synnott, *Half-Opened Door*, 67, 71, 87).

111. Ibid., 86.

112. For evidence that there was in fact considerable support among the students for Lowell's effort, see Harry Starr, "The Affair at Harvard," *Menorah Journal*, October 1922, 263–76, and Lipset and Riesman, *Education and Politics*, 148–49.

113. A. J. Hettinger Jr. and Edward Gay, "Statistical Report of Statisticians to the Subcommittee Appointed to Collect Statistics," 1922, HUA, 1–3; Synnott, *Half-Opened Door*, 107. See also the cover letter from A. J. Hettinger Jr. to Chester Greenough, chairman of the Subcommittee to Gather Statistics, 21 December 1922, HUA. On systems of classification and their relationship to systems of power, see David Karen, "Toward a Political-Organizational Model of Gatekeeping: The Case of Elite Colleges," *Sociology of Education* 63, October 1990; Pierre Bourdieu and Luc Boltanski, "Formal Qualifications and Occupational Hierarchies: The Relationship Between the Production System and the Reproduction System," in *Reorganizing Education*, vol. 1, ed. Edward Sage (Beverly Hills, Calif.: Sage, 1977); Luc Boltanski, "Taxonomies socials et luttes de classes: la mobilization de 'la classe moyenn' et l'invention des 'cadres,'" *Actes de la recherche en sciences socials*, September 1979; Michele Lamont and Virag Molnar, "The Study of Boundaries in the Social Sciences," *Annual Review of Sociology* 28, 2002; and Geoffrey Bowker and Susan Leigh Star, *Sorting Things Out: Classification and Its Consequences* (Cambridge, Mass.: MIT Press, 2000).

114. The report was compiled by two Harvard statisticians, Dr. A. J. Hettinger Jr. of the Graduate School of Business Administration and Edward R. Gay, a dean of Harvard College, who were not formal members of the subcommittee (Synnott, *Half-Opened Door*, 93).

115. These figures did not even include students classified as "J3s," estimated to make up about 2.5 percent of the student body between 1918 and 1923 (Hettinger and Gay, "Statistical Report," HUA, 3, 8.

116. Ibid., 28–29.

117. Lowell to Mack, 4 April 1922, HUA.

118. Synnott, *Half-Opened Door*, 60.

119. Lipset and Riesman, *Education and Politics*, 146.

120. Among students found guilty of "offenses involving dishonesty," 29 percent of the Jews were expelled or dismissed compared to 11 percent of non-Jews (Hettinger and Gay, "Statistical Report," HUA, 39, 44–45).

121. Hettinger to Greenough, 21 December 1922, HUA.

122. Synnott, *Half-Opened Door*, 85.

123. Totally absent from dramatics and barely represented on student papers and in class office (4 and 5 percent, respectively), Jews did, however, participate heavily in musical and debating activities (19 and 38 percent) (Hettinger and Gay, "Statistical Report," HUA, 48, 53, 57).

124. Between 1912 and 1921, the proportion of Jewish students at Harvard who were commuters exceeded 40 percent eight times, with the figure reaching a high of 49.5 percent in 1915 (the low was 29.1

580 Notes to Pages 98–104

percent in 1920). This was roughly double, and perhaps in some years triple, the proportion of non-Jewish commuters (ibid., 77–79).

125. Synnott makes a similar point, writing: "Although impossible to measure, Gentile social attitudes probably accounted for the limited participation in or exclusion of Jewish students from extracurricular activities" (Half-Opened Door, 101).

126. Nearly a quarter (23.8 percent) of Jewish students belonged to one of the six Jewish fraternities, bringing their total participation in social clubs to 27.4 percent (Hettinger and Gay, "Statistical Report," HUA, 61).

127. Only a handful of Jews managed to enter even the lower-ranking clubs, which included Owl, Delta Upsilon (DU), Phoenix, and Iroquois (numbers six, eight, nine, and ten, according to Boston Brahmin and Harvard alumnus Cleveland Amory) (ibid., 61–75; Amory, The Proper Bostonians (New York: Dutton, 1947), 300; Synnott, Half-Opened Door, 101.

128. Hocking to Lowell, 18 May 1922, HUA; David O. Levine, The American College and the Culture of Aspiration 1915–1940 (Ithaca, N.Y.: Cornell U.P., 1986), 155.

129. Synnott, Half-Opened Door, 78.

130. Ronald Steel, Walter Lippmann and the American Century (New York: Vintage, 1981), 191–92.

131. Ibid., 194.

132. Synnott, Half-Opened Door, 89; Steel, Walter Lippmann, 194–95.

133. Steel, Walter Lippmann, 195.

134. Grandgent to Lowell, 7 April 1923, cover letter to the Report of the Committee on Methods of Sifting Candidates for Admission, HUA.

135. Eliot had written to Greene of Lowell's "defects of judgment and good feeling" and had described "four generations of Lowells" as "eager to win in any controversy upon which they entered, credulous in regard to alleged facts which go their way and incredulous with regard to alleged facts which do not go their way." See Eliot to Greene, 7 June 1922, 25 January 1923, 17 February 1923, HUA; Greene to Eliot, 10 June 1922, 13 January 1923, 20 January 1923, 24 January 1923, 9 February 1923, HUA.

136. Synnott, Half-Opened Door, 88. Another prominent alumnus whose intervention influenced the committee's decision to oppose the Jewish quota was Learned Hand (B.A. 1893, LL.B. 1896). A widely respected federal judge who later became known as the "tenth justice" because of his profound influence on the Supreme Court, Hand wrote an eloquent and forceful letter to the committee on 14 November 1922. While acknowledging that Harvard's growing heterogeneity had created tensions, he believed that restricting Jewish enrollment was not an appropriate solution: "If the Jew does not mix well with the Christian, it is no answer to segregate him. Most of those qualities which the Christian dislikes in him are, I believe, the direct result of that very policy in the past. Both Christian and Jew are here; they must in some way learn to live on tolerable terms, and disabilities have never proved tolerable . . . But the proposal is not segregation or exclusion but to limit the number of Jews. That, however, is if anything worse. Those who are in fact shut out are of course segregated; those who are left in are effectively marked as racially undesirable. Intercourse with them is with social inferiors; there can be no other conceivable explanation for the

limitation." Hand also expressed his firm opposition to the use of nonacademic criteria such as "character," which were clearly designed to restrict Jewish enrollment by indirect means. Until someone should "devise an honest test for character," the only legitimate criterion for admission was scholarly excellence. "A college may gather together men of a common tradition," he concluded, "or it may put its faith in learning" (Irving Dilliard, ed., The Spirit of Liberty: Papers and Addresses of Learned Hand [New York: Knopf, 1960], 21). For more on Learned Hand, see the monumental biography by his former law clerk Gerald Gunther, Learned Hand; The Man and the Judge (Cambridge, Mass.: Harvard U.P., 1994).

137. Grandgent to Lowell, 7 April 1923, HUA.

138. On the controversy over the admission of blacks to the dormitories, see Nell Painter, "Jim Crow at Harvard: 1923," New England Quarterly 44, no. 4 (December 1971); Synnott, Half-Opened Door, 49–50, 81–84; and the eloquent letter to Lowell from Roscoe Conkling Bruce, an African American from the Class of 1902 who had graduated magna cum laude and Phi Beta Kappa (Bruce to Lowell, 4 January 1923, HUA).

139. "Report of the Committee Appointed 'To Consider and Report to the Governing Boards Principles and Methods for More Effective Sifting of Candidates for Admission to the University,'" 10 April 1923, HUA, 1–2.

140. Ibid., 3–6.

141. Synnott, "Social History," 432–34.

142. Ibid., 438.

143. Eliot to Greene, 13 January 1923, HUA.

144. "Report of the Committee on the Limitation of Students," 18 December 1923, HUA.

145. Synnott, "Social History," 441–46.

146. "Report of the Committee Appointed 'to Consider and Report to the Governing Boards,'" HUA, 2; "Report of the Committee on the Limitation of Students," 18 December 1923, HUA.

147. Lowell to Pennypacker, 24 March 1924, HUA.

148. Higham, Strangers, 282–85, 312–24; Neil Baldwin, Henry Ford and the Jews: The Mass Production of Hate (New York: Public Affairs, 2001).

149. For biographical profiles of Brigham, whose ancestors included William Brewster, the fourth signer of the Mayflower Compact, see Matthew T. Downey, Carl Campbell Brigham: Scientist and Educator (Princeton, N.J.: Educational Testing Services, 1961), and American National Biography.

150. Gerstle, American Crucible, 105.

151. Carl C. Brigham, A Study of American Intelligence (Princeton, N.J.: Princeton U.P., 1923), 189–90, 207–10. Seven years later, Brigham explicitly repudiated the conclusions about racial differences that he had reached in his book, writing that "one of the worst of these comparative racial studies — the writer's own — was without foundation." See Carl C. Brigham, "Intelligence Tests of Immigrant Groups," Psychological Review 37, 1930. For a sharp critique of Brigham's earlier work on intelligence, see Gould, Mismeasure of Man, 224–33.

152. Hendrick, Jews in America, 89, 134, 145, 168.

153. Among the most outspoken advocates of restrictive legislation was Henry Fairfield Osborn. Of the I.Q. tests that Brigham had used, Osborn wrote in 1923: "I believe those tests were worth what the war cost, even in human life, if they served to show clearly

to our people the lack of intelligence in our country, and the degrees of intelligence in different races who are coming to us, in a way which no one can say is the result of prejudice . . . We have learned once and for all that the Negro is not like us. So in regard to many races and subraces in Europe we learned that some which we had believed possessed of an order of intelligence perhaps superior to ours [read Jews] were far inferior" (Gould, *Mismeasure of Man*, 231).

154. Higham, *Strangers*, 319–24.

155. Gerstle, *American Crucible*, 109; Desmond King, *Making Americans: Immigration, Race, and the Origins of the Diverse Democracy* (Cambridge, Mass.: Harvard U.P., 2000), 191, 206.

156. Oren, *Joining the Club*, 320; *Freshman Herald: Class of 1927*, PU, 33; *Freshman Herald: Class of 1928*, PU, 31.

157. Lowell to Tucker, 20 May 1922, HUA.

158. Delmar Leighton to Lowell, memorandum, 9 November 1925, HUA.

159. In 1925, the top-seventh plan brought Harvard 91 Jews from New England and the Middle Atlantic states compared to a total of just 22 students (6 of them Jewish) from the western and South Central states combined ("Table II: Geographic Distribution of Schools from Which New Freshmen Were Admitted, Percentage of Jews in Each Group, and Award of Freshman Aid," 23 November 1925, HUA).

160. Williams (pseudonym)to Lowell, 17 December 1925, HUA. (To protect the privacy of alumni who sent private letters to Big Three administrators, I have generally used pseudonyms.) In implying that Jews, especially those from eastern Europe, were not "white," Williams was expressing a viewpoint common in the 1920s. Among the many scholars who have analyzed the fluidity of the position of Jews within the systems of racial classification of the period, see especially Jacobson, *Whiteness of a Different Color;* Karen Brodkin, *How Jews Became White Folks: And What That Says About Race in America* (New Brunswick, N.J.: Rutgers U.P., 1998), and Singerman, "Jew as Racial Alien." Among Jewish students themselves at the time was the category of the "white Jew" — those who accepted the dictates of the dominant student culture and "put themselves forward for judgment and acceptance by their Gentile peers" (Harold Wechsler, "The Rationale for Restriction: Ethnicity and College Admission in America, 1910–1980," *American Quarterly* 36, no. 5 [Winter 1984], 657–58). For a brief but fascinating discussion of the participation of a Jewish congressman in placing the Japanese in a stigmatized racial category totally ineligible to emigrate to the United States, see Gerstle, *American Crucible*, 118–22. According to Gerstle, Jewish complicity in the racial denigration of the Japanese helped consolidate their status as members of a single superior European race and their placement "on the right side of the racial divide."

161. Lowell to Williams, 18 December 1925, HUA. In another letter to an alumnus that same month, Lowell offered assurances that "the matter [of the Jews] is thoroughly understood by the authorities here," adding of his attempt at restriction in 1922, "My plan was crude, and its method was very probably unwise," Lowell to Cyrus Brewer, 11 December 1925, HUA.

162. As late as April 1925, Lowell was forced to reply to Eliot's request that he have the opportunity to meet with the Special Committee to present his views (Synnott, "Social History," 447).

163. James's biography of Eliot was published just five years after his service as chairman of the Special Committee on the Size of the Freshman Class. See Henry James, *Charles W. Eliot: President of Harvard University 1869–1909*, 2 vols. (Boston: Houghton Mifflin, 1930). For a brief profile of James, a prominent New York lawyer with close connections to the Rockefellers, see *WWA, 1944–1945*.

164. Lowell to James, 3 November 1925, HUA.

165. Ibid.

166. James to Lowell, 4 November 1925, HUA.

167. Lowell to James, 6 November 1925, HUA.

168. James to Lowell, 10 November 1925, HUA.

169. "Report of the Special Committee Appointed to Consider the Limitation of Numbers," 11 January 1926, HUA, 11–12.

170. Synnott, *Half-Opened Door*, 109–10.

171. After the passage of the Immigration Act of 1924, Ward wrote to President Coolidge to declare that "in signing the immigration bill you have approved one of the most important measures which has ever been put upon our statute books. You have done a very great service to the country. You have lived up to the words of your Message of last December, that America must be kept American" (quoted in King, *Making Americans*, 191). So loyal was Ward to the Immigration Restriction League that in nineteen years he missed only a single meeting except when he was away from Boston (Higham, *Strangers*, 102). For a portrait of Ward, a leader of the Immigration Restriction League for thirty years and an enthusiastic proponent of eugenics, see Solomon, *Ancestors and Immigrants*, 99–102, 104–5, 147–51, 168–69.

172. The membership of the Committee on Admission is listed in the "Report of the Committee on Admission, 1925–1926," HU, 297. An examination of the vote at the faculty meeting of 2 June 1922, at which the Henderson motion was defeated with 64 "nays" and 41 "ayes," reveals that four of its members (Pennypacker, Ward, Abbott, and Birkhoff) voted for the measure and none opposed it. "Minutes of the Special Meeting of the Faculty of Arts and Sciences," 2 June 1922, HUA.

173. Clarence Mendell, "Harvard," 8 December 1926, YUA.

4. The "Jewish Problem" at Yale and Princeton

1. In 1917, there were roughly 18,000 Jews out of New Haven's total population of about 160,000 (*American Jewish Year Book, 5681: September 13, 1920, to October 2, 1921*, vol. 22 [Philadelphia: Jewish Publication Society, 1920], 373).

2. Daniel A. Oren, *Joining the Club: A History of Jews and Yale* (New Haven, Conn.: Yale U.P., 1985), 320, and "Meeting of Association New England Deans Held in Princeton," minutes, 9–10, May 1918, YUA, 21–22.

3. The son of James Burrill Angell, who had served as president of both the University of Michigan and the University of Vermont, James Rowland Angell (1869–1949) graduated from the University of Michigan in 1890 and received a master's degree in psychology in 1892 from Harvard, where he studied under William James. A professor of psychology at the Uni-

versity of Chicago for many years before serving briefly as president of the Carnegie Corporation, he became president of Yale in 1921, the first man to hold that office who was not an alumnus. See George W. Pierson, *Yale: The University College, 1921–1937* (New Haven, Conn.: Yale U.P., 1955), 16–19.; *The National Encyclopedia;* and *WWA, 1944–1945.*

4. Oren, *Joining the Club,* 41–42; Marcia Graham Synnott, *The Half-Opened Door: Discrimination and Admissions at Harvard, Yale, and Princeton, 1900–1970* (Westport, Conn.: Greenwood Press, 1979), 139–40.

5. Synnott, *Half-Opened Door,* 138.

6. See the entry in the *Yale Class Book: Class of 1887; Vicennial Record: Class of 1887; Quarter Century Record: Class of 1887; Thirty-fifth Year Record: Class of 1887; Fiftieth Year Record: Class of 1887;* and *WWA, 1926–1927.*

7. Robert N. Corwin, "Memorandum on the Problems Arising from the Increase in the Enrollment of Students of Jewish Birth in the University," 12 May 1922, YUA.

8. Robert N. Corwin, "Memo on Jewish Representation in Yale," 26 May 1922, YUA.

9. Corwin, "Memorandum on the Problems." Corwin made a similar argument in support of a Jewish quota in a letter to the dean of Yale College Frederick S. Jones (Corwin to Jones, 3 May 1922, YUA).

10. Among those Yale administrators who referred to Jews as "Hebrews" were the registrar A. K. Merritt (who also referred to them, not without irony, as "the chosen race") and the director of the Sheffield Scientific School, Russell H. Chittenden. Both men were alumni, Merritt '93 and Chittenden '75. See Merritt to Corwin, 11 April and 25 May 1922, YUA, and Chittenden to Angell, 26 January 1922, YUA.

11. Corwin, "Memorandum on the Problems"; Corwin, "Limitation of Numbers," 9 January 1923, YUA.

12. Ibid.

13. Ibid.; Corwin, "Memo on Jewish Representation"; Corwin, "Memorandum on the Problems."

14. *WWA, 1926–1927.*

15. "Meeting of Association New England Deans," YUA, 21–22.

16. Ibid., 141–42, 268.

17. Ibid.

18. Jones to Corwin, 6 May 1922, YUA.

19. Jews and Scholarship Tables for 1924–1926, YUA.

20. Corwin, "Memorandum on the Problems." Ironically, in the very document in which Corwin proposed to further restrict the access of Jewish students to financial aid, he criticized local Jewish boys: "Those who have been refused scholarships usually maintain that they have been discriminated against and not infrequently threaten retaliating measures."

21. Oren, *Joining the Club,* 51.

22. Corwin, "Limitation of Numbers."

23. Frederick Jones, "Report on Jews, 1922," YUA.

24. Synnott, *Half-Opened Door,* 151.

25. Oren, *Joining the Club,* 54.

26. "Limitation of Numbers: The New Undergraduate Faculty," *YAM,* 16 October 1923; James Angell, "Current Conditions at the University," *YAM,* 2 March 1923.

27. Corwin, "Memo on Jewish Representation," YUA.

28. Oren, *Joining the Club,* 54, 320.

29. Corwin, "Memo on Jewish Representation," YUA.

30. Oren, *Joining the Club,* 320.

31. Ibid., 320–21.

32. "An Ellis Island for Yale," *YDN,* 30 March 1926.

33. "Applicants Submit Photographs," *YDN,* 29 March 1926; "An Ellis Island for Yale."

34. Angell to Mrs. George R. Faust, 10 June 1931, YUA.

35. George W. Pierson, *A Yale Book of Numbers: Historical Statistics of the College and University 1701–1976* (New Haven, Conn.: Yale U.P., 1983), 87–95.

36. Jerome Karabel, "Status-Group Struggle, Organizational Interests, and the Limits of Institutional Autonomy: The Transformation of Harvard, Yale, and Princeton, 1918–1940," *Theory and Society* 13, January 1984, 22.

37. Despite its claim to be a national institution, Yale had even fewer students from the South than from the West. In 1930, the 11 southern states of the Confederacy provided Yale with just 3 percent of its freshmen. In truth, Yale drew its students primarily from the Northeast, with just 5 states — New York, Connecticut, Massachusetts, Pennsylvania, and New Jersey — producing over 70 percent of the 1930 freshman class. See "Tables: Statistics, 1929–1938" in "Report to the Alumni Board of Yale by its Committee on Enrollment," 22 February 1940, YU; Pierson, *Yale Book of Numbers,* 95.

38. Ibid., 87–95.

39. Synnott, *Half-Opened Door,* 152–54.

40. Corwin to Board of Admissions, "The Admission Requirements as Applied to the Sons of Yale Alumni," memorandum, 28 September 1929, YUA.

41. Corwin to Parsons, 1 October 1929, YUA.

42. Ibid.

43. *The World Almanac and Book of Facts for 1931,* 190, 326; "Tables: Statistics, 1929–1938" in "Report to the Alumni Board of Yale," YUA.

44. Of the remaining 44 students in St. Paul's class of 1930, 26 went to Harvard and 15 to Princeton (Karabel, "Status-Group Struggle," 22).

45. *Yale Banner: Class of 1933,* YUA, 389–70; *WWA, 1984–1985;* and Todd Purdum, "Eugene Rostow, 89, Official at State Dept. and Law Dean," *NYT,* 26 November 2002.

46. Eugene Rostow, "The Jew's Position," *Harkness Hoot,* 23 November 1931, 51, 53, 55, YUA.

47. Clarence Mendell, "Harvard," 8 December 1926, YUA; Mendell, "Dartmouth," 8 December 1926, YUA.

48. Quoted in Marcia Graham Synnott, "A Social History of Admissions Policies at Harvard, Yale, and Princeton, 1900–1930" (Ph.D. diss., Univ. of Massachusetts, 1974), 544.

49. Angell to Corwin, 6 January 1933, YUA.

50. Richard Farnum, "Patterns of Upper-Class Education in Four American Cities: 1875–1975," in *The High-Status Track: Studies of Elite Schools and Stratification,* ed. Paul William Kingston and Lionel S. Lewis (Albany: State Univ. of New York Press, 1990), 160.

51. "Report of the President to the Board of Trustees, 1920–1921," PU, 39.

52. "Report of the President to the Board of Trustees, 1921–1922," PU, 38.

53. Office of the Secretary, "Analysis of Freshman Class," September 1921, PU, 1–2.

54. In addition, there may have been some Jews among the 27 members of the entering class of 1921

who did not state a religion; had Princeton used Harvard's system of religious classification, a few such students would probably have been placed in the "J2" or "J3" category. See "Report of the President to the Board of Trustees, 1921–1922," PU, 1–2, 12; Synnott, *Half-Opened Door*, 181–82.

55. Synnott, "Social History," 683.

56. "Princeton to Limit Students to 2,000," *NYT*, 24 June 1921.

57. Synnott, "Social History," 684.

58. On the admission policy of Dartmouth, which had adopted its own policy of limitation, see David O. Levine, *The American College and the Culture of Aspiration 1915–1940* (Ithaca, N.Y.: Cornell U.P.), 138–58. On the early history of the Rhodes Scholarships, see Frank Aydelotte, *The American Rhodes Scholarships: A Review of the First Forty Years* (Princeton, N.J.: Princeton U.P., 1946).

59. Between 1904 and 1939, Princeton led all American colleges with 61 Rhodes scholarships, followed by Harvard (46) and Yale (43) (Aydelotte, *American Rhodes Scholarship*, 126–30).

60. On the influence of Oxbridge on American undergraduate education since the late nineteenth century, see Alex Duke, *Importing Oxbridge: English Residential Colleges and American Universities* (New Haven, Conn.: Yale U.P., 1996). Both the Harvard house system and Yale's residential colleges were explicitly modeled on the residential colleges at Oxford and Cambridge.

61. The best biography of Cecil Rhodes is Robert Rotberg, *The Founder: Cecil Rhodes and the Pursuit of Power* (New York: Oxford U.P., 1988). Though there is no work of similar stature on Peabody, Frank S. Ashburn's biography offers a vivid picture of the man and his beliefs: *Peabody of Groton: A Portrait* (Cambridge, Mass.: Riverside Press, 1967).

62. Aydelotte, *American Rhodes Scholarships*, 4–5.

63. In 1901, perhaps in recognition of Germany's rising power as well as the "Teutonic idea of an eventual union of the white Anglo-Saxon entities," Rhodes added Germans to his list of nationalities eligible for scholarships (Ibid., 19; Rotberg, *Founder*, 668).

64. Though Rhodes's emphasis on "manliness" and sports was unremarkable for a member of the Victorian upper class, he did not fully conform to his own ideal. A sickly youth with health problems that plagued him throughout his life, he was "hardly distinguished for his love of or skill at sports." Though not lacking in physical courage, he died at the age of forty-eight without ever having participated in two of the pillars of conventional "manliness": marriage and fatherhood. Whether Rhodes was a practicing homosexual is a matter of debate among historians, but he did have a pattern of strong fondness for young men, which, at the very least, suggested powerful homosexual inclinations. See Rotberg, *Founder*, 31, 404–8; Robert Aldrich, *Colonialism and Homosexuality* (New York: Routledge, 2003), 91–93.

65. Rotberg, *Founder*, 667–68. In the final version of his will, Rhodes changed the weight of the various criteria, assigning three-tenths to scholarship, two-tenths to manly sports, three-tenths to concern about others, and two-tenths to character and leadership (Thomas Schaeper and Kathleen Schaeper, *Cowboys into Gentlemen: Rhodes Scholars, Oxford, and the Creation of an American Elite* [New York: Berghahn, 1998], 16–17).

66. The reference to "race and nationality" is drawn from "Amended Report of the Special Committee on Limitation of Enrollment," 21 March 1921, PUA.

67. Synnott, "Social History," 690–91.

68. Ibid., 692–93.

69. Ibid., 693–96; Synnott, *Half-Opened Door*, 191.

70. Don Oberdorfer, *Princeton University: The First 250 Years* (Princeton, N.J.: Trustees of Princeton Univ., 1995), 118; "Keeper of the Gate," *Newsweek*, 10 July 1950.

71. My portrait of Heermance is based on a number of sources, including the Williams College Class of 1904 yearbook; "Radcliffe Heermance: Dean of Freshmen and Director of Admission," *PAW*, 10 June 1932; "Dean Heermance," *Nassau Sovereign*, September 1946; "Dean Heermance of Princeton, 76," *NYT*, 31 October 1958; "Radcliffe Heermance," *PAW*, 6 February 1959; and a file kindly provided by the Williams College Archives.

72. A remarkably homogeneous institution even by the standards of the day, Williams was composed almost entirely of white Anglo-Saxon Protestants; Heermance's class had a total of one Catholic and one Jew. Yet despite the paucity of Jews on campus, Williams was the scene in 1910 of perhaps the first student demonstration against Jewish enrollment. A half-century later, a study of the alma maters of men listed in the New York *Social Register* showed Williams in fourth place, ahead of much larger institutions such as Columbia, Dartmouth, Cornell, Penn, and Brown. See Class of 1904 Yearbook, Williams College, 113; Synnott, *Half-Opened Door*, 150; Gene Hawes, "The Colleges of America's Upper Class," *Saturday Review*, 16 November 1963.

73. "Radcliffe Heermance," *PAW*, 10 June 1932, 802.

74. Ibid.; "Dean Heermance," *Nassau Sovereign*, September 1946, 14–15; "Radcliffe Heermance," *PAW*, 10 June 1932; Claude Fuess, "Memorial Tribute to Radcliffe Heermance," n.d., PUA; Frank Bowles to Beatrice Heermance, n.d. [c. 30 October 1958], courtesy of Williams College.

75. "Report of the President to the Board of Trustees, 1921–1922," PU, 2.

76. Collins to Henry Canby, 23 November 1922, PUA.

77. The one Jew in an eating club was a member of the Court Club, one of the newest and lowest in status of the eighteen eating clubs. See Synnott, *Half-Opened Door*, 194–95; William Selden, *Club Life at Princeton: An Historical Account of the Eating Clubs at Princeton University* (Princeton, N.J.: Princeton Prospect Foundation, 1994), 98; *1927 Freshmen Herald*, PU, 33.

78. Corwin, "Limitation of Numbers."

79. Synnott, *Half-Opened Door*, 195, 222; *Freshman Herald*s from 1922 to 1949, PU.

80. Over the course of his twenty-eight years as director of admissions, Heermance reportedly interviewed about 35,000 boys ("Keeper of the Gate").

81. "Report of the President to the Board of Trustees, 1921–1922," PU, 3–4; "Report of the President to the Board of Trustees, 1922–1923," PU, 18–19.

82. "Radcliffe Heermance."

83. "Report of the President to the Board of Trustees, 1922–1923," PU, 19; Heermance to Lowell, 2 December 1923, HUA.

84. Both Yale and Harvard believed that Princeton lowered its academic standards in its quest for tal-

ented athletes. After a visit to Harvard in 1926, Dean Clarence Mendell of Yale wrote: "Pennypacker is skeptical of Princeton standard — cites X, short of credits and refused at Harvard and Yale — accepted at Princeton. After a disgraceful year at Princeton he was fired and went to Penn who accepted him in spite of full knowledge and played him on the Freshman team . . . Incidentally Greenough and Moore are both extremely skeptical about the Princeton standards inside and cite the comprehensive exams which they believe are not comprehensive at all" ("Harvard").

85. In his letter, Marvin reported that his description was based on information provided by "one of the active Princeton trustees" (Marvin to Lowell, 12 January 1926, HUA).

86. Mendell, "Harvard"; Synnott, *Half-Opened Door*, 107–10.

87. F. Scott Fitzgerald, *This Side of Paradise* (New York: Scribner's, 1920); Upton Sinclair, *The Goose-Step: Study of American Education* (Pasadena, Calif.: Upton Sinclair, 1923).

88. Edmund Wilson, "Harvard, Princeton, and Yale," *Forum*, September 1923.

89. "How Shall We Limit Our Enrollment," *DP*, 27 January 1922; "Our Plan for Enrollment Limitation," *DP*, 28 January 1922; "The Claims of Princeton Men on Their University," *DP*, 30 January 1922. See also "Why More Than Two Thousand?" *DP*, 26 January 1922.

90. Selden, *Club Life*, 35.

91. Carol P. Herring to William G. Bowen, memorandum, 27 July 1978, PU; Selden, *Club Life*, 35–37.

92. *1930 Freshman Herald*, PUA, 29–32; "Report of the President to the Board of Trustees, 1929–1930," PU, 30.

93. Carl Brigham, "The Quality of the Classes Admitted to Princeton in the Years 1928 to 1935," n.d. [c. 1935], PU, 2–5.

94. Synnott, "Social History," 716. A similar decision was made at Dartmouth in March 1933, when Dartmouth faced a clear choice: either fail to fill the freshman class of 650 or waive the Jewish quota (set the previous year at less than 6 percent). President Ernest M. Hopkins did not hesitate to make a decision; better, he declared, not to accept a class of 650 than to violate the quota. The solution, he suggested to the director of admissions, E. G. Bill, was to consider admitting a number of "just the plain, ordinary bohunks such as it used to do" to meet the target figure. But Bill had already tried this; every Gentile applicant who had been judged capable of surviving academically had been admitted, yet the 650 mark could still only be reached by including 90 Jews (13.8 percent of the class). In the end, only 38 Jews entered Dartmouth in the fall of 1933; this figure remained constant for the rest of the decade. "I think," Hopkins wrote to Bill in 1933, "I would rather take the hazards of what appears to be a group of less scholastic promise, distributed among Anglo-Saxons, Hibernians, Scandinavians, and those from other outlying districts, than to let the Jewish proportion again rise" (Levine, *American College*, 153–57, 241).

95. Synnott, *Half-Opened-Door*, 196–97.

96. Randall Collins, *The Credential Society: An Historical Sociology of Education and Stratification* (New York: Academic Press, 1979); Joseph Ben-David, *Centers of Learning: Britain, France, Germany, United States* (New York: McGraw-Hill, 1977); Fritz K. Ringer,

Education and Society in Modern Europe (Bloomington: Indiana U.P., 1979); and Nira Kaplan, "A Changing Culture of Merit: French Competitive Examinations and the Politics of Selection, 1750–1820" (Ph.D. diss., Columbia Univ., 1999).

97. Harold Wechsler, *The Qualified Student: A History of Selective College Admission in America* (New York: John Wiley, 1977), 148–151.

98. Jones's innovative procedures met with the full approval of Columbia's president Nicholas Murray Butler, who in 1914 went so far as to suggest that each candidate for graduation be evaluated "on the basis of his character, personality, and general bearing while in college residence." In advocating such a procedure, Butler explicitly compared it to the credentials offered by "a candidate for admission to a Club, that is, having his personal qualifications examined" (ibid., 148–51, 162–63).

99. In explaining the new policy, Herbert Hawkes, who had become dean of Columbia College in 1918, explained that though "every college should be ready to admit as many divergent types of students as it can assimilate . . . [but] for a college to consist almost entirely of newly arrived immigrants makes it impossible for them to gain the contacts that they need and should have" (ibid., 135, 156–57, 163–64).

100. "Report of the Committee Appointed 'to Consider and Report to the Governing Boards Principles and Methods for More Effective Sifting of Candidates for Admission to the University,'" 10 April 1922, HUA, 2.

101. Lowell to Marvin, 10 June 1922, HUA; emphasis added.

102. As used here, "process of selection" refers to two separate, but related factors: the criteria (academic, cultural) that govern decisions of inclusion and exclusion, and the procedures used to see that the criteria are put into effect. An emphasis on religious origin would be an admissions criterion; an application form asking numerous questions about family religious background is a procedure set up to make possible the enforcement of a specific criterion.

103. Alfred Kazin, in his lyrical autobiographical memoir, *A Walker in the City* (New York: Harvest, 1951), offers a telling portrait of the terror that evaluations of "character" could arouse among children of eastern European Jews in the 1920s: "It was not just our quickness and memory that were always being tested. Above all, in that word I could never hear without automatically seeing it raised before me in gold plated letters, it was our character. I always felt anxious when I heard the word pronounced. Satisfactory as my "character" was, on the whole, except when I stayed too long in the playground reading; outrageously satisfactory, as I can see now, the very sound of the word as our teachers coldly gave it out from the end of their teeth, with a solemn weight on each dark syllable, immediately struck my heart cold with fear — they could not believe I really had it. Character was never something you had; it had to be trained in you, like a technique. I was never very clear about it. On our side character meant demonstrative obedience; but teachers already had it — how else could they have become teachers? They had it; the aloof Anglo-Saxon principal whom we remotely saw only on ceremonial occasions in the assembly was positively encased in it; it glittered off his bald head in spokes of triumphant light . . . Thus someday the hallowed diploma, pass-

port to further advancement in high school, but there — I could already feel it in my bones — they would put me through even more doubting tests of character; and after that, if I should be good enough and bright enough, there would be still more. Character was a bitter thing, racked with endless striving to please" (19–20).

104. In his letter to Lowell (9 June 1922, HUA), Marvin (Harvard A.B. 1898 and LL.B. '01) acknowledged that his idea of using the Rhodes criteria to limit Jewish enrollment had been influenced by an editorial in the *New York Herald Tribune* (7 June 1922) written by Nicholas Roosevelt (Harvard '14). Entitled "No Mere Bookworms," it called for "an end to the hysterical talk about race discrimination at Harvard" and advocated an admissions policy based on "the high standards set forth by the late Cecil Rhodes which govern the selection of Rhodes Scholars." Such a policy, it emphasized, would be a valuable correction to a policy that "has resulted in overemphasizing the intellectual abilities of students at the expense of character." For evidence that Princeton, too, was influenced by the Rhodes criteria, see the comments by President Hibben, who wrote that in implementing the new policy of limitation of numbers, "the Rhodes Scholarship requirements present an excellent precedent" (excerpts from the president's Annual Report in *PAW,* 9 February 1921).

105. On the sources of patrician anti-Semitism, see the classical works of Barbara M. Solomon, *Ancestors and Immigrants: A Changing New England Tradition* (New York: John Wiley, 1956); John Higham, *Strangers in the Land: Patterns of American Nativism, 1860–1925* (1955; New Brunswick, N.J.: Rutgers U.P., 1992); and Higham, "The Rise of Social Discrimination," in *Send These to Me: Immigrants in Urban America* (Baltimore: Johns Hopkins U.P., 1984), 117–52 (a different version of this chapter appeared as "Social Discrimination Against Jews in America, 1830–1930," *Publication of the American Jewish Historical Society,* September 1957); and E. Digby Baltzell, *The Protestant Establishment: Aristocracy and Caste in America* (New York: Vintage, 1964). Among the more recent literature, three of the most interesting works are Eric Goldstein, "The Unstable Other: Locating the Jew in Progressive-Era American Racial Discourse," *American Jewish History* 89, no. 4 (2002): 383–409; Matthew F. Jacobson, *Whiteness of a Different Color: European Immigrants and the Alchemy of Race* (Cambridge, Mass.: Harvard U.P., 1998); and George M. Fredrickson, *Racism: A Short History* (Princeton, N.J.: Princeton U.P., 2002).

106. Quoted in Levine, *American College,* 154–56. On the disproportionate success of Jews in scientific and scholarly pursuits, see Thorstein Veblen's provocative essay first published in 1919, "The Intellectual Pre-eminence of Jews in Modern Europe," in *Essays in Our Changing Order,* ed. Leon Ardzrooni (New York: Viking, 1934), 219–31.

107. Thomas G. Dyer, *Theodore Roosevelt and the Idea of Race* (Baton Rouge: Louisiana State U.P., 1980), 125.

108. While rarely excelling in outdoor sports, Jews were disproportionately prominent in basketball — an indoor sport centered in urban America. At Yale, when the varsity basketball team finished last in 1922, an independent committee found that there were no Jews on the team and that several Jewish candi-

dates claimed they had been discriminated against — the equivalent, writes Dan Oren, "of a modern-day charge of exclusion of blacks from a basketball team." One year later a new coach named Joseph Fogarty instituted a firm policy of nondiscrimination, selecting players whether they were "black or white, Jew or Gentile, so long as [they could] play basketball." Building his team around two Jewish players, Fogarty won league championships in both 1923 and 1924 (*Joining the Club,* 78–80). The quote from the Rhodes criteria is from Roosevelt, "No Mere Bookworms."

109. Edward A. Ross, "The East European Hebrews," in *The Old World in the New: The Significance of Past and Present Immigration to the American People* (New York: Century, 1914), 167.

110. On the connection between the expansion of the American state and the ideal of "manliness" in the late nineteenth and early twentieth centuries, see Gail Bederman, *Manliness and Civilization: A Cultural History of Gender and Race in the United States, 1880–1917* (Chicago: Univ. of Chicago Press, 1995), especially the chapter "Theodore Roosevelt's Manhood, Nation, and 'Civilization.'"

111. The full quote is: "For centuries the Jews of the Diaspora had no state identity and no military. They therefore developed no tradition of virile adventure — or at least no tradition that was dominant in their culture — such as the Western nations (following the English and the Dutch) developed in their imperial careers" (Martin Green, *The Adventurous Male: Chapters in the History of the White Male Mind* [University Park: Pennsylvania State Univ., 1993], 101).

112. According to Daniel Boyarin, a belief in nonviolence has been a powerful element in the Jewish masculine ideal since the Middle Ages (*Unheroic Conduct: The Rise of Heterosexuality and the Invention of the Jewish Man* [Berkeley, Calif.: Univ. of California Press, 1997]).

113. By 1921, accusations questioning the political loyalty of American Jews were so widespread that more than one hundred citizens of "Gentile birth and Christian faith," among them Woodrow Wilson and William Howard Taft, felt compelled to sign a public statement denouncing the "publication of a number of books, pamphlets, and newspaper articles designed to foster distrust and suspicion of our fellow citizens of Jewish ancestry and faith" and insisting that "the loyalty and patriotism of our fellow citizenry of Jewish faith is equal to that of any part of our people and requires no defense at our hands." For the full statement, see "Loyal and Intelligent Citizenship" in Samuel W. McCall, *Patriotism of the American Jew* (New York: Plymouth Press, 1924), 259–62.

114. Quoted in Levine, *American College,* 156–57.

115. Corwin, "Memorandum on the Problems," YUA. The sense of cultural revulsion felt by many high-status Protestants toward Jews was sometimes accompanied by feelings of physical revulsion. At Dartmouth, the requirement of a photograph was introduced, according to Director of Admissions Bill, to screen out "Jewish students of a physical type unattractive to the average Dartmouth student" (Levine, *American College,* 152).

116. This is not, however, to say that external pressures were so overwhelming that Big Three administrators had no choice but to impose a Jewish quota. In truth, a principled refusal to limit the number of Jews (such as that favored by Harvard's Eliot) would hardly

have caused the demise of their institutions; indeed, in all likelihood, it would not even have caused them to fall from the top tier of American higher education. Nonetheless, such a decision would almost certainly have had serious costs; accordingly, rational administrators need not have been anti-Semitic to conclude that, beyond a certain point, there was a genuine conflict between the principle of open access and the maximization of institutional interests.

117. In 1930, 498 of Harvard's 3,240 undergraduates (15.4 percent) held scholarships. At a time when the total cost of a year at Harvard was roughly $1,200, only 28 of these awards were over $600 (A. E. Hindmarsh, "The Cost of Going to Harvard College," *HAB*, 14 May 1931). See also "The Rich and the Gifted," *HAB*, 27 March 1930, 739–40.

5. Harvard's Conant: The Man and His Ideals

1. The best biography of Conant is James G. Hershberg's magisterial study, *James B. Conant: Harvard to Hiroshima and the Making of the Nuclear Age* (Stanford, Calif.: Stanford U.P., 1993). Though focused on Conant's role in developing the atomic bomb and in shaping nuclear weapons policy, Hershberg provides an insightful account of the man and his life. Conant's memoirs, written in the late 1960s, provide useful information about his early years and his Harvard career but are generally lacking in both introspection and revelation. See James Conant, *My Several Lives: Memoirs of a Social Inventor* (New York: Harper & Row, 1970). An excellent account of Conant's educational philosophy is contained in Jeanne Amster, "Meritocracy Ascendant: James Bryant Conant and the Cultivation of Talent" (Ph.D. diss., Harvard Univ., 1990). Thomas Grissom and Sam Bass Warner Jr. offer appraisals of Conant's writings, and Paul Douglass provides a good summary of Conant's life and works through 1953. See Grissom, "Education and the Cold War: The Role of James B. Conant" in *Roots of Crisis: American Education in the Twentieth Century*, ed. Clarence J. Karier, Paul C. Violas, and Joel Spring (Chicago: Rand McNally College, 1973), 177–97; Warner, "James Bryant Conant," in *Province of Reason* (Cambridge, Mass.: Belknap Press, 1984); and Douglass, *Six Upon the World: Toward an American Culture for an Industrial Age* (Boston: Little, Brown, 1954). Major journalistic pieces on Conant include a two-part article by Henry Pringle in the *New Yorker*, another two-part piece by Kermit Roosevelt in the *Saturday Evening Post*, and an unsigned cover story in the September 22, 1952, *Newsweek*, "U.S. Education's No. 1 Men." See Pringle, "Profiles: Mr. President," *New Yorker*, 12 and 19 September 1936; Roosevelt, "Harvard's Prize Kibitzer," parts one and two, *Saturday Evening Post*, 23 April 1949 and 30 April 1949; and Louis Menand, "The Long Shadow of James B. Conant," in *American Studies* (New York: Farrar, Straus, 2002), 91–111.

2. "Need-blind" admissions is a selection process that ignores the capacity to pay in determining who is admitted; "full aid" is a policy of providing sufficient financial assistance, calculated on a sliding scale according to need, to permit all those admitted to enroll.

3. Amster, "Meritocracy Ascendant," 81.

4. In 1933, when a year at Harvard cost roughly $1,100, only 6 students among well over 3,000 received

awards greater than $500; the other 487 scholarship recipients received awards as follows: $100 (89), $200 (129), $300 (108), $400 (134), $500 (27). See Amster, "Meritocracy Ascendant," 117; Marcia Graham Synnott, *The Half-Opened Door: Discrimination and Admissions at Harvard, Yale, and Princeton, 1900–1970* (Westport, Conn.: Greenwood Press, 1979), 12, and Seymour E. Harris, ed., *Economics of Harvard* (New York: McGraw-Hill, 1970), xxix, 108.

5. Conant, *My Several Lives*, 133.

6. "Memorandum on Harvard National Scholarships," n.d. [c. 1937], HUA.

7. Conant, *My Several Lives*, 129–30.

8. Ibid., 134; Claude M. Fuess, *The College Board: Its First Fifty Years* (New York: Columbia U.P., 1950), 141.

9. In his memoirs, Conant noted the impact of the adoption of the SAT: Harvard's "use of objective tests for selecting national scholars was an important factor in promoting the use of these tests for general purposes (*My Several Lives*, 134). See also Amster, "Meritocracy Ascendant," 83–84, 90–91.

10. Ibid., 90–91.

11. The responsibility of institutions such as Harvard was not only to identify and recruit such "natural aristocrats" but also to prepare them for the responsibility of leadership. To do this, the time-honored American tradition of students working their way through college was to be replaced, at least for the future elite of the meritocracy, with "a scholarship as large as is needed." "A promising student," Conant wrote in 1934, "should be able to devote his time to his studies without the distraction of trying to earn his living" (*My Several Lives*, 313).

12. Amster, "Meritocracy Ascendant," 89.

13. "U.S. Education's No. 1 Man," *Newsweek*, 22 September 1952.

14. Conant's critical role in the development of weapons in both world wars is discussed in great detail in Hershberg. For Conant's own account, see *My Several Lives*, especially chapter 5 and chapters 18–26.

15. Ibid., 3

16. Douglass, *Six Upon the World*, 331; Hershberg, *James B. Conant*, 12.

17. Vannevar Bush, "James Bryant Conant: President of the AAAS for 1946," *Scientific Monthly*, March 1946.

18. Douglass, *Six Upon the World*, 331; Hershberg, *James B. Conant*, 15.

19. "Harvard's James Bryant Conant," *Time*, 5 February 1934; Douglass, *Six Upon the World*, 330.

20. Amster, "Meritocracy Ascendant," 53. Douglass depicts Conant's childhood home as an "elm-shaded mansion near Peabody Square" with "a broad lawn down to the avenue" (*Six Upon the World*, 330). Hershberg however, simply describes the Conant domicile as a "two-story wood-frame house purchased in 1880" (*James B. Conant*, 13). Conant himself said that the "house had the spaciousness of another era" but characterized it as "not luxurious by the standards of the more modern houses of most of my friends" (*My Several Lives*, 7).

21. Amster, "Meritocracy Ascendant," 25.

22. Young Bryant insisted on going to Roxbury Latin despite his parents' preference for Milton because of his interest in science and his apparent awareness of Roxbury Latin's excellence in that area. "Harvard's James Bryant Conant," 26.

23. Amster, "Meritocracy Ascendant," 25.

24. Douglass, *Six Upon the World*, 332.

25. Ibid., 333; Amster, "Meritocracy Ascendant," 27; Conant, *My Several Lives*, 13–14.

26. Hershberg, *James B. Conant*, 16.

27. Conant, *My Several Lives*, 16.

28. Hershberg, *James B. Conant*, 16–19.

29. Ibid., 17.

30. Douglass, *Six Upon the World*, 333.

31. Hershberg, *James B. Conant*, 18; Pringle, "Profiles," 12 September 1936, 23.

32. Douglass, *Six Upon the World*, 332.

33. Hershberg, *James B. Conant*, 19.

34. Conant, *My Several Lives*, 31–33; Hershberg, *James B. Conant*, 28–29.

35. Amster, "Meritocracy Ascendant," 40; Douglass, *Six Upon the World*, 334; "Harvard's James Bryant Conant," 27.

36. Douglass, *Six Upon the World*, 334; Amster, "Meritocracy Ascendant," 40; Roosevelt, "Harvard's Prize Kibitzer," part 1, 72; "Harvard's James Bryant Conant," 27.

37. Of the 21 students who graduated with Conant from Roxbury Latin in 1910, 12 went to Harvard and 1 each to Yale, Amherst, Dartmouth, and MIT (Amster, "Meritocracy Ascendant," 26–29).

38. Hershberg, *James B. Conant*, 23–26. For a socially ambitious freshman, observes the historian Samuel Eliot Morison, "intellect was no handicap, provided it was tactfully concealed, and all the social taboos observed" (*Three Centuries of Harvard, 1636–1936* [Cambridge, Mass.: Harvard U.P., 1936], 422).

39. Conant, *My Several Lives*, 24.

40. Amster, "Meritocracy Ascendant," 36.

41. Ibid., 37–38.

42. Conant, *My Several Lives*, 24.

43. Ibid.

44. Morison, *Three Centuries of Harvard*, 427.

45. Hershberg, *James B. Conant*, 31.

46. Conant, *My Several Lives*, 24.

47. In 1906, four years before Conant entered Harvard, the Institute of 1770 (which merged with Hasty Pudding Club in 1926) enrolled slightly less than 20 percent of the sophomore class. From those selected, a smaller and more elite group was chosen for membership in the final clubs. At the apex of Harvard's social pyramid were two of those clubs, the Porcellian and the A.D. See Morison, *Three Centuries of Harvard*, 423–25, and Robert W. Merry, *Taking On the World: Joseph and Stewart Alsop — Guardians of the American Century* (New York: Penguin Books, 1996), 36–37.

48. Hershberg, *James B. Conant*, 31.

49. I am indebted to Amster for this observation on the link between Conant's public behavior and his scientific temperament. Amster, "Meritocracy Ascendant," 36.

50. Hershberg, *James B. Conant*, 26.

51. Douglass, *Six Upon the World*, 334.

52. Amster, "Meritocracy Ascendant," 35. Marquand was a small-town boy on a chemistry scholarship at Harvard and was less successful socially there than Conant. In several novels, the best known being *The Late George Apley* (Boston: Little, Brown, 1937), which won the Pulitzer Prize in fiction, Marquand satirized the snobbery pervading Brahmin Boston and undergraduate life at Harvard. Conant remained friends with Marquand, read his novels with relish, and "praised [his] penetrating sociological analysis of a highly interesting and complex bit of society" (Hershberg, *James B. Conant*, 24–26, 32–33, 786). See

also *Harvard Freshman Redbook: Class of 1915* and *WWA, 1944–1945*.

53. Douglass, *Six Upon the World*, 335; Univ. News Service, "James Bryant Conant, 23rd President of Harvard University (A Biographical Sketch — to June 1951)," n.d. [c. 1951], HUA, 7; Pringle, "Profiles," 12 September 1936, 24; Conant, *My Several Lives*, 39.

54. "Harvard's James Bryant Conant," 27.

55. Conant, *My Several Lives*, 32.

56. Ibid., 33; Hershberg, *James B. Conant*, 32, 36.

57. Conant, *My Several Lives*, 43; Hershberg, *James B. Conant*, 37–38.

58. Conant, *My Several Lives*, 43–44; Hershberg, *James B. Conant*, 37–38.

59. In the immediate aftermath, Loomis — who had been temporarily blinded by the blast but saved himself by rolling in the water — diplomatically refrained from giving Conant's name to the newspapers, and for many years, the tragic incident was not a part of Conant's biography. But in his twenty-fifth-year reunion report, written during his sixth year as Harvard's president, Conant gave an account of the explosion in Newark. While acknowledging that it "killed one of the three partners," he does not mention that two other people also died (Hershberg, *James B. Conant*, 39).

60. Ibid.

61. Conant, *My Several Lives*, 45.

62. Ibid.

63. Ibid., 47.

64. Hershberg, *James B. Conant*, 45; Conant, *My Several Lives*, 48–49.

65. Hershberg, *James B. Conant*, 44.

66. *Twenty-fifth Anniversary Report: Class of 1914*, HU, 165.

67. Hershberg, *James B. Conant*, 47.

68. Douglass, *Six Upon the World*, 337.

69. Hershberg, *James B. Conant*, 46–47.

70. Conant, *My Several Lives*, 49.

71. Hershberg, *James B. Conant*, 49.

72. "It is a severe blow to me . . . to the University of Chicago, and to the West at large," wrote his disappointed suitor from the University of Chicago Chemistry Department in February 1919, "that you are so rockbound in your provinciality to insist on Boston in spite of anything and everything" (Ibid., 54, 790).

73. Ibid., 50–52; Conant, *My Several Lives*, 54.

74. Richards, born into a patrician Philadelphia family in 1868, was the son of William Trost Richards, a renowned landscape painter, and Anna Matlock Richards, a pianist and poet. His mother tutored him at home, and he received his bachelor's degree from Haverford at seventeen, adding a second bachelor's from Harvard the following year. Receiving his Ph.D. at the age of twenty and becoming a full professor at thirty-three, Richards was the most famous chemist in the nation by the time Conant entered Harvard, and he was awarded the Nobel Prize in Chemistry in 1914. Charming and courteous, Richards has been described as displaying "the cool rationality and reserve that Americans often associate with the English gentry." See Hershberg, *James B. Conant*, 27, 59; Conant, *My Several Lives*, 28–29; Pringle, "Profiles," 12 September 1936, 24; *WWA, 1926–1927*.

75. Conant, *My Several Lives*, 52.

76. Hershberg, *James B. Conant*, 59; Pringle, "Profiles," 12 September 1936, 24.

77. Born in Lynn, Massachusetts, Henderson (1878–1942) graduated from Harvard College in 1898

and its medical school in 1902. A distinguished biochemist, he became interested in sociology and played a major role in introducing the works of Vilfredo Pareto, best known for his theory of the "circulation of elites," into American sociology. Henderson published his own book on the subject, *Pareto's General Sociology* (Cambridge, Mass.: Harvard U.P., 1935), and influenced the thinking of a number of sociologists, including Talcott Parsons, George Homans, and Robert Merton. In 1933, he became the first chairman of Harvard's elite Society of Fellows, whose early members included B. F. Skinner, W. F. Whyte, and C. M. Arensberg. See *International Encyclopedia of the Social Sciences*, vol. 6, "Henderson, L. J."

78. The final vote on the resolution was 41 in favor and 64 against ("Minutes of Special Meeting of the Faculty of Arts and Sciences," 2 June 1922, HUA). See also Hershberg, *James B. Conant*, 58–59.

79. Amster, "Meritocracy Ascendant," 51; Conant, *My Several Lives*, 74–75.

80. Douglass, *Six Upon the World*, 339; Richard N. Smith, *The Harvard Century: The Making of a University to a Nation* (Cambridge, Mass.: Harvard U.P., 1986), 103.

81. Pringle states flatly that Conant, had he remained a scientist, "would almost certainly have been a winner, ultimately, of the Nobel Prize" ("Profiles," 12 September 1936, 20). Smith claims that Conant's colleagues had "confidently forecast" a Nobel for him (*Harvard Century*, 104). Hershberg is more cautious, concluding that Conant had "at least a reasonable shot at a Nobel Prize" (*James B. Conant*, 69).

82. Pringle, "Profiles," 19 September 1936, 22.

83. Amster, "Meritocracy Ascendant," 56–59; Smith, *Harvard Century*, 101–5; Hershberg, *James B. Conant*, 68–75.

84. Conant, *My Several Lives*, 3–19; Hershberg, *James B. Conant*, 11–19; Amster, "Meritocracy Ascendant," 23–29.

85. Conant, *My Several Lives*, 82–83.

86. Ibid., 82–85.

87. Amster, "Meritocracy Ascendant," 56.

88. Curtis, a graduate of Groton and the son of a Harvard alumnus, had been a member of Conant's class at Harvard, (1914). In 1917, he graduated from Harvard Law School and immediately joined one of Boston's leading law firms. See *WWA, 1944–1945*.

89. Conant, *My Several Lives*, 87.

90. Perkins added that Conant was "intellectually first class, a first-class fellow, for his age a great scientist; and of course he might become just the man, but I suspect he has got to become it" (Amster, "Meritocracy Ascendant," 58).

91. Hershberg, *James B. Conant*, 73–74.

92. Conant, *My Several Lives*, 87–89.

93. During the latter stages of the search, Frankfurter had written to Grenville Clark that "all I have seen of Conant and all I have been able to learn about him from cross-examining others, he seems to me an essentially unperceptive mind, however distinguished in its own specialty . . . his own limited range hardly gives him the means of judging the range appropriate for the guidance of America's greatest university." See Hershberg, *James B. Conant*, 73–75; President's Report, 1932–1933, HU, 7–8.

94. President's Report, 1932–1933, HU, 7–8.

95. Ibid., 8–10.

96. Ibid., 10.

97. H. I. Brock, "Conant States His Creed for Harvard," *NYT*, 18 March 1934.

98. Ibid., 14–16; Conant's address to the Alumni Association on Commencement Day, *HAB*, 5 July 1935, 1128–32; President's Report, 1936–1937, HU, 7–8; James B. Conant, "Harvard Present and Future," *HAB*, 10 April 1936, 812–18.

99. President's Report, 1936–1937, 15.

100. Ibid., 8.

101. Conant, "Harvard Present and Future," 813. The 100 National Scholarships envisioned by Conant would have constituted a huge increase in the number of awards given annually; in the fall of 1935, only 11 entering students received National Scholarships, though their numbers increased to 17 in 1936 and 31 in 1937. "Prize Fellowships Awarded," *HAB*, 11 October 1935, 80–82; President's Report, 1935–1936, 19; President's Report, 1936–1937, 12–13.

102. James B. Conant, "The Mission of American Universities," *HAB*, 25 February 1938, 597.

103. Ibid., 598.

104. James B. Conant, "The Future of Our Higher Education," *Harper's*, May 1938, 563.

105. Ibid., 561.

106. Ibid., 570.

107. Ibid., 565.

108. Ibid., 566.

109. Ibid., 562.

110. Ibid., 564.

111. Ibid., 569.

112. In *Education in a Divided World*, Conant stated explicitly that "community colleges . . . should be defined as terminal two-year colleges," adding that "an occasional transfer to a university should not be barred" (Cambridge, Mass.: Harvard U.P., 1948), 200. For an account of his blueprint for junior colleges in the context of his larger plan for higher education, see Steven Brint and Jerome Karabel, *The Diverted Dream: Community Colleges and the Promises of Educational Opportunity in America, 1900–1985* (New York: Oxford U.P., 1989), 80–82.

113. Ibid., 565–66.

114. *Twenty-fifth Anniversary Report: Class of 1914*, HU, 164, 166. Though World War II had not yet begun when Conant wrote his statement for his reunion, he did not hesitate to describe Nazi Germany as totalitarian, writing that "no one concerned with the solidarity of the international community of scholars can be oblivious to the fate of those professors who have suffered by the destruction of the universities in the totalitarian states."

115. Hershberg, *James B. Conant*, 116.

116. William M. Tuttle Jr., "James B. Conant, Pressure Groups, and the National Defense, 1933–1945" (Ph.D. diss., Univ. of Wisconsin, 1967), 91.

117. Ibid., 92.

118. Smith, *Harvard Century*, 141. In November 1939, a *Crimson* poll of 1,800 students found that 95 percent opposed America's immediate entry into the war, with 78 still opposed even if France and Britain faced defeat. One student who was strongly opposed was a senior named John Fitzgerald Kennedy; in an unsigned editorial in the *Crimson*, "Peace in Our Time," he advocated the appeasement position endorsed by his father, Joseph P. Kennedy, the American ambassador to Britain (Hershberg, *James B. Conant*, 117).

119. James B. Conant, "Education for a Classless

Society: The Jeffersonian Tradition," *Atlantic Monthly,* May 1940, 593–602.

120. My portrait of the 1930s draws on a number of sources, including Eric Foner, *The Story of American Freedom* (New York: Norton, 1998), 195–218; Frances F. Piven and Richard A. Cloward, *Poor People's Movements: Why They Succeed, How They Fail* (New York: Vintage, 1979), 41–180; and Howard Zinn, *A People's History of the United States: 1942–Present* (1980; New York: Harper Collins, 1995), 368–97. The unemployment rate nationwide peaked at 24.9 percent in 1933 and stood at 17.2 percent in 1939 (U.S. Bureau of the Census, *Historical Statistics of the United States: Colonial Times to 1970,* part II [Washington, D.C.:. Department of Commerce, 1975], 135).

121. Dewey, quoted in Foner, *Story of American Freedom,* 211.

122. Conant, "Education for a Classless Society," 593.

123. Conant, "Future of Our Higher Education," 598.

124. Conant, "Education for a Classless Society," 597.

125. Ibid., 598.

126. Conant, "Education for a Classless Society," 599. Conant was, of course, aware that inequalities of wealth, power, and status were commonplace in the United States. Yet he persisted in calling America "classless" because of what he saw as a relative absence of hereditary privilege. "'Caste' and 'class' are equated by the average American," he argued, stating forthrightly that he would follow the lay usage. Thus when Conant declared that he rejected "the idea of an inevitable stratification of society," he was repudiating not inequality of *condition* but inequality of *opportunity.* From the perspective of modern sociology, Conant's ideal society would be a highly stratified, albeit fluid, social order.

127. Ibid., 598.

128. Ibid., 602.

129. The Jefferson quote is from Conant, "Future of Our Higher Education," 563.

130. Ibid., 597–99.

131. Ibid., 599.

132. Ibid., 602.

133. Ibid., 601.

134. Ibid., 598–99.

135. See Hershberg, *James B. Conant,* 135–257; Conant, *My Several Lives,* 234–360; and Tuttle, "James B. Conant," for detailed accounts of Conant's contribution to the war effort. Also useful are Vannevar Bush, "James Bryant Conant: President of the AAAS for 1946," *Scientific Monthly,* March 1946, 197–200, and Karl T. Compton, "James Bryant Conant," *Science* 103 (1946), 191–92. Both Bush, chairman of the Office of Scientific Research and Development and Conant's superior, and Compton, the president of MIT, were important collaborators with Conant in deploying the nation's scientific resources in the service of the Allies.

136. Bush reported in 1946 that during "the last two years of the war Dr. Conant spent an increasingly major portion of his time on the atomic bomb project, unbeknown to any except a few of his closest colleagues" ("James Bryant Conant," 192). On May 2, 1945, when Truman appointed a seven-member advisory group on atomic issues (the so-called Interior Committee), Conant was included, along with Bush,

Compton, and the committee's chair, Secretary of War Henry Stimson. The committee's primary task was to offer advice on whether the atomic bomb should be used — and, if so, how. At a critical meeting on May 31, the issue of a possible target was discussed. The minutes record that "at the suggestion of Dr. Conant the Secretary [Stimson] agreed that the most desirable target would be a vital war plant employing a large number of workers and closely surrounded by the workers' houses" (Hershberg, *James B. Conant,* 225–26). On whether to drop the bomb, the committee concluded that "we can propose no technical demonstration likely to bring an end to the war; we can see no acceptable alternative to direct military use." With only one member dissenting (Undersecretary of the Navy Ralph A. Bard), the committee recommended that the atomic bomb be used at the earliest opportunity (Conant, *My Several Lives,* 302). On August 6, the bomb was dropped on downtown Hiroshima; two days later a second bomb was dropped on Nagasaki. Conant, who died in 1978, never accepted the arguments of those who claimed that the use of the atomic bomb was immoral, believing (as he had during World War I on the issue of poison gas) that all war was immoral and that sometimes there was no alternative to the use of heinous means in defense of noble ends. Late in life, however, he acknowledged that the bombing of Nagasaki, which the Interim Committee had not discussed, might have been a mistake (Hershberg, *James B. Conant,* 228).

137. Though Conant retained his presidency, it was an open secret in Cambridge that he had delegated responsibility for its day-to-day administration to his loyal and energetic provost, Paul Buck. Buck, a Pulitzer Prize–winning historian, remained in office until Conant's resignation in 1953. See John T. Bethell, *Harvard Observed: An Illustrated History of the University in the Twentieth Century* (Cambridge, Mass.: Harvard U.P., 1998), 149.

138. James B. Conant, "Wanted: American Radicals," *Atlantic Monthly,* May 1943, 43.

139. Ibid., 44.

140. While clearly identifying with the "American radical," the ever-cautious Conant was at pains to declare that he did not "wish to give a blanket endorsement to his views" and did not believe "all his aims should be achieved" (ibid., 45). Nevertheless, anyone familiar with his earlier writings could have little doubt that he strongly sympathized with the "hypothetical gentleman" described in the *Atlantic Monthly* article.

141. Ibid., 43.

142. Ibid., 43, 45.

143. By the time Conant's article appeared in the *Atlantic,* Lamont had already pledged the funds for an undergraduate library (Conant, *My Several Lives,* 404). The contribution was not announced, however, until the end of the war. In 1949, Lamont Library opened in Harvard Yard just a few months after Lamont's death (Bethell, *Harvard Observed,* 189).

144. Lamont to Conant, 22 June 1943, HUA.

145. Conant to Lamont, 26 July 1943, HUA.

146. In Conant's view, World War II was rooted in "underlying forces of social dissatisfaction, of great power and transcending national boundaries." "The large maladjustment on which Marx centered his attention," he wrote, "has had a great influence in bringing about . . . the paralysis of France and the near pa-

ralysis of England." Conant concluded that "France fell largely because of the unresolved conflict between Left and Right" and that "England from the last war to the fall of Chamberlain suffered from paralysis in its foreign policy because the only alternative to the Tory party was the Labor party with its essentially socialistic basis." The clear implication of Conant's analysis was that if class lines continued to harden in the United States, it too would be increasingly wracked by bitter conflicts between Left and Right that would undermine its capacity to pursue the type of vigorous foreign policy necessary for the defense of freedom. See Conant to Lamont, 26 July 1943, HUA.

147. Ibid.

148. Ibid. In placing business and professional groups together in opposition to manual workers, Conant developed a sophisticated analysis of class that in many ways anticipated the theory of "professional and managerial class" (PMC) elaborated in the 1970s by John and Barbara Ehrenreich. See Pat Walker, ed., *Between Labor and Capital* (Boston: South End Press, 1979). Conant's formulation, which emphasizes that businessmen and professionals share a privileged position, also has striking affinities to Frank Parkin's theory of "social closure," which views the propertied and the credentialed jointly as constituting the dominant class in advanced capitalist societies (*Marxism and Class Theory: A Bourgeois Critique* [New York: Columbia U.P., 1979], 979).

149. Conant to Lamont, 26 July 1943, HUA, 8–9, 13.

150. Ibid.

151. Ibid.

152. Ibid. In his 1943 *Atlantic Monthly* article, written at the height of the American-Soviet alliance, Conant went so far as to refer to "the miraculous Russian state" ("Wanted: American Radicals," 42).

153. Conant to Lamont, 26 July 1943, HUA.

154. Tuttle, "James B. Conant," 31.

155. Though a registered Republican, Conant voted for James Cox in 1920, the Progressive candidate Robert La Follette in 1924, Al Smith in 1928, and Franklin D. Roosevelt four times between 1932 and 1944 (Tuttle, "James B. Conant," 23; Smith, *Harvard Century*, 108).

156. Tuttle, "James B. Conant," 33.

157. Hershberg, *James B. Conant*, 176.

158. Ibid., 175. In his letter to Lamont, Conant admitted that the "American radical" portrayed in the article is "an American type of thinker with whom I am in general sympathetic" and accurately described the article as "only an extension of what is implied in my earlier articles and speeches on a free and classless society" (Conant to Lamont, 26 July 1943, 14, 16).

159. William H. Claflin '15, Harvard's treasurer and a member of the Corporation, had been strongly opposed to Conant's interventionist stance. In May 1940, as France was falling, Conant's diary reports the following incident: "1 p.m. to New York for Ass. Harvard Club meeting . . . Black prophecy of French surrender. Bill Claflin particularly pessimistic after trip to Wall St. Told him I might urge USA to get in and help. He said, no, be realistic Hitler's going to win, let's be friends with him. Dinner at Lamont's." Two months later, after a dinner conversation with Claflin, Conant records in his diary that Harvard's treasurer was confident that America could "'get on' with a victorious Germany." In Conant's view, Claflin's position seemed "typical of business appeasement groups" (Hershberg, *James B. Conant*, 119, 129–30).

160. Paul H. Buck, interview by William Bentinck-Smith, June–July 1979, transcript of tape recording, HUA, 72.

161. Bethell states flatly: "From 1940 until the war's end, President Conant spent more than half his time in Washington as a government science adviser" (*Harvard Observed*, 149).

162. Ibid., 107; *WWA, 1944–1945*.

163. Shattuck to Conant, 8 September 1943, HUA.

164. Buck interview, 69–70.

165. Ibid.

166. It was not until August 1945, after the Japanese had surrendered, that Conant was able to inform the Corporation and Overseers why he had served in his "dual capacity." While the nation was still at war, he wrote in a confidential memo on August 25, 1945, he had not been able to "even hint to my closest Harvard advisors what stakes were involved." Conant had not wanted to force a change in Harvard's presidency during wartime, but a chief reason he did not resign, he acknowledged, was "the undoubted fact that the prestige of Harvard's name contributed much to my value in the work" (confidential memorandum, 25 August 1945, quoted in Hershberg, *James B. Conant*, 808).

167. James B. Conant, *Public Education and the Structure of American Society* (New York: Teachers College, Columbia Univ., 1946).

168. Ibid., 3–4.

169. Ibid., 6.

170. Ibid., 7.

171. Ibid., 37.

172. Ibid., 6.

173. Conant believed that commitment to the ideal of equality of opportunity "implies a high degree of competition." "Our problem," he wrote, "is to make these ideals operate as constructive social forces and to eliminate the anti-social aspects of the greedy side of competition," *Public Education*, 8).

174. Ibid., 43.

175. While criticizing those who failed to grasp the "significance of innate ability" and who decried "the reality of intellectual talent," Conant was careful not to push meritocratic ideology too far. As the president of a university committed ever since the appearance of the "Jewish problem" to the use of discretion in admissions, Conant was firmly opposed to selection on intellectual talent alone. Would such a system, he asked rhetorically, "result merely in a cutthroat competition among potential members of Phi Beta Kappa?" Worse still, "where would our future businessmen . . . obtain that *general* education we all admit they need?" (*Public Education*, 35, 37).

176. "Harvard's James Bryant Conant."

177. Conant, "Address to Rotary Club," Boston, 28 March 1948, quoted in Barry Jam Teicher, "James Bryant Conant and 'The American High School Today'" (Ph.D. diss., Univ. of Wisconsin-Madison, 1977), 151.

178. A reluctant Cold War warrior, Conant was still hopeful in 1946 that the Soviet Union could be made part of an international accord to control the atomic bomb. With this goal in mind, he had judged Churchill's "Iron Curtain" speech of March 5, 1946, "to be an error," for it threatened to close the door to fruitful contact with the Soviet Union. The coup in Czechoslovakia in February 1948 convinced Conant that the Cold War was unavoidable, but it was not until the North Korean attack on South Korea in June 1950 that

he converted to the view that the Soviets posed a direct and immediate military threat to the West. In response, he spearheaded the formation of the Committee on the Present Danger, a nonpartisan body of distinguished citizens whose purpose would be to strengthen "public support for such stern measures as may be necessary." When the committee's function was announced on December 12, 1950, its statement ended on an ominous note: "The bitter fact is that our country has again been thrust into a struggle in which our free existence is at stake, a struggle for survival. We have no time to lose." See Conant, *My Several Lives*, 505–14; Tuttle, "James B. Conant," 384–91; Hershberg, *James B. Conant*, 491–514.

179. Educational Policies Commission, *Education and National Security* (Washington, D.C.: Educational Policies Commission and American Council on Education, 1951), 60.

180. Educational Policies Commission, *Education for the Gifted* (Washington, D.C.: National Education Association, 1950), 88.

181. In his notebook for 1948, Conant wrote of his future ambitions: "Write a book for publication in January 1953 (after announcement of retirement on September 1, 1953, on 'The Principle of Equality (The Unique American Answer)')" (Amster, "Meritocratic Ascendant," 164). Conant claimed that he had made up his mind "shortly after taking office to retire from the presidency of Harvard soon after my sixtieth birthday" (*My Several Lives*, 496). On March 26, 1953, Conant turned sixty, having two months earlier left Harvard to become high commissioner (and later ambassador) to Germany.

182. Conant, *My Several Lives*, 469.

183. James B. Conant, "Education: Engine of Democracy," *Saturday Review*, 3 May 1952, 12.

184. Ibid., 13.

185. Conant, *My Several Lives*, 468.

186. See, for example, his ten-point plan for American education in *Education and Liberty: The Role of the Schools in a Modern Democracy* (Cambridge, Mass.: Harvard U.P., 1953), 56–58.

6. *The Reality of Admissions Under Conant*

1. Seymour Martin Lipset and David Riesman, *Education and Politics at Harvard* (New York: McGraw-Hill, 1975), 305.

2. Lipset and Riesman, *Education and Politics*, 190.

3. James G. Hershberg, *James B. Conant: Harvard to Hiroshima and the Making of the Nuclear Age* (Stanford, Calif.: Stanford U.P., 1993), 402, 67.

4. Nicholas Lemann, *The Big Test: The Secret History of the American Meritocracy* (New York: Farrar, Straus, 1999), 9, 44, 49.

5. Hershberg, *James B. Conant*, 80. Conant's decision to open Dudley House, a haven for commuters, many of whom were Jews, is often cited as additional evidence of his lack of anti-Semitism. In his book *In Search of History: A Personal Memoir* (New York: Harper & Row, 1978), Theodore H. White '38, an ambitious Jewish commuter from Boston, described Conant as "the first president to recognize that meatballs were Harvard men, too" (40–44).

6. Richard N. Smith, *The Harvard Century: The Making of a University to a Nation* (Cambridge, Mass.: Harvard U.P., 1986), 113. Lipset concurred, concluding

that "under Conant and Buck, Harvard was implementing the policy enunciated by Eliot that its officers are selected for their fitness only, without the least regard to their religious affiliation" (Lipset and Riesman, *Education and Politics*, 180).

7. Henry Rosovsky, "Then and Now: The Jewish Experience at Harvard," *Moment*, June 1980, 24.

8. The reference to Pennypacker's "manly character" is from the Committee on Admission, "Report of the Committee on Admission," 1934–1935, HU, 349. "The Minute on the Life and Services of Henry Pennypacker," *Harvard University Gazette*, 10 February 1934, also refers to his "manliness" as well as his "commanding presence," his "resonant voice," and his "high ideals." See also "Pennypacker, Noted Harvard Educator, Dead," *Boston Herald*, 28 November 1933; "Pennypacker Dies After Illness of Week at Stillman," *HC*, 20 November 1933; "H. Pennypacker, Educator, Dead," *NYT*, 20 November 1933.

9. Anne MacDonald, "Memorandum Concerning Admission Office," 7 April 1934, HUA.

10. According to E. Digby Baltzell, author of *The Protestant Establishment* and the man who introduced the word "WASP" into popular usage, the Gummeres "have been perhaps the leading Quaker family of educators in the nation's history." The family's first American ancestor was a French Huguenot who settled in the Germantown section of Philadelphia in 1719; the Gummeres went on to produce numerous educational leaders, including Samuel James Gummere, who in 1862 became the second president of Haverford College (Baltzell, *Puritan Boston and Quaker Philadelphia: Two Protestant Ethics and the Spirit of Class Authority and Leadership* [New York: Free Press, 1979], 444).

11. See "Dr. Gummere, 86, Harvard Dean," *Boston Herald Traveler*, 4 December 1969; "Richard M. Gummere Is New Admissions Head," *HC*, 18 May 1934; "More Poor Boys in Harvard Now Than There Were 17 Years Ago," *Boston Globe*, 14 October 1951.

12. Gummere to Pennypacker, 25 May 1922, HUA.

13. A 1921 graduate of Swarthmore, a Quaker, and a Rhodes Scholar, Valentine joined the Yale faculty as a professor in the History Arts and Letters Department in 1932. The author of *The English Novel* (1927) and *Biography* (1927), he left Yale in 1935 to become president of the University of Rochester.

14. Hanford to Conant, 8 March 1934, HUA.

15. "Richard M. Gummere," 18 May 1934.

16. Richard Gummere, "Confidential Report to President Conant on Harvard Admission Problems," 19 August 1934, HUA, 1.

17. Ibid., 15.

18. Ibid., 5.

19. Ibid., 3. Except in rare cases, Gummere believed that the public school boy, despite his high grades, "has no mental toughness or agility." Moreover, he was less likely to exercise leadership later in life: "It would incidentally be worth while to get up a list of young men in prominent positions of all kinds, and establish the ratio of public or private training" (ibid., 2).

20. Ibid., 13, 16.

21. Ibid., 16–17.

22. President's Report, 1932–1933, HU, 7–8. See also the discussion of this report in Chapter 5.

23. Gummere, "Confidential Report," 6.

24. The idea that Harvard's student body should

be "balanced" was articulated in Conant's Oration at Harvard's Tercentenary Celebration in 1936, his first truly major public address as president. Conant contended that several distinct streams "have watered the soil on which the universities have flourished." Among these currents was "the never-failing river of student life carrying all power that comes from the gregarious impulses of human beings." He continued: "The cultivation of learning alone produces not a university but a research institute; the sole concern with student life produces an academic country club or merely a football team maneuvering under a collegiate banner." The future of the university tradition, he concluded, depends on "keeping a proper balance," and it must include a "healthy student life." From "Oration at the Solemn Observance of the Tercentenary of Harvard College, Cambridge, Massachusetts, September 18, 1936," reprinted in James B. Conant, *My Several Lives: Memoirs of a Social Inventor* (New York: Harper & Row, 1970), 651–58. Paul Buck, in his influential article "Balance in the College" (1946), makes extensive reference to this address (*HAB*, 16 February 1946, 404).

25. Buck, interview by William Bentinck-Smith, June–July 1979, transcript of tape recording, HUA, 69–70.

26. Ibid. The Tavern was one of several exclusive social clubs frequented by Boston's Protestant upper class.

27. Gummere, "Confidential Report," 1.

28. Committee on Admission, "Report of the Committee on Admission," 1939–1940, HU, 161–62.

29. See Marcia Graham Synnott, *The Half-Opened Door: Discrimination and Admissions at Harvard, Yale, and Princeton, 1900–1970* (Westport, Conn.: Greenwood Press, 1979), 107.

30. MacDonald to Heermance, 7 March 1936, PUA.

31. William Johnson and James are pseudonyms. In the few cases where archival documents refer to individual applicants, I have used pseudonyms to protect their privacy while trying to communicate a sense of their ethnicity. I have also sometimes changed their place of residence (e.g., from Cleveland to Detroit). Hanford to MacDonald, 16 March 1939, HUA; Hanford to the Committee on Admission, n.d., HUA.

32. Irving B. Rosenstein, Goldberg, and Rabinowitz are pseudonyms. Hanford to Gummere, 11 May 1936, HUA.

33. Goldstein is a pseudonym.

34. Greene to Lynch, 31 July 1936, HUA.

35. For documentation of Harvard's Jewish quota from 1933 through 1942, see Synnott, *Half-Opened Door*, 112–20.

36. Those figures slightly underestimate the percentage of Jews in the freshman class because they include only those students who applied for residence in one of the residential houses after freshman year. Jews, however, were overrepresented among commuters, who generally did not live in the houses. Among freshmen in 1938, for example, Jews composed 22 percent of commuters but only 15.4 percent of those applying for a place in the houses (ibid., 115–20).

37. "Supplementary Memorandum Explaining Method of Arriving at Estimate of Size of Class of 1946," 3 April 1942, HUA, 2. Given Harvard's recurrent emphasis, visible in numerous internal documents, on the importance of attracting students who did not need scholarship assistance, the imposition of a quota

even on those Jewish applicants who could pay their own way clearly indicates the importance attached by the Conant administration to keeping the number of Jews down.

38. Helen E. Davis, *Getting into College* (Washington, D.C.: American Council on Education, 1949), 29.

39. For a discussion of this controversy, see the more detailed account in Nell Painter, "Jim Crow at Harvard: 1923," *New England Quarterly*, 1971, 627–34.

40. Woodward to Hanford, 28 February 1935, HUA.

41. Hanford to Woodward, 4 March 1935, HUA.

42. Hibbard to Birkhoff, 22 May 1939, and Hanford to Addison Hibbard, 31 May 1939, HUA. Figures for 1935–1936 from B. J. Hunt, memorandum, 3 June 1936, HUA. Dean Hibbard's inquiry was part of an investigation by a Senate Committee at Northwestern "appointed to consider our policy regarding dormitory space for colored students."

43. Synnott, *Half-Opened Door*, 83.

44. James B. Conant, "Confidential Memorandum concerning the 'size of the small pond in which the private colleges are fishing,'" n.d. [c. March 1938], HUA.

45. Throughout the Conant years and beyond, the internal documents of both the Harvard admissions office and the administration show a consistent preoccupation with attracting what they called "paying guests" and "paying customers." In the early part of this period, the term most commonly used was "paying guests" — which suggests an affinity with an exclusive hotel or resort. During the later years, "paying customers" — suggesting a business firm's transactions with those who wished to purchase its "product" — became dominant, though it never entirely displaced "paying guest" as the phrase of choice.

46. Bender to Lamont, 25 January 1957, HUA. During Conant's first eight years as president, the proportion of the freshman class who were legacies ranged from 23 to 28 percent. By 1951 and 1952, Conant's final two years, the proportion had dropped to 16.5 and 17.0 percent.

47. Data provided by Harvard's Office of Admissions.

48. Ibid.

49. "Freshmen Records," *HAB*, 24 April 1948.

50. Committee on Admission, "Report of the Committee on Admission," 1940–1941, HU, 149–51.

51. David Karen, "Who Gets into Harvard? Selection and Exclusion at an Elite College" (Ph.D. diss., Harvard Univ., 1985), 432.

52. "Comparison of New Freshmen in the Classes of 1931–32 with 1941–1942 on Basis of Admission Data," n.d., HUA.

53. The principle of geographical diversity became a standard means of limiting Jewish enrollment at elite private colleges. Laurence Veysey, a distinguished historian of American higher education, has put the matter bluntly: "The idea of recruiting students on the basis of geographical diversity emerged as an excuse to restrict the number of students from Jewish backgrounds who came from such places as New York City. Without that peculiar impetus, the otherwise innocuous logic of gaining national appeal and support would not have gained the prominence in certain institutional strategies that it did" ("Undergraduate Admissions: Past and Future," in *Marketing in College Admissions: A Broadening of Perspectives*, ed. Colloquium on Marketing, Student Admissions, and the

Public Interest [New York: College Entrance Examination Board, 1980], 9).

54. Conant, *My Several Lives*, 135.

55. In 1937, New York State alone contained 46 percent of the nation's Jewish population of 4.77 million. Combined with Pennsylvania and New Jersey, the three states included over 60 percent of the Jews in the United States; figures compiled from *The World Almanac and Book of Facts for 1946*.

56. "Memorandum to the Trustees of the Charles Hayden Foundation," 30 December 1937, HUA.

57. Wise is a pseudonym. Chauncey to Hanford, 13 August 1936, HUA.

58. Streator to Conant, 29 January 1934, HUA.

59. Monroe to Streator, 5 February 1934, HUA.

60. That Conant took for granted that blacks were not part of the pool from which Harvard drew its students (much less its National Scholars) is confirmed by his discussion to limit the number of "potential freshmen" to white males in his "small pond" memo of March 1938. Similarly, Hanford, in a letter to Conant estimating the number of National Scholarships to be awarded to each state based on its population, based his figures on the number of "male white school seniors" (Hanford to Conant, 11 August 1937, HUA). Though internal documents from this period reflect a clear presumption that blacks would not be among the winners of the National Scholarships, when Harvard sought outside funding for the program, it dropped all mention of whites and referred only to the "male senior high school population" ("Memorandum to the Trustees of Charles Hayden Foundation," 5).

61. Chauncey to Conant, 21 December 1938, HUA.

62. Amster, "Meritocracy Ascendant," 90–91.

63. Tobin, the son of the director of publicity for the Athletic Association at the University of Illinois, was the valedictorian of University High School in Urbana, Illinois, where he had edited the yearbook, led the junior class, and played on the basketball team ("Prize Fellowships Awarded," *HAB*, 11 October 1935, 811). A summa cum laude graduate in 1939, Tobin received a master's degree in 1940 and his Ph.D. in economics in 1947. After three years as a Junior Fellow at Harvard, he went to Yale as an associate professor in 1950, becoming a full professor in 1955 and Sterling Professor of Economics in 1957. At Yale, he chaired an influential key faculty committee on admissions during R. Inslee ("Inky") Clark's controversial term as director of admission (see Chapter 12). In 1981, Tobin was awarded the Nobel Prize in economics (see *WWA, 1990–1991*).

64. "National Scholars," *HAB*, 19 January 1946. From 1934 through 1942, almost 10,000 students entered Harvard College. The proportion of freshmen holding National Scholarships was thus well under 3 percent.

65. President's Report, 1936–1937, HU, 123.

66. This conclusion echoes that of Conant himself, who claimed in his memoirs that "Harvard's interest in the use of objective tests for selecting national scholars was an important factor in promoting the use of these tests for general admission purposes" (*My Several Lives*, 134).

67. For accounts of the role of the National Scholarship Program in the origins of these special scholarship examinations, which featured the Scholastic Aptitude Test and were administered nationwide at 118

centers throughout the country, see Claude M. Fuess, *The College Board: Its First Fifty Years* (New York: Columbia U.P., 1950), 141–42; Michael Schudson, "Organizing the 'Meritocracy': A History of the College Entrance Examination Board," *Harvard Educational Review*, February 1972; Lemann, *Big Test*, 38–39; and Conant's remarks in the President's Report, 1936–1937, HU, 119–20.

68. Committee on Admission, "Report of the Committee on Admission," 1940–1941, HU, 154. The state of Massachusetts, in addition to being particularly fertile ground for the type of patrician Protestant young men sought by all the Ivy League colleges, was of special political importance to Harvard. Always concerned about its relations with local and state authorities, Harvard had a long-standing policy of giving preference to boys from Cambridge, Boston, and the surrounding communities. As Conant wrote to Gummere in 1939, "The high schools of Massachusetts occupy a special place in our scheme of things . . . they are important to us as a matter of public relations — more directly important from this angle than the schools in other states" (Conant to Gummere, 16 January 1939, HUA).

69. President's Report, 1941–1942, HU, 146.

70. The population figures for New York and Massachusetts are from *The World Almanac and Book of Facts for 1946*. The figure on the proportion of Harvard freshmen from New York is calculated from the Committee on Admission, "Report of the Committee on Admission," 1940–1941, HU, 154.

71. Ibid, 151; Lemann, *Big Test*, 49.

72. See, for example, James Conant, "Mobilizing American Youth," *Atlantic Monthly*, July 1942, 50–52; Conant, "Wanted: American Radicals," *Atlantic Monthly*, May 1943, 43; and the interesting collection of essays, Conant, *Our Fighting Faith* (Cambridge, Mass.: Harvard U.P., 1942).

73. Committee on Admission, "Report of the Committee on Admission," 1942–1943, HU, 1.

74. Committee on Admission, "Report of Committee on Admission," 1943–1944, HU, 4; Committee on Admission, "Report of the Committee on Admission," 1944–1945, HU, 120.

75. Buck, who became Harvard's first provost in 1945 (while continuing as dean of the faculty), administered Harvard's daily affairs during the war and throughout the remainder of the Conant administration, which ended in January 1953.

76. Richard Gummere, "Problems of Admission to Harvard College," 25 August 1943, HUA, 6–7.

77. Ibid., 7.

78. Prototype of letter to "key-men" alumni from Richard Gummere, September 1942, HUA. Gummere, "Problems of Admission to Harvard College," 8.

79. "Supplementary Memorandum Explaining Method," HUA.

80. Richard Gummere, "Exhibit B," in "Problem of Admission to Harvard College," HUA. Of the 221 students who had been rejected as of May 1943, 189 (89.6 percent) were Group III. Though no Harvard documents ever stated explicitly that Group III referred to Jews, numerous pieces of evidence point to that conclusion. Apart from language suggesting that the issue was extremely sensitive ("a dangerous situation," "we are sitting on a volcano"), the very document that mentions Group III explicitly considers a "New York City quota . . . for the protection of the Committee's

free choices" (though Gummere rejects this proposal on the grounds that "the difficulties of such a policy outweigh the benefits"). In the minutes of the meeting at which Gummere presented his report, the same euphemistic tone is used: "A report was submitted containing certain *problems and figures* by the Chairman of the Committee on Admission"; see "Minutes of a Special Meeting held at the Faculty Club," 25 August 1943, HU, emphasis added. Evidence presented confirms that a "quota" was in place in 1942, and there is nothing in the statistics of the Committee on Admission, "Report of the Committee on Admission," 1943–1944, HUA, to suggest that this changed; on the contrary, the decline in the percentage of students from public schools in 1943 suggests that discriminatory measures against Jews may even have been strengthened. Additional, if indirect, evidence comes from the confidential annual reports of Harvard's chief rival, Yale, during this same period. According to Yale's report for 1943–1944, "Selective Services has increased the problem of Jewish applicants for Yale; as for many other colleges." The reason for this upsurge in Jewish enrollments, the report suggested, is that "Jewish boys apparently finish secondary school at an earlier age than Gentiles"; as a consequence of this jump in Jewish numbers, Yale deemed it "necessary for the Board of Admissions to adopt standards of selection from this group more severe than in the past" (for a fuller discussion of the case of Yale, see Chapter 7). Ironically, the availability of qualified Jews under draft age led to an increase in the percentage of Jews at Harvard despite its vigorous efforts to maintain a limit; while enrollments had fluctuated between 10 and 16 percent of the freshman class from the late 1920s through the 1930s, the entering freshmen of 1942 were at least 19 percent Jewish, and by 1943–1944, Jewish enrollment at three Harvard houses (Adams, Dunster, and Lowell) had reached the unprecedented level of 31.7 percent (Synnott, *Half-Opened Door*, 112, 122).

81. As early as March 8, 1943, *Time* reported that 2 million Jews had been murdered by the Nazis and that another 5 million were at risk of extermination ("Total Murder," *Time*, 8 March 1943, 29). That April, the *New York Times*, citing a report by the Inter-Allied Information Committee on conditions in the occupied territories based on evidence supplied by 10 governments, repeated the estimate of 2 million murdered, noting that "lethal gas and shooting were among the methods being used to exterminate the Jews" ("2,000,000 Jews Murdered," *NYT*, 20 April 1943). In a front-page story two days later, the *Times* reported on an uprising in the Warsaw ghetto:

Stockholm, Sweden, April 21 — The secret Polish radio appealed for help tonight in a broadcast from Poland and then suddenly the station went dead.

The broadcast, as heard here, said:

"The last 35,000 Jews in the ghetto at Warsaw have been condemned to execution. Warsaw again is echoing to musketry volleys.

"The people are murdered. Women and children defend themselves with their naked arms.

"Save us . . ."("Secret Polish Radio Asks Aid, Cut Off," *NYT*, 22 April 1943).

82. Founded in 1879 as the sister institution of Harvard College, Radcliffe had a comparatively tiny endowment and lacked its own faculty, relying instead

on an informal arrangement by which Harvard professors delivered their lectures twice — once to Harvard men and then to Radcliffe women. This arrangement lasted until the governing boards of both institutions signed the 1943 agreement described in the text (Calvin N. Moseley, "The Impact of the Merger of the Offices of Admissions and Financial Aids at Harvard and Radcliffe College" [Ph.D. diss., Harvard Univ., 1981], 15–24).

83. Conant, *My Several Lives*, 374–80.

84. Smith, *Harvard Century*, 168. Conant had not been alone in assuming that Radcliffe women would never be taught alongside Harvard men; the preeminent Harvard historian Samuel Eliot Morison wrote in 1936 that "no proposition to make Harvard College co-educational has ever been seriously entertained (*Three Centuries of Harvard, 1636–1936* [Cambridge, Mass.: Harvard U.P., 1936], 393). Other faculty members were overtly hostile to the very idea. One popular professor, Charles Townsend, was alleged to have declined to give a course in argument for Radcliffe women, saying, "How deplorable for women to become apt in argument. We can't obliterate a natural tendency, but why cultivate it?" (quoted in Conant, *My Several Lives*, 380).

85. Buck, interview, 65.

86. In addition to the 3,500 students who had left Harvard for military service, an additional 1,200 students had been accepted but went directly into the military (John Bethell, *Harvard Observed: An Illustrated History of the University in the Twentieth Century* [Cambridge, Mass.: Harvard U.P., 1998], 178).

87. Paul Buck, interview by Bentinck-Smith, 66.

88. Synnott, *Half-Opened Door*, 207.

89. Wilbur J. Bender, "Speech to Class of '27," 3 May 1947, HUA, 2. Among the many sources of information on Bender, the more important were Bender's own entries in the *Tenth Anniversary Report: Class of 1927, Fifteenth Anniversary Report: Class of 1927, Twentieth Anniversary Report: Class of 1927, Twenty-fifth Anniversary Report: Class of 1927*, and *Thirtieth Anniversary Report: Class of 1927*, HU; the entry on Bender in the *Harvard Class Album: Class of 1927*, HU; Bender, "Speech to the Class of '27," HUA; "Bender for Guarantee to Talented Students," *Boston Herald*, 27 November 1946; University News Office, "Dean Wilbur J. Bender — Harvard College (Biographical Sketch — September 1, 1957)," HUA; "Faculty Profile: Wilbur J. Bender '27, Dean of Harvard College," n.d. [c. 1952], HUA; Charles L. Whipple, "Many Are Called, Few Are Chosen," 15 May 1960, unmarked newspaper clipping; and the obituaries "Wilbur J. Bender, Harvard Ex-Dean," *NYT*, 1 April 1969, and "W. J. Bender, 65, Ex-Harvard Dean," *Boston Herald*, 1 April 1969. See also the biography of Wilbur Bender's brother, Harold Bender, who was for many years the leader of the Mennonite church (Albert N. Keim, *Harold S. Bender: 1897–1962* [Scottdale, Pa.: Herald Press, 1998]).

90. In his memoir, Conant discusses his decision to assign responsibility for developing the selection procedures for the National Scholarships to Bender and Chauncey: "I could not have put the fate of the idea in better hands" (Buck, interview, 66; Conant, *My Several Lives*, 130).

91. *Twentieth Anniversary Report: Class of 1927*, HU, 20–21; Buck, interview.

92. For reasons that remain unclear, Bender never

completed his dissertation. What does seem clear is that this failure caused him some regret; in 1947, in a speech to his classmates, he stated that "I am not a scholar or intellectual or philosopher, educational or otherwise, though I wish I were" (Bender, "Speech to the Class of '27," HUA, 3). Reminiscing about Bender some years after his death in 1969, Buck described him as "a great younger friend of mine [whom] I had great admiration for," but added that "he wasn't on the University level as a scholar" and "quite rightly went to Andover to teach" (Buck, interview, 65).

93. Bender to Buck, Hanford, Leighton, and Gummere, "Re: Harvard College Admission Policy," memorandum, 31 July 1945, HUA.

94. "Bender for Guarantee to Talented Students." The G.I. Bill (officially the Servicemen's Readjustment Act of 1944) paid for veterans' college education and offered a variety of other benefits, including medical care and low-rate mortgages. Conant, who is described by Lemann as "a (or maybe the) leading opponent of the GI Bill," believed that giving every veteran a chance to attend college was a grave mistake, given that higher education, in his view, already enrolled far too many students (Lemann, *Big Test,* 58–59).

95. Bender, "Speech to the Class of '27," 2–3.

96. Wilbur J. Bender, "Report on the Veteran: His Grades, His Difficulties, His Pressures and Enthusiasms," *HAB,* 11 March 1947, 464.

97. Wilbur J. Bender, "Speech for Harvard Club Annual Dinner," 20 March 1946, HUA, 4.

98. Ibid., 4.

99. Bender, "Report on the Veteran," 466.

100. Given their wartime experience, the fact that the veterans were exceptionally serious, hard-working, and mature was hardly surprising. Of the veterans enrolled at Harvard in 1946–1947, almost half had commissions and 329 had received the Purple Heart (ibid., 466).

101. Cited in Bender, "Speech for the Harvard Club Annual Dinner"; "Report on the Veteran," 466.

102. In *The Harvard Century,* for example, Smith portrays the arrival of the veterans as leading to a vast democratization of Harvard. As a symbol of their arrival, he notes that "Winthrops and Cabots and Lees were replaced on the Crimson football team by Dvarics, Gorzynskis, and Flynns." Summarizing his view of the Conant administration, Smith concludes: "In place of Lowell's emphasis on manners and breeding, the hallmarks of a gentleman, Conant and Buck had designed a program [General Education] in harmony with the president's belief in a casteless national family, led by its most academically gifted, yet purified of excess and hereditary pride" (169–70).

103. Cited in Bender, "Speech for the Harvard Club Annual Dinner"; "Report on the Veteran," 466.

104. Data provided by Harvard's Office of Admissions. The leading 12 prep schools are identified in Chapter 1; at the 6 most socially exclusive ones, commonly known as St. Grottlesex, the acceptance rate was 88 percent (64 of 72). Of the 36 applicants from the selective urban high schools, only 12 were admitted.

105. Paul Buck, "Who Comes to Harvard?" *HAB,* 10 January 1948, 314–15.

106. By fall 1950 and fall 1951, the proportion of veterans among admitted freshmen was down to 1.4 and 0.4 percent, respectively. See Committee on Admission, "Report of the Committee on Admission," 1945–1946, 1946–1947, HU; Committee on Admission, "Report of the Committee on Admission of Harvard College," 1947–1948 through 1950–1951, HU.

107. Buck, "Balance in the College," 404; Buck, "Who Comes to Harvard?"; Wilbur J. Bender, "To the Critics of Harvard," *HAB,* 9 April 1949, 545–48.

108. Buck, "Balance in the College," 405.

109. Ibid.

110. Sensing that his statement might arouse charges of anti-Semitism, Buck quickly added the following disclaimer: "A few may be quick to suspect, in any admission policy which deviates from absolute standards of scholastic excellence, some underlying implication or racial or religious prejudice. I wish at this point to be explicit in pointing out that I have no such implications in mind ("Balance in the College," 406).

111. Ibid.

112. Buck, "Who Comes to Harvard?," 314.

113. Buck, "Balance in the College," 406.

114. Buck, "Who Comes to Harvard?," 317.

115. Buck, "Balance in the College," 406.

116. Bender, "To the Critics of Harvard," 545.

117. In Bender's view, the only real alternative to discrimination in admissions would be to "admit solely on a basis of test scores and school marks, a highly unreliable basis for predicting success in college or later life." For this reason, he opposed anti-discrimination legislation, for any such law "with real teeth in it would completely destroy the admission policy I just described" (ibid., 546). In taking this position, Bender was echoing the stance of Harvard and other private schools in Massachusetts, including M.I.T., Tufts, and Williams. Among the grounds cited by Harvard's witness, Oscar Shaw '26, LL.B. '29, in opposing Senate Bill No. 133 was the absence of an "adequate need for the bill" and the likelihood that it would "prove costly, unworkable, and detrimental to the education institutions of the Commonwealth." Shaw claimed that Harvard was free of any discrimination and "does not maintain or operate, explicitly or implicitly, any quota or any other device . . . for the arbitrary limitation of the number of applicants to be admitted from any particular religious, racial, or national groups" ("Admission Criteria," *HAB,* 23 April 1949, 579–80).

118. Bender, "To the Critics of Harvard," 546.

119. Ibid. The University of Chicago, which had been a powerhouse in football in the early years of the twentieth century, eliminated its varsity program in the 1930s, thereby reinforcing, Bender believed, its image as a one-sided, intellectual institution.

120. Ibid., 546.

121. Harvard's ideal, Buck wrote, "was to blend democratic selection with aristocratic achievement." To realize this ideal, Harvard "deliberately sought to draw students from all sections of the country, all types of schools, and from all economic levels" (Buck, "Who Comes to Harvard," 313–14).

122. Bender, "To the Critics of Harvard," 545, 548. In this regard, it is worth remembering that Conant also believed that the proportion of the class reserved for brilliant students should be strictly limited. In a 1934 proposal for the fellowships that later became Harvard National Scholarships, he cautioned giving these academic awards to more than 10 to 15 percent of each class "lest our fellowships be so large in num-

ber that we pauperize the student body." Two years later, Conant apparently decided that 15 percent might be too high, suggesting that "the ideal . . . would seem to me to be something like a hundred National Scholarship holders in each entering class of a thousand." See "From President Conant's Report," *HAB,* 2 February 1934, 484; James B. Conant, "Harvard Present and Future," *HAB* 38, no. 25 (10 April 1936), 813.

123. Richard Gummere, "Harvard College," 1 October 1949, HUA.

124. Bender, "Speech to the Class of '27," 7.

125. "Meeting of Schools and Scholarships Committee Representatives," 4–5 November 1949, HUA, 78.

126. Bender, "Speech to the Class of '27," 16–17.

127. In enumerating the colleges with "snob appeal," Bender also listed as on the "fringe" of the group Dartmouth, Cornell, Bowdoin, Haverford, Brown, and Stanford (ibid., 17). Conspicuously absent from the list were Columbia, Penn, and Chicago, all of them urban institutions with sizable Jewish enrollments.

128. Data provided by Harvard's Office of Admissions.

129. Bender, "Speech to the Class of '27," 16.

130. Richard Farnum, "Patterns of Upper-Class Education in Four American Cities: 1875–1975," in *The High-Status Track: Studies of Elite Schools and Stratification,* eds. Paul William Kingston and Lionel S. Lewis (Albany: State Univ. of New York Press, 1990), 53–73.

131. "Harvard Prize Scholars," *HAB,* 28 October 1950, 110.

132. Henry S. Dyer to von Stade, 17 October 1951, HUA.

133. Data on Exeter and Andover from Harvard's Office of Admissions. For all applicants in 1950, both public and private, the rejection rate was 36.4 percent (calculated from the Committee on Admission, "Report of the Committee on Admission of Harvard College, 1949–1950," HU, 4).

134. Committee on Scholarships and Financial Aids, "Harvard College Admission Policy, Confidential for Use of Schools and Scholarship," 12 December 1949, HUA, 4. The Schools and Scholarship Committees, which played a critical role in Harvard's admissions process starting in the 1940s, were organs of the Associated Harvard Clubs, located in virtually all major American cities. The statement on "Harvard College Admission Policy" was written shortly after a meeting, the first of its kind, between the administrators most involved with Harvard's admissions and the representatives of many of the major Harvard Clubs. The meeting took place in Cambridge, and there is a transcript of its proceedings: "Meeting of Schools and Scholarship Committee Representatives," 4–5 November 1949, HUA. After the meeting, Bender drafted a statement on Harvard College admissions, which he sent to Gummere, Leighton, von Stade, and Dyer. This draft subsequently became the 12 December 1949 statement referred to above.

135. Bender to Thomas S. Lamont, 25 January 1957, HUA. The percentage for all applicants, including alumni children, rejected by Harvard in 1952 was 37 percent (Committees on Admission and on Scholarships and Financial Aids, "Report on the Office of the Dean of Admissions and Financial Aids for Students in Harvard College, 1952–1953," HU, 9).

136. Committee on Scholarships and Financial Aids, "Harvard College Admission Policy," 5.

137. Buck, "Who Comes to Harvard?," 317.

138. Bender, "Speech to the Class of '27," 8.

139. Gummere, "Harvard College," HUA.

140. "Scholars and Athletes: the Statement of the Three Presidents," *HAB,* 10 November 1951, 163.

141. Bender, "Speech for Harvard Club Annual Dinner," 5.

142. Wilbur J. Bender, "Speech to the Board of Overseers of Harvard University," 8 March 1954, HUA, 9.

143. Committee on Scholarships and Financial Aids, "Harvard College Admissions Policy," 4.

144. Charles C. Buell '23 was president of the Harvard Club of New Hampshire and played an active role in the Schools and Scholarships Committee. See Associated Harvard Clubs, "Digest of Schools and Scholarships Committee Meeting," 9–10 November 1951, HUA.

145. Hanford to Buell, 18 January 1946, HUA, 2; emphasis added.

146. The guidelines did hasten to add, however, that the existence of health problems "will not necessarily lead to rejection" and noted that the committee sometimes "has gone out of its way to admit applicants with certain kinds of physical hardships" (Committee on Scholarships and Financial Aids, "Harvard College Admission Policy," 3).

147. "Notes on North Shore Country Day Boys for Mr. Gummere and Mr. Leighton," n.d., HUA.

148. Bender to the Committee on Scholarships and Financial Aids, memorandum, 6 February 1952, HUA, 2.

149. See Richard Hofstadter's classic study, *Anti-Intellectualism in American Life* (New York: Knopf, 1970).

150. "Meeting of Schools and Scholarship Committee Representatives," HUA, 83–84.

151. The *Harvard Freshmen Red Book: Class of 1942; Harvard Class Album: Class of 1942;* Bethell, *Harvard Observed,* 242; and Smith, *Harvard Century,* 244.

152. In addressing a 1949 meeting of Schools and Scholarship Committee representatives, von Stade began by saying, "Gentlemen, may I summon Mr. Gummere's plea for paying guests," adding, "I'm even more inclined in the direction of paying guests than I used to be" ("Meeting of Schools and Scholarships Committee Representatives," 4–5 November 1949, Harvard University, 19).

153. Francis Skiddy von Stade Jr., "'Poore Scholars' and Good Students: The How and Why of Harvard's Scholarship Program," *HAB,* 25 May 1946, 657–60.

154. Associated Harvard Clubs, "Digest of Schools and Scholarships Committee Meeting," HUA, 25.

155. von Stade to Conant, 4 June 1948, HUA.

156. Associated Harvard Clubs, "Digest of Schools and Scholarships Committee Meeting," HUA, 3.

157. The equivocal fashion in which Conant handled the Jewish question was apparently not out of character. On the crucial matter of academic freedom, Hershberg offers an astute portrait of his behavior: "Repeatedly, Conant defined and adopted lofty principles, but his actions uncomfortably blended principle and pragmatism, courage and squeamishness, personal integrity and concessions to the constraints of his position" (*James B. Conant,* 84).

158. In February 1946, six months after the end the war, 55 percent of Americans agreed with the state-

ment "Do you agree that Jews have too much power in the United States?" This figure was up from March 1938 and February 1941, when 41 and 45 percent, respectively, agreed with the statement. See Leonard Dinnerstein, "Anti-Semitism Exposed and Attacked, 1945–1950," *American Jewish History* 71, no. 1 (September 1991): 135, and Samuel H. Flowerman and Marie Jahoda, "Polls on Anti-Semitism: How Much Do They Tell Us?" *Commentary* 1, no. 6 (April 1946): 82–86. In December 1947, a survey of anti-Semitism in higher education in the *New Republic* reported that Amherst, Bryn Mawr, Dartmouth, Haverford, Middlebury, Mount Holyoke, Northeastern, Princeton, Swarthmore, Williams, and Yale were among the colleges enrolling "conspicuously small numbers of Jews" (Bruce Bliven, "For 'Nordic' Only," *New Republic*, 18 December 1947, 18).

159. Students at Princeton and Williams "are both very polite and very genteel." But if those institutions did not appeal to certain upper-class families, they could send their sons "to Yale where they have Morys and the Whiffenpoofs and the Yale Fence and Boola-Boola." "Or," he added, "to Dartmouth with its rugged he-men and the great out-of-doors" ("Speech to the Class of '27," 16–19).

160. Bender turns out to have been correct in his impression that Yale surpassed the limit of 5 percent on Jewish enrollment. In 1947–1948, 9.4 percent of Yale freshmen listed themselves as Jewish when asked for "religious preference"; two years later, in 1949–1950, the proportion of Jews had increased to 12.3 percent (Marcia Graham Synnott, "A Social History of Admissions Policies at Harvard, Yale, and Princeton, 1900–1930" [Ph.D. diss., Univ. of Massachusetts, 1974], 740). As Bender had suggested, the Jewish percentage at Princeton was lower than that at Yale; in the freshman class of 1946, only 4.7 percent were listed as "Hebrew." By 1949, however, the proportion had reached 5.6 percent. See statistics of the Class of 1950 and 1953 in Princeton's *Freshmen Herald* and Daniel Oren, *Joining the Club: A History of Jews at Yale* (New Haven, Conn.: Yale U.P., 1985).

161. At a 1949 meeting with representatives of the Harvard School and Scholarship Committee, Bender admitted that "we are likely to take almost any boy from Mississippi who looks like he is a decent person who will make the grade" ("Meeting of Schools and Scholarship Committee Representatives," HUA, 56).

162. In the document reporting these figures, Dean of Freshmen Delmar Leighton, comparing statistics for applicants to the entering freshmen of 1950 and 1951, expressed his concern about an apparently unwelcome increase in applications from the Middle Atlantic states: "The imminent shift to the Middle Atlantic States should be noted in this comparison. I recommend that this shift be called to the Committee's attention in considering marginal cases" ("Committee on Admission Preliminary Screening 1951, Confidential," HUA, 2). The acceptance rate for the class as a whole is calculated from the Committee on Admission, "Report of the Committee on Admission of Harvard College, 1949–1950," HU, 4.

163. These population figures are based on the 1940 census. The figures on the geographical origins of Harvard's admits are calculated from the Committee on Admission, "Report of the Committee on Admission of Harvard College, 1948–1949," HU, 6.

164. Interestingly, all 6 of the applicants from New

Trier, a public high school in the northern Chicago suburbs that was at the time predominantly Protestant, were accepted by Harvard (figures provided by Harvard's Office of Admission).

165. Deborah Dash Moore, *GI Jews: How World War II Changed a Generation* (Cambridge, Mass.: Belknap Press, 2004), 256.

166. Sidney Kaplan (pseudonym) et al. to the President and Fellows of Harvard College, 2 October 1946, HUA.

167. Buck to Hanford, 17 August 1946, HUA.

168. Committee on Admission, "Fair Educational Practices Law," n.d. [c. 1949], HUA.

169. Among the groups participating in the National Community Relations Advisory Council were the American Jewish Committee, the American Jewish Congress, the B'nai B'rith, the Jewish War Veterans, and the Union of American Hebrew Congregations. For a detailed discussion of the postwar Jewish offensive against anti-Semitism, see Dinnerstein, "Anti-Semitism Exposed and Attacked, 1945–1950"; the movement against anti-Semitism in higher education is also discussed in Synnott, *Half-Opened Door*, 201–2, Harold S. Wechsler, *The Qualified Student: A History of Selective College Admission in America* (New York: John Wiley, 1977); and Stuart Svonkin, *Jews Against Prejudice* (New York: Columbia U.P., 1997).

170. U.S. President's Commission for Higher Education, *Higher Education for American Democracy* (New York: Harper & Brothers, 1947); Carey McWilliams, *A Mask for Privilege: Anti-Semitism in America* (Boston: Little, Brown, 1948); Helen E. Davis, *Getting into College* (Washington, D.C.: American Council on Education, 1949).

171. Dinnerstein, "Anti-Semitism Exposed," 142–49.

172. "Meeting of Schools and Scholarship Committee representatives," HUA, 46.

173. Ibid., 41, 46–47.

174. Ibid.

175. In 1949, 35.3 percent of Middle Atlantic applicants were accepted, compared to 55.8 percent for all applicants (a ratio of 0.63); in 1950, the comparable figures were 46.5 percent and 62.8 percent (a ratio of 0.74) (Leighton, "Committee on Admission Preliminary Screening 1951, Confidential," HUA). Consistent with this trend, the proportion of freshmen admits from the Middle Atlantic region increased from 21.5 percent in 1946 to 22.9 percent in 1950 and 24.4 percent in 1952. Data calculated from the Committee on Admission, "Report of the Committee on Admission, 1945–1946," HU; Committee on Admission, "Report of the Committee on Admission of Harvard College, 1949–1950," HU; and Committee on Admission, "Report of the Committee on Admission of Harvard College, 1951–1952," HU.

176. The other nine universities were Dartmouth, Fisk, Michigan, North Carolina, Texas, UCLA, Wayne, Wesleyan, and Yale (Lipset and Riesman, *Education and Politics*, 179). A separate study by Louise Epstein suggests that the figure of 25 percent for Harvard in 1952 is accurate; in her own empirical study of the entering freshmen of 1950, Epstein estimates that 26 percent were Jewish, compared to only 17 percent in 1935 ("Elitism, Diversity, and Meritocracy at Harvard: Changing Patterns of Achievement in College and Career" (undergraduate thesis, Harvard Univ, 1982), 35).

177. The figure of 28 percent for 1925 is from Synnott, *Half-Opened Door*, 107. The conclusion that Jew-

ish enrollments at Harvard increased in the wake of the 1949 Fair Educational Practices Act receives further confirmation from the fact that only 17 percent of the students in Harvard's Houses were Jewish as late as 1946–1947. Since Jews were overrepresented among commuters, however, their proportion of the student body as a whole in 1946–1947 may have approached 20 percent.

178. Cited in Dinnerstein, "Anti-Semitism Exposed," 148.

179. Hershberg, *James B. Conant*, 58, 82.

180. For the small number of institutions that can afford it, the preferred policy is not only "need-blind" admissions and "need-based" financial aid, but also "full aid" admissions: that is, all candidates judged worthy of admission are given sufficient financial resources to permit them to attend.

181. Hershberg, *James B. Conant*, 79. Relying on Conant's militant public rhetoric, Lemann draws a similar portrait, depicting Conant as a committed meritocrat who fervently wished "to unseat the Episcopacy" (*Big Test*, 49). For Lemann's definition of the "Episcopacy," the Protestant upper-class elite of which Lowell was a quintessential embodiment, see *Big Test*, 11–12.

182. Data provided by Harvard's Office of Admissions. In 1950, for example, the products of 12 top boarding schools were accepted at a rate of 88 percent (246 of 278), only a modest decline from the 95 percent rate (183 of 193) in 1930, when getting into Harvard was far less difficult. In 1952, the year of the last group of freshmen admitted under Conant, the rejection rate of 13 percent for sons of the alumni was less than one-third the rejection rate of 40 percent for applicants whose fathers had not attended Harvard. Committees on Admission and on Scholarships and Financial Aids, "Report on the Office of the Dean of Admissions and Financial Aids for Students in Harvard College," 1952–1953, HU, 18, 21. Still another indicator of Harvard's extremely close ties to its traditional constituencies during the Conant years is that 61 percent of the sons of Boston *Social Register* families who graduated from college in the 1940s had attended Harvard. No other major East Coast city had such close ties between its upper class and a particular college; the leading colleges for upper classes in the three other major cities in the Northeast in the 1940s were for New York — Yale, 25 percent, Philadelphia — Princeton, 35 percent, and Baltimore — Princeton, 25 percent (Farnum, "Patterns of Upper-class Education," 57–65).

7. Reluctant Reform Comes to Yale

1. According to George W. Pierson (*Yale: The University College, 1921–1937* [New Haven, Conn.: Yale U.P., 1955], 477), had Yale been willing, it could easily have doubled or even tripled its enrollment. In 1929, Yale accepted only 59 percent of its applicants, compared to 80 percent at Harvard. See Robert N. Corwin to Angell, 17 October 1930, YUA; Committee on Admission, "Report of Committee on Admission," 1928–1929, HU, 325.

2. Committee on Enrollment, "Report to the Alumni Board of Yale University," 22 February 1940, YUA, 1; Pierson, *Yale*, 656. In 1933, the national unemployment rate peaked at 24.9 percent, up from 23.6

percent in 1932 (Bureau of the Census, *Historical Statistics of the United States: Colonial Times to 1970*, part 1 [Washington, D.C.: Government Printing Office, 1989], 135).

3. Harold P. Rodes, "Educational Factors Affecting the Entrance Requirements to Yale College" (Ph.D. diss., Yale Univ., 1948), 199–200.

4. Ibid., 200–201; Pierson, *Yale*, 656. Of the last 145 candidates admitted in 1933, only about half continued into their sophomore year (Rodes, "Educational Factors," 200–201).

5. The estimate of 20 percent is from the Committee on Enrollment, "Report to the Alumni Board of Yale University," YUA, 61.

6. Geoffrey Kabaservice, *The Guardians: Kingman Brewster, His Circle, and the Rise of the Liberal Establishment* (New York: Henry Holt, 2004), also notes the peculiar fact that "almost a third of the Class of '41 came with a 'Jr.' or a number after their name, proclaiming each scion the second, third, fourth, or fifth of his line" (48). Figures on the percentage of alumni sons in every entering class from 1920 through 1957 can be found in George Pierson, ed., *A Yale Book of Numbers: Historical Statistics of the College and University, 1701–1976* (New Haven, Conn.: Yale U.P., 1983), 87.

7. August Heckscher, "Bulldog in the Nursery," in *My Harvard, My Yale*, ed. Diane Dubois (New York: Random House, 1982), 173. For a full account of how residential colleges came to Yale three years after Harvard opened its residential houses, even though Edward Harkness '87 first approached Yale, see Pierson, *Yale*, 207–52. According to Pierson, Yale's reluctant response to the offer of a huge gift was emblematic of larger differences between the institutions: "By the touchstone of a millionaire, Harvard and Yale seemed made of entirely different stuff — the one forward-looking, decisive, and successful; the other backward, hesitant, fumbling. The older university proved easy to help, the younger almost impossible to change. Yet it is to be noted that both institutions arrived at the same end" (594).

8. As late as 1951, Yale's scholarship policy stated that recipients needed to rank in the top quarter of their class to be sure that their awards would be renewed ("Terms of Admission to the Undergraduate Schools of Yale University, 1950–1951," n.d., YUA). Internal documents reveal, however, that scholarships could be awarded on a discretionary basis to students ranking in the top half of their class if they were judged to have "outstanding qualities of character and personal leadership" (Albert B. Crawford to Seymour, 25 April 1949, YUA).

9. Robert W. Merry, in his biography of Joseph Alsop (Harvard '32) and Stewart Alsop (Yale '36), contrasts campus life at the two institutions: "At Harvard, when the time came to judge potential initiates into the Porcellian and other exclusive clubs, it mattered more who you were, meaning who your parents were and your grandparents. But at Yale more emphasis was placed on campus accomplishment. As that fictional Yalie Dink Stover put it, one had to do something to be someone" (*Taking on the World: Joseph and Stewart Alsop — Guardians of the American Century* [New York: Penguin, 1996], 39).

10. Despite Yale's relatively democratic reputation, public school students were in fact much less likely to be members of its senior societies than their prep

school classmates. As late as 1942, public school graduates made up only 6 percent of society men compared to 25 percent of freshmen. By 1952, however, the senior societies had become more open, with 25 percent public school products compared to 35 percent of freshmen (Daniel A. Oren, *Joining the Club: A History of Jews and Yale* [New Haven, Conn.: Yale U.P., 1986], 163.

11. Yale's role as the number one undergraduate producer of American business executives is documented in George W. Pierson, *The Education of American Leaders: Comparative Contributions of U.S. Colleges and Universities* (New York: Praeger, 1969), 83–122.

12. Canby, *Alma Mater*, 75.

13. Paul Moore Jr., "A Touch of Laughter," in *My Harvard, My Yale*, 198, 203–4.

14. William Proxmire, "Blind Man's Bluff," in *My Harvard, My Yale*, 183–84, emphasis added.

15. In a comparative study of the classes that entered Yale and Harvard in 1937, Kabaservice found that 45.6 percent of Yale seniors, but only 29 percent of Harvard seniors, planned careers in business ("Kingman Brewster," 101–2). Law was popular at both institutions, but projected careers in medicine, science, journalism, government, and writing were more common at Harvard than at Yale.

16. In 1937, Boston's population included 118,000 Jews; New Haven's, fewer than 25,000. See *The World Almanac and Book of Facts for 1946*, and the *1943 Jewish Family Almanac* (New York: FFF), 44.

17. Pierson, *Yale*, 491.

18. F. Scott Fitzgerald, *This Side of Paradise* (New York: Scribner's, 1920), 25.

19. The number of public school applicants to Yale in 1929–1938 is listed in Alumni Board Committee to Committee on Enrollment, 22 February 1940, YUA, 53. The estimate of the number of male public school graduates is derived from Bureau of the Census, *Historical Statistics of the United States*, 379, and *Digest of Education Statistics, 1995* (Washington, D.C.: U.S. Department of Education, 1995), 108.

20. A native of New Haven, Edward MacArthur Noyes took a divinity degree from Yale in 1882 after graduating from the college three years earlier. A Republican, he was a member of several elite social clubs, including the Winthrop and the Charles River Country Club (*WWA, 1926–1927*).

21. The profile of Edward S. Noyes is based on several sources, including reunion reports of the Yale Class of 1913; "Edward S. Noyes, Educator, Dean," *NYT*, 19 December 1967; and "Two Former Faculty Members Die," *YAM*, February 1968, 17. A religious man, Noyes served as a deacon at the Church of Christ at Yale.

22. After Corwin's retirement, Alan Valentine, a professor in the Department of History, Arts and Letters and master of Pierson College, became the new chairman of the Board of Admissions. But he stayed in the job for only two years, leaving in 1935 to become president of the University of Rochester. In 1935–1936, the position was held on an interim basis by Perry Talbot Walden (Ph.B. '92, Ph.D. '96), dean of the freshmen year and professor of chemistry.

23. Board of Admissions, "Report to the President and Fellows of Yale University," 1936–1937, YU, 2.

24. Figures calculated from Kabaservice, "Kingman Brewster," 606–23. Harvard's top private feeder

schools in 1937 were Exeter (62), Milton (43), Andover (36), St. Paul's (25), and Middlesex (17). But Harvard also had several major public school feeders: Boston Latin (52), Cambridge Rindge and Latin (18), Brookline (13), and Newton (12) — all within commuting distance. Yale, in contrast, had only one public school feeder with over 10 students: New Haven (32).

25. Pierson, *Yale*, 489.

26. In the Board of Admissions, "Report to the President and Fellows," 1940–1941, YU, 3, Noyes suggests that the alumni representatives should be "on the look-out to encourage paying guests." Eight years later, in Board of Admissions, "Report to the President and Fellows," 1948–1949, YU, 2, he approvingly noted the position of the Corporation that, if scholarship funds were increased, "there should also be an increase in the number of paying guests."

27. Moore, "A Touch of Laughter," 197.

28. Edwin R. Embree, "In Order of Their Eminence: An Appraisal of American Universities," *Atlantic Monthly*, June 1935, 652–64.

29. Yale did boast a distinguished law school that some thought equal and perhaps superior to Harvard's, but its medical school was not quite as illustrious, and it lacked a business school altogether.

30. Figures calculated from Karabel, "Status-Group Struggle, Organizational Interests, and the Limits of Institutional Autonomy: The Transformation of Harvard, Yale, and Princeton, 1918–1940," *Theory and Society* 13, January 1984, 22. In 1940, only 21 percent of freshmen at Princeton and 25 percent at Yale had attended public high schools (Committee on Admission, "Report of the President to the Board of Trustees, 1939–1940," PU; Pierson, *Yale*, 671).

31. Harvard held a slight advantage over Yale in the competition for the scions of the most elite upper-class families, drawing 75 students in 1940 from the exclusive "St. Grottlesex" schools (St. Paul's, St. Mark's, St. George's, Groton, Middlesex, and Kent), compared to 65 at Yale; Karabel, "Status-Group Struggle," 22. In 1937, Harvard was also ahead of Yale in attracting St. Grottlesexers, 87–69. Kabaservice, "Kingman Brewster," 606–23. One indication that these schools drew from a much more socially elite milieu than did other leading prep schools comes from a study showing that in 1926, Groton and St. Mark's drew 74 percent of their students from families in the *Social Register*, compared to 28 percent at Hotchkiss and none at Andover. The same study also found that St. Grottlesex alumni dominated membership in the two most exclusive Harvard final clubs in 1926, filling 9 of 12 slots, compared to none for the other six leading boarding schools combined (Steven Levine, "The Rise of American Boarding Schools and the Development of a National Upper Class," *Social Forces* 28, no. 1 [October 1980], 75, 86).

32. Karabel, "Status-Group Struggle," 21–22.

33. Board of Admissions, "Report to the President and Fellows," 1940–1941, YU, 1.

34. Board of Admissions, "Report to the President and Fellows," 1946–1947, YU, 4–6.

35. Wilbur J. Bender, "Speech to the Class of '27," 3 May 1947, HUA, 16–19.

36. The figures on the graduates at Yale from public schools in New York City (pop. 6,930,446 in 1930) and Philadelphia (1930 pop., 1,950,961) from 1929 through 1938 are from the Committee on Enrollment, "Report to the Alumni Board," YUA, 56–57. The number of

Yale freshmen from St. Paul's was 26 in 1930, 27 in 1932, 21 in 1937, and 34 in 1940 (Karabel, "Status-Group Struggle," 22; Kabaservice, "Kingman Brewster," YU, 608; "Class of 1936," 12 January 1935, YUA).

37. Committee on Enrollment, "Report to the Alumni Board," YUA, 6.

38. Edward S. Noyes, "Brief Account of the Procedures of the Board of Admissions," 18 October 1939, Appendix A of the Committee on Enrollment, "Report to the Alumni Board," YUA, 31–33.

39. Bender, "Speech to the Class of '27," HUA, 16.

40. Richard Farnum, "Patterns of Upper-Class Education in Four American Cities, 1875–1975," in *The High-Status Track*, ed. Paul W. Kingston and Lionel Lewis (Albany: State Univ. of New York Press, 1990), 60.

41. Corwin to Francis Parsons, 1 October 1929, YUA.

42. Yale did not surpass the level of 13.3 percent Jewish students reached in the 1920s until 1962, when the proportion of Jewish freshmen reached 14.2 percent (Oren, *Joining the Club*, 320–21).

43. Synnott, *Half-Opened Door*, 139.

44. Angell to Valentine, 9 March 1934, YUA.

45. According to Professor Henri Peyre, anti-Semitic sentiments were common among Yale faculty members in the 1930s. As he remembered it, one joke circulating at the time went as follows: "If there are Jews who want to go to college, let them go to Harvard. Let Hitler be Harvard's president. He'll take care of them" (Oren, *Joining the Club*, 346).

46. Board of Admissions, "Report to the President and Fellows," 1938–1939, YU, 2.

47. Edward Noyes, "Memorandum to the President and Provost," 13 December 1941, YUA, 1.

48. Board of Admissions, "Report to the President and Fellows," 1943–1944, YUA, 4.

49. Feldman (pseudonym) to Seymour, 23 June 1944, YUA.

50. Seymour to Feldman, 7 July 1944, YUA.

51. Ibid. See also Oren, *Joining the Club*, 175–76, and Synnott, *Half-Opened Door*, 212.

52. Edward S. Noyes to Seymour, 10 July 1944, YUA.

53. Hotchkiss, which produced well under 100 graduates each year, sent 42, 32, and 40 students to Yale in 1930, 1932, and 1937, respectively. During these same years, the entire public school systems of New York, Boston, and Philadelphia produced, respectively, 23, 14, and 27 Yale freshmen. See Committee on Enrollment, "Report to the Alumni Board," YUA, 56–57; Karabel, "Status-Group Struggle," 22; Kabaservice, "Kingman Brewster," 608; and "Class of 1936," 12 January 1935, YUA.

54. During 1943–1944 and 1944–1945, Yale admitted students at three separate times: July, November, and March. Despite this increase in flexibility, the number of students who matriculated dropped to 678 in 1943–1944 and 642 in 1944–1945 (Rodes, "Educational Factors," YU, 249).

55. Board of Admissions, "Report to the President and Fellows," 1944–1945, YU, 3.

56. The concept of symbolic capital is central to the work of the French sociologist Pierre Bourdieu, who has discussed its various forms in *The State Nobility: Elite Schools in the Field of Power* (Stanford, Calif.: Stanford U.P., 1996) and *Language and Symbolic Power* (Cambridge, Mass.: Harvard U.P., 1991). For excellent discussions of Bourdieu's writings on symbolic cap-

ital, see David Swartz, *Culture and Power: The Sociology of Pierre Bourdieu* (Chicago: Univ. of Chicago Press, 1997), and the introduction to Pierre Bourdieu and Loïc J. D. Wacquant, *An Invitation to Reflexive Sociology* (Chicago: Univ. of Chicago Press, 1992).

57. Board of Admissions, "Report to the President and Fellows," 1944–1945, YU, 3. Even with continued restrictive measures, one could never be sure how many Jews were really enrolled; as Yale's secretary Carl A. Lohmann '10 put it: "A number of Hebrews record themselves among the Protestants, chiefly as Episcopalians, and some don't reply at all." Lohmann to Frederick W. Wiggin (chief of the law firm that provided Yale's legal counsel), 24 March 1945, YUA; Oren, *Joining the Club*, 178.

58. Oren, *Joining the Club*, 254–55.

59. Though Rostow's specific focus was on Yale Medical School's quota of 10 percent, he made it clear that the principles he espoused should apply across the campus.

60. Oren, *Joining the Club*, 178.

61. The averages for 1946–1950 and 1937–1941 are calculated from Oren (ibid., 321).

62. Kabaservice, "Kingman Brewster," 304–5.

63. In an interview with Dan Oren, Donald Walker, a member of the Board of Admissions in these years, insisted that Yale did not have formal quotas: "I could swear on the Bible; we never had quotas for anything. We didn't want to know the numbers." But he acknowledged that some Jewish students from schools such as Bronx High School of Science and Stuyvesant High School with relatively higher test scores were turned down because they "were not interested in contributing to Yale. They were interested only in getting what Yale had to offer: grades and a way to get into graduate school. This is a little characteristic of Jewish kids, and a fairly common thing in the New York Jewish boys" (Oren, *Joining the Club*, 371–72).

64. Bowles, in Henry G. Stetler, *College Admissions Practices with Respect to Race, Religion, and National Origin of Connecticut High School Graduates* (Hartford: Connecticut State Inter-Racial Commission, 1949), 5–6.

65. Signing the statement for Yale were the incoming president A. Whitney Griswold, Board of Admissions chair Edwards S. Noyes, university secretary Carl A. Lohmann, and university counsel Frederick H. Wiggin. Ten other leaders of Connecticut's private colleges and universities were also among the signatories ("Hearing Before the Committee on H. Bs. Nos. 1130, 1433 and S. Bs. Nos. 262, 411, 413. Relating to Claimed Discrimination in Admission of Applicants to Education Institutions"; "Memorandum in Opposition to the Bills Submitted in Behalf of the Catholic Colleges, Connecticut College for Women, Trinity College, Wesleyan University and Yale University," 14 March 1950, YUA).

66. "Hearing Before the Committee."

67. Among the rejected, the statement observes, there is always a "certain proportion of persons who may unreasonably consider that they have been unfairly treated." "This attitude of mind may be exaggerated in the case of one of the minority races," leading disgruntled members of such groups "to take advantage of the provisions of these bills and require the college to spend much time in lawsuits" (ibid).

68. Ibid.

69. Wiggin to Carl A. Lohmann, 5 February 1951.

70. In 1949, the percentage of Jews in the freshman class was 6.6 percent — the lowest figure since 1922 (Oren, *Joining the Club*, 320–21).

71. Gumbiner to Wiggin, 2 February 1951, YUA.

72. Anthony Astrachan, "Class Notes," in *My Harvard, My Yale*, 213.

73. Ibid., 214.

74. Oren, *Joining the Club*, 189.

75. These figures are from a memorandum of 27 November 1961 from Yale's Rabbi Richard J. Israel to Sidney Lovett, YUA. Princeton, long considered a citadel of anti-Semitism, had had an embarrassing incident as recently as 1958, when over half of the 23 men who failed to be invited into an eating club were Jews (see Chapter 10). And Dartmouth, the most rural of the Ivy League colleges, was still remembered for its legendary president, Ernest M. Hopkins, who in 1945 published a letter in a New York newspaper that defended Jewish quotas, stating flatly that "Dartmouth College is a Christian college founded for the Christianization of its students" (quoted in David O. Levine, *The American College and the Culture of Aspiration, 1915–1940* [Ithaca, N.Y.: Cornell U.P., 1986], 158).

76. Kabaservice, "Kingman Brewster," 351.

77. "Yale Men," *Ebony*, July 1950, 18.

78. Secretary's Office of Yale University [unsigned] to Mr. Spivak, 11 September 1945, YUA.

79. Rodes, "Educational Factors," 242–43.

80. Eugene H. Kone, associate director of the Yale News Bureau, to Sally Eaton of *Time* magazine, 21 April 1948, YUA.

81. Ibid.; "Yale Men," 20.

82. "Protestant, Catholics, Hebrews, Negroes — 1948–1949 — Second Terms," n.d., handwritten table found in YUA.

83. Jackson, a graduate of Hillhouse High School in New Haven, was the son of a master steward and chef at Yale's Pierson College. After serving in the army, where he attained the rank of sergeant, Jackson entered Yale in September 1946 on the G.I. Bill; he served as captain of the football team and also lettered in basketball (Synnott, *Half-Opened Door*, 135, 266; Oren, *Joining the Club*, 162).

84. E. Digby Baltzell, *The Protestant Establishment: Aristocracy and Caste in America* (New York: Vintage, 1964), 279.

85. The first Jew offered membership in Skull and Bones was Thomas H. Guinzberg, a Hotchkiss graduate who was also a member of the Fence Club and managing editor of the *YDN*, then edited by William F. Buckley Jr. (Oren, *Joining the Club*, 162).

86. Figures calculated from Pierson, *Yale Book of Numbers*, 95–98. The years 1941–1946 were excluded because the war led to wide fluctuations in enrollment, with 1941 and 1946 having exceptionally large freshman classes and 1942–1945 suffering from a shortage of students.

87. George Pierson, *Yale: The University College, 1921–1937* (New Haven, Conn.: Yale U.P., 1955), 95–98.

88. Board of Admissions, "Report to the President and Fellows," 1944–1945, YU, 1–2.

89. Figures calculated from Pierson, *Yale Book of Numbers*, 95–98.

90. Norman S. Buck, "What Kind of Boy Does Yale Want?" *YAM*, November 1950, 13.

91. Ibid., 9.

92. Ibid.

93. "How Undergraduates Get Their Scholarships," *YAM*, October 1951, 9.

94. Buck, "What Kind of Boy?" 13. According to Calvin Trillin, who entered Yale in 1953, "Most of the people sent from the public high schools of the provinces to places like Yale seemed to have been high-school heroes of one sort or another" (*Remembering Denny* [New York: Warner Books, 1994], 4).

95. Buck, "What Kind of Boy?" 14.

96. Pierson, *Yale*, 489–90.

97. Ibid., 490.

98. Committee on Enrollment, "Report to the Alumni Board," YUA, 61.

99. Homer D. Babbidge Jr., "Yale's Scholarship Program," *YAM*, February 1949, 1.

100. Ibid., 2–3.

101. Ibid., 2. The Board of Admissions under Edward S. Noyes was especially impressed with the accuracy of Yale's formula for predicting grades; it had, after all, predicted the averages of Noyes's own sons, who entered Yale from Exeter in 1936 and 1939, remarkably well — within one point in one case and precisely on target in the other (Rodes, "Educational Factors," YUA, 244). The formula, based on a combination of test scores and rank in class, claimed to predict freshman grades scientifically and reported a correlation in the vicinity of .70–.72. But as Kabaservice has pointed out, it was in fact biased against the great majority of high school applicants, for it applied a negative "correction" for candidates from schools that did not send many students to Yale (Kabaservice, "Kingman Brewster," 91).

102. Buck, "What Kind of Boy?" 13. Similarly, Homer D. Babbidge Jr., secretary of the Scholarship Committee, after affirming Yale's desire to enroll "applicants of *truly outstanding* intellectual capacity," quickly added, "and there are not as many as one might expect" ("Yale's Scholarship Program," 2).

103. And even the truly brilliant were sometimes rejected; as noted in Chapter 6, it was Harvard's official policy to reject even "mental giants" if they were judged to have "serious defects of character or personality." There is no reason to believe that Yale's policy was different from Harvard's, but Yale seems — not uncharacteristically — to have been more diffident on the matter than Harvard.

104. Babbidge, "Yale's Scholarship Program," 2.

105. Buck, "What Kind of Boy?" 14.

106. Albert B. Crawford, "Financing Him," in *Seventy-five: A Study of a Generation in Transition* (New Haven, Conn.: YDN, 1953), 34. That the "Jewish problem" may have been one of the reasons behind the reduction is suggested by the fact that the nearby northern New England region (Vermont, New Hampshire, and Maine) — whose population was well under 1 percent Jewish — was added to the program of University Regional Scholarships only in 1944, when there was intense concern about the growing Jewish enrollment. Also consistent with this interpretation is that the six northeastern states excluded from this program — states that together accounted for almost 70 percent of the nation's Jewish population — supplied Yale with 68 percent of its freshmen since 1951 but just over half of its scholarship recipients (Board of Admissions, "Comparative Inquiries on Geographical Distribution by Residence of the Classes of 1954 and 1955: Harvard, Princeton, Yale," 24 October 1951, YUA). For state-by-state statistics on the distribution

of Regional Scholarships between 1930 and 1953, see Pierson, *Yale*, 684; for state-by-state statistics on the Jewish population, see the *1946 World Almanac*.

107. Crawford, "Financing Him," 34.

108. "How Undergraduates Get Their Scholarships," 11.

109. Ibid., 10.

110. Crawford to Bender, 9 February 1955, YUA; Bender to Crawford, 14 February 1955, HUA.

111. Buck, "What Kind of Boy?" 15.

112. Babbidge, "Yale's Scholarship Program," 3.

113. "Terms of Admission," YUA, 22; Crawford to Seymour, 25 April 1949, YUA.

114. Babbidge, "What Kind of Boy?" 4.

115. "How Undergraduates Get Their Scholarships," 11. An earlier study of the entering freshmen of 1927, 1931, and 1936 had found a similar pattern, with 22 percent of scholarship men elected to Phi Beta Kappa or Sigma Xi, compared to only 8 percent of nonscholarship men (Ralph C. Burr, "Scholarship Students at Yale" [Ph.D. diss, Yale Univ., 1952], 62).

116. Crawford, "Financing Him," 34.

117. "Report of the Committee on Scholarship Aid," 9 January 1953, YUA, 6–7.

118. In 1930, the percentage of Yale freshmen from neither New York nor New England was 40 percent; by 1952, it had risen to nearly half (48.4%) (calculated from Pierson, *Yale*, 670–71).

119. "How Undergraduates Get Their Scholarships," 10.

120. William C. DeVane, "Report of the Dean of Yale College, Yale Report to the President, 1947–48" (Oren, *Joining the Club*, xiv). The Yale graduate schools, DeVane noted, admitted students on the basis of their college record and did not ask for "physical prowess or too much of that indefinable thing called personality" (Synnott, *Half-Opened Door*, 213).

121. Reflecting back on the late 1940s, the Yale historian Edmund Morgan described it as "so inbred, so dead that it was on the verge of ceasing to be a great university" (Kabaservice, "Kingman Brewster," 262–63).

122. The son of Thomas Day Seymour, Hillhouse Professor of Greek Language and Literature from 1880 to 1907, and the great-great-great-grandson of Joseph Coit, who received an M.A. in 1702 at Yale's first Commencement, Charles Seymour's Yale lineage was impeccable. Though he received a bachelor's degree from Cambridge in 1904, he returned to Yale as an undergraduate, getting his degree in 1908. A quintessential Yale man, he was active in the choir, glee club, and athletics and was elected to Skull and Bones. The author of a well-received book, *Diplomatic Background of the War* (1916), published shortly after he had turned thirty, and of *Woodrow Wilson and the World War* (1921), Seymour in 1922 became one of the youngest men to be appointed to a prestigious Sterling professorship (Holden, *Profiles and Portraits of Yale University Presidents* [Freeport, Me.: Bond Wheelwright, 1968], 120). Conservative in his views and gentlemanly in his appearance and demeanor, Seymour was, in the words of the Yale historian Brooks Mather Kelley, "an idealized version of a college president." See Kelley, *Yale: A History* (New Haven, Conn.: Yale U.P., 1974), 393–94, and Reuben A. Holden, *Profiles and Portraits*.

123. Seymour to Noyes, 20 December 1948, YUA. In the same folder is a document from the Board of Ad-

missions that offers proof of the depth of Yale's preference for athletes. Of the 48 men on the varsity football squad in 1948, 13 were admitted with predicted grades of 67 or below, 9 were admitted with no prediction whatsoever, and 9 were admitted with predictions at or above the Yale average (76 or higher) (Board of Admissions, "Varsity Football Squad," 12 January 1949, YUA).

124. Board of Admissions, "Report to the President and Fellows," 1948–1949, YU.

125. Board of Admissions, "Report to the President and Fellows," 1948–1949, YU.

126. It should be noted, however, that in 1951 Yale had the lowest acceptance rate for legacies among the Big Three: 73 percent, compared to 79 at Princeton and a remarkable 94 percent at Harvard (Board of Admissions, "Comparative Figures on the Classes of 1954 and 1955 in Harvard, Princeton and Yale," YUA; Bender to Lamont, 25 January 1957, HUA). If, as these figures suggest, Harvard's standards for admitting alumni sons were even more lax than those of Princeton and Yale, this may well have been because of its concern that it was attracting fewer of the sons of the eastern upper class than its rivals because of its reputation as a college filled with socially undesirable students, many of them "grinds." That Harvard's concern may not have been misplaced is suggested by the recollections of James C. Thompson Jr., Lawrenceville '49, who noted that Harvard's reputation was that it "was only a place for weenies, wonks, and weirdoes." In part for this reason, Thompson chose Yale ("Neither Here nor There," in *My Harvard, My Yale*, 224–25).

127. Leading the pack was Andover (46), Hotchkiss (38), Exeter (37), Taft (37), Lawrenceville (34), Choate (26), St. Paul's (24), and Deerfield (23). Even more striking was the high number from the less renowned boarding schools: Loomis (15), Brooks (13), Cheshire (13), Gunnery (13), Mercersburg (13), and Mt. Hermon (12) (Board of Admissions, "Report to the President and Fellows," 1949–1950, YU, 3, 6–7).

128. Alumni Board Committee, "The Operations of the Board of Admissions," YUA, 3. So fixated was Noyes on rank in class, claimed the report, that "if a boy ranking 180 in a class of 220 at Exeter is admitted, any applicant above him must also be admitted, unless he is a moral leper (and who is these days!), lest the school officials be offended."

129. Buck, "What Kind of Boy?" 14.

130. Calculated from Board of Admissions, "Choate Study," 14 November 1949, YUA.

131. Kelley, *Yale*, 420; Kabaservice, "Kingman Brewster," 229.

132. Kabaservice, *The Guardians*, 154.

133. Bender, who had just been appointed dean of Harvard College at the time of his remarks about Seymour, also delivered a pointed appraisal of Harvard's Conant. In Bender's view, Conant had three principal weaknesses: "he lacks magnetism and warmth . . . is not a very good administrator in the technical sense . . . [and] is not a superlative judge of men." Counterbalancing these weaknesses were several important strengths: "an absolutely first rate intelligence, a distinction of mind and character, an integrity and simplicity and selflessness, a realistic awareness of what is going on in the world." Together, these attributes, Bender believed, made Conant "a *great* president" despite his weaknesses. And compared to other presi-

dents, Conant loomed even larger. From Bender's perspective, Seymour was not the only president who failed to meet Conant's high standard; Dodds of Princeton was "a nice mediocrity" and Hutchins of Chicago a "perverse, egocentric screwball" (Bender, "Speech to the Class of '27," HUA, 11–12).

134. Until 1949, students were required to list their first choice of college on registering for College Board tests. Though they could name their second and third choices, colleges frequently refused to consider such candidates. Then the College Board introduced a complicated system in which candidates could list two or even three first choices, or two first choices and one second, or one first and two second, or a first, a second, and a third choice. This system proved unsatisfactory, and in 1951 applicants were asked to list the colleges to which their scores should be sent, with no requirement that they state a preference. The most detailed description of these changes, and of their consequences, is in the Committee on Admission, "Report to the President," 1948–1949 through 1951–1952, PU. See also the Board of Admissions, "Report to the President and Fellows," 1948–1949 and 1950–1951, YU.

135. Board of Admissions, "Comparative Figures on the Classes of 1954 and 1955," YUA.

136. Alumni Board Committee, "The Operations of the Board of Admissions," 21 February 1951, YUA, 1.

137. The portrait of Griswold is based on several sources, including Anne Rothe, ed., *Current Biography 1950* (New York: H. W. Wilson, 1950), 200–202; Holden, *Profiles and Portraits;* Kabaservice, "Kingman Brewster," 225–30, 296–305; Kelley, *Yale,* 425–59; and *WWA, 1952–1953.*

138. Kabaservice, "Kingman Brewster," 227.

139. Kelley, *Yale,* 427.

140. Ibid.

141. Kabaservice, *The Guardians,* 155.

142. Holden, *Profiles and Portraits,* 138.

143. Kabaservice, "Kingman Brewster," 305.

144. Roger Geiger, *Research and Relevant Knowledge: American Research Universities Since World War II* (New York: Oxford U.P., 1993), 89; Kabaservice, "Kingman Brewster," 207.

145. Kabaservice, *The Guardians,* 156.

146. Kabaservice, "Kingman Brewster," 301.

147. Ibid., 302. A devoted advocate of liberal education, Griswold seemed to identify the capacity to appreciate it with class and ethnic privilege. Through "lack of previous opportunity," he wrote, America's "foreign population failed to support it." And "for want of previous opportunity," blacks too "lacked comprehension of the liberal arts." Both African Americans and the "foreign-born and their children" were, therefore, "beyond the pale, so to speak, of the liberal arts" ("What We Don't Know Will Hurt Us: The Power of Liberal Education," *Harper's Magazine,* July 1954, 79).

148. William Butler (pseudonym) to Griswold, 29 November 1950, YUA.

149. Special Subcommittee #1 of the Committee on Enrollment and Scholarships, "Operations of the Board of Admissions," 1, 2.

150. Crawford to Noyes, June 1951, YUA; Crawford to Griswold, June 1951, YUA.

151. The conclusion that Crawford did not resign in the end is based on his presence at meetings of the Board of Admissions in 1951–1952 and 1952–1953. See

Board of Admissions, "Minutes of the Meeting of the Board of Admissions," 24 January 1952, YUA; Board of Admissions, "Minutes of the Board of Admissions," 23 October 1952, YUA.

152. Hopkins (pseudonym) to Griswold, 12 February 1953, YUA.

153. Board of Admissions, "Minutes of the Meeting of the Board of Admissions," 2 October 1953, YUA, which appointed Arthur Howe Jr. as acting chairman of the board effective that day (Board of Admissions, "Report to the President and Fellows," 1952–1953, YU).

154. Pierson, *Yale Book of Numbers,* 87; Office of Admission, "Report to the Faculty," 1967–1968, PU, Chart G; Bender to Lamont, 25 January 1957, HUA.

155. Pierson, *Yale Book of Numbers,* 96, 98; Committee on Admission, "Report to the President, 1952–1953," PU; Committees on Admission and on Scholarships and Financial Aids, "Report on the Office of the Dean of Admissions and Financial Aids for Students in Harvard College, 1952–1953," HU, 213.

156. Data on the number of students from various prep schools entering Yale in 1953 are derived from *The Handbook of Private Schools,* 35th ed. (Boston: Porter Sargent, 1954).

157. Crawford, "Financing Him," 34.

158. Oren, *Joining the Club,* 321.

159. Trillin reported that his entering freshman class included "perhaps half a dozen members of our class who could be considered people of color," including a Jamaican and two Asians (*Remembering Denny,* 36–37). Henry Chauncey Jr. remembers only one black student in the same class (interview by Geoffrey Kabaservice, 22 March 1992, transcript, YUA).

160. Pierson, *Yale Book of Numbers,* 96, 98.

161. Pierson, *Yale,* 670; Board of Admissions, "Report to the President and Fellows," 1952–1953, YU, 11.

162. "Report of the Committee on Scholarship Aid," YUA, 2, 6.

163. Pierson, *Yale Book of Numbers,* 87.

164. Calculated from ibid., 96, 98. Even the most distinguished boarding schools were not totally spared; the twelve leading institutions that provided 35 percent of the freshmen in 1937 contributed only 25 percent in 1953. The figures for 1937 are derived from Kabaservice, "Kingman Brewster," 606, 609; the figures for 1953 are derived from *Handbook of Private Schools.*

165. Trillin, *Remembering Denny,* 36, 37.

8. Princeton: The Club Expands Its Membership

1. James B. Conant, *My Several Lives: Memoirs of a Social Inventor* (New York: Harper & Row, 1970), 52. For an account of the political maneuverings that led to Conant's selection as president, see Chapter 5 of this volume.

2. Don Oberdorfer, *Princeton University: The First 250 Years* (Princeton, N.J.: Steering Committee for Princeton's 250th Anniversary, 1995), 131.

3. The portrait of Dodds includes information from *WWA, 1962–1963;* Alexander Leitch, ed., *A Princeton Companion* (Princeton, N.J.: Princeton U.P., 1978), 137–41; *The Presidents of Princeton University: 1746 to the Present* (Princeton, N.J.: Office of Communications/Publications, 1996), 21–22; and Oberdorfer, *Princeton University.*

4. Leitch, *Princeton Companion,* 137–41.

5. Bureau of the Census, *Historical Statistics of the United States: Colonial Times to 1970,* Part 1 (Washington, D.C.: Government Printing Office, 1989), 379.

6. According to the *Freshman Herald for the Class of 1936* (PU, 31), the 122 alumni sons who entered Princeton in 1932 were the offspring of fathers who had entered between 1886 and 1909, with many of them clustered between 1897 and 1903. Since the average number of freshmen in these years was no more than 300, the number of potential legacy applicants must have been very small. A remarkable proportion of them seem to have followed their fathers to Princeton; see Edwin E. Slosson, *Great American Universities* (New York: Macmillan, 1910), 109.

7. "Preliminary Analysis of Freshman Class," September 1932, PU, 2–3.

8. As late as 1959, the social critic Vance Packard could write, "I have found Princeton students able to list with impressive unanimity the status ranking of the clubs, from the highest down to seventeenth" with Ivy, Cottage, Cap and Gown, and Colonial the top four and Prospect, number seventeen (*The Status Seekers* [New York: Pocket Books, 1961 (1959)], 213).

9. The 90 percent figure for the 1930s is taken from Oberdorfer (*Princeton University,* 121), who estimates that only 75 percent of upperclassmen belonged to eating clubs in the 1920s.

10. Marcia Graham Synnott, *The Half-Opened Door: Discrimination and Admissions at Harvard, Yale, and Princeton, 1900–1970* (Westport, Conn.: Greenwood Press, 1979), 174–75.

11. "Preliminary Analysis of the Freshman Class," September 1932, PU, 5. Though Princeton's twentieth-century reputation as a southern institution was mythical, there had been a point in its distant past — 1848, according to Synnott (*Half-Opened Door,* 175) — when a majority of students did come from the South. More relevant in explaining Princeton's long-standing tradition of excluding blacks than its fabled southern demographic composition was the strong conservatism of its major constituencies: its trustees, its administration, its students, and its alumni.

12. Roman Catholics, particularly numerous in the Middle Atlantic states, from which Princeton drew the majority of its students, made up 10.5 percent of Princeton freshmen in 1932 (*Freshman Herald: Class of 1936,* PU, 28).

13. If contractors (7) are excluded from the category of "workers," then only 9 members of the entering freshmen of 1932 had fathers who were working men (ibid., 27).

14. Ibid., 28–30.

15. Committee on Admission, "Admission," in "Report of the President to the Board of Trustees," 1932–1933, PU, 7.

16 Carl C. Brigham, "The Quality of the Classes Admitted to Princeton in the Years 1928 to 1935 (Confidential Report to the Committee on Admissions)," 1935, PUA, 1.

17. "Academic Performance of Undergraduates," in "Report of the President to the Board of Trustees," 1931–1932, PU, 9.

18 Committee on Admission, minutes, 14 June 1935, cited in George E. Tomberlin Jr., "Trends in Princeton Admissions" (senior thesis, Princeton Univ., 1971), PU, 134.

19. Committee on Admission, minutes, 25 January 1938, PUA, and "Report of the President to the Board of Trustees," 1939–1940, cited in Tomberlin, "Trends in Princeton Admissions," 134.

20. Calculated from *Freshman Heralds* of the Classes of 1941 through 1945, PU. For the entire 1937–1941 period, the percentage of Jews among Princeton freshman was 1.6 percent (53 of 3,307 matriculants).

21. Leslie I. Laughlin, "Admission Without Examination," *PAW,* 1 December 1936.

22. Committee on Admission, "Admission and Freshman Year," in "Report of the President to the Board of Trustees," 1937–1938, PU, 56.

23. Committee on Admission, "Admission and Freshman Year," in "Report of the President to the Board of Trustees," 1938–1939, PU, 64.

24. "Preliminary Analysis of the Freshman Class," September 1936, PUA, 1; "Preliminary Analysis of the Freshman Class," September 1941, PU, 1.

25. Committee on Admission, "Admission and Freshman Year," in "Report of the President to the Board of Trustees," 1935–1936, PU, 70; Committee on Admission, "Admission and Freshman Year," in "Report of the President to the Board of Trustees," 1940–1941, PU, 56.

26. Committee on Admission, "Admission and Freshman Year," in "Report of the President to the Board of Trustees," 1936–1937, PU, 66–69.

27. Ibid.

28. Committee on Admission, "Admission and Freshman Year," in "Report of the President to the Board of Trustees," 1937–1938, PU, 56.

29. Committee on Admission, "Admission," in "Report of the President to the Board of Trustees," 1932–1933, PU, 23.

30. "Annual Giving," in Leitch, *Princeton Companion,* 21.

31. Ibid. Perhaps not coincidentally, at $1,097,978, Princeton's endowment was in 1999 the highest per student of any major American research university ($795,092 for Harvard and $661,572 for Yale; Rockefeller University, a graduate institution with only 140 students, ranked first at $7,197,143). In absolute dollars, Princeton ranked fourth, behind Harvard, the University of Texas system, and Yale ("Largest Endowments per Student, 1999," *Chronicle of Higher Education Almanac,* 1 September 2000, http://chronicle.com/prm/weekly/almanac/2000/facts/4801money.htm [accessed 2 June 2004]; "College and University Endowments Over $100-Million, 1999," *Chronicle of Higher Education Almanac,* 1 September 2000, http://chronicle.com/prm/weekly/almanac/2000/facts/4601money.htm [accessed 2 June 2004]).

32. Charles W. Edwards, "The Admissions Problem," *PAW,* 4 November 1955, 8.

33. Slosson, *Great American Universities,* 104.

34. Karen W. Arenson, "Princeton Honors Judge It Once Turned Away for His Race," *NYT,* 5 June 2001.

35. *Looking Back: Reflections of Black Princeton Alumni,* produced by Melvin McCray and Calvin Norman, Joint Project of the Association of Blacks Princeton Alumni, the Alumni Council, and the Office of the 250th Anniversary, 1996, PU.

36. Ibid.

37. Thomas (1884–1968), who left the ministry in 1931, was the leader of the Socialist Party after Eugene Debs's death in 1926 and its candidate for president in 1928, 1932, 1936, 1940, 1944, and 1948 (*WWA, 1952–1953,* and *The Columbia Encyclopedia*).

38. Norman Thomas, "Negroes," *PAW,* 29 March 1940.

39. Tomberlin, "Trends in Princeton Admissions," PU, 88.

40. Committee on Admission, minutes, 15 January 1941, cited in ibid., 87.

41. The estimate that about 85 percent of the students were Republican comes from the same panel of deans who wished to ensure that Princeton not be a university only for "high stand" men (Tomberlin, "Trends in Princeton Admissions," 87). A survey of students in 1947 revealed that 75 percent preferred to see a Republican in the White House in 1948 and only 25 percent a Democrat (only 1 percent supported the incumbent president, Harry Truman) ("The Sovereign Survey," *Nassau Sovereign,* March 1947).

42. "White Supremacy at Princeton: A Time to Decide," Part II, *DP,* 30 September 1942. See also "White Supremacy at Princeton: A Thousand Million Colored Allies," Part I, *DP,* 28 September 1942, and "White Supremacy at Princeton: We Make Answer," Part III, *DP,* 3 October 1942.

43. Benjamin H. Walker, "'Prince' Speakers Challenge on Policy of Discrimination," *DP,* 2 October 1942. Francis Broderick, an Andover graduate who became a professor at Lawrence College in Appleton, Wisconsin, and wrote a biography of W.E.B. Du Bois, flew more than sixty B-24 bombing missions in World War II. Powell Whitehead died in combat during the war (Walter White, "Princeton University Signifies Color Barrier is Crumbling There," *New York Herald Tribune,* 26 December 1948).

44. Walker, "'Prince' Speakers Challenge on Policy of Discrimination."

45. Joseph D. Bennet, letter to the editor, *DP,* 3 October 1942.

46. Harry R. Stack IV '46, Kenneth Gorman '46, W. Kennedy Cromwell II '46, and Chas. C. Fenwick '46, letter to the editor, *DP,* 5 October 1942.

47. "The Negro Question," *Nassau Sovereign,* October 1942. For a discussion of the method used in the survey, which sampled every tenth student in the directory and included 258 respondents (10 percent of whom offered "no opinion"), see John Bigelow '43, "Sovereign Speaks."

48. Of the classes that entered Princeton in 1939–1942, the proportion of Southerners (including the southwest region of Oklahoma and Texas) was 9.3 percent. Of these students, 175 came from Maryland, the District of Columbia, and northern Virginia (the "Potomac Region" in Princeton's classification). Only 72 students — 2.7 percent of the undergraduates — came from what might loosely be defined as the Deep South. These figures are calculated from the "Preliminary Analysis of the Freshman Class," 1939–1942, PU.

49. "Negro Question." In a separate survey conducted by the *DP,* 51 percent of undergraduates favored the admission of blacks, with 49 percent opposed ("Poll Indicates 51 Percent of Students Favor Proposal," *DP,* 22 October 1942).

50. "Council Vetoes Negro Admission to College Now," *DP,* 22 October 1942.

51. "'A Time for Greatness,'" *DP,* 22 October 1942. A careful reading of the article reporting the results of the faculty survey reveals, however, that there may have been more faculty opposition than suggested by the report of 79 for the admission of Negroes and 24 against, for 173 of the 285 faculty (61 percent) polled

did not respond, instructors (as opposed to assistant, associate, and full professors) were over-represented among respondents, and nine faculty members surveyed responded "no comment." See "Princeton Faculty Backs Move by More Than 3-to-1 Vote," *DP,* 22 October 1942.

52. "'Time for Greatness.'"

53. "Minutes of the Meeting of the Board of Trustees," 22 October 1942, PU.

54. Synnott, *Half-Opened Door,* 219–22; Oberdorfer, *Princeton University,* 144–145; Tomberlin, "Trends in Princeton Admissions," PU, 136–138. A letter to the *DP* of 3 June 1946 praising the enrollment of Negroes cites as evidence that their participation and contribution to Princeton life had been realized in a harmonious and satisfactory way to all concerned "the election of one of these Negroes to an Upper Class Eating Club." John H. Bunzel '46 and Charles R. Schwab '44, letter to the editor, *DP,* 3 June 1946.

55. Oberdorfer (*Princeton University,* 144–45) reports that though there were no blacks in his own entering class of 1948, three African-Americans entered the freshman class in 1949. On 1949, see also "Minutes of a Regular Meeting of the Executive Committee of the Board of Trustees of Princeton University," 23 September 1949, PUA. Tomberlin, "Trends in Princeton Admissions," PU, 139, reports that no blacks entered Princeton in 1953, 1954, and 1955.

56. In 1946, there were 4,564 applicants for a class numbering 776; in 1941, there were only 1,136 applicants for a class of 673. Edwards, "Admissions Problem." "During the twenty years from 1921 to 1941, the Committee on Admission always found a natural cleavage at some point between the well prepared candidates and the less well prepared; this point might be as low as 600 or as high as 700, but during those years we were never forced to refuse admission to boys with good character testimonials and adequate scholastic preparation." Committee on Admission, "Report to the President," 1947–1948, PU, 4–5.

57. Harold Dodds, "To All Princeton Alumni," 22 April 1947, PUA.

58. Graduate Council of Princeton University, "Review of Princeton's Current Admission Policy," 7 May 1948, PUA, 9; Edwards, "Admissions Problem," 2.

59. Edwards, "Admissions Problem," 9.

60. Next was Exeter (739), followed by Hill (443). Whereas a dozen prep schools sent over 190 students to Princeton between 1927 and 1946, the top public school in the country, New Trier, contributed only 91. See an untitled two-page document (begins "Show definite relationships with Private Schools"), 1947, PUA.

61. Graduate Council of Princeton University, "Review of Princeton's Current Admissions Policy," PUA, 5; Committee on Admission, "Report to the President," 1950–1951, PU.

62. Committee on Admission, "Report to the President," 1955–1956, PU. On Yale, see George Pierson, ed., *A Yale Book of Numbers: Historical Statistics of the College and University, 1701–1976* (New Haven, Conn.: Yale University Press, 1983), 98.

63. *The World Almanac 1946,* 571.

64. This portrait of the Princeton alumni is based on annual data presented in *Freshman Herald* and the *Nassau Herald* as well as on a perusal of the *PAW.*

65. Radcliffe Heermance, "Admission to Princeton, A Digest of Remarks Delivered at the Seventh Annual

Dinner in Honor of the Class Agent of the Princeton University Fund, The Princeton Inn," 4 October 1946, PUA, my emphasis.

66. Committee on Admission, "Report to the President," 1948–1949, PU, 6.

67. Calculated from Committee on Admission, "Report to the President," 1950–1951, PU, 9.

68. Between 1940 and 1950, the percentage of high school graduates grew from 20 to 39 percent, the number of secondary schools represented declined from 196 to 146, and the percentage of the class from outside New York, New Jersey, and Pennsylvania increased from 38 to 49 percent (ibid.).

69. Committee on Admission, "Report to the President," 1954–1955, PUA, 6.

70. Committee on Admission, "Report to the President," 1953–1954, PU, 16.

71. Heermance, "Admission to Princeton," PU. A slightly different version of these remarks was published as "Admissions Policies in the Demobilization Phase," *PAW*, 1 November 1946.

72. Dodds, "To All Princeton Alumni," PUA.

73. Graduate Council of Princeton University, "Review of Princeton's Current Admission Policy," PUA, 4.

74. Alumni Council of Princeton University, "Answers to your questions about the ADMISSION OF PRINCETON SONS," 1 June 1958, PUA, 3.

75. Ibid., 2.

76. "Getting into Princeton."

77. Graduate Council of Princeton University, "Review of Princeton's Current Admission Policy," PUA, 4.

78. Calculated from the Committee on Admission, "Report to the President," from 1948–1949 to 1953–1954, PU.

79. Beginning in 1922, the *Freshman Herald* listed "Princeton Classes with Sons" and "List of Colleges from which Mothers of Freshmen have Graduated" in addition to "Religious Preference," "Father's Occupation," and "List of Colleges from which Fathers of Freshmen have Graduated." In 1934, the *Freshman Herald* also began to list (by name) "Members of the Freshman Class whose Fathers Attended Princeton" (*Freshman Heralds* for Classes of 1926–1938).

80. In 1951, Princeton also admitted a lower percent of legacy applicants than Harvard (78.5 vs. 93.1 percent). The proportion of freshman who were alumni sons was, however, slightly lower at Harvard in the 1950s, averaging 17 percent in the early 1950s, compared to 18 percent at Princeton. On Princeton, see Committee on Admission, "Report to the President," 1951–1952 and 1952–1953, PU. On Harvard, see Wilbur J. Bender to Thomas S. Lamont, 25 January 1957, HUA.

81. Calculated from Pierson, *Yale Book of Numbers*, 87.

82. Graduate Council of Princeton University, "Review of Princeton's Current Admission Policy," PUA, 5.

83. "Preliminary Analysis of the Freshman Class," 1946, 1949, 1952, PU.

84. On Yale, see Pierson, *Yale Book of Numbers*, 96. On Harvard, see Committees on Admission and on Scholarships and Financial Aids, "Report on the Office of the Dean of Admissions and Financial Aids for Students in Harvard College," 1952–1953, HU, 19.

85. Committee on Admission, "Report to the President," 1951–1952, PU, 8.

86. Committee on Admission, "Report to the President," 1953–1954, PU, 1.

87. Committee on Admission, "Report to the President," 1952–1953, PU, 6–7.

88. Ibid. On Harvard, see Committees on Admission and on Scholarships and Financial Aids, "Report on the Office of the Dean of Admissions and Financial Aids for Students in Harvard College," 1952–1953, HU, 9.

89. Calculated from Committee on Admission, "Report to the President," 1955–1956, PU, 5.

90. Committee on Admission, "Report to the President," 1952–1953, PU, 6.

91. "Preliminary Analysis of the Freshman Class," 1940, PU, 2; "Preliminary Analysis of the Freshman Class," 1952, PU, 2–3. Interestingly, the decline between 1940 and 1952 in the number of freshmen from Exeter and Andover, generally considered the most meritocratic of the major private schools, was only 15 percent, compared to 39 percent for Lawrenceville and Hill.

92. Untitled document, 1947, PUA; "Preliminary Analysis of the Freshman Class," 1952, PU, 3.

93. Committee on Admission, "Report to the President," 1953–1954, PU, 5. Because fewer of the admitted high school boys actually matriculated at Princeton, a majority (55 percent) of the freshmen who entered in 1953 had attended private schools.

94. According to annual statistics reported in the *Freshman Herald*, the proportion of Jews at Princeton between 1924 (the year a strict quota was imposed) and 1941 ranged from a low of less than 1 percent in 1931 to a high of 3.1 percent in 1934, with most years over 2, but under 3 percent.

95. From the *Freshman Herald* for Classes of 1946, 1947, 1948, 1950, and 1951, PU.

96. Carey McWilliams, *A Mask of Privilege: Anti-Semitism in America* (Boston: Little, Brown, 1948), 136.

97. "Dean Heermance Denies Claim that Quota System Used Here," *DP*, 24 March 1948.

98. For an account of the political and legal struggle of Jewish organizations against anti-Semitism, see Leonard Dinnerstein, "Anti-Semitism Exposed and Attacked, 1945–1950," *American Jewish History* 71, no. 1 (September 1991): 134–149. One of the more important intellectual assaults on anti-Semitism was a seven-part series by Bruce Bliven in the *New Republic* in 1947. In the fourth article in the series, Bliven specifically discussed anti-Semitism in higher education and named Princeton as one of the several institutions that "enrolled conspicuously small proportions of Jews." See Bruce Bliven, "For 'Nordics' Only," *New Republic*, 8 December 1947.

99. "Anti-Discrimination," *PAW*, 15 October 1948.

100. Dinnerstein, "Anti-Semitism Exposed," 140. For an illuminating account of the events leading to the passage of the Fair Educational Practices Act by the New York State Legislature, see Harold S. Wechsler, *The Qualified Student: A History of Selective College Admission in America* (New York: John Wiley, 1977), 194–204.

101. Tomberlin, "Trends in Princeton Admissions," PU, 135.

102. Oberdorfer, *Princeton University*, 141. *Freshman Herald: Class of 1952*, PU, 37, includes figures on the number of "Hebrews" and the total number of students in the Class of 1952.

103. Quoted in William K. Selden, *Club Life at*

Princeton: An Historical Account of the Eating Clubs at Princeton University (Princeton, N.J.: Princeton Prospect Foundation, 1994), 45–46.

104. Oberdorfer, *Princeton University*, 142.

105. The "Dirty Bicker" of 1958, examined in Chapter 10, is described in great detail in Walter Goodman, "Bicker at Princeton: The Eating Clubs Again," *Commentary*, May 1958.

106. I have chosen to compare Princeton with Harvard rather than with Yale because of the sharper contrast — both in reputation and reality — between the two institutions. In virtually every salient dimension — geographical location, proportion of blacks and Jews, size of city, centrality of the club system to campus life, and percentage of the freshman class from private schools — Yale occupied an intermediate position between Princeton and Harvard.

107. "President Dodds Speaks," *PAW*, 19 July 1946, 7.

108. See especially James B. Conant, "Wanted: American Radicals," *Atlantic Monthly*, May 1943.

109. Calculated from "Preliminary Analysis of the Freshman Class," 1930, 1950, PU.

110. Data for 1930 provided by Office of Admissions, Harvard University. Data for 1950 provided by individual boarding schools and, in missing cases, by a face count of students listed in Harvard's *Freshman Facebook: Class of 1954*.

111. Lemann, *Big Test*, 9.

112. Bender to Lamont, 25 January 1957, HUA, 1.

113. Calculated from Committee on Admission, "Report to the President," 1951–1952, PU, 10, and Committee on Admission, "Report to the President," 1952–1953, PU, 10.

114. Between 1930 and 1932, just 1.4 percent of Princeton freshmen — 27 students of 1,930 students — were Jewish. See the *Freshman Heralds* for Classes of 1934, 1935, and 1936, PU.

115. Synnott, *Half-Opened Door*, 107–17.

116. The estimate that Harvard was 25 percent Jewish in 1952 is from Lipset (chap. 6, n. 176) and consistent with an estimate of 26 percent for the class that entered in 1950 by Epstein, "Elitism, Diversity, and Meritocracy at Harvard," 35.

117. Data for the specific public and private schools cited were provided by Harvard's Office of Admission. The overall rejection rate for 1950 of 36 percent is reported in Committee on Admission, "Report of the Committee on Admission of Harvard College," 1949–1950, HU, 4.

118. See the *Freshman Heralds* for Classes of 1952 and 1953, PU.

119. Goodman, "Bicker at Princeton," 409; "Incident at Princeton," *Newsweek*, 24 February 1958.

120. The estimate that the percentage of Jews was approximately twice as high at Harvard than at Princeton in 1953 is based on the figure of 25 percent at Harvard cited above and an estimate of about 12 or 13 percent at Princeton. While no figures are available for Princeton in 1953, we do know that the proportion of Jews had been rising since the mid-1940s and that the 14 percent figure for 1958 cited above is based on those students who entered Princeton in the years 1954 and 1957.

121. Tomberlin, "Trends in Princeton Admissions," PU, 137–38. As late as 1958–1961, Princeton averaged only one to two black entrants annually. See Commission of the Future of the College, *The Report of the Commission of the Future of the College* (Princeton, N.J.: Trustees of Princeton University, 1973), Table 28.

122. Wilbur J. Bender to Joseph H. Chadbourne Jr., 16 October 1951, HUA.

123. Committee on Admission, "Report to the President," 1952–1953, PU, 11; Committees on Admission and on Scholarships and Financial Aid, "Report of the Office of the Dean of Admissions and Financial Aids for Students in Harvard College," 1952–1953, HU, 27. Of the 29.9 percent of freshmen on financial aid at Harvard, only 24.1 percent received scholarship grants.

124. Committees on Admission and on Scholarships and Financial Aid, "Report on the Office of the Dean of Admissions and Financial Aids for Students in Harvard College," 1952–1953, HU, 11.

125. Committee on Admission, "Report to the President," 1952–1953, PU, 10.

126. Wilbur J. Bender, "Speech to Class of '27," 3 May 1947, HUA, 12.

9. Wilbur Bender and His Legacy

1. Henry Rosovsky, "Report of the Task Force on the Composition of the Student Body," March 1977, HU, 3.

2. "The University," *HAB*, 13 October 1951, 59.

3. Paul Buck to James Conant, 9 December 1947, HUA. One of several indications that Gummere remained out of step with Conant and Buck even as he left office was his remark, at a November 1951 meeting of the Schools and Scholarships Committee, that Harvard Clubs in several large midwestern cities were paying insufficient attention to "paying guests" and that they should "seek from their private schools more boys who could pay their own way, and not devote too much time to the scholarship boys" (Associated Harvard Clubs, "Digest of Schools and Scholarships Committee Meeting," HU, 37).

4. Paul Buck, interviewed by William Bentinck-Smith, Summer 1974, 66–67.

5. "The University," 59.

6. Figure calculated from the Committees on Admission and on Scholarships and Financial Aids, "Report on the Office of the Dean of Admissions and Financial Aids for Students in Harvard College, 1952–1953," HU, 18.

7. Paul Buck, HU.

8. Conant resigned as president in January 1953, and Nathan Marsh Pusey (B.A. '28, Ph.D. '37), the president of Lawrence College in Wisconsin, was named his successor on June 1, 1953 (John Bethell, *Harvard Observed: An Illustrated History of the University in the Twentieth Century* [Cambridge, Mass.: Harvard U.P., 1998], 191–92).

9. Wilbur J. Bender, "A Comprehensive Formal Statement of Harvard College Admission Policy (Confidential)," 18 September 1952, HUA, 9.

10. Henry Bragdon, "Conversation About Bill Bender, Mostly With E.T. Wilcox, But Sargent Kennedy Also Chiming In," 30 October 1971, HUA.

11. Ibid. The dinner at which the statement was discussed took place on October 1, 1952 — less than four months before Conant resigned as president.

12. For illuminating portraits of the atmosphere of the period, see James T. Patterson, *Grand Expectations: The United States, 1945–1974* (New York: Oxford U.P., 1996), 105–242, and Godfrey Hodgson, *America in Our Time: From World War II to Nixon — What Happened and Why* (New York: Vintage, 1976), 17–98. For a use-

ful chronology of events, see Laurence Urdang, ed., *The Timetables of American History* (New York: Simon & Schuster, 1996), 348–58.

13. McCarthy, quoted in Patterson, *Grand Expectations*, 196.

14. McCarthy, quoted in Seymour Martin Lipset and David Riesman, *Education and Politics at Harvard* (New York: McGraw-Hill, 1975), 192.

15. Ibid.

16. McCarthy, quoted in Hodgson, *America in Our Time*, 43.

17. In the parlance of contemporary sociology, Bender may be considered a gifted lay practitioner of what has come to be called institutional analysis — an approach that takes as its starting point organizations, which are viewed as pursuing their own distinct interests. Within the framework of institutional analysis, "organizational fields" — which may be defined as being composed of "those organizations that, in the aggregate, constitute a recognized area of institutional life: key supplier, resource and product consumers, regulatory agencies, and other organizations that produce similar services or products" — warrant special attention. Relations among organizations within the same field are often — albeit not always — competitive. In the case of Harvard admissions, for example, the relevant organizational field would be that of other selective private institutions of higher education with whom it competed for students. Much of Bender's behavior may be understood as a conscious attempt to improve Harvard's position within its field of peer organizations — an effort that required a firm grasp of power relations both within the organization and in relation to major actors outside it (e.g., alumni, key feeder schools, "paying customers," dominant social classes). In Bourdieuian terms, Bender's brilliant practical grasp of the complex dynamics of the "field" in which he was operating permitted him to accumulate for Harvard far more "capital" — both material and symbolic — than a less sophisticated analyst of fields would have been able to amass. For an example of institutional analysis, see Steven Brint and Jerome Karabel's account of the development of American community colleges (*The Diverted Dream: Community Colleges and the Promise of Educational Opportunity in America, 1900–1985* [New York: Oxford U.P., 1995]). For a discussion of the "new institutionalism" in sociology, see Paul DiMaggio and Walter W. Powell, eds., *The New Institutionalism in Organizational Analysis* (Chicago: Univ. of Chicago Press, 1991). On Bourdieu's concept of "field," see David Swartz, *Culture & Power: The Sociology of Pierre Bourdieu* (Chicago: Univ. of Chicago Press, 1997), ch. 6, and Pierre Bourdieu and Loïc J. D. Wacquant, *An Invitation to Reflexive Sociology* (Chicago: Univ. of Chicago Press, 1992), intro.

18. Bender, "Comprehensive Formal Statement," 2.

19. Ibid., 2–5.

20. Ibid., 7. For 1951 and 1952 combined, 64.4 percent of all applicants to Harvard College were accepted. See Committee on Admission, "Report of the Committee on Admission of Harvard College," 1951–1952, HU; Committees on Admission, "Report for Students," 1952–1953.

21. Ibid., 7, 29.

22. Ibid., 27.

23. Ibid., 29–30.

24. Ibid., 24.

25. Ibid., 28–29, 7.

26. Bender's use of the phrase "paying guests," the term used by Gummere, von Stade, and Buck, is noteworthy, for it metaphorically portrays Harvard as an exclusive club, resort, or hotel welcoming as "guests" the "Final Club group." Elsewhere in his report, however, Bender uses the metaphor of "paying customers" seven separate times. The metaphor of the "paying customer" typically used by Bender suggests that Bender had a different and more "modern" vision of Harvard, seeing it as a national, consumer-driven enterprise attentive to the needs of its customers rather than a private club.

27. "A Social Register family in the Northeast," Bender noted, "can send its son to Harvard or Yale or Princeton." "It isn't likely," he noted pointedly, "to send him to Rutgers or Penn" ("Comprehensive Formal Statement," 28).

28. Bender acknowledged freely that "certain factors . . . limit our freedom of choice." Harvard, he realized, faced constraints, including "what might be called political considerations, or perhaps institutional or public relations considerations." In enumerating these constraints, the affinity between Bender's analysis and that of contemporary "institutional analysis" is particularly striking. Among the "political factors" he cited were:

1. "the obligation to admit a number of Cambridge boys just because they live in Cambridge who might not be admitted on a strictly competitive basis"
2. placing "considerable weight" on the recommendations from "alumni and Harvard Club Schools and Scholarship Committees" because of their help in recruiting, screening, and the provision of scholarship funds
3. "preferential handling" of "fifteen or twenty schools, mostly private, each of which sends us regularly half a dozen or more students," most of them "paying customers"
4. the "related and sticky problem" of the "social and economic upper crust," also referred to as the "Final Club groups," which comprised "almost entirely paying guests"
5. "preference given to sons of alumni who constitute at present about 20% of our student body" (ibid., 26–29).

29. Ibid., 9–10.

30. Ibid., 35.

31. Ibid., 33–34.

32. Ibid., 36, 39.

33. Ibid., 15–16.

34. Ibid., 39. In his 1954 speech to the Board of Overseers, Bender sounded a similar theme in characteristically colorful language: "Do you turn down an apparently brilliant boy who looks like a fairy, or who appears to have a seriously warped psyche? . . . Do we want a student body of perfectly adjusted he-man extroverts with hair sprouting all over their chests or shall we leave this to Dartmouth?" ("Speech to Board of Overseers," HUA, 11).

35. Ibid., 13. In a 1955 letter to Conant's successor, Nathan Pusey, Bender made a similar point about Harvard's reputation, bemoaning the "the notion that we are just a grind factory full of goggle-eyed bifocal geniuses or precious effeminate types none of whom speak to each other, have any juice in their veins or give a damn about normal, healthy aspects of life"

(cited in Morton Keller and Phyllis Keller, *Making Harvard Modern: The Rise of America's University* [New York: Oxford University Press, 2001], 294, 546).

36. Bender, "Comprehensive Formal Statement," 32.

37. Ibid., 37. It is worth noting that in Bender's formulation the ideal of *service* ("contribute to American life") is conflated with the ideal of *power* ("influence . . . American life"). The same conflation of service and power occurs a second time in Bender's statement. Arguing against those who would focus primarily on academic ability in admissions, Bender maintained that "some people are going to contribute a lot more to society and have a lot more power and influence than others with the same I.Q." (ibid., 34). Any acknowledgment that these two orientations — to contribute to society and to exert power and influence — are not the same thing (and, indeed, might sometimes be in conflict) is altogether missing, not only from Bender's writings, but also from the writings of virtually all of the administrators concerned with admissions at the Big Three in the twentieth century. And while there is no reason to believe that the Big Three's characteristic emphasis on service was anything other than genuine, their admissions policy generally seems to have been driven far more by the recognition that remaining close to the nation's centers of economic and political power was essential to the advancement of fundamental institutional interests.

38. Ibid., 39.

39. Ibid., 8–9.

40. Ibid., 9.

41. Ibid., 16–17. The frequency with which Bender mentions specific rival institutions corresponds closely to its competition for the most "desirable" students: Yale (12), Princeton (10), Dartmouth (7), Williams (4), Amherst (2), with the "Little Three" (Williams, Amherst, and Wesleyan) as a group mentioned 4 times. Chicago and Pennsylvania, both urban institutions with large Jewish enrollments, are mentioned only as warnings of what Harvard could become if it followed the wrong policies. Columbia, one of America's top research universities and another urban institution with a large Jewish enrollment, is not mentioned at all.

42. Wilbur J. Bender, "Speech to Class of '27," 3 May 1947, HUA, 16.

43. Bender, "Comprehensive Formal Statement," 43. On the linkage between the politics of homophobia and the politics of anticommunism, especially in the early 1950s, see John D'Emilio, *Sexual Politics, Sexual Communities: The Making of a Homosexual Minority in the United States, 1940–1970* (Chicago: Univ. of Chicago Press, 1998), and Barbara Epstein, "Anti-Communism and Homophobia," *Critical Sociology* 20, no. 3 (1995).

44. Bender, "Comprehensive Formal Statement," 39.

45. In 1925, a national study of doctoral programs had ranked Chicago as the nation's leading research university (Raymond M. Hughes, *A Study of the Graduate Schools of America* [Oxford, Ohio: Miami U.P., 1925], cited in David S. Webster, "America's Highest Ranked Graduate Schools, 1925–1982," *Change* 115, no. 4 [May/June 1983], 17, 23). This result shocked Harvard, and it was an important backdrop to the Corporation's decision to select Conant, a brilliant scholar

who favored high standards for faculty hiring and promotion, as Lowell's successor. In 1935, two years after Conant took office, a study published in the *Atlantic Monthly* concluded that Harvard had regained its position as America's top research university but by only one point — 21–20 — over the University of Chicago (Edwin Embree, "In Order of Their Eminence," *Atlantic Monthly,* June 1935).

46. Setting aside issues of educational and social values, there may have been considerable truth to Bender's analysis of the cost to a major university of moving too far toward the pole of intellectualism. Whereas in 1930 the endowment of the University of Chicago was 56 percent of Harvard's, it had dropped to 35 percent of Harvard's by 1961 and stands at 18 percent today. See the, "Colleges With $2,000,000 Endowment or Over," *1931 World Almanac;*, "Colleges With $5,000,000 Endowment or More," *1962 World Almanac;* and "Largest Endowments Per Student, 1998," *Chronicle of Higher Education Almanac* 46, no. 1 (27 August 1999), 46. In 1940, according to one ranking of the social status of American universities, Chicago was in the fifth of 33 categories, ranking behind Harvard, Yale, and Princeton (Category 1); Dartmouth, Stanford, and Williams (2); Brown (3); and Columbia, Cornell, Johns Hopkins, MIT, and Penn (4) (Richard Coleman, *Report on College Characteristics* [Cambridge, Mass.: Harvard-MIT Joint Center for Urban Affairs, 1973]). Similarly, a study of the chief executive officers of 750 major corporations found that the University of Chicago ranked fourteenth with 14 CEOs, with Yale (85), Harvard (53), and Princeton (44) occupying the top three positions (George W. Pierson, *The Education of American Leaders: Comparative Contributions of U.S. Colleges and Universities* [New York: Praeger, 1969], 107). Interestingly, the issues Bender raised about the University of Chicago in 1952 resurfaced more than forty years later, during the presidency of Hugo Sonnenschein, who had come to Chicago in 1993 after serving as provost of Princeton. Faced with a small pool of applicants (acceptance rate of 60 percent vs. Harvard's 13 percent), a high dropout rate (17 percent vs. 3 and 4 percent, respectively, at Harvard and Yale), a low percent of alumni children (5 percent vs. 10–20 percent at the top Ivy League colleges), and an apparently widespread perception that life at the academically rigorous institution was monastery-like and something of a grind, Sonnenschein set out to make Chicago more consumer-friendly by reducing the requirements of the traditional core curriculum, building a $35 million swimming pool and sports center, renovating the student center, and increasing undergraduate enrollment from 3,500 to 4,500. His proposed reforms created great controversy among the faculty and students, and in June 1999 Sonnenschein announced that he would step down as president the following year and return to teaching (Ethan Bronner, "Winds of Academic Change Rustle University of Chicago," *NYT,* 28 December 1998; Bronner, "U. of Chicago President to Return to Teaching," *NYT,* 5 June 1999; Benjamin Gose, "'U. of Chicago Social Life' May No Longer be an Oxymoron," *Chronicle of Higher Education* [hereafter *CHE*], 15 November 1996; Gose, "U. of Chicago President to Resign, but the Battle Over His Policies Lives On," *CHE,* 7 June 1999; Gose, "U. of Chicago President's Plan to Resign Doesn't Quiet Debate Over His Agenda," *CHE,* 18 June 1999; "U. of Chicago Students and Alumni

Protest Planned Rise in Enrollment," *CHE,* 26 February 1999; and David Kirp, *Shakespeare, Einstein, and the Bottom Line: The Marketing of Higher Education* [Cambridge: Harvard U.P. 2003], 33–51).

47. In a 1947 speech, Bender had described Robert Hutchins, the renowned president of the University of Chicago who had made the decision to eliminate intercollegiate football, as "a perverse, egocentric screwball" ("Speech to Class of '27," 12). On the history of football at Chicago, see Robin Lester, *Stagg's University: The Rise, Decline, and Fall of Big-Time Football at Chicago* (Urbana: Univ. of Illinois Press, 1955).

48. Since the issue for Bender was Harvard's image as a place filled with effeminates, he emphasized that winning in just any sport would not address the problem: "Occasional reports of victories in crew and squash don't help much because these are exotics — un-American, effete, Eastern snob sports." Being constantly beaten in football, on the other hand, was viewed by Americans as "proof of unAmericanism, of our unsound and unhealthy state." And because of Harvard's reputation for intellectualism, the threat posed by losing a football game was "much greater . . . than at Yale or Princeton or Dartmouth" ("Comprehensive Formal Statement," 35–39). Perhaps not coincidentally, Harvard's fortunes in football improved considerably after Bender became chairman of the Committee on Admission. Between 1947 and 1952, while Gummere was still in office, Harvard's record had a combined winning record of 35 percent (18-33-1) and lost to Yale and Princeton ten times while winning only once and tying once. Between 1953 and 1960, with Bender as chair, Harvard's winning percentage improved to 51 percent (33-32-2), and near parity was attained with archrivals Yale and Princeton, with Harvard splitting the series with Yale, 4–4, and winning three of eight contests with Princeton (Sports Information Office, *1998 Harvard Football Media Guide,* 1998, HU, 92, 97–98).

49. And even the most brilliant applicants, Bender emphasized, should be rejected if "there is convincing evidence of serious defects of character or personality" ("Comprehensive Formal Statement," 31–33).

50. Ibid., 37.

51. Ibid., 32.

52. Committees on Admission, "Report for Students," 1952–1953, 1–2.

53. Bender, "Comprehensive Formal Statement," 3.

54. Ibid., 3–4. David Karen provides an excellent account of the increasingly professional and bureaucratic character of the admissions office under Bender. Professionalization, he notes, brings in its wake increased standardization and measurement of performance; one indication of it is the growth of the annual admissions report from 7 pages in 1951–1952, Gummere's last year in office, to 34 in 1952–1953, Bender's first. And of the most visible changes was a tremendous growth in the amount of statistical data included ("Who Gets into Harvard? Selection and Exclusion at an Elite College" [Ph.D. diss., Harvard Univ., 1985], 118–24). The admissions office under Bender was also subject to what Max Weber has called *rationalization* — the process whereby emotion and tradition are increasingly replaced by knowledge-based rational calculation (*Economy and Society,* 2 vols. [Berkeley, Calif.: Univ. of California Press, 1978]).

55. Bender, "Comprehensive Formal Statement," 40.

56. Ibid., 40. King was already part of the admissions process in 1952–1953, and Glimp joined the office on a part-time basis in 1954.

57. In 1952–1953, when Harvard had just under 3,400 applicants, 85 Harvard Club Schools and Scholarship Committees interviewed over 2,000 candidates for admission (*Schools and Scholarship Committee Handbook,* September 1953, HUA, 24).

58. Bender, "Comprehensive Formal Statement," 41.

59. Ibid., 41. As evidence that Bender took indoctrination seriously, the *Schools and Scholarship Committee Handbook* of 1953 devotes 3 pages (9–11) to an "Indoctrination of the Committees." On December 9, 1952, the first issue of the *Harvard College Admission and Scholarship Newsletter* appeared. On page 1 of the inaugural issue, members of the Schools and Scholarship Committee were informed that the *Handbook* was indeed a confidential document (as it had been marked), "a family publication which deals frankly with family problems." The *Handbook,* Bender declared, "should not be given to schools, to newspapers, or to candidates or their families," for it could "lead to misunderstanding" (*Harvard College Admission and Scholarship Newsletter,* HUA, 1).

60. *Schools and Scholarship Handbook,* 27–29.

61. Ibid., 29–30.

62. Ibid., 36–39. Harvard's grading system divided students into Rank Lists, from Group I (3½ A's and ½ B) to VI (three C's and one D), with those below Group VI classified as "Unsatisfactory." Until about 1948, students had to stand in Rank List III or higher to maintain a scholarship (about the top 40 percent of all students); the policy was then adjusted to permit students in Rank List IV to be eligible for renewal (about 50 percent of freshmen and 65 percent of all students). In 1952, only 3.6 percent of students stood in Rank List I, with 1.3 percent in Rank List VI and 6.8 percent compiling unsatisfactory records (ibid., 37–51).

63. "Invitation to Harvard," VHS (Cambridge, Mass.: Harvard Univ., 4 May 1951), HUA, 2. Bender's enthusiasm for public relations was one of many qualities that distinguished him from his predecessor. Whereas the aristocratic Gummere was not comfortable "selling" Harvard, Bender believed that "in a sense the whole admission job is a public relations job." What Harvard actually is, he observed, "only partly determined our drawing power." The most powerful force "is really what Harvard appears to be, what people think it is" ("Comprehensive Formal Statement," 4).

64. Ibid., 4, 12.

65. *Official Register of Harvard University: Information About Harvard College for Prospective Students* (also known as the Rollo Book), 24 October 1952, HUA, 39–43.

66. Ibid., 10.

67. Ibid., 61.

68. Committees on Admission, "Report for Students," 1952–1953, 10.

69. Ibid., 18.

70. Bender to Bundy, 19 January 1955, HUA, 5.

71. *Admission and Scholarships Newsletter,* 21 July 1954, 2.

72. Committees on Admission, "Report for Students," 1952–1953, 1953–1954, 1954–1955; ibid., 1955–1956, 1956–1957.

73. Ibid.

74. In 1955, 117 of 148 applicants from Exeter and Andover, 68 of 92 applicants from the St. Grottlesex schools, and 218 of 311 applicants from the top prep schools were accepted by Harvard (from data provided by the Office of Admissions, Harvard University).

75. Bender, "Speech to the Board of Overseers," 9.

76. Data provided by Office of Admissions, Harvard University.

77. Of 1,942 scholarship applicants, 24.2 percent received awards and registered, with an additional 235 registering despite being denied awards. This adds up to 34.6 percent, but Harvard elsewhere reported that a disproportionately high percentage of scholarship applicants were admitted but denied aid and declined to come. Assuming very conservatively, however, that they registered at the same rate as applicants awarded scholarships (67.2 percent), this would leave at least 115 additional scholarship applicants who were admitted but did not matriculate, for a total admission rate for scholarship applicants of over 40 percent. And this estimate is doubly conservative, for not all of the candidates from the three aforementioned high schools had requested scholarships (calculated from Committees on Admission, "Report for Students," 1954–1955, 2–3).

78. Bender to Bundy, 5.

79. Ibid.

80. Committees on Admission, "Report for Students," 1954–1955, 46, 38.

81. Data derived from Committees on Admission, "Report for Students," 1952–1953, 1953–1954, 1954–1955; ibid., 1955–1956, 1956–1957.

82. King to the Admission and Scholarship Committee, memorandum, 7 January 1958, HUA. In addition to the factors cited by King, another source of the declining number of disadvantaged students at Harvard was the decrease in the number of commuters. This decrease, which was associated with the movement of the children of immigrants to suburbs and the simultaneous decline of urban schools, deprived Harvard of its main sources of working-class students. Between the mid-1930s and the late 1950s, the percentage of students who were commuters dropped from over 20 to under 10 percent.

83. Committees on Admission, "Report for Students," 1956–1957, 13.

84. Ibid., 1954–1955, 50; *Admission and Scholarship Newsletter*, 1 January 1957, 2.

85. Ibid., 8.

86. Richard G. King, "Financial Thresholds to College," *College Board Review*, Spring 1957, 21–24.

87. Ibid., 23.

88. Monro, "Who Gets the Scholarships," 258.

89. Ibid., 258–59.

90. King, "Financial Thresholds," 23–24.

91. Monro to the Admission and Scholarship Committee, memorandum, 3 January 1958, HUA, 2.

92. Biographical data is drawn from Glimp's entry in the *Harvard Class Album: Class of 1954;* David McClintock, "Glimpses of a Half Century," *HM*, January–February 1997, 62–66; "Fred L. Glimp, A.B. 1950, Ph.D. 1964: A Celebration and Tribute," 2 November 1966, HUA; and *WWA, 1962–1963, 1978–1979, 1984–1985.*

93. Fred Glimp, memorandum, 7 January 1958, HUA. Neil McElroy '25 was president of Procter and Gamble; Roy Larsen '19 was president of Time Inc. (*WWA, 1944–1945*).

94. Glimp, memorandum, 7 January 1958, HUA, 1.

95. Ibid., 2.

96. As an undergraduate, Glimp worked part-time as a chauffeur for President Conant. Glimp remembered Conant as "very outspoken and kind of crusty — not a cold person, but just a reserved old New England Yankee." He also shined Conant's shoes — a task that began when he was waiting for the president one day and asked his wife if there was anything he could do while killing time. "After hesitating politely, she said, 'You know he's terrible at shining his shoes, would you mind doing that?' So I used to shine his shoes while I waited" (McClintock, "Glimpses of a Half Century," 63).

97. Christopher Jencks and David Riesman, *The Academic Revolution* (New York: Doubleday, 1968), 14.

98. Shortly after the end of World War II, Bender, then the counselor for veterans, forcefully emphasized the contribution of the brilliant young scientists — the very group whom he was accused of excluding from Harvard College as dean of admissions barely a decade later. In a memo to Provost Paul Buck, Bender wrote: "It is true that Harvard College is interested in attracting men of extraordinary talents who give promise of exceptional ability and in making it possible for such men to obtain a Harvard education regardless of their economic situation. The contributions of men of this type to society are most strikingly demonstrated by what was accomplished, for example, by the host of young college trained physicists who helped in the all-important war research in electronic physics and radar, to say nothing of research in atomic energy. It is doubtful if Harvard University would be in existence today if it had not been for the work of these young men in the dark days at the beginning of the war when the margin between victory and defeat, between survival and subjugation to Nazi rule, was so slim" (Bender to Buck, memorandum, n.d. [c. 1946], HUA).

99. Hugh Davis Graham and Nancy Diamond, *The Rise of the American Research Universities: Elites and Challengers in the Postwar Era* (Baltimore: Johns Hopkins U.P., 1997), 33; Alfred K. Mann, *For Better or Worse: The Marriage of Science and Government in the United States* (New York: Columbia U.P., 2000), 101.

100. Ibid., 100.

101. Graham and Diamond, *Rise of American Research Universities,* 34.

102. Born in 1922 in Berlin, Holton had received a bachelor's degree in 1941 from Wesleyan University and a Ph.D. in physics from Harvard in 1948. During World War II, he worked on radar with the Office of Scientific Research and Development (*WWA, 1962–1963*).

103. Holton to Bundy, 30 January 1958, HUA.

104. *WWA, 1962–1963;* Bethell, *Harvard Observed;* Richard Smith, *The Harvard Century: The Making of a University to a Nation* (Cambridge, Mass.: Harvard U.P., 1986); and James G. Hershberg, *James B. Conant: Harvard to Hiroshima and the Making of the Nuclear Age* (Stanford, Calif.: Stanford U.P., 1993).

105. Bethell, *Harvard Observed,* 143–44; James B. Conant, *My Several Lives: Memoirs of a Social Inventor* (New York: Harper & Row, 1970), 279.

106. Hershberg, *James B. Conant,* 231–34. When the blast went off, Kistiakowsky won a $10 bet from J.

Robert Oppenheimer (Harvard '25), who had wagered that it would fail to detonate (Smith, *Harvard Century*, 215).

107. A member of the president's Science Advisory Committee since 1957, Kistiakowsky became White House special assistant to President Eisenhower for Science and Technology in 1959.

108. Accounts of the faculty meeting at which the confrontation between Kistiakowsky and Bender took place are offered by Smith, *Harvard Century*, 215–16; Fred Glimp, interview by Henry Bragdon, 22 October 1971, transcript, HUA; and Wilcox, interview, HUA.

109. Glimp, interview, HUA.

110. Admission and Scholarship Committee, "Report on the Admission and Scholarship Committee," 1957–1958, HUA, 23–25.

111. Ibid., 27–28.

112. Ibid., 28–29.

113. Information on Bate, Brinton, Monro, Pappenheimer, and Wilson from *WWA, 1962–1963*; for Ford, *WWA, 1978–1979*. For members who were either Senior or Junior Fellows, see Crane Brinton, ed., *The Society of Fellows* (Cambridge, Mass.: Harvard U.P., 1959). For information on Stouffer, see the *International Encyclopedia of the Social Sciences*, vol. 15.

114. By "academic meritocracy," I mean an educational system that recognizes scholastic accomplishment (e.g., grades, test scores, rank in class) as the only legitimate form of merit. A more expansive definition could also recognize other forms of accomplishment such as athletic or musical ability, leadership in school and community activities, and personal qualities such as resilience, energy, persistence, and creativity. In the classical work that invented the term "meritocracy," merit is defined as "IQ + effort" (or I + E = M) (Michael Young, *The Rise of the Meritocracy, 1870–2033: An Essay on Education and Equality* [1958; New York: Penguin, 1961]).

115. H. G. Rickover, *Education and Freedom* (New York: Dutton, 1959), 157, 186. Most of the chapters in *Education and Freedom* had been presented as speeches between 1956 and 1958.

116. Roger L. Geiger, *Research and Relevant Knowledge: American Research Universities Since World War II* (New York: Oxford U.P., 1993), 161–66.

117. Seymour E. Harris, ed., *The Economics of Harvard* (New York: McGraw-Hill, 1970), 519.

118. Michael Schudson, "Organizing the 'Meritocracy': A History of the College Entrance Examination Board," *Harvard Educational Review* 42, no. 1 (February 1972): 34–69.

119. Admission and Scholarship Committee, "Report on the Admission and Scholarship Committee," 1957–1958, HU, 6. The largest SAT increase in a single year at Harvard was 53 points, between 1952 and 1953, when Bender succeeded Gummere as dean of admissions.

120. Ibid., 39.

121. *Admissions and Scholarship Newsletter*, 9 July 1958, 1. One of the twelve students admitted directly from his junior year in 1958 was a talented young man from a suburban public school near Chicago. A brilliant mathematician, he went on to earn a Ph.D. at the University of Michigan before joining the Berkeley faculty. His name was Theodore Kaczynski '62, and he later gained notoriety as the Unabomber.

122. Admission and Scholarship Committee, "Report on the Admission and Scholarship Committee,"

1957–1958, 15–16; *Admissions and Scholarship Newsletter*, 9 July 1958, 1. By way of comparison, the yield rate for Princeton for 1958 was 60 percent. Though Yale's "Annual Report to the President and Fellows of Yale University" for 1958 does not record a yield, the figure in 1957 was just over 58 percent. As recently as 1955, Harvard had lost 620 potential students to other colleges, over half of them to just six institutions: Yale (103), Princeton (85), Dartmouth (47), MIT (38), Amherst (32), and Stanford (23) (Admission and Scholarship Committee, "Report on the Admission and Scholarship Committee," 1954–1955, 45).

123. *Admissions and Scholarship Newsletter*, 9 July 1958, HUA, 1. Another factor that may have contributed to the increase in Harvard's yield rate (from 61 percent in 1955 to 74 percent in 1958) was the expansion of the ABC plan, carried out in cooperation with Yale and Princeton, of giving students from selected secondary schools formal preliminary estimates of their chances of admission. The system, which began as an experiment in 1955, seems by 1958 to have given Harvard — always the most prestigious of the Big Three — an added advantage in attracting candidates from the leading boarding schools. Harvard may also have benefited from a change in its financial aid policy in 1958. From that point on, an applicant accepted with financial aid could be secure in the knowledge that his scholarship would be renewed as long as he maintained a minimally satisfactory record (three C's and a D or better). This marked a sharp change from Harvard's scholarship policy before the war, when failure to be on the Dean's List (a B average) meant losing one's scholarship (Admission and Scholarship Committee, "Report on the Admission and Scholarship Committee," 1957–1958, 15–16, 30–31). Compared to Yale, which remained Harvard's chief rival, Harvard's scholarship recipients had for some time enjoyed the advantage of being able to maintain their scholarships (albeit at a reduced level) even if they refused to work during the school year; now they could assume that renewal of these scholarships would be almost automatic.

124. Admission and Scholarship Committee, "Report on the Admission and Scholarship Committee," 1957–1958, 18–19. *Admission and Scholarship Newsletter*, 7 January 1957, 2–3. Though MIT was second only to Harvard in admitting students with National Merit Scholarships and General Motors Scholarships, Bender did not consider MIT a serious threat to Harvard, writing that it "appeals only to a special and limited group" and is an institution "with which we do not seriously compete" ("Comprehensive Formal Statement," 13). The likely reason is that the students lost to MIT, though academically distinguished, were not as elite socially as many of the students lost to top Ivy League colleges or the Little Three and hence less likely to become the "men of action" Bender admired as projected leaders of the nation's major political and economic institutions. On the pattern of college choice of students who turned down Harvard's offer of admission, in 1957, when MIT placed fourth, behind Yale and Princeton, see Peter Briggs, "Why They Didn't Choose Harvard," *HAB*, October 26, 1957, 112–14.

125. Seymour Harris (A.B. '20, Ph.D. '26), a prominent economist who had joined the Harvard faculty in 1927, believed that Bender had done a "superb job," noting that "the gains had been especially great in the 1950's." Comparing admissions under Bender to

the regime of Henry Pennypacker, Harris recalled the days when "aptitude tests and motivation seemed to count for less, and good manners, blue eyes, charm and background for much more, than is true now." "A great democratization in our admission requirements," he maintained, had taken place in the Bender years (Harris to Pusey, Bundy, Bender, Monro, and Stouffer, memorandum, 15 January 1959, HUA).

126. Admission and Scholarship Committee, "Report on the Admission and Scholarship Committee," 1957–1958, 41.

127. Data provided by the Office of Admissions, Harvard University.

128. Of the applicants in 1956 who received an athletic rating of 1 (varsity athlete), over 72 percent (79 of 109) gained admission (*Admission and Scholarships Newsletter*, 17 January 1957, 9).

129. In a speech to the Board of Overseers, Bender did not mince words in describing the need to relax academic standards for athletes: "If we followed the [principle of] admitting people solely on the basis of relative verbal ability, we wouldn't be able to feel [sic] the football team that would beat Wellesley. This would be true in most other sports also . . . Right now, it is a fact that if we did not place considerable emphasis in our recruiting and admission and award of scholarship assistance on athlete ability we couldn't stay in the Ivy League, the road being what it is" ("Speech to the Board of Overseers," 9).

130. "Group Study: The Pigskin Tribe," 24 July 1958, HUA.

131. Wilbur J. Bender, "Confidential Memo by Wilbur J. Bender to the Committee on Admission and Scholarships," 17 November 1958, HU, 1.

132. Ibid., 3.

133. Ibid., 2.

134. Ibid.

135. In the preface to *The Protestant Establishment: Aristocracy and Caste in America* (New York: Vintage, 1964, x) E. Digby Baltzell writes: "A crisis in normal authority has developed in modern America largely because of the White-Anglo-Saxon-Protestant establishment's unwillingness, or inability, to share and improve its upper-class traditions by continuously absorbing talented and distinguished members of minority groups into its privileged ranks." See also Cleveland Amory, *Who Killed Society?* (New York: Harper & Bros., 1960).

136. Richard G. King, "Minutes of the First Meeting of the Faculty Committee to Consider Admissions Policies and the Future Composition of the College," 20 March 1959, HUA, 1–2. At this meeting, "committee members were asked to think about a formal name for the committee and make suggestions at the next meeting. It was suggested that the committee *not* be called the Committee on the Future Composition of the College, because of the similarity in name to that of a former committee, set up in the 20's to establish racial and religious quotas for the college."

137. Brinton, *Society of Fellows*, 263–64.

138. Richard G. King, "Meeting of the CEP Subcommittee on College Admission Policy (Confidential)," 3 April 1959, HUA, 4.

139. As secretary, King took the minutes. The one exception was a meeting on 29 October 1959, which he missed because of illness (see minutes of that meeting by Franklin Ford).

140. Richard G. King, "School Performance Study — Classes of '54, '55, and '57 (Confidential)," 22 Sep-

tember 1959, HUA; quote from King, "Minutes of the CEP Subcommittee," 6 October 1959, 2.

141. King, "School Performance Study," 2. In truth, the study almost certainly *underestimated* the performance differential between public and private school students because it excluded members of two of the three cohorts (the classes of '54 and '55) who did not graduate on schedule. Since private school graduates were overrepresented among students who dropped out or failed out, their overall performance was even weaker than the study indicated.

142. Of the 10 New York City schools, 2 were just outside the city limits in Long Island (Great Neck High School and Lawrence High School). All 8 of the remaining schools were in New York City proper: 5 public schools (Clinton, Erasmus Hall, Madison, Lincoln, Midwood) and 3 private schools (Friends Seminary, Horace Mann, and Polytechnic Prep). Judging from performance patterns, these students apparently faced even more discrimination than graduates of New York's most selective public schools: Bronx High School of Science and Stuyvesant, which ranked 21st and 23rd, respectively, out of the 79 schools analyzed.

143. King, "School Performance Study," 4.

144. As late as 1961, over 35 percent of all Jews in the United States — 1,940,000 — resided in New York City. An additional 328,500 lived in nearby Nassau County, for a combined total of 41 percent of all American Jews. Including other Jewish population centers in the metropolitan area brings the figure close to 50 percent ("U.S. Jewish Population in Large Cities," *World Almanac 1962*).

145. In 1961, the Middle Atlantic states (New York, New Jersey, Pennsylvania, Delaware, Maryland, and the District of Columbia) were the home of over 60 percent of the nation's Jewish population. Calculated from ibid.

146. Richard G. King, "Study of Magna, Summas, Flunk Out and Drop Outs: Classes of 1957 and 1958 (Confidential)," 22 September 1959, HUA. King reported that magnas and summas together made up 15 percent of the entering classes while the flunkouts and dropouts each represented about 10 percent.

147. Ibid., 2, 8.

148. Ibid., 10. The lowest groups of all — "laborer, factory hand" — reported 6 summas and magnas, compared to 13 flunkouts and 17 dropouts. King reported that "this last finding was surprising to me, but in line with Dean von Stade's observation that despite adequate financial aid and high aptitude the cultural jump is sometimes just too big" (ibid., 3). In a letter to Chairman Ford, von Stade wrote: "As you know, I have had a number of reservations about a) poor boys from very poor cultural background and b) negroes" (von Stade to Ford, 7 October 1959).

149. King, "Minutes of the CEP Subcommittee," 6 October 1959, 3.

150. Professor Samuel Stouffer, who taught at the University of Chicago before becoming professor of social relations at Harvard, also had a negative view of Chicago's policy; according to him, admissions there concentrated on the "intellectual" who turned out as often as not to be merely the "pseudo-intellectual" (King, "Minutes of the CEP Subcommittee," 3 April 1959, 4).

151. King, "Minutes of the CEP Subcommittee," 6 October 1959, 4. Evidence suggesting that Bender may have had a point about Chicago is that only 29 National Merit Scholars enrolled there in 1958–1959 com-

pared to 213 at Harvard, 62 at Yale, and 57 at Princeton. At the same time, however, several other schools noted for their heavy emphasis on academic qualifications and their lack of emphasis on athletes did attract large numbers of Merit Scholars — MIT (164), Cal Tech (66), and Swarthmore (52) (National Merit Scholarship Corporation, "Annual Report," 1959).

152. At one of the committee's earliest meetings, Bender raised the issue of Harvard's social standing explicitly: "There was an important political-institutional question of how much attention should be made to keep contact with the 'gentlemen' class of students, who are educated in many of the private schools. We had been told on more than one occasion that Harvard was no longer 'fit for gentlemen'" (King, "Minutes of the CEP Subcommittee," 13 April 1959, 4).

153. Ibid., 6 October 1959, 4.

154. Ibid., 29 October 1959, 1.

155. Ibid., 2. Special Committee on College Admission Policy, *Admission to Harvard College: A Report by the Special Committee on College Admission Policy*, February 1960, HU, 47.

156. King, "Minutes of the CEP Subcommittee," 29 October 1959, 3.

157. King to Ford, 23 October 1959, HUA.

158. According to the minutes, "the Subcommittee turned from the topic [alumni sons] with the apprehensive feeling that no portion of the final report will be read with greater interest, nor requires more careful drafting" (King, "Minutes of the CEP Subcommittee," 29 October 1959, 4).

159. Office of Admissions, "PRL Scores of Potential Freshmen Football Players," 8 November 1957, HUA.

160. Richard G. King, "Statistics for the CEP Subcommittee on College Admission Policy," 12 November 1959.

161. King, "Minutes of the CEP Subcommittee," 29 October 1959, 4.

162. Special Committee, "Working Notes for the Report," confidential, November 1959, HUA, 1.

163. Ibid., 4. Brinton's and Wilson's comments are recorded by Ford in handwritten notes in the margins of the "Working Notes."

164. Ibid., 4, 8.

165. Ibid., 9.

166. Ibid., 15.

167. Wilson to Ford, "Comments on 'Working Notes for the Report,'" memorandum, 20 November 1959, HUA, 1. Even Wilson, however, was not unequivocally against giving preference to the privileged in the admissions process: "Success often depends on family, wealth, and opportunity," he wrote to Ford a few days later. "If Harvard is to train intelligent leaders, the fact that a candidate comes from a family of wealth cannot be ignored" (Wilson to Ford, "Harvard Admission Policy," memorandum, 3 December 1959, HUA, 2).

168. Wilson to Ford, memorandum, 30 November 1959, HUA, 2–3. In this same memo, however, Wilson acknowledges that standardized tests have definite limitations: "I completely share the view that objective test scores can be very misleading and that they do not tell the whole story in very many cases."

169. Ibid., 3

170. Bundy to Ford, 17 December 1959, HUA, 3.

171. Ibid., 3.

172. Special Committee, *Admission to Harvard College*, 31.

173. Ibid., 11, 9.

174. Moreover, of the top 651 applicants (the top 15.7 percent), 204 (over 31 percent) were rejected, leaving 1,143 slots for applicants with lower PRLs. Calculated from ibid., 21.

175. King, "Minutes of the CEP Subcommittee," 20 April 1959, 3.

176. Special Committee, *Admission to Harvard College*, 39. When the issue of commuters was addressed by the committee in the spring of 1959, the statistics revealed that both the relative and absolute number of commuters had been in decline since the early 1930s. Among the most important reasons cited were "the increased pressure of more qualified candidates from other parts of the country and the consequent increase in selectivity for the class as a whole" and "a shift of some of the more energetic and successful families to the suburbs, whence it was more fashionable to send students 'away' to college." Data covering the classes admitted from 1937 to 1941, 1949 to 1953, and 1954 to 1957 showed that local feeder schools still enjoyed an advantage in admissions but that it had declined over time. During this period, the number of applications from Greater Boston actually declined while the total number of applicants increased (King, "Minutes of the CEP Subcommittee," 20 April 1959, 1–2).

177. Mimeographed draft of the Special Committee, *Admission to Harvard College*, 15 December 1959, 59; final published version, *Admission to Harvard College*, 40.

178. Ibid., 34. Note the contrast between the portrayal of private school students, who "are not interested in striving," and the portrayal of graduates of the big urban high schools, who are "tremendously competitive" and "ruthless in their demands on themselves" (ibid., 66–67). That these images, though stereotypical, may not have been devoid of empirical support is suggested by Charles McArthur, "Personalities of Public and Private School Boys," *Harvard Educational Review* 24, no. 4 (Fall 1954): 256–62.

179. Special Committee, *Admission to Harvard College*, 34.

180. Ibid., 49–50.

181. Ibid., 50. In its internal discussion about alumni sons, the committee reported that there was "concern at Columbia and Chicago that so *few* alumni sons appear to wish to enroll." On the other hand, two of the institutions that remained highly desirable included Harvard's principal rivals: Yale, which "remains the Ivy League college with the highest percentage of alumni sons attending," and Princeton, which had "an unusual degree of support" in the area of "alumni giving." Ford's conclusions about the admissions practices of other schools were based on trips to 11 institutions, including Columbia, Chicago, Yale, and Princeton (King, "Minutes of the CEP Subcommittee," 11 December 1959, 1–3).

182. As late as 1972, according to a study of the social status of institutions of higher education, Harvard, Yale, and Princeton remained alone in the highest category. In contrast, institutions such as Chicago, Columbia, MIT, and Penn were relegated to the third tier of social prestige. Between the first and the third tier were four schools: Brown, Dartmouth, Stanford, and Williams (Richard Coleman, "Report on College Characteristics," Harvard-MIT Joint Center for Urban Affairs, 1973).

183. Special Committee, *Admission to Harvard College*, 53–54.

184. In the section on athletes, Ford wrote in the margin "EBW against *any* weighting" (Special Committee, "Working Notes for the Report," 15).

185. Special Committee, *Admission to Harvard College*, 53.

186. Ibid., 36.

187. The definition of "working class" used here includes "skilled technicians," "foreman, factory supervisor," "laborer, factory hand," and "public worker." In 1954, 111 Harvard freshmen out of 1,160 had fathers in these occupations; by 1958, the number had dropped to 80 out of 1,155 freshmen. In contrast, 222 freshmen were sons of business executives in 1954, 250 in 1958. See Committees on Admission, "Report for Students," 1953–1954, 216; Admission and Scholarship Committee, "Report on the Admission and Scholarship Committee," 1957–1958, 42.

188. Special Committee, *Admission to Harvard College*, 36.

189. While the report did not propose the elimination of ability to pay as a factor in determining acceptance, it did call for an increase in the number of scholarships and a reduction in the size of the "admit-deny" category — those applicants who were admitted but denied needed scholarship assistance (ibid., 15–16).

190. Ibid., 28. In his "Working Notes for the Report" (8), Ford frankly discusses the issue of "weak admits": "With more scholarships and loan money, we can unquestionably bring here a larger number of high school graduates now in effect turned away by being admitted but denied scholarship aid. Presumably, these would replace some of our least promising 'paying guests,' and thus would almost certainly push the position of public school graduates increasingly ahead of those from private schools."

191. Wilson to Ford, memorandum, 30 November 1959, 1.

192. Special Committee, *Admission to Harvard College*, 35.

193. Ibid., 40, 50, 54, 34.

194. Ibid., 11.

195. McGeorge Bundy, "Admission to Harvard," *HAB*, 7 May 1960, 580. The goal of doubling the number of brilliant students from 1 to 2 percent was actually less ambitious than the one enunciated eight years earlier by Bender, who had proposed doubling the percentage of the freshman class taken almost exclusively on the basis of academic brilliance from 5 to 10 percent (Wilbur J. Bender, "A Comprehensive Formal Statement of Harvard College Admission Policy," 18 September 1952, HUA).

196. Bundy, "Admission to Harvard," 580. F. Skiddy von Stade Jr., then the dean of freshmen, had expressed similar sentiments ever more strongly in an article in the *HAB* just as the Special Committee was being formed: "Surely Cecil Rhodes was writing for today as well as for sixty years ago when he said in correspondence about his great Trust that he was looking for 'not merely bookworms, but the best men for the world's fight'" ("Balance in the College," *HAB*, 7 February 1959, 345).

197. Bundy, "Admission to Harvard," 581.

198. Special Committee, *Admission to Harvard College*, 11.

199. Bender's public comments after he left Harvard to become associate director (and then director) of the Permanent Charity Fund of Boston, were published as both the "Final Report of W. J. Bender, Chairman of the Admission and Scholarship Committee and Dean of Admissions and Financial Aids, 1952–1960," HUA, and Wilbur J. Bender, "The Top-One-Percent Policy: A Hard Look at the Dangers of an Academically Elite Harvard," *HAB*, 30 September 1961.

200. Wilbur J. Bender, "Comments on the Report of the Subcommittee on College Admission Policy," 7 January 1960, HUA, 6.

201. For an illuminating examination of the distinctive place of l'École Normale Supérieure in France's intellectual life, as well as an analysis of the relationship between the French system of elite schools ("grandes écoles") and the French power structure, see Pierre Bourdieu, *The State Nobility: Elite Schools in the Field of Power* (Stanford, Calif.: Stanford U.P., 1996). Among the many distinguished graduates of l'École Normale are Jean-Paul Sartre, Claude Lévi-Strauss, Raymond Aron, Michel Foucault, and Bourdieu himself.

202. Bender, "Comments on the Report of the Subcommittee," 6. Among American colleges and universities, Bender suggests, Swarthmore and Cal Tech come closest to the French model.

203. Ibid., 6.

204. Ibid., 7.

205. For Bender, as for Ford, the member of the Special Committee whose views embodied the model of academic meritocracy was Wilson. According to Bender, "If Bright Wilson had his way and decimated the Harvard son and private school group this would cut our Massachusetts delegation in half probably" (ibid., 12).

206. Ibid., 8–9.

207. Bender, "Comments on the Report of the Subcommittee," 9.

208. Ibid.

209. Ibid., 10.

210. Special Committee, *Admission to Harvard College*, 224.

211. Bender, "Comments on the Report of the Subcommittee," 10.

212. Special Committee, *Admission to Harvard College*, 54.

213. The other private schools represented were: St. Mark's (2), Milton (2), Pomfret (2), Choate (2), Exeter (2), Hill (2), Middlesex (1), Andover (1), and St. Louis Country Day (1). From "Footnote to My Comments," 15 January 1960, attached to Bender, "Comments on the Report of the Subcommittee," HUA.

214. The PRL standing by years of the 26 men was available as following (not available in some cases for the senior year): Group I — 1, Group II — 6, Group III — 15, Group IV — 27, Group V — 26, Group VI — 9, Unsatisfactory — 5 (ibid).

215. Ibid.

216. Wilbur J. Bender, "Some Observations and Questions About Admission Policy or Will I Want My Son to Go to Harvard in 1970?" n.d. [c. 1960], HUA. A revised and condensed version of the presentation, minus a number of its most revealing passages, was published as Bender, "Top-One-Percent Policy," *HAB*, 30 September 1961. A different version of "Some Observations," minus pages 17–20 of the original, appears as part of Bender's "Final Report to the President."

217. Bender, "Some Observations," 10. In his *HAB* article, Bender does not stop with the (unnamed) references to John F. Kennedy and Henry Cabot Lodge, asking whether the two preceding Harvard graduates in the White House, FDR and TR, would have been admitted to or would have wanted to attend an academically elite Harvard. According to Bender, "The answer is probably no" ("Top-One-Percent Policy," 23).

218. Admission and Scholarship Committee, "Final Report of W. J. Bender," 4. Bender's contention that 1952–1960 was the period of "the greatest change in Harvard admissions" in its "recorded history" is certainly debatable; my own candidate is the 1920s, when selective admissions was introduced and many of the criteria ("character," athletic ability, alumni parentage, geographical diversity) central to the admissions policy favored by Bender were invented.

219. Ibid., 2–8.

220. Ibid., 6. Between 1950 and 1960, the number of students accepted by Harvard from the leading prep schools had dropped just 9 percent at a time when overall applications had increased almost 100 percent. Figures on prep school applicants provided by Harvard's Office of Admissions; figures on applicants from the Committee on Admission, "Report of the Committee on Admission of Harvard College," 1949–1950, and the Admission and Scholarship Committee, "Final Report of W. J. Bender."

221. As the number of legacy applicants increased between 1952 and 1960 from 282 to 425, the percent accepted did, however, drop from 87.2 to 56.5 percent Admission and Scholarship Committee, "Final Report of W. J. Bender," 3).

222. Ibid., 14. In 1952, median family income was about $4,300 and in 1960, about $5,300.

223. Ibid., 15.

224. For a classic analysis of the Protestant upper class, written not long after Bender's departure, see Baltzell, *Protestant Establishment*. By the time Baltzell returned to the issue in 1976, he concluded that "what remains of the Protestant establishment has been watered down beyond recognition" (Baltzell, "The Protestant Establishment Revisited," *American Scholar* 45, August 1976: 499–518).

225. Alvin W. Gouldner, *The Future of Intellectuals and the Rise of the New Class* (New York: Oxford U.P., 1982). For an elaboration on his theme of the role of "cultural capital" in the transmission of class privilege, see Bourdieu, *State Nobility*.

226. Admission and Scholarship Committee, "Final Report of W. J. Bender," 20, 35.

227. Ibid., 31–32.

228. Ibid., 22–23.

229. Bragdon, "Conversation About Bill Bender." According to Wilcox, who had worked closely with Bender during the 1950s and discussed his recollections with the Exeter historian Henry Bragdon for a never-completed book on Bender, Bender's preconceptions were: "Farm boys better than city boys/West better than East/athletes better than ballet dancers (he had a hard time accepting figure-skaters) . . . He might suggest that a small-statured, highly intellectual, aesthetic boy would be happier at a small college." With respect to the Bronx School of Science, Wilcox, who in the interview emphasized repeatedly that he was exaggerating, reported that Bender was "not consciously anti-Semitic but anti-urban" and that he "never heard him use the term Jew in a derog-

atory way." In Bender's last year in office, 26 of 34 applicants from Bronx Science were rejected by Harvard compared to 4 of 19 at Groton and 4 of 17 at St. Mark's (data from Harvard's Office of Admissions).

230. Bragdon, "Conversation About Bill Bender."

231. One expression of the apparent ascendancy in 1958 of meritocratic ideology was the publication of Michael Young's classic satire, *The Rise of the Meritocracy 1870–2033: An Essay on Education and Equality* (1958; New York: Penguin, 1961).

232. "Ivy League Admissions," *NYT*, 14 May 1960.

233. Bender, "Comments on the Report of the Subcommittee," HUA, 7.

234. This profile is based on a variety of sources, including "Fred Glimp A.B. 1950, Ph.D. 1964: A Celebration and Tribute, Harvard University, 2 November 1996," HUA; *WWA, 1962–1963* and *1986–1987*; "Glimpses of a Harvard Half-Century," *HM* 99, no. 3 (January–February 1997); and E. J. Kahn Jr., *Harvard Through Change and Crisis* (New York: Norton, 1969), 38–39; and the entry in the Harvard Yearbook as well as several reunion reports.

235. A similar characterization of the Glimp years is offered in Jennifer Davie Carey, "Tradition and Transition: Achieving Diversity at Harvard and Radcliffe" (Ph.D. diss., Harvard Univ., 1995), 20–21.

236. Admission and Scholarship Committee, "Schools and Scholarship Handbook," September 1961, 15, 17.

237. *Information About Harvard College* [the Rollo Book], 1962, HUA, 77.

238. *Admission and Scholarship Newsletter*, 10 October 1960, 12.

239. In his "Final Report" (31), Bender also raises the issue of the bottom quarter, noting that even under a "top-one-percent policy," "there would still be a bottom half of the class and even a bottom quarter." He then raises the question: "Would the very able man who might have been the outstanding student at another college . . . but who was only average at Harvard, have his self-confidence destroyed, his ambition sapped, or his psyche seriously damaged?"

240. Admission and Scholarship Committee, "Report on the Admission and Scholarship Committee," 1960–1961, 197.

241. Stovault to Messrs. Briggs et al., "Financial Aid Available to Male Freshmen Entering Ivy League Colleges and MIT in September 1961," memorandum, 5 December 1961, Cornell University Archives.

242. Admission and Scholarship Committee, "Report on the Admission and Scholarship Committee," 1964–1965, 2. See also Humphrey Doermann, "The Market for College Education in the United States" (Ph.D. diss., Harvard Univ., 1967), 96–193.

243. The relationship between systems of classification and systems of power is a major theme in the work of Bourdieu and Foucault. Bourdieu has written that systems of classification are "instruments of power, subordinated to social functions and more or less openly geared to the satisfaction of the interest of a group" (quoted in Pierre Bourdieu and Loic J. D. Wacquant, *An Invitation to Reflective Sociology* [Chicago: Univ. of Chicago Press, 1992], 14). Foucault's interest in classification and power runs throughout his work; see, for example, Michel Foucault, *Madness and Civilization* (London: Tavistock, 1971), and *History of Sexuality*, vol. 1 (London: Tavistock, 1979). For an excellent discussion of struggles over classification and

elite college admissions, see David Karen, "Who Gets into Harvard? Section and Exclusion at an Elite College" (Ph.D. diss., Harvard Univ., 1985), 30–37.

244. On the history of racial classification, see Ian Haney Lopez, *White by Law: The Legal Construction of Race* (New York: NYU Press, 1998) and Margo Anderson et al., *Who Counts? The Politics of Census-Taking in Contemporary America* (New York: Russell Sage Foundation, 2000). On the politics of the multi-racial category, see Kim DaCosta, "Revealing the Color Line: Social Bases and Implications of the Multicultural Movement" (Ph.D. diss., Univ. of California, Berkeley, 2000).

245. As late as 1988, when the federal government launched an investigation of complaints that Harvard's Admissions Office was discriminating against Asian Americans, the docket system was still in effect. See Office for Civil Rights, U.S. Department of Education, "Statement of Findings, Compliance Review 01–88–6009," October 1990.

246. Office of Admissions, "Number and Quality of Applicants and Targets for the Class of 1970," 1966, HUA. Another indication of the privileged position of the New England boarding schools was that nearly two-thirds (184 of 291) of the students receiving A's early in their senior year, virtually guaranteeing their admission, were from Dockets L, M, and N.

247. Ibid. Between 1961 and 1965, Docket K (Exeter and Andover) consistently had a higher target than Docket S, which covered most of the public schools in the densely populated region from metropolitan New York City through metropolitan Philadelphia.

248. Feldman, "Recruiting an Elite," 34–41.

249. Office of Admissions, "Reading Procedures 1965–1966," 13 January 1966, HUA.

250. Ibid. An obvious typographical error in this document used the exact descriptions for an Academic 5 and 6 in describing a Personal 5 or 6. I have, accordingly, used the correct version, reported in the "Rating Code Guide for the Class of 1975," in Feldman, "Recruiting an Elite," App. 1.

251. Calculated from Office of Admission, "Comparative Summaries of Pre-Admission Ratings: Classes of '64, '65, '66, '67, '68," n.d. [c. 1965], HUA.

252. Admission and Scholarship Committee, "Final Report of W. J. Bender," 35.

253. Humphrey Doermann, memorandum, 25 January 1966, HUA.

254. Phillips Brooks House, an organization founded in 1900, was "dedicated to Piety, Charity, and Hospitality" and intended as a home for student religious and charitable organizations. See Samuel E. Morison, *Three Centuries of Harvard* (Cambridge, Mass.: Harvard U.P., 1936), 368. Over the course of the twentieth century, Phillips Brooks House developed a reputation as a center of liberal sentiment, with a special emphasis on the obligation that the children of the privileged had to improve the circumstances of the "less advantaged." For a discussion of Phillips Brooks House in relation to student politics, see Seymour M. Lipset and David Riesman, *Education and Politics at Harvard* (New York: McGraw-Hill, 1975), 115, 172, 175, 299.

255. "Taconic" refers to the name of the private foundation that, starting in the late 1950s, provided financial resources for Harvard's effort to bring more socially and culturally disadvantaged students to Cambridge.

256. The description of Type K is taken from "Typologies for Class of 1975." In the 1966 version, the reference was to "good athlete," but the 1971 reference to "prospective varsity athlete" is a more precise description of what the Admissions Office of the mid-1960s seemed to have in mind.

257. Reference to a very similar typology is made in the final report of the investigation of the Office of Civil Rights, "Statement of Findings, Compliance Review 01–88–6009."

258. Office of Admissions, "A Comparison Between Men with a 4 or 5 Academic Rating and the Total Class (Class of 1970)," n.d. [c. 1967], HUA.

259. Office of Admissions, "Harvard Son Applicants to Class of 1969," n.d. [c. 1966], HUA. The estimate of 25 percent for the overall admission rate for applicants with an academic rating of 2 in 1965 is derived from Office of Admissions, "Summaries of Pre-Admission Ratings: Classes of 1964, 1965, 1966, 1967, 1968," n.d. [c. 1966], HUA. In a 1965 memorandum to the admissions staff, Glimp acknowledged that "our policy of giving substantial preference to Harvard sons is roughly the same as it was ten years ago" (Glimp to the Admission and Scholarship Committee, 8 December 1965, HUA, 1–2).

260. Admission and Scholarship Committee, "Report on the Admission and Scholarship Committee," 1966–1967, HUA, 30. Here Glimp wrote that "no comparable (high-cost, selective) college I know of has that degree of contact with low-income families." By 1967, the number of students who qualified for Federal Educational grants had dropped to 8.5 percent (101 students) — still a relatively high figure for an Ivy League institution.

261. Doermann to Glimp, "Small Size of the Pool of Bright AND Prosperous College Candidates in the United States," memorandum, 2 November 1964, HUA.

262. In estimating that in 1964 only about 5 percent of American families (those with incomes over $5,000) could afford Harvard without financial assistance, Doermann was replicating a similar calculation made by Conant more than a quarter of a century earlier when he estimated that only 3 percent of American families (those with incomes over $5,000) could afford a Harvard education. More remarkable still, in attempting to estimate the number of high-scoring students nationwide from families that could pay for a Harvard education, Doermann was unknowingly replicating an identical exercise carried out by Conant in 1939; in Doermann's best estimate, there were 5,000–7,000 such students in the mid-1960s, while Conant guessed no more than 7,000–8,000 in the late 1930s. Apparently, Harvard's preoccupation with finding students who were both smart *and* well-to-do was a constant of its admissions policy. See James B. Conant, "The Future of Our Higher Education," *Harper's*, May 1938, 567; Conant, "Confidential Memorandum concerning the 'size of the small pond in which the private colleges are fishing,'" n.d. [c. March 1938].

263. As late as 1966, Harvard's procedures for reading the files of individual applicants distinguished between "paying guests" and other candidates. Among those students, most of them from private schools, who received early ratings from the "A. B. C." system, "Paying guest applicants rated A go directly to school man who makes *final* ratings . . . One reader only" and "Scholarship applicants rated A go first to school

man, then to HPB [Henry P. Briggs Jr., director of the Financial Aid Office]. Two readers only" (Office of Admissions, "Reading Procedures 1965–1966," 13 January 1966, HUA, 1).

264. Admission and Scholarship Committee, "Report on the Admission and Scholarship Committee," 1966–1967, 23.

265. Glimp to Members of the Admission and Scholarship Committee, memorandum, 7 February 1967, HUA, 1.

266. Admission and Scholarship Committee, "Report," 1966–1967, HU, 17. While it was true, as Glimp reported, that students from disadvantaged backgrounds were overrepresented among those with relatively low test scores, it was *not* true that the majority of students with such scores were from disadvantaged backgrounds. Of the 106 students (8.8 percent of the freshman class in 1965) coming from disadvantaged, rural, or blue-collar backgrounds, just 41 (38.6 percent) of them had SAT verbal scores in the bottom 30 percent of Harvard students (below 637). Such students would have made up no more than about one in seven of the 300 or so students in Harvard's "happy-bottom-quarter." See Doermann to Glimp, "Diversity in the Class of 1969," memorandum, 13 January 1966, HUA.

267. Though a document produced by the association of leading admission and financial aid officers at the eight Ivy League colleges and MIT reported that the number of African Americans entering Harvard in 1965 was 35, the more reliable figure is probably 42, cited in a 1967 dissertation by Humphrey Doermann, then Harvard's director of admissions. According to Doermann, half of the black students entering Harvard in 1965 came from families earning more than $5,000 (a modest income, but well above the poverty line), and 5 were from wealthy enough backgrounds not to even apply for aid (estimated family income in excess of $16,000). The median SAT verbal score for blacks in 1965 was about 600, and all 42 black entrants scored better than 500. See Doermann, "Market for College Education," 141–45; Derek Smith and Fred Glimp, "Meeting of the Order of the Misunderstood," Skytop, Pennsylvania," 16–18 May 1965, HUA, 3.

268. In 1964, 144 students were accepted with SAT verbal scores in the 500s, and an additional 21 were accepted with verbal scores in the 400s (Office of Admissions, "Comparative Studies of pre-Admission Ratings"). In his final report, Glimp noted that early in the 1960s, the Admissions Committee made "a conscious effort to try to maintain the range of measured ability in entering class" (Admission and Scholarship Committee, "Report on the Admission and Scholarship Committee," 1966–1967, 16).

269. Squeezing out the bottom tenth (roughly SAT verbal 450–575) would, Harvard estimated, reduce the national pool of male seniors from 350,000 to 80,000. Raising the SAT floor an additional 100 points, to 675 (roughly approximating the type of "top-one-percent" policy that Bender militantly opposed), would further reduce the pool from 80,000 to 22,000 (Admission and Scholarship Committee, "Report," 1966–1967, 18). For an internal discussion about the size of the pool, see Fred Glimp to Members of the Admission and Scholarship Committee, memorandum, 17 January 1966, HUA, 6.

270. Conant, "Confidential Memorandum concerning the size of the small pond."

271. Committee on Admission and Scholarships, "A Statement by the Committee," 13 April 1968, Harvard University. An identical sentence also appears in the slightly different 1960 version of "A Statement by the Committee."

272. Office of Admissions, "Comparative Summaries of Pre-Admission Ratings," HUA. In determining which students received an academic rating of 1 (89 in 1964 out of over 5,600 applicants), Harvard had at its disposal, not only such quantitative indicators as scores on standardized tests, rank-in-class, and PRL, but also qualitative indicators such as teachers' and principals' letters of recommendation, comments from staff and/or alumni interviewers, and the candidates' personal statements.

273. Bender, "Comprehensive Formal Statement," 31–32.

274. Glimp to Members of the Admission and Scholarship Committee, memorandum, 17 January 1966, HUA, 6. In his report to the president for 1964–1965, Glimp used the same estimate, stating that there were "as many as perhaps 100 to 150" students "whose intellectual potential will seem extraordinary to some part of the Faculty" (Admission and Scholarship Committee, "Report," 1964–1965, 14).

275. The figures reported are factor loadings from a technique called "factor analysis," which is explained in Dean K. Whitla, "Evaluation of Decision Making: A Study of College Admissions," 476–81. See also Whitla, "Admission to College: Policy and Practice," *Phi Delta Kappan* 46, no. 7 (March 1965): 303–6.

276. Office of Admissions, "Comparative Summaries of Pre-Admission Ratings," HUA.

277. In sharp contrast to the great urban public high schools, the elite New England boarding schools continued to enjoy a strong preference in the admissions process. Remarkably, the target for "Select New England Private Schools" (Docket M) actually rose during the supposed ascendancy of meritocracy, increasing from 104 to 130 between 1960 and 1965. In 1965, 71 of 130 applicants from the St. Grottlesex schools (all in Docket M) were accepted by Harvard. This was an increase of 6 over 1960, at the very time that three of the leading Middle Atlantic schools saw their number of acceptances plunge from 21 to 8. Calculated from data provided by the Office of Admissions, Harvard University.

278. Data calculated from National Merit Scholarship Corporation, "Annual Report," 1963.

279. Bender, "Comprehensive Formal Statement," 39. In 1961, Bender offered this dystopian vision of a Harvard College that admitted its students under a "top-one-percent policy": an institution dominated by an "army of future Ph.D.'s" who embodied a "high level of dull, competent, safe academic mediocrity" ("Top-One-Percent Policy," 22).

10. Tradition and Change at Old Nassau

1. Quote from Wilbur J. Bender, "Comprehensive Formal Statement of Harvard College Admission Policy (Confidential)," 18 September 1952, HUA, 16.

2. Wilbur J. Bender, "Speech to Class of '27," 3 May 1947, HUA, 19. Lumping Princeton together with Williams, Bender describes the students at both as "very polite and very genteel."

3. Committee on Admission, "Report to the President," 1950–1951, 1953–1954, PU.

4. See Edwards's entry in the Princeton Class of 1936 Yearbook, his entries in the Fifth and Fiftieth Reunion Reports of the Class of 1936, and press releases from the Department of Public Information at Princeton on his appointment to and retirement from the position of director of admissions.

5. Ibid.

6. Charles W. Edwards, "The Admissions Problem," *PAW*, 4 November 1955, 9.

7. Alexander Leitch, ed., *A Princeton Companion* (Princeton, N.J.: Princeton U.P., 1978), 21–22.

8. Committee on Admission, "Report to the President," 1954–1955, PU, 10.

9. *Freshman Herald: Class of 1958*, PU, 37–40.

10. Alumni Council of Princeton University, "Answers to your questions about the ADMISSION OF PRINCETON SONS," 1 June 1958, PUA, 3.

11. Committee on Admission, "Report to the President," 1958–1959, PU, 7.

12. The Converted School Grade (CSG) was a vehicle for predicting freshman grades developed by the Princeton psychologist Carl Brigham in the 1920s and the 1930s. The CSG ranged from a high of 1 to a low of 7, with 6 a failing grade. See Carl Brigham, "The Quality of the Classes Admitted to Princeton in the Years 1928 to 1935 (Confidential Report to the Committee on Admissions)," n.d. [c. 1935], PUA, 6–8. The CSG was used throughout Edwards's tenure (1950–1962) as director of admissions.

13. Committee on Admission, "Report to the President," 1954–1955, PU, 10.

14. Committee on Admission, "Report to the President," 1957–1958, PU, 6.

15. Office of Admission, "Report to the President," 1961–1962, PUA, 16.

16. Between 1958 and 1962, the admission rate for alumni sons was 67.3 percent (920 of 1367) and just 33 percent for other applicants. Had alumni sons been admitted at the same rate as the others, an average of over 90 additional places in the freshman class would have become available each year. Calculated from Committee on Admission, "Report to the President," 1958–1959, 1959–1960, 1960–1961, PU and Office of Admission, "Report to the President," 1961–1962, PU.

17. Martin Mayer, "How to Get into Princeton," *PAW*, 28 September 1962, 9.

18. "Analysis of Freshman Class," October 1954, PUA, 2–4.

19. Committee on Admission, "Report to the President," 1954–1955, PU, 12.

20. Committee on Admission, "Report to the President," 1957–1958, PU, 4.

21. "Heermance on Admissions," *PAW*, 30 January 1953, 5–6. On Heermance's report, see also "Criteria Set for Entry to Princeton," *NYT*, 25 January 1953.

22. Edwards to E. M. Gemmell, memorandum, 29 January 1958, PUA; untitled document to General Osborn, n.d. [c. 1957], PUA, 6. General Osborn, a Princeton trustee, was Frederick Osborn '10, a prominent New York banker who had served in World War II as a brigadier general heading the morale branch of the army. He was also a member of the Eugenics Society and wrote such books as *Dynamics of Population* (1934) and *Preface to Eugenics* (1940)(*WWA*, 1960–1961).

23. Mayer, "How to Get into Princeton," 14.

24. By 1955, just 10 percent of the freshmen had character ratings below 2; three years earlier, in 1952, 20 percent of the freshmen had such ratings. Calculated from Committee on Admission, "Report to the President," 1955–1956, PU, 4.

25. "Which of These Boys Would *You* Admit to Princeton? . . . ," *PAW*, 2 October 1959, 8; "Admissions Answers," *PAW*, 2 October 1959, 11; Charles W. Edwards, "If *You* Were Director of Admissions . . . ," *PAW*, 2 October 1959, 9–11. Though the interviewer classified the candidate as "narrowly bookish," the principal's report described the young man as "scholarly but not bookish as evidenced by participation in many school activities."

26. Committee on Admission, "Admission and Freshman Year," in "Report of the President to the Board of Trustees," 1940–1941, PU; Committee on Admission, "Report to the President," 1949–1950, 1957–1958, PU.

27. *Freshman Herald: Class of 1944*, PU, 24; Walter Goodman, "Bicker at Princeton: The Eating Clubs Again," *Commentary*, May 1958, 409.

28. Dean A. Allen, "History of the Undergraduate Social Clubs at Princeton," *Social Problems* 2, no. 3 (January 1955): 160–65; Goodman, "Bicker at Princeton."

29. According to one observer in the mid-1950s, "There is strong but minority opinion against 100% election among the students"; hence "it is not the case that a unanimous undergraduate body is being thwarted by the reactionary alumni." That said, he acknowledged that in a small town with no adequate student center, "being outside the clubs may amount to social ostracism" (Allen, "History of the Undergraduate Social Clubs at Princeton," 165).

30. Special Committee of the Graduate Inter-Club Council, "Report of the Special Committee of the Graduate Inter-Club Council of Princeton University," 4 June 1956, PUA, 3.

31. Ibid., 4.

32. Ibid., 2. From the perspective of the alumni, the nonacademic side of campus life was essential to the college experience, and its basis was "mutual groupings of congenial friends." So central was the notion of "congeniality" to the role of eating clubs that the word "congenial" appears seven times in their five-page report (the "most valuable asset" of the clubs, the report contended, was "their congenial membership"). But the ideology of congeniality cherished by alumni was in growing tension with the ideology of diversity, which by the 1950s was increasingly influential among university administrators. The latter emphasized that it was precisely through close contact with people very different from themselves in backgrounds, values, and interests that student growth and development during the college years would be maximized.

33. Ibid., 3.

34. Ibid., 4.

35. Ibid., 3.

36. Raymond W. Apple, "Study of This Year's Bicker Shows Extreme Difficulties of 100 Per Cent," *DP*, 16 March 1955, cited in William K. Selden, *Club Life at Princeton: An Historical Account of the Eating Clubs at Princeton University* (Princeton, N.J.: Princeton Prospect Foundation, 1994), 46. See also "Statement Released by Harold W. Dodds," 7 February 1956, PUA.

37. Frederick C. Rich, *The First One Hundred Years of the Ivy Club* (Princeton, N.J.: Ivy Club, 1979), 192. Though the undergraduates supported the 100 percent principle far more than the alumni, there was also considerable ambivalence and some outright opposition. As far back as 1953, the Undergraduate Inter-Club Committee qualified its support for the 100 percent principle by insisting that it be by "natural selection" and not forced measures; at the same time, the club presidents described Bicker that year as artificial and unrealistic and declared that "admission to the University does not constitute a guarantee of subsequent admission to a club." In 1955, a poll of students conducted by the *DP* showed that 61 percent favored the current club system at the same time that 68 percent supported a proposed university-sponsored social facility (Selden, *Club Life at Princeton,* 46).

38. Steven C. Rockefeller '58, "Reflections on the Princeton Club System and the 1958 Bicker," 22 January 1960, PUA, 18.

39. Selden, *Club Life at Princeton,* 48; Carol P. Herring to William G. Bowen, memorandum, 27 July 1978, PUA, 9. Ivy, the oldest and most prestigious of the eating clubs, did not follow the lead of the Graduate Inter-Club Council, informing the university that it would not amend its constitution to eliminate graduate representation. The governors of Ivy had rejected the 100 percent principle from the outset, denouncing the pledge signed by over 600 sophomores in 1949 as "an ultimatum by mass action and, as such, entirely inappropriate." In 1950, in a report to its membership, Ivy announced its intention "to retain the characteristics of a club in every sense of the word, and to elect sections from year to year of individuals closely united by a desire for congenial companionship in an association which will continue and strengthen through the years after graduation" (Rich, *First One Hundred Years,* 176–77, 191).

40. Just a few months earlier, Dodds had rejected the notion of an alternative facility, stating that the experience of Princeton's sister institutions demonstrated that such facilities "have not fulfilled expectations" and that "any 'solution' which led to a divisive outcome would at this stage be a retrogression." He then reaffirmed his position, viewed by many students and alumni as an evasion of responsibility by the administration, expressing "confidence in the capacity of the undergraduates themselves to conduct club elections satisfactory to all" ("Statement Released by Harold W. Dodds," PUA, 2). Six years earlier, Dodds had actually favored the construction of an eighteenth eating club open to all, but it had been voted down by the students as a "dumping ground." This rebuff reportedly led Dodds to state "I have felt like wiring President Truman telling him I'll settle the [national] steel dispute if he will come to Princeton to settle the club dispute" (Selden, *Club Life at Princeton,* 46).

41. Rockefeller, "Reflections," PUA, 21.

42. Rich, *First One Hundred Years,* 176–77.

43. Henry R. Blynn, "Are Princeton Eating Clubs Stereotyped?" (senior thesis, Princeton Univ., 1950), App. II, Table I; Thomas P. Elliott, "An Investigation of Reputation — An Index to the Campus Characteristics of Six Princeton Eating Clubs" (senior thesis, Princeton Univ., 1956), 19, 47.

44. Rockefeller, a graduate of Deerfield, was the son of Nelson Rockefeller and a nephew of John D. Rockefeller III, a Princeton trustee. At Princeton, he was a two-year letterman as fullback on the soccer team and a campus leader, serving as vice president of the junior class and secretary-treasurer of the Undergraduate Council. A history major, Rockefeller wrote a senior thesis, "A. A. Berle and the New Deal." After graduation, he took a master of divinity from Union Theological Seminary and a Ph.D. in the philosophy of religion from Columbia. Now a professor emeritus of religion at Middlebury College, where he served as dean of the college, he is the author of *John Dewey: Religious Faith and Democratic Humanism* (New York: Columbia U.P., 1991), and co-editor of *The Christ and the Bodhisattva* (New York: SUNY, 1987) (yearbook entry from the *Nassau Sovereign: Class of 1958,* and entry from www.earthforum.org/9904/rockefeller/biography.htm [accessed 10 August 2001; now discontinued]).

45. Geoffrey Wolff, *The Final Club* (New York: Knopf, 1990), 92. Though a work of fiction, the book was based in part on Wolff's own experience; he was half-Jewish and a member of the sophomore class that was the object of the "Dirty Bicker" of 1958. In his "Author's Note," he insists on the fictional character of the work but notes that "the institution of Bicker is too perversely odd for my fancy to have fabricated." In his memoir of his father, *The Duke of Deception* (New York: Random House, 1979), Wolff, a graduate of Choate, discusses his traumatic experience with Bicker, which he portrays as a major element in his decision to withdraw from Princeton in the winter of 1958. Having left as an apparent "100 percenter," Wolff later returned and was invited to join Colonial, one of Princeton's higher-status eating clubs (211–14).

46. Graduate Inter-Club Council, Undergraduate Inter-Club Committee, Central Committee on Clubs, "Now that You Are *Eligible* . . . A Sophomore Guide for the 1958 Elections to Princeton's Upperclass Eating Clubs," 1958, PUA, 7.

47. Ibid., 9. While the cost per term for Prospect was just $260, fees at the other clubs ranged from $340 to $391 per term, with 7 charging $374.

48. A list of the members of Prospect in the Class of 1958 is available in Graduate Inter-Club Council et al., "Now that You are *Eligible* . . . ," PUA, 27. The names of the high schools attended by these members is available in the *Nassau Herald: Class of 1958.* A club-by-club breakdown of the number of students who attended public versus private secondary school in the cohort that entered the eating clubs in 1958 is in Frank Deford, "Club Section Prep-High School Ratios," *DP,* 23 March 1959. As late as 1948, the number of prep school students in three of the Big Five eating clubs outnumbered public school students by a ratio of 65 to 1 ("Pride and Prejudice: A *Sovereign* Study of the Club System with Comments by Vernon M. Geddy, Chairman of the Interclub Committee," *Nassau Sovereign,* February 1949, 12).

49. "Plainfielder Joins Fight Against 'Bias' at Princeton," *Plainfield Courier News,* 12 February 1958. In choosing to attend Princeton on a scholarship, Margolin turned down scholarship offers from Harvard and Columbia.

50. Rockefeller, "Reflections," PUA, 74. At the time of the incident, it was reported that "Rockefeller conceded that perhaps five clubs set loose quotas" ("Incident at Princeton," *Newsweek,* 24 February 1958). According to *Commentary,* it was "widely, and openly,

acknowledged that . . . five clubs set more or less rigid quotas" (Goodman, "Bicker at Princeton," 410).

51. Quoted in Rockefeller, "Reflections," PUA, 71–72. Carnicelli, a Massachusetts native, was a graduate of Andover, where he was president of his class and a member of the varsity soccer and track teams. At Princeton, he was chairman of the *Nassau Lit* and an occasional columnist and theater reviewer for the *DP*. The president of the Elm Club, he also served as chairman of its Bicker Committee (*Nassau Herald: Class of 1958*).

52. Rockefeller, "Reflections," PUA, 9, 74; "Princeton's Head Decries Bias Talk," *NYT*, 13 February 1958. Ivy had two Jewish members — one of them the captain of the lacrosse team (Goodman, "Bicker at Princeton," 410).

53. "To Decide for Oneself," in *The Unsilent Generation*, ed. Otto Butz (New York: Rinehart, 1958), 69–72.

54. Rich, *First One Hundred Years*, 192–94.

55. Rockefeller, "Reflections," PUA, 8–9.

56. Goodman, "Bicker at Princeton," 411.

57. Rockefeller, "Reflections," PUA, 34.

58. Goodman, "Bicker at Princeton," 412.

59. Rockefeller, "Reflections," PUA, 41–42. Of the three clubs that refused to take a "100 percenter," one pledged that it would have if all of the clubs did so.

60. Ibid., 44–45.

61. Rich, *First One Hundred Years*, 195–97; James Ridgeway, "Much Ado About Bicker," *Ivy Magazine*, March 1958, 20; Goodman, "Bicker at Princeton," 412; Rockefeller, "Reflections," PUA, 51; "Incident at Princeton."

62. Rockefeller, "Reflections," PUA, 49–51.

63. Ibid., 53.

64. "Incident at Princeton." Apparently, 2 of the 7 Merit Scholars subsequently either accepted membership in Prospect or received a late bid from another club, reducing the number to 5 (Rich, *First One Hundred Years*, 197).

65. The estimate that 75 Jews joined eating clubs that year is from Goodman, "Bicker at Princeton," 414. But if *Newsweek* was correct that there were 100 Jews in the sophomore class (which was consistent with Goodman's own estimate that the class was about 14 percent Jewish), then as many as 85 Jews may have joined an eating club.

66. According to the schedule published in "Now That You Are *Eligible* . . . ," students had to sit in their rooms awaiting calls from Bicker delegations for nine straight evenings (five of them until midnight) and four late afternoons, for a total of over 42 hours.

67. Edward Said, *Out of Place* (New York: Vintage, 2000), 274–75.

68. Sophomore Class of 1958, "Common Sense about Clubs," *DP*, December 1955.

69. Said, *Out of Place*, 275.

70. Wolff, *Duke of Deception*, 212.

71. The term for groups of men who expressed a desire to belong to the same club was "preferential." The club leadership made clear, however, that the result of Bicker might be to fragment such groups: "it should be understood that there is nothing binding or irrevocable, TO EITHER THE ELIGIBLE OR THE CLUB, about such statements of preference" (Graduate Inter-Club Council et al., "Now that You are *Eligible* . . . ," PUA, 12). A few years earlier, a more solitary mode of handling Bicker called "Ironbound" ("a

group of two to six individuals . . . pledged to stick together and accept a bid from the same club") was not uncommon, but it apparently had virtually disappeared by the late 1950s ("Bicker Terminology," in the Sophomore Class of 1958, "Common Sense About Clubs"). In his memoir, Edward Said describes a poignant incident showing just how personally divisive Bicker could be: "My then roommate, a gifted but, alas, socially undeveloped musician, drove nearly all the committees off, though three of the middle-level clubs kept coming back to see me; they would encircle me at one end of our tiny living room and leave him sitting sadly alone at the other end. Finally, on the night when the entire class descended on Prospect Street to go to the clubs to pick up their bids, I was given three bids, my poor roommate none. Then one of the clubs, through its spokesman, a fat young man who was also a champion golfer, offered to strike an unappealing bargain with me: join here and, as an extra inducement, he said, we'll take your roommate too. As I was about to reject this offer and walk out of the place, I heard a heart-rending wail: "Oh Ed, please don't leave me. Please accept. What'll happen to me?" And so I accepted membership but I never enjoyed the club. I felt alienated and wronged by a publicly sanctioned university ritual that humiliated people in this way. From that moment on Princeton ceased to matter to me except as a place of study" (*Out of Place*, 275–76).

72. Wolff, *Final Club*, 90–99. Wolff's nonfiction account of his experience as a "100 percenter," in many ways even more chilling than the fictional version, may be found in *Duke of Deception*, 212–14.

73. Wolff, *Final Club*, 87.

74. The portrayal of both the ideal "top clubman" and the "100 percenter" comes from many sources, including Butz, *Unsilent Generation;* John McNees, "The Quest at Princeton for the Cocktail Soul," *HC*, 21 February 1958; Elliott, "Investigation of Reputation"; Goodman, "Bicker at Princeton"; and the works cited earlier by Wolff and Said.

75. Jews apparently were not the only Semites concentrated toward the bottom of the club hierarchy. Ralph Nader '55, a Lebanese American, was a member of Prospect. And Edward Said, who was of Palestinian origin, did not receive bids from any of the Big Five, though he was a decent athlete who had attended a good prep school (Mount Hermon) and came from a wealthy family. See Said, *Out of Place*, 275–76, and his entry in the *Nassau Sovereign: Class of 1958;* see Nader's entry in the *Nassau Sovereign: Class of 1955*.

76. Rockefeller, "Reflections on the Princeton Club System," 83.

77. Goheen, the son of a physician who was also a Presbyterian missionary, graduated from Lawrenceville in 1936. At Princeton, he was an outstanding student, graduating Phi Beta Kappa with high honors in classics and highest honors in the humanities. Goheen was also very active in campus activities, lettering on the varsity soccer team and serving as president of Quadrangle, an eating club of relatively high status with a reputation as a place for "Campus Wheels and Christers" (Goheen listed himself in the senior yearbook as an Anglican). After a year of graduate study in Princeton's Department of Classics, he enlisted in the army, where he rose to the rank of lieutenant colonel during World War II. He returned to Princeton after the war, receiving his master's degree in 1947 and

his Ph.D. in 1948. Immediately appointed as an instructor in the Department of Classics, Goheen was promoted to assistant professor in 1950. On December 7, 1956, the trustees appointed him to the presidency of Princeton at the age of thirty-six and at the same time promoted him from assistant to full professor. Profile derived from Leitch, *A Princeton Companion*, 218–21; and the entry on Goheen in the *Nassau Herald: Class of 1940;* and *WWA, 1962–1963.* Information on the Quadrangle Club is from Blynn, "Are Princeton Eating Clubs Stereotyped?" Appendix II, Table I, and Elliott, "Investigation of Reputation," 49–51.

78. "Princeton's Head Decries Bias Talk."

79. "President Goheen's Reply to UGC," *DP,* 19 February 1958.

80. "Plan Princeton Club Alternative," *New York Mirror,* 23 February 1958. See also "Princeton U. Plans Dorm," *Atlantic City Press,* 23 February 1958, and "Princeton Plans Eating Facilities," *Asbury Park Press,* 23 February 1958.

81. McNees, "Quest at Princeton," 3–4.

82. Ibid., 4.

83. Ibid.

84. A passage in Wolff's *Final Club* (74) captures the far more powerful role of the clubs at Princeton than at Harvard or Yale. Booth Tarkington Griggs, a graduate of St. Paul's and a roommate of Nathaniel Clay's, the novel's half-Jewish protagonist, explains the situation: "This Darwinian model of the feral would require fewer us's than thems, or why be an us? Up or out: the elevator to be mounted was not a greasy poll but a slick pyramid, with scant room at the apex — ninety Yale seniors, say of a class of a thousand. At Harvard or Yale so few made the final club, the secret society, that the many thems at least had the solace of their own great society." At Harvard, as far back as the 1930s, only 11 or 12 percent of the students joined final clubs, and in the 1950s, these clubs were even more peripheral to campus life than they had been before World War II (Marcia Graham Synnott, *The Half-Opened Door: Discrimination and Admissions at Harvard, Yale and Princeton, 1900–1970* [Westport, Conn.: Greenwood Press, 1979], 112).

85. Committee on Admission, "Report to the President," 1958–1959, 4.

86. Committee on Admission, "Report to the President," 1951–1952, 1955–1956, 1957–1958; Committee on Admission, "Report of the Committee on Admission of Harvard College," 1951–1592, HU; Admission and Scholarship Committee, "Report on the Office of the Dean of Admissions and Financial Aids for Students in Harvard College," 1955–1956, HU; Admission and Scholarship Committee, "Report on the Admission and Scholarship Committee," 1957–1958, HU.

87. In an internal study of why students admitted to Princeton in 1958 declined to attend, the second most commonly cited factor among the 95 men who gave a reason was the "social system, or clubs." Of the 18 students who referred to the social system, 10 went to Harvard and 7 to Yale. The top reason for the decline was "finances," cited by 24 students; of these, 8 went to Yale and only 1 to Harvard (Committee on Admission, "Report to the President," 1959–1960, 9).

88. Rich, *First One Hundred Years,* 195. Reflecting on the Bicker process, Rockefeller reached a similar conclusion: "The Admissions Office has been bringing into Princeton a rising number of students whose needs are incompatible with the club system. Some are just not suited for Princeton's clubs and cannot cope with the competition and requirements involved. It was this type of student who often became a one hundred percenter" ("Reflections," 84).

89. Committee on Admission, "Report to the President," 1958–1959; Admission and Scholarship Committee, "Report on the Admission and Scholarship Committee," 1958–1959, HU.

90. After Harvard, the leading schools were MIT (83), Radcliffe (40), Cal Tech (32), Stanford (28), Michigan (24), Swarthmore (22), Yale (20), and Northwestern (19)(National Merit Scholarship Corporation, "Annual Report," 1958).

91. Mayer, "How to Get into Princeton," 15.

92. Princeton was, of course, much smaller than Harvard and had no professional schools. But its graduate school was also tiny, enrolling only 660 students in 1958 (Leitch, *Princeton Companion,* 227). Perhaps as a result, Princeton was ranked seventh nationally in 1959, behind (in order) Harvard, Berkeley, Columbia, Yale, Michigan, and Chicago (David S. Webster, "America's Highest Ranked Graduate Schools, 1925–1982," *Change,* May/June 1983). For a general historical treatment of American graduate schools in this period, see Roger L. Geiger, *Research and Relevant Knowledge: American Research Universities Since World War II* (New York: Oxford U.P., 1993).

93. Mayer, "How to Get into Princeton," 7, 15.

94. The committee was clearly aware of the Harvard report and noted that "many of the difficulties described . . . in the recent Harvard report on admission policy will be recognized as being identical to those at Princeton" (Faculty Subcommittee on Admission Policy and Criteria, "Report to the President of the Subcommittee on Admission Policy and Criteria," September 1960, PUA, 3).

95. Ibid., 4–5. If the intent of the reference to "large schools" was to increase the number of students from the huge public high schools of nearby New York City, it did not have the desired effect. In 1961, only 8 students entered Princeton from the public schools of New York City, with none from the Bronx High School of Science and only 2 from Stuyvesant. That same year, New Trier, a high school in a predominantly non-Jewish suburb of Chicago, sent 11 students to Princeton ("Analysis of the Freshman Class," September 1961, PUA, 2–4).

96. Faculty Subcommittee, "Report to the President," 6–7.

97. Mayer, "How to Get into Princeton," 15.

98. Committee on Admission, "Report to the President," 1959–1960, 6.

99. Office of Admission, "Report to the President," 1961–1962, 19.

100. Mayer, "How to Get into Princeton," 7.

101. Office of Admission, "Report to the Faculty," 1962–1963, 11.

102. Committee on Admission, "Report to the President," 1960–1961, 11, and Office of Admission, "Report to the Faculty," 1962–1963, 5.

103. Ibid., 11; Admission and Scholarship Committee, "Report on the Admission and Scholarship Committee," 1962–1963, HU, 211.

104. The 9 feeder schools, Andover, Exeter, Lawrenceville, Hill, Hotchkiss, Deerfield, Choate, Gilman, and St. Paul's, are cited as sending the largest delega-

tions to Princeton in the Office of Admission, "Report to the President," 1964–1965, 3. The numbers are extracted from *The Handbook of Private Schools*, 42nd ed. (Boston: Porter Sargent, 1961). Because the schools analyzed were specifically selected as top Princeton feeders, they do not include minor feeder schools historically linked to Yale (Taft) and Harvard (Groton) and hence are a conservative estimate of Princeton's relatively weaker standing with the leading prep schools compared to that of its Big Three rivals. A second, smaller source of underestimate of the gap is that for both Harvard and Yale, one of the 9 schools sent so few students to Cambridge (Hill, fewer than 4) and Yale (Deerfield, fewer than 8) that they did not list statistics in *The Handbook of Private Schools*.

105. Mayer, "How to Get into Princeton," 8, 17.

106. Blynn, "Are Princeton Eating Clubs Stereotyped?" Appendix II; Elliot, "Investigation of Reputation," 43.

107. The profile of Dunham is based on a number of sources, including his entry in the *Nassau Herald: Class of 1953;* press release from Princeton's news office, 1962; reports from his Tenth, Twenty-Fifth, and Thirty-Fifth class reunion reports; entry from *Leaders in Education*, 5th ed. (New York: Bowker, 1974), 292; E. Alden Dunham, "A Look at Princeton Admissions," *PAW*, 19 January 1965; and "Princeton Admissions: Squeezing Through the Gates," *DP*, 31 October 1964.

108. Dunham, "Look at Princeton Admissions," 1; press release from Princeton news office, 1962.

109. James B. Conant, *My Several Lives: Memoirs of a Social Inventor* (New York: Harper & Row, 1970), 621–22.

110. Office of Admission, "Report to the Faculty," 1962–1963, 1–2. As befit a disciple of Conant, Dunham was a sophisticated and hard-headed analyst of campus politics, well aware that "admission policies affect every segment of the University" and hence "must be arrived at only after careful consideration of their effect on all parties involved in the life of the University." Concretely, this meant that "the Committee on Admission must work closely with representatives of the two other major interested parties — trustees and alumni."

111. "Princeton Admissions," 6. The *DP*'s conclusion was that "the [faculty] committee has in fact ceased to be a force in admission policy simply because it agrees so fully with Mr. Dunham."

112. "Getting into Princeton Under Dunham," *DP*, 31 October 1964. Dunham's apparent lack of warmth led one trustee to state flatly: "Alden Dunham scares people."

113. Office of Admission, "Report to the Faculty," 1962–1963, 17. In a 1965 article, Dunham explained Princeton's quest for black students as part of its long tradition of fulfilling "the nation's need for men who can fill important leadership roles." "From the national point of view," he wrote, "the call for Negro leadership at this time in our history is clear" ("Look at Princeton Admissions," 4).

114. Office of Admission, "Report to the Faculty," 1962–1963, PU, 17–18. In 1961, in response to a special effort by Princeton to learn why some Negro admits had decided to go elsewhere to college, one responded, "I don't think I want to be Princeton's Jackie Robinson" (Mayer, "How to Get Into Princeton," 9).

115. Office of Admission, "Report to the Faculty," 1962–1963, 17.

116. "Your Slant on the Admissions Picture . . . It All Depends on Your Point of View," *DP*, 31 October 1964.

117. Commission on the Future of the College, *The Report of the Commission on the Future of the College*, Table 2.8. Already in 1965, Harvard enrolled at least 40 African Americans (3.3 percent) in its entering class (Humphrey Doermann, "The Market for College Education in the United States" [Ph.D. diss., Harvard Univ., 1967], 141–45). In 1966, there were 35 blacks (3.4 percent) in Yale's entering class (Geoffrey Kabaservice, "Kingman Brewster and the Rise and Fall of the Progressive Establishment" [Ph.D. diss., Yale Univ., 1999], 697).

118. Leitch, *Princeton Companion*, 21–22.

119. Office of Admission, "Report to the Faculty," 1962–1963, 3.

120. Ibid., 6.

121. "Getting into Princeton Under Dunham."

122. Dunham had first raised the "possibility of a class composed entirely of university sons" in an interview with the *DP* ("Princeton Son Crisis Looms," *DP*, 25 October 1962). He raised it again in 1964 in the *DP* ("Getting into Princeton Under Dunham"), but the threat of a class composed entirely of legacies was grossly exaggerated. During Dunham's years, when the number of admissions annually exceeded 1,150 students, the number of alumni son applicants peaked at 355 in 1965 (Office of Admission, "Report to the President," 1966–1967, Chart G).

123. Office of Admission, "Report to the Faculty," 1965–1966, 9. The 1964 data are from Office of Admission, "Report to the President," 1966–1967, Chart G, 12.

124. Dunham, "Look at Princeton Admissions," 4.

125. Calculated from Office of Admission, "Report to the President," 1966–1967, Chart G.

126. Office of Admission, "Report to the Faculty," 1962–1963, 11.

127. "Getting into Princeton Under Dunham."

128. *Handbook of Private Schools 1955*, 36th ed., 343; *Handbook of Private Schools 1966*, 47th ed., 354.

129. The 15 schools are Choate, Deerfield, Groton, Hill, Hotchkiss, Kent, Lawrenceville, Middlesex, Milton, Andover, Exeter, Taft, St. George's, St. Mark's, and St. Paul's. Because *The Handbook of Private Schools* lists only the number of students enrolled at the most frequently attended colleges, Princeton and Harvard may have had as many as half a dozen additional freshmen from the 15 private schools analyzed.

130. Office of Admission, "Report to the Faculty," 1967–1968, 61.

131. Calculated from the Office of Admission, "Report to the President," 1966–1967, Chart L. In 1955, Harvard lost at least 85 admits to Princeton; in 1957, the number of Harvard admits who chose to enroll at Princeton was at least 62. By 1963–1966, the number of joint admits who selected Princeton over Harvard had plummeted to an average of 31 per year (Committees on Admission and on Scholarships and Financial Aids, "Report on the Office of the Dean of Admissions and Financial Aids for Students in Harvard College," 1954–1955, HU, 55; Peter Briggs, "Why They Didn't Choose Harvard," *HAB*, 26 October 1957).

132. Even among those outstanding students who did apply to Princeton, many in the end selected Harvard; of 38 University Scholars (Princeton's top academic award) in 1963, 14 chose Harvard, with only 3

enrolling elsewhere (Office of Admission, "Report to the Faculty," 1962–1963, 13).

133. Ibid., 12–13.

134. Office of Admission. "Report to the Faculty," 1965–1966, 16.

135. One indicator, albeit imperfect, of the number of top scholars in an institution is the number of students who win National Merit Scholarships. In 1968, the number of Merit Scholars enrolled (a figure that includes freshmen, sophomores, juniors, and seniors) was 169 at Princeton, 503 at Harvard, 296 at MIT, 278 at Yale, 229 at Stanford, and 187 at Michigan (National Merit Scholarship Corporation, "Annual Report," 1968).

136. Dunham, "Look at Princeton Admissions," 2.

137. Calculated from Office of Admission, "Report to the Faculty," 1965–1966, 16.

138. According to Dunham, "Interview reports are used to get at the nonacademic factors, as are the personal applications and, of course, the school recommendations" (Office of Admission, "Report to the Faculty," 1962–1963, 15). Alumni interviewers played a crucial role in this process, and in 1964, 1,300 active alumni on 129 local schools committees played a role described by Dunham as "more important than ever" ("Look at Princeton Admissions," 5).

139. Calculated from Office of Admission, "Report to the President," 1964–1965, 14.

140. Dunham, "Look at Princeton Admissions," 1, 3.

141. As late as 1964, an astonishing 250 students — over 30 percent of the freshman class — had played varsity football in secondary school (Office of Admission, "Report to the President," 1963–1964, 11).

142. Dunham, "Look at Princeton Admissions," 1.

143. Calculated from Office of Admission, "Report to the Faculty," 1965–1966, 16.

144. "Your Slant on the Admissions Picture . . . ," 4.

145. Office of Admission, "Report to the Faculty," 1965–1966, 16. From the point of view of the typical undergraduate, however, Dunham was apparently not tough enough on brilliant applicants who might not "fit in." According to the *DP*, 60 to 70 percent of 116 undergraduates interviewed were dissatisfied with Dunham because of the "type of class he is admitting." One of the most common undergraduate criticisms was that Dunham was trying to "outwonk Harvard." Said one student: "Under the policies of Dunham, the students seem to be less sociable; they're finks" ("Your Slant on the Admissions Picture . . . ," 4).

146. Office of Admission, "Report to the Faculty," 1965–1966, 16.

147. Dunham, "Look at Princeton Admissions," 3.

148. Of 4,908 applicants in 1964, Dunham reported that "4515 had predicted freshman averages that would see them safely through the freshman year" (ibid., 2).

149. Calculated from Office of Admission, "Report to the President," 1963–1964, 16, and Office of Admission, "Report to the Faculty," 1965–1966, 16.

150. Office of Admission, "Report to the Faculty," 1965–1966, 7.

151. There had, however, been a significant shift from private to public schools between 1951 and 1966, with the proportion of the freshman class comprised of public school graduates rising from 40 to 59 percent. But the public schools from which Princeton drew most often were heavily concentrated in the

affluent suburbs of major cities. Topping the list of public schools in 1966, for example, were New Trier (10 students) in suburban Chicago and Haverford (5) in suburban Philadelphia (ibid., 14).

152. The data reported here are from the results of a freshman survey conducted at Princeton in 1966 by the Office of Research of the American Council on Education. While the proportion of freshmen reporting a Jewish religious background was 11.7 percent, an additional 3.6 percent reported "none." If, as seems likely, some of these students were from secular families that would nonetheless have been deemed Jewish by Princeton in the past, then the decline in the proportion of the Jews under Dunham may in part be a product of a change in definition. The estimate that 15 percent of the undergraduates at Princeton in 1960 were Jewish is from Lawrence Bloomganden, "Our Changing Elite Colleges," *Commentary*, February 1960, 153. In 1966, Dunham's last year in office, not a single public high school in New York City or Philadelphia — not Bronx Science, not Stuyvesant, not Central — made the list of the top 22 public school feeders to Princeton, each of which sent at least 3 freshmen (ibid.).

153. Bureau of the Census, *Historical Statistics of the United States: Colonial Times to 1970*, Part 1 (Washington, D.C.: Government Printing Office, 1989), 297, 380.

154. "Your Slant on the Admissions Picture . . . ," 8.

11. Yale: From Insularity to Inclusion

1. An ordained Presbyterian minister, Arthur Howe Sr. was from 1931 to 1940 the president of Hampton Institute, one of the nation's leading black colleges (see *WWA, 1944–1945; Yale Banner: Class of 1912;* Howe, interview by Geoffrey Kabaservice, 18 July 1992, transcript, YUA, 1). Arthur Howe Jr. was also the nephew of Henry S. Howe '09 and the brother of Harold Howe II '40, who became U.S. commissioner of education under President Johnson.

2. Howe, interview, 18 July 1992, 28.

3. Howe, interview by Kabaservice, 1 April 1991, transcript, 15.

4. *Twenty-fifth Year Reunion Report: Class of 1943*, YU, 185. Other sources include *Yale Banner: Class of 1943*, YU, 442; and *Fiftieth Year Report: Class of 1943*, YU, as well as the previously cited interviews.

5. Howe, interview, 1 April 1991, 2, 3, 10.

6. Geoffrey Kabaservice, "Kingman Brewster and the Rise and Fall of the Progressive Establishment" (Ph.D. diss., Yale Univ., 1999), 262–63.

7. Ibid., 267.

8. Roger Geiger, *Research and Relevant Knowledge: American Research Universities Since World War II* (New York: Oxford U.P., 1993), 89–90.

9. Nicholas Lemann, *The Big Test: The Secret History of the American Meritocracy* (New York: Farrar, Straus, 1999), 141–42.

10. Data from *The Handbook of Private Schools*, 36th ed. (Boston: Porter Sargent, 1955).

11. Calvin Trillin, *Remembering Denny* (New York: Farrar, Straus, 1993), 39–41.

12. Ibid., 93.

13. Daniel Oren, *Joining the Club: A History of Jews and Yale* (New Haven, Conn.: Yale U.P., 1985), 162–63, 321. For the sources behind the estimate that Prince-

ton was 14 percent Jewish in the late 1950s, see Chapter 10, note 65. In a comparative study of the Ivy League colleges in 1961–1962, Yale remained at the bottom with 12 percent, followed by 15 percent at Princeton and Dartmouth (ibid., 196).

14. Office of Admissions and Freshman Scholarships, "Report to the President and Fellows of Yale University," 1953–1954, YU, 12; Committees on Admission and on Scholarships and Financial Aids, "Report on the Office of the Dean of Admissions and Financial Aids for Students in Harvard College," 1953–1954, HU, 213; Committee on Admission, "Report to the President," 1954–1955, PU, 13.

15. These qualities are specifically cited in the Office of Admissions and Freshman Scholarships and the Financial Aids Office, "Report of the Dean of Admissions and Student Appointments to the President and Fellows of Yale University," 1959–1960, YU, 2.

16. Office of Admissions and Freshman Scholarships, "Report to the President and Fellows," 1954–1955, 4.

17. Lemann, *Big Test,* 145.

18. Office of Admissions and Freshman Scholarships, "Report to the President and Fellows," 1954–1955, 5.

19. Lemann, *Big Test,* 145.

20. Data calculated from *Handbook of Private Schools,* 1956. The 15 schools studied included Deerfield, Taft, and Milton as well as the Big Twelve cited in earlier analyses. Over the three years, the leading schools were Andover (153), Exeter (114), Lawrenceville (69), Deerfield (59), Hotchkiss (54), St. Paul's (53), and Choate (49).

21. Office of Admissions and Freshman Scholarships and the Financial Aids Office, "Report to the President and Fellows," 1956–1957; Office of Admissions and Freshman Scholarships and the Financial Aids Office, "Annual Report to the President and Fellows," 1957–1958, 1958–1959.

22. "The Problem of College Admission III: Preparing for College," *Yale Reports,* 14 October 1956, transcript, YUA, 5. See also Arthur Howe Jr. "Who Gets into Yale?" *YAM,* April 1954, 9.

23. Howe, interview, 18 July 1992, 21–23.

24. Ibid., 29.

25. "Problem of College Admission III, 4.

26. "Admissions: I," *YDN,* 18 September 1957.

27. "Admissions: II," *YDN,* 20 September 1957.

28. "Admissions: III," *YDN,* 23 September 1957.

29. Herschel E. Post Jr., "Special Report: Yale Admissions, the Well-Rounded Myth," *YDN,* 23 November 1959.

30. Ibid. If the cutoff was set at $10,000 per year, which Yale considered the absolute minimum for a family to cover a year at Yale, then the proportion of eligible families would be closer to 10 percent. Howe's own estimate, however, was that only 5 percent of American families could afford Yale (Katherine Kinkead, *How an Ivy League Decides on Admissions* [New York: Norton, 1961], 27).

31. Board of Admissions, "Report to the President and Fellows," 1950–1951; Office of Admissions and Freshman Scholarships and the Financial Aids Office, "Report to the President and Fellows," 1956–1957; Committee on Admission, "Report of the Committee on Admission of Harvard College," 1950–1951, HU; Admission and Scholarship Committee, "Report on the Office of the Dean of Admissions and Financial

Aids for Students in Harvard College," 1956–1957, HUA.

32. Katherine Kinkead, "The Brightest Ever," *New York,* 10 September 1960; Kinkead, *How an Ivy League College Decides.*

33. Kinkead, *How an Ivy League College Decides,* 64.

34. Ibid., 55. Johnston, the son of Waldo Johnston '06, was a graduate of the Hill School and a member of Scroll and Key at Yale (*Yale Banner: Class of 1937*).

35. Howe was acutely aware of the political character of admissions policy and Yale's institutional interest in admitting certain types of students. In his report to the president for 1956–1957, he expressed his "hope that all the legitimately interested parties will be satisfied that their particular interests have been given thorough consideration by the Admissions Committee" (Office of Admissions and Freshman Scholarships and the Financial Aids Office, "Report to the President and Fellows," 1956–1957, 3). Describing the composition of the Admissions Committee in 1960, Kinkead noted that while it "varies annually, — it reflects as many as possible of the interests and pressures bearing on selection" (*How an Ivy League College Decides,* 63).

36. Ibid, 25.

37. Ibid., 71.

38. Ibid., 92.

39. Russell Inslee Clark Jr., interview by Geoffrey Kabaservice, 8 April 1993, transcript, YUA, 32.

40. Detailed information on the height and weight of Yale freshmen from 1879 through 1963 is available in George Pierson, *A Yale Book of Numbers: Historical Statistics of the College and University 1701–1976* (New Haven, Conn.: Yale U.P., 1983), 118–20. Yale was hardly alone among elite colleges in its interest in the physical characteristics of its entering students. From the 1940s well into the 1960s, Yale — along with Princeton, Smith, Vassar, Mount Holyoke, and other colleges — took nude photos of freshmen, ostensibly for the purpose of examining their posture (Harvard had a similar program going back to the 1880s, but it was discontinued in the 1940s). But the real purpose of the program, which was directed by the well-known psychologist W. H. Sheldon, was to link genetically based body types (endomorph, mesomorph, ectomorph) to types of temperament and personality. Like many of his contemporaries, Sheldon was influenced by the eugenicist views then current and adhered to the belief that "Negro intelligence" came to "a standstill at about the 10th year" and Mexicans at about age twelve. Yale continued to participate in the posture photo program until 1967, and in the mid-1990s, a writer for the *New York Times* found the negatives in a box whose contents were described as "Full-length views of nude freshmen men, front back and rear. Includes weight, height, previous or maximum weight, with age, name, or initials" (Ron Rosenbaum, "The Great Ivy League Nude Photo Scandal," *NYT Magazine,* 15 January 1995). Sheldon (1898–1977), a graduate of Brown with a Ph.D. and an M.D. from the University of Chicago, became a full-time researcher at Harvard in 1938 and later was affiliated with a number of institutions, including Columbia's College of Physicians and Surgeons, the University of California at Berkeley, and the University of Oregon (see "Sheldon, W. H.," *International Encyclopedia of the Social Sciences*).

41. Kinkead, *How an Ivy League College Decides,* 26.

42. Ibid., 67.

43. Ibid., 26.

44. Ibid., 48–49.

45. Ibid., 39.

46. Tuttle, who had prepared for Yale at Hotchkiss, later became an ordained Congregational minister and served for a time as the chaplain at Williston Academy (*Yale Banner Book: Class of 1945*).

47. Kinkead, *How an Ivy League College Decides*, 38.

48. Ibid., 55–56.

49. "The Problem of College Admissions II: The Scholarship Story," *Yale Reports*, 7 October 1956, transcript, YUA, 4.

50. André Schiffrin '57 recalls that "all of us on scholarship spent fourteen hours a week working, washing dishes for the first year, doing other jobs later." He acknowledges that "the university did save money in this way," but he believes that "far more important was the obeisance paid to puritanical doctrine. Work was necessary and would efface the stigma of poverty. Most important of all, students had to learn that you never got something for nothing." Kinkead reports that scholarship students worked only up to 10 hours a week in 1960, but Yale documents show that aid recipients still worked 12 hours weekly at that time, with the reduction to 10 hours beginning only in 1961–1962 (Schiffrin, "A World on Tenure," *Midway* 8, no. 4 [1968]: 41–42; Kinkead, *How an Ivy League College Decides*, 43; Office of Admissions and Freshman Scholarships and the Financial Aids Office, "Report of the Dean of Admissions and Student Appointments," 1960–1961, 4).

51. "Financial Aid and Renewal Standards," attached to "Minutes of the Governing Board of Admission and Student Appointments," 12 March 1957, YUA.

52. In a letter to an alumnus, Howe complained that Harvard was willing to admit academically weaker athletes than was Yale — a policy, he argued, that was made possible in part because "Harvard has no academic requirement for the renewal of financial aid above that regularly required for all candidates for continuation in the college" (Howe to Adams, December 1959, YUA).

53. In 1964, Horowitz decided to run for a position on the Yale Corporation, having earned a place on the ballot through the democratic loophole of collecting 250 signatures. But he did not succeed in becoming the first Jew in Yale's history to become a member of the Corporation, losing in 1965 to John V. Lindsay '44, the patrician future mayor of New York City. A year later, using the same technique to gain a place on the ballot, Horowitz — with the support of many alumni, both Jewish and gentile, who thought it was time to end the Corporation's tradition of excluding Jews — succeeded (Oren, *Joining the Club*, 273).

54. Horowitz to Griswold, 5 April 1960.

55. Griswold, memorandum that accompanied the letter from Horowitz, 5 April 1960.

56. This was apparently not the first time that Griswold explained that he considered to be Jews people who did not define themselves as such. A story illustrates his thinking: "At some point during the 1950's, long before Horowitz contemplated that he would ever want to run for the Yale Corporation himself, he went to see his classmate and friend, A. Whitney Griswold. Horowitz said, 'You realize, of course, Whit, that the members of the Corporation have never nominated a Jew for a successor trusteeship.' Griswold

thought for a moment and said, 'That's not true. We *have* nominated some.' 'Who?' 'Why, there was, uh, So-And-So,' said Griswold, mentioning the name of a wealthy New York banker, an 'Our Crowd' type who had long since lapsed into Episcopalianism. 'But, Whit,' Horowitz protested, '*we* don't think of him as Jewish.' The President of Yale said, without hesitating or smiling, '*We* do' (quoted in Mark Singer, "God and Mentsch at Yale," *Moment*, July/August 1975, 31). Howe's views on the issue seem to have been similar to those of Griswold. When Yale's new rabbi, Richard J. Israel, suggested to Howe that there were not as many Jews at Yale as he suspected, Howe demurred, producing a list that, in the rabbi's view, "presupposed every student with a German name to be Jewish and considered every student with a Jew lurking somewhere in the family tree to be a Jew" (Oren, *Joining the Club*, 191).

57. Basil D. Henning '32, Ph.D. '37, a graduate of Andover and a member of Wolf's Head at Yale, spent his entire adult life at Yale, where he became professor of history and master of Saybrook College from 1946 to 1975. See *Yale Banner: Class of 1932* and Thomas A. Bergin, *Yale's Residential Colleges: The First Fifty Years* (New Haven, Conn.: Yale U.P., 1983), 143.

58. Henning to Howe, 6 July 1955, YUA.

59. The "Don" cited in the letter is Donald K. Walker '26, assistant director of the Office of Admissions and executive secretary of the University Enrollment and Scholarships Committee. Walker, whose brother was Yale '09, attended Andover and was active in the Andover Club while at Yale (*Yale Banner: Class of 1926*).

60. Israel to Kahn, 23 November 1960; quoted in Oren, *Joining the Club*, 193–94.

61. Ibid., 194.

62. Ibid. In a conversation with Rabbi Israel, Howe claimed (in an assertion echoed by other admissions staff) that "when Harvard removed its quota it became 55% Jewish and was well on its way to becoming a Jewish school until the quota was re-established" (quoted in Oren, *Joining the Club*, 194). In truth, the proportion of Jews at Harvard peaked in 1925 at 27.6 percent — just half of the mythical figure that shaped Howe's belief that Harvard would become a virtually Jewish school without quotas. For the correct figure on Harvard, see Marcia Graham Synnott, *The Half-Opened Door: Discrimination and Admissions at Harvard, Yale and Princeton, 1900–1970* (Westport, Conn.: Greenwood Press, 1979), 107.

63. On Coffin, see *Yale Banner: Class of 1949* and the entry in *Who's Who in America, 1978–1979*. For information on his uncle Henry Sloane Coffin, who became president of Union Theological Seminary, see *Who's Who in America, 1944–1945*. A recipient of both an A.B. (1887) and an M.A. (1900) at Yale, Henry Coffin was a fellow of the Yale Corporation and listed his membership in Skull and Bones in *Who's Who in America*.

64. William Sloane Coffin Jr., *Once to Every Man: A Memoir* (New York: Atheneum, 1977), 137–38.

65. Ibid.

66. Ibid., 195–97. The estimate that Harvard was 21 percent Jewish in 1961–1962, it should be noted, is lower than all of the other available estimates. A 1952 survey cited by Lipset, for example, found that Harvard was 25 percent Jewish — this at a time when a clear majority of its students still came from private

schools. Other estimates, which refer to the 1960s and early 1970s, place the percentage at 25 percent (Riesman), 25–30 percent (Synnott), and 30 percent (Kahn). See Seymour M. Lipset and David Riesman, *Education and Politics at Harvard* (New York: McGraw-Hill, 1975), 179, 307; Synnott, *Half-Opened Door*, 209; and E. J. Kahn Jr., *Harvard: Through Change and Through Storm* (New York: Norton, 1969), 54.

67. Albert W. Griswold, "Undergraduate Admissions Policy," 9 March 1962, YUA, 3.

68. Clark, interview, 36–37.

69. Oren, *Joining the Club*, 200–201.

70. Ibid., 321.

71. Kabaservice, "Kingman Brewster," 267.

72. Clark, interview, 26.

73. Office of Admissions and Freshman Scholarships and the Financial Aids Office, "Report of the Dean of Admissions and Student Appointments to the President and Fellows of Yale University," 1959–1960, YU, 3–4.

74. Howe, interview, 1 April 1991, 7–8.

75. Ibid., 18 July 1992, 30.

76. Dean of Students to the Trustees of Phillips Academy, "College Admissions, 1959," memorandum, 23 October 1959, YUA.

77. Of the Big Three, Yale was the only one that gathered systematic data on the fate of applicants with a parent who had attended graduate or professional school there but not college. Yale gave these applicants preference as well (though probably not as much as those whose fathers attended Yale College); in 1960, 33 such applicants out of 71 gained admission, and 25 matriculated. When their numbers are added to Yale College legacies, the proportion of 1960 Yale freshmen with a parent who had attended Yale rises to well over 25 percent. Figures from Office of Admissions and Freshman Scholarships and the Financial Aids Office, "Report of the Dean of Admissions and Student Appointments to the President and Fellows of Yale University," 1959–1960, 7; Admission and Scholarship Committee, "Final Report of W. J. Bender, Chairman of the Admission and Scholarship Committee and Dean of Admissions and Financial Aids, 1952–1960," HU, 3; and Committee on Admission, "Report to the President," 1959–1960, PU, 12, 14–15.

78. Kinkead, *How an Ivy League College Decides*, 55.

79. Ibid., 49. Kinkead reports that only 1.7 percent of students failed out of Yale at this time.

80. Nicholas Lemann, "The Quiet Man: Dick Cheney's Discreet Rise to Unprecedented Power," *New Yorker*, 7 May 2001. After failing out of Yale, Cheney enrolled at the University of Wyoming, graduating in 1965. Though an Ivy League dropout, he benefited enormously on his route to political prominence from the patronage of a number of powerful men with Ivy League pedigrees, among them Donald Rumsfeld (Princeton A.B. '54), Gerald Ford (Yale LL.B. '41), George H. W. Bush (Yale A.B. '48), and George W. Bush (Yale A.B. '68, Harvard M.B.A. '75).

81. Among the students who remarked on the limited academic capabilities of some of their classmates was Calvin Trillin '57, who admitted that to this day, "if I meet someone who is easily identifiable as being from what was once called a St. Grottlesex background, my gut expectation — kicking in fast enough to override my beliefs about judging people as individuals, slipping in well below the level of rational thinking — is that he's probably a bit slow" (*Remembering Denny*, 41). R. Inslee Clark Jr. '57 recalled that even as an undergraduate, he "recognized that the student body was not as able as it should be" (Clark, interview, 28).

82. The Aurelian Society, "Academic Indifference at Yale," 1957, YUA, 1–2, 7, 9. Founded in 1910, the Aurelian Society was a Yale honor society (George Pierson, *Yale: The University College 1921–1937* [New Haven, Conn.: Yale U.P., 1955], 132). The president of the Aurelian Society in 1957 was André Schiffrin, and one of the other signers of the report was Henry Chauncey Jr., a longtime Yale administrator who in 1970 became director of university admissions.

83. John P. Miller, *Creating Academic Settings: High Craft and Low Cunning* (New Haven, Conn.: J. Simeon Press, 1991), 69, cited in Kabaservice, "Kingman Brewster," 306.

84. *Handbook of Private Schools 1961*, 80.

85. "Minutes of the Governing Board of Admission and Student Appointments," 9 January 1962, YUA, 3–4; Arthur Howe Jr. to the Governing Board of Admissions and Student Appointments, "Thoughts emerging from the Governing Board's 9 January, 1962, discussion concerning Mr. Ramsey's 15 December, 1961, letter on the recruitment of top graduates of independent schools," memorandum, 25 January 1962, YUA, 3–4.

86. On alumni concern, see Robinson (pseudonym) to Griswold, 4 December 1959, and James W. Crocker (pseudonym) to Waldo Johnston and Arthur Howe Jr., 7 June 1961, YUA.

87. Office of Institutional Research, "Yale College Admissions, Class of 1962–1982, Applicants, Admitted Applicants, and Matriculants, Total and Alumni Children," 2 April 1979, YUA; Admission and Scholarship Committee, "Report on the Office of the Dean of Admissions and Financial Aids for Students in Harvard College," 1955–1956, 1956–1957, HU; Admission and Scholarship Committee, "Report on the Admission and Scholarship Committee," 1957–1958, 1958–1959, HU; Admission and Scholarship Committee, "Final Report of W. J. Bender," HU.

88. Howe, memorandum, 25 January 1962, 3.

89. Ibid., 4.

90. In 1950, Yale's yield was 62.4 percent and Harvard's was 61.7 percent (Board of Admissions, "Comparative Figures on the Class of 1954 and 1955 in Harvard, Princeton, Yale," 24 October 1951, YUA).

91. Howe, interview, 18 July 1992, 39.

92. Committee on the Freshman Year, "The Education of First Year Students in Yale College" [The Doob Report], *YAM*, June 1962, 10.

93. Doob, Dartmouth '29 and Harvard Ph.D. '34, had been on the Yale faculty since 1934. During World War II, he served in a number of prominent positions, including chief of the Bureau of Overseas Intelligence of the OWI (*WWA, 1962–1963*).

94. Oren, *Joining the Club*, 254–55. On Rostow's letter to Seymour, see Chapter 7 of this volume..

95. Oren, *Joining the Club*, 202. Rostow, a graduate of New Haven High School who was appointed dean of Yale Law School in 1955, was born in Brooklyn to a left-of-center family that named its sons Eugene Victor Rostow (after Eugene Victor Debs, the leader of the Socialist Party) and Walt Whitman Rostow. Hutchinson, who was born in Cambridge, England, and graduated from Cambridge University, joined the

faculty at the age of twenty-five in 1928 and wrote numerous scientific books and papers (*WWA, 1962–1963*).

96. See Kabaservice, "Kingman Brewster," 307, and Oren, *Joining the Club*, 201.

97. "The Education of First Year Students," 9.

98. Ibid., 9–10.

99. Ibid., 11. According to Doob, many of the key sentences of the report were written by William DeVane, dean of Yale College. And DeVane's views had not changed since 1948, when he wrote approvingly of the admissions policies of Yale's graduate and professional schools, which focused on the college record and did not ask for "physical prowess, or too much of that indefinable thing called personality" (Synnott, *Half-Opened Door*, 213). See also Leonard Doob, interview by Geoffrey Kabaservice, 6 November 1990, transcript, YUA, 30.

100. Brooks M. Kelley, *Yale: A History* (New Haven, Conn.: Yale U.P., 1974), 451–51; Oren, *Joining the Club*, 203.

101. Ibid., 372.

102. Doob, interview, 31. The obvious subtext — which Doob made explicit when prompted — was that these "serious, lower-class, New York boys" were in many cases Jewish. Yet Yale at this time vehemently denied that it discriminated against Jews; indeed, an official statement from President Griswold stated: "Yale University does not discriminate in any way in its admission polices on account of race, creed, or color. It does not now and never has employed any quota system" (quoted in "Harvard and Yale Deny Discrimination in Admissions," *YDN*, 7 January 1960). But this claim was false, and in 1962 the issue of Yale's treatment of Jews was raised publicly by Paul Weiss, a well-known philosopher who had been the first Jew at Yale to hold the rank of full professor. Weiss, who had grown up on New York's Lower East Side and graduated from City College, had received the appointment in 1946 only after great internal debate about both his intellectual and his personal characteristics; a letter from Charles W. Hendel, titular head of Yale's Department of Philosophy, remarked that it was "difficult for men who like Weiss have been brought out of the lowliest social conditions to know how to behave in a society of genuine equality where it is not necessary to assert oneself" (Oren, *Joining the Club*, 261–63). For the exchange between Professor Weiss and Dean Howe on whether, as Weiss suspected, "White, non–New York Protestants are preferred as candidates," see "Professor Weiss Protests" and "Dean Howe Replies," *YDN*, 2 November 1962.

103. Oren, *Joining the Club*, 203.

104. The committee's rationale for making all jobs for scholarship students optional was straightforward: "some students of the highest intellectual potential decide not to come to Yale because of our present policy of demanding that all students on scholarship shall earn part of their expenses by a job, or in some cases a loan." Though Harvard is not mentioned, there can be no doubt that the committee was aware that Harvard made no such demands on its scholarship recipients (Committee on Freshman Year, "Education of First Year Students," 11).

105. Ibid.

106. Oren, *Joining the Club*, 204. Noting the lack of the kind of alumni opposition one might have expected to the Doob Report's proposal to change the character of the student body, Kelley suggests that Old Blues were distracted by the recommendation to admit women and by the awarding of an honorary degree to President Kennedy, who was intensely disliked by many conservative alumni (Kelley, *Yale*, 453).

107. Oren, *Joining the Club*, 204.

108. Howe, interview, 18 July 1992, 41. Though two other sources cited by Kabaservice also argue that Griswold did not support the Doob Report, Kabaservice himself concludes that "there is no way to know for sure" ("Kingman Brewster," 315–16).

109. Howe, interview, 18 July 1992, 41.

110. For a description of the shock and grief felt by many in the Yale community at Griswold's death, see Kelley, *Yale*, 457–58.

111. Doob, interview, 40.

112. Howe, interview, 18 July 1992, 47.

113. Arthur Howe Jr. to Members of the Governing Board, memorandum, 19 April 1963, YUA. According to Howe's own estimate, "approximately 95% of the families in the United States are not capable of meeting our present charges to undergraduates," meaning that about 65 percent of Yale's entering freshmen (those not on financial aid) came from families in the top 5 percent of the income distribution.

114. Kabaservice, "Kingman Brewster," 316. Though the Corporation approved the policy of need-blind admissions in May 1963, it was not until 1966 that "all mention of financial need was removed from the admissions docket."

115. Far and away the best source on Brewster is Geoffrey Kabaservice's meticulous and illuminating study, "Kingman Brewster." The first three chapters, in particular, are an especially rich source on his background, his childhood and youth, and his milieu. Other sources included the entries on him in *Yale Banner: Class of 1941; Twenty-fifth Reunion Report: Class of 1941; WWA, 1984–1985*; obituaries that appeared in the *New York Times* and the *Boston Globe* on 9 November 1988, and in the *Daily Telegraph* (U.K.) on 10 November 1988; and the portrait in Reuben Holden, ed., *Profiles and Portraits of Yale University Presidents* (Freeport, Me.: Bond Wheelwright, 1968), 146–54.

116. Kabaservice, "Kingman Brewster," 27. Brewster Sr.'s views on race and religion were similar to those of his good friend, the eugenicist Lothrop Stoddard, whose influential racist and anti-Semitic works are discussed here in Chapter 3. A list of the writings of Kingman Brewster Sr., as well as the names of the six social clubs to which he belonged, is included in his entry in *Who's Who in America, 1944–1945*.

117. Kabaservice, "Kingman Brewster," 6–28.

118. Ibid., 31–32.

119. Ibid., 34–35, 55–57.

120. Ibid., 35–37.

121. Loosely translated as "golden youth" or "gilded youth."

122. Kabaservice, "Kingman Brewster," 37–41.

123. See the *Yale Banner: Class of 1941*; Kabaservice, "Kingman Brewster," 59–63.

124. Ibid., 63, 91.

125. Long the pinnacle of Yale's social system, Skull and Bones (1832) remained central to campus life through the 1950s, declined in status in the 1960s, and by the 1970s had lost much of its luster. There are a number of suggestive journalistic pieces about Skull and Bones and/or Yale's senior societies; the best

known is Ron Rosenbaum, "An Elegy for Mumbo Jumbo," *Esquire,* September 1977. See also Stephen Prothero, "Skulls in the Closet," *Salon,* 21 January 2000; Jacque Leslie, "Smirk from the Past," *Salon,* 1 March 2000; Franklin Foer, "Tomb of Their Own," *New Republic,* 17–24 April 2000; and Alexandra Robbins, *Secrets of the Tomb: Skull and Bones, the Ivy League, and the Hidden Paths of Power* (Boston: Little, Brown, 2002). For a more scholarly history of one of the most prestigious senior societies, see A. Bartlett Giamatti, *History of Scroll and Key* (New Haven, Conn.: Scroll and Key Society, 1978). Giamatti, Yale '60 and a member of Scroll and Key, was president of Yale from 1978 to 1986.

126. Brewster had been president of Zeta Psi fraternity but had "later resigned in order to retain his freedom to criticize fraternities as a *News* editor" (Holden, *Profiles and Portraits,* 147). Oren observes that Brewster, in refusing to join Skull and Bones, "achieved a level of social eliteness even higher than the secret societies" (*Joining the Club,* 208).

127. As a prominent activist in the AFC, Brewster became friendly with Charles A. Lindbergh, the nation's most renowned foe of intervention, and his wife, Anne Morrow Lindbergh. In October 1940, Brewster arranged for Lindbergh — who had not yet given his famous Des Moines speech that identified Jews as a key source of the effort to push America into war — to speak at Yale before a packed audience. Before his lecture, Brewster and several faculty members attended a private dinner with Lindbergh at the home of President Griswold — who would later appoint Brewster Yale's provost and the man whom Brewster would ultimately succeed. Anne Lindbergh recorded in her diary her impression of Brewster during this period: "Kingman Brewster, a senior at Yale, comes down to see us . . . He is sensitive, very intelligent, with a precise, searching mind. I feel on my toes keeping up with it. He asks C. about the war and the after-the-war conditions. In our own country and abroad. He is worried (as I am) about the reaction which may take place here against the present party in power and against the Jews. He wishes we could do something to avert that bitterness and reaction — now. To plan for the future — for some kind of rapprochement of the opposing parties — with a constructive plan of reform for the United States. I like him — *how* I like him — his sensitivity, his earnestness, his intellectual integrity (hard as steel), and something soft, too, within, a gentleness, beside his hard thought" (Anne Morrow Lindbergh, *War Within and War Without* [New York: Harcourt Brace Jovanovich, 1980], 193–94, cited in Geoffrey Kabaservice, *The Guardians: Kingman Brewster, His Circle, and the Rise of the Liberal Establishment* [New York: Henry Holt, 2004], 76; see also Kabaservice, "Kingman Brewster," 136–38).

128. The *Atlantic Monthly* article by Brewster, co-authored with Spencer Klan, the president of the *Harvard Crimson,* appeared under the title "We Stand Here" in September 1940 (ibid., 139–49).

129. Kingman Brewster Jr., "Class Oration, as delivered on Class Day," YUA, 317.

130. Kabaservice, *The Guardians,* 90–94.

131. Quoted in Kabaservice, "Kingman Brewster," 178; see also 188, 219.

132. Ibid., 200–220. That Brewster became a full professor having written only a single article was not unusual at the time. Duncan Kennedy, a Harvard law professor appointed some years after Brewster's departure, describes the system that prevailed in the 1950s: "no elaborate formal appointments process at all. You just got hired through the old boy network. The crucial things were your transcript (your numerical average), your membership on the *Law Review,* and your clerkship or, in Kingman's case, your work with your professor after graduation. That was it. There was a tenure requirement in form. You had a three-year contract as an assistant professor, and you were not expected to publish. You were expected to be working on something which your colleagues who could vouch for you thought was interesting. Milt [Katz] decided that Kingman should be hired, he went to [Dean] Erwin Griswold, and that was that . . . It was a lifetime job based on your mentor saying to Griswold, 'This guy would be good'" (quoted in ibid., 220).

133. Ibid., 219–13.

134. Ibid., 60–62, 165, 225, 236.

135. Ibid., 161–65, 225, 233–36.

136. Ibid., 247–73. Though a liberal Republican who had twice voted for Eisenhower over Stevenson, Brewster supported his friend and fellow patrician Endicott Peabody Jr., a Democrat, for governor of Massachusetts and claimed he would have voted for Kennedy over Nixon in 1960 had he met Connecticut's residency requirements (ibid., 207, 243).

137. Himmelfarb (pseudonym) to Brewster, 27 October 1963, YUA; Brewster to Himmelfarb, n.d. (but after Howe's draft of 7 November 1963), YUA.

138. Robinson to Brewster, 21 October 1963, YUA.

139. Kingman Brewster Jr., "Speech to the 100th Anniversary Dinner of the Cincinnati Yale Club," 8 February 1964, YUA, 7–8.

140. Kingman Brewster Jr., "Address to the National Yale Alumni Meeting," 21 March 1964, YUA, 2. Frederick Barghoorn, a Soviet specialist, was professor of political science at Yale, and James Tobin was Sterling Professor of Economics.

141. O'Hearn, a graduate of Exeter and Yale '24, had been a star in three sports at Yale, once drop-kicking a 52-yard field goal against Carnegie Tech. For a brief portrait, see Jack Cavanaugh, "Charlie O'Hearn, 99, Kicker and Three-Sport Man at Yale," *NYT,* 27 April 2001.

142. Howe to Brewster, 2 January 1964, YUA.

143. Brewster to Howe, memorandum, 9 January 1964; emphasis added.

144. Kabaservice, *The Guardians,* 260.

145. Howe, interview, 18 July 1992, 48.

146. Hyatt, who served as acting dean of admissions until 1 July 1965, was captain of the university crew at Yale and a member of Delta Kappa Epsilon and the Elihu Club, a senior society (*Yale Banner: Class of 1918*).

147. Howe to Brewster, 2 January 1964.

148. The candidate did somewhat better in math, scoring 640, which would have placed him in approximately the 20th percentile of Yale freshmen in 1964 (Office of Admissions and Freshman Scholarships, Financial Aids Office, and Office of Enrollment and Scholarships, "Report of the Acting Dean of Admissions and Student Appointments to the President and Fellows of Yale University," 1963–1964, YU, 6).

149. George W. Bush was not alone in receiving preference in 1964; the admissions rate that year for the 523 legacy applicants was 47 percent compared

to 27 percent for nonlegacy applicants (from figures provided by the Office of Institutional Research, Yale University). In the fall of 1964, 30 of Bush's classmates from Andover joined him in New Haven (*Handbook of Private Schools*, 1965, 94). On Bush's three years at Andover and his application to Yale, see Bill Minutaglio, *First Son: George W. Bush and the Bush Family Dynasty* (New York: Three Rivers Press, 2001), 58–75; Nicholas D. Kristof, "Earning A's in People Skills at Andover," *NYT*, 10 June 2000; and Evan Thomas and Martha Bent, "A Son's Restless Journey," *Newsweek*, 7 August 2000.

12. Inky Clark, Kingman Brewster, and the Revolution at Yale

1. Kingman Brewster Jr., "Question and Answer Session Following the Annual Meeting, Yale Alumni Association of Cleveland," n.d., YUA.

2. University Council, "Report of the Council's Committee on Admissions to Yale College," May–July 1964, YUA, 8–9. Among the members of the committee were John Hersey (Hotchkiss '32, Yale '36), the renowned author of *Hiroshima* and a fellow of Berkeley College (and soon master of Pierson College), and Zeph Stewart (Hotchkiss '39, Yale '42; brother of Supreme Court Justice Potter Stewart), professor of Greek and Latin at Harvard and Griswold's first choice for provost. Both Hersey and Stewart had been members of Skull and Bones as undergraduates. See entries on Hersey in *Yale Banner: Class of 1936* and Stewart in *Yale Banner: Class of 1943*, as well as *WWA, 1978–1979*. On Griswold's decision to first offer the provostship to Zeph Stewart, see Geoffrey Kabaservice, *The Guardians: Kingman Brewster, His Circle, and the Rise of the Liberal Establishment* (New York: Henry Holt, 2004), 141–42.

3. Edward ("Ned") T. Hall, headmaster of the Hill School, was a graduate of St. Mark's and a classmate of Brewster's at Yale, where he was a member of Skull and Bones and the Aurelian Society. An Episcopalian from Manchester, Massachusetts, he belonged to the Century Association and the Elizabethan and Tavern clubs (*WWA, 1962–1963*).

4. Russell I. Clark Jr., interview by Geoffrey Kabaservice, 13 May 1993, transcript, YUA, 6–7. See also Clark, interview by Kabaservice, 9 April 1993, transcript, 21–22.

5. Clark, interview, 9 April 1993, 22.

6. The biographical profile of Clark is constructed from a number of sources, including *Yale Banner: Class of 1957*, 355; Clark., interview, 9 April 1993, 1–7; Derek Norcross, "'Inky' Clark: Most Popular Man in America," *Parade Magazine*, 16 March 1969; "New Admissions Dean," *YAM*, March 1965, 23; press release on R. Inslee Clark Jr. from the Office of Public Information, n.d., YUA; and Kabaservice, "Kingman Brewster," 317–18.

7. Clark, interview, 9 April 1993, 5–6.

8. Weiss to Brewster, 12 February 1965, YUA.

9. Vann Woodward added, not without irony: "I hope I am wrong and that in reality he bristles with intellectual interests and proletarian sympathies" (Woodward to Brewster, 4 February 1965, YUA). For another expression of similar concerns, see Richard B. Sewall (master of Ezra Stiles College) to Brewster, 12 February 1965, YUA.

10. In Coffin's view, Clark embodied "traditional Yale" (Clark, interview, 9 April 1993, 29–30).

11. Clark, interview, 13 May 1993, 1.

12. Ibid., 3.

13. "Ivy Overlap Study," 26 October 1965, HUA. Of the 244 students admitted by both Yale and Harvard, 210 ended up enrolling at Harvard.

14. Clark, interview, 13 May 1993, 3–4.

15. See, for example, Jeffrey Gordon, "'Inky's' Era," *YAM*, March 1970, 33–37.

16. "New Admissions Dean," 23–24.

17. Brewster's assistant, Henry ("Sam") Chauncey Jr. '57, reports that Brewster had Conant's admissions policies in mind when he decided to select Clark as the person most likely to improve Yale's undergraduate student body (Kabaservice, *The Guardians*, 263). Sam Chauncey is the son of Henry Chauncey Sr., who had worked with Conant on admissions as a junior dean at Harvard in the 1930s. Henry Chauncey Sr. went on to become the first president of the Educational Testing Service (see Nicholas Lemann, *The Big Test: The Secret History of the American Meritocracy* [New York: Farrar, Straus, 1999]).

18. Kingman Brewster Jr., "Speech Delivered By Kingman Brewster, Jr. at the Yale Club of Southern California," 10 November 1965, YUA, 1–2.

19. Admissions Policy Advisory Board, "Preliminary Report of the Admissions Policy Advisory Board to President Kingman Brewster Jr. and Dean R. Inslee Clark Jr.," 15 December 1965, YUA, 1–2.

20. Kabaservice's more general conclusion, which is consistent with the available evidence, is that "Clark abandoned the old geographic criteria" — a major change that reversed more than four decades of Yale policy ("Kingman Brewster," 320).

21. Admissions Policy Advisory Board, "Preliminary Report," 3–6.

22. Kabaservice, "Kingman Brewster," 320–21.

23. Clark, interview, 13 May 1993, 32; 9 April 1993, 62–63.

24. According to Kabaservice, "Clark retained the concept of predicted averages, but eliminated the huge deflation factor it applied to grades earned at schools which had sent few (if any) students to Yale." But the transcript of the Clark interview is ambiguous on the fate of the predicted grade average and is worth quoting: "And so we really had to get the predicted average out of there. Or, if it was going to be on the slate, we had to explain to the committee that in some cases, the predicted average was absolutely unreliable" (Clark, interview, 9 April 1993, 63). See also Kabaservice, "Kingman Brewster," 320–21.

25. Calculated from "Report of the Director of Financial Aid Office" for 1963–1964 and 1964–1965, YU, and from George W. Pierson, ed., *A Yale Book of Numbers: Historical Statistics of the College and University 1701–1976* (New Haven, Conn.: Yale U.P., 1983), 88.

26. Clark, interview, 9 April 1993, 62.

27. Ibid.

28. As late as January 1967, Humphrey Doermann, who served as Harvard's director of admissions through 1966, wrote that "about 50 needy students have enrolled in each of the recent years knowing that, while they were clearly admissible, insufficient scholarship funds were available to award them gift aid in the freshman year, or to make any financial commitment for the years following." But by the fall

of 1966, "the number of needy students entering Harvard College without financial aid virtually disappeared" ("The Market for College Education in the United States" [Ph.D. diss., Harvard University, 1967], 287–88).

29. The three staff members whose fathers had attended Yale were Charles F. Nelson Jr. '54 (son of Charles Nelson '25), Lawrence M. Noble Jr. '53 (son of Lawrence Noble '27), and Donald R. Williams (son of Donald R. Williams '27). Alton Hyatt '18, the acting dean of admissions, was the brother of Roswell Hyatt '03, Willard Hyatt '05, and I. Robert Hyatt '15. Information obtained from the *Yale Banner;* roster of members of the Admissions Committee for 1964–1965 listed in the Office of Admissions and Freshman Scholarships, and the Office of Enrollment and Scholarships, "Annual Report of the Acting Dean of Undergraduate Admissions and Student Appointments," 1964–1965, YU, 3–4.

30. Clark, interview, 9 April 1993, 32–33.

31. Kabaservice, *The Guardians,* 263.

32. Tom Herman, "New Concept of Yale Admissions," *YDN,* 16 December 1965.

33. Ibid.

34. Pierson, *Yale Book of Numbers,* 96–99. For Harvard and Princeton, see Committee on Admission, "Report of the Committee on Admission of Harvard College," 1947–1948 to 1951–1952, HU; Committees on Admission and on Scholarships and Financial Aids, "Report on the Office of the Dean of Admissions and Financial Aids for Students in Harvard College," 1952–1953 to 1954–1955, HU; Admission and Scholarship Committee, "Report on the Office of the Dean of Admissions and Financial Aids for Students in Harvard College," 1955–1956, 1956–1957, HU; Admission and Scholarship Committee, "Report on the Admission and Scholarship Committee," 1957–1958, 1958–1959, 1960–1961 to 1964–1965, HU; Admission and Scholarship Committee, "Final Report of W. J. Bender, Chairman of the Admission and Scholarship Committee and Dean of Admissions and Financial Aids, 1952–1960," HU; Committee on Admission, "Report to the President," 1947–1948 to 1961–1962, PU; Office of Admission, "Report to the Faculty," 1962–1963, PU; and Office of Admission, "Report to the President," 1963–1964, 1964–1965, PU.

35. Pierson, *Yale Book of Numbers,* 98–99.

36. *The Handbook of Private Schools* (Boston: Porter Sargent, 1966).

37. Clark, interview, 9 April 1993, 15.

38. Ibid., 65

39. Brewster publicly chided Harvard about its refusal to go along with Yale and Princeton in abolishing the ABC system, and the controversy reached the media (Sydney N. Schanberg, "Yale President Chides Harvard," *NYT,* 30 October 1965).

40. Clark, interview, 9 April 1993, 65–66.

41. Ibid., 66–67.

42. *Handbook of Private Schools 1967.* The 12 schools are the same as those identified in Chapter 1.

43. Warren to Brewster, 4 May 1966, YUA; Brewster to Warren, 12 May 1966, YUA.

44. Edward Palmer (pseudonym) to Kingman Brewster, 6 June 1966, YUA.

45. The figures on the number of students enrolled at Harvard and Yale, respectively, in 1966 seem consistent with Palmer's claim: St. Paul's, 18 and 6; Exeter, 45 and 19; St. Marks, 10 and 3; Andover, 47 and 22 (*Hand-*

book of Private Schools 1966). In part, it seems to have been a product of the "best boys" applying in greater numbers to Harvard than Yale; even before Clark was named dean, Yale was having internal discussions about "our image problem" with Andover and was making special visits in an attempt to correct it ("Minutes of the Committee of Admissions and Freshman Scholarships," 26 October 1964, YUA, 3–4). But the greater numbers of Harvard admits from the top prep schools also seem to have reflected a more generous treatment of applicants from these institutions than was the case at Yale under Clark.

46. Palmer to Brewster, 6 June 1966, YUA.

47. Ibid. All three of the most recently elected members of the Yale Corporation were, Palmer noted, alumni of St. Paul's, his own school: John Vliet Lindsay (St. Paul's '40, Yale '44), mayor of New York City and former Republican congressman representing Manhattan's Upper East Side; Frederick Baldwin Adams Jr. (St. Paul's '28, Yale '32), director of the J. Pierpont Morgan Library in New York City and a member of the Board of Directors of several major corporations; and Paul Moore Jr. (St Paul's '37, Yale '41), suffragan Episcopal bishop of Washington, D.C., and later Episcopal bishop of New York City. On Adams, see *WWA, 1962–1963;* on Lindsay and Moore, see *WWA, 1978–1979.*

48. Clark, interview, 9 April 1993, 16.

49. "Why Yale Turned Cool on Choate," *Choate News,* 27 April 1968; reprinted in Peter S. Prescott, *A World of Our Own: Notes on Life and Learning in a Boys' Preparatory School* (New York: Coward-McCann, 1970), 396–98.

50. Prescott, *World of Our Own,* 201–3. Prescott reported that Clark was "not impressed by the academic record of Choate boys taken by Yale several years ago before Yale became more choosy." In an interview with Geoffrey Kabaservice, Clark described schools such as Choate as not "diverse at all; in fact, they were terribly, terribly inbred." Explaining why Choate got battered, Clark recalled that while the top of the class was very strong, "the quality of the class fell off dramatically," with all kinds of Yale sons floating around in the middle and the bottom half of the Choate class who hadn't done an awful lot at Choate." During the Clark years, these students "weren't admitted to Yale any more as they had been" (Clark, interview, 9 April 1993, 16, 71).

51. Ibid., 35.

52. William Borders, "Ivy League Shifts Admissions Goals," *NYT,* 17 April 1967.

53. Terrer Ferrer, untitled newspaper clipping, unknown newspaper, n.d. [c. 15 April 1966], YUA.

54. Pierson, *Yale Book of Numbers,* 98–99; Admission and Scholarship Committee, "Report on the Admission and Scholarship Committee," 1966–1967, HU, 6. Princeton had roughly the same proportion of private school students as Harvard, averaging 41 percent for the classes that entered between 1966 and 1968. See Office of Admission, "Report to the President," 1966–1967, PU; Office of Admission, "Report to the Faculty," 1967–1968, PU; Office of Admission, "Annual Report," 1968–1969, PUA.

55. According to Clark, the abolition of the ABC system did not constitute discrimination against the prep schools but rather reflected that "the independent schools were now being placed on the same plane, in terms of the process, as the public schools.

Everybody was going to be dealt with the same; therefore, no more favoritism" (interview, 9 April 1993, 56).

56. In 1940, 213 Yale freshmen (out of 861) had graduated from public schools. That year, just five boarding schools — Andover (67), Hotchkiss, (59), Exeter (49), St. Paul's (34), and Choate (34) — sent 243 graduates to Yale. Overall, 35 percent of the freshman class came from a dozen boarding schools (Pierson, *Yale Book of Numbers,* 96; Jerome Karabel, "Status-Group Struggle, Organizational Interests, and the Limits of Institutional Autonomy: The Transformation of Harvard, Yale, and Princeton, 1918–1940," *Theory and Society* 13, January 1984, 22).

57. In 1960, in a freshman class of 1,000 students, Yale enrolled 235 sons of Yale College alumni and an additional 25 sons of alumni of a Yale graduate or professional school (Office of Admissions and Freshman Scholarships and the Financial Aids Office, "Report of the Dean of Admissions and Student Appointments to the Presidents and Fellows of Yale University," 1959–1960, 8).

58. Admission and Scholarship Committee, "Final Report of W. J. Bender," HU, 3; Committee on Admission, "Report to the President," 1959–1960, PU, 15.

59. Office of Admissions and Freshman Scholarships and the Financial Aids Office, "Report of the Dean of Admissions and Student Appointments to the President and Fellows of Yale University," 1962–1963, 3. The substantially higher rate of acceptance for the sons of Yale College alumni compared to the alumni of the graduate and professional schools was typical of this period; in the years from 1960 to 1964, Yale College sons were accepted at a rate of 58 percent (1,201 of 2,064) but only 40 percent (146 of 365) of the sons of graduate or professional school alumni were admitted (calculated from Office of Admissions and Freshman Scholarships and the Financial Aids Office, "Report of the Dean of Admissions and Student Appointments to the President and Fellows of Yale University," 1959–1960, 1960–1961, 1962–1963; Office of Admissions and Freshman Scholarships, Undergraduate Financial Aids Office, and the Office of Enrollment and Scholarships, "Report of the Dean of Admissions and Student Appointments to the President and Fellows of Yale University," 1961–1962; Office of Admissions and Freshman Scholarships, Financial Aids Office, and the Office of Enrollment and Scholarships, "Report of the Acting Dean of Admissions and Student Appointments to the President and Fellows of Yale University," 1963–1964).

60. Steven E. Carlson to Brewster, memorandum, 7 June 1974, YUA.

61. Ibid.

62. Ibid.

63. James Barrington (pseudonym) to Holden, 20 April 1966, YUA. That same year, a faculty member who had served on the Admissions Committee reported that Yale sons received "very little special consideration" and had "a much harder time of it" than he had expected (Charles E. Lindblom to James Tobin, memorandum, "Impressions of Yale Admissions Policies After Serving on the Admissions Committee — Spring 1966," 30 March 1966, YU).

64. Calculated from Carlson, memorandum, and Office of Admissions and Freshman Scholarships, "Report of the Dean of Admissions and Student Appointment to the President and Fellows of Yale University," 1965–1966.

65. "Report to Alumni on Alumni Board's Study of Admissions" (Cook Report), October 1967, YU, 5.

66. Ibid., letter on the cover page.

67. Ibid., 1.

68. Ibid., 5–6.

69. In a typical year, about 3 percent of Yale freshmen were sons of parents who had attended a Yale graduate or professional school but not Yale College (see Office of Admissions and Freshman Scholarships and the Financial Aids Office, "Report of the Dean of Admissions and Student Appointments to the Presidents and Fellows of Yale University," 1960–1961, 1962–1963; Office of Admissions and Freshman Scholarships, Undergraduate Financial Aids Office, and the Office of Enrollment and Scholarships, "Report of the Dean of Admissions and Student Appointments to the President and Fellows of Yale University," 1961–1962; and Office of Admissions and Freshman Scholarships, Financial Aids Office, and the Office of Enrollment and Scholarships, "Report of the Acting Dean of Admissions and Student Appointments to the President and Fellows of Yale University," 1963–1964; and Carlson, memorandum).

70. Carlson, memorandum.

71. Calculated from Admission and Scholarship Committee, "Report on the Admission and Scholarship Committee," 1965–1966, HU, 29; Office of Admission, "Report to the Faculty," 1965–1966, PU, 12; Office of Admissions and Freshman Scholarships, "Report of the Dean of Admissions and Student Appointment to the President and Fellows of Yale University," 1965–1966, 1; and Carlson, memorandum.

72. Letters by Joseph E. Muckley and Kenneth E. Ryan under "Reaction to Alumni Board Report," *YAM,* December 1967. For a thoughtful defense of Yale's admissions policies, see the letter by Stowe C. Phelps '39 in the same issue.

73. William Borders, "William Buckley Runs at Yale to Combat Liberals," *NYT,* 21 October 1967.

74. M. A. Farber, "Buckley 'Interferes,'" *NYT,* 29 October 1967.

75. Profile of Vance from *Yale Banner: Class of 1939* and *WWA, 1978–1979.*

76. William F. Buckley Jr., "What Makes Bill Buckley Run," *Atlantic Monthly,* April 1968.

77. William Borders, "Buckley Opposed by Cyrus Vance in Yale Election," *NYT,* 9 March 1968.

78. Lawrence Van Gelder, "Vance Tops Buckley in Election at Yale," *NYT,* 17 June 1968.

79. C. Tracy Barnes to Howard Phelan, Yale's director of development, 13 February 1968, YUA. The memorandum exhibits an awareness of, and a concern about, Buckley's forthcoming article in the *Atlantic Monthly.*

80. "Resolution of Yale Development Board," 15 November 1968, YUA.

81. Daniel A. Oren, *Joining the Club: A History of Jews and Yale* (New Haven, Conn.: Yale U.P., 1985), 321. Of the Yale undergraduate student body as a whole, Rabbi Israel estimated that 12 percent were Jewish in 1961–1962 (ibid., 196).

82. "U.S. Jewish Population in Large Cities," *World Almanac, 1962.* Adding New York's Westchester County and northern New Jersey to the New York metropolitan area brings the number of Jews there to over 48 percent of the nation's Jewish population.

83. Oren, *Joining the Club,* 208. The other region that vied with the New York–Long Island area for the

title of "crummiest" was the Northwest (also known as the "boondocks"), which lacked "posh hotels to stay in" as well as Yale alumni with whom a visiting member of the admissions staff could socialize.

84. Ibid., 196, 321.

85. For a vivid description of the anti-Semitic atmosphere of the Yale Admissions Office in the early 1960s, see Clark, interview, 9 April 1993, 36–37.

86. Ibid.

87. Admissions Policy Advisory Board, "A Preliminary Report," 5.

88. In a 1967 interview, Clark reported that Yale had almost completely abandoned the goal of geographical distribution (see Borders, "Ivy League Shifts Admissions Goals").

89. Clark, interview, 9 April 1993, 76; Oren, *Joining the Club*, 211.

90. Clark, interview, 9 April 1993, 76.

91. An early indication that Brewster was dissociating himself from the anti-Semitism common in his milieu was his participation in two extracurricular activities, the Yale Debating Association and the *YDN*, in which Jewish students played prominent roles. Another indication was Brewster's rejection of Skull and Bones (which did not accept its first Jew until 1949) at the same time that he accepted membership in a fraternity with two Jewish members (see Oren, *Joining the Club*, 162). At Harvard Law School, where Professor Milton Katz was his mentor, Brewster welcomed the hiring of large numbers of Jewish faculty members. According to Kabaservice, during his years at Harvard, "Brewster was, if anything, a pronounced philo-Semite")"Kingman Brewster," 124–25, 200–204, 223–24).

92. Charles H. Stember et al., *Jews in the Mind of America* (New York: Basic Books, 1966), 208–24. See esp. 208–9, 229.

93. Among the many fine books on the student movement of the 1960s, see James Miller, *Democracy Is in the Streets* (New York: Simon & Schuster, 1987), and Kirkpatrick Sale, *SDS* (New York: Vintage, 1974). For an illuminating general treatment of the period, see Todd Gitlin, *The Sixties: Years of Hope, Days of Rage* (New York: Bantam, 1987).

94. Borders, "Ivy League Shifts Admissions Goals"; Watzek to Brewster, 27 April 1967, YUA.

95. Arnold J. Wolf, "'Jewish Experience is Vividly Present at Yale,'" *YAM*, 14. In 1972, an article in *New York* magazine estimated the proportion of Jews at Yale to be 30 percent (14 August 1972, 28; cited in Lux et Veritas, "A Report on Yale Admissions 1950–1972," 1972, 11).

96. Letter by "Hal" to Richard E. Bishop, class secretary, cited in "Class of 1912S [Sheffield Scientific School] Notes," *YAM*, April 1973, 43.

97. Clark, interview, 9 April 1993, 68.

98. Frank D. Ashburn Jr., "The Essence of Yale," *YAM*, January 1949, 9.

99. Homer D. Babbidge Jr., "Yale's Scholarship Program," *YAM*, February 1949; see also "How Undergraduates Get Their Scholarships," *YAM*, October 1951, 9–11.

100. Katherine Kinkead, *How an Ivy League College Decides on Admissions* (New York: Norton, 1961), 26. See also the remarks by Howe in Office of Admissions and Freshman Scholarships and the Financial Aids Office, "Report of the Dean of Admissions and Student Appointments to the Presidents and Fellows of

Yale University," 1959–1960, 3–4, discussed in Chapter 11.

101. Admissions Policy Advisory Board, "Second Report," 6. Immediately after this cautionary statement, however, the board expressed its belief that "Yale's admissions procedures and the composition of the admissions staff now protect us from such distortion of values."

102. Russell I. Clark Jr., "Admission to Yale: Policies and Procedures," *YAM*, October 1966, 35–37.

103. University Council, "Report of the Council's Committee on Admission to Yale College," 7–8.

104. Stewart Alsop, "Yale Revisited," *Newsweek*, 19 May 1969, 120.

105. Robert Livingstone Jr. (pseudonym) to Clark, 30 August 1965, YUA.

106. Pierson, *Yale Book of Numbers*, 118–20. Interestingly, the second largest drop in average height during the 1883–1967 period occurred between 1942 (70.0 inches) and 1943–1945 (69.8, 69.9, 69.8 inches, respectively) — the very time when the dean of admissions was complaining about the growing number of Jews at Yale, many of whom were not yet eligible for the draft because they had graduated from high school early and were still under eighteen years old (see Chapter 7).

107. If one compares Clark's first class with the class admitted in 1958 (nearly midway through Howe's deanship), one can immediately see why so many Old Elis were upset by the new policy. For one thing, the admission rate for legacies plummeted from 66 to 37 percent over the eight years, with the proportion of Yale College sons in the freshmen class down from 21 percent in 1958 to 13 percent in 1966. Paralleling this decline was a sharp decrease in the percentage of freshmen from private schools, from 56 to 42 percent. Even more striking were the falling numbers of entrants from the top feeder schools between 1958 and 1966: from 53 to 22 at Andover, 24 to 7 at Lawrenceville, 21 to 6 at St. Paul's, 20 to 2 at Choate, 19 to 8 at Deerfield, and 19 to 7 at Taft (Office of Admissions and Freshman Scholarships and the Financial Aids Office, "Annual Report to the President and Fellows of Yale University," 1957–1958; Office of Admissions and Freshman Scholarships, "Report of the Dean of Admissions and Student Appointment to the President and Fellows of Yale University," 1965–1966). The figure on the percentage of Yale College sons in the freshman class of 1966 is from Carlson, memorandum. Prep school figures for 1958 are from Office of Admissions and Freshman Scholarships, "Annual Report to the President and Fellows of Yale University," 1957–1958; figures for 1966 from *Handbook of Private Schools 1967*, except for the figure on Choate (which did not list Yale as one of the six principal colleges attended by its 1966 graduates), which comes from Kabaservice, "Kingman Brewster," 327.

108. Pierson, *Yale Book of Numbers*, 102.

109. In comparison, Princeton and Harvard recorded an increase in the number of National Merit Scholars, from 123 to 169 and 344 to 503, respectively, during the same five years, but did not approach Yale's rate of increase (116 percent). The figures include the total number of National Merit Scholars on campus — that is, of all the undergraduates. By 1968, the year before Yale admitted women and hence was stable in the size of its student body, three of the four classes

had been admitted while Clark was dean of admissions. Statistics from the National Merit Scholarship Corporation, "Annual Reports," 1963, 1968.

110. According to Kabaservice, a feature of Clark's policies that was particularly galling to the prep schools was that Yale was often taking boys not recommended by the headmasters — "often the bright, single-minded 'abrasive' boys the College faculty preferred" ("Kingman Brewster," 329).

111. Kingman Brewster Jr., "Admission to Yale: Objectives and Myths," *YAM*, October 1966, 32–33.

112. Lindblom, "Impressions of Yale Admissions Policies," 1.

113. Lux et Veritas, "A Report on Yale Admissions 1950–1972," 10.

114. Gordon, "'Inky's' Era," 34.

115. Even at the end of the Howe era, in 1963, the number of young men from families listed in the *New York Social Register* (a standard indicator of upper-class membership) attending college at Yale dwarfed that of any other institution of higher learning: 173, compared to 123 at Harvard and 76 at Princeton. While no comparable data are available on the late 1960s, a number of trends — the sharp decline in legacies, the drastic drop in boys from the top boarding schools, and the sheer volume of irate alumni letters from Wall Street — strongly suggest that Inky Clark's Yale was no longer the top destination for the scions of New York's social elite (Gene Hawes, "The College of America's Upper Class," *Saturday Review*, 16 November 1963, 70).

116. Clark, "Admission to Yale," 37.

117. Gordon, "'Inky's' Era," 34.

118. Admission and Scholarship Committee, "Report on the Committee on Admissions and Scholarships," 1968–1969, HU, 2, 22. Calculated from Office of Undergraduate Admissions, "Report of the Dean of Admissions and Student Appointment to the President and Fellows of Yale University," 1968–1969, and Carlson, memorandum.

119. Data on Harvard supplied by its Office of Admissions; data on Yale from the *Old Campus: Class of 1972.*

120. Prescott, *World of Our Own*, 200.

121. Clark, interview, 9 April 1993, 57–58.

122. Pierson, *Yale Book of Numbers*, 102; Admission and Scholarship Committee, "Report on the Committee on Admissions and Scholarships," 1967–1968, HU, 97.

123. See the data in Office of Institutional Research, "Athletes and Non-Athletes in the Yale Class of 1958, 1962, 1967, and 1971," 8 August 1973, YUA; Arthur Howe Jr. to Andrew Robinson, December 1959.

124. Clark, interview, 9 April 1993, 17–18.

125. Doermann to Glimp, memorandum, "Diversity in the Class of 1969," 13 January 1966, HUA.

126. Lemann, who interviewed Tobin, described his views: "To Tobin the question of Yale admissions was a simple one. The world's great universities admitted students on the basis of their academic promise. That was what Yale should do" (*Big Test*, 146).

127. Gordon, "'Inky's' Era," 34. Of the 1,021 students who entered Yale in 1966, 42 percent held scholarships, but an additional 9 percent received other forms of financial assistance, mainly loans and jobs. See also "Report of the Director of the Financial Aids Office," 1966–1967.

128. Doermann, "Market for College Education in the United States"; Doermann, *Crosscurrents in Col-*

lege Admissions (New York: Teachers College Press, 1968), 48–49.

129. J. Richardson Dilworth (St. Mark's '34, Yale '38), the head of the Corporation's Ad Hoc Committee on Admissions and its Committee on Educational Policy, believed that "Clark was not only a menace but a real complication in terms of his subsequent efforts at fundraising — not so much because of what Clark was trying to do, but rather the arrogance and his way of doing it." He recalled that "I was so upset by the Inky problem that I arranged to go to an actual Admissions Office meeting so I understood what in the world was going on" (interview by Geoffrey Kabaservice, 26 March 1991, transcript, YUA, 17).

130. Brewster, "Admission to Yale," 33.

131. Admissions Policy Advisory Board, "Preliminary Report," 6–8. While reluctantly acknowledging that extracurricular activities might tell the Admissions Committee something about a candidate's "qualities of mind and character," the advisory board sternly reminded Brewster and Clark that "the central business of the university is the mutual pursuit of knowledge by students and teachers" and "not to produce newspapers, singing groups, or athletic teams."

132. The board, while acknowledging the need for some "subjective judgment," generally stressed the importance of objective indicators of academic achievement. "Experience shows," it wrote, "that the 'predicted scores' based upon them contain useful information. Certainly a candidate should not be scorned because he has an A grade record and 700–800 scores." Elsewhere in the same memorandum, the board mounted a further defense of objective measures of academic qualifications, reporting that it knew of no evidence that young men showing high intellectual achievement and promise are less likely to turn out to be socially responsible citizens and creative leaders in college and afterward than young men displaying less evidence of intellectual power. Indeed what evidence there is suggests that the correlation is the other way — the better the grades and test scores, the more likely the leadership contribution" (ibid., 7–8).

133. Gordon, "'Inky's' Era," 35.

134. Admissions Policy Advisory Board, "Second Report," 9.

135. "Report to Alumni," 4. Data for the class that entered in 1971 (one year after Clark's departure) reveal a 100-point gap in combined math and verbal SATs (1270 vs. 1370) between matriculants who were athletes and those who were not (Office of Institutional Research, "Athletes and Non-Athletes," YUA).

136. Admissions Policy Advisory Board, "Second Report," 3.

137. Lindblom, "Impressions of Yale Admissions Policies," 1–2.

138. The same Admissions Committee, Lindblom reported, did not see a similar problem with an applicant who had an equally "lopsided" commitment to swimming that took him away from his family to relatives in Southern California so that he could swim all the time. Later in the same interview, Lindblom recalled that "it was disillusioning to find at one of the world's great universities such an odd hostility toward a premature intellectual. It reminded [me] of the history of the Thirties when we used to talk about 'premature anti-fascists'" (interview by Geoffrey Kabaservice, 3 June 1991, transcript, YUA, 14–16).

139. Ibid., 15.

140. Pierson, *Yale Book of Numbers*, 614.

141. Admission and Scholarship Committee, "Final Report of W. J. Bender," 29, 35.

142. Pierson, *Yale Book of Numbers*, 611, 614.

143. Office of Admissions and Freshman Scholarships, "Report to the President and Fellows of Yale University," 1953–1954; "Annual Report of the Dean of Freshmen," 1955–1956, 14.

144. Bureau of the Census, *Historical Statistics of the United States: Colonial Time to 1970*, part 1 (Washington, D.C.: Government Printing Office, 1989), 379.

145. Office of Admissions and Freshman Scholarships and the Office of Enrollment and Scholarships, "Annual Report of Dean of Admissions and Student Appointments," 1964–1965.

146. Hugh D. Graham, *The Civil Rights Era: Origins and Development of National Policy 1960–1972* (New York: Oxford U.P., 1992), 173–74; John D. Skrentny, *The Ironies of Affirmative Action* (Chicago: U. of Chicago Press, 1996), 72.

147. Gitlin, *The Sixties*, 183.

148. Kingman Brewster Jr., "Speech in Philadelphia," 15 January 1965, YUA, 27.

149. Brewster to Muyskens, YUA, 1.

150. Clark, interview, 13 May 1993, 11–12; Brewster, "Admission to Yale," 31; Brewster to Muyskens, 1.

151. Kabaservice, "Kingman Brewster," 335.

152. As early as the spring of 1962, Daniel Bell — the person with whom the idea of the "post-industrial society" is most closely associated — presented a paper in Boston entitled "The Post-Industrial Society: A Speculative View of the United States in 1985 and Beyond." Bell then presented a version of this paper to the Seminar on Technology and Social Change at Columbia University the following winter. The paper began by boldly stating, "The post-industrial society is a society in which business is no longer the predominant element but one in which the intellectual is predominant" (Bell, "The Post-Industrial Society," in *Technology and Social Change*, ed. Eli Ginzberg (New York: Columbia U.P., 1964), 44. For Bell's account of the history of the idea of "post-industrial society," see Bell, *The Coming of Post-Industrial Society* (New York: Basic Books, 1999), 33–40; for a discussion of the idea's reception and impact, see the foreword to the same edition, ix–lxxxv, as well as the foreword to the 1976 edition, lxxxvii–c.

153. Kingman Brewster Jr., "Speech at the 100th Anniversary Dinner of the Cincinnati Yale Club," 8 February 1964, YUA, 7. Another factor pushing Yale and other elite private colleges toward a greater emphasis on "academic excellence" was the growing prominence in the 1950s and 1960s of elite professional and graduate schools as pathways to elite status. This change fundamentally transformed the character of the elite college, where by the mid-1960s perhaps three-quarters of students went on to a graduate or professional school after completing their B.A. degrees. Christopher Jencks and David Riesman captured this change when they wrote that an institution such as Yale College had become "a de facto prep school for a small number of graduate professional schools, in much the same way that Groton, Andover, and Farmington are prep schools for the Ivy League and Seven Sister colleges" (*The Academic Revolution* [New York: Doubleday, 1969], 24).

154. Kingman Brewster Jr., "Educational Goals Appropriate for Balance of Century," 11–12 March 1966, YUA, 1.

155. Brewster, "Admission to Yale," 31.

156. Oren, *Joining the Club*, 272. In a different version of the same incident, the Corporation member was a banker who "swept his hand to take in such figures as John Lindsay, mayor of New York, and William Scranton, Governor of Pennsylvania, both liberal Republican, Episcopalian boarding school graduates, either of whom at that point might possibly be the next President of the United States" (Lemann, *Big Test*, 150).

157. Wilbur J. Bender, "Some Observations and Questions About Admission Policy or Will I Want My Son to Go to Harvard in 1970?" 1960, HUA, 13–14. For a fuller account of Bender's views, see Chapter 9.

158. For a slightly different use of the metaphor of Brewster as an "investment banker," see Kabaservice, "Kingman Brewster," 337. To protect its institutional interests, Yale needed an admissions policy that predicted reasonably well, under conditions of rapid social change, which kinds of applicants *would* be most likely to be members of the elite thirty or forty years hence. But as an institution that prided itself on *shaping* the nation as well as responding to it, Yale also wished to have a say in determining who *should* lead the nation — that is, in identifying the kinds of qualities, both personal and demographic, that the next generation of leaders should possess. To a considerable degree, the shift in admissions policy under Brewster and Clark may be seen as a conscious attempt to grapple with both of these issues.

159. Brewster to Herbert Sturdy, 11 August 1966, YUA. The same theme, using some of the same language, is developed in Brewster, "Admission to Yale," 32.

160. Brewster to Spruille Braden, 19 June 1967, YUA.

161. James B. Conant, "Education for a Classless Society: The Jeffersonian Tradition," *Atlantic Monthly*, May 1940, 599; Conant to Thomas W. Lamont, 26 July 1943, YUA, 8–9, 13. See Chapter 5 for a fuller account of Conant's writings on education and their relationship to his larger vision of American society.

162. Clark, interview, 9 April 1993, 73.

163. For a similar interpretation, which focuses on the comparison between Brewster and Franklin D. Roosevelt, see Kabaservice, *The Guardians*, 289.

164. Clark, interview, 13 May 1993, 26.

13. Racial Conflict and the Incorporation of Blacks

1. Todd Gitlin, *The Sixties: Years of Hope, Days of Rage* (New York: Bantam, 1987), 81–82.

2. The Greensboro protest, which involved both a lunch counter sit-in and outside picketing, lasted six months and ultimately forced Woolworth's (which lost $200,000 in business) to accept the protestors' demands (Stephan Thernstrom and Abigail Thernstrom, *America in Black and White* [New York: Simon & Schuster, 1997], 119).

3. Douglas McAdam, *Political Process and the Development of Black Insurgency, 1930–1970* (Chicago: Univ. of Chicago Press, 1982), 138–40.

4. Philip A. Klinkner and Rogers M. Smith, *The Unsteady March* (Chicago: Univ. of Chicago Press, 1999), 242–43.

5. The boycott actually ended on November 13, 1956, when the U.S. Supreme Court ruled that the Montgomery ordinances on seating on buses violated

the Fourteenth Amendment. The Court declared that the old discriminatory rules had to be eliminated by December 20, and on December 21, 1956 — 381 days after the boycott had begun — Martin Luther King Jr. sat down in the front of a bus (James T. Patterson, *Grand Expectations: The United States, 1945–1974* [New York: Oxford U.P., 1996], 405).

6. Klinkner and Smith, *Unsteady March,* 247–49. Other works that emphasize the problems that racial injustice posed to the interests of the United States in the Cold War include Mary L. Dudziak, *Cold War Civil Rights* (Princeton, N.J.: Princeton U.P., 2000); Thomas Borstelmann, *The Cold War and the Color Line* (Cambridge, Mass.: Harvard U.P., 2001); and John D. Skrentny, "The Effects of the Cold War on African-American Civil Rights: America and the World Audience, 1945–1968," *Theory and Society* 27, 1998.

7. Klinkner and Smith, *Unsteady March,* 242–53.

8. According to Charles Puttkammer, approximately 165 African Americans had matriculated at Harvard College by 1941. He estimates that 37 black students entered between 1939 and 1949, with 34 of them graduating. Between 1950 and 1957, roughly 84 blacks (including foreigners) entered, of whom 67 graduated ("Negroes in the Ivy League," 1962, ERIC, ED150924, 13–17). At Yale, between 1874 and 1923 approximately 30 blacks received undergraduate degrees. The interwar period was generally one of decline in black enrollment, with just 7 African Americans graduating between 1924 and the end of World War II (Geoffrey Kabaservice, "Kingman Brewster and the Rise and Fall of the Protestant Establishment" [Ph.D. diss, Yale Univ., 1999], 351). Puttkammer estimates that roughly 15 blacks graduated from Yale between 1955 and 1961 ("Negroes in the Ivy League," 34).

9. The estimate that 9 black students entered Harvard in 1960 does not include foreign-born black students. According to a personal communication from Caldwell Titcomb, co-editor of *Blacks at Harvard* (New York: New York U.P., 1993), roughly 15 black students, both foreign and domestic, entered Harvard in 1960. If this estimate is correct, then excluding the 6 freshmen from nations in the Caribbean and Africa with predominantly black populations would leave 9 African Americans.

10. Kabaservice, "Kingman Brewster," 694–95. In addition to the 5 African Americans who entered Yale in 1960, 5 foreign black students matriculated — 3 from Nigeria, 1 from Sierra Leone, and 1 from Trinidad.

11. Commission on the Future of the College, *The Report of the Commission on the Future of the College* (Princeton, N.J.: Trustees of Princeton Univ., 1973), Table 2.8.

12. Yale's figure is calculated from Kabaservice, "Kingman Brewster," 83; Princeton's figure is from Commission on the Future of the College, *The Report of the Commission on the Future of the College,* Table 2.8; Harvard's figure is estimated from Committee on Race Relations, "A Study of Race Relations at Harvard College," May 1980, HUA, figure 4.

13. Arthur Howe Jr. to Connelly Edwards, 30 March 1960, YUA.

14. According to Nellie Elliot, who had worked in Yale's Admissions Office for more than four decades, few African Americans had failed out in recent years because "it would be so much worse for a Negro to fail" and, consequently, the committee had taken spe-

cial care in assessing black applicants to pick the "right boy" (Puttkammer, "Negroes in the Ivy League," 17).

15. Katherine T. Kinkead, "The Brightest Ever," *New Yorker,* 10 September 1960. Some of the details cited here are not included in the book version of the article.

16. For an account that stresses the limits of Kennedy's commitment to civil rights, see Kenneth O'Reilly, *Nixon's Piano: Presidents and Racial Politics from Washington to Clinton* (New York: Free Press, 1995), 189–237.

17. Thernstrom and Thernstrom, *America in Black and White,* 97, 125–27.

18. Biographical information on McCarthy from the *Yale Banner: Class of 1960.*

19. Kabaservice, "Kingman Brewster," 363–64. While remaining a part-time admissions officer at Yale, McCarthy became the first head of the Cooperative Program for Educational Opportunity.

20. The Seven Sister colleges were Smith, Wellesley, Mount Holyoke, Bryn Mawr, Radcliffe, Vassar, and Pembroke. The last three are now coeducational.

21. In addition to the 6 African Americans who entered Yale in 1962, there were 4 foreign black students, 1 each from Haiti, Jamaica, Nigeria, and Trinidad (Kabaservice, "Kingman Brewster," 695).

22. James B. Conant, *Slums and Suburbs* (New York: McGraw-Hill, 1961), 2.

23. Patterson, *Grand Expectations,* 478.

24. Ibid, 362.

25. James Baldwin, *The Fire Next Time* (New York: Dial Press, 1963). See also the reviews by Sheldon Binn in the *New York Times Book Review,* 31 January 1963, and by F. W. Dupee in the *New York Times Book Review,* 1 February 1963.

26. The influential *National Review* (edited by William F. Buckley Jr. '50), for example, was a consistently harsh critic of King and staunchly opposed the Civil Rights Bill of 1964.

27. Brewster to Brady, 25 June 1964, YUA.

28. *WWA, 1978–1979.*

29. J. Irwin Miller to John McKay, 2 October 1964, YUA.

30. Humphrey Doermann, "The Market for College Education in the United States" (Ph.D. diss., Harvard Univ., 1967), 60. See also Doermann, *Crosscurrents in College Admissions* (New York: Teachers College Press, 1968). Doermann's estimate was consistent with that of the Coleman Report, *Equality of Educational Opportunity,* which estimated that only 1 or 2 percent of black high school students would score 500 or more on the verbal section of the SAT (cited in Kabaservice, "Kingman Brewster," 362).

31. George W. Pierson, ed., *A Yale Book of Numbers: Historical Statistics of the College and University, 1701–1976* (New Haven, Conn.: Yale U.P., 1983), 102.

32. Doermann, "Market for College Education," 60.

33. In addition to the Cooperative Program for Educational Opportunity, Yale sponsored the Yale Summer High School Program for disadvantaged youth, both black and white, to help them meet its academic standards. It also actively cooperated with the program A Better Chance (ABC), founded in 1963 by 16 independent secondary schools, with the assistance of Dartmouth College and private foundations, to provide educational opportunity for promising minority

students. Through 1972, Yale was the seventh most popular college among ABC graduates, with 26; Harvard was first, with 54 graduates, and Princeton failed to make the list of the top 15 institutions. See Richard L. Zweigenhaft and G. William Domhoff, *Blacks in the White Establishment* (New Haven, Conn.: Yale U.P., 1991), 2–3, 72; Kabaservice, "Kingman Brewster," 364–65, 384–85.

34. Kabaservice, "Kingman Brewster," 696–97.

35. "Minutes of the Committee on Admissions and Freshmen Scholarships," 26 October 1964, YUA, 2.

36. "Minutes of the Committee on Admissions and Freshmen Scholarships," 16 October 1964.

37. John D. Skrentny, *The Ironies of Affirmative Action* (Chicago: Univ. of Chicago Press, 1996), 72; Thernstrom and Thernstrom, *America in Black and White*, 158–59.

38. In 1965, there were 23 racial disturbances in 20 cities, including Los Angeles (McAdam, *Political Process*, 222).

39. Charles E. Lindblom to James Tobin, memorandum, "Impressions of Yale Admissions Policies After Serving on the Admissions Committee — Spring 1966," 30 March 1966, YU, 3.

40. In his letter on the university's policy in admissions, Brewster wrote: "I do think that where social and economic and racial circumstance has made the testable strengths difficult to assess fairly, it is desirable to go as far as possible to uncover other evidence which might bear witness to special potentialities" (Brewster to John Muyskens Jr., 15 March 1967, YUA).

41. Admissions Policy Advisory Board, "Second Report," 31 October 1966, YU, 12–13.

42. Office of Admissions and Freshman Scholarships, "Report of the Dean of Admissions and Student Appointment to the President and Fellows of Yale University," 1965–1966, YU, 2. See also Clark, interview, 9 April 1993.

43. Financial Aids Office, "Report of the Director of the Financial Aids Office," 1965–1966, YUA.

44. Kabaservice, "Kingman Brewster," 384–85.

45. Coombes, "Making It at Yale," 52. The total number of freshmen entering Yale from 1909 through 1975 is in Pierson, *Yale Book of Numbers*, 94–99.

46. McAdam, *Political Process*, 222.

47. Ibid., 225. For a detailed account of the background to the Newark riot and of the riot itself, see National Advisory Commission on Civil Disorders, *The Kerner Report* (New York: Pantheon, 1988), 56–69.

48. William Lichten to Kingman Brewster Jr., 18 July 1967, YUA.

49. Thernstrom and Thernstrom, *America in Black and White*, 160. For a detailed account of the Detroit riot, see National Advisory Commission on Civil Disorders, *Kerner Report*, 84–108.

50. Cited in Klinkner and Smith, *Unsteady March*, 281.

51. Patterson, *Grand Expectations*, 656–57.

52. Among the most provocative of the young black militant leaders was H. ("Rap") Brown, who succeeded Stokely Carmichael as head of SNCC in May 1967. Brown referred to white people as "honkies" and police as "pigs." "Violence," Brown was fond of saying, was "as American as apple pie." And in one of his most famous speeches, delivered from the top of a car in racially tense Cambridge, Maryland, Brown proclaimed, "Black folks built America, and if America don't come around, we're going to burn it down."

Within hours a fire erupted, and when the firemen (who claimed they were afraid of snipers) were slow to respond, the heart of Cambridge's black neighborhood burned (ibid., 622).

53. For an illuminating discussion of the rise of the ideology of "black power," see Michael Omi and Howard Winant, *Racial Formation in the United States* (New York: Routledge, 1994), 101–4. The classic study of SNCC is Claiborne Carson, *In Struggle: SNCC and the Black Awakening of the 1960s* (Cambridge, Mass.: Harvard U.P., 1961). On the Black Panthers, see Hugh Pearson, *The Shadow of the Panther: Huey Newton and the Rise of Black Power in America* (Reading, Mass.: Addison-Wesley, 1994).

54. For one contemporary example of such thinking, see Gary Wills, *The Second Civil War: Arming for Armageddon* (New York: New American Library, 1968).

55. Kerner, Brown '30 attended Trinity College of Cambridge University before obtaining a J.D. from Northwestern in 1934. A trustee of Brown, he began his first term as governor of Illinois in 1961 (*WWA, 1962–1963*).

56. National Advisory Commission on Civil Disorders, *Kerner Report*, 23.

57. Skrentny, *Ironies of Affirmative Action*, 99–100.

58. National Advisory Commission on Civil Disorders, *Kerner Report*, 1.

59. Ibid., 2.

60. Ibid., 10.

61. Ibid., 205.

62. Ibid., 7.

63. Ibid., 204.

64. Ibid., 1.

65. Ibid., 25–26.

66. The meetings of the Admissions Committee began on March 4, 1968 (one day after the release of the full text of the Kerner Report), and continued through the early part of April (Office of Undergraduate Admissions, "Report of the Dean of Admissions and Student Appointment to the President and Fellows of Yale University," 1967–1968, YU, 6).

67. John Hay Whitney (1905–1982) — diplomat, sportsman, philanthropist, and one of Yale's greatest benefactors — was the inheritor of a large fortune and the grandson (on both sides) of men who had been Cabinet members. The son of Payne Whitney (Groton '94, Yale '98, and Harvard Law School '01), a banker and president of the Great Northern Railroad, he graduated from Groton in 1922. At Yale, he was a member of Scroll and Key and earned a "Y" as a member of the University Crew Squad. After a year at Oxford, Whitney returned home when his father died in 1927. An outstanding horseman and polo player, he was elected to the Jockey Club in 1928 — the youngest member ever. Whitney had a number of successful careers, serving variously as chairman of the board of Selznick International Pictures (which produced *Gone With the Wind* and *A Star Is Born*), ambassador to Great Britain during the Eisenhower administration, and publisher of the *New York Herald Tribune*. During World War II, he served as an air force colonel, was taken prisoner by the Germans in southern France, and managed to escape when his train came under Allied fire. He served as a member of the Yale Corporation from 1955 to 1973, contributing many major gifts, including the Payne Whitney Gymnasium, a memorial to his father. A descendant of John

Whitney, who settled in Massachusetts in 1635, Mr. Whitney was, according to his obituary, "so secure that he never allowed his name to be listed in the *Social Register,* which he called a travesty of democracy with absurd notions of who is and isn't socially acceptable." See "John Hay Whitney," *Philadelphia Inquirer,* 9 February 1982; Judith A. Schiff, "John Hay Whitney: Philanthropist, Film Producer, and the Father of the Crew Cut," *YAM,* April 2002; *Yale Banner: Class of 1926,* YU, 314–15; and *WWA, 1962–1963.* E. J. Kahn of *The New Yorker* has written a colorful account of Whitney in *Jock: The Life and Times of John Hay Whitney* (Garden City, N.Y.: Doubleday, 1981).

68. "How Black Studies Happened," *YAM,* October 1968, 23–24.

69. Ibid., 23.

70. Ibid.

71. Office of Undergraduate Admissions, "Report of the Dean of Admissions and Student Appointment to the President and Fellows of Yale University," 1967–1968, YU, 5.

72. Coombs, "Making It at Yale," 52. For the 15 colleges that made up the Ivy League and the Seven Sisters, the number of blacks admitted more than doubled between 1967 and 1968 — a remarkable increase for a single year and even higher than the rate of increase at Yale, which had mounted a vigorous effort to recruit African Americans earlier than most of its sister institutions. See "How Black Studies Happened," 1, and Fred M. Hechinger, "More Negroes Accepted by Ivy League Colleges," *NYT,* 14 April 1968.

73. Klinkner and Smith, *Unsteady March,* 281–82. An indicator of the truly national scope of the April 1968 riots is the fact that racial disorders were reported in 36 of the 50 states (McAdam, *Political Process,* 227).

74. Klinkner and Smith, *Unsteady March,* 282.

75. "'Take Everything You Need, Baby,'" *Newsweek,* 15 April 1968, 31.

76. In the end, it took 14,000 federal troops to restore order in Washington. Though shaken by the riots, President Johnson apparently did not lose his sense of humor. According to an anecdote by Joseph Califano, "When told of a rumor that black militant Stokely Carmichael was organizing blacks to march on Georgetown, home of Washington's elite, Johnson responded, 'God-damn! I've waited thirty-five years for this day!'" (quoted in Klinkner and Smith, *Unsteady March,* 282).

77. "Mobs Run Wild in the Nation's Capital," *U.S. News and World Report,* 15 April 1968, 10. See also in the same issue, "More Violence and Race War? Effects of Dr. King Tragedy," 31–34.

78. "'Take Everything You Need, Baby,'" 32.

79. Klinkner and Smith, *Unsteady March,* 282.

80. Among the many student revolts influenced by the events at Columbia was the famous May uprising in France, which began within days of the police bust that ended the Columbia occupation. For illuminating accounts of the "May events" — which, unlike the events at Columbia, came close to toppling the government and seemed pregnant with revolutionary potential — see David Caute, *The Year of the Barricades: A Journey Through 1968* (New York: Harper & Row, 1988), 209–55; and Ronald Fraser, *1968* (New York: Pantheon, 1988), 203–30. The inspiration for "two, three, many Columbias" was Che Guevara's famous appeal for "two, three, many Vietnams."

81. Caute, *Year of the Barricades,* 167. Other useful accounts of the Columbia protest include Kirkpatrick Sale, *SDS* (New York: Vintage, 1974), 430–51, and Fraser, *1968,* 195–200. The most detailed treatment is the volume (written by members of the *Columbia Spectator*) by Jerry L. Avorn et al., *University in Revolt: A History of the Columbia Crisis* (New York: Atheneum, 1970).

82. The phrase is from Gitlin, *The Sixties,* 306.

83. Fraser, *1968,* 197–99.

84. Ibid., 199.

85. Caute, *Year of the Barricades,* 195; Sale, *SDS,* 438.

86. In the weeks after the Columbia events, major demonstrations took place on at least 40 campuses. One study concluded, "College student unrest has escalated to the point where perhaps most officials responsible for the higher learning in America would now consider it their number one problem" (quoted in Sale, *SDS,* 445).

87. Geoffrey Kabaservice, *The Guardians: Kingman Brewster, His Circle, and the Rise of the Liberal Establishment* (New York: Henry Holt, 2004), 330.

88. Jeffrey Gordon, "'Inky's' Era," *YAM,* March 1970, 35.

89. Ibid.

90. Ibid.

91. Coombes, "Making It at Yale," 52; Pierson, *Yale Book of Numbers,* 99.

92. Kabaservice, "Kingman Brewster," 403.

93. Ibid., 391.

94. Kabaservice also points to Yale's admissions policy as a source of estrangement for many Old Blues, but he may exaggerate when he writes, "Race was perhaps the most important underlying factor distancing Yale's alumni from their *alma mater*" ("Kingman Brewster," 395). More important, in my view, was the radical reduction in preferences for alumni sons and graduates of private schools — policies that, judging from letters received by Brewster, had enraged many Old Blues in Clark's first year in office. Affirmative action for blacks was, to be sure, an issue, but it was pursued most vigorously *after* the alumni had become estranged and did far less direct damage to alumni interests than the decline in preference for legacies and prep school boys as well as Yale's alleged emphasis on "brains" over "character," see "Report to Alumni on Alumni Board's Study of Admissions" (Cook Report), October 1967, YUA.

95. "Admissions Down for Ivy League," *NYT,* 15 April 1966.

96. Office of Undergraduate Admissions, "Report of the Dean of Undergraduate Admissions to the President and Fellows of Yale University," 1969–1970, YU, 2.

97. In 1969–1970, for the first time, Yale paid for student recruiting trips by MECHA (Mexican-American students) and Asian-American students in addition to trips by the BSAY (Office of Undergraduate Admissions, "Report of the Dean of Undergraduate Admissions to the President and Fellows of Yale University," 1969–1970, YU, 6).

98. Don T. Nakanishi '71, recruitment chairman of the Asian American Students Association, to George Kehm of the Undergraduate Admissions Committee, 25 January 1970, YUA. For an illuminating account of Nakinishi's efforts to construct a Pan-Asian identity among students more likely to think of themselves as Japanese- or Chinese-American, see "The Invention

of the Asian-American" in Nicholas Lemann, *The Big Test: The Secret History of the American Meritocracy* (New York: Farrar, Straus, 1999), 174–85.

99. In 1971, Yale for the first time reported separate figures for Asian Americans, Mexican Americans, and Puerto Ricans in addition to those for blacks. See "Statistics — Class of 1975 — July 1 Release" in Office of Undergraduate Admissions, "Report of the Dean of Undergraduate Admissions to the President and Fellows of Yale University," 1970–1971, YU.

100. Writing in 1962, Charles Puttkammer, Princeton '58, claimed that "Princeton's long tradition as an exclusively white college is, even today, the outstanding reason why she does not attract a reasonable proportion of the best colored students" ("Negroes in the Ivy League," 27).

101. In 1961, when Princeton enrolled just 1 African-American freshman, 3 Nigerian students were enrolled under the auspices of the African-American Institute. From 1957 through 1960, a total of 6 American blacks enrolled at Princeton (George E. Tomberlin Jr., "Trends in Princeton Admissions" [Senior thesis, Princeton Univ., 1971], 137, 141).

102. William A. McWhirter, "On the Campus," *PAW,* 26 January 1962, 14.

103. Ibid.

104. Ibid.

105. According to Charles Puttkammer, who had firsthand knowledge of Princeton's policies, President Goheen "simply is not much interested in racial questions and would like to see Princeton avoid them whenever possible" ("Negroes in the Ivy League," 30.

106. McWhirter, "On the Campus," 14.

107. As originally planned, the March on Washington was to have been more militant, including a protracted sit-in at the Capitol until a satisfactory civil rights law was enacted by Congress. But President Kennedy was alarmed by the plan and succeeded in convincing Martin Luther King Jr., Whitney Young (Urban League), and Roy Wilkins (NAACP) to limit the events to one day and to tone down some of the speeches, including a fiery one that SNCC's leader, John Lewis (now a Democratic congressman from Georgia) intended to deliver. The crowd that finally gathered on August 28, 1963, was estimated at 250,000, including perhaps 50,000 whites. The March on Washington was, of course, the scene of King's historic "I Have a Dream" speech. What is less well known is that King also told the marchers that "those who hope that the Negro needed to blow off steam and will now be content will have a rude awakening if the nation returns to business as usual." A month later, after the Birmingham bombing, King warned, "Unless some immediate steps are taken by the U.S. Government to restore a sense of confidence in the protection of life, limb, and property, my pleas [for nonviolence] will fall on deaf ears and we shall see in Birmingham and Alabama the worst racial holocaust the nation has ever seen" (Klinkner and Smith, *Unsteady March,* 271–72).

108. "New Enrollment Grows for Princeton University," *Princeton Packet,* 9 September 1964.

109. "Ivy Colleges Encourage Negro Applicants," *DP,* 14 November 1963.

110. See Chapter 10 for a profile of Dunham.

111. Office of Admission, "Report to the Faculty," 1962–1963, PU, 18.

112. Conant referred to Dunham as "my right hand man in my educational inquiries" and credited him

for the phrase "social dynamite," which quickly became part of the national discussion about race after the publication of *Slums and Suburbs* in 1961 (see Conant, *My Several Lives,* 621–22).

113. Office of Admission, "Report to the Faculty," 1962–1963, PU, 17.

114. Paul Sigmund, "Princeton in Crisis and Change," in *Academic Transformation,* ed. David Riesman and Verne A. Stadtman (New York: McGraw-Hill, 1974), 251.

115. John Armstrong, "Group Promotes Segregation," *DP,* 13 March, 1964.

116. Fields, who served as assistant director of the Bureau of Student Aid at Princeton from 1964 to 1968 and as assistant dean of the college from 1968 to 1971, wrote several articles about his experiences, including Carl A. Fields, "One University's Response to Today's Negro Student," *University: A Princeton Quarterly,* Spring 1968, 14–19; Fields, "The Black Arrival at Princeton," *PAW,* 18 April 1977, 11–19; and Fields, "A Time of Adjustment," *PAW,* 25 April 1977, 15–20.

117. E. Alden Dunham, "A Look at Princeton Admissions," *PAW,* 19 January 1965.

118. Office of Admission, "Report to the President," 1964–1965, PU, 4.

119. Office of Admission, "Report to Faculty," 1965–1966, PU, 5. By 1967, even James B. Conant, archmeritocrat and one of the earliest and strongest supporters of the SAT, was calling for less reliance on standardized tests in college admission and greater emphasis on school records. In the years leading up to Conant's statement, noted the *New York Times,* "there has been much criticism of the college admission tests by those who believe they were geared to the middle and upper classes and are unfair to those with few cultural advantages" (see Gene Currivan, "Conant Criticizes Entrance Exams," *NYT,* 13 November 1967).

120. Of the 31 black students who entered Princeton between 1963 and 1966 for whom data are available, roughly two-thirds may be judged working class and one-third middle class, as determined by parental occupation, education, and income. Data from Office of Admission, "Survey of Secondary School and College Performance of Negroes Admitted to Princeton 1963–1967," December 1967, in "Minutes of Meetings of the Admissions Committee," n.d. [c. December 1967], PUA. According to an American Council on Education survey of freshmen entering Princeton in 1966, just 7.1 percent had fathers who were workers (skilled, semiskilled, or unskilled) and over 70 percent had fathers who were either businessmen (46.4 percent), lawyers (8), doctors or dentists (8.9), engineers (7.9), or college teachers (2.2) (American Council on Education Office of Research, "Summary of Data on Entering Freshmen, Princeton University," fall 1966).

121. Office of Admission, "Survey of Secondary School and College Performance of Negroes Admitted to Princeton 1963–1967," PU; Office of Admission, "Report to the President," 1966–1967, PU.

122. Office of Admission, "Report to the Faculty," 1965–1966, PU, 15.

123. Dunham, "Look at Princeton Admissions."

124. Office of Admission, "Report to the President," 1966–1967, PU, Chart B.

125. Landon Y. Jones '66, "On the Campus," *PAW,* 1 February 1966, 6. In 1966 and even more in 1967, the eating clubs found themselves subject to growing criticism, culminating in a September 1967 trustees' special report calling for "the creation of a variety of at-

tractive alternatives" so that no undergraduates "feel a compulsion to seek membership in private clubs because other social and dining facilities are undesirable." By the winter of 1967, the proportion of sophomores registered for bicker had dropped to about 70 percent, down from over 90 percent just a year earlier. Overall club membership, which had been 1,397 in 1965, dropped to a low of 838 in 1971 despite the expansion, beginning in 1969, of undergraduate enrollment due to coeducation. The breaking of the quasi-monopoly that eating clubs had held over student life rendered Princeton a far more hospitable environment to prospective black students than had been the case just a few years earlier and hence facilitated the massive increase in minority enrollment that began in 1968. On the history of the eating clubs in this period, see Carol P. Herring to William G. Bowen, memorandum, 27 July 1978, PUA, 10–13, and William K. Selden, *Club Life at Princeton: An Historical Account of the Eating Clubs at Princeton University* (Princeton, N.J.: Princeton Prospect Foundation, 1994), 42–60.

126. Fields, "One University's Response," 17–18; Fields, "Black Arrival at Princeton," 16–18.

127. Tomberlin, "Trends in Princeton Admissions," 145. The figures on the number of admits is from Table 2.8 in Commission on the Future of the College, *Report of the Commission.*

128. On the Newark riot, see Governor's Select Commission on Civil Disorder, State of New Jersey, "Report for Action," February 1968, 103–144; National Advisory Commission on Civil Disorders, *Kerner Report,* 56–69.

129. Office of Admission, "Report to Schools," 1967, 4.

130. Don Oberdorfer, *Princeton University: The First 250 Years* (Princeton, N.J.: Trustees of Princeton Univ., 1995), 199–200.

131. Office of Admission, "Report to the Faculty," 1967–1968, PU, 7–22; Tomberlin, "Trends in Princeton Admissions," 146; Commission on the Future of the College, *Report of the Commission,* Table 28.

132. Office of Admission, "Report to Schools," 1968, PU, 1.

133. John Thomas Osander, a graduate of Washburn High School in Minneapolis, was Princeton's first director of admission to have attended a public high school. At Princeton, where he was a member of the Tower Club and served as vice president and a member of its Bicker Committee, he was best known as president of the Triangle Club (the drama club). An athlete in high school, where he was captain of the golf team, he served on the *DP* in college, winning its outstanding achievement award for 1956–1957. An English major, his senior thesis was "The Religious Theme in the Novels of William Faulkner." When he became Princeton's director of admission in 1966, after serving as assistant director (1963–1964) and associate director (1964–1966), he was thirty-one years old. See *Nassau Herald: Class of 1961,* PU, 232, and Department of Public Information, press release, 9 May 1966, PUA.

134. In explaining its decision to adopt vigorous affirmative action programs for blacks, the Office of Admission explained in 1968 that it was "basically a response to two documents published this year": "The Report of the National Advisory Commission on Civil Disorders" [*Kerner Report*] and Governor's Select Commission on Civil Disorder, "Report for Ac-

tion." Office of Admissions, "Report to the Faculty," 1967–1968, PU, 7–10.

135. Ibid., 7, 19.

136. Ibid., 10.

137. Fields, "Time of Adjustment," 17–18; Oberdorfer, *Princeton University,* 205.

138. Fred M. Hechinger, "Ivy League and Big 7 Take Record Number of Nonwhites," *NYT,* 20 April 1969; Office of Admission, "Annual Report," 1968–1969, PU, 14–15.

139. Tomberlin, "Trends in Princeton Admissions," 147–48. Princeton's decision to accept late applicants in 1968–1969 followed a similar decision in 1967–1968. The decision to suspend the normal deadline for African Americans was one of the many signs of the sense of "social emergency" common among elites in the period between 1967 and 1969.

140. Alumni Council of Princeton University, "Answers to your questions about the ADMISSION OF PRINCETON SONS," 1 June 1958, PUA, 3–4. Princeton's policy of admitting all alumni sons who could "be expected to graduate" apparently was in place through 1962, when 68 percent of all legacies were accepted. See "Getting into Princeton Under Dunham," *DP,* 31 October 1964, 6, and Office of Admission, "Report to the President," 1963–1964, PU.

141. Tomberlin, "Trends in Princeton Admissions," 151. Of the 1,640 applicants to Princeton in 1969 rated as an academic 4 or 5, just 12.4 percent were admitted. Blacks, though composing just 5 percent of all applicants, made up 37 percent of all Princeton admits rated as an academic 4 or 5 in 1969. Though no specific figures are provided, the text of the annual report suggests that blacks would have been heavily overrepresented among students deemed "disadvantaged" even under a race-neutral definition. See Office of Admission, "Annual Report," 1968–1969, 11–15, E-7.

142. Ibid., 11–14.

143. Between 1953 and 1955, not a single black undergraduate entered Princeton. During the four ensuing years, a total of 7 black freshmen matriculated (Tomberlin, "Trends in Princeton Admissions," 137).

144. Office of Admission, "Report to the Faculty," 1967–1968, 55.

145. Ibid., 8; Office of Admission, "Annual Report," 1968–1969, PU, 15.

146. Office of Admission, "Report to the President," 1970–1971, 7.

147. Around this time, Princeton's Chinese Americans also began to organize, forming a Chinese club. See Tomberlin, "Trends in Princeton Admissions," 154, and Office of Admission, "Report to the President," 1970–1971, 7.

148. Office of Admission, "Report to the President," 1971–1972, 8–10. The proportion of the freshman class filled by alumni sons in these years ranged from a high of 20.3 percent in 1968 to a low of 15.1 percent in 1970.

149. See Office of Admission, "Report to the Faculty," 1965–1966, 1967–1968, PU; Office of Admission, "Report to the President," 1966–1967; Office of Admission, "Annual Report," 1968–1969, PU; Office of Admission, "Report to the President," 1969–1970, PU; and Commission on the Future of the College, *Report of the Commission,* Table 2.7.

150. Results of a survey of the freshman class that entered Princeton in 1970 by the Office of Research of the American Council on Education.

151. Ibid.; Bureau of the Census, *Historical Statistics of the United States: Colonial Times to 1970,* part 1 (Washington, D.C.: Government Printing Office, 1975), 290.

152. Office of Admission, "Report to the Faculty," 1967–1968, 57; Office of Admission, "Annual Report," 1968–1969, Appendix C, 2; Tomberlin, "Trends in Princeton Admissions," 152–53.

153. Richard T. Greener graduated from Harvard in 1870, having won the top undergraduate prizes in writing and speaking. He later became a professor of philosophy, a foreign diplomat, and a law school dean (Caldwell Titcomb, "The Black Presence at Harvard: An Overview," in *Blacks at Harvard: A Documentary History of African-American Experiences at Harvard and Radcliffe,* ed. Werner Sollors et al. [New York: New York U.P., 1993], 2).

154. Paul Davis, "Fair Harvard," *Harvard Guardian,* June 1941, 29.

155. Of the 97 black students who matriculated between 1939 and 1955, 14 (15 percent) did not receive degrees. In an analysis of the estimated 184 black students who entered Harvard between 1939 and 1961, Charles Puttkammer found that 22 were foreign (16 from Africa and 6 from the Caribbean) and that of the remaining 162, the largest group by far — 40 students — came from the Cambridge-Boston area. Next was the New York vicinity (21), the former Confederate states (21), and Washington, D.C. (15). Of the 175 students for whom secondary school information was available, 128 (73 percent) came from public schools and 47 (27 percent) from private schools ("Negroes in the Ivy League," 16–18).

156. Ibid., 17. A 1948 article from *Ebony* confirms Puttkammer's conclusion that Harvard enjoyed an elevated reputation in the black community. It begins by reporting that "Harvard is the alma mater of more distinguished leaders of Negro America than any other university" ("Harvard Men: Famed University Turns Out Some of Most Distinguished U.S. Negroes," *Ebony,* May 1948, 13–18).

157. See, for example, Nell Painter, "Jim Crow at Harvard: 1923," *New England Quarterly* 44, no. 4 (December 1971): 627–34.

158. David O. Levine, *The American College and the Culture of Aspiration 1915–1940* (Ithaca, N.Y.: Cornell U.P., 1986), 158–60.

159. Puttkammer, "Negroes in the Ivy League," 20.

160. Jennifer D. Carey, "Tradition and Transition: Achieving Diversity at Harvard and Radcliffe" (Ph.D. diss., Harvard Univ., 1995), 21.

161. Puttkammer, "Negroes in the Ivy League," 22. Instrumental in Harvard's early efforts to enroll black students was the work of John U. Monro, director of the Financial Aid Office from 1950 to 1958 and dean of Harvard College from 1958 to 1967. Monro (Andover '30, Harvard '34) left Harvard to take a position at Miles College, a black institution in Alabama (see Carey, "Tradition and Transition," 18–19, and Monro's obituaries in the *New York Times* and other newspapers).

162. Puttkammer, "Negroes in the Ivy League," 19.

163. Ibid., 21.

164. For Harvard students as a whole during this period, about 80 percent of freshmen graduated on schedule and 90 percent within six years (Doermann, "Market for College Education," 144).

165. Edward A. Grossman, "The Undergraduate:

Africans and Afro-Americans," *HAB,* 25 May 1963, 632–33; and Edward A. Grossman, "The Undergraduate: Africans and Afro-Americans — Recognition Scene," *HAB,* 11 January 1964, 302–3. The fact that the organization was composed of both Africans and American blacks reflected the demographic reality of Harvard in this period, when foreign black students were about as numerous as domestic ones. From 1959 through 1962, 28 students entered Harvard from African and Caribbean countries — roughly half the total of black undergraduates estimated at Harvard College in May 1963. Figures on foreign students from the Admission and Scholarship Committee, "Report on the Admission and Scholarship Committee," 1958–1959, 1960–1961, 1961–1962, HU; Admission and Scholarship Committee, "Final Report of W. J. Bender, Chairman of the Admission and Scholarship Committee and Dean of Admissions and Financial Aids, 1952–1960."

166. Admission and Scholarship Committee, "Report on the Admission and Scholarship Committee," 1960–1961, 197.

167. Doermann, "Market for College Education," 142; Coombs, "Making It at Yale," 52; Commission on the Future of the College, *Report of the Commission,* Table 2.8.

168. In the years immediately preceding 1965, verbal scores of 450–500 were represented among black and other entering students (Doermann, "Market for College Education," 142–44 and Doermann, *Crosscurrents in College Admissions,* 48–49). For all Harvard freshmen in 1965, a verbal score of 572 was in the tenth percentile, a score of 673 in the thirtieth percentile, and a score of 679 at the fiftieth percentile (Admission and Scholarship Committee, "Report on the Admission and Scholarship Committee," 1964–1965, 4).

169. Harvard estimated that a family income of approximately $16,000 was necessary in 1965 in order to pay full college expenses without scholarship assistance (Doermann, "Market for College Education," 142–43). Of all American families in 1965, only 9.2 percent reported incomes over $15,000 (Bureau of the Census, *Historical Statistics of the United States,* 290).

170. Doermann, "Market for College Education," 142–43; Bureau of the Census, *Historical Statistics of the United States,* 290.

171. Committee on Race Relations, "Study of Race Relations at Harvard College," 2.

172. Joel R. Kramer, "Blacks Get Changes Made Peacefully," *HC,* 13 June 1968.

173. Carey, "Tradition and Transition," 29–31.

174. According to the *Crimson,* other Afro demands included "an endowed chair for a black professor, more courses relevant to blacks, [and] more lower level black Faculty members" (Joel R. Kramer, "University Will Not Move on Afro's Focus Requests," *HC,* 11 April 1968; "Afro's Proposals," *HC,* 12 April 1968).

175. Chase Peterson was born in 1929 in Logan, Utah, the son of Elmer George Peterson, the president of Utah State (formerly Utah State Agricultural College), a bacteriologist with a Ph.D. from Cornell University and a member of the Mormon Church. Rather unusually for a Mormon, Chase was sent off to the exclusive Middlesex School, graduating in 1948. At Harvard, where he was a National Scholar, Peterson was a varsity tennis and squash player. A devout Mormon who neither smoked or drank, he became president of the Porcellian Club. After graduating from Harvard

Medical School in 1956, he served as a captain in the Army Medical Corps in Europe and then as assistant clinical professor of medicine at the University of Utah School of Medicine. There, Peterson had served for several years as chairman of the alumni group charged with identifying and interviewing promising candidates for Harvard, and it was apparently in this capacity that he came to the attention of the administration as it sought a successor to Fred Glimp. Asked why Harvard wanted Peterson, Glimp (who was himself from Idaho) said, "It's a preference I think Harvard has not to become too inbred." Peterson served as dean of admissions and financial aid for five crucial years, from 1967 to 1972, stepping down to become vice president for development and alumni relations. In 1978, he returned to Utah to serve as vice president of health sciences and professor of medicine, and in 1985 he became president of the University of Utah, a post he held until 1991. Biographical portrait compiled from a variety of sources including an entry for Elmer George Peterson, *WWA, 1944–1945;* Bertram G. Waters, "Meet Dr. Petersen, Restless New Dean of Harvard Admissions," *Boston Globe,* 28 August 1967; "New Dean of Admissions," *HAB,* 8 July 1967, 11; entry in *Harvard Class Album: Class of 1952;* "4th VP," *Harvard University Gazette,* 10 March 1972; *WWA,* 1999–2000.

176. Charles J. Hamilton, "Peterson Pledges Search for More Black Students," *HC,* 30 April 1968.

177. Ibid.

178. By the time negotiations at Harvard had been concluded and an agreement announced, the uprising at Columbia was in its seventh day. The following day (April 30, 1968), the New York City police removed the students from the five buildings they were occupying and cleared the campus. On the chronology of the events at Columbia, see Avorn et al., *Up Against the Ivy Wall,* 299–301.

179. Admission and Scholarship Committee, "Report on the Committee on Admissions and Scholarships," 1967–1968, 107.

180. Penny H. Feldman, "Recruiting an Elite: Admissions to Harvard College" (Ph.D. diss., Harvard Univ., 1975), 74–75.

181. According to Martin Kilson, "Militancy and political threats perpetrated by Negro students in 1968–1970 paved the way for major alternations in Harvard's recruiting and admissions policies toward blacks" ("Blacks at Harvard: Crisis and Change," *Harvard Bulletin,* April 1973, 25).

182. Admission and Scholarship Committee, "Report on the Committee on Admissions and Scholarships," 1968–1969, 14.

183. On the Harvard protest, see Lawrence E. Eichel et al., *The Harvard Strike* (Boston: Houghton Mifflin, 1970); Steven Kelman, *Push Comes to Shove: The Escalation of Student Protest* (Boston: Houghton Mifflin, 1970); and E. J. Kahn Jr., *Harvard: Through Change and Through Storm* (New York: Norton, 1969). A detailed account of the police assault appears in Eichel, *Harvard Strike,* 125–32.

184. Eichel, *Harvard Strike,* 287. Henry Rosovsky, chairman of the Academic Committee on African and Afro-American Studies, referred to the faculty vote as "an academic Munich" (see Morton Keller and Phyllis Keller, *Making Harvard Modern* [New York: Oxford U.P., 2001], 287; and Henry Rosovsky, "Black Studies at Harvard: Personal Reflections Concerning Recent

Events," *American Scholar* 38, no. 4 [Autumn 1969]: 562–72).

185. On the events at Cornell, see the illuminating account by Donald Alexander Downs, which places what happened there in April 1969 in the context of the racial politics of the time (*Cornell '69: Liberalism and the Crisis of the American University* [Ithaca, N.Y.: Cornell U.P., 1999]). There was, however, a seven-hour sit-in at Radcliffe, Harvard's sister college, in December 1968 in which 25 black students demanded that more blacks be admitted ("News at Harvard," HUA, 1968).

186. Carey, "Tradition and Transition," 30–32.

187. Admission and Scholarship Committee, "Report on the Committee on Admissions and Scholarships," 1969–1970, 96–97, HU.

188. Feldman, "Recruiting an Elite," 73–75, 246; Admission and Scholarship Committee, "Report on the Committee on Admissions and Scholarships," 1968–1969, 15.

189. Feldman, "Recruiting an Elite," 74.

190. Ibid., 75, 246; Committee on Race Relations, "Study of Race Relations at Harvard College," 4.

191. The historic high before 1969 was around 4 percent (Committee on Race Relations, "Study of Race Relations at Harvard College," 2–3).

192. Calculated from figures in Feldman, "Recruiting an Elite," 111.

193. Ibid.

194. In 1971, graduates of private schools with a rating of academic 2 and 3 were accepted at a rate 1.4 times higher than that of public school graduates (37 v. 27 percent) (Feldman, "Recruiting an Elite," 111). Graduates of the leading boarding schools may, however, have been given a "greater degree of preference."

195. Donald H. Smith, "Admissions and Retention Problems of Black Students at Predominantly White Institutions," *Metas,* Spring–September 1980, cited in David Karen, "Who Gets into Harvard? Selection and Exclusion at an Elite College" (Ph.D. diss., Harvard Univ., 1985), 147.

196. Eddie Williams Jr., "Professor Kilson's Contentions: A Reply," *Harvard Bulletin,* June 1973, 44.

197. Feldman, "Recruiting an Elite," 128.

198. Kilson, "Blacks at Harvard," 26.

199. Admissions Office, "Admissions: Some Questions of Policy," *Harvard Bulletin,* June 1973, 46.

200. Admission and Scholarship Committee, "Report on the Committee on Admissions and Scholarships," 1969–1970, 96.

201. Commission on the Future of the College, *The Report of the Commission,* Table 2.8; Committee on Race Relations, "Study of Race Relations at Harvard College," 4.

202. The National Achievement Scholarship Program, established in 1964–1965 and associated with the National Merit Scholarship Program, gave scholarships to "outstanding Negro students" based in part on their scores on the National Merit Scholarship Qualifying Test. The figures for 1970 are from the National Merit Scholarship Corporation, "Annual Report," 1970–1971, 27.

203. William G. Bowen and Derek Bok, *The Shape of the River: Long-Term Consequences of Considering Race in College and University Admissions* (Princeton, N.J.: Princeton U.P., 1998), 5.

204. In 1964, 58 of the 3,078 students — 1.9 percent

— who entered Harvard, Yale, and Princeton were African Americans. Of these students, 28 were at Harvard (of 1,201), 18 at Yale (of 1,061), and 12 at Princeton (of 816). See Committee on Race Relations, "A Study of Race Relations at Harvard College," 4; Coombs, "Making It at Yale," 52; Commission on the Future of the College, *Report of the Commission*, Table 2.8.

205. On the upsurge of white radicalism in the New Left in 1968, see Gitlin, *The Sixties*, 285–340, and Sale, *SDS*, 404–510.

206. Though the Newark riot was much larger and more highly publicized, the racial disturbance at Plainfield, just 29 miles from Princeton, was significant enough to result in 46 injuries and 152 arrests. On the riot in Plainfield, see National Advisory Commission on Civil Disorders, *Kerner Report*, 75–82, and the Governor's Select Commission on Civil Disorder, "Report for Action," 145–53.

207. Coombs, "Making It at Yale," 52; Committee on Race Relations, "A Study of Race Relations at Harvard College," 2. Office of Admission, "Report to the Faculty," 1967–1968, 12–19. In contrast, Yale and Harvard did not change nearly as rapidly, with Yale showing an increase of just 12 African Americans and Harvard actually registering a slight decline.

208. Princeton, which had moved to sharply increase black enrollments a year earlier than Yale and Harvard, experienced a somewhat smaller increase (46 percent) in the number of black admits in 1969 (Hechinger, "Ivy League and Big 7 Take Record Total of Nonwhites").

209. For purposes of comparison, the figure of 224 blacks in 1969 excludes the 25 black women who entered Yale and the 6 black women who entered Princeton in 1969. On 1964, see Committee on Race Relations, "A Study of Race Relations at Harvard College," HUA, 4; Coombs, "Making It at Yale," 52; and Commission on the Future of the College, *The Report of the Commission on the Future of the College*, Table 2.8. On 1969, see Feldman, "Recruiting an Elite," 246; Coombes, "Making it at Yale," 52; and Office of Admission, "Annual Report," 1968–1969, 15.

210. Between 1952 and 1967, the verbal scores of students in the tenth percentile of Harvard freshmen rose from 474 to 596 (Committee on Admission and on Scholarships and Financial Aids, "Report on the office of the Dean of Admissions and Financial Aids for Students in Harvard College," 1952–1953, 10; Admission and Scholarship Committee, "Report on the Admission and Scholarship Committee," 1966–1967, 4).

211. Doermann, "Market for College Education," 59.

212. Social closure, a concept most closely associated with the work of Max Weber, refers to "the process by which social collectivity seek to maximize access to resources and opportunities to a limited circle of eligibles" (Frank Parkin, *Marxism and Class Theory: A Bourgeois Critique* [New York: Columbia U.P., 1979]). See also Max Weber, *Economy and Society*, 2 vols. (Berkeley, Calif.: Univ. of California Press, 1978), and Raymond Murphy, *Social Closure* (New York: Clarendon Press, 1988).

213. The theme of the urgent need for black leadership was a particularly recurrent one in the writings of Alden Dunham, Princeton's dean of admissions from 1962 to 1966, and Kingman Brewster.

214. The Wilkins to whom Brewster was referring was Roy Wilkins, executive secretary of the NAACP

from 1955 to 1965 and (when the title of the position changed) executive director from 1965 to his retirement in 1967.

215. Later in the letter, Brewster expressed his belief that "it is a close thing whether the race problem will destroy any society which is unwilling or unable to give positive hope its cure" (Brewster to Block, 12 August 1964, YUA).

216. Kabaservice, "Kingman Brewster," 377. The quote within the quote is from Kingman Brewster Jr., "Admissions to Yale: Objectives and Myths," *YAM*, October 1966.

217. For a sophisticated expression of the view that the degree of group political mobilization is a major factor in explaining trends in access to higher education by race, gender, and class, see David Karen, "The Politics of Class, Race, and Gender: Access to Higher Education in the United States, 1960–1986," *American Journal of Education* 99, no. 2 (February 1991): 208–33, and Karen, "Toward a Political-Organizational Model of Gatekeeping: The Case of Elite Colleges," *Sociology of Education* 63, no. 4 (October 1990): 227–40. Efforts at mobilization do not, however, always succeed; at Harvard in 1970–1971, for example, the Chicano student organization demanded a Chicano admissions officer and a 5 percent quota for Chicanos in the freshman class, but both demands were rejected. According to Feldman, "Privately committee members expressed the belief that responsibility for Mexican-Americans lay primarily with Western and Southwestern universities and not on Harvard's New England shoulders" ("Recruiting an Elite," 75).

218. Office of Institutional Research, "Minority Groups," 25 September 1972, YU; Office of Admission, "Report to the President," 1971–1972, 83.

219. Admissions and Scholarships Committee, "Report on the Committee on Admissions and Scholarships," 1975–1976 and 1976–1977, 108.

220. Yale, which reduced considerably the degree of preference for alumni sons during the Clark years (1965–1970), is a partial exception here, though greater preference for legacies was restored after 1972 (see Chapter 15).

221. Other factors contributing to the rise of meritocracy in the 1960s were the greater availability of federal funds, the rise of an affluent upper middle class, and the sheer increase in the number of applicants.

222. Clark, interview, 13 May 1993, 25–26.

14. Coeducation and the Struggle for Gender Equality

1. On the link between the ideology of "domestic containment" (the relegation of women to traditional gender roles) and the Cold War ideology of the "containment" of communism, see Elaine T. May, *Homeward Bound: American Families in the Cold War Era* (New York: Basic Books, 1999).

2. Barbara M. Solomon, *In the Company of Educated Women* (New Haven, Conn.: Yale U.P., 1985), 199.

3. Patricia A. Graham, "Expansion and Exclusion: A History of Women in American Higher Education," *Signs* 3, no. 4 (Summer 1978).

4. Carnegie Commission on Higher Education, *Opportunities for Women in Higher Education* (New York: McGraw-Hill, 1973), 100.

5. Harvard, of course, did have a "coordinate" women's college in Radcliffe, whose students had attended classes with Harvard men since 1943. But Harvard and Radcliffe remained separate institutions, with separate endowments and admissions offices. In 1960, roughly four times as many men entered Harvard (about 1,200 Harvard freshmen, 300 Radcliffe freshmen). Other Ivy League colleges with similar arrangements were Columbia, with Barnard, and Brown, with Pembroke. This left only two Ivies — Cornell and Penn — in the ranks of fully coeducational institutions, although Cornell had policies that limited the number of women, as did Stanford, the West Coast institution most like the Ivies. See Carnegie Commission on Higher Education, *Opportunities for Women*, 52, and Charlotte W. Conable, *Women at Cornell: The Myth of Equal Education* (Ithaca, N.Y.: Cornell U.P., 1977), 140–42.

6. C. Wright Mills, *The Power Elite* (New York: Oxford U.P., 1956).

7. Richard L. Zweigenhaft and G. William Domhoff, *Diversity and the Power Elite: Have Women and Minorities Reached the Top?* (New Haven, Conn.: Yale U.P., 1998), 41–77.

8. Blanche Linden-Ward and Carol H. Green, *American Women in the 1960s: Changing the Future* (New York: Twayne, 1993), xii.

9. Ethel Klein, *Gender Politics* (Cambridge, Mass.: Harvard U.P., 1984), 39.

10. As Cynthia Harrison, the author of a major study of the politics of women's issues in the decades after World War II, observed, the 1957 launching of Sputnik by the Soviet Union "crystallized national apprehensions" about the capacity of the United States "to meet the challenges of its chief rival" and led Americans to ask, "Had devotion to a stable family life resulted in a complacent and insular society vulnerable to the threat of Russian domination?" (*On Account of Sex: The Politics of Women's Issues 1945–1968* [Berkeley, Calif.: Univ. of California Press, 1988], xi).

11. Geoffrey Kabaservice, "Kingman Brewster and the Rise and Fall of the Progressive Establishment" (Ph.D. diss., Yale Univ., 1999), 432.

12. Ibid., 433–34. On the National Manpower Council, see also Harrison, *On Account of Sex*, 48.

13. In good part in response to the scare created by Sputnik, Congress passed the National Defense Act of 1958. As noted by Barbara Miller Solomon, the legislation "was intended to recruit a wider spectrum of students, including women" (*In the Company*, 198).

14. Kabaservice, "Kingman Brewster," 433.

15. Sarah M. Evans, *Born to Liberty: A History of Women in America* (New York: Free Press, 1989), 265.

16. Ibid., 265–66.

17. Ibid., 265. Betty Friedan's classic *The Feminine Mystique* did not appear until 1963. By 1970, this work, which identified the "problem that has no name," had sold five million copies ("The Path of the Women's Rights Movement: A Timeline of the Women's Rights Movement 1848–2002," *Women's History Sourcebook*).

18. According to several Radcliffe alumnae, Jordan apparently delivered this speech to entering freshmen until the end of his tenure, in 1960 (Solomon, *In the Company*, 192, 252–53). For information on Jordan, a historian who had served as Radcliffe's president since 1943, see *WWA, 1962–1963*.

19. Geoffrey Kabaservice, *The Guardians: Kingman Brewster, His Circle, and the Rise of the Liberal Establishment* (New York: Henry Holt, 2004), 293.

20. Ibid., 233–34.

21. Alan S. Katz, "Women at Yale Proposed by Dean of Admissions Howe," *YDN*, 28 September 1956; "Yale College Advised by a Dean to be Modern and Admit Girls," *NYT*, 29 September 1956.

22. Arthur Howe Jr., interview by Geoffrey Kabaservice, 18 July 1992, transcript, YUA, 34–35.

23. Yale University News Bureau, 28 September 1956.

24. Ibid., 29 September 1956.

25. See Kabaservice, "Kingman Brewster," 423–26, for evidence that Griswold was unsympathetic to proposals for coeducation at Yale.

26. See, for example, the letter from Richard Lloyd '06 (pseudonym) to Griswold, 29 September 1956, YUA. In it, Lloyd wrote to Griswold (to whom he sent his "warmest personal regards") that "if such a disaster as is proposed should be visited upon Yale, 'Mother of Men,' it would be a good and sufficient reason for reconsidering any testamentary bequest I have in mind for Yale."

27. F. T. Rowe III (pseudonym) '35 to Arthur Howe Jr., 17 October 1956, YUA. Given the virtually total exclusion of women from the top positions in business, government, and the professions, the concern that coeducation (especially if it resulted in the admission of fewer men) might lead to a reduction in Yale's influence and prestige was not unreasonable.

28. Frederick Schmidt (pseudonym) to Griswold, 14 October 1956, YUA; Huntington Campbell '01 (pseudonym) to Griswold, 30 September 1956, YUA. In his response to the letters from Schmidt and the earlier letter from Lloyd, Griswold blamed "the recent publicity given to co-education to a garrulous faculty member" and enclosed statements from the Yale News Bureau (and, in the case of Lloyd, a clipping from the *NYT*) to "allay your fears in the matter" (Griswold to Schmidt, 22 October 1956, YUA; Griswold to Lloyd, 5 October 1956, YUA).

29. Kabaservice, *The Guardians*, 294.

30. Just how unfriendly the spirit of the times was to coeducation (and to gender equality more generally) is illustrated by the following poem by President Griswold, originally written for McGeorge Bundy '40, the dean of Harvard's Faculty of Arts and Sciences, and delivered in a speech to 200 alumni chairmen on October 19, 1956:

> By keeping in step with the male
> We fall in step with the snail,
> Let's keep our position
> Said the Dean of Admissions
> "And get some fast women at Yale."

Dorrit A. Cowan, "Single-Sex to Coeducation at Princeton and Yale: Two Case Studies" (Ph.D. diss., Teachers College, Columbia Univ., 1982), 157, and Reuben A. Holden, *Profiles and Portraits of Yale University Presidents* (Freeport, Me.: Bond Wheelwright, 1968), 136. See also "Griswold: A Poem on Coeds," *YDN*, 20 October 1956.

31. Committee on the Freshman Year, "The Education of First-Year Students in Yale College," *YAM*, June 1962, 11.

32. Ibid., 10. "Ultimate" recommendations were defined as goals "that should be envisioned now, but

for good reasons, usually financial, cannot be achieved for some time."

33. Leonard Doob, interview by Geoffrey Kabaservice, 6 November 1990, transcript, YUA, 40.

34. See, for example, the letters under the heading "Women" in the June 1962 *YAM*.

35. Leonard M. Chazen, "A Coeducational Yale?" *YDN*, 27 November 1961, 1, 3.

36. Howard F. Gillette Jr., "Freshman Report Stirs Controversy Among Students," *YDN*, 20 April 1962, 1, cited in Kabaservice, "Kingman Brewster," 437.

37. *Gate '67*, vol. 2, cited in ibid.

38. "Women at Yale College? Students Split on Issue, Cite Tradition, Standards," *YDN*, 9 October 1963. On the persistence of traditional attitudes among Yale men, see also the results of a 1962 survey of Yale, Cornell, and Mount Holyoke students by an employee of the Yale Sociology Department ("Yale Men Victorian?" *YDN*, 18 May 1962).

39. A particularly dramatic display of such attitudes occurred in the fall of 1963, when hundreds of students protested the decision to allow women to use the Linonia and Brothers Reading Room (commonly known as L&B), formerly restricted to men (Cowan, "Single-Sex to Coeducation," 167).

40. Kabaservice, "Kingman Brewster," 438; Cowan, "Single-Sex to Coeducation," 167.

41. "Dean at Yale Sees the Day When It Must Take Women," *NYT*, 23 May 1964.

42. The "first wave" of feminism generally refers to the generation that waged the successful fight for suffrage and to its activities after the passage of the Nineteenth Amendment, in 1920; the "second wave" typically refers to the young women, often active in the civil rights movement and the New Left, who created a new women's movement in the mid- and late 1960s (see Ruth Rosen, *The World Split Open* [New York: Viking, 2000], 27, 87). For an excellent study of the origins of second-wave feminism, whose first stirrings may be linked to the November 1964 SNCC Position Paper Number 24 ("Women in the Movement") and the fall 1965 "A Kind of Memo [Addressed to] A Number of Other Women in the Peace and Freedom Movements" (both by Casey Hayden and Mary King), see Sarah Evans, *Personal Politics: The Roots of Women's Liberation in the Civil Rights Movement and the New Left* (New York: Vintage, 1980). In 1966, the older and generally more conservative generation of feminists, many of them professional women, created the National Organization for Women (NOW; see Harrison, *On Account of Sex*, 192–209). For a detailed timeline on the history of American women, see Rosen, *The World Split Open*, xvii–xxxii.

43. "The Morals Revolution on the U.S. Campus," *Newsweek*, 6 April 1964, 52–56, 59.

44. Ibid., 56.

45. In 1965, for example, Frederick Taft, an undergraduate from one of Yale's most distinguished families, proposed a plan for bringing coeducation to Yale. The plan expressed the changing attitude of undergraduates toward women, arguing that Yale students "would relish the chance for more natural, more frequent, and more constructive contact with the opposite sex" ("A Transfer Approach to Coeducation," 8 May 1965, YUA). Brewster responded that Taft's plan was "too expensive" and would not admit enough undergraduates to foster a "natural mixed environment for Yale students" (Brewster to Taft, 8 June 1965, YUA).

In an undated and unsigned memo to "Kingman" regarding Taft's proposal now in the Yale archives, someone (presumably a member of the Yale administration) jotted at the bottom, "Maybe the Tafts will give us 10M."

46. "The Morals Revolution on the U.S. Campus," 55. According to Alan F. Guttmacher, president of Planned Parenthood, the sexual revolution on America's campuses was already under way by 1962–1963 (cited in Linden-Ward and Green, *American Women*, 90).

47. Cowan, "Single-Sex to Coeducation," 167–68. As late as the academic year 1963–1964, Yale students were still being expelled for violations of parietals (Kabaservice, "Kingman Brewster," 435).

48. In 1965, 86 percent of admissions at Harvard matriculated there; for Yale, the figure was 67 percent (Admission and Scholarship Committee, "Report on the Admission and Scholarship Committee," 1964–1965, HU, 2, and Office of Institutional Research, "Yale College Admissions, Class of 1962–1982, Applicants, Admitted Applicants and Matriculants, Total and Alumni Children," 2 April 1979, YU).

49. "Ivy Overlap Study," 26 October 1965, HUA.

50. Of the 478 students who had been accepted by Yale but chose to go elsewhere, 237 enrolled at Harvard and 241 at other institutions ("1965 Admit-Withdrawn Study," 24 June 1965, attached to the Office of Admissions and Freshman Scholarships and Office of Enrollment and Scholarships, "Annual Report of the Acting Dean of Undergraduate Admissions and Student Appointments," 1964–1965, YU).

51. Arthur Howe Jr., interview, transcript, 18 July 1992, 32.

52. Ibid.

53. "Corporation Statements Concerning the Admission of Women as Undergraduate Students at March 12, 1966, Meeting," YUA.

54. Kabaservice, *The Guardians*, 297.

55. Ibid., 194–95.

56. "Special Report to the Alumni," 2.

57. Kabaservice, "Kingman Brewster," 456–57.

58. Kabaservice, *The Guardians*, 324.

59. Admissions Policy Advisory Board, "Second Report," 31 October 1966, YU, 13–14.

60. Kabaservice, *The Guardians*, 324.

61. "Talk by J. Irwin Miller to Yale Alumni," 7 June 1967, YUA, 1.

62. Quoted in Kabaservice, "Kingman Brewster," 446.

63. Ibid., 472.

64. Kingman Brewster Jr., "An Institution for University Women at Yale: A Proposal," 13 May 1968, YUA.

65. Students for a Democratic Society (SDS), "Coeducation at Yale," n.d. [c. 15 October 1968], YUA. See Timothy Bates, "SDS Proclaims for Girls Next Year," *YDN*, 16 October 1968.

66. Jeffrey M. Stern, "Coed Rally Meets 'Brewster at Home,'" *YDN*, 7 November 1968.

67. Coed Action Group and Coed Steering Committee, untitled statement during "Coeducation Week," n.d. [c. 5 November 1968], YUA.

68. (SDS), "Coeducation at Yale."

69. On the conflict within the New Left during this period, see Evans, *Personal Politics*, 193–211, and Rosen, *World Split Open*, 94–140.

70. On the upsurge of radical feminist activity in 1968 — a wave of public actions that included the fa-

mous protest at the Miss America Pageant in 1968 — see Rosen, *World Split Open,* 159–64, 196–208.

71. For a list of some of the classic feminist works published in 1970 and 1971, see ibid., xxi–xxii.

72. Office of Undergraduate Admissions, "Report of the Dean of Admissions and Student Appointment to the President and Fellows of Yale University," 1967–1968, YU, 2–3.

73. Clark to Chauncey, 28 October 1968, YUA.

74. James F. Clarity, "Princeton Panel, Backed by Goheen, Urges Admission of Coeds," *NYT,* 16 September 1968; Gardner Patterson et al., "The Education of Women at Princeton: Report on the Desirability and Feasibility of Princeton Entering into the Education of Women at the Undergraduate Level," *PAW,* 24 September 1968.

75. Kingman Brewster Jr., "Higher Education for Women at Yale," 23 September 1968, YUA.

76. Like Yale, Princeton was also faring poorly in the competition for students accepted at Harvard, enrolling only 23 percent (129 of 549) of them from 1965 to 1968 (calculated from Office of Admission, "Report to the Faculty," 1967–1968, PU, 80).

77. Kabaservice, *The Guardians,* 368–69.

78. Kabaservice, "Kingman Brewster," 1.

79. Cowan, "Single-Sex to Coeducation," 188.

80. Brewster, "Proposal for Coeducation in Yale College," YUA, 1, 4; William Borders, "Yale Going Coed Next September," *NYT,* 15 November 1968.

81. Office of Undergraduate Admissions, "Combined Annual Reports of the Dean of Admissions and the Director of Undergraduate Admissions," 1968–1969, YU, 2.

82. Kabaservice, "Kingman Brewster," 473. Among the women who entered Yale in 1970, two out of five were National Merit Scholarship semifinalists — an honor which meant they scored in the top 0.5 percent of high school students (Elga Wasserman, "Coeducation 1969–1970," 1970, YUA, 6).

83. Calculated from the Office of Institutional Research, "Yale College Admissions," YU.

84. Jeffrey Gordon, "Blacks, Financial Aid Students, Public School Students Decline," *YDN,* 14 September 1970. By 1970, however, Radcliffe had regained a narrow lead, attracting 45 of the 88 students admitted to both institutions, with Yale enrolling 43.

85. Calculated from Office of Institutional Research, "Yale College Admissions," YU.

86. Elga Wasserman, "Coeducation Report 1968–1969," 29 May 1969, YUA, 1, 9.

87. Borders, "Yale Going Coed Next September"; "President Brewster's Remarks on Coeducation," YUA, 12.

88. Jeffrey Gordon, "Inky's Era," *YAM,* March 1970, 35.

89. Office of Undergraduate Admissions, "Report of the Dean of Admissions and Student Appointments to the President and Fellows of Yale University," 1969–1970, YU, 2.

90. Christ to President Brewster, deans, and faculty masters, 17 October 1969, YUA.

91. Johnson to Brewster, 27 March 1970, YUA.

92. Calculated from Office of Institutional Research, "Yale College Admissions," YU.

93. University Committee on the Education of Women, "The Admission of Women to Yale College," July 1974, YUA, 5–6.

94. Ibid., 7.

95. On the dynamism of the early years of the feminist movement, see Rosen, *World Split Open,* and Evans, *Born to Liberty.*

96. For examples of the early coverage of the women's movement in the mass media, see "The New Feminists Revolt Against 'Sexism,'" *Time,* 21 November 1969; "New Victory in Old Crusade," *Time,* 24 August 1970; "Who's Come a Long Way, Baby?" *Time,* 31 August 1970; and "The Women Who Know Their Place," *Newsweek,* 7 September 1970.

97. Evans, *Born to Liberty,* 290; see also Klein, *Gender Politics.*

98. Jane Mansbridge, *Why We Lost the ERA* (Chicago: Univ. of Chicago Press, 1986), 8–12. The ERA had been introduced into Congress almost half a century earlier in 1923.

99. Klein, *Gender Politics,* 90.

100. By 1973, the proportion of students at private universities agreeing with the statement had dropped five additional points, to 22 percent. And among women at highly selective private universities, the proportion was a mere 6 percent (American Council on Education, *National Norms for Entering College Freshmen — Fall 1967* 2, no. 7 [1967], 51; American Council on Education, *The American Freshman: National Norms for Fall 1972* 7, no. 5 [1972], 47; American Council on Education and University of California, Los Angeles, *The American Freshman: National Norms for Fall 1973* [Los Angeles: Cooperative Institutional Research Program, 1973], 47).

101. Klein, *Gender Politics,* 90.

102. Bates, "SDS Proclaims Girls Next Year."

103. Kabaservice makes a similar point, noting that Yale's admissions policy had two distinct missions: to allocate places in the freshman class on the basis of merit and to "seek out the leaders of thirty years hence and give them the education and certification which would help them towards membership in the elite" ("Kingman Brewster," 464).

104. Christ to President Brewster, deans, and faculty masters, 17 October 1969, YUA.

105. For evidence that women were still grossly underrepresented in the "power elite" in the mid-1990s, constituting well under 10 percent of corporate leadership and perhaps just over 10 percent of political leadership, see Zweigenhaft and Domhoff, *Diversity in the Power Elite,* 41–77.

106. "Admissions Group Protests Present Sex Quotas," *YAM,* January 1972, 31.

107. "Committee Urges More Women," *YDN,* 14 February 1972, 1.

108. In the same statement, Brewster said, "I do feel bound by the commitment made then [1968] that we did not intend to reduce the number of men simply because we initiated coeducation on a limited basis." Alumni confidence, he added, "obviously has special importance in a time like this when universities so badly need financial support and popular understanding" ("Brewster Vows Reassessment of Sex Ratio Next Fall," *YDN,* 14 February 1972, 1, 4).

109. Ibid.

110. Dahl, "Dahl Report," 23–24.

111. University Committee on the Education of Women, "The Admission of Women to Yale College," YUA, 8–11, my emphasis.

112. Ibid., 10–11.

113. Mary Arnstein to Worth David, 23 May 1973, YUA.

114. Describing the admissions process in 1973, Mary Arnstein wrote: "Though we never admitted to 'quotas,' it was certainly difficult to ignore the numbers given from previous years which then were presumably to be thought of as guidelines; or, not to have in mind that we were essentially trying to put together a class of 1300 students, of which 870 would be men and 430 would be women" (Office of Institutional Research, "Yale College Admissions," YU).

115. Between 1964 and 1968, an average of 1,037 men entered Yale annually (Office of Institutional Research, "Yale College Admissions," YU; George W. Pierson, ed., *A Yale Book of Numbers: Historical Statistics of the College and University, 1701–1976* [New Haven, Conn.: Yale U.P., 1983], 98–99).

116. In 1995, 694 women (50.7 percent) and 675 men (49.3 percent) entered Yale's freshman class (see Office of Undergraduate Admissions and Financial Aid, "Profile of the Class of 1999," September 1995, YU).

117. Cowan, "Single-Sex to Coeducation," 156.

118. Don Oberdorfer, *Princeton University: The First 250 Years* (Princeton, N.J.: Trustees of Princeton Univ., 1995), 182. In addition to Yale (included in Oberdorfer's estimate of 20 percent), the other Ivy League institutions with graduate and professional schools were Brown, Columbia, Cornell, Harvard, and Penn. Dartmouth, whose enrollment at the time was almost entirely undergraduate, was presumably not included in Oberdorfer's figure despite its being a member of the Ivy League.

119. Cowan, "Single-Sex to Coeducation," 74–75.

120. Quoted in ibid., 71.

121. Quoted in ibid., 82–83.

122. Committees on Admission and on Scholarships and Financial Aids, "Report on the Office of the Dean of Admissions and Financial Aids for Students in Harvard College," 1954–1955, HU, 45; Office of Admission, "Report to the President," 1964–1965, PU, 11.

123. Admission and Scholarship Committee, "Report on the Admission and Scholarship Committee," 1964–1965, HU, 2; Office of Admission, "Report to the President," 1964–1965, PU, 11.

124. Committee on Admission, "Report to the President," 1954–1955, PU, 14; Committees on Admission and on Scholarships and Financial Aids, "Report on the Office of the Dean of Admissions and Financial Aids for Students in Harvard College," 1954–1955, HU, 2.

125. "DP Asks Coeducation As 'Healthy' Move," *NYT,* 9 January 1965.

126. "Dr. Goheen Rejects Coeds at Princeton in Spite of Pleas," *NYT,* 8 February 1965.

127. Cowan, "Single-Sex to Coeducation," 88.

128. In truth, Yale still had a slight edge over Princeton, enrolling 53 percent (177 of 336) of students accepted by both institutions in 1965 and 1966 (Office of Admission, "Report to the Faculty," 1967–1968, PU, 80).

129. Michael W. Miles, "On the Campus," *PAW,* 17 January 1967, 4.

130. Luther Munford, "Coeducation at Princeton: The Struggle of an Idea at a University in Transition," *DP,* 21 October 1969. An abbreviated version of this extremely detailed and illuminating article was published as Luther Munford '71, "Anatomy of a Decision," *PAW,* 11 November 1969. Where possible, I refer to the *PAW* version.

131. Oberdorfer, *Princeton University,* 176.

132. In January, a group of students in favor of coeducation, calling themselves the "League for the Institution of Masculine Peculiarities," or "LIMP" for short, staged a mock protest in front of Nassau Hall (Munford, "Coeducation at Princeton").

133. Oberdorfer, *Princeton University,* 177–78.

134. Munford, "Coeducation at Princeton"; David Bird, "A Coed Princeton Urged by Faculty," *NYT,* 10 March 1967; Merrill Folson, "Sarah Lawrence Declines Merger," *NYT,* 3 June 1967.

135. Since this poll was designed with a political purpose in mind, it is quite possible that the 95 percent figure exaggerates the degree of undergraduate support for coeducation in the spring of 1967. A more scientific poll taken that fall found 82 percent of undergraduates in favor of coeducation (Munford, "Anatomy of a Decision," 10). For technical details on the Patterson Committee's poll in the fall of 1967, see "Appendix B, Questionnaire Distributed to Princeton Undergraduates and a Tabulation of Their Replies," in Patterson, "Education of Women," 12 July 1968. It is included in the full, 288-page version of the Patterson Report.

136. Munford, "Coeducation at Princeton."

137. "Princeton Told to Expect Coeds," *NYT,* 18 May 1967.

138. Munford, "Coeducation at Princeton"; Oberdorfer, *Princeton University,* 177–78.

139. Munford, "Anatomy of a Decision," 9.

140. Born in Burt, Iowa, in 1916, Gardner Patterson received a B.A. from the University of Michigan in 1938 and an M.A. in 1939. After service with the Treasury Department and the U.S. Naval Reserve in World War II, he completed his graduate education at Harvard, receiving a Ph.D. in 1949. A member of the Princeton faculty since 1949, Patterson was promoted to full professor in 1954 and served as director of the Woodrow Wilson School of Public Policy and International Affairs from 1958 to 1964 (*WWA, 1978–1979*).

141. Munford, "Anatomy of a Decision," 10.

142. Gardner Patterson, "Coeducation — An Interim Report," *PAW,* 12 March 1968.

143. Ibid., 6, 8.

144. Patterson, "Education of Women," 8; Munford, "Anatomy of a Decision," 10.

145. John T. Osander to William G. Bowen, 11 March 1968, YUA.

146. Office of Admission, "Report to the Faculty," 1967–1968, PU, 55.

147. Fred M. Hechinger, "More Negroes Accepted by Ivy League Colleges," *NYT,* 14 April 1968.

148. Office of Admission, "Report to the Faculty," 1967–1968, PU, 50–53, 80.

149. Munford, "Anatomy of a Decision," 10.

150. Ibid.

151. Ronald Sullivan, "Princeton Alumni Group Set Up to Oppose Coeds and Protests," *NYT,* 13 March 1969.

152. Arthur Horton '42 grew up in New York and attended Polytechnic Preparatory Country Day School. At Princeton, he was a member of the Cannon Club, listed himself in the yearbook as an Episcopalian and a Republican, and graduated with honors in architecture. In 1954, he returned to Princeton to serve as the Director of Annual Giving and was Director of Development at the time of the debate over coeducation. Munford, "Coeducation at Princeton"; *Nassau*

Herald: Class of 1942, PU, 239; *Reunion Class of 1942*, June 1967, PU, 159; *Reunion Class of 1942*, June 1979, PU, 57.

153. Prescott Jones (pseudonym) to Jerry Horton, 5 February 1968, PUA.

154. "Terry" (pseudonym) to Jerry Horton, 16 March 1968, PUA.

155. Chase Putnam (pseudonym), non-addressed letter, n.d., PUA.

156. "Letter to the Editor, From Fifteen Ohio Alumni," *PAW*, 28 May 1969.

157. Quoting a letter from E. Alden Dunham, Princeton's previous Director of Admission, Patterson noted that "Princeton loses one third of its admitted to other colleges . . . all too often the very people we want most." "There is no doubt whatsoever in my mind," Dunham added, "that coeducation is very much a factor in their decision not to attend Princeton." Patterson, "Education of Women," 7.

158. Ibid., 9. See also Humphrey Doermann, "The Market for College Education in the United States" (Ph.D. diss., Harvard Univ., 1967), 241; Doermann, "The Market for College Education," *Educational Record*, Winter 1968, 55.

159. Munford, "Anatomy of a Decision," 12.

160. Arthur Horton, "Statement of Mr. Horton," *PAW*, 24 September 1968, 55, and also "Statement of the Faculty Administration Committee," *PAW*, 24 September 1968, 55.

161. "Statement of the Faculty-Administration Committee."

162. Cowan, "Single-Sex to Coeducation," 108.

163. Helm, who had spearheaded a successful "$53 million for Princeton" drive early in Goheen's tenure, also served as Chairman of the Trustees' Executive Committee. Munford, "Anatomy of a Decision," 12.

164. Ibid.

165. Ibid.

166. Ibid.

167. John Davies, "'Coeducation — A Self-Evident Conclusion,'" *PAW*, 26 November 1968, 11.

168. Cowan, "Single-Sex to Coeducation," 113.

169. Munford, "Anatomy of a Decision," 12, 18.

170. Cowan, "Single-Sex to Coeducation," 115.

171. Munford, "Anatomy of a Decision," 18.

172. "The Education of Undergraduate Women at Princeton: An Examination of Coordinate Versus Coeducational Patterns," March 1968, PUA, 9–10.

173. Ibid., 8–13, 20. The figure on the female-male ratio at Stanford refers to undergraduates in the School of Humanities and Sciences (Patterson, "Education of Women," 21).

174. Ibid., 12–13.

175. Cowan, "Single-Sex to Coeducation," 115.

176. "Princeton Will Add Graduate Trustees and Admit Women," *NYT*, 21 April 1969; Munford, "Anatomy of a Decision," 18–19. In the end, 135 women were admitted to the entering class of 1969 (out of 505 applicants) and 102 enrolled (Office of Admission, "Annual Report," 1968–1969, PUA, E-2).

177. Calculated from Office of Admission, "Report to the President," 1969–1970, PU, B-5. Figures for 1967–1972 are available in Commission on the Future of the College, *The Report of the Commission on the Future of the College* (Princeton, N.J.: Trustees of Princeton Univ., 1973), Table 2.5.

178. Calculated from Office of Admission, "Report to the President," 1969–1970, PU, B-2.

179. David Swartz offers an illuminating definition of cultural capital. Bourdieu's "concept of cultural capital," he writes, "covers a wide variety of resources including such things as verbal facility, general cultural awareness, aesthetic preferences, information about the school system, and educational credentials. His point is to suggest that culture (in the broadest sense of the term) can become a power resource . . . Bourdieu's concept of cultural capital emerged initially from his research to explain unequal scholastic achievement of children originating from families with different educational though similar social origins. He sees the concept as breaking with the received wisdom that attributes academic success or failure to natural aptitudes, such as intelligence or giftedness. School success, Bourdieu finds, is better explained by the amount and type of cultural capital inherited from the family milieu than by measures of individual talent or achievement" (*Culture and Power: The Sociology of Pierre Bourdieu* [Chicago: Univ. of Chicago Press, 1997], 75–76; see also Pierre Bourdieu, "The Forms of Capital," in *Handbook of Theory and Research for the Sociology of Education*, ed. J. G. Richardson [New York: Greenwood Press, 1986], 241–58).

180. American Council on Education, "Summary of Data on Entering Freshmen, Princeton University," fall 1970, 2.

181. The son of Henry H. Callard, from 1943 to 1963 headmaster of the Gilman School in Baltimore (a major feeder school to Princeton), Timothy C. Callard graduated from Gilman in 1959. He then entered Princeton, where he served as president of the Ivy Club, captain of the lacrosse team, won all-Ivy honors in football, and graduated with honors in religion in 1963. He went on to receive his M.A. in religion from Columbia University and Union Theological Seminary in 1966 before becoming a faculty member and college placement officer at Phillips Academy, Andover. At the age of twenty-nine, he was appointed by Goheen to replace John Osander as the director of admission ("Callard to Head Admissions for Princeton University," *DP*, 3 March 1971; "Timothy Cooley Callard," *Nassau Herald*, 1963, PUA; "Callard Moving to Gilman School," *Princeton Packet*, 25 November 1978, PUA).

182. Office of Admission, "Report to the President," 1971–1972, PU, 6, 16.

183. Ibid., 16.

184. Discrimination against women in admissions was already prohibited by Title IX at *public* educational institutions (Commission on the Future of the College, *The Report of the Commission*, 81).

185. According to Margaret C. Dunkle and Bernice Sandler, Title IX specifically exempted certain types of institutions, including private undergraduate institutions, from the requirement of nondiscriminatory admissions because of "pressure from parts of the educational community" (*Sex Discrimination Against Students: Implication of Title IX of the Education Amendments of Association of American Colleges* [Washington, D.C.: Association of American Colleges, 1975], 8). Yet until it was clear that that the Green Amendment had failed, there was widespread concern that even private institutions like Princeton and Yale, once having admitted women, would be forced to adopt sex-blind admissions or lose federal aid. See, for example, William V. Shannon, "Diversity Endangered," *NYT*, 1 October 1971.

186. Born in Cincinnati in 1933, Bowen graduated from Denison College, where he was a top scholar, an Ohio Conference tennis champion, and co-chairman of the student body. He went to Princeton in 1955 as a graduate student in economics and Woodrow Wilson Fellow. In 1958, he joined the faculty as an assistant professor of economics and won an appointment as the Jonathan Dickinson Preceptor a year later. The director of graduate studies in the Woodrow Wilson School at the age of thirty, Bowen became professor of economics and public affairs at thirty-one, provost of Princeton at thirty-three, and president of the university at thirty-eight. The author of numerous works in labor economics, the economics of education, and the economics of culture, he served as Princeton's president from 1972 to 1987. In 1987, he became president of the Andrew W. Mellon Foundation, where he wrote (with Derek Bok) the landmark study of affirmative action, *The Shape of the River: Long-term Consequences of Considering Race in College and University Admissions* (Princeton, N.J.: Princeton U.P., 2000) ("Bowen, William Gordon," in *A Princeton Companion*, ed. Alexander Leitch [Princeton, N.J.: Princeton U.P., 1978], 61–62; *WWA, 1999–2000*).

187. Marvin Bressler, professor of sociology at Princeton and the chairman of the Commission on the Future of the College, astutely described how things had changed between 1968 and 1973:

The Patterson Report gives one the clear impression that to exercise direct control over the sex composition of the student body was thought by the Committee to be entirely natural and in no way objectionable. Such was the temper of the time. Realistically speaking, in 1968 there was no chance whatever of opening up admissions to the College on a freely competitive basis and the issue simply did not arise. Hence, any difficulties concerning this matter that might have been felt in the early stages of coeducational planning passed almost unnoticed, perhaps as minor necessary disadvantages of a project whose overall benefits were overwhelming. Of equal importance, however, is the fact that societal aversion to quotas — and especially to quotas based on sex — was not as strong in the late 1960's as it has become in the early 1970's.

Commission on the Future of the College, *The Report of the Commission*, 80, PU.

188. Ibid., 81.

189. Ibid.

190. "Equal Access: Some Questions and Answers," 31 January 1974, PUA, 5.

191. As late as 1973, Princeton used the waiting list to admit extra men in order to meet its quota of 800 men (Office of Admission, "Report to the President," 1972–1973, PU, 2).

192. Board of Trustees to Alumni, 24 January 1974, PUA.

193. Princeton University News Bureau, 19 January 1974, PUA.

194. Calculated from Office of Admission, "Report to the President," 1973–1974, 1974–1975, 1975–1976, 1976–1977, 1977–1978, PU.

195. Office of Admission, "Report to the President," 1973–1974, PU; Office of Undergraduate Admissions, "Report of the Dean of Admissions to the President and Fellows of the Yale Corporation," 1973–1974, YU; Admissions and Scholarships Committee, "Report on the Committee on Admissions and Scholarships," 1973–1974, HU.

196. Calvin N. Moseley, "The Impact of the Merger of the Office of Admissions and Financial Aids at Harvard and Radcliffe Colleges" (Ph.D. diss., Harvard Univ., 1981), 17–20. The Conant quote is from p. 7.

197. Ibid., 27. It was not until 1962 that the Corporation voted to admit women to the Graduate School of Arts and Sciences, thereby discontinuing the Radcliffe Graduate School (Strauch Committee, "Report of the Committee to Consider Aspects of the Harvard-Radcliffe Relationship That Affect Administrative Arrangements, Admissions, Financial Aid, and Educational Policy," 26 February 1975, HU, 4).

198. Moseley, "Impact of the Merger," 27.

199. Ibid., 28.

200. Gordon, "Blacks, Financial Aid Students, Public School Students Decline"; Office of Admission, "Report to the President," 1969–1970, PU, 15.

201. *Admissions and Scholarship Newsletter* 17, no. 3 (July 1969); Commission on the Future of the College, *The Report of the Commission*, Table 2.5.

202. Admission and Scholarship Committee, "Report on the Admission and Scholarship Committee," 1958–1959, 1960–1961, 1961–1962, 1962–1963, 1963–1964, 1964–1965, 1965–1966, 1966–1967, HU; Admission and Scholarship Committee, "Final Report of W. J. Bender, Chairman of the Admission and Scholarship Committee and Dean of Admissions and Financial Aids, 1952–1960," HU; Admission and Scholarship Committee, "Report on the Committee on Admissions and Scholarships," 1967–1968, 1968–1969, 1969–1970, HU.

203. Chase N. Peterson, "The Harvard-Radcliffe Relationship: Admission and Financial Aid," 30 January 1970, HUA. The 36-member committee included 11 representatives of the Associated Harvard Alumni Schools Committee and several prominent faculty members, including Richard J. Herrnstein (Psychology) and Ernest May (History). May was the only member who abstained, with one other member (Anthony G. Oettinger) dissenting.

204. Ibid., 2, 10.

205. Ibid., 15.

206. Peterson was referring primarily to greater racial and class diversity, but he also mentioned the need for "the raw-boned and unsophisticated rural students" and "more sons of alumni" (a peculiar argument, given that alumni sons constituted 19 percent of the freshman class in 1969). The claim that a reduction in the number of men would reduce diversity, Peterson recognized, "assumed, perhaps debatably, that men and women students are not fully interchangeable within 'delegations.'" Peterson did not explain why this assumption was correct, but stated simply "we believe it is" ("Harvard-Radcliffe Relationship," 10–11).

The belief that reducing male enrollment would reduce diversity was not limited to Harvard; Princeton's director of admissions, Timothy Callard, also worried that "the desired diverse composition of the student body would be difficult to maintain in all respects if the size of the undergraduate college were to remain the same and male enrollment were reduced in order to increase female enrollment." But Princeton's logic was different from Harvard's; it was based on the belief that recruiting minority and working-class females would prove more difficult than attracting their male classmates. And in contrast to Peterson, Callard favored sex-blind admissions as well as further expansion of the freshman class (see Office of Admission, "Report to the President," 1971–1972, PU, 17).

207. Peterson, "Harvard-Radcliffe Relationship," 11–12.

208. "Our independence," Peterson wrote, "is directly proportional to the strength and coherence of the community which supports us," with the "alumni/ae . . . the most conspicuous members of this community, but by no means the only element" (ibid., 3).

209. Dean Whitla, "Some Data on the Male-Female Admissions Ratio," n.d. [c. 1970], HUA. In 1969, 8,424 men applied to Harvard and just 2,723 to Radcliffe (Admission and Scholarship Committee, "Report on the Committee on Admissions and Scholarships," 1968–1969, HU, 2; "Radcliffe College — Report of the President 1967–1972," HU, 96).

210. Peterson, "Harvard-Radcliffe Relationship," 3, 15.

211. "Sex Discrimination, I," *HAB*, 2 March 1970, 12.

212. Edward Bok became editor of the *Ladies' Home Journal* in 1889, at the age of twenty-six, and in 1896 married Mary Louise Curtis, the daughter of Cyrus Curtis. Curtis was the head of the Curtis Publishing Company, which published (among other magazines) the *Saturday Evening Post*. Bok was the author of several books, including *Successward* (1895), *The Young Man in Business* (1900), and *The Americanization of Edward Bok* (1920), which was a top-ten bestseller for three years in the early 1920s. Edward Bok's son, Curtis Bok, became an associate justice of the Pennsylvania supreme court (*WWA, 1926–1927;* University News Office, 11 January 1971, HUA; Michael Korda, *Making the List: A Cultural History of the American Bestseller 1900–1999* (New York: Barnes & Noble, 2001), 46–48; and "Edward William Bok: Biographical Data," Bartleby.com, www.bartleby.com/197/103.html, accessed 1 August 2002).

213. "How Harvard Chose Bok," *Change*, March/April 1971, 19–21; University News Office, 11 January 1971, HUA; Robert Reinhold, "New Harvard Head Will Seek Unity," *NYT*, 12 January 1971; and *WWA, 1978–1979*.

214. Admission and Scholarship Committee, "Report on the Committee on Admissions and Scholarships," 1968–1969, HU, 2; Admission and Scholarship Committee, "Report on the Committee on Admissions and Scholarships," 1970–1971, HU, 2.

215. "Reardon Named Admissions Director," *HC*, 20 October 1971; Moseley, "Impact of the Merger," 85.

216. "Reardon Named Admissions Director"; Admission and Scholarship Committee, "Report on the Committee on Admissions and Scholarships," 1970–1971, HU; Admissions and Scholarships Committee, "Report on the Committee on Admissions and Scholarships," 1971–1972, 1972–1973, 1973–1974, HU.

217. "Radcliffe College — Report of the President 1967–1972," HU, 96; Strauch Committee, "Report of the Committee," A4–9.

218. A graduate of Taunton High School in Taunton, Massachusetts, Lester Fred Jewett received a scholarship from Harvard. A government major, he was a member of the Young Republicans as a student, graduating Phi Beta Kappa and magna cum laude in 1957. He then traveled to France for a year of study on the Tower Fellowship before returning to Harvard Business School, where he received his M.B.A. in 1960.

Before becoming dean of admissions, Jewett accumulated much experience in freshman admissions as an assistant dean of freshmen, assistant director of admissions, and director of freshman scholarships. Jewett served as dean of admissions at Harvard from 1972 to 1985 (University News Office, 15 August 1972, HUA; *Harvard Class Album: Class of 1957*, HU).

219. Among the groups mobilizing for greater gender equality was Women Employed at Harvard (WEH), which was founded in May 1973 and specifically called on Harvard to admit more undergraduate women (Michael Massing, "Women Employee Organization Criticizes Unequal Admissions," *HC*, 30 November 1973; "Jewett Replaces Peterson as Admissions Dean," *HC*, 15 August 1972).

220. Ibid.

221. "One-to-One," *HC*, 11 April 1973.

222. Ibid., 12 February 1974.

223. Moseley, "Impact of the Merger," 29. Among those worried about the consequence of reducing the number of men was the former dean of admissions Chase Peterson, who in his new capacity as Harvard's vice president for Alumni Affairs and Development expressed his concern that fewer men might mean a serious reduction in alumni donations. Echoing this view was David Riesman, the Henry Ford II Professor of Social Sciences, who, according to the alumni magazine, opposed a change in the 2.5–1 ratio on the grounds that "men will continue to provide the lion's share of financial support for higher education" (H. Jeffrey Leonard, "Strauch Committee Studies Future Admissions Alternatives," *HC*, 16 September 1974; "Woman and Man at Yale, and Elsewhere," *HM*, May 1974).

224. Robin Freedberg, "The Century-Old Merger Issue," *HC*, 16 September 1974.

225. Charles E. Shepard, "Bok to Reserve Opinion on Admissions," *HC*, 21 November 1973.

226. Among the members of the Strauch Committee were a number of influential members of the administration, including Fred Glimp (Associated Harvard Alumni), Charles Whitlock (dean of Harvard College), and Alberta Arthurs (dean of admissions at Radcliffe). The other faculty members were Roger W. Brown (Psychology), Doris Kearns (Government), and Stephen Thernstrom (History).

227. Freedberg, "Century-Old Merger Issue."

228. Leonard, "Strauch Committee Studies Future Admissions Alternatives."

229. Strauch Committee, "Report of the Committee," 9. In a major speech to the alumni in June 1974, Bok had foreshadowed the major arguments of the Strauch Committee, noting that women were "the only category of students who are subject to a fixed ceiling on the number that can enter the undergraduate body" (University News Office, speech by President Derek C. Bok at the Annual Meeting of the Associated Harvard Alumni, 12 June 1974, HUA).

230. Strauch Committee, "Report of the Committee," 15.

231. Ibid., 10. Historically, Radcliffe had been far less wealthy than Harvard, and as late as 1973, only 30 percent of Radcliffe students received financial aid compared to over half to Harvard undergraduates ("Colleges Seek Funds for Radcliffe Scholarships," *HM*, November 1973).

232. Moseley, "Impact of the Merger," 74–76; see also "Harvard-Radcliffe Combined Admissions,"

Harvard-Radcliffe Admission and Scholarships News-letter, August 1975, HUA, and "The Strauch Commit-tee Recommends Equal Access in Undergraduate Ad-missions," *HM*, April 1975, 12c-12d.

233. "Coeducation at Harvard: 'Equal Access is the Word,'" *HM*, February 1975, 12c. Still, it was a not insignificant drop from 1975, when 70 percent of the freshman class was male (Admissions and Scholar-ships Committee, "Report on the Committee on Ad-missions and Scholarships," 1975–1976 and 1976–1977, HU, 95).

234. Office of Admissions and Financial Aids, "Re-port on the Office of Admissions and Financial Aids," 1979–1980, HU, 113.

235. Admission and Scholarship Committee, "Re-port on the Committee on Admissions and Scholar-ships," 1967–1968, HU, 94; Admission and Scholarship Committee, "Report on the Committee on Admis-sions and Scholarships," 1975–1976 and 1976–1977, HU, 95.

236. Kabaservice, *The Guardians*, 293.

237. In his classic essay, "The Social Psychology of World Religions," Weber wrote: "Not ideas, but mate-rial and ideal interests directly govern man's conduct. Yet very frequently the 'world images' that have been created by 'ideas' have, like switchmen, determined the tracks along which action has been pushed by the dynamic of interest" (H. H. Gerth and C. Wright Mills, eds., *From Max Weber: Essays in Sociology* [New York: Oxford U.P., 1946]).

238. University News Office, speech by President Derek C. Bok, HUA.

239. At Yale in 1970–1971, when blacks composed roughly 6 percent of the student body, they absorbed almost half of Yale's financial aid budget (Kabaservice, "Kingman Brewster," 391). On Harvard, where 88 per-cent of black freshmen were on scholarships in 1965–1966, compared to a third of all freshmen, see Doer-mann, "Market for a College Education," 142–43. In the first class admitted under sex-blind admissions, just 35 percent of women received scholarships com-pared to 41 percent of men (calculated from Admis-sions and Scholarships Committee, "Report on the Committee on Admissions and Scholarships," 1975–1976 and 1976–1977, HU, 95).

240. Office of Institutional Research, "Minority Group Students," 16 February 1972, YU. Office of Ad-mission, "Annual Report," 1969–1970, PU, B-2; Office of Admission, "Report to the President," 1977–1978, PU, B-4. Harvard also showed a similar decline, drop-ping from a peak of 8 percent in 1970 to 6 percent in 1973. By 1976, however, it had rebounded back to 8 percent (Committee on Race Relations, "A Study of Race Relations at Harvard College," May 1980, HUA, 2).

241. Office of Institutional Research, "Minority Group Students"; Office of Admission, "Report to the President," 1969–1970, PU, E-2; Office of Admission, "Report to the President," 1977–1978, PU, B-4. Har-vard exhibited a parallel pattern, with women rising from 21 percent of the freshmen class in 1970 to 37 percent in 1978 (Admission and Scholarship Commit-tee, "Report on the Committee on Admissions and Scholarships," 1969–1970, HU, 81; "Radcliffe College — Report of the President 1967–1972," HU, 96; Office of Admissions and Financial Aids, "Report on the Office of Admissions and Financial Aids," 1977–1978, HU, 90).

15. The Alumni Revolt at Yale and Princeton

1. Brooks Mather Kelley, *Yale: A History* (New Ha-ven, Conn.: Yale U.P., 1974), 277.

2. Ibid., 326.

3. According to the University of Wisconsin histo-rian Merle Curti, the Alumni University Fund at Yale marked the beginning of "the organized effort to institutionalize philanthropic support" for colleges (quoted in ibid., 277).

4. Marcia Graham Synnott, *The Half-Opened Door: Discrimination and Admissions at Harvard, Yale, and Princeton, 1900–1970* (Westport, Conn.: Greenwood Press, 1979), 152.

5. By 1939, the proportion of the Yale freshman class composed of sons of alumni had reached 31.4 percent. According to a 1940 report of the Yale Alumni Board, alumni sons were "a substantially larger proportion of the undergraduates at Yale than at Harvard, Princeton, or Dartmouth" ("Report of the Alumni Board of Yale University," 22 February 1940, YUA, 6). For figures on the proportion of alumni sons in the Yale freshman classes from 1920 through 1975, see George W. Pierson, *A Yale Book of Numbers: Historical Statistics of the College and University, 1701–1976* (New Haven, Conn.: Yale U.P., 1983), 87–88.

6. Since many alumni gifts, however, were not put to current use but were made part of the endowment or used for other purposes, only about 4–5 percent of annual expenditures came directly from alumni con-tributions (Pierson, *Yale Book of Numbers*, 611, 617).

7. Called the Graduate Council for almost fifty years, the body changed its name to the Alumni Council in the late 1950s (Alexander Leitch, ed., *A Princeton Companion* [Princeton, N.J.: Princeton U.P., 1978], 10–13).

8. For an examination of Princeton's eating clubs in the 1950s, see Chapter 10.

9. Though the late 1960s was also a period of tre-mendous political turmoil at Harvard, it did not eventuate in an alumni revolt, as at Yale and Prince-ton. In contrast to Yale, Harvard did not move sud-denly to curtail the privileges of elite constituencies such as the alumni and major boarding schools. And in contrast to Princeton (and Yale as well), Harvard had long since abandoned its exclusively male tradi-tion at the undergraduate level, with Radcliffe women attending classes with Harvard men since World War II. Finally, for historic reasons related to both its lib-eral reputation and its demographic composition, the Harvard alumni had always had a smaller proportion of ardent political conservatives — the social basis of the alumni revolt at both Yale and Princeton.

10. Edwin E. Slosson, *Great American Universities* (New York: Macmillan, 1910), 72–73.

11. Richard W. Goldman, "Class of 1970: Accent on Variety," *YDN*, 15 April 1966.

12. See, for example, James Hill (pseudonym) to Reuben A. Holden, 20 April 1966, YUA; Edward Palmer (pseudonym) to Brewster, 6 June 1966, YUA; and Herbert Sturdy to Brewster, 22 June 1966, YUA.

13. Brewster to Sturdy, 11 August 1966, YUA.

14. Brewster to Nathaniel Hawkins (pseudonym), 5 October 1966, YUA.

15. Kingman Brewster Jr., "Admission to Yale: Ob-jectives and Myths," *YAM*, October 1966.

16. Sanford Dickson to David Martin, 6 January 1967, YUA. The letter was mistakenly dated 6 January

1966 but refers to articles that appeared in the October 1966 *YAM*.

17. Ibid. Dickson's decision to withhold contributions from Yale was not an isolated act.

18. Turner Dunbar to Brewster, 13 June 1967, YUA. See also David Meyer to Dunbar, 29 April 1967, YUA, and Barton Schwab to Brewster, 7 July 1967, YUA. Dunbar, Meyer, and Schwab are pseudonyms.

19. For a more detailed discussion of the Cook Committee and its findings, see Chapter 12.

20. In a letter to Barclay Hawkins, Brewster wrote: "Happily, since we talked, I have had positive feedback on Ink's recent visit to Andover. Happily he did much to restore us to the grace we had traditionally and which Yale deserves" (Brewster to Hawkins, 4 November 1966, YUA).

21. Minutes from a meeting of the Alumni Board Committee raise the question of whether Clark had "gotten the message" and suggested that the composition of the class of 1971 "would provide an answer" (Alumni Board Committee, minutes, n.d. [c. February 1967], YUA).

22. Brewster to Muyskens, 15 March 1967, YUA.

23. Nicolas Lemann has aptly described Muyskens as "a deeply reassuring and moderate older gentleman from Canada" whose appointment was designed to communicate "to the alumni that he [Brewster] was going to rein Clark in" (*The Big Test: The Secret History of the American Meritocracy* [New York: Farrar, Straus, 1999], 151).

24. A copy of Brewster's letter to Muyskens was enclosed with his responses to Turner Dunbar and Ashby Porter '09 (pseudonym); see Brewster. to Dunbar, 26 June 1967, YUA, and Brewster. to Porter, 9 June 1967, YUA, as well as Porter to Brewster, 27 April 1967, YUA, and Dunbar to Brewster, YUA. The letter from Porter, which described Jews as "clannish, self-centered, [and] rather selfish," must have been painful to Brewster, who had long been a principled opponent of anti-Semitism. But as president of Yale, Brewster was concerned about growing alumni disaffection and responded diplomatically, telling Porter that he was "grateful for the concern which prompts your letters" and affirming that his "loyalty means a great deal to everyone who knows how much you have done for Yale."

25. The figure of 12 percent includes only the sons of alumni who attended Yale College. Adding legacies whose fathers attended a graduate or professional school, the percentage rises to 14 percent (Pierson, *Yale Book of Numbers*, 88).

26. Office of Admissions and Freshman Scholarships and the Office of Enrollment and Scholarships, "Annual Report of the Acting Dean of Undergraduate Admissions and Student Appointments," 1964–1965, YU, 3; Office of University Development, "The Development Reporter," 1968, YUA.

27. For an account of the publication of *God and Man at Yale* and the reaction (including a sharply critical review in the *Atlantic Monthly* by McGeorge Bundy) that it provoked, see John Judis, *William F. Buckley Jr.: Patron Saint of the Conservatives* (New York: Simon & Schuster, 1988), 17–34, 83–98. The first chapter of this excellent study is called "The Counterrevolution."

28. "Buckley Seeks Trusteeship," *YDN*, 20 October 1967.

29. Admission and Scholarship Committee, "Report on the Committee on Admissions and Scholar-

ships," 1967–1968, HU; Office of Admission, "Report to the Faculty," 1967–1968, PU; Office of University Development, "The Development Reporter," YUA.

30. Because of the quota on the number of women in 1969, the admission rate of alumni daughters was just 20 percent (Office of Undergraduate Admissions, "Combined Annual Reports of the Dean of Admissions and the Director of Undergraduate Admissions," 1968–1969, YU, 3).

31. Lemann, *Big Test*, 149.

32. Orde Coombs, "Making It at Yale," *Change*, June 1973.

33. "Dwyer Commission Completes Major Report on Alumni Relations with Yale," *YAM*, February 1971, 35. A graduate of Montclair Academy in New Jersey, Dwyer was a member of the football and track teams and a member of Zeta Psi (*Yale Banner: Class of 1944*, YU, 321).

34. Pierson, *Yale Book of Numbers*, 611, 613, 618.

35. Office of Undergraduate Admissions, "Combined Annual Reports of the Dean of Admissions and the Director of Undergraduate Admissions," 1968–1969, YU, 5.

36. Clark's official reason for consolidating the Alumni Schools Committees (ASCs) was "to achieve greater efficiency and closer rapport with alumni aiding the Admissions process," but it was also clearly an attempt to consolidate control over the admissions process by placing the ASCs under the supervision of the Office of Admissions (Office of Admissions and Freshman Scholarships, "Report of the Dean of Admissions and Student Appointment to the President and Fellows of Yale University," 1965–1966, YU, 1).

37. Office of Undergraduate Admissions, "Report of the Dean of Admissions," 1967–1968, YU, 5.

38. Lux et Veritas, "A Report on Yale Admissions 1950–1972," 1972, YU, 7. See also Charles Cuneo, "Research on Interviews Illustrates Discrepancies," *YDN*, 20 September 1972.

39. Lux et Veritas, "Report on Yale Admissions," 7.

40. B. H. Prentice, letter to the editor, *YAM*, December 1966, 7.

41. Robert H. Kilpatrick, "Dwyer Commission Completes Major Report on Alumni Relations with Yale," *YAM*, February 1971, 37.

42. Russell I. Clark Jr., interview by Geoffrey Kabaservice, 9 April 1993, transcript, YUA, 74. In a second interview, however, Clark seemed less certain about whether he would have been reappointed: "I also know that for me personally, another five years as Dean of Admissions, had I wanted it and had Brewster given it to me — and that's speculative on both sides — would not have been rewarding" (Clark, interview by Kabaservice, 13 May 1993, transcript, YUA, 25).

43. Ibid., 25, 55.

44. Geoffrey Kabaservice, "Kingman Brewster and the Rise and Fall of the Progressive Establishment" (Ph.D. diss., Yale Univ., 1999), 515–28. The Brewster quote is from page 523.

45. M. A. Farber, "Brewster Tells Friendly but Questioning Yale Alumni He Cannot Be 'Personally Neutral' on Public Issues," *NYT*, 14 June 1970.

46. The following paragraphs draw extensively on the excellent account of events surrounding May Day at Yale in Geoffrey Kabaservice, *The Guardians: Kingman Brewster, His Circle, and the Rise of the Liberal Establishment* (New York: Henry Holt, 2004), 404–18.

47. William Sloane Coffin Jr., interview, 9 Decem-

ber 1991; cited in Kabaservice, "Kingman Brewster," 537.

48. Farber, "Brewster Tells Friendly but Questioning Yale Alumni."

49. Kabaservice, *The Guardians*, 415.

50. Brewster to Albert Van Sinderen, 1 June 1970; cited in Kabaservice, "Kingman Brewster."

51. Brewster to John Mitchell, 28 November 1969, cited in Kabaservice, *The Guardians*, 395.

52. Kabaservice, "Kingman Brewster," 533.

53. See, for example, the concessions described in "Response of the Yale Administration to the Proposals of the Action Committee of the Black Student Alliance of Yale," 23 April 1970, YUA, and the account of the assistance that Brewster received from Kurt Schmoke, a black student leader (and later a Rhodes scholar), in helping the situation at Yale stay calm as May Day approached (Kabaservice, *The Guardians*, 406–7).

54. Kabaservice, "Kingman Brewster," 514.

55. In 1971, the Yale University Study Commission on Governance, a 60-member commission that included 24 faculty and 24 students, concluded that the Corporation was a self-perpetuating body drawn from a "narrow stratum of society" and excluding, until very recently, "women, blacks, Jews, Catholics, and other persons, however distinguished, who are not members of the more favored groups in society" (M. S. Handler, "Study Concludes Yale Trustees Perpetuate Their Own Stratum," *NYT,* 10 April 1971).

56. Joseph B. Treaster, "Trustees Praise Brewster's Rule," *NYT,* 28 September 1970; "Trustees Give Brewster Tenure," *YAM,* October 1970, 39.

57. Lux et Veritas, "A Statement of Objectives," n.d. [c. October 1970], YUA; "Lux et Veritas, Inc.," *YAM,* January 1971, 33; Louis M. Loeb et al. to Brewster., 5 November 1970, YUA.

58. "Lux et Veritas, Inc."

59. Ibid.; "Joseph W. Stack Jr.," *Yale Banner: Class of 1940,* YU; "John Wesley Castles III," *Yale Banner: Class of 1943,* YU.

60. "Lux et Veritas, Inc." A graduate of Andover, Charles Stafford Gage was a member of Skull and Bones and captain of the varsity track team. John Dorsey Garrison, a son of Elisha Eli Garrison 1897 and a graduate of the Taft School, was a member of Wolf's Head and the Sword and Gun Club. Louis Melville Loeb, the son of a Jewish immigrant from Heidelberg, was a graduate of Exeter and a member of the varsity swimming team at Yale, where he belonged to the Exeter club and Alpha Delta Phi (see *Yale Banner: Class of 1919, Yale Banner: Class of 1925,* and *Yale Banner: Class of 1931*).

61. "A Statement of Objectives."

62. Buck, "What Kind of Boy Does Yale Want?", quoted in Lux et Veritas, "Report on Yale Admissions 1950–1972," 1–2.

63. Ibid., 8–12.

64. Ibid., 2, 11, 16.

65. Lux et Veritas, "Coeducation at Yale," 1972, YUA, 2–3, 10.

66. Ibid., 9.

67. Ibid., 11–12.

68. Brewster to Lux et Veritas, 18 November 1970, YUA. Copies sent to Louis M. Loeb '19, John D. Garrison '31, J. William Stack Jr. '40, and John W. Castles III '43.

69. Brewster to Charles S. Gage, 7 December 1970, YUA.

70. Jonathan Straus (pseudonym) to Lux et Veritas, 24 January 1973, YUA; Henry Chauncey Jr. to Straus, 24 January 1973, YUA.

71. Pierson, *Yale Book of Numbers,* 613, 618.

72. M. A. Farber, "11 College Presidents Caution Money Crisis Imperils Future," *NYT,* 13 July 1970.

73. "Yale Alumni Schools Committee Memo: September 1970," YUA; see also Lemann, *Big Test,* 152.

74. A member of the varsity hockey team and of the Aurelian Society (an academic honor society), Chauncey was tapped for Wolf's Head, which was just a notch below Skull and Bones and Scroll and Key in the campus hierarchy (*Yale Banner: Class of 1957,* YU).

75. Lemann, *Big Test,* 146.

76. Daniel A. Oren, *Joining the Club: A History of Jews and Yale* (New Haven, Conn.: Yale U.P., 1986), 372.

77. In 1971, a record 887 of those admitted to Yale chose to attend other colleges, including 441 who went to Harvard-Radcliffe and 113 to Princeton. Of those who picked Harvard, 10 percent cited financial considerations as the primary factor (Charles Cuneo, "887 Yale Admittees Choose Other Colleges," *YDN,* 13 October 1971). In 1972, Yale acknowledged that the "self-help gap" in its financial packages was a factor in its relatively low yield and admitted that it was "not competitive with our major rivals" (Office of Undergraduate Admissions, "Report of the Dean of Undergraduate Admissions to the President and Fellows of Yale University," 1971–1972, YU, 9).

78. Henry Chauncey Jr., "Yale Undergraduate Admissions," 12 January 1972, YUA, 2, 7, 9.

79. Ibid.

80. Pierson, *Yale Book of Numbers,* 618.

81. John E. Ecklund to Chauncey, 10 January 1972, YUA, 2, 5–6.

82. Henry Chauncey Jr., "Excerpts From the Chauncey Speech on Admissions Reforms," *YAM,* August 1972, 23; see also "Chauncey Cites New Reforms Affecting Admissions Policies," *YDN,* 22 May 1972.

83. Scott Herhold, "Admissions: 'An Element of Humanity and Order,'" *YAM,* August 1972, 22.

84. Office of Undergraduate Admissions, "Combined Annual Reports of the Dean of Admissions and the Director of Undergraduate Admissions," 1968–1969, YU, 3; Office of Undergraduate Admissions, "Report of the Dean of Admissions and Student Appointments to the President and Fellows of Yale University," 1969–1970, YU, 3; Office of Undergraduate Admissions, "Report of the Dean of Undergraduate Admissions to the President and Fellows of Yale University," 1970–1971, YU, 9; Office of Undergraduate Admissions, "Profile of the Yale College Class of 1976," 1 July 1972, YU, Table IV.

85. Following his resignation from Yale, Muyskens moved to Stanford to become associate dean of admissions (*Alumni Schools Committee Newsletter,* September 1972, YUA).

86. *Yale Banner: Class of 1956,* YU, and "Worth David: New Dean of Admissions," *YAM,* August 1972, 26.

87. Worth David to Alumni Schools Committees, *ASC Newsletter,* September 1972, YUA.

88. Worth David to Yale Corporation Sub-Committee on Admissions, memorandum, 25 January 1973, YUA.

89. David to Brewster, memorandum, 23 February 1973, YUA.

90. Parker Williamson III is a pseudonym.

91. Williamson to J. Richardson Dilworth, 6 December 1972, YUA. So concerned was Dilworth about Williamson's letter that he forwarded it to his friend Endicott Peabody Davison (whom he addressed as "Dear Cottie"), then serving as the officer of the Yale Corporation for Institutional Development and Capital Support. He wrote that "in view of Parker's long connection with the Development Board I felt it was important that you and Kingman [who also received a copy of Williamson's letter] be aware of this." Dilworth concluded by admitting that he "cannot escape the feeling that . . . we have a real problem of timing that we have got to face frankly." Davison, a graduate of Groton, Yale '48, and the grandson of Groton's founder, Endicott Peabody, was a partner in the New York law firm of Winthrop, Stimson, Putnam, and Roberts (see Dilworth to Davison, 12 December 1972, YUA, and *WWA, 1978–1979*).

92. Caldwell B. Wellington to Paul R. Moritz, 23 April 1973, YUA. Wellington is a pseudonym for an old-stock Yale family.

93. David to the Yale Corporation Sub-Committee on Admissions, YUA.

94. Calculated from Office of Undergraduate Admissions, "Profile of the Yale College Class of 1977," 1 October 1973, YU.

95. Chauncey to Dilworth, 25 June 1973, YUA. In the letter, Chauncey refers to a letter from an 1938 alumnus that apparently raised several issues, including that of "policy with regard to minorities, Jewish students in particular."

96. Jay Hirshfield et al. to Kingman Brewster, Horace Taft, and Henry Chauncey, 24 May 1973, YUA, 6–7.

97. Pierson, *Yale Book of Numbers*, 613.

98. Another promising young Yale humanist, a professor of English and comparative literature, A. Bartlett Giamatti was also considering an offer from Princeton at the time. In 1978, he was named Brewster's successor as president of Yale (John P. Miller, *Creating Academic Settings* [New Haven, Conn.: J. Simeon Press, 1991], 212–13).

99. "Speech by Kingman Brewster to 1973 Yale Assembly Corporation Dinner," 26 October 1973, YUA.

100. Ibid.; "Brewster's Speech to Alumni" (excerpts), *YAM*, January 1974, 19.

101. Brewster's letter to David also reaffirmed that the Corporation wished "to encourage outstanding athletes to apply" and had instructed "everyone engaged in the admissions process to give positive weight to athletic distinction" (Brewster to David, 14 November 1973, YUA).

102. Office of Undergraduate Admissions, "Profile of the Yale College Class of 1978," 1 July 1974, YU.

103. Including the children of alumni of Yale's graduate and professional schools (Yale's traditional way of reporting on the issue), the proportion of legacies rose to 20 percent of the freshman class (Pierson, *Yale Book of Numbers*, 88).

104. Ibid.; Office of Undergraduate Admissions, "Profile of the Yale College Class of 1978," YU.

105. Even during the Clark-Muyskens period, legacies still received considerable preference. A study of the entering class of 1971 by Robert Sternberg, then a student working in the Office of Institutional Research and currently the IBM Professor of Psychology and Education at Yale, was conducted in a context of "considerable . . . alumni pressure to ease standards of admission for Yale affiliates . . . or even to declare open admission for those Yale affiliates who meet certain very minimal entrance requirements." Sternberg found that alumni children had a substantially higher probability of admission, given the same level of "merit" as judged by the academic and personal ratings of the two readers who had evaluated the candidates. In the case of male candidates with average ratings, the probability of acceptance for an alumni son was 30 percent — six times higher than the probability of 5 percent for candidates without Yale parentage (Robert Sternberg to Sam Chauncey, memorandum, "Comparative Expectancies of Admission for Yale Affiliates and Non-Affiliates," 3 September 1971, YUA; see also "Admissions Edge for Alumni Children," *YAM*, December 1971, 24).

106. Steven E. Carlson to Brewster, 7 June 1974, YUA. The letter is the cover note attached to a memorandum of 26 April 1974 on "Alumni Children Admissions Statistics" from Steven E. Carlson to William Lyons.

107. It is worth emphasizing that the degree of preference reported here for 1973 — including candidates designated by the Development Office as three, four, or five stars — was almost certainly *less* than in 1974, when the admission rate for legacies increased from 39 to 49 percent (Carlson to Lyons, "Alumni Children Admissions Statistics," YUA).

108. Carlson to Brewster, YUA.

109. Office of Admission, "Report to the President," 1964–1965, PU, 9; Office of Admission, "Report to the Faculty," 1967–1968, PU, 77.

110. "Dissident Alumni Organize," *Princeton Packet*, 19 March 1969, PUA; "Letter from ACTION to the *PAW*," *PAW*, 22 April 1964, 5, 18.

111. Ronald Sullivan, "Princeton Alumni Group Set Up to Oppose Coeds and Protests," *NYT*, 13 March 1969.

112. Patterson was born in Chicago in 1917 and graduated from the Chicago Latin School for Boys. A Rhodes Scholar, he served with the OSS and the AUS from 1944 to 1946 before embarking on a successful business career. In 1958, he became a senior partner in Jere Patterson & Associates, an international consulting firm in New York City. His views on the issues facing Princeton appear in "Thunder on the Right: An Interview with Jere Patterson '38, Chairman of ACTION," *PAW*, 20 October 1970; biographical information from *WWA, 1978–1979*).

113. Ronald Sullivan, "Princeton Alumni in Poll Opposed to Disorders," *NYT*, 11 November 1969.

114. Sullivan, "Princeton Alumni Group Set Up."

115. See, for example, 23 September 1968 radio editorial (PUA), written shortly after the release of the Patterson Report, by Herbert W. Hobler '44, one of the founders of ACTION and president of the Nassau Broadcasting Company: "Editorial Broadcast Over WHWH and WTOA." Hobler, a graduate of the Hill School who was a member of the Princeton basketball, football, and track teams and Tiger Inn, was preceded at Princeton by two brothers, Edward W. Hobler '39 and Wells A. Hobler '41. On January 15, 1969, Hobler presented the Board of Trustees with a petition against coeducation signed by 250 alumni (see Hobler to Harold Helm and James Oates, 15 January 1969, PUA). The letter was dated just three days before the trustees announced their decision to admit

women. On Hobler's undergraduate career, see *Nassau Herald: Class of 1944*, PU, 247.

116. Robert H. Frazier et al., letter to the editor, *PAW*, 22 April 1969.

117. Sullivan, "Princeton Alumni Groups Set Up."

118. "'Ohio Alumni' Poll," *PAW*, 1 July 1969, 9–10; Dorritt A. Cowan, "Single-Sex to Coeducation at Princeton and Yale: Two Case Studies" (Ph.D. diss., Teachers' College, Columbia Univ., 1982), 135–36.

119. "Princeton Will Add Graduate Trustees and Admit Women," *NYT*, 21 April 1969; Luther Munford, "Anatomy of a Decision," *PAW*, 11 November 1969, 18–19; Office of Admission, "Annual Report," 1968–1969, PU.

120. Cowan, "Single-Sex to Coeducation," 135–36.

121. Goheen to Hobler, 20 March 1969, quoted in Cowan, "Single-Sex to Coeducation," 134.

122. "Dissident Alumni Organize," PUA; George A. Hamid Jr., "Doubts on Coeducation," *Daily Princetonian*, 11 April 1969; "ACTION Meeting," *PAW*, 1 July 1969, 9.

123. "More Candidates," *PAW*, 22 April 1969, 7. Arthur S. Langlie, a trustee of Seattle's Lakeside School (from which he graduated in 1948), was the son of Arthur B. Langlie, the Republican governor of Washington from 1941 to 1945 and 1949 to 1957. On Arthur S. Langlie, see *Nassau Herald: Class of 1952*, PU, 205; on Arthur B. Langlie, see *WWA, 1962–1963*.

124. "For Alumni Trustee," *PAW*, 4 March 1969, 10–11; "New Trustees," *PAW*, 1 July 1969, 9–10.

125. "ACTION Meeting," PUA, 9.

126. "ACTION Poll" and "Goheen Response," *PAW*, 11 November 1969, 4–5. Despite having denounced the ACTION poll as biased, Goheen conceded that there was a "split in opinion on many sensitive issues, which seems to pertain on the basis of age."

127. "Thunder on the Right," 10.

128. "Goheen Says Princeton Expects $2.4 Million Deficit This Year," *NYT*, 25 October 1970.

129. "Thunder on the Right," 11–12.

130. Shelby C. Davis, "Silent Majority," *PAW*, 22 February 1972, 3. On the founding of CAP, see Cole Bunzel, "'Prospect': Publication Starts; Copies Mailed Free to Alumni," *Daily Princetonian*, 5 October 1972.

131. Shelby C. Davis, "Homogeneous or Heterogenous?" *PAW*, 2 May 1972, 3.

132. See E. J. Kahn Jr., "Annals of Higher Education: A Tiger by the Tail," *New Yorker*, 23 May 1977, 90–92.

133. The biographical portrait of Davis comes from several sources, including *Nassau Herald: Class of 1930*, PU; *Reunion Class of 1930: 25th Reunion*, June 1955, PU; *WWA, 1944–1945*; *WWA, 1978–1979*; Kahn, "Annals of Higher Education"; and the Selected Funds, "Our Research Methodology," www.selected funds.com/sdidmp3.html (accessed 15 October 2002).

134. Shelby C. Davis, "Caesar's Wife," *PAW*, 10 October 1972, 4–5. A public university just 18 miles from Princeton, Rutgers was much more heterogeneous than its more prestigious neighbor and enrolled far more students from families of limited means and low-status religious and ethnic backgrounds. Apparently, it had long been a symbol in the Ivy League of a university populated by too many students of low-status background. In 1952, Harvard's dean of admissions, Wilbur Bender, noting with approval that "we are one of the few colleges to which scions of the social and economic crust go as a matter of course," observed tartly, "A Social Register family in the North-

east can send its son to Harvard or Yale or Princeton" but "isn't likely to send him to Rutgers or Penn." As the only Ivy League college never to have had a quota on the number of Jews, Penn also suffered from some of the same status problems afflicting Rutgers. The difference between Princeton and its neighbors to the north and south was visible as early as 1918, when the proportion of Jews was 2.6 percent at Princeton, 9.1 percent at Rutgers, and 15.7 percent at Penn (see Wilbur J. Bender, "Comprehensive Formal Statement of Harvard College Admission Policy," 18 September 1952, HUA, 28; Richard A. Farnum, "Prestige in the Ivy League: Meritocracy at Columbia, Harvard and Penn, 1870–1940" [Ph.D. diss., Univ. of Pennsylvania, 1990]; and *American Jewish Year Book, 5681: September 13, 1920 to October 2, 1921*, vol. 22 [Philadelphia: Jewish Publication Society of America, 1920]).

135. *Nassau Herald: Class of 1921*, PU; *Reunion Class of 1921, 1966*, PU; *WWA, 1962–1963*.

136. Kahn, "Annals of Higher Education," 93–96; Ronald Smothers, "Princeton Alumni Scorn Liberalism," *NYT*, 25 December 1972; and Bunzel, "'Prospect': Publication Starts." On Jones, see *Nassau Herald: Class of 1972*, PU.

137. Just how strongly Davis agreed with Jones's perspective on the faculty was apparent in a fundraising pamphlet he wrote for CAP in 1973: "A left-wing, anti-business anti-establishment attitude permeates much of America's intelligentsia today . . . The Administration at Princeton today is likewise permissive and liberal-radical . . . The unannounced goal of the Administration, now achieved, of a student population of approximately 40% women and minorities, will largely vitiate the alumni body of the future . . . The permissive, liberal-radical faculty is continuously indoctrinating students along the permissive, liberal-radical lines . . . If Princeton cannot be salvaged for free thinking and free enterprise, what educational institution in America can be salvaged?" (quoted in Kahn, "Annals of Higher Education," 98).

138. "Why CAP? Why Prospect?" *Prospect*, 9 October 1972.

139. "Bradley Does Not Concur," *Prospect*, 4 December 1972, 12.

140. See, for example, John Thatcher Jr., "Scholarships . . . Can We Still Compete?" *Prospect*, 13 November 1972; John H. Thatcher Jr., "Evaluating Student Applicants," *Prospect*, 29 October 1973; "Opinion Research Corporation Polls Alumni [Poll on Admissions]," *Prospect*, 29 October 1973; John Thatcher Jr., "Reviewing Princeton's Admission Policy," pt. 1, *Prospect*, 15 September 1974; Thatcher, "Princeton's Admission Policy," pt. 2, *Prospect*, 9 October 1974; "Admissions and Princeton," *Prospect*, 15 December 1975; "Can You Pick a Princeton Student?" *Prospect*, 15 September 1976.

141. "Our Objectives," *Prospect*, 29 October 1973, 7.

142. "Opinion Research Corporation Polls Alumni," 10–13.

143. Shelby C. Davis, "Preserving the Spirit of the Princeton Alumni Body," *Prospect*, 7 May 1973, 8–9. In a 1974 interview with the *Daily Princetonian*, Davis elaborated on his vision of Princeton's distinctive position within the Big Three: "'Goheen wanted Princeton to be a little Harvard,' Davis said. 'I don't think this is Princeton's role. I think Princeton's role is educating not geniuses so much but turning out well-rounded people; some will be Secretary of State, but a

lot more will go back to Akron, Ohio, and be good citizens there'" (quoted in Kahn, "Annals of Higher Education," 102).

144. John H. Thatcher Jr., *Prospect*'s point man on the issue of admissions, was the son of John H. Thatcher '26. A member of the Charter Club (the same eating club to which Davis belonged), Thatcher was also a member of the Republican Club and listed himself in the yearbook as an Episcopalian (*Nassau Herald: Class of 1953*, PU).

145. Thatcher, "Evaluating Student Applicants," 14.

146. "A Statement of the Concerned Alumni of Princeton Executive Committee," *Prospect*, 17 December 1973, 14.

147. Board of Trustees to "Princetonians," 24 January 1974, PUA.

148. As at Yale, the Princeton administration, while acknowledging that there had been an understanding with the alumni that coeducation would not lead to a reduction in the number of men, insisted that "there was never a formal commitment to that effect" (News Bureau, "Equal Access at Princeton," 19 January 1974, PUA, 3).

149. Office of Admission, "Report to the President," 1971–1972, PU, 5; Office of Admission, "Report," 1972–1973, PU, 8; Office of Admission, "Report," 1973–1974, PU, 10; Office of Admission, "Report," 1974–1975, PU, 4.

150. Office of Admission, "Report," 1973–1974, PU, 6–7.

151. John H. Thatcher Jr., "The Decline of Princeton Athletics," *Prospect*, 18 December 1972; Laurence B. Chollet, "Rah! Rah! Tiger! Tiger! Tiger! Football's Worst Record — A Dismal Autumn," *Prospect*, 17 December 1973; "The Strange Decline of Princeton Football," *Prospect*, 30 November 1976, 5.

152. Office of Admission, "Report," 1974–1975, 9.

153. Office of Admission, "Report," 1975–1976, 4–6.

154. The estimate that the Princeton class entering in 1976 was 19 percent Jewish is based on the number of students who described their mother's religious preference as Jewish. However, given that 8 percent of the students checked the box "none," it is very possible that 19 percent was an underestimate if one counts as a Jew — as was historically the pattern at Princeton — any student with even partial Jewish ancestry (American Council on Education and the University of California, Los Angeles, "Princeton University, Summary of Data on Entering Freshmen for Fall 1976").

155. Office of Institutional Research, "Yale College Admissions, Classes of 1962–1982," 2 April 1979, YU.

156. Office of Admission, "Report to the Faculty," 1965–1966, PU, 12; Office of Admission, "Report to the President," 1966–1967, PU, Chart G; Office of Admission, "Report to the Faculty," 1967–1968, PU, 25; Office of Admission, "Annual Report," 1968–1969, PU, E-2.

157. The lowest ratio at Princeton of legacy-nonlegacy applicants was 1.84 in 1973 (Office of Admission, "Report to the Faculty," 1965–1966, 1967–1968, PU; Office of Admission, "Report to the President," 1966–1967, 1970–1971, 1971–1972, 1972–1973, 1973–1974, 1974–1975, PU; Office of Admission, "Annual Report," 1968–1969, PU; Office of Admission, "Report to the President," 1969–1970, PU).

158. Office of Undergraduate Admissions, "Profile of the Yale College Class of 1980," September 1976, YU; Oren, *Joining the Club*, 321; Arnold Jacob Wolf, "Jewish Experience Is Vividly Present at Yale," *YAM*, January 1973, 14.

159. Lemann, *Big Test*, 152.

160. Kingman Brewster Jr., "Johns Hopkins Commencement Address," 6 June 1968, cited in Kabaservice, "Kingman Brewster," 387.

161. The son of Reuben Andrus Holden Jr. '11, Reuben ("Ben") Andrus Holden IV '40 prepared for Yale at the Cincinnati Country Day School, the Institute La Ville in Lausaune, and the Asheville School. An English major, he was managing editor of the *Yale Daily News* and a member of Skull and Bones, the Aurelian Society, and Phi Beta Kappa. After graduation, he served for five years in the AUS before returning to Yale, where he served in a variety of administrative posts and received a Ph.D. in 1951. In 1953, he was named Secretary of the University (*Yale Banner: Class of 1940*, YU, and *WWA, 1962–1963*).

162. Quoted in Kabaservice, *The Guardians*, 413.

163. In a forthright letter to the president of Amherst, Brewster acknowledged that "we were very apprehensive about what the coeducating of Yale's undergraduate mission would do to alumni feelings." Admitting that "it was the trustees who led me, not vice versa" in deciding to admit women directly to Yale College, he continued: "The immediate alumni response was mixed. Numbers are misleading, no poll or head count has ever been taken. But if I had to use fractions for illustrative purposes I would surmise that one third were really enthusiastic, partly on the merit, partly because of what they thought was Yale 'leadership.' Maybe a half were their usual apathetic or deferential selves; assuming that whatever the faculty, administration, and trustees did was probably correct. That would leave about a sixth who were outraged — clustered discernibly toward the higher level of the age graph. They were more grumbling than boisterous. Often the outrage was couched in terms of failure of consultation or the precipitate style of the decision, but fundamentally they were against the desecration of their Yale by females." While Brewster's estimate that only about a sixth of Yale alumni were vigorously opposed to coeducation seems on the low side, he was almost certainly correct on two key points: that a substantial proportion of the alumni supported coeducation (and, more generally, the new Yale admissions policy) and that support increased as age declined (Brewster to John W. Ward, 17 November 1972, YUA).

164. Among those alumni opposed to CAP was one Cullom Davis '57, the nephew of Shelby Cullom Davis, who in the notes about his class in the February 9, 1976, *PAW* wrote, "My longest and earliest contribution yet . . . I support the Bowen administration and deplore the costly ego-tripping of its CAP antics" (quoted in Kahn, "Annals of Higher Education," 106).

165. The term "Progressive Establishment" is borrowed from Kabaservice. Though Kabaservice distinguishes the group from liberals, for our purposes it stands for the liberal wing of the Progressive Establishment as opposed to the conservative wing represented by such men as Shelby Cullom Davis (see Kabaservice, "Kingman Brewster," 2–7).

166. David Gelernter, "How the Intellectuals Took Over (And What to Do About It)," *Commentary* 103, no. 3 (March 1997), 36.

167. E. Digby Baltzell, "The Protestant Establishment Revisited," *American Scholar* 45, Autumn 1976,

505. See also his classic work, *The Protestant Establishment: Aristocracy and Caste in America* (New York: Vintage, 1964), as well as *Philadelphia Gentleman: The Making of a National Upper Class* (Glencoe, Ill.: Free Press, 1958), reprinted as *An American Business Aristocracy* (New York: Collier Books, 1962); *Puritan Boston and Quaker Philadelphia: Two Protestant Ethics and the Spirit of Class Authority and Leadership* (New York: Free Press, 1979); *The Protestant Establishment Revisited*, edited and with an introduction by Howard Schneiderman (New Brunswick, N.J.: Transaction, 1991).

168. The person who planned and directed the Bay of Pigs invasion was the CIA's director of covert operations, Richard M. Bissell Jr., Groton '28, Yale '32. Yet it is also worth noting that it was two archetypal members of the Protestant Establishment, Archibald Cox and Elliot Richardson, who resigned from the Nixon administration in response to the Watergate scandal. In the words of Baltzell, "The class code of Cox, of Saint Paul's and Harvard, and Richardson, of Milton and Harvard, would no longer allow them to go along with the team." On Bissell, see *WWA, 1962–1963*, and Bart Barnes, "Richard Helms Dies; Founding CIA Member Led Agency Six Years," *Washington Post*, 24 October 2002. On Cox and Richardson, see Baltzell, "Protestant Establishment Revisited," 503.

169. See David Halberstam, *The Best and the Brightest* (New York: Random House, 1972).

170. James Fallows, "What Did You Do in the Class War, Daddy?" *Washington Monthly*, October 1975, 15.

171. Kahn, "Annals of Higher Education," 107.

172. Ibid., 101.

173. While it failed in its attempt to change Princeton's basic direction, the alumni revolt had more success in helping to create a counterintelligentsia that would combat the alleged liberal and leftist bias of American intellectuals. Among the prominent right-wing intellectuals who worked at *Prospect* were Dinesh D'Souza, the editor from 1983 to 1985 and Terry Eastland, the managing editor in 1975. Among D'Souza's many books are *Illiberal Education: The Politics of Sex and Race on Campus, Ronald Reagan: Spirit of a Leader*, and *Letters to a Young Conservative*. Eastland, who served for a time as publisher of the *American Spectator* (which led the media campaign to impeach President Clinton and is now the publisher of the *Weekly Standard*), is the author of *Ending Affirmative Action, Counting by Race* (with William Bennett) and *Conservatives in Power: The Task of Governing*. For a useful account of the rise of the conservative counterintelligentsia, see Sidney Blumenthal, *The Rise of the Counter-Establishment: From Conservative Ideology to Political Power* (New York: Harper & Row, 1988).

174. According to Brooks ("David Rockefeller's 'Memoirs': Born to be Mild," *NYT Book Review*, 20 October 2002), "For 200 years a certain sort of people with a certain culture occupied the commanding heights of American society. Then suddenly sometime around the 1960s . . . poof! . . . they were gone. Within a historical instant most of the power networks, codes of conduct and institutions the Protestant Establishment built were eliminated or transformed beyond recognition. And the amazing thing is that its members didn't even put up a fight." For Brooks's own account of how the elite has changed in recent decades, see *Bobos in Paradise: The New Upper Class and How They Got There* (New York: Simon & Schuster, 2000).

175. Wilbur J. Bender, "Confidential Memo by Wilbur J. Bender to the Committee on Admission and Scholarships," 17 November 1957, HUA, 2.

16. Diversity, the Bakke *Case, and the Defense of Autonomy*

1. Commission on the Future of the College, *The Report of the Commission on the Future of the College* (Princeton, N.J.: Trustees of Princeton Univ., 1973); Orde Coombs, "Making It at Yale," *Change*, June 1973; and Caldwell Titcomb, letter to Jerome Karabel, 18 August 1999. Titcomb is an editor of the book Werner Sollors et al., eds., *Blacks at Harvard: A Documentary History of African-American Experience at Harvard and Radcliffe* (New York: New York U.P., 1993).

2. Data from Office of Admissions, Harvard Univ.; Daniel A. Oren, *Joining the Club: A History of Jews and Yale* (New Haven, Conn.: Yale U.P., 1985), 188–201, 321.

3. Admissions and Scholarships Committee, "Report on the Committee on Admissions and Scholarships," 1975–1976, 1976–1977, HU; Office of Undergraduate Admissions, "Profile — Class of 1979," September 1975, YU; Office of Admission, "Report to the President," 1975–1976, PU; Cooperative Institutional Research Program, "Summary of Data on Entering Freshmen, Princeton University," fall 1976; Arnold J. Wolf, "'Jewish Experience Is Vividly Present at Yale,'" *YAM*, January 1973, 14.

4. Morton Keller and Phyllis Keller, *Making Harvard Modern: The Rise of America's University* (New York: Oxford U.P., 2001), 466.

5. Office of Admission, "Report to the President," 1969–1970, 1970–1971, 1971–1972, 1972–1973, 1973–1974, PU.

6. In the parlance of sociology, it was a period of growing institutional "isomorphism" — a process in which organizations facing similar environmental conditions come increasingly to resemble one another (Paul J. DiMaggio and Walter W. Powell, "The Iron Cage Revisited: Institutional Isomorphism and Collective Rationality in Organizational Fields," *American Sociological Review* 48, April 1983, 149).

7. Office of Admission, "Report to the President," 1974–1975, PU, App. B. At Harvard, too, the personal rating was a better predictor than the academic rating of whether an applicant would be admitted, with a correlation of 0.40 compared to 0.36 (Penny H. Feldman, "Recruiting an Elite: Admission to Harvard" [Ph.D. diss., Harvard Univ., 1975], 106).

8. Apparently confirming the perception that scholastic excellence was a poor predictor of success in later life was a study of 2,678 men who had entered Yale between 1927 and 1933. Thirty years later, their careers revealed that the most successful businessmen tended to be those with the worst academic records (Paul S. Burnham and Benjamin A. Hewitt, "Thirty-Year Follow Up of Male College Students" [Washington, D.C.: Dept. of Health, Education, and Welfare, May 1967]). But it is an open question whether such a pattern would have prevailed in the 1970s, when firm leadership was less frequently handed down from father to son and postgraduate training was common among corporate executives. For suggestive evidence that a different pattern may already have emerged at

Harvard in the 1950s, see Louise K. Epstein, "Elitism, Diversity, and Meritocracy at Harvard: Changing Patterns of Achievement in College and Career" (undergraduate thesis, Harvard Univ., 1982).

9. Wilbur J. Bender, "The Top-One-Percent Policy: A Hard Look at the Dangers of an Academically Elite Harvard," *HAB*, 30 September 1961, 23. On the case of George W. Bush, see Chapter 11.

10. The source of the figure of 150 "academic superstars" (out of 2,195 students admitted) was Assistant Dean of Admissions Seamus Malin '62, who told a *HC* reporter, "We've seen enough high-scoring people do abysmally here." An administrative intern on admissions added, "We have a real bias against those who sat in their high school libraries grinding out their A's" (Jaleh Poorooshasb, "The Tip Factor," *HC*, 13 April 1978).

11. In 1976, only 152 of the more than 11,000 students who applied to Harvard received an academic rating of "1." Of these 152 students, 14 were nevertheless rejected. But it was in the next category — the academic "2's" who were still among roughly the top 20 percent of all candidates — where Harvard's willingness to reject students who would have been accepted on purely academic criteria was most apparent. In 1971, 51 percent of academic "2's" were rejected, though there would have been room for all of them under a policy of academic meritocracy (that year 1,480 students were admitted, and the number of applicants with academic ratings of "1" or "2" was 1,381). Calculated from the "Report of the Faculty Task Force" HUA, 30–31; Admissions and Scholarships Committee, "Report on the Committee on Admissions and Scholarships," 1975–1976, 1976–1977, HU; and Feldman, "Recruiting an Elite," 102.

12. Ibid.

13. Ibid., 222.

14. See, for example, "Report of the Faculty Task Force," 14.

15. Walter Goodman, "The Return of the Quota System," *NYT Magazine*, 10 September 1972; Sidney Hook, "Discrimination Against the Qualified?" *NYT*, 5 November 1971; Brewster C. Denny, "The Decline of Merit," *Science* 186, December 1974, 875; John Bunzel, "Do Colleges Practice Reverse Bias?" *Wall Street Journal*, 27 July 1972; Nathan Glazer, "A Breakdown in Civil Rights Enforcement?" *Public Interest*, Spring 1971; Sidney Hook and Miro Todorovich, "The Tyranny of Reverse Discrimination," *Change*, Winter 1975; Paul Seabury, "The Idea of Merit," *Commentary*, December 1972.

16. A white Jewish man of Spanish-Portuguese heritage whose family had been in the United States for several generations, DeFunis had graduated magna cum laude from the University of Washington as a political science major with a GPA of 3.6. But his first two scores on the LSAT were 512 (average) and 566 (above average, but well below the top level). DeFunis took the LSAT a third time, receiving a 668 (placing him among the top 7 percent nationwide), and the University of Washington Law School (UWLS) at this point averaged his three scores, assigning him a 582 [Allan P. Sindler, *Bakke, DeFunis, and Minority Admissions: The Quest for Equal Opportunity* (New York: Longman, 1978), 38–39].

17. Ibid.

18. Ibid., 194. In addition to Sindler, illuminating discussions of *DeFunis* may be found in Joel Dreyfuss

and Charles Lawrence III, *The Bakke Case and the Politics of Inequality* (New York: Harcourt Brace Jovanovich, 1979), and Timothy J. O'Neill, *Bakke and the Politics of Equality* (Middletown, Conn.: Wesleyan U.P., 1985).

19. Sindler, *Bakke, DeFunis*, 194–98.

20. Ibid., 201–2.

21. Ibid., 202.

22. H. Jeffrey Leonard, "Harvard Joins in the Defense," *HC*, 9 February 1974.

23. Robert M. O'Neil, *Discriminating Against Discrimination: Preferential Admissions and the DeFunis Case* (Bloomington, Ind.: Indiana U.P., 1975), 180–81, 196–97.

24. Having clerked for the renowned federal judge Learned Hand and joining the prestigious Boston law firm of Ropes, Gray, Best, Coolidge, and Rugg, Cox served in the office of the solicitor general and as associate solicitor of the Department of Labor during World War II. In 1946, he became a professor of law at Harvard Law School, becoming Royall Professor of Law in 1958. From 1961 to 1965, he served as solicitor general under Kennedy and Johnson, and in 1965, he returned to Harvard as Williston Professor of Law in 1965 and was made Loeb University Professor in 1976. An expert on constitutional and labor law, Cox wrote many works, including *Civil Rights, the Constitution, and the Courts* (1967), *The Warren Court* (1968), and *The Role of the Supreme Court in American Government* (1976). See Ken Gormley, *Archibald Cox: Conscience of a Nation* (Reading, Mass.: Addison-Wesley, 1997); *WWA, 1978–1979*; Association of American Law Schools, *The AALS Directory of Law Teachers, 1999–2000* (Eagan, Minn.: West Group, 1999), 369.

25. Perhaps unbeknownst to him, Cox himself had been the beneficiary of a very different — and much older — form of affirmative action as a young man. In April 1926, when he was thirteen, his father had written to St. Paul's, worried that his son would fail to gain admission. Writing to an administrator, he emphasized the boy's lineage: "'I am told that, other things being equal, relationship to Alumni may count something in favor of a boy on the waiting list. If so, my boy can claim, in addition to his father and four uncles, a grandfather and five or six grand-uncles, and a Trustee in the generation before that.' A representative of St. Paul's quickly wrote back reassuringly: 'You are right in understanding that relationship to Alumni counts in a boy's favor when he is trying for admission to the School. Your boy should score heavily in this regard when the time comes.'" Young Archie was ultimately admitted and was a great success at St. Paul's, where he performed well academically, excelled at squash and tennis, and won the top prize for public speaking. At Harvard, he roomed with two classmates from St. Paul's, continued to move in St. Grottlesex circles, and joined the Delphic Club, one of the more prestigious Harvard final clubs (Gormley, *Archibald Cox*, 11–20).

26. "Brief of the President and Fellows of Harvard College, Amicus Curiae," in *DeFunis versus Odegaard and the University of Washington: The University Admissions Case*, vol. 2, ed. Ann F. Ginger (Dobbs Ferry, N.Y.: Oceana, 1974), 1–2.

27. In terms of connections to Harvard and Yale, Justice Rehnquist (Stanford '48, LL.B. '52) received an M.A. in government from Harvard in 1949, and Justice Douglas (Whitman College '20, Columbia, LL.B.

'25) had served as a member of the Yale Law School faculty from 1928 to 1934. Of the nine justices, only two — Burger and Marshall — had no affiliation with either Harvard or Yale (*WWA, 1978–1979*).

28. "Brief of the President and Fellows," 2.

29. Ibid., 19, 12, 5; my emphasis.

30. Sindler, *Bakke, DeFunis,* 202–6.

31. O'Neil, *Discriminating Against Discrimination,* 257.

32. Sindler, *Bakke, DeFunis,* 206.

33. O'Neil, *Discriminating Against Discrimination,* 243–44. For a vivid account of just how agonizing *DeFunis* was to Douglas (who went through eleven drafts before issuing his opinion), see Nicholas Lemann, *The Big Test: The Secret History of the American Meritocracy* (New York: Farrar, Straus, 1999), 205–8. On Douglas's dissent in *DeFunis,* see also O'Neil, *Discriminating Against Discrimination,* 40–43.

34. Ibid., 247.

35. Bakke's scores on the Medical College Admissions Test (MCAT) were good but not outstanding: 72nd percentile in general knowledge, 96th percentile in verbal ability, 94th percentile in mathematics, and 97th percentile in scientific knowledge. Nevertheless, those scores were higher than the average for students admitted to Davis (Dreyfuss and Lawrence, *Bakke Case,* 16).

36. Bakke's age may in fact have been the chief obstacle to his admission; in his interview at UC Davis, Dr. Theodore West, a member of the faculty, described him as a "pleasant, mature person . . . tall and strong and Teutonic in appearance . . . a well-qualified candidate for admission whose main handicap is the unavoidable fact that he is now 33 years of age" (UC San Francisco, which also turned Bakke down, cited his age as a factor in its letter of rejection). Not until the Age Discrimination Act of 1975 was put into effect in January 1979 was discrimination based on age declared illegal at any institution, including medical schools, that received federal funds (ibid., 17; Sindler, *Bakke, DeFunis,* 65–67).

37. In 1973, when Bakke was first turned down by UC Davis, he was also rejected by UCLA, UC San Francisco, Stanford, Georgetown, Wake Forest, the University of Minnesota, Wayne State University, the University of South Dakota, the University of Cincinnati, and the Mayo Medical School. Of these 11 schools, Bakke was interviewed at 4: UC Davis, Minnesota, Mayo, and Stanford (Dreyfuss and Lawrence, *Bakke Case,* 16).

38. O'Neill, *Bakke and the Politics of Equality,* 26.

39. Quoted in Dreyfuss and Lawrence, *Bakke Case,* 63.

40. Quoted in Sindler, *Bakke, DeFunis,* 62.

41. Ibid., 223.

42. Quoted in O'Neill, *Bakke and the Politics of Equality,* 43.

43. Ibid.

44. Dreyfuss and Lawrence, *Bakke Case,* 93–94.

45. O'Neill, *Bakke and the Politics of Inequality,* 135–36.

46. Ibid. The only other Ivy League institution to involve itself in the Harvard-Penn-Columbia-Stanford effort was Brown, which — along with Duke, Georgetown, MIT, Notre Dame, Vanderbilt, and Villanova — attached a prefatory note announcing "general support for the arguments advanced in the brief and join the *amici* in urging reversal of the judg-

ment of the California Supreme Court" (brief of Columbia University, Harvard University, Stanford University, and the University of Pennsylvania in Alfred A. Slocum, ed., *Allan Bakke versus Regents of the University of California,* vol. 3 [Dobbs Ferry, N.Y.: Oceana, 1978], 319).

47. William G. Bowen, "Admissions and the Relevance of Race," *Princeton Alumni Weekly,* 26 September 1977, 7–13. It is unclear why Yale, one of the Ivy League's earliest and strongest supporters of affirmative action, did not join in the brief, but it is possible that Kingman Brewster's departure from Yale to become U.S. ambassador to Great Britain may have left a temporary vacuum at the top of the administration.

48. O'Neill, *Bakke and the Politics of Equality,* 136.

49. Brief of Columbia et al., in Slocum, *Allan Bakke versus Regents,* 323–25.

50. Ibid., 314.

51. Ibid., 336–37.

52. Ibid., 338, 344, 351.

53. Sindler, *Bakke, DeFunis,* 241. Minority organizations had suggested Nathaniel Colley, a Yale graduate and a prominent black attorney in California, and William Coleman, the African-American secretary of transportation during the Ford administration, but the Regents wanted to avoid any impression that their lawyer represented minority interests rather than the general interests of the University of California and of higher education. From this perspective, the appointment of Cox was the logical choice (Dreyfuss and Lawrence, *Bakke Case,* 177).

54. John C. Jeffries Jr., *Justice Lewis F. Powell Jr.* (New York: Scribner's, 1994), 469.

55. Sindler, *Bakke, DeFunis,* 242.

56. McGeorge Bundy, "The Issue Before the Court: Who Gets Ahead in America?" *Atlantic Monthly,* November 1977. The report that Blackmun was influenced by this article is from "The Landmark Bakke Ruling," *Newsweek,* 10 July 1978, 25, cited in O'Neill, *Bakke and the Politics of Inequality,* 166, 295.

57. The account of the oral argument reported here is drawn from three sources: Jeffries, *Justice Lewis F. Powell Jr.,* 478–82; Dreyfuss and Lawrence, *Bakke Case,* 172–202; and Sindler, *Bakke, DeFunis,* 252–58.

58. Quoted in Dreyfuss and Lawrence, *Bakke Case,* 177.

59. Quoted in Sindler, *Bakke, DeFunis,* 255.

60. Dreyfuss and Lawrence, *Bakke Case,* 187, 179, 180.

61. Ibid., 200.

62. Jeffries, *Justice Lewis F. Powell Jr.,* 494.

63. "Opinion of Mr. Justice Stevens, with whom the Chief Justice [Burger], Mr. Justice Stewart, and Mr. Rehnquist join, concurring in the judgment in part and dissenting in part," *Regents of the University of California v. Bakke,* No. 76–811, Argued 12 October 1972 — Decided 28 June 1978, 421.

64. "Opinion of Mr. Justice Brennan, Mr. Justice White, Mr. Justice Marshall and the Mr. Justice Blackmun, concurring in the judgment in part and dissenting in part," *Regents of the University,* No. 76–811, 325–27.

65. "Opinion of Mr. Justice Marshall," *Regents of the University of California,* No. 76–811, 400.

66. "Opinion of Mr. Justice Blackmun," *Regents of the University of California,* No. 76–811, 407. Himself a summa cum laude graduate of Harvard College

'29 and Harvard Law School '32, Blackmun was well aware that colleges and universities had long given preference to a number of groups, many of them privileged. In his opinion, he noted: "It is somewhat ironic to have us so deeply disturbed over a program where race is an element of consciousness, and yet to be aware of the fact, as we are, that institutions of higher learning, albeit more on the undergraduate than the graduate level, have given conceded preferences up to a point to those possessed of athletic skills, to the children of alumni, to the affluent who may bestow their largess on the institutions, and to those having connections with celebrities, the famous and the powerful" (ibid., 404).

67. I am indebted here to Jeffries's excellent biography, *Justice Lewis F. Powell Jr.* On Powell's year at Harvard and its impact on him, see pp. 39–43.

68. For a colorful account of Powell's experiences in Army Air Force intelligence from 1942 to 1946, see ibid., 60–114.

69. Ibid., 2.

70. Ibid., 234, 172.

71. Ibid., 235.

72. Lewis Powell, "Confidential Memorandum, Attack on American Free Enterprise System," *Washington Report* 11, no. 23 (23 October 1972), 2, 4, 7. Powell's little-known memorandum first came to my attention in David Hollinger, "Money and Academic Freedom a Half-Century After McCarthyism: Universities Amid the Force Fields of Capital," in Peggie Hollingsworth, ed., *Unfettered Expression: Freedom in American Intellectual Life* (Ann Arbor, Mich.: Univ. of Michigan Press, 2000), 161–84. For useful discussions of the conservative countermobilization, see Sidney Blumenthal, *The Rise of the Counter-Establishment: From Conservative Ideology to Political Power* (New York: Harper & Row, 1986), and Jerome Himmelstein, *To the Right: The Transformation of American Conservatism* (Berkeley, Calif.: Univ. of California Press, 1992).

73. For evidence of sharp racial divisions on the issue of affirmative action, see Seymour M. Lipset and William Schneider, "The Bakke Case: How Would It Be Decided at the Bar of Public Opinion?" *Public Opinion* 1, no. 1 (March–April 1978): 38–44.

74. The quotes are cited in Jeffries, *Justice Lewis F. Powell Jr.*, 497.

75. "Opinion of Mr. Justice Powell," *Regents of the University of California*, No. 76–811, 289, 290, 296.

76. Jeffries, *Justice Lewis F. Powell Jr.*, 499.

77. Ibid., 470.

78. "Opinion of Mr. Justice Powell," *Regents of the University*, No. 76–811, 311.

79. "Harvard College Admission Program," appendix to Sindler, *Bakke, DeFunis*, 323–25. Harvard's description of its admissions policy had originally been filed as an appendix to the amicus brief submitted by Columbia and the other private universities.

80. Bowen's article is cited in "Opinion of Mr. Justice Powell," 312–13, 317; Jeffries, *Justice Lewis F. Powell Jr., Regents of the University*, No. 76–811, 484–85.

81. Jeffries, *Justice Lewis F. Powell Jr.*, 485.

82. Among the many articles criticizing Powell's opinion as lacking intellectual rigor, one of the most penetrating was Ronald Dworkin, "The Bakke Decision: Did It Decide Anything?" *New York Review of Books*, 17 August 1978.

83. Quoted in Jeffries, *Justice Lewis F. Powell Jr.*, 497.

84. "Opinion of Mr. Justice Brennan et al.," *Regents of the University*, No. 76–811, 325.

85. "Opinion of Mr. Justice Powell," 307, 313.

86. I am indebted here to Charles R. Lawrence III, "Two Views of the River: A Critique of the Liberal Defense of Affirmative Action," *Columbia Law Review* 101 (2001: 928–75, a brilliant and sympathetic critique of Bowen and Bok's landmark study of affirmative action, *The Shape of the River: Long-Term Consequences of Considering Race in College and University Admissions* (Princeton, N.J.: Princeton U.P., 1998).

87. Derek Bok, "Open Letter on Issues of Race at Harvard," 27 February 1981, HUA, 3.

88. Largely as a result of the mobilization of Asian Americans on campus, the number of Asian-American freshmen at Yale increased from 11 in 1969 to 35 in 1970 (Office of Institutional Research, "Minority Group Students," 16 February 1972, YU). For an illuminating treatment of the Yale case, see "The Invention of the Asian-American" in Lemann, *Big Test*, 174–84. On Princeton, which as late as 1972 referred to students of Asian heritage as "Orientals," see Office of Admission, "Report to the President," 1971–1972, PU, 2. Of the 74 "Orientals" admitted in 1972, only 27 planned to enroll at Princeton.

89. Jane Bock, "The Model Minority in the Meritocracy: Asian-Americans in the Harvard/Radcliffe Admissions Process" (senior thesis, Harvard University, 1981), 28; Nicole Seligman, "Asian-Americans Seek Minority Status," *HC*, 15 October 1976.

90. At Yale and Princeton, where Asian Americans had been recognized as minorities much earlier, the rate of increase from 1976 to 1978 was much lower: 4.1 to 5.2 percent at Yale and 3.6 to 4.1 percent at Princeton (Office of Undergraduate Admissions, "Profile of the Yale College Class of 1980," September 1976, YU; Office of Undergraduate Admissions, "Profile — Class of 1982," September 1978, YU; Office of Admission, "Report to the President," 1975–1976, 1977–1978, PUA).

91. Quoted in Ron Takaki, *A Different Mirror: A History of Multi-cultural America* (Boston: Little, Brown, 1993), 400–401.

92. The proportion of immigrants who came from Europe and Canada was 68 percent in the 1950s but plunged to 21 percent in the 1970s ("Immigration by Country of Last Residence 1820–1979," *World Almanac and Book of Facts 1982*).

93. Ibid., 351; Bureau of the Census, *Historical Statistics of the United States: Colonial Times to 1970*, pt. 1 (Washington, D.C.: Government Printing Office, 1989), 14; "Resident population of the U.S., by Race and Hispanic Origin, 1990–2000," *NYT Almanac 2002*; "Black and Hispanic Population by States," *World Almanac 1982; American Jewish Year Book, 5681: September 13, 1920, to October 2, 1921*, vol. 22 (Philadelphia: Jewish Publication Society of America, 1920), 247. Between 1980 and 2000, the Hispanic population (which may be of any race) grew from 14.6 million to 35.3 million.

94. For data on academic achievement patterns among Asian Americans, see Grace Kao, "Asian Americans as Model Minorities? A Look at Their Academic Performance," *American Journal of Education* 103, no. 2 (1995): 121–59; L. Scott Miller, *An American Imperative: Accelerating Minority Educational Advancement* (New Haven, Conn.: Yale U.P., 1995).

95. Admissions and Scholarships Committee, "Report on the Committee on Admissions and Scholar-

ships," 1975–1976, 1976–1977, HU, 108; Office of Admissions and Financial Aid, "Report on the Office of Admissions and Financial Aid," 1984–1985, HU, 135.

96. David A. Bell, "The Triumph of Asian-Americans: America's Greatest Success Story," *New Republic*, 15 and 22 July 1985, 24–31.

97. Dana Takagi, *The Retreat from Race: Asian-American Admissions and Racial Politics* (New Brunswick, N.J.: Rutgers U.P., 1992).

98. "Report to the Corporation Committee on Minority Affairs From Its Subcommittee on Asian American Admissions," 10 February 1984, Brown University, 2, 4. For a discussion of Brown's COMA Report, see John Bunzel and Jeffrey Au, "Diversity or Discrimination? Asian Americans in College," *Public Interest* 87, Spring 1987, 49–62; Takagi, *Retreat from Race*, 27–29; and Michael Winerip, "Asian-Americans Question Ivy League's Entry Policies," *NYT*, 30 May 1985.

99. On Princeton and Stanford, see Takagi, *Retreat from Race*, 38–42, and Bunzel and Au, "Diversity or Discrimination?"

100. Takagi, *Retreat from Race*, 26–27, 30–33.

101. Lawrence Biemiller, "Asian Students Fear Top Colleges Use Quotas," *CHE*, 19 November 1986.

102. Robert Lindsey, "Colleges Accused of Bias to Stem Asians' Gains," *NYT*, 19 January 1987.

103. Takagi, *Retreat from Race*, 56–57.

104. The data are for 1982, when the Asian-American admission rate was 74 percent of the white admission rate (14 vs. 19 percent) (Bunzel and Au, "Diversity or Discrimination?" 54–55).

105. For an analysis of Asian-American admissions between 1976 and 1980, when they also lagged behind white admission rates, see Chapter 4 in Bock, "Model Minority in the Meritocracy."

106. Office of Admissions and Financial Aid, "Report on the Office of Admissions and Financial Aid," 1986–1987, HU, 2.

107. Takagi, *Retreat from Race*, 70.

108. Spencer Hsu, "Asian-American Admissions," *HC*, 11 February 1988.

109. David Karen kindly provided copies of the OCR documents.

110. Barbara Vobejda, "Harvard, UCLA Admissions Policies Probed; U.S. Investigating Whether Colleges Limit Asian American Students," *Washington Post*, 18 November 1988.

111. Thomas H. Moore, "Some Top Colleges Admit More Asian Americans, but Deny that the Increase Is the Result of Pressure," *CHE*, 28 June 1989.

112. In 1990, the Asian-American admission rate was 98 percent of the white admission rate (Office of Civil Rights [OCR], U.S. Dept. of Education, "Statement of Findings, Compliance Review 01–88–6009," October 1990, 4–5; calculated from Office of Admissions and Financial Aid, "Report on the Office," 1989–1990, Table XV, and Office of Admissions and Financial Aid, "Report on the Office," 1991–1992, Table XV).

113. William R. Fitzsimmons to Thomas J. Hibino (acting regional director, Office of Civil Rights, 5 December 1988, 1 February 1989, HUA, and Thomas J. Hibino to William R. Fitzsimmons, 1 March 1989. In his letter of 1 March 1989, Hibino rejected Harvard's proposal to carry out statistical analyses for OCR while keeping the data, noting, "To rely on analyses conducted by University staff would, at best, give the

appearance of collusion or the lack of an independent investigation and, at worst, compromise the integrity of OCR's review."

114. Fitzsimmons to Hibino, 21 March 1989.

115. Office of Civil Rights, "Statement of Findings," 45.

116. Ibid., 46.

117. Ibid., 43.

118. Scott Jaschik, "Doubts Are Raised About U.S. Inquiry on Harvard Policies," *CHE*, 6 February 1991.

119. Office of Civil Rights, "Statement of Findings," 37.

120. Further evidence of the weight given to athletic prowess comes from OCR's analyses of the difference between the candidates provisionally accepted at the end of subcommittee meetings and "the final admit/reject decisions which resulted from the full committee meetings," when institutional interests exerted their most powerful influence. Whereas only 13 percent of all ultimately accepted applicants had not been admitted at the subcommittee stage, the figure for recruited athletes was 28 percent (ibid., 29–30).

121. Ibid., 26–27.

122. Ibid., 35–37.

123. "TRs" refers to transcripts and "Alum IV" to alumni interviews.

124. Office of Civil Rights, "Statement of Findings," 27–28.

125. Ibid., 28.

126. Karen's study also showed that legacies with a sibling who attended Harvard had a 52 percent admission rate, compared to 40 percent for those whose only connection was a parent (David Karen, "'Achievement' and 'Ascription' in Admission to an Elite College: A Political-Organizational Analysis," *Sociological Forum* 6, no. 2 [1991], 367–68).

127. Office of Civil Rights, "Statement of Findings," 41.

128. Ibid., 40–41.

129. "Is Harvard Really Innocent?" *HC*, 10 October 1990; Jerome Karabel and David Karen, "Go to Harvard, Give Your Kid a Break," *NYT*, 8 December 1990; John Larew, "Why Are Droves of Unqualified, Unprepared Kids Getting into Our Top Colleges?" *Washington Monthly*, June 1991. See also John D. Lamb, "The Real Affirmative Action Babies: Legacy Preferences at Harvard and Yale," *Columbia Journal of Law and Social Problems* 26, no. 3 (Spring 1993): 491–521, and Mark Megalli, "So Your Dad Went to Harvard: Now What About the Lower Board Scores of White Legacies?" *Journal of Blacks in Higher Education* 7, Spring 1995, 71–73.

130. "Is Harvard Really Innocent?"; Joshua P. Gerstein and Philip P. Pan, "Education Dept. Findings Dispute Harvard's Claims," *HC*, 1 November 1990; "The Cat Is out of the Bag," *HC*, 8 November 1990; William R. Fitzsimmons '67 et al., "The Admissions Office Strikes Back: The Process Is Fair," *HC*, 26 November 1990.

131. "Admissions for Fun and Profit: Why Byerly Hall Won't Tell All," *HC*, 27 November 1990.

132. Fitzsimmons, "Admissions Office Strikes Back."

133. While statistics affirming Harvard's leading position were generally absent from previous annual reports of the Admissions Office, the one for 1989–1990 was full of statistics, even noting that 11 of the 20 seniors cited by *USA Today* as members of its

"all U.S.A. academic first team" were reported to be bound for Harvard (Office of Admissions and Financial Aid, "Report of the Office of Admissions and Financial Aid," 1989–1990, HU, 2).

134. Neil Rudenstine, *The President's Report 1993–1995*, January 1996, HU, 3. The son of a first-generation Italian mother and a Russian-Jewish immigrant father from Kiev, a guard in the Connecticut state prison system, Rudenstine was born in 1935 and attended the Wooster School in Danbury, Connecticut, on a scholarship. In 1952, he entered Princeton, where he wrote his senior thesis, "The Use of Myth in the Poetry of John Keats, Matthew Arnold, and T. S. Eliot," graduated summa cum laude, and was a member of the Quadrangle Club. After Princeton, Rudenstine attended Oxford on a Rhodes scholarship and then earned a Ph.D. in English literature at Harvard in 1964. He became assistant professor of English at Harvard but returned to his alma mater to serve as the dean of students (1968–1972), dean of the college (1972–1977), and provost (1977–1988), as well as professor of English (1977–1988). In 1988, he turned down an opportunity to become president of Princeton, instead following William Bowen to the Andrew W. Mellon Foundation, where he was executive vice-president. In 1991, he was appointed president of Harvard College and served for ten years (*Nassau Herald: Class of 1956*, PU; Fox Butterfield, "Man in the News: Top Man at Harvard: Neil Leon Rudenstine," *NYT*, 25 March 1991; *WWA, 1990–1991*; and Liz McMillen, "For the Harvard Presidency, an American Success Story," *CHE*, 3 April 1991).

135. Rudenstine, *President's Report 1993–1995*, 3–5.

136. Ibid., 44, 38.

137. Ibid., 45, 50, 53.

138. Quotes from handwritten comments by readers of files examined during the OCR investigation. Raw data, courtesy of David Karen.

139. Even today Harvard requires an interview of all applicants — a clear indication of the importance that it continues to accord personal characteristics as judged subjectively. According to Dean of Admissions William Fitzsimmons, interviews can sometimes reveal that candidates with strong qualifications on paper are personally arrogant, fragile, or simply less interesting than expected. In 2002, only two or three students, all of them foreign, were admitted without an interview (William Fitzsimmons, phone interview by author, 18 December 2002).

140. Calculated from Office of Admissions and Financial Aid, "Report on the Office," 1990–1991, HU, Table XV.

141. COFHE data from "Report Discloses SATs Admit Rate," *HC*, 7 May 1993. While the black-white gap in 1992 was smaller at Harvard than at competing institutions (95 at Harvard vs. 150 at Princeton and Brown and 171 at Stanford), the Asian-white SAT gap was larger (65 at Harvard v. 40 at Princeton and Brown and 58 at Stanford). The figures for 1992 reveal that Harvard was by far the most successful of the elite private colleges in attracting high-scoring African Americans, with mean black SATs 1305 at Harvard compared to 1172, 1164, and 1160 at Princeton, Stanford, and Brown, respectively. COFHE data cited in Richard J. Herrnstein and Charles Murray, *The Bell Curve: Intelligence and Class Structure in American Life* (New York: Simon & Schuster, 1994), 452, and Stephen Thernstrom and Abigail Thernstrom, *America*

in *Black and White: One Nation, Indivisible* (New York: Simon & Schuster, 1997), 408.

142. Between 1991 and 1997, the Asian-American/white admission rate ranged from a low of 0.82 to a high of 0.92. Calculated from Office of Admissions and Financial Aid, "Report on the Office," 1989–1990, 1990–1991, 1991–1992, 1992–1993, 1993–1994, 1994–1995, 1995–1996.

143. Office of Admissions and Financial Aid, "Profile — Admits — Class of 2002," April 1998, HU; Office of Admissions and Financial Aid, "Profile — Admits — Class of 2003," September 1999, HU; Office of Admissions and Financial Aid, "Profile — Admits — Class of 2004," September 2000, HU; Office of Admissions and Financial Aid, "Harvard Admissions Profile — Class of 2005," n.d., HU; Office of Admissions and Financial Aid, "Profile — Admits — Class of 2006," September 2002, HU. Whether the 2001 figure paralleled a decline in the Asian-American/white admission ratio is not known because Harvard's tradition of making its annual report on admissions available to the public was discontinued in 1997.

144. Admissions and Scholarship Committee, "Report on the Admissions and Scholarship Committee," 1966–1967, HU, Table I; Admissions and Scholarships Committee, "Report on the Committee on Admissions and Scholarships," 1975–1976 and 1976–1977, HU, 95; Office of Admissions and Financial Aid, "Report on the Office of Admissions and Financial Aid," 1981–1982, HU, Table I.

145. Office of Admissions and Financial Aid, "Report on the Office," 1985–1986, HU, 115–16.

146. Office of Admissions and Financial Aid, "Report on the Office," 1994–1995, HU, 4.

147. Mary Madison, "Best, Brightest Bypass Stanford: More Students Prefer Harvard," *San Francisco Chronicle*, 23 September 1994.

148. Office of Admissions and Financial Aid, "Report on the Office," 1994–1995, HU, 6.

149. A graduate of Archbishop Williams High School in Braintree, Massachusetts, William Robert Fitzsimmons entered Harvard in 1963 and was a recipient of a scholarship from the Harvard Club of Boston. A Social Relations major and a member of the varsity hockey team, he also belonged to the Young Democrats and the Catholic Student Association. After graduating cum laude in 1967, he entered the Harvard Graduate School of Education, where he earned an Ed.D. in the sociology of education in 1971. Following brief stints teaching at Holy Cross and Boston College, he joined the Admissions Office as associate director in 1972. He then served as director of admissions from 1975 to 1984, leaving for two years to serve as executive director of the Harvard College Fund. In 1986, he was named dean of admissions and financial aid, a position he holds today. (*Freshman Face Book*, 1967, HU; University News Office, press release, 24 March 1986, HU; *Harvard Class Album: Class of 1967*, HU).

150. Office of Admissions and Financial Aid, "Report on the Office," 1981–1982, HU, 2–3.

151. Office of Admissions and Financial Aid, "Report on the Office," 1986–1987, HU, 4.

152. Office of Admissions and Financial Aid, "Report on the Office," 1991–1992, HU, 4; Mary Jordan, "'Need-Blind' Admissions Policy at Top Private Colleges Losing Favor to Wealth," *Washington Post*, 26 April 1992.

153. Committees on Admission and on Scholarships and Financial Aid, "Report on the Office of the Dean of Admissions and Financial Aid for Students in Harvard College," 1952–1953, HU, 20; Office of Admissions and Financial Aids, "Report on the Office," 1995–1996, HU, Table XII.

154. Committees on Admission and on Scholarships and Financial Aid, "Report on the Office," 1953–1954, 216; Office of Admissions and Financial Aids, "Report on the Office," 1995–1996, HU, Table XIII.

155. Wendy D. Widman, "Harvard Students Awarded Fewer Pell Grants," HC, 7 November 2002; "Low-Income Let Down," HC, 13 November 2002.

156. Table, "2001–2002 Scholarship Holders by Income, All Classes," in Office of Admissions and Financial Aid, "Profile — Admits — Class of 2006," HUA.

157. Ibid. The estimate that an income of $100,000 was roughly in the top 10 percent of the American income distribution is extrapolated from figures in Statistical Abstract of the United States: 2001 (Washington, D.C.: Dept. of Commerce, 2001), 438.

158. Kate L. Rakoczy, "College Enrolls Fewer Blacks," HC, 21 October 2002.

159. Office of Admissions and Financial Aid, "Profile — Admits — Class of 2006," HUA. In recent years, Harvard has attracted more than two-thirds of joint admits to Stanford, which annually draws 70–90 students admitted to Harvard. A roughly similar ratio prevails at Harvard's other main competitors, Yale, MIT, and Princeton, which each attract 40–60 Harvard admits annually (Fitzsimmons, interview, 18 December 2002).

160. Office of Budget and Financial Planning, "Harvard University Fact Book, 2000–2001," Harvard University, vpf-web.harvard.edu/budget/factbook/00–01 (accessed 1 June 2004).

161. Dan Rosenheck, "The Back Door to the Yard," HC, 6 June 2002. See also Zachary S. Podolsky, "Veritas Has No 'Z,'" HC, 17 October 2002.

17. Money, the Market Ethos, and the Struggle for Position

1. Between 1980 and 2000, prices rose roughly 207 percent, but the Dow rose 1,544 percent (The World Almanac and Book of Facts 2005 [New York: World Almanac Books, 2005], 109, 124).

2. The NASDAQ and the Dow had dropped to lows of 1,114 and 7,286, respectively, during 2002 but had bounced back to highs of 2009 and 10,453 in 2003 (ibid., 124–25).

3. One measure of the growth of huge fortunes during the period is that in 1982 the first Forbes list of the 400 richest people in America identified 13 billionaires, compared to 102 individuals whose net worth was $2 billion or more in 2003 ("The Forbes 400," Forbes Special Edition, 6 October 2003; Kevin Phillips, The Politics of Rich and Poor: Wealth and the American Electorate in the Reagan Aftermath [New York: Random House, 1990], as cited in Martin Marger, Social Inequality: Patterns and Processes [London: Mayfield, 1999], 386).

4. David Kirp, Shakespeare, Einstein, and the Bottom Line: The Marketing of Higher Education (Cambridge: Harvard U.P., 2003); Derek Bok, Universities in the Marketplace: The Commercialization of Higher Education (Princeton U.P., 2003); David Hollinger,

"Money and Academic Freedom a Half-Century after McCarthyism: Universities amid the Force Fields of Capital," in Unfettered Expression: Freedom in American Intellectual Life, ed. Peggie Hollingsworth (Univ. of Michigan Press, 2000).

5. Quoted in Kirp, Shakespeare, 11.

6. On Yale's historical contribution to the American elite, see George W. Pierson, The Education of American Leaders: Comparative Contributions of U.S. Colleges and Universities (New York: Praeger, 1969); on the centrality of the leadership ethos to Yale's identity in the twentieth century, see Geoffrey Kabaservice, The Guardians: Kingman Brewster, His Circle, and the Rise of the Liberal Establishment (New York: Henry Holt, 2004).

7. George W. Pierson, ed., A Yale Book of Numbers: Historical Statistics of the College and University 1701–1976 (New Haven, Conn.: Yale U.P., 1983), 618.

8. Princeton's endowment grew during that time as well, from $173.3 million to $403.4 million (Council for Financial Aid to Education, Voluntary Support of Education 1974–1975 [New York: Council of Financial Aid to Education, 1976], 11, 13; Council for Financial Aid to Education, Voluntary Support of America's Colleges and Universities [New York: Council for Financial Aid to Education, 1966], 23).

9. "Kingman Brewster," Daily Telegraph, 10 November 1988, 23.

10. John P. Miller, Creating Academic Settings: High Craft and Low Cunning (New Haven, Conn.: H. Simeon, 1991). George H. W. Bush, the forty-first U.S. president, graduated from Andover in 1942 and immediately enlisted in the navy, where he served as a fighter pilot, flying 58 missions and winning the Distinguished Flying Cross. He then entered Yale, where he was a member of Skull and Bones, captain of the varsity baseball team, and a member of Phi Beta Kappa, earning an A.B. in economics in 1948 (Bill Minutaglio, First Son: George W. Bush and the Bush Family Dynasty [New York: Three Rivers Press, 2001], 22).

11. "A New Record for the Fund," YAM, October 1980, 21.

12. Margaret Corvini, "Admissions Office Accepts More Yale Alumni Children," YDN, 3 October 1980.

13. Ibid.; Pierson, Yale Book of Numbers, 88.

14. Office of Admission, "Report to the President," 1969–1970, PU, B-5; Office of Admission, "Report to the President," 1979–1980, PU, A-7.

15. Office of Admissions and Financial Aid, "Report on the Office of Admissions and Financial Aid," 1980–1981, HU, Table A1; Office of Undergraduate Admissions, "Profile — Class of 1984," YU; Office of Admission, "Report to the President," 1980–1981, PU, Table A-1.

16. Data on Stanford's yield rate provided by the Office of Undergraduate Admission, Stanford University.

17. Office of Admission, "Report to the President," 1981–1982, 1982–1983, 1983–1984, PU; Admission Office, "Report to the President," 1984–1985, 1985–1986, 1986–1987, 1987–1988, PU; Admission Office, "Admission Office Annual Report to the Dean of the College," 1988–1989, PU; Admission Office, "Admission Statistics," in "Report of the President," 1989–1990, PU.

18. National Merit Scholarship Corporation, "Annual Report," 1978; "Colleges with Most Freshman National Merit Scholars," CHE, 1988.

19. Liz McMillen, "Yale U. Buffeted by Storm Over Its Fiscal Problems," *CHE*, 4 December 1991; "Yale Lays Off 140," *CHE*, 7 August 1991; Douglas Lederman, "Yale U. Drops Its Varsity Wrestling and Water-Polo Teams," *CHE*, 1 May 1991.

20. Richard Bernstein, "The Yale Schmidt Leaves Behind," *NYT Magazine*, 14 June 1992.

21. The son of Benno Charles Schmidt, a prominent lawyer who in 1946 had joined the legendary Yale Corporation member John Hay Whitney to start one of the nation's leading venture capital firms (J. H. Whitney & Co.), Benno Charles Schmidt Jr. graduated in 1959 from Exeter, where he had a reputation as a prankster. From there, he went to Yale, where his undergraduate career was, he told the *NYT*, "marked more by gregariousness and play than by sustained intellectual inquiry." But after graduating from Yale in 1963, he attended Yale Law School, where he reported experiencing a "tremendous release of intellectual energy" that propelled him into an academic career. Schmidt went on to clerk with Supreme Court Justice Earl Warren, followed by two years in the Department of Justice. In 1969, he joined the faculty of Columbia Law School, where he was appointed dean in 1984. As Yale searched for a successor to Giamatti, Schmidt came to the attention of the Corporation, which was impressed by his reputation as a humanist who had brought Columbia's law school into closer contact with the rest of the university, including the faculty of arts and sciences. Schmidt was named Yale's twentieth president in December 1985 and took office in July 1986 ("Yale Said to Pick Benno Schmidt as President," *NYT*, 10 December 1985; David Margolic, "Man in the News: Benno Charles Schmidt Jr.; Constitutional Scholar," *NYT*, 11 December 1985; Edward Fiske, "Schmidt, Named Yale Chief, Looks to 'Challenge,'" *NYT*, 11 December 1985; Michael Freitag, "A Special 'Old Blue' Is Returning to Yale," *NYT*, 15 December 1985; and *WWA, 1990–1991*).

22. Bernstein, "The Yale Schmidt Leaves Behind."

23. Ibid.

24. Marc Wortman, "Getting into Yale Today," *YAM*, March 1993, 35; Office of Undergraduate Admissions, "Admissions Profile — Yale Class of 1994," YU, September 1990; Office of Undergraduate Admissions, "Admissions Profile — Yale Class of 1996," YU.

25. "The College Welcomes the Class of 1998," *YAM*, November 1994, 15.

26. In good part because of sharp cuts in federal aid that began under the Reagan administration, the proportion of Yale's financial aid budget that came from federal funds dropped from 24 percent in 1979–1980 to 6.2 percent in 1992–1993 (Marc Wortman, "Can Need-Blind Survive?" *YAM*, October 1993, 66).

27. Kingman Brewster Jr., "Admission to Yale: Objectives and Myths," *YAM*, October 1966, 33.

28. For endowment per capita figures for 1992, see CHE, *The Almanac of Higher Education, 1994* (Chicago: Univ. of Chicago Press, 1994), 72.

29. Julie L. Nicklin, "Yale Opens a Campaign for $1.5-Billion: Largest Drive in U.S. Higher Education," *CHE*, 13 May 1992; Kit Lively, "Yale Plans to Spend $500-Million on Science and Engineering," *CHE*, 28 January 2000.

30. Office of Undergraduate Admissions, "Undergraduate Admissions and Financial Aid — Profile of the Class of 1997," September 1993, YU; Wortman, "Can Need-Blind Survive?" 64.

31. Office of Admissions and Financial Aid, "Report on the Office of Admissions and Financial Aid," 1989–1990, HU, 3.

32. The son of a sales executive for a liquor importer, Richard Charles Levin was born in 1947 in San Francisco, where he attended public schools and graduated from Lowell High School (San Francisco's closest equivalent to Bronx High School of Science). He went to Stanford and majored in history, graduating in 1968. Levin then enrolled at Oxford, where he studied politics and philosophy, receiving a B.Litt. in 1971. That same year, he enrolled as a doctoral candidate in economics at Yale, receiving his Ph.D. in 1974. He has been at Yale ever since, joining the Economics Department in 1974 and serving as chair from 1987 to 1992. In 1992, Levin was named the Frederick William Beinecke Professor of Economics and dean of the Graduate School of Arts and Sciences. Though his administrative experience was relatively modest, Levin was the Corporation's choice because his talent for conciliation, combined with his reputation for openness and affability, was thought likely to heal the breach between the administration and both faculty and students that had opened up under Schmidt. A Democrat and a Jew with a strong loyalty to Yale, Levin was a clear departure from Schmidt, who had continued to live in New York during his tenure. In praising the choice of Levin, the Corporation's Calvin Trillin '57 described him as a "mensch . . . someone whose basic honesty and decency are just the first things people mention when they talk about him" (Troy Flint, "He's Not a Typical President — The Man in Charge," *YDN*, 5 October 1995; Maria Newman, "After National Search, Yale Picks Its Graduate Dean to be President," *NYT*, 16 April 1993; N. R. Kleinfeld, "Man in the News; Sharp Mind Minus Rough Edges: Richard Charles Levin," *NYT*, 16 April 1993; William Honan, "Yale Inaugurates Dean and Economist as Its 22nd President," *NYT*, 3 October 1993; Carolyn Mooney, "Yale's Next President," *CHE*, 28 April 1993; *WWA, 1998–1999*).

33. Mark A. Branch, "A More Global Yale," *YAM*, November 2001.

34. Carter Wiseman, "'I Must Say I'm Very Optimistic,'" *YAM*, October 1993, 50.

35. Office of Undergraduate Admissions, "Admissions Profile — Yale Class of 1986," October 1982, YU; Office of Undergraduate Admissions, "Admissions Profile — Yale Class of 1994," September 1990; Office of Undergraduate Admissions, "Admissions Profile — Yale Class of 1995," September 1991; Office of Undergraduate Admissions, "Admissions Profile — Yale Class of 1996," September 1992, YU; Office of Undergraduate Admissions, "Undergraduate Admissions and Financial Aid — Profile of the Class of 1997," YU; David Karp, "Applicants Drop Again This Year," *YDN*, 25 March 1993.

36. When the final figures came in for 1993, it was reported that over 1,100 students had declined Yale's offer of admission, resulting in a yield rate of 54.6 percent, the third consecutive year of decline (Office of Undergraduate Admissions, "Undergraduate Admissions and Financial Aid — Profile of the Class of 1997," YU).

37. "A New Dean's First Crop of Freshmen," *YAM*, November 1993, 12; "Faces: A Coach, Three Deans, and a 'Genius,'" *YAM*, October 1992, 34.

38. David Karp, "Admissions Alters Recruiting

Strategy," *YDN,* 24 September 1993, 1, 3; Wortman, "Getting Into Yale Today."

39. Wiseman, "'I Must Say I'm Very Optimistic.'"

40. Office of Undergraduate Admissions, "Undergraduate Admissions and Financial Aid — Profile of the Class of 1997," YU; Office of Undergraduate Admissions, "Undergraduate Admissions and Financial Aid — Profile of the Class of 1998," September 1994, YU.

41. "A New Dean's First Crop of Freshmen."

42. "3 in Ivy Group Add Early Admissions," *NYT,* 15 February 1976.

43. Ethan Bronner, "Colleges Are Altered by Early Admissions," *NYT,* 26 December 1997.

44. Stewart Ugelow, "Yale Drops Early Action Admissions," *YDN,* 1 March 1995.

45. Office of Admissions and Financial Aid, "Report on the Office of Admissions and Financial Aid," 1993–1994, HU; Office of Undergraduate Admissions, "Undergraduate Admissions and Financial Aid — Profile of the Class of 1998," YU.

46. James Fallows, "The Early-Decision Racket," *Atlantic Monthly,* September 2001, 40. As James Shulman and William Bowen note in the preface to the paperback edition of their important book, *The Game of Life: College Sports and Educational Values,* "While presidents universally dismiss the [*U.S. News and World Report*] rankings as shallow and thoroughly flawed, many are with the other hand manipulating their schools' data in such a way that they can climb a notch" (Princeton, N.J.: Princeton U.P., 2001), 84. For evidence that the *U.S. News* rankings do affect student and institutional behavior, see Ronald Ehrenberg, "Reaching for the Brass Ring: How the *U.S. News and World Report* Rankings Shape the Competitive Environment in U.S. Higher Education," paper prepared for the Macalester Forum on Higher Education, "Competitive Advantage and Common Purpose in American Higher Education," Macalester College, 12 June 2001; James Monks and Ronald Ehrenberg, "The Impact of *U.S. News and World Report* College Rankings on Admissions Outcomes and Pricing Policies at Selective Private Institutions," National Bureau of Economic Research Working Paper No. 7227, 1999; Monks and Ehrenberg, "*U.S. News and World Report's* College Rankings: Why Do They Matter?" *Change* (November/December 1999).

47. Joining Yale and Princeton in adopting an early decision program was Stanford, which — unlike its eastern counterparts — had previously held to a single notification date (Ugelow, "Yale Drops Early Action Admissions"; Bronner, "Colleges Are Altered").

48. Ibid.

49. Loren Brody, "Low Minority Admissions at Yale This Year Concern Many," *YDN,* 2 February 1996; Office of Undergraduate Admissions, "Undergraduate Admissions and Financial Aid — Profile of the Class 2000," September 1996, YU.

50. Office of Undergraduate Admissions, "Profile of the Yale College Class of 1978," YU; Office of Undergraduate Admissions, "Undergraduate Admissions and Financial Aid — Profile of the Class 2000," YU.

51. Andrea Gabor, "Best Big Universities," *U.S. News and World Report,* 15 October 1990; Jeffrey Sheler et al., "The Best Big Schools," *U.S. News and World Report,* 16 October 1989; Betsy Bauer et al., "The Best Big Schools," *U.S. News and World Report,* 10 October 1988.

52. Beverly Waters, "Yale University, Summary of Endowment, 1900–2000," Office of Institutional Research, Yale Univ., October 2001, www.yale.edu/oir/book_numbers_updated/M1_Endowment_Table.pdf.

53. Mark A. Branch, "Deciphering the Admissions Map," *YAM,* November 2000.

54. Branch, "A More Global Yale"; Elyssa Folk, "Yale to Go Global in its Fourth Century," *YDN,* 20 April 2001.

55. Beverly Waters, "Yale University, Summary of Yale College Admissions, 1979–2001," Office of Institutional Research, Yale University, October 2001, www.yale.edu/oir/book_numbers_updated/D7_Summary_YC_Admissions_1979_2001.pdf; Bridget Kelly, "Aid Changes Diversify Yale Student Body," *YDN,* 26 May 2002.

56. Donald Heller, "Pell Grant Recipients in Selective Colleges and Universities," in *America's Untapped Resource: Low Income Students in Higher Education,* ed. Richard Kahlenberg (New York: Century Foundation Press, 2004), 157–66.

57. "News and Views: The Progress of Black Student Enrollments at the Nation's Highest-Ranked Colleges and Universities," *Journal of Blacks in Higher Education,* no. 37 (31 October 2002): 8; Office of Admissions and Financial Aid, "Report on the Office of Admissions and Financial Aid," 1992–1993, 1993–1994, 1994–1995, HU.

58. Daniel Golden, "Family Ties: Preference for Alumni Children in College Admission Draws Fire," *Wall Street Journal,* 15 January 2003; Office of the Dean of the College, "Report on Undergraduate Admission and Financial Aid," 2001–2002, PU; Jon Cohen, "Scrutinizing Special Admissions Policies," *Yale Herald,* 1 November 2002; Jacques Steinberg, "Of Sheepskins and Greenbacks: College-Entrance Preferences for the Well Connected Draw Fire," *NYT,* 13 February 2003. Unlike the statistics for Harvard and Princeton, the figures for Yale include applicants whose parents attended graduate or a professional school there.

59. Cohen, "Scrutinizing Special Admissions Policies"; "Class of '06 Chosen from Record Pool of 19,605," *Harvard Gazette,* 2002; William F. Buckley Jr., "Civil Rights for the Old Boys," *NYT,* 24 January 2003; Steinberg, "Of Sheepskins and Greenbacks"; Office of the Dean of the College, "Report on Undergraduate Admission and Financial Aid," 2002–2003, PU.

60. Office of Undergraduate Admissions, "Undergraduate Admissions and Financial Aid — Profile of the Class of 2006," September 2002, YU; "Directory of Colleges and Universities," in *U.S. News & World Report: America's Best Colleges,* 2003 ed., 154.

61. Office of Institutional Research, "Common Data Set 2002," YU.

62. Office of Undergraduate Admissions, "Undergraduate Admissions and Financial Aid — Profile of the Class of 2006," YU; Office of the Dean of the College, "Report on Undergraduate Admission and Financial Aid," 2002–2003, PU, A-3; Office of Admissions and Financial Aid, "Harvard Admissions Profile — Class of 2006," n.d., HUA.

63. "Admission Statistics," in "Report of the President," 1990–1991, PU; Admission Office, "Admission Office Annual Report to the Dean of the College," 1993–1994, 1994–1995, 1995–1996, PU; "Admission 1997: Class of 2001," Princeton University, www.princeton.edu/pr/facts/profile/97/09admiss.html;

"Profile 98–99 — Admission and Enrollment," Princeton University, www.princeton.edu/pr/facts/profile/98/08-adm.html; "Profile 1999–2000 — Admission and Enrollment," Princeton University, www.princeton.edu/pr/facts/profile/99/08.htm; "Profile — The Undergraduate College and Enrollment," 2000–2001, Princeton University, http://www.princeton.edu/pr/facts/profile/00/09.htm.

64. Karen Arenson, "Yale Changes Its Approach to Admissions," *NYT,* 7 November 2002.

65. Chaitanya Mehra, "Ivy League Weighs Pros and Cons of Early Programs," *Yale Herald,* 21 November 2002. The study to which Levin referred was Christopher Avery, Andrew Fairbanks, and Richard Zeckhauser, "What Worms for the Early Bird: Early Admissions at Elite Colleges" (working paper, Kennedy School of Government, Harvard Univ., August 2001). See also Christopher Avery et al., *The Early Admission Game: Joining the Elite* (Cambridge, Mass.: Harvard U.P., 2003).

66. See Admission Office, "Admission Office Annual Report to the Dean of the College," 1995–1996, PU; Office of the Dean of Admission, "Report on Undergraduate Admission," 1996–1997, PU; Office of the Dean of the College, "Report on Undergraduate Admission and Financial Aid," 1997–1998, 1998–1999, 1999–2000, 2000–2001, 2001–2002, PU.

67. Office of the Dean of the College, "Report on Undergraduate Admission and Financial Aid," 2000–2001, PU; Office of Undergraduate Admissions, "Undergraduate Admissions and Financial Aid — Profile of the Class of 2005," YU; "Best National Universities," *U.S. News & World Report: America's Best Colleges,* 2001 ed., 32.

68. Calculated from "Largest Endowments Per Student, 2000," *CHE,* chronicle.com/weekly/almanac/2001/nation/0103301.htm (accessed 27 February 2003).

69. Office of Admission, "Report to the President," 1976–1977, PU.

70. Ibid., 11–12.

71. Office of Admission, "Report to the President," 1973–1974, 1974–1975, 1975–1976, 1976–1977, PU.

72. After Harvard and Yale, it was MIT, not Stanford, that attracted the most Princeton admits (64 in 1976 vs. 61 to Stanford). But in the case of MIT, Princeton did garner a clear majority of admits: 108 of 172 (63 percent in 1976) (Office of Admission, "Report to the President," 1978–1979, PU, App. A-8).

73. Of the 11,106 students who applied to Princeton in 1979, just 5 percent received academic "1"s. Of these, 76 percent were admitted. In that same year, 68 applicants were admitted with a 2/1 (nonacademic/academic) rating, and just 12 ultimately enrolled at Princeton (ibid., 19, App. A-8).

74. Office of Admission, "Report to the President," 1980–1981, PU, 4–5.

75. Nancy Jeffrey and Lisa Eichhorn, "Faculty Members Criticize New Academic One Definition," *DP,* 6 March 1985, 1.

76. William K. Selden, *Club Life at Princeton: An Historical Account of the Eating Clubs at Princeton University* (Princeton, N.J.: Princeton Prospect Foundation, 1994), 74–88.

77. Office of Admissions, "Report to the President," 1979–1980, PU, 22.

78. Jeffrey and Eichhorn, "Faculty Members Criticize"; Office of Admissions, "Report to the President," 1982–1983, PU, A-9; Admission Office, "Report to the President," 1984–1985, PU, A-9.

79. Office of Admission, "Report to the President," 1980–1981, PU, 9.

80. Michael Winerip, "Asian-Americans Question Ivy League's Entry Policies," *NYT,* 30 May 1985; Dana Takagi, *The Retreat From Race: Asian-American Admissions and Racial Politics* (New Brunswick, N.J.: Rutgers U.P., 1992), 41–42, 67–68.

81. Office of Admissions and Financial Aid, "Report on the Office of Admissions and Financial Aid," 1986–1987, HU, 2.

82. Admission Office, "Report to the President," 1984–1985, PU, A-3.

83. James W. Wickenden Jr., "To: All Princeton Alumni," *PAW,* 22 October 1979. The legacy advantage was most pronounced at the margins, and there it was often the decisive factor. Wickenden explained how the system operated: "In a process where very fine lines must be drawn, the advantage Princeton children receive can perhaps be best appreciated when one analyzes the admissions ratios of candidates with certain rankings. For instance, of all candidates with 3/2 ratings, only 21 percent were admitted. However, 100 percent of the Princeton children with this combination of ratings gained admission. Similarly, 29 percent of all candidates with 2/3 ratings were admitted, as compared to 89 percent of all Princeton children in this category. Finally, only 6.7 percent of all applicants with 3/3 ratings were offered admission, as compared to 28.8 percent of the alumni children." "To make fine distinctions" among marginal candidates, including even those with 2/4 [nonacademic/academic] ratings, the Office of Admission "solicited and received a great deal of information from the Alumni Council, the Development Office, and the Annual Giving Office." Such information, Wickenden noted, "proved to be most helpful" (Office of Admission, "Report to the President," 1979–1980, PU, 17).

84. Office of Admission, "Report to the President," 1977–1978, PU, 8, B-4. How far was Princeton willing to go in its effort to recruit talented athletes? In 1975, it admitted 156 athletes with academic ratings of "4" or "5," and 97 of them enrolled; that same year, Old Nassau turned away 61 applicants with academic ratings of "1" — a figure that would rise to 212 by 1983. A year later, the mean SAT scores for enrolled athletes were 1190 (557 verbal and 623 math) — 90 points lower than the freshman average of 1280 (623 verbal and 657 math). Particularly weak academically were the recruited football players, of whom there were 80 in 1979, and the hockey players, whose academic records were the worst of all (Office of Admission, "Report to the President," 1979–1980, PU, Table A-5). In his 1981 "Report to the President," Wickenden stated: "It is my opinion that Princeton can recruit football players whose Academic Index falls within one standard deviation of the class mean for the Class of 1986. I would not, however, share such optimism with respect to those recruited to play hockey" (Office of Admission, "Report to the President," 1980–1981, PU, 15).

85. According to Princeton's review of the class that entered in 1981, it appeared that Ivy institutions fell into two groups: "Brown, Columbia, University of Pennsylvania, and Cornell seem to admit more students with lower academic indices than did Harvard, Yale, Dartmouth, and Princeton" (Office of Admission, "Report to the President," 1980–1981, PU, 12).

86. Office of Admission, "Report to the President," 1979–1980, 1980–1981, 1981–1982, 1982–1983, 1983–1984,

PU; Admission Office, "Report to the President," 1984–1985, PU.

87. Office of Admissions and Financial Aids, "Report on the Office of Admissions and Financial Aids," 1983–1984, HU; Office of Undergraduate Admissions, "Admissions Profile — Yale Class of 1989," September 1985, YU; Admission Office, "Report to the President," 1984–1985, PU.

88. Admission Office, "Report to the President," 1987–1988, PU, Table 20. On Harvard's positive reputation among blacks, see Charles Puttkammer, "Negroes in the Ivy League," 1962.

89. Office of Admissions and Financial Aids, "Report on the Office of Admissions and Financial Aids," 1986–1987, HU; Admission Office, "Report to the President," 1986–1987, PU.

90. Admission Office, "Report to the President," 1984–1985, PU, Table 15.

91. Another non–Ivy League university that emerged as a rival in the mid-1980s was Duke, which by 1985 ranked sixth (after Harvard, Stanford, Yale, MIT, and Brown) as the institution that attracted the most Princeton admits. In 1976, Duke ranked fifteenth among Princeton's competitors and attracted only 8 joint admits. By 1985, however, 20 students accepted by Princeton matriculated at Duke, which was more than the number that enrolled at four other Ivy League institutions: Dartmouth (17), Columbia (11), Penn (11), and Cornell (7). Though no figures are available on the decisions of students jointly accepted by Duke and Princeton, Admissions Office statistics reveal that — unlike the cases of Harvard, Stanford, and Yale — the majority of applicants jointly admitted by MIT (118 of 176) and Brown (103 of 136) attended Princeton (ibid., 7, A-7, Table 15; Admission Office, "Report to the President," 1985–1986, PU, A-7; Ibid.," 1986–1987, App. B, B-7).

92. Ibid.," 1984–1985, 5, A-7.

93. Ibid., 1986–1987, 6.

94. Ibid., 5–6.

95. Though the first Jewish president of a Big Three school, Shapiro was not the first Jewish president in the Ivy League. In 1970, Penn — the only Ivy League institution that never attempted to limit Jewish enrollment — appointed Martin Meyerson president. Seven years later, Yale — then seeking a replacement for Kingman Brewster — offered the presidency to Henry Rosovsky, the dean of Harvard's Faculty of Arts and Sciences. But Rosovsky, born in 1927 in Danzig and a 1940 immigrant to the United States, chose to remain at Harvard. In 1980, Columbia — which had taken drastic measures to limit the number of Jews in the 1920s and 1930s — appointed Michael Sovern as its first Jewish president. Even Dartmouth — a rural institution that historically had relatively low Jewish enrollments but that nevertheless imposed a quota on Jews in the 1930s — appointed a Jew as president (James Freedman) in 1987. By 1993, all three presidents of the Big Three — Levin at Yale (1993–present), Rudenstine (whose father was Jewish) at Harvard (1991–2001), and Shapiro at Princeton (1988–2001) — were of Jewish background. On Penn's policy of nondiscrimination, see E. Digby Baltzell, Allen Glicksman, and Jacquelyn Litt, "The Jewish Communities of Philadelphia and Boston, 1740–1940: A Tale of Two Cities," in E. Digby Baltzell, ed., *Judgment and Sensibility: Religion and Stratification* (New Brunswick, N.J.: Transaction, 1994), 229–66, and Richard Farnum, "Prestige in the Ivy League: Democratization

and Discrimination at Penn and Columbia, 1890–1970" (Ph.D. diss., Univ. of Pennsylvania, 1990), 75–103. On Yale's offer to Rosovsky and his decision, see Daniel A. Oren, *Joining the Club: A History of Jews and Yale* (New Haven, Conn.: Yale U.P., 1985), 274–78. On the history of discrimination against Jews in admissions at Columbia and Dartmouth, see, respectively, Harold S. Wechsler, *The Qualified Student: A History of Selective College Admission in America* (New York: John Wiley, 1977), 131–85, and David Levine, *The American College and the Culture of Aspiration 1915–1940* (Ithaca, N.Y.: Cornell U.P., 1986), 151–58.

96. Edward B. Fiske, "The Talk of Princeton University; a New President in a Week of Rallies and Parties," *NYT,* 30 April 1987.

97. The son of a delicatessen owner, Harold Tafler Shapiro was born in 1935 in Montreal. After receiving his Ph.D. in economics from Princeton and joining the faculty of the University of Michigan, he spent his entire career there, from 1964 to 1987. Becoming a full professor in 1970, he was named chairman of the Economics Department in 1974 and vice president for academic affairs in 1977. While at Michigan, he served as an adviser to the Bank of Canada and a consultant to the U.S. Treasury Department. In 1980, he became the tenth president of the University of Michigan, a position in which he remained until he assumed the presidency of Princeton in January 1988 (ibid.; "New Princeton President," *Washington Post,* 29 April 1987; *WWA,* 1998–1999).

98. "College Board Officer Named Dean of Admission," *PAW,* 20 April 1988.

99. Bill Paul, *Getting In: Inside the College Admissions Process* (Reading, Mass.: Addison-Wesley), 28–29.

100. "College Board Officer Named Dean of Admission."

101. Admission Office, "Report to the President," 1987–1988, PU, Table 15; Admission Office, "Admission Office Annual Report to the Dean of the College," 1988–1989, PU.

102. Fred Hargadon, "The Changing Face of West College," *PAW,* 9 November 1988, 22.

103. Admission Office, "Report to the President," 1987–1988, PU; Admission Office, "Admission Office Annual Report to the Dean of the College," 1993–1994, PU, A-3.

104. Admission Office, "Admission Statistics," in "Report of the President," 1989–1990, PU, 9–10.

105. Hargadon, "Changing Face of West College," 19.

106. Admission Office, "Admission Office Annual Report to the Dean of the College," 1988–1989, PU, 10; my emphasis.

107. Admission Office, "Admission Statistics," in "Report of the President," 1989–1990, PU, 6.

108. The structure of the Admission Office under Hargadon became highly stratified, with five separate titles — dean, associate dean (2), associate director (3), assistant director (5), and admissions officer (6) — arrayed in a clear bureaucratic hierarchy (ibid., 3).

109. Ibid., 5.

110. Ibid., 5–6.

111. Undergraduate Admission Study Group, "Report to the Princeton University Faculty on Undergraduate Admission and Financial Aid," 1 December 1997, PU, App. 3, Table 10.

112. Ibid.

113. American Council on Education Office of Re-

search, "Summary of Data on Entering Freshmen, Princeton University," Fall 1968; Undergraduate Admission Study Group, "Report to the Princeton University Faculty," PU, App. 3, Table 14.

114. In part, the decline between the late 1970s and mid-1980s may have reflected a change in the wording of the question about religion. In 1978, only 6.7 percent of freshmen reported no religion, but by 1985 that number had risen to 20.4 percent (ibid).

115. Undergraduate Admission Study Group, "Report to the Princeton University Faculty," PU, App. 3, Table 14.

116. Another rival institution in a small-town location (albeit one in the Philadelphia suburbs) was Swarthmore, where Jews made up 20 percent of the student body (Richard Just, "For the Jewish Community, Low Numbers and a Search for Answers," *DP*, 27 April 1999; Just, "For Some Faculty, Enrollment Drop Has Roots in Approach to Admissions," *DP*, 28 April 1999; Just, "Old Image, Current Social Scene May Deter Jewish Prospectives," *DP*, 29 April 1999; Just, "Beyond Search for Explanations, Jewish Community Ponders Future," *DP*, 30 April 1999).

117. Ibid.

118. American Council on Education Office of Research, "Summary of Data on Entering Freshmen, Princeton University," 1970–1971, 1971–1972, 1972–1973, 1973–1974, 1974–1975, 1975–1976, 1976–1977, 1977–1978, 1978–1979, 1979–1980; Undergraduate Admission Study Group, "Report to the Princeton University Faculty," PU, App. III, Table 14.

119. Just, "For Some Faculty."

120. Hargadon, "Changing Face of West College," 22.

121. Calculated from Office of Admissions, "Report to the President," 1983–1984, PU; Admission Office, "Report to the President," 1984–1985, 1985–1986, 1986–1987, 1987–1988, PU; Admission Office, "Admission Office Annual Report to the Dean of the College," 1988–1989, PU; Admission Office, "Admission Statistics," in "Report of the President," 1989–1990, 1990–1991, PU.

122. One faculty member later likened Hargadon's tight control of the admissions process to that of a "czar." Just, "For the Jewish Community."

123. Admission Office, "Admission Office Annual Report to the Dean of the College," 1993–1994, PU, 1, A1.

124. Ibid., 1994–1995, 1.

125. Ibid.; Office of Admissions and Financial Aid, "Report on the Office of Admissions and Financial Aid," 1993–1994, HUA.

126. Between 1995 and 1996, the number of Princeton admits enrolling elsewhere dropped from 219 to 169 at Harvard, 86 to 70 at Yale, and 109 to 47 at Stanford (Admission Office, "Admission Office Annual Report to the Dean of the College," 1994–1995, 1995–1996, PU).

127. Karen Arenson, "Youths Seeking Early College Entry Are More Likely to Get In, Study Says," *NYT*, 24 December 2001; Avery et al., *Early Admissions Game*.

128. For a powerful and widely read critique of early decision, see Fallows, "Early Decision Racket."

129. Cornell's Web site flatly stated in 2002 that it gives preference to early applicants while Penn — which acknowledged in the 1997 *U.S. News Guide* and in the September 2001 *Atlantic Monthly* that it gives early applicants extra consideration — was silent on

the issue. Princeton's Web site offered a particularly ambiguous statement, though Dean Hargadon did vigorously defend the early decision program in 2001, contending that it helped Princeton put together a well-rounded class and saved it from wasting valuable decision-making time and scarce admissions slots on students who hoped to attend Yale or Harvard (Avery et al., *Early Admissions Game*, 80–82; Fallows, "Early Decision Racket").

130. Between 1996 and 2002, the admissions rate for early decision applicants ranged from 27.6 to 38.2 percent, compared to 8.1 to 10.0 percent for other applicants (Admission Office, "Admission Office Annual Report to the Dean of the College," 1995–1996, PU; Office of the Dean of Admission, "Report on Undergraduate Admission," 1996–1997, PU; Office of the Dean of the College, "Report on Undergraduate Admission and Financial Aid," 1997–1998, 1998–1999, 1999–2000, 2000–2001, 2001–2002, PU).

131. Avery et al., *Early Admissions Game*, 152–56.

132. Of the 14 schools studied, the greatest difference in percentage points (though not ratio) was at Columbia (25.4 vs. 85.3 percent) (ibid., 156–61).

133. Office of the Dean of the College, "Report on Undergraduate Admission and Financial Aid," 1999–2000, PU; Office of Undergraduate Admissions, "Undergraduate Admissions and Financial Aid — Profile of the Class of 2004," September 2000, YU.

134. Karen Arenson, "Yale President Wants to End Early Decisions for Admissions," *NYT*, 13 December 2001; Eric Hoover, "Yale's President Proposes Abandoning Early-Decision Admissions," *CHE*, 14 December 2001.

135. Barbara Kantrowitz, "The Early Decision Rebellion," *Newsweek*, 18 November 2002.

136. Kat Liu, "Early Decision Policy to Stand," *DP*, 9 October 2002; Jane Gross, "Brown and Princeton to Restrict Early Applications," *NYT*, 2 October 2002.

137. Ronald Ehrenberg and Susan Murphy, "What Price Diversity?" *Change*, July/August 1993, 71.

138. Council for Financial Aid to Education, *Voluntary Support of Education 1990* (New York: Council of Financial Aid to Education, 1991), 7, 9; "Largest Endowments Per Student, 2000."

139. Florence Olsen and Kit Lively, "Princeton Increases Endowment Spending to Replace Students' Loans with Grants," *CHE*, 9 February 2001.

140. Office of the Dean of the College, "Report on Undergraduate Admission and Financial Aid," 1998–1999, 1999–2000, 2000–2001, 2001–2002, 2002–2003, PU.

141. Ibid., 2000–2001, 2001–2002, PU.

142. Admission Office, "Admission Office Annual Report to the Dean of the College," 1994–1995, PU; Office of the Dean of the College, "Report on Undergraduate Admission and Financial Aid," 2001–2002, PU; Office of Admissions and Financial Aid, "Profile — Admits — Class of 2006," September 2002, HU.

143. In 2004 and 2005, Harvard joined Princeton in a tie for the top slot in the *U.S. News* rankings. "Best National Universities," *U.S. News & World Report: America's Best Colleges*, 2001 ed., 82; ibid., 2002 ed., 82; ibid., 2003 ed., 82; ibid., 2004 ed., 82; ibid., 2005 ed., 82.

144. For evidence that Princeton may in fact be behind Yale in head-to-head competition for students, see the innovative study by Christopher Avery, Mark Glickman, Caroline Hoxby, and Andrew Metrick, "A

Revealed Preference Ranking of U.S. Colleges and Universities," National Bureau of Economic Research, Working Paper 10803, September 2004, 5–7, 26. This same study makes the provocative claim that Princeton practices "strategic admissions" to increase its yield rate, admitting a lower proportion of students as combined SATs rise from the 93rd to the 98th percentile. The author's reasoning is that such students are particularly likely to be admitted to — and to attend — institutions such as Harvard and MIT, leading Princeton to reject them preemptively. Parallel analyses for Harvard and MIT show no such decline in the 93rd to 98th percentile, but all the schools show a higher admission rate for the "stars" above the 98th percentile.

145. Additional evidence that there was widespread worry among elite private universities about Princeton's willingness to deploy its tremendous financial resources to "buy" students was provided by Peter Conn, deputy provost of the Penn, who was quoted in a *NYT* article about an organizing drive among graduate teaching assistants as saying that "what keeps me up at night is not the union. It's Princeton. Princeton provides students with better financial support than anybody. Princeton has a lot more money and it worries me" (Daniel Duane, "Eggheads Unite," *NYT Magazine*, 4 May 2003).

146. Karen Arenson, "Leading Colleges Adopt New Guidelines for Awarding Financial Aid," *NYT*, 6 July 2001; "Financial Aid Enhancements Improve Accessibility," *Princeton Weekly Bulletin* 92, no. 1 (9 September 2002); Rich Tucker, "Expanded Aid Packages Lure Large, Diverse Freshman Class," *DP*, 22 September 1998; Eric Hoover, "28 Private Colleges Agree to Use Common Approaches to Student Aid," *CHE*, 20 July 2001.

147. Charles Forelle, "Ivy Imbroglio: Princeton Admits It Spied on Yale Admissions Site," *Wall Street Journal*, 26 July 2002. The incident generated a great wave of adverse publicity nationwide for Princeton; see, for example, Karen Arenson, "Princeton Pries into Web Site for Yale Applicants," *NYT*, 26 July 2002; Michael Barbaro, "Bush Niece's Files Among Targets of Alleged Princeton Snooping," *Washington Post*, 27 July 2002; Jeffrey Young, "Princeton Admissions Official Breaks into Yale Admissions Site," *CHE*, 26 July 2002.

18. The Battle over Merit

1. Office of Admissions and Financial Aid, "Harvard Admissions Profile — Class of 2004," n.d., HU.

2. In 1999, Harvard's Hillel chapter estimated that 21 percent of the undergraduate student body was Jewish (Richard Just, "For the Jewish Community, Low Numbers and a Search For Answers," *DP*, 27 April 1999). The figure for 1900 is from Marcia Graham Synnott, *The Half-Opened Door: Discrimination and Admissions at Harvard, Yale, and Princeton, 1900–1970* (Westport, Conn.: Greenwood Press, 1979), 96.

3. In 2000, 34 percent of Harvard freshmen were members of minority groups (17 percent Asian American, 8 percent African American, 7 percent Hispanic, and 1 percent Native American and other minorities). In addition, roughly 21 percent were Jews and 6 percent foreign. This leaves approximately 40 percent of the remaining places in the freshman class for Ameri-

cans of Christian background, and nearly half of these students were women. Of the 20–22 percent left who were male and Christian, perhaps a fifth were Catholic rather than Protestant, leading to my conclusion that fewer than 20 percent — and perhaps less — of Harvard freshmen in 2000 were males of WASP origin (Office of Admissions and Financial Aid, "Harvard Admissions Profile — Class of 2004," HU).

4. The proportion of Big Three students on scholarship in the entering class of 2000 ranged from a high of 48 percent at Harvard to a low of 35 percent at Yale, with Princeton occupying an intermediate position at 40 percent. In 2004, the proportion of students on scholarship remained steady at 47 percent at Harvard, but had risen to 44 percent at Yale and 52 percent at Princeton (Office of Admissions and Financial Aid, "Harvard Admissions Profile — Class of 2004," September 2000; "Harvard Admissions Profile — Class of 2008," September 2004; "Undergraduate Admissions and Financial Aid — Profile of the Class of 2004," September 2000; Office of Undergraduate Admissions, "Undergraduate Admissions and Financial Aid — Profile of the Class of 2008," September 2004; Office of Undergraduate Admissions, YU; Office of the Dean of the College, "Report on Undergraduate Admission and Financial Aid," 2000–2001, September 2000; Office of the Dean of the College, "Report on Undergraduate Admission and Financial Aid," 2003–2004, September 2004, PU).

5. See the study of 19 "elite colleges" (5 Ivy League universities, including the Big Three, 10 selective private liberal arts colleges, and 4 leading state universities) in William Bowen et al., *Equity and Excellence in American Higher Education* (Charlottesville: Univ. of Virginia Press, 2005), 95–100.

6. By 2004, well over a third of Harvard scholarship recipients came from families with incomes over $100,000, and the median family income of all freshmen was roughly $150,000 (Office of the Dean of the College, "Report on Undergraduate Admission and Financial Aid," 2000–2001, PU, 5–7; Office of Admissions and Financial Aid, "Harvard Admissions Profile — Class of 2004," HU; Office of Admissions and Financial Aid, "Harvard Admissions Profile — Class of 2008," HU; David Leonhardt, "As Wealthy Fill Top Colleges, New Efforts to Level the Field," *NYT*, 22 April 2004.

7. Office of Institutional Research, "Common Data Set 2002," YUA.

8. "Brief of Harvard Univ., Brown Univ., the Univ. of Chicago, Dartmouth College, Duke Univ., the Univ. of Pennsylvania, Princeton Univ., and Yale Univ. as Amici Curiae Supporting Respondents," in *Grutter v. Bollinger et al.*, and *Gratz and Hamacher v. Bollinger, et al.*, Nos. 02–241 and 02–516 (2003).

9. Robert Shireman, "Campus Richies Need Archies," *Los Angeles Times*, 1 March 2002; "'Campus Richie Riches Need Archies: Irvine Program Director Bob Shireman Compares the Economic Diversity of Colleges in a *Los Angeles Times* Op-Ed," press release, James Irvine Foundation, 1 March 2002; Robert Shireman, "Enrolling Economic Diversity," *NYT*, 4 May 2002. See also Donald E. Heller, "Pell Grant Recipients in Selective Colleges and Universities," in *America's Untapped Resource: Low Income Students in Higher Education*, ed. Richard Kahlenberg (New York: Century Foundation Press, 2004), 157–66, and the recent study by Carnevale and Rose, which finds that only

3 percent of the freshmen at the nation's 146 most selective colleges and universities come from the bottom 25 percent of the income distribution (Anthony Carnevale and Stephen Rose, "Socioeconomic Status, Race/Ethnicity, and Selective College Admissions," in *America's Untapped Resource,* Richard Kahlenberg, ed. [New York: Century Foundation Press, 2004]).

10. Among the 8 colleges listed in the highest selectively level (SEL-1) in Bowen and Bok's study are Princeton, Yale, and Stanford. In their analyses of the national population, 28 percent of families are classified as having low socioeconomic status (SES), 9 percent as high, and 64 percent as middle. Though only 1 percent of white matriculants at SEL-1 schools were from low SES backgrounds, the proportion of blacks at SEL-1 colleges from low SES backgrounds was 12 percent (*The Shape of the River: Long-Term Consequences of Considering Race in College and University Admissions* [Princeton, N.J.: Princeton U.P., 1998], 48–50).

11. Bowen and Bok, *Shape of the River,* 288, 50. My own position, which argues for class-based affirmative action in addition to (and not as a substitute for) race-based affirmative action, is laid out in Jerome Karabel, "Freshman Admissions at Berkeley: A Policy for the 1990s and Beyond; A Report of the Committee on Admissions and Enrollment, Berkeley Division, Academic Senate, University of California," 1989, Univ. of California, Berkeley; Jerome Karabel, "No Alternative: The Effects of Color-Blind Admissions in California," in *Chilling Admissions: The Affirmative Action Crisis and the Search for Alternatives,* ed. Gary Orfield and Edward Miller (Cambridge, Mass.: Harvard Civil Rights Project and Harvard Education Publishing Group, 1998), 34–50. The most sophisticated argument in favor of substituting class-based affirmative action for race-based affirmative action is Richard D. Kahlenberg, *The Remedy: Class, Race, and Affirmative Action* (New York: Basic Books, 1996).

12. Data on SAT scores by family income, parental education, and race calculated from data kindly provided by the College Entrance Examination Board. It should be noted that the large number of non-respondents on the questions on race (19.1 percent), parental education (24.4 percent), and family income (41.8 percent) means that the estimates of the numbers of minority and low-socioeconomic-status students with high SAT scores are almost certainly well below the actual numbers.

13. Based on a simulation, Bowen and Bok concluded that a race-neutral admissions policy would reduce the proportion of blacks at the most selective colleges to 2 percent (Bowen and Bok, *Shape of the River,* 41).

14. As an example of this mobilization, see the statement in favor of diversity in university admissions, reprinted in the *New York Times,* that was approved by all 62 member institutions of the Association of American Universities (Association of American Universities, "AAU Diversity Statement on the Importance of Diversity in University Admissions," 14 April 1997, www.aau.edu/issues/Diversity 4.14.97.html [accessed January 15, 2004]).

15. Bowen, *Equity and Excellence,* 175–83.

16. "President Lawrence H. Summers Remarks at ACE: 'Higher Education and the American Dream,'" 29 February 2004, http://www.president.harvard.edu/speeches/2004/ace.html; see also Lawrence H. Summers, "Committing to Equal Opportunity," *HM,* January–February 2005, 83. President of Harvard since October 2001, Lawrence Summers was born in New Haven in 1954, the son of two Jewish economists (professors at the University of Pennsylvania) and the nephew of two Nobel Prize–winning economists: Paul Samuelson (on the side of his father, whose original name was Robert Samuelson) and Kenneth Arrow (on the side of his mother, Anita Summers). A 1975 graduate of MIT (which he entered after eleventh grade, having been turned down by Harvard), he received his Ph.D. in economics from Harvard in 1982. In 1983, he became one of the youngest tenured professors in the history of Harvard, and in 1993 he was awarded the Bates Medal, given every two years by the American Economics Association to an outstanding American economist under the age of forty. After a stint from 1991 to 1993 as the chief economist for the World Bank, he joined the Treasury Department under the Clinton administration, becoming secretary of the treasury in 1998. In March 2001, the Harvard Corporation, with strong support from the former treasury secretary Robert Rubin (also a member of the Corporation), selected Summers as Harvard's 27th president (John S. Rosenberg, "A Worldly Professor," *HM,* May–June 2001; Morton Keller and Phyllis Keller, *Making Harvard Modern* [Cambridge: Harvard U.P., 2001], 489; Richard Bradley, *Harvard Rules* [New York: HarperCollins, 2005], 1–37; *WWA 1998–1999*).

17. For a similar perspective on access to elite colleges, see an important article by David Karen, which concludes: "Groups that mobilized made inroads even into elite institutions, while the group that did not mobilize appeared to make no such gains" ("The Politics of Class, Race, and Gender: Access to Higher Education in the United States, 1960–1986," *American Journal of Education,* February 1991, 227).

18. Committee on Admission, "Report of the Committee on Admission of Harvard College," 1951–1952, HU, 20; Admission and Scholarship Committee, "Report on the Admission and Scholarship Committee," 1962–1963, HU, 22.

19. See Bureau of the Census, *Historical Statistics of the United States: Colonial Times to 1970,* pt. 1 (Washington, D.C.: Government Printing Office, 1989), 379, 383.

20. Admission and Scholarship Committee, "Report on the Office of the Dean of Admissions and Financial Aids for Students in Harvard College, 1955–1956," HU, 233; Admissions and Scholarships Committee, "Report on the Committee on Admissions and Scholarships, 1975–1976," HU, 105.

21. The data for 1954 are from the *Freshman Herald,* which did not publish statistics on "father's occupation" after that year. The 1976 data are from a survey of the freshmen class conducted jointly by the American Council of Education and UCLA ("Statistics of the Freshman Class-1958," *Freshman Herald: Class of 1958,* PU, 36; American Council on Education and the University of California, Los Angeles, "Princeton University — Summary of Data on Entering Freshmen for Fall," Cooperative Institutional Research Program [1976].)

22. Alvin W. Gouldner, *The Future of Intellectuals and the Rise of the New Class* (New York: Oxford U.P., 1982). For a useful, if critical, discussion of the theory of the new class, see Steven Brint, *In an Age of Experts:*

The Changing Role of Professionals in Politics and Public Life (Princeton, N.J.: Princeton U.P., 1994).

23. Eliot, *Man and His Beliefs*, 110.

24. Quotes cited in William Tuttle, "James B. Conant, Pressure Groups, and the National Defense, 1933–1945" (Ph.D. diss., Univ. of Wisconsin, 1967), 31.

25. James B. Conant, "Education for a Classless Society: The Jeffersonian Tradition," *Atlantic Monthly*, May 1940, 598.

26. James B. Conant to Thomas S. Lamont, 26 July 1943, HUA. For a detailed account of Conant's educational and political views as well as his correspondence with Lamont, see Chapter 5.

27. Kingman Brewster Jr., "Admission to Yale: Objectives and Myths," *YAM*, October 1966, 32. Brewster's educational and political philosophy as well as his policy innovations at Yale are discussed in Chapter 12.

28. Kingman Brewster Jr. to Herbert Sturdy, 11 August 1966, YUA.

29. For an analysis of how the structure of American higher education serves to reinforce meritocratic ideology and legitimate inequality, see Steven Brint and Jerome Karabel, *The Diverted Dream: Community Colleges and the Promise of Educational Opportunity in America, 1900–1985* (New York: Oxford U.P., 1989), 220–25.

30. Sweezy continues: "It is this aspect of the American educational system, involving as it does fairly generous scholarship and other forms of assistance for the bright poor, which is most often and least deservedly praised as democratic" (*Marxian Socialism: Power Elite or Ruling Class?* [New York: Monthly Review Press, 1956], 29).

31. *Grutter v. Bollinger et al.*, 539 U.S. 982 (2003), 20.

32. Ibid., 16–17.

33. Allan P. Sindler, "Appendix: Harvard College Admissions Program," in *Bakke, DeFunis, and Minority Admissions: The Quest for Equal Opportunity* (New York: Longman, 1978), 323–25.

34. *Grutter v. Bollinger et al.*, 25.

35. Among the best of the insider accounts of elite college admissions are books by two journalists (Paul at Princeton, Steinberg at Wesleyan) and two former admissions officers (Hernandez at Dartmouth, Toor at Duke): Bill Paul, *Getting In: Inside the College Admissions Process* (Reading, Mass.: Addison-Wesley, 1955); Jacques Steinberg, *The Gatekeepers: Inside the Admissions Process of a Premier College* (New York: Viking, 2002); Michele A. Hernandez, *A Is for Admission: The Insider's Guide to Getting Into the Ivy League and Other Top Colleges* (New York: Warner, 1997); Rachel Toor, *Admissions Confidential: An Insider's Account of the Elite College Selection Process* (New York: St. Martin's, 2001). But see also the revealing statistical studies of admissions at Harvard by Feldman and Karen and the neglected Final Report filed by the Office of Civil Rights of the U.S. Department of Education after a two-year investigation of allegations of discrimination against Asian Americans at Harvard (Penny Hollander Feldman, "Recruiting an Elite: Admission to Harvard" [Ph.D. diss., Harvard Univ., 1975]; David Karen, "Who Gets Into Harvard? Selection and Exclusion at an Elite College" [Ph.D. diss., Harvard Univ., 1985]; Office of Civil Rights, U.S. Department of Education, "Statement of Findings, Compliance Review 01-88-6009," October 1990).

36. Undergraduate Admission Study Group, "Report of the Undergraduate Admission Study Group," 5 October 1998, Princeton Univ., 2–4.

37. For a fascinating article on the role of the development office in admissions at Duke, where the university "has accepted 100 to 125 underqualified applicants annually due to family wealth or connections," see Daniel Golden, "How Much Does It Cost to Buy Your Child In?" *Wall Street Journal*, 12 March 2003.

38. Office of Admission, "Report to the Faculty," 1967–1968, PU, 3–4. There is every reason to believe that Princeton's description of its admissions process as one that is highly responsive to various internal and external pressures holds equally well for Harvard and Yale. At Harvard, a prestigious faculty committee, after discussing the "rough target figures" for each docket, described the admissions process as follows: "All these analytic breakdowns by origin as well as personality type have facilitated the Committee's task of representing the major interest groups who are important in the mix to be represented at Harvard such as alumni, private schools, scientists, blacks, athletes or the like. These and other constituencies with supporters among the Harvard administration, the faculty, the alumni, or in the public scene cannot be ignored. The result is a process wherein the Admissions Committee . . . weights an applicant's individual strengths carefully while also considering his membership in some broader constituency" ("Report of the Faculty Task Force on the Composition of the Student Body," March 1977, HU, 14). And at Yale, the longtime administrator Henry Chauncey, who served for a time as director of university admissions, said simply, "No Yale president was ever so unrealistic as to believe that there were not institutional reasons for admitting certain people" (quoted in Daniel A. Oren, *Joining the Club: A History of Jews and Yale* [New Haven, Conn.: Yale U.P., 1985].) In an internal document, Chauncey endorsed an essentially interest-group model of admissions, suggesting: "The Corporation sub-committee on admissions of the Educational Policies Committee should establish the groups who need to be represented at Yale. The Committee should then give the Admissions Office and Committee some indication of the number in each group. And finally, as there will be changes in the groups which need to be represented at Yale, over time, the Committee should review, at regular intervals, the question of which groups need to be represented" ("Yale Undergraduate Admissions," 12 January 1972, YUA, 4).

39. In his great work, *Economy and Society*, Max Weber emphasized the "need of any power, or even of any advantage in life, to justify itself . . . Simple observation," he continued, "shows that in every situation he who is more favored feels the never ceasing need to look upon his position as in some way 'legitimate,' and the other's disadvantage as being brought about by the latter's fault." This need for legitimation "makes itself felt in the relations between positively and negatively privileged groups of human beings . . . Every highly privileged group develops the myth of its natural, especially its blood, superiority," and "under conditions of stable distribution of power . . . that myth is accepted by the negatively privileged strata." But there are also times when the distribution of power is in flux, and in these times "the class situation" can "become unambiguously and openly visible to everyone as the factor determining man's individual fate." At such historical moments, "that very myth

about everyone having deserved his particular lot has often become one of the most passionately hated objects of attack" (*Economy and Society*, vol. 2, ed. Guenther Roth and Claus Wittich [Berkeley, Calif.: Univ. of California Press, 1978], 953).

40. This point was made with particular force in the Michigan case in a brief submitted by a group of retired military officers, who argued persuasively that "in the 1960s and 1970s, the stark disparity between the racial composition of the rank and file and that of the officer corps fueled a breakdown of order that endangered the military's ability to fulfill its missions" ("Consolidated Brief of Lt. Gen. Julius W. Becton Jr., Adm. Dennis Blair, Maj. Gen. Charles Bolden, Hon. James M. Cannon, Lt. Gen. Daniel W. Christman, Gen. Wesley K. Clark, Sen. Max Cleland, Adm. Archie Clemins, Hon. William Cohen, Adm. William J. Crowe, Gen. Ronald R. Fogleman, Lt. Gen. Howard D. Graves, Gen. Joseph P. Hoar, Sen. Robert J. Kerrey et al. as *Amici Curiae* in Support of Respondents" in *Grutter v. Bollinger, et al.,* and *Gratz and Hamacher v. Bollinger, et al.,* Nos. 02–241 and 02–516 [2003], 28).

41. Robert Worth, "For $300 an Hour, Advice on Courting Elite Schools," *NYT,* 25 October 2000; Emily Nelson and Laurie P. Cohen, "Why Grubman Was So Keen to Get His Kids Into the Y," *Wall Street Journal,* 15 November 2002; Michael Wolff, "The Price of Perfection," *New York,* 2 December 2002; Tamar Lewin, "How I Spent My Summer: At Getting-Into-College-Camp," *NYT,* 18 April 2004; Jodi Wilgoren and Jacques Steinberg, "Under Pressure: A Special Report; Even for Sixth Graders, College Looms," *NYT,* 3 July 2000; Hannah Friedman, "When Your Friends Become the Enemy," *Newsweek,* 19 April 2004.

42. Parental anxiety about their toddlers' future has become so severe that Harvard's dean of admissions, Bill Fitzsimmons, felt compelled to tell the press, "The idea that you need to have attended a brand-name kindergarten doesn't conform to reality at all" (Judith Gaines, "Admissions Tussle at an Early Age," *Boston Globe,* 15 February 1994).

43. The debate on whether coaching produces significant gains in scores on the SAT and similar tests remains unresolved, though the bulk of the evidence suggests that gains may be relatively modest. For some of the better scholarly studies of the issue, see Betsy Becker, "Coaching for the Scholastic Aptitude Test: Further Synthesis and Appraisal," *Review of Educational Research* 60, no. 3 (1990): 371–417; James Kulik et al., "Effectiveness of Coaching for Aptitude Tests," *Psychological Bulletin* 95, no. 2 (1984): 179–88; and Donald R. Powers, "Effects of Coaching on SAT I: Reasoning Test Scores," *Journal of Educational Measurement* 36, no. 2 (1999): 93–118.

44. On the growth of the private college counseling industry, see Patricia M McDonough et al., "Access, Equity, and the Privatization of College Counseling," *Review of Higher Education* 20, no. 3 (Spring 1997): 297–317; Ben Gose, "Anxious College Applicants Seek Edge by Hiring Consultants," *CHE,* 24 January 1997; Carol Loewith, "Independent Consultants and the College Selection Process," *Los Angeles Times,* 29 December 2002; and Ralph Gardner Jr., "The $28,955 Tutor," *New York,* 16 April 2001, 32–36. See Kate Zernike, "Ease Up, Top Colleges Tell Stressed Applicants," *NYT,* 7 December 2000. For the original paper, see William R. Fitzsimmons, Marlyn Lewis, and Charles Ducey, "Time Out of Burn Out for the Next Genera-

tion," Harvard University, http://admis.fas.Harvard .edu/timeoff.htm (accessed 13 December 2000).

45. Daniel Golden, "Prep Schools Buff Images to Boost College Admissions," *Wall Street Journal,* 23 January 2001.

46. Calculated from statistics reported in *The Handbook of Private Schools* (Boston: Porter Sargent, 1955 and 2001). Between 1998 and 2001, 94 of the 100 schools nationwide that sent the highest percentage of graduates to Harvard, Yale, and Princeton were private institutions (Reshma Memon Yaqub, "Getting Inside the Ivy Gates," *Worth,* September 2002, 94–104).

47. Committees on Admission and on Scholarships and Financial Aids, "Report on the Office of the Dean of Admissions and Financial Aids for Students in Harvard College," 1953–1954, HU, 216; Office of Admissions and Financial Aid, "Report on the Office of Admissions and Financial Aid, 1996–1997," HU, Table 13; "Statistics of the Freshman Class-1958," *Freshman Herald: Class of 1958,* PU, 36; Office of the Dean of the College, "Report on Undergraduate Admission and Financial Aid," 2001–2002, PU, 8–9.

48. In 2004, Princeton joined Harvard and Yale in admitting international students without regard to financial need ("Princeton Univ. Report on Undergraduate Admission and Financial Aid," September 2004, 2–3).

49. Quoted in John T. Bethell, *Harvard Observed: An Illustrated History of the University in the Twentieth Century* (Cambridge, Mass.: Harvard U.P., 1998), 22.

50. Conant, "Education for a Classless Society," 595–98. Also, James B. Conant, "The Future of Our Higher Education," *Harper's,* May 1938, 563.

51. Pierre Bourdieu, *The State Nobility: Elite Schools in the Field of Power* (Stanford, Calif.: Stanford U.P., 1996), 287.

52. For the notion that the educational system transforms privilege into merit, I am indebted to the work of Pierre Bourdieu and Jean-Claude Passeron. See especially *The Inheritors: French Students and Their Relation to Culture* (Chicago: Univ. of Chicago Press, 1979) and *Reproduction in Education, Society, and Culture* (Beverly Hills, Calif.: SAGE, 1977), and also Bourdieu's later works, *Distinction: A Social Critique of the Judgment of Taste* (Cambridge, Mass.: Harvard U.P., 1984) and *The State Nobility.*

53. Undergraduate Admission Study Group, "Report of the Undergraduate Admission Study Group," 5 October 1998, 10.

54. At Princeton in 2002, legacies were admitted at a rate of 35 percent, compared to 11 percent for non-legacies (Daniel Golden, "Family Ties: Preference for Alumni Children in College Admission Draws Fire," *Wall Street Journal,* 15 January 2003). According to evidence from a study of 13 highly selective institutions, legacy status increased an applicant's chance of admissions by an average of 20 percentage points even when controlling for SAT scores, race, income, parental income, early application, and other variables (Bowen, *Equity and Excellence,* 105).

55. Jacques Steinberg, "College-Entrance Preferences for the Well Connected Draw Ire," *NYT,* 13 February 2003; Daniel Golden, "No More Boost for 'Legacies' at Texas A&M University," *Wall Street Journal,* 13 January 2004; Jerome Karabel, "The Legacy of Legacies," *NYT,* 13 September 2004.

56. In a letter to *HM* concerning Lawrence Sum-

mers's recent defense of preference for alumni children, two graduates expressed their disagreement, arguing that legacy preference was incompatible with Harvard's public commitment to addressing the issue of educational inequality. They write: "Coming from well-educated and wealthy parents, our [future] children will already have an enormous advantage in the college admissions process. Should they ever decide to apply to and be accepted at Harvard, we would not want them to have any doubt in their minds that it is because of their abilities and future potential — not because their parents are Harvard alumni. We urge Harvard to end its policy of favoring children of alumni in the college admissions process" (Gernot Wagner '02 and Siripanth Nippita '00, "End Legacy Admission," *HM*, September–October 2004). Summers is hardly alone, however, among Big Three administrators in defending the positive weight given to legacy status in the admissions process; see, for example, the interview with Yale's president, Richard Levin; Katherine Lassila, "Q&A: Rick Levin, Why Yale Favors Its Own," *YAM*, November/December 2004, 28–29.

57. Alvin Powell, "Endowment Posts Positive Returns," *Harvard Univ. Gazette*, 16 September, 2004; "Yale Endowment Gains 19.4%; Total Assets Reach 12.7 Billion," *Yale Bulletin and Calendar*, 22 October, 2004; "The Endowment," www.princeton.edu/pr/facts/profile/04/30.htm, September 2004.

58. Daniel Golden, "Bill Would Make Colleges Report Legacies and Early Admissions," *Wall Street Journal*, 29 October 2003.

59. Edwards, quoted in "The Curse of Nepotism," *Economist*, 8 January 2004, 27.

60. For an excellent study of early admissions programs that includes an insightful discussion of the policy dilemmas they pose, see Christopher Avery et al., *The Early Admissions Game: Joining the Elite* (Cambridge, Mass.: Harvard U.P., 2003).

61. Karen Arenson, "Youths Seeking Early College Entry Are More Likely to Get In, Study Says," *NYT*, 14 December 2001; James Fallows, "The Early Decision Racket," *Atlantic Monthly*, September 2001; Christopher Avery et al., "What Worms for the Early Bird: Early Admissions at Elite Colleges" (working paper, JFK School of Government, Harvard Univ., Cambridge, August 2001).

62. Karen Arenson, "Yale President Wants to End Early Decisions for Admissions," *NYT*, 13 December 2001.

63. "Yale Changes Its Approach to Admissions," *NYT*, 7 November 2002.

64. See Avery et al., *Early Admissions Game*, especially the concluding chapter.

65. A recent study by *The* (London) *Times Higher Education Supplement* (*THES*) lists the Big Three as among the world's leading universities; Harvard ranked first, Yale eighth, and Princeton ninth. The other universities in the top ten of the *THES* rankings were UC Berkeley (#2), MIT (#3), Caltech (#4), Oxford (#5), Cambridge (#6) Stanford (#7), and ETH Zurich (#10) ("The World's Top 200 Universities," *THES*, 5 November, 2004). A separate study conducted in 2003 in Shanghai reported similar findings; Harvard once again ranked first, with Princeton seventh, and Yale eighth ("Academic Raking of World Universities — 2003," Shanghai Jiao Tong Univ. Institute of Higher Education, ed.sjtu.edu.cn/rank/2003/2003main.htm [accessed 21 December, 2004]).

66. James L. Shulman and William G. Bowen, *The Game of Life: College Sports and Educational Values* (Princeton, N.J.: Princeton U.P., 2001), 34.

67. Craig Lambert, "The Professionalization of Ivy League Sports," *HM*, September–October 1997; James L. Shulman and William G. Bowen, "A Gladiator Class?" *YAM*, April 2001; Louis Menand, "Sporting Chances: The Cost of College Athletics," *New Yorker*, 22 January 2001; Paul E. Steiger, "The High Cost of Winning," *YAM*, September/October 2003.

68. Shulman and Bowen, *Game of Life*; William G. Bowen and Sarah A. Levin, *Reclaiming the Game: College Sports and Educational Values* (Princeton, N.J.: Princeton U.P., 2003).

69. Ibid., 89–94. At every SAT level at Ivy League institutions, recruited athletes enjoy a massive advantage over nonathletes. For male applicants with SATs between 1300 and 1399, for example, the admissions rate is over 60 percent compared to 10 percent for other applicants; among females in the same SAT range, the gap is even larger — just under 70 percent for recruited athletes and about 15 percent for nonathletes (Bowen and Levin, 75–76; see also Thomas J. Espenshade et al., "Admission Preference for Minority Students, Athletes, and Legacies at Elite Universities," *Social Science Quarterly* 85, no. 5, December 2004).

70. Welch Suggs, "Ivy League Votes to Raise Academic Standards for Athletes," *CHE*, 19 June 2003.

71. For a vivid recent account of the lengths to which Ivy League schools will go to recruit athletes, see Chris Lincoln, *Playing the Game: Inside Athletic Recruiting in the Ivy League* (White River Junction, Vt.: Nomad, 2004).

72. MIT already follows such a policy, and it has done so while retaining 41 varsity teams — one of the highest numbers in the nation (Bowen and Levin, *Reclaiming the Game*, 55). MIT's policy of giving no discernable preference to athletes is part of a larger admissions policy that more closely approximates the meritocratic ideal than those of Harvard, Yale, and Princeton. In their study of early action and early decision programs, Avery et al. found that MIT gave far less preference to early applicants than the Big Three and other Ivy League institutions, and at MIT "little if any preference is given to legacies" (ibid., 68). In addition to being more meritocratic, MIT is also more socially inclusive, with more Pell Grant recipients than Harvard, Yale, and Princeton (Heller, "Pell Grant Recipients," 160–61).

73. "Brief of Harvard Univ. et al.," 2, 10.

74. Neil Rudenstine, *The President's Report 1993–1995*, January 1996, HU, 53.

75. Carnevale and Rose, "Socioeconomic Status, Race/Ethnicity," 106–7. For evidence that the proportion of wealthy students at the nation's most selective institutions increased substantially between 1985 and 2000, see Alexander Astin and Leticia Oseguera, "The Declining 'Equity' of Higher Education," *Review of Higher Education* 27, no. 3 (2004): 321–41.

76. Bowen, *Equity and Excellence*, 166. The boost for underrepresented minorities was 28 points — less than for athletes, but more than for legacies (ibid., 105). Early applicants received a boost of 20 points — the same degree of preference given legacies (ibid.).

77. After decades of neglect, there have been signs that the leaders of the Big Three were finally acknowledging the magnitude of the problem of class inequality in access to higher education. In 2001, Princeton

announced a series of initiatives, including a more generous scholarship policy and the adoption of a no-loan initiative, designed to increase the number of low-income students. Harvard moved quickly to improve its financial aid packages, and in 2004, President Summers announced new policies exempting families with incomes under $40,000 from having to make a financial contribution to their child's education and increasing aid to families with incomes between $40,000 and $60,000. These changes were adopted partly in response to data showing that almost three-quarters of Harvard students came from families in the top quartile of the income distribution, and the median family income hovered around $150,000. Finally, Yale, acting in response to pressures from Princeton and Harvard, announced its own new financial aid policy for students from low-income families in March 2005 (Bill Beaver, "Univ. Approves 'No-Loan' Financial Aid Program," *DP*, 5 February 2001; Eunice Kim, "Report Gauges Impact of Aid," *DP*, 27 September 2001; Karen Arenson, "Harvard Says Poor Parents Won't Have to Pay," *NYT*, 29 February 2004, 12; Office of the Dean of the College, "Report on Undergraduate Admissions and Financial Aid," September 2004; Lawrence Summers, Commencement Address, delivered at Harvard, 10 June 2004, www.president.Harvard.edu/speeches/2004/commencement.html; David Leonhardt, "As Wealthy Fill Top Colleges, New Efforts to Level the Field," *NYT*, 22 April 2004; Yassmin Sadeghi, "Yale Pressured by Rivals' Aid Changes," *YDN*, 1 March 2005; Raymond Pacia and Yassmin Sadeghi, "Yale Announces Financial Aid Plans," *YDN*, 3 March 2005).

78. Carnevale and Rose, "Socioeconomic Status, Race/Ethnicity," 130.

79. For a provocative attempt at a performance-based redefinition of "merit" that better serves the interests of minority and working-class students than current test-based definitions, see Susan Sturm and Lani Guinier, "The Future of Affirmative Action" and the ensuing discussion in Lani Guinier and Susan Sturm, *Who's Qualified?* (Boston: Beacon Press, 2001), as well as Lani Guinier, "Admissions Rituals as Political Acts: Guardians at the Gates of Our Democratic Ideals," *Harvard Law Review* 117, no. 1 (September 2003).

80. Yet it is unclear whether the Big Three would pay much of a price if they eliminated early admissions. Harvard's William Fitzsimmons has said: "If we gave it up, other institutions inside and outside the Ivy League would carve up our class and our faculty would carve us up." Yet Stanford, a close competitor, did not even have an early admission program until 1995–1996, but it continued to do well in the competition for top students, ranking number one in the *U.S. News and World Report* in 1987 and number two in 1990 (Avery et al., *Early Admissions Game*, 272; U.S. News and World Report, *America's Best Colleges and Professional Schools* [Washington, D.C.: U.S. News and World Report, 1987]; U.S. News and World Report, *America's Best Colleges and Professional Schools* [Washington, D.C.: U.S. News and World Report, 1990]. The phrase "positional arms race" is drawn from Robert Frank, "Higher Education: The Ultimate Winner-Take-All Market?" (paper, Forum for the Future of Higher Education, Aspen, Colorado, 27 September 1999).

81. Buckley, who has long defended the preference for legacies, did so most recently in "Civil Rights for Old Boys," *NYT*, 24 January 2003. For a learned, if ultimately unconvincing, defense of the hereditary transmission of privilege, see Adam Bellow, *In Praise of Nepotism: A Natural History* (New York: Doubleday, 2003).

82. Michael Young, *The Rise of the Meritocracy, 1870–2033: An Essay on Education and Equality* (London: Thames & Hudson, 1958; Harmondsworth, U.K.: Penguin, 1961). Citations are to the Penguin edition.

83. Ibid., 94, 48–49.

84. Young, *Rise of the Meritocracy*, 123–24. The quote referring to the "best geniuses" is from Thomas Jefferson, *Notes on the State of Virginia*, and is quoted in Nicholas Lemann, *The Big Test: The Secret History of the American Meritocracy* (New York: Farrar, Straus, 1999), 44. Conant, who was fond of quoting Jefferson, writes, "I was never so tactless as to quote these particular words, of course" (*Thomas Jefferson and the Development of American Public Education* [Berkeley, Calif.: Univ. of California Press, 1962], 54).

85. In his magisterial book, *A Theory of Justice*, John Rawls makes a similar point, writing, "Equality of opportunity means an equal chance to leave the less fortunate behind in the personal quest for influence and social position" ([Cambridge, Mass.: Belknap Press, 1971], 106–7). John Schaar also offers a penetrating philosophical and political critique of the principle of equality of opportunity in his essay "Equality of Opportunity and Beyond." In it, he writes: "The doctrine of equality of opportunity is the product of a competitive and fragmented society, a divided society, a society in which individualism . . . is the reigning ethical principle . . . It views the whole of human relations as a contest in which each man competes with his fellows for scarce goods, a contest in which there is never enough for everybody and where one man's gain is usually another's loss. Resting upon the attractive conviction that all should be allowed to improve their conditions as far as their abilities permit, the equal opportunity principle insists that each individual do this by and for himself . . . It breaks up solidaristic opposition to the existing conditions of inequality by holding out to the ablest and most ambitious members of the disadvantaged groups the enticing prospect of rising from their lowly state into a more prosperous condition. The rules of the game remain the same: The fundamental character of the social-economic system is unaltered. All that happens is that individuals are given more of a chance to struggle up the social ladder, change their position on it, and step on the fingers of those beneath them (in J. Pennok, John Chapman, ed., *Equality* [New York: Atherton Press, 1967], 237). For an elegant critique of the argument that contemporary societies, including the United States and Great Britain, are in fact becoming more meritocratic, see John Goldthorpe, "The Myth of Education-Based Meritocracy," *New Economy* 10 (2003), 234–39.

86. Young, *Rise of the Meritocracy*, 140.

87. Ibid., 106–8.

88. Ibid., 176.

89. Everett Carl Ladd and Karlyn H. Bowman, *Attitudes Toward Economic Inequality* (Washington, D.C.: AEI Press, 1998), 118–21. See also Gordon Marshall et al., "What Is and What Ought to Be: Popular Beliefs about Distributive Justice in Thirteen Countries," *European Sociological Review* 15, no. 4 (1999): 349–67, and

Seymour M. Lipset, *American Exceptionalism: A Double-Edged Sword* (New York: Norton, 1996), 287.

90. Ibid.

91. In a survey conducted in the 1980s, only 33 percent of low-income Americans agreed with the statement "Government should provide everyone with a guaranteed basic income," compared to 80, 71, 66, and 58 percent, respectively, in Italy, Great Britain, West Germany, and the Netherlands. Parallel national differences appeared among those with high incomes, with only 12 percent of upper-income Americans supporting a guaranteed basic income, compared to 39 to 53 percent in the four other countries studied. Similar results were reported on the proposition "The Government should provide a decent standard of living for the unemployed," with fewer than a quarter of high-income Americans expressing agreement in contrast to well over half of high-income respondents elsewhere (Karlyn H. Keene and Everette Carl Ladd, "America: A Unique Outlook," *American Enterprise* [March/April 1990], 118, cited in Seymour Martin Lipset and Gary Marks, *It Didn't Happen Here: Why Socialism Failed in the United States* [New York: Norton, 2000], 289). For evidence that rates of social mobility in the United States are similar to those in other advanced industrial countries, see Anthony F. Heath, *Social Mobility* (London: Fontana, 1981); Karin Kurtz and Walter Muller, "Class Mobility in the Industrial World," *Annual Review of Sociology* 13 (1987), 417–42; Jesper B. Sorensen, "Locating Class Cleavages in Inter-Generational Mobility: Cross-National Commonalities and Variations in Mobility Patterns," *European Sociological Review* 8 (1992): 267–81; and Robert Erikson and John H. Goldthorpe, *The Constant Flux: A Study of Class Mobility in Industrial Societies* (Oxford: Clarendon, 1993).

92. A *Time*/CNN poll cited in Nancy Gibbs and Michael Duffy, "Two Men, Two Visions," *Time*, 6 November 2000.

93. Harold L. Wilensky, *The Welfare State and Equality* (Berkeley, Calif.: Univ. of California Press, 1975). See also Arnold J. Heidenheimer, "Education and Social Security Entitlements in Europe and America" in *The Development of Welfare States in Europe and America*, ed. Peter Flora and Arnold J. Heidenheimer (New Brunswick, N.J.: Transaction, 1981), 269–304.

94. Lipset, *American Exceptionalism*, 289; Lipset and Marks, *It Didn't Happen Here*, 281–83.

95. Michael Young, "Down with Meritocracy," *Guardian*, 29 January 2001.

Selected Bibliography

Abramson, Rudy. *Spanning the Century: The Life of W. Averell Harriman, 1891–1986*. New York: William Morrow, 1992.

"Admissions and Princeton." *Prospect*, 15 December 1975.

Allen, Dean A. "History of the Undergraduate Social Clubs at Princeton." *Social Problems* 2, no. 3 (January 1955).

Amory, Cleveland. *The Proper Bostonians*. New York: Dutton, 1947.

Amster, Jeanne. "Meritocracy Ascendant: James Bryant Conant and the Cultivation of Talent." Ph.D. diss., Harvard University, 1990.

Armstrong, Charles F. "The Lessons of Sports: Class Socialization in British and American Boarding Schools." *Sociology of Sport Journal* 1, no. 4 (December 1984).

Ashburn, Frank D. *Fifty Years On: Groton School, 1884–1934*. New York: At the Sign of Gosden Head, 1934.

———. *Peabody of Groton: A Portrait*. Cambridge, Mass.: Riverside Press, 1967.

Ashburn, Frank D., Jr. "The Essence of Yale." *Yale Alumni Magazine*, January 1949.

Astin, Alexander, and Leticia Oseguera. "The Declining 'Equity' of Higher Education." *Review of Higher Education* 27, no. 3 (2004).

Avery, Christopher, et al. *The Early Admissions Game: Joining the Elite*. Cambridge, Mass.: Harvard University Press, 2003.

Baker, Ray Stannard. *Woodrow Wilson: Life and Letters*. Garden City, N.Y.: Doubleday, Page, 1927.

Baltzell, E. Digby. *Philadelphia Gentleman: The Making of a National Upper Class*. Glencoe, Ill.: Free Press, 1958.

———. *The Protestant Establishment: Aristocracy and Caste in America*. New York: Vintage, 1964.

———. "The Protestant Establishment Revisited." *American Scholar* 45, Autumn 1976.

———. *Puritan Boston and Quaker Philadelphia: Two Protestant Ethics and the Spirit of Class Authority and Leadership*. New York: Free Press, 1979.

Banks, Roger. "When Ivyish Eyes Are Smiling: The History and Practice of Marketing in Harvard College Admissions." Ph.D. diss., Harvard University, 1995.

Beisner, Robert L. *Twelve Against Empire: The Anti-Imperialists, 1898–1900*. New York: McGraw-Hill, 1968.

Bell, Daniel. *The Coming of Post-Industrial Society*. New York: Basic Books, 1999.

Bender, Wilbur J. "Speech to Class of '27," 3 May 1947. HUA.

———. "Comprehensive Formal Statement of Harvard College Admission Policy," 18 September 1952. HUA.

———. "The Top-One-Percent Policy: A Hard Look at the Dangers of an Academically Elite Harvard." *Harvard Alumni Bulletin*, 30 September 1961.

Bernstein, Mark F. *Football: The Ivy League Origins of American Obsession*. Philadelphia: University of Pennsylvania Press, 2001.

Bethell, John. "Frank Roosevelt at Harvard." *Harvard Magazine*, November–December 1996.

———. *Harvard Observed: An Illustrated History of the University in the Twentieth Century*. Cambridge, Mass.: Harvard University Press, 1998.

Bliven, Bruce. "For 'Nordics' Only." *New Republic*, 8 December 1947.

Bloomganden, Lawrence. "Our Changing Elite Colleges." *Commentary*, February 1960.

Bok, Derek. "Open Letter on Issues of Race at Harvard." *Harvard Gazette*, 27 February 1981.

Bourdieu, Pierre. *Distinction: A Social Critique of the Judgment of Taste*. Cambridge, Mass.: Harvard University Press, 1984.

———. "The Forms of Capital." In *Handbook of Theory and Research for the Sociology of Education*, ed. J. G. Richardson. New York: Greenwood Press, 1986.

———. *The State Nobility: Elite Schools in the Field of Power*. Stanford, Calif.: Stanford University Press, 1996.

Bourdieu, Pierre, and Jean-Claude Passeron. *Reproduction in Education, Society, and Culture.* Beverly Hills, Calif.: SAGE, 1977.

——. *The Inheritors: French Students and Their Relation to Culture.* Chicago: University of Chicago Press, 1979.

Bowen, William G. "Admissions and the Relevance of Race." *Princeton Alumni Weekly,* 26 September 1977.

Bowen, William, and Derek Bok. *The Shape of the River: Long-Term Consequences of Considering Race in College and University Admissions.* Princeton, N.J.: Princeton University Press, 1998.

Bowen, William G., and Sarah A. Levin. *Reclaiming the Game: College Sports and Educational Values.* Princeton, N.J.: Princeton University Press, 2003.

Bowen, William G., Martin Kurzweil, and Eugene M. Tobin. *Equity and Excellence in American Higher Education.* Charlottesville: University of Virginia Press, 2005.

Bragdon, Henry W. *Woodrow Wilson: The Academic Years.* Cambridge, Mass.: Belknap Press, 1967.

Branch, Mark A. "Deciphering the Admissions Map." *Yale Alumni Magazine,* November 2000.

Brewster, Kingman, Jr. "Admission to Yale: Objectives and Myths." *Yale Alumni Magazine,* October 1966.

——. Letter to John Muyskens, 15 March 1967. YUA.

"Brewster's Speech to Alumni." *Yale Alumni Magazine,* January 1974.

Briggs, Peter. "Why They Didn't Choose Harvard." *Harvard Alumni Bulletin,* 26 October 1957.

Brigham, Carl C. *A Study of American Intelligence.* Princeton, N.J.: Princeton University Press, 1923.

——. "The Quality of the Classes Admitted to Princeton in the Years 1928 to 1935 (Confidential Report to the Committee on Admissions)." 1935, PUA.

Brint, Steven, and Jerome Karabel. *The Diverted Dream: Community Colleges and the Promise of Educational Opportunity in America, 1900–1985.* New York: Oxford University Press, 1989.

Broun, Heywood, and George Britt. *Christians Only: A Study in Prejudice.* New York: Vanguard, 1931.

Buck, Norman. "What Kind of Boy Does Yale Want?" *Yale Alumni Magazine,* November 1950.

Buck, Paul H. "Balance in the College." *Harvard Alumni Bulletin,* 16 February 1946.

——. "Who Comes to Harvard?" *Harvard Alumni Bulletin,* 10 January 1948.

Buckley, William F., Jr. "What Makes Bill Buckley Run." *Atlantic Monthly,* April 1968.

Bundy, McGeorge. "Admission to Harvard." *Harvard Alumni Bulletin,* 7 May 1960.

——. "The Issue Before the Court: Who Gets Ahead in America?" *Atlantic Monthly,* November 1977.

Burr, Ralph C. "Scholarship Students at Yale." Ph.D. diss., Yale University, 1952.

Canby, Henry S. *Alma Mater: The Gothic Age of the American College.* New York: Farrar & Rinehart, 1936.

Carnevale, Anthony P., and Stephen J. Rose. "Socioeconomic Status, Race/Ethnicity, and Selective College Admissions." In *America's Untapped Resource: Low-Income Students in Higher Education,* ed. Richard D. Kahlenberg. New York: Century Foundation Press, 2004.

Carson, Claiborne. *In Struggle: SNCC and the Black Awakening of the 1960s.* Cambridge, Mass.: Harvard University Press, 1961.

Caute, David. *The Year of the Barricades: A Journey Through 1968.* New York: Harper & Row, 1988.

Chauncey, Henry, Jr. "Excerpts from the Chauncey Speech on Admissions Reforms." *Yale Alumni Magazine,* August 1972.

Clark, Russell I., Jr. "Admission to Yale: Policies and Procedures." *Yale Alumni Magazine,* October 1966.

Coffin, William Sloane, Jr. *Once to Every Man: A Memoir.* New York: Atheneum, 1977.

Cohen, Jon. "Scrutinizing Special Admissions Policies." *Yale Herald,* 1 November 2002.

Collins, Varnum Lansing. *Princeton.* New York: Oxford University Press, 1914.

Committee on Race Relations. *A Study of Race Relations at Harvard College.* Cambridge, Mass.: Harvard University, May 1980.

Conant, James B. "The Future of Our Higher Education." *Harper's,* May 1938.

——. "Education for a Classless Society: The Jeffersonian Tradition." *Atlantic Monthly,* May 1940.

——. "Wanted: American Radicals." *Atlantic Monthly,* May 1943.

——. *Public Education and the Structure of American Society.* New York: Teachers College, Columbia University, 1946.

——. *Education and Liberty: The Role of the Schools in a Modern Democracy.* Cambridge, Mass.: Harvard University Press, 1953.

——. *Slums and Suburbs.* New York: McGraw-Hill, 1961.

——. *Thomas Jefferson and the Development of American Public Education.* Berkeley, Calif.: University of California Press, 1962.

——. *My Several Lives: Memoirs of a Social Inventor.* New York: Harper & Row, 1970.

Cowan, Dorritt A. "Single-Sex to Coeducation at Princeton and Yale: Two Case Studies." Ph.D. diss., Teachers College, Columbia University, 1982.

Davis, Shelby C. "Silent Majority." *Princeton Alumni Weekly,* 22 February 1972.

———. "Preserving the Spirit of the Princeton Alumni Body." *Prospect,* 7 May 1973.

D'Emilio, John. *Sexual Politics, Sexual Communities: The Making of a Homosexual Minority in the United States, 1940–1970.* Chicago: University of Chicago Press, 1998.

DiMaggio, Paul, and Walter W. Powell. "The Iron Cage Revisited: Institutional Isomorphism and Collective Rationality in Organizational Fields." *American Sociological Review* 48, April 1983.

Dinnerstein, Leonard. "Anti-Semitism Exposed and Attacked, 1945–1950." *American Jewish History* 71, no. 1 (September 1991).

Doermann, Humphrey. "The Market for College Education in the United States." Ph.D. diss., Harvard University, 1967.

Domhoff, G. William. *Who Rules America?* Englewood Cliffs, N.J.: Prentice-Hall, 1967.

Dreyfuss, Joel, and Charles Lawrence III. *The Bakke Case and the Politics of Inequality.* New York: Harcourt Brace Jovanovich, 1979.

Dudziak, Mary L. *Cold War Civil Rights.* Princeton, N.J.: Princeton University Press, 2000.

Duke, Alex. *Importing Oxbridge: English Residential Colleges and American Universities.* New Haven, Conn.: Yale University Press, 1996.

Dunham, E. Alden. "A Look at Princeton Admissions." *Princeton Alumni Weekly,* 19 January 1965.

Edwards, Charles W. "The Admissions Problem." *Princeton Alumni Weekly,* 4 November 1955.

———. "If You Were Director of Admissions . . ." *Princeton Alumni Weekly,* 2 October 1959.

Eichel, Lawrence E., et al. *The Harvard Strike.* Boston: Houghton Mifflin, 1970.

Eliot, Charles. "Why a Student Should Choose Harvard." *Harvard Graduates' Magazine,* September 1914.

———. "Three Lines of Action for American Jews." *Menorah Journal,* February 1918.

———. "The Evils of College Football." In *Charles W. Eliot: The Man and His Beliefs.* Vol. 1, ed. William A. Neilson. New York: Harper & Bros., 1926.

———. "The Function of Education in Democratic Society." In *Charles W. Eliot: The Man and His Beliefs.* Vol. 1, ed. William A. Neilson. New York: Harper & Bros., 1926.

———. "Inaugural Address as President of Harvard College, October 19, 1869." In *Charles W. Eliot: The Man and His Beliefs.* Vol. 1, ed. William A. Neilson. New York: Harper & Bros., 1926.

Embree, Edwin R. "In Order of Their Eminence: An Appraisal of American Universities." *Atlantic Monthly,* June 1935.

Espenshade, Thomas J. "Admission Preference for Minority Students, Athletes, and Legacies at Elite Universities." *Social Science Quarterly,* December 2004.

Evans, Sarah M. *Personal Politics: The Roots of Women's Liberation in the Civil Rights Movement and the New Left.* New York: Vintage, 1980.

Fallows, James. "The Early-Decision Racket." *Atlantic Monthly,* September 2001.

Farnum, Richard, Jr. "Patterns of Upper-Class Education in Four American Cities: 1875–1975." In *The High Status Track: Studies of Elite Schools and Stratification,* ed. Paul W. Kingston and Lionel S. Lewis. Albany: State University of New York Press, 1990.

Feldman, Penny H. "Recruiting an Elite: Admissions to Harvard College." Ph.D. diss., Harvard University, 1975.

Fields, Carl A. "One University's Response to Today's Negro Student." *University: A Princeton Quarterly,* Spring 1968.

———. "The Black Arrival at Princeton." *Princeton Alumni Weekly,* 18 April 1977.

Fitzgerald, F. Scott. *This Side of Paradise.* New York: Scribner's, 1920.

Fitzsimmons, William R., et al. "The Admissions Office Strikes Back: The Process Is Fair." *Harvard Crimson,* 26 November 1990.

Foucault, Michel. *Power/Knowledge: Selected Interviews & Other Writings, 1972–1977.* New York: Pantheon, 1980.

Freidel, Frank. *Franklin D. Roosevelt: The Apprenticeship.* Boston: Little, Brown, 1952.

Fuess, Claude M. *The College Board: Its First Fifty Years.* New York: Columbia University Press, 1950.

Gardner, Ralph, Jr. "The $28,995 Tutor." *New York,* 16 April 2001.

Geiger, Roger L. *Research and Relevant Knowledge: American Research Universities Since World War II.* New York: Oxford University Press, 1993.

Gerstle, Gary. *American Crucible: Race and Nation in the Twentieth Century.* Princeton, N.J.: Princeton University Press, 2001.

Gerth, H. H., and C. Wright Mills, eds. *From Max Weber: Essays in Sociology.* New York: Oxford University Press, 1946.

"Getting Into Princeton." *Nassau Sovereign,* April 1949.

"Getting Into Princeton Under Dunham." *Daily Princetonian,* 31 October 1964.

Gitlin, Todd. *The Sixties: Years of Hope, Days of Rage.* New York: Bantam, 1987.

Glimp, Fred, and Dean K. Whitla. "Admissions and Performance in the College." *Harvard Alumni Bulletin,* 11 January 1964.

Golden, Daniel. "Family Ties: Preference for Alumni Children in College Admission Draws Fire." *Wall Street Journal,* 15 January 2003.

———. "How Much Does It Cost to Buy Your Child In?" *Wall Street Journal,* 12 March 2003.

Goodman, Walter. "Bicker at Princeton: The Eating Clubs Again." *Commentary,* May 1958.

Gordon, Jeffrey. "'Inky's' Era." *Yale Alumni Magazine,* March 1970.

Gouldner, Alvin W. *The Future of Intellectuals and the Rise of the New Class.* New York: Oxford University Press, 1982.

Graham, Patricia A. "Expansion and Exclusion: A History of Women in American Higher Education." *Signs* 3, no. 4 (Summer 1978).

Grant, Madison. *The Passing of the Great Race.* New York: Scribner's, 1924.

Guinier, Lani. "Admissions Rituals as Political Acts: Guardians at the Gates of Our Democratic Ideals." *Harvard Law Review* 117, no. 1 (2003).

Gummere, Richard. "Confidential Report to President Conant on Harvard Admission Problems," 19 August 1934. HUA.

Harris, Seymour E., ed. *Economics of Harvard.* New York: McGraw-Hill, 1970.

Hawkins, Hugh. *Between Harvard and America: The Educational Leadership of Charles W. Eliot.* New York: Oxford University Press, 1972.

"Heermance on Admissions." *Princeton Alumni Weekly,* 30 January 1953.

Herman, Tom. "New Concept of Yale Admissions." *Yale Daily News,* 16 December 1965.

Hershberg, James G. *James B. Conant: Harvard to Hiroshima and the Making of the Nuclear Age.* Stanford, Calif.: Stanford University Press, 1993.

Hettinger, A. J., Jr., and Edward Gay. "Statistical Report of the Statisticians to the Subcommittee Appointed to Collect Statistics," 1922. HUA.

Higham, John. *Strangers in the Land: Patterns of American Nativism, 1860–1925.* New Brunswick, N.J.: Rutgers University Press, 1992 (1955).

Hoftstader, Richard. *Anti-Intellectualism in American Life.* New York: Knopf, 1970.

Hoganson, Kristin. *Fighting for American Manhood: How Gender Politics Provoked the Spanish-American and Philippine-American Wars.* New Haven, Conn.: Yale University Press, 1998.

Hollinger, David. "Money and Academic Freedom a Half-Century After McCarthyism: Universities amid the Force Fields of Capital." In *Unfettered Expression: Freedom in American Intellectual Life,* ed. Peggie Hollingsworth. Ann Arbor: University of Michigan Press, 2000.

Honey, J. R. de S. *Tom Brown's Universe: The Development of the English Public School in the Nineteenth Century.* New York: New York Times Book Co., 1977.

"How Black Studies Happened." *Yale Alumni Magazine,* October 1968.

Hughes, Raymond M. *A Study of the Graduate Schools of America.* Oxford, Ohio: Miami University Press, 1925.

Hughes, Thomas. "The Public Schools of England," Parts I and II. *North American Review,* April and July 1879.

Isaacson, Walter, and Evan Thomas. *The Wise Men: Six Friends and the World They Made.* New York: Simon & Schuster, 1986.

Jacobson, Matthew Frye. *Whiteness of a Different Color: European Immigrants and the Alchemy of Race.* Cambridge, Mass.: Harvard University Press, 1998.

James, Henry. *Charles W. Eliot: President of Harvard University, 1869–1909.* Boston: Houghton Mifflin, 1930.

Jencks, Christopher, and David Riesman. *The Academic Revolution.* New York: Doubleday, 1968.

Johnson, Owen. "The Social Usurpation of Colleges: Part I — An Introductory Article to a Series Disclosing the Growth of Snobbery at American Universities." *Collier's,* 18 May 1912.

———. "The Social Usurpation of Colleges: Part II — Harvard." *Collier's,* 25 May 1912.

———. "The Social Usurpation of Colleges, Part III — Yale." *Collier's,* 8 June 1912.

———. "The Social Usurpation of Colleges, Part IV — Princeton." *Collier's,* 15 June 1912.

———. *Stover at Yale.* 1912; New York: Collier Books, 1968; Simon & Schuster, 1988.

Just, Richard. "For the Jewish Community, Low Numbers and a Search for Answers." *Daily Princetonian,* 27 April 1999.

Kabaservice, Geoffrey. "Kingman Brewster and the Rise and Fall of the Progressive Establishment." Ph.D. diss., Yale University, 1999.

———. *The Guardians: Kingman Brewster, His Circle, and the Rise of the Liberal Establishment.* New York: Henry Holt, 2004.

Kahlenberg, Richard D. *The Remedy: Class, Race, and Affirmative Action.* New York: Basic Books, 1996.

———, ed. *America's Untapped Resource: Low Income Students in Higher Education.* New York: Century Foundation Press, 2004.

Kaplan, Nira. "A Changing Culture of Merit: French Competitive Examinations and the Politics of Selection, 1750–1820." Ph.D. diss., Columbia University, 1999.

Karabel, Jerome. "Status-Group Struggle, Organizational Interests, and the Limits of Institutional Autonomy: The Transformation of Harvard, Yale, and Princeton, 1918–1940." *Theory and Society* 13, January 1984.

——. "Freshman Admissions at Berkeley: A Policy for the 1990s and Beyond." Report of the Committee on Admissions and Enrollment, Berkeley Division, Academic Senate, University of California, 1989.

——. "No Alternative: The Effects of Color-Blind Admissions in California." In *Chilling Admissions: The Affirmative Action Crisis and the Search for Alternatives*, ed. Gary Orfield and Edward Miller. Cambridge, Mass.: Harvard Civil Rights Project and Harvard Education Publishing Group, 1998.

——. "The Legacy of Legacies." *New York Times*, 13 September 2004.

Karen, David. "Who Gets into Harvard? Selection and Exclusion at an Elite College." Ph.D. diss., Harvard University, 1985.

——. "Toward a Political-Organizational Model of Gatekeeping: The Case of Elite Colleges." *Sociology of Education* 63, no. 4 (October 1990).

——. "'Achievement' and 'Ascription' in Admission to an Elite College: A Political-Organizational Analysis." *Sociological Forum* 6, no. 2 (1991).

——. "The Politics of Class, Race, and Gender: Access to Higher Education in the United States, 1960–1986." *American Journal of Education* 99, no. 2 (February 1991).

Keller, Morton, and Phyllis Keller. *Making Harvard Modern: The Rise of America's University.* New York: Oxford University Press, 2001.

Kelley, Brooks M. *Yale: A History.* New Haven, Conn.: Yale University Press, 1974.

Kinkead, Katherine. *How an Ivy League College Decides on Admissions.* New York: Norton, 1961.

Krumpe, Elizabeth. "The Educational Ideas of the Clarendon Headmasters from 1860 to 1914." Ph.D. diss., Boston University, 1983.

Lamb, John D. "The Real Affirmative Action Babies: Legacy Preferences at Harvard and Yale." *Columbia Journal of Law and Social Problems* 26, no. 3 (Spring 1993): 491–521.

Lambert, Craig. "The Professionalization of Ivy League Sports." *Harvard Magazine*, September–October 1997.

Lambert, Jeremiah D. "Princeton Proletarianized." *Princeton Alumni Weekly*, 21 November 1972.

Leitch, Alexander, ed. *A Princeton Companion.* Princeton, N.J.: Princeton University Press, 1978.

Lemann, Nicholas. *The Big Test: The Secret History of the American Meritocracy.* New York: Farrar, Straus, 1999.

Levine, David O. *The American College and the Culture of Aspiration 1915–1940.* Ithaca, N.Y.: Cornell University Press, 1986.

Levine, Steven B. "The Rise of the American Boarding Schools and the Development of a National Upper Class." *Social Problems* 28, no. 1 (October 1980): 63–94.

Lincoln, Chris. *Playing the Game: Inside Athletic Recruiting in the Ivy League.* White River Junction, Vt.: Nomad Press, 2004.

Link, Arthur. *Wilson: The Road to the White House.* Princeton, N.J.: Princeton University Press, 1947.

Lipset, Seymour M. *American Exceptionalism: A Double-Edged Sword.* New York: Norton, 1996.

Lipset, Seymour M., and David Riesman. *Education and Politics at Harvard.* New York: McGraw-Hill, 1975.

Lowell, Abbott L. "Inaugural Address." *Harvard Graduates' Magazine*, December 1909.

Ludmerer, Kenneth. "Genetics, Eugenics, and the Immigration Restriction Act of 1924." *Bulletin of the History of Medicine* 46, no. 1 (January/February 1972).

Lux et Veritas. "A Report on Yale Admissions 1950–1972," 1972. YU.

——. "Coeducation at Yale," 1972. YUA.

MacDonald, Anne. "Memorandum Concerning Admission Office," 7 April 1934. HUA.

Mangan, J. A. *Athleticism in the Victorian and Edwardian Public School: The Emergence and Consolidation of An Educational Ideology.* Cambridge: Cambridge University Press, 1981.

Marquand, John P. *The Late George Apley.* Boston: Little, Brown, 1937.

Marsden, George. *The Soul of the American University: From Protestant Establishment to Established Nonbelief.* New York: Oxford University Press, 1994.

"May Jews Go to College?" *Nation*, 14 June 1922.

Mayer, Martin. "How to Get into Princeton." *Princeton Alumni Weekly*, 28 September 1962.

McAdam, Douglas. *Political Process and the Development of Black Insurgency, 1930–1970.* Chicago: University of Chicago Press, 1982.

McDonough, Patricia M., et al. "Access, Equity, and the Privatization of College Counseling." *Review of Higher Education* 20, no. 3 (Spring 1997).

McLachlan, James. *American Boarding Schools: A Historical Study.* New York: Scribner's, 1970.

McNees, John. "The Quest at Princeton or the Cocktail Soul." *Harvard Crimson*, 21 February 1958.

McWilliams, Carey. *A Mask of Privilege: Anti-Semitism in America.* Boston: Little, Brown, 1948.

Megalli, Mark. "So Your Dad Went to Harvard: Now What About the Lower Board Scores of White Legacies?" *Journal of Blacks in Higher Education* 7, Spring 1995.

Menand, Louis. "Sporting Chances: The Cost of College Athletics." *New Yorker,* 22 January 2001.

———. "The Long Shadow of James B. Conant." In *American Studies.* New York: Farrar, Straus, 2002.

Mills, C. Wright. *The Power Elite.* New York: Oxford University Press, 1956.

Monro, John U. "Who Gets the Scholarships?" *Harvard Alumni Bulletin,* 10 December 1955.

Morison, Samuel E. *Three Centuries of Harvard, 1636–1936.* Cambridge, Mass.: Harvard University Press, 1936.

Munford, Luther. "Anatomy of a Decision." *Princeton Alumni Weekly,* 11 November 1969.

"Negro Question, The." *Nassau Sovereign,* October 1942.

Oberdorfer, Don. *Princeton University: The First 250 Years.* Princeton, N.J.: Trustees of Princeton University, 1995.

O'Neill, Timothy J. *Bakke and the Politics of Equality.* Middletown, Conn.: Wesleyan University Press, 1985.

Oren, Daniel A. *Joining the Club: A History of Jews and Yale.* New Haven, Conn.: Yale University Press, 1985.

Oriard, Michael. *Reading Football: How the Popular Press Created An American Spectacle.* Chapel Hill: University of North Carolina Press, 1993.

Patterson, Gardner, et al. "The Education of Women at Princeton: Report on the Desirability and Feasibility of Princeton Entering into the Education of Women at the Undergraduate Level." *Princeton Alumni Weekly,* 24 September 1968.

Pierson, George W. *Yale College: An Educational History, 1871–1921.* New Haven, Conn.: Yale University Press, 1952.

———. *Yale: The University College, 1921–1937.* New Haven, Conn.: Yale University Press, 1955.

———. *The Education of American Leaders: Comparative Contributions of U.S. Colleges and Universities.* New York:. Praeger, 1969.

———, ed. *A Yale Book of Numbers: Historical Statistics of the College and University, 1701–1976.* New Haven, Conn.: Yale University Press, 1983.

Poorooshasb, Jaleh. "The Tip Factor." *Harvard Crimson,* 13 April 1978.

Post, Herschel E., Jr. "Special Report: Yale Admissions, the Well-Rounded Myth." *Yale Daily News,* 23 November 1959.

Powell, Lewis F. "Confidential Memorandum, Attack on American Free Enterprise System." *Washington Report* 11, no. 23 (23 October 1972).

Putney, Clifford. *Muscular Christianity: Manhood and Sports in Protestant America, 1880–1920.* Cambridge, Mass.: Harvard University Press, 2001.

Pyle, Ralph E. *Persistance and Change in the Protestant Establishment.* Westport, Conn.: Praeger, 1996.

Rawls, John. *A Theory of Justice.* Cambridge, Mass.: Belknap Press, 1971.

Rodes, Harold P. "Educational Factors Affecting the Entrance Requirements to Yale College." Ph.D. diss, Yale University, 1948.

Rosen, Ruth. *The World Split Open: How the Modern Women's Movement Changed America.* New York: Viking, 2000.

Rotberg, Robert. *The Founder: Cecil Rhodes and the Pursuit of Power.* New York: Oxford University Press, 1988.

Rotundo, E. Anthony. *American Manhood: Transformations in Masculinity from the Revolution to the Modern Era.* New York: Basic Books, 1993.

Said, Edward. *Out of Place.* New York: Vintage, 2000.

Saveth, Edward N. "Education of an Elite." *History of Education Quarterly* 28, no. 3 (Autumn 1988).

Schaar, John. "Equality of Opportunity and Beyond." In *Equality,* ed. J. Pennock and John Chapman. New York: Atherton Press, 1967.

Schaeper, Thomas, and Kathleen Schaeper. *Cowboys into Gentlemen: Rhodes Scholars, Oxford, and the Creation of an American Elite.* New York: Berghahn, 1998.

Schudson, Michael. "Organizing the 'Meritocracy': A History of the College Entrance Examination Board." *Harvard Educational Review* 42, no. 1 (February 1972).

Selden, William K. *Club Life at Princeton: An Historical Account of the Eating Clubs at Princeton University.* Princeton, N.J.: Princeton Prospect Foundation, 1994.

Shand-Tucci, Douglass. *The Crimson Letter: Harvard, Homosexuality, and the Shaping of American Culture.* New York: St. Martin's, 2003.

Shulman, James L., and William G. Bowen. *The Game of Life: College Sports and Educational Values.* Princeton, N.J.: Princeton University Press, 2001.

Sinclair, Upton. *The Goose-Step: Study of American Education.* Pasadena, Calif.: Upton Sinclair, 1923.

Sindler, Allan P. *Bakke, DeFunis, and Minority Admissions: The Quest for Equal Opportunity.* New York: Longman, 1978.

Singer, Mark. "God and Mentsch at Yale." *Moment,* July/August 1975.

Singerman, Robert. "The Jew as Racial Alien: The Genetic Component of American Anti-Semitism." In *Anti-Semitism in American History,* ed. David Gerber. Urbana: University of Illinois Press, 1986.

Skrentny, John D. *The Ironies of Affirmative Action.* Chicago: University of Chicago Press, 1996.

——. "The Effects of the Cold War on African-American Civil Rights: America and the World Audience, 1945–1968." *Theory and Society* 27, 1998.

Slosson, Edwin E. *Great American Universities.* New York: Macmillan, 1910.

Sollors, Werner, et al., eds. *Blacks at Harvard: A Documentary History of the African-American Experience at Harvard and Radcliffe.* New York: New York University Press, 1993.

Solomon, Barbara M. *Ancestors and Immigrants: A Changing New England Tradition.* New York: John Wiley, 1956.

——. *In the Company of Educated Women.* New Haven, Conn.: Yale University Press, 1985.

Special Committee on College Admission Policy. "Admission to Harvard College: A Report by the Special Committee on College Admission Policy," February 1960.

Steiger, Paul E. "The High Cost of Winning." *Yale Alumni Magazine,* September/October 2003.

Stimson, Henry, and McGeorge Bundy. *On Active Service in Peace and War.* New York: Harper & Bros., 1948.

Stoddard, Lothrop. *The Rising Tide of Color Against White World-Supremacy.* New York: Scribner's, 1922.

Swartz, David. *Culture and Power: The Sociology of Pierre Bourdieu.* Chicago: University of Chicago Press, 1997.

Synnott, Marcia Graham. "A Social History of Admissions Policies at Harvard, Yale, and Princeton, 1900–1930." Ph.D. diss., University of Massachusetts, 1974.

——. *The Half-Opened Door: Discrimination and Admissions at Harvard, Yale, and Princeton, 1900–1970.* Westport, Conn.: Greenwood Press, 1979.

Takagi, Dana. *The Retreat from Race: Asian-American Admissions and Racial Politics.* New Brunswick, N.J.: Rutgers University Press, 1992.

Thatcher, John, Jr. "Reviewing Princeton's Admission Policy." Parts 1 and 3. *Prospect,* 15 September 1974; 9 October 1974.

Thelin, John R. "Images of the Ivy League, 1890 to 1960: The Collegiate Ideal and the Education of Elites in American Culture." Ph.D. diss., University of California at Berkeley, 1973.

"Thunder on the Right: An Interview with Jere Patterson '38, Chairman of ACTION." *Princeton Alumni Weekly,* 20 October 1970.

Veysey, Laurence R. "Yale Students in a Changing Society." *Yale Alumni Magazine,* November 1969.

von Stade, F. Skiddy, Jr. "'Poore Scholars' and Good Students: The How and Why of Harvard's Scholarship Program." *Harvard Alumni Bulletin,* 25 May 1946.

——. "Balance in the College." *Harvard Alumni Bulletin,* 7 February 1959.

Weber, Max. *Economy and Society,* ed. Guenther Roth and Claus Wittich. Berkeley: University of California Press, 1978.

Webster, David. *Academic Quality Rankings of American Colleges and Universities.* Springfield, Ill.: C. C. Thomas, 1986.

Wechsler, Harold. *The Qualified Student: A History of Selective College Admission in America.* New York: John Wiley, 1977.

——. "The Rationale for Restriction: Ethnicity and College Admission in America, 1910–1980." *American Quarterly* 36, no. 5 (Winter 1984).

"Which of These Boys Would You Admit to Princeton? . . ." *Princeton Alumni Weekly,* 2 October 1959.

"White Supremacy at Princeton: A Thousand Million Colored Allies." Part I. *Daily Princetonian,* 28 September 1942.

"White Supremacy at Princeton: A Time to Decide." Part II. *Daily Princetonian,* 30 September 1942.

"White Supremacy at Princeton: We Make Answer." Part III. *Daily Princetonian,* 3 October 1942.

"Why CAP? Why Prospect?" *Prospect,* 9 October 1972.

Wickenden, James W., Jr. "To: All Princeton Alumni." *Princeton Alumni Weekly,* 22 October 1979.

Wilson, Edmund. "Harvard, Princeton, and Yale." *Forum,* September 1923.

Wolff, Geoffrey. *The Final Club.* New York: Knopf, 1990.

Wortman, Marc. "Getting into Yale Today." *Yale Alumni Magazine,* March 1993.

——. "Can Need-Blind Survive?" *Yale Alumni Magazine,* October 1993.

Yeomans, Henry A. *Abbot Lawrence Lowell, 1856–1943.* Cambridge, Mass.: Harvard University Press, 1948.

Young, Michael. *The Rise of the Meritocracy, 1870–2033: An Essay on Education and Equality.* New York: Penguin, 1961.

——. "Down with Meritocracy." *Guardian,* 29 June 2001.

Zweigenhaft, Richard L., and G. William Domhoff. *Blacks in the White Establishment.* New Haven, Conn.: Yale University Press, 1991.

——. *Diversity in the Power Elite: Have Women and Minorities Reached the Top?* New Haven, Conn.: Yale University Press, 1998.

Acknowledgments

Recent research on what psychologists call "subjective well-being" and the rest of us call happiness reports that the simple act of thanking those to whom we are indebted is beneficial to our mental and physical health. Whether this claim is true or not, thanks are certainly owed to the numerous people who helped make this book possible. It is a genuine pleasure to express my gratitude to them.

All scholarly work builds on the cumulative labors of others, and this book is no exception. In researching elite college admissions, I had the good fortune to be the beneficiary of a superb body of work from which I was able to draw. I am particularly indebted to Marcia Graham Synnott's pioneering dissertation "A Social History of Admissions Policies at Harvard, Yale, and Princeton, 1900–1930" (1974) and to her landmark book, *The Half-Opened Door: Discrimination and Admissions at Harvard, Yale, and Princeton, 1900–1970* (1979); to Geoffrey Kabaservice's meticulous dissertation, "Kingman Brewster and the Rise and Fall of the Progressive Establishment" (1999) and his masterful work, *The Guardians: Kingman Brewster, His Circle, and the Rise of the Liberal Establishment* (2004); to Dan Oren's pathbreaking examination of the history of Jews at Yale, *Joining the Club* (1985); to Penny Hollander Feldman's elegant dissertation, "Recruiting an Elite: Admission to Harvard College" (1975), reprinted as a book by Garland Publishing in 1988; to Harold Wechsler's seminal *The Qualified Student: A History of Selective College Admissions in America* (1977), which includes an outstanding chapter on the history of admissions at Columbia; to David O. Levine's *The American College and the Culture of Aspiration, 1915–1940* (1986), which provides an illuminating account of the history of admissions at Dartmouth; and to Richard Farnum Jr.'s unjustly neglected dissertation, "Prestige in the Ivy League: Meritocracy at Columbia, Harvard and Penn, 1870–1940" (1990), and his fine pair of articles that examine the connection between elite colleges and the American upper class. Those interested in elite college admissions will also want to read the revised and expanded edition, currently in preparation, of Marcia Graham Synnott's *The Half-Opened Door.*

In addition to this remarkable body of scholarship on elite college admissions, the writings of four great sociologists, all of them now deceased, exerted a profound influence on me. I am referring here to Max Weber, Pierre Bourdieu, Michael Young, and E. Digby Baltzell, all of whom helped me situate the particular cases of Harvard, Yale, and Princeton in comparative and historical perspective. Four very different men from four distinct national traditions of sociology who disagreed on many matters of politics and philosophy, they nonetheless shared an abiding commitment to sociological scholarship that is theoretically grounded, historically informed, and politically engaged.

But my deepest debt, both personal and intellectual, is to David Karen, with whom I have been in constant dialogue about the issues addressed in this book since 1978. The author of a notable 1985 dissertation, "Who Gets into Harvard? Selection and Exclusion at an Elite College," as well as a series of justly influential articles in the sociology of education (above all, "Toward a Political-Organizational Mode of Gatekeeping: The Case of Elite Colleges"), David has been an unending source of ideas and inspiration. At this point, it is impossible to identify a dividing line between the ideas that are his and those that are mine. All I can say is that I am grateful for his intelligence, his friendship, and the constant support that he has provided since this project first began more than a quarter of a century ago.

In the intervening years, I have conducted research and published on many subjects far afield from elite college admissions. Yet the issue has never been far from my mind. In 1977, shortly after returning from graduate study in Paris and Oxford and completing my doctoral dissertation at Harvard, I began research on the history of admissions to Harvard, Yale, and Princeton as part of a larger project on politics and inequality in American higher education. At the time I was a senior research associate at the Huron Institute in Cambridge, Massachusetts, and was a participant in a multiyear seminar on education, politics, and inequality. Its members included (at various times) Steven Brint, Paul DiMaggio, Kevin Dougherty, David Karen, Katherine McClelland, David Stark, David Swartz, and Michael Useem. Our sometimes heated discussions generated ideas that played a formative role in my thinking about higher education and continue to influence me today.

At the Huron Institute, I was able to draw on a pool of exceptionally talented Harvard undergraduates to serve as research assistants. Among what was, in retrospect, a remarkably distinguished group, I would especially like to thank Louise Epstein, Gerald LeTendre, Steven Levine, and Maureen Scully. Each of them provided crucial assistance for a paper I published in 1984 on the history of admissions at Harvard, Yale, and Princeton between 1918 and 1940.

In the fall of 1984, I became a member of the Sociology Department at the University of California at Berkeley, a vibrant community of scholars with a long tradition of engagement in great public issues. By this time, I was working primarily on a study of institutions at the opposite end of American higher education's implicit tracking system from Harvard, Yale, and Princeton — the nation's community colleges. In 1989, I published a book (co-authored with Steven Brint) summarizing this research, *The Diverted Dream: Community Colleges and the Promise of Educational Opportunity in America, 1900–1985.*

As I was completing this work, I was asked to join the Admissions and Enrollment Committee of the Academic Senate at Berkeley. This was the body that set admissions policy for the Berkeley campus, and what I learned while serving on it for three years gave me an insider's view of the vexing admissions issues facing highly selective colleges and universities. In 1988–1989, I was asked to serve as chair of the Admissions and Enrollment Committee and, drawing on research that I had been conducting over the previous two decades, to write a report reviewing

Berkeley's admissions policy and offering specific recommendations. In May 1989, the Senate formally approved the committee's report, "Freshmen Admissions at Berkeley: A Policy for the 1990s and Beyond." The report recommended that Berkeley admit an academically stronger student body while extending the process of diversification begun in the mid-1960s; toward this end, it proposed that Berkeley institute a program of class-based affirmative action alongside its long-standing policy of race-attentive affirmative action.

Working on the report proved immensely helpful in thinking about admissions issues, for it put me for the first time in the position of policy-maker — a very different vantage point from that of the scholar. Equally helpful was the intense and often acute criticism that I received from colleagues, students, administrators, and interested citizens. Though this criticism was at times painful, responding to it led me to reflect on the social and political consequences of different admissions policies in ways that I had not prior to my service on the committee.

Having spent many years working on issues of politics and inequality in American higher education, I was ready after 1989 to turn my attention to other issues, above all, a long-delayed project on intellectuals and politics in Eastern Europe. But the battle over opportunity in higher education intensified during this period, with an increasingly visible intellectual and political assault on affirmative action gaining momentum. By 1994–1995, California had become the epicenter of this movement, and I found myself increasingly drawn into the debate. The situation escalated in July 1995, when the Regents of the University of California voted to eliminate affirmative action at all nine of the system's campuses. I decided at this time to do what I could to contribute to the struggle to preserve the autonomy of the University of California from regental intrusion (I was joined in this effort by the former UC chancellor Clark Kerr) and protect the gains in minority enrollment that were in obvious danger of being reversed. I did so first as a leader of the faculty movement to persuade the Regents to rescind their decision and later as a consultant to the movement to defeat Proposition 209 (a 1996 measure banning race-based affirmative action in public education, employment, and contracting). Both these efforts failed.

Defeat concentrates the mind. As I reflected on my experiences in the protracted battles over admissions at the University of California, I decided that the time had come to step back and take a deeper look at the roots of the contemporary conflict. Returning to my earlier research on the history of conflicts over access to Harvard, Yale, and Princeton and carrying it forward to today would, I thought, illuminate what is at stake in contemporary struggles over admissions, for it is at these institutions that the battle for places in the freshman class has been most intense over the course of the twentieth century. This book is the result.

Perhaps the greatest privilege of being a member of the Berkeley faculty is the opportunities it provides for interchange with an extraordinary group of students. Over the year, a goodly number of these students, both graduate and undergraduate, worked with me as research assistants. Among the graduate students, Emily Beller, Ben Moodie, Stephanie Mudge, Michele Rossi, and Lisa Stampnitzky deserve special mention for their superb work; so too does Trinh Tran, who came to the project as a volunteer. I was also assisted by a small army of undergraduates, who worked with me under the auspices of Berkeley's Undergraduate Research Apprentice Program (URAP) — an innovative program connecting faculty and students initiated and directed by Terry Strathman. Among the URAPs who made especially important contributions to these books were Lupe Carrillo, Joanna Chan, Su Jin Gatlin, Joshua Guetzkow, Jin Im, Sean Jaquez, Vandana Kapur, May Liao, Adelaide Nalley, Lisa Nguyen, Alyson Paul, Nisha Ramachandram, Nicole Rogers, Alex Strassman, Karen Teresi, Scott Washington, and Ursula Yearwood.

In preparing the manuscript, I was also the beneficiary of outstanding work from a series of special assistants — all Berkeley undergraduates — who performed a variety of complex administrative, research, and clerical tasks, including organizing a vast body of archival materials. More than anyone else, Fiona Chong, Stacey May, and Julie Pham know that I could not have completed this book without them. I hope they realize how deeply I appreciate their efforts.

Working parallel with my staff in Berkeley was a talented team of students in the archives of Harvard, Yale, and Princeton. I would especially like to thank Yael Schacher, Caitlin Anderson, June Kim, and Zach Heineman (at Harvard), Denise Bossy, Daniel Lanpher, Charles Keith, and Thomas Whitney (at Yale), and Nicole Esparza and Joshua Guetzkow (at Princeton). Their work was tremendously facilitated by the generous cooperation of the archive staffs. I am especially grateful to Dan Linke (Princeton), Bill Massa (Yale), and Harley Holden, Brian Sullivan, Megan Sniffin-Marinoff, and Andrea Goldstein (Harvard) for their kind assistance.

A number of friends and colleagues read part or all of the manuscript, in a few heroic cases more than once. I would especially like to thank Emily Beller, Carolyn Bond, Michael Burawoy, Miguel Centeno, Bill Domhoff, Troy Duster, Peter Evans, Josh Guetzkow, Geoffrey Kabaservice, David Karen, David Labaree, Kristin Luker, Isaac Martin, Irv Muchnick, Naomi Schneider, David Swartz, Eric Simonoff, Lisa Stampnitzky, and Loic Wacquant. I was not able to do justice to all their excellent criticisms and suggestions, but their engagement with the manuscript made the book far better than it would have been otherwise.

In revising the book, I benefited tremendously from the editorial assistance of Jane Cavolina. From the moment she received the manuscript, she communicated an understanding of what I was trying to do and an enthusiasm for the project that helped sustain me through many difficult moments. Jane's astute editorial eye, her commitment to clear language and strong argument, her evident disdain for academic equivocation, and her willingness to tell me — politely but firmly — when I was wrong made this book different from (and, I hope, better) than anything I had written previously. Jane also introduced me to my agent, Eric Simonoff, whose intelligence, integrity, diplomacy, and plain good sense have helped me navigate between the very different worlds of academe and commercial publishing. It has been a privilege to work with him.

My talented editor at Houghton Mifflin, Amanda Cook, gave me the gift of a careful, clear-eyed, and insightful reading of the manuscript. Thanks are due as well to her able assistant, Erica Avery, to Luise Erdmann, whose meticulous eye and love of the English language made her an exceptional copy editor, and to Mary McClean, who directed the search for photographs.

I am also indebted to Lana Muraskin, who as a program officer at the National Institute of Education many years ago took a chance on a young scholar and awarded me a grant for a project on power and inequality in higher education. This grant permitted me to undertake the research program that eventuated in both *The Diverted Dream* and this book. Since 1996, the project has been housed at the Institute for the Study of Social Change at UC Berkeley, where Janice Tanigawa and David Minkus have provided a supportive atmosphere for the many students who have worked with me.

Above all, I would like to thank my wife, Kristin Luker, whose steadfast intellectual and emotional support over the years has meant so much more than I could possibly articulate. I would also like to express my love and gratitude to my children, Sonya and Alex, for their humor, their kindness, their patience, their quirks, and their affection. Their love has sustained me since their birth thirty-seven minutes apart in 1996. Finally, I would like to thank my parents, Dorothy Karabel (1916–1975) and Henry Karabel (1916–1982), now long gone, but whose presence is still felt.

Photo Credits

Index